THE ORIGINS OF THE KOREAN WAR

II. THE ROARING OF
THE CATARACT
1947–1950

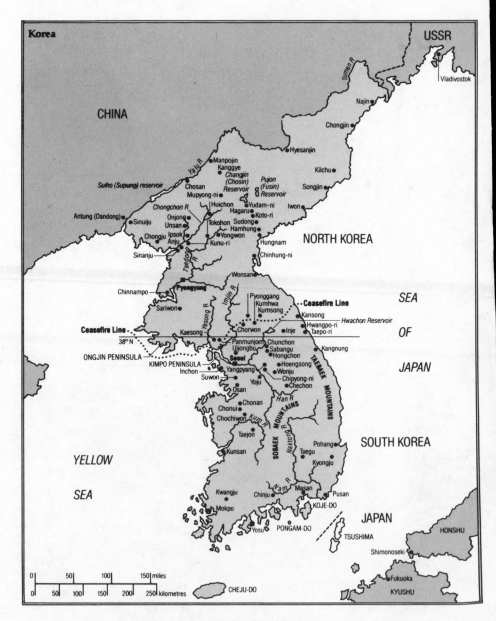

Map 1. Korea
SOURCE: Halliday, Jon, and Bruce Cumings. *Korea: The Unknown War*.
London: Penguin Books, 1988.

THE ORIGINS
OF THE
KOREAN WAR

Volume II
The Roaring of the Cataract
1947–1950

Bruce Cumings

PRINCETON UNIVERSITY PRESS
PRINCETON, NEW JERSEY

Copyright © 1990 by Princeton University Press

Published by Princeton University Press, 41 William Street,
Princeton, New Jersey 08540
In the United Kingdom: Princeton University Press, Oxford

Library of Congress Cataloging-in-Publication Data
(Revised for volume 2)

Cumings, Bruce, 1943–
The origins of the Korean War.
(v. 1: Studies of the East Asian Institute, Columbia University)
Bibliography: v. 1, p. 565–588; v. 2, p.
Includes indexes.
Contents: v. 1. Liberation and the emergence of separate regimes, 1945–1947—
v. 2. The roaring of the cataract, 1947–1950.
1. Korea—History—Allied occupation, 1945–1948.
2. Korean War, 1950–1953—Causes. I. Studies of the East Asian Institute.
DS917.55.C85   951.9042   80-8543

Library of Congress Cataloging-in-Publication Data

ISBN 0-691-09383-0 (v. 1)
ISBN 0-691-10113-2 (v. 1. : pbk.)
ISBN 0-691-07843-2 (v. 2 : alk. paper)

This book has been composed in Linotron Baskerville

Princeton University Press books are printed on acid-free paper,
and meet the guidelines for permanence and durability of the
Committee on Production Guidelines for Book Longevity of the
Council on Library Resources

Printed in the United States of America by Princeton University Press,
Princeton, New Jersey

10   9   8   7   6   5   4   3   2   1

Dedicated to the Reconciliation and Reunion of the Korean People

ABBREVIATIONS USED IN THE TEXT

ACJ	American Council on Japan
CCF	Chinese Communist Forces
CDP	Chosŏn Democratic Party (North)
CIA	Central Intelligence Agency
CIC	Counter-Intelligence Corps
CINCFE	Commander in Chief, Far East
CHŎNNONG	National League of Peasant Unions
CHŎNP'YŎNG	National Council of Labor Unions
DNF	Democratic National Front (South)
DPRK	Democratic People's Republic of Korea
ECA	Economic Cooperation Administration
G-2	Army Intelligence
JCS	Joint Chiefs of Staff
KCP	Korean Communist Party (South)
KDP	Korean Democratic Party (South)
KLO	Korean Liaison Office
KMAG	Korean Military Advisory Group
KNP	Korean National Police (South)
KNY	Korean National Youth
KPA	Korean People's Army (North)
KPR	Korean People's Republic (South)
KVA	Korean Volunteer Army (China)
KWP	Korean Worker's Party
NEUDA	Northeast United Democratic Army
NKWP	North Korean Worker's Party
NSC	National Security Council
NSRRKI	National Society for the Rapid Realization of Korean Independence
NWY	Northwest Youth (South)
OCMC	Oriental Consolidated Mining Company
OIR	Office of Intelligence Research
OPC	Office of Policy Coordination
OSS	Office of Strategic Services
PC	People's Committee
PLA	People's Liberation Army (China)
PPS	Policy Planning Staff-State Department
PRC	People's Republic of China

ROC	Republic of China (Taiwan)
ROK	Republic of Korea
ROKA	Republic of Korea Army
SACO	Sino-American Cooperation League
SANACC	State-Army-Navy Coordinating Committee
SCAP	Supreme Command, Allied Powers
SKIG	South Korean Interim Government
SKILA	South Korean Interim Legislature
SKWP	South Korean Worker's Party
SOE	Special Operations Executive
SWNCC	State-War-Navy Coordinating Committee
UN	United Nations
UNCOK	UN Commission on Korea
UNCURK	UN Commission on the Unification and Rehabilitation of Korea
UNTCOK	UN Temporary Commission on Korea
USAFIK	U.S. Armed Forces in Korea
USAMGIK	U.S. Army Military Government in Korea
USFIK	U.S. Forces in Korea
YHD	Yi Hong-gwang Detachment

ABBREVIATIONS USED IN SOURCES

ATIS	Allied Translator and Interpretor Section
CP	Carrollton Press
CRC	Carrollton Retrospective Collection
MA	MacArthur Archives, Norfolk, Va.
RG	Record Group
RG242	Captured Enemy (DPRK) Documents
FO	British Foreign Office
FR	*Foreign Relations of the U.S.*
HST	Harry S. Truman Library
HST, PSF	Truman, Presidential Secretary's File
HGND NDSM	*Hamgyŏng Namdo Worker's Daily* (North)
NDSM	*Nodong Sinmun* (Worker's Daily, North)
USFIK	U.S. Armed Forces in Korea

My thanks for their intellectual stimulation and friendship go to Dan Chirot, Tom Ferguson, Jon Halliday, Harry Harootunian, Jim Kurth, and Jim Palais. Others who have aided my thinking in this volume include Chung Kyung Mo, Barton Bernstein, Jang Jip Choi, Roger Dingman, Peter Katzenstein, Kevin Marchioro, Gavan McCormack, John Merrill, Joel Migdal, Pang Sun-joo, Elizabeth Perry, Michael Schaller, Englebert Schucking, Robert Strong, William Stueck, Dae-sook Suh, Gayle Turner, Haruki Wada, and Immanuel Wallerstein. Gregory Henderson's early passing in 1988 was an irreplaceable loss to the field; I had so looked forward to his reading of my book. My father also passed on in 1988, after a long life, but depriving me of another cherished reader. Sandy Thatcher of Princeton University Press was once again most helpful in guiding this book to publication, with welcome support from Margaret Case. I would like to thank Lesley Beneke for her painstaking copyediting and Richard Boscarino for his excellent map-drawing skills. The love and friendship of Jackie Cumings meant so much to me as always, but especially when this project drew so heavily on my reserves of time and patience. My greatest debt is owed to my wife, Jung-en Woo: scholar, interlocuter, editor, friend, helpmate.

I began the research for this volume in 1977 and completed most of it in 1985. During much of that period a grant from the Henry Luce Foundation allowed release time from teaching and research funds for travel, microfilming, and the like. An individual fellowship from the National Endowment for the Humanities made possible a leave year in 1983–1984. The Korean Studies Committee of the Social Science Research Council provided two summer grants to aid my research, and I also benefitted from summer grants from the Graduate School Research Fund of the University of Washington and from Dr. Kenneth B. Pyle, director of the Jackson School of International Studies at the University of Washington. Dr. George M. Beckmann, provost of the University of Washington, arranged a travel grant to the Public Record Office in London. I have been to so many archives and libraries that I cannot acknowledge all those who have aided my research; but John Saunders went beyond the call of duty and deserves a special thanks. Thanks is also owed to research assistants who tracked down materials for me: Moon Young Park, David Satterwhite, Michael Robinson, and Hui-yun Wang. It should go without saying, of course, that I bear sole responsibility for the interpretations, arguments, judgments, and facts to be found in this book, and any errors herein. As before, translations from Korean and Chinese are my own, except for a few handwritten or scrawled documents that I checked with Dae-sook Suh or Jung-en Woo. Unless otherwise noted, dates and times refer to the time zone in which the events described occurred; the reader should remember that Korea was about fourteen hours ahead of Washington, D.C.

To avoid misunderstanding, I should say that the large number of North Korean documents that I have used came from captured materials that John Saunders and I discovered in the National Archives and had declassified in 1977; I have received no help in my research from North or South Korea—quite the contrary. The captured archive extends from top secret documents to the full range of published materials circulating in the North in the late 1940s. Until 1977 scholars of North Korea did not even have a good run of the party newspaper from before the war; this archive includes that, as well as provincial newspapers and nearly a full run of the *Haebang ilbo* (Liberation daily) published in Seoul during the northern occupation. As the reader will see, it also includes heretofore unavailable documentation on a wide range of issues, including the start of the war itself; however, there are few central state, party, or military documents (although more of these may have been held back by declassification authorities).

From 1982 to 1988 I visited London frequently to help in the making of a documentary entitled *Korea: The Unknown War*. The originator and writer of the series, Jon Halliday, has a rare talent for wide reading in a number of languages, from which he has gleaned useful sources and interpretations, data, and odd tidbits relating to the Korean War. I have learned much from our many conversations, and have gained much from his warm friendship and encouragement. The way in which Thames Television goes about making documentaries enabled my participation in many seminars, interviews, and discussions that have bolstered my knowledge of the war. I also accompanied a Thames crew to North Korea, from which we brought back twenty-five interviews and a lot of rare newsreel footage, as well as some indelible impressions about the destructiveness of the war. I would like to thank in particular the producer, Phillip Whitehead, co-producer Max Whitby, Sue Lockett, Jill Service, and seminar participants General Sir Anthony Farrar-Hockley, Rosemary Foot, Lawrence Freedman, John Gittings, Kim Chong Hwi, Peter Lowe, Callum MacDonald, and Robert Oliver.

This book contains a variety of arguments that will unsettle and discomfit some readers, more so than my first volume. I have been stunned by some of the evidence I found in the archives and paper collections. The book has been delayed because I had to shine flashlights down dark alleys and into murky affairs about which I knew nothing. But there is also a matter of method and temperament here: I am not interested in writing a book that gathers dust in libraries; the politics of Korea and America at midcentury are too fascinating for that. A more sober and sedate approach might produce a safer and more acceptable interpretation, but this would necessarily leave too much in the realm of questions left moldering in the dustbin of "history." I would instead take a lesson from Paul's epistle to the Ephesians (5:11–13):

> Take no part in the barren deeds of darkness, but show them up for what they are. The things they do in secret it would be shameful even to mention. But everything, when once the light has shown it up, is illumined, and everything thus illumined is all light.

The scholar's only concern must be with truth as he sees it, pursuing that truth wherever it takes him. I have found that this nice homily, on which we all can agree, calls forth in this case a ferment in the mind which asks, does this task require faith in reason, or the incredulity of the detective? Temerity or foolhardiness? Joy in discovery, or dark nights of the soul? Especially is this so with a vicious civil war that still smolders, or an American politics that in 1950 was shrill, raucous, turbulent, and unrestrained in ways that astonish young people today. Our knowledge advances more quickly by probing questions that are contentious, even if by their nature they ultimately escape an excavation with only the tools available to the scholar. But in any case I cannot work in any other way; closure of questions draws the curtain down on desire, inquisitiveness, the energy to sustain one's project.

The structure of presentation begins with some methodological and theoretical considerations, which impatient readers may wish to skip; part I elaborates on the theoretical argument about America's relation to the world in the late 1940s. It seeks to retrieve an America that, in my view, has been either forgotten or mystified in much of the literature. In the period covered by my first volume, events in Korea governed the developmental logic of the origins of the war, but in 1947 the center of gravity shifted to Washington, so it is appropriate to dilate on the American side of the equation. Like part II, this section proceeds less chronologically than to take the 1947–1950 period in one bite; both parts represent an extended clearing of the throat that establishes common ground for assessing the main event. Part II returns us to the internal milieu in Korea, assessing the nature of the two "sides" and their foreign alignments. The third part is an overture to the main event; each chapter is meant to conjure waves rolling forward, observed from different vantage points, gathering force before an early summer crash on the shore. Thus each chapter moves back and forth over the months, weeks, and days immediately preceding June 25, 1950. Chapter 18 ("Who Started the Korean War?") is the point of departure for the conventional tale of the Korean War, but the denouement to mine. An epilogue follows, where I bring out aspects of the war that reflect back on its origins, or that help to make my case that it was a civil and revolutionary war.

The subtitle of this volume expresses my judgment that a bit over five years after American ships first sailed into Inch'ŏn Harbor on a warm and sunny day, the Siberian winter descended upon a Korea and a United States both peering into an appalling abyss, reflecting back to Koreans the true audacity and peril of their attempt at self-determination after the liberation from Japan, and to Americans the full measure of their aleatory pursuit of global hegemony. The phrase comes from Dean Acheson, who, as he readied himself for a congressional appearance in 1950, ruminated on the sanctuary from predatory forces that the barrier of Europe and two great oceans had provided America since the country's founding. Now all that had ended. As the United States grasped for world leadership amid the regression of the British empire, it was for the first time in the position of a person who, "on the death of a parent, hears in a new way the roaring of the cataract."[1] There our study of the origins of the Korean War ends, but the war goes on today, and so does the quest.

THE ORIGINS OF THE KOREAN WAR

II: THE ROARING OF
THE CATARACT
1947–1950

Chapter One

INTRODUCTION: RECOLLECTIONS ON METHOD AND A THEORY OF AMERICAN FOREIGN POLICY

> [Historical activity] is governed in its entirety by the basic conditions, the structures of materiality, the initial situation, the continuous action of external and internal factors, and the balance of the forces involved.
>
> *Jean-Paul Sartre*

Science and Mystery: "A Highly Nonlinear Unstable Free Boundary Problem"

AMONG the most inaccessible of scientific secrets is the reason for the breathtaking symmetry of snowflakes, combined with their seemingly endless variation. As each flake falls to the ground, it obeys an unknown dictum that mingles randomness and determinism. None will be as another, yet all will have harmonious structure. As one piles on another, the unique constituents transform the whole into a field of soft beauty, covering the ground with a uniform brilliance: it has snowed.

The intractable problems in figuring out snowflakes include their free-fall promiscuity: "a snowflake records the history of all the changing weather conditions it has experienced." Not only that, but interventions occur along the way: floating in the wind, "the choices made by the branching tips" at any instant depend on many things, such as temperature, humidity, or impurities in the air. Snowflakes meander along different paths amid unmeasurable "variables." And yet each one has an unvarying pattern of six arms—a mysterious hexagon to a scientist, a magnificent lacework to an artist. Many are thus led to think that there must be "some mechanical equivalent of somebody sitting at the center of the snowflake and telling all of them to do the same thing." What nature made most beautiful, it also made most unpredictable.

Or so it would seem, until scientists armed with supercomputers attacked "a highly nonlinear unstable free boundary problem," otherwise known as the snowflake, utilizing the heuristic principle that if we know little now, we may someday know enough to explain and predict such

3

"pattern formation." First they found that under the gaze of a powerful microscope, it turns out that snowflakes are not quite symmetrical, after all. Second, there is more uniformity in their structure than meets the naked eye.

Snowflake research has yielded mathematical models that seek to bring together and analyze forces that create and give predictability to the six-legged structure, and also that destabilize it—"large-scale processes and microscopic processes" that forge what we might call a determined random outcome—and that break it up. Each outcome can be subjected to minute examination, its common structure and variant physiognomy laid bare. But in spite of the advance of science, the "large-scale processes" remain unknown, or at least unpredictable.[1] Some readers will take heart in learning that the problem of randomness and determinism is still not solved, so that the snowflake may remain an object of study for science and for art.

Observers of postwar American foreign policy might be forgiven if they sometimes sense that somebody is "sitting at the center, telling all of them to do the same thing." Something seems to produce a determined random outcome: a Bay of Pigs, a Tonkin Gulf incident, or a "Contra" war; a Col. Preston Goodfellow or a Col. Oliver North (the latter quickly labeled a "flake" by his superiors). But politics more generally is this way, producing predictable if variant results, a repetition that is not quite exact but reminiscent enough to suggest common authorship or to loose legions of would-be scientists in search of political regularities. Louis Bonaparte may not be Napoleon; the nephew is lesser than the uncle. A farce recapitulates and illuminates a tragedy, but it is a predictable if variant result. Ronald Reagan may not be Dwight Eisenhower, the "hidden hand" turned out to be palsied or absent, but no other president since 1960 comes as close.

Each political event is both structured and random; each is both regular and unpredictable; each sums up the history it has experienced and goes beyond it; each is subject to unpredictable interventions, called choices; each comes from a particular field, and each event, piled on another, also creates a political field; each can be dissected and understood, but only in retrospect. If we were to stop here in this analogy, it would be obvious that we are still far from a science or a mathematics that can predict and explain political events.

But there is much more to say, because politics is about human beings. We can paraphrase Marx to say that while no human being can create the intricate and variant filigree of falling snowflakes, no snowflake can conceive of itself or its choices. Snowflakes obey physical laws, however impenetrable their secrets may be; humans obey human laws, and thus politics will always retain an incorrigible residue of mystery and unpredictability. Snowflakes react against each other within confines of universal law; people act and react against each other and against the laws, fashioning new ones as they act. Even the retrospective objectivity and understanding implied by the tale of Minerva's owl flying at dusk is denied to people, for they cannot comprehend their own history without a preexisting subjectivity that tells them *this* history but not *that* history. The discrete political event that can be held still and examined under glass does not exist, but if it did, it still could not be understood apart from the passions and interests of the human peering through the microscope, through a looking glass that we call theory.[2] Every political analyst is thus a participant-observer.

Sartre makes this point in a remarkable passage.

> From my window, I can see a road-mender on the road and a gardener working in a garden. Between them there is a wall with bits of broken glass on top protecting the bourgeois property where the gardener is working. Thus they have no knowledge at all of each other's presence. . . . Meanwhile, I can see them without being seen, and my position and this passive view of them at work situates me in relation to them: I am "taking a holiday" in a hotel; and in my inertia as witness I realize myself as a petty bourgeois intellectual. . . . Hence my initial relation to the two workers is negative: I do not belong to their class, I do not know their trades . . . I do not share their worries.
>
> But these negations have a double character. . . . I could not contrast their ends with mine without recognizing them as ends . . . in order to differentiate their ends from mine, I realize myself as a member of a particular society which determines everyone's opportunities and aims. . . . In this way, the affective quality of my perception depends both on my social and political attitude and on contemporary events.[3]

In other words, the two workers, separated from each other by a special type of wall, sum up in themselves, their work and their location a particular history, social structure, and politics. That is, according to Jean-Paul Sartre (and that is the point).

Elsewhere Sartre takes up the problem of determinism and randomness in history; more precisely, Marx's famous judgment that men make their own history, but not under circumstances of their own choosing.[4] If this statement is true, he says, then determinism must be rejected. At the same time, "if we imagine that every one simply follows his inclinations and that these molecular collisions produce large scale effects, we will discover average or statistical results, but not a historical development." This collision is, rather, a "dialectical movement" of people acting as and against people, which will often have the quality of the free fall of random snowflakes (if not usually the beauty). But this activity will be conditioned by a deep structure "[that] is governed in its entirety by the basic conditions, the structures of materiality, the initial situation, the continuous action of external and internal factors, and the balance of the forces involved."

That structure is ultimately a specifiable condition of scarcity and necessity, within which operates a human dialectic.

> The dialectical movement is not some powerful unitary force revealing itself behind History like the will of God. It is first and foremost a resultant; it is not the dialectic which forces historical men to live their history in terrible contradictions; it is men, as they are, dominated by scarcity and necessity, and confronting one another in circumstances which History or economics can inventory, but which only dialectical reason can explain.[5]

An individual does not live merely in a condition of scarcity, within a particular mode of production. He lives in a milieu of interacting influences, a specific life lived in interaction with other humans, in a field that we call society or culture. To grasp history in this sense means to grasp a *total field* "in all its complexity," to grasp the human being "produced" by all the influences in a field, and the human influencing his field and storing it up, summing it up, much as a snowflake buffeted by the winds.

The method must be one which, in principle, as Sartre says, makes use of "the whole of contemporary knowledge . . . to elucidate a given undertaking or social ensemble. . . . Far from assuming, as certain philosophers have done, that we know nothing, we ought as far as possible (though it is impossible) to assume that we know everything." The investigation should make use of "everything that comes to hand," because that is the way an individual lives his life. Such a total investigation ought in the end to "reveal certain structures, relations and meanings which necessarily elude all positivism." The result ought to be a new interpretation which, like the human being constantly bringing novelty into the world, partially or completely reorganizes "the practical field" in which we live.[6]

Sartre without saying it intuits here the direction and method of inquiry of people like Kurt Levin, who elaborated field theories of psychology to grapple with all those influences on an individual, and of the individual on the field, which combine to shape his psyche. The principle is to cast one's net widely enough to gather in "everything that comes to hand" in shaping events. But more deeply a "total field" approach, or what is sometimes called "totalizing history," recapitulates what the person knows about the inner self: that it always sits uneasily amid the generalizations made about it, especially the social science generalizations of our time, because they violate a law that every human intuits: "that every man is a unique miracle . . . [and] that in being thus strictly consistent in uniqueness he is beautiful, and worth regarding, and in no way tedious." That is, a human snowflake. It is quite remarkable that Nietzsche—such a fully "Western" man—goes on in this passage to remark that "Orient and Occident are chalk lines drawn before us to fool our timidity."[7]

People know that they are a mosaic of interacting influences. In our vanity we may single out a single cause of our success; but always our failure has a multiplicity of authors and extenuating circumstances. It is the opposite for our detractors. Still, this mosaic is not happenstance, it registers one's environment, it exists within a larger field or structure, and the imperatives of the latter may often yield good predictions about people in spite of their mosaic-like humanity. The broader level of humans interacting, that is, history, will also have its mosaics and its outer limits, its indeterminacy and its regularity.

Elsewhere Nietzsche writes that our explanations of causality are better at the descriptive level than earlier stages of knowledge; but this means merely "a manifold one-after-another," which we *call* cause and effect, but which "does not involve any *comprehension* [sic]." In chemical experiments, for example, qualitative change still appears as a "miracle"; we can predict when it happens, but not comprehend why. Instead we give the process a name. He then suggests that perhaps cause and effect does not exist: "In truth we are confronted with a continuum out of which we isolate a couple of pieces." Something appears suddenly and we assign a name to its "cause"; but "in this moment of suddenness there is an infinite number of processes that elude us." He suggests that cause and effect should be seen as "a continuum and a flux," not "in terms of an arbitrary division and dismemberment."[8]

It is difficult to speak of "total history" and retain any modesty, but Eric Wolf has done so in exploring "the totality of interacting processes" that make up our human world, incorporating those who rarely speak, and therefore all the more rarely write history. Perry Anderson has done so as well, in a cogent defense of a method that does not assume that truth is revealed only in the abstract categories that march forth as science; "there is no plumb-line between necessity and contingency of historical explanation, dividing separate types of enquiry." That which is known is what is established by historical research, and "the latter may be either the mechanisms of single events or the laws of motion of whole structures."[9]

The method derived from such assumptions does not mean including everything but the kitchen sink, with no principle of selection. It is founded instead on a persistent back-and-forth dialectic between the observed fact and one's theory, back to fact, back to theory—what ought to be expected of every inquiry, which, Sartre wrote elsewhere, must acknowledge the "indissoluble unity" between the given conditions men find themselves in and the actions they take. But before showing "their substructural conditioning," the inquirer must see people as they are, neglecting nothing, pursuing a conscious empiricism that leaves the outcome open-ended.

> For he will be obliged to account for everything, for the necessity and the finality which are so strangely intermingled. . . . The more easily he has at his disposal a philosophy, a point of view, a theoretical basis of interpretation and totalization, the more he will force himself to approach these ends in a spirit of absolute empiricism; he will allow them to develop, to release by themselves their immediate meaning, for he will have the intention of learning, not rediscovering.[10]

Once the net is cast widely, it may then be drawn tight to disclose the essence of things. In Marx's complicated thought there is still the desire to get to the bottom of it all, an assumption that prolonged inquiry and probing can uncover hidden forces that are startling in their simplicity. The essence of a commodity, or the essence of man as maker: *homo faber*.[11] When Karl Polanyi wrote that "the snapping of the golden thread was the signal for a world revolution," he summed up his entire understanding of how the system of 1815 finally unraveled in the 1930s,[12] as well as his own proclivity for mixing theory, concrete history, and metaphor to achieve a desired result. In the work of all three men (Sartre, Marx, and Polanyi), there is an indefinable mix of objective inquiry, subjective belief or theory, and human intuition, not to mention literary flourish and allusion.[13]

Sartre illustrates this combination in the simple observation that every human, including small children, intuitively grasps that "a straight line which intersects a circle at any given point must also intersect it at another point." The child will need empirical observation, but will not need geometric theory: he will know from the structure of the circle itself. On the one hand there is a figure going round on a page, called a circle, and on the other there is the logic of the circle, which is to contain and confine. There is also the line, and its tendency is to extend, it "shatters obstacles in its path." Both are not simply things, but movements in relation to each other, each with an antagonistic logic. It requires no detailed inquiry, no knowledge of geometry, for a person to grasp this logic. It is immanent in the "circle-gestalt," or what might be called the "circleness" of the circle in its field of interaction.[14]

Marx's method in his best historical works, like *The Eighteenth Brumaire*, was precisely to account for what happened "in its detail and in the aggregate," to discover the facts by means of the totality and the totality by means of the facts. In *The Grundrisse*, Marx at first suggests we should begin with the "the real and the concrete," but then he tells us people cannot be studied apart from the social classes they inhabit; to begin with an undifferentiated population "would turn out to be a chaotic conception of the whole." So one would "move analytically toward ever simpler concepts, from the imagined concrete towards ever thinner abstractions until I arrived at the simplest determinations. From there the journey would have to be retraced until I had finally arrived at the population again, but this time not as a chaotic conception of the whole, but as a rich totality of many determinations and relations."[15] Ultimately what is sought by such a method is comprehension, in the dual meaning of the word: a comprehensiveness that grasps the totality of relevant experience, and the achievement of a new understanding.

My digression on method is meant as an exercise in explaining what I have sought to do, history and the doing of it as "learning." Sartre puts it, "my knowledge must be dialectically conditioned by my ignorance," which I take to mean among other things that the inquiry must always be open, seeking new questions as it finds answers. This book begins, proceeds, and ends with a combination of theory, mystery, old questions answered and new ones left exposed, a text conditioned by its own ignorance.

The Korean War was a *resultant*, but was taken in the West to be the "initial situation" that subsequently governed events. June 25, 1950, thus was a *denouement* mistaken for a beginning. This has been my position from the outset, and by making this simple statement I join a dispute over what manner of war it was, who bears responsibility for it, and what its causes and effects were. I make a political statement. So does all the remaining literature, whether explicitly or not. To treat the Korean War as a matter of political conflict, great-power rivalry, diplomatic or military history, deterrence or decision-making theory, is to accept a particular viewpoint, and to make a partial inquiry. It was all of those, but it was much more.

In my view, the "initial situation" of the Korean War was the liberation in 1945, itself a product of forces set in motion earlier, ultimately going back to the irruption of the capitalist market and the modern world system in East Asia. But a Korean War was only conceivable after August 15, 1945, and a new war has been conceivable ever since. Why?

We may take the thirty-eighth parallel, drawn in 1945, as the equivalent of Sartre's straight line, carrying an immanent energy that violated the unitary and confining entity known historically as Korea; from the partition forward, war was predictable if not inevitable. But unlike the child with the line and the circle, we cannot know this without a certain subjectivity, by grasping the Korean gestalt, or what the writer Paek Ki-wŏn meant when he remarked, "when the unified life of our country is cut in two . . . our country will be like a nail stuck in the flow of history."[16] The national division festered then and festers today, ever calling forth a new war.

This we may call an appropriately "Korean" rendering. Both South and North date their histories of the war from 1945, not 1950. But we need to know more. I also had to look at the population—where it was in 1945 (Japan, Manchuria, northern Korea), why it was there, and what happened when the colonial diaspora returned home. In this I discerned a social movement, a movement of humans in the original sense of Vico,[17] that played upon Korea after the division—strong here, weak there. We move from the aggregate account to a peasant seizing grain stocks and back again. In this inquiry we add a social and political struggle to the national division. And then an American and a Soviet occupation, divergent policy choices that are also residuals of American and Soviet society, a series of diplomatic maneuvers, and the like.

The first volume attempted to integrate four levels of analysis: the local, the nation/state, the regional, and the world. It seemed as important to grasp why peasants were stoning cops in some southern village, as it was to interpret Roosevelt's trusteeship policy, a vintage example of American hegemonic statecraft; as important to understand how two state systems emerged on the peninsula, as it was to grasp Japan's regional empire, Korea's place in it, and what happened when it ruptured in 1945. But this dawned all too slowly, only through a constant dialogue between the evidence and my assumptions and hypotheses.

The volume at hand continues these themes for Korea. The peasant question becomes the guerrilla question, the social question becomes the upheavals during the North's occupation of the South. We will also examine the two state systems on the peninsula, their foreign alliances, and the manner in which American hegemony both substituted for Japanese imperialism, and provided an umbrella under which Japanese industrial might could resuscitate. Within Korea, the analysis I used for the early period after liberation proves predictive of much that happened thereafter, and it will not be necessary to revive my account of why that might be so. But that is not the case for explaining the American side of the Korean dialectic.

1945 was also the "initial situation" for the United States, a founding moment, but it was not recognized as such; instead 1947 was taken to be the beginning of the cold war. The Korean War, moreover, was by no means a denouement for the United States. It was instead the palpable birth of interventionist policy abroad and a state apparatus to go with it at home; ever since, this state and its matrix of decision has been with us.

The initial situation in 1945, in Korea, prompted the Occupation's policy of de facto containment. By 1947 this became established policy for the world, affairs in Korea now appearing premature rather than mistaken. We might liken the lines of containment to Sartre's circle; the purpose was to confine and corral the vectors of a different movement. Through most of the postwar era, containment has been the stable logic of imperial America confronting its enemies. But from 1947 to 1950 the containment circle was unstable, its logic confounded not so much by the world at large as by a vector with a different logic at home, called expansionism or rollback. We will need to probe at that intersection from every angle, because it deeply affected the course of the Korean War and American politics, and remains with us today—as ill-understood as the war itself.

In the earlier volume, the goal was to subject all sides of the Korean political spectrum, and the American occupation, to an empathetic but also critical and occasionally unpitying examination. I will do the same in this account. But the method must also be applied to all sides of the American political spectrum. There is a tendency for conventional scholarship to deal coldly or harshly (or at least without empathy) with the perceived extremities in American politics, but to be understanding if not solicitous of the central tendencies, typified by Harry S. Truman and Dean Acheson. The variant treatment of isolationism and internationalism would be two good examples. In my view a mix of *verstehen* and cold judgment should be applicable to all.

Another point that is particularly relevant to the volume at hand is the distinction between structural and empirical arguments, or what could be called structural and "smoking gun" arguments. If Sartre is right in seeking to "reveal certain structures, relations and meanings which necessarily elude all positivism," one also grasps that he has trampled on the dominant standards of proof, especially in American social science: empirical evidence, the stuff of positivism. Freud could never verify the existence of the id to the satisfaction of a positivist, but he nonetheless considered himself a scientist. Marx's entire discussion of capital rests less on empirical evidence than on a relational analysis of the movement of capital; he also believed that he founded a science.

This volume will adduce empirical evidence in defense of the analysis, but ultimately the argument must rest both on this evidence, and on theory, on logic, on assumptions, on relationships, and on conceptions that illumine the terrain. The reader looking for "smoking guns" will find some, but will also be disappointed—for example, on the question pregnant with politics, "who started the Korean War," or on the ultimate intent of Acheson's architecture for Korea and East Asia. There are perhaps a hundred lines of inquiry in this volume that one could spend years pursuing, but ultimately a dogged empiricism becomes a kind of misguided zealotry. During an interview with Dean Rusk, he asked me if his answers to my questions squared with the documents I had seen. After we discussed that for a moment, he counseled that written documents were useful, but far less so than the daily, ongoing discussions of all sorts, hardly any of them recorded for posterity. If he is right, and I think he is, this expresses the limits of an inquiry based on the written record. But by careful and full use of this record, and by trying to think through problems to the underlying logic or structures, we can hope to make an advance in the literature.

TOWARD A THEORY OF
AMERICAN FOREIGN POLICY

Sometimes the piling on of empirical evidence merely adds to our problems, rather than solving them; we need theory to sort it all out and make sense of it. In my view the continuous misunderstanding of the forces making American foreign policy derives from bad theory. Thus each time a disaster occurs—the march to the Yalu, the Bay of Pigs, the Vietnam defeat, the revolution in Iran, or "Irangate" in the Reagan administration—it is treated as sui generis, a temporary aberration that contains no rule of its own, only an exception to the rule of how American foreign relations are conducted. But the disasters do have a logic, and become predictable when we look beneath the surface pattern of events. For this, in other words, we need a theory of American foreign policy, tested continuously against the evidence.

The existing theories tend to highlight decision making, bureaucratic politics, perceptions, conceptions of deterrence or credibility, and the like.[18] Although this volume has much to say about how foreign policy issued forth from American political struggles, bureaucratic conflicts within the American state, deterrence, and perceptions and world views of major actors, such perspectives are not sufficient to account for the field of forces affecting decisions, or the fundamental direction of American foreign policy, nor can that basic direction be understood apart from the structural position of America in a distinct world system that had its own identifiable imperatives. We must situate the United States in the nature and dynamics of that system, lest we present a partial account; that is what I sought in the first volume, that is why the account stretched from agricultural transformation to population shifts to industrialization to the quality of Japanese imperialism and how it ended before I ever considered the Korean-American interaction. The world market system placed similar but unequal burdens on states and societies, with economic competition the driving force, but with the nation-state being a prime vehicle of conflict, and with society reacting to market penetration in different but always significant ways.

Otto Hintze thought that two phenomena condition the organization of the state: "first, the structure of social classes, and second, the external ordering of the states—their position relative to each other, and their over-all position in the world."[19] This is a very good statement, a beginning at trying to develop a world system theory that does not slight domestic societies, but integrates three levels of world position, state, and social situation. This is what Polanyi sought, to harmonize several levels of analysis: the world market system as the total field, nations opening and closing within that field depending on their interests, the state as protector of society in the wider field, societies and peoples reacting to the impact of the market, the importance of timing in all this (when did it happen in world time, how fast or slow did the market mechanism proceed).[20] We will see that such a conception can be applied to America at midcentury.

Robert Cox, another world system theorist, has cogently argued that hegemonic powers are always carriers of an economic and social revolution—England, the Soviet Union, and the United States being examples. Hegemonic power will not only interact with foreign social systems that are more or less resistant to it, but will interpret such resistance in terms of the immanent revolution (liberal, socialist) seeking to impose itself abroad, and always achieving some partial, deformed, or abortive result.[21] We might add that this revolutionary thrust will not be uniform, but will inherit domestic conflicts over how to define the essence of the revolution (Stalin vs. Trotsky, Beard vs. Roosevelt).

A full grasp of the field of American foreign policy will thus require a consideration of its sources at home, and how they effect the state apparatus. The late Theodore White once said that "Pekingology" is like watching two great whales do battle beneath the ocean; occasionally they surface and spout a bit, which is your only evidence on what the trouble might be. But American politics, too, is often like "Chinese" politics: you need to do some "Washingtonology," read newspapers carefully, watch the rise and fall of key figures, look for power struggles. Yet to say these things runs deeply against the grain of American thought. It violates our conceptions of politics, history, of human action. It conjures up conspiracy theory. A people with a built-in ahistoricity is ill-accustomed to retrospective digging, to lifting up rugs, to searching for subterranean forces and tendencies. It is only among radicals of the Left and Right that one finds a passion for excavation, for first causes; a Nietzschean "predestination for the labyrinth" is alien to the American soul.

In 1974 Franz Schurmann wrote a book that opened on a note of mystery, Tacitus' *Arcana Imperii*—empire and its method as a "hidden thing," shrouded above all from the people it ruled. Mostly lacking in sources and footnotes, this was nonetheless a deeply learned and observant book, by far the best study of postwar American foreign policy, and theoretically at the cutting edge. Schurmann did for American imperialism and world politics what Karl Polanyi did for the world economy, in a somewhat similar way and with a big debt to Polanyi. But it is in explaining postwar events that his analysis proves itself. The more one knows about the postwar period at the empirical level, the better this book appears; the less one knows, and the more captured one is by conventional conceptions, the more incomprehensible this book becomes. *The Logic of World Power* is now out of print.[22] It is rarely cited, and usually the citations are odd, to the point of misreading. The book suffered a fate for which its own analysis is predictive: if the empire it analyzed is arcane to its own people, so will be the best accounts of it. But, we will resurrect his theory and seek to fill it out.

One initial, mundane observation we may make is that critical turning points in postwar American foreign policy seem to occur in Democratic administrations and spawn major new programs that are then ratified and carried on by Republican administrations; furthermore these shifts seem mostly independent of presidential elections. This is true of the most important turning point in 1950, but also of 1947 and the Truman Doctrine, also 1968, when Democrats anticipated basic moves later accomplished by Nixon in drawing down the Vietnam War and beginning to solve the gold and dollar crises, and 1979, when a critical shift occurred within the Carter administration, anticipating much of the Reagan foreign policy.[23]

Another simple observation is that in each case there was a symbolic bipartisan accommodator: a middleman who goes both ways politically and can accomplish what most people take to be "consensus." Sen. Arthur Vandenberg is best known for this role, but John Foster Dulles was the archetype in 1950, achieving the best of both worlds by helping to hold together a Democratic administration, then going on to become secretary of state in the Eisenhower administration. Clark Clifford would be the key figure in 1968, although Henry Kissinger would run him a close second. Clifford substituted for the roundly loathed Robert MacNamara (excoriated by the military branches and leftist students alike), and provided stability through the Johnson resignation. In 1979, Zbigniew Brzezinski would be the best candidate. The foreign policy crises of the Carter period were the tools that he used to assert his power with the president, to best his bureaucratic rivals in the State Department (Cyrus Vance and his cohort of establishment types who had "lost their nerve," according to Jeanne Kirkpatrick), and to inaugurate the fundamentals of the Reagan foreign policy.[24]

So, the argument thus far is that critical shifts in one administration, usually Democratic, are ratified in the successor administration, usually

Republican; there will be a prominent person who symbolizes and helps to accomplish the accommodation. Elections and party politics seem to have little do with it. But the causes of this pattern remain to be assessed. What explains those critical shifts that do occur? What accounts for the apparent insulation of foreign policy from the electoral process?

Incomprehensible Incrementalism and the American Egg

Few foreign countries replicate the American passion for area studies, but when they do send their "American studies" experts to our shores, the typical remark is that American elections, party conventions, indeed the political system itself, are strange, mysterious, incomprehensible. One hears this most from communist travelers, but also from garden-variety Europeans. What can Americans possibly find interesting in the (to a European) manic competition between candidates differing infinitesimally on the issues? Why all the hoopla amid all the incrementalism? The answer begins our theoretical sketch: incomprehensible incrementalism is the result of marginal adjustments and trade-offs in a nation that disagrees fundamentally about next to nothing. America is the most thoroughly capitalist of all societies, and is in that sense unique. Furthermore its bourgeois freedom was mostly a "found" freedom, found by migrants escaping a far more complex and historical class structure.

As Louis Hartz argued,[25] the absence of feudalism in America predicted the absence of socialism and a rooted political Left. A "born free" country has little comprehension of unfree societies, and vice-versa. A deep, abiding, and largely unexamined "consensus" is so rooted that it is not a matter for conscious reflection (i.e., it is a species of Gramscian hegemony), and therefore Americans conceive of themselves as people without ideology. The Hartzian argument ignores episodic/spasmodic class conflict, and the regions (more often islands) in the United States where class conflict is evident. Nonetheless wherever one looks on the American Left in the past century, on inspection one finds European peasants and immigrants (the Wobblies); dying, dependent peripheries (the Non-Partisan League); collective upward mobility for aggrieved minorities (Jews or blacks in the American Communist Party in the 1930s); isolated places that are exceptions proving rules (Harlan County); or morally outraged students and intellectuals. In all cases, the leftism seems to disappear in the solvent of second generations, personal "maturity," individual and collective mobility, and the immense capacity of American productive forces to continue expanding the economic pie. Viewed *comparatively*, America is unquestionably what Hartz said it was.

The relative absence of sharp class conflict gives you an incremental politics. We may liken this to a shifting oval, or egg, around a mix of states and markets within an advanced capitalist system.[26]

Does this have anything to say about foreign policy? For Hartz, his conception predicted a sharp clash of America with the rest of the world, each incapable of comprehending the other. He hoped—it was no more than a hope—that as America interacted with the world at large, it would develop that "spark of philosophy," that relative sensibility, that would enable Americans to live with and in the rest of the world, and ultimately to transform the unique qualities of the United States about which Hartz was so deeply ambivalent. The problem is in convincing a people that thinks its goals are self-evident and universal, that it is bound by its history and particularity. Benedict Anderson writes that "no nation imag-

Figure 1. The Limits of American Politics

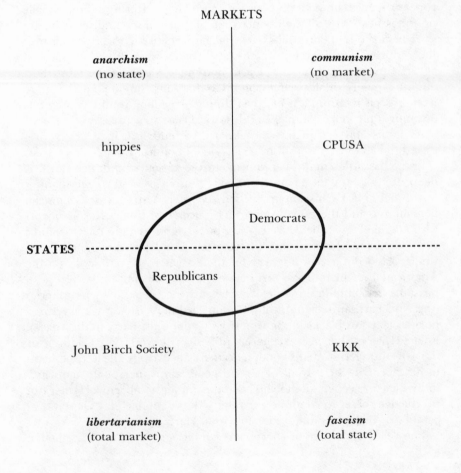

ines itself coterminous with mankind," the imagined community of the nation is finite in this sense.[27] But the minute he says it, it occurs that the United States might be the exception to that rule.

The struggle against communism, Hartz thought, would take a peculiar form because Americans had no comprehension of why anyone would be a communist. "There is more than a touch of irony in the fact that circumstances of national power should have made of America the leader of the resistance to the Bolshevik revolution. It is as if history actually had an interest in the vivid doctrinal contrast. For a fragmented liberalism is of course the most powerful manifestation of the bourgeois tradition that can be found."[28]

The external world is both an abstraction and a source of events that detonate crises at home, indeed those events that are utilized in domestic conflicts over power. The external crisis has never yet taken the form of all-out struggle with the uncomprehended global adversary. If one did not know this, it would be very difficult to explain the fixation of the Truman years on "Formosa," of the Eisenhower years on Quemoy and Matsu, of the Kennedys on Cuba, of Lyndon Johnson on Vietnam, of Carter on an Islamic Republic in Iran, or of Reagan on Nicaragua or Grenada. Why else would a hegemonic power successively repeat this remarkable diversion of its attentions to the peripheral, indulge this instinct for the toenail? Thus, as a first approximation, we may say that the world is the source of harsh reality and conflict that does not exist, in great measure, at home. World events do not cause crises, so much as detonate raw material at home; and after the explosion, what we call "foreign policy transition" is the output of that domestic conflict, the events of the rest of the world still remaining basically an abstraction. Foreign crises also tip the balance of power within the state toward the executive, who potentially can use crises to best his enemies.

The best example of this conception is the "China" issue in the early postwar period, which was not really about who lost China, but about power struggles and alternative conceptions of the American political economy going back to the early 1930s, that is, it was also a struggle over the New Deal and the role of the state in American society. Its virulent proponent, Joseph McCarthy, sought a purge within the state. Events in China (and Korea) were the ostensible causes of this power struggle, but they really were blasting fuses for gunpowder that was very dry in domestic politics.

Now, we seem to have a contradiction in the argument: on the one hand, Americans scrap over incremental issues, and class struggle is muted or nonexistent. On the other, alternative conceptions of political economy compete and conflict, not an incremental matter. We can resolve this seeming contradiction by looking at the American state.

The State as Object and Result
of Class Conflict

American society did have a critical turning point in the early 1930s, when the manifest class conflict during the depression produced a basic change in the party system and the relationship between state and society. The Republicans remained a party of business (Ferguson), "the interests" (Schurmann), or accumulation (Wolfe et al.). The Democrats, however, turned into a business/labor party (Ferguson), the "party of ideology" (Schurmann), or the party of legitimation (Wolfe).[29] In the elaboration of the New Deal bureaucracies, the state became an object of class struggle, as well as an arena of upward mobility for minorities. The demands of workers and minorities were expressed through political parties and branches of the state administration; the state was not the agent of a ruling class so much as the object and resultant of a conflict of interest among different classes and groups, especially between capitalist attempts at control from above and people's attempts at control from below. At the same time, the New Deal state expressed the interests of and functioned to give cohesion to the hegemony of a rising group of capitalists, which Ferguson calls an "hegemonic bloc." It guaranteed the interests of a new, multinational capitalism conceived of as a holistic, structural entity, rather than this owner or that firm. This bloc needed the state to support its outward thrust to the world. But the state also extended downward through the reaches of American society to absorb and protect working-class and minoritarian interests against a weaker form of capitalism that could not abide unions or civil rights. This is what is meant by the "relative autonomy" of the capitalist state (open to the assertion of interests by both the ins and the outs, but still functioning to preserve capitalism as a system).[30]

Since the 1930s the state has thus been an arena of conflict within the capitalist class (although by no means just that alone), the two sides resolving to an advanced-technology, labor-accommodating, national and international capital increasingly organized into huge bureaucratic hierarchies called corporations, seeking profits and taking the world market as the target; and declining, labor-sensitive (and therefore union-hating) local and national capital organized in small and often individually-held firms, seeking control and taking the American market as its target.[31]

The foreign policy output of these two tendencies is said to be, in the conventional account, responsible internationalism versus irresponsible isolationism, but Schurmann is correct to term the two tendencies imperialism/internationalism and expansionism/nationalism. The isolationists just wanted isolation from Europe; they tramped through Central America and Asia in search of markets, minerals, and cheap labor. The internationalists were imperialists, we might say high imperialists: their model was England, and their goal was the organization of great spaces in the world (what the Council of Foreign Relations called in the early 1940s our "Grand Area"[32]) for profit and enlightenment. They looked after the whole.

Viewed in this manner, American politics is indeed a hidden politics; we do not hear about all this on the evening news. Yet such conflict has shaped every administration since 1932. Here we also find the delicious, often hilarious, and yet mysterious vignettes of our politics that seem "crazy"; the spoutings of these two whales are as strange as Chinese two-line struggles. H. L. Hunt, an archetype of the nationalist current, spent millions of his billions bankrolling groups and propaganda arguing that the Rockefellers were communists engaged in a global conspiracy; the hard fact at the bottom of this line was national oil versus world oil, Texas capital versus New York capital. John Maynard Keynes and, let us say, Sumner Welles, were British or British-mimicking homosexuals who were architects of the New Deal political economy and of internationalist foreign policy, respectively. J. Edgar Hoover (chief gendarme of the ex-pansionists—at home and in Latin America) sent his men to spy on Welles's liaisons in Washington's public toilets, thereby accumulating the essential evidence that there was, indeed, the pinko-queer global conspiracy that right-wingers talked about.[33]

The humor (and cruelty) of this raucous politics obscures an important analytical point. It all takes place within the American egg, about issues that take on world-historical importance to those involved, even though all sides agree on what Europeans would take to be "the fundamentals." The vehemence over incrementalism is therefore incomprehensible to foreigners. The battles are, moreover, fought with a European vocabulary, so that an effete Eastern blue-blood capitalist like Alger Hiss becomes a "communist," and the sphinx-like, unprepossessing, and shy billionaire H. L. Hunt becomes a "fascist." Yet the truth is, the vast majority of Americans have never seen a communist or a fascist.

This conflict over alternative conceptions of the American political economy expressed itself within the American state, indeed within its important bureaucracies, which often either took sides in the struggle (Commerce vs. Treasury), or had contradictory tendencies within (the Agriculture Department during the New Deal; the Central Intelligence Agency in the 1950s, the latter actually being several CIAs: the CIA of the liberal, academically-inclined intellectuals; the CIA of the clandestine cowboys in East Asia; elements linked to the FBI who mistrusted elements linked to the British and allegedly to the Philby conspiracy, and so on). The knock-down, drag-out conflicts of the Navy and the Air Force in the early postwar period also reflected alternative world views and alliances with the two sides.

The strife also led to rumors of that thing least associated with stable American democracy: the coup d'etat. It is interesting for the subject of this book that the rumors came first in the alleged conspiracy against FDR in the mid-1930s to which Douglas MacArthur was purportedly linked;[34] and again when MacArthur was sacked by Truman in April 1951. In other words the rumors flew at the time of the greatest domestic crisis, the depression, and the greatest postwar foreign policy crisis, called the "Truman-MacArthur controversy." One could also cite Robert Kennedy's worries about a military coup during the Cuban Missile Crisis, or Watergate at another critical turning point, thought by many foreigners (especially the Chinese) to have been a coup against Nixon.

The Executive and the Interests

If one looks at the American state this way, then the question of who is president becomes important: not because of elections, but because of the requisites of fighting the struggle within the state. The president, unlike the vested and particular interests represented by the bureaucracies, speaks for the nation and has an autonomy, a realm of action, that no one else has. The executive therefore becomes, in Schurmann's theory, the analogue of the Schumpeterian entrepreneur in the economy: he stirs up the interests (or smashes them, like Stalin), breaks the routine, introduces new ideas, reflects and draws upon new currents and interests in the society at large. Not all presidents do this, of course: in fact several do not.[35]

The executive—the president and his staff in the American system, although a member of the staff may now and then become the "executive"—differs from other elements in the state and the society by having a complex and often indeterminate relationship to particular interests. The chief executive embodies the national will, represents the aspirations of the broad society, symbolizes an "imagined community" of nationhood,[36] or may act on behalf of "interests" that arise outside the national boundaries. The maximum leader may be anointed or elected by a set of particular interests, but he must reach beyond them to a larger constituency that does not necessarily share those interests. The recent structuralist literature develops this insight, emphasizing an autonomy for the state that somehow is concerned with system maintenance, with the broad field in which activity occurs, not just the pursuit of individual or class interest. The state is not simply the executive arm of the bourgeoisie, but guarantees the field on which the bourgoisie plays. The executive's key role inheres in his sway over the whole field.

In his long dialogue with Marx and Hegel, Max Weber elaborated on states as forms of domination and bureaucracies as rational-legal mechanisms of rule, of typically-defined form. But he said little about what larger interest or agent the state and the bureaucracies would serve, indeed what the relationship was between the state and civil society. But from Weber's work onward it was simple to construct a model of rationality for the bureaucrat, and to understand that particular bureaucrats would pursue interests that would benefit particular bureaucracies.

From this we get various conceptions of how "bureaucratic politics" explain foreign policy decisions. The best-known example is Graham Allison's model of bureaucratic organization and process, as applied to the Cuban Missile Crisis.[37] This postulates among other things that where bureaucrats *sit* in the state bureaucracy will determine where they *stand* on foreign policy decisions, and that those decisions will therefore take on the character of a mosaic, the resultant of a process of decision in which various departments are represented. The Navy will have different interests than the Army, or the State Department, and as they interact to make policy, no one will get all of what they want, but each will get some of what they want.

Allison shrewdly used his conception to criticize, if not completely to bury, the notion that something called the "national interest" (his "Model I") can be rationally known. For if foreign policy decisions are merely a mosaic of competing interests, there is no such thing as the national interest. Such a model, however, has difficulty in accounting for the role of the president in foreign policy, and indeed Kennedy's decisions over Cuba in 1962 seem to betray a conception more general than the sum total of the advice he got. The state is not just a set of institutions, but has an executive who is charged with looking after the whole, and who effects decisions that may look quite unlike a mosaic of summed-up interests.

The executive also has a different relationship to nation and society, to political constituencies, when compared to other elected officials. He is the only one responsible to the whole. But more than that, the executive may in a sense deploy the whole to get his way, by reaching over the state bureaucracies to society and building support for his policies through the use of ideology, the rhetoric of patriotism, personal style—that is, charisma in some form. The chief executive has the potential for charisma built into his office, which he may or may not be effective in using. Some executives are charismatic in themselves (Roosevelt, Mao Tse-tung, Reagan) while some may use the office to "achieve" a charismatic presence (perhaps Dwight Eisenhower or Deng Xiaoping).

Charisma is a name we may use to signal that the relationship between the leader and the masses is, as Marx says, vexed; that both in the acceptance of a leader (Roosevelt) and in his rejection (Nixon), no simple theory of interest can grasp the totality of that relationship—for it may involve one's relations to one's parents, a Jungian archetype of the father figure, the myriad ways in which humans respond to the cloak of authority, or the inexplicable way in which community is (or is not) established between a particular leader and an entire society.

Schurmann's model of the executive is taken from his study of China, and of Mao Tse-tung. When Mao said before the Cultural Revolution, "I am alone with the masses, waiting," that epigram symbolized his determination to mobilize society against "the interests," against the encrusted privilege of a new stratum of party and government bureaucrats. But Schurmann's rendering of this relationship does not get us beyond Marx's early formulation; he merely substituted words like "ideology" and "vison" to denote but not further to explain the reasons why executives come to symbolize a common weal, or how they may deploy civil society against the state.

The executive may also respond to supranational considerations, exemplified by statements that such-and-such piece of geography is vital to the national interest, or that a distant event forces unpopular decisions at home, or that for insufficiently stated reasons it is no longer important to maintain a direct relationship between the dollar and gold. This will often prompt domestic opponents to charge that the executive is the agent not just of domestic but of foreign interests. Yet executives somehow are among the only people to escape the dire penalties placed on citizens for serving foreign interests. In some sense the postwar American president has also been the executive of the world (that world identified for example as the "free world"); and to those who take the American nation as their "unit of analysis," such an executive may look to them like an international construct. So, an executive looks after the whole, is somehow above narrow interest, is somehow both outside and inside what we call the state, and if we define the state as a set of relationships, those relationships may even mean that an American chief executive is an executive for some larger world.

Truly dominant executives will fight on two fronts: domestic policy and international policy. There have been only two of these, FDR and Nixon. Reagan fought on the domestic front, launching assaults against various bureaucracies; he succeeded against the weaker ones, like the Department of Education and the National Endowment for the Humanities. But he rarely fought on the foreign front (except for the bizarre forays of Oliver North), which requires dramatic initiatives, new alliances, wars. The Truman period is most interesting in this sense because there was one dynamic executive, Acheson, fighting on the foreign front (while Truman tried to hold onto a modified New Deal on the domestic front); yet the domestic opposition had an archetypal heroic executive who was exclusive suzerain of Japan and his "Anglo-Saxon lake" (the Pacific), and who wanted to rule all East Asia. Thus it was that MacArthur and his backers mounted the strongest assault against liberal or internationalist hegemony in the postwar period.

Internationalism / Imperialism and Expansionism / Nationalism

Internationalism or imperialism is not difficult to define. It is Polanyi's "liberal creed" writ large, resting on indirect rule and the principles of the market, the open door, "relying on the support of the trading classes, and using largely *laissez-faire* and free trade as its methods."[38] We might add that in the postwar period the hidden hand emerged as a set of regulatory rules and institutions from Bretton Woods in 1944 onward, the New Deal extended to the world to create a regulated open door, but otherwise Polanyi's conception is apt.

Polanyi contrasts the liberal creed to "the principle of social protection," aiming to conserve man and nature but also "productive organization"; here the state is not the facilitator and organizer of an outward thrust into the world market but the agency for protecting society against the backwash of world competition. This is the theory of the state, how ever much it may be unconscious, carried by the expansionist/nationalist current. The state should protect against the world, or aid in the conquest of chunks of it, but should stay out of the domestic market. Thus American expansionists could call for a minimal state at home while demanding protective tariffs and while supporting agencies of the state that threaten liberty: a strong FBI (often to guard against combination at the workplace), a strong intelligence agency (to spy on enemies at home and abroad, the preferred apparatus being military intelligence), and strong Marines (to intervene abroad). Out of this we get the genus *Americanus nationalisticus*, a seeming contradiction in terms from 1945 to 1980, but now with us again.

Expansionism expresses the direction, motive, and content of nationalists abroad. It moves like an amoeba, attaching contiguous territory and possessing it exclusively, growing out of an inclination to see economic and national competition as a zero-sum game. The empirical and incremental quality of such an orientation begets an inherently illogical, contradictory motion wholly alien to a hegemonic internationalist. We will have occasion to explore this illogic later on, but here we may simply mention card-carrying American nationalist John Wayne, who committed apostasy on his constituency by supporting the Panama Canal Treaty during the Carter administration. Why? Because he was a personal friend of Omar Torrijos, president of Panama.[39]

Expansionists look West, toward the frontier and Asia, and sometimes South, mainly to Central America and the Caribbean; imperialists look East, toward Europe, or to the "Far East" as an extension of the interest in Europe. They meet (and will meet in this volume) in those distant regions where, in John Hay's words, "the Far West becomes the Far East." Schurmann hints at this perspective, but the best account is Richard Drinnon's *Facing West*. His is the story of an empire chasing the setting sun, and in our time, finding a set of rising suns in Asia: "a straight line of march drawn by its length almost into a circle."[40]

It will not surprise the reader to say that the domestic expressions of the internationalist and nationalist currents squabbled at home and in the state apparatus over domestic issues, such as the role of the state in the economy. But the scrapping over foreign policy was less intense, more of an abstraction. The curious "lateness" of America's full involvement with the world, coming only in the 1940s, meant that foreign policy had a remarkable autonomy within the American state. Those bureaucracies that dealt with it were manufactured overnight from 1941 to the early 1950s, except for the British-modeled and often ineffectual Foreign Service.

This relative lateness derived from the protection of the British Navy and two great oceans and the still unplumbed, immense, and productive national market; most American capitalists in 1950 did not care much about investments in the world market. Only certain capitalists did: international oil companies, industries facing competition in Europe (like chemical firms), various trading outfits, and so on. For most Americans, the business of America was business in America. Thus "foreign policy" often was the mere reflex of special interests: oil companies in the Middle East, banana companies in Central America, trading firms in East Asia. Foreign policy experts were mostly products of the Eastern establishment, not rooted in broad social forces in America, and often resembling foreign (i.e., British) implants or what Maurice Meisner in a different context has called "internal foreigners."[41] Thus foreign policy makers had tremendous autonomy most of the time, but significant vulnerability in crises. In the early postwar period, autonomy and vulnerability meant that those state bureaucracies dealing with foreign policy would be the objects of power grabs and internecine rivalry, which indeed they were.

The Parameters of American Foreign Policy:
Internationalism, Containment, Rollback

Since Aristotle it has been recognized that political conflict will often be resolved through a conflict of threes: there will be two "extremes" shaping a middle, or vice versa. In bureaucratic politics, the most banal form of this discord, policy options will take the form of option A and option C, both of them unacceptable and extreme, leaving the preferred option, "B " as the obvious choice. Among our presidents, Richard Nixon was most wont to think in such manner, in syllogisms like this: "Well, some people want me to bug out of Vietnam today. Others say, bomb 'em back to the Stone Age. Now, I'm taking the middle course. Tomorrow we will invade Cambodia." In the crisis of 1949–1951—the crucible from which foreign policy has issued forth ever since—there was also a conflict of threes.

One "extreme" was left-internationalism, really globalism or one-worldism, symbolized by Henry Wallace and attractive enough to FDR to make him appear to his opposition as the leading symbol of this current. The other "extreme" was rollback, the ultimate goal being the erasure of communism and the obviating of alliances, toward an ideal of global American unilateralism. Both are capitalist views: Wallace wanted world markets for Midwestern grain surpluses, although of course not only that; rollback meant American national capital in world-ranging conflict with everyone else for scarce goods. Henry Wallace was vice-president in 1944. By 1948 he was in eclipse, ridiculed mercilessly for his association of convenience with some American communists. In 1947 James Burnham published a book arguing for an American world empire, based on exclusive possession of the atomic bomb. The book was widely thought to be hysterical if not insane. By early 1950, Burnham's rollback views had significant influence in the Pentagon and other bureaucracies.

In the late 1940s and early 1950s, this conflict-of-threes shaped the consensual midpoint of the American political spectrum: it shifted it decisively rightward, excluding the Wallaces and including the Burnhams; the parameters of acceptability by 1950 ran from cold war liberals like Hubert Humphrey or Americans for Democratic Action (although ADA was on the borderline, just as it sought to draw a line excluding those to its left) to Burnham and William F. Buckley, both of whom founded *The National Review* in 1956. Curtis LeMay was in and Sumner Welles was out. In the critical arena of atomic weapons, Edward Teller was in and Robert Oppenheimer was out.

But it is rare to find mention of rollback as having any centrality in this period; if it is mentioned, it is seen as an extreme that had little influence, something demented, or something associated with the post-1952 hysteria and bombast of John Foster Dulles. Only observant foreigners, like Godfrey Hodgson, have understood how central rollback was in the 1949–1951 crisis.[42]

Now, this anecdotal account is not enough to make our point. If internationalism and expansionism were the two broadest tendencies, if foreign policy had great autonomy within the American state, if the state was the object of intraclass struggle; and if two "extremes" shaped the center and therefore the matrix of acceptability and decision, how can we conceptualize the three tendencies? I would sketch them out as follows.

INTERNATIONALISM / IMPERIALISM

We might simply call this Roosevelt's New Deal for the world: a regulated, managed world market system; the open door or "Grand Area" mixed with regulation, the openness or absence of obstacles being essential to free trade and economic growth, the regulation necessary to tame economic depression and unruly nations. The essentials of this world vision would be:

Metaphor: the open door

Economic Content: Nonterritorial imperialism, a regulated open door, a world economy made safe for free trade, an absence of obstacles (i.e., protectionism), a grand area encompassing the globe with the United States as the hegemone looking after the whole—the supreme regulator so disastrously absent in the 1930s, a bloc of high-tech, competitive industries as the engine of expansion.[43]

Political Content: A world under regulated law (the United Nations) with four regulators (U.S., USSR, England, China) looking after the peace through collective security; the Yalta decisions symbolized the practical content, envisioning both trade-offs for Soviet and Western security and an enmeshing of the USSR in multilateral, criss-crossing ties that would hamstring its insurgent impulses (containment by embrace and envelopement); practical U.S. dominance assured through proxy-voting allies and clients in the UN and elsewhere.

Strategic Content: The United States looks after the whole, the allies the parts; joint world policing, with the Soviets recognized as a great power (but known to be merely a regional power) and welcomed into security arrangements; high-technology and maneuverable Navy, Air Force, and atomic capabilities more important than exclusive control of territory and military bases.

Ideological Content: A Hartzian convex mirror radiating classic Wilsonian idealism, masquerading as universalism; human rights and democratization; free trade as the (regulated) hidden hand that would bring progress everywhere and liberalize both transnational intercourse and domestic political and social structures.

Role of the State: The executive predominates within the state, at the expense of vested interests in the State Department and the military branches; presidential foreign policy direction; innovative and dynamic leadership; liberalization of target authoritarian states abroad.

Social Constituency: Eastern bankers, high-technology industries that can compete in the world market, pro-British ethnic groups and regions, liberal Democrats, Navy and Air Force (depending on budgets), intellectuals.

I AM WELL aware that this sketch will please no readers in entirety, and some readers not at all. But it does get us closer than usual toward understanding an internationalist current in American foreign policy that won power in the mid-1930s, fought over foreign policy in the 1940s, and returned in the alpenglow of its decline in Nixonian détente, the Trilateral Commission, and the Carter administration of the 1970s.

CONTAINMENT

Containment was fundamentally a compromise between internationalism and nationalism, a second-best world in which both the United States and the USSR erected political and economic barriers and blockades that made a mockery of Rooseveltian enmeshment. Instead there arose two blocs, the United States organizing by far the stronger one in those (substantial) parts of the "grand area" still left to it, the Soviets attempting to create a socialist political bloc and an economic common or alternative market system. The United States got much, but by no means all of what the internationalist vision had promised: free trade and open systems in the capitalist realm, the rapid revival of Japan and West Germany as motors of the world economy. But bulwarks of defense had to be created, usually with expensive American ground forces; enormous bureaucracies proliferated at home to service the containment bridge-heads. Containment was "option B," between internationalism and the positive nationalism of rollback. Therefore many of FDR's followers retreated and joined Republican internationalists (Vandenberg, Dulles) in a domestic coalition, but this was not a stable realignment before the 1949–1951 crisis. The containment sketch is as follows:

Metaphor: bulwarks

Economic Content: A second-best world of regional blocs, but with open systems outside socialist boundaries and the potential for reintegrating selected socialist states into the capitalist world economy (Yugoslavia, China); economic aid to states on the containment periphery or to defeated rivals bolsters grand area economy and security; a period of de facto unilateralism from 1947–1960 as the dollar holds sway; defense expenditures to maintain containment bulwarks create deficits that prime the economic pump at home (military Keynesianism).

Political Content: The UN as an American instrument, collective security becomes American policing; Yalta assumptions give way to Riga assumptions regarding the USSR[44]; model of Soviet expansion as a mechanical wind-up car (Kennan's metaphor) requires bulwarks all along Soviet-bloc borders, thus reinforcing state structures in Iran, South Korea, Taiwan, and elsewhere; counterrevolution in Greece, Korea, Vietnam, Guatemala.

Strategic Content: The United States looks after the whole and most of the parts; exclusive control of territories and bases near the containment periphery; ground forces constitute bulwarks and require immense expenditures for maintenance, necessitating huge defense budgets and transfer payments to pay for a far-flung empire; allies corralled and disciplined by the communist threat and U.S. military presence in Germany, Japan, elsewhere; various alliance systems dominated by the United States proliferate. The Army prospers, the Navy and Air Force fight.

Ideological Content: Progressivism giving way to freedom and democracy as code words for anticommunism; anticommunism to forge alliances at home and abroad, but muted nationalism to keep opponents in line; realpolitik praxis with idealist rhetoric of justification; sacrifice of means to ends.

Role of the State: Executive-dominant at the inception (Acheson present at the creation), but giving way to vested interests in the bureaucracies as the national security state emerges; development of a Schumpeterian perpetual-motion-machine political economy fed by defense dollars, leading to permanent empire;[45] controlled reinforcement of security agencies at home; abroad, alliances with authoritarian anticommunist states with legitimation provided by periodic human rights salvos and campaigns (the weak, liberalized states envisioned by FDR give way to state bulwarks).

Social Constituency: Initially unstable containment compromise (1947) giving way to stable coalition between Democratic and Republican middle after 1952, with boundaries of consensus drawn by the failed rollback of 1950 and McCarthyism; bankers, advanced industries, agriculture interests get most of what they wanted, but retain potential interest in Soviet bloc; national and declining industries restive and critical, but conflict muted during long revival of Japan and Germany.

CONTAINMENT WAS the resultant of sharp conflict within the American state. This historical compromise established foreign and domestic alliances that were relatively stable after the 1949–1951 crisis, during the long period of American hegemony lasting until Nixon's withdrawal from Vietnam, his détente toward the USSR and China, and his New Economic Policy in 1971. Pleasing no one in entirety, it gave almost every interest something of what it wanted and therefore persisted longer than internationalism or rollback. Given a restive right-wing, trade-offs were required, going by the names of Taiwan, Guatemala, Cuba, the Dominican Republic, and the like.

ROLLBACK

Rollback was the preferred strategy of those elements wholly dissatisfied with internationalism and mostly dissatisfied with containment; it got its strongest voicing in the 1950s, but its only actual (and disastrous) implementation in the march to the Yalu, that is, the only thorough attempt to displace on ongoing socialist system; next in importance would be the Bay of Pigs, an abortive version. But rollback remains to this day a powerful shaping force on U.S. foreign policy, and reemerged dramatically in the Reagan administration, the episodes this time known as Grenada, Nicaragua, Libya, and Surinam, along with the reinvigoration of covert capabilities. The "Irangate" episode that burst forth in November 1986 was a classic rollbacker's calamity, comprising just about all of the qualities of the 1950 debacle, but with the first-time-tragedy, second-time-farce quality that so marked the Reagan period. Col. Oliver North distrusted not simply the State Department, but also the CIA, the Pentagon, and most of the foreign policy establishment—as does the rollback constituency.

Since it barely exists in both theory and practice, and therefore contains many contradictory elements, the rollback current is the hardest of the three visions to sketch satisfactorily. Its ideal was a world absent of communism (communism being the apotheosis of society reacting against the market or the entrepreneur), leading to ominous compromises on other fronts: just as New Dealers and internationalists would flirt with socialism, 1950s rollbackers and 1930s isolationists would flirt with fascists: Hitler, Mussolini, Franco. The American heartland of rollback was the oil belt and the Sun Belt, and of course the right wing of the Republican party. Its stalwarts were industrialists like H. L. Hunt and Robert Wood, military men like Curtis LeMay or John Singlaub, politicians like Patrick McCarran, and political groups like the John Birch Society. Dulles gave voice to this current, as did Nixon, but both were opportunists who moved fluidly through all three tendencies during their careers, riding circuit on the American oval as it were. The grand hero of this current was Douglas MacArthur, but he lacked organic ties with its constituency and functioned as a party of one, which explains in part the 1951 failure of expansionism (Chinese "volunteers" explain the major part of this failure). The sketch looks like this:

Metaphor: positive action

Economic Content: Classic, not Wilsonian, imperialism, territorial instead of nonterritorial, resting on expansion by agglomeration and direct controls rather than indirect, economic levers; exclusive grasp of raw materials and markets (because of inability to compete in world markets); opposition to competition from revived Japan and Germany.

Political Content: Opposition to the UN and collective security; Soviets functioned diabolically, not mechanically; bulwarks were means to an end (rollback), not the ends in themselves; Yalta signifies treason and Riga signifies appeasement (since Riga axioms emphasized Russian expansionism instead of global communist conspiracy); counterrevolution moves from Soviet periphery to Soviet heartland; anticommunism by whatever means necessary means support for reaction everywhere (Rhee, Chiang, Battista, Trujillo, et al.).

Strategic Content: Asia-first, not Europe-first; away from old-world, immoral diplomacy; toward new-world, moral imperialism; exclusive control of territories and bases as means and not ends; hatred of taxes and communists leads to fascination with cheap, high-tech weaponry for obliterating the enemy, thus desire to use the atomic bomb and the Air Force, or another panacea like "Star Wars"; allies dominated and if recalcitrant, abandoned for fortress America.

Ideological Content: Rampant American nationalism, chauvinism with high (if specifically American) moral content; eruptive anticommunism; loathing of unions; frontier expansionism and Indian Wars as models; idealist rhetoric, but a non-Wilsonian idealism resting on entrepreneurial virtues and a restless search for new ventures, markets, and raw materials; Friedrich List or Adam Smith as ideologues, depending on market position.

Role of the State: Strong military departments but weak regulation of the economy; a heroic executive, a gutted State Department; strong FBI and covert action capability; war capitalism is necessary, vast reinforcement of the military branches in the meantime (often as a way to pork barrel for local constituencies). Neomercantilist in its conception of relations between states, but hostile to state interventions in markets at home.

Social Constituency: Declining national-market firms; labor-sensitive industries, especially textiles; independent oil companies; Republican Party right-wing, especially Western and Sun Belt constituencies resentful of Eastern establishment dominance, Rockefeller wing, and Eastern banks that control and provision credit; fundamentalist religious groupings that hate liberal theology or liberals; ethnic groups that resent England or hate the Soviets.

IN HARTZ'S TERMS, internationalism reflects the liberal impulse to transform the world in the American image; isolationism the liberal impulse to withdraw from a recalcitrant world; rollback, drawing upon 1930s isolationist currents in the changed circumstances of the 1950s, represents a reaction against both, caused by the perception of the communist threat as diabolical, and yet sharing with isolationists of the 1930s a general lack of real interest in or connectedness with the rest of the world. Rollbackers are thus true "red-blooded" Americans, the provincial residue of America's "late" enmeshment with the world. This lack of real connectedness explains the habitual propensity of rollbackers toward a self-protective withdrawal in the face of a recalcitrant world, or in view of the hegemonic containment–liberal dominance of foreign policy after 1952. The utter unrealism of rollback policies (proved in the frozen wilderness of North Korea) and the predilection for losing gloriously instead of winning shrewdly (MacArthur) expresses the typical lack of interest in or knowledge of the world at large for these quintessential American nationalists.

The above three sketches are approximations that simply seek to explain more of the variance in American foreign policy than do other conceptions, especially conventional ones that take neither Wallaceite globalism nor rollback nationalism seriously. We may hedge by calling them Weberian ideal types; to some extent the three visions—especially the first and third—may even be mythical, abstracting as they do from a reality that is never neatly configured. But that does not invalidate the hypothesis that people acted on the assumptions. Myths, ideal types, visions, ideologies, and interests mingle together in the mind and in the real world as they shape history.

In any case, the proof of this pudding will be its utility in explaining the course of United States policy toward East Asia and Korea, and the critical and defining crisis of the postwar era, that of 1949–1951. The general categories of internationalism, containment, and rollback give us a new way to order Korean-American relations. The first formal Korea policy, a commitment to a multilateral trusteeship from 1943 until early 1947, marks the internationalist phase. Trusteeship did not work because Koreans did not like it and neither did the Americans in the Occupation, who hammered out a de facto containment policy in the weeks and months after Japan's defeat. Containment won formal sanction in the spring of 1947, garbed in the internationalist clothes of United Nations collective security, but partaking of all the containment realpolitik found in Greece and Turkey. That phase lasted through the withdrawal of American troops from Korea in the summer of 1949; but just as they departed, the rollback option was placed on the table. This had its only postwar praxis in the fall of 1950, but it was incipient in 1949, and it was born by ostensibly strange patronage. One of the first rollback documents surfaced within the State Department in the late summer of 1949, in that den of iniquity inhabited by agrarian-reformer China hands, and penned by none other than John Paton Davies, soon to have his career and livelihood destroyed by Joe McCarthy. But first, let us have a look at containment.

Part I

AMERICA

Chapter Two

CONTAINMENT AND INTERNATIONALISM

It is no longer the case that we can lie in the sun without having to
worry about the Koreans and the Azerbaijanis.

Henry Luce

Please have plan drafted of policy to organize a definite government of So. Korea and *connect up* [*sic*] its economy with that of Japan.

George Marshall, January 1947

FOR A FAMOUS fifteen weeks in early 1947, Washington was witness to a
reorientation of American policy on a world scale. The enunciation
of the Truman Doctrine and the Marshall Plan proclaimed to the public
what insiders had known for a year: that Rooseveltian internationalism
was dead, containment was the policy, and the cold war was on. Like
another critical transition three years later, in the spring of 1950, the
1947 shift adumbrated the analytical elements that signify momentous
structural change in American global strategy. Tremors reverberated
through all levels, from the world system to regional economies to bureaucratic conflict and personnel shuffles in the American state, to exec-
utive-legislative relations, to the political coalition behind the administration, finally to the typical patterns of interaction between the American
state and its public.

It had become apparent that the hegemonic rules and systems enunciated at Bretton Woods in 1944 would not suffice to revive Europe, and
that the British could not handle the problem unilaterally. The inherent
multilateralism of those arrangements would not work with prostrate European states, England was weak, and so the Americans would have to
take on a unilateral and expensive role if European industrial economies
were again to become engines of growth in the world economy. This critical problem spanned Western Europe and Japan, detonating basic shifts
in 1947 that led to the revival and flourishing of the German and Japanese economies as engines of world economy growth, but shorn of their
former military and political power.[1]

From a world system perspective, the United States was the one great
power with the central economic, financial, and technical force to restore
the health of the world economy. Although hegemony usually connotes

"relative dominance" within the group of core states,[2] by 1947 it was apparent that the United States would have to exercise unilateral dominance for some time, given the gross asymmetry between the robust American industrial system and the poverty of nearly all the others. Furthermore, Soviet-American conflict in Central Europe had erected barriers to almost any exchange, a great divide known to Americans as the iron curtain. The original Rooseveltian idea of entangling socialist states in the world economy had been defeated by two critical factors: the slim base of free-trading internationalists in American politics, and the comparative weakness and insecurity of Stalin's Russia, which preferred the sanctuary of a neomercantilist type of industrialization (once socialism in one country, now socialism in one bloc) to the perils of letting the greatest capitalist power get a foot in the door. Maximizing its power close to home through contiguous bloc dependencies, the Soviet program was, as Mao Tse-tung later put it, to build two separate markets, two world-economies, two alternative world systems in globe-ranging competition.[3]

At the level of the nation-state system, the dialectic of conflict between the two superpowers forced nationalist solutions everwhere, hardening the battle lines of military, political, and ideological conflict. In the postwar period it seems the case that periods of sharp bipolar conflict tighten hegemonic controls and alliances, spawn enhanced mobilization in all domestic spheres, encourage political consolidation and repression in affected political systems—that is, two tightly-unified blocs simultaneously polarize global and domestic politics. During periods of thaw and détente, alliances weaken, allies get off the mark and deal with the other side, and domestic political coalitions oriented toward the superpower conflict weaken or crumble. Generally speaking, the 1950s demonstrated the first pattern and the 1970s the second pattern.[4] In the case of Korea, the decisions of 1947 sanctioned and deepened the nationalist actions of the previous eighteen months, making Gen. John R. Hodge look less like a premature cold warrior and more like a sage. Inside south Korea political conflict polarized and repression intensified, with the emergence for the first time of a potent rightist politics. Within north Korea, Soviet controls became more pronounced, and the ruling elements stamped out the opposition. As neighboring China turned from attempts at negotiations and coalition government to bloody civil war, north Korea took upon itself an internationalist duty by dispatching large numbers of Koreans to fight with the Chinese Communists—the first large contingent of soldiers crossing into China precisely in March 1947.[5]

The perfect expression of the way in which containment synthesized world economy and security concerns, and internationalism and nationalism, however, is to be seen in the continuing stress on *interdependence* by high policy makers. They opposed purely national solutions and state-controlled economies, and pursued *regional* economic integration. This, in turn, required the revival of regional motors of growth, leading to support for the reindustrialization of Germany and Japan.

Soviet-American conflict broke up marketing and exchange patterns that had underpinned important regional economies. The bulwarks dropped across the central front in Europe and the developing cold war in Asia cut the Western European and Japanese economies off from peripheral and semiperipheral sources of food, raw materials, and labor—in Eastern Europe, grain from Poland and Hungary, meat and potatoes from Poland, oil and coal from Rumania and Silesia; in East Asia, rice and minerals from Korea, sugar from Taiwan, coking coal from Manchuria, tungsten from South China. With the European recovery so sluggish, Japan still dormant, and communist parties threatening in Italy and France, China and Korea, this structural problem was newly perceived and demanded action in 1947.

Much of the security program established in early 1947 was a ratification and public airing of previous decisions, something Truman noted in April 1947 when he remarked that people seemed to think the contest with the Soviets accelerated suddenly into the Truman Doctrine, when in fact it had been developing since his talks with Molotov in April 1945.[6] But at the level of the state and the bureaucracies in Washington, the enhanced commmitments of early 1947 met continued low defense appropriations, which detonated brawling over budgets between the State and War Departments, and internal wrangling in military agencies in the Pentagon. This struggle also reverberated back to Korea, deeply affecting American policy there: the War Department, tired of footing the bill for a very expensive occupation that was subject to frequent criticism by the State Department, developed a plan to quit Korea.

Personnel shifts accompanied strategic change. The State Department, charged with constituting global policies, came to be dominated by two brilliant minds: Dean Acheson, often functioning as de facto secretary of state under George Marshall (secretary of state from January 1947 onward), and George Kennan as head of Policy Planning. Kennan, of course, is widely known as the architect of the containment doctrine. Acheson, together with Clark Clifford and William Clayton, developed much of the policy and wrote the key Truman Doctrine and Marshall Plan speeches.[7] Both Acheson and Kennan had well thought out and articulated visions of the politics of containment; both understood the world better than the world (and the bureacuracies) understood them.

Another personnel change that had both substantive and symbolic meaning was the appointment on March 5, 1947, of Dean Rusk to replace Alger Hiss as director of the Office of Special Political Affairs. Rusk, one of two men who drew the original line at the thirty-eighth parallel in August 1945, was an archetypal containment bureaucrat; he took on direct responsibility thereafter for United Nations affairs.[8] Hiss was an archetypal internationalist who, in the peculiar European-derived but misplaced political argot of America, would be seen as a communist by his enemies. The change was appropriate, since the United States pursued its containment policies in Korea through the internationalist device of the UN, as we will see, with Rusk nearly always involved.

The foreign policy crisis detonated political conflict between parties and politicians in Washington, with most of the fault lines going back to the 1930s trench warfare between internationalists and isolationists, New Dealers and Hooverites. The administration achieved a great coup in gaining the assent of Sen. Arthur Vandenberg for the new policies; we may take him as our paragon of the bipartisan accommodator in 1947. Behind Vandenberg's shift was an implicit political economy: his state, Michigan, was typical of the Midwestern isolationist constituencies, except for its preeminent automobile industry—which did not fear world competition and thus could benefit from the muted internationalism of Truman, and could lose if the nationalist policies of old isolationists were to win out. (When the automobile industry began losing out to foreign competition in the 1970s, the Michigan congressional delegation shifted toward protection with an alacrity that would make an economic determinist blush.)

The move to containment, as we would predict, produced more repression at home, and detonated new ideological currents. In March, Truman established by executive order loyalty boards to inquire into the political behavior of government employees.[9] In 1947 the Americans for Democratic Action organized themselves as exemplars of a liberal anticommunism that would establish itself as the consensual political preference of most educated Democrats. The central text here was Arthur Schlesinger, Jr.'s, *The Vital Center*, a book full of arguments for detaching American liberals from the Left; the central doctrine was Reinhold Niebuhr's realpolitik morality for the man of the world. Yet just as these views gained ascendancy, an incipient text for a subsequent synthesis appeared: James Burnham's *The Struggle for the World*, coining the term, "cold war," but presciently thinking beyond it toward rollback.[10]

The fifteen weeks also underlined the extraordinary autonomy of foreign policy in the American polity, and the fundamental irrelevance of the American public to its critical shifts—the public as shaped rather than shaper. The United States had real problems on its hands: the decline from empire of England, the intractibility of the world economy, stagnant industrial allies, and at least one "grand area" of the world now removed from capitalism: the Soviet sphere. But only the fourth problem got through loud and clear, and in crude form. Policy makers chose frankly to simplify the major theme to "communism vs. democracy," the better to "sell the public" on it. Truman's salty aide, Admiral Leahy, said in a March 7 meeting, "the people of the U.S. should be brought in and told—it is Communism or free enterprise" (a crudity with a different nuance).[11] Much like the NSC 68 period three years later, congressional and bureaucratic opponents of the new policy were cowed by exaggerated fears of the Soviet threat, ones that went quite beyond the personal views of people like Kennan and Acheson, and that crowded out alternative voices and the other, deeper causes of the shift. During his tenure as secretary of state, Acheson once noted that "leadership requires understanding, responsibility, discipline. The flatulent bombast of our public utterances will lead no one but fools," a stark distinction among what leadership does, what it says, and what Acheson thought about the public.[12]

As far as most people knew, the ostensible crisis was in Greece and Turkey, where through civil war and aggressive intent the Soviets were seeking to bring both nations into their camp. England was no longer able to bear the burden of the Greek civil war, and so the United States had to step in. British representatives touched off the fifteen weeks by reporting that they could no longer pay for the war in Greece, or security in Turkey.[13] But behind this Mediterranean crisis was England's decline from empire, something of dire moment without American cushioning and substitution.

Acheson "carefully kept the central economic factors" out of the Truman Doctrine speech and the general discussion. According to LaFeber, "the economic interests were nevertheless crucial." Truman's address instead focused on communist expansionism, and a defensive American response. "I believe that it must be the policy of the United States to support free peoples who are resisting attempted subjugation by armed minorities or by outside pressures. . . . I believe that our help should be primarily through economic and financial aid." It was George Kennan, of course, who expanded this to a doctrine that became, according to Ambrose, "the touchstone of American policy," requiring "the adroit and vigilant application of counter-force at a series of constantly shifting geographical and political points, corresponding to the shifts and maneuvers of Soviet policy."[14]

Truman openly referred to stopping the proliferation of state-controlled economies in a speech at Baylor University in early March, however, saying that the open world marketplace had to be restored lest a depression occur; the Baylor speech was written by Acheson and William Clayton. The oil of the Middle East was also behind the new policy.[15]

We may say that Greece and Turkey (what Zbigniew Brzezinski later termed the first zone of containment) were to the 1947 crisis as Afghanistan was to the late 1970s Persian Gulf crisis, Brzezinski's "third zone." Whereas policy makers and commentators in 1979 imperturbably linked this third zone to the oil resources of the gulf, in 1947 only radical critics on the Left and Right, and unusually frank businessmen, noted the relationship between the energy needs of the European economies, cut off from Eastern European sources of supply, and the vast oil resources of the Middle East.[16]

Worldly men like William Donovan linked containment and the oil problem straightaway. In a memorandum by Charles Prince on Soviet policies and Middle Eastern oil, Donovan underlined a portion arguing that "oil politics have become power politics," and another passage asserting that the Soviets were trying to organize a "hegemony" over the entire oil-producing region. Prince, who had security clearances sufficient to make him aware of Lavrenty Beria's central role in the Soviet atom bomb project, contended that Middle East oil would be a crucial source of supply for industrial economies in Europe and the Far East, given "the interdependence of all nations as far as oil is concerned."[17]

Barron's magazine in a lead editorial in March 1947 argued more generally that the Truman Doctrine would enhance productivity at home and abroad, and caught the dialectic between our three currents in U.S. foreign policy, labeling them "three roads": one road was to keep trying to make friends by offering concessions to enemies, which it identified with Roosevelt's policies and now with Henry Wallace (internationalism), another road was "to withdraw within our shell" (isolationism-cum-rollback), and the third was "the one upon which we are about to embark." Noting the appealing realism of containment, the editorial said that the two other courses share "a certain emotional affinity . . . [in] a search for utopia." Such utopians failed to take into account that "much of the production and employment which will be stimulated here by our proposed new undertaking in Greece, Turkey and elsewhere will tend to sustain the level of American business, which in recent months has definitely levelled off." Therefore, "Mr. Truman cannot be thanked too gratefully . . . for embarking on a course so alien to that of his widely worshipped predecessor." *The Commercial and Financial Chronicle* supported Truman's external policies but said that the United States must get its fiscal house in order at home, and simultaneously "abolish the New Deal and all its works"—thereby expressing the degree to which business liked Truman's foreign policy and loathed his domestic policy, a distinction that increasingly became the main difference between moderate Republicans and Democrats.[18]

No one expressed the containment compromise and synthesis—fashioning a concord to agree to disagree at home and to intervene abroad—better than Henry Luce in his June 1947 editorial called "The U.S. Opportunity." This was, like his famous "American Century" text, an early brief for multinational corporate capitalism. Americans must become "missionaries of capitalism and democracy," he said, and used as his "classic current example" the archetypal multinational corporation, the American international oil firm. Aramco, he noted, not only developed Middle Eastern oil but built schools, water works, even whole cities where there had only been desert. His next exemplar was an individual named Nelson Rockefeller, whose far-flung activities in Latin America exemplified "the traditional internationalism of the oil business." Nelson was "fired with a great idea": the transformation of Latin America by American capital. In the past American business had been content to exploit "the world's greatest free trade area," the American national market; now, however, big corporations constituted the "front-line soldiers and batallions in the battle of freedom." Among these "great corporations," he listed exclusively high-technology, competitive firms with large international markets: Standard Oil, General Motors, General Electric, ITT, Pan American Airlines, Westinghouse. Here "at the top," he said, American business was "already international." He also mentioned a second-tier group consisting of smaller industrial and sales firms already marketing abroad, like Singer Sewing Machines, Sears Roebuck, and Woolworth. And so, it was "no longer the case that we can lie in the sun without having to worry about the Koreans and the Azerbaijanis."[19]

In defending the Point Four program against right-wing attacks, *Fortune* said it was not "the final projection of New Deal statism"; rather, private capital was the main force behind it. Which of the "good internationalist" firms did he speak of? Standard Oil, Texaco, Socal, Shell, Gulf, Socony, United Fruit, Westinghouse, Singer, Pan Am, General Electric, IBM, and Coca Cola, which was "pursuing the 'Coca-colonization' of the world."[20]

The main arena of expansion for Henry Luce, of course, was Asia. His argument had a particular appeal in the American domestic context, linking multinational corporations to traditional expansionism, that is, linking internationalism and nationalism, Europe and Asia, in a way that isolationist currents could understand. Although widely ridiculed for his frothy rhetoric and his diehard support of the Chinese Nationalists, Luce symbolized better than anyone else the interventionist compromise that grew out of the clash of the containment, rollback, and internationalist currents.

Charles Beard joined this spring 1947 discourse with his interesting study of Pearl Harbor, intended also as a commentary on Truman's policies. The newfound internationalism of American business, he said, "does not, as often claimed, rise wholly above the special economic interests into the pure empyrean of world welfare. If 'greedy' and 'purblind' manufacturers for the domestic market are to be found supporting high tariff rates . . . manufacturers for the export market are likewise to be discovered using money, influence and politics on their side." In his conclusions he said, Truman had now "set out on an unlimited program of underwriting, by money and military 'advice,' poverty-stricken, feeble and instable [*sic*] governments around the edges of the gigantic and aggressive Slavic Empire." In such manner, "the domestic affairs of the American people became appendages to an aleatory expedition in the management of the world." He counseled "a prudent recognition and calculation of the limits on power," lest the United States suffer "a terrible defeat in a war"—like the "wrecks of overextended empires scattered through the centuries." The analysis was penetrating and the prediction accurate, but next to no one was listening on this birthday of American interventionism, which over the next quarter-century placed an average of a million American soldiers a year at some four thousand military bases in thirty countries.[21]

ACHESON AS STATESMAN

No figure is more important to this study, and none more misunderstood, than Dean Acheson. He was the greatest of postwar secretaries of state. Like other accomplished and self-confident men, a mask of himself, indeed several masks, paraded before the public and the different friends and antagonists who knew him. His personality and his policies have thus been subject to constant and enduring misinterpretation. But unlike another controversial and influential figure from the period, George Kennan, Acheson never seemed overly concerned with unveiling himself, clarifying his true meaning, or elucidating historical events. He had an easy contempt for his enemies, few qualms about remaining ambiguous to the *incogniscenti*, and the skills to write history from his viewpoint, as he did in a fine and fascinating memoir that, nonetheless, retains a shroud on several critical episodes in the early postwar period.

Acheson was an American aristocrat, in the domain of ethos if not necessarily material things (although he never wanted for money). His father, Edward Campion Acheson, was bishop for Connecticut in the church and the moral vision of the Eastern establishment, high Episcopalianism.[22] Foster Dulles also had a cleric for a father (in his case Presbyterian). But unlike Edward Acheson's moral calling in the spiritual world, or Dulles's stiff morality in the political world, Acheson's calling was the pragmatic in the material world, with at best a remnant Calvinism—of proving one's mettle in the real world. His self-conception, judged from his voluminous papers and correspondence, came closest perhaps to Aristotle's notion of the magnanimous soul, responsible and

purposive to a fault in one's own behavior, loving and loyal to one's inti-
mates and friends, harsh but just in giving one's enemy his due.[23] On
Wall Street he was known for his "ruthlessly logical mind," an apt char-
acterization of his diplomacy as well. He became a lifelong friend of Felix
Frankfurter, and an intimate of A. Whitney Griswold—historian of
American diplomacy with East Asia and later, president of Yale.

He was also known as part of the Winthrop Aldrich camp, that is, the
Rockefeller camp; he spent many years as a Standard Oil lawyer. Like
John J. McCloy after him, he combined a lawyer's career for multina-
tional oil with central statecraft. Like McCloy and his association with the
Democratic party, or Dulles and the Republican party, political affiliation
was less important to Acheson than charter membership in a bipartisan
internationalist coalition that conferred comprehensive hegemony. Like
Dulles, Acheson would not have been called a premature antifascist.
Charles Higham has numerous examples of Acheson's opposition to
State Department attempts to investigate corporate ties to the Nazis.[24]

Acheson's self-assured pride often made him the best interlocuter of
his own world view; he was, as he said, "present at the creation," and
more than anyone else he articulated a realpolitik credo for a developing
world-system centered on America. His favorite sermon plugged the
multiple virtues of a holistic outlook. He never tired of saying that problems must be looked at in the round, in their comprehensive fullness. He
had an international banker's completeness; the world was his oyster, his
"unit of analysis." His hubris bred condescension for alternative views,
and scorn for the hopes and fears of the unwashed mass. Much like Karl
Polanyi, he began his memoirs with a discussion of the "century of international peace" after Waterloo and the Congress of Vienna in 1815.
"Economically, the globe was indeed 'one world.' The great empires of
Europe, through their colonies and spheres of influence, spread authority, order, and respect for the obligation of contract almost everywhere;
and where their writs did not run, their frigates and gunboats navigated."
He was, of course, a strong advocate of the "wecipwocal twade agwee-
ment pwogwam to weduce tawiffs." Acheson both parodied Cordell
Hull's speech impediment and praised him for "a reversal of a hundred
years of American policy." Acheson was also a charter member of a min-
uscule fraternity, those diplomats who self-consciously followed the foot-
steps of Henry Stimson.[25]

If in 1947 the problem was the Greek civil war, Acheson tutored that
"the picture should be seen as a whole"—if Greece fell, "the whole of
Western Europe was threatened."[26] If in 1947 the problem was worry-
warts who deemed Vietnamese nationalism formidable, French colonialism abominable, Acheson instructed that he could not conceive of any
setbacks to the French that would not also be setbacks to the United

States. If in 1950 the problem was the Korean civil war, Acheson would judge it a war about Europe, or the world, that happened to occur in Korea.

Henry Kissinger became an Acheson enthusiast, and he probably thought of him (as well as himself) when he said that power in foreign policy decisions depends not on process or bureaucratic locus, but on superior capacity to know and interpret the world; a person with this will find his own center of gravity. Certainly this was Acheson's conviction, and his property in the Truman administration. Nothing was in more short supply in a virgin Washington just coming to grips with unprecedented "responsibilities" than a man with a holistic world view, and so Acheson's ascent was swift.

Acheson was Harry Truman's vicar for foreign policy, the executive for the world in Schurmann's sense. Although he did not become secretary of state until 1949, he was the point man for the Truman Doctrine and the Marshall Plan; some also gave him credit as the "chief force" behind Bretton Woods.[27] Acheson was also, we will argue, the architect of Korea policy from the important transition point in early 1947 to the momentous American intervention in 1950.

Acheson outlasted several secretaries of defense, two of them direct antagonists (Forrestal, Johnson); astutely cloaked his own ideas in the persons and prestige of Truman, General Marshall, Arthur Vandenberg, and others; and deftly got his views across to the influential Eastern media, often through the columns of James Reston of the *New York Times*. Always loyal to his president and finding in him an exemplar of plebeian American virtue, Acheson nonetheless was a constant tutor to Harry Truman, an inexperienced man in foreign affairs. The tutelage continued in emeritus as Truman wrote his memoirs, Acheson gently but carefully reminding him of what really happened during his presidency. In a remarkable series of seminars at Princeton, Acheson also coached his former colleagues, like Nitze and Kennan, and shaped the historical record of the Truman foreign policy.

His enemies thought they saw through Acheson's masks, uncovering an Anglophile with a phony British accent who cultivated a dandy's moustache, a silk stocking who seemed so at home in top hat, tails, and striped pants as to be plainly un-American. If he was Anglophile he must be internationalist; if he was internationalist he must be arrogant and effete; if he was effete there was an outside chance that he was homosexual; if he was all of the above he was clearly a communist. After all, he did look to most Americans like the portrait of a Red sketched by Anglophobe Senator McCarthy, like a parody of what isolationists thought about the Foreign Service. Furthermore he proudly named among his friends John Maynard Keynes, Alger Hiss, and Harry Dexter White; he even went with Hiss to brief Roosevelt before Yalta.[28] It would seem an open and shut case. But all this simply skimmed Acheson's surface; the "unmasking" was simultaneously so easy and so off the mark.

What the exterior camouflaged was a sharp, shrewd, formidable defender of Western civilization in the moral realm, and the interests of the American state and multinational capital in the material realm; what captures him so precisely is his inability to distinguish the two. Arrayed against the West and his conception of the good life Acheson, like the old Chinese emperors, saw only varieties of barbarism. Most formidable was the barbarism of Soviet communism. Most irritating and despicable, because it was so stupid, was McCarthy's style of "primitivism." Most irrelevant, to the point of being the butt of his jokes, was the barbarism of Moslems and peoples inhabiting the Middle East and Africa, unless they were active against American interests, in which case they were fanatics. Most mysterious to him was the combined barbarism/fanaticism of revolutionary nationalism in the third world, which Acheson made the dire mistake of underestimating in China, Korea and Vietnam.[29]

I. F. Stone caught this complexity in a fine portrait of Acheson: "nothing could be more dangerous to a public figure in America," he wrote in 1952, "than the mere suspicion of an urbane and compassionate view of history and humanity," which Acheson retained. At the same time, he recalled that Roosevelt had brought him into public service mainly for bipartisan reasons, as the war approached.

> Only in the heat-distorted vision of cold-war America could Acheson be seen other than as he was: an "enlightened conservative"—to use a barbarous and patronizing phrase. . . . Who remembered in these days of McCarthyism that Acheson, on making his Washington debut at the Treasury before the war, had been denounced by New Dealers as a "Morgan man," a Wall Street Trojan Horse, a borer-from-within on behalf of the big bankers?[30]

THE "GREAT CRESCENT":
ACHESON DRAWS THE LINE IN KOREA

In 1947 Acheson established and sustained a containment logic for the next three years that ultimately governed American intervention in the Korean War, regardless of military and congressional opposition. In essence we may say that the de facto containment that the Occupation realized from 1945 to 1947 became in Acheson's mind and practice a de facto commitment to include South Korea in the Truman Doctrine from 1947 onward.

Support for a separate government in the south had welled up to the highest levels in early 1947, coterminous with Syngman Rhee's visit to the United States. At the end of January 1947, Secretary of the Army Robert Patterson had told an interdepartmental meeting that "he was growing increasingly alarmed" about Korea; it "presents the most urgent of any of our occupation problems by far." Some people, he said, think it might be better "to pull out [rather] than to let the situation blow up in your face." The Moscow Decision ought to be abandoned, he said, the alternative being "to set up a South Korean Republic." General Eisenhower responded that he "was inclined to favor a separate republic," because the long-run costs of a "retreat from Korea" would be far worse than the appropriations "to maintain ourselves there."[31]

It was Acheson and the State Department, however, who pushed for a commitment to containment in Korea, reflected best in an interdepartmental report of March 27, 1947, which Acheson personally approved.[32] It began by saying that in the event of general hostilities, "Korea would be a military liability," and thus the United States had "little strategic interest in maintaining troops or bases in Korea." Nonetheless, "control of all Korea by Soviet or Soviet-dominated forces . . . would constitute a strategic threat to U.S. interests in the Far East." In particular, this "would constitute an extremely serious political and military threat" to Japan.

After this preamble, the report bluntly applied containment to Korea.

It is important that there be no gaps or weakening in our policy of firmness in *containing* the U.S.S.R. because weakness in one area is invariably interpreted by the Soviets as indicative of an overall softening. A backing down or running away from the U.S.S.R. in Korea could very easily result in a stiffening of the Soviet attitude on Germany or some other area of much greater intrinsic importance to us. On the other hand, *a firm "holding of the line" in Korea* can materially strengthen our position in our other dealings with the U.S.S.R. (emphasis added).

The timing and context of this weighty paper link it directly to Truman Doctrine planning for Greece and Turkey. Indeed, the impetus for the study came from Robert Patterson's letter to Acheson of March 5, saying that Greece and Turkey were "only part of a much larger problem growing out of the change in Great Britain's strength"; thus it was "important and urgent that study be given . . . to situations elsewhere in the world which may require analogous financial, technical, and military aid on our part."

The planners recommended "an aggressive, positive, long-term program" for Korea, estimated to cost $600 million over the next three years for political, cultural, and economic aspects alone, not counting military expenditures. (Truman asked only $400 million for Greece and Turkey combined.) American troops, the paper said, could not come home before several "safeguards" were in place: a representative government chosen in proportion to the populations of both zones, "some type of guarantee by the United Nations," an "effective Bill of Rights," and, last but never least, "financial assistance and supervision by the World Bank." It was also at this time, with the trusteeship plan foundering, that thought was first given to turning the Korean problem over to the United Nations.

The State Department recognized in early 1946 that the Soviets would not accept the proportional population formula, since the 1945 division of the peninsula established Soviet-American parity, not a one-third, two-thirds split. The Bill of Rights reference underscored State's distaste for Korean leaders whom the Occupation had supported. In an appendix the planners declared the "Kim Koo–Syngman Rhee group" to be extremist, and not "representative" of the Korean people; Kim Kyu-sik was the preferred model of a proper politician, the one leader who seemed to realize the liberal principle. Not so prominent in this document, but obvious in many other deliberations was a bureaucratic struggle by liberal internationalists to take the Occupation away from Hodge, the Army, and "the military minds" that they blamed for the problems in South Korea. This took the form of plans to appoint a civilian "Commissioner," which never came to fruition because Ambassador John Muccio came to play the role instead.[33]

The political recommendations made clear the degree to which the new policy sought to retain some of the reformist bent of earlier State Department planning. But this remained now in muted form, with containment the more important goal, in other words, here was an excellent demonstration of the residual internationalism of the Truman Doctrine. The important mention of World Bank supervision had to do with a corollary of the plan, which was in turn a corollary to the developing momentum for the "reverse course" in Japan: land reform and the revival of Korean industry, with the guidance of "well-trained, top-level management and technical personnel," provided by the United States.

Lloyd Gardner points out that the British "were amazed at the audacity of American policy shifts toward Korea"; M. E. Dening of the British Foreign Office immediately grasped that all this represented "a bold move." In a memo of March 26, 1947, Dening remarked, "I cannot help wondering whether they have thought this all out. But the grant-in-aid to Korea does suggest that the challenge is of world-wide application." It is also interesting that in 1947 Foreign Minister Bevin discussed with Soviet Foreign Minister Molotov places such as Turkey and Austria which Bevin said were off limits for Russian expansion; then he exclaimed to Molotov, "Do you want Korea? You can't have that."[34]

If this interdepartmental study is not the smoking gun, it would be Acheson's testimony in executive session before the Senate Foreign Relations Committee in March 1947 to the effect that Korea is a place "where the line has been clearly drawn between the Russians and ourselves," sending the nonplussed senators into the historical oblivion of discussions "off the record" (forever). But as usual the smoking gun is less important than the logic behind it.

Acheson, like Kennan, always favored limited containment, applying the medicine only where it would work (e.g., not mainland China). The context of the colloquy with the senators concerned those places where containment was merited, and where it was not. After mentioning a couple, Acheson said, "There are other places where we can be effective. One of them is Korea, and I think that is another place where the line has been clearly drawn between the Russians and ourselves."[35] The point was never that the Korean peninsula was vital strategically, but rather that it invoked American prestige and the credibility of its commitments, precisely in the sense Acheson pondered on Sunday afternoon, June 25, 1950, that prestige is "the shadow cast by power."[36] As soon as Acheson sampled the Pentagon's distaste for remaining in Korea, in a meeting with Forrestal and Patterson, he responded that neither Marshall nor he favored a retreat because American prestige "would greatly suffer if we should withdraw." After Congress had enacted aid for Greece and Turkey, he wanted a bill for Korea as well.[37]

The distinction was between what we might call Korea's *military-strategic* significance and its *political-strategic* significance.[38] Regardless of whether Korea was a good place to fight a war or not, the United States was there and committed, and thus had to emerge as a good doctor or cause a perceived weakening of its stand elsewhere. Such logic could survive every military argument that Korea was not important strategically (including the ones made by General Bradley at Blair House in June 1950), because the premise was psychological and political, not material or martial.

In sustaining a containment logic for Korea for the next three years, regardless of military and congressional opposition, Acheson had the support of the president. When he girded his loins for congressional criticism after the Korean War began, Acheson told his staff, "Korea might be expanded. (ie, case for Korea) [*sic*] John Hilldring's letter to me. Barbara has it—gives the story of our plan of 1947, rejected by Vandenberg in 1947." And in his account of a National Security Council (NSC) meeting, also in the summer of 1950, Acheson wrote, "The President asked that we talk with Mr. Pauley and Mr. Harriman and . . . work up the steps which came from Mr. Pauley's report and Mr. Hilldring's recommendations of 1947, and have our records show what we had recommended and the President had approved in regard to Korea—steps which had been rejected by the 80th Congress."[39]

This cryptic reference to Pauley is a tip-off to his thinking. The foundation of Achesonian containment in East Asia was a world economy logic, captured by his metaphor of a "great crescent" stretching from Japan through Southeast Asia and around to India. Although mostly incipient as 1947 dawned, here was the crucial background to Acheson's extension of containment to southern Korea, his later elaboration of a "defense perimeter" in Asia, and his decision to intervene in the Korean War.

A regional economy driven by revived Japanese industry, with assured continental access to markets and raw materials for its exports, would kill several birds with one stone: it would link together nations threatened by socialist state-controlled economies, weave sinews of economic interdependence with Japan and the United States, make Japan self-supporting, and help draw down the European colonies by getting a Japanese and American foot in the door of the pound and franc blocs in Asia. All this fits nicely with a world-system conception of multiple, overlapping, tripartite hierarchies: if the United States was the dominant core economy in the world, Japan and Germany would underpin regional core systems, and help reintegrate peripheral areas as exclusively-held empires disintegrated.[40] The world-competitive American industries had nothing to fear from Japan and Germany, as long as they were kept on capital, technology, defense, and resource dependencies. Korea was in the contingent semiperipheral zone, of upward and downward mobility within the system and palpable threats from the antisystem. If Roosevelt was the architect of policy for a single world, when that conception failed Acheson and others devised a second-best strategy of regional concentrations of strength within the noncommunist "grand area," to forestall the greater catastrophe of exclusively-held, independent, state-controlled economies.

Oilman Edwin Pauley, as we saw in volume 1, led a mission to survey reparations from a defeated Japan in the late spring of 1946, touring Korean and Manchurian industry. He impressed Truman with his argument that since Japan had done much to develop the Korean peninsula, it would be a shame to let its industry and modern facilities fall into the hands of the people's committees, who in his view had done nothing to earn them. He recommended instead developing Korea on "a democratic (capitalist) basis." Herbert Hoover also played an important role, criticizing reparations policies after touring Japan and Korea in May 1946, and arguing against ceilings on heavy industry in Germany and Japan in early 1947. In May 1947 he wrote to Patterson urging leniency for Japanese war criminals and "no further industrial repressions," thus to hold Japan "as a bulwark against the Communist invasion of Asia."[41]

The prime movers during the fifteen weeks, however, were Acheson, Kennan, and Draper. Secretary of State Marshall himself scribbled a note to Acheson in late January that said, "Please have plan drafted of policy to organize a definite government of So. Korea and *connect up* [*sic*] its economy with that of Japan," a stunning mouthful. Army department proponents of withdrawal from Korea on budgetary grounds sometimes wanted a substitution of Japanese influence: Draper said, "over a period the Japanese influence may again develop, since Korea and Japan form a natural area for trade and commerce."[42]

They all thought the solution to the "dollar gap" and the sluggish European and Japanese recovery lay in lifting restrictions on heavy industry, and finding ways to combine Germany and Japan with their old providers of raw materials and markets. Borden wrote that Germany and Japan thus formed "the key to the balance of power," and shrewdly observed that whereas Germany was merely "the pivot" of the larger Marshall Plan program, "the Japanese recovery program formed the sole large-scale American effort in Asia."[43] Germany was divided and held by multiple foreign occupants, and thus remained a pivot; unitary Japan under American unilateral dominance became the centerpiece of the Asian crescent. After the fall of China, Japan's hinterland came to mean mostly Southeast Asia, but in 1947–1948 Korea, Manchuria, and North China were all targets of potential reintegration with Japan. Acheson gave rare public voice to the formula in a speech in Cleveland, Mississippi, on May 8, 1947, where he said that the United States would reconstruct two great workshops, upon which two continents were dependent. The insiders also had help from the outside, as a "Japan Lobby" including Averell Harriman, *Newsweek* magazine, Harry Kern, and various others began beating the drums in January 1947 for ending Occupation reforms of the *zaibatsu* (conglomerate) groups.[44]

The logic for the application of containment to Korea thus unfolded from two premises: the prestige of American commitments, and the reverse course in Japan, making southern Korea a hinterland for Japanese industry and a frontyard of Japanese defense. State Department officials generally identified as "pro-Japan" in the early 1940s urged a nonpunitive occupation and tied Korean security to that of postwar Japan, as we saw in volume 1. Japanophiles could not think of Korea without caricaturing it as a "little Japan," much as supporters and opponents of the Nationalists saw Rhee as "little Chiang," differing only on whether this was good or bad. Hugh Borton helped draft both the early plans and the 1947 document—except that this time he and others consulted with Japanophile heavyweights like Harriman, Hoover, and Joseph Grew.[45]

The interdepartmental report was basically ratified in early May. During a meeting between departmental secretaries on May 7, Acheson described as "decisions" the following: a request that Congress approve a one-year program for Korea "as soon as possible" after the Greece-Turkey bill passed; the appointment of a civil commissioner with the State Department assuming responsibility for the nonmilitary aspects of the Occupation; and this: "the Provisional Government for Southern Korea [to be] set up as soon as possible following the passage of a suitable electoral law." Two days later, as we will see, a cable went to Hodge telling him to defend the South from attack. Acheson recommended a $215 million program for fiscal year 1948 alone. Forrestal and Patterson agreed to the one-year program, with Patterson still arguing that the military forces had to come out (Marshall disagreed with him).[46] Thus the War Department assented to the new program, at least for a year.

Although opposition quickly surfaced to this plan in the military and in Congress, it governed American policy for the next three years. It enunciated assumptions under which the State Department took over the Army's responsibility for Korea in 1948 and developed a Marshall Plan aid mission and a military advisory group that became the largest in the world, bigger than those in Greece and Turkey. It prefigured elections held in the South alone. Whether Congress liked it or not, Korea became one of three centerpieces of the Truman Doctrine—at least in Acheson's head.

The program also surfaced publicly. A big article on Korea in Luce's *Fortune* in June 1947 opened with the line, "After Greece and Turkey . . . comes Korea." It referred to a "new $540 million program" prepared by John Hilldring which would "give the country sovereignty in almost everything but fact," after the United States "forget[s] Russia and does the U.S. best in the U.S. zone." *Fortune* plumped for reviving the Korean economy, especially "eight large and twenty small textile plants." Korea would need oil, electricity, and chemical fertilizer, which the United States was well fitted to provide. Korea was now "the particular proving ground for United States policies and intentions in the Far East."[47]

Interestingly, the secret American planning to extend containment to Korea was reported in Korea. A book published in early 1948 by a leftist aligned with the (southern) Korean People's Republic quite remarkably pinpointed Washington's plans, apparently on the basis of a close study of newspaper accounts. The author, Yi Ch'un-sik, linked the new policy to Syngman Rhee's long visit to Washington (see below) and his desire for a separate southern government; citing articles in American newspapers, Yi thought that the United States also was pushing for a separate government and an army for the South. On the basis of Associated Press reports of March 21 and 25, he said quite accurately that Acheson, Forrestal, Patterson, and Hilldring had discussed a three-year program for Korea amounting to $600 million, that the same policy for Greece and

Turkey was being advocated for Korea, but that more total aid was being asked for the latter. He also asserted that in testimony before the Senate Acheson had linked Korea to the Truman Doctrine.[48]

Although Congress would not fund the full $600 million program, State Department officials came to speak of the country as if it were included in the new doctrine. Thus, for example, Kennan wrote a memorandum to Kenneth Lovett on June 30, 1947, in which he said: "The [Policy Planning] Staff sees only two areas outside of Europe where this Government is committed to the continuation of large-scale economic assistance of the sort envisaged here for Europe. These are Korea and Japan." Likewise, in some notes for Marshall on July 21, 1947, Kennan said: "European situation no precedent for other areas. Suggestions made in Harvard speech [i.e., the Marshall Plan speech] applicable to Europe alone. Problems elsewhere require different approach, main exceptions being Korea and Japan."[49]

But perhaps the best evidence for State's position is precisely the perceptions of the American military, reflected in a memorandum some months later. "You may be interested in knowing," an aide wrote to Secretary of the Army Draper, that

> there is still a strong feeling in some parts of the State Department that we should draw the line against Communist aggression, and that in the Far East the 38th parallel is that line. They consider the Army desire to withdraw as a form of "appeasement," forgetting two overriding factors: (1) holding Korea is useless when we have given up Manchuria, (2) we haven't got enough troops to hold places where we must fight, and Korea is a place were *we must run if war comes* (italics in original).[50]

In spite of military and Congressional opposition, the United States meant to fight there anyway in 1947, should an attack come. That is, the relevant orders to defend South Korea went out during the same Truman Doctrine period in the spring. On May 9, 1947, the Joint Chiefs of Staff (JCS) authorized Hodge to maintain "internal order and authority of the military government . . . using the means available," should the North Koreans attack. Some months later Hodge indicated just what that authorization meant: in a top secret cable he said that "pursuant to" the May 9 directive, "I contemplate prompt positive aggressive action, utilizing the full military strength of all forces, both American and Korean, at my disposal for the purpose of opposing any actual or attempted egress of military or quasi-military strength from north of the 38 Degree North Parallel."[51] In a conference with Hodge on August 27, Gen. Albert Wedemeyer asked if there was a possibility of American involvement should the North Koreans invade. "That is correct. There is," said Hodge. "I got a radio about three months ago [May 1947] which was very specific in answer to that very question." Hodge said he also had discussed the possibility with MacArthur. Wedemeyer asked, "What responsibilities does General MacArthur have . . . in case the Soviet troops are still in power and the Korean troops move south of the 38th? Have you a plan that contemplates his moving troops over here?" Hodge responded, "Yes, we have a plan."[52]

This commitment, about which Congress knew nothing, and about which the existing literature is silent, lasted at least until the last American combat forces left Korea in July 1949. The mission of the commander of U.S. forces in Korea in December 1948, for example, included the following:

> So long as [the] United States remains a tactical military force in [Korea], ultimate responsibibility for defense of Korea south of 38 parallel will continue to fall on United States. This force should therefore be prepared . . . to take appropriate action to repel attack by external hostile forces, such action to be taken upon direction by higher authority unless time and exigencies of the situation will not permit delay.[53]

If that commitment seemed linked to the continued presence of American troops in Korea, in August 1948 Dean Rusk developed another rationale. He remarked that the United States had to "bear the responsibility for the external security of Korea" for the duration of the UN deliberations on the Korean question, because "any attack which might come from the north during this period would be an attack against us and not against the Koreans."[54] Later on we will consider the possibility that such a commitment might also have extended from July 1949 to June 1950.

Acheson never intended an automatic commitment of American troops to defend South Korea. But then containment did not mean that in Greece and Turkey, either. The point instead was to identify American credibility and prestige with those anti-communist forces who could and would fight effectively; American aid and help through military advisory missions and the like would constitute an earnest of American intentions and reliability. Acheson's line drawing in Korea fit with his deeply held view that containment should help only those nations that helped themselves, and that the commitment need not be public or even communicated, necessarily, to the endangered nation. Too many nations along the Soviet periphery were threatened, he thought, for the United States to extend guarantees to all of them; to make a commitment required effective action both by the United States (including a reluctant Congress) and the threatened country; to make all this public only telegraphed high policy to the Soviets, and convinced leaders of smaller nations that the United States would protect them no matter what they did. Both would then encumber the United States such that it could not make its own decisions.

Acheson sought to get these points across, indirectly, to representatives of the regime not on the containment line, Nationalist China. Wellington Koo, Chinese ambassador to the United States, met with Acheson and John Carter Vincent on March 11, seeking to get China included in the new policy. When he asked whether the policy would include the Far East, Vincent replied that MacArthur in Japan and Hodge in Korea were taking actions "to check the expansion of Soviet influence." They also told Koo that containment would be the policy where you have states or forces capable of containment, and that was up to the Nationalists. If China wished to check the communists "in her own way," then the United States "would not bring pressure to bear on her."[55] Acheson, of course, had little hope for Nationalist success. In a cabinet meeting in March 1947, when queried as to why, if containment were the policy, the United States would want to pull out of China, he responded, "Fundamentals of problems the same [in China]. The incidences are different."[56] The "incidences" in Korea were such that containment might work, but they were not so in China.

KENNAN'S ENGINEERING

If Acheson was the architect of containment, Kennan was the engineer. He articulated ideas and developed plans that gathered under and filled Acheson's architectonic vision. Kennan could never look after the whole, he could never substitute for Acheson, for he lacked the latter's skills at statecraft, his Wall Street experience, and at bottom, a hegemonic conception of the political economy of America's world position. But he was a master at placing the parts, at engineering the blocks in Acheson's world city.

The core of Kennan's containment vision was a parsimonious theory of industrial structure. Like Acheson, he was a bit of a technological determinist. Whereas Acheson shaped the grand area into which marched the bloc of world-competitive industries, Kennan had a realpolitik conception of *national* industry: an advanced industrial base was essential to war-making capacity and great power status. We had four and they had one and things should be kept that way. That is, containment meant defending the United States, England, Western Europe, and Japan, but not worrying about every brushfire war or revolution in the preindustrial underbelly, and especially not in distant and depraved Asia.[57] Here was the core assumption that gave a muted nationalist tendency to the 1947 doctrine.

Kennan mixed his determinism with a fond appreciation of Western culture. He reversed the classic imagery of the Chinese emperors: Asia for him was the far periphery of a high civilization that radiated outward from Western Europe. The first drop down was in Eastern Europe, the next was in Russia, most of whose vices were "Oriental," and when one reached China and its little brother, Korea, one truly scraped the barrel of civilization and found mostly barbarity. Japan was the exception in Asia, not because of its petite culture, but because it had an industrial base.

These concise views remained firmly fixed in Kennan's mind, giving his policy recommendations a curious prescience founded in anachronism. Thus on the China issue he arrived at the right conclusions for the wrong reasons: the United States should not intervene in the civil war because China was incontinent and how could you have containment with incontinence? China was "a country with a marvelous capacity for corrupting not only itself but all those who have to do with it"; "you can help any government but one which does not know how to govern." The day would come when those Chinese who now revile American "imperialism" would "long bitterly" for its return. In the meantime, the West should keep out. His opposition to the Vietnam War drew upon the same wellsprings, although few knew it.[58]

This vintage Orientalism existed side-by-side with a shrewd grasp of the limits of American power: "we must realize that there are in China tremendous deep-flowing indigenous forces which are beyond our control." Then there was the simple fact that China had no integrated industrial base, which he thought basic to any serious capacity for warfare. When David Nelson Rowe argued in 1949 that the United States should intervene to stop the advance of the Communists, Kennan responded, "China doesn't matter very much. It's not very important. It's never going to be powerful."[59]

Some places in the world, Kennan once remarked, get Russian domination and "deserve it."[60] Asia was where most of those places were. If China was an opaque miasma for Kennan, too amorphous and corrupting even to make a good colony, Korea was even less capable of acting in history—and therefore it *could* make a good colony. After all, his beloved Theodore Roosevelt, and the scholar he liked to quote, Tyler Dennett, had both termed Korea incapable of striking a blow in its own defense, in rationalizing Japanese control; his cousin George Kennan, whom he idolized, had penned racist caricatures of Koreans in defending Japan's presumed civilizing mission.[61] In the elder Kennan's time few progressives cared much about Japan's annexation of deprived and depraved old Korea—including Sydney and Beatrice Webb.[62] What is amazing about Kennan is that he preserved such a viewpoint in the late 1940s, and even sought to base policy on it. Thus he informed Rusk and Jessup in September 1949:

The day will come, and possible sooner than we think, when realism will call upon us not to oppose the re-entry of Japanese influence and activity into Korea and Manchuria. This is, in fact, the only realistic prospect for countering and moderating Soviet influence in that area. . . . The concept of using such a balance of power is not a new one in U.S. foreign policy, and the [Policy Planning] Staff considers that we cannot return too soon, in the face of the present international situation, to a recognition of its validity.

Kennan went on to footnote Roosevelt's letter of 1905 to Sen. Henry Cabot Lodge, saying that it is best that Russia "should be left face to face with Japan so that each may have a moderative effect on the other," and Dennett's judgment that "Japanese ascendancy in the peninsula" was preferable to "Korean misgovernment, Chinese interference, or Russian bureaucracy."[63]

With American friends like this Korea hardly needed enemies. Here was the author of containment, four years after liberation, arguing for a reimposition of Japanese domination in Korea. Both for imperialists and expansionists, mainland Asia was empty: people without history, people who cannot make history. The difference was that imperialists were content with a vacuum that was "open," expansionists wanted American control.

Only Japan held Kennan's attentions in East Asia, and his new notoriety and strategic placement in 1947 made it possible for him to author the "reverse course," or what we may call the Kennan Restoration—even if he was helped along mightily by Max Bishop and various others in the Japan Lobby. If Acheson wanted Japan revived as an industrial power of the second rank and posted as an engine of world-economy accumulation, Kennan wanted it restored as a regional power of the second rank, hamstrung by the hegemonic power but free to dominate its historic territory. Acheson and other internationalists had a world-economy conception of how Korea and other places in the pullulating Asian hinterland could be hinged to the revival of Japan. Kennan wanted the Japanese back in to butt up against the Soviets, thus to establish a balance of power like that at the turn of the century, and to save the needless spillage of American blood and treasure.

The operative document for the reverse course, developed in draft form under Kennan's aegis in September 1947, opened with a cogent analysis remarkably similar to the Stalinist Zhdanov's conception at the same time, of a two-bloc world.

The present world situation is characterized by the fact that there resulted from World War II a concentration of power in two centers—the US and the USSR; that the relationship between these two powers is one of struggle, with the USSR on the offensive and the US basically on the defensive; that there is now no third center of power to which individual states could gravitate; and that, therefore, a process of political division is occurring, with states thus far uncommitted to either side tending to succumb to the Soviet offensive or to seek refuge in defensive assocation with the US.

The paper envisioned a Japan that would be "friendly to the United States," amenable to American leadership in foreign affairs, "industrially revived as a producer primarily of consumer's goods and secondarily of capital goods," and active in foreign trade; militarily it would be "reliant upon the U.S. for its security from external attack." The paper reserved to the United States "a moral right to intervene" in Japan should "stooge groups" like the Japanese Communist Party threaten stability. Leaving little to the imagination, it went on: "Recognizing that the former industrial and commercial leaders of Japan are the ablest leaders in the country, that they are the most stable element, that they have the strongest natural ties with the US, it should be US policy to remove obstacles to their finding their natural level in Japanese leadership."[64]

Thus Kennan called for an end to the purge of war criminals and business groups who supported them, a bilateral U.S.-Japan peace treaty to be "initiated in the immediate future," "minimum possible reparations," and, in general, an integration of Japan into the bipolar global structure. Later on, Kennan did not shrink before etching out Japan's presumed need for an economic hinterland. In October 1949 he referred to "a terrible dilemma" for American policy.

> You have the terrific problem of how then the Japanese are going to get along unless they reopen some sort of Empire toward the South. Clearly we have got . . . to achieve opening up of trade possibilities, commercial possibilities for Japan on a scale very far greater than anything Japan knew before. It is a formidable task. On the other hand, it seems to me absolutely inevitable that we must keep completely the maritime and air controls as a means . . . of keeping control of the situation with respect to [the] Japanese in all eventualities . . . [it is] all the more imperative that we retain the ability to control their situation by controlling the overseas sources of supply and the naval power and air power without which it cannot become again aggressive.

As if the listener might mistake his intent, he went on,

> If we really in the Western world could work out controls, I suppose, adept enough and foolproof enough and cleverly enough exercised really to have power over what Japan imports in the way of oil and such other things as she has got to get from overseas, we would have veto power on what she does need in the military and industrial field.[65]

It was a masterful performance, this, elaborating in detail what Japan Lobby figure Harry Kern meant when he said of the U.S.-Japan relationship, " 'remote control' is best."[66]

In April 1949 Kennan explored the idea of raising "limited Japanese armed forces" again "for the establishment and use in the event of war or emergency . . . for the defense of Japan, as well as for the maintenance of internal security."[67] A Korean patriot reading these papers (this one was quickly leaked) would have thought them grounds for another war against Japan, and perhaps that is why Kennan, ever the introspectionist, has doggedly held to the view that the Korean War was started because of Japan's resurgence—a hypothesis we discuss later.

In a long discourse on Asia just two days before the Korean War began, he said the United States did not have the capacity to influence Asia, even though many Americans thought it did. "Our public opinion on this subject should be corrected as soon as possible."[68] This was really how Kennan thought about the struggle between Europe- and Asia-firsters in the United States: the latter, like students, needed to be "corrected." It is the view of someone wholly alien to the political process of his own country.

Even in his brilliance, Kennan never could avoid prejudiced asides about "Asiatics."[69] His views on Asia thus melded an anachronistic ethnocentrism, a simple version of the theory of Oriental despotism, a limited grasp of the region's diplomatic history, and his typical belief in the primacy of industrial structure and power politics. It was this strange mélange that informed a draft speech that he wrote for Acheson to use on January 12, 1950, at the Press Club no less. It was more a discourse on history and the mysterious East than a guide to policies that the United States might reasonably follow. He ruminated on "the nature of man," on the "xenophobic," "exotic," and "despotic" character of Asian government (a contradiction in terms for him), and on the balance of power. "Military balance in northern Asia, as Theodore Roosevelt clearly saw, lay with Russian and Japan. You could not lay prostrate Japan without creating vast alteration in that balance to favor of Russia."[70] This was classic Kennanism, but it also marked his differences with Acheson. Kennan could be an engineer in the late 1940s, but never an architect. This was about the last draft he wrote for Acheson, Nitze replacing him shortly thereafter.

THE POLITICS OF STRATEGY: STATE AND WAR SQUABBLE OVER KOREA

The new policies and interbureaucratic struggles of early 1947 set a pattern for Korea policy that persisted down to the outbreak of the war. The

State Department argued for the political-strategic importance of Korea, while military departments argued that the military-strategic value of Korea was nil: it would be bypassed in a general war, and so American combat troops should come out. As Lynn Eden cogently argues, the American military was mostly outside the 1940s debate between internationalists and nationalists, preferring to base its judgments on considerations of war-fighting strategy, budgetary entitlement, and departmental prerogative.[71] Korea policy was no different.

State would combine its high evaluation of Korea's place in American strategy with the fairly unsubtle suggestion that the Occupation was botching the political aspect by ignoring established policies and supporting self-defeating rightwingers in Seoul. The War Department and the Army, however, had tired of depleting strained budgets and footing bills for an Occupation engaged in a highly political struggle in Korea, getting little but criticism from State for its efforts. The Occupation was costing about $100 million per annum. Their hope was for a "graceful exit" from Korea,[72] and so the military retreated to a narrow, general-war based definition of Korea's value to the United States. As often as not, one suspects, military planners hoped that in so doing, they could stick a bullet in State's teeth and see if it would bite. In any case, the military sought to put the brakes on.

The military saw Acheson making explicit and implicit commitments around the globe, with little attention to whether the funds or forces would be available to implement the commitments. The pattern, which continued down to the Blair House discussions in June 1950 and which deeply structured the Vietnam debate in the 1960s, was one in which relatively "liberal" civilian advisors expanded the scope of American commitments, while presumably "conservative" military figures dragged their feet, aware that they would have to implement the commitments—and that if the forces were insufficient to do so, they would be blamed for any failures. The disagreements were not really substantive, but about departmental prerogative and budget lines. Many military figures were conscious of Korea's strategic importance. In February 1947, for example, S. J. Chamberlin, War Department director of intelligence, asserted that Korea had "high strategic value to the USSR," completing "a perfect outer perimeter protecting the Siberian Maritime Province" and especially the base of Vladivostok; it put Soviet ground and air forces "within easy striking distance of the heart of the Japanese islands."[73]

In the absence of congressional backing or sufficient funds, however, military planners had to make realistic assessments and tough choices about the global deployment of America's limited forces, and so they demurred on new commitments to Korea, threatening to "haul freight" as a way of placing the problem in State's lap. Some military people also thought China much more important than Korea, and did not want funds expended that might better go to the Nationalists.

Military opposition to new commitments for Korea burst forth most clearly on April 4, when Patterson asserted that the United States should "get out of Korea at an early date"; all measures should have withdrawal as their goal. He argued that the Occupation was a great drain on departmental funds, that Congress was unlikely to provide $600 million for Korea, and that if it did, this would sap other needed monies. He suggested either that the United States set up and recognize a separate southern government or turn the problem over to the United Nations, both as a means of getting out. An important consideration for Patterson, in addition to the general sense that the War Department was paying mightily for a thankless struggle in Korea, was the likely call on U.S. resources for the conflict in China. The possibility of substantial aid to the Nationalists was still high.[74]

The Army compromised in early April when Patterson agreed to support the State Department program if Congress would put up the funds, and if this would "assure at least a very substantial reduction at an early date of [Army] commitments in Korea,"[75] and as we have seen he agreed to a one-year program in May. But by September, the Joint Chiefs of Staff had concluded that "from the military point of view," Korea was "of little strategic interest to the U.S.," and no strategic purpose would be served by "maintaining the present troops and bases" on the peninsula.[76] The JCS definition of Korea strategy continued to be based on an assumption of general hostilities in the Far East.

The received wisdom on the origins of the war misconstrues certain meaningful distinctions, especially in regard to war-fighting strategy. First, the State Department and the president, together with the National Security Council later on, made American policy. And to make policy, one must consider many things, of which only one is the military judgment on whether war can be fought or is an effective means of policy in a given situation. Second, not only before the Korean War, but also after it, purely military strategy dictated a rapid withdrawal of American forces from Korea in a global war and their redeployment to Europe, something known as the "swing" strategy. Third, a general war-based definition of strategy is a blunt instrument indeed for deciding policy; what would happen if war broke out in Korea but nowhere else? It was never the case in the period 1947–1950 that Korea policy was defined either by the military or by its unwillingness to fight in Korea if war with the Soviets raged elsewhere. Policy remained in the bureaucratic hands of the State Department and the personal hands of Acheson.

The shift of the Korean problem to the United Nations was the means by which the State-military stalemate on Korea was ultimately resolved, but that did not end the essential differences. Until 1949 the basic argument over Korea within official circles continued to revolve around the military consideration that Korea was not a good place to fight in time of general war, versus State's political consideration that the loss of Korea would threaten Japanese and Pacific security and call into question American prestige and credibility. The military never had the upper hand, and there was but one moment when its views were taken seriously at State: when George Kennan briefly sided with the military argument that the United States should cut bait and get out.

Kennan came to agree with the military that Korea was not a good place to make a stand in the cold war, but for reasons the military had never contemplated. In September 1947, he noted that the armed services were leaving "the impression" that Korea was not "regarded as militarily essential to us." About the same time he found "a real likelihood that Korea will eventually become a Soviet satellite" and recommended putting it "at the bottom of the list," meaning after Japan and China.[77]

Kennan thought the military's strategic judgment was important, and had to be taken seriously, even though he disliked their propensity always to think in terms of global war. But more important, of course, Kennan hoped that a revived Japan would again serve as the balancer to the Soviet Union in Northeast Asia. In late September, Kennan recommended that "our policy should be to cut our losses and get out of [Korea] as gracefully but as promptly as possible."[78] A rare consensus between the State Department and the military seemed to have latched onto a stunning option: the elegant bugout. Alas, this point of congruence merely underlined Kennan's perennial inability to read the mind of Dean Acheson; soon Korea was in the lap of the United Nations, and the containment logic persevered.

THE RHEE LOBBY IN WASHINGTON: "I HAVE REAL DOPE RHEE IN DEEP"

The decision on containment for Korea coincided with Syngman Rhee's presence in Washington, and so one naturally asks the question, did he have any influence on it? Traditionally Korea had seen itself as China's little brother, and in one case the Rhee forces sought an unfeigned recapitulation of Chinese politics, in respect to the truly extraordinary influence in American politics wielded by the China Lobby. The "Rhee Lobby," however, consisted of a claque of cheerleaders and hangers-on whose primary attribute was the absence, with one exception, of any significant influence in the United States; most of its members were so inconspicuous that they remain mostly anonymous today. This does not mean that the miniscule lobby exercised no influence, however. In Seoul it had extraordinary access to the presidential office, and in 1947 it played an interior role in the emergence of Korean containment in Washington.

Simply to list the most prominent members of this lobby is to underline their obscurity: John W. Staggers, Jay Jerome Williams, Robert T. Oliver, Harold Noble, Samuel Dolbear, Henry DeYoung, Ben Limb, Harold Lady, Frederick Brown Harris. Only one stalwart, Col. Preston Goodfellow, could be dubbed a man of influence in the United States. Several members went back to the 1920s with Rhee; before Pearl Harbor they established the Korean Commission, a Washington lobby not so much for Korea as for Rhee.[79]

Jay Williams was a Hearst correspondent who began helping Rhee publicize the cause of Korean independence during the March 1 uprisings in 1919. Samuel Dolbear was well-known as a mining engineer, and had been associated with British gold mines in northern Korea in the 1930s. In 1945 Rhee named him "minerals advisor" to the "Korean Provisional Government" and got him to lobby the State Department on Rhee's behalf. Staggers had been a lawyer for Rhee before the war, and Lady was his brother-in-law. Henry DeYoung and Ben Limb were Korean-American followers of Rhee from Hawaii. The Rev. Frederick Brown Harris was minister of the Foundry Church in Washington, D.C., and chaplain to the Senate—which is probably why Rhee chose to join his flock, which also included U. Alexis Johnson, consul in Seoul in the late 1930s, and later an influential State Department officer.[80]

Harris used his publication "Foundry Facts" to trumpet Rhee's case, typifying the breathless and fairly ridiculous quality of much Rhee Lobby publicity. On Rhee's eightieth birthday he vouchsafed that Rhee was "a God-intoxicated man, praying with Christian love even for his enemies . . . [God] is for him the reality behind every sham, the dynamic behind every thought of his brain, every beat of his heart, every breath of his body."[81]

The modus operandi of the Rhee Lobby can be seen in the case of Ray Richards, a Hearst correspondent whom Rhee employed from November 1949 to June 1950. Rhee paid him the sum of $850 per month in addition to his Hearst salary, to write articles through the "Cultural Research Foundation." In return, Richards did public relations from his post in Tokyo on behalf of "purely rightist loyal citizens of Korea" living in Japan. He sent his articles to Rhee's office for clearance, then published them in the Hearst press.[82]

The one figure in the Korea Lobby who can unequivocally be termed prominent and influential was Colonel Goodfellow. His name comes up in just about every significant change in American policy in Korea from 1945 to 1950, from Rhee's return in 1945, which he personally arranged, to the planning for a separate southern government in 1945–1946, to the de facto containment decision in early 1947, and finally to the border fighting in 1949 and the outbreak of the war itself in 1950. Goodfellow is the one member of the "Korea Lobby" worth keeping a close eye on.

Of particular interest to the events of early 1947 and thereafter is Goodfellow's claim that he was personally friendly with Dean Acheson. In an undated telegram to Rhee, sent after Acheson became secretary of state, Goodfellow remarked that "Acheson will be helpful. I used to walk to work with him from 'I' street and had many opportunities to talk with him about Korea." He also termed Max Bishop "a good friend of mine."[83] There is no reference to Goodfellow in the Acheson papers held at the Truman Library and at Yale, and Robert Oliver thought Goodfellow a bit of a boaster, always seeking to impress Rhee with his high-level contacts. However, Acheson says he had close interaction with Herbert Hoover in 1947–1948, and Goodfellow knew Hoover well.[84] Moreover, given Goodfellow's many intelligence ties it is not likely that a researcher would find much mention of him; in any case there is no question of his access to men of power like William Donovan.

Robert Oliver was a professor at Penn State University and prolific author of books on public speaking. Unlike most of the other lobby members, he abjured economic speculation in Korea and stayed within the law, registering himself as a Korean agent with the Department of Justice. When questioned about the speculative activities of others in the Lobby, he expressed little knowledge but no surprise.[85] Other Americans who generally supported Rhee's efforts and occasionally lobbied on his behalf included the influential Republican newspaperman, Roy Howard, the Hearst correspondent Richards, and George Maines of the Johnson newspapers in Michigan.

Several of the lobbyists were classic American expansionists, pursuing a gold mine here or a tungsten contract there, with Rhee willing to trade Korean concessions for their loyalty and whatever influence they could muster in Washington. The Staggers group, including John Staggers, Harold Lady, and some other hangers-on, was frequently absorbed in one or another scheme to profit from their Rhee connection. A State Department official later called them "carpet-baggers who operate at a high level," who were "most active in exploiting [Rhee's] friendship through participation in several highly lucrative ventures in Korea."[86]

Although Harold Lady was just as interested as the others in making money in Korea, he also ended up in a position of rare political influence as a member of Rhee's informal group of American advisors. Generally loathed by the embassy (Ambassador Muccio particularly disliked Lady and sought to keep him out of Korea),[87] Lady and a few other Americans constituted an American embassy within an embassy, if not a state within a state. Answerable to no one but Rhee, and paid by him, they had extraordinary access at the highest levels, often more than his own cabinet.

In 1947 Rhee was not yet president, of course, and the Rhee Lobby had as its main goal the recognition of a separate southern government by the United States: immediately, if possible; through State Department procedure, if necessary; or through United Nations action, if that did not conflict with Rhee coming out on top. This separate government, John Staggers thought, would be prelude to a unified Korea. "Let's get this Government [*sic*] recognized then let the Korean people in the South take care of [the communist] problem," he said in late 1946. The United States should "forget about the Russians" and recognize a southern government. "Then we will take care of the northern situation."[88]

The centerpiece of these plans was Rhee's visit to the United States, from December 1946 through March 1947—he was also present at the creation. Rhee parlayed the minimal influence of his lobbyists and hangers-on to gain access to high-level officials. Rhee even had Secretary of War Robert Patterson thinking he was already "president of Korea."[89] George Maines utilized his acquaintance with his home-state senator, Arthur Vandenberg, to get Rhee an audience with this critical bipartisan swing man. Reverend Harris wrote to Vandenberg, saying Rhee had the backing of Herbert Hoover and Henry Luce, and recommending that Goodfellow be made "high commissioner to Korea." Oliver, Goodfellow, Williams, Louise Yim, and others made the rounds on Capitol Hill.[90]

Perhaps the most significant access Rhee had was to Gen. John Hilldring, whom Acheson found instrumental in the application of containment to Korea. A friend of MacArthur's, Hilldring was "well disposed to deal with Syngman Rhee as the presumptive leader of the south Korean people." Like the "governing commission" proposal a year earlier, the basic idea was to substitute a separate southern government for multilateral trusteeship. Hilldring was deeply opposed to the Moscow accords, remarking that the only way for the United States was "the painful and perhaps hazardous process of renouncing an agreement only recently arrived at to which Russia was a party." Rhee's trip was "a great crusade," Hilldring said, and later told Oliver that "persistent and patient efforts" by Rhee and his lobbyists had "converted first one and then another official." On March 22, 1947, while high officials deliberated on the interdepartmental study for Korea, Rhee released a statement saying that "independence for south Korea will soon be an accomplished fact," citing a confidential meeting with Hilldring.[91]

From that point on, Rhee regularly claimed that he had secret assurances that the United States would back a separate southern government. Although Oliver thought in retrospect that Rhee might have misinterpreted Hilldring's words,[92] it is unquestionable that Hilldring joined others in high positions in Washington who hoped to draw the line in Korea; he probably erred in stating this too frankly to the voluble Rhee. In one of his periodic blasts at Rhee and his lobbyists, Hodge later urged Army Department officials to "have nothing to do" with them; meetings that Rhee had with officials in Washington, Hodge thought, "have contributed greatly to enhancing Rhee's position in Korea."[93]

Meanwhile back in Korea, Hodge thought Rhee was seeking to pull off a coup to go with his Washington entreaties. The general wrote to Goodfellow in January, saying that the Kim Ku group was planning a coup attempt, with Rhee's apparent backing. "Either Rhee doesn't know developments here or he is guilty of heinous conspiracy against American efforts. I believe the latter. Kim Koo [*sic*] gang moving in fast claiming Rhee's mantle . . . I have real dope Rhee in deep."[94]

THE UNITED NATIONS COMPROMISE

In much of the existing literature, the American decision to turn the Korean question over to the United Nations is regarded as the inevitable result of American desires for Korean independence and reunification, and for multilateral solutions backed by the Allies, pursued against Soviet intransigence and its appetite for a unilateral solution that would result in a divided Korea—manifest in the second round of Joint Commission (JC) meetings in 1947, just as it had been in the first round a year earlier.[95] In fact the decision to seek UN backing for America's Korea policy long predated the breakdown of the second Joint Commission, expressed the new American commitment to containment in Korea, was taken unilaterally, and was essentially the product of the State-military stalemate over how to defend southern Korea. Instead of an internationalism that abjured containment—the standard interpretation—American policy garbed containment in internationalist clothes.

As we saw in volume 1, as early as March 1946 an unnamed but important policy maker conceived of the UN as a means of pulling American chestnuts out of Korean fires. The drafters of the interdepartmental study that pushed for a containment commitment to Korea suggested that the United States might want to try another attempt at direct negotiations with the Soviets through a reconvened Joint Commission, not so much because they believed it would bear fruit, but because the Korean problem could not be referred to the UN until Soviet obstructionism was "conclusively demonstrable." Even at this late date the drafters still thought "a period of trusteeship" was necessary because without it "there is likely to be widespread civil war and chaos in Korea." But by now the internationalist device of trusteeship was coming to mean the invocation of the prestige and aegis of the United Nations.[96]

A study on how the UN might help conduct elections and establish "a provisional government in southern Korea" was begun in early April 1947 and was forwarded to the secretary of state by Dean Rusk in early May. Some weeks before the second Joint Commmission opened, the study asserted that negotiations with the Soviets on a provisional government for all of Korea had failed. It noted suggestions that "the United States might initiate steps to set up a provisional Korean government in Southern Korea alone," and that elections toward that end "should take place under international auspices," to avoid "possible charges of 'fixed elections' or a 'puppet government.' " It recommended an electoral commission or corps of observers chosen through UN procedures, composed of "a relatively small number of representatives or nationals of 'neutral' states." To preserve "the desired atmosphere of impartiality," the United States would not formally propose the members of such a commission, but the American delegation to the UN "would probably wish to exercise informal influence" on the selection process to assure that the commission would be "impartial in its composition." The United States would be ready to bear "the entire cost" of such a commission, if necessary. The objective of this policy would be "to secure the widest possible mobilization of public opinion behind United States policy."[97]

The planners described this document as merely informal and exploratory. But, of course, it delineated the basic procedure for the elections that were eventually held in May 1948, as well as the goal of utilizing the UN to mobilize world opinion behind a unilateral American policy for southern Korea alone. Although the Americans thought the Soviets had been intransigent at the first Joint Commission, and by early 1947 expected little agreement with the Soviets anywhere in the world, the move to the UN really came from other motivations. It was, in fact, a nice synthesis of basic conflicts in American policy—the differences between Seoul and Washington, and between departments in Washington. By getting Korea policy deposited under the aegis of the United Nations, the State Department could reassert the virtues of internationalism without paying the costs, that is, gain an image of multilateralism and reasonableness without having to negotiate real trade-offs with Moscow, thus preserving the existing situation in Seoul. It could have containment and call it internationalism.

Within the American state, Acheson could bring the prestige of the UN to bear on his desire to maintain American credibility in Korea, in the face of military and congressional unwillingness to back the $600 million program for Korea. He later noted that the problem was turned over to the UN because the military was pressing to get its troops out of Korea, something that "we delayed until June 29, 1949." In midsummer 1947, the War Department also perceived the virtues of the UN for solving the interdepartmental battles over Korea: if the problem were submitted to the UN, "the United States might be able to prevent Soviet domination of the entire peninsula, while simultaneously withdrawing from what is rapidly becoming an untenable position."[98] Although military opposition to the new policy remained substantial, the UN compromise became inevitable with congressional refusal to fund a big Korea program. The remove to the UN thus became both a means of delaying the troop withdrawal, and a way to pursue containment on the cheap, through a type of collective security.

The nuts and bolts documents that finally ratified this policy show that a classic bureaucratic "option B" came to govern American policy for the next two years. Instead of cutting losses through complete withdrawal (option A), or jumping in with both feet for a big program and a direct, public guarantee of south Korean security (option C), the middle road of maintaining existing troop commitments and a more modest political and economic program persisted as the consensual compromise position, and was enshrined in NSC 8, which governed policy until the troop withdrawal beckoned in 1949.[99]

The United Nations stamp of approval, John Allison told the British, would mean that "the Soviet Government would not then take positive action against the resulting government, for example by invasion of South Korea, because they would not care to flout the United Nations to that extent." The British, however, failed to grasp that UN action was a substitute for the limits of American military power within the general policy of containment. F. S. Tomlinson of the Foreign Office, when informed that Wedemeyer had told British officials "in strictest confidence" that the American military thought its position in Korea untenable, rightly concluded that "this suggests that the whole American policy of American reference to the United Nations . . . was fundamentally dictated by strategic realities and not at all by political morality." But then he wrongly inferred from Wedemeyer's information that the Americans were concealing their intentions: "they are knowingly abandoning their Korean proteges to inevitable Sovietization."[100]

Tomlinson was right, however, to register the unilateralism behind the UN policy. First, it finally abrogated the Moscow Accords. These agreements had, of course, effectively foundered in early 1946 in Korea, but they had been negotiated in Moscow and the United States ostensibly remained committed to them in 1947. Second, as the State Department's David Mark later noted, the United States did not just "divest itself" of the Moscow Accords, but also of the presumed British and Chinese participation in a four-power trusteeship—"without their prior consent" (but then the United States had not bothered to consult them before the Moscow agreements, either).[101] Third, American planners unilaterally ended the procedure to be followed in setting up a southern government under the Moscow Accords. Thus the UN decision on Korea was a ratification of Washington's policy, which was in turn, as we have seen, a post-facto ratification of containment policy of the Occupation going back to the liberation.

Instead of Korea being a neglected backwater in 1947, the new policy was the modal example of the Truman Doctrine as it should have been. As Warren Cohen points out, "the largest outcry against the Truman Doctrine focused on the administration's failure to work through the United Nations." Dean Rusk had encouraged Acheson to rely on the UN in the case of Greece, hoping that it could be turned into an instrument "for preventing or stopping indirect aggression [i.e., civil wars]." Arthur Vandenberg likewise saw the failure to consult and use the UN in the spring crisis of 1947 as "a colossal blunder." Acheson and Kennan were "generally contemptuous of the UN," Cohen writes, which was true.[102] But Acheson's contempt for the UN was just part of the point. For him the UN was unnecessary in regard to Greece and Turkey because the military went along and Congress provided the funds; it was necessary in Korea because they did not.

We may leave it to the forthright General Hodge to imagine the type of government likely to result from American-designed United Nations procedure. First, he assumed rightly that the UN would establish a southern, not a unified government. Then he predicted that leftists would boycott the election, which would give Rhee and his supporters "the majority of the seats in the new assembly." This would then "lead to the establishment of what even we (to say nothing of the Soviets) would call a reactionary Fascist government with which it might be very difficult if not impossible to deal." Thus, he thought, it is probable that "only the fortunes of war will permit a reunion of the North and South. . . ." All this Hodge said half a year before the elections were held.[103]

THE SECOND JOINT COMMISSION

After the new policies in Washington were effectively worked out, Marshall sent a letter to the Soviets on April 8 asking for a reconvening of the U.S.-Soviet Joint Commission. The second negotiation merely parodied the first in 1946; the Soviets in effect demanded the unilateral inclusion of left-wing parties and groups in North and South, by refusing to consult with parties that did not support the Moscow decisions; the United States argued in turn for an inclusion of just those parties, and an exclusion of major leftist mass organizations, all of whom did support the Moscow decisions. The Soviets asked why they should consult with the Right on "how not to implement" the Moscow Accords, and the

United States interpreted this to be a free speech issue, saying any and all should be consulted regardless. By September 1947, USAFIK intelligence put the net result of two years of Commission meetings at "exactly zero," and Hodge told a group of visiting congressmen that he was "very anxious" to see the Joint Commission end, since it was accomplishing nothing except to give the Russians an excuse to keep people in Seoul to organize subversion. At the session on September 5 both sides acknowledged that they could not agree, and stopped meeting regularly. At length the Soviets entrained for P'yŏngyang on October 22, never to return.[104]

The tactics and the relative strengths of Left and Right also supplied a repeat performance of 1946. The Right called major demonstrations against the Moscow agreements in late June, but they got little support; the Right then splintered into its respective factions, some of which were willing to talk to the Joint Commission and some of which were not. Meanwhile truckloads of rightist youths, most of them said by U.S. intelligence to be refugees from the north, raced through the streets reviling the Russians, pausing now and then to fling rocks at their headquarters. Some 425 "political parties" registered with the Commission, their membership said to total 62 million, or roughly four times the population of southern Korea; nonetheless the U.S. delegation argued that refusal to consult all of them constituted denial of free speech. Meanwhile internal reports found rightist parties resting on "an insecure foundation," whereas the "bulk" of leftist parties were "highly organized to the lowest levels of Korean society." The Left had a program and appeal for every class of Koreans, whereas the right-wing "fails utterly in its appeal to the lower classes, since they do not promise them a pot of gold." Kim Ku had mostly lost out to Syngman Rhee, but Rhee's continuing intransigence played into the hands of the Left. "Probably more than any other person, [Rhee] has increased the power of the Communists. He has labelled all those who would cooperate with the Joint Commission, as Communists," and this had resulted in making the Democratic People's Front "the most powerful single group in [south] Korea." United States intelligence estimated in late June, 1947 that "the power of the left wing is steadily increasing in South Korea."[105]

Just before the Commission breakdown, Undersecretary of State Robert Lovett addressed a letter to Molotov calling for a four-power conference to resolve the Korean problem,[106] something no one in Washington expected the Soviets to accept; it was merely the last prelude to moving the problem to the UN. The United States was not prepared for the Soviet response, however: on September 26 the Soviets called for an immediate withdrawal of all foreign troops from Korea. In the absence of documentation, it is difficult to know what the Soviets had in mind. As early as October 1946, Soviet political advisor Gerasim Balasanov had told Arthur Bunce that "the Soviet government was very anxious to have a withdrawal of both Soviet and American troops from Korea." Balasanov's statement was widely discussed in Washington at the time, and had prompted Hilldring's suggestion that the United States simply agree and "haul our freight." In July 1947 I. A. Shabshin, a Korea expert and member of the Soviet delegation, told an American naval officer that both the Soviets and the United States should come to an agreement and withdraw and wash their hands of Korea, allegedly saying that if only the Soviets were to withdraw, then the north Koreans "will overrun South Korea and kill you."[107] Such statements would fit with other evidence, discussed in volume 1, pointing to the low priority placed on Korea in Soviet global policies, and the typical Soviet desire that the great powers decide amongst themselves the fate of small nations, so that the latter do not disrupt the peace.

The United States had already announced that it planned to refer the Korean problem to the UN, so the Soviets may have sought to avoid that by a dramatic demarche; they may also have known about bureaucratic conflicts in Washington that were coincident with their proposal, such that it might swing the balance toward an American decision to withdraw. In retrospect this was the last opportunity before the formal establishment of the two Korean regimes to seize upon a policy urged both by Moscow and some bureaucracies in Washington. But whereas Moscow and the internationalists in Washington had forged the agreement on Korea in December 1945, now it was the military bureacracies who wanted a pullout, and the internationalists had mutated into advocates of containment. When Commission member Shtykov explained the Soviet proposal publicly, moreover, he homed in on the critical issue in southern politics since the liberation, about which the Soviets and Americans could never agree. "The Korean people had set up the People's Committee[s], Central People's Committee and the People's Republic on their own initiative before . . . [the arrival of foreign armies and he] condemned the American action in south Korea of not allowing these committees to participate in the political, economic and livelihood problems of south Korea."[108] So, no agreement was possible, but Moscow caught the United States off balance and gained a propaganda victory just before the United States put the Korea problem on the UN agenda.[109]

The United Nations and the 1948 Elections

On October 17 the United States urged the United Nations to set up a commission that would observe an election that would produce a national assembly for all of Korea. Once this assembly was elected it would establish a new government, which would then negotiate the withdrawal of foreign troops—an implicit answer to the Soviet demand for immediate withdrawal. Dean Rusk played a key role on the Korea issue at the UN and in bringing in the preeminent Republican diplomat to be the American chief delegate: John Foster Dulles.[110] In Dulles's experienced legal hands the Korean question could be negotiated in a rarefied, abstracted atmosphere where the realities of Korea disappeared and the country became just another bone of contention with the Soviets, like the Polish or the German question.

Dulles was always a legalist and a moralist, of course, but in the Asian context the legality was Western and the morality was paternal. Dulles had attended the Hague Convention in 1907 as a young secretary, a gathering at which a Korean patriot committed suicide when he was not allowed to present the case for his nation's independence. Dulles prized a portrait of his grandfather, John W. Foster, negotiating the Treaty of Shimonoseki that ended the Sino-Japanese War and gave Japan a leading hand in Korean affairs. (The *Christian Science Monitor* had depicted his grandfather poised between the Japanese and Chinese delegates "with his arms stretched out, apparently laying down the law between them." The grandson, however, saw in the portrait America's "quality of righteousness and justice.")[111] Foster Dulles, his funereal style and lack of "come-hither"[112] masking one of America's most effective international lawyers, moved his case through the UN so well as to become, at least in the eyes of some South Koreans, the Father of the Republic of Korea (ROK).

The Soviet delegate to the UN was Andrei Vyshinsky—also a bit of an undertaker, having cut his Stalinist teeth in sinister bullying of old Bolsheviks in the show trials of the late 1930s. He deployed the usual Soviet argument that the Moscow Accords remained valid, and could not unilaterally be abrogated by one side (although he said in October 1947 that a four-power forum would be a better venue than the UN, an interesting sidelight on the earlier United States proposal for a four-power conference on Korea, which the United States never pushed). Nationalist China also thought the Moscow agreements should not be abrogated, presumably because they gave China a role in deciding Korea's fate.[113]

The United Nations was the more advantageous forum because the United States dominated it. The many nations dependent on the United States could be counted on to provide an image of multilateralism and internationalism far better than a four-power conference in which the United States might get trouble not just from the Soviets, but from the British or the Chinese Nationalists. As Shirley Hazzard put it,

> The almost unbounded power of the U.S. at the United Nations was in the first place financial, in a world-wide as well as a parochial budgetary sense; it was numerical, consistently commanding the majority

in UN councils; it was psychological, in that the UN was sited in New York and cast in an American mould; and it was potentially moral— the U.S. then being regarded as the stable, prosperous, beneficent centre of democratic energies.

Sen. William Fulbright remarked in 1972 that, "Having controlled the United Nations for many years as tightly and as easily as a big-city boss controls his party machine, we had got used to the idea that the United Nations was a place we could work our will."[114] As early as March 1947, UN staffers revolted against a "surreptitious understanding" that UN civil service procedures should conform to American directives; in 1949 Trygve Lie secretly agreed with the State Department to have U.S. agents screen those Americans who worked at the UN. The U.S. government soon secretly controlled hiring and promotion decisions for a majority of the UN staff.[115] It was to much of the world, however, an organization for collective security, guaranteed by U.S. military might, carrying commensurate moral authority.

In southern Korea, the decision to go to the UN caused "wide jubilation throughout the rightist ranks"; Syngman Rhee now looked forward to both American and UN backing for his plans. He dispatched his sidekicks Ben Limb and Louise Yim to the UN, their "official credentials" coming from the Representative Democratic Council, long thought to be defunct. Louise Yim then claimed that she had Military Government recognition as an official delegate to the UN.[116]

The UN approved the establishment of a United Nations Temporary Commission on Korea (UNTCOK) on November 13, 1947; the countries sending delegates were Nationalist China, Canada, Australia, the Philippines, France, India, El Salvador, Syria, all but India and Syria being allies of the United States, with India receiving substantial amounts of American aid. Kim Il Sung predictably declared the delegates to be "running dogs" of the United States, but exhibited a rare eloquence in saying the Chinese participants were members of a government now little more than "a candlelight flickering in the wind."[117] Perhaps so, but the flame still burned brightly at the United Nations.

The assistant secretary-general of the UN and head of the UNTCOK Secretariat was Victor Hoo (Hu Shih-tse), a former vice-minister of foreign affairs for the Nationalists;[118] of seven other Secretariat members, two were Chinese. British Foreign Office sources found it "remarkable" that Victor Hoo "should so consistently intrigue behind the backs of the Commission, which he is surely intended to serve"; they reported "intricate" maneuvers between Hoo, Rhee, and the Nationalist ambassador, Wellington Koo. The Australian delegate to UNTCOK said that the American command in Seoul appeared to use Mr. Hoo "as go-between with the Korean leaders," and asserted that Hoo had "private plans for [a separate] election with Rhee, Kim Koo, and Kim Kyu-sik." The Nationalist delegate on UNTCOK was Liu Yu-wan, who held his position down to June 1950 and who had been consul-general in Seoul; in 1948 he sought to assure his Korean friends that the Kuomintang would be the real "guiding influence" on the Commission. He often met Koreans in the company of rightist youth leader Yi Pŏm-sŏk, a protégé of Chiang Kai-shek.[119]

The UNTCOK delegates arrived in Seoul just after the New Year. Peter Lowe aptly captured their situation.

> The challenges facing [UNTCOK] were daunting: a considerable proportion of the UN was opposed to its existence; the predominant political forces in south Korea regarded it simply as providing a veneer of international respectability for the creation of a south Korean state; north Korea had no intention of helping it in any way and the United States believed the commission should complete its task swiftly and without answering awkward questions.[120]

For the most part, internal documents do not support the prevalent notion that most of the Korean political spectrum applauded the Commission and the elections it was to observe. British sources estimated that "only the extreme right wing welcomes the Commission," with the moderate Right and the center "anxious" and everyone else opposed. The CIA predicted in late 1947 that "the rightist leadership is so single-mindedly bent on dictatorial control that following its accession to power," the moderates would "join the leftist camp."[121] This proved true, except that the moderates joined the leftists before the election was held. On January 14, 1948, Cho Pyŏng-ok presided over an official welcome for UNTCOK. He was the National Police chief who, one may remember, organized the welcome for American forces in October 1945. Cho's address harshly attacked north Korea and the Soviets, calling for an election in the South alone if necessary. Victor Hoo made the ceremony compulsory for UNTCOK members, prompting British speculation that he had worked together with Cho.

Many of the delegates were uncomfortable in their role, which was mostly thankless and gave them little autonomy. They also found Korea, and one another, noisome. "I have no desire to stay here," delegate Jackson of Australia remarked to an American; "I don't like Korea, I don't like Koreans, I don't like Seoul and I don't like the food." The Costa Rican soon was "so homesick he can hardly eat." The Syrian delegate was an unfortunate alcoholic, given to dozing through meetings; he had a notorious affair with a Rhee myrmidon, the redoubtable Mo Yun-suk. The Philippine member, Melecio Arranz, hailing from a country that had

been an American colony until 1946, stopped off on his way to Seoul to
see former Philippine commander MacArthur and told reporters that he
and the general saw eye-to-eye on Korea. He was a rotund, bombastic,
self-important man given to uttering fatuous irrelevancies; his loud snor-
ing led the French delegate to demand separate quarters.[122]

In spite of the remarkably skewed membership of the Commission,
which might be expected to do American bidding with nary a whimper,
and thorough massaging and prompting by the Occupation command,
most of the members did not like what they found in Korea. They soon
discovered, for example, that twelve of fifteen members of the original
National Election Committee were either Korean Democratic party
(KDP) members or close associates of Kim Sŏng-su; when new nominees
were added, they always seemed to be described as "conservative" or
"rightist." American internal sources said all but one of the Committee
members was rightist; the remaining member, Kang Ki-dŏk, was a signer
of the March 1, 1919, declaration and a "former leftist" from north Korea. An Election Review Board established to assess the propriety of the
May elections had five members, including Chang Myŏn, Kim Yong-mu,
and Kim Ch'an-yŏng, all KDP members. The latter two were early U.S.
Army Military Government in Korea (USAMGIK) appointees to high positions in the courts.[123]

The National Election Committee judged the fitness of individuals for
candidacy in the projected elections. Among its rulings was the disquali-
fication of candidate Pak Jae-hong of Kŭmhae, because he had never
finished an eighteen-month sentence under the Japanese "Total Mobilization Order" of 1944 for protesting to local police about "recruiting
Koreans for forced labor" while Japanese citizens were left alone. The
committee ruled that this was not a "political crime" and therefore his
incarceration made him unfit for election.[124]

When the Commission arrived in Seoul, the State Department representative, Joseph Jacobs, told the press that the United States had no desire to influence its deliberations in any way. But UNTCOK was completely dependent on the Occupation for facilities, communications, and
transportation. The Occupation went all out to shelter and cajole the delegates, using every organization and medium at its command to publicize, support, and push for an "observed" election that could be declared
free and fair. The delegates spent many hours in Seoul, much like the
Joint Commission before them, hearing streams of witnesses from across
the political spectrum. When the delegates toured rural areas, it was
through the careful shepherding of American and Korean officials.
Other "observers" shadowed the UNTCOK observers, sending daily reports to the Occupation command about their activities, what they saw,

and their attitudes. The Korean National Police censored mail sent by Koreans to UNTCOK.[125]

Brig. Gen. John Weckerling, the key officer in USAMGIK dealing with UNTCOK, hectored and lobbied with the various delegates. When he found out that the Syrian delegate was partially responsible for a clause stating that UNTCOK would only observe the elections if a free atmosphere prevailed, Weckerling accosted him: "Have you been instructed to find them [conditions in Korea] not free?" "Are your intentions entirely sincere in this or do you intend to obstruct the observance of the elections?" Yasin Mughir responded that he had no such instructions, and that he was not trying to spite the United States over its position on the Palestine issue. When Gen. William F. Dean appeared before the Commission on March 5 and got some sharp questions about the national police, youth groups, and whether a free atmosphere could be created before May, he exploded and accused UNTCOK of interfering in Occupation affairs—an interesting judgment given the Commission's charge to examine political conditions then extant in Korea. The alternate French delegate, however, confided to Weckerling that Dean was "foolish" to get angry: "We are not going to insist on any police reform . . . we are not going to ask that even one police official be removed . . . right now everything is very favorable for the United States . . . Gen. Dean should realize that and not abuse it."[126]

The Occupation also withheld crucial information from UNTCOK. For example, Weckerling told Hodge that UNTCOK election registration statistics showed that 95.9 percent of eligible voters had registered by the end of April; this figure, however, was based on then-outdated 1946 population figures, and the real percentage was under 80. But he deemed it "inadvisable" in inform UNTCOK of this fact.[127]

Australia, Canada, and India decided in early February that they could not carry out their mandate, since they would only be able to observe elections in the South. They reported this back to the Interim Committee for instructions (the Interim Committee functioned when the General Assembly was not sitting). On February 26, the Interim Committee nonetheless approved holding elections in South Korea alone.[128]

Thereafter the delegates began debating resolutions that sought to remedy the structure of southern politics, calling for reorientation of the National Police, placing rightist youth groups outside the election process, and the like. On March 10 the Australian delegate, S. H. Jackson, wrote a resolution that in effect would have denied both the UNTCOK function and the validity of any elections. "It appears that the elections are now under the control of a single party," the KDP, it said; conditions were not suitable in either north or south to hold an election; the UN General Assembly "should not be drawn into a position where it may be held responsible" for an election in the South alone. He recommended that UNTCOK leave Korea and report this to the UN, and then return in August 1948 to reexamine the situation. The next day Patteron also spoke on behalf of the resolution (in paraphrase): "From all available evidence this separate course is opposed by [the] overwhelming majority of [the] Korean people, Dr. Rhee notwithstanding. . . . Let not [the] prestige of [the] UN, the body that enshrines the hopes of mankind, founder on rocks so barren of moral fiber and fundamental principle." The resolution, of course, was not adopted.[129]

If an UNTCOK delegate criticized Occupation policies, he was likely to be thought a leftist or a communist. When Patterson told Weckerling that "the Korean problem is not the business of the U.N., which was brought into a situation that can only be decided by [the U.S. and the USSR]. U.N. has no business here," Weckerling thought this indicated that Patterson's opinions "had all the essential elements of Henry Wallace in the U.S. and the South Korean Labor Party in South Korea." When the ineffectual Mughir urged reform of the police and youth groups, Weckerling suspected he might be a communist. The French delegate told Weckerling that Jackson was working in the Soviet interest, but also that his resolutions were meaningless; Hodge would continue to have a free hand to do what he wanted. Some of this percolated up to Washington, such that Kenneth Royall described the Australian and Canadian delegates as "most uncooperative," with "distinct signs of Leftist tendencies."[130]

Olivier Manet, the alternate French delegate, was a worldly man, anything but a leftist, who approached his duties with a cheerful cynicism. Weckerling thought him "extremely" favorable to the U.S. position. Manet assured him on March 8 that "The right will have a strong anti-communist government. That is best for the U.S. and in the long run, best for Korea. To try to put liberal ideas into it would only more quickly cause its downfall." He thought the question of a Korean bill of rights, which had come up in UNTCOK deliberations, would best be left "in the hands of the military authorities." He did hope, however, that the Occupation might do something about basic freedoms, so that he would have something to take back to Paris "to show to the General Assembly that [a free] atmosphere did exist." He dutifully kept Weckerling informed about UNTCOK activities, telling him after a visit to Pusan that "there was no one anti" on the trip; "we had no trouble" with the delegates, and "even Mughir . . . was leaning way over on our side."[131]

The number of observers was miniscule compared to previous examples of foreign-observed elections. In the Saar in 1936, some two thousand observers were on hand. In Korea by comparison the supervision of the elections had to be "of an extremely cursory nature," as Peter Lowe put it.[132] UNTCOK members took quick chaperoned trips through the countryside to check on election procedures. Mostly they did not like what they found. The assistant secretary of UNTCOK, J. F. Engers, visited Inch'ŏn to examine election preparations and declared himself "very unfavorably impressed"; out of eighteen candidates whom he met, sixteen described themselves as rightists. When he told this to Ernst Fraenkel, USAMGIK legal advisor, Fraenkel asked him if he had evidence of anyone having placed "pressure" on people to obtain such a result. Having never been to Inch'ŏn before, Engers naturally said he had none (nor did Fraenkel mention the reams of internal reports to which he was privy which might help Engers with such evidence).[133]

In an interview, an American who guided the delegates through the Chŏlla provinces referred to the Australian and Canadian delegates years later simply as "the two communist members." They had asked him some pointed questions, he recalled, but "I worked out answers that deliberately gave them the wrong information." Without a trace of irony, he went on to say that he did not think the delegates "had really seen, heard, or learned much about the people or the situation."[134]

In reporting back to Weckerling on a journey to Taegu, Kyŏngju, and Pusan with some of the other delegates, Olivier Manet said that everyone who went along had "either an open mind or a pro-United States mind." When he arrived in Kyŏngju, according to a reporter who accompanied him, Korean officials loyal to Rhee immediately took him in hand, showing him the sights of the ancient Silla capital and putting him up for the night at a hotel near the renowned Sŏkkuram grotto—along with lots of beer and *kisaeng* girls.

In spite of such hospitality, however, Manet was constrained to tell Weckerling that the Koreans they interviewed "seem so anxious to lie," and appeared "too determined to cover up something." He thought it had been drummed into them "to give the answer that they think the authorities want." Manet thought the pressure brought to bear on Korean respondents was mainly "social," not a result of terrorism or denial of ration stamps. "Everyone thought that if he didn't go down to register, as a voter, he would be taken as a Communist and because of this something would happen to him later."

Manet told Weckerling that the KDP was "the only [party] that has a machine . . . it would make no difference whether or not the moderates or even the leftists ran . . . the Hankook Party will still win." "We have a very hard time finding anyone who supports Kim Koo," he said, "Its the same with Kimm Kiusic." All this was really a moot point, Manet admitted, because the delegates wanted to get out of Korea as soon as possible. And so he told Weckerling, "You will have your United Nations observed election. You can take these representatives and form a National Government," and from there on things will be in the hands of the General Assembly in Paris.[135]

That is about what happened. The election was held, the United Nations gave its imprimatur, and Acheson had won the first round of Korean containment, Truman Doctrine style.

Chapter Three

ROLLBACK AND NATIONALISM

The rest of the world—ah! There's the rub.
Franklin D. Roosevelt, 1936

I want especially to see your Japan, Korea, one city in China, Manila, Bangkok and India. I do not want to see the mess in Europe.
Robert R. McCormick to MacArthur, 1947

THE "Truman-MacArthur controversy" was, presumably, about the chain of command in time of war, civilian supremacy over the military, and various things that divided Democrats and Republicans on foreign policy. These differences had vaguely to do with whether emphasis should be placed on Europe or Asia, whether there was "a substitute for victory" in Korea, what to do about sanctuaries in China, or what "limited war" meant in a nuclear age. The established historiography has it that Truman was right and MacArthur was wrong: a courageous decision by a beleagured president cut the Gordian knot, and MacArthur came back to fade away into a well-deserved obscurity.

Meanwhile, a bizarre sideshow in Washington pitted an ignorant, even barbaric inquisitor, Sen. Joseph McCarthy, against a multitude of innocent liberals who had been taken for communists, and a minority of Stalinists who got what they deserved. The "vital center" prevailed, fortunately, and McCarthy died a broken man, his "ism" a nasty but temporary episode. Assorted crackpots and clinical paranoiacs ranted for a while longer about communists in government and conspiracies on Wall Street, but that, too, finally passed into the dustbin of history.

One would never begin to understand early postwar America if this construction were fact rather than fantasy, if this liberal discourse were taken to be the truth. Yet it is the dominant interpretation, if exaggerated a bit here. The source is an incapacity to take the American right-wing seriously, an inability to fathom why they think what they think: they must be crazy. But such people were as American as apple pie, modal to its politics. The extant literature is so suffused with the contrary view that we will have to undertake an extended reconstruction of the two sides, to provide a scorecard as it were.

The Truman-MacArthur clash abroad and McCarthyism at home mirrored the surface spouting of two whales doing battle in the depths of state and society, pitting individuals, bureaucracies, interests, and parties against each other, and forming alternative conceptions of political economy and America's role in the world. This conflict ran back to the nineteenth century and goes forward to the 1980s, if in vestigial and nostalgic form, but its main heyday was a twenty-years crisis from 1930 to 1950. At bottom the conflict was rooted in different sets of capitalist and bureaucratic interests, producing variant world views and political coalitions.

The foreign policy expression of this antagonism produced what the Chinese would call a two-line struggle, between what we would call internationalism and rollback. Internationalism on the "Left" and rollback on the "Right," through sharp political struggle, forged a shifting consensual midpoint along the American political spectrum. This dialectic etched the parameters of foreign policy choice throughout the postwar period and down to the present. Truman and Acheson were the archetypes of containment, MacArthur the archetype of rollback. The outcome in 1947 was a compromise embodied in the Truman Doctrine. By 1949, however, a rollback alternative had gotten sufficient backing to become a formidable competitor with containment, within and without the bureaucracies that produce foreign policy. The substance of the "Truman-MacArthur controversy" was in place at least a year before the Korean War, and simply awaited an external crisis to detonate an explosion in the American body politic. By early 1950, rollback had emerged as the clear antagonist of the containment policy, with liberal internationalists increasingly excluded from inner circles of decision. The debate had changed from "accommodation or containment?" to "containment or rollback?" and as it did so the consensual midpoint shifted sharply to the right, excluding not liberals like Henry Wallace—he got excluded by 1947—but marginalizing (if not wholly excluding) centrists and containment advocates like George Kennan, and stretching to include rollbackers like Curtis LeMay and James Burnham.

These interpretations remain to be demonstrated, but the evidence is substantial and, in my view, definitive. Yet there is a much harder phenomenon to explain, because it does not begin to fit the labels and symbols with which Americans think about their politics. The rollback strategy emerged within the bureaucracy not just among people who can be labeled "rightists." John Paton Davies, who later had his career ruined by McCarthy's scattershot volleys, produced one of the first major papers advocating rollback in the Far East. Douglas MacArthur, presumed darling of the rollback crowd, was often more conservative in his recommendations than Dean Acheson, Anglophile internationalist. John Foster Dulles, with whom most historians associate the term rollback, was in fact a centrist seeking to channel and constrain raucous rollback constituencies.

Why are the labels inapt? First, because Americans think about a non-

European politics with a European political vocabulary, as we asserted earlier. If H. L. Hunt found his oil interests infringed by the Rockefellers, or his credit strangled by New York banks, his inclination was to call them communists; their inclination was to call him a fascist. If Henry Wallace wanted to sell midwestern grain to the Soviets, he might be a communist; if Richard Nixon wanted to, he was a statesman. If Hubert Humphrey wants to jail American Communists, he is a liberal; if Richard Nixon wants to, he is a fascist.

The comparatively narrow circumscription of the American experience makes for a politics of mistaken identity, as people who (by European standards) agree on all the fundamentals sling mud at each other. The bedrock of consensus is so deep, people know each other so well (actually or figuratively), that differences must be grossly magnified, caricatured grotesquely, to make a point or build a constituency. In a world-comparative sense the label for central participants in American politics, whether of "right" or "left," is *liberal*, reflecting the constrained politics of a thoroughly bourgeois democracy.

Second, all that exists most of the time in American politics is different brands of anticommunism. The absence of a rooted American Left that persists over time (indicated by labels like "New Left") leaves most Americans with no conception of socialism or communism, they tend to grow aphasic or blabber inanities when asked to define such terms; this was especially so in 1950. So, we have the Roosevelt/Nixon anticommunism of envelopment, enmeshment, containment-by-embrace, détente, seeking to win communists over by the example of liberalism or the subtle charms of the market; we have the Acheson/Rusk/Nixon anticommunism of containment by building dikes and drawing lines in the dirt, while splitting the Left from liberals at home; and we have the Burnham/Hunt/Nixon anticommunism of rollback, which seeks the erasure of communism abroad and of liberalism at home. (Nixon can be present at all creations, because he was an opportunist and because the differences are not fundamental.)

All this is evident when one witnesses, for example, a cold war liberal trying to muster a comeback to the rollback argument that we should obliterate communism; the response is usually that it would be infeasible or unrealistic, not that it would be morally wrong or genocidal, because anticommunism is the consensual foreign policy morality of the postwar period. Thus in the 1950s one could make arguments for preventive thermonuclear war and still command the U.S. Air Force, but one could never argue for wide-ranging accommodation with Moscow and hope to hold high position. One could push for attacking North Korea and become a protected confidant of Americans in Seoul, or advocate recognition of the People's Republic and be sent home on an early ship.

But a deeper reason why the labels are so confusing is that within the broad consensus on capitalism there *are* serious differences of political economy, germinating in different sets of interests, which in turn make for different conceptions of states and markets, and of the proper American role in the world. This is the substance of the conflict between "two lines," but there is no vocabulary for it; it can hardly be discussed seriously in the United States without risking calumny or oblivion, usually taking the form of assertions that one has a conspiracy theory. At least this was true before the 1970s and 1980s. Now the crisis of American decline and the shifting of whole congressional delegations from free trade to protection in the wink of an eye has brought home, to some at least, the virtues of a theory of class interest and world economy for explaining our predicament.

A half-century earlier, in the 1930s, such thinking was commonplace as a rising set of interests and a new conception of states and markets, known colloquially as the New Deal, displaced a waning set of interests and a failed conception of states and markets, labeled Hooverism. Although the battle was lost in the economic realm by the late 1940s, the remnants of the earlier coalition still held political position and they sought to reverse the verdict of the 1930s through an assault on their political opposition within and without the American state. Standing behind all the mystifying and inane blather about who lost China, Reds in the Foreign Service, Acheson's pinstripes, Gen. George Marshall serving the communist conspiracy, and the like, was the attempt by the losers to refight the battles of the 1930s. And the losers had a foreign policy preference: rollback or right-isolationism, two sides of the same political/economic coin.

Nothing can be understood about how rollback currents shaped high policy and the course of the Korean War without probing into what Franz Schurmann called the arcana of empire and the mysteries of the state. But we also need to probe for hidden interests and conceptions of political economy, something Schurmann neglects. This chapter will begin that task by seeking to understand the primitives (Acheson's term), paranoiacs (Richard Hofstadter's term), the group that Peter Viereck called "the same old isolationist, Anglophobe, Germanophile revolt of radical Populist lunatic-fringers."[1] When liberals take commonplace Americans and call them insane, we all should pay attention.

American Nationalism Revisited: The Political Economy of Isolationism / Rollback

In the introduction we presented a sketch of the rollback tendency, which readers can refer to as the skeleton or lattice-work of concepts presented in this chapter. The world outside the confines of the United States was mostly unknown to the advocates of this current, especially the Asia they coveted. Like their patron saint, Joe McCarthy, most of them possessed an "organic innocence";[2] they were original Americans, classic Hartzians, members of America's universal class, the petite bourgeoisie, believing in an American dream, in Charles Beard's words, of "the embourgeoisement of the whole society—a universality of comfort, conveniences, security, leisure, standard possessions of food, clothing and shelter."[3]

In an essay written more than 130 years ago, entitled "Bastiat and Carey," Marx argued that the North Americans belonged to

> a country where bourgeois society did not develop on the foundation of the feudal system, but developed rather from itself; where this society appears not as the surviving result of a centuries-old movement, but rather as the starting-point of a new movement; where the state, in contrast to all earlier national formations, was from the beginning subordinate to bourgeois society, to its production, and never could make the pretence of being an end-in-itself; where, finally, bourgeois society itself, linking up the productive forces of an old world with the enormous natural terrain of a new one, has developed to hitherto unheard-of dimensions . . . and where, finally, even the antitheses of bourgeois society itself appear only as vanishing moments.

Thinkers like Henry C. Carey (whom Marx deemed the only original American economist), desired both society's emancipation from the state, and state intervention to aid society, in the form of protection against foreign competition. Carey was simultaneously a free trader and a protectionist: laissez-faire in the national market, protection in the world market against the earlier and more competitive industrializer, England. He saw economic conflicts "as soon as they appear on the world market as English relations," not as something integral to the workings of the world economy: the British disrupted the natural order of things.[4]

That natural order was a deeply contradictory one, in which American capitalists wanted simultaneously to be left alone to exploit the home market, and to be left alone in expanding elsewhere in the world. But the smaller ones differed with workers or bankers over how to do it, especially in regard to the general abstraction that was American foreign policy. One would not call their foreign policy preferences subtle or fine tuned. In effect they had no foreign policy, something that was perfectly predictable given the structure of their interests: coming mostly from independent capitalist stock, they cultivated the home market, and thought about the rest of the world only when there was foreign competition or war. The great obstacle to outward expansion was the British Empire.

Whereas Acheson and other internationalists took the British as their exemplary model, this current hated England. Their ideal was a self-contained America, and their economic theory was mercantilism. Less obvious, often, was a conception of the United States as a "late" industrializer and developer, with so much of the world already spoken for by England. Lynn Eden has aptly termed this group "business nationalists," and found them in several regional economies within the national market: the corn belt, central plains, Rocky Mountain and intermountain areas. Their leader in the Senate was Robert Taft of Ohio, for whom liberty connoted "local self-reliance," and who stood for a self-contained America, based in the home market.[5]

An example of such thinking is Samuel Crowther's *America Self-Contained*,[6] a book written in 1933, the moment of Polanyi's snapping golden thread. When I checked it out of an enormous university library in 1980, it was the first time anyone had done so since 1949—a nice symbol of the moribund status of Crowther's political economy by the time of the Korean War. Crowther was a publicist for Henry Ford, himself an industrialist with decidedly bizarre views from a liberal standpoint.

Crowther led off by saying that "We in the U.S. have today no friends among the nations of the earth. But we have many bitter enemies," a nice mercantilist view that Hofstadter would perhaps find paranoid. In Crowther's world nothing existed beyond the nation-state; this was his unit of analysis. He thought the United States should make its isolation more complete, "shape our own destinies," instead of doing a lot of "sordid international shop-keeping" in that "old system of world economy." Continuing to do so would only lead to an American standard of living "fixed by the [world's] lowest common denominator."

The logic of the system of world economy, he said, would inevitably lead to a "world super-state with a planned economy," a preference internationalists hid under code words like "economic interdependence" and Adam Smith's notion of an international division of labor. If the state of the world were as Smith described it, Crowther wrote, his counsel would be wholly logical. But the world was carved into feudatories called nations. Crowther identified internationalism and the New Deal with a dying "old order," an Anglophile foreign policy, and a state meddling in the economy in *the wrong way*—mainly to redistribute wealth. Instead of a New Deal, the United States needed a new order. It was such thinking, of course, that led isolationists to flirt with European fascism.

The American nationalist was always made to seem "the boorish provincial" instead of the patriot, while free traders lowered tariffs and let foreigners "cavort without an admission fee in the largest market in the world." The hallowed ground upon which internationalists trod was prepared by cosmopolite college professors at Eastern universities, all Anglophiles who deemed Adam Smith a genius. Crowther, however, thought the internationalists, economists, and world bankers displayed "a strange dementia" that assumed that the world of their theories was the world that existed. Crowther merely put in simpler terms Polanyi's notion that the world market and free trade constituted an elaborate fiction, "a stark utopia," ultimately incapable of holding national interest at bay.[7]

Crowther preferred German mercantilism. Remembering that Friedrich List had lived in Pennsylvania for a while and was a confidant of James Madison and Andrew Jackson, Crowther sought to Americanize Listian thought. List had helped Germany set up its railroad system, a good "national" industry, and had recommended that the American South stop shipping cotton to England, since the exchange put the United States in a dependency relationship. Only one American economist could measure up to List, he said, and that was none other than Henry C. Carey.

Sounding like Kim Il Sung expounding on the "Juche" idea, Crowther invoked List to the effect that a high tariff policy has the advantage of "securing the interior market against all events, fluctuations of prices, and against all changes in the political and economical conditions of other nations." Like Kim, Crowther also defined "freedom" as America's national freedom to do what it wanted and to maintain its independence of action. Early Americans had the right idea, viewing imports as destructive and exports as constructive: "We don't need to import a nickle's worth." He even used family analogies, like Kim Il Sung. Internationalists saw the world as "one big happy family," but it was actually a feuding nightmare—better to make a happy family at home, "giving over America to the Americans."

England was for him the great antagonist of the American political economy, with New England its regional expression in the national market. All the panics and depressions of the nineteenth century were British-induced, he thought; cotton exports put the United States "exactly in the position of any one-crop country, such as Cuba or Brazil today;" the advanced technology and superior position in the world economy of England meant that, as a late developer, the United States had to import-substitute in glass, tin, and various other industries, with high tariffs essential lest the industries "could not get a start." Furthermore England kept the United States on raw materials dependence, even when American industry was competitive. Germany had suffered from British dominance, and thus put great effort into its chemicals industry—seeking to make synthetically what it could not import. The United States could do the same: "by chemical means we freed ourselves from every material foreign clutch."

The United States could not hope to sell in markets dominated by England and, the implication was, it would have to find regions where England was not dominant (which tended to be the Americas and East Asia), or stay at home. The free traders and internationalists did not understand this, and pinned their hopes on cooperation with England. Their fantastic theories had finally, in the depression, led America to ruin. "Grouping bankers and socialists together as, to be elegant, the morticians of an era, is in no sense cynical but a plain statement of fact."

In another book, written with George Peek, Crowther remarked brilliantly of Roosevelt and other New Dealers, "they would remake the United States as an incident to remaking the world," something rather close to the truth. Peek and Crowther spoke of foreign intercourse weakening "our self-reliance," worried about the Japanese textile industry, referred to FDR's reciprocal trade agreements as "internationalism gone wild," and described New Dealers as "a curious collection of socialists and internationalists . . . fanatic-like."

Internationalists in the Agriculture Department wanted "socialized farming," and those in the State Department (Cordell Hull being the archetype) wanted free trade, with bizarre notions that this would lead to world peace. Henry Wallace roamed both agencies, with "an elastic and fantastic mind capable of any stretching." For "America's choice" in coming years, the authors provided a Chinese menu: Column A was internationalism and Column B "policy for America," meaning high tariffs, control over capital export, a good Navy to defend the Panama Canal, and so on.[8]

Rarely has a man conjuring a new order been so brilliantly illustrative of a dying past. Crowther had the uncommon talent of clear exposition, pinned on a theory of industrial structure. He assayed the implications of his thought with a ruthless logic, foundering only on the question of labor cost: he was less opposed to unions than desirous of building up the buying power of the national market—thus to put Fords in the hands of workers, no doubt. Had Henry Ford been a textile man, we imagine, Crowther would have added to his theory demands for a minimal state, restrictions on the combination of labor, and a strong policing authority (Hoover's FBI). He then would have summed up the mostly unarticulated assumptions of the American Right at midcentury.

A less sophisticated view of a self-contained America is available in a magazine called, appropriately enough, *The National Republic*. Publishing from 1928 until the late 1950s, it pushed a hard domestic line. It described itself as a magazine of "fundamental Americanism," explaining what it meant with a credo on its inside cover. It called for unimpaired American nationality, expulsion of "alien agitators," protection of family and religion, unrestricted property rights, and "complete American independence from Old World political or economic domination." In the

1930s it embodied all the elements of McCarthyism, with frequent articles on alleged Reds in the government and in academia—"the long arm of Satanic Russia" creating "an enemy within"; one of its heroes was Douglas MacArthur. In the 1950s, *The National Republic* carried extensive and detailed articles dealing with McCarthyite attacks on academics in the China field and Foreign Service officers with East Asian experience, including a long one on the Canadian scholar-diplomat E. H. Norman. Most of its advertisers were small businesses selling their wares in the American market; its board of patrons included smaller Texas and Oklahoma oil firms, and steel and tool companies selling at home.[9]

Another example would be a journal called *The Protectionist*, which stopped publishing just after Pearl Harbor. It carried numerous articles in the 1930s calling for protection against "destructive Japanese competition" and "unfair dumping" in textiles, shoes, and other American industries just beginning a long decline. It viciously attacked Roosevelt as a "New Deal Caesar," lambasted "Reds in Government," and termed the Wagner Act "an expression of socialist-communist class conflict." All of its advertising came from small industries under foreign threat.

The deep hostility to the New Deal and its foreign expression even raised the specter of that "Banana Republic" event thought so alien to the United States, the coup d'etat. Right-wingers associated with the Liberty League reportedly sought to oust "Franklin Stalino Roosevelt," as they liked to call him, in 1934, by seeking support within the American military from Douglas MacArthur, Hanford MacNider, and Smedley Butler. Although no one has proved the existence of such a plot, the names connected with it figured directly in the politics of 1950: Louis Johnson, allegedly involved with other American Legion leaders and DuPont interests in the coup, and Douglas MacArthur, the unwitting choice to replace Roosevelt.[10] It is the case that from the crushing of the Bonus Marchers onward (in which Patrick Hurley was also involved) the extreme right seemed always to look to MacArthur as a man-on-horseback who could save the day. The notorious anti-Semite Father Coughlin urged just after Pearl Harbor that MacArthur be made supreme commander of all U.S. military forces; in 1949 and 1950 rollbackers demanded that MacArthur be made a kind of high commissioner for Asia and Asian policy, as we will see.[11]

Many isolationists and rollbackers were much less coherent than Crowther or the *National Republic* crowd; we do not speak here of introspective and thoughtful people given to explication of their motives. But it is the self-contained political economy, with a unilateralist foreign policy, that structures the fundamental conceptions of the isolationist/rollback current, and of American nationalism. Isolationists did have a foreign policy: it was expansionism in regions "open" to their interests. They tended to support Roosevelt's Latin American policies, but always hoped to avoid British empire-building.[12]

In an important analysis, Gareth Stedman Jones found the nonterritoriality of American imperialism abroad to be "founded on an unprecedented territorialism 'at home' "; which was "one vast process of territorial seizure and occupation."[13] Still, even if they were connected, there were two distinct types of imperialism. New England, in particular, originated a British-style imperialism of free trade, akin to a foreign or at least regional implant, placing primacy on Europe; here was the fount of the "open door."

After the closing of the frontier it was Asia that held expansionist attentions, an extension of the westward march to the frontier—"a straight line of march drawn by its length almost to a circle," as Richard Drinnon put it. The American empire pushed toward the setting sun, toward "those distant regions where the Far West becomes the Far East," in John Hay's phrase. Walter LaFeber found the same expansionist thrust westward, linking Frederick Jackson Turner's frontier theses, the imperialism of the 1890s, and Woodrow Wilson's "new frontiers" in "the Far Pacific."[14] The distinction, however, is that expansionists preferred unilateral American sway in the Pacific, whereas internationalists favored cooperation with Britain.

Much of this account would be familiar to historians of the 1930s. But the idea that concrete interests and a very different conception of political economy motivated rollbackers and the right-wing rarely penetrated comment on the political conflicts of the early postwar period. Instead the dominant interpretation was a psychological one: Hofstadters's paranoid style, or Daniel Bell's judgment that the "radical right" was fighting a rear guard action against "modernity," frustrated and discomfited by a new world they did not understand. "Insofar as there is no real left to counterpose to the right, the liberal has become the psychological target of that frustration," he wrote, a statement that implicitly assumed liberal innocence. At times Bell hinted at a political-economic basis for this frustration, linking rightists to "the automobile dealers, real estate manipulators, [and] oil wildcatters,"; Alan Westin noted that John Birch Society members tended to come from the textile industry, carpet manufacturers, small railroads, and independent oil companies.[15] But the modal emphasis among sociologists and political scientists studying the right-wing was to seek psychological explanations for aberrant viewpoints, rather than to probe into economic interests or conceptions of political economy.

A particularly good example is a study by Bernard Fenstwerwald in the *Journal of Conflict Resolution*. In the first part he provided a fine analysis of what we have called expansionism, a movement by unilateral agglomeration of nearby territories or concessions, usually in a westward direction toward the frontier and Asia. "Aloofness toward Europe and expansionism elsewhere are both attitudes of [American] nationalism." Fensterwald's own view was that internationalism pointed in "the right direction," and so he condemned MacArthur and James Burnham as "new imperialists." In the second part of the article, however, he deduced a psychological test: the "W Scale" to detect those who look West, toward Asia, and the "E Scale" for those who look East, toward Europe. The results proved that West-lookers were bigoted, ethnocentric, and anti-Semitic, whereas East-lookers were enlightened and liberal. Fensterwald even derived an argument on "potty training and politics," to show that West-lookers may have gotten their unfortunate orientation from indelicate early handling of this basic function.[16]

Seymour Martin Lipset argued that the "financial support" of the radical right came from "newly acquired wealth, and from small business"; he thought that "new wealth most often tends to have extremist ideologies" (a generalization that would hardly apply to the 1980s Silicon Valley). He was closer to the truth in saying that small business had been squeezed both by foreign competition and by the great corporations, and therefore disliked the status quo and had trouble tolerating unions. He thought the base of the radical right was to be found among traditional isolationists, depicted as "rooted in ethnic prejudices or reactions, ties to the homeland, and populist xenophobia."[17] It is amazing how such caricatures can pass for social science.

Historians with some empathy for isolationism have done better. Justus Doenecke wrote properly that the received wisdom about isolationism has been the verdict of "the winners of a complex and bitter battle" and in passing he linked many isolationists to particular industries: William Regnery to textiles; Ernest Weir to national steel; Col. Robert Wood of *America First* and Sears, Roebuck to his clientele among small businessmen and farmers in the Midwest (but also to expansion southward into Central and South America—Sears had moved southward by the 1940s, and Wood had also been a director of the United Fruit Company); the isolationist-turned-internationalist Arthur Vandenberg to the changing world market fortunes of American automobiles. But Doenecke's dominant interpretation is to link isolationists to Midwestern farm constituencies, or to find such diversity as to see no links at all. The same is generally true of Wayne Cole's monumental work, although both he and Doenecke occasionally hinge isolationism to a political economy of self-containment.[18]

It is hard to remember in our worldly and interdependent era, but as recently as the 1930s many regions in the Midwest still were not integrated into the world economy, with local markets running on principles of barter. States like North Dakota were classically dependent grain-producing peripheries, with farm credit provisioned by Eastern banks. Major media, like the *Chicago Tribune*, and major providers of consumer goods, like Sears, were run by isolationists (Robert C. McCormick and Robert Wood), who parleyed news, clothes, and politics to a vast farming and small-business clientele. So it is true, as many analysts have argued, that the Midwestern farming and small business community was a homebase for isolationism and later for McCarthyism and rollback.[19] But this usually derived from hatred of snooty Eastern internationalists, bankers who denied credit, fear of foreign competition, or a steady diet of the McCormick and Hearst press—not pathology or indelicate potty training.

The South, on the other hand, if anything more conservative than the Midwest, rarely joined the McCarthyite and "who lost China" bandwagon. The main reason was its historic internationalist position going back to the early nineteenth century: it sold cotton in the Empire of free trade. Dean Acheson, to whom industrial-structure thought came naturally, said in 1960 that the southward movement of American textile firms, in search of cheaper labor cost and nonunion areas, "had subverted the last stronghold of liberal trade policy."[20]

If one takes a theory of industrial structure that would seek to differentiate industries on the basis of an index of their world-market competitiveness and their sensitivity to labor costs, as Thomas Ferguson has done, then isolationists have a distinct tendency to group around industries producing either for the national market or for American-controlled markets (often in Central America), and industries where labor is a big component of total costs. Internationalists tend to form around 1930s–1940s capital-intensive "high-tech" industries that can compete in world markets, such as international oil and banking, communications, aircraft production and airlines, and automobiles. Ferguson demonstrates how a "hegemonic bloc" of world-competitive industries and their investors structured the New Deal coalition, encouraged strong state promotion of external business, and enabled decades of Democratic party dominance after 1932.[21] But it was really in the 1940s that this bloc marched outward to the rest of the world—first through the productive effects of the war and the British decline, than through hegemonic statecraft and economic mechanism.

Charles Beard in the 1930s had contrasted an "industrial thesis" with an "agrarian thesis" in American history: the former is our internationalism/imperialism, the latter is our nationalism/expansionism. The first assumed that American industry produced a surplus that required expansion into foreign markets if stagnation were to be avoided; the advocates of this course were free traders who will export, say, both cotton and the machinery to finish cotton, even if it provides foreign-based industry with a competitive edge. Beard recognized that the maturing of American industries in the mid-1930s had produced a coalition for "outward thrust" (Ferguson's "hegemonic bloc").

The agrarian thesis was "intra-nationalist and anti-imperialist," opposing England and the imperialism of free trade; it represented national rather than international interests, but to the extent that it had a foreign tendency, it favored "the annexation of contiguous unoccupied [*sic*] territory which . . . can be exploited by self-governing farmers and planters." The agent of expansion was the individual, not the corporation. Beard aptly noted that each tendency produced different systems of thought, "intricately interwoven with a system of active interests."[22] This is precisely the way I would put the argument in this chapter.

Beard found a type of isolationist who favors "the anarchy of the acquisitive instinct at home and abroad," and who sounds like a rollbacker:

> They believe that the U.S. Government should make no treaty commitments to peace which would interfere with American capitalists in the enjoyment of protective tariffs, in pushing foreign trade and investments, and in enforcing their interests abroad by engines of coercion, by war if necessary. They favor the anarchy of the acquisitive instinct at home and abroad, with the government as an adjunct, not a control—an adjunct to employ force and violence whenever those private interests are seriously thwarted in obtaining concessions, pushing trade, and making collections.[23]

Carrol Quigley linked such a conception to the great political struggles of the early postwar period, seeing them as "centering on the rise and decline of unilateralism and neoisolationism." The basic assumptions of neo-isolationism, he thought, were American omnipotence, unilateralism in foreign policy, unlimited and Utopian goals (such as erasing communism), and internal treason conceived as a greater problem than external threat. Behind all this was a ruthless pursuit of economic advantage: prominent neoisolationists "had no conception of any man who placed objective truth higher than subjective interests." They hated taxes and unions, because both cut into profits; the logic extended to strong opposition to big defense budgets, something that never troubled centrist conservatives. Newer wealth in Texas and California practiced a "ruthless exploitation of natural resources" such as oil and gas, and was "unbelievably ignorant and misinformed" on the world outside their locale. They were thoroughly petit bourgeois, as opposed to the semiaristocratic Eastern establishment.[24] All this was true, and possesses far more explanatory power than a conception of the isolationist/rollback current as paranoid and pathological.

Former isolationists like Robert Wood became big backers of McCarthy and MacArthur, as did Texas oil men like Hunt, Clint Murchison, and Hugh Roy Cullen; whereas General Electric head Philip Reed, Paul Hoffman of Studebaker, and other leaders of industries with international markets did not.[25] Alfred Kohlberg, the leader of the "China Lobby," was a textile man. William Regnery, likewise a textile man, published many right-wing books in the 1950s. H. L. Hunt and the Pew family of Pittsburgh, both in independent national oil, bankrolled right-wing groups. Railroad and steel interests, wholly national for the most part, tended to the Right. Arthur Vandenberg of Michigan was a fence sitter in the late 1930s, never a pure isolationist, and of course he became the symbol of bipartisanship in 1947. It just so happened that Michigan's political economy was split at that time between an automobile industry which was the standard for the world, and which, in Vandenberg's words, had been "most generously and sypathetically treated by the State Department"; and an agricultural sector that opposed free trade and the State Department run by Cordell Hull.[26]

Certain industries were borderline, like American chemicals, which both took German chemicals as its model and was a late-developer facing German technical advantage and its huge presence in the world chemicals market. DuPont was a big supporter of MacArthur and other right-wingers, for example, although that had in part to do with the feudal-industrial setting of its fief in the state of Delaware, big investments by T. V. Soong, and its history of profiting from every war since 1812 through government contracts for gunpowder and other explosives.[27] Certain industrialists did not follow the tendency of their industry: railroads were usually national by definition, and labor-sensitive. But one railroad family was inveterately internationalist—the Harrimans, because they built railroads abroad. Of course, no one is a mere reflex of their economic interest—although as we will see some of our protagonists come rather close, especially those interested in minerals.

The corporate and state capitalism of the New Deal heralded a new political economy that rendered individualism little more than a fond memory of the nineteenth century. Bureaucratization of both the corporation and the state produced an organization man, a bureaucrat, who was the antithesis of the swashbuckling individualist.[28] The new corporate synthesis of state and multinational corporation made a mockery of the axiomatic ways that Americans thought about state and civil society. Internationalization of business spun its own webs of enmeshment and dependence. Roosevelt's new domestic bureaucracies, and the Anglophile State Department "fudge factory," seemed to epitomize these trends. American nationalists thus reacted against almost everything that had happened in recent decades, harking back to a simpler time, and searching restlessly for an arena where the old virtues held sway.

For them, Europe (or at least northern Europe) symbolized all that was wrong with Roosevelt's America. The New Deal had even imported none other than John Maynard Keynes, socialist, Bloomsbury intellectual, and homosexual, a far more threatening British economist than Adam Smith. It had also seemed to import "socialism," meaning strong state intervention at home, and a weak and enmeshed multilateral diplomacy abroad, hinged to cooperation with discredited British imperialists.

Europe was thick, clustered, hamstrung. Its markets were filled, as were those of its colonies—it was like a bureaucracy. Central America and East Asia, however, seemed open. Indeed, nations like Cuba, Nicaragua, and the Dominican Republic were open to almost anything Americans wished to do, as long as the Marines were nearby. The image of Asia (racist and utterly uninformed), was of a region with vast resources and opportunities, populated by dutiful and cringing peoples who followed white leadership. It was thought to be wide-open, policed by Britain only in its southern reaches, placing few external restraints on one's ambition. Of course, East Asia had closed, revolutionary nationalism had filled it in the 1940s, but rollbackers did not know this (anymore than Roosevelt did with his trusteeship policy). That they were wrong about East Asia, however, was not proved until the Korean War, so this assumption animated expansionists who sought an escape from Europe and from Eastern establishment dominance of foreign policy.

The material base for the isolationist, self-contained world view evaporated in the 1940s boom, as an America mostly undamaged by the war straddled the globe. But it persisted in the politics of Congress, the Republican party and the ideological realm, and structured the right-wing's attempts to counter internationalism. The vocal rightists in the 1950s functioned much like the "Gang of Four" in China in the 1970s: engaging in opaque ideological polemics ("the anti-Lin Piao, anti-Confucius campaign"), scrapping over control of the superstructure (the state), lobbing wild charges in a vain attempt to preserve a particular (and dying) conception of political economy, seeking to win back in the ideological and political domain what they had lost in the material domain.

John Flynn, a propagandist for the rollback current, an Asia-firster, and a strong supporter of MacArthur, wrote in 1952 (not in 1932) that New Dealers had carried out a "sneak attack" on the American way by secreting socialists in the bowels of the bureaucracy, bringing in Fabianism "on the British gradualist model." At home their goal was state guidance of the economy, shown by a "cult of national planning" imported from England via Harvard. Abroad, they pursued an "insane adventure in world salvation"—these "eager revolutionaries," whose "interests are in other lands," used the world crisis "to destroy our way of life." Flynn liked purely national industries, such as railroads, mines, and steel, which he argued should be kept from nationalization.[29]

Rollbackers and isolationists habitually engaged in venomous attacks on prominent internationalists and the institutions they represented; Wall Street itself was often a target. H. L. Hunt was a great opponent of "world government," which he took to be the end goal of both internationalists and communists. In this he was simply a bit more eccentric than most isolationists and rollbackers, who never recognized an entity greater than the nation-state, and who identified bankers, internationally-oriented firms, and international or stateless people (especially Jews), as advocates of a superordinate world authority.

Robert Wood loathed Dewey for his ties to Wall Street and "our Jewish friends," saw Eisenhower as "a stooge for the late F.D.R.," and expressed a virulent hatred of Harry Truman. Frazier Hunt, another strong MacArthur backer, lumped together "the Internationalists, the Europe-Firsters, the Red appeasers, [and] the United Nations worshippers," a typical formulation. Anthony Kubek, one of the few China scholars to defend the McCarthy/McCarran inquisition, declared himself in favor of "national independence," as against the internationalism and globalism of FDR and the "self-appointed One World planners." Ideologues of this current frequently associated a hated globalism with high-technology and exporting firms, as when Joseph Kamp linked support for the United World Federalists to Standard Oil, General Mills, and cotton tycoon W. T. Holliday. H. L. Hunt could barely think of the major oil firms and banks without a knee-jerk outburst along these lines, referring to the chairman of the board of Standard Oil of Ohio as "interested in some sort of World Government."[30]

Gen. Charles A. Willoughby, MacArthur's intelligence chief, shared the same assumptions, at one point finding the Carnegie Foundation full of "one-world fanatics, hell-bent to put up a tyrannical U.N." A friend of Willoughby's thought that "the Communists are not too far away from fact when they say this country is controlled by Wall Street." John Flynn linked Acheson, Alger Hiss, John Vincent, and Averell Harriman to "the One-Worlders and pro-pinks," who supported FDR's "grand design" for "a world federation, with himself sitting in majestic and historic eminence at the top." A broadside blaming Roosevelt for Pearl Harbor written by Ivan Yeaton, a man with Army intelligence connections, referred to the following "stooges" of Wall Street: FDR himself, Harry Hopkins, John J. McCloy ("the War Department Watchdog"), Harriman ("the State Department Watchdog"), "the EPICENTER [sic], the Chase Bank of New York," and "their paper, the Wall Street Journal."[31]

The mainstream literature places such views on the margins, in a lunatic fringe incorrigibly given to conspiracy theories, thus ignoring the centrality to American politics of such people and such ideas. Herbert Hoover and MacArthur were in extensive contact with isolationists and rollbackers, people like Wood, Hunt, Willoughby, Flynn, and many others. The belief that New Dealers constituted a pink if not Red influence within government penetrated almost every important state bureaucracy, pitting internationalists against nationalists; the intelligence agencies were particularly prone to such splits. If it is difficult to imagine that a man of Harriman's great wealth and cold war temperament might be a hidden communist sympathizer, it is also important to remember that James Angleton, long the head of CIA Counter-Intelligence, launched his "Project DINOSAUR" to smoke Harriman out as the long-sought Soviet mole within the intelligence "community."[32]

Great banking houses have been repositories of a sort of one-worldism: that single world called the capitalist world system. Polanyi took the Rothschild family as the metaphoric microcosm of the internationalist world view, the gold standard their lifeline because it was the lifeline of the world economy. Quigley found the great banking families to be cosmopolitan, internationalist, close to the state and its regulation of credit and debt, tending to invest in freely-circulating commodities like money, stocks, and bonds rather than fixed goods or real estate, and also noted their concern with the gold standard. Such investments encourage free-flowing, rapid circulation, and underpin a world view that abhors obstacles to exchange—such as nation-states. Quigley also remarked upon another characteristic of banking interests, which prompted conspiracy theories of the Right and Left: bankers "were almost equally devoted to secrecy and the secret use of financial influence in political life."[33]

Internationalist interests, of course, took a proprietary view of American foreign policy, establishing a tradition of selecting foreign service officers from the Ivy League, and secretaries of state and treasury from Wall Street. An observant Englishman remarked that the Eastern establishment was "fondest of scoffing at the very idea that it exists." He then went on to say, "To an extent that is quite astonishing to Europeans, who are brought up to think of the U.S. as a great populist democracy with a strong anti-aristocratic bias, the foreign policy of the U.S. as a great world power over the whole seventy years from 1898 to 1968 was a family affair." He noted that the foreign policy establishment since 1941 was fully unified on one point: oppose isolationism. He might have added: support interdependence and the cultural homogeneity that went with it.[34]

This ingenious combination of establishment dominance of foreign policy and incessant denial that any such thing existed drove isolationists and rollbackers to distraction, looking for the nearest carpet to gnaw. This mostly hidden conflict in part explains the Hiss case and the morbid fascination it held for Americans of all stripes. Alger Hiss rolled together

in his minor and thus vulnerable person all the establishment characteristics loathed by the Right: good breeding, an aristocratic demeanor, a
tutored mind, intellectual arrogance, Anglophilia, a deep commitment to
a world under law and internationalist rule-making, connections to numerous Wall Street stalwarts (like Dean Acheson), and errant flirtations
with the Left.

The establishment always took England and northern Europe as its
model, whether it was a Harvard professor emulating an Oxford don, a
graduating senior salivating after a Rhodes scholarship, Acheson admiring British diplomacy, Kennan ruminating on civilization and its barbarian peripheries, or a durable goods exporter looking for consumer buying power. Asia for them was at best a potential market or dependency
and at worst either an upstart enemy (Japan)³⁵ or a pathetic running sore
(China or India). In any case Asia was always subordinate to Europe in
foreign policy concerns.

The isolationist and rollback currents, however, saw Asia, especially
those parts of it not controlled by England, as barbarian but *obedient*, incontinent but *profitable*, secondary to Europe but therefore *open*. For
them East Asia was a Western extension of Indian country. Much of this
was fantasy, but fantasy becomes reality on a tabula rasa. It would not,
however, be fair to say that they disliked all of Europe. They simply differed from internationalists in preferring mercantilist and authoritarian
Germany, Italy, and Spain to England, France, and other northern European countries. In Asia, the country that caught expansionist imagi-
nations was China; internationalist attentions went to Japan, because it
was rather an honorary European country, clean and fastidious, long the
repository of a high culture, and most important, it deployed an industrial base and thus military might.

MacArthur, as the introductory chapter quotation suggests, symbolized
the virtues of an Asia-first, unilateral foreign policy. Herbert Hoover
wrote to him in 1947 that Japan was "the only area [in the world] where
the United States is in dominant action,"³⁶ an apt characterization of
MacArthur's imperious position and the unilateralism that characterized
American policy in East Asia in the postwar period. General Wedemeyer
summed up the world view of expansionists in a letter to MacArthur,
saying America's two major objectives should be "a free competitive cap-
italistic system" at home, and "placing America's interests first in all international organizations and agreements."³⁷ Such people were indeed
"America firsters," in the 1950s as in the 1930s.

In MacArthur's conception, it was Truman and Acheson who were the
isolationists: they expanded their world only to Europe, and "never com-
prehended the world as a whole. They never understood the enormous
forces of Asia." This was, of course, poppycock; Acheson had an inte-

grated conception of the globe which happened to place Asia as secondary or tertiary to Europe. Where they really differed was in the direction of American expansionism: MacArthur saw Asia as a new frontier. Over and over, his rhetoric placed America's destiny to the West, and there was much to support him in traditional American expansionism. George Washington, it may be remembered, warned only of involvement in Old World diplomacy, but expansion to the West was "new world" and a different sort of imperialism than the European variety. MacArthur's father, too, a veteran of the Civil and Indian wars, had spoken of currents sweeping "this magnificent Aryan people across the Pacific."[38]

MacArthur's sidekick Willoughby loved to quote Commodore Matthew Perry's 1856 statement that "the people of America will, in some form or other, extend their dominion and their power, until they shall have . . . placed the Saxon race upon the Eastern shores of Asia." MacArthur also assumed that America would have a tutelary role to play, and that he in particular would be the tutor: he prided himself on his command of "Oriental psychology," which reflected nineteenth-century renderings of Asians as obedient, dutiful, child-like, and quick to follow resolute leadership. He loathed the British presence in Asia, seeking to keep them out of his area of command. He also disliked the American agencies that he thought were Anglophile: the State Department, of course, but also the Office of Strategic Services (OSS) and the CIA, which he rightly knew were modeled on British intelligence practice.[39]

The Republican party leadership, however, split cleanly on the issue of Europe versus Asia. Expansionists took it as an article of faith that moderate Republicans like Dewey, Dulles, Eisenhower, and Nelson Rockefeller were Europe-firsters, and mostly they were right. Dewey was "steeped in the internationalism of the Eastern seaboard, suspicious of the Tafts and MacArthurs who proclaimed the primacy of Asia over Europe," and the same could be said of Dulles.[40] This cleavage often seemed as great as that dividing Republicans and Democrats, perhaps greater.

EXPANSIONISM AND MINERALS

If the mode of expansion is through agglomeration and unilateral sway, and if the entrepreneur wishes to control his investment with no interference, and if capitalism is assumed to be a zero-sum game (instead of the internationalist assumption that a rising tide hoists all ships), then the mine or concession is the proper symbol. Over and over we find an association between mineral deposits abroad and expansionism.

If expansionists seem to have an affinity for "found" wealth—usually found in the ground—and an especial fondness for gold, the American expansionist with an eye cast westward had an uncommon affection for silver. Key Pittman of Nevada, chairman of the Senate Foreign Relations Committee, had "a passionate devotion to the silver interests of America's West," and was an "economic nationalist and protectionist." He hated Cordell Hull and, in Wayne Cole's words, was "obsessed with silver." He was an important opponent of reciprocal trade in 1934, defending American mining interests against the import of foreign mineral products. Father Coughlin supported him in the 1934 silver purchase program. Much the same was true of other "silver senators" from the West. At the same time that they opposed Rooseveltian free trade, such isolationists sought markets abroad for American mineral exports.[41]

The unlikely grand inquisitor of the China field, Sen. Patrick McCarran of Nevada, was little more than a knee-jerk reflex connected to silver mine interests. His interest in the China issue seemed to resolve to some scheme to sell minerals in China, like getting the Kuomintang (KMT) to use silver specie. A classic expansionist, he loved generalissimos and hated one-worlders, and mixed together silver, air power, and rollback. He loathed the United Nations, calling it "a haven for spies and Communists," and despised immigrants to America (those who came after the Irish).

McCarran was nothing if not devoted to the interests of his constituency. Bashing China hands was an aberration beside his three loyalties: shepherding, silver, and gambling, which just happened to be the three most important businesses in Nevada. At one point he offered Generalissimo Franco an exchange of Basque shepherds for silver bullion loans. Although he schooled himself in handling China experts by shearing sheep as a young man, in maturity his real love was silver. His first political race found him both on the Democratic and the "Silver" ticket. He liked to intone that silver was not a commodity: "Silver is a monetary unit."[42]

Well, it had been in China at least, and in 1949 Nevada had a big silver surplus and the Kuomintang had a big need for a stable currency. "I think Senator McCarran's principal interest [in China] is providing a market for surplus silver," Sen. Theodore Green observed in 1949,[43] and that went for most of the representatives of the Western-state "silver bloc." When they eyed China, the glint was silver. D. Worth Clark of Idaho, like McCarran, was close to the China Lobby, getting involved in the provision of an informal military advisory group to the KMT. But perhaps our best prototype would be Sen. Elbert Thomas of Utah—often considered among the more enlightened of the silver state people. In some Senate hearings in 1949 he first turned to cotton exports, repeating verbatim the old yarn about adding an extra inch to every Chinese shirt; but he also opined that "the Chinaman put his profits in little silver balls," hanging them on his cotton shirt as a hedge against the fates. "A Chinese village could be destroyed, a Chinese house could be torn down, but always the Chinaman could go in the ashes and find a little bit of silver . . . and he started life over again."[44]

Now Nationalist China was itself "starting life over again," on Taiwan; it adopted a new silver specie in the summer of 1949. Its proposal in August for how the United States ought to aid it uncannnily caught Thomas's drift: $40 million in silver for the currency, $12 million in coarse cotton, out of a total request of $90 million (military aid comprised most of the remainder). The impetus for the KMT's "currency reform" came from McCarran's China aid bill in the spring of 1949. By the end of July, American mints had cut fifteen million silver pieces for the Nationalist government. The KMT thought that its most beneficial congressional combination would be "Republicans, southern Democrats, and members from the silver states."[45]

A different example is William Pawley, an important CIA figure who linked Asian experience to Central America. Pawley was born in 1896 into a family with Cuban business interests, and Pawley himself became extraordinarily wealthy on various Central American investments. He had been a Flying Tiger in China, and ran an airline in Cuba in the 1930s. He met the dictator Rafael Trujillo at that time, and became Trujillo's advisor on "mining and oil ventures." Soon he had achieved "spectacular" results, and came to own large nickle mine concessions in the Dominican Republic. Later on Pawley owned bus lines in Havana, helped overthrow the Arbenz regime in Guatemala, and played an important role in the initial planning for the Bay of Pigs.[46]

General Willoughby also tried a mining venture, in Mexico, finding a good model in the infamous Peruvian Cerro de Pasco mine, long held by the Republican Right. The products in Mexico were gold, tungsten, and other minerals. His associates included one Peter O'Crotty, who tended to rail on about "pinkoes" in the Mexican government (so influential as perhaps to necessitate its overthrow, he thought), and Roberto Fierro, who ran Fierro Tungsten and whose involvement in airpower led Willoughby to call him the "Mexican Lindbergh."[47]

The one form of American imperialism that Korea had directly experienced before 1945 was the expansionist variety—concessions on gold mines given out by King Kojông in the 1890s to Horace Allen, almost to Herbert Hoover in 1910, then passing into different American hands until 1939 when the lucrative mines in northern Korea were sold to the Japanese. We will come back to the Korean specifics in a later chapter. Here it is useful to note that several prominent Republican families, all conservative and aligned with Herbert Hoover—those of Ogden Mills, J. B. Haggin, and William Randolph Hearst—dominated the ownership of the Korean gold mines in the early part of the twentieth century. They also held interests in the Homestake Gold Mine in South Dakota and the Cerro de Pasco copper mines in Peru. Hearst also had interests in the Philippines, and his ranches employed great numbers of Chinese laborers.[48] M. Preston Goodfellow, Syngman Rhee's key American ally, was a pint-sized Hearst, combining publishing with mineral interests—in his case, mainly tungsten and gold.

The mineralist conception of interest was national in two senses: it wanted to exploit the American market without interference from foreign imports, but it also wanted a nationalist, unilateral defense of American rights to minerals abroad. Independent oil firms were very similar. Joseph Pew of Sun Oil was associated in 1946 with Robert Wood, John T. Flynn, Robert McCormick, and Merwin K. Hart (the latter a flamboyant anti-Semite) in something called the American Action Committee, an intensely nationalist grouping. But H. L. Hunt was the archetype of this current, loathing the Rockefellers and loving generals, and believing only in the tangible wealth of mineral commodities—oil, gold, and, fatefully for his sons who later sought to corner the world market, silver. Robert Wood, who ought to know, described Hunt as "a fanatical admirer of General MacArthur," and worked with him to try to get the 1952 Republican presidential nomination for MacArthur.[49]

ROLLBACKERS AND AIRPOWER

The rollback current drew upon unilateralist assumptions that, like Right-isolationism, went back to a political economy of self-containment, associated with industries and enterprises fearing foreign competition. Mineral politics was a good symbol of this. At the same time, however, one finds over and over an association between rollbackers and the high-technology of the midtwentieth century, airpower. A kind of technological fetishism drew rollbackers to panaceas that would obliterate threats to Americanism, especially the Soviets. This ostensibly contradictory position owes to their lack of enmeshment and connectedness with the rest of the world. They were far less consistent in their logic than internationalists; Acheson looked after the whole, he had to have a logic. They looked after the parts, pursuing quintessential "special interests."

An ineffable ignorance of the world beyond America's borders also led rollbackers to fantasies of an ultimate American freedom to do anything it wanted in the world, regardless of the consequences; the extraordinary prowess of the world's central technological power seemed to provide the means to make any fantasy conceivable. Curtis LeMay's Strategic Air Command (SAC) was the agency of rollback panaceas in the 1950s, with SAC's exclusive hold on delivery methods for atomic weapons the destructive but ultimate power—just as the Star Wars program expressed the same fantasies in vestigial form in the 1980s. If the Navy symbolized internationalism and the Army, containment, then rollback had its symbol in the Air Force, the one military capability that would enable the leapfrogging and rolling back of cold war boundaries.

Airpower may also be taken as a symbol of the contradictions and transformations of the isolationist/rollback current in the postwar period. Long having preferred a minimalist state, governmental funding of airpower and defense industries led rollbackers to change their attitude toward one aspect of state intervention: an enormous defense budget. Since 1950, the Right has maintained a deafening silence about this brand of state intervention in the "natural" workings of the market, separating it decisively from the outmoded but more consistent and honest views of fiscal conservatives like Robert Taft.

Lloyd Gardner was among the first to grasp the interaction of airpower and politics, arguing that it extended the open door to the skies and bridged cleavages between different interest aggregations (such as, we might say, the Europe-first versus Asia-first cleavage).[50] We may take it as a symbol of the 1950 compromise on interventionism. The American state subsidized the expansion of firms like Pan American into Latin America and East Asia, an early version of the extraordinary state involvement in and funding of the entire aerospace industry in the postwar period, much of it going to rollback constituencies in the Sun Belt.

The contradictions induced by airpower and state involvement were reproduced in individual rightists. Whereas Claire Chennault was a rollbacker pure and simple, making his reputation and his alliance with Chiang Kai-shek through daring exploits in the air, and always proferring airpower as the decisive panacea for the Chinese civil war, airpower entrepreneurs like Juan Trippe of Pan American or Howard Hughes shared part of the rollback vision but by no means all of it, mainly because both prospered so mightily from close connections to the American state.

A man like Bonner Fellers, part of the MacArthur entourage, fits the Chennault pattern. Fellers was a member of William Donovan's "planning group" in the OSS, having earlier been a military attache in Franco's Spain. In 1943 he joined MacArthur's staff. Always an advocate of the virtues of air power, he frequently called for rollback policies in the 1950s, and thought the CIA harbored "a group of Marxist-Socialist pro-Communists," including John Paton Davies, whom he alleged to be on the CIA payroll even during his forced exile in Lima, Peru. Fellers participated with Robert Wood, Generals Wedemeyer and Van Fleet, Frank Gannett, and others in an organization called For America.[51]

William Pawley, combining minerals and airpower, would be closer to the postwar mainstream than Fellers, even though his political views were, if anything, more virulently anticommunist. Pawley had helped Pan American set up air services in the Far East in the 1930s, and also inaugurated air services in Central America and helped build an airplane factory in India. In the late 1940s he was ambassador to Peru and then to Brazil. He had central access to the highest levels of the American government, and was a friend of CIA director Allen Dulles. With his interests in East Asia and Central America, profitable investments in minerals and airpower, and his deep intelligence connections, he may be taken as the quintessential rollbacker with central political credentials.[52]

Another good example would be Whiting Willauer, cofounder of the Flying Tigers, close associate of Chennault, and ambassador to Honduras and Guatemala in the 1950s. He and Pawley were deeply involved in the overthrow of the Arbenz regime in 1954. The ultimate airpower/rollback figure was of course Gen. Curtis LeMay, who as late as the 1960s continued to call for "nuking the Chinks" and other such elegantly expressed rollback adventures.[53]

MacArthur and Willoughby: The Local Rollback Headquarters

The hero of the rollback current, and indeed of the Republican right-wing going back to the Bonus March, was Gen. Douglas MacArthur. He and his intelligence chief, Gen. Willoughby, were flypaper for rollbackers visiting East Asia. Willoughby, as we will see, was an unreconstructed fascist. MacArthur's views were eminently more complex, as was his relationship to the rollback constituency in the United States.

MacArthur was an "untimely" character, an eighteenth-century pretense for contemporary national, patriotic imaginings, always striking his fellow Americans as "larger than life."[54] He was the ever-victorious conqueror on the white horse; the embodiment of past, present and future martial honor; the keeper of an occult, concealed national grail; the patriot of reflection rather than the patriot of lathered, unconsidered belief; the artist of the inner secrets of self-mastery that so escaped "modern" man, and thereby the master of himself. Whether he remained off on the Western frontier (the Pacific) for long years, or sequestered in his inner sanctum at the Dai Ichi Building for long days (as was his wont), this self-removal was prerequisite to his mask and his mystery. Forced up against the demands of daily life in the capitalist bazaar of our century, his veil could only drop to reveal a naked, frail human being.

Clayton James, MacArthur's learned biographer, thought the general "intensely conscious of himself as a 'man of destiny,'" but also found him full of complex, contradictory traits, that he himself never mastered. In any case no one else did. Most people thought him "the most complicated person they had ever met"; some thought him "charming, amiable, tactful and considerate"; whereas "others saw him as obnoxious, haughty, and calloused." Like another elderly patriot, Ronald Reagan, MacArthur spoke often of God but never attended church.[55]

MacArthur grew up hearing his father espouse views that long anteceded the rollback current, especially a bias against Europeans as decadent and conspiratorial, and a deep hatred of England as the center of gold power, responsible for the financial panic of 1893. As early as 1906 he had become an "Asia firster," saying that "the future and, indeed, the very existence of America, were irrevocably intertwined with Asia and its island outposts."[56] MacArthur's policy suggestions before the Korean War were often more moderate than those of State Department planners, and he was less favorable to the revival of Japanese industrial and military power than the centrist members of the Japan Lobby.

On the record, MacArthur did comparatively little to push the idea of rollback in the Far East before the Korean War. In talks with Kennan in early 1948 he supported "all-out aid" to the Chinese Nationalists, and urged Washington to place Asia above Europe in its strategy, thus to bring democracy and Christianity to Asia and "fundamentally alter the course of history." In late 1949 he continued to urge a commitment to the Nationalists, in effect backing the Chennault plan for continental rollback. Arguing that the Chinese communists "are grossly overrated," he called for hitting them "where they are weakest, namely in the air and on the sea." The United States ought to place "500 fighter planes in the hands of some 'war horse' similar to Gen. Chennault." Just before the Korean War, MacArthur's important memorandum on the peace treaty with Japan called for overcoming Soviet dynamism in Asia through "the drama of a reassertion of positive leadership, the regaining of forceful initiative."[57] But the "positive action" envisioned here seemed merely to be a quick conclusion of the peace treaty.

MacArthur kept close company, however, with an abominable assortment of cryptofascists and anti-Semites, and his backers in the United States came mostly from the Right-isolationist, rollback tendency. One close friend, Gen. George Van Horn Mosely, thought that organizers of the American working class in the 1930s ought to be gathered up and "segregated," either to be shipped off to Russia or held in island camps. He hoped MacArthur would run for president in 1944, thus to halt the "mongrelization" of the United States by Blacks, Jews, leftists, and "lowbred" immigrants—something that might require MacArthur to "restore our Republic by the temporary institution of the most drastic methods" (if, as Mosely expected, MacArthur lost the election because of the activities of "subversives"). In other words, a military coup. As if to leave nothing to the imagination, Mosely said after the war that although Hitler by then had "few friends" in the United States, "one hears on all sides today that Hitler was right in one thing he did—that is, in getting rid of the Jews."⁵⁸

Mosely's idea was that dissent and ethnic pollution could be dealt with by expulsion and amputation from the body politic, something characteristic of MacArthur's world view and especially his constituency in the United States. Robert Wood, former head of the America First Committee, was his biggest backer for the presidency in 1944 and 1948; by 1952 he left this quixotic activity to H. L. Hunt, often described as a "fanatic" admirer of MacArthur. Other powerful right-wing forces supporting a MacArthur candidacy in 1944 and 1948 included the Hearst and Gannett presses, Colonel McCormick, the Pew family and another important Republican newspaperman, Roy Howard.⁵⁹

Still, Gen. Charles A. Willoughby, chief of Supreme Command, Allied Powers (SCAP) intelligence, was closer to the hearts of rollbackers than was MacArthur. An odd and little-known man, MacArthur liked to call him "my little fascist." It was an apt characterization. Willoughby was born in Heidelberg to Junker stock, being the son of Freiherr T. von Tscheppe-Weidenbach. He came to the United States at the age of eighteen and changed his name to Willoughby. He graduated from Gettysburg College in 1914, and served with the American expeditionary force that sought out Pancho Villa in 1917–1918. He was MacArthur's intelligence chief all through the Pacific War and up to his removal from the Korean command in 1951. Thereafter he maintained close and public ties to extreme-Right groups like the John Birch Society and the Billy James Hargis Crusade; for a decade (1961–1971) he wrote an "intelligence digest" for the latter's *Weekly Crusader*. He carried himself like a Prussian officer, as if he were "looking out over a high board fence." During the Pacific War he got a reputation for "vainglorious" and highly inaccurate intelligence communiqués.⁶⁰ Willoughby spent much of his life trying to reproduce his kind in the United States, and found them, imperfectly, in the rollback constituency.

Willoughby was a profound racist and anti-Semite who saw the Soviet bloc as "the historical continuity of 'Mongoloid-PanSlavism.'" He once wrote that "when the teeming millions of the Orient and the tropics got their hands on magazine rifles, Kipling's white man was on the way out." He deplored Asian wars in which "illiterate Chinese coolies" wiped out American draftees, given that "the white man is an expensive and limited commodity." When *The American Mercury* was filled with virulently anti-Semitic tracts, Willoughby wrote articles for it—referring to the New York press as a "stronghold of Jewry" and the like.⁶¹ His "intelligence digest" recommended all through the 1960s that various "weapons of mass destruction," unspecified, be used against the Vietnamese people. It is hard to find something nice to balance this account. Willoughby was a thoroughly loathsome person whose entire world view consisted of piles of ethnic stereotypes; he was apparently capable of anything.

He also was one right-winger who fit Hofstadter's paranoid politics like a glove. When it looked like Eisenhower might get the Republican nomination instead of MacArthur or Taft in 1952, Willoughby told MacArthur that this proved the Republicans were part of "a clever conspiratorial move to perpetuate the vampire hold of the Roosevelt-Truman mechanism." After reading Chalmers Johnson's *An Instance of Treason*, he described Johnson and his colleague Robert Scalapino, two scholars of East Asia who could hardly be accused of left-wing sentiments, as "pipsqueak Frankensteins" trying to "whitewash" the record of Ozaki Hatsumi, a person whom Willoughby held responsible for the Chinese revolution.[62] His paranoia extended to the destruction of classified documentation so that it would not fall into the hands of evil malefactors like Gordon W. Prange, the great historian of Pearl Harbor,[63] a matter of great moment also for the classified record of the Korean War—with which Willoughby tampered, as we will see.

Willoughby's revered hero, besides MacArthur, was Gen. Francisco Franco. He claimed to have met Franco during the "campaign against the Riff" in Spanish Morocco in 1923. He admired how Franco had "settled the Communist fifth column, once and for all," and saw the Spanish Civil War as the opening shot in a fifteen-year battle against communism, the last chapter of which, for him, was the Korean War—which he frequently likened to the Spanish conflict. He spent taxpayer's money during the Occupation to produce a private edition book, *Bailen and the Spanish Bridgehead*, on Franco's military campaigns; he claimed that James Forrestal had suggested this project to him. During the Occupation he and MacArthur maintained close ties to the Spanish and Portuguese embassies in Tokyo.[64]

During the Occupation of Japan and the Korean War Willoughby maintained clandestine ties to Japanese militarists, including the bacteriological warfare criminal General Ishii; in the 1950s and 1960s he claimed to have close ties to Reinhard Gehlen and other former Nazi officers then being used by United States intelligence in the cold war.[65]

After MacArthur's sacking, Willoughby frequently visited Spain, and claimed to have been involved in the American military base negotiations with Franco. He set up a kind of right-wing internationale called the "international comité," using money from the Hunt brothers in Texas, linking Spain and Portugal together with German right-wingers, the Hargis Crusade, and others. He was an agent for Hunt Oil in seeking offshore oil rights in the Portuguese colony of Mozambique.[66]

It is impossible to argue that this fascist and, it would appear, clinical paranoiac was a marginal figure in MacArthur's eyes. He was the only high officer who had access to MacArthur without having to go through his chief of staff: he and his boss discussed intelligence affairs in total privacy. Observers described Willoughby as "very close" to MacArthur, and Willoughby followed MacArthur with a devotion that might put Kim Il Sung's scribes in the pale. In 1947 he wrote to the general,

> There is no contemporary figure comparable to yours . . . ultimately [people] have been attached to a great leader, to a man and not an idea, to a Marlbrough [*sic*], to a Napoleon, to a Robert E. Lee. Underneath it all, these are age-old dynastic alliances. . . . A gentleman can serve a grand-seigneur. That will be a good ending to my career . . . and as I scan the world, the grands-seigneurs are leaving the arena, fighting a bitter rear-guard action against the underman, the faceless mob driven by Russian knouts.

On MacArthur's seventieth birthday, Willoughby again likened him to Napoleon, to men who "have always known how to inspire personal devotion . . . and [to] respond with paternal benevolence, the essence of personal leadership."[67]

Willoughby inspired personal revulsion. He prided himself on possessing the high qualities of the Junker ruling class, people to whom Nietzsche referred when he once said "the mere proximity of a German retards my indigestion."[68] An organic reactionary, Willoughby was an island alone in the sea of American liberalism, seeking to reproduce himself in the rollback constituency. He did not serve his chief well. Perhaps Willoughby was right in likening the Korean civil war to the one in Spain, but in likening MacArthur to Napoleon, he might have served his boss better by reminding him, before he embarked on the march to the Yalu, of what happened to Napoleon in Spain.

THE CHINA LOBBY, MCCARTHYISM, AND ROLLBACK

One day in 1949, Patrick Hurley appeared with I. F. Stone on "Meet the Press." In the course of tough questioning about his experience in China and the issuance of the State Department's China "White Paper," Hurley boiled over, "shook his finger at Stone and bellowed over the air, 'Okay, kid! You go back to Jerusalem, and I'll go back to the oilfields.' "[69] A foreigner would need at least an hour's tutoring before that exchange could be made remotely intelligible; why Jerusalem, why oilfields, why was an Oklahoma oilman appointed wartime ambassador to China, why was he the first publicly to charge certain State Department officers with procommunist leanings, why in a democratic society was Stone almost alone in his spirit of principled dissent? American politics had an inscrutability in the early postwar period, as subterranean conflicts and schemes gave off rumblings and burps that only sometimes breached the surface; an Aesopian political language masked fissures that could not be interpreted in liberal or pluralist terms. It was like a Chinese two-line struggle, it was the stereotype of Oriental politics in our own backyard.

But we did have "Chinese politics" in our own backyard. One important element of this hidden conflict was the extraordinary influence of Nationalist China on the ordinary politics of the Republican right-wing, a relationship that could not stand the light of day and, apparently, still cannot in the 1990s. The China Lobby itself was a rather minor effort, led by people of little influence and obvious self-interest. The Kuomintang was losing the civil war in China and seemingly had few strings to pull in Washington. Its foreign policy agenda was pure and simple: rollback on the mainland. Yet this seemed utterly infeasible before June 1950.

Its remarkable if temporary influence emerged because China became "China." China, little known to most Americans, an opaque, inscrutable vastness, could become "China," an issue that people could be mobilized around because it stood for nothing in the American mind and therefore could stand for everything—it was a tabula rasa on which the right-wing and the expansionists could write. The "China" issue became an unwobbling pivot in the attempt to reverse the verdict of the 1948 election, and beyond that the New Deal and the victory of internationalism—unwobbling because unknown and mysterious, and therefore not subject to refutation. (Richard Nixon pivoted nimbly with the "China" issue his entire career: early architect of "who lost China," nervy opponent of "Peiping," august statesman of the reconciliation with "Beizhing," politically resurrected by Deng Xiao-ping.)

A vast indigenous revolution, culminating a century of disorder in old China, could be rendered as a diabolical creature of Moscow or American fifth-columnists; a failed nationalist revolution turned into a nauseating dictatorship presiding over a miasma of corruption and ruin could become a Christian democracy, all in the waving of a Hearst wand, because nobody knew anything about China. The basic conflict was in American state and society, but "China" provided conservative and rightist Republicans with their first galvanizing issue since the New Deal itself (the attempt at pinning Pearl Harbor on Roosevelt having failed). The Nationalists and their minions were glad to oblige, desperate as they were for U.S. backing, and so a network of relationships, funds, and probably treasonable activities mushroomed overnight, giving a moribund exile regime an extraordinary influence on American politics.

Powerful Republicans (and sometime Democrats, like William Pawley) backed the China Lobby effort, but in predictable fashion the conspicuous activists were an odd lot. The public leader of the China Lobby was Alfred Kohlberg, who had garnered about $1 million per year in passing Irish linens through the delicate embroidery and decidedly cheap labor of "an Army of Chinese women" until they became "Kohlkerchiefs." He was a typical if peculiar expansionist, looking after the parts in the form of a minor textile business that was major for his personal fortunes. Although a Jew, he associated with many public anti-Semites. He was assisted by William Goodwin, who had been connected to American fascist groups before Pearl Harbor, and was a paid lobbyist of the Nationalists.[70]

Kohlberg began peddling his conspiracy theories about China experts in and out of the State Department in the mid-1940s, specializing in attacks on the Institute for Pacific Relations. But few were listening. When he wrote to John Foster Dulles requesting a meeting to fill him in on Alger Hiss—whom Dulles had handpicked to head the Carnegie Foundation—Dulles refused to see him. Two years later after the China issue had heated up, however, Dulles could not ignore him and granted him an audience.[71] By this time "China" had become a way perhaps to reverse the effects of Dewey's narrow loss to Truman, and major figures in the Republican party began backing the China Lobby.

A top secret cable just before the 1948 election explains the Nationalist interest in Dewey. It said Dulles would be Dewey's secretary of state, and he and other Republicans, including Styles Bridges and Walter Judd, would then seek "to induce Dewey to send a special investigating group to China right after the election."[72] Chiang was desperate for American aid; Dewey's hair-whisker loss to Truman unquestionably panicked the Nationalists.

Soon Kohlberg and others got high-level Republican backing. For example, Kohlberg participated with Roy Howard, Henry Luce, General Wedemeyer, Walter Judd, and other prominent Republicans in a private "study group" on China and the Far East organized by William Pawley; Kohlberg was also close to the caustic newspaperman William Loeb, and to many senators and congressmen. The Scripps-Howard newspaper chain hawked Chiang's line to the point that Truman labeled its owner "Roy Chiang Kai-shek Howard"; Howard had extensive contacts with wealthy Nationalists like T. V. Soong, H. H. Kung, Hollington Tong, and the tungsten magnate K. C. Li, as well as political figures like Hu Shih, K. C. Wu, and T. F. Tsiang. He arranged for H. H. Kung to meet with Willoughby in Tokyo on at least two occasions, in June and September of 1950. Howard was one of the few China lobbyists with ties to the Rhee camp, mainly through Louise Yim. Another major activist and financial backer was Frederick C. McKee, an eccentric Pittsburgh industrialist and casket maker.[73]

Various sources suggest that the major part of China Lobby funding, besides that from the Nationalist regime, came directly from T. V. Soong, one of the wealthiest men in the world at the time. Wellington Koo's papers show that the Nationalists directly funded Kohlberg's *Plain Talk* and *The National Republic*, which perhaps explains why the latter took such an unexpected interest in the China hands. Nationalist officials gave one Norman Paige $2,000 a month to serve as a publicist, and scripted articles by Hearst correspondents like Ray Richards. Wellington Koo funded Freda Utley's mudslinging broadsides against China experts in the State Department and academia (as did Robert Wood and H. L. Hunt).[74] Drew Pearson wrote that "more money had been spent on bribes on behalf of the China lobby than any other major matter in Washington," and asserted that Louis Johnson had offered him $10,000 if he would make favorable references to H. H. Kung.[75]

General Willoughby was an eager supporter of Kohlberg and the Lobby, supplying them with his conspiratorial fantasies about various itinerant leftists. Just before McCarthy's inquisition began, Willoughby wrote Kohlberg to congratulate him on "the relentless stand" *Plain Talk* had been taking on "the China betrayal [from] 1943 onward," and on unmasking the "foul intrigues" of Hiss and the China hands.[76]

Into this undulating mire stepped Sen. Joseph McCarthy, who told a reporter in early 1950, "I've got a sock full of shit and I know how to use it." Kohlberg, Willoughby, J. Edgar Hoover, and other rightists provided most of the shit, and McCarthy supplied what the Soviets called "amateur night in an insane asylum," rising to denounce 207, or 55, or, as it happened, a handful of vulnerable liberals in the State Department and elsewhere as "Communists and queers who have sold 400,000,000 Asiatic people into atheistic slavery." Meanwhile, for his patriotic efforts he had to suffer the slings and arrows of "egg-sucking phony liberals." "Tailgunner Joe" was a brute, but he knew how to stampede the rollback constituency.[77]

For Americans who had to be told what a communist looked like,[78] McCarthy supplied plausible models: mainly Eastern establishment blue bloods, but also Foggy Bottom scribblers, tweedy professors, closet-bound homosexuals, and China experts who had been abroad too long— anyone who might be identified as an internal foreigner, alien to the American heartland. (*The Freeman* once said that Red propaganda appealed only to "Asian coolies and Harvard professors.") Almost anybody with a good education might qualify; thus the bane of the liberal in the 1950s was the threat of mistaken identity.

After McCarthyism had seemingly run its course, it was easy to interpret it as a populist aberration, the dominant social science interpretation until the late 1960s. Richard Rovere found the pathology mostly on the Right. "McCarthy drew into his following most of the zanies and zombies and compulsive haters who had followed earlier and lesser demagogues in the fascist and semifascist movements of the Thirties and Forties." Peter Viereck thought the aberration was both Right and Left, that McCarthy drew upon an "enormous, gullible mass base," hiding a "leftist instinct behind a self-deceptive rightist veneer." Never one to mince words, he thought McCarthyism brought together

> The nationalist alliance between the sticks and the slums, between the hick-Protestant mentalities in the West (populist-progressive on the Left, know-nothing on the Right) and the South Boston mentalities in the East. The latter are, metaphorically, an unexplored underground catacomb, long smoldering against the airy, oblivious palaces of both portions (liberal and Wall Street) of the Eastern upper world.[79]

In this *pasticcio* of bilious elitism and mixed metaphor there is a truth. As a first approximation, McCarthyism was an attack against the Eastern establishment, what Viereck called "our old ruling class," including "Eastern, educated, mellowed wealth—internationalist and at least superficially liberalized, like the Achesons of Wall Street or the Paul Hoffmans of the Easternized fraction of Detroit industrialists." Rovere wrote that this class "maintains effective control over the executive and judicial branches of government . . . dominates most of American education and intellectual life . . . has very nearly unchallenged power in deciding what is respectable opinion . . . [and] is absolutely unrivaled in controlling foundations." He nominated John J. McCloy as chairman of the board of this establishment, Reinhold Neibuhr as its "official establishment theologian," and he might have added Arthur Schlesinger, Jr., as its court historian.[80] One may quibble about establishment "control" of all this, but it is hard to deny its dominance of the foreign policy process for decades before 1950.

McCarthy unquestionably drew upon the historic grievances of the right-isolationist and rollback tendency. He himself came from a farm constituency of Catholics and German-Americans, giving colorful voice to their hatred of the British and Anglophile easterners, for whom Acheson, with his phony British accent, waxed moustache, top hat, and tails, was the flypaper. On the very day McCarthy first rose in the Senate to denounce communism in government, Sen. Homer Capehart of Indiana exploded, "How much more are we going to have to take? Fuchs and Acheson and Hiss and hydrogen bombs *threatening outside* and New Dealism eating away at the vitals of the nation! In the name of Heaven, is this the best America can do?" [emphasis added][81]

A bizarre sexual politics attended this farcical drama. McCarthy lumped "communists and queers" together, of course, but also managed to make anyone with a Boston blue-blood accent, or with intellectual pretensions or worldly knowledge, seem like a sissy if not a homosexual. Everett Dirksen, a centrist, referred to the "Lavender Lads" in the State Department, and indeed the period saw widespread purges of homosexuals in government.[82]

Washington gossips had unquestionably tutored McCarthy in tales of J. Edgar Hoover's G-men catching card-carrying internationalists like Sumner Welles in public toilets, the real or alleged homosexuality of Keynes, Harry Dexter White, and Lauchlin Curry, and of course some believe to this day that Alger Hiss (or his son) and Whitaker Chambers had a homosexual relationship.

Two other deep structures take this sexual politics beyond the realm of cruel gossip. First, British spies known by 1951 if not earlier to have infiltrated American intelligence included homosexuals like Guy Burgess and Donald McLean, and the CIA was often thought to harbor many homosexuals. Second, there was scuttlebutt that McCarthy himself was a homosexual, Whittaker Chambers was gay, and of course J. Edgar Hoover's relationship with Charles Tolson was the subject of similar conjecture. McCarthy's youthful myrmidons, Roy Cohn and David Schine, were also suspect; Lillian Hellmann referred to the three of them as "Bonnie, Bonnie, and Clyde."[83] This all belongs in a trashy gossip column, of course, were it not isomorphic to an interesting aspect of the period: homosexuals covering their predilection by fingering other homosexuals; traitors hiding their activities by alleging treachery.

McCarthyism was not pathological. It was American politics, part of an ever-present tendency that comes forward in crises, taking always strange and unpredictable forms—the Red scare after World War I, McCarthyism after World War II, Jerry Falwell and Jesse Helms after the Vietnam War. It is a central tendency, rooted in the conservative wing of the Republican party but getting critical help from centrist Republicans and Democrats. As Michael Paul Rogin put it, "McCarthyism was not a mass protest; it flourished within the normal workings of American politics, not radically outside of them"; it was an attack "made by one section of the political elite against another and was nurtured by the very elites under attack."[84] It was also a purge within the state.

Domestic politics in America is like rugby, slouching toward the goal line, hamstrung by constituents and the pulling-and-hauling of a thousand bargains, lacking autonomy. Foreign policy is like ballet, or the long pass from quarterback, or the boxer with a knockout punch. McCarthy was a nihilist who believed in nothing; a breaker of Senate rules, he also broke free of the webs of domestic politics, taking a foreign policy issue that hardly anyone understood and running with it. He escaped the slogging politics of Congress, which he disliked; drawing upon an aggrieved mass base, he launched ideological attacks on the Truman-Acheson executive, thus limiting their extraordinary autonomy.

McCarthy (and later, Senator McCarran) were supplied documentation on alleged subversives, most of it classified, by J. Edgar Hoover, Willoughby and Whitney of MacArthur's staff, and even Walter Bedell Smith of the CIA. In 1953 the Justice Department worked with Willoughby, Ho Shih-lai, and Chiang Ching-guo on the cases of Lattimore and John Davies—Chiang, of course, being the son of Chiang Kai-shek, with long experience in the KMT secret police. Perhaps most shocking, it is now clear that several of these cases were faked.[85] Willoughby had begun McCarthy-style investigations of his own in 1947, especially of scholars working for "the extremely leftist" Institute for Pacific Relations; his first case was Andrew Grajdanzev, author in 1944 of what remains today the best English-language account of Japanese rule in Korea. Willoughby had him tailed, read his mail, and determined that he might be "a long-range Soviet agent"—the evidence being that Owen Lattimore had written a recommendation for him, and that he wanted to purge Japanese that MacArthur and Willoughby did not.

Willoughby fingered Anna Louise Strong and Agnes Smedley as crafty subversives who somehow, despite their blanketed obscurity, brought Mao to power by remote control. In a letter of May 1950 to the head of the House Un-American Activities Committee—one that might well have investigated Willoughby were it truly looking for "unAmericans"—Willoughby said that "American Communist brains planned the communization of China," fellow-traveling people who have "an inexplicable fanaticism for an alien cause, the Communist 'Jehad' of pan-Slavism for the subjugation of the Western world." Willoughby paid particular attention to names and birthplaces that might indicate Jewish origin.[86]

Major Republican publishers also aided McCarthy. He won the support of all the big Republican chains: Hearst, Scripps-Howard, McCormick, and Gannett. The Hearst press assigned Ray Richards to help him with investigations that were meant to prove his allegations about communists in government; Richards had worked with Congressman George Dondero on the 1945 *Amerasia* case, and took as his particular target Owen Lattimore. Richards was also a friend and lobbyist for Syngman Rhee.[87]

Beyond the general interest of Republican elites in reversing the 1948 election and hacking away at the New Deal, McCarthyism served narrower interests as well. As Thomas C. Reeves notes, among McCarthy's first "anti-communist" acts was a September 1949 attempt to impose import quotas on Russian furs, thus to protect Wisconsin's fur industry. When his inquisition got going, he quickly accumulated the support of independent oil barons such as Hunt, Hugh Roy Cullen, and Clint

Murchison; he frequently vacationed at Murchison's estate and became known as the "third Senator from Texas."[88] He also was said to have benefitted from a Chinese soybean conspiracy just before the Korean War began, as we will see.

The case of Owen Lattimore says much about McCarthyism, the China Lobby, and its relationship to Korea. It is usually forgotten that McCarthy began his attacks well before the Korean War, that Lattimore's views on Korea were one of McCarthy's central subjects, and that by June 1950 McCarthyism seemed to be losing its momentum—its capacity to establish "China" as an issue in American politics. McCarthy first attacked Lattimore indirectly on March 13, 1950, then alleged that he had found a "chief Russian spy" on March 21, and finally named Lattimore when information leaked from his committee. Beyond Lattimore he was after Philip Jessup, "a dangerously efficient Lattimore front," but ultimately his object was Acheson, whom McCarthy termed "the voice for the mind of Lattimore."[89] Acheson was his final target: why? In part it was because, by the spring of 1950, as we will see, Acheson was the last high official, besides Truman himself, standing between the Kuomintang and the American backing it desperately needed to survive an impending communist invasion.

In early April McCarthy claimed to have a document incriminating Lattimore as a Soviet agent, prompting Lattimore to release it to the press—a memorandum he wrote in August 1949, arguing that "the United States should disembarass itself as quickly as possible of its entanglements in South Korea." Lattimore saw Korea as "little China," and Rhee as another Chiang: if we could not win with Chiang, he said, how could we win with "a scattering of 'little Chiang Kai-sheks' in China or elsewhere in Asia." The argument was cogent, and hardly treasonable: this was a common theme of anti-Chiang liberals from 1945 on. Of greater moment, Lattimore's memo also implicitly criticized the developing bureaucratic momentum for rollback in the summer of 1949, which we will survey later.

> It certainly cannot yet be said . . . that armed warfare against communism in the Far East . . . has become either unavoidable or positively desirable. Nor can it be said with any assurance that . . . the Far East would be the optimum field of operation. There are still alternatives before us—a relatively long peace, or a rapid approach toward war. If there is to be war, it can only be won by defeating Russia—not northern Korea, or Viet Nam, or even China.[90]

This document was part of a general reassessment of East Asian policy, bringing in outside consultants such as Lattimore for their views. It reads as if Lattimore were aware of the developing dialectic between containment and rollback in the Far East.

In mid-May 1950 McCarthy again attacked the "Acheson Lattimore axis" (or, the "pied pipers of the Politburo") on Korea policy, saying Lattimore's plans for Korea would deliver millions to "Communist slavery." Taking direct aim at the Nationalists' principal antagonist, Acheson, he blared, "fire the headmaster who betrays us in Asia."[91]

Lattimore's fuller views on Korea were given in the fall of 1949 when the State Department called in experts to consult with them on the new Asian policy. Generally speaking, liberal scholars such as Lattimore, Cora DuBois, and John K. Fairbank sought merely to point out that the revolution sweeping much of East Asia was indigenous, the culmination of a century of Western impact. Conservative scholars like Phillip Taylor, William Colegrove, and Bernard Brodie sought instead to argue that Soviet machinations were behind Asian revolution; Taylor and Colegrove were particularly anxious to reestablish Japan's position in East Asia, Taylor saying that "we have got to face it head on. We have to get Japan back into, I am afraid, the old co-prosperity sphere . . . and include India in it." The liberal wing was dominant within scholarly circles, however, and in these meetings a consensus emerged looking forward to the establishment of relations with the People's Republic of China (PRC). Taylor and the others were in the distinct minority.

Lattimore sought to make some simple and obvious points. The United States should stand with progressive and liberal forces in Asia, where they existed, but should not place itself in the path of changes that were already fait accompli, such as the Chinese revolution. This he saw as self-defeating and stupid. His views were reasonable and well informed; they would have been centrist in 1945 and acceptable in 1947, but by 1950 he had not tacked properly to the new winds blowing in Washington. That, in essence, was Owen Lattimore's crime. If we must make the point in legalistic terms, everything he said was protected by First Amendment guarantees, there is not the slightest evidence that he had connections with the Soviets, and in any case Acheson, Kennan, Rusk, and the others hardly waited with baited breath for the views of outside consultants.

Lattimore's views on Korea during these sessions were prescient. "Korea appears to be of such minor importance that it tends to get overlooked, but Korea may turn out to be a country that has more effect upon the situation than its apparent weight would indicate." After this prophetic mouthful, he went on to say accurately that the ROK politically was "an increasing embarassment," an "extremely unsavory police state" where the chief power is concentrated in the hands of people who were collaborators of Japan. . . . Southern Korea, under the present regime, could not resume close economic relations with Japan without a complete reinfiltration of the old Japanese control and associations . . . the kind of regime that exists in southern Korea is a terrible discouragement to would-be democrats throughout Asia. . . . Korea stands as a terrible warning of what can happen.

Once the war began, however, Lattimore expressed his support for the American intervention.[92]

McCarthy's information on Lattimore was little more than the welter of lies, half-truth, and fantasy that Kohlberg had been peddling unsuccessfully for years. Willoughby supplied Kohlberg and McCarthy with his conspiratorial rantings, but he had nothing concrete on Lattimore—even after searching French police files and Japanese *kempeitai* (secret police) intelligence files from China in the 1930s. And so he sent one of his agents to Formosa: "that slippery snake in the grass is bound to show up somewhere." But according to high CIA authority, Willoughby never dug up anything of importance on Lattimore (or anyone in the State Department), and the same was true of McCarthy. The FBI solicited information from both Willoughby and Kohlberg, and also gave that to McCarthy. Other members of the China Lobby collaborated with McCarthy, including Victor O'Kelliher, a close aid to Louis Johnson, who solicited Kuomintang information on Lattimore in April 1950.[93]

In spite of the obviously political and mendacious nature of McCarthy's witch-hunt against Lattimore, within a few weeks liberal organs of opinion were already giving the classic formulation that enabled them to escape McCarthy's gunsights: supporting Lattimore's right to his opinions, but condemning them as irresponsible or extreme. In mid-April the *New York Times* singled out his "unsound" position on Korea; it found Lattimore's view "quite shocking," saying that the State Department had "rejected flatly Mr. Lattimore's advice to cut and run in Korea" (a good indication of the perception of the ROK's importance by this time).[94]

In this assembled procession of liberals toward the comfortable neo-center we witness the consequences of the absence of a rooted Left in American politics, leaving left-liberals on shifting ground, extraordinarily vulnerable to being tossed out of the Americal oval, the hallowed realm of political inclusion. McCarthy's assault on Lattimore drew precisely the new boundaries of acceptability: a left-liberal China scholar was out, Freda Utley was in.[95] Mary McAuliffe is quite right to say, "One of the major ironies of the period was the unexpected role which liberals played, first in constructing a new liberalism which rejected the American left, and then in accepting some of the basic assumptions and tactics of the Red Scare itself."[96] In foreign policy, the effect was to tie off and cauterize any thought of internationalist accommodation, and to push through to acceptability the rollback alternative—just in the weeks before the Korean War began.

Tailgunner Joe was a good marksman: he left a generation of liberals looking over their shoulders to the right, fearing yet another case of mistaken identity.[97] This is the real source of liberal outrage against McCarthyism: not that thousands of American leftists and communists were unfairly and unconstitutionally persecuted, but that liberal innocents got caught in his gunsights. McCarthyism was an intraelite struggle, with most of the issues going back to the 1930s. Joe McCarthy popped up as the point man of the conflict, because he was an opportunist, a nihilist, the quintessential extremist who stands out front and takes positions that clear the path for what established elites want—he was to American politics what a Qaddafi is to Arab politics. The public was involved when the senator and his allies sought to mobilize masses of people from the isolationist-rollback constituency, and hurl their concentrated strength at the executive.

But there is another point to note. Although it cannot be proved here, it is probable that a core issue in the intraelite conflict was treasonable activity by McCarthy's main supporters. In the late 1930s many of his backers had been pro-German, including several participants in the America First Committee and the American Bund. Pearl Harbor left them all in an extraordinarily precarious position; they may have feared postwar inquiries into their prewar activities. The best defense being a good offense, this would explain part of the motivation for the Pearl Harbor inquiries, New Dealers being the common target. Of particular interest would be the cases of Harry Dexter White and Lauchlin Currie, who in the early 1940s were key antagonists of American firms still dealing with the Nazis during wartime, who knew where all the bodies were buried, and who were targets of the McCarthyites in the 1950s.[98]

In the 1950s McCarthyism served to draw attention away from the corruption and intrigue of high officials with the Nationalists and the China Lobby, including, as we will see, the filching of top-level secrets on behalf of a foreign government. Through McCarthyism a narrow set of interests combined to achieve (not singlehandedly, of course) the result of maintaining American-Taiwan ties for two decades, wrecking the careers of nearly all government officials who had spoken the truth about the Nationalists, and enriching the pockets of numerous expansionists. Congress and the Justice Department should have been investigating this, and perhaps still should; but McCarthy's ferocious and wild attacks diverted all attention to the other direction.

JAMES BURNHAM: IDEOLOGUE OF INTERVENTIONISM

In Alfred Kohlberg's little-known magazine called *Plain Talk*, a rude and crude vehicle mostly for his China Lobby views, we find Isaac Don Levine arguing in June 1948 that the goal of American strategy must be "the disgorging by the imperialists of Moscow of the illicit trophies they had amassed," the "foundation-stone" of which must be *action*—"not where Russia is strongest, but where she is weakest, not on her threshold but in her hinterland, in the Pacific and not in the Atlantic sphere." He suggested that the United States arm two hundred Chinese Nationalist divisions "to regain Manchuria," which would have the virtue of drawing Soviet attentions away from Europe, while depriving them "of the one great industrial bastion available to her in the Far East." In October 1948, Kohlberg and Levine called for a general policy of "liberation," in Eastern Europe as well as Asia. But it would be difficult to say that such views had more than a fringe following in 1948; most of *Plain Talk*'s support came from the Chinese Nationalists. Kohlberg's call for rollback in Northeast Asia fell on the same deaf ears that would not listen to his charges about Alger Hiss.[99]

By 1950 *Plain Talk*'s fortunes had changed: it now was a glossy magazine called *The Freeman*, an organ of neoconservative (or merely ever-conservative) opinion—the *Commentary* of that era. Kohlberg's attacks on Hiss, Lattimore, the Institute for Pacific Relations (IPR), and the rest now got a respectful hearing throughout the nation's capital; and so did rollback. But Kohlberg, his best efforts notwithstanding, was merely the Norman Podhoretz of his time, not the George Kennan of the rollback strategy. That title fell to a far more formidable mind.

In 1947, just at the time of the announcement of the Truman Doctrine, James Burnham published *The Struggle for the World*, a critique of the containment thesis and a harbinger of its antithesis, rollback. In 1950 Burnham became the synthesis. He was a former Trotskyite from a wealthy Chicago family, known for his brilliant intellect both at Princeton and in his 1930s Marxist writings. Later he produced an influential book, *The Managerial Revolution*, celebrating bureaucratic modernism and his decoupling from Marx and the Left. He subsequently became for rollback what Kennan had been for containment: its theorist, its Zvengali. He was the most effective and analytical advocate of rollback because he articulated its logic so well.

More importantly, though, Burnham's thought decisively rejected isolationism and provided a bureaucratic rationale for the national security state, thus bridging the obsolescent isolationists and the Sun Belt, defense budget–hungry rollbackers. Burnham was also an important influence on the political go-between cum odd fellow who in his congenial amorality symbolized the realpolitik world view of the national security manager, Richard Nixon; Nixon's recent books seem strangely animated by Burnham's concerns, cadences, and theories, as if four decades had not passed. James Burnham should be seen as the intellectual architect of a historic compromise between nativist rollback and cold war containment: a meld that we will call *interventionism.*

Burnham was widely credited in the spring of 1947 with coining the term, "cold war," yet typically he was already moving beyond the Truman Doctrine accommodation. He thought that by then the United States was "committed everywhere, on every continent," such that it "can never again withdraw." Yet America was immature, possessing the resources for global power with a distinctly provincial and outmoded world view. The United States and the USSR he perceptively likened to "two mighty, semi-barbarian super-states of the periphery," now dividing the globe between them. "One of the two power centers is itself a child, a border area, of Western civilization. . . . The U.S., crude, awkward, semi-barbarian, nevertheless enters this irreconcilable conflict as the representative of Western culture."

He found three tendencies in American foreign policy. First was the internationalist view, which he thought represented appeasement and error. Next was the isolationist view, placing centrality on the conquest of the American internal market and frontier, but which now had become "distorted and degraded by the inexhorable pressure of a historical reality in which they can have no natural outlet," an eloquent and accurate comment. Isolationism was belligerently nationalist, and purely unilateralist ("it refuses to intervene responsibly"). What was the third tendency? It would be a mix of containment and rollback, premised upon the immanent reality of an American imperium. Instead of world government or nationalist withdrawal and self-containment, the United States should pursue a "world empire."

Such an empire was and would be established "at least partly through force and the threat of force." Since the United States in 1947 possessed exclusively the ultimate weapon, the atomic bomb, this monopoly should be used—it "makes politically possible . . . the domination of the world by a single sufficiently large state." World empire would be the goal and atomic weapons the means in the Third World War, which he thought had already begun. The inescapable condition of the world was conflict, indeed irreconcilable struggle between the two superpowers. Thus, "in the creation of this Empire there would be necessarily involved the reduction of Communism to impotence" at home and abroad—something possible given the American atomic monopoly (and a strong FBI, one assumes).

An important start had been made with the Truman Doctrine, Burnham thought, which established a defense holding back Soviet expansionism. But such a policy "leaves unresolved the problems which generate the crisis in world politics." Instead a "bold," "positive" policy that "takes the initiative" should be established, such that the direction of the thrust to empire is reversed, "turning the [Soviet] expansive advance into a demoralizing retreat." He therefore recommended that "the defensive policy" (containment) be merged with the "offensive policy" (rollback, although he did not then use the word), thus to undermine Communist power "in East Europe, northern Iran, Afghanistan, Manchuria, northern Korea and China." Never one to mince words, at the end of the book he pointed to the ultimate objective: "the policy aims not at the defeat of Russia, but at its liberation."

Time and *Life* gave the Luce imprimatur to the book, the latter running a condensation, with laudatory hyperbole. Arthur Schlesinger, Jr., thought Burnham might not make a good secretary of state, but nonetheless Schlesinger preferred his thesis to the "confusion and messy arguments of the appeasers."[100] Still, Burnham was on the sidelines in 1947, his influence miniscule compared to, say, the architect of containment, George Kennan.

By 1950 a reversal had occurred, with Kennan's influence waning and Burnham's waxing. In *The Coming Defeat of Communism*, published with great Luce fanfare in early 1950, he argued forcefully for rollback. Containment was "too defensive," it could never be "more than a partial and temporary expedient." The United States faced a "dynamic enemy" on all world fronts. The only answer to this was "the turn to the offensive."

Burnham and his friend, William F. Buckley, Jr. (with whom he established *The National Review* in 1956) had intelligence connections and seemed well aware of internal shifts in the American state.[101] Burnham wrote that by 1949, "cooperation and appeasement [read internationalism] . . . had been laid aside by almost all except the Communists, their hangers-on, and the self-deluded." He was correct, the consensual midpoint had shifted sharply to the right, eliminating Roosevelt's policy of containment-by-embrace, accommodation and enmeshment of the Soviets, and opening the way to a new synthesis. Burnham also was aware of the NSC-68 deliberations, saying that "a plan of military rearmament and development is at present going forward." Perhaps most important, in discussing resistance and rollback strategies, he turned first to Albania, which had already been subject to various covert Bay of Pigs–style rollback attempts, each of them about as successful as the Cuban venture, but highly secret at the time (and since). He went on to argue for support of Chiang Kai-shek in his resistance to communism, which at an appropriate point "will be able to join the offensive . . . when the wheel enters another cycle," thus to "throw the Communists back out of China." In Korea, he said, the United States "has already been fighting . . . the probing into southern Korea has begun."

Burnham carefully distanced himself from right-isolationism by arguing for free trade and reformist labor unions. But his true heroes were "the managers," his new ruling class in America, which in the case of foreign policy would be the national security professionals. This was music to the ears of the emerging managerial class in the growing security bureaucracy, giving them a rationale for their new-found status and an ideology in service to empire: global interventionism, justified by the diabolical Soviet menace, but underpinned by the extensive clusters of interest arising around far-flung foreign commitments and domestic bureaucratic and economic fractions.[102]

This second book had far more influence than the earlier one. Burnham's arguments fell on willing ears in 1950, as Americans in and out of government grew increasingly frustrated with a passive containment. His views found much favor in the national security bureaucracy in the early months of 1950. In late January, a top secret account of State Department discussions with unnamed senators indicated that several were ready to fight: they said their constituents would "back to the hilt" a preventive war, even if the Soviets had taken no overt action against the United States; one was quoted as saying, "why don't we get into this thing now and get it over with before the time is too late?" *Life* ran an account of the decision to proceed with the hydrogen bomb, accompanied by a broadly grinning picture of John J. McCloy captioned, "if there were an oxygen bomb that would be bigger than the H-bomb, I would build it."[103]

R. A. Wormser, a member of a Wall Street committee on foreign policy, wrote to Gen. William Donovan, A. A. Berle, Joseph L. Broderick and others on the same committee in February 1950 that "the appearance of Burnham's book coincidental with the creation of our sub-committee is encouraging. I am so convinced that we in the U.S. need to revise our thinking." Wormser thought the peace had been too punitive on Germany and Japan. He argued for a united Germany, a restoration of "the eastern borders," and an offensive strategy against the Soviets: "Surprise after surprise, blow after blow, attack after attack. In every geographical area and in every political and economic and social area. Energies spent on defense and blocking are lost to the offense, and we cannot only contain Russia, but [must] drive her back." The United States had simply been "waiting always for their next move," and while "there are limits," morality must give way to realism. Thus, the members should prepare a list of cold war strategies and tactics—"including everything we can think of, however extreme."[104]

William Buckley was once asked what position in the executive branch he would most covet: he shot back, "ventriloquist." This was Burnham's role in national security affairs. He coined one catchy term or phrase after another, beginning with "cold war." Taking "the offensive," "seizing the initiative," "positive action," "rollback"—most of these terms redolent of the 1949–1950 turn in American strategy were Burnham's inventions or usages.

Americans who never knew a communist when they saw one were forced to rely in these years on reformed or recanted communists, who parleyed bitter personal experience into high-level ventriloquy, writing on the blank sheet of Hartzian man. Of these, Burnham was the best. He had the finest mind, and the requisite ambition. He etched a consensus on interventionism, bridging containment and rollback at the level of strategy and articulating an ideology of justification for the managers of the incipient national security state. Only eccentric, recalcitrant critics were willing to blast this neoorthodoxy in the 1950s atmosphere, like Harry Elmer Barnes, who saw Burnham as the ideologue of "perpetual war for perpetual peace" and "military managerialism," cheered on by court historians like Samuel Eliot Morison and Arthur Schlesinger, Jr.[105]

We will examine how the rollback doctrine penetrated the bureaucracies of the national security state shortly, but first we need to put in place some people, places, and things that often have eluded inquiry.

Chapter Four

PREDESTINATION FOR
THE LABYRINTH: SPIES AND
SPECULATORS

> One must be honest in intellectual matters to the point of harshness . . . one must have become indifferent, one must never ask whether truth is useful or a fatality. . . . Strength which prefers questions for which no one today is sufficiently daring; courage for the *forbidden*; predestination for the labyrinth.
>
> *Nietzsche*

THE ROLLBACK impulse and the beginnings of the Korean War are inexplicable apart from familiarity with a mostly hidden intelligence politics, and a fevered speculation, combining clandestine activity with rank cupidity. This is, by its nature, the most inaccessible and speculative aspect of our inquiry; nonetheless it is an essential part and we must do our best to excavate the remains of an ulterior history. Richard Rowan once wrote that "spies and speculators for thirty-three centuries have exerted more influence on history than on historians."[1] We hope that will not be the case with this volume.

Here we will do little more than establish lineages and interests, to put in place the dramatis personae of a murky politics and the stakes it held for them. We will try to retrieve a few personalities who held the attentions of Acheson and MacArthur, Chiang and Rhee, but who have barely made it into the postwar literature. We will examine some deals, scams, and speculations that set the stage for the later chapters, and for the onset of the war itself.

The rub in all this is that scholars are trained to trust only the verifiable printed word, the document solemnly committed to the historical record. A deeply inbred assumption tells us that if something happened, the causes and considerations ought to be duly and honestly recorded for posterity. Yet those in the political arena do not share the same respect for the record, and those in intelligence work usually have no respect for it, consigning facts (and their consciences) to a never-to-be opened dustbin of history. Erasure is as common as preservation. Even in hallowed academe, however, decisions are sometimes made for reasons quite unlikely to be put down on paper, but this commonplace, everyday occurrence does not much enter into the scholarly consciousness. So we will have to make do with the available documentation, stick closely to it, while not fainting before some speculation of our own.

Consider the following statement from a person whose career placed him at a critical node in the American state: that "the deep party line" (knowledge of the real causes of events) is known only to a select few, and that much of what passes for contemporary history is "pure propaganda and close to brainwashing." Fletcher Prouty, who was a key liaison and briefer between intelligence agencies and politicians in the White House and elsewhere, thinks that much of postwar history is hidden, that a "secret team" has influenced events far out of proportion to their numbers. He gives us a primer in how conspiracies work, by someone presumably expert in them (the book itself may be some kind of black operation). Likewise, one can learn much from another ex–intelligence operative's account, William Corson's *Armies of Ignorance*; it is only in such accounts, for example, that a person like M. Preston Goodfellow merits attention.[2]

Consider the following facts: George Blake, the Soviet mole thought to have done more damage to Western interests than the Philby conspiracy, was chief of British intelligence in Seoul when the war began. Kim Philby and Donald McLean sat astride the flow of top secret documents in Washington in 1950, while Guy Burgess ran the Far Eastern department of the Foreign Office in London. That is, the CIA was penetrated; it also fought with Hoover's FBI, and was itself split into several different tendencies, ranging from Wall Street internationalism to a cowboy-style expansionism. Its founder, William Donovan, ran a personal cold war-central from his Wall Street offices. MacArthur kept the CIA out of his territory of command, and Willoughby destroyed documents rather than let them fall into the hands of the "communists" in the CIA—a crackbrained conspiracy theory, unless we remember the British spies.

The China Lobby infiltrated the CIA, and vice versa. On Taiwan, the CIA funded pro-Chiang rollbackers. The brother of T. V. Soong mounted a corner on the soybean market timed for the outbreak of some expected event on the weekend of June 25, 1950; Joe McCarthy was reportedly a beneficiary. Gold and tungsten mingled with anticommunism in the minds and exploits of archetypal expansionists like Goodfellow, a former top official in the Office of Strategic Services (OSS); just as Wall Street speculation and global intrigue met in the person of Allen Dulles. So, at the empirical level we have much that remains to be explained about the mysterious realm of intelligence politics.

Even today, much of central importance to understanding the events of 1950 both at home and abroad is either generally unknown, or generally inaccessible because of declassification restrictions. But enough is known to raise important new questions about the American role—or should we say the role of Americans?—in the beginning of the Korean War. It would be irresponsible not to probe these questions.

CENTRAL INTELLIGENCE

In the 1940s when it originated, the purpose of "central intelligence" was to sift the information vacuumed in by America's far-flung but splintered collecting agencies, and then turn this scattered information into finished intelligence products for the president and his advisors. But such a text-book description of intelligence in the Truman era would strike knowledgeable observers as barely more plausible than belief in the tooth fairy.

At the analytical level we may say that the extraordinary autonomy of the foreign policy organs in the American state, discussed earlier, had even greater expression in the various intelligence agencies. They were among the newest of the proliferating bureaucracies of the national security state, with munificent budgets and critical tasks that made intelligence work prestigious and politically sensitive; they were arenas of political conflict between expansionists and internationalists, operating with great power and next to no scrutiny. Our hypothesis has been that the American state was both the object and the subject, the arena and the residuum, of a power struggle. In the clandestine agencies of state, therefore, the struggle would be more intense, less subject to scrutiny, more open to forays from without. The novelty of the agencies reinforced a pattern that always marks intelligence mechanisms, at the shadowy point where official and unofficial, formal and informal action meet. Informal actors hostile to established routine, in and out of government office, mounted stark power grabs and may have held a whip hand in central events of 1950.

Intelligence in the Truman period also bears inquiry because the president, unlike Roosevelt, liked to read his intelligence after it had been digested by underlings, relying on final intelligence products "which had been carefully screened for his consumption."[3] In other words a hegemonic executive who understood the shaping of information gave way to someone who did not, thus opening a larger realm for unsanctioned maneuver.

The Office of Strategic Services was the mother of the postwar American intelligence network, minus a year or two when the very idea of central intelligence was in abeyance and when the father of it, William Donovan, was in eclipse. But in 1947, coterminous with the deepening of the cold war, Truman set up a Central Intelligence Group, soon to become the CIA, and in June 1948 he added a covert capability by establishing the Office of Policy Coordination (OPC) under Frank Wisner. The OPC had a discretionary budget of $4.7 million in 1949, $84 million by 1952.

Wisner was, as they say, "of the moneyed New York legal establishment," a Wall Street lawyer from the firm of Carter, Ledyard, and Milburn who had worked with Donovan in the Balkans in World War II, and with Allen Dulles in, among other things, the reestablishment of Hitler's Gehlen organization as part of the American cold war effort in Europe. Acheson had brought him into the State Department in 1947 for an unknown "intelligence assignment" in the occupied areas.

Foster Dulles and George Kennan also worked closely with OPC. In his fine and often shocking account, Christopher Simpson establishes that the Dulles brothers directed much of the OPC's campaign against the Italian Communist Party in the 1948 elections from their Wall Street firm, and that both they and George Kennan were deeply involved in the use of the dreadful Gehlen organization. The Far East division chief of OPC was Col. Richard Stilwell, who would for decades thereafter have a deep, if mostly unknown, involvement with Korea.[4]

Wisner was what we might call a Wall Street cowboy, combining the internationalism and Europe-first sentiments of the financial community with a taste for clandestine missions and a belief in the virtues of covert action. In other words he was much like Donovan. As head of OPC he routinely (Corson says "completely") bypassed the CIA chain of authority under the ineffectual and overwhelmed director, Roscoe Hillenkoetter.[5]

We might take it to be coincidental that a remarkable number of Wall Street stalwarts held high position in the CIA, as in the State Department. Such indulgence of the improbable could not be expected of the Soviets, however, who must have thought the instrumental theory of the state too subtle to capture the reality of early postwar Washington, especially when the Dulles brothers divided up State and CIA.[6] Yet these same capitalists drew fire from the American Right, which tended to see the CIA as a hotbed of liberalism, maybe harboring communists or Soviet moles.

Bonner Fellers, MacArthur myrmidon, belched redundantly that the CIA had in its depths "a group of Marxist-Socialist pro-Communists," naming once again the unfortunate John Paton Davies. When William Bundy joined the CIA in the early 1950s, McCarthy demanded of Allen Dulles that he reveal Bundy's exact duties, since he had contributed to the Hiss defense fund. When Dulles responded that Bundy's background had been fully checked, McCarthy accused him of "protection and cover-up."[7]

The CIA held no communists in its midst, but it did hold such a congeries of tendencies that it could be seen by liberals as a refuge from McCarthyism, by conservatives as a hotbed of radicalism, by radicals as the essence of American imperialism, by some China lobbyists as the enemy and by others as an ally. The depths of this conflict may be seen in the story of James Kellis, an intelligence operative with a background in

OSS activities in China in 1944–1945, the Greek civil war, and intelligence-gathering inside North Korea before June 1950.

Kellis thought the CIA was "rotten to the core," harboring "pinkos, homosexuals, [and] incompetents," and that the operational side of the CIA "had a definite left wing tinge." At the same time, he thought that after 1950 the CIA was "run without interference from the White House by Republicans, Smith, Jackson & Dulles." He said in letters to General Donovan in 1954 that Senator McCarthy "had 4–5 good penetrations of the agency [CIA]," and that Kellis, then in the CIA, did nothing about McCarthy's agents "because they aimed at the same thing, on a different way [sic]." McCarthy's people, Kellis said, "had access to some very sensitive information we could not get." When one suspect CIA employee was let go, Kellis noted, the man "was soon presented with a subpoena by the Senator's committee."

Kellis sought to purge the CIA of presumed leftists by forming an internal cabal of trusted allies, drawing up a report, then making an end run around the higher CIA leadership directly to President Eisenhower. The venue for this end run, according to Kellis, was Richard Nixon, who always took a close interest in intelligence matters. Nixon gave the report to Ike and to Allen Dulles, who then sought out Kellis, especially to ascertain if his report had gotten into Senator McCarthy's hands. Kellis said the report was only for Nixon and Eisenhower, but that Nixon's copy might have gone to McCarthy.[8]

There is obviously much more to this story than is revealed in the scattered information in the Donovan Papers. Here we merely document the degree to which the McCarthy-style conflicts of the early 1950s penetrated all sensitive agencies, including the CIA; it also illustrates again the impoverished vocabulary of this conflict, in which one's political enemies, all sharing common assumptions, nevertheless materialize as pinkos and commies. McCarthyism was not new and not aberrational, but central to American politics. Walter Bedell Smith, among the most powerful men in the CIA and the director before Dulles, was, according to Ambrose, "about as right-wing as a professional Army officer was ever likely to get," telling Eisenhower once that he thought Nelson Rockefeller was a communist.[9] James Angleton, head of counter-intelligence, was probably to the right of Smith. Although Corson is correct to emphasize the great damage that McCarthyism did to the CIA, that merely underlines its centrality to the era.[10]

Allen Dulles played upon the bizarre cleavages of American politics with great skill. He ran the Gehlen gang in Europe, but fought with Mac-Arthur in Asia. He kept in touch with Willoughby long after MacArthur's sacking, and at the same time convinced many liberals that the CIA "had become a sort of refuge for the freethinkers and liberals who had been driven underground by the McCarthyites." He presided over joint CIA-Nationalist guerrilla forays into the China mainland and apparently funded some China Lobby activities, while lending help to liberals attacked by the China Lobby.

For many years one of the few good sources on the China Lobby was a long two-part article in *The Reporter*, a magazine that could be found on every good liberal's coffee table in the 1950s. It also published a big exposé of General Willoughby. Yet it ran articles faked by the CIA (one of them purporting to come from a Soviet defector who helped build up the North Korean army), and its crusading editor, Max Ascoli, had Allen Dulles (then a top aide in the CIA) check the page proofs of the China Lobby articles; this leads one to speculate that elements in the CIA informed parts of the exposé which did, indeed, contain much new information.[11]

Perhaps the most significant intraintelligence conflict was that between the CIA and MacArthur. Both understood that knowledge is power, and saw each other as threats of the first order. MacArthur and Willoughby accomplished an "absolute interdiction" of OSS activity during the war;[12] MacArthur had commanded a brigade, Donovan a regiment, in the Rainbow Division, which many thought to be the origin of their rivalry. MacArthur's intelligence operations always left a bit to be desired; Willoughby had aircraft nicely huddled together in the Philippines on Pearl Harbor Day, leaving them at the mercy of Japanese Zeroes winging in from Taiwan, the first but decidedly not the last of Willoughby's "intelligence failures." MacArthur and his G-2 chief trusted only themselves, and had an intuitive approach to intelligence that mingled the hard facts of enemy capability with hunches about the enemy's presumed ethnic and racial qualities. Corson called it MacArthur's "personal infallibility theory of intelligence," in which he "created his own intelligence organization, interpreted its results and acted upon his own analysis."[13]

When the CIA was formed, it threatened MacArthur's exclusive intelligence theater in the Pacific and J. Edgar Hoover's in Latin America. But this did not owe merely to bureaucratic prerogative and institutional loyalty; MacArthur and Hoover were heroes and chief gendarmes of the American Right, and perceived the CIA as the executive arm of the Eastern establishment. MacArthur and Willoughby thus continued their "interdiction." Although the CIA did function in Japan and Korea before June 1950, operatives either had to get permission from Willoughby or hide themselves from MacArthur's G-2 as well as the enemy target. Effective liaison in the handling of information barely existed.

At the late date of March 1950 some minimal cooperation was achieved, when General Collins of the Joint Chiefs of Staff asked that MacArthur share with them Willoughby's reports on China and areas near to it, and also transmitted Wisner's request that an OPC office be approved for Japan. In both cases MacArthur gave his approval, while asserting that his G-2 had always "promptly furnished reports" when asked about "specific items."[14] The exchange was suggestive of negotiations between foreign intelligence agencies.

Even during the pressing period of the Pusan Perimeter, MacArthur—and, it seems, military intelligence in general—withheld "planning and operational information" from the CIA.[15] But with the debacle of the Chinese entry into the war, the power struggle finally ended with a clear CIA victory. In January 1951, as Sino–North Korean forces pressed southward from Seoul, Walter Bedell Smith journeyed to Tokyo and the *merde* hit the fan. Smith was personally forbidding: a small, tough man with steely eyes, he was "an acknowledged master in the military's fine art of chewing ass." In a scene that probably resembled the boardroom meeting in *The Godfather*, Smith cut the CIA in on Supreme Command, Allied Powers (SCAP) intelligence traffic for good, while propelling Willoughby and MacArthur further down the path that would end in April 1951.[16]

China's entry into the war was, of course, Willoughby's career-ending "intelligence failure," and he never recovered from it. Just after the Chinese came in, he drew up a document, "Aid and Comfort to the Enemy," where he attacked "sly and inaccurate" press reporting by "traitorous idiots [who] go out of their way to create defeatist thought-patterns." The CIA fueled this treacherous journalism, he thought, by strategic leaks casting blame on Willoughby for an event that no one predicted. He later claimed that Truman "impounded" thirty-two footlockers of his G-2 records, which perhaps had to do with charges by Army historians that MacArthur and Willoughby sought to destroy documentation from their command.

At any rate, Willoughby excluded the CIA from his bailiwick, intelligence was not routinely shared, CIA liberals thought Willoughby a fascist and leaked stories to the liberal press, Willoughby thought CIA liberals were subversives and sent reports on them to McCarthy and Allen Dulles; both failed to predict the Chinese entry, but the CIA succeeded in shaping a historical verdict that it was all Willoughby's fault, and he spent the rest of his life gnawing the carpet. Willoughby's later writings for the *Intelligence Digest* show a highly-developed case of paranoia, but of the most excruciating kind: the paranoia of one with much to be paranoid about.[17] For his part MacArthur took the high road after his dismissal, telling congressmen that any and all reports about difficulties between his G-2 and the CIA were "all tommyrot"—"pure bunkum, Senator."[18] It was a gallant effort to bury in history an extraordinary internecine conflict that shaped the Korean War and American politics.

MacArthur also told the members of the Senate Committees on Armed Services and Foreign Relations that he had nothing to do with intelligence collection in Korea before the war—a falsehood. Korea was a microcosm of the MacArthur/CIA conflict. Willoughby maintained something called the Korea Liaison Office (KLO), with a mission to penetrate North Korean "governmental, military, and industrial agencies." It was established in June 1949, when American troops were withdrawn, and headed by Leonard J. Abbott; it filed an average of three reports per day for the next year. At the Washington end some saw the KLO as "a brazen, extralegal creation," but Willoughby later averred, "I could not be indifferent to that area; I maintained intelligence elements [in Korea] with spectacular results."[19]

Simultaneously, the CIA worked with the regular USAMGIK and KMAG G-2 organizations, under the leadership of the G-2 operations head Gen. John N. Robinson and CIA man James Kellis. The latter described this joint effort as "an effective machine that was capable in [*sic*] penetrating the Soviet forces in North Korea, the Korean Communist Forces, the North Korean Administration and to a limited degree Manchuria and the Maritime Provinces of Siberia."[20] Like British intelligence in 1950 and Japanese intelligence before them, the Americans used South Korea as a collection point for information on much of the Northeast Asian mainland.

DONOVAN'S COLD WAR CENTRAL

When entering the foyer of the Central Intelligence Agency, so I am told, the visitor is greeted by a portrait of its founding father: that is, the head not of the CIA but of the OSS, Gen. William "Wild Bill" Donovan. Although exiled to Wall Street in the postwar period, thence to the ambassadorship of Thailand in 1952, Donovan played an important and mostly unappreciated role in the CIA and the cold war in the period when containment and rollback currents fought for hegemony in Washington. Although a good Europhile internationalist, Donovan crossed over the divides of strategy to become a strong advocate of rollback. That is, like Henry Luce he merged the two currents as a modal interventionist.

Donovan was an Irish-Catholic born in Buffalo in 1883. He studied at Columbia, and commanded a regiment of troops in the Rainbow Division in World War I. Like Willoughby, he chased Pancho Villa along the Mexican border with the "silk stocking boys." A power in New York Republican politics after that, everyone thought he would be attorney-general in the Hoover administration, given their long personal friendship; but he did not get it. In 1932 he ran for the governorship of New York vacated by Roosevelt, and lost that, too. Identified with the Morgan interests from the 1920s onward, he was a founder of the powerful Wall Street firm, Donovan, Leisure, and was also a charter member of the bloc of high-tech firms of the 1930s, defending the new multinational oil firms against antitrust suits, and establishing close connections with International Telephone and Telegraph and its German partners.[21]

Donovan visited Japan, Korea, and Siberia in 1919. He was cheerleading for Kolchak's anti-Soviet troops and at the time got off an early stanza of his favorite tune: "we can prevent a shooting war [with the USSR] if we take the initiative to win the subversive war." Much like Dulles, Kennan, and other cold warriors, he combined a disgust for the Soviets with admiration for the Japanese, finding the big *zaibatsu* groups in 1919 to be "the liberal business interests of Japan. They are pro-American."[22] From that period onward, he parleyed a deep hatred of Bolshevism and a penchant for secret action into the "general belief," as Cave Brown put it, that Donovan "was the point man of the force that led to America's emergence as a superpower."[23] He was America's premier anticommunist.

International business and world politics went hand in hand on Wall Street, making it an island of riveted attention to global information in the sea of American indifference. From the 1920s onward Donovan had "a rare hunger for exotic intelligence"—and a penchant for exotic behavior. He cultivated an aura of intrigue, with "exceedingly mysterious" peregrinations, "difficult to track," according to Cave Brown. His wife shared in the mystery, believing he was off to Hawaii when he was actually bound for Europe. He seemed to materialize at every front line trouble spot from Abyssinia in 1936 to Hungary in 1956. "Nobody could be more elusive than Donovan," Brown wrote, "and nobody was better at the craft of not letting the left hand know what his right hand was doing."[24]

In the early postwar period, in spite of Truman's distaste for him, Donovan played a major role in American intelligence and covert operations. From 1947 to 1952, and especially under Bedell Smith's directorship, Donovan "was in constant communication and saw [Smith] frequently. He submitted planning and policy papers on request or on his own initiative." He was a fanatic believer in the value of covert operations and guerrilla struggle. Smith wrote that in the early postwar period, "the Donovan group was always at hand, claiming that it had great expertise in shadow warfare."[25]

In 1942 Donovan had defined "Special Operations" as follows:

They may take the form of offensive or defensive measures. These operations may be direct, indirect, or under cover. They may or may not involve physical action and may be conceived with a view to affecting the mind or body. In the accomplishment of the foregoing it may be necessary or advisable, among other things: To corrupt and control enemy organizations and enemy dominated agencies; to fabricate propaganda, rumor and news, and to disseminate the same, whether true or false; to promote or incite resistance, revolution, and sabotage of all kinds . . . generally to . . . conduct against the enemy and its adherents special forms of subversive warfare.[26]

Donovan's files, or what of them are available, show that his attentions to the anticommunist effort in the early postwar period ranged far and wide. He seemed to be involved in everything, however distant from his ostensible Wall Street calling. In 1948 he met frequently with Evron Kirkpatrick and officers of the Rockefeller Foundation, seeking to set up a national foreign area studies program, the progenitor of a far-flung effort eventually funded by the Ford Foundation; his attentions even roamed to Seattle, where he helped the president of the University of Washington prepare a famous case against several dismissed professors who had refused to say whether they were members of the communist party or not.[27]

In the period before the Korean War Donovan made several trips to East Asia and became a powerful advocate of rollback. Ostensibly his only purpose was to pursue his legal defense of General Chennault, who was seeking the return of a set of China National Air Corporation (CNAC) planes that the British had sequestered in Hong Kong; in fact, as we will see, this was merely a convenient cover for his covert lobbying efforts, seeking to turn the United States away from containment and toward rollback. He took a seven-week trip to Asia in 1949–1950, which we will examine in a subsequent chapter.

Wall Street lawyers and bankers, with Acheson in the lead, sketched a vision for postwar America's role in the world.[28] But Donovan's role as an outsider in the recasting of American strategy in 1949–1950, and the role of Wall Streeters like the Dulles brothers, Wisner, Paul Nitze, and others on the inside, make the distinction between "high" policy and covert action seem less important, and render the following colloquy between Kennan and Adam Malik of some moment. In the spring of 1951, Kennan visited him at the Soviet mission's Long Island estate, seeking to get peace talks started on Korea. Toward the end of their discussions Kennan remarked that the Soviet idea that Wall Street ran American foreign policy was nothing more than a fantasy, a "dream," and he asked Malik how they could justify spouting such poppycock. Malik replied that it was not a dream, but "the deepest reality."[29] Whether it was or not, Donovan made it seem so.

INFORMAL ACTORS IN EAST ASIA:
CHENNAULT, PAWLEY, WILLAUER, COOKE,
AND OTHER NOTABLES

If we may take Donovan as the king of the informal intelligence actors in Washington, then in East Asia we would nominate General Chennault, his sidekick Whiting Willauer, William Pawley, and Adm. Charles Cooke. Their contribution was to provide ostensibly unoffical, informal military backing for the Chiang regime in 1949–1950, while seeking the full official backing of the Truman administration. In so doing they made major strides in the privatization of foreign policy. Chennault, Willauer, and Cooke attached themselves to the Chiang regime much like Goodfellow and others did to Syngman Rhee, a coterie that defined patriotism as service to a foreign government, subversion as the normal output of the State Department. Operating outside formal procedures but with the backing of important officials, they were yet another aspect of the extraordinary internecine struggles within the emergent national security state.

Chennault's real love was airpower and the particular air service that was his claim to fame, the Flying Tigers, and thereafter Civil Air Transport (CAT)—the latter being both lucrative and bound to sink with the Kuomintang, should Taiwan be attacked. The CAT crowd and its successor, Air America, marked the apotheosis of the rough-hewn, hell-bent-for-leather bravado and terminal ignorance of American expansionists in East Asia. "Weird Neil" Hansen, for example, a pilot for CAT, was "tall, lean, and laconic," the sort of character "who can be imagined hitching his horse to a post and kicking open the swing doors of a saloon in some dusty cowboy town." CAT pilots liked the "high adventure" of life in the Orient, according to an admiring author; the rollicking good times included nights in Rangoon where the pilots "got drunk and ripped the sarongs off the Burmese women in the street, and were arrested for wearing their high Texas boots into the pagoda."[30] Anyone who has walked the streets of Seoul, Taipei, or Manila in the late evening hours can fill in all the blanks of such escapades; here is the sordid underbelly of the assumption that Asia is open, an arena for American action.

More interesting than the Pat Butram–like pilots was Whiting Willauer, Chennault's key aide and coowner of CAT. Willauer, like William Pawley, typified the common links between backers of Chiang and anticommunists in Central America, the model region of American foreign policy for the expansionist current. He became an important CIA operative who was asked by Bedell Smith in 1953 to take the ambassadorship in Honduras, where with Pawley and others he helped to overthrow the

Arbenz regime in Guatemala the following year. He and Pawley were also instrumental in planning for the Bay of Pigs.[31]

CAT helped evacuate the Nationalists southward and thence to Taiwan in 1948–1949, and formed "an extensive system of intelligence and security" in the late 1940s, information from which was routinely transmitted to the American Marine base at Tsingtao.[32] In 1949–1950 Chennault and Willauer were prime advocates of American bolstering of Taiwan and rollback on the mainland—that is, Chiang Kai-shek's policy—a predictable result of their close ties and the money that reportedly flowed between them.[33]

But was CAT an informal or formal actor? The State Department did not like Chennault, to be sure, but the CIA did. In the summer of 1948 Wisner's Office of Policy Coordination "took increasing control of the airline, which it looked upon as having perfect cover"; CIA funds flowed to it by the summer of 1949, if not earlier, through a dummy corporation set up by Tommy "The Cork" Corcoran, T. V. Soong's agent in Washington.[34]

William Pawley also got his start with air power, helping to establish air links in China and Central America in the 1930s and, with Chennault, the Flying Tigers. Like Willauer, he merged support for Chiang with cozy relations with Central American dictators. But unlike most, Pawley had powerful friends among centrists and liberals in Washington even though his views were just as unreconstructed as any rollbacker. George Marshall was an old friend, as was Robert Lovett; Vernon Walters, among the most important of CIA troubleshooters, was a Pawley disciple. Pawley had access to Truman's office on several occasions before the Korean War, and Truman made him ambassador to Brazil in 1948.

Pawley carried out many sensitive missions for the CIA in the early 1950s, according to his own account, appraising CIA operations in East Asia for Wisner in 1951, joining with James Doolittle to investigate the operational side of the CIA, negotiating with India on the purchase of raw materials for the atomic bomb, and finally planning the 1954 Guatemala intervention with Allen Dulles, Wisner, Willauer, and others. Later on Eisenhower asked him to be under-secretary of state for the Western Hemisphere (opposition was too great for him to get it); soon he and other CIA figures began planning for the Bay of Pigs. He was a long-time friend of Richard Nixon, and rumors linked him to Mafia leaders having investments in Cuba.[35]

In late 1949 Pawley became the point man for an end run around American policy toward Taiwan, carrying military aid and advisors to the Kuomintang (KMT); this group came to be led by Adm. Charles Cooke. Cooke was born in Arkansas in 1886, and had a distinguished naval career. He was chief of staff to Adm. Ernest W. King during the Second

World War, then deputy chief of Naval Operations, and finally commander of the Western Pacific Fleet before his retirement. He was also involved with Naval intelligence in China, through the Sino-American Cooperation League (SACO). Like the leader of SACO, Adm. Milton "Mary" Miles, Cooke was friendly with the unsavory chief of the KMT secret police, Tai Li; indeed the latter had been meeting with Cooke just before his fatal plane crash in March 1946.[36]

In a later chapter we will rejoin the activities of Donovan, Pawley, Chennault, Willauer, and Cooke. In the meantime, let us examine their counterpart in Korea.

Special Activities: Goodfellow

On a sticky afternoon in the dog days of August 1935, Herbert Feis plunged into the refreshing waters of a lake in the improbably named Connecticut town of Silvermine. His neighbor, a Wellesley girl named Florence Haeussler Goodfellow, observed that Feis had no clothes on. Quick to uphold proper standards for the wealthy residents near her summer home, she brought charges against Feis and three friends for skinny-dipping.[37] It was a minor battle won in the clash of internationalists and expansionists.

Florence Haeussler of Silvermine was wife to Millard Preston Goodfellow, a pretender to the Eastern establishment who also had Western, mineral (although gold, not silver) and thus expansionist, credentials. Goodfellow was born in 1892, and began working for the *Brooklyn Eagle* in 1907. He purchased the *Eagle* in 1932 from Frank Gannett, the conservative Republican publisher who later became an important supporter of the Chinese Nationalists. If the politics of the paper were middle-of-the-road, Goodfellow's were similar to Gannett's, and to another stalwart of New York Republican politics and Wall Street—William Donovan.[38]

Like Donovan, much about Goodfellow's career remains obscure. But in the 1940s he held positions that were among the most sensitive in the American state. When "Wild Bill" set up the Office of Strategic Services, Goodfellow was the person Donovan called upon to organize the "special activities" so dear to his heart. A deep believer in covert action and guerrilla warfare, Donovan put Goodfellow in charge of an OSS department called simply SA/G, "Special Activities/Goodfellow." Goodfellow was also a longtime advocate of experimentation in unconventional methods of warfare; he personally selected land in the Washington area for the establishment of training camps for sabotage, subversive activities, and guerrilla action, later taken over by the CIA. Goodfellow also had an important but unilluminated role in protecting the interests of Army intelligence within the OSS.[39]

Goodfellow was one of two men (the other was David K. E. Bruce) selected to accompany Donovan to London in June 1942, to establish liaison and, with the Special Operations Executive (SOE) of British intelligence, to divide the globe into British and American areas of responsibility—a mission of extraordinary responsibility and secrecy. Donovan did not attend the meeting where the details were negotiated, but left them to Goodfellow, and W. T. Keswick on the British side, along with another unnamed Englishman. Some sources also place one Col. Garland Williams at the meeting. As William Corson puts it in his very good book on the history of American intelligence, "In the course of their conversations, the participants quite literally reviewed the world and divided it up in terms of how their organizations, separately and jointly, would carry out subversive and special operations." The importance of the "notes" negotiated at this meeting "cannot be overstressed," according to Corson.

Donovan and Goodfellow also arranged for a number of Americans to get training in England in "dirty tricks" and the like. One result of these negotiations was to leave China, Manchuria, and Korea as "an American sphere of influence" for intelligence work; another result, no doubt, was to bring Goodfellow to the attention of Soviet intelligence and its agents in England, such as Kim Philby and Guy Burgess, both of whom worked in SOE at about that time.[40] Burgess had been in the the Special Operations department, which was responsible for sabotage and resistance, since 1939, and when it changed to the Special Operations Executive, Philby joined it. After Pearl Harbor, "the extraordinarily intimate association between the two major Western intelligence organizations was beginning and Philby was in on the ground floor." The OSS men were inexperienced in spying, but had good Establishment-Anglophile educations; they "modelled themselves so closely on the British" that the SOE and OSS "could be regarded as the same service."[41]

Goodfellow remained in the OSS throughout the war, rising to become its deputy director under Donovan. His prime territory was the Far East, where he ran guerrillas into Burma, and where, according to Bradley F. Smith, the OSS developed "extensive intelligence operations in occupied China . . . using business operations as a cover." There is some evidence that Goodfellow was involved with Tai Li, Milton Miles, and the Chinese tungsten magnate K. C. Li.[42]

In the early postwar period Goodfellow maintained a residence on Foxhall Road in Washington, D.C.; for some time in 1947–1949 he also lived in Pocatello, Idaho, where he owned the *Pocatello Tribune*. Like many other American expansionists, he combined associations with right-wing regimes in Asia with interests in Central America: in March 1957 he was awarded a "freedom" medal by El Jefe, Rafael Trujillo of the

Dominican Republic, for unknown services rendered. He presided over the Overseas Reconstruction Corporation from the late 1940s to the early 1970s, a firm incorporated in Delaware about which information is nil. It may have been a Central Intelligence Agency proprietary company. A biographical statement likewise refers to his having served on "a board" for twenty years with J. Edgar Hoover or Herbert Hoover, but it is not identified. He was on a first-name basis with John J. McCloy, according to letters exchanged between the two. When Goodfellow died in 1973, at the age of 81, he was still head of the Overseas Reconstruction Corporation.[43]

Goodfellow went back and forth from Washington to Pocatello on a monthly basis; he told Herbert Hoover in late 1947 that he was located in the West because "the next war, if it comes, will be nearer the West than the East."[44] By early 1949, however, Goodfellow was with Donovan's World Commerce Corporation, seeking to become Rhee's principal American advisor,[45] and pursuing the typical Donovan combination of business and clandestine activities. From the fall of 1949 to the mid-1950s, Goodfellow succeeded in becoming a key agent for Korean-American business deals, a modern-day and highly successful Horace Allen.

In October 1949 he and John Staggers dickered with Rhee in trying to establish "Forwarding Houses" in Korea, two months later he developed the first American trade delegation to visit postwar South Korea. In February 1950 he hoped to bring the director of the Bank of Korea, Chae Sŏn-ju, to the United States, the next month he presented Chae with his plan for Korean-American "reciprocal commerce"; soon Chai became the Republic of Korea's (ROK) Finance Minister (April 1950). In April 1950 Goodfellow arranged for an RCA engineer to come to Seoul as part of some communications deal. In December 1950, with Seoul in ruins, he told his secretary to "find a man who wants to buy a lot of scrap of all kinds . . . Korea is so full of it." In 1952 he sought to arrange Japanese and Korean purchases of baking machinery, with a plan to get them both to eat more bread (a constant theme, since the United States had so much wheat to sell); in 1953 he and his "engineer associate" Rear Adm. Warren S. Parr (retired) sought cost estimates on a flat glass plant; in 1954 he helped an OSS friend establish the first tungsten sintering mill in Korea; in 1956 and 1957 he sought to interest Rhee in buying nuclear power generation equipment.[46]

The trade delegation in early 1950 was a good example of Goodfellow's operations. Goodfellow convinced a number of Seattle businessmen to tour Korea, Taiwan, and the Philippines, led by the mayor of Seattle. Rhee personally received the delegation with great pomp and ceremony in late January 1950. United States embassy materials on the visit treat it as purely a matter of Korean-American business. In the embassy list of delegates, only businessmen and Seattle officials are included. However, Goodfellow also placed on the delegation Henry F. Shoemaker, a veteran of the OSS-SACO operation in China, and much of the Seattle end was taken care of by Col. David R. Girdwood, also an OSS veteran. Both Girdwood and Shoemaker were interested in doing business in Korea; they may have had no intelligence connections in 1950. But it is interesting that their names do not make the embassy list, nor is Goodfellow's role in arranging the delegation mentioned.[47]

Girdwood established Girdwood Shipping Company in Seattle in 1930, and was active in North Africa and Italy with the OSS during the war. In April 1950 John Staggers, "under the authority given him by Dr. Rhee," made this company one of Korea's two shipping forwarders to the American West Coast. Girdwood toured Japan, Korea, Taiwan and the Philippines in May 1950, describing himself as the representative of Pacific Coast Fertilizer Company, with letters of introduction from Goodfellow; as we will see, Goodfellow used this same company as a cover for visits to Taiwan at about the same time.[48] When Shoemaker went to Seoul, Goodfellow gave him a letter that said "he represents very powerful people on the West coast." He met with Rhee at that time, and by September 1950 was involved in Goodfellow's RCA communications deal.[49] Later on we will have another look at Goodfellow's activities in 1949–1950, when, like Donovan, he spent several weeks in East Asia.

MOLES IN THE LABYRINTH: THE BRITISH SPIES

If the CIA did not hide communists, it did hide spies—and not our own. By virtue of taking most of its cues from British intelligence since the early 1940s, the OSS/CIA developed relationships that could be exploited by Philby and the other British moles. This most privileged of conspiracies could not have been better pitched to cultivate right-wing phobias about an Anglophile-Establishment-communist-homosexual bacillus swimming in the central bloodstream of the American state. The Philby gang confirmed as if in caricature the prejudices of the rollbackers: they were British, socialists, a couple were homosexuals, all were well bred— just the sort of things that lead to treachery. The British moles (Guy Burgess in particular) made these biases come alive, step out of a Lewis Carroll story as a tale from an inconceivable reality; if it were a novel, no one would believe it.

The clandestine history of postwar intelligence coups by the Russians bears directly on the Korean War. Kim Philby had extraordinary access to American intelligence before and during the war. Guy Burgess ran the Far Eastern office in London, then moved to Washington in August 1950. Donald MacLean was positioned nicely by the middle of 1950. And

George Blake was the intelligence chief in the British embassy in Seoul when the war started. According to a senior intelligence official for the Joint Chiefs of Staff (JCS), "it would appear that very nearly all U.S./U.K. high-level planning information prior to 25 May 1951 [the date Burgess and MacLean fled] must be considered compromised."[50] MacLean betrayed atomic secrets to the Russians in 1947, helping their bomb program, but he thought his "greatest coup" was his disclosure to Stalin of "Truman's orders to General MacArthur during the Korean War."[51] Philby tipped Albania to Bay of Pigs–style rollback efforts, first by British intelligence and then by joint British-American teams in the spring of 1950, when rollback was bubbling up in Washington (Wisner's OPC was behind these efforts to "detach" Albania from the Soviet bloc).[52]

Guy Burgess claimed to be a descendant of Huguenot settlers named de Bourgeois, and carried on in the profligate fashion of a *haute bourgeois* bad boy—routinely drinking to stupefaction, flamboyantly homosexual ("I could never travel by train," he used to proclaim at parties, "I would feel obliged to seduce the engine-driver"), mixing a seedy incontinence with sharp and worldly intelligence, which some found overpoweringly charming and others grotesquely appalling. But no one could believe him capable of high treason, so adept was he at molding outrageousness to a cover. Unbeknownst to many, he was also remarkably well-read, especially in history and Marxism, and an avid fan of Jane Austen and George Eliot.[53]

Burgess displayed a superior analytical ability in his work, despite legendary drinking bouts, unexplained absences, and memorable slothfulness. Many of his "minutes" on the covers of Foreign Office documents were discerning and subtle. His comments in early 1950 first show up in regard to the Sino-Soviet Treaty, which he thought the Americans were purposely misinterpreting for public consumption, playing upon alleged differences between Beijing and Moscow that he and other British analysts discounted—mainly the alleged Soviet designs on Manchuria. Burgess had contempt for MacArthur's G-2, saying SCAP was always finding "documents" (his quotes) issued by the Soviets, telling the Chinese what to do and when. "They have seen things that no one else to my knowledge has and which would be of the greatest interest. I wish . . . we were given the documents."[54] P. W. Scarlett called Acheson's Press Club speech "hogwash," and Burgess remarked that it was "wishful thinking . . . I am certain of expensively bought information designed by the KMT to please the assumed view of the purchasers."[55] He was right, we will learn, even though the disinformation came from Acheson, not the KMT; we will also follow Burgess's close reading of the Taiwan situation as June 1950 appoached.

Burgess stayed with the Foreign Office in London until August 1950, when he was sent to Washington as second secretary of the British Embassy, with special responsibility for East Asian affairs. A friend told him to watch his step in the United States: "Don't be too aggressively left-wing. Don't get involved in race relations. And, if you can, avoid homosexual incidents." To which Burgess replied, "In other words, Hector, you mean I mustn't make a pass at Paul Robeson."[56]

In the fall of 1950 Burgess correctly predicted that the United States would cross the thirty-eighth parallel. Michael Straight wrote that Burgess must have known about "our plans to advance into North Korea," and related a conversation in March of 1951 in which, when asked if he filtered documents on the march north to the Soviets, Burgess said, "everyone knew about" the plans; MacArthur thought the Chinese were bluffing, and "Acheson and the C.I.A. agreed with him."[57]

Burgess was right, MacArthur and Acheson both failed to predict the Chinese entry. But what Burgess's blithe reply to Straight's allegation of treachery screened is something known to every intelligence officer: that access to closely-guarded secrets is essential to sorting out the welter of reports, rumors, and opinions that appear in the press or in Washington gossip, to judge which ones are correct. This Philby, Blake, and Burgess were positioned to do from January to June 1950. The reader will want to keep this in mind for later chapters.

Whereas Philby, Burgess, and MacLean functioned as a gang-of-three, George Blake apparently did not know them and tended to act alone, making him the most enigmatic figure. He went out to Seoul in the summer of 1948, to spy on Manchuria, North Korea, and the Soviet Far East, remaining there until the U.K. embassy was captured by the North Koreans, and he and his ambassador, Vyvyan Holt, were taken to the North. He is well remembered by those in Seoul before the war began as an intelligent man and bon vivant who had utter contempt for American policy in the South; some analysts say he was working for the Soviets at this time, others that he was converted during three years in a Korean prison camp. Intelligence specialists believe that he did more damage than any other mole, including Philby; one example is his tipping the Russians to a tunnel in Berlin used to intercept East German and Soviet electronic communication, for which he won the Lenin Prize, a higher decoration than Philby ever got.

Unlike the other defectors, the Soviets refuse access by Westerners to Blake, who still lives in Moscow. It is impossible to get much information on Blake during his time in Seoul, both because he cannot be interviewed and because documents from the British embassy in Seoul were burned or captured; and since Blake was the MI6 chief, his reports do not show up in Foreign Office files, which do not declassify intelligence materials.

Philby, according to a high CIA officer, could get access to almost any information: "The sky was the limit. He would have known as much as he wanted to find out." He lunched every week with James Angleton, and was often briefed by Bedell Smith "on top policy." At one point he was codirector of the attempts to roll back the Albanian regime.[58] Blake was sitting in Seoul for two years before the war, and all the Far Eastern information flowed through Burgess in London. Yet even those positioned amid the flow of secrets still differ on the true meaning of the conspiracy.

Perhaps Philby's greatest coup was to turn the CIA into a pretzel by manipulating its counterintelligence chief, Angleton, leaving this master spy to spend the rest of his life trying to convince people he ran Philby instead of vice versa, and with an advanced case of paranoia. Thus he turned the agency upside down in search of moles and fake defectors (like Averell Harriman, or the famous Yuri Nosenko). The British spies cut the intelligence bureaucracy at a nodal point of conflict: the internationalist, Ivy-educated, orchid cultivator Angleton failed to grasp Philby's game; the Midwestern, paunchy, sweaty, FBI gumshoe William Harvey revealed Philby, and demonstrated for every right-winger to see that the intelligence community did harbor Reds—whom the Anglophile liberals had failed to spot.

Was the communication route merely one in which Western secrets were transmitted to Moscow, or was there a complicated back-and-forth dialectic of information, disinformation, and double agentry? Angleton and his backers claim that Israeli intelligence, with which Angleton was intimate, fingered Philby, Burgess, and MacLean early on, "providing them with intelligence disinformation to mislead the Soviets." Others say it was Harvey who discovered the conspiracy, in the spring of 1951, and that Angleton was completely had by Philby. The available evidence tends to support the second interpretation.[59]

Regardless of who ran whom, anyone who read the documentation leading up to and including NSC 68 would have predicted American involvement in the Korean War. Anyone with access to Angleton and high CIA and State Department intelligence would have been most interested in the activities of Donovan, Pawley, Cooke, and Goodfellow; anyone with good knowledge of the inner Washington scene in 1950 would never have taken Acheson's Press Club speech as an earnest of American intent. If, however, Angleton specifically told Philby that the United States would not defend South Korea, as a piece of disinformation, this might have influenced Stalin in what the Soviets told the North Koreans about American intentions.

What can be said with certainty is that Philby and Burgess both were intimately aware of the origin and development of American intelligence capabilities, especially those "special activities" loved by Donovan; and that Burgess showed extraordinary interest in American policy toward East Asia in the months before the Korean War, keeping careful track of the "informal" actors in Taiwan and elsewhere, such as Admiral Cooke, as we will see.

CRIPPLE CREEKS ALL OF THEIR OWN?:
GOLD, TUNGSTEN, BLACK SAND, AND BEANS

In 1950 Korea did not, on the face of it, have much to offer the American speculator. With the peninsula wrenched in half, the South seemed an economic basket case. Only visionary internationalists understood the virtues of bringing the South back into connection with Japan and the world economy. But it did have minerals, and expansionists understood minerals. As it happened, they also understood commodities speculation. And somehow, whether it was the gold or the lowly soybean or the highly-valued uses of tungsten and monazite "black sands," these four commodities attracted a bizarre collection of spies and speculators, and establish for us the stake, the interest, of expansionists: gold, tungsten and monazite because of their value, but also because they tend to be found in the same geological deposits; whereas the modest soybean, robust only as a "future," opens an unlikely window on a shrouded past.

Preston Goodfellow was involved with three of the four commodities. Yoshio Kodama, dark knight of Japanese politics, also turns up in three of the four. T. V. Soong turns up in two if not more, and dramatically so. So does the U.S. government, whose internationalism gave way to expansionism where strategic minerals were concerned. We will not get to the bottom of it. But we will shine some probing lights.

Korean gold attracted foreigners from earliest antiquity. No less than Kija, whom the Chinese claim to have been the founder of the Land of the Morning Calm, arrived in 1122 B.C. from China, and soon applied the latest methods to extract Korean gold. The ninth-century Arab traveler Ibn Khordadzbeh noticed that "at the extremity of China, opposite Kancu, there is a mountainous country named Sila . . . gold abounds there."[60]

In 1894 Leigh S. J. Hunt, founder of the *Seattle Post Intelligencer*, found his plans to turn this verdant, lake-rimmed city into the "Pittsburgh of the West" ruined by the panic of 1893 (to the eternal benefit of its citizens, one might add). He sold the newspaper to John D. Rockefeller, and left Seattle—and several rather large bad debts—posthaste. However, as a friendly biographer wrote, all was not lost. His father had followed the hordes out to California in the gold rush, and Leigh would continue the Westward march:

He resolved to enter Corea and begin the search for gold. Thru untracked lands, over mountain passes, thru the fiery ranks of brigands of all kinds . . . thru the frowning battelions of the adventurers that pour into Corea from the robber spirits of China and Japan; thru all these terrific perils Leigh Hunt had made his way . . . untill at last he found gold; and then, coming back to London with his wondrous tale, met great capitalists to back him and unearthed a great gold mine, which still, I believe, pours forth its yearly treasure and gives big dividends to its fortunate owners. Fragil, kindly, vigilant, delighted above all things to entertain his friends, and pursuing in the intervals the modern Holy Grail of the American—silently, without haste, without rest [sic—all].[61]

In 1897 Hunt hit paydirt, hooking up with James R. Morse to establish the Oriental Consolidated Mining Company (OCMC). King Kojŏng's family had owned most of the Ŭnsan district and its fabulous gold mines. In 1895 Morse got the first concession to work them, owning rights for the next quarter-century on Ŭnsan's gold. Shortly Hunt bought Morse out and joined up with two powerful New York Republicans, J. Sloat Fassett and Ogden Mills, Jr.; Hunt and Fassett became known as "the fathers of modern mining in the Far East." Fassett had intermarried with the San Francisco Crocker family that built the Southern Pacific railway, and raised his Korean ante of $100,000 through Crocker relatives.

As the new century dawned, Korean gold was bringing in tens of millions of dollars, it attracted other powerful gold expansionists, and thus the one form of American imperialism that Korea directly experienced before 1945 was the expansionist variety. (The initial ventures were the subject of Fred Harvey Harrington's splendid chapter, "A Cripple Creek All of Their Own.")[62] Herbert Hoover was what we might call a technician of mineral expansionism, having gotten an engineering degree at Stanford and then, in 1897–1899, making his fortune in the Australian outback pursuing gold mines and new techniques of recovering minerals for the great British firm, Bewick, Moreign. At the time of the Japanese Annexation he turned his attentions to Korean gold: "A group of Japanese bankers approached me with an invitation to join in what they considered was a large and rich group of copper and gold mines in Korea. I journeyed both ways over the Trans-Siberian Railway. The only profit was a view of the magnificent scenery of the Yalu River. . . . We went up the Yalu River in a junk." Hoover failed to mention that he visited the Ŭnsan mines, where he left unpaid a large liquor bill. Later on, Hoover created a "small syndicate for preliminary exploration" for gold in Siberia, together with George Kennan, elder cousin to our George Kennan and a racist disparager of Koreans. They found high quality ore, but were never able to exploit it. The Bolshevik Revolution intervened, prompting Hoover to write in 1951, "So far as I know, none of [the gold mines] is today even supporting the jackals [Soviets]. Had it not been for the First World War, I should have had the largest engineering fees ever known to man."[63] This excursion is merely to establish Hoover's background, and to suggest that Hoover provided an example to other conservative Republicans.

The peninsula became widely known for its most valuable mineral export. Like Ibn Khordadzbeh, investors would scratch their heads when they heard the word Korea and say, "they've got gold there, don't they?" That is, until the partition of Korea, for all the good gold was in the North. By 1916, nine million tons of ore had been recovered from the Ŭnsan mines, a gross value of $56 million on which the handsome profit was $15 million. By the early 1930s, OCMC milled an average of 600 tons of gold ore per day. The company was a fine investment, paying $12 million in dividends over the period 1900 to 1933, with a 9 percent per annum average profit.

Upwards of fifty thousand Koreans were directly dependent on gold mining companies for their livelihood; Americans trained "a small army of efficient native miners," Korean gold mine labor being considered the best in the Orient, and certainly among the cheapest in the world: 60 sen per day, about 35 Mexican centavos (amazingly, the mine used Mexican dollars as currency in this period). Ŭnsan had its own residences, schools, hospitals, foundries, machine shops, and electric-generating capacity (the power generation systems alone being worth about $1 million). The company's schooners brought supply materials up the coast from Ch'innamp'o to a small rail spur line. The gold went out on horseback convoy, sixty miles overland to the Manchurian rail system, well protected from "the fiery ranks of brigands." "It was reminiscent of the rear guard of a Mexican expeditionary force. The party consisted of five Europeans—all sharp shooters—and five special Japanese policemen—as good riders and seasoned gunmen—armed with the best make of rifles and carrying ammunition enough 'to wreck the forts of Verdun.' "[64]

Several prominent Republican families, all conservative and aligned with Herbert Hoover, dominated the ownership of the Korean gold mines in the early part of the twentieth century. The William Randolph Hearsts and the Ogden Millses, both of whose fortunes had originated with the gold rush, were the principal ones; they "became deeply interested in the OCMC." Ogden Mills, Jr., joined the OCMC board of directors in 1897, and from that time until the Japanese bought out the company in 1939, the Mills, Fassett, and Hearst interest was continuous. The great sociologist Ferdinand Lundberg listed the Hearst and Mills families in his famous *America's Sixty Families*; their wealth in classic expansionist fashion was centered on mining and publishing.[65]

The Mills, Fassett, and Hearst interests interlocked the boards of four companies, each a prime example of the history of American expansionism: OCMC in Korea, the Homestake Mine in Nevada, the Cerro de Pasco copper mines in Peru, and the Insular Lumber Company, the largest lumber firm in the Philippines. Homestake and Cerro de Pasco were notorious for harsh conditions and ruthless strike-breaking; the Hearst and Mills interests made Homestake the biggest gold producer in the United States, but not without bitter battles with the Wobblies. Hearst and Mills were also the largest stockholders in Cerro de Pasco, followed by J. P. Morgan interests; the mine was a symbol of American imperialism throughout Latin American. Drew Pearson developed information that MacArthur's key aide, Courtney Whitney, had an interest in Insular Lumber in the 1940s; Hearst also had interests in the Philippines, as did the Hearst-aligned First National City Bank, which dominated the islands.

In Lundberg's book the Millses are mentioned prominently in mining, but of course with Reid interests they also owned the *New York Herald-Tribune*, a paper influenced by J. P. Morgan. Lundberg also mentions Goodfellow in his book, as publisher of the *Brooklyn Eagle*, but not as one of the prominent families. William Donovan knew Ogden Mills well, from the time they both helped found the American Legion. Adolph Coors, of another right-wing family without tender mercies for labor, also owned gold mines in Korea. It is perhaps interesting to note that one of the only American publications reviewed in the North Korean party journal was Lundberg's *Sixty Families*.[66] Until 1939, Korean gold was mostly a wholly-owned subsidiary of the Republican right-wing.

The Japanese allowed American expansionists to profit from Korean gold mines because they needed American technology. Foster Bain noted that Japan occupied "an intermediate position" in mining, being an imperial power with mines, but requiring advanced technology it did not have. That is, Japan was still "semi-peripheral" in mineral extraction (just as North Korea was in 1987, when it asked the Japanese to return and try to revive the Ŭnsan mines). An expert stated that Korea was the only Far Eastern country where the mechanical extraction of gold had become well-established, and the only one with successful foreign concessions.[67] After the establishment of Manchukuo the Japanese embargoed the export of gold except through Japanese hands, thus establishing price controls on the American mines and forcing sales to stay within the empire. But as the price of gold rose during the 1930s, the mines remained profitable. In 1939, with World War II in the offing, the Japanese purchased OCMC's properties for $8 million, payable in annual sums—a price that would seem to have been under the market, suggesting a forced sale.[68] Thus a case could be made that the Japanese had unfairly pressured the sale at a bad price in wartime conditions, and that the mines ought to revert to American ownership after the war.

The Soviets also took a political interest in gold, especially Hoover's leading "jackal," Joseph Stalin. He got interested in the California gold rush in 1927 and "began to read every book he could get on the subject."

> Stalin showed an intimate acquaintance with the writings of Bret Harte. . . . Without going into technical details, he said that the [Western] districts of the U.S. were opened up from the beginning by gold and nothing else. On the tracks of the gold hunters came other mining industries, zinc, lead, copper . . . "this process [Stalin said], which really made up the history of California, must be applied to our outlying regions in Russia."[69]

Stalin's interest had another purpose: he feared Japanese expansionism after the debacle of the Chinese revolution in 1927 and the rapid development of Japanese interests in Manchuria, into a region of extraordinary mineral wealth and few defenses: the Soviet Far East. The morbid Russian fear of invasion is well known, and replete with historical justification. Napoleon and Hitler invaded from the West, with disastrous results. But the underpopulated, vast East was vulnerable, exposed to entry from the rear. This was precisely the region of joint Japanese-American exploitation of gold, and the one that drew the attention of inveterate anticommunists like Hoover and Donovan.

Perhaps the murkiest aspect of the speculation in Korean gold was the role of a scoundrel named Serge Rubinstein. He was the son of Dmitri Rubinstein, Petrograd banker, money-lender to the last Russian czar and an intimate of Rasputin (I understand that this account is beginning to sound like a novel); the family fled Russia after the revolution, and Serge accumulated great wealth through mining and other investments in Paris and London, through the Banque Franco-Asiatique, which had branches in Manchuria and Shanghai.

He met Chiang Kai-shek and T. V. Soong in 1936, when he sought to build a gold mining consortium with House of Peers' Viscount Inouye Kyoshiro; some of the mines were in Korea, others in Manchukuo. Apparently Rubinstein later got a gold concession on the Sungari River through the venue of Emperor Henry P'u-Yi's family.[70] He came to New York at about the same time, traveling on a passport given him by the Salazar regime, and calling himself Serge Manuel Rubinstein de Ravello. He quickly gained notoriety with his money, his flashy night life, and a court case written up lengthily in the newspapers, in which he was accused of "looting" the Chosen Corporation of $5.9 million; the money came from the sale of Korean gold mines to the Japanese. He acquired the successful Texas oil firm Midway-Victoria in 1939, and was known for his close ties to Central American ambassadors in Washington.

Rubinstein had been involved in espionage in France in 1933, and apparently had links to British intelligence during the war. In the late 1940s he was involved in scams to lease war-surplus aircraft. By 1949 he was in prison, accused of a $3 million stock fraud and facing deportation; he beat the first rap in April 1949 and successfully resisted deportation through the early 1950s. William Donovan kept a file on him; in his diary on the day after the Korean War broke out is the notation, "call Rubinstein." (It may not have been Serge.) In January 1955 someone entered Rubinstein's Fifth Avenue home, formerly the residence of Jules Bache, trussed him up like a pig and strangled him, leaving him in his black pajamas at the foot of his own portrait, in which he was accoutered as Napoleon. The murder has never been solved.[71]

Those connected with OCMC interests say that the Japanese made all their payments on time, in spite of Pearl Harbor, and that the Americans lost interest in the Ŭnsan mines after 1945, believing that most of its gold had been recovered.[72] But there is no question that the mines remained valuable after 1945. North Korean gold output was substantial, the mines important enough to be run directly by Russians. North Korea exported significant amounts of gold in the late 1940s, and P'yŏngyang later accused Moscow of taking much Korean gold at below market prices. There is also, of course, the geological fact that tungsten and certain radioactive materials tend to be found near gold deposits.[73]

When I wrote the first volume, I was unaware of the importance of this concession and Goodfellow's attempt to get it back. In 1945 the Reid-Mills interests retained ties to the OCMC board of directors, and to other concessions in East Asia directed by the OCMC group (such as Insular Lumber in the Philippines). Ogden Mills, treasury secretary during the Hoover administration, had been on the OCMC board, and the Reids also maintained influence on the OCMC Board through family members and through Roy C. Gasser, a Wall Street broker who represented Mills-Reid interests. It would seem likely that Goodfellow would have known the Reids before the war, when he owned the *Brooklyn Eagle*, they the *Herald-Tribune*.

In any case it so happened that Ogden Mills Reid materialized in Seoul just as Rhee returned in October 1945, lunching with Rhee and attending the October 20, 1945, Welcoming Ceremony in which Gen. John R. Hodge, commander of the Occupation, introduced Rhee to the Korean people. (Reid thought Rhee was "General Hodge's white hope.") Reid then traveled on to Chungking, where he met with Chiang Kai-shek and T. V. Soong on October 26. In the Reid family papers there is no evidence to suggest continuing interest in Korean gold mines, however, and it seems doubtful that this wealthy family with diversified investments really cared much anymore about Korean gold.[74] But others did, mainly Rhee and his lobby, and a group of businessmen in Elmira, New York, who were OCMC investors and remained on the board of Insular Lumber.

Preston Goodfellow spirited Rhee back to Korea in October 1945 and helped to establish a separate government, but he was forced to leave Korea on May 24, 1946, after he sought to revive the north Korean gold mine concession. Rhee himself was forced to take a temporary leave of absence from the Representative Democratic Council in March 1946 after news appeared that he had promised gold mining concessions to the OCMC. The Korean press reported that Rhee had sold the Ŭnsan mining rights to "an American businessman," naming Goodfellow; at a news conference on May 27 Rhee said he had formed a "Korean-American Economic Institute," with which Goodfellow was involved. It had been established to develop the Ŭnsan mines. If Goodfellow had not come to the attention of the north Koreans and Soviets before, he was certainly noticed after this episode.[75]

A man named Mervin R. Arick owned mines near Seoul and was heavily involved in OCMC in the 1930s; he also worked with the Insular Lumber interests in the Philippines. He spent eighteen months in Army intelligence in Korea in 1945–1946. At least two prominent Koreans who were close to Americans had interests in Korean gold: Cho Pyŏng-ok, who managed a gold mine from 1937 to 1945, and Herbert Kim, recommended to Donovan for intelligence work in 1948.[76]

Korean gold is interesting also because other minerals appear with it, tungsten and monazite. Tungsten was by far the most important of South Korea's exports by the 1950s, accounting for 17 percent of total exports and 42 percent of mineral exports in 1960. Its export value by 1953 was about $30 million. Although paltry by world standards, this was a tidy sum as mineral deposits go, touching off a scramble for tungsten contracts amongst Rhee's cronies and political friends. Tight world supplies in 1950 and 1951 also drew in the attention of the U.S. government, which cornered the entire South Korean supply for itself, while seeking to fight off a corner by John Staggers and a company with links to the Japan Lobby.

Tungsten became a critical strategic mineral by the 1950s for two reasons. First, when it is alloyed to steel the result is sharp and highly heat resistant, like a man-made diamond, making it essential in antitank devices, and especially for the new, high-speed jet engines, just produced since the mid-1940s, and for Werner Von Braun's missiles. Second, the Allies had gotten 90 percent of their supply from southern China during

the war, via the Wah Chang Trading Company, led by tungsten magnate
K. C. Li. The PLA's march into South China had a predictable effect on
the world tungsten market; by 1950 most of China's tungsten supply had
been diverted to the Soviet Union. China shipped five million pounds to
the United States in 1949, only 350,000 pounds in 1950, and almost all
of it before the June trade embargo. By late 1952 the price of tungsten
had tripled.[77]

During World War II the Japanese also designated tungsten a strategic
war mineral, and upped Korean output in the early 1940s. As supplies
tightened and as Japan pushed the development both of jet engines and
atomic bombs, in 1944–1945 none other than Yoshio Kodama was put in
charge of Korean tungsten mines, and the monazite "black sands" that
were found with it.[78] K. C. Li was close to Chiang Kai-shek, and also knew
most of the prominent Americans with interests in China; he was a strong
backer of the Institute for Pacific Relations. Goodfellow also approached
him for help in clandestine warfare behind Japanese lines, Li recommending to him Tu Yueh-sheng, leader of the ill-famed "Green Gang."[79]

South Korea became the main alternative source of tungsten supply
after the Communists occupied the mainland. The Sangdong mine was
among the world's best. Located in the rugged hills of Kangwŏn Province
near Yongwŏl, it had known reserves making it one of the largest in the
world and good for at least a century of mining, with an ore deposit "very
rich by American standards." It was in disrepair during the Occupation,
and the work force was strongly leftist (one report noted difficulties in
keeping a work force due to "wholesale arrests"). A smaller mine was
located at Talsŏng, near Taegu; the Kobayashi Mining Company had
worked it for gold until 1939, tungsten thereafter. Guerrillas destroyed
its surface plant in July 1949, but at Sangdong American engineers used
new processes to double the output of this mine in 1949.[80]

In April 1951 the State Department stated that "tungsten [was] in desperately short supply and potential Korean production [was] essential";
Muccio reported that Sangdong alone could furnish a quarter of the annual American requirement for tungsten. Acheson personally urged that
Sangdong be exploited fully in the fall of 1951, with American loans to
rehabilitate it. Thus the U.S. government came to act like the expansionists. Willard Thorp of State said, "we've got to get the tungsten and
soon," urging that the U.S. military run the Sangdong Mine for five
years—a relationship that was "one-sided," "pretty tough" on Korean interests, to be sure, but "if we can get away with it, fine." The United States
wanted American control and supervision, as much controlled Korean
labor as necessary, and no taxes, duties, or levies of any kind on exports.
By early 1952, the U.S. Defense Procurement Agency was getting the
entire production of the ROK's tungsten mines, except for limited do-

mestic needs. Sangdong by then had 2,300 workers, with security provided by a battallion of American troops; the local commander said the mine could not operate without such protection, owing to "guerrillas and poachers," and looting by ROKA soldiers, who would take "all food supplies" if given the chance.[81]

Still, a private American firm was needed to work the mine under military protection. And Rhee would choose the one to do it. All the firms who came out on top of the bidding had some personal connection with Rhee or his lobby. Behre Dolbear of New York made the low bid, and seemed the likely choice, its president being Samuel Dolbear, Rhee's "minerals consultant." But then there were Rhee myrmidons John Staggers and Harold Lady, described by the embassy as "keenly interested in mining deals in Korea," and now associated with Eichelberger Mining Company, a firm put together just for this tungsten bid. Its chairman was Frank Eichelberger, brother of Japan Lobby figure Gen. Robert Eichelberger. Richard Burwell was the metallurgist in Eichelberger's company, and happened to be a friend of Frank Crampton, Rhee's "engineering advisor." A Pinkerton report described Crampton as a "mental case" having some sort of "pull" with Senator Knowland, and connected to "political groups in Central America"; he also coveted Korean tin and made "extravagant claims" about Korea's rather meager tin deposits.[82]

K. C. Li's Wah Chang was also interested, through a subsidiary called Blackrock Mining. Most of the major American tungsten firms did not make bids, perhaps because they knew the likely outcome. In September 1952 Rhee drafted an agreement with Eichelberger's firm, a decidedly unequal arrangement guaranteeing a payment of $1.25 million with various bonuses for the firm, no liability for nonperformance, no possibility of lawsuits, and the like, leading a UN reconstruction official to comment that the contract "leaves me a most unfavorable impression of the 'Eichelberger Mining Company.' "[83]

Muccio, the State Department, and the General Services Administration blocked this contract, but Rhee and his cronies continued well into 1953 trying to arrange a deal with Eichelberger's firm. By that time, tungsten was no longer critical to the United States and so Rhee's shenanigans were less obnoxious.[84] A year later, Staggers and Goodfellow interested none other than Firth Sterling, one of the world's largest consumers of tungsten, and through their efforts the president, Kenneth Mann, set up the first tungsten carbide sintering mill in Korea. Goodfellow was on a first-name basis with Mann, and letters in July 1954 make clear his involvement in Firth's plans for Korean tungsten (earlier he had corresponded with Francesca Rhee about Staggers' tungsten deal with Eichelberger). Although information on his involvement is sketchy, it is likely that OSS connections between Goodfellow and Mann helped Firth in obtaining concessions with Rhee.[85]

The United States also got tungsten during this period through the good offices of Kodama Yoshio, supplying the Occupation in Japan with tungsten smuggled out of mainland China on Nationalist warships;[86] one assumes Kodama's experience would also have been useful in Korea. Eugene Dooman of the Japan Lobby was also "hired by the CIA, apparently in late 1950," one of his missions being a $2.8 million project to buy tungsten through a Japanese supplier. Kodama was also long rumored to have been a confidant of CIA people in Japan.[87]

It is a geological curiosity that tungsten is found with gold, and that a material called monazite is found with both of them; it is a political curiosity that Kodama handled the procurement of these scarce minerals for the Japanese war effort in 1944–1945. Monazite is a black sand that bears small amounts of radioactive material that can be made into thorium, which can be used for constructing an antique but potent version of the atomic bomb. Gen. Leslie Groves began a highly secret program in 1944, therefore, to control thorium supplies on a world scale. According to Jonathan Helmreich, efforts to keep thorium and other rare ores from the Soviet Union "took high precedence in the thoughts of American officials"; the United States retained an interest in preempting thorium through the early 1950s even though it was never used for an American bomb, because it was thought that the Soviets wanted it. Brazil and India were the main sources of high-grade monazite sands, and William Pawley was involved in attempts to corner both supplies.[88]

Korea was the center of Japanese attempts to acquire fissionable material and build a bomb. Because of intense Allied bombing in the last years of the war, northern Korea produced more electricity than all of Japan. Atomic weapons require huge electrical generating capacity, and so Japan's bomb project was moved to Korea. It centered on the great chemical factories built by Noguchi Jun in Hŭngnam; here the Japanese processed more than 90 percent of the monazite mined in Korea in 1944, seeking to recover sufficient amounts of thorium for a bomb. By the end of the war, the Japanese had stockpiled another 1,000 tons of monazite for processing. Although Robert K. Wilcox claims that the Japanese actually exploded some sort of atomic device off a Korean island in August 1945, this seems far-fetched and most unlikely. But the limited evidence available does suggest that Kodama, the Noguchi interests, and Japanese militarists put a major effort into a thorium bomb made from the raw material of Korean monazite.[89]

The Noguchi complex and most of the monazite deposits fell into North Korean and Russian hands after 1945, but the Americans got the documents on Japan's bomb project. Although little is known about how the United States used this information, it would appear that intelligence circles were convinced that the Soviet atomic bomb program was built in part upon Japanese efforts. USAFIK G-2 records show continuing interest in the Hŭngnam complex and in north Korean radioactive minerals. In May 1947, for example, two Korean agents were dispatched to collect and bring back samples of uranium ore from mines near Chŏngjin and Nanam, with unknown results. Various G-2 reports cite agent accounts of highly secret and closely guarded activity at the Hŭngnam complex.[90]

In March 1950, American intelligence cited unverified information suggesting that the Hŭngnam installation was being used for the production of atomic weapons using Japanese and German technicians (there was also interest at this time in Taiwan's monazite deposits, which were plentiful but apparently not rich enough to yield thorium). The United States sought monazite deposits with a thorium content of 8 percent or more; apparently the percentage content of North Korean monazite was unknown. But in early June 1950, SCAP intelligence reported that monazite was being recovered at five or six mines in the North and shipped to the USSR.[91]

It is worth noting that Donald MacLean collected detailed intelligence on "extensive metallurgical research" by the British and Americans "aimed at extracting large quantities of low grade uranium from Witwatersrand gold ore" in South Africa, which he apparently kept the Russians informed about from 1947 onward.[92] Perhaps the British spies followed the monazite trail as well.

Once the war began, the United States faced a dilemma were it to cross the thirty-eighth parallel. Dean Rusk in late July said that "the Soviet interest in thorium, which was to be found in North Korea," would have an influence on their attitude toward future control of the peninsula, in other words they might fight to keep the United States out. On the other hand, a march North would have the possible virtue of weakening the Soviet bomb program. At some point in August the JCS made a decision to hit the Hŭngnam plant, "used to process monazite" and termed a "critical target"; on August 24 American bombers destroyed most of it.[93] It is an indication of the extraordinary caution of the Soviets during the Korean War that they took this lying down.

Once the United States occupied the North and inspected the Hŭngnam facility, it learned that the Japanese had guarded every window of the plant in 1945, and had brought in large amounts of lead, probably for shielding; some informants also claimed that it had been used to make "rocket fuel." In 1946 the Russians reportedly removed all the equipment from the plant, workers and all, and took them to the Soviet Union.[94]

Meanwhile mining of monazite continued. In the Ch'ŏlsan mining area (a small peninsula south of Sinŭiju), some 23,000 workers dug out monazite on a round-the-clock basis in 1949 and 1950, yielding 18,000 tons of black sand concentrate annually, about half the North Korean total. This was crudely refined and then shipped by train to the USSR, in return for tanks, machine guns, trucks, and other materiel.[95]

Although much remains obscure about Korean "black sands," it is apparent that American intelligence paid attention to the mining of monazite and its refinement into thorium in the North, and that in the period 1945–1951 two of our cast of rogues again turn up with this business: Kodama and Pawley. The monazite went together with tungsten, and both were found with gold. It must be just a coincidence, but when Chinese soldiers first joined the battle in Korea in October 1950, they came roaring out of the Ŭnsan fastness.

The Soybean Caper

Freedom of speech and a fairly extensive disclosure of foreign policy secrets exists in the United States, but one wonders now and then if this is because no one is listening, or if listening, not remembering. A remarkable aspect of Hartzian America is its ineffable capacity to forget those secrets that do happen to penetrate the media, salient facts that surface but quickly waft to the briny deep, owing to a lack of context or perhaps an absence of the political sensibility that likes to seek out patterns in the events of the day.

A soybean conspiracy occured just before the Korean War began, according to Dean Acheson. But we are not supposed to think about conspiracies, so no one but the unflagging I. F. Stone ever took it seriously. During the MacArthur hearings in 1951, a senator asked Acheson if he had heard anything about a corner on the soybean market in June 1950. Acheson replied blandly, "there was, I recall, a very serious situation created by a group of Chinese buying and taking delivery of a certain amount of soybeans, which gave certain controls over prices." The secretary of agriculture had called this to his attention, he said, and had taken unspecified "remedial steps." But, Acheson did not quite recall who might have been involved, could not really say if perhaps the China Lobby had something to do with it, and the legislators went on to a new line of questioning, leaving Senators Wayne Morse and Brian McMahon lonely figures in demanding an investigation of the China Lobby.[96]

The *New York Times* reported that a total of fifty-one Chinese, all but fourteen residing in the United States (the rest were in Hong Kong), operating through a Hong Kong company, had cleared a profit estimated at $30 million by pushing the price of soybean futures from $2.32 to $3.45 per bushel, that is, a 50 percent increase. The Agriculture Depart-

ment had the names of those involved, "but the law forbids their publication." One who disposed of 500,000 bushels was identified as a wealthy
relative of Chiang Kai-shek's; a Chinese woman in New York held a million bushels. The *Times* noted that the corner had "aroused official suspicion that they had advance knowledge of a war that caught this country
wholly unprepared." Some senators were said to be "upset" about all this;
rumor had it that $200 million in "hard gold" given to China by the
United States during World War II had turned up in the accounts of
"wealthy Chinese" in the United States.[97] The law did not forbid investigation, indictment, and trial of the individuals, but that never happened.

The Japanese had developed Manchurian soybeans during the colonial
period into a major cash crop for export. After the assumption of power
by Kao Kang's Northeast government, soybeans still poured forth into
the world market. Before the Korean War, export totals were worth upwards of $400 million annually.[98] A crisis in the Far East would disrupt
exports of Manchurian soybeans, thus forcing the world price up. Donovan's World Commerce Corporation was known to be involved with
Manchurian soybeans, with Japan Lobby figure Joseph Grew one of its
trade representatives in the Far East. In late May 1950, Congressman
Fred Crawford of Michigan charged that World Commerce had reaped
$2.7 million in a "fantastic deal" in which Manchurian soybeans worth
$4.6 million were bartered for cotton worth $7.6 million. He criticized
the Agriculture Department for doing nothing about this deal; a spokesman for Agriculture replied that Crawford had exaggerated World Commerce profits. Of both this case and the soybean caper, Agriculture Department records in the National Archives show no trace.[99]

The Chinese individual in the United States with the financial wherewithal to corner markets was, of course, T. V. Soong. It was he who had
diverted $200 million in gold to his California acounts, held in part by
the Bank of America (which became, understandably, a strong backer of
the China Lobby) and managed by Tommy Corcoran. Simply this
amount would make him among the richest men in the world in 1950,
and he had more: Dean Rusk estimated, in a memo for Acheson, that
T. V. controlled $1.5 billion. And his relatives had more. Two of his sis-
ters were married to Chiang Kai-shek and H. H. Kung, as a starter. Furthermore T. V. and his brother T. L. Soong were very active in the spring
of 1950 in the United States, meeting with congressmen to discuss a mysterious "plan" T. V. had for rollback on the mainland, and along with his
brother-in-law, H. H. Kung, bankrolling Kohlberg and McCarthy in their
attacks on alleged procommunists in government. Robert Blum includes
all of them in a grouping around Madam Chiang, who was then in the
United States.[100]

On June 10, T. V. announced that he would not return to Taiwan, as

Chiang had requested, and articles in the press linked this to an impending invasion of Taiwan. Shortly thereafter Chiang removed him, his brother T. L., and H. H. Kung from the board of directors of the Central Bank of China. At this time, H. H. Kung was in Tokyo visiting Willoughby. Wen Ying-hsing, who had been T. V. Soong's commander of the Salt Revenue Guards and who was close to Gen. Sun Li-jen, left New York for Hong Kong in a big flurry in late May.[101]

Soybean futures fluctuated unusually in these weeks, as the following table indicates:

	May price (dollars per bushel)	July futures (dollars per bushel)
May 9	$3.16	$3.14
May 18	$2.92	$2.92
May 29		$3.21
June 1		$3.27
June 8		$3.15
June 16		$2.93
June 24		$2.92

The Commodity Exchange Authority reported "heavy" activity in soybeans on June 15, noting that recent speculation totaled $1.2 billion, or "six times the size of the crop." This was a 170 percent increase over 1949, coming in months that were not usually heavy ones for soybean trading, because most farmers had already sold off their crop.[102] Three days later, soybean authorities found "radical changes," and a "severe price recession." The day the war began, Associated Press reported that in final trading before the weekend soybeans were hit by "steady selling," with pressure coming from "the East." One unconfirmed rumor said that 500,000 bushels of Manchurian beans had been offered for sale in the United States on Friday. The following day more heavy selling off was reported to have occured, before word of the war came. And then, of course, sharp rises in price began with the war news, obvious by June 27: the war "may result in shutting off the only other available supply of this commodity." The amounts sold in the two weeks before the war were three or four times the comparable 1949 levels.[103]

Someone had dumped large amounts of soybeans on the market to force the price down, while holding much greater accounts in July futures. The speculation began in March, but sell-offs were targeted particularly on the weekend of June 24–25, that is, not in anticipation of some June or July crisis in East Asia, but specifically timed for big selloffs at the end of the week before that fateful Sunday. The Commodity Exchange Authority later said that by June 30, fifty-six Chinese held nearly half of all open contracts for July soybean futures—all "on the long side," meaning they were playing for a rise in price.[104]

At the time I. F. Stone named T. L. Soong as a party to this conspiracy, and documents quietly declassified recently and buried in the economic files of the Office of Chinese Affairs also name T. L.—then alternate governor of the World Bank, and termed "the worst of the Soongs" by Amb. Leighton Stuart. Indeed, this was known within a month of the outbreak of the war, when the name "John L. Soong" turned up on the list of those "suspected of commodity speculation on the Chicago grain market." John L. Soong just happened to list as his address the domicile of T. L. Soong.[105]

In early August, Oliver Edmund Clubb observed that, "Soybeans in the past few months have enjoyed a spectacular speculative rise on the Chicago market, created largely by activities of a group of Chinese speculators among whom has been identified T. L. Soong, brother of T. V. Soong, and an Alternate Governor for China of the World Bank."[106] When I wrote to Clubb in 1985 about the soybean case, he said he had no knowledge of it. Within a few months he was the target of McCarthy's attacks, which ruined his State Department career.

According to several sources, Joe McCarthy profited from the soybean corner. Drew Pearson wrote in his diary, "McCarthy was buying soybeans" at the time when "the Chinese Nationalists did just about corner the market before Korea"; Stone said McCarthy had "a successful flier in soybeans" later on in 1950.[107] In May of 1951, after the war had been going almost a year, Colonel Goodfellow sent Herbert Hoover a sample of soybean meal. Of all the things Goodfellow might choose to send to a friend, why would he choose this?[108]

WHAT IS the significance of this soybean scam? It might mean that someone acquired advance knowledge of an impending North Korean invasion. However, it requires a daunting leap of the imagination to think that fifty-one Chinese could have foreseen the onset of the Korean War when American intelligence said it did not. P'yŏngyang's mobilization (and not necessarily for aggression) did not begin before June 15, as we will see. Even if aggression was planned, who would know P'yŏngyang's timing? Foreknowledge is only plausible in two hypothetical scenarios: human intelligence within the North or South Korean regime which would predict timing, or advance knowledge of a crisis involving Taiwan, also giving the timing. A Taiwan crisis could mean a Communist invasion that the United States would in fact resist, or it could mean a coup against Chiang Kai-shek which, as we will see, was being mounted in the weekend the Korean War began. In the Korea and Taiwan scenarios one would also have to predict U.S. involvement (without an American response, Manchurian soybean exports might continue even if the Communists took South Korea or Taiwan, or if Chiang or Rhee provoked a war.) But then, a coup against Chiang also would not cut off soybean exports—unless it were the signal for an American defense of Taiwan. Finally, timing would be known best to that person who controls it, and does not need to rely on someone's prediction.

We are then left with three possibilities of foreknowledge, in declining order of probability: (1) a coup against Chiang, followed by a commitment of American defense of Taiwan and an embargo against the mainland; (2) the provocation of a war in Korea, which would also lead to an embargo; (3) evidence of a coming North Korean attack, with the timing known and the American response known. Speculators are gamblers, of course, and might have bet that one of these three scenarios would eventuate. Or perhaps, a handful of witting people might have anticipated that all three would, or could, occur.

CONCLUSION

The careful and skeptical reader will now come forward and declare, not proved. We have, indeed, failed to show that this riveting but murky business of spies and speculators had clear effect on the origins of the Korean War. But we have done what we set out to do, to establish lineages and retrieve personalities and peculations, so that we may at minimum ask better questions about our dramatis personae, and the origins of the war. As we will see, our knaves and villains appear and reappear in the later narrative.

Chapter Five

ROLLBACK PERCOLATES IN
THE BUREAUCRACY

> In the war in which we are presently engaged, we should fight with
> no holds barred. We should find every weak spot in the enemy's
> armor, both on the periphery and at the center, and hit him with
> anything that comes to hand. Anything we do short of an all-out
> effort is inexcusable. We should cause them trouble wherever we
> can.
>
> *Robert Lovett, March 1950*

O UR ARGUMENT to this point has dealt with the rollback constituency, and its fringe elements in intelligence work and pecuniary speculations. What remains to be explained is how a rollback vision once on the periphery of American politics became a central contender with the containment strategy among national security elites in 1950. McCarthyism played a major role in preparing the domestic scene for a new accommodation. But rollback was not the preferred strategy of the blue bloods in the State Department, and indeed most accounts of the period continue to place this tendency in the pale of unacceptability, ruled out-of-bounds, too extreme.¹ As it happened, however, the containment decisions of the first Korean War were prefigured in the summer of 1949, and the rollback option of the second Korean War bubbled up in the subsequent six months. And the eventual implementation of the march North germinated amongst the faint-hearted, striped pants crowd at Foggy Bottom. How so?

Six months before the Korean War, Harry Truman signed a highly-classified document, NSC 48, that introduced a new logic into the East Asian and Korean situation. Whereas in 1947 the issue between Acheson and the military was whether to contain communism in Korea (Acheson was for it) or to cut bait and withdraw (the military's preference), by the end of 1949 the issue was whether to contain communism in East Asia or to roll it back, if an opportunity presented itself. Again it was Acheson for containment: in Korea, but not in Taiwan. Again it was the rollback constituency that wanted first containment and then rollback, in Taiwan and China. But a new element entered, which was a rationale for a Japan-centered rollback, to secure a larger hinterland for the revival of the Japanese economy.

For very different reasons, a coalition formed behind a rollback logic:

in our terms, the essential difference was between expansionist rollback (MacArthur) and internationalist rollback (various pro-Japan figures). In regard to areas on the periphery of China, except for Japan, the basic options had been three: withdrawal (the military's preference for Korea, but usually not for Taiwan), containment (Acheson's preference for Korea but not for Chiang's Taiwan), an ironclad guarantee of American protection (desired by Rhee, Chiang, and their backers). In the summer of 1949 the new option was added: a reduction of communist territory, that is, rollback. One phrase captured this logic: "to check and reduce" communism, embodied both in NSC 68 and NSC 48 (which might be called the NSC 68 for Asia). It is the process leading to NSC 48 and NSC 68 that demonstrates how rollback logic percolated up in the bureaucracy, and, later, how it provided a rationale for transforming the Korean War from a war for containment to a war for rollback.

The year 1948 changed the East Asian context of American policy profoundly. Most importantly, the Nationalists lost the civil war in China. Next in importance, the reverse course for Japan had begun, giving the United States a strong commitment there and raising old fears among Japan's neighbors and former enemies. For containment advocates like Kennan, both of these changes suggested the necessity for a stiffened policy in the region. Spring crises in Czechoslovakia and Berlin shook the United States and suggested to Americans a Soviet strategy willing to probe with force at the periphery of its empire. As Americans contemplated the prospect of a Eurasian land mass under what appeared to be unified communist control, with an ostensible dynamic expansionism in contrast to the passivity of a defensive containment, they began to think of alternative strategies. But the rollback option did not become a serious alternative at high levels until after June 1949, by which time a somewhat curious figure, Louis Johnson, had replaced James Forrestal as secretary of defense.

Johnson was born in Roanoke in 1891, and boxed and wrestled his way through the University of Virginia. In 1932 he became commander of the American Legion, and as we have seen, was rumored to have been implicated in a plot against Roosevelt. As assistant secretary of war in 1937–1940 he advocated an expanded air force but in 1940 he lost the top spot to Henry Stimson and thus resigned. He became secretary of defense in March 1949 and held that position until September 1950 (Truman owed him one for Johnson's stupendous fundraising efforts in the 1948 campaign).[2]

Johnson did not leave much of a paper trace. His collection at the University of Virginia is virtually useless. If one were to judge by the weight of his files, he paid more attention to the annual gathering of bigwigs at Bohemian Grove, the ruling class retreat in California, than to East Asian policy.[3] However little Johnson may have left for the historian, he was (for better or worse) a much more commonplace American leader than Acheson or the man he replaced, Forrestal. David Lilienthal penned this acidic portrait of Johnson and his cronies:

> The "characters" . . . hovering around the outer office . . . [had] the overfed, cigar-chewing, red-faced glum look that you see hanging around the courthouse and the city hall all over the country. The vultures who gather where there is dead meat (in the way of public contracts) and who think they know how to get a hunk of the same.[4]

Acheson held Johnson in deep contempt, thinking him foolishly ambitious in campaigning openly for the 1952 presidential nomination (to which Acheson attributed his niggardliness on defense spending), incapable of subtle policy analysis, and one supposes, rather stupid. But he was a bit more than that. As Robert Donovan described him, "Bald and square-shouldered, Louis Johnson, two hundred pounds of power, competence, acerbity, wile, and bumptiousness, hit the Pentagon like a thunderstorm."[5] Johnson unnerved people with his wide, round, yet somehow beady eyes, poking from under wrinkled-up eyebrows like half-inch drill bits. Loud, abrasive, cocksure, this antithesis of Acheson was also formidable enough to be his nemesis.

In contrast to many Democrats, he was a China-firster, thinking it more important than Japan. He initiated a general review of East Asian policy soon after taking office, and was a key person in bringing the Taiwan question to the center of America's concerns in East Asia. He was also, on the available record, involved in activities with the Nationalists that would be treasonable by some definitions. He (or his close underlings) slipped national security documents of the highest classification to Nationalist sources, both directly (to the ambassador, Wellington Koo) and indirectly (through back-channel communications with Chiang Kai-shek). Sometimes the Chinese would know about top secret deliberations the next morning, if not sooner. This is perhaps one reason for taking what he knew to the grave with him, rather than leaving his papers to inquiring scholars.

His trusted aide, Paul Griffith, frequently informed Wellington Koo about matters of the highest classification; he also used other go-betweens, like Victor O'Kelliher and Leslie Biffle, to keep the Nationalists informed. Johnson also operated through back-channel communications with Taipei that bypassed the Nationalist embassy.[6] At the same time Johnson prided himself on keeping secrets from the State Department, as if Chiang were an American patriot and Acheson a foreign implant. (Probably that is what Johnson thought.) He also schemed with T. V. Soong and conservative congressmen.[7] Warren Cohen is right to say that

Johnson and his aides in the "highest echelons" of the Defense Department were "in collusion with Chiang's agents," yet even that may put the case mildly. Kennan later remarked that the Kuomintang (KMT) had "intrigued in this country in a manner scarcely less disgraceful to it than to ourselves," probably a reference to Johnson's activities.[8]

The emergence of Johnson as a top policy advocate and antagonist of Acheson did two things. First, Johnson's desire to apply containment to East Asia dovetailed with Acheson's views on Korea going back to 1947. The problem was that Johnson wanted containment for Taiwan—perhaps also for Korea, but Taiwan came first; Acheson wanted containment for Korea but not for Taiwan if that meant a commitment to the Chiang regime. Second, Johnson's connections with rollback currents brought the new logic into the top levels of the administration. We may say that containment in East Asia won high-level sanction in the summer of 1949, not the summer of 1950 as the conventional historiography suggests. Even more, it won sanction in a rollback package, as containment became a comfortable option B between two "extreme" alternatives: withdrawal and rollback.

To use the football metaphors so dear to Johnson's heart, we may say that rollback ran interference for containment. But, again, there were two kinds of rollback: liberal rollback anchored on Japan, and conservative rollback anchored on Taiwan. Johnson supported the latter, and *some* officials in the State Department and elsewhere were at least conjuring with the former. Acheson, however, on the available record remained committed to containment until the Korean War. For him, the best offense was a good defense. For Johnson, the best defense was a good offense. The question was which team to get across the goal line, China (Nationalist version) or Japan. Johnson looked after the parts and quarterbacked the Nationalists, Acheson quarterbacked the whole and looked after a part named Japan. Johnson was an expansionist, Acheson was an internationalist.

On June 10, 1949, Johnson wrote that the recent course of events in Asia required new National Security Council (NSC) deliberations, toward a general, correlated policy for Asia. The objective would be "to contain communism in order to reduce its threat to our security." He wanted an "action plan." A secret Joint Chiefs of Staff (JCS) history of the Korean War is correct in saying that this document stimulated the NSC 48 process, resulting in a final document whose "general effect was to apply the doctrine of 'containment' to the Far East."[9]

In June and July of 1949 Acheson, Dulles, and Kennan also fretted about communist advances in East Asia. Dulles told Acheson that "if the Chinese Communists were not stopped, they would go beyond China, and the U.S. had to stop them somewhere and sometime." Dulles related

to Wellington Koo that Acheson "shared this view." During NSC deliberations in early June, Kennan had said that the Soviets "were probably
turning to the East where they had revolutionary possibilities," and a
month later he offered his "personal view" that in the wake of the Chinese Communist victory on the mainland, "our situation in the Far East
will not permit further inaction in areas where our military and economic
capabilities would be adequate to meet the possible commitments flowing
from intervention." Kennan stated, however, that if the military departments continued to think that global limits to U.S. power forbid a defense
of Taiwan (and by implication, South Korea) then the United States
should reconcile itself to an ultimate takeover. He implied that the military, while wanting to make a commitment to Taiwan, did not wish to
take the responsibility for what might happen if such a commitment were
made.[10]

Kennan had frequently chided the military for thinking always in
terms of general war, rather than planning for the realities of cold war
politics in which smaller wars might break out. It so happened, however,
that in late June the JCS concurred in a Department of Army study that
both sketched the scenario followed a year later in Korea, and intruded
the notion of a "police action" or limited war. This was a top secret scenario of options in the events of "a possible full scale invasion from
North Korea subsequent to withdrawal of U.S. troops from South Korea"—a withdrawal that was to be completed exactly three days later.

The possible courses of action included (a) emergency evacuation of
American nationals in Korea; (b) presentation of the problem to the UN
Security Council for emergency consideration; and (c), "To initiate *police
action* with U.N. sanction by the introduction of a military task force into
Korea composed of U.S. units and units of other member nations of the
U.N. with the objective of restoring law and order and restoration of the
38th parallel boundary inviolability" [emphasis added]. The authors recommended adopting options (a) and (b) as policy, but option (c) was
deemed "unsound militarily" and should be considered only if "all other
methods failed." Although the paper was not forwarded to the NSC, it is
noteworthy that the military stuck to its longstanding judgment that Korea was the wrong place to make a stand—but now with the signal caveat,
unless all else fails.[11]

A month later the CIA also referred to "the U.S. objective of containing Communism in Asia," and praised American aid to the Republic of
Korea (ROK): "Communist domination of southern Korea would have
convinced many people that even U.S. assistance is not capable of halting
the growth of Communist power in Asia."[12]

Dean Rusk, increasingly important in East Asian deliberations and con-
genitally a containment thinker, definitively laid down the State Depart-

ment's logic of containment in midsummer 1949. Written for Acheson, the document called for "a program of action" on East Asia, envisioning the establishment of domestic bipartisanship, no recognition of Communist China, aid for Indochina "to help seal off [the] China border and prevent the spread of Communism into Southeast Asia," "political support for the Bao Dai regime," and an implied commitment to defend Taiwan. On Korea, he suggested more experts be sent, more military aid, stronger diplomatic backing, "stimulation of Korean-Japanese trade," and the "presentation to SC [Security Council] of any serious case of incursions across 38 parallel from the North."

Acheson responded two days later that "it is a fundamental decision of American policy that the U.S. does not intend to permit further extension of Communist domination on the Continent of Asia or in the Southeast Asian area," a precise formulation that included Korea but excluded Taiwan (although he mentioned neither). Backing Rusk in calling for a program of action to be drawn up, Acheson said the United States must "make absolutely certain that we are neglecting no opportunity that would be within our capabilities to achieve the purpose of halting the spread of totalitarian Communism in Asia."[13]

State Department sources saw Acheson's response as the basis for inaugurating a full review of East Asia policy, something Johnson had called for a month earlier. After John Foster Dulles declined Acheson's invitation to supervise the review, it fell to Ambassador-at-Large Phillip Jessup, Acheson's close friend, professor of international law, and charter internationalist. Two outsiders assisted him: Everett Case, president of Colgate University, and Raymond Fosdick, formerly head of the Rockefeller Foundation. Amid attacks on the administration's China policy, Jessup began work on the famous China White Paper, and Acheson and Rusk opened "a bipartisan offensive"; Truman and Acheson brought in Senate Foreign Relations committee head Tom Connally to work out a Congressional strategy.[14]

Precision is important here. As these deliberations ensued, South Korean forces instigated attacks against the North, and plans began in Washington for a possible clandestine overthrow of Chiang Kai-shek, as we will see. Many of the events of June 1950 were thus prefigured, except that North Korea invaded the South, instead of vice versa. These documents also presage and predict the American entry into the Korean War a year later. In fact Acheson's 1947 logic had not changed, even if it had been reinforced by containment-advocate Rusk. Nothing in these papers required a direct application of American military force, but instead posited collective action under the UN. But they do make indelible the application of Truman Doctrine containment to Korea—which, as in Greece, meant miltary advisory groups, aid and expertise, support for "free peoples," collective security through the UN, and the like. This is exactly what Acheson was *not* willing to do for Taiwan. As for the use of American military force, it would be in Acheson's mind just what it was in the Army study of a possible North Korean invasion: something to be invoked when all else failed, and with United Nations sanction.

American troops were withdrawn from Korea at the end of June 1949, placing Korea in a contingent status. Whereas before MacArthur had elicited a direct commitment to defend southern Korea as long as U.S. troops were on the ground, now Korea entered the status of Greece or Turkey, the indirect style of Truman Doctrine containment, fixed precisely on the premise that one did not vow to contain communism everywhere and always with U.S. troops, but only in selected spots and with resources short of combat intervention, if at all possible. Instead of marking a sharp change, these 1949 deliberations followed on Acheson's 1947 logic of containment in Korea (which *did* presage the June 1950 decision). In his mind, containment for Korea was nothing new.

Toward the end of the NSC 48 process, those involved presented an "Outline of Far Eastern and Asian policy for Review with the President," which embodied a direct commitment to containment. It read as follows: "*Containment of communism*: An immediate objective of the U.S. in Asia must be to check the spread of Soviet communism beyond the countries where it already has seized power . . . this objective must be achieved principally by means other than arms." It went on to say, "the U.S. will deal with any direct aggression against an Asian state through the machinery of the United Nations."15 This was Achesonian containment: the moderate position by late 1949.

The final, approved version of NSC 48 said of Korea that the United States should continue strengthening the ROK "to the point where it can (1) successfully contain the threat of expanding Communist influence and control . . . and (2) serve as a nucleus for the eventual peaceful unification of the entire country on a democratic basis." That is, a continuance of Truman Doctrine–style containment, with no clear provision for the use of American forces, although this was always implied in the containment doctrine, if native forces could not hold.

But this is still just containment. What is so fascinating about the extensive reevaluation of America's East Asia policy that ensued from July through December 1949 is that as soon as it got going, rollback was thrown on the table as well: first by likely people, then by unlikely people.

Acheson's policy review and "action program" were intended to counter Louis Johnson's; from this point until the Korean War Acheson sought to contain not just Asian communism, but a rollback offensive by hard-liners in the administration. Indeed, he personally intervened to change NSC 48 language, muting rollback and underlining containment.

Above all, Acheson had to worry about a president who was temperamentally closer to the hard-liners.[16] It was this internecine conflict that explains why both NSC 48 and NSC 68 seemed equivocal about whether "checking" or "reducing" communism was the main point.

With Johnson running the Defense Department, conservative, China-linked rollback got a hearing—initially in the form of top-level consideration of a crackpot scheme by an archetypal rollbacker, Gen. Claire Chennault. In the late spring of 1949 this Asian swashbuckler peddled his plan all over Washington, which envisioned the use of airpower, warlord armies, and Islamic loyalties to halt the southward march of the communists. He hoped to cut China in half from Ninghsia in the Northwest to Yunnan in the Southwest, to contain Mao and save Southeast Asia. The resources for the scheme were to be his then-idle Civil Air Transport (CAT) airplanes, a collection of ersatz armies run by warlords and Muslim chiefs (the numbers and tenacity of which he grossly inflated), and, needless to say, a resuscitated Nationalist army led by Chiang Kai-shek.

Although this effort was to be the mere prelude to a general rollback of communism on the mainland, when he came to the State Department Chennault modestly noted that he was not then considering a "grand offensive" to retake "all of China," but merely to divide it.[17] This half-baked, pathetic scheme demonstrated little more than Chennault's abysmal ignorance of the course of events on the mainland, and the degree to which almost anything could be poured into the vacuum in the American mind that was "China." Yet it garnered support from Luce publications, prompted several hearings in Congress, audiences at the Pentagon and State Department, and even Oval Office attention. Truman seemed momentarily taken by it, showing just what Acheson had on his hands in trying to keep his chief on the beam. But then the two leading Chinese generals headed off to Mecca, and that was the end of it.[18]

Johnson thought Chennault's plan should not be categorically rejected, given that the Defense Department was "actively pursuing its studies of feasible military means to achieve the objective of denying to Chinese Communist forces those parts of China still remaining free from Communist control"; he then referred to the various drafts of NSC 48, a final decision upon which "would greatly facilitate governmental consideration of such means."[19]

Rollback emerged as a real policy option, however, in the course of interdepartmental deliberations leading up to NSC 48—a more workable sort of rollback than the Chennault plan, limited to feasible means and potential opportunities. An August 16, 1949, paper, one of the first in the NSC 48 series, titled "A Survey of the Strategic Importance of Asia to the U.S." (top secret but unsigned and with no department of origin), inaugurated basic themes that would continue down to the final approval of the document. It dilated frequently on the necessity to take the offensive, used the term "rollback," and sought to include Taiwan in the American defense line.[20]

Shortly thereafter John Davies wrote to Kennan that the United States could no longer afford "to follow indefinitely a policy of avoiding risks of conflict with [the Soviets] at whatever cost to us." He thought the initiative now rested in the "reckless hands" of the Communists, but that the United States could reverse that through the use of covert means, "coercion by punitive action," "coercion through a selective use of air power" (including limited airstrikes on Manchuria), and the like. Airpower, he thought, provided a better means than the outmoded gunboat diplomacy and small-scale expeditionary forces of the Boxer era. He added the interesting observation that the United States "could not embark on such a course [intervention], even on a limited scale, until the Communists have *so acted as to justify our retribution* along the lines of this paper" [emphasis added].[21]

In late August, the State Department review committee (Jessup, Fosdick, and Case) had produced the phrase that would later be embodied in NSC-48 and that would symbolize the conjoining of containment and rollback. An unsigned paper on East Asia policy said the overall objective of the United States should be to establish "free and independent governments," but "the objective of the immediate policy of the U.S. was to *check and roll back* in the [Asian] area the threat of Soviet Communism." The Communists had seized the initiative, and the United States should get it back.

But this was to be liberal rollback, Kennedy-style cold war interventionism. The United States should back Asian nationalist aspirations, help correct "social and economic disadvantages," urge states in the area "to join in a reaffirmation of the traditional policy of the 'Open Door,' " and seek multilateral instead of unilateral approaches. On China, the United States should seek every opportunity "to drive a wedge between China and the Soviet Union" (a good reason not to support Taiwan); in Indochina "steady pressure" should be brought to bear on the French "to interpret liberally" their rule.[22] Much like the 1947 ushering in of containment in internationalist clothes, State Department liberals sought to accommodate the rising demands for rollback by giving the notion an internationalist twist. It was, however, the "check and rollback" phrase that stuck.

An October 14 draft stated that the United States should recognize "the great advantages in cold war tactics of seizing and retaining the initiative through the prosecution of a coordinated [six spaces still classified] cold war offensive." A later draft argued that Asia had "indigenous forces" which, "if effectively developed in aggressive pursuit of the cold war should be able by means short of war to *commence the roll-back* of Soviet control and influence in the area" [emphasis added]. When this paragraph made its way into the final draft, however, after Acheson's revisions, it had evolved to say that Asian indigenous forces could "assist the U.S. in *containing* Soviet control and influence in the area" [emphasis added]. In other words containment had to be added to an original draft thinking only of some sort of rollback.

Another part of this early draft stated that American control of the situation in Asia "may be adequately established . . . only if the area of communist control is reduced." More generally, the draft urged a "dynamic program" that would be "a springboard for positive action in Asia,"[23] using typical rollback code words.

Max Bishop, a key figure in this planning, wrote on October 21 in a memorandum for Rusk that military aid should be given to the Nationalists, "in consonance with our overall policy of containing communism." But he also suggested that it might still be possible for capable Chinese leadership "to retain footholds in South China," which could be "rallying points susceptible for use in future efforts to deliver the country from Communism." He then suggested "a program of special operations in China," referring specifically to "covert operations."[24]

In the final version of NSC 48, the critical phrase became "to contain and where feasible to reduce" communist power in Asia. In other words, it collapsed the concern for rollback and for reducing the area of communist control into a realm of feasibility (where rollback might happen if it seemed likely to work), and reintroduced containment as the main point.

The various drafts of NSC 48 expressed the atmosphere of crisis that permeated the weeks and months following the victory of the Chinese revolution and the explosion of the Soviet atomic bomb. Americans sensed an expansionist pressure all along the Soviet perimeter, but especially in Asia, indicating the necessity for the United States to apply counterpressures everywhere. The October 26 draft asserted that "the United States for its part must be able to apply pressure on any front at a time of its own choosing if it is not to lose the advantages of the initiative." In the final draft, this paragraph instead warned about the United States "spreading itself thin," an Achesonian intervention.

The October 26 draft also blurted mouthfuls of ambition that revealed the degree to which Achesonian deftness and concern for proper limits was being undermined from below. The draft conclusions called for a Pacific association, a regional pact of noncommunist states (something Rhee and Chiang pressed for all through the summer of 1949), and said, "The United States should obtain title to Formosa and the Pescadores and transfer them to the trusteeship of the Pacific Association." Both Japan and Formosa were to be available to American forces in the event of war in this original draft; in the case of Japan this meant use of "its territory, manpower, industrial and communications facilities."

An October 25, 1949, draft was remarkably explicit on the uses of island bases to the United States, not just for containment purposes, but to project American power. It referred to the "island chain," including Japan and Taiwan, as "our first line of defense and, in addition, our first line of offense from which we can seek to reduce the area of communist control, using whatever means we can develop, without, however, using sizable U.S. armed forces."[25]

Many readers will perhaps think that these must have been mere contingency plans, that no one in State or the NSC really thought about offensive "positive action" at this time; indeed, the idea that American planners, let alone State Department liberals, contemplated Asian rollback in the fall of 1949 would have been treated, at any point before the declassification of these documents, as the wildest radical claptrap. But the evidence is unimpeachable.

That this NSC 48 thinking was seen as new, serious, and a clear departure from previous assumptions is manifest in internal critiques at the time. None of the dissent was directed at the application of containment to East Asia (except containment for Taiwan). But the new emphases on rollback drew immediate fire. S. C. Brown wrote on October 24 that NSC 48 reflected "an imposing collection of logical absurdities." The "reduction" of Soviet influence, he said first off, was "quite different from the concept of 'containment' of Soviet power." This, he said, "is made perfectly clear by the reference to a possibility of 'rolling back' communism." Noting that the areas cited for rollback included Manchuria and the Shanghai-Nanjing-Beijing-Tianjin area (i.e., the major industrial areas of China, not mentioned in any draft I have seen, and therefore probably excised by declassification censors), he remarked, "This concept of 'reduction' goes far beyond anything I have ever seen used to describe current U.S. policy toward the USSR, and clearly implies military action of some sort." The basic purpose of the drafts, in his view, was "to see communism (i.e. Soviet power) forced back in Asia." Even though the drafters stated that military force should not be used for rollback, he rightly noted that such goals could be achieved "only by military action."[26]

At this time John Allison also made a number of objections to earlier NSC 48 drafts, criticizing the "sense of imminent danger and urgency" that he thought permeated the drafts. Indeed, Acheson had appointed Allison to head a committee, in Michael Schaller's words, "to emasculate NSC 48 before it caught the president's fancy." But Allison did not object to the phrases about rollback; all the October drafts contain the reference to NSC 48 as "a springboard for positive action in Asia." Allison objected instead to the business about "securing title to Formosa" and blockading China, which would play into Chiang Kai-shek's hands.[27]

Acheson, in typical fashion, played a dual game. At the same time that he put his charter internationalists to work in toning down NSC 48, he also acquiesced in covert plans to run guerrillas into China and give aid to the Nationalist regime, as we will see. His goal was to control the process, and leave the options open on containment and rollback. In the event, the document itself was the end product of a half-year's conflict between State and Defense, like a Rorschach inkblot that registered the relative weight of competing perspectives.

Containment and Rollback: The Japan Link

We learned earlier that Korean containment was linked to the security of Japan, and that security concerns mingled intimately with the economic revival of Japan, centerpiece of the "great crescent." For now-jaded, fallen internationalists, the needs of the Japanese economy also implied a Japan-linked rollback strategy. Various plans along these lines bubbled up at the end of 1948, that is, the time when it was obvious that the Nationalists had lost the civil war.

The CIA had issued new estimates in the light of the "fall" of China and the revival of Japan. Its estimate of "the strategic importance of Japan" in mid-1948 argued that the extension of Soviet control over North China, Manchuria, and "the whole of Korea" would result in "an incalculable loss of U.S. prestige throughout the Far East;" it linked the revival of the Japanese economy to the need for a hinterland. "The key factor in postwar development of Japan is economic rehabilitation. As in the past, Japan, for normal economic functioning on an industrial basis, must have access to the Northeast Asiatic areas—notably North China, Manchuria, and Korea—now under direct, indirect, or potential control of the USSR." Southeast Asia might be able to compensate for the loss of Japan's old colonies, but there the Japanese would face European competition and indigenous anticolonial nationalism. Furthermore, Japan had to export and Southeast Asia would only suffice if native industry remained undeveloped there.

Thus, "geographical proximity and the character of its economic development make Northeast Asia [more] complementary to the economy of Japan," the CIA argued, mentioning markets and raw materials as the key elements; among them were Manchuria's iron ore and north Korea's ferro-alloys. An integration of these areas "could provide the largest industrial potential of any area in the Far East." But if Japan were "excluded from Northeast Asia" over a long term, this "would so drastically distort Japan's natural trade pattern that economic stability could be maintained only if the US were prepared to underwrite substantial trade deficits on a continuing basis." The report went on to say that the United States would also have to supply Japan with "many essential raw materials," such as lumber, pulp, and coking coal. Were the United States not to do this, Japan might "align itself with the USSR as the only means of returning to economic normality."[28]

Another important CIA study on the troop withdrawal from Korea linked security and economics, saying that were the Soviets to take over the South, the "political and psychological consequences" would be felt most acutely in Japan, and that "the USSR would be able to develop bases in the South from which they could launch air, airborne or amphibious attacks on Japan, Formosa, and the Ryukyus"; as for economic relations, the ROK economy could be transformed from an American liability to an asset with "integration of SK economy with that of Japan, Formosa, and the Philippine Islands [which] would help economic stability in all the countries."[29]

Soon the American desire to recouple South Korea's economic fortunes to Japan was palpable, ongoing, and, as we shall see, may have been a central *casus belli*. The industrial and mineral resources of northern Korea were also well known to American planners, and were one reason for the coalescing of conservatives and liberals around rollback in the fall of 1950. But it was only expansionists who focused directly on the Korean economy or its resources, people with specific and narrow interests. The internationalist position emphasized instead the broader question of securing for a revived Japan a hinterland (or periphery) for raw materials, labor, and markets, in which Korea played merely a secondary or complementary role. It was this broad concern that suggested a Japan-linked rollback of communism, in both Southeast and Northeast Asia.

Max Bishop, often thought to be a member of the State Department's "pro-Japan" contingent, was among the first to discern the new, postcontainment logic. As chief of the Division of Northeast Asian Affairs, he argued in December 1948 that the changed situation of East Asia necessitated a careful review of NSC-8, the operative document on Korea policy. "Should communist domination of the entire Korean peninsula become an accomplished fact, the islands of Japan would be surrounded on three sides by an unbroken arc of communist territories . . . we would be confronted with increasing difficulties in attempting to hold Japan within the U.S. sphere." If South Korea should fall, the United States "would have lost its last friend on the continent"; failure to face this problem in Korea "could eventually destroy U.S. security in the Pacific." It was the ancient strategic logic of Hideyoshi, and the Meiji *genro*: Korea as a dagger at the heart of Japan.

Bishop suggested a "positive effort," in Truman Doctrine language, "to develop in non-Soviet northeast Asia a group of independent people . . . who, on an economically viable basis, are capable of successfully resisting communist expansion." Paraphrasing Kennan's logic, he noted that Northeast Asia constituted "one of the four or five significant power centers in the world." And so he asked the *containment* question: "whether communist expansion in northeast Asia had already reached the point at which the security interests of the U.S. required positive efforts to prevent further expansion." But then, he went on to ask a *rollback* question: "whether the communist power system, already brutally frank and outspoken in its hostility to the U.S., must be caused to draw back from its present extensive holdings."[30]

At the same time perhaps the most stunning example of such thinking appeared, written by an unnamed person in the liberal Economic Cooperation Administration (ECA). It identified North China and Manchuria (by then under the consolidated control of the Chinese Communists) as the one area on the mainland "of vital importance to the U.S."; the Japanese had "proved it to be the key to control of China," and the United States ought to regard it in the same light. The region contained most of the heavy industry and "exploitable natural resources." Nearly 90 percent of China's coal came from here, and it also exported foodstuffs, especially soybeans. The nearest source of coking coal for Japan's steel mills would be West Virginia if Chinese resources were not available. Thus, "without the resources of this area, there would be literally no hope of achieving a viable economy in Japan." If the Soviet Union were to control this region, "Japan, Korea, and the rest of China would be doomed to military and industrial impotence except on Russian terms."

The author accordingly recommended a new, "limited" policy for the United States: "our first concern must be the liberation of Manchuria and North China from communist domination." This would require a "far-reaching commitment for American assistance" on the pattern of Greece, including the training and equipping of "a Chinese army capable of recovering and holding Manchuria and North China." Once the region were secured, the United States could pour in investment (it would not take so much, since the Japanese had earlier made the region "a going concern"); this should be accompanied by extensive reforms of land, tax, and credit arrangements. Here was liberal rollback, "limited" rollback, and it was Japan-linked rollback: "the strategic and economic relationship of North China and Manchuria with Korea and Japan is especially clear." Acheson's reaction is not known, but a covering memo informed him that the document "has met with such approbation in a number of quarters that you might be interested in reading it."[31]

John Davies weighed in with another rollback scheme in the same month. It called for holding offshore island points "from Hokkaido to Sumatra," but also looking beyond containment to "vigorous measures of political warfare to reduce" communism in Korea, China, and Southeast Asia, as well as building "an apparatus which will enable us to employ our and Japan's economy as an instrument of political warfare."[32]

These papers are important less for their action programs than for the assumptions that drove them, a logic that could potentially unite competing currents within and without the American state in a drive through North Korea into Manchuria, should NSC 48's realm of feasibility open: the China Lobbyists because it would reestablish Chiang Kai-shek on the mainland, internationalists because it would install Japan back on the mainland. But Japan-linked rollback was less important in 1948 and 1949 than the florescence of planning for "the great crescent."

THE WIDENING CRESCENT

We have dealt with the dialectic between containment and rollback in the NSC 48 deliberations on East Asian security. But in many ways the most interesting and most important part of these drafts was the underlying economic conception that linked power and plenty which, more explicitly than the 1947 planning we surveyed earlier, embodied a design for an Asian "grand area," a regional hierarchy of core, semiperiphery, and periphery in the broader world system. A revived industrial core in Japan came first; keeping South Korea, Taiwan, and Southeast Asia (including especially Indochina) in the world market system came next; then there was the question what else might be brought in if conditions permitted.

With Acheson's support, George Kennan and William Draper were the big guns in pushing the revival of Japanese industry. Ralph Reid, an economic advisor under Draper, was also an important participant, working closely with Joseph Dodge, father of Japan's 1949 austerity program that put it on the path of export-led growth. In February 1949, Reid and Tracy Voorhees worked out a "Marshall Plan for the Far East," as they called it, linking Japan "to a ring of Asian states capable of resisting communism."[33] At about the same time, Truman approved NSC 41, "Trade with China." It said that whereas American economic interest in China was not high, the Japanese economy "is to a degree dependent on access to the export surpluses of north China and Manchuria"; were these cut off, the United States would face "indefinite support" of Japan. Thus, Japan should reestablish "its natural trade relations with the Northeast Asia mainland," and in pursuit of this the United States should not isolate or blockade China, but instead try to drive a wedge between the USSR and the Chinese Communists, and then seek to render China dependent on the United States and Japan. The document said nothing about rollback, preferring the seductions of the market to the uses of positive action. Acheson later followed this logic point-by-point in his early-1950 attempts to split the PRC and the USSR.³⁴

The principal planning for incorporating parts of Asia in Japan's regional sphere occurred, like so much else, in the turning-point summer of 1949. A CIA paper in mid-July brought power-and-plenty arguments together, saying that the United States had "no vital economic requirements from the Far East," but it had "an important interest . . . in retaining access to Southeast Asia, for its own convenience and because of the great economic importance of that area to Western Europe and to Japan." It said trade with China would also help Japan and Western Europe, and thus it was important to draw China away from the USSR. It suggested "positive action to ensure the political and military security of Japan and Southeast Asia," the means being primarily political and economic, but with "potential military support for anti-Communist nations of the Far East."³⁵

American planners did not worry about declining industries. Their vision was the Smithean, internationalist creed of a world of interdependent free trade, encouraging the export of American plants and technology that Samuel Crowther found so demented. The core thinking for the whole of the new policy appeared first in an August 31 NSC 48 draft, again unsigned and with no departmental identification, entitled "Asia, Economics Section."³⁶ It began by saying that American economic policy should be "measured against principles." What were the principles? First: "the economic life of the modern world is geared to expansion"; this required "the establishment of conditions favorable to the export of technology and capital and to a liberal trade policy throughout the world."

Second principle: "reciprocal exchange and mutual advantage." Third principle: "production and trade which truly reflect comparative advantage." Fourth principle: opposition to "general industrialization"—that is, Asian countries do, indeed, possess "special resources" and the like, "but none of them alone has adequate resources as a base for general industrialization." India, China, *and Japan* merely "approximate that condition." And then the injunction against self-containment and *Juche*: "General industrialization in individual countries could be achieved only at a high cost as a result of sacrificing production in fields of comparative advantage."

Fifth principle: certain parts of the world, such as Southeast Asia (but also parts of South America and Africa), are "natural sources of supply of strategic commodities and other basic materials," giving the United States "a special opportunity for leverage" as a "large and very welcome customer." Sixth principle: "in trade with countries under Soviet control or domination, the above principles are not applicable." The United

States must instead find means of "exerting economic pressure" on such countries (the germ of embargoes against Soviet-aligned economies).

The paper went on to mention things like Japan having gotten 80 percent of its coal from North and Northeast China and from northern Korea; that Japan's economy, to be viable, must quickly realize "an enlargement of foreign trade"; it should also revive steel production—but only to a level of four million tons or so, for domestic market needs; it should revive merchant shipping (but only to Asian countries); and it should find its markets in Asia. Japan, too, was unfit for comprehensive, world-class industrialization.

Succeeding drafts embodied these ideas. An October 14 draft stated,

> The economic life of the Western world is geared to expansion. Historically, the development of less advanced areas has not only contributed to the well being of those areas themselves but has also provided the markets and opportunity for useful employment of productive facilities surplus to more advanced countries.

It also elaborated on the virtues of a triangular, hierarchical structure, which

> would involve the export from the U.S. to Japan of such commodities as cotton, wheat, coal and possibly specialized industrial machinery; the export from Japan of such items as low-cost agricultural and transportation equipment, textiles, and shipping services to Southeast Asia; and the export from the latter of tin, manganese, rubber, hard fibers, and possibly lead and zinc to the U.S.

Anticipating nationalist objections in the grand manner of the nineteenth-century Rothschilds, the paper remarked,

> The complexity of international trade makes it well to bear in mind that such ephemeral matters as national pride and ambition can inhibit or prevent the necessary degree of international cooperation, or the development of a favorable atmosphere and conditions to promote economic expansion.[37]

It was enough to set any free trader's heart to pounding. It was also precisely the sort of thinking to make Samuel Crowther or Kim Il Sung reach for his revolver. But it was deeply reflective of postwar American theory about what makes the world go round, a creed for internationalists, even if the rendering here was unusually explicit.

The October 26 draft stated that Japan can be self-supporting only if it were able to secure "a greater proportion of its needed food and raw materials (principally cotton) imports from the Asiatic area, in which its natural markets lie." Southeast Asia was the best regional candidate, with

South Korea and Taiwan offering "limited" help. The draft referred to "certain advantages in production costs of various commodities" in the United States, Japan, and Southeast Asia, which "suggest the mutually beneficial character of trade of a triangular character [*sic*] between these three areas."

In other words, the theory of comparative advantage and the product cycle, elaborating a tripartite hierarchy of American core heavy industries, Japanese light industries and heavy industries revived to acceptable ceilings, and peripheral raw materials and markets. This section was left out of the final draft, not because of the bad English or its irrelevance, but because it was simply too unseemly to state how much American policy now hinged upon the just-defeated Japanese industrial base, how much it now sought the revival of Japan's former imperial relationships, if on a modified basis. Earlier drafts contained the phrase that "before its defeat Japan was a strong anti-communist force in Asia," something also too bald for the final draft, but reflective of core assumptions. This was not to be an imperium, but "a strong trading area,"[38] what we would call a "grand area."

Southeast Asia was to be a pivot for both the Japanese and the Western European economies, each having important sources of raw materials and markets such that the revival of industry in Northeast Asia dovetailed with revival in Europe. Japan, however, was in the region of unilateral American dominance, whereas Southeast Asia had been held exclusively by the European imperial powers. The reentry of Japan would thus benefit the United States *and* draw down the competing European empires, while allowing the United States an entry into previously off-limits markets—"for its own convenience," as the CIA nicely put it. The French and Dutch were happy, the Germans uninvolved, but the British resisted both the Japanese revival and its linkage to Southeast Asia.

The essential reason for British opposition was its declining textile industry. The British complained mightily about American policy and about a Japan that harmed "orderly world trade" through "dumping," "collusive uniform pricing," and tax laws that closed its own market to British goods. Textile interests said that "the new Japanese theorists are more violently opposed to the participation of Allied nationals in Japanese life than were their predecessors before the war," suppressing British banks in particular. It was essentially a matter of old-world imperialism against new-world imperialism.[39] Free traders like Acheson, of course, did not care about the decline of the American textile industry, especially since textile interests bankrolled the right-wing onslaught against his policies.[40] Anyway, Japanese textiles had little impact in the vast American market.

The final version of NSC 48 dropped some of the more flamboyant and ambitious aspects of American strategic and economic policy for East

Asia, but retained the core phrases reflective of the conjoining of containment and rollback, and the emphasis on a grand area underpinned by a triangular hierarchy placing Japan at its core, as a revived industrial economy but not one that would compete directly with the United States, except in declining sectors like textiles. When one digests the full plate of assumptions behind NSC 48, of course, it makes the Korean and Vietnam wars into a struggle for the periphery of the core industrial powers, in America, Japan, and West Europe.

The irony is that Japan never really developed markets or intimate core-periphery linkages in Southeast Asia. The Korean War gave the critical boost to its economy, and thereafter Japan succeeded in penetrating the American and other Western markets. But the logic of an Asian hinterland persisted through the Korean War; it is remarkable to see how vexed the Eisenhower administration still was with "the restoration of Japan's lost colonial empire."[41]

THE JAPAN LOBBY AND AMERICAN POLICY

It is common knowledge that an influential China Lobby pushed rollback policies on the U.S. government. Only recently has it become clear that a Japan Lobby functioned at the same time, less visibly but probably more effectively. Pioneering work by Howard Schonberger and John Roberts uncovered this effort.[42] Like the China Lobby, it functioned both outside and inside the American state.

Schonberger and Roberts both identify the American Council on Japan (ACJ) as the organizational vehicle for the Japan Lobby, bringing together "old Japan hands" in the State Department, several high officials in the Truman administration, and various American business interests anxious for trade with or investment in Japan. The "Japan hands" included people like former Ambassador Joseph Grew, Max Bishop (described by Roberts as "a key figure in AJC strategy"), Eugene Dooman, Joseph Ballantine, and John Allison. The higher officials were James Forrestal, William Draper, Robert Patterson, Kenneth C. Royall, Robert Lovett, Lt. Gen. Robert L. Eichelberger, and John Foster Dulles. Roberts even describes George Marshall as "a bulwark of the Japan Lobby."

The American business interests were almost exclusively in world market-competitive industries with nothing to fear from Japanese revival, such as General Electric, Westinghouse, Reynolds Aluminum, Standard Oil, Socony-Vacuum, and various Wall Street banking and investment interests, including the Chase, First National City, and Chemical Banks. Whereas representatives of declining American industries like textiles had influenced the early, punitive occupation, the reverse course was backed by mostly "high-tech" firms.[43] The latter looked to Japan as a source of markets, did not fear Japanese competition, and hoped to use

Japan's docile cheaper labor (thus the AJC tended to oppose a strong position for Japanese unions).

Newsweek was represented on the AJC by Harry Kern, its foreign affairs editor from 1945 to 1954 and the primary AJC activist. There is also circumstantial evidence suggesting Kern worked with American intelligence, something he has denied.[44] Schonberger notes that he undoubtedly had the backing of Averell Harriman, "a founder, large stockholder, and former member of the board of directors of *Newsweek*," who frequently met with Kern to discuss Japan and to urge its economic rehabilitation.

In several cases, government officials merged the public and private impulses of the AJC. Grew was a cousin of J. P. Morgan, who had strong interests in Japan through banks and through General Electric; Draper was a vice-president in the Dillon, Read Wall Street firm, deeply involved in Japan Lobby efforts; Lovett was a high executive in Brown Brothers, Harriman. Lovett was a childhood friend of Harriman's; his father was E. H. Harriman's right-hand man.[45]

Herbert Hoover was also a strong backer of the Japan Lobby, frequently in contact with Kern and others in the AJC. In 1945 Hoover was alone in advocating the retention of Korea as Japan's colony; his close friend, W. R. Castle, under-secretary of state during the Hoover administration, was a stalwart of the Japan Lobby. Both had been close to Ogden Mills, investor in Korean gold mines. Japan's militarist record was less important to Hoover than its anti-Sovietism, and he urged a nonpunitive occupation from 1945 onward. In June 1947 Adm. William V. Pratt, another activist in the Japan Lobby, wrote to him that the Pacific War was a war "we need never have been involved in." Hoover scrawled in the margins of the letter, "the truth."[46]

The general goal of the Japan Lobby was to bring to an end the "democratization and demilitarization" emphasis of the early occupation, and instead revive the Japanese industrial economy. This led them to oppose the purge of wartime business leaders linked to Japanese militarism, and the dismantling of the major *zaibatsu* groups. Kennan and Draper, the most important people connected to the reverse course, "frequently listened to the counsel of [Harry] Kern's group," according to Clayton James.[47]

Japan lobbyists urged not simply the revival of the Japanese economy, but a reconstitution of its ties to the Asian mainland as well. A privately circulated paper by Kern written sometime in 1948 said, "the development of other Pacific raw material sources should be pressed," including iron ore on Hainan Island (which the Japanese had been developing before 1945), Malayan bauxite (which had been used in Taiwan's colonial aluminum industry); he remarked also that "Southern Korea has neglected mines and other natural resources now being surveyed by ECA."

Kern told General Eichelberger in 1948, "we have destroyed the only force in Asia that kept the Russians out of Manchuria and North China. That force was the Japanese Army."[48]

There seems little doubt that Schonberger and Roberts are correct about the connection of officials like Bishop, Draper, Royall, and others to a decidedly pro-Japan position. Bishop had been in the Tokyo embassy before the war, and played a major role in planning for the economic rehabilitation of Japan. He frequently accompanied Royall and Draper on trips to Japan. As we have seen, he had a key role in the NSC 48 planning.[49] Draper wrote later that the ideas behind the Greater East Asia Co-Prosperity Sphere included the notion that the food and raw materials of less developed regions would be exchanged for Japanese machinery, textiles, and manufactured goods. "These economic objectives were generally sound, and if peaceably and fairly pursued could have increased the per capita wealth and raised the standard of living throughout the area . . . [but Japan sought] to carve out her co-prosperity sphere with the sword, and to dominate its economic life by force."[50]

Although the Japan Lobby had different interests than the China Lobby, and rarely pushed Taiwan's case vigorously, there was a political affinity between some members of both groups. A 1947 issue of Luce's *Fortune* that urged Korean economic development also called for the revival of Japanese industry and especially its exporting industries. Kohlberg's *Plain Talk* and its successor *The Freeman* tended to be pro-Japan, one article in the middle of the Korean War blandly calling for the peninsula to revert to Japan, since "its people have never been able to establish effective independence"; furthermore Japanese "effective sovereignty" over Korea would greatly aid "in making Japan self-supporting." Kohlberg and other China lobbyists also frequently called attention to alleged "purges" by left-wingers of conservative State Department people like Joseph Grew, Eugene Dooman, and Everett Drumwright. Harry Kern thought the State Department harbored procommunists who had undermined Chiang, and William McGovern, one of the few academics working on Asia who testified against Lattimore during the McCarthy inquisitions, was a strong supporter of the revival of Japan and an end to the purges. Lattimore, however, had urged the Pauley commission to promote "a vigorous antimonoply program and massive industrial transfers." So both Asian lobbies looking for a change in U.S. policy could find reasons to hate him.[51]

CONTAINMENT AND ROLLBACK in NSC 68

As the deliberations on NSC 48 proceeded, American policy entered what we may call the "NSC 68 period," dating from the explosion of the Soviet atomic bomb in late August 1949 to the beginning of the Korean

War. NSC 68 was by far the most important cold war document of the era, perhaps of the entire postwar period.[52] A brief look at some of the commentary connected to it illustrates that the new element in strategy was, just as with NSC 48, the conjoining of containment and rollback.

In the terms of our analysis, we should expect to find the new strategy resulting from shifts in global politics and economics, domestic coalitions, and reflecting itself in bureaucratic changes. The critical global shifts were the Soviet atomic bomb, the victory of the Chinese Revolution, the industrial revival of Japan and Germany, and the Sino-Soviet alliance established in February 1950. The new domestic coalition merged containment and rollback currents and constituencies toward what we have called interventionism.

The bureaucratic shuffle meant key personnel replacements, of which the most important were Paul Nitze for George Kennan, the entry of bipartisan accommodator Dulles into the Truman administration, and the search for another Arthur Vandenberg in Congress, with H. Alexander Smith the most likely candidate. If one person were chosen, however, whose star rose and who would best symbolize the new currents, it would again be William Donovan.

Kennan's fortunes ebbed with Acheson as the NSC 68 period got going, and in early 1950 Paul Nitze replaced him. Acheson loved him,[53] and their association launched Nitze on a career that made him central to U.S. foreign policy for the next forty years. Nitze wrote most of NSC 68, working closely with Acheson. In early February 1950 Nitze saw the Soviets "animated by a general sense of confidence," a result of the Soviet A-bomb and the Chinese Revolution; he thought the Soviets now were ready to take "aggressive action against all or most soft spots on its periphery." In early 1950 American officials thought that the communist world was on a roll.

But such estimates also projected American strategic thinking onto the Soviets. The director of the Office of East European Affairs, Charles Yost, wrote in mid-February of the necessity "for holding firmly the line around the present peripheries of the Soviet sphere," arguing that the United States should continue to provide economic and military aid to "the numerous 'soft spots' on our side of the periphery." In a top secret meeting two weeks later, the president of Harvard University, James Conant (apparently possessing rather exhalted security clearances), argued for "a twenty-year containment on present lines, without a war." But Nitze responded that "we must capitalize upon the desire of the Poles, etc. for liberation. A purely defensive objective may deny us their assistance."[54]

Referring in mid-March to "the war in which we are presently engaged," wise man Robert Lovett said,

We should fight with no holds barred. We should find every weak spot in the enemy's armor, both on the periphery and at the center, and hit him with anything that comes to hand. Anything we do short of an all-out effort is inexcusable. We should cause them trouble wherever we can. There are plenty of partisans and dissidents on the enemy's borders and within his camp who are willing to fight . . . if we give them some leadership.

The vast defense expenditures projected by NSC 68 did not bother Lovett, since the U.S. economy "might benefit from the kind of build-up we are suggesting."[55]

This hint of military Keynesianism indicates an additional goal for the new program: pump-priming for the American and allied economies through defense spending, at a time when worries surfaced about continuing stagnation in export markets. The American economy was robust after the first postwar recession in 1949, but elites feared that it could not sustain its allies and markets around the world without major infusion of new funds. Big defense budgets could square the circle by meeting security contingencies and boosting the American and the global economy.[56] The United States also needed a vast array of national security expertise if it were to meet the enhanced commitments of NSC 68, requiring equivalent expansion of the security bureaucracies.

An intelligence estimate done by the U.S. embassy in Moscow in late April thought the United States had already entered "total war" with the Soviets, and asserted that containment was "too defensive and static a concept for winning either the public or the war itself"; all measures—economic, political, military—should be "put to work in accordance with plans devised to seek out and destroy the foe at his weakest points." Noting that intelligence estimates said that the Soviets did not now want a global war, therefore, "a judicious use of military power can have a salutary effect in stopping certain forms of Soviet aggression in the near future . . . such action should be taken without hesitation or apology . . . [because] in a deeper sense a state of war has already been in existence for years."

What sort of action? "Every occasion should be sought not only for checking Soviet aggression but for forcing a retreat"; "a properly designed counteroffensive launched at that point [where the Soviets are weak] would thereby have some chances of rolling them back as the Russians rolled the Germans after Stalingrad." In China the Soviets might quickly become overextended, so opportunities for "inflicting dramatic reverses" might exist there.[57]

For NSC 68, containment was to be global, all along a communist periphery perceived to be incontinent at the boundaries, spilling over first here, then there. Soviet mischief might lead to global war, or might have "limited objectives"; in any case the United States had to "apply force" to counteract such activity. Containment was no longer passive and reactive:

> As for the policy of "containment," it is one which seeks by all means short of war to (1) block further expansion of Soviet power, (2) expose the falsities of Soviet pretensions, (3) induce a retraction of the Kremlin's control and influence and (4) in general, so foster the seeds of destruction within the Soviet system that the Kremlin is brought at least to the point of modifying its behavior.

The syllogism was the same as in NSC 48, containing and reducing the Soviet sphere. Later on the document referred to "the checking and rolling back" of the Kremlin's drive, "to check and to roll back" its putative attempt at world domination, and the inauguration of "dynamic steps to reduce the power and influence of the Kremlin."[58]

Leaks to public media also reflect this discourse. A front-page article in the *New York Times* spoke of a policy effort "many weeks old" in which the "major theme" was liberation in Eastern Europe, a campaign to win over "satellite" peoples, with "political warfare maneuver[s] to support its anti-Communist military preparations . . . calculated to divide the peoples of Communist Eastern Europe from their Soviet satellite governments." *Barron's* wrote that Paul Nitze, formerly a vice-president at Dillon, Read, was "the active director" of the new foreign policy effort, and urged the maintenance of "the Pax Americana without which all talk of freer trade and the development of backward areas is vain."[59]

As with NSC 48, strong dissent emerged within the bureaucracy to the new policies. The most cogent and prescient came from William Schaub of the Budget Bureau, who thought that NSC 68's "free" and "slave" distinction ignored the appeals of communism to peoples suffering economic and social deprivation; American support for anyone calling himself an anticommunist had led to "associations which are exceedingly strange for a people of our heritage and ideals." Schaub caught the eruptive American nationalism of the document, arguing prophetically that "an upsurge of unadulterated nationalism might for the time being lessen or remove the military threat of Russia, but it would over time tend to accentuate the subtle undermining of our own system and guarantee the eventual loss of the Cold War through the proliferation and subsidization of unstable tyrants." Schaub also thought that the United States was vastly stronger than Russia in every respect except manpower, and therefore questioned the need for a huge buildup. Other estimates showed that Schaub was right.

Willard Thorp, for example, put Soviet "gross investment" for 1949 at $16.5 billion compared to $34 billion in the United States; Soviet defense spending he estimated at $9 billion compared to the American $16 billion. A major CIA estimate of the relative military and industrial strengths of the two blocs had the West in the lead in everything but artillery, tanks, and manpower; even with the latter the two sides were about equal at some 25 million men under arms, and the Soviet bloc estimate included 10 million from Mao's underequipped peasant army. Western GNP was $441 billion compared to the Soviet bloc's $119 billion, oil production was more than ten times as high, machine tools more than double; the West had overwhelming advantages in steel, coal, and aluminum. Later scholarship has shown that most of these estimates still exaggerated Soviet bloc strength.[60]

Acheson and Nitze could not deny these disparities. Instead they argued that the Soviets were rapidly closing gaps, such that a window of vulnerability would soon open. By 1953 or 1954, Acheson thought, "the balance of forces might induce the USSR to take or threaten to take hostile measures."[61]

NSC-68 had an hysterical view of the Soviets that Acheson usually reserved for the public, adopting the diabolical imagery favored by the rollback current. It coined a new term for the Soviet public: the "totalitariat." Some have argued that this was merely designed to scare bureaucrats and Congressmen into appropriating the enormous defense spending increases envisioned in the document. That may be so, but the imagery was nothing new. Two years earlier George Kennan's Policy Planning Staff produced an important document describing communists as deviates produced through "a natural mutation of [the] species," leading to "congenital fifth-columnism." The Soviet political process was "strange and inscrutable," run by "a desperate, conspiratorial minority"; the world could not be at peace until communists in and out of the Soviet Union changed their entire world view.[62] This sort of morbid Orientalism and dehumanization suggests that NSC 68 had no corner on diabolical imagery.

CONCLUSION

This chapter posited that schemes for rolling back communism were not the exclusive province of the extreme right-wing. Instead, from the establishment of containment in 1947 to the destruction of rollback in the fall of 1950, centrist elites took containment as their starting point but differed over whether a defensive strategy was sufficient to counter their perception of the threat of communism. They also disagreed over whether rollback in East Asia was feasible, and if so, whether it should benefit Japan or Nationalist China.

Did NSC 48 and NSC 68 represent an Achesonian viewpoint, or the hollowing out beneath Acheson of an alternative vision—the active move to the initiative instead of a passive containment? Acheson sculpted much of the documentation and herded it through the opposition to, in his view, final approval in April 1950, in spite of the absence of Harry Truman's signature.[63] So, one must conclude that he supported the move toward joining containment and rollback. He was an anticommunist and an interventionist, and his vision since 1947 unilaterally asserted American goals, cloaked in a garb of multilateralism and internationalism. Always, his great concern was with the health of the American and, therefore, the world economy, looking after the whole. The question was how power could best serve plenty. His difference with centrist rollbackers was primarily tactical. Like eminent Americans before him, he preferred to leave the initiative in the hands of the enemy. He knew the United States played the role of aggressor badly.

During this period, sober, thoughtful anticommunists like George Kennan moved from centrality to the edge of the shadows, as a sense of crisis gripped prominent Americans. The ideal hopes of 1945 had given way in a few short years to apocalyptic fears. We might illustrate this in closing with the following colloquy from a Policy Planning Staff meeting, a year before the Korean War. Coca-Cola magnate Robert Woodruff mused that perhaps the United States needed a rectification of names: "History of the world shows to me [*sic*] that always the strongest nations in the world broke the world, and didn't ask people about it. Couldn't you best go about it by developing a new name for it—benevolent imperialism, if you like." Walter Bedell Smith worried about "what sort of hegemony of forces" the United States could "set up"; but he also thought Woodruff's question premature, the Americans first had to answer this: "Are we or are we not going to war with Russia?" To which Woodruff ejaculated yet a prior question: "Are we going to instigate it or are they?"[64]

Part II

KOREA

Chapter Six

THE SOUTHERN SYSTEM

> Imagine how the peaceful garden of the world has been deserted
> by the cold wind of capitalism and how it has been destroyed by
> the storms of communism. . . . Let us, the thirty million people,
> combine together under one principle. We Koreans are not a het-
> erogeneous race of two or more different peoples, but a homoge-
> nous race. . . . And now, it is the supreme command of our nation
> and the sacred obligation of our people to rise and smash the par-
> tition of the 38th parallel line, which was erected by the hands of
> the foreign forces, by our own hands and unify the divided terri-
> tories and combine the divided people together into one people.
>
> *An Ho-sang*

T HE SOUTHERN political system issued forth in the first few months after liberation, and did not substantially change until the 1960s. Under American Occupation auspices, Koreans captured the colonial state
and used its extensive and penetrative apparatus to preserve the power
and privilege of a traditional landowning elite that had been tainted by
its associations with the Japanese. The one reliable and effective agency
of this restoration and reaction was the Korean National Police (KNP).
The one viable political party was the Korean Democratic Party (KDP),
not because it organized a mass constituency but because it organized the
elite, and captured central positions in the state. The effective opposition
to this system was almost wholly on the Left: the Korean People's Republic and the people's committees in 1945–1946, the South Korean Worker's Party (SKWP) and various mass organizations, especially the
Chŏnp'yŏng labor union, in 1947, and most important, a mass popular
resistance that from 1945 to 1950 mingled raw peasant protest with organized union activity and, finally, armed resistance in the period 1948–
1950.

The elemental conflict in the South, then, pitted a ruling class with
control of a strong and effective state—one that had been remarkably
autonomous of society during the colonial period—against a leftist and
communist leadership with less certain control of its main resource, a
restive and aggrieved mass that had been severely dislocated by Japanese
imperialism and its demise, and that strongly resisted the assertion of
conservative power.

All this was, of course, a main theme of the first volume of this study
and it does not need much recital. It is unlikely that the system we ob-

served in 1946 would suddenly change in the years that followed; instead there was an entrenchment of the basic structures. It is gratifying, however, to find internal American reports in 1947 and 1948 that attest to this reality—that one could write oneself, as it were. Maj. Gen. Albert Brown, for example, sketched the southern system as follows:

> The most powerful group in [south] Korea today is the rightist group. Their power derives from the fact that they control most of the wealth of Korea. They occupy strategic positions in government both at Headquarters and in the field, as well as in police. To a large extent they have the power to dictate policy for control of Korea.[1]

CIA analyses were even more blunt. South Korean political life was "dominated by a rivalry between Rightists and the remnants of the Left Wing People's Committees," the latter persisting doggedly in demands for American recognition—which the Americans would never give, of course, even though the CIA recognized the imprimatur of this movement: a "grass-roots independence movement which found expression in the establishment of the People's Committees throughout Korea in August 1945," led by "Communists" who based their right to rule on the resistance to the Japanese.

The CIA lamented the absence of "articulate proponents of capitalism among the Koreans," a remarkable intelligence disclosure comparable to the Korean CIA determining that only a handful of errant Confucianists are to be found in America (mainly in departments of East Asian studies). Instead of entrepreneurial capitalists, a semifeudal landed class sought to control everything (strangling rather than unleashing capitalism, that is):

> The leadership of the Right [sic] . . . is provided by that numerically small class which virtually monopolizes the native wealth and education of the country. Since it fears that an equalitarian distribution of the vested Japanese assets [i.e., colonial capital] would serve as a precedent for the confiscation of concentrated Korean-owned wealth, it has been brought into basic opposition with the Left. Since this class could not have acquired and maintained its favored position under Japanese rule without a certain minimum of "collaboration," it has experienced difficulty in finding acceptable candidates for political office and has been forced to support imported expatriate politicians such as Rhee Syngman and Kim Koo. These, while they have no pro-Japanese taint, are essentially demagogues bent on autocratic rule.

Thus, "the extreme Rightists control the overt political structure in the U.S. zone," mainly through the agency of the National Police, which had been "ruthlessly brutal in suppressing disorder." The CIA went on to say,

The enforced alliance of the police with the Right has been reflected in the cooperation of the police with Rightist youth groups for the purpose of completely suppressing Leftist activity. This alignment has had the effect of forcing the Left to operate as an underground organization since it could not effectively compete in a parliamentary sense even if it should so desire.

Although membership in the South Korean Worker's Party (SKWP) and other left-wing mass organizations was ostensibly legal under the American Occupation, "the police generally regarded the Communists as rebels and traitors who should be seized, imprisoned, and sometimes shot on the slightest provocation." The structure of the southern bureaucracy was "substantially the old Japanese machinery"; the Home Affairs Ministry, an agency that E. H. Norman had described as a base for forces of the darkest reaction in prewar Japan, exercised in south Korea "a high degree of control over virtually all phases of the life of the people." With crucial support from the director of the National Police, Cho Pyŏng-ok, whom many thought to be the most powerful Korean after Syngman Rhee, the Korean Democratic Party "built up its membership within the ranks of the police and local governments." (Some Americans disliked Cho "for harsh police methods directed ruthlessly against Korean leftists," but most found him to be a capable and intelligent official.)

As for the ersatz parliament then in existence, the South Korean Interim Legislative Assembly (SKILA), it operated on "the line laid down by Syngman Rhee," acting "as the parliament of [all] the Korean nation, in open defiance of both the US and Soviet occupation," indeed as if they did not exist. Like many other such reports, the CIA tendered the analysis as if the Americans had been watching it all unfold like innocent bystanders since their arrival in September 1945.[2]

Gen. Albert Wedemeyer reported much the same evidence during his tour of Korea in late 1947. The Korean Democratic Party, he wrote, held "the active membership or tacit support of the large majority of the administrative officials of the interim government." It was the party of "the land-owning community," led by Kim Sŏng-su, "one of the greatest landholders" in the southwest, and by Chang Tŏk-su, Kim's inseparable companion and the "dominating intellect" of the KDP, albeit somewhat constrained in public by his "strong support" to the Japanese regime. As a political party, however, the KDP left much to be desired: "it is not organized in the provinces, except in the leading cities." Wedemeyer found in conversations with Koreans that many had turned to the Left because they could not stomach pro-Japanese collaborators, not because they were communists. The notable literateur Chŏng In-bo told the general that communists had their hold on people not because of northern intrigue, but because of the lingering memory of their anti-Japanese patriotism: "communism here has been nurtured with the fertilizer of nationalism." Furthermore, Chŏng observed pointedly, for decades "only Russia, contiguous to us, shared our enmity against Japan."

The novelist Younghill Kang, an anticommunist, wrote to Wedemeyer that "Korea was one of the worst police states in the world"; the struggle in Korea, he said, was "a fight between the few well-fed landed and the hungry landless. These few today control [the KDP] and the mass of people want to rectify these ancient wrongs." Kang predicted that Rhee wanted the blessing of the UN so he could then "kick the Russians out of the north." Several other prominent Koreans told Wedemeyer that the inevitable result of Korea's stalemated politics would be civil war.

An American advisor to the police, David Fay, told Wedemeyer that "by definition a national police organization is synonymous with the police state." He thought the KNP were largely autonomous of American influence: in his province a new Korean police chief had taken charge some weeks before, but "not one problem of police administration has been presented to the Americans for discussion." Statistics given to Wedemeyer by the director of the Justice Department showed that 63,777 criminal cases had come before the southern court system in 1946, compared to 52,455 for all of Korea in wartime 1944. Southern jails held 17,363 prisoners in July 1947 compared to 16,587 in June 1945, by his count; most of the swelling of judicial work, of course, was for political cases.[3]

An experienced observer of Korea, the Yale anthropologist Cornelius Osgood, made many analogous points in trying to get Army Secretary William Draper to comprehend the situation in Korea in late 1947. He remarked on the patriotic aura surrounding leftists and communists, the similarity between stated American objectives and Soviet reforms of land and labor conditions in the North, and the way in which "a hated group . . . is taking advantage of the Military Government with the same classical self-interest characteristic of Yi Dynasty politicians"—having learned "an added cunning developed by subservience under the Japanese." Most Koreans, especially the majority in the villages, never saw Americans, only the local elite of Koreans (in many cases the same elite as under the Japanese). Reunification is what Koreans care most about, he related, and they would never support a separatist policy. The only course for the United States, Osgood argued, was quickly to eliminate police who had served the Japanese, carry out land reform, and move toward "a strongly supported 'middle' in politics."[4]

Relatively disinterested foreign observers frequently expressed their aversion to the southern system. An Australian dispatch in 1949 said that the authority of the Rhee regime "rested on the machinery of a police state"; apart from officials of the regime, no one believed that it was "extending the basis of its popular support"; missionaries in villages reported on repressive KNP activity, teachers "spoke of the activity of provocateurs and spies in the universities." The police, the dispatch said, resembled the Japanese *kempeitai*. British observers noted that Rhee's picture was in nearly every police station in South Korea in February 1948, months before his election. The police needed Rhee to protect them from reprisals, given that most of the officers had served the Japanese. Rhee for his part needed the police "because they alone can decide the course of elections and keep him in power."[5]

More evidence could be adduced on the nature of the southern system, but why be tiresome about an obvious reality? More interesting perhaps was the range of American attitudes, moving from cynical support of the system, to a tepid distance that disclaimed fatherhood of an unpleasant offspring, to demands for reform that never got beyond the limits of the American spectrum, a Graham Green–like "Quiet American" project of reform that sought to bolster a middle that barely existed. A centrist and modal position in American society became in Korea a quixotic and weak posture, while exposing one to charges of procommunism. The dog that so rarely barked was any sign of American support for a thorough renovation of Korean society. The harsh truth is that the United States as a matter of high policy vastly preferred the southern police state to any sort of serious revolutionary regime. The repression of the Rhee regime, in other words, had a joint Korean-American authorship.[6]

At the same time that American officials publicly praised and privately censured the southern regime, they nonetheless misconstrued the reality. The South did have a police state, and it was an agent of a small class of landlords. But it was more than that, or it could not have survived even to June 1950. The landlord class held both obtuse reactionaries and vibrant capitalists. Korean capitalism may not have had articulate proponents, but it had impressive practioners, of which the Kim Sŏng-su group was the most formidable. This was hardly the visionary entrepreneur, however, looking for the main chance; the main chance had been the Japanese regime and the opportunities that close alliance with it brought to this, Korea's first *chaebŏl* (conglomerate).[7]

Americans found this sort of capitalism hard to dignify or legitimate, as did Koreans, seeing little virtue in business that hewed close to the state. But it was a source of dynamism in the Korean economy, this state-led capitalism implanted by a Japanese imperialism different from more stagnant varieties, such as the Dutch in Indonesia or the Portuguese in Angola. It laid the foundations for the economic growth of the 1960s. But it did not fit a textbook description of capitalism, anymore than the Standard Oil Trust did in America.

Just as it is wrong to underestimate the economic resources of the Korean Right, it would be wrong to misconstrue its political resources. It is a curiosity of Korean politics going back several centuries that the *yangban* (aristocracy) and landowning class was capable of marginal change and adjustment in the longrun interest of preserving its position, as James Palais has shown, but was remarkably weak and brittle when faced with external challenge. The Yi Dynasty persisted for half a milennium, and only broke down under the onslaught of the modern world system. But then it capsized quickly, abruptly in light of its remarkable longevity. A Korean of 1392 would be less shocked by the changes he would see in 1865, than would a Korean of 1865 witnessing the mise-en-scène of 1940. When observed in comparative perspective, Korea is a remarkable example of internal strength and external weakness, of indigenous stasis and exogenously-induced change.

This same pattern has marked the postwar period. By 1950 the South Korean state impressed observers with its relative stability, especially as the first glimmerings of economic dynamism came to light. Yet in 1950 a well-placed military thrust demolished the regime overnight. In the late 1970s various pundits likened the Republic of Korea (ROK) to another Japan in glowing accounts of its economic prowess and political stability. Yet an assassin's bullet, combined with mass unrest in Kwangju and elsewhere, caused the temporary collapse of the southern system. The more knowledge one has of this polity, the less weight one places on externals: its strong exterior hides a flimsy interiority—a house of cards masquerading as a pyramid of power.

But a house of cards can stand if a strong glue holds it together. Most of what held it together was at the top: the central state in Seoul, its executive, and its claim of legitimacy. It is only when this is lopped off that the disintegration begins. The Korean superstructure—state, culture, ideology—is remarkably tenacious. It has great staying power if not challenged from without by dynamic social and economic forces. The politics of stasis rests on a hegemony of traditional ethos coming down from on high, a philosophy that good things flow from good ideas, and a praxis in which ideas emerge at the apex of the system. The politics that the old guard covets rests on a hierarchical unity and ethic deriving ultimately from the model of the well-run family, finding its plausibility and appropriateness in a homogenous people for whom race and nation and family mean about the same thing. The object of every Korean ruler is to inculcate proper ideas in everyone in the realm, to push a uniform pattern of thought to the point that it becomes a state of mind, and therefore impervious to logic and argument. This is taken to be the essence and ideal of stable rule. The modal foreign policy is the Hermit Kingdom option, an exclusionism that seeks to control and ward off external shocks that can detonate collapse, or encourage heterodoxy. The paradigm of all Koreans thinking and acting alike is never met, and in postwar South Korea is so far from being met as to mislead some observers into asserting that an individual-based scramble for personal ambition has atomized the whole society. But it comes closer to being met in Korea than in most other twentieth-century societies.

This is not a "cultural argument." The pattern of Korean political culture is remarkably persistent, but springs most generally from the unique homogeneity and long-term isolation of this nation, and the relative stability of its mode of production over centuries. This can denature many solvents, perhaps even the solvent of twentieth-century socialism. But it cannot denature the ultimate modern solvent, industrial capitalism. In the final analysis, as it is said, it was the irruption of the world market system on Korean soil that began—and has not yet completed—the transformation of old Korea. It is this that makes southern Korea the most dynamic and revolutionary portion of the peninsula in the recent period, through the incessant change detonated by a potent and wholly new economic dynamic and social formation. It is so potent because it is incipient, the material and social foundations of capitalism are still new, vibrant, and at the same time weak. As this dynamic proceeds, it erodes and ultimately will transform the cultural fabric.

All this sketches the antithesis of liberalism: an organic politics. For Western individualists who cannot imagine that human beings find solace and fulfillment in giving oneself over to a family, a group, a society, or to a shared state of mind, the Korean monolithic ideal will be repellent, especially its apotheosis in Kim Il Sung's North Korea. It is bound to seem pathological, just as the Yi Dynasty did to early Western travelers. For liberals who have not peered into their own assumptions, because their liberalism is also a state of mind and they cannot do it, this entire discourse will be alien.[8] But if one wants to understand the pattern of Korean politics, it hardly helps to indulge one's own ethnocentrism when the point is to unravel another.

Perhaps the best proof of these assertions is the testimony that South Korea offers in the late 1940s. Those political leaders who succeeded in organizing masses of people drew upon the same sources of strength as did the North, an appeal to complete unity at home and resistance to penetration from abroad, an assertion of a Korean essence against all the rest. Their ideal was similar to Kim Il Sung's, minus the revolution—a way to weld together a nation under one's own leadership. We are not talking here about Korean Democratic Party leaders, situated to control the means of production and the state, and therefore finding utility in silence and withdrawal. Instead we speak mainly of leaders of mass organizations of the Right like Yi Pŏm-sŏk, who may have served KDP interests but also had a certain autonomy from them.

We have thus far assayed the continuity in southern politics. In 1947 and thereafter, however, an important change occured that gave the regime more strength. This was the development of a mass politics of the Right, which rested on a myriad of youth groups, an incipient corporatist organization of the working class, and a set of Korean political ideas that were illiberal to the point of being fascist, but that were far more potent than the tepid and pro-American liberalism of a handful of middle-road politicians. In his homespun way, Gen. John R. Hodge in late 1947 instructed some visiting Congressmen on the dilemmas he faced in Korea:

> We always have the danger of Fascism taking over when you try to fight Communism. It is a very difficult political situation that we run into. Germany was built up by Hitler to fight Communism, and it went to Nazism. Spain the same thing. On the other hand, when the Communists build up—when Communism builds up—democracy is crushed, and the nation goes Communist. Now, what is the answer on the thing? How in the dickens are you going to get political-in-the-middle-of-the-road out of the mess. Just bring it up for discussion. I don't know the answer. I wish I did.[9]

The Lockean American knows what he likes ("political-in-the-middle-of-the-road") and what he dislikes ("Communism and Fascism"), but knows not whence any of the three tendencies come. An amnesiac ahistoricity combines with a congenital distaste for introspection, such that the spark of relativity or philosophy that Louis Hartz kept searching for can hardly be struck. Cursed with a European political vocabulary in the fragmented American setting, Hodge as archetypal American can only grasp nonliberal politics as a pathology of the Left or Right, two things beyond the pale and one in the familiar middle. Stuck with this conceptual baggage in Korea, Rhee becomes Hitler, Kim Ku becomes Al Capone, Kim Kyu-sik becomes Henry Wallace, and Kim Il Sung becomes a pint-sized Stalin. And the Good that Hodge sought, the elusive middle-of-the-road, recedes ever into the horizon because he has not thought: What road? What middle? Kim Il Sung and Yi Pŏm-sŏk were far closer to the middle of the Korean road than was Kim Kyu-sik, and so they got mass support. Syngman Rhee was closer to King Kojŏng than he was to Hitler, and so he knew how to manipulate conservative Korean politics.

To liberal Americans the Rhee system looked like Nazism, but if we wish to classify it comparatively in European terms, it was closer to Franco's Spain or Salazar's Portugal (without the glue of the Catholic church), a diffuse authoritarianism that fell short of total control, in spite of its desires to have it, and that lacked the demonic energy of the Nazis. Juan Linz's Iberian-derived portrayal of fascism fits Rhee's Korea well: a negative ideology, knowing better what it is against than what it is for, growing out of a gnawing fear of the Left; an antiliberalism that is also partly antiproletarian and antibourgeois, and that can barely dignify capitalism; corporative forms of interest aggregation and representation, designed to overcome class cleavages; reliance upon paramilitary organization and street activists; exaltation of the authority of the nation and the state; voluntarism in theory and political style; a concern for grassroots organization that conservative notables typically disdain; an opening to upward mobility and access to power for aggrieved nonelites; a single mass party that obliterates the opposition. Linz speculated that in countries where secondary associations were weak, a type of fascism might result from the introduction of "a relatively widespread suffrage," if such countries were also characterized by "large rural populations, economically dependent on noble and particularly bourgeois landowners, societies with a large illiterate [group], and in which, in addition, the centralized bureaucratic Napoleonic type of state made local government dependent on the decisions of the central administration and the prefects."[10]

South Korea did not have a single mass party, and its landowners were both noble and bourgeois in Linz's sense, poised between the two and in transition; but most of the other characteristics fit the South from 1947 onward. South Korea also had episodes reminiscent of the rural fascism of Italy's *squadrismo* in the 1920s, and of Franco's Spain in the 1930s. After the upheaval and catharsis of the Korean War, the ROK was more like postcivil war Spain, a diffuse authoritarianism following on the resolution of a central crisis in the body politic—a mundane politics of the Right that no longer demanded the thunder of the street, content with acquiescence instead of positive support.

Still, the European categories do not capture the full Korean reality. South Korean "fascism" was much like North Korean "communism," an adaptation of Western ideas in a non-Western context, vetted through China. Rhee and Yi Pŏm-sŏk modeled their right-wing politics most closely on the experience of Chiang Kai-shek, and like the Kuomintang system and Chiang's pastiche of new/old ideas, Rhee filtered the dimly perceived European fascist model through a prism of Eastern tradition and Confucianism. The result was less a Koreanized version of fascism than a fascistized version of Korean politics. Let us now sample this right-wing stew: the emergent youth groups, incorporated labor, and the ideas that bubbled to the top.

THE RISE OF KOREA'S YOUTH GROUPS

The autumn uprisings of 1946 had marked a stunning assault against the southern system, striking fear in the hearts of the privileged and powerful. When the rebels retreated, the Right began a general movement to organize a politics of the street, mass organizations to fight fire with fire. South Korea's youth groups are an unstudied phenomenon, but they were a potent form of political organization that belies the factious, politically-impotent stereotype of Korean politics. The raw material came in the greater part from young men who were refugees from the North, although unemployed and marginal elements of southern society, as well as a corps of elite students, also participated. In the cities, youth groups served as police auxiliaries, strikebreakers, or plain clothes thugs who broke up opposition demonstrations (still a common feature of ROK politics today). In the countryside, depending on the social complexion of villages, youth groups might defend prominent clans, or side with marginally richer peasants, or indeed organize whole villages to fight against neighboring leftist villages or to protect against guerrillas and bandits.

Nearly every political party of any significance had a "youth" auxiliary, defining youths as roughly between the ages of eighteen and thirty-five. The Left had a mass organization of youths formed in late 1945, named the *Chosŏn ch'ŏngnyŏn ch'ong tongmaeng* or General Federation of Korean Youth. On the Right, the most important groupings were the Korean National Youth (KNY), the Northwest or *Sŏbuk* Youth (NWY), the *Taedong* Youth, the *Kwangbok* Youth, and Rhee's NSRRKI Youth (*Taehan tokch'ŏk ch'ŏngnyŏn ch'ong yŏnmaeng*). Most of them were organized in the aftermath of the autumn uprisings; one, the Korean National Youth led by Yi Pŏm-sŏk, was an official agency of Military Government (MG), funded by Hodge.[11]

The youth groups were set in motion at the top by the most powerful rightists: Rhee, Yi Pŏm-sŏk, Cho Pyŏng-ok, and Chang T'aek-sang. The Korean National Police, led by Cho and Chang, was the general patron of rightist youth, relying on the groups time and again as auxiliary strong-arm forces. Youth group offices were often next door to police stations (and sometimes inside). People flowed out of the youth groups into the police and the army, and vice versa. Chang T'aek-sang, the head of the Seoul Metropolitan Police, was on the board of directors of at least two youth groups, and as early as November 1946 was said to be encouraging joint police–youth group operations. Chang's conspicuous role in running the groups occasionally approached black comedy, as in his remarks on September 11, 1947 (deemed "unfortunate" by the G-2): Chang announced a "crackdown" on terrorism regardless of politics, and then remarked, "During the past two months, the police have allowed several young men's groups and parties to perform terroristic activities, explaining to them their unlawful actions, and hoping they would repent their past errors." American authorities noted that "practically all rightist organizations maintain their headquarters and branch offices in vested property," that is, buildings controlled by the Occupation.[12]

In November 1947, the G-2 intercepted a memo from the Seoul Metropolitan Police to the provinces, indicating that the police were training two hundred members of the *Taedong* Youth in each of the following cities: Seoul, Taegu, Taejŏn, and Kwangju. Once the ROK was established, the tie between the police and youth groups no longer needed to be hidden. In December 1948, for example, the Metropolitan police trained six hundred members of the Northwest Youth, then dispatched them to riot-torn areas "equipped with police uniforms and on regular police status." The Army took much larger numbers of youth group members into its ranks in mid-1948. No one was safe from the terrorism. In September 1947, an assistant district attorney in Pusan, Chŏng Su-bak, an employee of the Military Government, sought to prosecute four members of a rightist youth group for terrorism. He was assassinated, and no one was brought to justice for the murder.[13]

The officially-supported Korean National Youth melded Chinese influences with Japanese methods of dealing with political recalcitrants. Yi Pŏm-sŏk was a fierce Korean nationalist, except where the Chinese Nationalists were concerned. Born in 1899 in Kyŏnggi Province, he went to China during World War I. He fought the Japanese as a guerrilla along the Sino-Korean border in the early 1920s. In 1933 he visited Germany to study military affairs; later he worked with German and Italian advisors to the Nationalists. By 1937, he was in the Office of the Chief of Staff of the KMT 51st Army, and by 1938, was a company commander at the KMT Military Academy in Hangchou. He was widely known in Korea as a follower and admirer of Generalissimo Chiang Kai-shek.[14]

Chiang and his secret police chief, the unsavory Tai Li, organized a youth wing called the "Blue Shirts" in the 1930s, a fascist-style paramilitary force that chose the color blue, it would appear, because brown, black, and green were already spoken for. Yi worked with this group, and wrote in 1947 that the Germans and the Italians were "pioneers" in youth movements, and also cited the Kuomintang's good experience with youths. He originally termed his own youth group "the Blue Shirts," and the KNY, as an American delicately noted, had "distinctive blue uniforms."[15]

American sources in Shanghai reported that Yi had been "working for Tai Li" during the war, and thought he had been involved with a group of young men who "persecuted all Korean residents of Shanghai and other Eastern cities without discrimination." Tai Li had been a confidant of the Office of Strategic Services (OSS) chief in China, Adm. Milton "Mary" Miles. In August 1945 ten OSS agents in Shanghai flew Yi into Seoul briefly, than took him back to Shanghai for reasons that have never been clear.[16] Whatever the OSS may have thought of Yi, by 1950 the CIA termed him "a man of little imagination and mediocre intelligence," possessing a forceful personality, "great political ambitions, and an intensely nationalist viewpoint." He thought and acted "like a traditional Chinese war lord," and remained deeply under the influence of Chiang Kai-shek. The CIA thought his future was limited, in part because he could not speak English.[17] It was probably Yi's nationalism that the Americans disliked the most, however, for it meant he could not be trusted.

Yi became known for his use of the Chinese slogan, "*minjok chisang, kukka chisang*," meaning nation first, state first. He got the slogan in China, which probably got it from Germany. In his mind nation and race were synonymous, just as they were in Hitler's; the difference was that in Korea the distinction between race and nation was minimal, *minjok* (ethnic people) often connoting both. His 1947 book is interesting for its anachronisms, its "untimely" quality; coming two years after the Holocaust it is a bit much to hear someone prattling on yet again about race, nation, and blood lines. At one point he lauds the Jews for preserving their identity for centuries, at another he remarks that "the exclusion of the Jews was quite efficacious for [German] unity." In classic corporatist fashion, he called upon Koreans to forget class conflicts, distinctions between superior and inferior, and to unite as one family.

But the book is really a text on what it means to be a Korean, with "being Korean" the essence of citizenship and nationhood. He even uses the term *Juche*, (*chuch'e*), by which he meant something like being ever subjective where things Korean are concerned, always putting Korea first. This is the cornerstone of Korean nationalism, just what one would expect from an ancient, homogeneous people long subject to outside threat. For the American who has rarely had to think about how to preserve a nation surrounded by predators, such views are bloody-minded, solipsistic, utterly recalcitrant, obnoxious, doing violence to reason at every turn. But these are popular ideas in Korea, and also a realm where Left meets Right.[18]

If this is a type of fascism, perhaps no national elite would be more receptive to such appeals than right-wing Koreans; if not that, still far more receptive than to liberal ideas. Fascist doctrine in politics lauds unity, and most Koreans thought disunity had brought on the disaster of colonialism; in economics it posits autarchy, a traditional fact and ideal in Korea; it likes a strong leader, and no people seems to praise and respect a leader more than Koreans (even if much of the flattery may be false); it conflates ethnicity and nation, which coincide almost exactly in Korea but hardly anywhere else. It was common in Seoul in the 1960s to see *Mein Kampf* in Korean translation displayed in one bookstall after another, and secondary school students would often name Hitler the man they respected most amongst twentieth-century leaders. One can condemn this all one wants, but it is clear that Yi Pŏm-sŏk and others like him spoke to Koreans in a way no liberal ever could. He just did not speak as forcefully as did Kim Il Sung. Kim drew upon a quite similar conception of Korea's needs, eventuating in his *Juche* doctrine, but with him the empty talk about abjuring class differences in a family-style national unity became a praxis seeking widespread egalitarian reforms that would, in fact, seek to make one Korean equal to the next.

The Occupation's rationale for sponsoring the Korean National Youth was both the threat from the Left, which always seemed better organized than the Right, and the proliferation of youth groups in the fall of 1946. A year earlier Hodge had violated established policy to begin building a Korean army, in part because of the propagation of personal private armies. The youth groups were similar, with each of them identified with a particular strong man. So Hodge violated State Department admonitions again, to set up the KNY. Hodge wanted the KNY to be an additional basis for the establishment of a southern military, along with the Constabulary; he also perhaps hoped that the KNY would be something wholesome like the Boy Scouts or a police auxiliary. It turned out to be a vehicle for Yi Pŏm-sŏk to become the second most powerful leader in the South by 1948, after Syngman Rhee.

Hodge originally authorized 5 million *wŏn* (about $330,000) from the MG budget to start up the Korean National Youth on October 9, 1946, and additional funding came from sponsors in each county, drawn from "the upper classes . . . business men, merchants, professionals, wealthier farmers, and teachers." Col. Ernest Voss, an OSS man with China background, was attached as the top American advisor, and together with Yi Pŏm-sŏk presided over a quick expansion of the KNY, to a membership of 30,000 by March 1947. MG officials noted its "rightist orientation," but gave all official support to the KNY in the interests, as Hodge put it, of establishing a youth movement "upon a decent basis."[19]

The KNY had grown to 200,000 members by September 1947, with six classes of officers having graduated from its Suwŏn training center, each with about 175 members. By then the MG had put in almost 20 million *wŏn*, plus assorted donations of army equipment; precisely at this time G-2 also reported the KNY to be engaged in political terrorism in South Chŏlla Province. An American reporter who visited the Suwŏn center in May 1948 was given a membership figure of 800,000, probably an exaggerated total, and noted that the MG had donated "thousands of dollars" worth of trucks, beds, tents, and other equipment over and above the regular subsidy to the KNY.[20]

Official KNY reports show that by mid-1948 there were sixty-three provincial and local training posts, where officers from Suwŏn would go to give two-week training courses. Recruits were drawn from "large floating populations" in the cities, especially Seoul, which necessitated "unusual vigilance" in the screening of recruits. Given its status as a stalking horse for a future enlarged army, the KNY had "maritime" and "air" sections; during the early part of 1948 the maritime section "was repeatedly rescreened" because of fears that people with "radical leftist tendencies" might infiltrate. The organization in the countryside began with groups of ten members each at the village level, ten of these groups then forming a unit of one hundred at the township level, and so on, a procedure probably modeled on the Chinese *pao-chia* system and designed to counter communist cell structures. The local groups held weekly discussions, using material provided by the American Office of Civil Information. Industrialists used the KNY "to counteract subversive influences" in factory unions, and the members were expected to "infiltrate and neutralize" radical (i.e. leftist) youth groups.

Another KNY duty was the "infiltration of trouble spots," often using "converted" leftists in their cause. The notoriously radical Hwasun mines near Kwangju, for example, had 1,500 KNY members on hand, who claimed (it was an exaggeration) that "all Communists have been eliminated from that industry"; the Samch'ŏk mines were hoping to follow the Hwasun example. KNY educational efforts included holding some 13,080 neighborhood discussion groups in the first six months of 1947; a focus of the program was to give "the full facts about Communism and its menaces." In addition to their political activities, members helped with harvests, repaired roads and bridges, aided homeless refugees, and the like. The American advisor, Ernest Voss, referred to the KNY's "continuous effort to counteract radicalism in all its forms," thus to provide "a powerful but quiet influence that is cooperating with the forces of law and order in Korea."[21]

THE NORTHWEST YOUTH

If the Korean National Youth represented something obnoxious to a liberal but modal for Korean nationalism, the Northwest or *Sŏbuk* Youth was merely obnoxious. Named for the region in north Korea that many of its members hailed from, it was a nasty but classic example of terrorist reaction, pure and simple. Most of its members were recruited from dispossessed refugee families fleeing the northern revolution, it was purely negative in its direction, and it shamed the Korean people. It was the main shock force in the slaughter of thousands of people on Cheju Island, as we will see in the next chapter, and was hardly less constrained in other parts of southern Korea.

Like the KNY, this organization got going in the aftermath of the autumn uprisings, having been inaugurated on November 30, 1946. A special report by American military intelligence pronounced it "a terrorist

1. Members of the Northwest Youth demonstrate on May 31, 1948

group in support of extreme Right Wing political figures"; it was organized by bringing together several groupings of northerners on a provincial-tie basis. At the beginning, "the members had all been refugees from North Korea, with real or imaginary grievances against the Soviets and the Korean Communists." No group matched them in "their vindictive hostility" to the Left. Another account by U.S. intelligence described the NWY as "by far the most virulent of the rightist youth organizations"; it merited "first place" in numbers of "beatings, terrorisms, and minor disturbances." It had "influential" sponsors, and the "tacit" backing of the police. Indeed, but the backing was scarcely tacit. At its first anniversary celebration, the honored guests on the podium were Rhee, Kim Ku, and the two top police officials, Cho Pyŏng-ok and Chang T'aek-sang.[22]

The leader was Mun Pong-je, a refugee from the North and confidant of Rhee. Some scholars have used him as a source on things like the responsibility for political assassinations, rather like asking Göering who started the Reichstag Fire. Other leaders included Sŏnu Ki-sŏng, Im Il, Kim Sŏng-ju, and Chang Yun-p'il. At first the major deployments of NWY were just below the thirty-eighth parallel, where "they aid[ed] the Korean police by screening travelers and apprehending known North Korean Communist young men." The NWY operated an underground network in the North as well, and by April 1947 had branch offices in all major southern cities. Often it shared office space with Rhee's political group. Its funds came from wealthy refugees, and businesses who used the members as strikebreakers. It used "special storming groups" to attack leftist party offices and newspapers, routinely beating anyone found there. It put out a periodical that was one part propaganda broadside and one part comic book, indulging in virulent attacks on the North, the Soviets, and the Left in general; this and propaganda leaflets wafted into the North engaged in precisely the kind of poisonous slander and wild charges that the Americans thought so characteristic of communist propaganda—exhibiting drawings of disemboweled babies and mutilated grandparents, and the like.[23]

In the spring of 1947 the reconvening of the Second Joint Commission was the occasion for *Sŏbuk* and other youth groups to ignite a binge of terrorism, and the MG was forced to act. In early April it banned a group called the Korean Democratic Youth Alliance (*Taehan minju ch'ŏngnyŏn tongmaeng*), after a G-2 report had described it as "a rightist terrorist group," with a thousand member–strong "shock squad"; its members "reported to police boxes to receive orders." It ignored the ban, whereupon Counter-Intelligence Corps (CIC) agents raided its headquarters on April 21, and found its leader, Kim Tu-hwan, personally leading the torture of ten leftists. One man was already dead, another died a week later, and the remaining eight were seriously injured (one was emasculated).

The day after the raid, a branch of the organization again defied the ban by holding a meeting in Chŏnju; local police were observed handing out new armbands to group members, giving a different title to the group, and deputizing members as police auxiliaries. At the trial of Kim Tu-hwan, the presiding judge, Yi P'il-bin, did not call the CIC agents as witnesses, even though they had taken photographs, supervised autopsies, and the like. The court merely listened to Kim's confession and then sentenced him to 160 days hard labor or a 20,000 *wŏn* fine; needless to say, Kim's backers paid the fine and he was free.[24]

The Left's main youth group by 1947 was the Korean Democratic Youth (*Chosŏn minju ch'ŏngnyŏndan*] which CIC sources estimated at 826,940 strong, with 17,671 branches. In the eyes of conservative Koreans and many Americans, it was just as bad and terroristic as any group on the Right. It engaged in many pitched battles with the rightist groups, and several murders were laid to its members. It was thought to be the main action arm of the SKWP, and certainly supported SKWP positions. But there is little evidence of a pattern of organized terrorism coming from this group in the American intelligence files; it certainly did not have the patronage of the police nor the support of some of the highest Korean officials in the bureaucracy. Nonetheless, in a show of impartiality and evenhandedness, General Lerche banned it as well in early May, 1947.[25]

After the MG crackdown, rightists gathered to form a new youth organization, which, it was hoped, would incorporate all the others. From this effort came the *Taedong* Youth. Its leader was Yi Ch'ŏng-ch'ŏn, another ally of Chiang Kai-shek whom Rhee brought home from Chungking after his meeting with Chiang in April 1947. Like Yi Pŏm-sŏk, Yi Ch'ŏng-ch'ŏn had fought the Japanese along the Manchurian border in the 1920s, and then became an officer in the Nationalist Army. He led the Korean Provisional Government's "Kwangbok Army," which we treated in volume 1.

In early August 1947 Yi announced that he had succeeded in uniting nineteen various youth organizations under his leadership, and in late September the *Taedong* Youth was inaugurated. Rhee, Kim Ku, and other China-aligned leaders were present, and Yi Ch'ŏng-ch'ŏn announced that he supported Rhee's program for an election in the South alone. But few members of the Northwest Youth or the Korean National Youth switched allegiances, and Yi Pŏm-sŏk became an intense rival of Yi Ch'ŏng-ch'ŏn. Rhee, who was thought by Army intelligence to be the hidden hand behind the Northwest Youth, probably did not try to get it to merge with Yi's group, but approved the creation of yet another paramilitary force. The CIA said Yi Ch'ŏng-ch'ŏn controlled a "secret organization composed of extreme nationalists." Army intelligence thought

Yi's "only motive" was to further "the creation of a [south] Korean Army" sufficient to confront the north.[26] This would seem to be the case, since at the same time that the *Taedong* Youth appeared, Yi sent a lengthy memorandum to Hodge laying out a plan to commence a general war against communism in Korea and Manchuria, which we will treat in a later chapter.

Those who led the most powerful youth groups—Yi Pŏm-sŏk, Mun Pong-je, Yi Ch'ŏng-ch'ŏn—all became prominent figures in the Rhee regime. The organizations were excellent vehicles for personal power. In March 1948, for example, the Standing Committee of Rhee's political organization included Mun and the two Yis among its five members. Yi Pŏm-sŏk became the first Minister of Defense in the ROK, and then Prime Minister; Mun Pong-je was director of the National Police in 1952. Just as Hodge had supported the KNY, so the embassy's Everett Drumwright later supported Rhee's conception of the uses of such paramilitary organizations. In early 1949 he wrote,

> The only answer to the Communist threat is for non-Communist youth, after weeding out, to be organized just as tightly and for just as ruthless action as their Leftist counterparts. This, in turn, means a really united youth movement, strongly centralized, controlled by a strong Government official, and trained in rudimentary military ways and in anti-guerrilla or subversive tactics.[27]

During the Korean War, rightist youth groups were the main organizational force countering communists in POW camps, and thus came to the attention of American social scientists. A careful study done at that time offers a window on the character of the ROK's youth groups. Within the camps, the youth groups of both Right and Left were organized "like little police states." "Each was geared for quick, effective action under the command of a single person with enormous powers. Each was capable of multifaceted control of the lives of the mass of PWs." The communist organizations, however, "showed a far greater ability to separate functions and to organize them rationally with a minimum of confusion and overlapping," whereas "the rightist groups caused widespread demoralization by massive corruption and profiteering on the part of the leadership." Although both sides beat and maltreated POWs, South Korean authorities—presumably under the command of the United Nations—engaged in widespread use of brutality and torture against communist prisoners. The study found that "generally speaking, brutality was most evident in the anti-Communist South Korean compounds"; communist violence was "purposeful and minimal in contrast to the vengeful brutality of the anti-Communist leaders," a "disproportionately large number [of whom] came from backgrounds with high prestige and authority" in the prewar social order.²⁸

The youth groups contributed many members to the ROK Army. After the May 1948 elections, enlistments for the USAMGIK Constabulary suddenly ballooned. Twenty thousand young men a week joined up under recruiting campaigns inaugurated on May Day. Its ranks swelled from then onward by the incorporation of members of the KNY, NWY, and *Taedong* Youth. On August 15, tens of thousands of soldiers marched by reviewing stands, ripping off the Constabulary insignia and proclaiming themselves members of the Republic of Korea Army (ROKA). Hodge's Constabulary, established in violation of existing policy in November 1945, proved to be the mother of the ROKA, as he had hoped. This unorthodox way of building an army meant that youth group leaders had strong personal followings inside the military, leading to endless personal clashes between Yi Ch'ŏng-ch'ŏn, Yi Pŏm-sŏk, and various army commanders.²⁹

CORPORATIZED LABOR

From 1945 to 1947 Korean labor was thoroughly organized by the indigenous leftist *Chŏnp'yŏng* union, a subject treated in volume 1. The year 1947 witnessed the effective demise of *Chŏnp'yŏng* and its replacement by the General Federation of Korean Labor (*Taehan nodong ch'ong yŏnmaeng*, or *Noch'ong* as it was colloquially known), a regime-controlled organization exercising top-down coordination of workers in the interests of business and the state. This remains the major union in South Korea today.

A careful study of Korean labor in mid-1946 had found that *Chŏnp'yŏng* was "the only union federation," there being "no record of any bona fide labor union which is not affiliated" with it. It had grown out of worker's committees set up in most Korean factories just after the liberation, and was not, according to this report, dominated by communists. It was "left wing," but not "party line," and its politics differed from factory to factory and region to region. *Noch'ong*, which began organizing in mid-1946, operated "under the guise of trade unionism without performing any normal union functions." The key figure in *Noch'ong* was Chŏn Chin-han, a former schoolteacher who, according to USAMGIK information, received 500,000 *wŏn* from Syngman Rhee and 250,000 *wŏn* from Kim Ku in 1947 to use for *Noch'ong* organization. In addition to money from Rhee and Kim, the organization was said to be "financed and controlled by employers."³⁰

The suppression of the general strike that touched off the autumn uprisings in 1946 severely damaged *Chŏnp'yŏng* and brought many factories under *Noch'ong* control. The leftist union mounted a one-day strike on

March 22, 1947, leading to 2,718 arrests of striking workers and, again, a general replacement of *Chŏnp'yŏng* organizers by *Noch'ong* people. In April 1947 Arthur Bunce estimated current *Chŏnp'yŏng* strength at 80,000, *Noch'ong* at 90,000; he remarked that the latter "was organized by Rightist political parties," was usually "management-dominated," and "acts as a company union." The KNP assisted *Noch'ong*, Bunce said, by "a policy of hands off wherever they have been concerned," whereas *Chŏnp'yŏng* was "subject to strict police surveillance," arrests, and "roundups following strike activity." As the American G-2 put it, the strikes in October 1946 and March 1947 "gave the Right Wing labor unions an opportunity to act as strikebreakers and seize a great deal of power in important industries and utilities."[31]

Hugh Deane interviewed some *Chŏnp'yŏng* organizers during this period. Many of them had been part of the labor movement since the 1920s; Han Ch'ŏl, for example, was a miner in the 1920s and later became a labor organizer. The Japanese authorities arrested him three times for labor agitation, and he served a total of fourteen years in colonial prisons. Yi In-dong, "big, heavy-set, with a large, dark face," talked "rough worker talk" to Deane. His head was "slightly twisted in relation to his body, the result of torture by the Japanese." Deane tried to interview Pak Pong-u, another labor organizer, but terrorists had knocked all his teeth out so he couldn't talk too well. Mun Ŭn-jŏng, a *Chŏnp'yŏng* organizer, had been in jail from August 1946 to April 1947, and was tortured for two months of that time: "hung by his heels, given the water cure, beaten, and had his face smeared with a mixture of ashes and human waste." He could not see or hear when he was released, but an American doctor partially restored his senses. These organizers told Deane that fifteen thousand of their members had been arrested from 1945 through June 1947.[32]

The American command did nothing about the widespread pattern of arrests and violence directed at *Chŏnp'yŏng* by the police, strikebreakers, and rightist youth groups working in concert. Commenting on a series of work stoppages at the Seoul Electric Company in the summer of 1947, in which strikebreakers beat workers with clubs labeled "correct one's mental attitude," and culminating in an agreement of August 13 that *Noch'ong* would be the sole legal bargaining agent for workers in this large public utility, the American G-2 said,

> Since Chawn Pyawng [*sic*] members are universally disloyal to the Seoul Electric Company, and to the SKIG, their subversive acts have prevented them from holding important positions . . . it is not strange that [*Noch'ong* organizers] receive the support of the Korean police. Not justifiable, though understandable, are the strong arm methods they ex-

ercise to prevent infiltration into the Company of menial Chawn Pyawng adherents.

Hodge said somewhat later that the company had been plagued by slow-downs and minor sabotage until *Noch'ong* "cleaned out the leftists." MG officials thought it was appropriate to support *Noch'ong*, "in default of a group which can be better worked with."³³

By 1949 the CIA found that *Noch'ong* controlled labor organization in "all significant industries" in South Korea. Just before the war the American embassy noted that the ROK had enacted no "modern social-indus-trial laws," or indeed any "basic labor law"; *Noch'ong* leaders were de-scribed as "neither competent nor seriously interested" in such things. In 1951 Chŏn Chin-han still ran the union, and was described by the CIA as "a close friend of Syngman Rhee." In 1952 the Americans sought to encourage "orthodox labor unions," given the "deplorable" weakness of labor; but the Rhee regime and Korean industrialists looked askance at U.S. Information Agency films depicting "the role of labor unions in free societies."³⁴ It is truly an American oddity, a sign of structural amnesia, that just a few years after an American Occupation had presided over the systematic destruction of representative labor organization, other Americans could come along and deplore the absence of unions.

Roger Baldwin, for many years the head of the American Civil Liber-ties Union, toured Korea in May 1947. "The country is literally in the grip of a police regime and a private terror," he wrote to friends; "you get the general impression of a beaten, discouraged people." He saw a prison where one thousand people were held for labor and strike orga-nizing. Koreans "want all foreigners to get out and let them build their nation," but were the Americans to pull out, he thought, a civil war would result. After the American G-2 chief showed him intelligence reports on the countryside, however, Baldwin concluded that "a state of undeclared war" already existed in Korea. He spoke with Yŏ Un-hyŏng, 1945 leader of the Korean People's Republic, who told him that the government was "full of Quislings" and "toadies to the Americans"; it was the American retention of the colonial police, Yŏ thought, that was the key to the "pres-ent chaos."³⁵

On a quiet, sultry afternoon a few weeks later, Yŏ picked up the editor of the Indendence News, Ko Kyŏng-hŏm, and motored over by the an-cient Ch'anggyŏng'wŏn Palace to meet another American, Edgar John-son, an Economic Cooperation Administration (ECA) official. Johnson later recalled,

I remember how impatiently I waited, with my interpretor, that after-noon of July 19, 1947. I had been told by messenger that Lyuh would come about four o'clock. Four o'clock came, four thirty, and then a furiously driven car swerved into the muddy lane leading up the hill to our house . . . a man jumped out and ran stumbling up the hill. Breathlessly he told me that Lyuh had been assassinated less than half a mile from my house.³⁶

The driver had slowed to negotiate the *Haehwadong* traffic rotary, when the murderer mounted the running board and pumped three bullets from a .45 automatic into Yŏ Un-hyŏng's head, killing him instantly. G-2 investigators pinpointed the site "within a stone's throw of a police box," but said that police "made no effort to apprehend the assassin."³⁷

The executioner, nineteen-year old Han Chi-gŭn, belonged to a small group of right-wing terrorists; like Japanese hotheads in the 1930s, he reckoned that his act would make him a national hero. Upon his capture he told police he had acted at the instigation of a man in P'yŏngyang named Pak Nam-sŏk. After plotting to assassinate Kim Il Sung,³⁸ Han had come down from P'yŏngyang a month before the murder, residing at the home of Han Hyŏn-u, who was then doing a life sentence for the 1945 murder of Song Chin-u; living in the same house was none other than Kim Tu-hwan, whom CIC agents had caught torturing leftists just a few weeks before. Although Han denied any political affiliation, he and his group "acknowledged adherence" to Kim Ku. General Hodge and other knowledgeable Americans in the Occupation thought that Kim Ku was responsible for the murder; Leonard Bertsch believed that Kim had first cleared the act with Syngman Rhee.³⁹ But there is evidence for another possibility, one that Hodge and Bertsch would hesitate to assert: that the National Police engineered it.

By the summer of 1947 Yŏ Un-hyŏng was "the most shot at man in South Korea," according to a U.S. Armed Forces in Korea (USAFIK) historian, who counted nine attempts on his life since liberation. In July 1946 several thugs had tried to lynch him; in October 1946 leftists detained him for two days, after which he entered a hospital suffering from "nervous shock." For months before his death, Yŏ complained that police followed him everywhere and periodically searched his home; but since these same police would not protect him from attack, he asked Americans for permission to carry a weapon and to arm his bodyguards.⁴⁰

Bertsch visited Yŏ's country home in March 1947 and found that police had arrested Yŏ's bodyguards after searching his house and finding weapons; Yŏ was in hiding, fearing an assassination. The American advisor to the provincial police, a Colonel Stone, defended the arrests and said he would not indulge in "groundless prognostications" about whether Yŏ was a target for assassination. Two weeks later Yŏ's home was wrecked by a bomb.⁴¹

In the same period, American G-2 reports carried many rumors of assassination plots by rightist groups, including one that targeted Maj. Gen. Albert Brown, head of the American team at the Joint Commission. In late May, the G-2 cited the existence within the Korean National Police of a "Black Tiger Gang," run by the Seoul police director, Chang T'aek-sang; this gang was "reliably reported" to have met with leaders of the Northwest Youth on or about May 13, to plot "a terroristic campaign aimed specifically" at Yŏ Un-hyŏng, Kim Kyu-sik, and Wŏn Se-hun. A week before Yŏ died, American intelligence found "serious unrest" in police ranks over the pro-Japanese, antitraitor bill then before the SKILA; "several ranking members of the police force," whom the Americans termed "old pro-Japs," were "attempting to coerce all police into direct action." SKILA legislators expressed fear for their own safety, while Yŏ Un-hyŏng and Kim Kyu-sik again asked the Americans to supply bodyguards. None were provided.[42]

Of those politicians with whom the Americans were willing to deal, Yŏ Un-hyŏng was the most vocal critic of the retention of hated Korean police who had done Japanese bidding. He was also, as the CIA later acknowledged, the only noncommunist southern leader capable of challenging Syngman Rhee for power. His daughter, Yŏ Yŏn-gu, told me that Chang T'aek-sang ordered the murder.[43] Either the police arranged his assassination, or looked the other way so that it could happen. It is remarkable, for example, that the murderer could live at the home of Song Chin-u's assailant for a month with Kim Tu-hwan, and not be detected by the police. It is even more remarkable that the American command dealt so cavalierly with Yŏ's many requests for protection, and so leniently with his police and rightist adversaries.

In 1945 Yŏ Un-hyŏng was a gifted, fitting leader for liberated Korea. A hardy man and charismatic orator, he reflected the aspirations of the great majority of the Korean people, and in his person embodied the peculiar class structure of Korean society as it emerged from the Japanese grip: at home with the vast peasantry, he also had a bit of the bourgeois gentleman about him. He was an ardent nationalist, a staunch resister during the colonial period who also kept his distance from General Hodge, earning the latter's enmity. Yŏ also developed a bit of camaraderie with Kim Il Sung, something that still carries a hint about how Korea might have been unified without civil war.[44] But by 1947 the national division had hardened, separate states had arisen, and in retrospect it is difficult to imagine how a man of his magnanimous qualities could have survived the deepening strife.

The British epitaph was that Yŏ "tried to ride all the horses at once in order to be sure of coming home on the winner,"[45] which has an unkind measure of truth in it, were Korea England or America. But in the Manichaean world of postwar Korean politics, a man who sought to bridge differences and unite parties was rare indeed. Yŏ Un-hyŏng remains about the only politician from the 1940s who is honored both in South and North Korea. That itself is an eloquent epitaph.

On the third anniversary of liberation in 1948, the remnant *kŏn'guk tongmaeng* faction sought to hold a memorial service for Yŏ: Rhee had ninety-six of them arrested.[46]

At the end of 1947 KDP stalwart Chang Tŏk-su was also assassinated, rather a replay of the murder of Song Chin-u two years earlier. In both cases the assassins were traced to Kim Ku, the motives were the same, and the Occupation did nothing but put the underlings in jail. One of the assassins, P'ae Hŭi-bŏm, said that during World War II Chang had been an advisor to the Headquarters of the Japanese Army in Korea, had mobilized many youths for wartime service, and ran a "reeducation" institute for political prisoners; since 1945 he "had been plotting to establish a separate government in South Korea." All this appears to have been true, but Hodge did not take kindly to the murder of one of his closest advisors; he came to think that Kim and Syngman Rhee were behind the murders of both Chang and Yŏ. For weeks he pondered the arrest of Kim Ku, and some sort of exile for Rhee, but ultimately Hodge merely got Kim to testify in the case, whereupon Kim predictably denied involvement. The British attaché thought "it would be a happy day for Korea if these senile power-holders [Kim and Rhee] could be extracted from its head."[47]

THE IDEOLOGY OF THE SOUTHERN SYSTEM

It was, of course, Syngman Rhee and not Yi Pŏm-sŏk or another radical nationalist who achieved power in the South, and so it is appropriate to begin our consideration of southern ideology with him. To read some American accounts, one would think Rhee's forty years in the United States had turned him into a Christian democrat, suffused with Wilsonian idealism. What is more remarkable, really, is the virtual absence of evidence that Rhee imbibed in those four decades any trace at all of American ideals of democratic rights, fair play, or tolerance of the minority. However, like his northern counterpart Kim Il Sung and like any Korean chief of state, he took ideas seriously. His Confucian heritage would tell him that a well-run polity proceeds from a correct set of ideas; divining right ideas, in turn, is thought much harder and more important than deciding right action. He would agree with Chiang Kai-shek that "to act is easy, to think is difficult," and would find Mao's reverse dictum—"to think is easy, to act is difficult"—a barbarism.

Such assumptions gave to his regime, and to much of southern politics ever since, a pronounced voluntarism in theory and hypocrisy in action.

The first principle of rule was to found good ideas, and it mattered little that the ideas often bore little resemblance to political reality. The ruling doctrines of the Rhee regime, in theory and practice, combined a pastiche of Korean Confucianism, Western fascism, democratic slogans, Chinese Nationalist pretentiousness and haplessness, and effective Japanese method. The Confucian and Nationalist Chinese influence was palpable and something to be proud of; good traditional Koreans had always got their political models from China. The Japanese influence was never mentioned, but it was of central importance, given its entrenchment in bureaucratic practice.

Rhee's inaugural address manifested his capacity to draw tears from older Koreans, as he portrayed himself "shaken to the core with emotions" at the prospect of Korean independence. Organizing the government, he thought, was a matter of finding "good men":

A man may be either too big or too little for a [government] position. But a truly great man is able not only to cover a big thing, but also a small one and, above all, not to be ashamed of doing a small thing well. With such true great souls coming forward to fill a position with a will . . . the attainment of our ultimate objects will be made possible. Such men of genuine character alone will make the government work like a clock.

The president told the audience that the government would be endangered if power were "monopolized by one party or one group of politicians," and then dwelt on the duties of citizens.

Good citizens must be protected, while bad ones [are] curbed. Selfishness must make room for justice. Formerly the state used to decline by the monarchs upholding the unworthy and estranging the wise. But in these times when it is the people that elect their own officers, it is up to them to exercise the judgement to distinguish between the good and bad, between the competent and the incompetent.

A new constitution, a new government, he said, were less important than "a new people . . . we cannot make a holy state out of a corrupt people." So, with "a rejuvenated national spirit blasting away all the old corrupt practices," the ROK could become a "new rising nation whose foundation should be on the rock of ages never to be washed away by the torrent of world events."[48]

This somewhat tepid and windy beginning gave way shortly to a pet doctrine, termed *Ilminjuǔi*, or "The One-People Principle." This was, needless to say, a take-off on Sun Yat Sen's "Three People's Principles" (*San Min Chu I*), which the historian Gabriel Kolko once described as a vague paraphrase of the Gettysburg Address. The "one people" was, of course, the Korean people; like Yi Pŏm-sŏk, Rhee used nation and race as synonymous terms, and saw himself embodying "the will of the nation" (or the race, take your pick). "Our race has been one race," he opined; "our territory has been one unity, and our *Volkgeist* has been one, and one has been our economic class." This mouthful connoted the four "sub-principles" of the doctrine: elimination of class distinctions, an end to factionalism, equality of men and women, and Korean national unity. The nation ought to be an organic whole, a body politic akin to the corporeal man.[49]

Rhee's ideologues broadened this organic argument to include the family: according to *Ilminjuŭi*, "a nation is an enlarged home and its people are an extended family. . . . The people must live together in the spirit of one family." Father should not fight son, nor brother fight brother, so why do Koreans fight with each other? If a father should not exploit a son, why should the wealthy class exploit the poor? Or, "in plainer words, no home can be said to be perfect if within it the father, the mother, and the sons and daughters should stand against each other." If this was ersatz Confucianism, it was also a bit odd coming from Rhee, who married an Austrian woman and never had children. Nonetheless *Ilminjuŭi* was the answer to Korea's problems, if not to Syngman Rhee's, according to his prime minister. Indeed, Koreans had been hoping

> for a most rational and excellent theory which is based on a philosophy and which is urgently needed to march toward the goal. . . . The theory of *Ilminjuŭi* has appeared to meet the requirements of the times. The learned people will admit that this theory is most suitable to lead the whole nation. . . . President Rhee made a minute review of the philosophical basis of the principle of one people and refined it so as to conform with the current thoughts of the world and the historical background of our country. Consequently, the principle has not a single demerit.[50]

With this example and numerous others that might be submitted, the reader will remain somewhat unclear about the content of Ilminjuŭi; but if the reader will compare this to North Korea's mountains of verbiage about *Juche*, or indeed Reverend Sun Myung Moon's much-bruted "divine principle," one will begin to understand that the ideas are less important than their fount of origin. If one follows the fount one embraces the ideas; and the ideas, however vague, when read over and over again will result in a state of mind that brooks no alternatives and that breeds unquestioning loyalty. In other words, this is vintage Korean politics.

Rhee's allies came out of the woodwork to trumpet the idea, and to praise the learned thought that had gone into it, but not as much as the learned person who had presumably thought it all up, that is, the maximum leader. Yi Hwal, for example, an early KDP member and wealthy landowner who had his palatial home destroyed in the 1946 uprisings, became the head of The Society for the Diffusion of the *Ilmin* Principle. Yang U-jŏng, editor of the most pro-Rhee newspaper, wrote many articles and a couple of books extolling its virtues, and Syngman Rhee's, whom Yang likened to Korea's "Messiah" and "Moses." By early 1950, hundreds of middle and high school principals were being drilled in the doctrine, which they then propagated to students during daily hours set aside for "moral education."[51] But of all the adherents of this doctrine, none was so interesting or so singular as its real author, Rhee's first minister of education.

An Ho-sang as Educator

An Ho-sang was something of a philosopher, having studied continental thought at Jena University in Germany in the late 1920s. Also something of a mystic, he frequently evoked old Korean mythology, such as the *Tan'gun* fable about the birth of the Korean people, or the *Hwarang* spirit of Silla warriors, to peddle his ideas on the uniqueness of the Korean race and to encourage an armed conquest of North Korea, on the model of the Silla unification (668 A.D.). He frequently used the *Juche* term to refer to a Korean essence, a subjective appreciation of what it meant to be a Korean. Many Americans were sure he was a bona fide Korean Nazi; Richard Robinson said he modeled his youth organizations after the Hitler *Jugend*, Gregory Henderson thought wrongly that he had studied in Germany during the Nazi era, and even Drumwright, with a strong stomach for right-wing politics, remarked upon the similarity between An's racial doctrines and "the Herrenvolk concept." But his views were as Korean as *kimch'i*. He was a mostly homespun fascist, exemplifying an attempt by a traditional and compromised elite to find a usable past and to establish a doctrine that might somehow compete with the dynamism of communist theory.[52]

In his speeches and his books, An propounded the One People doctrine, usually in prose like this:

Historically speaking the philosophy of *Ilminjuŭi* originated already in the Tan'gun era and developed later in the Silla era, when *Hwarangism* was in full sway throughout the country. But patriotism is greater than the idea of duty. The doctrine that for the sake of one's nation and people everything selfish should be sacrificed, which our honorable President embodies in his philosophy, has been historically handed down to this nation from father Tan'gun. The fact that Korea has been called the nation of civility in the Orient has, therefore, a deeply rooted historical foundation.

If, then, we value justice more than death, there is a question: Why do we oppose Capitalism and Communism? That is because the two doctrines lack justice. . . . The doctrine of Communism is nothing but Capitalism pulled back to old feudalism. But our philosophy, *Ilminjuŭi*, is deeply rooted philosophically with public-mindedness as its principle. To be ultimately just and public-minded is to be fair. . . . From both philosophical and scientific points of view, this is a very systematic and harmonious truth. This is why I agree to call it a theory of greater truth than any other theories.[53]

An was a bit clearer in a speech to the *Taehan* Youth Corps in December 1949. "Democracy is very hard to comprehend," he contended; "I think the best principle is *Ilmin*." Anyway, with their "strong fists," the *Taehan* Youth "will beat down the crazy Communists under the *Ilmin* flag, and we will have our second anniversary meeting under Moran Hill in P'yŏngyang."[54] And he was perfectly clear in his policies within the Ministry of Education, which were designed to achieve totalitarian control of what he thought was the best venue for inculcating his ideas, the South Korean school system.

As soon as An took up his duties in the fall of 1948, he launched a widespread purge of heterodox teachers and implemented methods for checking (and correcting) the thoughts of teachers and students throughout the system. He rejected American suggestions that the Japanese-built structure be decentralized, arguing that local school board elections, for example, "would produce many undesirable and Communist school officials."[55] Thus the Ministry retained its colonial-style central controls, on everything from teacher appointments to the content of textbooks. Male students continued to wear Japanese-style black military uniforms to school, and were required to continue the 1930s militarist practices of shaved heads and early morning mass-formation drills. Even into the 1970s, South Korean schools were little museums of the colonial era in form, if not necessarily in content (anti-Japanese attitudes were drummed into the students, often by the same teachers who had taught in the colonial system).

An Ho-sang moved the youth group conception into the school system, inaugurating a "Student National Defense Corps" in March 1949 designed to gain government control of student organizations, most of which had been leftist. He appointed himself its "National Commander." All male secondary school students automatically became members, and underwent periodic examinations of their thoughts and compulsory military training. Members were routinely mobilized for massive government-sponsored political demonstrations. All other student organizations were outlawed. Although Muccio sought to depict the organization as akin to ROTC outfits in American schools, at least for the consumption of the State Department, within weeks of its inauguration the embassy knew An was using it to "purify thoughts" throughout the system; "arrests of leftist teachers continued all over the country."[56]

An Ho-sang and other ROK officials also ended the pronounced leftist bias of much of the media in the south, with a thorough system of censorship. An American survey of translated political writings found that almost all publications in 1945 and 1946 were leftist; what they termed "Communist publishing" continued "comparatively strong" in 1947, but it virtually ended with the accession to power of Rhee. Rhee's press law, passed in 1948, outlawed statements that were "contrary to policy," "detrimental" to the ROK, "approving" of North Korea, or "agitating" to the public mind. The CIA noted that the regime was not organized well enough "completely to control the flow of information," even though that was its obvious intent. The press in the period 1948–1950 was freer, perhaps, than the ROK during the last years of Park Chung Hee's rule, but it was less free than during the Occupation.[57]

Just before the war began, An Ho-sang superintended the first anniversary of the Student National Defense Corps. With Arthur Jamieson, a UN Commission on Korea (UNCOK) delegate, and James L. Stewart of the U.S. embassy present on the podium, he introduced *Ilminjuŭi* as the "torchlight of the human race," derived from "a synthetic unification theory developed from all the theories old and new in the East and in the West," termed Rhee "the supreme leader of our nation," and urged students to swear to "recover the lost territories," i.e., the North. "You students, the warriors of the nation, should fight bravely," he said.

> Imagine how the peaceful garden of the world has been deserted by the cold wind of capitalism and how it has been destroyed by the storms of communism. . . . Let us, the thirty million people, combine together under one principle. We Koreans are not a heterogeneous race of two or more different peoples, but a homogenous race. . . . And now, it is the supreme command of our nation and the sacred obligation of our people to rise and smash the partition of the 38th parallel line, which was erected by the hands of the foreign forces, by our own hands and unify the divided territories and combine the divided people together into one people.

The forum adopted messages to Harry Truman, "the great leader of the United States," cited the ROK as the "Citadel of democracy in Asia" and the Student Corps as "the vanguard of the Citadel." It was some citadel, this—an American emissary and a United Nations delegate identifying themselves with the most elemental urges of a frightened and ultimately pathetic elite. In May 1950 An Ho-sang left the educational citadel to become the chief of the *Taehan* Youth Corps. If there is something called a Korean Confucian fascist, he was it.[58]

Speaking with those Americans who knew Korea in the 1940s, or An Ho-sang, or Yi Pŏm-sŏk, or for that matter Syngman Rhee, one has the sense that they found this pasticcio of native fascism, and its practitioners, rather humorous. Embarrassing, to be sure, but one really should not take them too seriously, these posturing and flatulent windbags.[59] It is true that Korean fascism was not well organized, it was often a hapless, Keystone Cops fascism, if there is such a thing. But this made its violence even more indiscriminate and purposeless. And behind the American chuckling at these figures is not merely a deep cynicism, but a contempt for Koreans that assumes they cannot do anything right—they can't even run a proper police state. Such attitudes ignore the experience of a vast bureaucracy under people who did know how to run a police state, the Japanese colonizers.

If the youth groups were the main vehicle of irregular repression, the bureaucracy was the agent of effective repression. Under the imperative direction and in the interests of the class represented by Cho Pyŏng-ok, Chang T'aek-sang, and the rest, state bureaucrats in the Home Ministry, the police, the justice and court system, the educational system, and the army dispatched their duties. Compared to other postcolonial nations, Korea had a rich bureaucratic experience and was well ahead of many developing countries by 1950. Many skilled, honest, and unpretentious career professionals labored at extraordinarily low pay to deliver public services to citizens; indeed, one is so often struck by the contrast between their sincerity and the people who command the state. In the economic sphere, had it not been for the war the state would have arrived much sooner at the position it has held since the mid-1960s, a technically competent and often dynamic coordinator of planned economic activity. But in the political sphere, this bureaucracy functioned to give coordinated, coherent, penetrative, effective structure, a powerful backbone, to the frequently incontinent Rhee regime. As the CIA recognized, this was the ROK system's forte.[60]

We have witnessed this in the police, judicial, military, and educational realms during the Occupation. All functioned to promote rightist political goals, and this only deepened in the Rhee period. But the Americans did blanch at clearly totalitarian methods of controlling and correcting thoughts, something that Korean conservatives frequently cited as a big failure of the Military Government. The American philosophical assumption is that a political system should be premised on the failings of humans; in the famous words of the Federalist Papers, "men are not angels," and so their passions and interests must be confined and corralled by a separation and balancing of power. The Korean philosophical assumption is that a good political system must be premised on good men, and that good men are created through correct thought. So, during the Rhee period the bureaucracy was used to examine, monitor, and correct heterodox thought which, given Rhee's style of orthodoxy, meant very widespread attempts at control and conversion.

These methods were learned from the Japanese, even though they would smack of Chinese "brainwashing" to many Americans. Rhee set up a National Guidance Alliance in 1949, to do conversion and reeducation work among alleged communists. To be cleared and able to join this organization as a repentant convert required complete admission of guilt (even though the allegation of communism might be false), written confessions and recantations, and complete information on all associates and past activities. The Alliance frequently made claims that it was converting as many as three thousand people per week, as many as ten thousand converts per province. Its chief, Pak U-ch'ŏn, explained to an embassy officer how the process worked.

> In order to be sure that conversions are sincere and complete, each individual upon surrendering himself to the Alliance is required to prepare a complete written confession. . . . Most important, he must set down the names of all individuals who served in the same cell. . . . For a period of one year confessions are subject to constant recheck, largely by matching name lists. If a confession proves false or deficient at any time during the year, the person who made it becomes liable to the full legal penalty for his action and for his leftist affiliations.

Court procedures did not try to hide political intent, but began with it. For example, when Rhee trumped up charges of procommunism against several National Assembly members in 1949, a judge began the questioning of one of them as follows: "What is your personal history? What is your personal belief? What is your ideology?" During the Korean War Americans captured "enemy documents" that they thought were communist confessions of political sin, but they were in fact vows of allegiance to the ROK required of former leftists; the documents are replete with oaths of fealty, pledges to repent and "rectify errors," and promises loyally to fight communism in the future. In spite of the sweep of this effort to make people repent and convert their politics, however, one must also remember that in 1949 large numbers of people were simply shot for their beliefs.[61]

The national school system was a prime vehicle for monitoring hearts and minds under An Ho-sang, as we have seen. Anticommunism was the leitmotiv of political education, drummed into the students' heads on a daily basis by rote recitation and memorization, by periodic drilling and marching, and by frequent political campaigns that festooned schools everywhere with banners and slogans; to a foreigner the schools often looked like counterparts in communist countries. When I taught at a Seoul middle school in 1968, for months the gates were draped with banners proclaiming a campaign to smash communism and catch spies; President Park's calligraphic phrase "obliterate communism" [*myôlgong*] was stamped in many books. English lessons incorporated phrases like "smash the Red cloven hoof that annihilates the people"; essays from students evinced dark, inchoate fears of communists as the devil incarnate. Children would wake up from nightmares, screaming about the "*kong-sandang*" (communist party). Anyone who showed the slightest liberal or social-democratic tendency ran an immediate risk of being labeled a communist, and if the label stuck at all, the student would be systematically ostracized. Students from "bad families," meaning families with a heterodox political background, were prevented from studying abroad, or would be required to work at radio stations shrieking into the night at North Korea before getting a passport. Spies and informants roamed high school and college classrooms at will; one could be turned into the authorities for little more than a careless remark.

All this is second nature to Koreans who grew up in the system, but hardly any Americans seem to know about it, or be willing to talk about it. It is the result of state methods of political and thought control that belie any "Keystone Cop" image of South Korea. Of course, the country has never been totalitarian, and young people in particular have courageously resisted the self-interested orthodoxy of the regime in power. But in my experience the fetters on South Korean political thought are remarkably strong when compared to other countries; to say that they are stronger in North Korea does not justify such a system. Koreans on both sides have had their creative and fertile intellects badly blighted and deformed by the struggle that has engulfed the peninsula since 1945. And one half of Korea has been under the constant care and protection of an America that has rejected such practices for two centuries, and that fought against the same Japanese militarists who taught Koreans how to suppress dissent by any means necessary.

In the 1950s, the United States used the manifold powers of its worldwide publicity networks to picture the ROK, always, as a free-world democracy, or something developing toward a democracy, with some unfortunate backsliding here, a bit short of the mark there. Even the most liberal of Foreign Service officers, deeply critical of this regime in their memorandums, still believe it was a start toward liberal democracy, something dashed by the military coup of 1961 and the Yusin System of 1972. South Korea has always had an authoritarian system, the legacy of the colonial period and American midwifery. But nothing in the 1970s or 1980s compares to the terror of the Rhee regime.

Internal American data on political prisoners placed 21,458 in prison in December 1947, under the U.S. Occupation, compared to 17,000 in southern Korea in August 1945 by this estimate; Consul William Langdon lied through his teeth in saying "none are listed for political offenses." Two years later, 30,000 alleged communists were in Rhee's jails, with proceedings against suspected communists constituting 80 percent of all court cases. "Guidance camps" held those additional prisoners unable to be placed in the grossly overcrowded prisons. "Repentance" campaigns in November 1949 were followed in December by "Extermination Weeks," in which as many as a thousand people a day were rounded up. An embassy political officer summarized this as follows:

> The suppression of Communism appeared to be increasingly successful. The government had mobilized its forces in many ways. Security forces were ruthlessly stamping out the Communist party organization and guerrilla resistance, using whatever methods were considered necessary. . . . The Great Korean Youth Corps [*Taehan* Youth] and Student's National Defense Corps were instilling patriotism and teaching military drill. Agents were everywhere watching actions and conversations; every organization had its watchers for communist behavior.[62]

Top-level Korean police officials told Americans privately that they considered torture the only way to deal with political prisoners. The vice-minister of Home Affairs said "communists will not always confess unless we torture them." The home minister, Kim Hyo-sŏk, lauded by Muccio in an internal memorandum for doing "a most effective job of cleansing the Seoul area of communist subversive groups," told newspapers in mid-December that police torture of communists was "unavoidable" in interrogating communists: "However, it is strictly prohibited to torture good citizens." British sources reported that a "routine entry" in the police registry was "died under torture." It all is reminiscent of Guatemalan president Rios-Mont's statement in 1982 that "we don't have a scorched-earth policy, we have a scorched-communist policy."[63]

For the record and out of decency, one would like to list all those "communists," as opposed to "good citizens," who were arrested and often put to death. But a few names will have to suffice: Cho Yun-je, dean of the College of Literature and Science at Seoul National University, arrested as a communist on December 9, 1949; Kim Chin-hong and seven other judges, arrested as communists, December 28, 1949; Professor Chang Hyŏn-du, tortured to death, December 1949; Ko Hŭi-du, politician, dead under the application of electric torture machinery, October

1949; an unfortunate policeman, tortured to death in a case of mistaken identity.[64]

A woman in Rhee's inner circle named Angela, wrote on official presidential stationery in early 1950 that most good citizens lived in fear of the police, that 80 percent of those jailed for political offenses were innocent, and that hundreds had been beaten to death. She could not believe the president countenanced all this, and blamed it on Madame Rhee who, she said, protected the police chief.[65]

KOREAN LIBERALISM AND THE OPPOSITION TO RHEE

To the extent that there was an opposition to the Rhee regime, it came from the Korean Democratic Party. From its inception until the early 1970s, when younger leaders untainted by the Japanese era came to maturity (such as Kim Dae Jung), the original set of leaders who were prominent in the 1940s formed the backbone of this tepid opposition even though the party changed its name from time to time. In the literature on the ROK, the KDP is often depicted as an advocate of basic freedoms and human rights, and of parliamentary prerogatives against Rhee's dictatorial executive power. Many Americans remember Cho Pyŏng-ok and Chang T'aek-sang in the 1950s as good, well-spoken liberals, when they frequented Seoul cafes and tearooms as stalwarts of the Rhee "opposition."

Behind the formal democratic facade of the First Republic, however, traditional politics motivated the political elite. The KDP was the organ of landed wealth and local power, and like the old *yangban* aristocracy from which most of its members came, it fought with central executive power over the allocation of resources and the control of wealth. The tension between Rhee's presidency and the KDP mimicked James Palais's analysis of state-society conflicts in the Yi Dynasty, with Rhee playing the king and the legislature aggregating the interests of the landed nobility; it was, in typical Korean conservative fashion, old wine in new bottles. For those KDP elements who had cut their tie to the land and invested in industry, this tension was not as great, because the state bureaucracy was their ally in distributing vested properties and erecting walls of protection to incubate native industry through a nascent import-substitution industrialization program. But wealth still required a state guarantee or bureaucratic tie, as in the past, and in any case most KDP industrialists were like Kim Sŏng-su, interested in combining the traditional privilege and status of landed power with the greater return of industrial investment.

The relationship between Rhee and the KDP was the same during the First Republic as it had been in 1945: a tempestuous marriage of convenience. As the CIA put it in the autumn of 1948, KDP leaders "dare not overthrow him but must maintain an uneasy coalition with him since they need his political prestige," the latter a reference to the collaborationist background of most KDP leaders and Rhee's role in protecting them; "at the same time, since [Rhee] requires their money and ability, he cannot ignore their demands."[66]

Rhee's position on the independence of the legislative branch, called for in the Constitution, was contradictory. He tolerated a good bit of noisy debate and interpolation, within the narrow limits of the parties and individuals who made up the National Assembly. The CIA was right to see the National Assembly as "the locus of democratic spirit" in the ROK, with legislative debate often bringing heated exchanges with government officials, but also right that it did not "approximate any typical democratic Western legislature," and was no obstacle to "Bonapartism," since it had no effective checks on executive power.[67] It was a legislature that perched on the state system like a rowdy ski lodge on the slopes of an avalanche-prone mountain.

Rhee had no compunction about jailing its members and, of course, closing it as he did during the Korean War. In late 1949 thirteen members of the Assembly were arrested under the National Security Law; Ernst Fraenkel, formerly with the Occupation's Justice Department and then serving in the ECA mission, said that those Assembly members indicted ran afoul of an article of the law making it illegal to join a group having the purpose of "disturbing the tranquility of the nation." In their trial, from November 17, 1949, to February 4, 1950, the judge refused to call witnesses nominated by the defense, since "these witnesses might make false statements in an effort to protect the accused"; the prosecutor relied on confessions extracted by torture; the bias of the presiding judge, Fraenkel said, was obvious "time and again." Just as the trial came to an end, the judge elaborated a remarkable new wrinkle in conspiracy theory: even if the defendants had done "good" things, it was a punishable crime to do good things if it were at the direction of the South Korean Worker's Party. Among other things, the accused had sought to express opinions critical of Rhee to UNCOK, had called for the withdrawal of American troops, and, according to the indictment, had opposed the "invasion of North Korea by South Korean forces."[68]

The KDP, now called the Democratic Nationalist Party, continued to penetrate the commanding heights of the state bureaucracy, just as it had during the Occupation. A listing of provincial governors, city mayors, and county magistrates in early 1949 shows remarkable continuity with 1945 and 1946 lists of local officials, the same people being switched to different locales through the old law of avoidance, having a higher velocity in Korea than in China. Given the pattern established in 1945 it is hardly surprising to find KDP predominance in the bureaucracy under the Rhee regime.[69]

It will be remembered that for a brief time in mid-1946, the Occupation sponsored talks between moderate leftists and rightists in something called the Coalition Committee. This broke up amid the autumn 1946 unrest, and never again did the United States pursue a coalition policy in Korea to bring extremes together in the "middle." In July 1947 the leading leftist in the group, Yŏ Un-hyŏng, was murdered, and by early 1948 Kim Kyu-sik, spokesman for the moderate right, had spent his capital with Hodge by supporting the P'yŏngyang Unity Conference.

Nonetheless, many American officials continued to think that the United States was wrong to back Rhee and the extreme Right. The logic of their situation was remarkably simple, embracing the American experience in Korea, Vietnam, Guatemala, the Dominican Republic, Cuba, and now Nicaragua and El Salvador. It was expressed best by John F. Kennedy, when he remarked that we don't like Trujillo and we do like the Dominican moderates, but we can't oust Trujillo until we're sure we won't get the communists. This is the Achilles heel that condemns the quest for the middle to eternal replication and eternal failure, unless that middle has a solid social base. Bourgeois democracy without a bourgeoisie is bad policy, but the quest for it is as American as apple pie, because only this quest legitimates the involvement.

If one can imagine an omniscient and prescient American policy for liberated Korea, it would have been to turn over the government to Yŏ Un-hyŏng and his Republic. Yŏ knew how to lead and he represented broad social forces, he *was* the middle of the Korean political spectrum, he was a patriot and he was sympathetic enough with Western liberalism to listen politely to Americans. If he bested the communists in some form of coalition, Korea would have tended toward social democracy and either neutrality or alignment with the United States. If the communists bested him (which was more likely), the United States could then have taken its troops home and washed its hands of the involvement. A regime of socialist nationalism, national socialism, and national solipsism under Kim Il Sung would have been the likely result, not pro-American but, as years passed, a barrier to Soviet expansionism as well. Either way, millions of lives and decades of conflict would have been avoided. Instead, of course, the United States sought to be a good doctor in the South, ever producing a deformed or aborted offspring. After each debacle would begin another quest for a liberal or moderate alternative, at least among those Americans who were not purely cynical.

In 1947, Kim Kyu-sik was the odds-on favorite for this role among anti-Rhee Americans. Before he proved unreliable by flirting with the North, Army G-2 described him as follows: "Least heroic, most sound, infinitely more conciliatory than either Rhee or Kim Koo. . . . Constantly maligned by the extreme rightists, self-termed 'sacrificial goat' of US-inspired coalition efforts, Kim Kyu Sik has been the most important Korean to cooperate with the American Occupation."[70] Kim was a mild-mannered, experienced, erudite, scholarly person who had functioned in the independence movement since the early 1920s; he was not a strong nationalist, but he was capable of a principled independence in regard to American demands. But unlike Rhee, Kim Ku, or Yŏ Un-hyŏng he did not have a strong coterie of personal followers, and did not represent broad social forces. The CIA in early 1948 was correct to say that Kim and a handful of other moderates "represent perhaps the only democratic force in Korea today," but also to note that "they are not a cohesive group but a loose assemblage of splinter parties with a relatively small popular following."[71] Kim's worldly savoir faire and excellent English were qualities that endeared him to Americans, just as they estranged him from the average Korean. He was elderly and out of touch with the strong tides sweeping Korea; when he went to P'yŏngyang he actually thought he would be able to sway the premier, Kim Tu-bong, because Kim had been his student at Chosŏn Christian College.[72]

The more he got in touch with Korean realities, the less the Americans liked him. He was impressed with what he saw in North Korea: not by Kim Tu-bong, whom he found "much too narrow-minded and doctrinaire," but by Kim Il Sung, in whom he saw "a ray of hope," since he was "a good guerrilla leader" who was popular among younger Koreans, even though Kim told Americans he thought Kim Il Sung was being "misled" by the Russians; he tried to get Hodge to understand Kim's strong nationalism. The North's industrial diligence also impressed him. In any case, his principles prevented him from supporting a separate southern government, and after that American policy never took him seriously. During the war he went to the North, voluntarily it would appear, and lived out an honorable if politically irrelevant last few years.[73]

Another pro-American moderate who labored as the South Korean Interim Government (SKIG) Civil Administrator for many months, An Chae-hong, retired from the government in June 1948. Accurately described by a reporter as a "weary and timid" man, almost "rabbit-like" in his cautiousness, An Chae-hong nonetheless told *Agence-France Press* that he could not serve the new government because it was "a creature of the extreme rightists," brought to power through youth groups "guilty of tens of thousands of acts of terrorism" who had "forced people to vote." An also ended up in the North after the war.[74]

Those moderates and liberals who were well known to Americans were often barely known to the mass of Koreans, to whom their Western learning and cultivation simply seemed alien. Leftist leaders who did move among large constituencies could not operate openly after 1947, so the U.S. conception of the political spectrum was often simply the spectrum of politicians in Seoul, all of whom knew each other. A long series on postliberation politics that ran in a Seoul newspaper in early 1950 spoke exclusively of the convoluted party politics of Seoul politicians, as if nothing else had happened since 1945, pausing only to say that the mass public scarcely noticed it at all, "hardly deigning to lift an ear to their innumerable statements and clamors." The CIA stated correctly in 1950 that "the political contest" in the ROK was "among conservative leaders and is almost entirely a struggle for power," with few issues dividing the participants. As for the population as a whole, "the regime and its policies command little positive support."[75]

It is daunting for the typical American image of North Korea to realize that many moderates chose it over the American-sponsored South. Most of Yŏ Un-hyŏng's family ended up there, with one of his daughters being prominent in the regime today. Many moderate National Assembly members cooperated with the North after Seoul was taken, as we will see. In 1948 Hong Myŏng-hŭi chose to stay in P'yŏngyang and join the regime; he had been an important figure in the South, a noncommunist whose politics were somewhere between those of Yŏ and Kim, although he associated with the latter. A CIA biography described him as a classical scholar, widely regarded as "a man of prudence and integrity" by associates in the South. His father was of the "petty nobility," perhaps in other words a *hyangban*, who committed suicide at the Japanese Annexation. In the 1920s he worked on the *Tonga ilbo* staff, the Japanese imprisoned him for anti-Japanese activities in South Chŏlla in the early 1930s, and later on he published a multivolume novel about a mythical peasant bandit in the Koryŏ period. The CIA wrongly thought that his eldest daughter had become Kim Il Sung's second wife in 1950; his descendants remain prominent in North Korea today.[76]

In seeking a moderate alternative to Rhee, Hodge actually sought to get the aged Philip Jaisohn (Sŏ Chae-p'il) to return to Korea and run for president, something that still seems hard to believe. Jaisohn had spent half a century in the United States after his early exploits in the attempted coup d'etat of 1884 and with the Independence Club in the 1890s; he went to medical school, became thoroughly Americanized, and served as a local draft board physician during World War II. He arrived at Inch'ŏn in July 1947, getting off to a bit of a bad start by telling assembled reporters that Koreans did not know how to make a simple bar of soap; how could they expect to have an independent government? He served as a personal advisor to Hodge, who sought to get him to run against Rhee in the 1948 elections. But he was already ill with the cancer that took his life shortly after his return to the United States.[77]

With the assumption of power by Rhee, the American moderate favorite became KDP leader Chang Myŏn. Chang was a well-educated man from a landed family who spoke English fluently, a devout Catholic (something of a rarity among Korean leaders), and the Korean ambassador to the United States when the war broke out. He was almost always described in American materials as intelligent, capable, reasonable, and docile, lacking in the strong nationalism that characterized so many other Koreans. As we will see, he drew the attention of high American officials to the near-collapse of the Rhee regime just before the war began; in January 1951 Muccio asked Dean Rusk to urge Chang to hurry back to head up a War Cabinet, thus "to guide the Princetonian," Muccio's moniker for Rhee. When Chang Myŏn finally guided a weak interim regime in 1960-61, it would seem that he hardly made an important move without consulting the embassy and the Seoul station chief of the CIA. He was a decent man and a sincere if weak democrat; but his relations with Americans represented a classic example of *sadae* (serving the great).[78]

The legal scholar and KDP member Yu Chin-o was another American favorite. Considered by some to be Korea's leading liberal, he wrote much of the 1948 Constitution—a document that was formally democratic, but that gave with the right hand what it took away with the left, in the form of broad loopholes through which Syngman Rhee could drive a truck (if he chose to respect the Constitution, which he rarely did). Yu, like Chang, had some unfortunate relations with the colonial administration, although neither was a prominent collaborator. He was reminiscent of Chinese Nationalist legal scholars, of whom R. H. Tawney once wrote, they were so adept and learned, so professional, that the only marvel was how little they had to do with the reality of Kuomintang rule. Yu was also capable of profound illiberalism, however, demonstrating the slim pickings Americans found in Seoul. In some advice to a team of American social scientists on "political reorientation campaigns in North and South Korea," he advised that committed communists can only be converted "by torture and severe punishment"; communism is like a religious faith, he thought, and "there is no way to prevail upon them except the above-mentioned two methods."[79]

RHEE'S LEADERSHIP

Syngman Rhee's statecraft and personality require careful study and thought because of his dominant position in the South, his contribution to the developing civil war, and the intrinsic interest of a man who, against formidable odds, moved from isolated exile in Washington, D.C., to fifteen years of political success, on his terms, at an age when most people retire. The existing literature is not much help. It is small, and most of it was written by a regime capable of outlandish hagiography, by people who were in his pay, or by American Asia-firsters for whom Korea and Rhee were abstractions, Rorschach ink-blots upon which they projected their fantasies. The regime would tell you he was always known as the Father of his country, an intrepid independence fighter; his publicists constructed an elaborate tissue of special pleading and labored mythology; Asia-firsters like Henry Luce featured his handsome face on the covers of magazines: a democrat and a Christian with the American point of view.

Then someone would actually talk to Rhee, and come away convinced of his senility; or Rhee would show his anger to Americans in private sessions by dissolving into what one of them called a "frothing drivel";[80] or he would turn up in Congress and advocate thermonuclear war, embarrassing even the China Lobby Congressmen. Rhee also had plenty of American critics, but they likewise knew very little about him, viewing him as a pint-sized Chiang Kai-shek, but at the same time accepting more of the Rhee mythology than they realized, because they had nothing else to go on. Was he a Wilsonian genius or in senile dementia, the father of Korea or another Chiang Kai-shek, Muccio's "Princetonian" or Hodge's "old bastard"?[81]

The first approximation is to say none of the above. Rhee was no more widely known in Korea before 1945 than Kim Ku, Kim Il Sung, Kim Wŏn-bong, or Kim Kyu-sik. He was a publicist for Korean independence, but remained safely distant from the Japanese for four decades. If he knew Woodrow Wilson, as he always claimed, it was probably from hailing him on a campus walk in 1911. When Americans thought he was saying his Christian prayers, he was more likely practicing calligraphy. His apparent frothing drivel and senility were useful ploys to mask his purposes or bargain with Americans. Nor was he another Chiang Kai-shek, an inapt comparison; Chiang had far more political and military experience than Rhee, had governed millions of people for decades, had a relatively independent regime that resisted the Japanese after its fashion, and was not deeply under the influence of Americans, at least not from 1927 to 1941. Rhee had political experience only in running coteries of followers, governed no one before 1945, presided over a regime populated by colonial servants, and was heavily influenced by both an official and an unofficial American presence. Nonetheless, Rhee was a formidable and effective leader. On paper he looked like a marionette. But the strings were more like hamstrings, and he could pull on them, too.

We might begin with some hard facts about what experienced Americans really thought about their erstwhile Free World ally. In small doses, Rhee came off as a handsome, warm, charming gentleman; he was a past

2. Yun Chʼi yŏng reads a eulogy at Chang Tŏk-su's funeral, December 8, 1947; Syngman Rhee and Francesca front right, Kim Sŏng-su over Rhee's left shoulder.

master of flattery and disarming, endearing use of the democratic sym-
bolism that stirs American hearts. It took a measure of experience with
Rhee to disabuse Americans of their first impressions of him. Hodge
knew him best, and by 1948 their relationship did have a certain similarity to Chinese experience: Hodge thought of Rhee about what "Vinegar
Joe" Stilwell thought of Chiang. Hodge's politics in the abstract were similar to Rhee's, he had a typical American's visceral disgust for anything
that looked like communism.[82] But he was an honest, unpretentious career military officer who, though he occupied the palatial Governor-
General's residence, moved several of his staff in with him and was well
known for hard work and plain living. Within a year of his arrival in
Korea, if not earlier, he developed a profound disgust with and distrust
of Rhee; it is the measure of his bone-hard pragmatic anticommunism
that he backed him anyway, having no alternative.

Hodge had plenty of information on Rhee's corrupt political funds, his
deals with his American coterie, his involvement in terrorism and assassination. Several times, according to Leonard Bertsch, he determined to
arrest Rhee and throw him in jail, always to stay his hand at the last minute. One time he sent a jeep screaming across Seoul to grab Rhee and jail
him, an order countermanded by military radio. He had long, emotional,
bitter sessions with Rhee where these two hard-bitten men went at each
other without restraint. As Hodge put it once, "Rhee cannot get through
his thick skull (he is aided and abetted by his wife in this) that in negotiating with me, he is negotiating with the U.S. Government." When Rhee
assumed power Hodge remarked that Rhee and Francesca ("particularly
the latter") retain "all the bitter hate fixation for me that they have ever
had." After the May 1948 elections, he had asked MacArthur to relieve
him as quickly as possible, saying he would soon be "persona non grata,"
and did not want to be around anyway when Rhee "bring[s] in his gang
of carpet baggers from the States, Hawaii, and China." Hodge wanted to
go quietly, with no fanfare, no "local political chicanery."

Syngman and Francesca, head of Korea's "Capone Gang" in Hodge's
eyes, reciprocated by telling incredulous listeners that Hodge was a communist. In letters to Oliver and others the Rhees repeated this theme,
even claiming that Hodge was supporting the *Chŏnp'yŏng* union over
Rhee's *Noch'ong* ("our rightist labor union was absolutely sidetracked").
Unlike Stilwell, Hodge did not have the experience with Asian politics to
seek to remove American support as a way to discipline Rhee; perhaps
he was more realistic than Stilwell in thinking that Washington would not
back him up.[83]

The CIA estimate of Rhee just after he assumed power said,

Rhee has devoted his whole life to the cause of an independent Korea
with the ultimate objective of personally controlling that country. In

pursuing this end he has shown few scruples about the elements which he has been willing to utilize for his personal advancement, with the important exception that he has always refused to deal with Communists. . . . Rhee's vanity has made him highly susceptible to the contrived flattery of self-seeking interests in the U.S. and Korea. His intellect is a shallow one, and his behavior is often irrational and even childish. Yet Rhee, in the final analysis, has proved himself to be a remarkably astute politician.

The conclusion of this "personality" study was prophetic: "The danger exists . . . that Rhee's inflated ego may lead him into action disastrous or at least highly embarrassing to the new Korean Government and to the interests of the U.S."

By 1950, the CIA found him "senile," strongly influenced by a small coterie of advisors, "indomitably strong-willed and obstinate" with "great powers of persuasion," possessing an "absolute and uncompromising" fear and hatred of the Soviet Union, tolerant of "collaborators with Japan in his cabinets and in key positions," a man with no understanding or patience with the idea of a legitimate opposition who "has not hesitated to use such totalitarian tactics as stringent censorship . . . police terrorism, and the use of extra-governmental agencies such as youth corps and armed 'patriotic' societies to terrorize and destroy non-Communist opposition groups and parties."[84]

Representatives of close American allies like Canada, Australia, and England were if anything more scathing than this; Kermode of the British Consulate littered his memorandums with harsh characterizations of Rhee as a dangerous fascist, or lunatic. Rhee's own letters to Robert Oliver and others show signs of clinical paranoia, terming anyone who opposed him a communist—including T. V. Soong, a capitalist who made Pak Hŭng-sik look like Little Lord Fauntleroy. Rhee terrorized his own cabinet, alternating a calm and fatherly demeanor with shrieking hysteria.

But how can one simultaneously be senile, dangerous, paranoid, obstinate, strong-willed, greatly persuasive and "remarkably astute?" Rhee was not senile and he was not crazy. Robert Oliver and others remember Rhee in the late 1950s, when he was pushing eighty-five, possessing the same mixture of calm lucidity and mercurial outbursts that had always characterized him.[85] If the CIA thought him monumentally obstinate in 1950, so did Koreans who knew him in the 1920s. Rhee had nothing but a handful of followers and a precarious dole throughout his decades of exile; an ambitious man thrown on nothing but his own resources, functioning always as a party of one, will survive and dominate by cultivating extraordinary willpower, fierce determination, and acute dissembling and acting skills. Rhee was, moreover, a Korean without a family, a clan, a web of affiliations. In a society with such strong family traditions, to be a loner is itself an act reflecting courage and determination, and Rhee was a loner in an alien land for most of his life. He married an Austrian and adopted a son, that was his family. Once he mastered his loneliness, he could be a free bird, a manipulator of others caught in the web of affiliation, an executive above the fray and vested interest. (It is remarkable that amid the vast corruption of his regime, Rhee and his wife took next to nothing for themselves.)

These qualities also, however, made him alien to Korea. Many Koreans who did not leave their country during the colonial period were absolutely appalled to have a president who spoke a strange and obsolescent Korean, who had no clear lineage or extant family line, and who had taken a foreign wife, the latter often being the greatest outrage.[86] Rhee was a strange hybrid, thoroughly Korean to Americans and thoroughly alien to many Koreans. His personality however, does seem modal for elderly Korean men of responsibility. It is quite common to witness in the same person, sometimes on the same day, ineffable charm and outrageous crudity; an icy Confucian demeanor of utter self-control and dignity at one point, giving way to a show of raging insanity or puerile inanity. This is often what it takes to maintain a patriarchy whose legitimation is purely traditional.

Rhee added to this patriarchal quality a Machiavellianism that was second nature to him, coming not from his intellect but his viscera. The CIA was right to say that Rhee's intellect was shallow; his publications and private communications, at least the ones available, betray few hints of a contemplative mind and every evidence of a calculative ambition. Time and again Rhee would cow American officials by throwing a tantrum, proclaiming that he was ready to die in the streets with his hardy youths, or commit some kind of mayhem if he did not get his way. He personified a quality that Daniel Ellsberg called the "madman theory" of the rationality of irrationality—convincing an adversary that you are capable of anything, probing at or crossing outer limits of behavior for effect and intimidation, to get the adversary to cease and desist. Richard Nixon is said to have first learned this tactic from Rhee, after a visit in which he found Rhee to have "what might be described as a conspiratorial mind, not unlike that of a Communist."[87]

Rhee was an inveterate gambler (Oliver said he could play poker with two deuces and come away with the pot[88]) with a penchant for getting his way through wild threat, an eruptive bottle of nitroglycerin who seemed always to require care in handling. The Americans tried to pin him down six ways to breakfast, to get basic controls on his behavior that would render a lesser man an abject puppet, but he never succumbed because he was willing (or appeared to be willing) to pull the whole structure down with his personal fortunes. He needed the Americans badly, but they needed him, and he knew it—for after him there was an abyss: an aged Philip Jaisohn, an ineffectual Chang Myŏn, a dangerous Kim Ku or Kim Il Sung, authentic and profoundly misjudged Koreans instead of a cranky hybrid who at least understood plain English and knew American politics.

Rhee's techniques were also used against Koreans in his cabinet and in the bureaucracy, but with less effect. A people that has survived for centuries under arbitrary rule and a perennial foreign threat will have many Syngman Rhees, just as shrewd, just as Machiavellian, just as willfull. Rhee formally dominated the administration and sought to centralize everything in his own office; most officials cringed before him and were afraid to do anything without his approval, from major decisions to daily items like the issuance of passports, which Rhee or his close associates reviewed. Rhee personally appointed most officials at the national and provincial levels, operated a highly centralized and personal spoils system, and, the CIA said, treated the prime minister like his own executive assistant.[89] But all this does not mean that everyone marched in lockstep at Rhee's order. The facade of top-down control masked a fractured regime that frequently splintered into competing clusters of power, and it is not the case that Rhee was in thorough control, even though that was his goal. He sheltered his own actions from real and presumed antagonists, and they did the same to him.

Rhee and the Americans

The important and critical influence on Rhee was a personal cabinet within a cabinet, his "kitchen cabinet" of long-time associates who were almost all either Americans, or Koreans who had spent years in the United States. After he achieved power Rhee brought several people from his "Korea Lobby" into the inner sanctum, and several of them became more influential than the ambassador, Muccio. Nowhere in the literature is this phenomenon treated with any comprehension of its significance. If one can imagine Kim Il Sung having lived in the Soviet Union for forty years, then bringing back with him a European wife and a close informal court of Russians and Russo-Koreans, most of whom spoke broken Korean, with names like Vladimir Kim and Ivan Lee, placing these people in his inner sanctum and between himself and the Soviet embassy, himself and his own cabinet, and staying mostly in their company, one would come close to Rhee's situation. The commanding heights in the Rhee regime were something very close to a foreign implant, no less important simply because the Americans were unofficial, in Rhee's pay, and often disliked by the embassy.

The CIA thought that if any group succeeded in influencing this solitary president, it was his kitchen cabinet. It tended perhaps to overemphasize the influence of Francesca Rhee, seeing her as a major and clever figure, an Austrian Empress Dowager; Rhee found it convenient to make people, especially Koreans who well know the inner-sanctum power of wives, think that she was formidable. Muccio said that she "had a great deal to say as to what non-Koreans got to see him," and did much of his paperwork. But Robert Oliver thought Rhee never paid much attention to her views, thinking she hopelessly misunderstood Korean politics. Oliver himself wrote many of Rhee's speeches, as did another long-time Rhee associate, Harold Noble; Oliver had far easier access to Rhee's office than most of his cabinet ministers or, indeed, the American embassy.[90]

Harold Noble was from an old missionary family in Korea; his father had taught Rhee at the Paejae School in the 1890s. Noble served in Army intelligence and frequently acted as a go-between in Rhee's negotiations with Hodge and with Muccio, and he personally wrote Rhee's speech delivered before the UN Command when Seoul was retaken in September 1950. Indicative of the way in which Rhee played one person off against another is that Oliver and Noble disliked each other, nor did Oliver get along with Preston Goodfellow, the most important member of Rhee's inner circle.

Another American of great effect on Rhee was Harold Lady, described in a *Chicago Daily News* account as "one of the most influential men in the South Korean Government," responsible for key trade negotiations between the ROK and Japan in 1949–1950. The ECA reported in March 1950 that "the influence of Mr. Lady appeared to carry much more weight with the President than the advice of his own Cabinet Ministers, who customarily supported the position of the [U.S.] Mission" (an interesting observation in itself). Lady often appeared in Rhee's office whenever embassy officials came in for tough negotiations.[91]

Several other American advisors came and went during the Rhee years, most of lesser importance than those above. Charles W. Dewing, for example, worked for Rhee as a consultant in the Office of Public Information in 1949; John Lasher was an advisor on "youth group affairs"; Jay Jerome Williams worked both in Washington and in Seoul as an advisor to Rhee, using the diplomatic pouch for exchanges. Several Americans usually accompanied Rhee on his provincial speaking forays; when he toured in April 1949 to popularize his "One People Principle," Williams, Oliver, and Francesca accompanied him.[92]

The presidential entourage also included Koreans and Korean-Americans who had spent long years in the United States. Rhee's accession to power was a dream come true to his old cluster of supporters in the Korean National Association. Ben Limb (Im Pyŏng-jik) was the best known of these, moving from selling *Ajinomoto* in Hawaii in the early 1940s to being Rhee's foreign minister from 1948 to 1951. He was born in 1893 into a wealthy landowning family from Puyŏ in South Ch'ungch'ŏng Province; his father had been a provincial governor. He was Rhee's long-time secretary and advisor, working with him first as a teenager in YMCA activities. He followed Rhee to the United States, studying at Mt. Herman School for Boys in Massachusetts and spending a year at Ohio State University. Rhee made him a "colonel" in the nonexistent KPG Army in 1919. He was with Rhee when he met Goodfellow and William Donovan in 1942, seeking to organize underground work in Korea. A CIA biography described him as Rhee's "alter ego," liked by most Americans but sometimes given to "ungoverned emotional outbreaks." He sometimes expressed bitterness to Americans about racial discrimination he long felt in the United States; some Korean groups regarded him as an outsider and foreigner, too.[93]

The head of the powerful Ministry of Home Affairs was Yun Ch'i-yŏng, a KDP member who had studied at Waseda University and Columbia University, described by the CIA as an "intimate associate and former personal secretary" to Rhee in Hawaii, who, during World War II, "participated actively in Japanese-sponsored commercial and war support enterprises." Yun's relative, Brig. Gen. Yun Ch'i-wang, was surgeon general of the ROK Army, and the latter's daughter was married to "Montana" Chang, another Rhee intimate whom we will hear more of later. Louise Yim (Im Yŏng-shin), a Rhee sidekick, became head of the Commerce Department, where she played a major role in dispensing vested Japanese firms and factories to Rhee supporters, and was the first cabinet member to step down under charges of corruption.[94]

Others in this category included Henry De Young, who prepared many of Rhee's official letters, whose Korean Rhee described as "inadequate"; Chang Ki-yŏng, an American citizen who was also a close Rhee associate in the United States, and who, after renouncing his U.S. citizenship, replaced Louise Yim when she lost her Commerce Department position; and Clarence Rhee (Yi Ch'ŏl-wŏn), Syngman Rhee's press secretary, who also attended the Mt. Herman School and then went to Columbia University. He was district manager of the American Cash Register office in P'yŏngyang, 1938–1943.[95]

The inexperience of Rhee and his *Kyŏngmudae* (presidential mansion) entourage in running a complex executive meant that they depended on the aid and expertise of the embassy and a host of American military and economic advisors; this does not of course mean that they necessarily got on well together. Rhee's explosive volatility led the official American presence to seek extraordinary controls on the new government, such as operational control of military and police units. The proper image here would not be the outer-limit controls on defense and resources that the United States forged in Japan, although those were present in Korea as well. Rhee could not be trusted, so there had to be close supervision, direct embargoes of means of aggression, controls on the expenditure of aid funds and currency transactions, scripting of policy documents, constant collection of intelligence on him and his government (the United States maintained several CIC, G-2, and CIA operations in Korea after the Occupation ended), even the transporting of all Korean foreign and gold reserve holdings to the American Federal Reserve after the war began and repeated hints, threats, and actual plans to remove Rhee.

It was a bizarre relationship that defies easy categorization: the American giants sought to throw a net on this Korean Lilliputian, still worried that he would get free. It was a fascinating dialectic between hand-wringing overlords and a palsied gambler, none knowing for sure what was happening today, what might happen tomorrow. Rhee could reach outside the official net to his paid Americans, or to MacArthur, or to Chiang, or to Republican Congressmen, or to allies in American intelligence, or to deeply experienced former Japanese colonialists; this was no one-way street. Yet at the same time, Rhee often seemed like a tethered hound, constantly pushing the leash to its limits until he nearly strangled.

If we move from the subjective, personal level to the objective, it is unquestionable that Rhee and his regime could never have survived without American backing. This regime was more an American creation than any in postwar Asia, eminently more so than Chiang's Nationalist government. Furthermore Rhee was willing to barter pieces of Korean sovereignty that the North has given to no one, such as operational control of his army and police, and the offer of naval and air bases to both the United States and Nationalist China before the Korean War. Like King Kojŏng, he also offered Americans key concessions of Korea's basic resources.[96] The CIA put the situation properly, from the official American perspective, when it said that "the policies of the ROK Government are conditioned and shaped by its dependence upon the U.S.;"[97] most of the time the relationship was one of shaping and cajoling rather than American domination of the situation. But, as in the Central American situations which Muccio knew so well, imperial dominance also had its place.

Muccio surmised that "Rhee really trusted no one—not even his wife." But it would appear that Rhee had reason to mistrust her, since she had the habit of tipping Muccio to Rhee's actions: "She quite frequently telephoned just to tip me off that he was about to do something that she thought I should know about." A Catholic, Francesca also passed information to Muccio through the Apostolic Delegate, Father Patrick Byrne. Muccio explained this by saying she felt alone and afraid as a "white Austrian" in Korea, but he did not grasp the implications of such behavior.[98] Perhaps he would if Bess Truman had the habit of ringing up the British ambassador or the Archbishop of Canterbury to let them know when old Harry was about to go off the deep end. This is just another vignette of the American habit of treating as perfectly natural their desire to monitor Rhee's every action; after all, it was the Russians who ran the Bunraku show in Korea.

On the surface, the relations between the ROK and the United States often seemed abjectly subordinate. Korean officials fawned shamelessly on important Americans; public meetings would adopt messages to "the great leader," Harry Truman, saying things like the ROK "owes her development in the political, economic and other fields entirely to your Excellency and the people of the United States."[99] The North Koreans did the same Humble Julius routines for Stalin and the Russians. This is merely polite behavior in the Korean context; it says very little about what Koreans really think. But there is little question that Rhee and his allies did hold one American in total awe, as did many Americans: General of the Army Douglas MacArthur. MacArthur's lustrous career and his stately, patriarchal bearing deeply impressed Koreans. He had laid imperial Japan low, a conquerer who looked the part. Muccio remarked that Rhee "had a very genuine awe of MacArthur," and more interestingly, said, "The similarities and the relationships between MacArthur, Chiang Kai-shek, and Syngman Rhee, intrigued and baffled me. I think they were all of the same school. Egomaniacs, if you want to use that term."[100]

The available evidence is insufficient to grasp Rhee's relationship to MacArthur. He held a number of meetings with MacArthur from 1945 to 1950 for which no record exists, one of many gaping holes in the documentation of MacArthur's activity. MacArthur met Rhee on his return to Korea in October 1945, providing his plane, The Bataan, for his flight from Tokyo to Seoul. Hodge was in Tokyo at the time; no one knows the substance of the meetings. MacArthur met Rhee again in December 1946, when Rhee journeyed to Washington via Tokyo. MacArthur bestirred himself to make one of only two trips outside Japan between 1945 and June 1950, to speak at the inauguration of the ROK in August 1948, throwing his arm around Rhee and telling him and those nearby that if North Korea were to attack, "I would defend Korea as I would California." Since at the same time he was complaining mightily to Washington that he did not want the responsibility of defending Korea, and given his contradictory personality, it is difficult to know which statements he meant, which he did not. But Rhee met him again in Tokyo in October 1948, when MacArthur sent The Bataan to get him; there is no doubt that he both told reporters and authorized Rhee to say that he would defend the ROK as he would the United States, apparently trying to leak publicly the secret American plans to defend the ROK as long as American troops were there.

On his return Rhee told reporters of MacArthur's pledge; Alvary Gascoigne, a very reliable interpretor of MacArthur who talked with him frequently, said MacArthur told him he had authorized Rhee to make the statement, but said he did so in his capacity as CINCPAC (Commander in Chief, Pacific), which Rhee left out, thus distorting the idea "somewhat." The most important meeting between Rhee and MacArthur occured in February 1950, which the North Koreans have always cited as the time when an attack on the North was planned; we will come to that later.[101]

THE PROBLEM OF COLLABORATION

The absence during the Occupation of any serious removals of Koreans who served the Japanese meant, of course, the perpetuation of the power of a colonized elite in every walk of South Korean life. Rhee reinforced and protected pro-Japanese elements, especially in the police and the military, something he sought to camouflage with noisy bluster against the Japanese. It is not suprising that there would be bureaucratic continuity into the postcolonial era and the ROK, this is a typical pattern in most colonies. But the relatively unique and intense nature of the Japanese-Korean experience, discussed in volume 1, made the pro-Japanese issue perhaps the most important of all issues in the early postwar period; furthermore in the colonial forces of order there were Koreans who, under the American Occupation in Japan, would have been purged and prosecuted for crimes. So, this was not an idle issue, but went to the heart of what it meant for Korea to again become an independent nation.

The police were completely officered by collaborators, and the newly-formed army was not much better. Constabulary "detachments" were renamed "brigades" in 1948 and then "divisions" in May 1949, but American sources reported that there were few changes "in actual organization." Whereas the Constabulary had been used mostly for tactical interventions in bad disorders in the countryside during the Occupation, under Rhee its political powers were extended, utilizing articles 147 to 149 of the Japanese criminal code, which had provided the hated *kempei-tai* "with authority in civil matters where national security was involved." There were six brigades at the start, led mostly by officers who had served the Japanese. These would include (as of December 1948) Kim Sŏk-wŏn, First Brigade Commander; Kim Paek-il, Wŏn Yong-dŏk, Ch'ae Wŏn-gye and Yi Chun-shik; Ch'ae Pyŏng-dŏk, an enormous man known to Americans as "Fattie Chae," was overall commander.[102] Rhee promoted officers with three characteristics: slavish loyalty to him, particularly notable reputations with the Japanese, and northern Korean background; each reinforced the other, made Rhee their protector, and helped to head off coups by leaders such as Yi Pŏm-sŏk with real following in the South.[103]

As soon as Rhee's cabinet appointments were announced in August 1948, charges started flying in the National Assembly that many were pro-Japanese. Yu Chin-o, head of the Office of Legislation, was charged with promoting the doctrine of Japanese-Korean unity (*Naisen ittai*) during the war, and with advocating the abolishment of the Korean language. The vice-minister of Commerce and Industry was said to have been a secretary to the governor-general and to have informed on Korean patriots, and so on. Given the nature of the personnel in the bureaucracy, the list of charges could have been very long. But the National Assembly was also full of such people, and so when Yu Chin-o was again attacked a few days later, a voice called out to his accuser, "You were also a pro-Jap, so why don't you shut up!" Whereupon, one imagines, a stunned silence enveloped the legislature.[104]

With a daily clamor to do something about the "pro-Japs," in late August several high prosecutors and some twenty police chiefs who had served the Japanese tendered their resignations. A few days later, however, Yi Pŏm-sŏk told the chiefs to keep at their work, but to "reflect" sincerely on their colonial background—and incidentally to stop drinking in public, and extorting free meals in restaurants.[105] Although the Assembly passed an "anti-traitor" law and set up a committee to investigate and make recommendations for arrests, and several particularly treacherous secret police were incarcerated in early 1949 (Yi Chin-ha, Kim Pyŏng-gi, Yi Tae-u, and others), Rhee obstructed their prosecution, according to American embassy information. In June 1949 police invaded the investigation committee headquarters two days after another handful of collaborationist police were arrested; they assaulted and jailed the committee's guards, and British information had it that Rhee ordered the assault.[106]

By September 1949 only one of 241 people indicted as "national traitors" remained in jail; 116 were on bail, 124 were at large but subject to trial. In the same month, General Wŏn Yŏng-dok, an officer in the Japanese Army, presided over the military trial of nine captured guerrillas, all of whom were sentenced to death. By November, Muccio reported that the trials of national traitors, "begun with a fervor," had come "to a virtual end with some of the most notorious collaborators escaping scot free." He also noted that the ROK government now "seemed clearly to recognize the desirability of close economic relations" with Japan, but was moving cautiously because of lingering anti-Japanese public opinion. In

February 1951 as the war raged, the National Assembly ultimately repealed the 1948 anti-traitor law; the CIA remarked that "the Korean collaborators are now forgiven." There ended the issue, thus vindicating those wealthy collaborators who had begun bankrolling Rhee in December 1945.[107]

The blatantly Japanophile industrialist, Pak Hŭng-sik, widely thought to be the richest man in Korea, was also brought to trial. Among other charges it appeared he never paid a 10 million yen fine levied against him in 1945 for accepting a 20 million yen bonus payment from the departing Japanese—for services rendered, such as devoting his airplane parts factory near Suwŏn to the war effort. In April 1949, however, this shameless but wily entrepreneur coughed up a 1 million *wŏn* bail note and never saw the inside of a jail again. He had bankrolled Rhee from 1945 on, and was a close friend of several American officers in the Occupation.

Important bankers who had served the Japanese also continued in their positions. As General Wedemeyer had noted after meeting with Ku Yong-sŏ and Chang Pong-ho, high officers in the Bank of Korea and the Choheung Bank, these were "representatives of the general category of Korean bankers, all of whom were necessarily deeply involved in the Japanese financial system, and most of whom believe in the eventual necessity of orienting Korean commerce again into alignment with Japan." The president of the Choheung Bank, a friend of Chang's, was Kim Han-gyu, who had been a member of the Japanese Central Privy Council.[108] Thus, in the economy as well, a pro-Japanese elite was ready again to do business, the necessary complement to the American regional strategy.

Chapter Seven

THE RESISTANCE
TO THE SOUTHERN SYSTEM

The people were usually more important than the leaders. The deeper I have excavated, the more I have satisfied myself that the best was underneath, in the obscure depths. And I have realized that it is quite wrong to take these brilliant and powerful talkers, who expressed the thought of the masses, for the sole actors in the drama. They were given the impulse by others much more than they gave it to themselves. The principal actor is the people.

Michelet

IN THE IMMEDIATE aftermath of World War II, the collapse of the state apparatus left political space everywhere. Leftists succeeded in organizing all levels of the Korean administration, from the center to the periphery, from Seoul to the smallest villages. Much of this was spontaneous, proceeding outward and downward in wave-like fashion. But as time passed a descending bureacratic displacement shrank the realm of political spontaneity. When the forces of order reasserted themselves, they consolidated their power first at the center, making the life of the Seoul people's committee a brief one, then proceeding to root out the Left at successively lower levels of the state apparatus. Thus the conflict between Left and Right was located at the national level in 1945, at the provincial and county levels in 1946, and at the village level in 1947.

The autumn harvest uprisings were the last nationwide, spontaneous politics of the Left in southern Korea. As the rebellion undulated through the Kyŏngsang and Chŏlla Provinces, it punctuated a thousand agonies over the events of the year after liberation, above all the destruction of the people's committees. Based in frustration, it looked not ahead, but backward to the dashed hopes of 1945. It was met with a scourge of repression, sending the mass of participants scurrying for cover only to find none. Thus it was the Left that was the big loser in 1946, and the Right that was invigorated. Peasant mobilization became much more difficult, while colonial employees in the national police, in particular, found that the American Military Government relied on them.

1947: A YEAR OF NO SIGNIFICANCE

These events polarized Korean politics, leading eventually to a rebellion in South Chŏlla and a guerrilla movement that waxed and waned from early 1948 until the Korean War. But that was after a year of sporadic protest that played out the failures of 1946 in parodied form; a year that was central to American policy was merely redundant in Korea. Furthermore, when the Left revived mass agitation in 1948 it did so in the southwest, a region remote from the communist base in the North, separated from succor and reinforcement by mountain, ocean, and the core area of Seoul.

The repression at the end of 1946 radicalized Korean politics and led to the ascendance of the South Korean Worker's Party (*Nam Chosŏn nodong-dang*, SKWP), South Korea's first effective communist party. But leftist leaders continued to focus on political organization, strikes, and the like, rather than armed resistance. As they trooped through the streets of the cities, or tried to, their experience was rather like that of Korean student protesters in the 1970s and 1980s: their mobilization usually was preempted by police obstruction and massive arrests. Meanwhile in the countryside the contest descended to the village level, where local leftists brawled with right-wing youth groups in skirmishes that often recapitulated traditional clan and village rivalries.

Some 585 people congregated in Seoul on November 23–24, 1946, to found the Worker's Party, a year almost to the day after the last national gathering of people's committee leaders. Hŏ Hŏn and Pak Hŏn-yŏng chaired the meeting. Although most of the left-wing parties were represented, communists ran the show. Internal communist materials traced the decision to form the party to the "lessons" of the October uprisings, which were expressed in the stock phrase that "the struggle had reached a new stage," requiring "a broader mass party" to direct the course of southern politics.[1] This is about what the North said when it set up the North Korean Worker's Party (NKWP) in August 1946. The important point is that the SKWP founding marked the radicalization of politics in the South, and an attempt to organize and coordinate the Left from a central locus.

Although no accurate membership figures are available for 1947, the CIA estimated that about 10,000 cadres carried SKWP cards in 1948, and classified another 600,000 people as associated "activists"; it thought about 10 percent of the population (2 million) belonged to SKWP front organizations. This estimate came at a point after the Yŏsu rebellion when communist capabilities were thought to be "at a low level."[2] It is unlikely that the SKWP grew much after the Rhee regime took power, so it would appear that the acceleration of this rather substantial membership occurred in the eighteen months after the party was formed.

The party was always indigenous to the South, but it was more independent of northern or Soviet influence in 1947 than after the formation of the Democratic People's Republic of Korea (DPRK) government.

3. ROK police and Constabulary block a leftist demonstration in downtown Seoul, April 1947

USAMGIK intelligence got information that as many as three hundred agents were being trained in Hamhŭng in 1946 for dispatch to the South, and daily reports and rumors asserted northern or Soviet manipulation of southern communists. But in mid-1947 the G-2 had still not authenticated most of these; for example, it still did not have one proven case of illegal radio contact with the North, which was assumed to be an important mode of communication. Only vague and unreliable evidence existed on northern or Soviet provision of funding for the party, and G-2 sources did not believe that the North directed SKWP activity—instead that the two worked toward common goals.[3]

By late 1948, however, the CIA had concluded that the party was "under the direct control of Soviet agents in North Korea," and that Chinese Communist agents had "appeared in South Korea on both commercial and intelligence missions."[4] Captured documents from the southern underground tend to support the second part of this judgment; the few that we have show some Chinese Communist influence, including Maoist texts translated into Korean. To my knowledge nothing demonstrates Soviet control of the SKWP, however.

Intelligence materials support the conclusion that by mid-1948, if not earlier, the SKWP was under North Korean guidance. Intercepted instructions from the North urged members to infiltrate into "all important bureaus" of the Rhee government, secrete food and other supplies for guerrillas in the mountains, and, interestingly, to "infiltrate into the South Korean Constabulary and begin political attacks aimed at causing dissension and disorder." By late 1949 captured materials disclose that southern communists had accepted the Kim Il Sung line on numerous issues, which indicated both the eclipse of southern communist leader Pak Hŏn-yŏng and the degree of northern control.[5]

Up to the Korean War, however, it cannot be said that southern communists were mere creatures of Kim Il Sung. Pak Hŏn-yŏng and other southern leaders were in command in 1947, and thereafter a sharp internecine struggle ensued between followers of Pak and followers of Kim. The history of the guerrilla struggle, as we will see, does not suggest either North Korean direction or substantial support.

The SKWP's relation to the Soviets is more complex. Pak Hŏn-yŏng was an old-line, orthodox Marxist-Leninist without armed support: precisely the sort of communist Stalin liked to have running foreign parties, because their loyalty to and dependence on Moscow would be more secure. An important retrospective intelligence study of North Korea found that Pak was particularly admired by Soviet-Koreans; it hinted that his purge became possible only after Stalin passed from the scene.[6] On the other hand, Pak himself never gave much indication that he accepted this role, and he was often unfairly maligned as a Stalinist stooge who wanted to make Korea a Soviet republic. Internal SKWP materials betray the same meld of national communism that one finds in the North, and indeed throughout the Korean left.[7]

Regardless of its subsequent evolution, when the SKWP got started in late 1946 it was a valid extension of the southern left, self-portrayed as a product of the struggle to set up people's committees and the heir of the autumn uprisings, and basing its authenticity in the spontaneous popular support for the Left that developed after the liberation. It still got the patronage, if not the membership, of moderate leftists like Yŏ Un-hyŏng.[8] Needless to say, it still attracted the untender mercies of the Korean National Police (KNP).

In the urban areas, 1947 was a year of SKWP initiatives and KNP preemption. A full coalition of the Left announced that it would protest working conditions and union repression by holding big work stoppages on March 22, 1947. The police called out maximum force to prevent workers from striking, and proceeded to make almost three thousand arrests, many in advance of the strikes, collecting "virtually all the leftist leaders" except Yŏ and Hŏ Hŏn.[9]

The liberation anniversary had degenerated from a time of celebration to a spectacle of mass arrests. When leftists announced that mass demonstrations would be held on August 15, 1947, to head them off the police arrested several thousand people in the first week of August. Those for whom warrants were issued included the top leadership of the SKWP, the Democratic National Front (DNF), the *Chŏnp'yŏng* labor union, and the *Chŏnnong* peasant union. American officials acknowledged that the arrests were preemptive, but generally supported the action. Gen. John R. Hodge prohibited any celebrations of Liberation Day besides the official one, which was itself organized specifically as a countermeasure to leftist plans. Military Government (MG) sources thought the arrests "greatly affected the political situation," pushing the Left into "relative inactivity" through the end of 1947.[10]

Chang T'aek-sang organized the preemptive arrests, and it seems likely that he did so in an attempt to torpedo, yet again, the second U.S.-Soviet Joint Commission talks. The Soviet representative, Terenti Shtykov, railed against the repression and accused Hodge of bad faith; Hodge responded with charges that the Soviets were directing subversive activity in the South.[11] The moderate *Seoul Times* editorialized that

While the police were making efforts to arrest a great number of leftist leaders . . . several terroristic groups belonging to youth parties not only continuously attacked newspapermen, politicians, and students who were considered by them as Leftists, but they also destroyed many printing plants . . . everybody in South Korea lives in fear of terrorists.

In Taejŏn, rightists tortured six leftists on August 14 by pumping water into them, preparatory to suspending them from the ceiling; they went unpunished.[12]

Journalist Hugh Deane happened to be in Chŏnju, the provincial capital of relatively quiescent North Chŏlla Province, in mid-August. Local American officials told him that south Korea was like a watermelon (Asian variety): white on the outside, red on the inside. The "whites" ran Chŏnju. The police chief was Song Pyŏng-sŭp, "a wealthy landowner" from Puan and a member of the Korean Democratic Party. Robert Ferguson of the 96th MG Company, a veteran policeman from St. Louis, counseled chief Song "always to stick to the middle of the road," but other American officers said the KDP ran the province.

According to Ferguson, there were about twice as many police in 1947 compared to the colonial period; he found their ways repugnant. The police had a favorite torment, he said, in which they "put a gas mask on a victim and then shut the breathing tube." His explanation for this? "Orientals are accustomed to brutality such as would disgust a white man." One would have thought Ferguson an interloper in the Korean midst like Hugh Deane, instead of the responsible officer of American Military Government. On Liberation Day Chŏnju police arrested 150 alleged subversives, while American fighter planes buzzed the crowd.[13]

In late August, DNF leader Hŏ Hŏn wrote a personal letter to Hodge, saying that "all the organizations of the democratic camp have been occupied and closed by force"; he asked Hodge to safeguard him from assassination, and to "protect human rights." But things only got worse. In October, DNF and *Chŏnp'yŏng* headquarters "were a shambles," according to State Department political advisor Joseph Jacobs. "Some fire had occurred, doors, windows and furniture were smashed. . . . Rightist parties and youth groups, by contrast, work from well furnished offices, with plenty of financial and tacit Korean Government [*sic*] official backing."[14]

THE VILLAGE FIGHTING

The autumn harvest uprisings in 1946 consolidated state control in the county seats, making the seizure of power by county people's committees unlikely thereafter. At that point, most Korean administrations would have stopped; the county level was the pivot of central and local power in the old system, and penetration below it was rare. The county magistrate was a remote figure to peasants living in the villages, a potentate of the center who displayed his authority in the villages every few years, if that. Furthermore, the Korean law of avoidance had a higher velocity than in China, circulating elites through the county magistracy every few

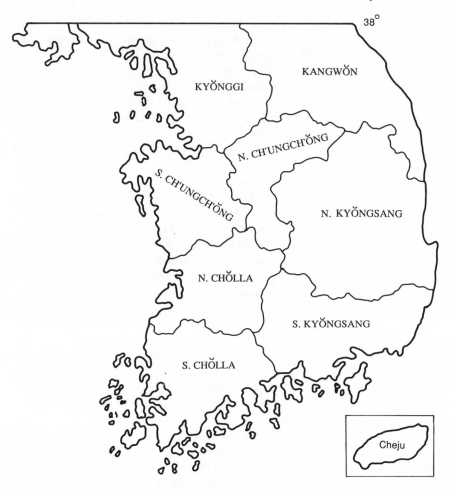

38°

KANGWŎN

KYŎNGGI

N. CH'UNGCH'ŎNG

S. CH'UNGCH'ŎNG

N. KYŎNGSANG

N. CHŎLLA

S. KYŎNGSANG

S. CHŎLLA

Cheju

Map 2. Provincial Boundaries in South Korea

months, placing high value on loyalty to the center and little on local responsiveness.

But what accrued to the center in this top-heavy system likewise debited the watchfulness and extractive capacity necessary for control at the bottom. The agrarian-bureaucratic pattern was weak at the periphery. Villages existed in isolation from central power; politics signified the exercise of informal power by village elites. Rudimentary transportation facilities meant that covering the distance from county seat to village was more time-consuming than going between the county and the provincial capital. In China the revolution failed in the cities but succeeded in the unintegrated rural areas by learning how to mobilize the ill-attended peasantry; traditional and Kuomintang politics had only jerry-rigged and mostly exploitative local stuctures with which to counter it.

In Korea the Japanese had remedied the local inadequacies of the old system with the modern apparatus of trained bureaucracy, most importantly a national police network, to push below the county level. They combined this with the traditional mechanism of landlord influence to keep the countryside quiet. The Americans continued this structure in place, but only after the disruption of a revolutionary ferment that greatly heightened the requisites of political order, necessitating a move below the county level if the threat was to be ended. Leftists understood this, of course, and given the high repressive capacity of the colonially-built state they naturally migrated downward through the bureaucratic reaches of the system in search of unattended space. After the bloodletting in the fall of 1946, this meant Korea's multitudinous and mostly isolated villages, home to the majority of the population.

In the highly mobilized postcolonial setting the national police were not sufficient to control the villages, which would have required permanent stationing of police. Thus, Syngman Rhee utilized irregular youth groups to confront the Left. The year 1947 was of little significance in postwar Korean history, but that may be because much of the class conflict ensued in the physically and bureaucratically distant villages, with much of it escaping the written record. As with other forms of rural political conflict in Korea, the village battles of 1947 followed the seasons: starting in the spring and ending in the late autumn, and reaching their maximal force in the summer months.

At first, 1947 promised to continue the 1946 pattern, with urban conflict that would subsequently spread to the rural areas. On the anniversary of the March 1, 1919, uprising, police fired on a crowd of eight thousand in Pusan and killed five people; in the third week of March an attempt at a general strike led to thousands of arrests in the major cities.[15] But there was no rural corollary to these events, as there had been in 1946.

Instead the pattern of 1947 is first instanced in late May, when "a totally leftist village" near Chŏngju booted seven members of the Northwest Youth (NWY) who had arrived on an "enlightenment" mission. For the next six months reports of village fighting filled police and intelligence reports. Roy Roberts of the Associated Press wrote in August that USAMGIK G-2 got an average of five KNP reports a day, "telling of fights in villages, fights between villages, beatings of rightists, beatings of leftists, burning of granaries, attacks on village officials, attacks on police, stoning of political meetings."[16]

The Left showed particular strength in the belt of counties leading west from Pusan; several incidents involving crowds of more than one thousand people were reported in this region in early July. The police even requested the intervention of American tactical troops in an incident in Sach'ŏn, although for reasons that are unclear the Americans stayed out of the fray. Most incidents involved conflicts with members of right-wing youth organizations; leftists called for power to return to the people's committees, so strong in this region.[17]

The empirical accounts are much too numerous to recapitulate here, but we can get a bit of their flavor. Here is an example of how the Northwest Youth acted:

> A roving band of 37 rightist-terrorist NWY Association members, armed with clubs, two short swords and three pistols . . . attacked and beat several villagers in Chinjan myun . . . one man was seriously wounded and three other young men were injured. In Hakka ri the group attacked the village master's home and stole 3 kwan of potatoes. They also took down the signboard over the Chosun Democratic Youth Alliance headquarters and broke the village bell. Leftists complain about police turning [their] backs.[18]

In South Kyŏngsang Province in mid-July, three hundred leftist youths attacked an office of the *Kwangbok* Youth in Changsŏngp'o; on Kŏje Island members of the NWY destroyed the fishing equipment of some leftists, and one hundred of the latter beat them up in response; in a town near Yŏngdŏk in North Kyŏngsang, some three hundred leftists staged antipolice and anti–grain collection demonstrations on July 15. "After being ordered for the third time to disperse, the excited mob attacked the police with Japanese swords, bamboo spears, clubs and shovels. Police fired thirty-two rounds into the mob, killing three rioters outright. . . ." Two days later police also fired into a crowd of one thousand leftists gathered just northeast of Kwangju in Sinan village, killing one. Two days after that, one hundred peasants in Sinan attacked a police box, seeking to free arrested prisoners from the previous demonstration.[19]

On July 24, four hundred leftist and rightist youths battled through the strongly leftist town of Kangnŭng; on July 27 in Hadong, police fired on a group of three hundred gathered to hear leftist appeals for land reform, killing two, and in Okch'ŏn, a town southwest of Taejŏn, five thousand peasants marched on a police station with clubs and spears, prompting the police to open fire and kill four of them. Peasants stole grain collection records in a town near Masan, and some seven hundred peasants assaulted county officials and police who were collecting grain near Kunsan. On an island off Mokp'o, three hundred peasants beat police and *myŏn* (township) officials who were enforcing the grain collection program.[20]

In early August Counter-Intelligence Agency (CIC) agents were able to rescue a number of leftists who were being tortured at NWY offices in various parts of the country. In a village west of Taejŏn, two hundred rightists surrounded a leftist village, searched many houses and beat many of the occupants; eight of the latter were subsequently reported near death. On August 5 some one thousand peasants gathered in Anŭi, in South Kyŏngsang Province near the Chŏlla border; they demonstrated against the intrusion of one hundred members of a rightist organization. Police fired on this crowd, too, wounding four people. Just southwest of Kwangju, villagers beat *myŏn* officials and police seeking to collect grain; a few days later a mob of one thousand "irate" peasants carrying spears, clubs, and farm implements atacked a police station in Taesang, a village in South Kyŏngsang; police fired on them, killing ten.[21]

In another small village near Taejŏn, on August 9 peasants corralled twenty-nine NWY members who had sought to reorient the villagers; police intervened and killed three peasants, and then escorted the NWY people, termed "terrorists," out of town. On August 15, village clashes were reported throughout South Kyŏngsang and South Chŏlla. In one such incident, near Kosŏng in South Kyŏngsang, fully four thousand peasant union members gathered to assault local police. Two peasants died in this clash. Peasants demonstrated against grain collections on Kŏje Island, and reports of pitched battles between police and leftists came in from Cheju Island.[22]

A relatively extended account of one of these battles, dated August 19 from a small town near Masan, can be considered representative. Some one thousand peasants gathered to hear officials talk about the grain collection program, and then

> became hostile and started stoning the speechmakers. The police present were forced to fire into the mob, to give the township officials a chance to retreat across the rice fields. The retreating policemen passed a police box, and stopped long enough to secure additional rifles and ammunition. The mob overran the police box, seized documents and demolished the box completely. They then split into two parts, one part erecting road blocks, and the other destroying telephone communications.

Soon, police reinforcements arrived from Masan and T'ongyŏng; they fired into the mob, dispersing it and leaving four peasants dead.[23]

In September there were numerous accounts of village fighting between leftists and members of rightist youth groups, most often the Northwest Youth. Typically elements of the latter group would enter a left-wing village, seek out its leaders to deliver a good beating, which would then be followed by peasant attacks on the invaders. Sometimes the incidents looked like simple shakedowns. On August 4, members of Rhee's National Society for the Rapid Realization of Korean Independence (NSRRKI) youth group came through Samgil village, near Chŏnju, demanding five hundred *wŏn* per family. Villagers resisted, whereupon the youths looted several homes, beating up women as they went along. "Now all doors in the village bear the [youth group] sign. . . . Nominally, all are members."²⁴

The police and intelligence records from the summer of 1947 read like unceasing journals of village anarchy, with countless little struggles that recapitulated in microcosm the cleavages that tore Korea apart in these years. Peasant grievances remained what they had been earlier: hatred of landlordism and tenancy, and the official matrix of bureaucrat, grain collecter, and policeman that put political muscle behind this agrarian system. In the summer the specific issues were the harsh methods of collecting summer grain, mentioned over and over again in the records, and the political attempt by the Right to organize irregulars and auxiliaries to control villages. In this period it is very rare to see rightists numbered in more than a few tens; leftists are usually in the hundreds or thousands. Yet official accounts often lay the blame for initiating incidents on rightists.²⁵ Why?

The answer is that the Right, meaning mainly Syngman Rhee and his friends in the police, sent members of youth groups—mostly paramilitary political activists, the majority from north Korea—into towns and villages known to have strong left-wing sympathies, seeking to reorient them. This was a general policy begun in the summer of 1946, but it began to achieve success in 1947, when the Right for the first time achieved formidable organization through a number of youth groups. They were vigilantes, police deputies in effect if not in name, seeking to compete with the Left for mass loyalties in the streets and villages. They did not have great numbers compared to the leftist organizations, but they were markedly swelled by the influx of refugee families from the North, bearing deep grievances against communism. It often resembled the *squadrismo* of rural Italy in the 1920s, when Mussolini carved a name for himself; recent research has demonstrated the importance to fascist movements of a grassroots substitution of fascist for traditional or communist leadership.²⁶

This stirred chaos in the villages, and many deaths, but it should be marked as an early success in what became a standard feature of South Korean politics thereafter: the mobilization of a powerful politics of the Right, through ubiquitous assemblage of plainclothesmen, irregular youths, strong-arm squads, and ordinary thugs. It became an effective style of politics, giving the lie to the idea that Korea always produces weakness and factionalism. For the first time, the Right competed with the Left for mass sympathies.

These irregulars were meant to be the village counterparts of underground people's committees and labor party cells. Initially the youths seem to have come largely from without and were merely predatory, but by the time of the Korean War most villages had a protective cordon of rightist riflemen, recruited locally, reasonably well organized, and capable of controlling the situation as long as they had the backing of the national police. One American survey team described the village fighters-cum-sentinels as "compulsory, government-directed organizations for male youth so common in totalitarian countries," but a better comparison would be the protective/predatory pattern of rural conflict that E. J. Hobsbawm found in Italy and Elizabeth Perry found in China.[27]

The timing of the summer anarchy, however, was accounted for by the grain collection program, bringing peasant grievances over the land system to a fever pitch. By the end of July, only 12 percent of the summer grain harvest quota had been collected—except for peasants on land still owned by the New Korea Company, which had secured compliance by threatening tenants with eviction. The National Food Administration reported that big landlords had succeeded in avoiding heavy grain collection quotas, because local officials "were reluctant to assign proper quotas to the rich, influential farmers." This, of course, led to proportionately larger exactions from small peasants: "In some instances practically the entire amount [quota] of rice was collected from small farmers." Another source of grievance was the privatization of the rationing system. Local officials would appoint favored individuals to run state ration stores, with "political considerations" usually being paramount. Sizeable "ghost" populations on the ration rolls and severe regional imbalances in the amounts of grain rationed would then emerge, with many peasants getting little or nothing. If rice collections were poor in a given region, rations would also be lowered accordingly, adding insult to injury for small peasants.[28]

For their part, leftists acknowledged that it was easier to organize at the village level because of the absence of potent bureaucracy.[29] It was considerably safer; the police didn't show up often, and when they did, you could run for the hills. But a safe haven in an isolated village is a far cry from a revolutionary movement. By the summer of 1947 many leftists were taking refuge in the villages, rather than knitting them together. Village isolation was both their protection and their undoing, as attempts to go beyond the villages met with effective repression. Whereas the substantial rural unrest in 1946 spread in undulating waves as one village or region nudged another into action, a billiard-ball pattern, a year later organizers were mostly left with the immobile billiard balls. Marx's famous metaphor of encapsulated peasants as potatoes in a sack would be just as apt. In either case the isolated village begat no community of interest that could be sustained as politics.

The involuted character of Korean villages often merged traditional and communist leadership. Korean peasants were householders in their work, and in their politics: the family was the smallest unit, not the individual. An elder who moved leftward would bring along the whole family, or clan. Many villages were dominated by one clan. If the leading family wanted a redistribution of landholding, typically the rest of the village would follow, creating what the authorities called a communist village. The police thus practiced a type of guilt-by-association in which one leftist in a family could subject all relatives to surveillance. However repellent the technique (it is standard operating procedure in both Korean states to this day), it is effective.

Korea also has many two-clan villages, in which one group may be dominant and the other disadvantaged for centuries. Dominant clans tended to be "rightist," and therefore something would have to happen to disrupt clan rule and provide space for the disadvantaged clan to take power—usually in the guise of "the left." That is, being "leftist" in such villages often merely marked membership in a disadvantaged clan. Such turning of the tables happened in the year after liberation, and during the North Korean occupation in 1950. In one well-studied example, the SKWP leader in a village came from the only family not belonging to the dominant group; instead his family was "the hereditary servitor of the clan," made up of former slaves and "base" people (*ch'ŏnmin*).[30] By 1947 traditional clan dominance in two-clan villages had solidified or been restored; thus one got a pock-marked pattern of "leftist" villages here, "rightist" villages there—sometimes just next door, as the CIA noted.[31] And "class conflict" often took the traditional Korean form of neighboring villages gathering to fling rocks at each other, the Kims against the Paks instead of the Hatfields and the McCoys.

The village battles mirrored the staying power of the Left in regions of previous people's committee strength. A CIC survey in September 1947 found that "an underground People's Committee government exists in certain parts of south Korea," with strength in the Chŏlla and Kyŏngsang Provinces, and in towns along the upper East coast (Samch'ŏk, Kangnŭng, Chumunjin, etc.).[32] The most violent and sustained strife in 1947 occurred in the region east of Pusan; after that South Chŏlla was the strongest area. A survey team sent to South Chŏlla in July termed it "perhaps the most Leftist area in South Korea"; it estimated that 15 to 20 percent of the communities visited "were openly hostile to the Americans. Leftist activity all over was evident."[33]

In North Kyŏngsang, which had fewer disorders in 1947, the G-2 nonetheless cited "a smoldering situation," with the province judged "extreme left"; provincial officials were "of the opposite faction." "The left remains extremely well organized," but lacked leadership because of the "purge" after the autumn uprisings in 1946. The leftist Women's Alliance was still quite active, in contrast to rightist women—"who appear reluctant to take an active part in politics" (whereas "no such inhibitions deter leftist women"). The police were counteracting the left's dominance by using the Northwest and *Kwangbok* youth groups, in seeking "the complete suppression of the left, in spite of its widespread organization."[34]

In North Chŏlla, by contrast, not a strong people's committee province after the initial ferment of liberation, an extensive American survey of sixty villages between Chŏnju and Kunsan in late August determined that "rightist groups completely dominated the political activity of the area," and rightist youths groups "were practically the only organizations with strength." Although there were several of these, they did not compete: one group "would completely dominate one area"; in adjacent areas, a different rightist group would dominate. Of course, "the relationship between the youth groups and the police and local officials was extremely close."[35]

THE CHEJU INSURGENCY

During a spell of lovely, warm, clear weather in June 1972, I flew on an old plane from Kwangju to Cheju Island. As we left Kwangju, the stewardess required everyone to close their window shutters for "security reasons," even though we were as far from North Korea as one could get and still be on the peninsula. Soon we touched down on a small landing strip, sprouting from a barren field. I walked around Cheju City, a small and somnolent place washed with pastels and hot sunlight. I then took a small bus south across the island to the port town of Sŏgwip'o, skirting the volcano called Hallasan that left the island with its ubiquitous black rock, casting a beautiful yet foreboding aspect, as if the island had the power and the secrets of a shiny obsydian stone. Blaring from the summit of the mountain were giant red letters: *sŭnggong*, "down with communism." The interior of the island lacked the thick settlement usually found in Korea.

I hopped on a local bus that went round the circumference, touching most of the towns and villages and making the circuit in a few hours time. Most of the population lived near the ocean, in traditional homes lashed by persistent winds cut only by barriers of carefully placed black stone, walls that nevertheless had an anarchic quality that one would never see, say, in Japan. By the road dark-skinned women in blue muslin trudged

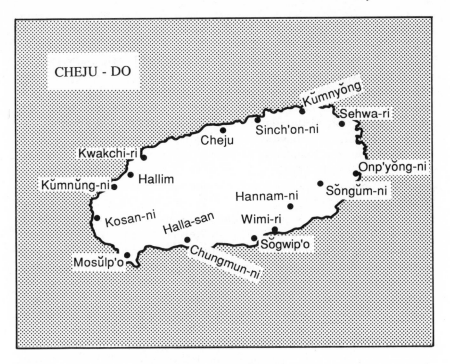

Map 3. Cheju Island

along, their faces grizzled by the hot sun, their backs bent under weighty loads. Little kids rubbed the hair on my arms in wonder, or peered into my hazel eyes and asked if I could see out of them. I bit into a hard candy and pulled a filling out of a tooth.

There was not much to see on Cheju, apart from the physical aura of the island. The state was busy turning it into a tourist "paradise," with inns for newlyweds, casinos for the rich, and whorehouses for American and Japanese businessmen. Indeed, the Cheju I was interested in was long gone, gone with the multitude who died, gone with the tens of thousands who fled to Japan, or muted in the bitter stares of the remnant older generation.

BEFORE 1950 no place suffered the political conflicts of liberated Korea like Cheju. During the Korean War no place was more quiescent. But then no place so deserved serenity. Cheju had its war earlier, a war over the people's committees that was a harbinger of the conflict to come, and that best expressed its civil and revolutionary character. Cheju is a magnifying glass, a microscope on the politics of postwar Korea, for in no place else were the issues so clear and the international influences so tangential as in the peasant war on this windswept, haunted, magnificent island.

The effective political leadership on Cheju until early 1948 was provided by strong people's committees that first emerged in August 1945. The American Occupation preferred to ignore Cheju rather than do much about the committees; it appointed a formal mainland leadership but let the people of the island run their own affairs. The result was an entrenched left-wing, having no important ties to the North and few to the SKWP on the mainland. In early 1948 as Rhee and his American supporters moved to institute his power in a separate southern regime, the Cheju people responded with a strong guerrilla insurgency that soon tore the island apart.

Before Rhee came to power, silenced his officials, and blamed the rebellion on alien communist agitators, Koreans in the Military Government attributed the origins of the insurgency to the tenure of the Cheju committees and subsequent police terrorism. An official investigation by USAMGIK Judge Yang Wŏn-il conducted in June 1948 found that "the People's Committee of Cheju Island, which was formed after the Liberation ... has exercised its power as a de facto government." He also found "the police have failed to win the hearts of the people by treating them cruelly." A Seoul prosecutor, Wŏn T'aek-yun, said the troubles began through official incompetence, not "leftist agitation." Lt. Col. Kim Ik-yŏl, commander of Constabulary units on the island when the rebellion began, said that the blame "should be laid entirely at the door of the police force."

Hodge told a group of American Congressmen in October 1947 that Cheju was "a truly communal area that is peacefully controlled by the People's Committee without much Comintern influence." Shortly thereafter a USAMGIK investigation estimated that "approximately two-thirds of the populace" on the island were "moderate leftist" in their opinions. The chairman of leftist organization, a former Cheju governor named Pak, was "not a Communist and [was] very pro-American." The people were deeply separatist and did not like mainlanders; their wish was to be left alone.

The survey determined, however, that Cheju had been subjected to a campaign of official terrorism in recent months. According to CIC information, the current governor, Yu Hae-jin, was an "extreme rightist," a mainlander with connections to the *Kwangbok* and *Taedong* youth groups; he was "ruthless and dictatorial in his dealing with opposing political parties." He thought anyone who did not support Rhee's NSRRKI or Kim Sŏng-su's KDP was "automatically leftist"; for months in 1947 he had sought to prevent "any meeting by any party except those he definitely approves."

Governor Yu had filled national police units on the island with mainlanders and north Koreans, who worked together with "ultra rightist party terrorists." Some 365 prisoners were in the Cheju city jail in late 1947; an American investigator witnessed thirty-five of them crowded into a ten-by-twelve-foot cell. "Direct control of food rationing" had also been placed in the hands of "politicians" responsive to Yu, who operated out of *myŏn* (township) offices. Unauthorized grain collections had been five times as high as official ones in 1947.

When Americans interviewed Governor Yu in February 1948, he acknowledged that he had utilized "extreme rightist power" to reorient the Cheju people, "the large majority" of whom were leftist. He justified this by saying that "there was no middle line" in Island politics; one supported either the Left or the Right. He said the police controlled all political meetings, and would not allow the "extreme leftists" to meet. Although the author of the survey called for Governor Yu's dismissal, Gen. William F. Dean decided in late March not to do it.[36]

After a March 1, 1948, demonstration against the separate elections on the mainland, the police arrested 2,500 young people; islanders soon fished the dead body of one of them out of a river: he had been tortured to death. This, Colonel Kim thought, was the incident that provoked the original rioting on April 3 that subsequently marked the start of the insurgency. We should add that his report goes a long way toward explaining the Yŏsu Rebellion, when Constabulary elements mutinied rather than fight the guerrillas on Cheju.[37]

Perhaps the affair that most inflamed the island population was the unleashing of the Northwest Youth to reorient leftists. In late 1947 the CIC had "warned" the NWY about their "widespread campaign of terrorism" on Cheju. Under the American command, these same youths joined the police and Constabulary in the Cheju guerrilla suppression campaigns. A special Korean press survey put it this way in June 1948:

> Since the coming of a youth organization, whose members are young men from Northwest Korea, the feeling between the [island] inhabitants and those from the mainland has been growing tense. . . . They may have been inspired by the Communists. Yet, how shall we understand how over 30,000 men have roused themselves to action in defiance of gun and sword. Without cause, there can be no action.

The Northwest Youth was said to have "exercised police power more than the police itself and their cruel behavior has invited the deep resentment of the inhabitants."[38]

The April 3 rebellion occured mostly along the north coast, with attacks on eleven police stations and various other incidents—roads and bridges destroyed, telephone wires cut. The demonstrators denounced the separate elections and called for unification with the North. Three rebels died, as did four police and twelve rightists. When news of the rebellion spread to the mainland, signal fires were lit in the hills near the port of Mokp'o, and demonstrators came out to shout huzzahs for "the Korean People's Republic."

About fifty more deaths occurred by the end of April, in attacks on police and "rightists" (most of the latter were youth group members), whereupon Constabulary units joined police in organized operations against what were now termed "guerrillas." Dead policemen were found run through with spears, hung by their heels, or decapitated. In May as the election proceeded on the mainland, the rebellion spread to the west coast of the island, with some thirty-five police and rightists dead by May 15; the next day police began rounding up civilians, taking 169 prisoners in two villages thought to have assisted the guerrillas. No election could be conducted on the island. By the end of May the violence had left only the eastern coast untouched; Constabulary units swept the mountains from east to west.[39]

A month later an American colonel, Rothwell H. Brown, reported that Korean and American military units had interrogated fully four thousand inhabitants of Cheju, determining that a "People's Democratic Army" had been formed in April, composed of two regiments of guerrillas; its strength was estimated at four thousand officers and men, although less then one-tenth had firearms. The remainder carried swords, spears, and farm implements. In other words this was a hastily-assembled peasant army. Interrogators also found evidence that the SKWP had infiltrated "not over six trained agitators and organizers" from the mainland, and none from north Korea; with some five hundred to seven hundred allies on the island, they had established cells in most towns and villages. Sixty to seventy thousand islanders had joined the party, Brown asserted, although it seems much more likely that such figures refer to longstanding membership in people's committees and mass organizations. "They were for the main part, ignorant, uneducated farmers and fishermen whose livelihood had been profoundly disturbed by the war and the post-war difficulties."[40]

The North Koreans subsequently said that the rebellion had been led by Yi Tŏk-ku, Kim Sam-dal, and Kang Kyu-ch'an, who touched it off at the Worker's Party direction. This may be true, or it may indicate that the North Koreans sought later to take credit for the events. In any case outside leadership was far less important than the revolutionary conditions on the island. Yi Tŏk-ku was indeed the commander of the rebels; he had been born in Shinch'on village on the island in 1924 into a family of poor fishermen-peasants. He subsequently went to Osaka as a child laborer, as did his brother and his sister. He returned to Sinch'on just after the liberation, and became a Worker's Party activist in Choch'ŏn township. He was a thus good example of our profile of Korean radicals. He was arrested and tortured for three months in 1947, and thereafter began organizing guerrillas.[41]

The guerrillas generally were known as the *inmin-gun* or People's Army, estimated to be three to four thousand strong. But they were not centrally commanded and operated in mobile units (*kidong pudae*) eighty or a hundred strong that often had little connection with other rebels. This, of course, was one of the elements that made the movement hard to suppress. An account of one unit of eighty men and women pictured them housed in a campsite in the hills of Hallasan, in eight round huts topped by pyramidal thatched roofs, with one guard tower protecting them; reveille was at 6:00 A.M., followed by an hour of physical training, a breakfast of millet, and political indoctrination. CIC elements found no evidence of North Korean personnel or equipment.[42]

The Japanese had left a honeycomb of caves, tunnels, and defensive bunkers on the island, constructed when Cheju was thought to be an important redoubt in the never-to-be-fought battle for the Northeast Asian mainland. Caches of small arms were also left behind, which the guerrillas utilized. Rebels hid in these same emplacements, striking from mountains that commanded the coastal road and low-lying villages. The island was not heavily forested, but tall grass easily hid guerillas. Mountain roads and trails were often impassable, or easily blocked; steep ravines and gullies made the movement of troops difficult. Food came from sympathetic islanders in an elaborate supply system that proved difficult to eradicate. By early June, most villages in the interior were controlled by the guerrillas; roads and bridges were destroyed throughout the island.[43]

Cheju, as we saw in volume 1, had a comparatively low rate of tenancy; most peasants owned their own land, and even though the soil was not particularly productive it was a stable area. Koreans often said that "feudalism" had never developed on the island. Income distribution was relatively equal. Peasants grew sweet potatoes, millet, and just a bit of rice; women collected seaweed and shellfish, and there was a substantial fishing industry. The Japanese had far less difficulty with the island than, say, South Chŏlla. But during World War II, an enormous percentage of the population had been mobilized for labor in Japan and for the war effort. Cheju women bulked larger in the population than males, and were particular objects of the most repulsive form of mobilization, forced prostitution as "comfort girls" for the Japanese Army. Population traffic between Cheju and Japan was very high in the 1930s and 1940s. (In 1948 the population of the island was about 250,000.[44])

The National Police refused to admit any responsibility for the eruption of the violence, blaming agitators from North Korea for the trouble.

They were able to stir up the population because "the learned and wealthy" had the habit of removing to the mainland, leaving "only the ignorant" on Cheju. It was necessary to appoint officials from the mainland, the police said, because local people were all interrelated and would not work "strongly and resolutely" in dealing with unrest. The KNP superintendent recommended that "patriotic young men's associations" be promoted, and the institution of "assembly villages" to drain the rural population away from the guerrillas.[45]

In his report Colonel Brown found that two successive regimental commanders of the Constabulary had refused to work with the police, had negotiated with the rebel leadership, and had adopted "stalling tactics where vigorous action was required." The rebellion had already led to "the complete breakdown of all civil government functions." People on the island were panicked by the violence, but also would not yield to interrogators: "blood ties which link most of the families on the Island . . . make it extremely difficult to obtain information."

On May 22, 1948, Colonel Brown adopted the following procedures to "break up" the revolt:

Police were assigned definite missions to protect all coastal villages [from guerrillas]; to arrest rioters carrying arms, and to stop killing and terrorizing innocent citizens.

The Constabulary was assigned the definite mission of breaking up all elements of the People's Democratic Army . . . in the interior of the Island.

He also ordered widespread, continuing interrogation of all those arrested, and efforts to prevent supplies from reaching the guerrillas. Subsequently, he anticipated a long-range program "to offer positive proof of the evils of Communism," and to "show that the American way offers positive hope" for the Islanders. From May 28 to the end of July, more than three thousand islanders were arrested. Other evidence demonstrated active American involvement in attempting to suppress the rebellion: daily tutoring of counterinsurgent forces, interrogating prisoners, and using American spotter planes to ferret out guerrillas. One newspaper reported that American troops intervened in the Cheju conflict in at least one instance in late April, and a group of Korean journalists charged in June that Japanese officers and soldiers had secretly been brought back to the island to help in suppressing the rebellion.[46]

Bad weather and impossible road conditions during the rainy season kept the Constabulary confined to the Island's perimeter in July and August, and the rebels mounted few operations. Col. Kim Yong-ju brought three thousand soldiers in the 11th Regiment back to the mainland in early August, and told reporters that "almost all villages" were vacant, residents having fled either to the protection of guerrillas in the interior, or to the coast. He implied that far more had gone into the mountains. "The so-called 'mountain man' is a farmer by day, rioter by night," the Cheju Constabulary commander said; "frustrated by not knowing the identity of these elusive men, the police in some cases carried out indiscriminate warfare against entire villages." When the Constabulary refused to adopt such tactics, the police called them communists.[47]

In late August the trouble started again, and a number of police died in mid-September. Attacks on police and rightist homes and organizations rose markedly during the Yŏsu Rebellion in October. By the end of 1948, the KNP had recorded 102 battles, more than 5,000 combatants on both sides, nearly 6,000 islanders in custody, and a claimed total of 422 dead insurgents. But Americans thought the total casualty figure was over 5,000 by December 1948, according to a "thoroughly reliable unofficial source." By that point it seemed as if "the main power" of the guerrillas had been broken. Yi Pŏm-sŏk attributed the successes to the regrouping of villagers in coastal towns, widespread defoliation of trees and bushes, and a so-called *pogap* system of joint community responsibility—which consisted of holding entire villages responsible for the transgressions of individuals within. The 9th Regiment of the Constabulary had gotten control of several points in the highlands, and had herded village people toward the coasts, which enabled them to starve out guerrillas and push them out of their mountain redoubts. Naval ships had completely blockaded the island, making resupply of guerrillas from the mainland impossible.[48] A Korean Military Advisory Group (KMAG) account in late 1948 cited "considerable village burning" by the suppression command; three new Constabulary batallions were being recruited, "mainly from Northwest Youth." Islanders were now giving information on the guerrillas—apparently because their homes would be burned if they did not.[49]

The proclamations of success proved premature. A typical winter lull set in, followed in March and April 1949 by the high-water mark of the Cheju insurgency, with Americans reporting the situation as "if possible, worse than before." In March guerrillas "roved at will throughout the island's center," with only "short strips of coastline" safe for "non-Communists." More than 70 percent of the island's villages had been burned, and tens of thousands of refugees packed the coastline. In April it was worse. "Chejoo [*sic*] Island was virtually overrun early in the month by rebels operating from the central mountain peak . . . rebel sympathizers numbering possibly 15,000, sparked by a trained core of 150 to 600 fighters, controlled most of the island. A third of the population had crowded into Chejoo town, and 65,000 were homeless and without food."[50] By this time twenty thousand homes on the island had been destroyed, and one-third of the population (about one hundred thousand) was concentrated in protected villages along the coast. Peasants were only allowed to cultivate fields near perimeter villages, owing to "chronic insecurity" in the interior and the fear that they would aid the insurgents.[51]

In March 1949 four Republic of Korea Army (ROKA) batallions mounted a big suppression campaign and succeeded in driving the rebels back into the mountains. About four hundred guerrillas were said to have been killed in March and April and more than two thousand captured; an amnesty program got another 5,404 to surrender. By the end of April, Everett Drumwright reported that "the all-out guerrilla extermination campaign . . . came to a virtual end in April with order restored and most rebels and sympathizers killed, captured, or converted." Muccio told Washington that "the job is about done." Shortly it was possible to hold a special election, thus finally to send a Cheju Islander to the National Assembly; none other than Chang T'aek-sang arrived to run for a seat.[52]

By August 1949 it was apparent that the insurgency had effectively ended. The rebel leader Yi Tŏk-ku was finally killed. Few if any guerrilla incidents occurred between June and the late fall of 1949, when there were some isolated skirmishes. Just before the war began in June 1950, an embassy survey found the island peaceful, with no more than a handful of guerrillas. It was the peace of a political graveyard.

The people of the island bore the worst of the Cheju violence. American sources thought that 15,000 to 20,000 thousand islanders died, but the ROK official figure was 27,719. The North said that more than 30,000 islanders had been "butchered" in the suppression. The governor of Cheju, however, privately told American intelligence that 60,000 had died, and as many as 40,000 had fled to Japan; officially 39,285 homes had been demolished, but the governor thought "most of the houses on the hills" were gone: of 400 villages, only 170 remained. In other words one in every five or six islanders had perished, and more than half the villages were destroyed.[53]

Over a six-month period in 1949, 2,421 guerrillas had been killed and 4,630 captured, according to KMAG sources; but only 230 rifles were recovered, indicating that the figures included many island peasants.[54] Most Cheju islanders have appalling atrocity stories to tell, if one can get them to talk. A Korean who comes from one of the few wealthy families on the island, now living in the United States, related to me an incident that he had witnessed in 1949 in which thirty or forty guerrilla suspects were roped together and placed on a barge, dragged offshore, and then shoved into the ocean. He thought that this was not an isolated case. Merrill documented two atrocities, one in which ninety-seven men, women, and children were massacred at Ora village, near Cheju City, and another in which American advisors stumbled upon right-wing youths slaughtering seventy-six villagers with bamboo spears at Todu-ri.[55]

The Northwest Youth now ran Cheju and continued "to behave in a very arbitrary and cruel manner" toward the islanders; "the fact that the Chief of Police was a member of this organization made matters even worse." By the end of 1949, three hundred of the Northwest Youth had joined the island police, and two hundred were in business or local government: "the majority have become rich and are the favored merchants." The senior military commander and the vice-governor were also from north Korea. The NWY controlled the newspapers, which "print only what they desire." Of course, "the rich men of the island" were once again influential, too, "despite the fact that governmental control has changed three times." About three hundred "emaciated" guerrillas remained in the Cheju city jail, and another two hundred were thought to be still on the loose, but inactive. Peasants and fishermen had to have daily police passes to work the fields or the ocean.[56]

During the warfare at the Pusan perimeter in the summer of 1950, an American survey reported that police had collected radios from the entire island population, so they could not find out about the North Korean progress on the mainland; the only telephone network was controlled by the police, and would be the main means of communication should the North Koreans seek to invade the island. A "subversive potential" still existed on Cheju, because of "an estimated 50,000 relatives of persons killed as Communist sympathizers in the rebellion." Fully 27,000 of the islanders had been enrolled in the National Guidance Alliance, an organization for leftist converts run by the state. Only three guerrilla incidents had been reported since the war began. In 1954 an observer of Cheju wrote, "village guards man watchtowers atop stone walls; some villages have dug wide moats outside the walls and filled them with brambles, to keep bandits out."[57]

THE YŎSU REBELLION

As the Cheju insurgency progressed, an event occurred that got much more attention, indeed international coverage: a rebellion at the port city of Yŏsu that soon spread to other counties in South Chŏlla and South Kyŏngsang, and that for a time seemed to threaten the foundations of the fledgling Republic. The proximate cause of the uprising was the refusal on October 19 of elements of the 14th and 6th Regiments of the ROK Army to embark for a counterinsurgency mission on Cheju, which in turn reflected the deeper problem that the Army, based on the Constabulary, had within it disparate political tendencies, unlike the National Police, including leftist elements that traced their origin back to the at-

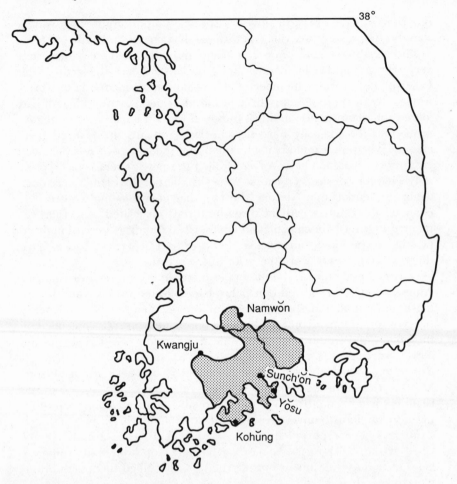

38°

Namwŏn

Kwangju

Sunch'ŏn

Yŏsu

Kohŭng

Map 4. Yŏsu Rebellion Area

tempt in 1945 to field an army for the Korean People's Republic. A week before the rebellion began, the regimental commander and one of his battalion chiefs had been arrested for alleged "subversive activities," which may have set the events in motion.[58]

On the evening of October 19, a Sargeant-Major named Chi Chang-su, with six confederates, began haranguing other elements in the 14th Regiment to take the unit over, arguing that it should not be used to suppress Korean brethren on Cheju. They won over some forty soldiers, who then seized an ammunition warehouse and began distributing weaponry to the rapidly swelling insurgents. By dawn on October 20, the group (numbered then at two thousand) had seized control of Yŏsu; they overwhelmed the town police station and seized its weapons. Some elements then entrained for the nearby town of Sunch'ŏn and took it over by the early afternoon. Soon rebels had spread out to Kwangyang, Kurye, Posŏng, and Namwŏn. The leader was now said to be Lt. Kim Chihwi, a native of South Hamgyŏng Province who had graduated from a Japanese Air Force school and who fled North Korea in August 1945, later graduating from the 3rd officer class in the Constabulary.[59]

The causes of the rebellion ultimately return to 1945 and the frustrated politics of a region that had strong and lasting people's committees. Yŏsu, Sunch'ŏn, Kwangyang, Posŏng, Namwŏn, Naju, and other affected counties were strongly oriented to the Left throughout the interwar period. The peculiar character of the events, however, owed to a Constabulary (now an Army) that had a history of conflict with the police organizations throughout South Korea, and that unlike the KNP, carried many leftists and communists within it. In May 1947 various arrests of alleged leftists and subversives were made in the Constabulary, in June several hundred police and Constabulary people brawled in Yŏng'am in South Chŏlla, leaving several dead and wounded, and by August American intelligence reported that police and constabulary feuding had been ensuing for months, creating a "house divided against itself" in the security organs. One CIC report said that in May 1948 some members of the Constabulary in Pusan, home of the 14th Regiment, had visited Cheju and had urged the guerrillas to attack the police, not the Constabulary; then the Constabulary would leave the guerrillas alone.[60]

Within hours of the regimental revolt, large numbers of people were parading through Yŏsu, waving red flags and shouting leftist slogans; at a mass meeting on October 20 the town people's committee was restored and hastily assembled people's courts proceeded to try and execute a number of captured policeman, as well as some other ROK officials, landlords, and people termed "rightists." People's committees were also restored in numerous small communities and islands near Yŏsu. Rebel leaders told followers that the thirty-eighth parallel had been done away with, and that unification would soon follow.[61]

On the afternoon of October 20 some two thousand citizens in Sunch'ŏn joined rebels in a mass meeting, sweeping up with it two Americans in KMAG, Lt. Stewart Greenbaum and another officer named Mohr. Although "a very strong anti-American feeling prevailed throughout the crowd," they were not harmed and later found refuge in the home of a missionary. Soon a Sunch'ŏn People's Committee was proclaimed, from "men who had sprang up from the folds of the public." Weapons were distributed, and, according to a Korean agent working for the American CIC, people "ran off in twos and threes, to kill the rich, the well-dressed, the landowners . . . some citizens in fine clothes were shot on the spot."

Speakers called for a "Korean People's Republic," using the 1945 term rather than the DPRK designation used in the North. (But some demonstrators also showed the DPRK flag, and pledged loyalty to Kim Il Sung.) As many as five hundred members of the KNP may have lost their lives, often through brutal atrocities. But American G-2 sources nonetheless reported that the attacks on the police met with "the satisfaction of a large portion of the [local] population." Students of the Sunch'ŏn Middle School avidly joined in the assaults on police.[62]

The hastily issued Yŏsu Inmin ilbo (People's Daily) promised "to protect and dedicate our loyalty to the Korean People's Republic." It referred to a "three year fight" against the American Occupation, and demanded that all Americans leave Korea forthwith. It announced that all agencies of government should be handed over to the Yŏsu People's Commmittee, and held out the classic Korean People's Republic (KPR) reform program: land redistribution without compensation to landlords, a purge of police and other officials who had served the Japanese, and opposition to a separate government for the South. Leaders who were mentioned in the press were all local: Mun Sŏng-hwi of the Yŏsu branch of the SKWP; Hong Ki-hwan, head of the local Chŏnp'yŏng union; Kim In-ok of the leftist youth organization; the principal of the Yŏsu Girl's Middle School, a graduate of Posŏng College. One article in this issue also pledged loyalty to Kim Il Sung, but that does not mean the insurgents were DPRK-controlled. In fact an intercepted radio message from the rebels related that "we received instruction from North Korea to the effect that North Korea will help us, but we refused it."[63]

Much the same process ensued in the next few days in the nearby towns of Kwangyang, Posŏng, and Kurye; many reports cited people's courts and executions of ROK police and other officials. As suppression forces converged on Sunchŏn, about two hundred members of the 4th Army Regiment dispatched from Kwangju also went over to the rebels, and soon insurgents were reported in Changhŭng, Namwŏn, Kohŭng, and Hadong. Underground members of the SKWP, Chŏnp'yŏng, and local people's committees surfaced and sought to lead the movement. By October 23, rebels were said to be "governing" parts of Kurye and Kwangyang.[64]

Northern internal materials shortly after the fact gave a generally accurate account of what happened, claiming no credit for themselves. Somewhat later they stated that Kim Chi-hwi was the Korean Workers Party (KWP) cell chief in the 14th Regiment, and that he was subsequently given a medal by the DPRK. But the account indicates that this was because of his later guerrilla activities. There is evidence that for the first time the North sought to infiltrate groups of guerrillas into the South, but this was after the rebellion had run its course, and probably was connected to the mainland insurgency that sprouted from the Yŏsu events. About sixty southerners who had trained for two months near P'yŏngyang were sent south in early November 1948. During the rebellion the North was very cautious; American intelligence noted that the thirty-eighth parallel was "astonishingly quiet" in the week that Yŏsu was held, marking "by far the longest period" on record with no incidents.[65]

The main reason for assuming a local inspiration, however, is the spontaneous and poorly-planned character of the rebellion. It went from six people to forty to two thousand within hours, showing the tinderbox at hand in South Chŏlla. But it did not bear the mark of experienced revolutionaries with clear goals in mind; indeed most of the rebels quickly wound up dead or in jail. Like so many other outbreaks in postwar South Korea, it bore the signs of a mutiny, not a movement, a last-ditch stand born of both outrage and futility, taken on the spur of the moment with little hope of success. It was what had happened over the past three years that mattered, and if it could not be undone it could at least be invoked and memorialized with a harrowing event. Yŏsu was held for a week, just as nearby Kwangju was held for about a week in 1980; and then came the predictable bloodletting by the forces of order—not a slaughter of innocents, true, but nonetheless a slaughter of alternative dreams and hopes that could find no outlet in the political system, only a doomed protest.

The timing of the rebellion may perhaps be explained by Rhee's absence from Korea. He flew to Tokyo to see MacArthur on the nineteenth, on "The Bataan," and the rebellion broke out that night; he returned to Seoul the next day. Rhee appointed General Song Ho-sŏng to head the suppression forces; no shrinking violet, he hailed his own arrival in South Chŏlla: "the Commander-in-Chief whom you have been waiting for has come here now, and is here with you. Now, I myself stand in the front lines with my real national army to induce, by any means, the rebellious elements to return to the right path." General Song proved a dismal failure, however, racing crazily along the front in an armored car, lunging first at the rebel line, then at his friendly forces, machine guns blazing all the while.

Another worthy who sought to distinguish himself at Yŏsu was "Tiger" Kim, Captain Kim Sŏk-yun of the 5th Regiment from Pusan, and formerly a sergeant in the Japanese Army in the Philippines. He sought to make an amphibious landing at Yŏsu on October 23, against American advice; his troops hit the beach in an LST, firing wildly, and were then forced to withdraw. When they finally succeeded in disembarking, some days after the rebellion was quelled, Kim's forces shot "wildly and aimlessly in all directions. . . . The main objective was the sacking and raping of now over-powered Yŏsu."[66]

The commanders who actually subdued the rebels were Americans, assisted by young colonels: Chŏng Il-gwŏn, Ch'ae Pyŏng-dŏk, and Kim Paek-il—even though the Occupation had ended and the United States ostensibly had no mandate to intervene in Korean internal affairs. But secret protocols placed operational control of the ROK military in American hands. Gen. W. L. Roberts ordered Americans to stay out of direct combat, but even that injunction was ignored from time to time. American advisors were with all ROK Army units, but the most important were a Col. Harley E. Fuller, named chief advisor for the suppression, Capt. James Hausman from KMAG G-3, and Capt. John P. Reed from G-2.[67]

On October 20 the USAFIK intelligence chief recommended that KMAG "handle [the] situation" and direct the Army in restoring order "without intervention of U.S. troops." Roberts told General Coulter that he planned "to contain and suppress the rebels at [the] earliest moment," and formed a party to fly to Kwangju on the afternoon of October 20 to command the operation. It consisted of Hausman, Reed, and a third American from KMAG; also an American in the Counter-Intelligence Corps, and Col. Chŏng Il-gwŏn. The next day Roberts met with Song Ho-sŏng and urged him "to strike hard everywhere . . . and allow no obstacles to stop him." Roberts's "Letter of Instruction" to Song read, "Your mission is to meet the rebel attack with an overwhelmingly superior force and to crush it. . . . Because of their political and strategic importance, it is essential that Sunchon and Yosu be recaptured at an early date. The liberation of these cities from the rebel forces will be moral and political victories of great propaganda value." American C-47 transports ferried Korean troops, weapons, and other materiel; KMAG spotter planes surveilled the area throughout the period of the rebellion; American intelligence organizations worked intimately with Army and KNP counterparts.[68]

Because the rebellion was spontaneous and unorganized beyond the immediately affected region, it was relatively easy to contain and suppress. About the only evidence of coordinated action elsewhere was a spurt of rebel attacks on Cheju as the Yŏsu events unfolded; some five hundred reinforcements had to be dispatched to Cheju city and Hamdŏk on October 23, for example, and the next day forty-eight police communication lines were cut, numerous roads were blocked, and as many as fifty rebel signal fires were observed around the island. But otherwise the rebellion did not spread beyond South Chŏlla and westernmost South Kyŏngsang. American air observers judged that rebel strength at Yŏsu was comprised of two military companies and about one thousand civilians; it was less at other occupied points. Sunch'ŏn was attacked on October 22 and retaken the next day by regular Army elements; they found about one hundred dead policemen in the town. Rebels fled in the

direction of Hadong; a sharp battle with six hundred ROK soldiers occurred there on October 25.[69]

When Posŏng was retaken on October 24 by elements of the 4th Regiment under the command of O Tŏk-jung, rebels were found to have
been in control of the county office, police station, and other government
offices; they had told the local citizenry that North Korean forces had
attacked the South. DPRK flags were hanging in the town. 150 ROK soldiers and 100 policemen were found dead. In Changhŭng, a G-2 road
patrol witnessed many people cheering for "the People's Republic."[70]

ROK forces fought over strategic ridges near Yŏsu for a couple of
days, and then attacked the city itself on October 26. "The rebels were
now fighting as a well-organized unit, and it was apparent that they were
under the control of a trained military leader. Every step on the way was
bitterly contested . . . [in] a house-to-house struggle." By noon, however,
the rebels had been beaten. Col. Kim Paek-il led the restoration of order;
"practically all of the people in the town were rounded up for questioning and screening." Only sixty-three Army rebels were recaptured; the
rest had fled into nearby mountains. About a fourth of Yŏsu was destroyed in the fighting, mostly by fire. Rebels still held Kwangyang and
Kurye at this time. Troops sent by train from Chŏngju converged on
Kurye on October 26; about 450 rebels burned the Kurye police station
that day, and then marched into the Chirisan fastness when Yŏsu fell,
leaving the town in control of a people's committee. Most towns were
abandoned by rebels by October 28.[71]

The revolutionary terror of the rebels met its opposite as loyalists took
their awful retribution. Keyes Beech observed the roundup at Yŏsu: the
rebels and the local people were aligned in perfect squares, sitting down.

> Before each square stood the police, some attired in old Japanese uni-
> forms and wearing swords. One by one, the citizens were called for-
> ward, to kneel before the police. Every question was punctuated by a
> blow on the head or back, sometimes from a rifle butt, sometimes from
> the edge of a sword. There was no outcry, no sound at all except for
> the barked questions and the thud of blows.[72]

"Tiger" Kim's forces were among the worst, according to eyewitness
American accounts; captured prisoners—about two thousand people
were in custody on October 28—"were mercilessly beaten with cot
rounds, bamboo sticks, fists, etc." The objects of the terror included
"poor farmers and fishermen," and many women and children. American sources reported that "loyal troops were shooting people whom they
had the slightest suspicion . . . of giving cooperation to the communist
uprising." The KMAG G-2 commented that "many innocent people have
been killed or jailed in the thorough measures" employed by the military

and police; people thought to have been leftists before the uprising "will receive little mercy." Roberts ordered General Song to "take strong positive measures to prevent executions and control National Police," but there is little evidence of any restraint. Hausman reported that police in Sunch'ŏn were "out for revenge and are executing prisoners and civilians. . . . Several loyal civilians already killed and people beginning to think we are as bad as the enemy."[73]

Official estimates of casualties from the rebellion at the end of November listed 141 loyalist soldiers dead, 263 missing, and 391 having joined the rebels; 821 rebels killed and 2,860 captured; a total of 3,700 rebels were said to have existed by this account, yet at least 1,000 remained in the hills, now functioning as guerrillas. Civilian casualty totals are unavailable, but American sources thought 500 civilians died in Sunchŏn alone, a higher number in Yŏsu. By the end of November 1,714 accused rebels had been tried in military courts, with 866 given the death sentence. The bodies of the executed were often burned, a sacrilege in a culture in which ancestor worship remained strong. At the end of the same month 2,591 prisoners were still in jail from the rebellion, including about 2,000 ROKA soldiers and 88 officers. According to British sources, "wholesale political arrests" went on in the first ten days of November, with 3,000 arrested in Kwangju alone. Executions of convicted rebels continued well into 1949.[74]

Some rebels were given lenient treatment in return for helping to hunt down their comrades: one of these allegedly was Park Chung Hee (Pak Chŏng-hŭi, later president of the ROK). His participation in the rebellion is documented in KMAG files, but his role in tracking down rebels, including his own brother as the story had it, cannot be documented except in newspaper accounts of questionable reliability. But when he made his coup in 1961, the Yŏsu background turned up in CIA files, causing momentary worry that he might be a communist.[75]

ROK Army morale and effectiveness were, of course, called severely into question by the Yŏsu events. Army strength had been 54,228 when the rebellion broke; two months later it was down to 45,000, suggesting a much wider purge than the above figures indicate. But ROK and American officials also thought the rebellion and its aftermath greatly strengthened the army and the ROK itself against internal strife and dissent.[76] Rhee returned from Tokyo and used the rebellion to launch an assault on his opposition.

Just before Yŏsu, Rhee had been in the process of closing down any newspapers that gave vent to opposition sentiments, except for the sanctioned *Tonga ilbo*. In September and early October he closed four newspapers, including the *Chungang sinmun* and the *Segye ilbo*. He defended this action, according to Muccio, by citing "a 1906 law of the Yi Dynasty making it illegal for the press to publish stories damaging the country's international relations."[77] This, of course, was under the Protectorate, when Imperial Japan ran Korea's foreign relations, and the offending newspapers were Korean ones criticizing Japanese imperialism; this time they were calling for the withdrawal of American troops.

After the rebellion, Rhee issued an unpublicized order to the press prohibiting any editorials opposing the retention of American troops in Korea; he also decreed that "puppet" should always be used in reference to the North Koreans. Rhee arrested as many as one thousand politicians in one weekend alone in early November, including Yŏ Un-hong and Ŏm Hang-sŏp; most were subsequently released. At about the same time he rammed a "public safety law" through the National Assembly that, according to Muccio, "so loosely defined groups seeking to disturb the national tranquility" that Assembly members thought it might be used against them; in December it was, as nineteen assemblymen were jailed. About twenty-three thousand political prisoners were held in Rhee's jails by late November.[78]

Within a few weeks of the end of the rebellion, members of the Northwest Youth were undergoing training by the National Police, for dispatch to Yŏsu and Sunch'ŏn; they were given regular KNP status and uniforms when the training (which lasted twelve days) was finished. By early December 1948, some 600 NWY "police" were on duty in the two troubled towns.[79]

The Yŏsu Rebellion was a fierce storm for a week or so, but ultimately it was a tempest in a teapot that Rhee utilized to clamp down upon any resistance to his rule, save that tepid and unthreatening, if nonetheless clamorous, dissent registered by the Democratic Party opposition. Yŏsu cannot be compared to the autumn uprisings in 1946 in extent and importance; it was a spontaneous and ultimately foolish mutiny by disgruntled soldiers that merely brought down an enhanced repression on the strong leftist base in South Chŏlla. Indeed, one incarcerated member of the SKWP told authorities that the rebellion had been "premature," the implication being that the Party was unprepared for it and unable to give it leadership. Nonetheless SKWP activists joined the rebellion, he said, because the uprisings were "a reflection of the mind of the people," and the people were "ready for revolution." He said the Party would be ready to lead the people the next time around.[80] This report has the ring of truth, it fits the evidence; we might take it as an epitaph for the southern Left: a mass base lacking leadership, with activists trailing after mutinies and calling them revolutions. It is this mutinous quality that gives Yŏsu its historical significance, ringing down the curtain on three years of left-wing failure. But it had a catalytic effect as well, in extending the guerrilla conflict to the mainland.

Chapter Eight

THE GUERRILLA CONFLICT

Large sections of South Korea are darkened today by a cloud of
terror that is probably unparalleled in the world. . . . Nights in the
hundreds of villages across the guerrilla areas are a long, cold vigil
of listening.

Walter Sullivan, March 1950

AFTER the village fighting of 1947, South Korea was relatively quiescent until April 1948, when the Cheju insurgency broke out. In October, the Yŏsu Rebellion unfolded. Before that point, few if any guerrillas existed in the South; after Yŏsu, and for the remaining time before
June 1950, guerrillas were a continuous problem.

In January 1948 the American G-2 surveyed the Left in the South, and
found that South Chŏlla was "truly the most leftist province . . . with a
virtual honeycomb of SKWP branches operating underground." North
Chŏlla was thought to have a reasonably strong underground as well, but
little showed up "on the surface." In the Ch'ungch'ŏng Provinces the left
was not strong; the G-2 noted in North Ch'ungch'ŏng "an abrupt decline
in all political activity." In Kangwŏn, "rightists" had thoroughly consolidated their power, except for the East coast; presumably it was not even
necessary to mention that they had done the same in Kyŏnggi. North
Kyŏngsang, however, still witnessed a continuing struggle between the
extremes of left and right, and South Kyŏngsang was "basically extreme
leftist."[1] This 1948 account parallels our own rendering of the political
complexion of the southern provinces in 1945–1946. But it does not
speak of guerrillas.

By the summer of 1948, however, American intelligence had picked
up numerous reports of guerrilla organizing. One or two North Korean
officers were reportedly in mountainous areas of several provinces, but
otherwise it was a southern effort. Most of the activity involved provision-
ing supplies, especially food, in mountain hideouts; operatives entered
villages at night and asked for gifts of food as an earnest of support.
Central Intelligence Agency (CIC) accounts acknowledged that "many of
the villagers are in sympathy with the guerrillas," but they rarely gave
food "for fear of police reprisals." The main focus was South Chŏlla,
which the organizers had divided into four separate operating areas with
four or five counties in each; four guerrillas corps of one hundred armed
members each were to be supported by about one thousand unarmed

members. Weapons were scarce, however, most carrying clubs or spears. Although the emphasis was on recruiting and screening existing members of left-wing organizations, bandits were getting in as well.

In the Ch'ungch'ŏng Provinces guerrillas were said to be concentrated in Yŏngdong county, at the confluence of the Kyŏngsang, Ch'ungch'ŏng, and Chŏlla province borders. Here the Sŏbaek mountains have their northern border, extending south to Chiri Mountain, which later became the most famous guerrilla redoubt. Some reports placed two thousand rebels in this area in mid-summer 1948, with South Korea Workers Party (SKWP) activists scouring mountains for hideouts and strongholds. Another training center existed in mountains in Sŏsan county in South Ch'ungch'ŏng; the regimen lasted forty days and was modeled on Chinese Eighth Route Army procedure. CIC sources thought more than one thousand recruits had already passed through that center. In the Ch'ungch'ŏngs, Yŏngdong and Sŏsan had the strongest people's committees in a generally conservative region.[2]

These reports suggest that the mainland insurgency had a less spontaneous origin than the guerrillas on Cheju. In long articles in early 1950, Pak Hŏn-yŏng and Yi Sŭng-yŏp traced the beginnings back to the aftermath of the autumn uprisings in 1946; the Cheju insurgency and the Yŏsu events gave a big boost to the effort, but it all went back to the autumn of 1946. In materials for party activists, the North Koreans dated the "armed guerrilla struggle" from the April 3 uprising on Cheju, extended to the mainland in the course of the Yŏsu Rebellion. The key goal of the guerrillas was said to be "the restoration of the people's committees."[3] There is really no conflict among the accounts. The guerrilla struggle was continuous with the events of 1945–1946, as the physiognomy of the movement will make clear, especially the suppression of the committees which was at the root of the autumn uprisings; at the same time some North Korean and SKWP activists sought to organize and direct it.

Open guerrilla war began after the Yŏsu rebellion. As the year 1948 drew to a close, G-2 sources reported guerrilla skirmishes all over South Chŏlla: attacks on villages, sabotage of rail and telegraph lines, and "heavy" Army losses in a particular battle on December 17 in Naju county. In both Kyŏngsang provinces similar raids occurred on a lesser level. Some of this was undoubtedly a response to another Korean National Police (KNP) crackdown in the first week of December, resulting in the arrest of two thousand leftists throughout the country.[4]

In early 1949, Korean Military Advisory Group (KMAG) intelligence compiled a map showing the areas of guerrilla operation (see map 5). At the same time, CIA information placed large units (numbering five hundred to one thousand each) at Cheju, Chiri-san, and Odae-san; and small

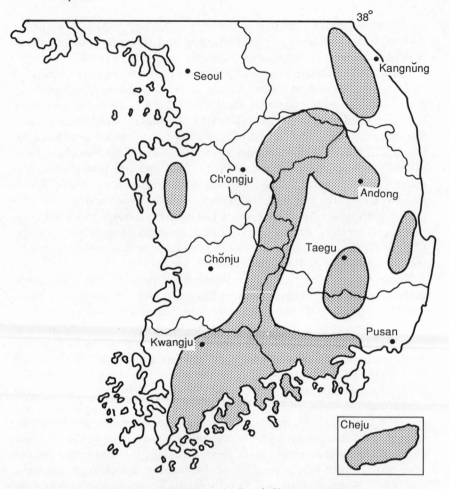

Map 5. Guerrilla Areas in South Korea, 1949

units (three hundred to five hundred) at Yŏngdong. An estimate a few months later by Hŏ Hŏn was very similar; with some exceptions North Korean published accounts of guerrilla activities correlate well with those of the KMAG G-2, allowing crossverification to the scholar.[5] These renderings correspond to counties where strong people's committees existed in 1945–1946. The CIA estimate would suggest that the total number of guerrillas in the South in early 1949 was somewhere between 3,500 and 6,000, not counting several thousands on Cheju, and leftist supporters in the counties indicated.

Qualitative evidence suggested an even greater problem for the estab-

Topography of Korea, 1948-1950

Map 6. Korean Topography
SOURCE: Halliday, Jon, and Bruce Cumings. *Korea: The Unknown War.*
London: Penguin Books, 1988.

lished authorities. Two vice-consuls from the embassy toured the countryside in early 1949 and found that in South Chŏlla, "the government has lost control outside of the cities and larger towns." Police stations in the province were "universally protected by huge stone walls of recent construction or by high mounds of sand bags. . . . Each police box resembles a medieval fort." The authorities had carried out extensive tree cutting in the hills to deny cover to the rebels, and all travel at night was prohibited. In Kurye, nearly all villages had been attacked by guerrillas or police. County officials thought that 90 percent of the people in Kurye were "Communist." The province governor said there were one hundred thousand refuges from the guerrilla fighting in the province—many of them created by authorities who emptied villages. In recent months nearly every police box had been attacked; fifteen had been overwhelmed and burned to the ground. At least one hundred police had died, apart from those killed during the Yŏsu Rebellion. Just after the counsuls arrived in Kwangju, guerrillas ambushed a police truck and killed twenty-five officers.[6]

A detailed North Korean account of the guerrilla fighting from December to March (1948–1949) listed incidents in most counties of South Chŏlla, including a major engagement with several hundred on each side in Kwangyang in mid-December, the annihilation of forty police in a "south river crossing operation," the occupation of several villages in Hwasun county by guerrillas, and attacks on communication lines at the Hwasun mines; it claimed that people's committees had been restored in mountainous villages near Chirisan, and a contemporaneous article claimed that PCs were again functioning in "liberated areas" in Kurye, Hamyang, and Sanch'ŏng counties.[7]

North Korean sources claimed that guerrilla activity grew during 1949 from 77 affected counties in February to 118 in August, with a total of 9,067 guerrillas fighting. They placed 3,122 of these in the Honam or southwest region, 2,642 in North Kyŏngsang, and the rest scattered around. This exaggerates the number of counties affected, but the total numbers are about right; there is no question that the movement mushroomed to its highest point in late summer. Furthermore the exaggeration has unaffected counties mostly in North Chŭngch'ŏng and Kyŏnggi, as we would predict.[8]

North Korean and American accounts depict a similar pattern of incidents escalating from April through October 1949, and then tapering off in November. In an important account, Yi Sŏng-yŏp listed numbers of guerrillas and active supporters, incidents, and number of enemy "annihilated" (see Table 1).

Although this is an exaggerated total, it nonetheless shows the same pattern as the KMAG evidence. Yi attributed the November decline to the guerrillas making preparations for winter, and denied that South Korean suppression measures were effective.[9]

THE GUERRILLAS IN THE CHŎLLAS

The transition to the Rhee regime in 1948 made little difference in Chŏlla politics. Perhaps the repression got more intense, but otherwise the settlement in 1945–1946 was highly predictive of the mise-en-scene

TABLE 1

THE GUERRILLA MOVEMENT IN 1949

Month	guerrillas[a]	incidents	enemy casualties[b]
April	16,257	482	716
August	44,200	759	1,203
September	77,900	1,184	2,104
October	89,900	1,330	2,415
November	77,900	1,260	2,213

SOURCE: Yi Sûng-yôp; "The Struggle of the Southern Guerrilla for Unification of the Homeland," *Kûlloja* (January 1950), p. 21.

[a] people who participated in all types of battles and actions
[b] killed and wounded; the number killed is about two-thirds of the total

in 1948. American surveys always deemed South Chŏlla the Reddest province in the South. The opposition rested precariously in cities and county seats. One survey done on South Chŏlla on the eve of the Yŏsu Rebellion found the police "engaged in a vigorous campaign to stamp out all leftist organizations and sympathizers," by now a mere litany. Sŏ Min-ho from Kwangju, a wealthy backer of Rhee since 1945 and a provincial governor under USAMGIK, was the big power in the province; his brother, Sŏ Kwang-sun, was provincial chief of detectives in the KNP. The Korean Democratic Party (KDP) was the big victor in the May elections, just as it controlled most county seats in the spring of 1946; otherwise no opposition was tolerated.[10]

In North Chŏlla, a weaker left-wing underground organization was thought to exist in late 1947; otherwise the Right was dominant. In Chŏngŭp, for example, ten political parties existed, nine following Rhee and one backing Kim Sŏng-su. Police had arrested 850 leftists in August 1947, and most were still in jail by the end of the year. If elections were to be held in North Chŏlla, the G-2 thought, the Right would completely dominate the whole process.[11]

Organized guerrilla activity in the Chŏllas concentrated in the Chiri mountains. These mountains rose to as much as seven thousand feet, and unlike lower foothills, were heavily forested. Roy Appleman described the area as an "almost trackless waste of 750 square miles." A key leader of the Chirisan guerrillas was Yu Il-sŏk, originally named Yun Chae-uk, a communist intellectual who studied at Keijo Imperial University, led left-wing students at Seoul National University after the liberation, and then became a labor organizer in the Seoul suburb of Yongdŭngp'o. He went into the mountains after the Yŏsu rebellion, and was killed in fighting in 1949. Other leaders included Kim Se-t'aek from South Kyŏngsang, thought by Americans to be the overall commander; Yi Hyŏn-sang, alias No Tong-mu, a Seoul native about forty years old, who headed the Chirisan guerrilla 6th regiment; Pak Chŏng-hae, from Kurye county, led the 7th Regiment.[12]

In the early months of 1949 Yi Pŏm-sŏk estimated that there were 3,500 guerrillas in South Chŏlla, with 1,224 more already killed and 3,293 "prisoners of war." They operated in almost every county in the province.[13] One hundred and twenty partisans battled police in Pŏlgyo in mid-February; in early March guerrillas carried out a major raid in Koksŏng county, killing as many as one hundred police and disrupting communications. There were many smaller incidents in Posŏng, Hwasun, Sunchŏn, Naju, Hamp'yŏng, Kurye, and Yŏnggwang during the next couple of months. According to a North Korean citation of a published account from Seoul, in May 1949 Gen. Wŏn Yong-dŏk "graded" the security situation in South Chŏlla townships, finding 28 "grade A" townships, 85 "negatively cooperating," and fully 130 as "grade C," or unpacified. The only counties affected in North Chŏlla, by North Korean accounts, were contiguous counties, Koch'ang and Sunch'ang. Their accounts seem to grasp at straws to find things to report elsewhere in North Chŏlla.[14]

The mining town of Hwasun was always a running sore for the rightwing in the 1940s, and it had its share of guerrillas. In mid-August 1949, three hundred guerrillas joined up with miners in a major battle with counterinsurgent combat police, cutting communication and rail lines, breaking into the mine offices, burning buildings, and killing many police. Large caches of mine supplies were lost in the fires. A week later, two hundred guerrillas joined with local people in Koch'ang to destroy the police station, torch government offices, seize weapons, and release about eighty prisoners from the jail. Among twelve guerrillas found dead two were women; many women were active fighters in the southern guerrillas, something unheard of on the ROK side. At the end of August KNP and Republic of Korea Army (ROKA) units fought guerrillas for several days in Hwawŏn-myŏn; at least twenty policemen and thirty guerrillas died; seven captured guerrillas were brought back to the spot where the KNP was first ambushed, and executed on the spot in front of local people. In July and August there were many smaller, if often bloody, incidents in most counties of South Chŏlla; Naju was particularly affected.[15]

In mid-September several hundred guerrillas attacked in Kwangyang and Yong'am counties, and continued smaller engagements in Sunchŏn, Naju, and other towns; on October 8, two hundred guerrillas attacked Koksŏng-ŭp from three different directions, destroying police stations and rightist homes. The fighting tapered off as winter drew near; most activity involved guerrillas foraging supplies to tide over the cold months, often resembling a type of peasant banditry in which noncooperating villages would be sacked for rice, bedding, and other supplies.[16] In early 1950 as a major suppression campaign and the winter reduced active guerrilla forces, Chŏlla peasants returned to their anomic pattern of unconnected village uprisings—attacking police and landlords, holding rudimentary people's courts, and the like. Landlords gathered in Kwangju in fear of "peasant riots," according to North Korean sources.[17]

THE KYŎNGSANG GUERRILLAS

As guerrilla strength waned in the Chŏllas, it grew in North Kyŏngsang, the home of the 1946 autumn revolt. Here, as in the Chŏllas, the guerrillas grew out of the leftist politics of 1945–1946, especially the people's committees. A CIC account afforded a rare glimpse of this continuity, near the ancient Silla capital at Kyŏngju.

> Shortly after the liberation in 1945, Lee Chung Won and his followers organized the People's Committee in Kyongju Gun for the purpose of eventually establishing a People's Republic. This group was the activating force behind the October 1946 riots and the 10 May disturbances of the South Korea Labor Party in Kyongju Gun. In February 1948, Lee Kyu Hak, leader of the SKWP in Kyongju Gun organized the Guerrilla Corps to provide a haven for those persons wanted by the various law enforcement agencies. . . . It is believed that the plans for the organization of the Guerrilla Corps came down from a higher headquarters.[18]

Guerrilla ranks apparently swelled in early 1949 when many soldiers from an ROKA unit defected to the guerrillas, shouting "long live the People's Republic." In March 1949 a major attack in Miryang killed sixty-seven police and rightists in a two-day battle, and guerrillas were active in many places in the Kyŏngsangs in March, April, and May, according to North Korean accounts: Koryŏng, Kŭmch'ŏn, Sŏnsan, Ŭisŏng, Andong, Yŏngdŏk, Yŏng'il, Ch'ilgok, Ch'ŏngdo, Yech'ŏn, and Kyŏngju. From March 14 to March 31, there were daily battles in Yechŏn. Guerrillas in the T'aebaek mountains also struck in the northeastern and mountainous counties, Ponghwa, Yŏngju, and Mun'gyŏng.[19] The main guerrilla force in North Kyŏngsang was named for the mountains they hid in, Ilwŏl-san; they were led by a famous southern partisan named Kim Tal-sam. He had divided the guerrillas into six battalions, one each for Ponghwa, Andong, Mun'gyŏng, Kyŏngju, Uljin, and

Yŏngdŏk; each batallion had about two hundred guerrillas, with thirty-five to eighty rifles, all Japanese or American.[20] An American account of a survey of North Kyŏngsang in July, 1949 related, "Small attacks and ambushes punctuated by larger attacks characterized almost every locale. Police boxes were barricaded to the roof, trees everywhere were cut down within 100 meters of the roads, local officials and policemen felt compelled to move nervously from house to house at night." Although this situation was "chronic" throughout the province, it was especially marked in the northeast counties of Ponghwa, Yŏngdŏk, and Yŏngju. Local police stated that "on the whole, the majority of the guerrillas appeared to be from South Korea," but they thought there might be a "North Korean nucleus."[21]

A month later Muccio reported that "guerrillas ruled at night, while police holed up in barricaded stations," and cited a particularly bad incident on July 19 in which guerrillas ambushed an ROKA infantry company in a mountain pass, killing forty-one of them. The next day one hundred miners armed with iron bars killed a mine owner and several assistants, destroyed mine buildings, and retreated to the hills. Police tried to keep young people out of guerrilla units by requiring all of them to join right-wing youth groups.[22]

Most incidents typically involved a group of one hundred or so guerrillas descending from the hills and attacking police stations, government offices, rail lines, and the homes of wealthy landlords. But in one episode near Andong in early June, guerrillas destroyed the homes of 123 people, and in Ponghwa county a couple of weeks later, guerrillas destroyed 219 homes and killed many police. The police responded with concerted attacks on caves hiding guerrillas and their supplies—and their families as well. The large number of homes destroyed in these cases suggests that whole villages were subject to attack by both sides.[23]

On August 19, 200 guerrillas joined with three hundred peasants in Ŭisŏng in an attack on local police that killed fifty-seven of them, and released sixty-three prisoners from the local jail; many government offices were destroyed. KMAG sources described guerrillas near Kyŏngju as organized into a "Field People's Army" and a "Training Army," with each unit having rifles for about 30 percent of the guerrillas. They spent most of their time destroying rail and electric lines, and attacking police stations. They told the local people that the North Korean Army would soon join their struggle by coming South. A flurry of reports in mid-September asserted that the Korean People's Army (KPA) was about to invade, provoking a war scare that we will treat in a later chapter.[24]

Three hundred guerrillas attacked police near Taegu on September 1, and then launched a major assault near Andong, a strategic town at the confluence of rivers, mountains, and railways on September 15; the next day they ambushed police in Mun'gyŏng. Many policemen died in these encounters. October saw guerrilla assaults throughout the province. In early October about four hundred guerrillas attacked Andong, including police and army positions and the local jail, prompting an extensive fire-fight. Nine public buildings, seven homes, a bus station, and a drug store were burned. Some days later, rebels burned an American USIS office, one of the few attacks on American facilities throughout the guerrilla struggle. In late October guerrillas launched a major assault on Chinju, a powerful leftist town west of Pusan. About three hundred guerrillas dressed in Japanese-style uniforms ran through Chinju, attacking a ma-rine barracks, a prison, burning down the city hall and a county office; Americans thought their goal was to seize the city. Some of the fires were set by townspeople supporting the guerrillas. After a few hours the guer-rillas retreated, losing only two men. North Korean sources said that the 2nd ROKA division was mobilized during the Chinju attack. In one grisly incident in a small village in N. Kyŏngsang, guerrillas beheaded 32 young men accused of aiding the police. Other significant guerrilla assaults oc-curred in Koksŏng, Muju, and in towns on the upper east coast.[25]

About this time, G-2 sources got their first good evidence that some of the Kyŏngsang guerrillas were being supplied from boats anchored off of Yŏngdŏk, presumably from North Korea. The American heavy cruiser USS St. Paul, with two destroyers accompanying, put in at Pusan shortly thereafter; I do not know if the two events were related.[26] On December 5, 150 guerrillas attacked Sanjung-myŏn, just north of Chinju, burning the *myŏn* office and other buildings; American sources reported that villagers "declined to assist our [*sic*] troops with information on en-emy movements." When the Army moved in, the guerrillas disappeared, and when the Army moved out, the guerrillas returned—and beat those who gave information. Most attacks were between midnight and dawn. In one case, some 130 guerrillas were right in the middle of territory occupied by an ROKA battalion for three days, "but no information was received from civilians . . . the majority of civilians in the outlying dis-tricts seem to be in sympathy with the guerrillas."[27]

As the winter of 1949–1950 blew in, guerrillas in the Kyŏngsangs be-gan foraging to put away supplies for the winter. Village grain stocks were seized, or landlords were attacked; on New Year's Day, 1950, near Andong, guerrillas or peasant rebels surrounded and burned the homes of twenty landlords, and executed several "in the name of the people."[28]

As 1950 dawned, Drumwright said that North Kyŏngsang had re-placed South Chŏlla as "the most flourishing guerrilla-infested area." The mountainous and wooded physiognomy of the region made it easy for guerrillas to conceal themselves. Taegu, he said, "was considered a Communist stronghold even during the Japanese occupation"; about one fire a day occurred there, most considered to be sabotage. Police abuses helped the guerrillas; residents in Taegu and the villages were required to contribute money to the police, or else be labeled a communist.[29]

American and North Korean accounts cited many guerrilla incidents in North Kyŏngsang in various counties in early 1950. At the end of March P'yŏngyang claimed there had been some 1,300 guerrilla actions since mid-February, with T'aebaek-san and North Kyŏngsang being the center. The party newspaper mentioned the Chirisan and Honam guerrillas, but gave no details on incidents in that region—meaning that there were few if any. The North Koreans claimed that Roberts was directly involved in the counterguerrilla campaign, and that the ROK Navy had blockaded the east coast from Pusan to Uljin. In April 1950 the North listed fewer incidents in the Kyŏngsangs, but once again cited many incidents of guerrilla activity in South Chŏlla. The truth, however, was that the guerrillas were seriously weakened and on the run by this time.[30]

Outside of the Chŏllas and Kyŏngsangs, guerrillas were only active in Kangwŏn on the upper east coast, and in Yŏngdong county in Ch'ungchŏng-do. There were one or two reports of guerrilla activity in Sŏsan and T'aechŏn in South Ch'ungch'ŏng; none of this was serious, but it is true that this was the only region of people's committee strength in the province. North Korean acounts never mentioned any serious guerrilla activity in the Ch'ungch'ŏngs; although some towns would be listed, they never gave details on the engagements.[31]

The Ch'ungch'ŏng pattern is far better represented by the county of Nonsan, where an American survey found in late 1947 that "extreme rightist groups appear to have complete control in Nonsan gun." Rhee's National Society for the Rapid Realization of Korean Independence (NSRRKI) had branches in thirty-eight of forty-four villages surveyed, and apart from the KDP and some right-wing youth groups, no other parties existed. The left had "never been strong" in South Ch'ungch'ŏng, but nonetheless the police were "now undertaking to wipe away the last vestiges." It would appear that they were taking no chances. One police officer told the Americans, "almost forty percent of the government officials in the area were imprisoned and interrogated [at one time or another] upon suspicion of having communistic thoughts and plan[s] to destroy the rightists."

Nonsan was a major rice-producing county with high rates of tenancy. Peasants told American officials that the grain collection program was unfair, with forcible removals of rice. The Americans concluded that what opposition existed owed to this problem, and "underground leftists" who exploited it. Local people said that the rightist parties provided two services: help with the rice collection, and aid to the police. In other words, they helped with the two things most peasants told the Americans that they hated the most.

The collected data on Nonsan county depicted a social structure which was about 65 percent rural, with landlords constituting 0.8 percent of the agrarian population, tenants and part-owners 86 percent, and smallholding peasants 13 percent. Of the remaining 35 percent, two-thirds were laborers, and the rest were office workers, businessmen, and shop owners. The result of the American Occupation in Nonsan, in other words, was to sponsor and defend a politics that looked after the interests of perhaps 2 or 3 percent of the population, and to leave the rest unrepresented, if not positively repressed. Two-thirds of the local citizens had not heard that the United Nations Commission was observing Korean elections, nor did they see this as an important issue.[32]

The exception that proved the rule of politics in the Ch'ungch'ŏngs was Yŏngdong county, a rebellious pudenda of the province that partook more of Chŏlla and Kyŏngsang politics: it was thoroughly red, and had guerrillas running in its hills and villages from 1948 well into the Korean War. Dr. Clesson Richards ran a Salvation Army hospital in Yŏngdong, arriving in 1947 and leaving just before the war. He told a *New York Times* reporter that "guerrilla warfare was around us all the time." He thought they were "North Korean Communists," or perhaps that was what he was told. "We had many Commies as patients. . . . The police would keep an eye on them, grill them and when they had all possible information, take them out and stand them before a firing squad. This wall was near the hospital. We could hear the men being shot." In Dr. Richardson's opinion "the Commies were ruthless"—although they "had no anti-foreign feeling and did not bother us."[33]

North Korean accounts of guerrilla activity in the Ch'ungch'ŏngs mostly cited incidents in Yŏngdong, grasping at straws elsewhere. Outside of Yŏngdong, partisans were confined to the mountainous counties of Tanyang and Koesan, the former more than the latter. Most of this was a spillover from mountain fighting in North Kyŏngsang.[34] Guerrillas were inactive in Kyŏnggi Province, surrounding the core region of Seoul, except for two counties that were remote and contiguous to the North: Ongjin and Yŏnbaek. In Kangwŏn, rightist power was secure in the capital at Ch'unch'ŏn and in nearby counties, but tenuous in the heavily leftist coastal counties. USAMGIK sources were proud to point to Ch'unch'ŏn in late 1947, where "rightist political groups have consolidated their position thoroughly," Rhee's NSRRKI being dominant amongst them.[35]

Kangwŏn was the obvious candidate for North Korean "infiltration," and here the guerrilla activity melded local partisans with units crossing the thirty-eighth parallel. In late 1948 an engagement occured near Yongwŏl, with about 150 guerrillas; some of their number were captured and they "all agreed that their group . . . is the only group which has entered South Korea"—although more were scheduled to follow. They were mostly southerners from the Chŏllas and Kyŏngsangs who had been trained at the P'yŏngyang Political Institute in the North.[36] These units operated together with local people from a base at Odae-san, west of Kangnŭng. Most of their attacks occurred in Kangnŭng and Samch'ŏk counties, both strongly left-wing in 1945–1946, and the latter having a big left-wing mining population. But incidents in this region were not on the scale of those in the southeast and southwest.[37]

METHODS OF THE GUERRILLAS

Much of the guerrilla activity in Korea followed peninsular geography, just as it had in the 1930s when guerrillas and Red Peasant Unions survived only in wild, mountainous, or remote counties. One American who helped track down the guerrillas later wrote that it was "an almost impossible task" to destroy guerrillas in the mountains.

> The mountains were thickly wooded with trees and underbrush, precipitous and extremely rocky and rough in nature, which not only provided excellent cover for the guerrilla groups, but confined troops movement to single trails and made ambushing a constant threat. Maps of the area [that we used] were of Japanese origin and only reasonably accurate. Communications were limited and difficult. For every trail used by the troops, there were a dozen other trails on which the guerrillas could bypass and escape the pursuers. Spotting the guerrillas by air was almost an impossibility.[38]

Mountain redoubts that the guerrillas were forced to live in were distant from significant centers of population, except perhaps in North Kyŏngsang. Guerrillas descended from the mountains into nearby villages, avoiding large plains and areas with modern transportation, where they would be subject to effective police or army action. Except in remote and underpopulated places, they were not able to hold several towns at the same time, or create base areas outside the mountains. They would enter a village at night, call out the population, give speeches, and secure food and other supplies. As their situation got more desperate, especially as the winter of 1949 arrived, they would attack whole villages and lay them waste in search of supplies. Attacks on police boxes were the most common sort of activity, both because of widespread hatred for the National Police, and because records of leftist families were kept at stations.[39]

An account of a village attack related to touring embassy officials by an American missionary gives the flavor of these little struggles, and an insight into American attitudes.

> One of the shrewdest American observers encountered during the trip was Mr. Linton, Presbyterian missionary at Chonju, who described in some detail a raid on a fairly large village. . . . Seven or eight young men of the village were taken into a Communist organization and made into trained agitators and rabble-rousers. These men capitalized on a general discontent with the situation then existing. . . . On the set date they egged most of the young men of the town into an attack on a police box. . . . The young men, filled with promises of what would happen when the police were defeated and the Communists took over, charged manfully upon the box, armed with clubs and wooden spears. . . . The police opened fire into the crowd, and as the casualties mounted the organizers melted away into the hills.

The women of the village proceeded to attack the homes of the absent organizers; "Communism in the village ended forthwith." The embassy people thought that such attacks on the police freed them to act decisively, "whereas previously the American [*sic*] ideas of habeus corpus and freedom of thought had greatly hampered police activities."[40]

Taken on their own terms, North Korean descriptions of guerrilla activity often sounded more like peasant rebellions. In early 1950 Yi Sŭng-yŏp wrote,

> With the help of the guerrillas, everywhere the broad peasant masses stir up struggles to eradicate the evil landlords who have oppressed them for centuries. They burn down their houses, destroy land documents, and attack the township offices which hold the land registers [*t'oji taejang*]. They hold peasant meetings and put out proclamations demanding land [reform] without compensation [to the owners].

He cited forty-six incidents of what he called "peasant riots" in North Kyŏngsang in November 1949; he related an account of one big rebellion in Subuk-myŏn, Tamyang county in late October, in which more than four thousand peasants from forty-six villages, aided by seventy guerrillas, set up a people's court for "evil landlords," meting out harsh punishment to them, and then "enforcing" land reform. American sources confirm that guerrilla incidents occured in Subuk-myŏn at this time, but they are short on details.[41]

Even on Yi Sŭng-yŏp's evidence, this is a myriad of peasant wars, not a guerrilla movement. As before, it suggests a pattern of high levels of class struggle and low levels of organization. That the organizers also engaged in self-defeating terror is alluded to in North Korean published accounts, and discussed critically in private ones. In a long account of the guerrillas, Hŏ Hŏn, another SKWP leader, remarked that "to answer terror with terror cannot be avoided."[42] Guerrilla violence often had the telltale quality of classic peasant retributive justice—apolitical, unthinking of the consequences. An American described one incident, for example, in which guerrillas attacked a police box in Kurye: a police lieutenant was "taken captive, tortured, and then killed by lashing one hand and arm to a tree and one hand and arm to a truck and driving the truck away."[43]

All this is little different from the autumn uprisings in 1946, and sounds like the situation in China in the 1920s that Mao criticized in his famous "Hunan Report," where organizers allowed or encouraged peasants to engage in unrestrained (and essentially unpolitical) violence against landlords, and trailed along behind a strong mass movement, failing to harness its energy and unable to protect poor peasants from the inevitable retaliation. The fractured structure that plagued leftist activities in 1946 also affected the guerrillas; the bands tended to operate separately from each other, rarely carrying out coordinated operations that would scatter the suppression forces.

EXTERNAL INVOLVEMENT AND COUNTERINSURGENCY

Hugh Deane argued presciently in March 1948 that Korea would soon come to resemble the civil wars in Greece or North China: as in Greece, "North Korea will be accused of sending agitators and military equipment south of the 38th parallel and the Korean problem will be made to look as if it were simply southern defense against northern aggression." Yet the worst problem, he thought, would come in the Chŏllas, as far from North Korea as any region save Cheju—which developed the biggest insurgency of all.[44] As it happened Deane's prediction was right on all counts: this was where the insurgency was strongest, and this became the American line—and not only that, but the judgment of history. To the extent that anyone knows about the guerrilla conflict, it is assumed to be externally induced, by North Koreans with Soviet backing and weapons, with the Americans standing idly by while the Rhee regime fought the infiltrators.

Yet the evidence shows that the Soviets had no involvement with the southern partisans, the North Koreans connect mainly to attempts at infiltration and guerrillas in Kangwŏn province, while the seemingly uninvolved Americans organized and equipped the southern counterinsurgent forces, gave them their best intelligence materials, planned their actions, and occasionally commanded them directly.

To my knowledge, no one has ever demonstrated any level of Soviet involvement with the southern guerrillas. Soviet arms were never captured in the South, except from small numbers of infiltrators along the parallel. Infiltrating guerrillas were not trained by Soviet advisors. The North Koreans trained them, in a school for partisans and agents called the *Kangdong hakwŏn*, and South Korean historiography has predictably declared this to be the original locus of the conspiracy: the conflict was caused by outside agitators, therefore no conditions promoting guerrilla activity existed in the south, and therefore no true southerners were ever guerrillas.[45]

American intelligence picked up evidence in late 1948 that some one thousand recruits were being trained at Kangdong for dispatch to the south, most of them said to be members of the SKWP. As we have seen, guerrillas in the Odae-san area either were infiltrated from the North, or got supplies from there. Such units always were better equipped, and always were better organized into staff sections, companies, and platoons.[46]

In early 1949 as the guerrilla struggle developed, the CIA was unable to confirm "a centralized coordinating authority" higher than the provincial level, nor the extent to which the SKWP (let alone the North Koreans) "issues specific directives to the guerrillas." A year later in April 1950 the Americans found that the North Koreans had supported guerrillas in Kangwŏn and the upper coast of North Kyŏngsang with weapons and supplies, but "almost 100 percent of the guerrillas in the Chŏlla and Kyŏngsang Provinces have been recruited locally." American intelligence had documented no more than 2,000 recruits passing through Kangdong, of which perhaps 1,800 had sought to infiltrate the South—most of them unsuccessfully. No Soviet weapons had ever been authenticated in South Korea, except near the parallel; most guerrillas had Japanese and American arms. Captured radio transmitters, with one exception, were not powerful enough to receive signals from the North. Guerrillas were usually reduced to foraging for food and other supplies, necessitating frequent depradations against the local population. Another report found that the guerrillas "apparently receive little more than moral support from North Korea."[47]

For American intelligence the question was not what the North Koreans had done, but why they had not done *more*. No good explanation presented itself as to why this particular dog did not bark, and so the Americans fell back on their usual crutch: it must be another deceptive

"Soviet strategy" (undefined).[48] The North Korean press paid much attention to the guerrillas, of course, but tended to let southern communist leaders analyze what was going on. They occasionally said that the southern guerrillas expressed fealty to Kim Il Sung and emulated his experience in Manchuria, but they never emphasized this in the manner that they would have had they believed—or desired others to believe—that it was true. Indeed, the party told its own propagandists that the North sent its "warm encouragement" to the southerners, but by implication, little else.[49]

In late 1948 as the guerrilla movement unfolded, American Counter-Intelligence Corps sources uncovered a tantalizing report, deemed highly reliable, saying that the North had ordered the SKWP to reorganize itself, such that "only ardent and able members" of the present SKWP cells would remain; the purpose of this was "to prepare the SKWP for military action in South Korea. There will be *no military training and the members will not be armed*, but when the North Korean forces invade South Korea they will be utilized by the North Korean Army to the fullest extent" (emphasis added).[50]

If northern and southern communists were united in a strategy to reunify Korea, a protracted armed struggle internal to the South would be the best bet, since it would be much less likely to bring in American military forces. Indeed, the CIA continued to take this as the best estimate of communist intentions up to June 1950. If on the other hand the northern guerrillas around Kim Il Sung wished to reunify Korea, they could kill two birds with one stone by doing little to support the southern guerrilla struggle, while laying its failure at Pak Hŏn-yŏng's door.

The evidence we have here hardly proves this point, it merely is the deduced logic. But it is suggestive: the Kim Il Sung leadership would stand back from the fray, and let the "domestic" communists like Pak Hŏn-yŏng and Yi Sŭng-yŏp take responsibility for the fate of the southern partisans. If they succeeded, so much the better for a unified Korea . . . and so much the worse for a unified communist leadership. If they failed, so much the better for the Kim Il Sung leadership, which had its own army and its own guerrillas (the latter fighting in China), fully capable of unifying Korea on their own terms. We will return to this possibility in a later chapter.

The principal source of external involvement in the guerrilla war was American. It is still the case that Americans, scholars included, perceive an hiatus between the withdrawal of U.S. combat forces in July 1949 and the war that came a year later, such that the question becomes, why did the Americans return? The point here is, they never left. American advisors were all over the war zones in the South, constantly shadowing their Korean counterparts and urging them to greater effort. The man who distinguished himself in this was James Hausman, one of the key organizers of the suppression of the Yŏsu Rebellion, who spent the next three decades as the most important American operative in Korea, the liaison and nexus point between the American and Korean militaries and their intelligence outfits. A wily operator who hid his skills behind the mannerisms of an Arkansas hayseed, he was the Edward Lansdale of Korea, without the latter's human touch or concern for civic action. Hausman termed himself the father of the Korean Army in an interview, which was not far from the truth. He said that everyone knew this, including the Korean officers themselves, but could not say it publicly. In off-camera remarks, Hausman said that Koreans were "brutal bastards," "worse than the Japanese"; he sought to make their brutality more efficient, by showing them, for example, how to douse corpses of executed people with gasoline, thus to hide the method of execution or blame it on communists.[51] Back in his homeland, hardly anyone has heard of him.

IF THE RHEE regime had one unqualified success, viewed through the American lens, it was the apparent defeat of the southern partisans by the spring of 1950. A year before it had appeared that the guerrilla movement would only grow with the passage of time; but a major suppression campaign begun in the fall of 1949 resulted in high body counts and a perception that the guerrillas could no longer mount significant operations when they would be expected to—as the spring foliage returned in early 1950.

Both Dean Acheson and George Kennan saw the suppression of the internal threat as the litmus test of the Rhee regime's continence: if this worked, so would American-backed containment; if it did not, the regime would be viewed as another Kuomintang. Col. Preston Goodfellow had told Rhee in late 1948, in the context of a letter where he referred to his "many opportunities to talk with [Acheson] about Korea," that the guerrillas had to be "cleaned out quickly . . . everyone is watching how Korea handles the Communist threat." A weak policy will lose support in Washington; handle the threat well, and "Korea will be held in high esteem."[52] American backing was thus crucial to the very willingness of the ROKA to fight the guerrillas.

Americans sang the praises of the Rhee regime's counterinsurgency campaign, even as internal accounts recorded nauseating atrocities. As early as February 1949, Drumwright reported that in South Chŏlla "there was some not very discriminating destruction of villages" by the ROKA; but a week later he demonstrated his own support for such measures (if discriminate): "the only answer to the Communist threat is for non-Communist youth, after weeding out, to be organized just as tightly and for just as ruthless action as their Leftist counterparts." He even suggested that American missionaries be utilized for information on the guerrillas.[53]

The Americans and the Koreans were in constant conflict over proper counterinsurgent methods, but out of this tension came a meld of American methods and the techniques of suppression the Japanese had developed in Manchuria, for combating guerrillas in cold-weather, mountainous terrain, implemented by Korean officers who had served the Japanese (often in Manchuria).

The method was premised on using climate, terrain, and unflinchingly brutal methods to separate the guerrillas from their peasant constituencies. Cold weather would deny them the protection of thick foliage and undetected movement, military encirclement and blockade would isolate base areas and prevent resupply of food and weaponry, and draconian methods would break the guerrilla/people nexus. Winter drastically shifted the advantage to suppression forces. Large armies would establish the blockades, usually between the mountains and the low-lying fields and villages; small search and destroy units would then enter the mountains to ferret out guerrillas, often by tracking them in the snow. As former Japanese army officers put it, winter made guerrillas stationary and the counterinsurgents mobile; the guerrillas holed up in winter shelters that well-supplied and protected troops sought out and burned. Rebuilding them was next to impossible "because everything is frozen."[54]

During the Pacific War Japanese imperial forces were willing to go to any lengths to break the relationship between guerrillas and the sea of people that they swim in. The methods consisted of slaughtering suspected peasant collaborators (millions of Chinese died in so-called "kill-all, burn-all, loot-all" campaigns), relocating large populations into protected villages, and either executing or "converting" captured guerrillas. Kwantung Army counterinsurgency experts advised Americans that because of the close relations between guerrillas and peasants, "semi bandits [*sic*] must be abolished."[55] "Semi bandits" they defined as peasants who supported guerrillas by refusing to pay taxes or to give information on guerrillas; in other words, almost anybody in a peasant village. Once guerrillas were captured, they were either routinely shot or put through intensive "thought reform" methods to turn them around (the Japanese term is *tenko*); they would then become leaders or members of anticommunist groups, or of so-called "Concordia" associations promoting Japanese-Korean unity.[56]

The Manchurian guerrillas still bogged the Japanese down. The sustenance of the movement for almost a decade owed to Japanese inability to establish effective integrated control over all of Manchuria or to cut resupply from North China or the Soviet border areas, to novel techniques of small unit guerrilla fighting, and to the existence of large numbers of fire-field farmers who could not be isolated in the plains and valleys. But ultimately the suppression techniques proved effective, against both Korean and Chinese guerrillas. Maoist mobilization techniques worked in the remote and vast areas of North China, but not in Manchuria.

In South Korea the same suppression techniques had utility because of the climate and mountainous terrain, and the difficulties of resupplying guerrillas. The peninsula had seas on both sides, offering no escape across international boundaries or into dense jungle (as in Vietnam, for example). Blockading the coasts was relatively easy. The mountainous eastern part of the thirty-eighth parallel was the best venue for resupply or infiltration of guerrillas, but a combination of effective ROKA blocking and P'yŏngyang's seeming indifference to the guerrilla struggle made that venue of marginal use.

If the methods were the same, so were the personnel. Kim Paek-il, one of three top suppression commanders (the other two being Chŏng Il-gwŏn and Paek Sŏn-yŏp), was a former officer in the Japanese Kwantung Army who had five years of experience in Manchurian counterguerrilla operations. Kim was born in the town of Myŏngch'ŏn, North Hamgyŏng Province. He was a classmate of Chŏng Il-gwŏn in the Manchukuo military academy, and left the North in early 1946 together with Paek Sŏn-yŏp. He distinguished himself in the suppression of the Yŏsu Rebellion.

Chŏng Il-gwŏn hailed from Kyŏngwŏn in North Hamgyŏng Province, and after graduating from the academy in 1938 he went into the Kwantung Army, where he remained until 1945. He returned to his hometown, but fled south at the end of 1945. By late 1947 he was Chief of Staff of the Constabulary. He became a favorite among Americans; after the war he held many high positions in the Park regime, including prime minister.[57]

This analysis is backed up by American internal evidence, as we will see, but perhaps more interesting is the corresponding communist perception of the difficulties of guerrilla fighting in the South—enunciated in the spring of 1950. In an important article published at the end of March, Yi Sŭng-yŏp, a southern communist, said that Rhee waited for the leaves to fall in 1949 before launching his suppression campaign (*t'oböl*); he mobilized five of the eight ROKA divisions (sixty thousand troops by Yi's count), combat units of the National Police, and right-wing youth groups. The commander Yi mentioned most frequently was Kim Paek-il, head of the Chirisan task force. The ROK used American naval vessels to patrol the coast, and American spotter planes to search out guerrillas. The five divisions corresponded to five suppression areas (*t'obŏl chigu*): Honam, Chiri-san, Yŏngnam, T'aebaek-san, and the "*chungbu*" or central area; the program placed ten suppression soldiers against each guerrilla (the classic counterinsurgency formula). Large units patrolled outer blockade lines, keeping the areas (and thus the guerrillas) separated; first one area was emphasized, then another (Honam, the worst area, was the main target in October and November 1949). Small units ran "daily searches" in the mountains. When they met guerrillas, they expended enormous firepower—Yi said the soldiers were "armed to the toenails" with American weapons.

Winter, he said, is the toughest time for guerrillas to fight, with both temperatures and foliage low; he also thought ROKA troops were afraid to fight the guerrillas in the warm months, preferring to corral them and starve them out. The blockade of the mountains, he asserted, was combined with a "scorched earth" policy in nearby villages, slaughtering or "driving away" large numbers of peasants. If there was suspicion that peasants were in contact with guerrillas, villages were burned and the population moved. He cited an incident in Pallidong, Yŏnggwang-gun, in which soldiers lined up all villagers between the ages of eighteen and forty, asked them questions about local guerrillas, and shot all those who refused to cooperate—32 in all. If peasants remained in their villages, a curfew was imposed during hours of darkness. Movement along certain roads was prohibited. Thorough records were kept on all families, and right-wing youths were posted as guards and informers.

Yi discussed the ROK's establishment of "encirclement nets" (*p'owimang*), something reminiscent of Chiang Kai-shek's German-directed encirclement and eventual defeat of Maoist forces during the Kiangsi Period in the early 1930s; but mostly he traced the techniques back to the Japanese. He alleged that "our sworn enemy, the Japanese militarist clique," was advising the ROK on suppression techniques.[58]

Although Yi's account was full of predictable outrage and hyperbole, it was a reasonably accurate rendering of the suppression campaign. The historical analogies were also correct. Rhee probably had in his mind the 1920s experience of Chiang Kai-shek, only reversed: if in China it was a northern expedition (*pukbŏl* in the Korean pronunciation of the Chinese characters Chiang used), followed by a communist repression (*t'obŏl*), it would be a *t'obŏl* followed by a *pukbŏl* in Korea. But the important lineage was from the Japanese experience in Manchurian counterinsurgency.

In the spring of 1949, with newly-leaved forests, the Chirisan guerrillas reactivated their struggle and won some quick victories, as we have seen. Rhee dispatched the young colonel of Japanese Army background, Chŏng Il-gwŏn, to command a three thousand-man suppression force, of whom about half were line ROKA troops. The guerrillas operated in small units, running hither and thither in the heavily wooded terrain.

Hong Sun-sŏk, aged twenty-four, led one unit; Kim Chi-hwi (twenty-three) and his wife (a former nurse from Cheju) led another. Colonel Chŏng set up a pass system requiring citizens in the area to hold identity cards, and established a civilian defense corps in each village, posting sentries, armed with bamboo spears, in village watchtowers. He told his troops not to requisition supplies without payment, and not to molest local peasants, especially women.

On March 12 Chŏng began an all-out offensive against the Chiri guerrillas with four battalions of soldiers; within a month they had succeeded in killing Hong Sun-sŏk and capturing Kim Chi-hwi's wife. By May the embassy thought that Chŏng had achieved a big victory, in suppressing guerrillas if not in keeping his troops in line.[59] But the success was short-lived. As we have seen, by the end of the summer the guerrillas operated in large areas of southern Korea and appeared quite formidable. Therefore the Americans decided to step in directly, and inaugurate a major winter suppression campaign. Beginning in the late fall of 1949, it lasted almost down to the outbreak of the war.

CONCLUSION

Walter Sullivan was almost alone among foreign journalists in seeking out the truth of this guerrilla war. Large parts of southern Korea, he wrote in early 1950, "are darkened today by a cloud of terror that is probably unparalleled in the world." In the "hundreds of villages across the guerrilla areas," local village guards "crouch in pyramided straw shelters," and nights "are a long, cold vigil of listening." Guerrillas make brutal assaults on police, and the police take the guerrillas to their home villages and torture them for information. ("They never say anything anyway, no matter how much they are tortured," one informant related.) Then the police shoot them, and tie them to trees as an object lesson.

The persistence of the guerrillas, he wrote, "puzzles many Americans here," as does "the extreme brutality" of the conflict. But Sullivan went on to argue that "there is great divergence of wealth" in the country, with both middle and poor peasants living "a marginal existence." He interviewed ten peasant families; none owned all their own land, and most were tenants. The landlord took 30 percent of tenant produce, but additional exactions—government taxes, and various "contributions"—ranged from 48 to 70 percent of the annual crop. Sullivan concluded from his observations that the ROK's optimistic reports of a thorough guerrilla defeat were wrong. Cold weather was the main reason for the recent abatement of guerrilla activity, and thus the winter offensive had failed.[60]

Whether it failed or not is a critical question in the origins of the war and the frontal, conventional assault in June 1950. Was the movement eradicated or not? What role did the winter suppression campaign play in the North-South conflict? We will leave to a later chapter the ultimate fate of the guerrilla struggle as the war approached.

Chapter Nine

THE NORTHERN SYSTEM

> The sublime good fortune of our guerrilla detachment was to have at our center the Great Sun. Our general commander, great leader, sagacious teacher, and intimate friend was none other than General Kim Il Sung. Our unit was an unshakeable one, following General Kim and having General Kim as the nucleus. The General's embrace and love are like the Sun's, and when our fighters look up to and receive the General, their trust, self-sacrifice and devotion are such that they will gladly die for him.
>
> *A follower of Kim, 1946*

THE EAST is forever being viewed through lenses forged and polished in the West, a deep, pervasive and often unconscious "Orientalism" that brings the familiar into focus just as it obscures indigenous authenticity. Americans sought a replicated liberalism in the South, and got isolates like Kim Kyu-sik, or empty formalism, like the 1948 Constitution. It is no curiosity that the original political model through which Western experts interpreted the Democratic People's Republic of Korea (and the People's Republic of China) was the East European one of "people's democracies." That is, the DPRK and the PRC were impositions of a Soviet-derived system lacking legitimate revolutionary credentials. Wlodzimierz Brus saw the people's democracy form as "a *model* [sic] of socialist structure," a transplantation and "concentrated form" of Stalinism; he also refers to the People's Democracies as "brutal instruments of foreign domination," opposed ipso facto to nationalist ideologies of legitimation.[1] This was the dominant paradigm of interpretation, the accepted wisdom, about China throughout the 1950s and early 1960s, and it was unlearned very slowly, and only through the clear emergence of the Sino-Soviet conflict and the many labors of China scholars. This remains today the dominant interpretation of the DPRK.

In nearly all the Western literature North Korea is depicted as a classic Soviet satellite and puppet in the 1940s and 1950s; only in the late 1950s did the DPRK flirt with emulating another foreign model, the Chinese, and only in the 1960s did it seek an independent path to building socialism. Few grant that North Korea even in the recent period has developed much independence, and it is routinely called a Soviet satellite.

Although this judgment could be documented ad nauseum in the literature written by professional anticommunists, its prevalence is reflected in the judgment of one of the very best Soviet specialists, Robert C. Tucker, that among different paths to communist revolution, North Korea fits the East European pattern, especially the East German pattern: both "belong to the imposed variety." Contrasted to this would be Russia, China, Vietnam, Yugoslavia, Albania, and Cuba, where the revolutions took place "fundamentally as an indigenous process involving a substantial level of mass participation." Tucker hypothesizes that the imposed regimes would have problems of legitimacy, would be dependent on Soviet succor, and would not reflect native national-cultural "domestication." Finally, he asserts that no real revolutionary situation existed in the nations of foreign imposition, whereas with the indigenous category, "it was only by happenstance . . . that the Communist revolution did not take place over the entire national territory (speaking of Vietnam and China).[2]

DPRK internal politics is also thought to be as Soviet-influenced as any European socialist regime, a pure form of "Stalinism in the East."[3] This is given an added filip with the assumption, most often tacit, that Stalinism itself is "Oriental," and that "Kimilsungism" is a wretched excess of the Stalinist-Orientalist tendency. One can hear this from Soviet as well as American specialists, and from British leftists. Trotsky, Bukharin, Isaac Deutscher, and Karl Wittfogel all likened Stalin to Eastern potentates, especially Genghis Khan and Tamerlane, and thought his system a species of Oriental despotism, the worst features of the Asiatic mode of production coming to the fore. It is stunning to see Trotsky open his biography of Stalin with a first sentence remarking that the old revolutionist, Leonid Krassin, "was the first, if I am not mistaken, to call Stalin an 'Asiatic,' " and he goes on to talk about "Asiatic" leaders as cunning and brutal, presiding over static societies with a huge peasant base.[4] Perry Anderson once wrote that in the night of our ignorance, all forms take on the same hue; in this case, the portrait contains the people's democracy model, Stalinism, Genghis Khan, Tamerlane, and Kim Il Sung.

China in the 1980s was lauded for its turn outward and its movement toward some form of market socialism, with various American media cheerleading for Deng Xiaoping's capitalist-road pragmatism (until June 1989), yet it is one of the few remaining socialist states that routinely displays Stalin's picture (Albania and Soviet Georgia, I believe, are the only other examples). "Stalinist" North Korea has not displayed his picture since the Korean War, and its leaders have nothing kind to say about his legacy. More importantly, there is no evidence in the North Korean experience of the mass violence against whole classes of people or the classic, wholesale "purge" that characterized Stalinism, and that has been particularly noteworthy in the land reform campaigns in China and North Vietnam and the purges of the Cultural Revolution. Nonetheless

North Korea remains everyone's example of worst-case socialism and Soviet stoogery, leading American observers whether at the time or since to deem it unlikely that the DPRK had any capacity for independent action in 1950.

The DPRK is thus badly understood whether on its own terms or in comparative perspective. It is well beyond the scope of this work to provide a full picture of the North in the period 1947–1950. But it is essential to grasp the nature of this regime and its foreign alliances, which bear directly on the origins of the war. The following generalizations may be made at the outset, and applied to the 1940s, the hardest test for my theses, that is, the period of presumed major and shaping Soviet influence:

(1) North Korea evolved an indigenous political system in the late 1940s; its basic structure has not changed substantially, so that in the fundamentals what you see in 1949 is what you get in 1989.

(2) Soviet influence was *always* in competition with Chinese influence in Korea, and both were in conflict with indigenous political forms and practices. But the foreign model that has been more influential on Kim Il Sung, since the 1930s, has been the Chinese. Since the experience of the Korean War, Kim Il Sung has hated the Soviets. They reciprocate with an undisguised contempt, except in public discourse.[5] Each sees it necessary to get along with the other, for different reasons, but their interactions are mainly cool, state-to-state relations.

(3) North Korea generally corresponded little to the East European experience, and the closest comparisons were Rumania and Yugoslavia— not the states under complete Soviet hegemony such as East Germany. It has been much closer to a form of *revolutionary nationalist corporatism*. Its industrial structure, however, is comparatively well developed and here there is comparison with the economies of several East European countries, and a sharp divergence from the Asian socialist states of China, Vietnam, and Mongolia.

(4) Ultimately the DPRK was and is perhaps the most divergent of all established Marxist-Leninist systems, and represents a profound reassertion of native Korean political practice, from the role of the leader, to his self-reliant ideology, to the independent foreign stance.

In recent years a mass of new materials, captured in the North, has been declassified and provides solid evidence for such interpretations. On a number of central issues, the new documentation undermines accepted wisdom. North Korea was not simply a Soviet satellite, but evolved from a somewhat decentralized coalition regime based on widespread "people's committees" in 1945–1946, to a period of relative Soviet dominance in 1947–1948, thence in 1949 (i.e., well before the Chinese intervention in the Korean War and the time from which Wlodzimierz Brus dates the Stalinization of East Europe⁶) to important ties with the PRC, which in turn provided a realm of maneuver for the DPRK between the two communist giants. The northern system in the late 1940s was a meld of Korean, Soviet, and Chinese experience, with much of the selection of models rooted in Korean political culture. The North also diverged significantly from the USSR and China, especially in its party structure and its leadership system.

Kim Il Sung was by no means a handpicked Soviet puppet, but maneuvered politically first to establish his leadership, then to isolate and best the communists who had remained in Korea during the colonial period, then to ally with Soviet-aligned Koreans for a time, then to create a powerful army under his own leadership (in February 1948) that melded Koreans who had fought together in Manchuria and China proper with those who remained at home. The "Kimilsungist" system and the self-reliant ideology are artifacts of the 1940s, not the 1960s. Whatever one may think of the northern system, it cannot be said that its distinctive features have changed for forty years.

Among these influences, the Army was the backbone of Kim's dominance. Its leaders were hardbitten guerrillas with as much as twenty years experience; as the civil war grew in China, these men came to command tens of thousands of soldiers. They were steely and determined people whom the Soviets could not impose effective controls upon, except in the fantasies of Western scholarship. The point is that in northern Korea a core leadership formed in rural guerrilla struggle won the cities with hardly a shot fired, by virtue of the Japanese collapse and the Soviet entry; it then moved outward and downward to encompass and channel a spontaneous politics welling up from the people's committees, taking what it needed or had to take from the Soviets, and rejecting much of the rest.

In the realm of Marxism-Leninism, Koreans were mostly content to reiterate Soviet, which meant by that time Stalinist, formulations. The reason, perhaps, was that this theory, Western and often alien to conditions in Korea, meant little to them. Lecture notes from Party schools show straightforward presentations of Lenin's theory of imperialism (often with a high level of sophistication), carried extensive quotation from Lenin and Stalin, and relatively little attention to Marx. The Marxist-Leninist classics were widely translated and studied in the late 1940s, however, including much from Marx. Unlike China, a transliterated terminology was often used (e.g., *p'ŭroret'ariat'ŭ*, proletariat, instead of *musan'gyegŭp*, property-less class), and the Koreans never seemed to show the qualms Mao did about the vanguard role of the party, fastening instead on its practical uses as an organizational weapon.⁷

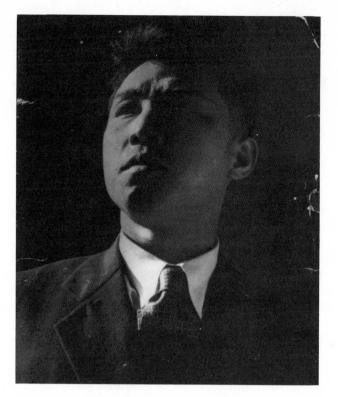

4. Kim Il Sung in the late 1940s

Kim Il Sung's thought was rarely presented as a separate wellspring of ideas in the late 1940s, as it was later on when his *Juche* ideology was placed on a par with Marxism-Leninism. In the 1940s *Juche* existed, but it was part of the general Korean desire, shared across the spectrum, for self-reliance and independence. The words then were *chaju*, *tongnip*, *charip*, *chach'e*, all words connoting some self-generated, autonomous, independent action. This was the source of most ideological divergence, and Kim Il Sung was behind much of it.

One long text for use by lecturers in Party schools, for example, followed contemporary Soviet lines, quoting from the *History of the Bolshevik Party—Short Course*, Lenin's *What is to be Done*, Engels's *Peasant War in Germany*, and then dilating in typical Soviet fashion on the "revisionism" of Karl Bernstein, Rosa Luxembourg, and others. When this same document comes to the Korean revolution, however, the dry tone disappears. The previous section is a preamble to the important thing, the purest Kim Il Sung line.

The text proceeds to dwell on the differing conditions in Korea when contrasted to other countries, how all methods of organization and work must be made to conform to the concrete historical situation in Korea, how the only "independent" [*chajujŏgin*] anti-Japanese movement, unaided by foreigners, was Kim's; how other Korean communists were petit bourgeois factionalists who had no contact with the masses, and how the North must be the base for preparing "a unified, self-reliant, independent country."

Until liberation, the text said, no Korean communists were able "to organize a revolutionary, vanguard party." Instead of a unified party, there were two types of communists: those who talked a lot about communism, but only "verbally" participated in the struggle, and the real activists, people who fought hard and went among the masses. They lacked theory but had good praxis. The first group ended up being unable to resist the Japanese, and thus after the mid-1930s quit the struggle, or did flip-flops under Japanese pressure and betrayed their comrades. The second group was best exemplified by Kim and his guerrillas. After liberation, the first group threw obstacles in the path of the revolution with endless haggling over Korea's historical stage, the correct line for the revolution, and so forth, engaging in "bourgeois personal heroism." It went on to quote Kim as saying, "whosoever has close ties with the masses, that person will be victorious."[8]

The Marxist-Leninist portion of this study moves on an abstract, disengaged track; when it turns to Korea, it forgets about the theory, even depicts Kim as lacking in theory (but so what?), and goes on to discuss actual conditions in Korea with the ring of authenticity, and with a devastating and often apt critique of the "domestic" communists and, by implication, Pak Hŏn-yŏng.

As much as any socialist system in the world, the DPRK has paid little attention to Marx and Lenin and overweening attention to its own peculiar problems. In terms of the iconography of the communist world, it is shocking to go from Moscow, where great, brilliant red and black banners of Marx and Lenin flap in the breeze, to P'yŏngyang where two almost invisible, tattered portraits of the same people hang on a downtown building—and nowhere else. They took from the Soviets and the Chinese what was useful, what was practical, and rejected the rest.

Stalinist ideology did have one thing to teach the Koreans that fit like a glove with their own preconceptions. This was the Platonism of Stalin, the architectonic, engineering from-on-high quality that marked his thought and his praxis. Stalin was a hegemon in the era of "late" heavy industrialization, and his discourse, like his name, clanked with an abased, mechanical imagery that valued pig iron over people, machines over bread, bridges over ideas, the leader's will over the democratic instincts of Marx. When he had Zhdanov impose his suffocating doctrine of socialist realism on the cultural realm in 1932, the metaphor of choice was that artists and writers should be "engineers of the soul," and that may serve as a general metaphor for Stalin's rule.

Koreans think that a maximum leader should be an engineer of the soul, too, but through exemplary behavior instead of by ramming it down your throat. They think a leader should be benevolent instead of brutish. And they think good ideas come from right thought—rectification of the mind—proceeding from the leader down through the masses, who learn the teaching by rote mastery of received wisdom. These Confucian residues melded with Soviet doctrines to make Kim a kind of benevolent Stalin, the fount of ideas, leading to a profound idealism and voluntarism at opposites with the materialism of Marx. The Koreans still refer to artists as engineers of the soul. They still surround Kim with a cult of personality. They still depict him as the source of all good ideas. This aspect of Stalinism stuck like glue in Korea, and if it had not existed in Moscow, it would have had to be invented in P'yŏngyang.

Such "top-downism," as we might call it, is one of the key characteristics of Korean politics, reinforced in the South by Japanese rule and in the North by Stalinism. Once the Koreans established centralized, imperative coordination of the political structure in late 1946, they reversed the flow of energy in the people's committees (PCs). Whereas it had been a bottom-up, spontaneous, percolating politics with variety and authenticity at the local levels, new regulations emphasized a structured control from above, top-heavy with bureaucratization and candid without mincing words about who ran the show.

Committee organizational regulations required "obedience" all the way down the line: provincial PCs "shall be obedient to" the center, and county PCs obey the provinces. Article 5 gave each PC authorization "to proclaim a decision and to impose it on the people under its jurisdiction"; there is little suggestion even of the questionable procedures of Leninist democratic-centralism.[9] This, of course, is not just a reflex of Stalinism. If the Japanese taught the Koreans in North and South one thing, it was how to use a state bureaucracy to impose the leadership's will, something much easier in North Korea because the old tension between state bureaucracy and landed wealth disappeared with the land revolution.

Kim Il Sung never, from the beginning, trucked with Maoist ideas about the spontaneity and creativity of the masses, the peasantry, or proletariat as the epistemological source of good ideas, and so on. Kim's use of Maoist techniques of leadership was not a reflex of a radical epistemology, but for implementation of what the Party wanted. It was always, for him, the passive tense: "the political level of the working class has been comprehensively raised"; educated people "are being turned into

5. People's Committee leaders commemorating their administrative training, June 1946, South P'yŏngan Province, North Korea

new intellectuals," peasants are being "working-classized." Party cadres were not to be tested by the masses; instead Kim used the Stalinist phrase, "cadres decide everything." Kim was completely orthodox in following a Soviet conception of the role of the leader and the party center which, as Merle Fainsod once put it, was "saturated in elitism."[10]

THE MASS PARTY

Korean communism in the late 1940s differed most from Soviet practice, perhaps, on the critical question of the proper role of the party. The Soviets wanted a bureaucracy based in urban proletarians and intellectuals; they wanted an institution that would have two prime characteristics: it would not be a vehicle of personal political power, and it would be penetrable by Soviet agents. Instead the North developed a party whose social base was the vast peasantry, and whose inner circle was constituted by the Kim Il Sung group.

Soviet doctrine in the 1940s called on countries as yet unripe for socialism, with class structures unready for either a bourgeois or a socialist revolution, to create coalitions of workers, national bourgeois, and peasants in so-called worker's parties, not communist parties. Thus Vietnam,

Poland, and Korea got "worker's parties." But the inner core was to be constituted by party bureaucrats, with at least a fiction of proletarian origin and leadership. These countries were not to talk about socialism; the Soviets were building that, and elsewhere the forces of production were insufficiently developed for a transition to socialism. The Soviets were thus far ahead of all the rest and leading the world revolution, and therefore they were in a position to provide tutelage.

The practical core of this position took the form in economics, for example, of Soviet opposition to rapid collectivization in the Asian countries, before the industrial revolution could provide mechanized agrarian production. Machines always came before men for Stalin.[11] The political corollary meant that "worker's parties" should be strong at home and weak abroad, that is, highly articulated organs of total power vis-à-vis their own societies, but permeable by Soviet control and influence.

The Kim leadership responded to this in typical Korean fashion: they gave the Soviets the form they wanted, and denied them the substance. The Koreans never spoke publicly of socialism as a goal in the 1940s. Like Poland, they left land in private hands and did not push collectivization; nonetheless the land could not be bought and sold, and village-level mutual aid and cooperation began quickly.

The Koreans called their organization a worker's party, and adopted a three-class alliance as per Soviet doctrine, symbolized by a hammer, a sickle, and a writing brush: workers, peasants, and a category, *samuwŏn*, that swept up all the rest: bureaucrats, clerks, teachers, experts, intellectuals. All this was formally correct.

The pro-Soviet man Hŏ Ka-i was a key agent in party building, occupying a critical position in the Organization Department. His orthodox conception placed a legal-rational Secretariat at the center of power, systematizing recruitment and promotion within the party apparatus. In a top secret report on party organization in late 1946, he began with many of the same things Kim Il Sung always said: too many reactionaries and impure elements had entered the party, there should be more "checkup" or inspection work on members, good statistics should be kept, policies of the center were poorly implemented locally, cell life was "generally weak," and so on. But then he dwelt on the basic class character (*sŏngbun*) of the party, implying that too many peasants had entered it, whereas its basis had to be the working class. Furthermore, too many landlords, entrepreneurs, and businessmen had entered the party; these should be "purged."[12]

Kim Il Sung's conception was rather different. He and his allies used the party apparatus to recruit a mass base for his rule, an open-door policy in which almost anyone could be a party member, regardless of class background. Attitude was far more important than class. Bad theory from a Marxist standpoint, it was good politics. It sought to organize all who could be organized, including members of "bad classes." But above all, the logic of this policy, given Korea's class structure, brought masses of poor peasants into the party ranks. Instead of a vanguard party constituting 2 or 3 percent of the population, Korea got a party encompassing 12 to 14 percent, meaning perhaps a quarter or more of the entire adult population; the "vanguard" was not proletarian, but an inner core bound together by personal loyalty to Kim Il Sung.

It is not hard to discern what the Soviets think about such a party. K. V. Kukushin wrote that in 1935 the Chinese Communist Party committed a "right opportunistic blunder" by setting forth "the very dangerous proposition that all who 'want to fight for the Communist Party's principles whatever their social origin' should be admitted to party membership," which meant in practice that proletarians would be "swallowed up" by the peasant and petit bourgeois masses.[13] This is precisely the quality that characterized Kim's party-building as well.

A careful American intelligence study noted Kim's "obsession to recruit membership at the lowest levels," and the Soviet opposition that this produced. By mid-1947, an intimate of Kim, one of a handful of people able to refer to him with the familiar sobriquet "Il Sung," Chu Yong-ha of the so-called "Yenan faction," said the North Korean Workers Party (NKWP) had become a "mass party" already 700,000 strong; using the organic language Kim favored so much, he said the party now had "blood-line like relations" with the masses. The latter, in turn, were being carefully "reared" by the party through a host of "study sessions," "debate meetings," "lecture meetings," "criticism and self-criticism" sessions, all part of a "broad educational network." In other words if poor peasants were not ready for the revolution, they could be made so by mass tutelage. Chu traced the origin of this conception directly to Kim's rise to power at the December 1945 meeting of the northern branch of the Korean Communist Party (KCP); this was when the organizational principles of the party were laid down.[14]

The tendency of underdevelopment is to produce distensions and deformations through uneven industrialization—a foreign-imposed infrastructure, for example, running ahead of society's capacity to react, to accommodate change. Thus in mid–twentieth century Korea if "modern" classes did not exist to complement newly-born means of production, the regimes would make them. The southern state was the midwife of a new bourgeoisie in the years after the Korean War. The North took poor peasants and made them over as proletarians. It is also predictable that a society emerging from a Confucian past would believe that modern, in this case revolutionary, consciousness can be taught, inculcated, and that education or "rearing" (yangsŏng) comes before material forces, that is, changes in social formations that presumably produce revolutionaries with automaticity. The Leninist conception was that if the proper social forces did not exist, then a tightly disciplined highly-organized vanguard would bring consciousness to people from without. Kim's conception was rather more like Mao's, except that the Korean Workers Party (KWP) was much larger in proportion to the society, and if anything more voluntarist in its belief in the infinite malleability of the human mind apart from social and material forces.

A book on peasant associations provided an argument for relying on poor and middle peasants in organization work, saying that they were not only the vast majority in Korea, but that the rich peasant or *kulak* class had not had significant development owing to the Japanese having "pushed them down" and taken the best lands; much like Mao, this book argued that although poor and middle peasants would be the base, rich peasants and even some landlords could be won over to the revolution because they had suffered at the hands of the Japanese.[15]

Such thinking led to an inclusive policy toward "bad classes," often enrolled through an elastic use of the *samuwŏn* category. Internal party organization materials provided a justification for opening the door to the bourgeoisie, such as it was in Korea. Because of Japanese laws limiting percentages of Korean capital in firms, and state bureaucratic controls on so much economic activity, the argument went, Korea's capitalists either prospered in league with the Japanese or became intensely antiimperialist by watching the Japanese trample their interests. The latter group was more numerous and could be worked with, and "played a significant role in postwar north Korean development."[16]

Internal evidence makes clear the extraordinary bulk of poor peasants in this party. At the time of NKWP formation in late 1946, workers constituted 20 percent of the membership, poor peasants 50 percent, and *samuwŏn* 14 percent. A year later, workers were still at 20 percent, but peasants were at 53 percent, *samuwŏn* at 13 percent (the latter probably reflected the movement southward of educated Koreans). From the fall of 1946 to the spring of 1948, whereas the number of workers in the party doubled, the number of poor peasants more than tripled. Figures for North Ham'gyŏng Province, which had a significant proletariat, show that in 1946 43 percent were workers and 26 percent poor peasants; a year later workers had dropped to 30 percent, poor peasants had gone up to 37 percent. At the end of 1947, only 10 percent of the party membership had schooling above the elementary level, with fully one-third illiterate—that is, a rather unenlightened vanguard.[17]

Even among cadres responsible for this massive mobilization and education campaign, poor peasant background was common. In a top secret compilation of data on some 1,881 "cultural cadres" in late 1949, 66 percent came from poor peasant background, 19 percent from proletarian background. Data on individual class, a category in which the Koreans defined class by occupation as opposed to the family's social situation, show 37 percent were proletarians and 25 percent were poor peasants; 23 percent were *samuwŏn*. Interestingly, 422 of these cadres had experience in the Chinese Eighth Route Army, a different route to education and upward mobility.[18]

This may be compared with Soviet data from the decade of the 1920s, showing the class composition of the Bolshevik Party ranging from 44 to 61 percent for workers, 19 to 29 percent for all peasants (i.e., not just poor peasants). Educational levels were much higher than in Korea, with only 3 percent illiterate, and 63 percent having at least elementary schooling.[19]

Qualitative information on individual poor peasants demonstrates the extraordinary change in personal fortunes that came with Kim's open-door policy, a kind of instant upward mobility that made most of them grateful for his "benevolence." Song Yun-p'il, for example, was born into a "miserable" poor peasant family in 1920; his father died in 1925. His mother slaved to feed her kids and put Yun-p'il through elementary school. There, he was influenced by communists, and spent eighteen months in a Japanese jail for it. In the 1930s and 1940s he worked as a tenant farmer. In December 1945 he became a "candidate" member of his local party branch, and in March 1946 was placed on the township committee responsible for enforcing the land reform. In early 1950 he was a county-level KWP cadre.

Kim Chu-suk, a woman born into a poor peasant family also in 1920, worked as a tenant farmer during the war. In 1946 she joined the Women's League as a "propagandist." The next year she attended the provincial party cadre school, and on graduation became a statistician in a township party branch office. By 1950 she had also been promoted to the county level.

Kim Ch'ŏl-gŭm fits nicely our pattern of mobilized worker-peasants. Born into a poor peasant family in 1910 in Sihŭng near Seoul, he farmed as a tenant and became responsible for the family when his father died in 1925; during the depression the family suffered greatly and his mother died. He took his sister to northern Korea, when industrial jobs started opening up. He got work on Japanese fishing trawlers as a boiler-room man, suffering "contemptuous treatment" at the hands of the colonizers, but managing to learn some skills. In 1942 he was "forcibly drafted" and sent to Singapore where he worked in merchant shipping for three years. In April 1945, with British airpower attacking every day, he decided he "did not want to die for the Japanese" and ran away. Three days later he was caught and thrown into a military prison. He joined the NKWP in 1946, as did four of his remaining five relatives, then living in Wŏnsan.

Tong Hak-jŏng, from a family whose entire extended group or clan were poor tenants, was also a classic worker-peasant. During the depression his father could not sustain a farming livelihood, and so when he was thirteen, Hak-jŏng went with the family from Myongch'ŏn County in North Ham'gyŏng Province to Ch'ientao in Manchuria, where they remained until 1945. His father worked in a Japanese textile factory, he in a mine. The son went to Seoul in 1946, trying to get into high school. Failing that, he returned to Susang and joined a *poandae* (peace-keeping) unit in October 1946. After two months of training in 1947, he became a deputy detachment head (*pudaejang*) in the *poandae*, and by 1950 was a Korean Peoples Army (KPA) officer.[20]

These cases delineate the microcosmic evidence of a thorough social revolution, a class structure stood on its head. At any time before 1945 it was virtually inconceivable for uneducated poor peasants to become county-level officials or officers in the army. But in North Korea such careers as the above were modal; multitudes of similar biographies could be presented that conform to this pattern. Even something as fundamental as Korean marriage patterns began to change quickly. It became important to marry a woman with the proper class background, meaning poor peasant or worker, because this was a ticket to better life chances.[21]

Americans would look at North Korea and say, so what? What is the quality of their political participation in this regime? But Americans make the implicit (and often false) assumption that their own society is somehow made up of a multitude of Thomas Jeffersons, all anxious to defend their rights and participate freely in politics without fear or favor—and so should everyone, everywhere. North Koreans made the assumption that their society was, or could be, made up of little Kim Il Sungs: people with no formal education who can overcome poor backgrounds on the basis of changed attitude. The "mass party" conception provided millions of poor peasants with status and position hardly dreamed of by their parents, thus forming a popular basis for Kim Il Sung's political power.

These cadre records also contain a fascinating biography of a south Korean communist of landlord background, later taken into the KWP. Kim Mun-sik (I have changed the name) was born as the only child into a *yangban* and landed family in Kyŏngju, North Kyŏngsang Province. His family, he said, was "undeserving of its wealth"; no one worked, but instead employed tenants and hired laborers who "lived like slaves." His grandfather occupied his time "reading the words of the old sages, and had the moral outlook of the Confucian." His father "did nothing but drink alcohol, write Chinese poetry, and wander around with his friends in the pattern of the country *yangban*."

His grandfather taught him the one thousand-character classic as a child, he went to elementary school, but then twice failed the exams for middle school. After another year of study with his grandfather, he passed the exams and entered a school where all but seven of the students were Japanese. After several beatings by Japanese teachers, he took after one with a club and was thrown out. He then led a "degraded life" in Taegu in the late 1930s. Meanwhile his family's wealth had improved considerably in the mid-1930s, a common pattern for landlords, which, he said, simply encouraged the "profligacy" of his relatives, and himself. During the war he did little else besides read books and take a wife. In 1943 he opened a store in Taegu with family money, but it failed and he began drinking heavily. In 1944 a friend got him a job in the city government. In December 1944 he received a draft order and fled to a mountain village, where he stayed until the liberation.

Kim then sought to open another store in Taegu, but it also failed and he returned to his family home. His politicization began with the Autumn Harvest Uprisings, the suppression of which appalled him; he joined the South Korean Workers Party (SKWP) in January 1947, and became organization chief in his local township. He was forced underground after the March 22, 1947, strike. On May Day 1947, he shot and killed two policemen who fired on a group of peaceful demonstrators. The authorities did not know this, and jailed him on other charges in October 1947. He came out two months later, worked against the May 1948 elections and then continued underground activities. Arrested again in February 1949, he spent eight months in prison. In late 1949 he became a military intelligence operative for the SKWP, and in March 1950 was swept up and given an indeterminate sentence in Seoul's West Gate Prison. North Korean tanks burst through the gates on June 27, 1950, and set him free.

Kim Mun-sik's extended family came to harbor several SKWP operatives. One male of Mun-sik's age had gone to Osaka where he labored in an iron works; on his return to Taegu he joined the SKWP. Another SKWP relative had been a textile worker before and after the liberation. Another had been a peasant farmer before 1945, and joined the SKWP after prolonged unemployment in postliberation Taegu. A thirty-six-year-old relative had been a factory head in Yŏn'il, but nonetheless joined the SKWP. The oldest male relative listed, a forty-two-year-old landlord, joined Yŏ Un-hong's Laboring People's Party.[22]

Kim Mun-sik is a good example of the typical pattern of southern communists, many of whom came from educated or landed backgrounds. Failing in Korean society in spite of their station, frustrated in school or business, they rebel because of downward mobility or real or imagined oppression. Their tendency was toward an intellectual Marxism and political infighting, or, if they became activists, toward urban politics and reliance on terrorist violence rather than on patient organizing of masses of people—which, in any case, was nearly impossible under the formidable police apparatus. But Kim Mun-sik is an utter contrast with the poor peasant cadres that filled the ranks of Kim Il Sung's party—a policy the southern communists would likely see as reflecting Kim's low theoretical level.

Americans later collected information from POWs and intelligence studies indicating that although many respondents disliked the tight controls of the regime, most were laudatory of the social revolution, which opened new careers to millions and raised the educational level of the entire population within a few years. The opening of the educational system to children of the poorest classes was frequently cited, given the importance Koreans place on education and the traditional elitism of the system. People did not cower under a totalitarian dictatorship, but tended to support the regime willingly because they got concrete status and material benefits from it; most had little understanding of "communism," but they did like to get land and jobs.[23]

CORPORATISM AND REVOLUTIONARY NATIONALISM

The greatest divergence in North Korean socialism came at the commanding heights of the regime, the core leadership that constituted the real vanguard of the revolution. Instead of a bureaucratic hierarchy, the organizational principle was personal loyalty among a tightly-knit inner circle, which then became the nucleus of ever-widening concentric circles radiating outward. The conception was less rational-legal than charismatic, less bureaucratic than organic. The glue holding that core together has been personalistic, based on the charisma of the guerrilla struggle against Japan; the ideology has been revolutionary nationalism; the political form best approximates a type of corporatism; the result is also something we might call national solipsism.

Kim's leadership system has changed little since the 1940s, or perhaps the 1930s. The extravagant praise surrounding him has grown as he has reached his later years, but the change is merely one of degree. Utterly obnoxious to a Western liberal, denounced as a ridiculous "cult of personality" surrounding a man of dubious achievement, this politics takes Kim's early years and makes them into a national legend, a founding myth, a fount of legitimacy. It is not a politics alien to Korea.

Although Kim became chairman of the North Korean Interim People's Committee in February 1946, his particular leadership style does not appear until mid-1947. But by then the evidence of a hagiographic and grandiose style was almost as palpable as it is today. Beginning in 1947, agents making forays into North Korea reported that pictures and posters of Kim festooned telephone poles and the like with tales of how "wise, clear-sighted, spirited, wonderful," Kim Il Sung was. At the same time, articles appeared describing him "the Sun of the Nation," "a beautiful new red star in the sky," wisely guiding things with his "brilliant, scientific" methods.[24]

The original source of this "red star" was, of course, the 1930s guerrilla struggle. A document unavailable to me when I discussed Kim's background in volume 1 demonstrates that there is more to his past than legend. This is a study by two Japanese Kwantung Army Colonels in 1951, men who chased Kim in Manchuria and who provided Americans with their experience and their racist judgments on how to fight Korean guerrillas. They depicted Kim Il Sung as "the most famous" of Korean guerrilla leaders in the late 1930s. "Kim Il Sung was particularly popular among the Koreans in Manchuria. It is said that there were many Koreans who praised him as a Korean hero and gave him, secretly, both spiritual and material support."

Although Kim and other Korean guerrillas cooperated with Chinese leaders like Yang Ch'ing-yu, they were under no one else's effective command. "They did not care about the relation of their command organ with the Soviet Army or the Chinese Communist [army]." They ran back and forth across the Soviet border to escape counterinsurgency units, but the Soviets provided no weaponry or material aid. "When they were attacked by a subjugation unit, they had to move like monkeys through the woodmen's paths in the dense forest."

They never established permanent positions and fought in small units of fifty or one hundred, something that was termed "natural" because larger groups would be much more liable to attack and capture. Instead, they "always make [a] surprise attack on the enemy with resourceful plans and tactics." Local police "were at the complete mercy" of the guerrillas until 1939, when extraordinary counterinsurgency campaigns began. The army sustained major losses in 1938–1939: "not infrequently, units under the command of the Kwantung Army . . . were annihilated by bandit [guerrilla] ambush." Entire convoys and companies were destroyed in the spring of 1939. The guerrillas got the aid of the local Korean population time and again; Ch'ientao, the home of hundreds of thousands of Koreans, was "a very safe place for Korean bandits." The Japanese officers described the Korean population as "depraved, rebellious, and anti-Japanese." There were "only a few good people" amongst this "rebellious, crafty and lazy," indeed "very discontented race." Their nasty habits included appearing "very gentle outwardly," while they nonetheless "harboured ill feeling against Japan." They would give no information on guerrillas to the Japanese, another index of their general depravity, one would assume.[25]

Original research by Haruki Wada has suggested that when the Manchurian guerrillas returned to Korea, the top leaders such as Kim Il Sung, Kim Ch'aek, and Ch'oe Hyŏn agreed amongst themselves to promote Kim Il Sung as the maximum figure, for reasons that of course remain unstated; but they may include his wider reputation and his personal force. By some indexes the others outranked him; Kim Ch'aek and Ch'oe Hyŏn were higher than Kim in the Chinese Communist hierarchy. In any case they did support Kim with unstinting loyalty for the rest of their lives, and with other Manchurian guerrillas became the core of the North Korean hierarchy.

In an important interview with Kim's first biographer in 1946, an unnamed member of his guerrilla unit promoted a Kim Il Sung line that remains the official history today. Kim set the following sort of example:

> This sort of person naturally has an extremely strong power of attraction to others. . . . And it goes without saying that a guerrilla organization with such a person at the center is incomparably strong. The sublime good fortune of our guerrilla detachment was to have at our center the Great Sun. Our general commander, great leader, sagacious

6. Kim Ch'aek, Kim Il Sung's right-hand man, with a child, perhaps his own, circa 1949

teacher, and intimate friend was none other than General Kim Il Sung. Our unit was an unshakeable one, following General Kim and having General Kim as the nucleus. The General's embrace and love are like the Sun's, and when our fighters look up to and receive the General, their trust, self-sacrifice and devotion are such that they will gladly die for him.

The detachment's "philosophy of life" was their willingness to follow Kim's orders even to the death; "its strength is the strength deriving from uniting around Kim Il Sung . . . our guerrillas' historical tradition is precisely that of uniting around Kim as our only leader."

Kim loved and cared for his followers, and they responded with an iron discipline for which "a spirit of obedience is needed, and what is needed for that is a spirit of respect. . . . Above all, the spiritual foundation [of our discipline] was this spirit of respect. And the greatest respect was for General Kim Il Sung. Our discipline grew and became strong amid respect and obedience for him." This officer then went on to recommend the guerrilla tradition as a good principle for party and mass organizations; he might have added that it would be the principle for the organization of the entire North Korean state.

The language used by this man is fascinating. It is all moral language, bathing Kim in a hundred virtues, almost all of which are Confucian virtues—benevolence, love, trust, obedience, respect, reciprocity between leader and led. It is a language of circles: the phrase "uniting around Kim" uses a term, *chuwi*, that literally means circumference; in a neighborhood it means living around a center or *chungsim*, which literally means a "central heart." Synonyms for this, widely used in the North Korean literature, are "core" and "nucleus." The Party center was also a euphemism for Kim and his closest allies, just as it became the euphemism for Kim's son in the 1970s when the succession was being arranged.[26]

This is also a language with religious resonance, both Shamanist and Christian. The term that the North Koreans translate as "to hold [Kim] in esteem," *urŏrŏ patta*, literally means "to look up to and receive," and is used religiously for receiving Christ. It is also used in the sense of esteeming one's father. The term "Great Sun" resonates with Western usages placing a king in communion with the Sun, or by extension with God, and with Japanese usages regarding the emperor. To my knowledge, the first statue of Kim erected in the North was unveiled on Christmas Day 1949, something that suggests a conscious attempt to present him as a secular Christ, or Christ-substitute.[27]

The style is also paternal, with Kim depicted as the benevolent father of the nation, and the nation compared to one large family. The strongest of emotional bonds in Korea is that of filial piety, and Kim and his allies sought to weld the nation together by drawing on vast reservoirs of duty and obligation toward one's parents, seeking to have them transferred to the state through Kim's auspices. North Korea always has been remarkable in its treatment of children; Kim personally identified himself with orphans of revolutionary fighters or, after 1953, of Korean War dead; a major school for orphans of important leaders was located at his birthplace. Kids routinely called him "our father."

The process of burnishing Kim's image and uniting around him also suggests an element of chivalry, of men and women bound together by oaths of fealty, duty, obligation, and possessing among them uncommon virtues of courage, daring and sacrifice. It is the language of feudal warlords, and indeed Kim in the early period always used the title *changgun*, translated as "general," but using the same characters as the Japanese term *shogun*.

The dynamic of this politics is centrifugal-centripetal, concentric circles radiating outward from the core, embracing first the Manchurian guerrillas and their families, then the Party hierarchy, then the Army, then the people; it then falls back upon itself as each outer circle returns trust and loyalty to the center. Somewhere in between there arose a plodding, dense bureaucracy that does the day-to-day administration. But at the commanding heights this was a charismatic politics, its legitimacy resting in an overblown history and a trumpeted mythology about men with superhuman qualities.

It is characteristic of the North Koreans, then and now, that they simultaneously paper the walls with hagiography and mythology about Kim and his guerrillas, while caring little to provide any evidence that would convince an independent observer. This speaks to another characteristic of the Kim leadership, a profound solipsism, indeed a *national solipsism* that is also connected to the theme of concentric circles. Kim's legend and mandate would seem to stop at the national border, non-Koreans cannot be expected to appreciate its virtues. Even prewar Japan did not try to sell *kokutai* to the *gaijin* (foreigners). But the circles keep on extending, to encompass foreigners and get them to see the virtues so obvious to North Koreans. This is far more pronounced today, when the regime organizes and funds "*Juche* study groups" all over the world, treating group leaders like heads of state, but it existed in the 1940s in a solipsism which seemed to think all eyes were on Korea as the Kim leadership blazed a trail for postcolonial revolution, providing a model to emulate. It is a Korean microcosm of the old Chinese world order, radiating outward from the Middle Kingdon or central source.

Another interesting element in the 1947 interview is implicit, the suggestion that Kim Il Sung is being put forward as "Kim Il Sung," a figure larger than life, as an example for all to emulate. If all are to emulate' him, he cannot put his pants on one leg at a time like anyone else, he has to be perfect. But in the conjuring of that perfection, the real man Kim Il Sung, nee Kim Sŏng-ju, runs the risk of being himself a symbol of power rather than holding it, being put forward by shadowy figures as the source of everyone's legitimacy. There is a hint of an Emperor system here, a figure being created who would have to be mysterious and remote.

Another person who articulated this vision of leadership was Kim Ch'ang-man, who like Chu Yong-ha used the familiar "Il Sung" in his writings, and who became for a time Kim Il Sung's ideological sidekick. Kim Ch'ang-man was a Yenan Korean and, like Kim Il Sung, melded Maoist and Korean leadership methods. In a critically important article entitled "Several Questions in Methods of Leadership in Party Work,"[28] Kim argued that two methods of leadership were central. The first is the mass line, and in discussing it he directly plagiarized Mao's famous 1942 speech, attributing the words to Kim (see chapter 9). The second was fostering or rearing core leadership. "This is the leadership method of forming in party branches and work units . . . leading nuclei [haeksim] based on a small number of active elements, and then tightly uniting this core and the broad masses." The mass line linked the core and the mass, likened to "blood lines" within a family. How is core leadership formed? It "must always be formed in a real struggle. . . . In an actual struggle, active elements are continuously born, while from among the original leading core a portion is cast off. . . . This is the natural growth of an organization." Workers and peasants with low theoretical and cultural levels, he said, can be fashioned into core elements through struggle; so can all of Korea, even though it is short on a history of struggle and has many people, even cadres, who are poorly educated and culturally backward.

Koreans are nothing if not eclectic in their foreign borrowing; among other things we may see in such statements a metaphor of atomic nuclei being born and dying. But anyone familiar with Mao's writings will see in this analysis a voluntarism that assumes a people who are "poor and blank" can be honed into revolutionaries through class struggle and specific methods for attitudinal change, such as small group criticism and self-criticism. The basic materialism of Marx, which assumes that class world views are ultimately formed through epochal change, through an ethos that is inseparable from a class's historical relationship to means of production, such that one's assumptions and premises are not a matter of conscious reflection, would treat of Korean efforts to remold millions of peasants overnight as the basest left-wing infantilism.

Kim and Mao made the idealist assumption that class consciousness can metamorphose through struggle and various forms of "consciousness raising." For Mao this was supposed to be something that people would be brought to through class struggle. But for Kim and for North Korea, where class struggle was telescoped (for example in the quick land reform) and where a Marxist conception of structuring from below gave way to a Hegelian conception of structuring from above, the borrowing from China melded with Kim's benevolent engineering conception. If Koreans were "poor and blank," he and his "core" would write on this tabula rasa.

Koreans have always assumed, implicitly and often explicitly, that the fount of wisdom, the spark of philosophy, occurs in the mind of the leader—that it resides in an exceptional person. One genius is at the core, one philosopher-king, and he tutors everyone else. But if Kim was at times an engineer from above, he also descended to the lower levels to observe his engineering through incessant "on-the-spot guidance." If he was often a remote emperor, protected by moats of security and mystery, he was also an emperor who pressed the flesh.

It is the engineering of the soul with a human touch. It is Platonism for the masses. It is Hegelian populism. It is the Confucian mass line. Indeed, hardly a cornerstone can be laid, a tunnel dug, a building topped off, without the genius-leader being present to sanctify it. The uniting of theory and practice is the catalytic action of the leader interacting with the led. His teaching was studied over and over, everywhere, in inner sanctum–like rooms where a ghostly white bust presided, until it was established as a state of mind.

There is not just a Hegelian idealism here, but a kind of individual heroism, focused on the extraordinary "I". Korean child-rearing patterns would reinforce such a conception, where the first son is both pampered and spoiled, by non-Korean standards, and given solemn responsibilities for rearing the other children. The eldest son is nurtured entirely within the nuclear family, living with the parents under the same roof after he gets married; at a certain point in his maturity he then becomes the family patriarch. When Kim's son finally (and predictably) came forward to assume the mantle in the 1980s, the universal line was that he, personally, was a genius; traditional first-son patterns explained the careful rearing and unveiling. But such family patterns also tend to produce first sons who think they can be anything; it is often said that every first son wants to be President in Korea. Kim Il Sung was a first son who got his wish.

In Kim's praxis as with Confucianism the family unit becomes a model for structuring the state, the ultimate metaphor for organizing everything under heaven, including international relations. True, the North Koreans have always called for equality and independence in state-to-state relations. But that is not the behavior that has governed their most important relationship, with China. The borrowing and emulating of China is extraordinary—"the Arduous March" for the Long March, concentric circles that mimic China's world order conception, rank plagiarism of Maoist classics, Kim even appearing in Mao cap and greatcoat looking just like the Helmsman. North Korea was China's little brother just as in the familial-based traditional system, if with even more autonomy, and with a contemporary argot that would make North Korea an extension of the Chinese revolution. China responded in traditional form: with obligatory reciprocity in crises, and with benign neglect as one humdrum year turned into another.

No communist inner core is more permeated with family connections than the North Korean; although the guerrilla tie is the innermost core of power, Kim's family is next. His entire lineage was, from the time of his return to Korea, projected as a model revolutionary family. His first wife (the mother of Kim Jong Il), became the model woman guerrilla. Presumably alien and un-Marxist to Western communists, this practice fits nicely with East Asian politics: Taiwan, for example, with Chiang Kaishek giving way to his son; Mao or Marcos trying to pass power onto a wife; any of the big South Korean conglomerates, about two-thirds of which are held within founding families.

Such systems, traditionally in East Asia and markedly in North Korea, seem to lack a political process (at least to any public scrutiny). Always it is the absence of conflict that the regime seeks to project, all for one and one for all, a much-bruted "monolithicism." (Trotsky notes how appalled he and his Bolshevik allies were when Stalin began using this term, but the Koreans use it all the time.)[29] How could there be a political process, when the leader is perfect? What is the "political process" of the Japanese emperor system? This is one reason, perhaps, for the absence of much public conflict since 1946, a remarkable phenomenon even when Korea is compared to other communist states.

By the 1960s Kim Il Sung had made everyone willing to listen aware of his *Juche* idea, including readers of the *New York Times* who would frequently be treated to full page advertisements for the concept. Kim's use of the term is thought to have begun with a December 1955 speech that, coming well before de-Stalinization and the Sino-Soviet conflict, was remarkable in its criticism of Koreans who mimic things Russian. The existing literature depicts Kim as a dependent Soviet toady who, somehow, burst his bonds and began sharp criticism of his former masters. But newly available materials, including originals of Kim's speeches in the 1940s that cannot have been tampered with retrospectively by regime ideologues, make clear that the elements of self-reliance and revolutionary nationalism in this concept were present from Kim's emergence as a leader in his own right in the summer of 1947.

The Koreans call it "the great *Juche* idea," but it is less an idea than a state of mind. The term literally means being subjective where things Korean are concerned, putting Korea first in everything. The second character, *ch'e* in the Korean pronunciation, is found in the famous Chinese term of the late nineteenth-century self-strengthening movement, *t'i* of *t'i-yung*, meaning Chinese learning for the base (*t'i*) and Western learning for use; it is also the *tai* of *kokutai*, a concept promoted in Japan in the 1930s that meant, in essence, what it means to be Japanese as opposed to everything else, what is authentically Japanese. It was deeply identified with the prewar emperor system and with ultra-nationalism. Japanese scribblers would write on and on about "getting *kokutai* firmly in mind," once you have it firmly in your mind all else follows.[30] The Koreans use *Juche* in much the same way, its goal being a subjective, solipsistic state of mind, the correct thought that must precede and that will then determine correct action. The term is really untranslatable; for a foreigner its meaning is ever-receding, into a pool of everything that makes Koreans Korean, and therefore ultimately inaccessible to the non-Korean.

It is from this basic philosophical stance, which can be linked to a doctrine of essences, that the rest of Korean voluntarism flows—all the talk about ideas come first, the leader comes first. In discussing "how to study appearances to reach essences," Mao once said that you start with appearances, observations, and then go on "to reveal the substance and contradictions of objective things and events." And once the essence is grasped, one can then act in the real world, linking theory or essence to concrete praxis.[31] Kim Il Sung thinks the same way, except with less emphasis on praxis. This is an Asian way to think, it is not in the least surprising. If Asians place too much emphasis on states of mind, Westerners place too little.

Although one can find uses of the term *Juche* in the 1940s in North and South, no one would notice were it not for its later prominence. But Kim's rhetoric rang with synonyous language; a variety of terms translating roughly as self-reliance and independence structured Kim's ideology in the 1940s: *chajusŏng* (self-reliance), *minjok tongnip* (national or ethnic independence), *charip kyŏngje* (independent economy). All these terms were antonyms of *sadaejuŭi*, serving and relying upon foreign power, which had been the scourge of a people whose natural inclination was toward things Korean. Kim at this time was a modal if early variant of third world revolutionary nationalism, reinforced by the Korean "Hermit Kingdom" past toward a left-isolationist tendency.

Kim was always the major interpretor of Korean self-reliance. In July 1982 he gave a vintage discussion of his ideology: Korea should not become "a plaything of great powers"; "I say to our officials: if a man takes to flunkeyism [*sadaejuŭi*] he will become a fool; if a nation falls into flun-keyism, this nation will go to ruin; and if a party adopts flunkeyism, it will make a mess of the revolution." "Once there were poets who wor-shipped Pushkin and musicians who adored Tschaikovsky. Even in cre-ating an opera, people patterned it on Italian ones. Flunkeyism was so rampant that some artists drew foreign landscapes instead of our beau-tiful mountains and rivers. . . . [But] Koreans do not like European artis-tic works." Koreans, he said, should always "hold fast to *chajusong*." Inter-estingly, in this same discussion he referred to Soviet efforts to prevent Korea from collectivizing agriculture before mechanization was avail-able,[32] a frequent complaint of the Maoists as well.

Although Kim muted his nationalist self-assertion when Soviet troops were on the ground, similar ideas are not hard to find in the 1940s. In his speech on the second anniversary of liberation in 1947, he began by thanking the Soviets profusely for their aid in defeating the Japanese. But soon he began discussing the need for an independent economy, "an economic foundation to make our Motherland a wealthy and powerful, free and independent country"; in spite of extended efforts toward this goal, he said, enemies in the south say we "intend to make [Korea] a political and economic dependency of a certain country." He went on to call for the construction of "a unified, self-reliant, independent state free of foreign interference." In another speech in the same month, he went on about the glorious traditions of Korea, and made a big pitch for young people to get educated so that "with our own hands" we can make everything we need ourselves—daily necessities, automobiles, trains, even aircraft, thus to realize "the complete independence of our Motherland." In a June 1946 speech, Kim referred to Koreans as "a superior people" whose contemporary backwardness was wholly attributable to Japanese oppression; unification, he said, was "a matter of restoring a free and independent state, without the interference of foreign countries, and guaranteeing the fundamental interests of our nation [*minjok*, nation or ethnic people]." Various ideologues drew attention to speeches earlier in 1947 where Kim called for "an independent national economy."[33]

Just before the Korean War, the KWP Agit/Prop Department put out a guide for propagandists that began by referring to Korea having "lost its *chajusŏng*" during the Japanese period, and, in the post-1945 period, having constructed an economic and political base "that firmly guaran-tees our nation's interests and *chajusŏng* on the world stage." The exis-tence of the Soviet Union and other socialist countries was the external condition that guaranteed Korea's position, and the economic basis at home would "build a rich and strong state that can guarantee our nation's *chajusŏng*." The document said explicitly that central planning "was a means of guaranteeing the *chajusŏng* of a democratic state's economy and ensuring that it does not become subordinated to a foreign economy."

In spite of praise for Soviet efforts in this document, it underlines the manner in which the Koreans took Japanese and Soviet state structures and ideas and turned them toward an autarkic conception of a self-contained national economy; it clearly referred to all foreign nations by using the term "foreign" instead of "imperialist."

Kim Il Sung was quoted many times in the document on the necessity "to build our own democratic homeland independently using our own strength and our own assets." Korea must use "our own domestic resources and our own strength," thus to avoid dependency on external sources of supply: this, too, would guarantee "the *chajusŏng* of our national economy." Perhaps most important, this document dates the adoption of these "basic principles" [*wŏlli*] from 1949, signaling the break toward an independent trajectory that occured after Soviet troops left Korea.[34]

Kim Il Sung's ideas resonate with the Left-isolationism, predicated on a withdrawal from the world economy, that European leftists popularized in the 1930s when the world economy collapsed and some sort of withdrawal and restructuring was on the agenda of every nation (a New Order, a New Deal, socialism in one country). In Kim's system in the 1940s, one discerns the rudiments of a type of *neosocialist corporatism*, going back to the Rumanian Mihail Manoilescu, whose fundamental depar-

7. Celebrating the establishment of the DPRK, September 1948

ture from Marxism was to substitute national struggle for class struggle, and to suggest that dependent, peripheral socialist nations unite horizontally in common cause.[35] This was precisely the Korean departure as well, incipient in the 1940s and trumpeted for all to hear by the 1960s.

For Manoilescu, "the organic, 'productivist,' vertically structured metaphors of a harmonic political-economic order" should characterize the system at home, a unity forged in struggle with a world system viewed as bent on subordinating Rumania.[36] Kim Il Sung has always thought the same thing; if the unit of struggle is the nation, then class conflict and division should give way to mass unity, the national people distilled from world-ranging conflict. This is another key reason for Kim's incessant emphasis on unity, and the relative absence of revolutionary class struggle. Given Korea's traditional background and the intensity of geopolitical and world-system pressure on North Korea, the corporatist outcome seems overdetermined.

Manoilescu and other such writers ended up in the fascist camp, something not surprising because there is a curious realm where Left and Right meet in theories emphasizing organic unity at home and national conflict abroad. The one place where Kim's ideas resonate in South Korea, interestingly, is on the extreme right, especially with the 1940s right-wing youth group leaders Yi Pŏm-sŏk and An Ho-sang. This does not make Kim a fascist or An a communist, but it does unite them in contempt for liberalism and makes of them all rock-ribbed Korea-firsters and bloody-minded nationalists, probably hated as much by Soviet internationalists as by American free traders. A self-reliant, self-contained Korea with a strong state and popular unity is an ideal that united masses of Koreans in the 1940s.

POLITICAL REPRESSION

In 1946 and 1947 the north Koreans eliminated all nonleftist political opposition with a remarkable thoroughness. The intent was the same as that of the right-wing in the South, to squash alternative centers of power. But the northerners did it much more effectively, because of their superior organization and the general weakness of the opposition. Neither North and South had qualms about using violence toward political ends, but the North tended to be more discriminating, in part because its enemies were numerically small classes and groups, and also because of a political practice, perhaps growing out of the Korean leadership's experience with Chinese Communism, of seeking to reeducate and reform political recalcitrants.

Those who did not go along with the regime's will, or those thought to be lagging ideologically—which meant just about everybody—were required to engage in small-group criticism and self-criticism sessions much as in China; these also were conduits of regime policies and occupied significant amounts of almost everyone's time. Internal party documents and party newspapers show a ubiquitous group life, with constant attention to holding meetings at all levels—in government offices, workplaces, schools, and villages. An article on the party cell in Sangsŏng village, Hamju county, referred to "political discussion meetings," "lesson and debate meetings," and the like, the usual story being that the theoretical level of members is low, but they enthusiastically participate in discussions.

Kim Ha-rin, a KWP cadre in a small village in Samsa township, ran a "democratic propaganda office," organizing meetings with peasants to discuss politics and exchange experiences from their work, such as in methods of irrigation; he also held "people's assemblies" at the neighborhood level every two weeks, and got peasants to do "beautification" work such as planting trees or flower beds. Many small-group meetings were held for group reading of the party newspaper. "Inner-party democracy," was taken to mean the encouragement of discussion and debate, so that people will understand the reasons why they should participate actively in local groups. Internal documents suggest less a draconian atmosphere than the mundane problems of getting people to come to meetings, be punctual, speak up, and so on. Group leaders spent a lot of time combatting "liberalism" [*chayujuŭi*], which seemed to be defined as skipping meetings, coming late or leaving early, "going out at night," remaining silent, and so on. Through these total methods, the regime achieved the result that almost everyone became a member of some organization, subject to the ever-present group life.[37]

In 1945–1946 there were a number of noncommunist parties and groups—nationalists, Christians, and followers of the native Ch'ŏndoggyo religion. The Kim leadership adopted a "united front" policy toward two major parties, the Chosŏn Democratic Party (CDP) and the Chŏngu-dang or "Friends Party" of the Ch'ŏndoggyo. In national people's committee elections in November 1946, the CDP elected 351 members, the Chŏngu-dang 253, and the KWP 1,102, with 1,753 of those elected listed as belonging to no party.[38]

Kil Il Sung publicly justified the presence of these parties in the united front by saying that the CDP opposed foreign interference in Korea, and therefore was antiimperialist; the Chŏngu-dang "consists largely of peasants, and therefore we can always maintain a coalition with this party."[39] But this united front policy gave no real power to these parties. It did take account of the rootedness in the peasantry of the Ch'ŏndoggyo religion, and the significance of urban Christian power, especially in P'yŏngyang. But the regime subjected these parties to the same top-down control everyone else got.

Kim Il Sung installed his close ally, Ch'oe Yong-gŏn, as the leader of the Chosŏn Democratic Party (CDP). It is perhaps significant that one of his first major speeches took place on Christmas Day, 1946. He berated CDP members for being insufficiently active, for not sending enough reports to the party center, for petit bourgeois attitudes, and for the "disease of our nation," factionalism. He urged the members to get rid of "bad, feudal influences," one example of which was CDP criticism of the Worker's Party (a good indication of Ch'oe's views on party competition). "Not a few" capitalists in the CDP carried around bad ideas in their heads, he said, and members should urge these recalcitrants to change their ways. Businessmen and merchants in the party should strive to develop the national wealth, not their own; profiteering was a major threat to the economy. Fund raising also lagged; CDP members had more money than anyone else, so why were there not more contributions? Only that which strengthens organization and the united front is good, he said, and not getting out among the masses is bad: "one who simply relies on others, does not work, and sits around eating *ttŏk* [rice-cake]—who will give this person *ttŏk*?" The membership should reflect on all this, and criticize their bad ways.[40]

The Chosŏn Democratic Party by this time was merely a transmission belt for regime policies, another of the ubiquitous organizations that did the bidding of the center. It is for this reason that the regime prodded CDP members to be more active, rather than less, the opposite of what would happen in a competitive party system. A secret KWP investigation of a CDP branch in Namp'o in 1947 found that members did hardly anything to bolster membership, get out the vote, or organize more branches. "Democratization" of the party was taken to mean weeding out landlords and pro-Japanese, not getting it mobilized.

The report said that the backgrounds of local members were uniformly bad, "every one of them was a pro-Japanese," and several had been removed from local committees for just that reason. Christians joined the CDP exclusively, and most of them were from landed backgrounds. Thus, "democratization" of the CDP was difficult, because "bad landlords" and "Christian believers" were not being "purged" [*sukch'ŏng*]. Furthermore, "they always say they will cooperate with us, but in reality they don't do so." They don't get out and run for elections, either, another bad thing—indicating that the regime saw CDP participation as legitimating the election process rather than providing electoral competition.

This investigation included "top secret" data on the class background of Democratic Party members in Namp'o, showing that of some 2,974 members, 625 were workers, 486 were peasants, 493 were clerks or bureaucrats, and 1365 were "other," which in the individual breakdowns tended to mean landlords, teachers, lawyers, businessmen, and other professional occupations. It almost reversed the KWP stratification, which always had poor peasants bulking the largest. Only 187 women were members of the CDP, whereas women often constituted one-quarter or more of KWP rosters.[41]

The Kim regime wanted the Democratic Party to be the never-victorious class representative of landlords and capitalists, who would slowly put their own class out of business by reflecting on their transgressions and rectifying their thoughts. The Chŏngu-dang was perhaps different, since the regime did not seek to extinguish this religion, a reflection of its nativism and its strength among the peasantry. But the few extant versions of its party newspaper demonstrate a similar pattern, in which the Chŏngu-dang became a mere conduit of regime policies.[42]

Press freedom also ceased to exist in 1946, with all newspapers—central and local, communist and noncommunist—carrying essentially the same news, with some local coloring thrown in. Furthermore, Soviet-aligned Koreans tended to predominate in the cultural organs; all three of the editors of the party journal, *Kŭlloja*, were Soviet-Koreans in 1945–1950.[43]

Christians were a particular target of the general coordination. Christianity took hold in Korea in a way that it did not in Japan or China, and even if the number of believers in the general population was not more than 2 percent in 1945, they were numerous and influential in P'yŏng-yang, and had a long association with American missionaries. American sources thought Christian churches were the strongest opposition to the regime, and scattered evidence suggests that many pastors were imprisoned in the late 1940s—including Rev. Sun Myung Moon, who ran a sect called the Israel Church and who was imprisoned on charges of fornication and adultery in 1948 and 1949. According to Haruki Wada, in one particularly bloody incident police fired on a crowd of Christian protesters in Sinŭiju, killing twenty-three people; Ham Sŏk-hŏn, the famous Quaker human rights figure, was then in the Provincial People's Committee, but he was beaten and arrested after this incident. Kim Il Sung personally visited Sinŭiju, seeking to mend rifts between communists and Christian nationalists.[44] Another Christian human rights activist in the South, Rev. Ch'i Hak-sŏn, remained in the North until 1948, when his Christian group was suppressed. Christian churches remained open until the war, and worship was allowed, but Christian political activities were stamped out.[45]

All this is hardly a record to be proud of, but the northern regime did not engage in massive slaughters against its enemies, such as those carried out in the USSR in the early 1930s, or China and Vietnam in their bloody land reform campaigns. Furthermore, with a few exceptions leadership purges were neither fatal nor permanent. O Ki-sŏp, for example, was purged in 1948 but then headed a Joint Stock Company, and came back to relatively high position in the mid-1950s. The southern leadership under Pak Hŏn-yŏng, however, was mercilessly destroyed, its main leaders executed, in scapegoating that followed the end of the Korean War.

POLICE AND INTELLIGENCE

Within a year after liberation the north Koreans had completely eliminated Koreans who had served the Japanese from the forces of order, a thoroughing renovation of the most hated and feared of colonial institutions. They did not replace it with a system that any American would wish to live under. The north Korean security apparatus, judging by existing documentation, was an agency of revolutionary justice, a thorough, often total system of control and surveillance. Those who staffed and benefitted from it believed it to be a vast improvement over the previous system; those who suffered from it thought it to be a draconian network that denied all freedom to the individual. It was unquestionably a more discriminating institution in its use of violence than the southern system, both by the nature of the enemies each faced and because, unimpeachable internal evidence shows, the north Koreans sought to reform people through persuasion, and tutored policemen toward eliminating historical abuses of citizens, such as arbitrary beatings, and confessions obtained through torture.

The security apparatus was very large in the North. An "extremely secret" document on the people's committee adminstrative structure shows that the intelligence [*chŏngbo*] section of each provincial committee always had more members than any other section, about 20 per province, with the provincial PC staff totalling 353 to 362, depending on the region. In city PCs, 55 members of the Ministry of the Interior (*naemuwŏn*) were attached to each PC, PCs varying from 141 members in Nanam to 185 in Sinŭiju, excluding the capital which had 341 members. P'yŏng-yang appeared to have 218 *naemuwŏn* in addition to the ordinary PC staff members. At the county level, of a total of 10,499 staff, more than one-third (3,732) were *naemuwŏn*. These personnel, of course, included ordinary neighborhood police, and even the intelligence function encompassed routine things like control of narcotics and poisons, that is, it was not just oriented to political cases. Furthermore the total numbers of police appear much smaller than in the south.[46]

A secret report in 1947 by Pak Il-u of the Department of Peace Preservation (*poan'guk*) made clear that political cases were a matter of direct concern. He admonished province chiefs, "in spite of your awareness of political criminals, [your] struggle against profiteers and evil capitalists is weak." The chiefs should be sure "to examine the class background and the thoughts" of all neighborhood leaders (*panjangs*) in their jurisdiction, and bring problem cases to the attention of the people's committee. Apparently discipline was lax among provincial police, for he said they were not paying enough attention to laws and directives from the center, and did not keep proper records. The class enemy was, obviously, given next to no rights under this system.

In the same document, however, Pak urged the chiefs to develop "the character of all-around revolutionaries"—people who abjure improper or immoral behavior, dispense justice in a strict but impartial manner, and relate means to the ends revolutionaries should seek. They were to "serve the people," he said, using the same characters that Mao did, earn their trust and the trust of the whole country. Weekly meetings should be held to explain policies, the political situation, and to conduct "thought training" (*sasang hullyŏn*): "protect our intimate ties with the people, the political parties and social organizations, especially lower-level people's committees." Pak even appreciated the weaknesses policemen are sometimes prone to, and urged them to repent. "Everyone has an appetite for food, and loves the opposite sex. But this is something that the patriot conquers. Debauchery, indolence . . . are just for the benefit of one's self, and are in opposition to patriotic thought."[47]

Internal documents on the training regimen for *naemuwŏn* personnel show similar emphases. The northern system of justice was described as "a new-born, new form of police," which was "completely dependent upon the people and their direct participation." "We must arm ourselves even more with the spirit of serving the people," and get rid of the old attitudes of "high-handedness, arrogance, selfishness, and self-aggrandizement." The document stated, "we must respect human rights . . . beatings, torture and other inhuman evils must not be used." Instead of beating people, be an example for them, try to explain things to them with patience and sincerity. All policemen should be "models of respect for the law as a guide to the people." Among the virtues of a good policeman, it said, are loving to serve, mutual comradely love, purging "unclean" things from one's life, and being disciplined, resourceful, and willing to face hardship. Only in capitalist countries, it was said, are the forces of order the enemies of the people; in north Korea the police must "serve the people," otherwise it cannot be called a people's state; security personnel defend "the people" and fight against the enemy, defined here as "traitors and pro-Japanese."[48]

This cannot be dismissed as propaganda, since it is taken from secret internal documents. At a minimum it suggests that, whatever the excesses of individual police personnel, the leadership sought to change some of the worst abuses of the old system. These and other materials also make it apparent that the term translated as "liberalism," *chayujŭui*, means to Koreans a kind of license in which the individual departs from the group, benefits his interests at the expense of others, and lacks a proper conception of morality. Pak frequently referred to getting rid of *chasa* and *chari*, which would translate literally as self-interest or self-profit, and of course the character *cha* is common to all these terms, symbolizing something produced out of the individual self rather than out of the group, and therefore selfish or immoral or hard to control, or all of the above. By contrast, the "all-around revolutionary" (*man'nŭng hyŏngmyŏngga*) possesses manifold moral virtue, like the Confucian ideal of the *chüntze* or true gentleman.

However virtuous these new policemen were, their functions included a total system of thought control and surveillance that would horrify a believer in basic political freedoms. The regime organized secret networks on a grand scale to report political statements, including rumors and hearsay, both as a means of checking on citizen loyalty and of providing the leadership with rudimentary guidance to public opinion. One internal directive from the occupation of the south in August 1950, which can be assumed to be representative of North Korean practice, if in wartime conditions, says the following:

> The most important mechanism for impressing the masses with the correctness and superiority of people's sovereignty is the question of grasping what their opinions are, and how they can be changed. Therefore, it is of the utmost importance to strengthen the organized collection network . . . and through it broadly to collect and report mass opinion, so as to sweep away anti-democratic phenomena and incorrect thoughts among the village people.

The document called for the organization of inspection networks that would ascertain the names, addresses, class backgrounds, party affiliations, pre-Liberation activities, and good and bad attitudes of everyone— to be reported as they are, without editorials.

One example was a report on a "small landlord," Yi P'an-gŭn, who was ecstatic that big landlords had their land confiscated, but felt that there was no reason to take any of his land, since he worked it himself.[49] Similar reports on mass opinion in Haeju, marked "absolutely secret," gathered together comments of various citizens, such as one who responded to a South Korean propaganda leaflet barrage by saying, "Sons of bitches! They're always dropping leaflets, to no purpose. I hope they're used by people to blow their noses." A group of workers were heard to say that "peaceful unification" will never work; Rhee rejects everything we offer, so "we'll have to attack." Some documents reported opinion on whether Kim Il Sung was an imposter or not, and quoted one man as saying, "Ch'oe Yong-gŏn is a superior man to Kim Il Sung." A laborer lamented, "If I don't work on a farm, I have to work in the factory, and either way my problems are so bad I might as well die—so why should I participate in elections? I just have to die."[50] With such materials, the leadership got feedback and complaints from citizens. One hesitates to ask what a citizen got for denigrating Kim Il Sung.

People who had suspect backgrounds were subject to frequent surveillance. These included dispossessed landlords, former officials of the colonial regime, capitalists, and especially families with relatives in the South (the South was equally concerned about families with relatives in the North). Data on nineteen people under observation in Anju County showed that even members of people's committees came under surveillance; of this group, thirteen had poor peasant or proletarian class background; sixteen were members of the KWP. Reasons given for the surveillance included relatives who went South, and unspecified "reactionary activity." Obviously "good" class background or party membership did not provide an escape from supervision.[51]

Individual records of people under surveillance show a similar pattern. Kim Chae-gi, for example, was a former agricultural laborer who became chief clerk in a township people's committee and was a KWP member; the father of three children then in school, no reason was given for classifying him as a person requiring "top-grade surveillance." Another person in the same category was Chang Myŏng-nyŏng, a proletarian who labored in a Kap'yŏng factory from 1934 to 1943, and who then became a member of the KWP and a PC official in Ch'ŏrwon. He had a brother in the South, which, combined with his position in a town near the thirty-eighth parallel, probably made him untrustworthy. Another case involved a township PC secretary, Yi Sŏng-hi, who was under surveillance because he had been a township official in the Japanese regime; the report noted his "zeal for work." Chŏng Wŏn-mo had been a tenant farmer and then a factory worker before 1945, then was a PC activist in 1945–1947 and a minor government functionary in 1947–1949. His surveillance owed to his being a member of the Chosŏn Democratic Party.

Although common criminals were watched, so was Sim Ki-sŏk, a county PC finance chief of poor peasant background. His transgressions consisted of slurping 120 *wŏn* worth of dog soup without paying for it at a local restaurant, and selling his wife's rubber shoes on the black market. These documents routinely listed the names of all relatives of those under supervision.[52]

Policemen themselves were subject to surveillance, which at least suggested that the regime spared no one. Meng Mun-ok was evaluated through a "*p'yŏngjŏngsŏ*" or consultation report; it listed his work qualities (gentle, composed, earnest, but lacks originality), his "political, ideological and training level" (he is resolute in working to raise his political level), and his "relations with the masses" (calm and collected, likes to play "petit bourgeois" sports with the people). He had been a patrolman under the Japanese; at that time he did not have the "broad trust" of the people, but his neighbors thought well of his work, he was himself of working class background, and he always sought self-improvement. Thus, the investigation concluded, he is a policeman "capable of serving the people."[53]

Studies done using POW interviews during the war bore out this general picture of law and order in the North—a highly penetrative structure that required correct behavior, as the regime defined it, of everyone. At the same time, most citizens seemed to believe that this apparatus was a distinct improvement over that of the Japanese period. One POW said the police were "severe," but "no third degree measures were ever used"; the result was that people came to look upon the police as "guardians of peace."[54] It was not a system any American would wish to live under. But it did provide what it claimed to provide: revolutionary justice.

Chapter Ten

THE SOVIETS AND NORTH KOREA

Stalin is our patron of Liberation, our lodestar, our master teacher, our intimate friend, who has the heart-felt respect and limitless love of our people.

Yi Sŭng-yŏp

FROM the standpoint of the world economy and American internationalists, Washington's containment strategy in the early months of 1947 reflected a move toward a second-best world. It signaled the end of the détente of the early and mid-1940s, a finale for Roosevelt's conception of a single world system embracing socialist as well as capitalist states. In the same period, the Soviets came to accept the reality of a globe divided into two camps. As late as 1950 a few prescient but isolated internationalists still hoped to bring People's China into the American-managed "grand area." But the emergence of a strong rollback current in 1949 drew the curtain down on the Rooseveltian conception for China—not to be revived for a quarter-century, and then through the ironic vehicle of Richard Nixon.

It is doubtful that Roosevelt's program for the Soviet Union would have succeeded, even if we discount the limits placed by a raucous domestic politics in the United States. The Soviet Union is a continental, almost completely self-sufficient economy and rendering it tractable would have been extraordinarily difficult, even for a Roosevelt who would have dominated the American scene had he lived. Furthermore Stalin's conception of industrialization, fashioned when the Soviet Union was weak and vulnerable, was a form of neomercantilist withdrawal from the world system, predicated on a go-it-alone strategy. Stalin probably felt that the USSR was still not strong enough to allow an open door intercourse with the West in the postwar period; in any case the Soviets rejected this course in the dialectic of early postwar interaction with the leading capitalist power. It is not important for us to assess the relative blame for the emergence of a bipolar world. In Western Europe, where the United States played such a stong hand, it was the Soviet Union that felt threatened by internationalist open systems. In East Asia and especially Korea, it was the United States, playing a weak hand, which moved first to consolidate an anticommunist bloc.

We examined the year after liberation in the North in the first volume of this study. At the world level, Soviet policy was marked by a desire to continue "the spirit of Yalta," to fulfill great power agreements worked out before Roosevelt died. The theories of Eugene Varga, arguing against the possibility of beneficial economic ties with the United States, were condemned. A period of "domesticism" characterized these months, as the Soviets began to reconstruct a country devastated by war. Soviet policy abjured involvement in the conflict in China, supported democratic or coalition governments in Czechoslovakia and Hungary, evacuated northern Iran under forceful American pressure, and did not seek to reconstitute the Communist International (Comintern).

In northern Korea and Manchuria the Soviets had no settled policy, instead following a kind of slash-and-burn strategy, suggesting that they did not have long-range plans to stay. This explains the widespread looting, pillage, and rape in both Korea and Manchuria, followed by the carting off of some $2 billion in Manchurian industry and an undetermined number of whole plants from Korea. The Soviets removed ground troops from Manchuria in 1946 and in 1947 announced their intention to withdraw from Korea. The best comparison for this policy might be Austria, where the Soviets also raped and looted, seemed indifferent to the native regimes when compared, say, to Poland or Czechoslovakia, and eventually left in 1955.

The changes in American policy of early 1947 affected the Soviets most directly in regard to their two antagonists, Germany and Japan. Both began to be organized into an hegemonic system that projected a revival of their industrial economies as engines of growth in the world economy. The Soviets responded by tightening controls on Eastern European countries, although by no means to the degree of the early 1950s. Most analysts date this from the famous Zhdanov report in September 1947, at the information conference of the Communist Parties, which inaugurated the Cominform, a weak version of the Comintern. Zhdanov said that now "two principal camps" had formed in the world, the imperialist camp and the anti-imperialist (Soviet) camp. Doctrinal uniformity was the most obvious result of the new bipolarism, important both to solidify the socialist bloc ideologically, and to impose conformity on regimes that had pretensions to ideological independence, such as China. But Eastern Europe was the main focus.[1]

As the cold war deepened American officials frequently charged that the Soviets also sought to dominate Northeast Asia, and indeed an intertwined political, economic, and military logic can be discerned for such a strategy, at least in 1947. Korea was effectively divided. China, Stalin seemed to think, was also likely to be divided, or to carry on a prolonged civil war that would keep China weak for years. "North China" could thus be linked with North Korea, both in conflict with anticommunist regimes to the south; both could be hinged to an international division of labor in which the Soviets supplied higher-technology industrial goods and military supplies in return for labor and raw materials. The United States had moved toward reviving the Japanese industrial economy in early 1947; to a Stalinist this would immediately suggest a return to formidable war-making potential and the economic reintegration of southern Korea and those parts of China available to Japan and the United States with the Japanese economy and the broader world economy. The maximal strategy would therefore be to carve out a transnational satellite system linked to and dependent upon Moscow, a buffer to Japan and a help to the Soviet economy.[2]

Soviet logic also grew from the existence of a potent transnational unit linking Northeast China with Korea. The Japanese had carved out a formidable political economy, linking the countries of the region together with rapidly growing industrialization, new trading patterns, railways, roads and ports, and common bureaucratic and military systems. The Soviets would naturally seek to direct joint Sino-Korean efforts in the region, especially since they had little other choice. MacArthur's intelligence, along with the Nationalist Chinese, always exaggerated the degree to which Northeast Asia was a single bloc controlled by Moscow, since this served their purposes; but in 1947–1948 there was a distinct transnational unit linking Kim's regime, Kao Kang's, and the Soviet command in a formidable but probably uneasy coalition.

The Chinese military was deeply marked by regionalism, enabling the Soviets and the North Koreans to deal directly with the Northeastern command, rather than going through Yanan or Beijing. The Soviets coordinated Sino-Korean exchanges of personnel and materiel, and they provided technical and military help to both parties. In September 1947, for example, the Northeastern Combined Command Army Headquarters put out a military training manual in Chinese, based on a translation of an official Soviet manual, "The General Principles of Army Group Tactics."[3]

There was an obvious consonance between Soviet and Korean strategic interests in 1947–1948. From Kim Il Sung's perspective, dependency on the Soviets was strategically necessary. The Chinese Nationalists occupied much of Manchuria at the start of this period. Were they to maintain control, Kim would have a tiger at the front door and a wolf at the back. Chiang and Rhee would unquestionably seek to squeeze north Korea like an irritating pimple. Years or decades more of guerrilla struggle in the mountains would beckon. But a reversal occurred in 1948–1949, as Chinese and Korean soldiers swept the Nationalists from Northeastern China: now it was southern Korea that looked like a boil ready for lancing. Mao's victory dramatically changed North Korea's situation, and also raised the ante for the Soviets. Northeastern Asia was now occupied by formidable native communist armies, something Stalin would see as a distinctly mixed blessing, signaling the end of anything but indirect attempts to control the native regimes.

After Soviet troops came out of Manchuria, Stalin sought influence indirectly through political controls and leaders that would do his bidding. The Chinese had set up a Northeast Provinces People's Republic in 1946 under Kao Kang, an interesting leader who some charged with being a pro-Soviet stooge, and who committed suicide in 1954 after being accused of running an "independent kingdom" in the Northeast, a charge probably much closer to the mark. The Kao Kang affair has never been definitively explicated in the literature. Many sources noted that Liu Shao-ch'i and Kao Kang arrived in Moscow in advance of Mao in late 1949; the Soviets concluded separate trade agreements with Kao Kang's Northeast administration, and delegations from this government made frequent visits to North Korea.[4] American intelligence in the late 1940s was convinced that a pro-Soviet faction competed for power with the Maoists, the former including Liu Shao-ch'i, Kao Kang, Jao Shu-shih, and Li Li-san; Li had been head of the "returned students" in the early 1930s, and, after a period of obscurity, returned to reasonably high position in the Northeastern regime in the late 1940s. An American ranking listed Liu forth, Kao Kang eleventh, Jao thirteenth, and Li fourteenth in the leadership in February 1950. One can find this argument throughout the available intelligence on the Chinese leadership, but in retrospect it is clear that it grossly overestimated both the pro-Soviet proclivities of such people and Moscow's capacity to manipulate Chinese politics. Still, the Soviets probably did influence Chinese politics through Kao Kang, if not the eclipsed and ineffectual Li Li-san.[5]

Interestingly, the available evidence shows that the Northeastern regime followed policies similar to those in North Korea. A document on land reform in the Northeast noted the similarity in land reform programs between the two administrations. The leadership decided to implement land reform in July 1946, a few months after Korea's began, and carried it out quickly, with a minimum of class struggle and revolutionary violence, just as in Korea. Within six months, 4.2 million peasants had received land. "Village committees" (*nongch'ŏn wiwŏnhoe* in the Korean) were set up to implement the reform, relying on poor peasants, hired laborers, and middle peasants. There is no reference to Maoist practices such as "settling accounts," "speaking bitterness," and the like, methods used in other parts of China. Ongoing research by Elizabeth Perry and others has found that land reform in North and Northeast China tended to be top-down, quick, and with less class struggle than in regions under Maoist control.

Like North Korea, the Northeastern regime also saw itself as an initiator of reform programs "showing the way in the East for oppressed peoples," a typical Soviet formulation. Other regions in China were presumably "following after" the Northeast. Again like North Korea, the Soviets helped get industrial production going again after 1946, and most sources agree that the Northeast did grow rapidly in the years thereafter.[6]

Whatever Stalin's goals may have been in the region, he failed to establish docile satellite regimes. Both American and British intelligence were, at some levels, aware of Soviet divergences in Northeast Asia from the satellite model in Europe, lessons that were later unlearned because of the political necessity during the Korean War to view China and North Korea as tools of Moscow. The CIA said in 1947, "Soviet policy in Korea is directed toward the establishment of a friendly state which will never serve as a base of attack upon the USSR. In order to attain this objective at a minimum cost to its own scanty resources in the Far East, the USSR has attempted to make North Korea economically self-sufficient though politically subordinate." The CIA amended the political subordination conclusion by saying that the Soviets had given north Korea "a semblance of autonomy by entrusting the administration to a hierarchy of people's committees dominated by the Korean Communists." The same report also argued that Soviet long-term goals were "to integrate the entire peninsula" in the Soviet defense system, a questionable assertion.[7] But the essence of this CIA argument was true. The Soviets had a low-risk strategy of the best gains possible given "scanty resources" and the necessity of minimal costs.

R. S. Milward of the British Foreign Office wrote a year later that north Korea had

an apparent similarity to the more autonomous western Communist states such as Yugoslavia. Kim Il Sung . . . was built up during the war into an almost legendary guerrilla hero . . . a Korean Tito. The Russians moreover are proposing to withdraw their forces from Korea, seeming to trust their puppets . . . [to] rule the land in the interests of Russia without direct Russian interference.

This "facade of autonomy," Milward thought, was more pronounced "than in almost any other country in the Russian orbit." The internal contradictions in this report (similar to Yugoslavia, yet a puppet that would rule in Moscow's interests) reflected inability to believe that Koreans could be independent, and the absence of experience at that point with communist regimes that had directly defied Moscow.[8]

Another CIA study in July 1949 made sharp distinctions between the Euro-Mediterranean region and East Asia, citing "a generally detached attitude" toward communism in East Asia in 1945–1949. The looting of Manchuria, the CIA thought, suggested that the Soviets did not want to build a dependent economic complex, and had problems controlling Asian nationalism and "Titoism." In early 1950 an estimate of Soviet intentions in Korea found that the Soviets had thus far "not made much effort to organize lateral trade between Korea, Manchuria and China."9 Still, such reports make no distinction between 1946 and 1950. In my view the Soviets lacked long-run plans in 1945–1946, developed them in 1947–1948 as bipolarity deepened, then had to abandon them in the face of Chinese and Korean resistance.

In Korea there is some evidence of enhanced Soviet dominance in the 1947–1948 period, mainly in the installation of Soviet-aligned Koreans in the ideological and cultural journals, and the downplaying of Maoist themes. The party journal ran articles on "democratic patriotism," quoting Stalin several times and saying, "the excellent point of socialism is [precisely its combining of] patriotism in regard to one's own Motherland [with] the political and moral uniqueness of the Soviet system." Another article sought to explain why Korea remained divided, utilizing "the science of Marxism-Leninism" and the ideas of "Great Marshal Stalin, leader of the science of the current era" to explain the situation. Many similar examples could be cited. Soviet magazines, books, and films flooded into the North.10

Kim Il Sung had been less doctrinaire and pro-Soviet in his public speeches in 1946 than, say, Kim Tu-bong. But his speech in August 1947 on the second anniversary of the Japanese defeat said, "We will never forget the sacrifices of the Soviet Army and people for our liberation," and went on for several pages to laud the Soviets, to refer to "new democracies" and "democratic reforms" in Eastern Europe, clearly identifying Korean policies with them. The imperialists, he said, are "beginning to form" a new fascist and reactionary alliance. He also quoted Tito, in saying "we go forward with the Soviet alliance. Why? We always hear the voice of peace coming from the Soviet alliance," whereas from the Western alliance, "we hear always about the atomic bomb and the danger of war."11

Even in the period of presumed Soviet dominance, however, Soviet policy was contradictory. Perhaps uniformity was achieved in the cultural and ideological sphere, but as any Marxist knows that is a weak and superficial reed upon which to base domination. H. de Galard is correct to see in Soviet policy during 1947–1948 "a kind of politico-diplomatic 'war of movement,' " seeking to get the Americans to respect, often with "brutal arguments," Soviet power and the Soviet desire to have a compromise of long enough duration to allow the USSR to recover from the war, that is, a policy that would above all avoid global war for the foreseeable future. This led to a number of changes, including the destruction of democracy in Czechoslovakia in February 1948. From June 1948 to May 1949 the Soviets pursued direct confrontation with the United States over Berlin. But, as de Galard said, the Soviets still did not "envisage precipitating affairs and falling back on military solutions," and thus "they withdrew almost everywhere" in 1949, abandoning the blockade of Berlin and the Greek insurgents.[12] We find a similar pattern in Korea, of attempts at dominance and the stirring up of crises in 1947–1948, followed by Soviet withdrawal.

Soviet strategy had a low-risk/high-gain quality in the region. The maximal strategy of integrating Korea, China, and the Soviet Far East would require a lot from the USSR. A very low-cost, minimal strategy might also evolve: the emergence of regimes that always would have one virtue, they would be organically anti-Japanese, and thus constitute long-term buffers against a revived Japan. The Japanese used to station the fiercest Korean soldiers along the narrow Russo-Korean border in the 1930s, human tigers who would defend the border at all costs. The Soviet minimal strategy would reverse this: install Korean tigers in P'yŏngyang, people who had grown to maturity fighting Japanese imperialism. Comintern Koreans, dependent on Moscow and unskilled in warfare, would not suffice; anyway Stalin had purged or shot most of them in the late 1930s. Anti-Japanese fighters in P'yŏngyang and Harbin would assure the most basic Soviet goal: a guarantee that an enemy would not again use the peninsula as a jumping off place for continental aggression.

A Korean veteran of the China campaigns who returned to his homeland in early April 1950, was told by his superiors that Stalin had said this: "To establish and forever protect Korea's unity [*t'ongil*], your duty is to build a steel-like people's army (Korean independence is up to the Koreans) [*sic*] and then the Koreans will become the masters of the house in Korea."[13]

But guerrilla fighters who are not dependent on Moscow do not make good satellite leaders. And it was this, combined with low-risk Soviet realpolitik, that was the undoing of the Soviet maximal strategy by 1949. A complex politicomilitary struggle in the late 1940s left Northeast Asia with independent kingdoms, not Soviet fiefdoms. A Sino-Korean united front from below undermined an attempted united front from above, so to speak.

THE SOVIET-KOREANS

If Kao Kang, Li Li-san, and others were the putative vehicles of indirect Soviet controls in China, people termed "Soviet-Koreans" were the presumed agents in North Korea. Anyone with knowledge of Koreans' interaction with foreigners should be wary of attributing agency to someone who happened to reside in one or another country during the Japanese period; as we have seen, even with Syngman Rhee having spent forty years in the United States, he was by no means merely an American agent. But since most of the available literature accepts the existence of Soviet-Korean penetration of the northern regime, what can we say about it?

Wild figures circulated in the 1940s on the number of Soviet-Koreans in Korea—fifteen thousand, thirty thousand, and more. Dae-sook Suh, however, found only about three hundred Soviet-Koreans, and included Kim Il Sung's following in that number. A German Benedictine priest who lived in the North from 1945 to 1949 said there were only a few Soviet-Koreans, and never any Soviet-Korean troops quartered there. Russian-speaking Koreans tended to come from Manchuria or from the small Russo-Korean border area, he said.[14]

A retrospective State Department study done in 1963 asserted that a group known as "the forty-three," forty-three Koreans who were born in or resided in the Soviet Union, most of whom were Communist Party of the Soviet Union (CPSU) members in 1945, constituted the core of the Soviet-Korean group; but even according to this official account, they played only "secondary roles" until after the Korean War, with Kim Il Sung's main competition coming from the domestic and Yenan groups. Although their power rose briefly in the early 1950s, they "were virtually eliminated" by 1956. The head of this group was Hŏ Ka-i, the proponent of Soviet models of organization described here as "a disciplinarian in the best Bolshevik tradition," working closely with the Soviet embassy. The CIA put great emphasis on Hŏ Ka-i, viewing him as a key liaison between the Soviets and the Koreans, and, according to hearsay evidence, an "enormous" behind-the-scenes influence. He was born in Russia in 1904, and spoke Russian in the home.

The CIA also thought a mysterious person named Kim P'a was in the bowels of the P'yŏngyang regime, "the most feared man in North Korea." Kim was born in the Soviet Far East in 1917, and was "reported to have been" a secret police agent in Kazakhstan during World War II; he became chief of counterintelligence operations in the North, and was one of the few Koreans that the Soviets really trusted—indeed, the CIA thought the Soviets consulted him before Kim Il Sung. The chief of the Security Bureau, Pang Hak-se, was also a Soviet-Korean; born in 1910, he graduated from a Soviet law college and served in the Red Army in the war. He was an interpreter and intelligence agent for Soviet forces after their entry into Korea in 1945. The CIA in 1951 thought that Soviet-Koreans occupied "a possible 200 critical positions." The 1963 State Department study argued, however, that Kim Il Sung's faction liked to place figures from other factions in charge of security bureaus, so their "hatchet-man functions" would taint their hands and keep Kim's clean. Available Korean-language documents captured in the North do not offer good evidence on the relative strength of the Soviet-Koreans.[15]

Recent, careful work suggests a different picture. The leading scholar on Soviet-Korean relations, Prof. Haruki Wada, found that among Stalin's large grouping of international communists in Moscow, not a single Korean communist or nationalist existed who clearly "was a trusted Soviet man." In 1937 Stalin ordered the forced deportation of some two hundred thousand Koreans from the Soviet Far East to Central Asia, on the racist grounds that they might harbor pro-Japanese seditious elements. "At the same time all Korean communists who were working in the Comintern were arrested and killed as [potential] agents of Japanese militarism." Dr. Wada also suggested that the Soviets may have subjected Kim Il Sung and other Korean guerrillas to investigation and severe interrogation when they moved back and forth across the Soviet-Manchurian border in the 1940s, keeping them under surveillance for a long time. In extant Soviet studies of Manchuria under the Japanese, and North Korea after 1945, Kim Il Sung is given distinctly short shrift for an alleged Soviet puppet.[16] This evidence suggests that the Soviet-Korean relationship was bloody and difficult, full of mutual mistrust and, often, marked Soviet racism toward Koreans.

This summarizes most of what is known about the Soviet-Koreans. Hŏ Ka-i and Pang Hak-se were unquestionably important figures in the regime. Kim P'a is an enigmatic figure, but shows up in a recent and equally enigmatic book as a member of Kim Il Sung's partisan detachment, not as a trusted Soviet man.[17] The evidence does not suggest that the Democratic People's Republic of Korea (DPRK) was under the control of Soviet-Koreans. Given Eastern European experience, if they were it would be inconceivable that Kim Il Sung could get away with purging prominent members of the group and virtually eliminating it by 1956. In countries like Poland, Soviet citizens held some of the highest positions, such as K. Rokossovsky, who became defense minister in 1949; some seventeen thousand Soviet officers held "command posts" in the Polish Army alone in 1948. The first premier of Bulgaria, Georgi Dimitrov, was a Soviet citizen who headed the Comintern; the Czech leader Klement Gottwald was hand-picked by the Soviets in 1929 and was a devoted follower of Stalin thereafter; most East bloc leaders had been either Comintern or NKVD operatives.[18] In Korea, Kim Il Sung's guerrilla allies have long outlasted other factional opponents, including all the Soviet-Koreans. Although that is not good evidence for the nature of the regime in 1950, it does retrospectively suggest a different situation than obtained in Eastern Europe.

North Korea did not become a satellite, but the Soviets wanted as much control as they could get for as little cost as possible. Although the Koreans never write candidly about this period, one knowledgeable North Korean said, when I asked him if the war was the most difficult time for the North, "No, the most difficult time was the 1940s. They didn't care to help us much, so we had to build everything from scratch. At the same time, they wouldn't let us do what we wanted."

Recent research has isolated certain key figures in the Soviet effort in the late 1940s. The commander of the Soviet Twenty-fifth Army, in occupation of north Korea, Gen. Ivan Chistiakov, had on his staff Maj. Gen. Nikolai Lebedev, described in Soviet sources as a distinguished political officer of considerable experience. Later, Maj. Gen. Andrei Romanenko became chief of Civil Administration, and brought with him one Col. Ignatiev; both were experienced political officers, Romanenko having spent long periods in the Soviet Far East. Ignatiev became particularly important in Korean political affairs, and died in P'yŏngyang during the bombing campaigns of the Korean War. According to Haruki Wada, however, the most important person in the Soviet presence was Gen. Terentii Shtykov, a former commander of the First Far Eastern Front; he headed the Soviet delegation to the Joint Commission and later became Soviet ambassador to the DPRK. Lebedev wrote in a memoir, "not a single measure was taken without his commitment at the time," even if he happened to be in Moscow rather than P'yŏngyang.

Shtykov was a typical Stalinist apparatchik, according to Wada. During Stalin's purges in 1938, he became second secretary of the Leningrad Party Committee, under Stalin's henchman, Zhdanov. He came into contact with Otto Kuusinen during the war, who had been an old Comintern contact with Korean communists, and who headed the puppet Finland Democratic Republic. Through this, Wada thinks, Shtykov became expert in using Soviet citizens to form puppet governments.[19]

In spite of the presence of such people, and unquestionable Soviet attempts at control, the North Korean relationship with Moscow was closer to the China model. Although a consensus of specialists now understands that no Sino-Soviet monolith under Moscow's imperative coordination ever existed, from 1949 to 1956 one could easily be fooled because on the surface, in the economic and cultural realm, Soviet influence was pervasive. Ambassador Leighton Stuart described Mao's China in July 1949, months before the People's Republic of China (PRC) was established, as giving every evidence of "unswerving allegiance to the doctrine of world revolution by violence, of devotion to the USSR . . . of destructive hatred of all opposing forces." He thought Mao was a thorough Stalinist. A month before the inauguration of the PRC, the American embassy deemed the Chinese "more papist than the Pope" in following the Soviet lead. A well-informed Englishman who spent the two years before the Korean War in Shanghai said that "thousands" of civilian-clad Russian bureaucrats "took command of the life of the city with cold efficiency." Translated Soviet materials flooded China, the embassy reported, with the Soviets having "a monopoly of foreign press news reaching China." During this early period the Chinese press was full of precisely the kind of slavish sycophancy toward the Soviets that critics find so significant in P'yŏngyang. Yet it is obvious in retrospect that the Soviets did not penetrate and control the inner core of Chinese political and military power.[20]

The surface Soviet presence tended to blind most observers to the real differences between Korean and Soviet socialism and the tensions in the relationship with Moscow. Internal CIA reports noted, for example, that a substantial private sector remained in the Korean economy before the war, with farms and small businesses owned or operated by individuals rather than the bureaucracy. A careful study of Korean communism by the forerunner of the RAND Corporation found that only 6 percent of North Korean respondents in extended interviews thought that there was any "foreign control" of North Korean politics.[21] But even such usually observant American agencies missed key aspects of the North that made it closer to Maoism than to Stalinism, as we will see.

The DPRK Political Economy and the USSR

The DPRK has always been a "late-late" industrializing socialist political economy, suffused with that strange ambition of the industrial epoch to outdistance all rivals, come hell or high water. It also has tried to be doggedly self-reliant, well beyond the point where its own interests are hurt. But that is because the Koreans do not believe in what Karl Polanyi called the "glorious fiction" that an international system of exchange will solve everyone's problems; they prefer industrialism in half-a-country.

Three characteristics pithily sum up the North Korean political economy that developed in the late 1940s, and distinguish it from China: heavy industry/labor shortage/postcolonial. North Korea has from the beginning conceived of itself as an industrial economy. Unlike the South, which had mostly light industry and agriculture in 1945, the North had heavy industrial complexes and energy sources that were quite formidable. Furthermore this complex was barely touched by American bombing in World War II; in the last stages of the war the north Korean economy was stronger than Japan's, with much more energy output (double that in Japan), that Japan's atomic bomb project was moved to Korea to make use of these facilities.[22] The DPRK National Seal, adopted in September 1948, places a star, meant to symbolize Kim Il Sung, above a hydroelectric dam and an electric transmission tower. We might say that socialism in North Korea has been "Kim Il Sung plus electricity."

It is always heavy-industry first in the DPRK. Here North Korea is preeminently Stalinist, but in the special sense in which Daniel Chirot calls Stalinism a strategy of late industrialization on a pattern of withdrawal from the world-system and self-reliant development. Chirot also rightly notes that this industrialization pattern has a certain resonance with Japan's in the prewar period, a type of industrialization that has been an important model for both North and South Korea.[23]

The DPRK has also always been relatively labor-short, when compared to China or Vietnam. The Koreans who worked in northern industry during the war were mostly from the South, surplus peasants forced into industry by direct and indirect structures of mobilization. Japanese managers and technicians ran the industries. After the liberation, the northerners watched worker-peasants stream south by the hundreds of thousands toward their homes, and Japanese experts flee in fear of their lives. The land reform turned the class structure on its head, so that after 1946 a stigma attached to landlord status and lineage; the majority of Korean experts and intellectuals came from this class, and so they also fled to the South. The regime was one of worker-peasants, most of them illiterate before 1945. The absence of expertise required an open-door policy toward intellectuals, who have never been denigrated in the DPRK the way they were in Mao's China.

With natural population patterns putting much of the surplus in the South, and political changes emptying factories of workers, the North faced a labor shortage, especially in skilled jobs. The North, of course, has always used large quantities of cheap human labor for construction projects and the like. But the percentage of peasants in the social structure was smaller than other Asian socialist countries, enabling the North to mechanize agriculture and dovetail the flow of peasants off the land with rising industries. The "red-expert" problem here was how to find the Reds and the experts in the first place, how to keep and build a proletariat that was very new and still suspended between farm and factory. Nothing can be understood about the northern political economy without grasping these simple facts, which account for much of the difference between Korean and Chinese socialism.

The DPRK has always been the most industrialized of the Asian communist countries. In a 1985 lecture at the University of Washington, Alexander Woodside pointed out that industrial production accounted for less than 2 percent of GNP in Vietnam in 1975, compared to 17 percent of China's GNP in 1949, and 28 percent in North Korea in the 1940s. Vietnamese economists in the mid-1980s questioned whether an economic model founded on Soviet and East European development had relevance for them and whether Vietnam should remain a member of COMECON (the Soviet-bloc common market), or instead seek to overcome problems of underdevelopment or even "undevelopment" unlike those in the comparatively industrialized socialist countries. These debates in Hanoi mirror Korean debates in the mid-1950s, when the *Juche* idea was first broached and when North Korea decided not to join COMECON, probably a courageous decision on its part. But they also underline the different character of North Korea's economy in the late 1940s, which was far better poised than any other Asian socialist state to pursue the classic Stalinist model.

Although the Soviets gave aid and advice up to a point, as we will see, skilled Koreans with experience in the Japanese period came to dominate the development of the economy. Chŏng Il-yong, termed the "king of North Korean industry" by State Department intelligence, had been an engineer under the Japanese. The same was true of another powerful figure, Chŏng Chun-t'aek. The first two-year plan (1947–1949) was drawn up under the direction of a former economics professor at Keijo Imperial University, Kim Kwan-jin. Yi In-uk had twenty-five years of experience in the construction of northern factories. Of ninety-three Koreans on a partial listing of the North's Industry and Engineering Federation in 1950, 35 had more than five years of experience, all with former Japanese industries. Japanese technicians who did not flee were also used throughout the economy; in 1947 some of them wrote home that industrial production was in full swing, expressing surprise at the Korean workers' "eagerness for production"; it apparently surprised them that Koreans would work diligently for themselves, since they evidently had not for the Japanese.[24] Paradoxically, by accomplishing a quick postcolonial social revolution, the north was able pragmatically to use Korean and Japanese expertise from the colonial period with little criticism, whereas the South tended to employ Korean experts from the agencies of law and order, with no legitimacy.

Finally, north Korea was postcolonial, and consciously so to a remarkable degree. In the economy the DPRK was one of the earliest examples of rapid industrial development on the radical model of withdrawal from the world economy and self-reliant development, postcolonial neomercantilism and import-substitution, noncapitalist style. Such a policy meant overcoming the distortions and deformations of colonial underdevelopment, and trying to prevent new dependency relationships. For a small economy it was much easier to talk about self-reliance than to accomplish it, but North Korea's extant heavy industrial base made such a policy far more possible than in most developing countries.

These three characteristics combine to explain the early economic program, and much else since. Economic plans focused on classic Stalinist

principles giving priority to heavy industry and to agricultural mechanization; they began in 1947 and have never ceased. Recruitment campaigns and crash education programs created a hybrid regime, where
overnight people became proletarian cadres, workers, or technicians,
coming overwhelmingly from Korea's most numerous class of poor peasants.

The commitment of the regime to postcolonial policies meant that the
Koreans would expect help from the Soviets, but would resist the establishment of a new dependency. The Korean desire to construct an independent national economy runs like a lietmotiv through the early plans;
Americans noted the frequent talk about this in discussions of the 1947
plan, and references to the second two-year plan beginning in 1949 refer
to the necessity to overcome the economic and cultural "backwardness"
of the colonial economy and to "build ever stronger the foundation for a
completely self-reliant and independent state and for the unification of
our territory."[25]

Qualitative observations of the northern economy found a pattern of
heavy-industrial prowess, squeezing out consumer goods and spending
to achieve high rates of savings for investment on the Stalinist model. A
reporter for a northern newspaper told an American in mid-1947 that
the regime rationed food in six categories, workers doing heavy labor
getting the most and collaborators with Japan the least; wages varied
from 950 to 3,500 wŏn, with four categories: technicians, managers,
skilled workers, and ordinary workers. Employment centers all over the
country recruited industrial technicians and workers. Women workers
had increased rapidly, with "equal pay [for equal work] and special treatment." Some 1,200 cooperatives distributed goods to workers and peasants; they bought 100 percent of the output of state factories, 90 percent
of that from privately-owned factories, with the remaining portion being
sold on a free market. The average wage was low, "barely permit[ing]
workers to live."[26] The result of this extraordinary effort to get the industrial economy functioning again was that, from the 1940s into the
mid-1960s, minus the period of the war and recovery from it (1950–
1956), North Korea grew far more rapidly than did the South, as rapidly
perhaps as any postwar industrializing regime.

Americans captured the top secret text of the 1947 plan during the
Korean War, giving a rare, full picture of the DPRK economy. About
one-fifth of the total budget went for industrial construction and one-
fifth for defense. Among top-grade experts, 105 of 1,262 were Japanese;
245 of the middle-grade experts were Japanese. No Russians were listed.
Seventy-two percent of all children were in elementary school, compared
to 42 percent in 1944; some 40,000 adult schools across the country held
basic literacy classes for workers and peasants. American data on the

economy gotten from internal North Korean sources show pig iron production going from 6,000 metric tons in 1947 to 166,000 in 1949; steel billets from 61,000 tons to 145,000; common steel products from 46,000 to 97,000, with the latter two figures surpassing Japanese production in 1944 when Korean industry was pumping the war effort; industrial production rose 39.6 percent in 1949 and, interestingly, figures for 1950 show that northern industry had almost reached 1949 totals in the first three quarters, before the heaviest American bombing began. Indeed, targets for the first year of the second two-year plan were surpassed early in 1950, causing a revision upward of targets for the rest of the year.[27]

As always, Americans found it difficult to believe that Koreans could be responsible for such success. Drumwright noted in March 1950 that "there is considerable industrial potential in North Korea"; its plans were "remarkably lucid, consistent and well organized . . . so well prepared as to suggest they were written by Soviet 'advisors.' " The northern program, he thought, did not seem to be "seriously hampered by Korean inexperience, ignorance, obstinacy, corruption, and other failings which plague the American program."[28]

Some Americans detained in Chinnamp'o for three months in September 1949 reported that people were generally less well-clad than in the South; pens, watches, and leather shoes were rare; shellfish were abundant but meat was rare; railroads were very active at night; electric power was abundant, as was coal, the latter being used even to power cars and trucks, since petroleum was in short supply; a steel mill in the port ran around-the-clock shifts, as did a coal yard; the streets were clean and well maintained, but sparsely populated and few workers loitered as they usually do in port towns. This account is convincing, and accords with my own observations of the port of Wŏnsan thirty-five years later.

A speech by Kim Il Sung in late 1949 cited many problems in the economy, in spite of strong growth rates. Referring to "complicated, troublesome difficulties," he said some industries had by September 1949 increased production 50 to 60 percent over 1948 figures, but some grew only by 20 percent, and "worst of all" were small increases in coal and metallurgy that did not meet plan targets. He noted that many workers had been peasants just a few years before; they came in from the countryside and "would take any job they could get." Many had been "forced to work by the Japanese imperialist bastards," who had exploited labor at the cheapest cost. The Japanese had starved people to the point that they had to work, he said, but now with no threat of starvation, workers consumed too much of the surplus; some workers simply went back to their villages because agricultural conditions were good, and only a small supply of labor now came from the rural areas. Labor power is not fixed to the factory, so workers move from place to place as they wish. He gave an example from the Hwanghae Iron Works, which got seven hundred new workers in August 1948, but could not supply more than three hundred of them with housing, so the rest left within a couple of days. Labor, therefore, "does not automatically supply itself."

What was to be done? First, in typical fashion, he called for better work with people, "a new style of leadership," and individual "rectification of work," using the Maoist characters *kai tsao* (*kaejo* in Korean). But, "above all, we must correctly organize the wage system for workers, and stimulate production efficiency," fighting "a merciless struggle against the average wage system," that is, a system that would equalize all at the expense of incentives. "It is a principle that those workers who produce more must also receive more in wages."[29]

There can be few better examples of the way in which Kim borrowed voluntarist methods from China and materialist methods from the Soviet Union, always with a pragmatic eye toward what worked in the Korean context. The Koreans accepted the socialist principle, from each according to their ability, to each according to their work (Lenin gave it a Biblical flourish: "he that does not work, neither shall he eat") and have never challenged it as the Maoist radicals did. An early statement of this principle argued that "our system is not one of general equality"; we have political equality, equality of work and equality of rest, but "people work according to their abilities and are paid according to the quality and quantity of their work."[30] But they also accepted the Maoist principle that work with people, leadership styles, and mass rectification campaigns also can help stimulate production.

Beginning with the first multiyear plan in 1947, typical Soviet practices and policies emerged, along with the potential of an international division of labor seeking to keep the North dependent on the USSR. The Soviet model had a powerful undertow, since only the Bolsheviks had filled in the opaque Marxist prescriptions for socialism. As Ben Anderson put it, "Without such plans and programmes a revolution in a realm barely entering the era of industrial capitalism was out of the question. The Bolshevik revolutionary model has been decisive for all twentieth-century revolutions because it has made them imaginable in societies still more backward than All the Russias."[31] This would predict heavy Soviet influence, and conflict with the DPRK's postcolonial nationalism. In 1964 in a burst of candor made possible by the Sino-Soviet conflict, the North Koreans said, "You [the Soviets] have sold us facilities . . . and materials at prices far above those prevailing in the international market, while taking from us in return many tons of gold, huge quantities of precious metals, and other raw materials at prices substantially below those prevailing in the international market." Furthermore, the Koreans said, the Soviets did so "at a time when our life was most difficult to bear."[32]

But in spite of such talk, there is not much evidence that the Soviets ever dominated the Korean economy, and the push for an international division of labor came under Khrushchev more than Stalin, explaining Korean and Chinese disgust with his "revisionism." Soviet influence is obvious in some of the Korean policies toward industry, particularly the conception of a planned, command economy emphasizing heavy industry, the one-man management industrial system, and the use of material incentives and piece-rates, all obvious by 1947. This makes North Korea no different from China in the early 1950s; the Koreans and Chinese had little but Japanese industrial experience to go on.

Yet throughout the Soviet realm in the late 1940s, Stalin pursued an unexpected policy of one, two, many strategies of import-substitution, a literal modeling of Soviet practices from the 1930s in very different circumstances: "general industrialization," the American economic planners would call it, and so most socialist countries got steel mills and machine-building industries. It is one thing for the Soviets to build a thoroughly integrated industrial base, capable of supplying its own needs. It is quite another to attempt the same strategy in Poland, Rumania, North Korea, and most other socialist states. And then there is the question, is this any way to run an empire? A well-developed international division of labor would provide the sinews of economic dependency, but import-substituting strategies putting heavy industry first merely cloned the Soviet pattern, and bequeathed the basis for independent action and self-reliance. This is what happened in those socialist countries where the Soviets did not maintain heavy troop commitments to control the situation over the long term.

Such a strategy was just what the Koreans craved. Any regime in North Korea would have pushed its comparative advantage in heavy industry. Furthermore the conception of a single person responsible for meeting production targets (and just about everything else) in a factory accorded well with traditional Korean hierarchical coordination, and the "top-downism" that characterized Kim's regime. Yet in early discussions of such quintessentially Stalinist policies one finds them placed within the context of building the requisites for an independent economy, and with an admixture of typically Maoist phrases about responsible factory leaders learning from the masses, reminding them that "leaders do not fall from the sky"; they must understand that "one who is today the leader [may] tomorrow [be] the one receiving leadership."[33]

The real test of Soviet influence would not be these policies, followed almost everywhere by Marxist-Leninists in the period, but evidence of extensive Soviet penetration of the Korean economy. In the late 1940s the relationship between North Korea and the Soviet Union was unquestionably one in which the Koreans exchanged precious minerals and raw materials for Soviet finished goods and items lacking in the Korean economy, such as coking coal and petroleum, that is, it resembled a colonial exchange relationship. Furthermore, the Koreans claim that the Soviets sought to structure their economy to fit a Soviet-defined conception of economic internationalism and division of labor, thus discouraging self-reliance and central industries like machine-building, which create other industries and provide autonomous developmental capability.

Captured internal documents demonstrate the trade pattern. A top secret memorandum from Ko Hi-man, vice-minister of industry, to Kim Ch'aek lists Korean exports to the USSR in 1949; these include copper, lead, zinc, tungsten, silicon, carbon, pig iron, high speed steel, fertilizer, carbide, cement, magnesite, anthracite, and other ores. According to this document in 1949 the Koreans sold a total value of 39,053,523 *wŏn* in gold to the Soviets, priced at 5,962,370 *wŏn* per ton; this was 86 percent of the total gold delivered to the Korean government, valued at 45,314,012 *wŏn*. The total of all North Korean exports in value was 264,085,224 *wŏn*—far higher than the planned amount of 161,576,863 *wŏn*; the heightened exports were used mostly to purchase military equipment. The absence in this documentation of useful exchange rates between the Korean currency, Russian rubles, and American dollars makes it very difficult to assess the real value of Korean exports.[34]

Internal materials also document the shipment of Korean laborers to work on the Kamchatka Peninsula in 1948, much as Vietnamese workers are exported today; according to these documents the laborers were healthy, with no great grievances about pay or working conditions.[35] Hearsay evidence, however, suggested that thousands of Koreans were sent to hard labor in the Soviet Maritime Provinces, probably recalcitrants and members of "bad classes."

The Soviets also set up Joint Stock companies in Korea, as they did in Northeast China and Sinkiang; usually the head man was a Russian. In 1947, for example, the general manager of the Wŏnsan Oil Refinery, a joint company, was a Russian named Rozanov; his Korean deputy was Kim Sŏng-gun. The refinery had been installed by the Japanese, using American oil company "blueprints and consultations," a reflection of American dominance in the world oil regime in the 1930s. This arrangement was originally to have lasted for thirty years, the Soviet interest being a reward for "services rendered in connection with the liberation" of northern Korea, according to U.S. Army intelligence. I do not know if the company lasted past 1950. The refinery had been run by a worker's committee until the fall of 1947.[36]

Another joint stock company, having the short title "Mortrans," provided for common use of the Korean ports of Najin, Chŏngjin, and several others; the Soviets ran Korean ports directly before their troops departed, it would appear, but on April 7, 1949, this company was established to supersede earlier arrangments. It is interesting that O Ki-sŏp, a "domestic" communist who ran afoul of Kim Il Sung almost immediately, was the Korean president of this firm (the general director was a Russian), perhaps reflecting Kim's desire to put his antagonists in positions where they would bear the onus of activities resented by Korean citizens. Share capital in this company was divided fifty-fifty between the USSR and the DPRK, and the Board of Directors was evenly split between Koreans and Russians. However, the group originating the company had four Soviets and two Koreans.

This company was, judging by the documentation, purely commercial and controlled sea traffic between Soviet and Korean ports, and governed arrangements for Soviet commercial use of several ports. It allowed both rental and purchase of port facilities. The constitution of the firm required publication of company balance sheets a week before the shareholders met; it says nothing about Soviet military use of Korean ports, and there never has been evidence that the Soviets acquired military bases or naval ports on Korean soil, in spite of much South Korean bluster to the contrary.[37]

Although the Kim regime was reluctant to emphasize such relationships with the Soviets, there was an occasional airing of the touchy issues they raised. Chang Si-u, a key economic planning official, for example, argued at the 5th Session of the Supreme People's Assembly in February 1950 that all possible domestic raw materials should be mobilized for export so that needed items could be imported and foreign exchange could be garnered, and he justified this as necessary to build the foundation for "an independent economy" and to overcome colonial distortions from the Japanese period. Chŏng Chun-t'aik gave a long list of what the Soviets shipped to Korea in return for Korean exports—coking coal, crude oil, lubricating oils, agricultural sulfur, rubber tires and hoses, machine-building tools, and the like—although with no statistics; but again, such trade was justified as necessary to overcome "feudal backwardness" and "colonial deformation," thus to lay the basis for "an independent economy" (*charip kyŏngje*).[38]

Even in this early period, the Koreans were able to diversify imports by balancing Soviet trade with China trade, much as they have done in recent decades. In 1946, internal documents show that north Korea imported more than twice as much from China as from the Soviet Union; in 1947 imports from and exports to China were about equal to imports and exports to and from the USSR. Although much of this China trade probably came from Soviet-influenced Manchuria, once Chinese Communist hegemony was established in Manchuria it gave the Koreans an alternative source of trade.[39]

The number of Soviet advisors was never very high in the North, even in the military. British sources estimated that Soviet advisors to the central government dropped from two hundred in 1946 to only thirty in April 1947, the greatest number of those, predictably, being in the Ministry of the Interior. Provincial governmental advisors were exceedingly few by 1950, it would appear, with only one or two for provincial and city people's committees. A report on the large Hŭngnam explosives factory showed that personnel were all Korean from 1946–1950, except for two Soviet advisors. Military advisors were more numerous, but they did not go down below the battalion level, where there would typically be two or three Soviet advisors. This Soviet presence simply cannot be compared to fully-functioning satellites in Eastern Europe, which had thousands of Soviet staff people and advisors.[40]

In late February 1949, Kim Il Sung left P'yŏngyang for his only official visit to the Soviet Union before the Korean War. Six Koreans accompanied Kim to Moscow: his foreign minister, Pak Hŏn-yŏng; economic and trade specialists Chang Si-u and Chŏng Chun-t'aek; and three cultural affairs figures, the economic historian Paek Nam-un, southern politician and scholar Hong Myŏng-hŭi, and Kim Chŏng-ju. No Korean military figures were part of the delegation, except for Kim himself. The entourage arrived in Moscow by train on March 3, with Kim delivering a friendly speech that contrasted markedly with Mao Tse-tung's clipped remarks in December 1949 (Mao said simply, "I am here to negotiate the interests of my country"). Kim gave effusive thanks for the Soviet liberation of Korea, spoke highly of Stalin, but also lauded the Soviets for withdrawing their troops. Kim met Molotov on March 4 and Stalin on March 5, the first meeting of these two leaders. Soviet officials who participated in the negotiations included Anastas Mikoyan, Andrei Vishinsky, an official of the trade bureau, M. A. Menshikovich [transliteration from Korean], and the Soviet ambassador to Korea, Shtykov. The talks went on between working delegations until March 17. Kim had a final dinner with Stalin that same day.

When he returned in March, Kim brought with him an economic and cultural agreement and, intelligence rumor had it, a secret military agreement. Several accords resulted, all of them having to do with economic and cultural affairs: trade, navigation, technical aid, scientific and artistic exchanges, by the Korean account. Soviet technical advisors were to be dispatched to the Ch'ŏngjin ironworks, the Waeryŏng rolling mill, an unnamed truck factory, and several other factories. Kim said these advisors would be under the management of the DPRK government, and would get the same treatment and pay as Korean technicians, including the same food ration (a most doubtful statement); the Soviet government would take care of their needs over and above that. Kim went on to contrast this negotiation negatively with U.S.-ROK agreements, and one publicist said it was the first Korean agreement with a foreign nation that was not an unequal treaty.[41]

The fact was that the agreement was neither generous nor equal. The Soviets made the Koreans pay for everything, including the 220 million-ruble loan; they charged 2 percent interest, which was about what mortgages returned to American banks in 1949, that is, there was profit in it. By contrast, in early 1950 Poland got a loan of $450 million at no interest, and the loans provided to China in February 1950 carried a 1 percent rate.[42] South Korea was getting about $100 million a year in economic aid at this time in outright grants, and in June 1949 the Americans left $110 million in military equipment. The defensiveness of the delegation members was palpable, seeking to show that they did not sell their country down the river, and got something in return for their concessions. So, the Soviet-Korean relationship was less an example of comradely internationalism than hard bargains won by a conservative and distrustful Stalin; the quality of the interaction is perhaps best appreciated in Kim Il Sung using his most trusted lieutenant, the tough-as-nails Kim Ch'aek, in secret negotiations with the Russians, including revisions of the March 1949 agreement.[43]

The most important indication of the nature of the Soviet-Korean relationship, of course, was the failure to sign a mutual defense pact. By the spring of 1948 Poland, Czechoslovakia, Hungary, Bulgaria, and Rumania all had agreements with the Soviets to come to each other's defense in case of external attack;[44] a similar treaty between the Soviets and the Chinese was concluded in early 1950. East Germany did not get a mutual defense treaty, since it had no army of its own, merely legions of Soviet soldiers and total penetration of its security system. A high-level American study after the Korean War began said, "there is no evidence to indicate the existence of a mutual assistance pact similar to those existing between the USSR and China and East European satellites." This judgment is reinforced by the semantics of the Soviet-Korean relationship. The Koreans never used the terms *tongmaeng* (alliance) or *choyak* (treaty) to refer to the agreement, but did so with the later Soviet-Chinese treaty.[45]

KOREAN VIEWS OF THE SOVIETS

The received verdict on North Korea is that Kim Il Sung was either a puppet or an imposter who owed his position to Moscow. This is a key reason to assume that North Korea is closer to the East European pattern, and to deny its revolutionary-nationalist credentials and its capacity for independent action. The corollary is that South Korea in the 1940s was the legitimate heir of Korean anti-Japanese nationalism, and that the two sides in Korea were very different than the two sides in Vietnam (Rhee equals Ho, Kim equals Bao Dai). The story in the West remains that the Soviets were everything in 1945 and the North Koreans nothing; the Soviets installed a pliable stooge-imposter in power and he has been, or should have been, grateful ever since. The North Korean conception is rather different.

From a global standpoint, the contribution of the Soviet Union to the victory in World War II was far greater than that of any other country; the Soviet armies and people bore the brunt of the struggle against Germany, which was by far the strongest Axis power. But from a regional standpoint—which, after all, is the way Koreans and Japanese perceived World War II, calling it the Pacific War (the Americans do so too, emphasizing their defeat of Japan and downplaying the role of the Soviets in Central Europe)—an entirely different conception emerges.

In the 1930s the Soviets were alone among the great powers in willingness to confront Japanese expansion directly, doing so in skirmishes along the Korean and Mongolian borders in 1938 and 1939. But this was not much of a sacrifice, and anyway the Soviets needed to convince the Japanese to turn south rather than north. There is no evidence of substantial Soviet support to Korean and Chinese anti-Japanese guerrillas thereafter, yet they bore the brunt of the struggle to keep Japan from a northward instead of southward strategy. A leading Japanese scholar of the Pacific War says it was precisely the Manchurian guerrilla quagmire that constituted the longest battle of this war, which he dates from 1931, and which was instrumental in the turn toward the south.[46]

Furthermore, after Kim Il Sung, Kim Ch'aek, Mu Jŏng, and other Korean guerrillas had been fighting the Japanese for a decade, the Soviets signed a neutrality pact with Japan, which they did not break until 1945. There were good Soviet reasons of state for this policy; they had their hands entirely full with Hitler's legions. But this meant that the Soviets were careful not to arm guerrillas against Japan. Koreans who had long fought the Japanese awaited what everyone thought would be a prolonged struggle to throw Japanese power off the Asian mainland. Suddenly in August 1945 the war ended overnight, and the Soviets marched in first. Then, they stopped at the thirty-eighth parallel when the peninsula was theirs for the taking. The end of the war was, therefore, a mixed blessing for Korean guerrillas.

What fighting did the Soviets do in liberating Korea, precisely? According to a U.S. Army intelligence account unavailable to me when I wrote the first volume, Soviet amphibious forces left Vladivostok and landed at Ŭnggi on August 9, taking this Korean port without a shot; on August 12, the Soviets lost thirty men in fighting for the port of

Ch'ŏngjin; on August 13 Soviet units were "badly mauled," until Soviet marines landed that evening. The war ended the next day.[47]

By comparison, according to a formerly classified study of the Manchurian guerrilla campaigns by two excolonels in the Japanese Kwantung Army, also unavailable to me when I wrote the first volume, in August 1939 the Japanese mobilized six batallions of the Kwantung Army and twenty thousand men of the Manchurian Army and police force in a six-month guerrilla suppression campaign, the main target being guerrillas led by Kim Il Sung and Ch'oe Hyŏn. In September 1940 an even larger force embarked on a counterinsurgency campaign against Chinese and Korean guerrillas. It was described as follows: "The punitive operation was conducted for one year and eight months until the end of March 1941, and the bandits, excluding those led by Kim Il Sung, were completely annihilated. The bandit leaders were shot to death or forced to submit."[48]

Thus massive conterinsurgency ensued for more than two years, until the eve of the German onslaught against the Soviet Union. Thousands of guerrillas were wiped out, and could be added to the estimates of about two hundred thousand slaughtered by the Japanese going back to the Manchurian Incident in 1931. Kim Il Sung, Kim Ch'aek, Ch'oe Hyŏn, and several other key North Korean leaders, and of course many Chinese counterparts, were the survivors.

These guerrillas, the former Japanese officers said, "were a great menace to the Kwantung Army because the Army had planned an offensive operation against the Soviet Union, and especially [so] because the Army intended to fight the main decisive battle in East Manchuria." This same source noted that the Manchurian guerrillas got no weapons or aid from the Soviets; instead the guerrillas took weapons, ammunition, and other supplies from the Japanese armies.

Without denigrating the Soviet war effort, it is not surprising that these guerrillas would believe that they helped the Soviet Union by preventing a Japanese northward advance and a two-front war in 1941, and would look askance at Soviet sacrifices in Manchuria and Korea in August 1945. This experience has gnawed at Soviet-Korean relations ever since; even in the 1980s both regimes still needle each other about who liberated Korea.

In spite of the heavy Soviet presence in the North after the war, one finds evidence even then of this perspective in internal north Korean sources. A lecture outline from a Korean People's Army (KPA) unit in May 1950 cited two key difficulties facing Kim's guerrillas: the strength of the Japanese enemy and "the absence of armed aid from international sources." Similar lecture notes from January 1950 state that in 1945 after Germany surrendered, Japan was "fighting the whole world," including the United States, England, and China; "it was in these conditions that the USSR . . . declared war on Japan on August 8." In secret materials prepared by the Interior Ministry for propaganda workers in the South, Kim Il Sung's struggle was placed before the Soviet contribution; although it said that the Soviets played the leading role in defeating Japan, it then immediately pointed out that they only began fighting on August 8. Ch'oe Ch'ang-ik, who fought in Yanan with the Chinese communists, clearly stated in 1947 that "the Korean people at home and abroad overthrew Japanese imperialism." After acknowleding the Soviet role in the final liberation of Korea, he remarked immediately, "Of course, it is a fact that the Korean people fought Japan for a half-century."[49]

The Soviet involvement in dividing Korea also came in for indirect criticism, or labored explanation. Kim Il Sung's report to the Second Party Congress in April 1948 said Korea was divided at the thirty-eighth parallel "because of an unavoidable international situation and because of military necessity"; hand-printed KWP Central Party School lecture outlines in 1948 said that the USSR and the United States occupied Korea under mutually-agreed terms at a time when they were allies; they were to disarm and oust the Japanese, and outside of these "they could have no other goals."[50] Public materials, however, always placed exclusive blame on the United States for the national division.

Stepping into the shoes of the northern leadership, then, provides a rather different perspective on the Soviet liberation of Korea, and explains in part why Koreans in the 1960s and 1970s rarely referred to any Soviet help, and why the Soviets reciprocate by totally ignoring the role of Kim Il Sung and other guerrilla leaders, even in histories of Manchuria in the 1930s and 1940s.

All this was obscured, of course, behind a smoke screen of nauseating adulation for Stalin and the Soviets in the late 1940s. Koreans, whether in South or North, are past masters at exaggerated flattery; nothing is more common to a foreigner in Korea than the experience of receiving outlandish praise, while suspecting that hardly any of it is meant seriously. But in the case of Stalin, a person of enormous prestige in the late 1940s by virtue of the Nazi defeat, with a multitude of myrmidons indulging the cult of personality, it was completely predictable that the Koreans would gladly join in this, since this is the way they tend to treat their own leaders.

Thus we find Yi Sǔng-yǒp referring to Stalin on his seventieth birthday as "our patron of Liberation, our lodestar, our master teacher, our intimate friend, who has the heart-felt respect and limitless love of our people." This sort of rank toadying went on for several more paragraphs—and it is one example culled from a thousand. Kim Il Sung was rarely heard saying such things, nor were his close allies; Yi was a member of the southern faction and people like him were probably given the task of wooing Stalin with blather that few Koreans believed, or they may have sought to pull on a Soviet connection to compete with Kim.[51] Pictures of Stalin and Kim hung all over the North, peering down from government buildings, railway stations, party meeting halls. Was North Korea unique in this Stalin-worship in the 1940s?

When Mao entrained from Moscow on February 17, 1950, he referred to Stalin as "the master teacher (*susŭng*) of the world revolution and the most intimate friend of the Chinese people," and said the Soviet experience "serves as a model" for China. The Chinese frequently referred to the "faithful love and respect" of the Chinese people for Stalin. Even before the PRC was established, pictures of Mao and Stalin appeared just as ubiquitously as in Korea. And Kuo Mo-jo, the leading Chinese Communist cultural figure, wrote odes to Stalin that surpassed the Koreans in sycophancy.[52]

The Soviet-Korean relationship, then, seems in retrospect to have been more complex and troubled than usually thought; the proper image is not some sort of puppetry, but a wary duet between two distrustful associates. This becomes even clearer when we examine the North's other foreign link: China.

Chapter Eleven

NORTH KOREA'S
CHINA CONNECTION

Comrade Il Sung always teaches us, go down to the lower levels,
take a look; go among the masses, listen to their opinions, study
directives and unite concrete leadership with general directives.
Kim Ch'ang-man

WHEN AMERICAN UNITS first joined the Korean People's Army (KPA)
in combat, they discovered that standard Soviet infantry procedures mingled with unexpected flanking and envelopment tactics. They
would prepare for frontal battle, only to find themselves surrounded.
American soldiers paid with their lives for the myopia of their superiors,
who did not know the enemy they faced. The KPA mixed Soviet tactics
with Chinese communist warfare: but this was only one aspect of a general phenomenon. Korean communism is, first, Korean. But after that,
we may say that it has learned most from China, while taking what it
wants and doing what it must with regard to the Soviets. This is what a
long view of the Sino-Korean relationship would predict, Korean emu-
lation of things Chinese, albeit with a certain reluctance—but not the
pure recalcitrance Koreans reserve for other foreign things.

North Korea was in great measure a mix of Korean authenticity and
Chinese influence. If all this seems perfectly predictable, one can search
the literature and find hardly a word about it—let alone the intelligence
estimates that could have prepared soldiers and presidents for what they
got in Korea. There are many "hidden histories" in the Korean War, but
North Korea's China connection is among the most important. The owl
of Minerva may fly at dusk, but it cannot even take wing in a vacuum of
ignorance and failed thought. This was a history available before the autumn of 1950 and the grave American failure to estimate Chinese and
Korean intentions. So, instead of an "intelligence failure," one had an
incapacity to conceive, first, that Chinese influence was superior in the
North to Soviet influence; second, that ties of revolutionary reciprocity
bound Koreans and Chinese together; third, that these ties were strong
enough such that, in retrospect, what an historian would have trouble
explaining is why the Chinese did *not* intervene in the Korean War.

The reasons for the obscurity of North Korea's China involvement are
typical: the North Koreans have sought to hide it so that Kim Il Sung's

legend may be intact; the Soviets tried to keep Chinese influence out, so it had to be infiltrated; South Korean scholarship has sought to dwell on purported Soviet puppetry; Americans who until the 1970s held to a conception of monolithic communism, have hardly thought to ask the question.

In this chapter we will see that the existence of tens of thousands of Korean "volunteers" in the Chinese civil war provided a potent base for Kim's power; that Kim worried about this army, too, and therefore sought to bolster and burnish the *Kapsan* legacy; that Kim Il Sung and his closest allies emulated aspects of Chinese practice, to the point of rank plagiarism; that Chinese Communist victory on the mainland had an extraordinary refractory effect on Korea; and finally that Chinese influence competed with Soviet before the Korean War began.

A few random comments in American intelligence documents grasp aspects of this North Korean mise-en-scène before June 1950. For example, in the CIA's estimate of North Korean intentions a week before the war began, it said the USSR would not want to use its own troops in Korea for fear of general war, and "its suspected desire to restrict and control Chinese influence in northern Korea would militate against sanctioning the use of regular Chinese Communist units in Korea."[1] The document was right about Soviet desires to "restrict and control" Chinese influence, but wrong about its power to determine the situation.

The CIA's nemesis, General Willoughby, typically was less perspicacious. In 1948 his G-2 developed a file, "Communist Far Eastern Ring," which consisted of innocuous letters from Anna Louise Strong to Hugh Deane, intercepted by Supreme Command, Allied Powers (SCAP) intelligence. Both were simply assumed to be communists by Willoughby, who never let the problem of evidence get in the way of his predilections. The letters dealt with her visit to North Korea in the summer of 1947. In the course of many interesting observations, she said, "Russian diplomacy treats the Chinese Communists as an unrecognized, outlaw regime, and maintains a blockade against them, hence Korea has no direct contact with the tremendous civil war on her border or with the thinking of Mao Tse-tung."[2] Unfazed by this revelation of Soviet-Chinese tension, Willoughby had his G-2 censor and suppress Deane's attempt to publish parts of the letter in Japan.

But Strong erred in saying that the Koreans had no contact with the Chinese revolution or the thought of Mao. In the 1940s it was easy to find references, for example, to Kim Il Sung's own membership in the Chinese Communist Party (CCP) in the 1930s, something never mentioned today. Some notes for a political lecture on Kim's background state that he joined the CCP in 1931, and formed "intimate ties" with the Chinese people, as the best way to resist the Japanese; the notes say nothing about the Soviets until they join the war in 1941.³ Hŏ Chŏng-suk, Hŏ Hŏn's daughter, said in an important speech published in 1946, but apparently first given in 1940, that Kim Il Sung was Korea's "national hero," embodying the "excellent revolutionary traditions of the Korean people," and then proceeded to laud Mao as China's "great leader," and to say that Korea's fate was intimately tied to that of the Chinese Communists.⁴

Kim Il Sung told his early hagiographer, Han Chae-dŏk, that he and his allies constantly sought to foster Sino-Korean unity in the 1930s; he referred to the creation of a "Chinese volunteer army" (*Chungguk ŭiyong-gun*) that his own guerrilla brigade joined up with in 1932. A Korean report on the twenty-sixth anniversary of the founding of the CCP in 1947 went far beyond Soviet materials in referring to the Chinese revolution as "under the guidance of Mao Tse-tung thought," saying that the past quarter-century had proved "the correctness of his thought and his line"; Mao's ideas now constituted the CCP's "leading thought, the guide to all party work . . . this is a very important milestone in history."⁵

Until 1949, however, Chinese influence had to be infiltrated under the noses of Soviet ideologues. Moreover, it was Kim and his allies who did it. In 1947 and 1948 some Yanan Koreans, such as Mu Chŏng, were in eclipse.⁶ Either the Soviets or Kim, or both, feared his personal influence and, perhaps, his ties to powerful Chinese military men like Chu Teh. Instead, the agent of infiltration was primarily an important man named Kim Ch'ang-man, a speechwriter for Kim Il Sung and one of two or three people who could refer to him in print by his first name. Kim Ch'ang-man was of key importance in the emergence of China-linked ideological themes in 1947, and again in the early 1960s when the Democratic People's Republic of Korea (DPRK) expressly sided with China in the Sino-Soviet conflict.⁷

The timing of this Maoist emphasis begins precisely with the emergence of Kim's particular brand of leadership, in the summer of 1947. On the first anniversary of the founding of the North Korean Worker's Party (NKWP), Kim Il Sung said that NKWP cadres are "always among the people, taking the interests of the people as their own, gathering together the demands and calls of the people and making policies in the interests of the people." Party "work style" (*ch'akp'ung*; *tso-feng* in Chinese) must be one of "living in the midst of the masses," "becoming one with the masses" (literally, becoming one lump with the masses, *kunjung kwa han tŏngŏri toeda*). Leaders must all "go among the masses"; they must correct errors through "the method of rectification" (*kaejŏng*); all must be subject to criticism and self-criticism (*cha-a pip'an*). The meaning and the terminology were directly out of Chinese Communist practice.⁸

Kim Ch'ang-man followed this with an important article, entitled

"Theory and Practice." He argued in good Korean fashion that the experience of foreign countries must be "absorbed" solely from the standpoint of Korea's own experience, what is useful to it. But nonetheless, studying and absorbing foreign experience was "the key" to victory. This should not mean studying foreign communist theory "for the sake of theory," something "abstract and blind," with no concrete application. Instead, Marxism-Leninism must be merged with the actual movement for Korean independence and democracy, he said. Then he made clear what this actually meant:

> We must follow and learn the method of thought and work of Comrade Kim Il Sung, letting it serve as a model and pattern . . . [this model] always takes advanced scientific theory and method as its principle, creatively examines and utilizes foreign experience, which is relevant to Korean reality, merges theory and practice, [and] applies the universal truth of Marxism-Leninism to the concrete practice of today's Korean movement.

This article appeared in the theoretical journal of the NKWP, preceded by a lead editorial calling for "intimate ties with the masses." It said, "We must establish the basic principles in our work of leading the masses, teaching the masses, and learning from the masses." It went on to quote Kim Il Sung, "We must establish the work method of going among the masses and to the lower levels, explaining things to them, studying their feelings, leading them to achieve goals." At these lower levels, opinions, work experience, and revolutionary practice must be "gathered together," returned to the leadership, then again returned to the masses. Then, "the masses will mobilize themselves through their own consciousness, and have the capacity to carry out decisions." People should never be "bossed around," but neither should activists who "go down to the lower levels" allow themselves to be led by the masses—this is "tailism" (*mihaengjuŭi*). Yet another article in this same issue linked "the new democracy" (*sin minjjuŭi*) and Korea.[9]

Anyone reading this prose or hearkening to the particular use of language will see the distinct Maoist resonance; in some cases the cadences are identical. Yet Mao's name never appears; his language is put in Kim Il Sung's mouth. Was this accidental? Did they do the same with Stalin? The answer is a categorical no in both cases. Kim Ch'ang-man was a ventriloquist taking Maoist verbiage and casting it to Kim Il Sung's mouth, without ever invoking Mao's name. Stalin, by contrast, was rarely cited by either Kim, nor was his thought plagiarized. Above all, Maoist influences were inserted at the critical point of supreme leadership and its methods, the political fount of towering importance to Koreans. It is also typical for Koreans to take models from the Chinese classics and apply them in the Korean context; but now the classics were Maoist.

In the issue of *Kŭlloja* that followed the one discussed above, the lead editorial again dwelt implicitly on Maoist thought and leadership. It urged NKWP cadres to "go among the masses," organize small-group discussions (*t'amhwa*), and avoid bureaucratism and a "work-style" that divorces one from the masses. Kim Ch'ang-man's article followed, entitled "Several Questions on Methods of Leadership in Party Work."[10] Much of it reads like a take-off on Mao's classic mass-line text, "On Methods of Leadership" (1943). Kim wrote, "Comrade Il Sung always teaches us, go down to the lower levels, take a look; go among the masses, listen to their opinions, study directives and unite concrete leadership [at the lower level] with general directives [from the center]." He said leading nuclei should insert themselves in party branches and work units (Chinese term, *danwei*), and tightly unite this core with the masses—thus linking Kim Il Sung's notions on core leadership and concentric circles with the mass line.

In a paraphrase of Mao, Kim wrote that "you can always divide a group into three parts": an active element, those in the middle, and those who are comparatively backward. Leadership consists of uniting with the first, leading the second, and drawing in the third. Leading nuclei "must always be formed in a real struggle." Even more interesting, however, is this statement.

> In all our party's practical work, correct leadership must be the leadership method of "from the masses, to the masses." This means taking the scattered, unsystematic opinions of the masses, collecting them, systematizing them, and studying them, making their ideas into a system, and then going back to the masses to explain and popularize them, and make the masses take the ideas as their own and thus support them.

All this must be done continuously, once, twice, thrice, and then again. Later in the article this is called "the mass line" (*kunjung nosŏn*).

This is a direct quotation from Mao's classic mass-line text, without a hint that it comes from there. Instead the ideas are attributed to Kim Il Sung. Here is how the Maoist text reads, in the usual English rendering:

> In all practical work of our party, correct leadership can only be developed on the principle, "from the masses, to the masses." This means summing up (i.e., coordinating and systematizing after careful study) the views of the masses (i.e., views scattered and unsystematic), then taking the resulting views back to the masses, explaining and popularizing them until the masses embrace the ideas as their own.[11]

Kim Il Sung's basic difference with Mao is implied, however, in the emphasis on core leadership. Instead of "from the masses, to the masses,"

Kim's principle would be "to the masses, from the masses, to the masses," the epistemological source of good ideas being the core leadership.

A few months later, Kim Il Sung used similar mass-line phraseology in his report to the Second NKWP Congress.

> We must establish the work method of going among the masses and going to the lower levels, explaining things to them, studying their feelings, and guiding them toward the achievement of our goals. It is not a matter of giving orders to the masses but of becoming one with the masses, teaching them, becoming friends with them, winning them over.[12]

This emphasis on "going among the masses" was frequently cited thereafter, as exemplifying Kim's leadership; use of mass-line rhetoric became synonymous with the promotion of Kim as the supreme leader.[13] Notice, however, that whereas Kim Ch'ang-man had said the masses "are our teachers, the source of our strength, our wisdom, and our creativity," this Maoist emphasis drops out of Kim Il Sung's presentation; instead the concern is with explaining policy and guiding people toward fulfillment of the goals of the top leadership. Kim's conception is that core leadership is catalytic: by coming into contact with it, the creativity of the masses is stimulated. The term is usually *chŏpch'ok*, which means both to touch or contact, and in chemistry to be a catalyst.

If readers trying to figure out the Korean War may find this all a bit esoteric, it is not so to communists. Soviet ideologues paid minute attention to ideological heterodoxy, and would immediately pick up such Maoist emphases, not to mention articles depicting Mao's thought as the guiding doctrine for China and Asia, thereby putting him on a par with Stalin. Their legitimate fear was that Mao and his doctrines would capture the leadership of the Asian revolution. It is interesting, therefore, that the Yanan-aligned Koreans who referred to "Il Sung" and put Maoist words in his mouth were in eclipse or even dropped from the leadership in 1948. Kim Ch'ang-man disappeared for a while; Ch'oe Ch'ang-ik, who toward the end of 1947 had likened the "great patriot, perspicacious leader" Kim Il Sung to Lenin and Stalin, also went into eclipse.[14] But when Soviet troops left Korea, these same emphases came back, deeply identified with Kim's leadership.

THE SOVIET TROOP WITHDRAWAL AND THE FLOWING IN OF CHINESE INFLUENCE, 1949–1950

At the end of 1948 Stalin withdrew the two remaining Red Army divisions from North Korea, and they never returned—a stark contrast with Soviet satellite policies in Eastern Europe at the time. This marked a crucial turning point in North Korean history: Soviet troops withdrew, and tens of thousands of Koreans who fought in China returned. During the World War, when informed of the global influence of Catholicism, Stalin responded, how many divisions does the pope have? In 1945 he remarked, "whoever occupies a territory imposes his own social system." For this hardbitten realist the placement of military force was the guarantee of everything. He could not have mistaken the effects of the removal of Soviet force and its substitution by China-linked Korean divisions; he must have done it because of the limits to Soviet power in the Far East, and perhaps, a desire to distance the USSR from a volatile Korean charge. From that time on, Kim Il Sung not only had one of the most potent armies in the world at his command, but gained room to maneuver between the two communist great powers.

In an interesting analysis, George Kennan argued that ideological and political controls were not enough to hold a country in the Soviet sphere; there has to be "the shadow or the reality of military domination."[15] Once the reality ended with the departure of Soviet troops, was there a "shadow"? There was in the presence of Soviet forces across the Russo-Korean border. But such forces would have to contend with an independently controlled and locally much larger force of Koreans, capable of winning Chinese backing. Soviet-Korean military relations thus were different than the satellite pattern; different than in Austria until the treaty in 1955, since Austria possessed no such military force; perhaps Finlandization is the best European approximation of the relationship, but even then the northern army was more formidable, and had the recourse of Chinese backing.

The Soviet withdrawal from Korea was complete; there is no evidence that armed forces remained in Korea surreptitiously. Nor did the Soviets get the warm-water naval base they were presumed to covet in Korea. Army G-2 sources said only Soviet military advisors remained in the North after December 1948; some one hundred towns continued to have one to three Soviet civilian "Kommandatura" members. Korean naval personnel captured during the war reported that no Soviet military vessels anchored in the key East coast port of Wŏnsan after 1948, nor did submarines come into the harbor.[16] Yanan-linked allies of Kim such as Ch'oe Ch'ang-ik were soon vociferous in lauding the Soviet withdrawal, saying it would "hasten the realization of the complete, self-reliant independence of our Motherland." Another high leader, Chŏng Chun-t'aek, said the withdrawal meant that the Soviets "respected our nation's *chajusŏng.*"[17]

We have sought to suggest that Soviet strategy in 1947–1948 pointed toward a transnational sphere of influence in Northeast Asia embracing north Korea, Manchuria, and the Soviet Far East. Stalin did not believe that the Chinese Communists would win the civil war, but probably looked forward instead to a communist North China and a noncommunist South China, or to a protracted struggle with indeterminate outcome. In either case, the preferred strategy would be to maintain the Soviet position in the critical industrial regions in the Northeast, preserving their links with north Korean energy sources, rail lines, and ports. This could not have been a critical goal of Soviet strategy, for otherwise he would not have withdrawn Soviet divisions from Manchuria in 1946. It was rather more like tsarist policy, seeking political influence and economic concessions in a region of great power conflict, but one removed from central Soviet concerns.

When the Chinese-Korean communist armies cleared Manchuria of the nationalist forces, however, Stalin could not hope to dominate the situation. The same would be true of North Korea once the Korean CCF troops returned home. (CCF means Chinese Communist Forces, the intelligence agency term for this multinational army made up mostly of Chinese and Koreans.) So, Stalin relied on attempts to establish economic dependencies and political controls. The first meant unequal exchange of raw materials and foodstuffs for Soviet finished goods; the second meant dealing directly with Kao Kang's "independent kingdom" in the Northeast, and seeking to counter Chinese influence in North Korea. This was a low-risk strategy, reflecting the low priority of Manchuria and Korea in Soviet global calculations. It could not survive the consolidation of Maoist control throughout China in 1949 which, in turn, had a powerful refractory effect on the Korean situation.

The relationship was not one in which the Soviets could push buttons and get the Korean army to do its bidding. Furthermore the Koreans made veiled but explicit references to a big change having occurred in 1949 in the "basic principle" of guaranteeing Korea's *chajusŏng* (independence) against becoming subordinated "to a foreign economy," and the same may be said of the military relationship.[18] This reality is perhaps reflected in contemporary Soviet writings on East Asia, which make no mention of Kim Il Sung or Mao Tse-tung in the 1940s, and denigrate Kim's anti-Japanese effort to the point of saying, "anti-Japanese actions [in Korea] took place predominantly in the cities."[19]

The truly big change in Korea after the Soviet withdrawal was the substitution of Chinese-linked military force for the Red Army troops, and the inevitable flowing in of Chinese influence thereafter. One can find next to nothing in the literature either on the growth of the Korean participation in mainland warfare, the return of these Koreans in 1948–1950, or the extraordinary significance of these events for the eventual course of the Korean War. Thus it is necessary to provide a detailed recapitulation.

Korean forces in China originated from various units that fought in

Manchuria or Yanan in the 1930s. The two units that survived into the late 1940s were the Korean Volunteer Army (*Chosŏn ŭiyong-gun*—KVA) and the Yi Hong-gwang Detachment (*Yi Hong-gwang chidae*—YHD). The Yi Hong-gwang Detachment was named for a Korean guerrilla who died in Manchuria in 1935. Some sources say the KVA dropped its name in April 1946, to be integrated into Korean units in the Northeast United Democratic Army (NEUDA), a title similar to ones used in the 1930s; but use of the KVA name continued after that date. The KVA apparently was inaugurated in 1941, but until August 1945 it had probably no more than three to four hundred members. Its ranks swelled rapidly, however, as Korean soldiers demobilized from the Japanese Army came in and as civil war grew in China; G-2 sources cited Kuomintang abuses of the local Korean population, including lumping them together with the Japanese for postwar reprisals, as "one of the costliest errors of the civil war," bringing in many Korean recruits to the Communists.[20]

Kim Il Sung sensed the immense strategic blessing of a Chinese Communist victory, and therefore in early 1947 he began dispatching tens of thousands of Koreans to fight with Mao and to swell the existing Korean units to division size, a "volunteer" army that prefigured the Chinese "volunteers" that returned the favor in the fall of 1950. This came at a time of crisis for the Chinese Communists. According to William Whitson, in March 1947 People's Liberation Army (PLA) morale was "very low because of a succession of defeats and heavy losses in all theaters"; aggressive Nationalist offensives meant that "the fate of the entire war seemed to hang in the balance."[21] Kim, or the Soviets, most likely both since their different strategies would predict it, supplied the Chinese communist armies with food and raw materials, and opened the North as a place for regrouping military forces in the Manchurian fighting, and for rest and recreation. The border towns of Antung and Sinŭiju became central switching points for communist soldiers.

Army intelligence in Seoul and Tokyo paid much attention to this transnational network in succeeding months and years. But British intelligence was better, because it did not take for granted a monolithic unity among the communists. What little we have of this, given England's tight declassification policies on intelligence materials, shows a good awareness of the realities of Northeast Asian power relationships in the late 1940s, and reasonably full knowledge of the Korean contribution to the Chinese civil war.

R. S. Milward, a perspicacious observer, remarked in mid-1948 that the Koreans were then "gaining battle experience" in China.[22] British intelligence reported that the entire North Korean rail network was devoted to the movement of CCF troops in December 1946 and January 1947 and that North Korea was a "reliable rear area" for the CCF, providing grain and other materials, rest and recreation, and the quartering of large numbers of troops. G-2 sources also noted that "during the period of the deepest Chinese Nationalist penetration into Manchuria, North Korea was a secure zone of communications for the CCF." In May 1947, the PLA used northern Korea to billet soldiers and exchanged Korean grain and minerals for Chinese manufactured goods. Furthermore, most of the output of the big Hŭngnam explosives plant was shipped to China, especially dynamite and blasting fuses.[23]

USAMGIK G-2 paid close attention to troop and materiel movements across the Sino-Korean border in early 1947, dating the origins of the cooperation from the fall of the border city of Antung in October 1946, and suggesting that by May 1947 15 to 20 percent of CCF forces in Manchuria were Koreans. It said north Korean military forces expanded rapidly in late 1946 within Korea, preparing for a spring offensive in Manchuria. Some thirty thousand Koreans under the command of Kim Ch'aek moved into Manchuria during April 1947. G-2 sources identified Mu Chŏng, the Korean guerrilla leader who joined Mao and Chu Teh in the Ch'inggangshan and who made the Long March, as Korean chairman of a Joint Military Council (*Kunsa hapjak wiwŏnhoe*) which included six Koreans, six Chinese, and two Soviets. It controlled all movements of troops and materiel across the Sino-Korean border.[24] The balance of Koreans and Chinese reflected the relatively equivalent contributions that Chinese and Koreans made in the anti-Japanese struggle in Manchuria.

One report also indicated that the Koreans and the Chinese signed a "defense" agreement on May 17, 1947, stipulating the levels of Korean assistance to China, and Chinese quartering rights in the North. Later reports, more numerous if not necessarily more reliable, said that the North Koreans and the Chinese signed a secret mutual defense pact in March 1949, that is, the month of Kim's visit to Moscow. The former warlord Yen Hsi-shan said in July 1950, according to Radio Taipei, that secret documents his agents captured during fighting in Shansi "revealed a secret pact between the Korean Communists and the Chinese Communists." It called for the dispatch of seventy thousand Korean troops to China, with China pledging in return that it would send two hundred thousand Chinese to Korea, if needed in a war.[25]

The G-2 quoted a pregnant statement by Ch'oe Yong-gŏn, given to the Americans by an informant who said he was present at a meeting of Korean CCF leaders on May 10, 1947: "Korea will soon be ours. At present there is not a single unit in the United Democratic Forces now driving the Kuomintang from Manchuria that does not have my troops in it. At the end of the Manchurian campaign these troops will be seasoned, trained veterans. When the Americans and the Russians withdraw, we will be able to liberate [south] Korea immediately."[26]

8. Defense Minister Ch'oe Yong-gŏn, 1948

Order of Battle intelligence on the PLA in July 1947 carried the KVA and a "Korean column" under Mu Chŏng headquartered at Shulan in Manchuria; the KVA was headquartered at Yenchi and was said to be commanded by Chiang Hsin-t'ai; American military attaches estimated that fully seventy thousand Koreans were fighting in Manchuria by that time.[27]

The Yi Hong-gwang Detachment (YHD) returned to Korea and was incorporated in the KPA at its inaugural meeting on February 8, 1948. It was thought to be ten thousand strong at the time. Although Yi Hong-gwang had died in 1935, the Chinese Nationalists were not aware of this. They thought he was the commander of the Koreans in Manchuria, and even placed him at a meeting in August 1950. Captured documents contain a photograph of this unit on the march, displaying pictures of Marx, Engels, Mao, and Kim Il Sung. One extant training manual from the

9. Koreans in the Chinese People's Liberation Army, circa 1947

YHD included Sino-Korean translations of Mao's "Combat Liberalism," and two other pieces by him on the mass line and on military doctrine; also nine essays by Liu Shao-ch'i, and even an attack on the intellectual Wang Shih-wei, who was a target of criticism during the Yanan rectification campaigns in 1942. When Chinese forces entered the Korean War, the People's Daily specifically cited the contributions of this detachment in the anti-Japanese resistance and the civil war.[28]

One of its key generals was Pang Ho-san, who later had a distinguished record in the the Korean War. He had attended the Whampoa Military Academy, and had been a member of the Chinese Communist Party since at least 1933. He was an instructor at a Yenan military school, where he was known as Yi Ch'un-bok. He then fought extensively in Manchuria and North China with the Yi Hong-gwang Detachment and other units, and was the commander of the PLA's 166th division, made up mostly of Koreans. The 166th became the basis for the KPA 6th Division. American sources described Pang as an intelligent, systematic military man, highly respected within KPA ranks.[29] Kim Ŭng, another commander, had also studied at Whampoa. Roy Appleman described him as "a spectacular soldier," "energetic and harsh," and the ablest of KPA commanders.[30]

Veterans of the China fighting, not Soviet-aligned Koreans, dominated the Korean People's Army. Mu Chŏng, of course, did not hold high position until the war began, mainly because of the threat he posed to Kim Il Sung, given his fine anti-Japanese record and his long participation in the PLA. He was a northern version of Kim Ku, a dedicated patriot of rough mien and little apparent political acumen. Pak Il-u, interior minister and a confidant of Kim Il Sung, spent much of his life in China. He was deputy head of the Korean military-political school at Yanan, and later helped Mu Chŏng reorganize the KVA. The top leaders of the KPA 3rd Division in April 1948, Pang Ho-san, Wang Cha-in, Hong Rim, and No Ch'ŏl-yong, were all China veterans. Ch'oe Tŏk-jo, another CCF veteran, led the KPA western command headquartered at Chinnamp'o; he was apparently a lieutenant colonel in the 8th Route Army, and his chief of staff, Kwak Tong-sŏ, was also a KVA veteran. Pak Hyo-sam, another China-aligned Korean, had also studied at Whampoa. Other KPA leaders with CCF experience included Yi Ho, Han Kyŏng, O Hak-yong, Ch'i Pyŏng-hak, Ch'oe A-rip, Kim Kwang-hyŏp, Yi Ik-sŏng, and Ch'oe Kwang. Like Kim Il Sung, most of these people were in their thirties. Army G-2 sources thought upwards of 80 percent of KPA officers had served in China.[31] This does not include, of course, the Manchurian guerrillas from the 1930s who also worked with the Chinese, such as Kim Ch'aek, Ch'oe Yong-gŏn, Kim Il, and of course Kim Il Sung. We have by now listed almost the entire high command of the KPA, all veterans of Sino-Korean joint fighting. There is no evidence of high-ranking officers with experience in the Soviet Army.

From 1948 until the autumn of 1950, Korean units that had fought in China filtered back home. The total numbers were at least one hundred

10. The Yi Hong-gwang detachment marching in Manchuria, circa 1947

thousand. Koreans fought all the way down to the "last battle" for Hainan Island in May 1950. This is mostly an unknown phenomenon. Even official sources with top secret clearances mention it only in passing.[32] When I discussed Korean involvement in the Chinese civil war at a panel of the Association for Asian Studies in 1979, one of the leading American scholars on China in the 1940s told me he had never heard a thing about the Korean veterans. The intelligence apparatuses who monitored the Koreans in the CCF were in Tokyo, Seoul, and Taipei, and their reports were apparently discounted in Washington. But this made the multinational CCF force well known to MacArthur and Willoughby, one of many reasons why they came to think that the Yalu River border was not one worthy of their respect.

The total numbers vary in the data. Intelligence estimates in the late 1940s and retrospective information gotten from POWs identified several waves: a unit 10,000–strong from the YHD returned for the initial formation of the KPA in February 1948; 30,000 to 40,000 returned in the period from July to October 1949; 40,000 to 50,000 returned in February and March 1950. Koreans in the 164th and 166th Divisons of the PLA crossed the border in July 1949 and formed the basis of the KPA Fifth and Sixth divisions. Many reports of arriving returnees came through intelligence networks in October 1949; the 155th Division of the 16th Army returned to Korea in February 1950, to become the 7th KPA Division; irregular units from China returned and constituted the new 10th Division in March 1950.[33]

Several intelligence sources put the total for all Koreans in the Fourth Field Army alone at 145,000; this army under Lin Piao was, of course, the crack force of the PLA, having never lost a battle as it swept southward from Manchuria. The Chinese Nationalists estimated that 50,000 Koreans fought below the Great Wall. Other estimates ran to a total of 200,000; some of the discrepancies may result from Koreans in the Ch'ientao minority area of China having been included, and from double-counting as units moved back and forth across the Yalu. The total was probably between 100,000 and 150,000. Intelligence estimates placed the KPA total at about 95,000 in June 1950, of which 40,000 to 50,000 were thought to be China veterans. That meant that an even larger force of Koreans was still in reserve or in China when the war began.[34]

POW interrogations and order of battle data developed during the Korean War found that Koreans in the CCF came from the following groups: the KVA, the YHD, and the Northeast Democratic United Army in China; Korean troops transferred from the North; and graduates of military training schools in Chiamassu and Lungch'ingtsün in Manchuria. Still, this war-garnered data probably underestimated the totals, because China veterans were integrated into the KPA well before 1950.

Diaries of individual Korean CCF soldiers show a mix of Chinese and

Korean experience.³⁵ One had pictures of Mao and Chu Teh plastered against the front and back; as the soldier moved from China to Korea in the spring of 1950, his diary entries changed from Chinese to Sino-Korean script. He inscribed pledges of loyalty to the DPRK and to Kim Il Sung (while complaining that Korean officers were less egalitarian than Chinese). "I, as a citizen of the DPRK, have solemn duties to my Motherland. Thus I will enter the KPA and faithfully devote myself to the homeland, the people, and the democratic people's government. I pledge this solemnly before our great forefathers. If I disobey any of my pledges, I will be dealt with mercilessly by a people's court." The pledges went on, "serving the people is the most glorious task"; we "fight for our Republic's freedom and our beloved and respected supreme leader [*suryŏng*], General Kim Il Sung."

One Fourth Field Army soldier, Kim Ho-il, joined the CCF in June 1947, and fought from Beijing down to Canton; assigned to Changsha in Hunan Province in February 1950, he then received orders to march north. He crossed the Yalu at Antung on March 17, 1950, changing his uniform that night. He was captured during fighting in northern Korea on October 17, 1950. Chŏn Chae-ro fought in China, then returned to P'yŏngyang where he studied with 1,200 other KPA members at the Second Central Political School, located at Kim Il Sung's birthplace, Man'gyŏngdae. Upon graduation the students received commissions as second lieutenants. Chŏn was stationed with the KPA Fourth Division at Chinnamp'o until June 16, 1950, when the division marched to Yŏnch'ŏn near the thirty-eighth parallel, arriving on June 20. He was captured during the Pusan perimeter fighting in mid-August.

Other captured materials show the influence of this Chinese background. The general staff of the KPA put out a Korean translation of Sun Tzu's *Art of War* in 1949, and a collection of documents from the Chinese civil war in 1950; guerrillas in the South carried Maoist texts on guerrilla war under fake covers, and Kim Il Sung was apparently forced to develop his own "seven points for attention," so deeply did soldiers have in their minds Mao's "eight points for attention" (don't steal even a needle, pay for everything you take, and so on).³⁶ And, of course, more than half of all KPA soldiers had their military experience in the Chinese civil war, thus carrying in their heads a deep Maoist influence.

So, more than 100,000 Koreans fought in the Chinese civil war, gaining battle experience that enabled them to crush the Republic of Korea (ROK) Army and humiliate an American army with far superior firepower until they were outnumbered in September 1950. Perhaps just as important, this blood contribution to the Chinese revolution placed a powerful call on Chinese help during the American march to the Yalu.

The Question of Military Control

After Soviet divisions departed Korea and tens of thousands of officers and soldiers crossed from China back to Korea, Kim Il Sung and his Manchurian guerrilla allies faced a formidable challenge to their power. In 1946, it may be remembered, Kim, or the Soviets, or both, refused to allow KVA returnees to enter the North with their accoutrement of weapons and equipment. Instead they urged them to continue fighting in China. This was widely thought to be the consequence of Kim's fear of Mu Chŏng and other Yanan Koreans. But it is just as likely that the Soviets were the party who blocked the entry of Chinese-linked Koreans. Kim later demonstrated little difficulty in working with Yanan Koreans and, as we have seen, several were his interlocutors in adapting Maoist practices to Korea in 1947. Given Kim's own membership in the CCP in the 1930s, it is likely that the Soviets feared an alliance between Kim's group and the Yanan Koreans. Once the Soviet troops were gone, Kim and his allies brought the CCF Koreans back.

An armed force like this would be a threat to any political leadership. It is fascinating to see how Kim and his allies retained control at the commanding heights. One aspect has already been mentioned: the oaths of loyalty not just to the DPRK but to Kim, on penalty of people's court retribution, and the quartering of officer recruits in Kim's birthplace, thus bringing CCF officers to graduate via "the bosom of the Fatherly Leader." One of Kim's techniques has been figuratively to preside over a paternal, intense rearing and education of selected young Koreans at or near his birthplace, especially party and military trainees and orphans of perished guerrillas and army officers. They all become, in effect, his children, thus drawing upon the deep wells of filial obligation bred into Koreans, but transferring them from the family to Kim, and thence to the state.

A more important aspect was the promotion of Kim Il Sung as "Kimilsung," that is, as a symbol of the power and legitimacy of the Manchurian guerrillas. At the same time, the *Kapsan* guerrilla tradition came to be the main historical theme and model for the DPRK, much as it is today. At the founding of the KPA on February 8, 1948, only Kim Il Sung's picture was displayed, whereas usually he was put in tandem with Stalin; the KPA was said to have emerged from the traditions set by the Kim Il Sung guerrilla detachment. Kim's speech laid emphasis on the necessity for a self-reliant nation to have its own army: "At all times and in all places our Korean people must take their fate into their own hands and must make all plans and preparations for building a completely self-reliant, independent nation in which they alone are the masters, and a government unified by their own hands." The KPA, he said, grew out of the

Manchurian guerrilla struggle, with a tradition of "100 battles and 100 victories." He made no reference to Soviet help in building the KPA.[37]

At the first anniversary of the founding of the KPA, Kim was for the first time referred to as *suryŏng*, a title meaning supreme or maximum leader that had been reserved for Stalin until that time. It has been his title ever since. *Suryŏng* is an ancient Korean term for a chief or conquering hero, common in the Koguryŏ period; its use for Kim was no accident, since North Korea has identified itself with Koguryŏ, just as the South has linked itself to the Silla legacy. At the second anniversary in 1950 the emphasis on Kim as *suryŏng* was even more palpable, and day after day newspapers ran articles glorifying the Manchurian guerrillas. To call Kim by this title was a form of nationalist heresy to Soviet ideologues; their formula was Stalin as world leader of the revolution, Dmitrov and Mao and Kim and all the rest as "national leaders." The Koreans had honored this until the Soviet troops left, by calling Stalin the *suryŏng* of the world's working people, Kim the *chidoja* (leader) of the Korean people.

It was within the military, more than any other institution, that Kim and his guerrilla comrades invoked the imagery of a maximum leader at the center, with concentric circles spreading outward to encompass the membership in an organic, personal relationship with Kim. Kim and the other Manchurian guerrillas were revolutionary warlords, uniting a hardy band of followers around one individual leader, with no clear hierarchy among the units and leaders. This both facilitated their survival, since large units would be discovered by Japanese forces, and coincided with the Korean preference for patron-client organizations linked by personal relationships.

The first evidence of the burnishing of the guerrilla tradition came, appropriately, in 1946 through Han Chae-dŏk, Kim's hagiographer. A member of the Kim Il Sung guerrilla unit told Han how the guerrillas were always "in the bosom of the masses," with "blood ties" linking the guerrillas and the people, a "unity formed in blood"; the tale was shot through with mythology about the worshipful love for Kim and the guerrillas on the part of peasants, and the benevolent, paternal leadership Kim gave in return. The guerrillas themselves were said to be bound by "a spirit of comradely love . . . like that for one's family." They shared life and death, the bitter and the sweet, trusted and respected each other like brothers. This type of organization was a good model, the text said, for party and mass organizations as well. Within the guerrilla units, much education and "rearing" went on, as younger or inexperienced people were inducted into the guerrilla customs. The small base areas often held the family members of the guerrillas, self-sufficient and self-supporting units where "the Japanese dogs did not walk." Here is the origin of the

DPRK's "national solipsism," the ideal of an untainted, self-contained community of Koreans.[38]

Here is also the model of organization for the DPRK ever since, a guerrilla unit as a family, a family within it that is superior (every member of Kim's family was a revolutionary, his mother fashioned special shoes that he could use in the Manchurian forests, so on and so forth in an endless gush of heroic tales), a person within the family that stands out, the exemplary eldest son (since the father had died). This is the Mother organization and Mother tradition for everything else, and it just happens to be where the new leader of the DPRK was born in 1941; Kim Jong Il's rise to power was always marked by invocation of the guerrilla tradition. It is all as Korean as *kimch'i*.

Yet these typically North Korean emphases were hard to find in 1948. Even Kim's speech at the founding of the KPA in February only brought in the guerrilla tradition as a minor emphasis. Shortly after the Soviet force withdrawals, the imagery came back again. The Kim cult and the China influence waxed from mid-1947 to the start of 1948, then went into eclipse, then returned again in 1949. A newspaper editorial in mid-1949 said, the KPA "was organized under the leadership of our nation's peerless patriot General Kim Il Sung, and has as its marrow [*kolgan*] fine, revolutionary and patriotic fighters from the anti-Japanese armed struggle." It included a song about the KPA with the title, "Through Love and Respect." A week later the paper greeted the twelfth aniversary of the Poch'ŏnbo incident, an engagement that is treated in North Korea like a major battle of World War II, as follows: "The more than ten-year guerrilla struggle of the Kim Il Sung partisan detachment was a protracted war longer than that of any country in the world, a glorious, proud, brilliant struggle unknown in the history of guerrilla warfare anywhere else, where for 100 battles there were 100 victories."[39]

For weeks leading up to the second anniversary of the KPA, the party newspaper burnished the reputations of the Kim-aligned guerrillas by giving their biographies or publishing accounts of their exploits. Kim-aligned partisans dominated the media, linking the KPA not with the tens of thousands of CCF returnees then flowing in, but with the *Kapsan* background. Kim Il, third in the leadership before his death in 1985 and a close confidant of Kim Il Sung since the 1930s, wrote that the KPA was "the new-born baby" of the Kim guerrilla detachment, which in turn formed the marrow of the new army. It had "blood relations" with the people, who "love and respect" it. The KPA, unlike most armies, had "lofty virtues," all of which derived from "the glorious victory achieved in the arduous armed struggle of General Kim Il Sung, peerless patriot." The KPA inherited and carried on the guerrilla tradition, having "the lofty patriotic thought of boundless loyalty to one's own people and one's own homeland." Kim Il said KPA soldiers emulate the Soviet soldier as well as the 1930s guerrillas, and made no mention of the Korean military experience in China.[40]

Kang Kŏn was born in 1918 in Sangju, North Kyŏngsang, went with his poor peasant family to Manchuria to escape the Japanese, and joined Kim Il Sung in 1933. He wrote that the Kim group was the backbone of the Manchurian resistance and was now the center of the KPA. In the 1930s varieties of mass organizations, youth volunteers, women's groups, and the like "united around" the leader; Kim was said to have "in a revolutionary way, rendered into practice the Lenin-Stalin proposition on the national question," that only a revolutionary struggle against imperialism "will liberate the oppressed masses" from colonialism and dependency. The Kim partisans "fought against the Japanese dwarfs for a longer period than any other [group], making its military accomplishments known throughout the world."

Ch'oe Hyŏn, another intimate of Kim's, said he joined the anti-Japanese struggle at the age of twelve, and worked with Kim from 1932 onward; he emphasized the strong belief in themselves possessed by the guerrillas. Pak Hun-il, who ran his own detachment in tandem with Kim, said the Japanese police "trembled at the sound of Kim Il Sung's name." He and Wang Yŏn dwelt on the tight unity of the Korean and Chinese guerrillas, but never mentioned Soviet aid.

O Paek-ryŏng, later a high leader in the North, went with his family to Manchuria after his father was oppressed for his participation in the March 1, 1919, movement. Like the others, he lauded Sino-Korean cooperation against the Japanese, and noted how Kim always set up "study groups" whenever possible, making the guerrilla detachments into floating schools.

Other articles glorified Kim-aligned guerrillas who perished in the 1930s, such as Pak Kil-song: a youth "reared" by Kim, he came from a "revolutionary family," joined Kim in 1934 at age seventeen, and fought only for a "self-reliant, independent" Korea. He died in battle in 1942. Hŏ Hyŏng-sik was from Sŏnsan, North Kyŏngsang; his father had his land stolen away by "the thieving Japanese imperialist aggressive bastards," so the family crossed the Yalu. He was tortured to death by the Kuomintang, the article said.

Ch'oe Yong-gŏn, who led a detachment independent of Kim's, nonetheless wrote on the second anniversary of the founding of the KPA that the Kim detachment was the center of the Manchurian resistance, and now of the KPA. He seemed to differ from Kim's closest allies, however, by downplaying people's war and quoting Stalin to the effect that "modern war is mechanized war," and so the KPA arms itself with "advanced military science." The one writer who said least about the Kim guerrillas was none other than Mu Chŏng, who dwelt on his own struggle in South and North China, noted that he began fighting in 1930 (that is, two years before Kim), said his units were "victorious everywhere," and linked the KVA to Kim's presumed leadership of the anti-Japanese guerrillas in a perfunctory way. Apart from this article, the rest were either written by or about the Kim guerrillas, and clearly were meant to demonstrate who controlled the top levels of the KPA.[41]

References to Kim as *suryŏng* were frequent in early 1950, especially around the time of the KPA anniversary. Ch'oe Yong-gŏn's speech used this title for Kim, and at the end he hailed, in the following order, the DPRK, Korean unification, Kim Il Sung, "the founder of the KPA and the *suryŏng* of the Korean people," and Stalin, "intimate friend of the Korean people and *suryŏng* of the Soviet people," thus placing Kim on a par with Stalin.[42] Such titles are the subject of the most careful orchestration. In the 1980s when Kim's son had his unveiling as successor to his father, he was always the *chidoja*, his father the *suryŏng*. Just as the 6th Party Congress in 1980 heralded the son's official successor role, the KPA anniversary in 1950 was Kim Il Sung's coming-out party as the Korean maximum leader, beholden to no one including Stalin. Internal materials demonstrate Kim's dominant position. Political lectures in the KPA in May 1950 dwelled on the Kim tradition, occupying three hours of the four and one-half hours devoted to the colonial period.[43] This was the origin of the practice of adumbrating all of post-1919 history with Kim's own anti-Japanese struggle, indeed going so far as to view all Korean history before 1919 as what Marx would have called "prehistory."[44]

The leadership also drew upon wellsprings of peasant obeisance to the king, urging citizens always to give thanks to the *suryŏng*'s benevolent largesse, and requiring oaths of loyalty and obedience from soldiers, almost all of whom were of poor peasant background: "We soldiers in the KPA, who always receive your unbounded love . . . standing before you, again pledge our fealty." "All actions in our daily life must conform to General Kim Il Sung's orders and wishes." Recruit interviewers asked questions like, "who is the greatest patriot in our country," which, needless to say, had but one answer.[45]

THE REFRACTORY EFFECT OF MAO'S VICTORY: THE EAST IS RED?

If the returning CCF veterans gave the North Koreans a potent, battle-tested army, the Chinese communist victory in 1949 gave them a secure rear area and turned South Korea into a dangling and eminently vulnerable pudenda. The decisive outcome on the mainland was the headiest thing since liberation, and the Koreans began crowing about it as soon as it was in sight.

In March 1949, the party journal said the liberation of North China had taken nearly twelve years, illustrating the Sino-Korean perception of how the guerrilla struggle of the 1930s fit with the denouement in 1949. Quoting Mao many times, the article attributed the approaching PLA victory to an army "born among the people, tightly united with the people, and serving the interests of the people." A month later, a delegation of Koreans visiting Beijing referred to an "alliance" [*tan'gyŏl*] between the Korean and Chinese people, forged by those Koreans who fought with the Chinese, beginning with Kim Il Sung. The coming Chinese victory had given a great boost to the DPRK, and "we are sure that the US imperialists and country-selling criminals [in the South] will meet a fate like they did in China."[46] (The term *tan'gyŏl* does not mean a military alliance, more like a unity between Korea and China; it was not used in regard to the Soviet Union, however, which was always depicted as "friendly" to Korea, or providing "selfless aid.")

In January 1950, coterminous with the promotion of the Kim guerrillas, North Korean publications began drawing exceedingly direct analogies between the final outcome in China and the Korean civil war. The New Year's issue of the party newspaper said that the Communist victory "cannot be underestimated," and took a distinctly non-Soviet line in depicting the Chinese revolution as guided by the correct leadership of the CCP since the 1920s (while "cleverly using the experience of the Bolshevik Party"). The "decisive element" in the Chinese revolution was the founding of the Red Army by Mao and Chu Teh, it said, placing Mao in control from 1927 onward. Two weeks later the newspaper exclaimed, "Look! How strong is the power of a people united! In China, the US imperialists supplied Chiang Kai-shek with [weaponry] . . . and generally interfered in China's civil war, but the united Chinese people destroyed US imperialism's aggressive plans." A few days later, in another publication, "Look! Wasn't the united strength of the Chinese people enough to achieve a brilliant victory . . . history has already passed a death sentence on reactionary influence. Chiang Kai-shek, who ran amok asking for the aid of the US imperialists, has ended up in defeat. The Rhee clique . . . simply awaits the same fate."[47]

On January 17, 1950, the DPRK appointed Yi Chu-yŏn to be its first ambassador to the PRC, and at the end of the month established diplomatic relations with the Democratic Republic of Vietnam. A lead editorial in the party newspaper said that the United States wants to make both South Korea and southern Vietnam into "aggressive bases for confronting the People's Republic of China." The DPRK's response to Dean Acheson's famous Press Club speech, about which more later, included a remarkable statement that Acheson sought to oppose "all those peoples who fight for their independence and freedom, following the Soviet

Union and the great Chinese people, and moreover, [those peoples who] follow the example of China."[48] In other words, the Chinese were a great people (the Soviets were not?); China had a model (the USSR did not?).

As the war approached this drumbeat got louder. Yi Sŭng-yŏp, who became mayor of Seoul during the northern occupation, wrote a key article at the end of March. It was about the southern guerrilla struggle, but in the course of it he pointed instead to the Chinese example and the power of the KPA.

> The same fate as that of Chiang Kai-shek awaits those who sell off the nation and slaughter the people. With a great victory like that of the Chinese people standing before a people fighting for the homeland and for justice, who can possibly doubt that a similar victory will not occur . . . the Korean People's Army is maturing and strengthening as an indomitable force, stands like an armed wall for the homeland and the people, and is growing into the great armed force of the people.[49]

THE SOVIET ATOMIC BOMB

The North Korean preference for China over the Soviet Union, and the superior influence of China on the DPRK, expresses the essence of Korea's position between the two communist giants. But in the confrontation with the capitalist world system, the Korean predilection has been for joint backing by the USSR and China. Kim has always wanted to have his cake and eat it too: free to be independent, free to invoke Chinese and Soviet support. As 1949 turned into 1950, it appeared that this best of all possible worlds had dawned.

The Soviets tested an atomic device in August 1949, touching off the "NSC 68" period and upsetting the 1947 containment compromise in Washington, as we saw. The Soviet bomb also rumbled through the communist world, having especially significant effect in Korea where, combined with the Chinese victory, it emboldened the leadership and inaugurated a period which we might call an early version of the "East is Red" theme of the late 1950s, prompted then by the Soviet launching of Sputnik.

Moscow exploited its great coup in producing an atomic bomb well ahead of the predicted schedule with a dual campaign: it inaugurated a world-wide peace movement through the Cominform and allied communist and leftist groups, which lasted through the start of the Korean War. But it also projected an aura of confidence, as if "history" had swung to its side. In November 1949 Georgi Malenkov gave a controversial speech that, in some eyes, seemed to point toward a more aggressive

Soviet course—wearing the A-bomb ostentatiously on his hip, to para-phrase Henry Stimson.

At the time and in their recollections, key American officials pointed to Malenkov's speech as heralding a change in Soviet policy. Paul Nitze, architect of NSC 68, wrote in February 1950 that Moscow "appears to be animated by a general sense of confidence"; Nitze mentioned Indochina, Berlin, Austria, and Korea as possible Soviet targets. George Kennan paid close attention to Malenkov's speech at the time, and later remarked that Malenkov "so far as we know" had always been "rather for an active policy in the Far East." Acheson wrote that Malenkov gave "a cocky and aggressive speech," mentioning three places where Soviet interests would soon triumph: Yugoslavia, Berlin, and Korea.[50]

Walter LaFeber, however, has argued that Malenkov in fact signaled a retreat from Stalinism, challenging the West to "peaceful competition with socialism." A few weeks later, hard-line ideologue Mikail Suslov "lashed back" at Malenkov, warning that because of recent Soviet victo-ries, there would be "war-mongering" attempts to alter the balance of power, and in LaFeber's words, "could lead to Western attacks on Eastern Europe, Communist China, and North Korea."[51] Perhaps what is most striking in this indeterminate business is the frequent mention of a com-ing crisis in Korea.

Whatever Malenkov's rhetoric may have meant, internal intelligence estimates still predicted that the Soviets were years away from a capability for global war, they had only a handful of atomic bombs, and lacked the capacity for effective delivery of them. But there is evidence that Soviet expressions of boldness had an effect on the North Koreans, who quite predictably interpreted the Chinese victory and the Soviet bomb as proof that the communist world was on a roll. The Koreans probably also hoped, quite wrongly, that Moscow would extend an atomic umbrella to the peninsula, especially since the Russians had apparently gotten aid in their bomb project from the Japanese facilities in Hŭngnam.

The first reference I have found to the Soviet bomb came in October 1949, when the Koreans interpreted it as proof of the advanced science produced by the premier socialist power, while putting the event in the context of the developing global peace campaign. In Kim Il Sung's speech on the Cominform in December 1949, he quoted Kremlin ideo-logue Suslov on the peace campaign, gave praise to "the unstinting aid" of the Soviets to Korea, and urged that Koreans heighten "the spirit of proletarian internationalism, people's democracy and socialism." It was rare for Kim to go on like this, suggesting that he was seeking to ingra-tiate himself with the Soviets now that they had the bomb. But he re-ferred to Malenkov's speech only in passing, quoting it to the effect that possession of the atomic bomb means both that the Russians do not want war, but do not fear it, either.[52]

As the New Year dawned, however, bold editorials in party newspapers in Moscow, Beijing, and P'yŏngyang blared forth the news that "the camp of peace and socialism is immeasurably stronger today than the camp of capitalist reaction," prompting ambassador to Moscow Alan Kirk to remark that "the Kremlin is now more expansively confident than at any time since the end of World War II." The *Nodong sinmun* greeted the New Year with an editorial calling attention to "the great victory" in China, and to Soviet successes in "the utilization of atomic energy"; an article on Syngman Rhee's "funeral march" said he would no longer be able to threaten the North "with talk about American atomic weapons," thus assuring that his "country-selling clique" would soon be "sent to the crematorium."

Yi T'ae-jun argued that "history is flowing to the advantage of the people," and said bluntly, "America, breathing its last and with benumbed morality, has used atomic power evilly as a tool of annihilation to intimidate and threaten the world and humanity, but the Soviet Union has used this power for peaceful construction, and has *forever rendered ineffectual* the Americans' shameful, inhuman madness [of atomic blackmail]" (emphasis added).[53]

An article a few days later by *Nodong sinmun* commentator Kim Sŏk-san discussed recent "collusion" between Chiang and Rhee toward "provoking war," but said, the "democratic camp is incomparably stronger than the imperialist camp now, stretching from Berlin to Canton, from Murmansk to Tirhana," just as "the Korean democratic forces, tightly united around Kim Il Sung and with the international democratic camp, are much stronger than the reactionary camp." Kim Il Sung said much the same on January 20, and in an important article at the end of March, the party newspaper said the United States is getting more dangerous, "especially because of the great victory of the Chinese Revolution," because of the Sino-Soviet Treaty which put eight hundred million people in the "peace camp," and because "the Soviet Union already possesses atomic power . . . last August TASS reported that [the USSR] had dealt a mortal blow to the US imperialists who had made the 'atomic bomb' into a means for unilateral threats."[54] In early 1950, then, the Koreans preened and pounded their chests over precisely what the United States feared the most: a presumably united and formidable Eurasian communist monolith, backed with atomic weapons.

It is still difficult to estimate whether this version of the "East is Red" theme represented propaganda or a harbinger of conflict. It is likely that the Kim leadership overestimated Soviet strength, and in good Korean fashion hoped to bait Stalin into coming to the Korean defense, or at least holding the Americans at bay. But the ebullient tone of early 1950 editorials was not really so different from those a year earlier, which suggested that the North was on something like a war footing.

Whereas in early 1948 Kim had described the Korean situation as "complicated," the problems not easily solved, getting more complex all the time, and the like, after Soviet troops departed the tone changed dramatically. In his 1949 New Year's address, Kim called upon the KPA to "always be ready" to protect the North, wipe out "aggressive foreign influence," and "unify the territory." He went on, "One of the country-selling traitors is talking about a 'northern expedition' [*pukbŏl*] and a civil war, like a puppy who doesn't know enough to fear a tiger. But, the Korean people are one . . . and cannot be divided." He said the day was not far off when all Koreans would unite under the DPRK.[55]

On June 25, 1949, a year to the day before the war began, Kim Tu-bong listed three tasks for the nation: kick the United States out, overthrow the Rhee regime, and unify the territory. Hŏ Hŏn ended his speech of that day by saying, "If unification cannot be arrived at through peaceful methods, then we must achieve it through methods of struggle," given that Rhee was openly calling for a "northern expedition." Amid increased defense mobilization taxes and army conscription, party newspapers remarked that a handful of "bad elements" were spreading rumors that "strengthening the KPA means a war will occur."[56]

By January 1950 this atmosphere of threat had deepened to the point that KPA soldiers were being urged to be "completely prepared to fight at any time," for the enemy might strike at will, at any place.[57] But this sort of thing was also said over and over again during the border fighting in the summer of 1949. On the face of it, North Korea seems to have adopted a belligerent rhetoric and a near-war footing almost from the time Soviet troops departed at the end of 1948.

CONCLUSIONS

Our consideration of North Korea's foreign involvements should not blind us to this cardinal fact: the DPRK was run by former guerrillas who, even by world-beating Korean standards, were fierce and hard-bitten nationalists. Most had come of age in the harsh Manchurian milieu where they carried out a protracted, thankless struggle to organize anti-Japanese resistance among dirt-poor Koreans, most of whom had picked up their families and fled Korea, in many cases to work in the self-reliant, hardy, but unforgiving task of slash-and-burn agriculture.

A Korean informant who had lived in Manchuria told Americans that 95 percent of the Koreans there had as their "first and foremost thought" a desire for Korean independence and were thoroughly anti-Japanese; they saw Koreans as "one people," and thus "did not establish ties in

Manchuria." Five percent of the population were educated or business-oriented; they were all "collaborators."

Yet North Korea's leaders were nationalists among Korean nationalists, zealots among Manchurian-Korean zealots. Used to bitter hardship and violence, they were people who make the most bloody-minded, gut-fighting American "rollbacker" look like a moderate. They had complete contempt for the internationalism both of Moscow communists and Wall Street internationalists—denouncing in their press the "cosmopolitanism" of the latter and their idea that "nationalism is dead." Even Chinese Communists, not well known for proletarian internationalism, found fault with Koreans in the CCF for their "rigidly nationalist views," who were said to mistrust Soviet-Chinese cooperation in the region.[58]

North Korea's preference for China among its socialist allies grew directly out of the joint battle against the Japanese and the Chinese Nationalists in Manchuria, an allied experience of almost two decades among the leadership. It also drew upon wellsprings of traditional Korean preference for China among its neighbors, and China's history of aloof, superior, but dignified treatment of Korea, a cultural and political hegemony of "benign neglect" in which Korea was left alone as long as it emulated China in its statecraft and its culture, and did not transgress outer limits by allowing an enemy of China to occupy its territory. This relationship was quite in contrast to that of China and Vietnam, where the Vietnamese nurtured a tradition of resistance to Chinese. Koreans, by contrast, had to worry about the Japanese, the Russians, and the Americans, placing Sino-Korean ties in a distinctly different light.

Hardly one to trust in tradition, however, Kim Il Sung shrewdly dispatched legions of Koreans to fight in the Chinese civil war, aiding the creation of a reliable rear area and thus transforming North Korea's strategic position, while giving tens of thousands of young Koreans the indispensable tempering of actual battle. While Syngman Rhee blustered emptily, turned his army over to a discredited and generally incompetent officer corps, and sought vainly to get the United States to fight his battles for him, the northerners built a war-tested and formidable army in the space of three years. For the first time in half a milennium, Korea had an army that could defend it against foreign predators.

Perhaps most important, the Koreans placed a call on China's vast resources that was anything but empty bluster and baiting. One hundred thousand or more Koreans had fought under PLA leadership, one-third of them moving below the Great Wall, some all the way to Hainan Island in the crack 4th Field Army. Kim had also provided a sanctuary for Chinese Communist troops during the fighting for Manchuria in late 1946 and throughout 1947, giving over the rail network to troop movements, quartering thousands of soldiers in Sinŭiju, and the like. Kim Il Sung could invoke both the traditional reciprocity of the Chinese world order, and this very recent experience, as a hole card against the chance of American entry into the Korean civil war. Korean "volunteer" (*ŭiyong*) guerrillas had fought in Manchuria in the 1930s, the Korean Volunteer Army made formidable contributions to the victory on the mainland in the late 1940s; why should not Chinese "volunteers" (*ŭiyong*) return the favor in the fall of 1950?

The Americans never grasped this history and these relationships. But their failure to foresee the coming of the war and the Chinese entry owed less to bad information and more to stereotypes of Koreans. Dealing mostly with an elder generation in the South that had either collaborated with the Japanese, mildly resisted, or remained at a safe distance, the Americans had trouble taking Koreans seriously. They grossly misjudged the Koreans in P'yŏngyang. Everett Drumwright, among the most experienced of embassy officers, was capable of writing in January 1950 that there was no reason to suppose that the DPRK leadership "contains any schisms or 'nationalistic tendencies' of importance"; the party was "merely an instrument of Soviet control." He also thought "one of the lessons learned in China during the past year" was fully applicable to North Korea as well: "namely, that the forces of Chinese nationalism . . . are far too weak to clash with the Kremlin."

Some Americans who knew how strongly nationalist most Koreans were still interpreted this in racist terms. One who had served in the Occupation told the *Far Eastern Economic Review* that Koreans were "a hard, fierce and cruel people . . . they possess a ferociousness and wildness," which American missionaries thought came from "an arrested mental development" caused by inbreeding. Koreans "detest" being told what to do by foreigners, he said; even America's "best friends" would say, "when are you going to leave; please hurry and let us alone." The only Koreans who did not want the Americans to depart, he said, were "the businessmen and the intellectuals." The British were no better. Kermode remarked callously, "While other nations made sacrifices in blood to win the war, the Koreans were wholly spared. They had cried for the removal of the Japanese yoke, and it was removed at no cost to themselves. The time for payment is now upon them. Whichever side gains the upper hand the price will be paid in blood."59

This from the representative of a nation that did nothing when the Japanese invaded Manchuria. In the wealth of documentation now available, there is rarely a departure from this sort of prejudice and myopia. One contrary example, however, came from the American scholar Claud Buss, who suggested that after the withdrawal of Soviet troops, the initiative might pass to the hands of Kim Il Sung and his allies, "volatile, physically strong, and tough-spirited." He judged that "blood will flow in Korea" unless "wise statesmanship" grasped hold of the situation.60

Part III

OVERTURES TO JUNE 1950

Chapter Twelve

DECENT INTERVAL: AMERICAN WITHDRAWAL, THE BORDER FIGHTING, AND THE GUERRILLA SUPPRESSION

> The Koreans contemplated the withdrawal of the U.S. task force with genuine fear—even jitteriness in certain circles. They moved heaven and earth to have withdrawal deferred. There were even elements that were preparing to instigate an incident with the North with the hopes of embroiling the U.S. task force to thwart withdrawal.
>
> *John Muccio*

A RMED CONFLICT in Korea began in the summer of 1949 and the summer of 1950 with incidents at Ongjin and Kaesŏng. The locale was about the same, dramatis personae were about the same, the initial skirmish was about the same. But one incident led to war and the other did not. In this chapter we will assay the 1949 fighting and the issues that provoked it, during the one year in postwar history when the Republic of Korea (ROK) did not appear to have a guarantee of American defense, or American joint command of its military.

In the historiography and bestiary of the American and Korean Right, MacArthur is the hero, defending the interests of a threatened free Korean Republic; Acheson is the bête noire, fixated wrongly on Europe, foolishly withdrawing troops from Korea and giving "the green light" to the Communists to attack. The truth is quite the reverse. It was Rhee's champion MacArthur and elements in the Pentagon who pushed an American withdrawal of troops from Korea, even at the cost of communization of the peninsula, and it was the lily-livered State Department that continually sought to delay the moment when the Rhee regime would be left without the protection of American combat troops. But when the pressure for withdrawal could no longer be resisted, the troops came out.

The logic of deterrence in a civil war is to deter both the enemy and the ally, which can best be done by controlling the ally's armed forces. When the last American forces withdrew from Korea, however, the United States was left without the protection of operational control of Rhee's military. This prompted Acheson to devise a careful but less predictable plan of defense and deterrence, reflected in his Press Club speech, which we will treat in chapter 13.

We saw earlier that the military in Washington, meaning mainly the Department of the Army, began seeking a withdrawal of American troops from Korea conjointly with the development of the Truman Doctrine in the spring of 1947. NSC 8 sought to resolve these bureaucratic conflicts by a compromise: a slow withdrawal, combined with military and economic advisors and aid to contain communism in Korea through indirect, Truman Doctrine methods.

It is noteworthy that the main proponents of withdrawal in 1947–1949 were Japan-firsters temporarily off Wall Street and in the Pentagon, such as Robert Patterson, William Draper, Kenneth Royall, and Robert Lovett. They represented the Army's desire to get its troops out of a costly and much-criticized occupation, true, but their strong backing for withdrawal must also have carried with it assumptions about Japan. For example, that Japan, not South Korea, should have the highest call on limited American resources; also that later on, when Japan was revived, it could substitute for American power in Korea. At least one high official made this explicit, as we have seen: George Kennan, architect of the reverse course.

We may resume the narrative on planning for withdrawal in March 1948, when Royall remarked that it was "highly important" that the Army "insist with the State Department that our troops be removed from Korea as soon as the election there is over." When Royall pushed a rapid withdrawal again in a National Security Council (NSC) meeting in April, Robert Lovett countered that "there must be a decent interval before our withdrawal,"[1] a mouthful that carried precisely the connotation McCarthy found so treacherous in Owen Lattimore's recommendations: let South Korea fall without it appearing to have been pushed.

Subsequently the military hoped the withdrawal would come with the establishment of the Rhee regime and the termination of USAMGIK. In August 1948, Draper told Muccio in a top secret conference that the northern army was no more than 50,000, not the 125,000 bruited about in the press; American arms given the South were far better than Soviet arms given the North. "Parity had now been achieved." Thus the United States could withdraw. But the withdrawal was successively postponed from August to December 1948, when the Russian troops were to be withdrawn, thence to March, May, and finally June 1949. In each case the State Department was the agency of delay. First it was the Yŏsu Rebellion in October 1948, then the inadequacy of the southern army, then worries about the North; behind it all was State's continued commitment to the idea that the loss of Korea could not be sustained without enormous damage to American credibility.[2]

The State Department view was reinforced by frequent pressure from Seoul, Muccio being a strong backer of direct containment through American combat troops, and of adding air and naval capabilities to the ROK accoutrement. Yŏsu caused Muccio to question the capacity of "loyal government forces to maintain even internal order should American troops finally be withdrawn"; in May 1949 he was more sanguine about internal security, but thought Seoul could not resist the North unless additional naval vessels, arsenals, and planes were provided.[3] Muccio was one of the key agents of troop withdrawal delay.

Royall, secretary of the Army, continued to oppose further postponement. In January 1949 he urged that all troops come out by the end of March. He gave way under MacArthur's argument that for "psychological reasons," the withdrawal should not occur until May 10, the anniversary of the first National Assembly elections. A few weeks later, Royall journeyed to Korea and, in a top secret meeting, heard this from Rhee:

> He said he would like to increase the Army, provide equipment and arms for it, and then in a short time move north into North Korea. He said the United Nation's recognition [*sic*] of South Korea made it legal to cover all Korea and that he saw nothing could be gained by waiting. . . . I told the President that, of course, no invasion of North Korea could in any event take place while the U.S. had combat troops in Korea, and that his request was in my opinion tantamount to a request that we should have all American combat troops removed.

This sort of aggressive threat in secret talks with ranking Americans was far different from Rhee's public bluster about a "northern expedition," and it scared Royall. He ended his account of the meeting by saying "I certainly do not feel we should wait until 10 May." Muccio quickly got from Rhee a promise that the Americans judged most important: "he would refrain from any action that might embarrass the U.S. position in the Far East and . . . would not take any offensive action against north Korea that might possibly embroil the U.S. forces there."[4]

The withdrawal was again put back, this time to the end of June. In May Muccio and State brought pressure to delay even the June schedule, prompting the acting secretary of the Army, Gordon Gray, to tell Louis Johnson that State had "caused three delays in military withdrawal completion dates which have created serious morale, budgetary and logistical problems."[5]

The military was hardly unaware of the northern threat. JCS and CIA estimates in early 1949 asserted that an invasion following the American withdrawal was highly probable. But Royall was apparently willing to live with this. MacArthur's G-2 in Tokyo thought that "South Korea probably will be subjugated" in the event of northern aggression, with the Russians "tak[ing] no active part in a military operation other than to provide logistical assistance and advice." MacArthur's staff even urged that "the Japanese must be conditioned to [the] prospect of [a] Soviet-dominated mainland," with American naval and air forces being Japan's "only firm long-range basis for maintaining Japanese orientation to US."[6] This accorded with MacArthur's belief that Japan could be protected without having combat troops on the ground, through naval and air forces stationed on Okinawa, something he changed his mind about shortly before the Korean War. But in 1949 the general apparently did not intend to use these same forces to back South Korea, were it to be attacked.

Acheson took the bull by the horns on May 9, 1949 and said there could be no more delays; the withdrawal could not wait for the naval vessels Muccio wanted. He asked Muccio if he had changed his earlier assent to the withdrawal, based on the ROK's ability to defend itself with American aid and advice; if he had, this would reopen "the entire question [of] withdrawal." Muccio responded that the vessels were needed, but the policy need not be reappraised.[7] Thus the withdrawal finally was consummated.

The last American combat soldiers (1,500 of them) steamed out of Inch'ŏn harbor on June 29, and USAFIK was officially deactivated at midnight the next day. This left the Korean Military Advisory Group (KMAG), 500 strong in officers and men, along with 150 U.S. Air Force personnel who ran Kimp'o Airport.[8] With the termination of USAFIK, the United States apparently lost its operational control of the ROK military and police, but close coordination between KMAG and Korean officers continued up to the Korean War, and Americans continued to maintain as many as fifteen intelligence bureaus and committees keeping watch on Korea. The Department of the Army also hedged against an invasion and conjured up rollback in promoting, simultaneous to the withdrawal, a program of covert warfare against the North: it recommended the inauguration of "a Korean underground task force in North Korea," giving the United States "the initiative in the formation of a counter-revolutionary effort," and helping to prevent "North Korean aggression."[9] Meanwhile in Washington the deliberations began that ended up in NSC 48 and a sharp change in the logic of America's Asian policy.

Rhee was implacably opposed to the withdrawal of American forces, despite his occasional public denials and indications of unconcern. In the summer of 1949 he mounted a dual diplomatic-military strategy to force an American commitment to his regime. The diplomatic drive promoted the creation of a NATO-like "Pacific Pact" of anti-Communist states, including the ROK, Republic of China (ROC), the Philippines, and any other countries that could be gotten to join. Rhee and his scribes spilled oceans of ink in tracts and speeches calling for a Pacific treaty. He raised the possibility with the Philippines delegate to the UN Commission on Korea (UNCOK) in April 1949, and "shocked" Muccio in May by issuing a press release demanding inclusion of the ROK within the American "first line of defense" after the troops go home, through a Pacific defense pact involving Japan and the ROK. Rhee got Chiang's agreement to such a pact during their talks in August 1949, and they both urged Elpidio Quirino, president of the Philippine Republic, to join up.[10]

The Pacific Pact never got very far, but not for the absence of American backing. The United States did not want to extend public defense guarantees to Rhee and Chiang, it is true, but it did look favorably upon a defense pact initiated by the East Asian nations themselves.[11] The problem was that Rhee, Chiang, and Quirino all had separate and unequal communist problems: Rhee had the greater part of a divided country, Chiang had an island off the mainland, Quirino had Huk guerrillas. Each wanted the United States to pull his chestnuts out of the fire, and saw any other call on American resources as a threat; each doubted the others' capacities to resist communism; for each it was a zero-sum game, and thus no pact eventuated.

Left alone with his Korean problems, Rhee's preferred strategy was to provoke a war, or at least major fighting along the thirty-eighth parallel, thus to convince the Americans to keep their troops in Korea. Several sources point to the Rhee regime being in a state of "panic and bravado" (Australians), "mass hysteria" (the CIA), "crisis bordering on panic" (Muccio), or "climactic insanity" (the North Koreans).[12] The Rhee forces knew they could not hold the line against the North Koreans; the panic in June 1949 prefigured the collapse of June 1950. But it is likely that Rhee, at least, manipulated the appearance of panic to try and bait the Americans into staying on. More importantly, he instructed his commanders to provoke incidents along the parallel.

We will have occasion to go into the border fighting later in this chapter. For now we can merely reproduce Muccio's analysis of Rhee's actions in the summer of 1949. During May and June, he said, "the Koreans contemplated the withdrawal of the U.S. task force with genuine fear— even jitteriness in certain circles. They moved heaven and earth to have withdrawal deferred. There were even elements that were preparing to instigate an incident with the North with the hopes of embroiling the U.S. task force to thwart withdrawal."[13]

This actually puts the situation somewhat mildly; the Ongjin and Kaesŏng fighting in the summer of 1949 was often provoked by elements in the ROK Army. The North Koreans, however, were not ready for war in the summer of 1949. They had recognized as early as 1947 that the Rhee regime would seek to provoke conflict to get the American troops to stay, and presumably they limited their attacks and counterattacks in 1949 such that the American forces would, in fact, withdraw.[14] And so they did withdraw, and for the only year in the past four decades, the ROK was apparently without the protection of American combat troops, or American operational control of the Army.

I say apparently because there may have been a highly secret plan to defend South Korea with American forces in the event of a northern attack, in place one year before the war came. Wellington Koo had various emissaries bringing high-level secrets to him, including people in Secretary Johnson's office. A mysterious but well-informed man identified as Capt. Ross Jung appeared at Koo's embassy on June 29, 1949, and told him that "the North Koreans were now invading South Korea," and although U.S. troops were quitting Korea, they would only go "as far as Japan." Were the North Koreans to push further south at some point in the future, "the U.S. troops would move into South Korea again to protect it, as their obligation to the South Korean people remained valid." Jung thought that if another world war began, "he was sure it would start in the Far East, and that Korea was likely to be the scene of its outbreak." Jung was departing for the Far East, and asked for an introduction to Chiang Kai-shek, and also told Koo that "his department is entirely aware of the strategic importance of Manchuria to whole U.S. defense position in NE Asia and the Pacific." Koo immediately wired this information to Taipei in a top-secret cable.

Ross Jung had excellent connections: on February 8, 1949, he apprised the Nationalist Embassy of NSC decisions taken the previous day; in June 1949 he knew about the American protection of General Ishii, who ran Japan's genocidal bacteriological warfare projects in Manchuria, and showed interest in the effectiveness of such warfare and what the Russians knew about it; Jung also told Koo of American operational planning for the use of nuclear weapons in November 1950, a secret of the highest order. There is also a cryptic note in the Koo diaries suggesting that Jung was in touch with Acheson: a June 28, 1949, entry read, "[Jung] appreciates my help but Acheson has found a way out for his wife to go to Tokio." This would suggest Acheson's knowledge of Jung's trip—taken on the last weekend in June 1949, just at the point when the last U.S. combat troops came home from Korea, and when UNCOK was going off to Ongjin to report on the latest fighting (see below). Jung's trip, judged by the information, included stops in Tokyo and Taipei.

Wellington Koo said that Ross Jung was working with State Department intelligence. Although I have not conclusively identified Ross Jung, I believe he was Wing Fook Jung, by 1950 the only colonel in the Army with this Chinese name; routine G-2 documents just at the time the Korean War began list one "Col. Jung, G-2" on the distribution list.[15]

KOREA ON THE CONTAINMENT LINE

In spite of the withdrawal of American combat forces, South Korea still boasted the two largest Economic Cooperation Administration (ECA) and military advisory missions in any country. KMAG had more than five hundred officers and men, compared to 378 in the advisory group in Greece. It bears repeating that military advisory groups were part of the Truman Doctrine containment policy of posting advisors as an earnest of American intent, in lieu of the basing of American combat forces.[16]

Acheson and Truman frequently put Korea in the same category as Greece and Turkey, but always refused to do so for Taiwan. Acheson opposed an "FMAG" (Formosan military advisory group) precisely on the grounds that it would be "widely interpreted as evidence of [an] American intention to underwrite mil[itary] defense of [the] Island. Damage to US prestige w[ou]ld be very great if notwithstanding such advisors, Island's defenses collapsed."[17] Interpolating: KMAG would therefore be widely seen as evidence of an American intention to underwrite the military defense of the ROK. The damage to American prestige would be very great if, notwithstanding KMAG, the ROK's defenses collapsed. Although he never put it this explicitly, this was Acheson's Korea policy.

Acheson also got this across to Senator Vandenberg. In some hearings in June 1949, the senator aptly remarked that "it is such a strange thing that people way off yonder should be looking to us to save them." But he went on to say that Korea was "the only symbol left of any constructive interest on the part of the Government of the US . . . to contain the Communist menace in Asia." The ROK had been founded "under the aegis of the United Nations," he said, "and any gobbling which can be identified as external aggression is just a fundamental challenge to the entire United Nations, and I doubt whether that will be lightly undertaken."[18]

The assumption that South Korea was part of global containment was also palpable in the mind of that figure who first drew a line in the dirt across the peninsula, Dean Rusk. In October 1949 he said, "we must support against agressive pressure from the outside even states which we regard unfavorably. *We must preserve them merely as states.* This we have done in Greece, Korea and Yugoslavia" (emphasis added). At about the same time the CIA said the following: "The ROK is wholly dependent on US economic and military aid for its survival. The severe psychological effect of a reduction [in aid] would lead in a straight line to Communist domination" (one paragraph deleted by declassification censors).[19] The Truman administration bolstered South Korea during this period with visits by high civilian and military officials and some flag-showing by the Seventh Fleet, something they would not allow for Taiwan. The North

Koreans kept careful track of all this, including "informal" visits by pro-Chiang figures like Air Force General Russell E. Randall.[20]

Limited War and General War

The literature remains confused on the nature of the American deterrent in Korea before the war because it has failed to distinguish between situations of limited war and global war, and because it has not understood the civil origins of the war, and therefore has not grasped the specific nature of deterrence in civil war conditions. The latter point has been emphasized repeatedly, but we may view its logic in the clipped prose of a cable in October 1949, referring to the shipment of military aid to Korea. The equipment was "not believed sufficient to prov[ide] stocks to encourage SKSF [S. Korean security forces] to at[tac]k North Korea. In event unprovoked at[ac]k on South Korea and if US policy indicated all out spt [support] nec[essary], issues from Eighth A[rmy] stock might be authorized without regard to MAP funds."[21] You wanted containment of the enemy *and* containment of the ally.

If a general war were to break out, almost everyone knew that American troops in Korea would be a liability. In December 1948 MacArthur said he assumed that the "concept of [his] ultimate responsibility for [the] defense of South Korea does not contravene provisions of CINCFE emergency plan . . . for expedited withdrawal of U.S. forces in Korea."[22] This is not particularly remarkable, however. The same plans held true for Japan. The emergency war plan from the late 1940s on to the Carter administration called for a "swing strategy" in which American forces would be withdrawn from Japan and swung around to defend Europe in the event of global war. The logic, presumably, was that the Soviets were stretched and weak in the Far East, and Japan could be defended by air and naval power.[23]

This said little about what American forces might do in a conflict short of World War III. By the standards of global war, Indochina was far less important strategically than Korea, yet the United States gave military aid or fought there for a quarter-century. The Joint Chiefs expressed the logic clearly in 1950, and the same could be said of Korea: "There is an important difference between the strategic importance of Indochina to the US in a major war and its strategic importance in a Cold War." The United States would not fight there in the first condition, but in the second it becomes important, owing to the domino theory, considerations of prestige and credibility, and the like.[24]

There is also a political element at stake. Liberals wanted a flexible American strategy, whereas conservatives tended to think there was no substitute for victory: war was war, and should be fought in a total way to achieve victory as soon as possible. This is a commonplace in strategic debate, captured in the contrast between Dulles's "massive retaliation" and Kennedy's "flexible response." Yet this issue predated the Korean War, and shaped both how it was fought, and the historical verdict. It was the "best and the brightest" who articulated flexible response *before* June 1950. In April, McGeorge Bundy and Arthur Schlesinger, Jr., among others, argued for a military capacity to respond in limited ways, rather than relying on the atomic bomb; otherwise the United States simply invited limited types of aggression. Once the Korean War began, Schlesinger wrote that "events in Korea have lent force to our contention" regarding "guerrilla warfare and internal revolt in marginal areas."[25] This is merely one more way in which the logic of decision circa 1950 established a matrix of choice ever since.

Kennan's prescience in engineering so many aspects of cold war strategy is really rather daunting; in January 1947 he had already enunciated the logic of flexible response. The United States, he said, should maintain highly trained and combat-ready ground forces "which would be in a position to be moved anywhere on short notice," a kind of rapid-deployment force for plugging leaks in the containment periphery:

> It might be necessary for us on very short notice to seize and hold . . . outlying bases or peninsular bases on other continents. . . . If we do not maintain such forces, there will always be an incentive to unruly people elsewhere to seize isolated and limited objectives on the theory that we would be able to do nothing . . . [we need] a compact, mobile, and hard-hitting task force which could make American power felt rapidly and effectively on limited fronts almost anywhere in the world within reach of the seven seas.[26]

Kennan said in October 1949 that the military "have been basing all their plans on the use of the bomb," that is, global war, whereas "limited rather than total warfare should be our objective."[27] The military departments thought about Korea exclusively on the premise of general war, their dogged illogic masking a desire to get out of an expensive and thankless conflict and turn it over to State Department responsibility, as well as marking the limits of American conventional power.

Acheson completely agreed with Kennan. He said in 1953 that all Pentagon thinking "had been related to the contingency of general war, rather than a localized war." Someone else jumped in and said, this was related to "whether you keep a regimental combat team in Korea then. If you decided this was a matter of general war, you've got one kind of conclusion. If you thought about it as a centrally political problem you might come to another decision."[28] Exactly so.

THE BORDER FIGHTING IN 1949

The war that came like a thunder clap in June 1950 was immanent in the fighting of the previous summer. Border battles lasted from early May until late October, taking hundreds of lives and embroiling thousands of troops. The reason that war did not come in 1949 is at once simple, and essential to grasping the civil origins of the Korean conflict: the South wanted a war then, the North did not, and neither did the United States. A year later this had changed.

The border battles of 1949 established the setting for June 1950. The fighting did not start all at once in the early morning hours, but began in the remote Ongjin Peninsula, spread to Kaesŏng, thence to Ch'unch'ŏn, and finally to the East coast. June 1950 was the microcosm of the summer of 1949, collapsing it in time but not changing its character: the difference was that now the North was ready to fight.

In most histories of the war there is next to no reference to the 1949 fighting, and if there is, the initiation of all battles is routinely blamed on the North, with the South portrayed in a state of original innocence, arrayed defensively and either unwilling or incapable of threatening anyone. One stalwart Korea hand told me, "I certainly hope you're not going to take Rhee's threats to march North seriously! Why, his commanders used to laugh behind his back when he said those things."

Formerly classified sources, however, tell a different story. An Army G-2 study stated that South Korean forces "took advantage of the withdrawal of the U.S. forces to become more aggressive," and that leaders of the ROK government "will go to any ends to insure the continued presence of U.S. forces upon which their own positions, fortunes, and perhaps even their lives depend." Thus, the study said, various border incidents in the summer of 1949 were "not only encouraged, but probably even initiated by certain members" of the ROK government. That was an understatement.

General Roberts, KMAG commander, said that in the numerous clashes in August, "Each was in our opinion brought on by the presence of a small South Korean salient north of the parallel. . . . The South Koreans wish to invade the North. We tell them that if such occurs, all advisors will pull out and the ECA spigot will be turned off." Roberts went on to say that "both North and South are at fault" in the back-and forth "needling" along the parallel.[29] But according to captured documents sent to the United Nations by North Korea, in an August 2, 1949, meeting with Republic of Korea Army (ROKA) divisional commanders, Roberts said that "almost every incident has been provoked by the South Korean security forces," a stronger allegation; but in the atmosphere of

1950 about the only American newspaper willing to bring these allegations out was *The Daily Worker*.[30]

During this period Rhee rapidly expanded the Army. Two new divisions (the Capital and the 8th) were activated in June 1949; Army strength was at 81,000 by the end of July, and 100,000 by the end of August.[31] By then it was much bigger than the accepted strength of the North Korean army; the subsequent buildup and the return of China-linked soldiers could thus be viewed as the North's attempt to establish a balance (U.S. intelligence thought the KPA was 95,000 strong in June 1950).

Rhee also brought into the Army officers who had served the Japanese and who were refugees from the North, at the expense of nationalist figures who had fought with the Chinese Nationalists; the main reason was to surround Rhee with military people who owed everything to him, and who could be counted on not to mount a coup (and to loath communists). Two Paek brothers, Sŏn-yŏp and In-yŏp, led a northwest faction in the Army, which also included Generals Yang Kuk-jin, Kim Sŏk-bŏm, and many members of the Northest Youth. Both Paeks were born near P'yŏngyang a few years after Kim Il Sung, and had been Japanese Kwantung Army officers. Chŏng Il-gwŏn, also an officer in the Kwantung Army, led the northeast or *Tongbuk* faction. Chŏng was thirty-two, and Paek Sŏn-yŏp thirty, in 1950.[32]

The border had been a potential flash point since late September 1945, when the United States and the Soviets erected check points and barriers that exemplified the developing division of the peninsula. But for the next three years little serious fighting occurred, and the border points served to exchange millions of people backwards and forwards, as well as a considerable amount of North-South trade. Fighting flared up in early 1948, however, Gen. John R. Hodge reporting that although the South "invariably" placed the blame on the North, much of it occurred because of provocations by elements of the Northwest (*Sŏbuk*) Youth. After the May 1948 elections a number of border incidents were provoked by both sides. In August 1948 the ROK set up a "Korean Research Bureau," patterned after the American Counter-Intelligence Corps; it routinely sent agents into the North on spying and sabotage missions, assisted by rightist youth organizations, of which the most prominent was the Northwest Youth (NWY). According to American Counter-Intelligence Corps (CIC) findings, in January 1949 elements of the NWY formed a special crack brigade in the ROK Army, given the best equipment and supplies, and posted near the parallel—thus to act as "the spearhead in the event that the [ROK] Army invades North Korea." In other words, the border fighting, like just about everything else on the peninsula, illustrated the continuing pattern of revolution and counterrevolution.[33]

The border also served as a bellwether of Northern intentions. During the Yŏsu-Sunch'ŏn Rebellion, as we have seen, it was exceedingly quiet. In the summer of 1949 the North wanted the American troops to leave, and so was less aggressive than the South, which wanted to provoke enough fighting to make them stay. Nonetheless, the North was hardly passive, and mixed the fighting with a unification politics that also presaged June 1950.

The 1949 battles began at Kaesŏng on May 4, in an engagement lasting about four days and taking an official toll of four hundred North Korean and twenty-two South Korean soldiers, as well as upwards of one hundred civilian deaths in Kaesŏng, according to American and South Korean figures. The South committed six infantry companies and several battalions, of which two defected to the North.[34] It is unlikely that the South killed so many northern soldiers since later reports said the southerners were badly mauled.

Months later, the North Koreans alleged that several thousand troops led by Kim Sŏk-wŏn attacked across the parallel on the morning of May 4, near Sŏng'ak Mountain.[35] Kim was indeed the commander of the critically-important First Division. He was a former north Korean who had tracked Kim Il Sung in the Manchurian wilderness in the late 1930s as the head of the "Special Kim Detachment" in the Kwantung Army. He was known then as Kaneyama Shakugen; Emperor Hirohito decorated him with the Order of Merit for "bravery" in campaigns in Shansi Province. He sported a Kaiser Wilhelm moustache, and was widely thought to be responsible for numerous atrocities against Chinese citizens during the war. Kim was close to Rhee, Louise Yim, and Yi Ch'ŏng-ch'ŏn, among others. On June 2, 1948, Kim had led 2,500 veterans of the Japanese Army through the streets of Seoul, their wartime uniforms now shabby but their goose-stepping smartness still impressive; Yi Ch'ŏngch'ŏn was on the reviewing stand and described the group as the nucleus of the ROK army. Kim's son told a reporter that Yi and his father were good friends in spite of Yi being on the other side in the war, since they once attended the same Japanese military academy.[36]

Roberts seemed to confirm the North Korean charge, by later writing that the "flare-up" at Kaesŏng resulted from "needling" of the North Koreans by Kim Sŏk-wŏn—"stuffed-shirt, blown-up, Japanese-trained friend of the President, who commands the 1st Division there. We Americans and the Korean staff are all after his scalp, as he has all his B[attalio]ns now on line of the Parallel and one Co[mpany] in reserve. He snow jobs the [KMAG] Advisors and does as he pleases."[37]

The defectors were from the 1st and 2d battalions of the 8th ROKA regiment, a total of about 245 soldiers, led by Majors P'yo Mu-wŏn and Kang T'ae-mu. During interviews with northern reporters, the two majors said that "the majority of ROK Army officers had been running dogs of Japanese imperialism," of whom the most notorious was Kim Sŏk-wŏn, who "forcibly mobilized Korean youths to fight Japan's aggressive war in China," and "slaughtered the Chinese people." ROKA officers fighting under him were his "clients," former officers in the Japanese Army. The head of the 6th Division was Kim Paek-il, who, they said, had been head of "a special detachment of the Japanese Army in China."[38] Although the reader already knows the background of Kim Sŏk-wŏn and Kim Paek-il, it is significant that these names come up in the early fighting in May 1949.

In mid-May the North Koreans noticeably escalated their propaganda rhetoric, saying that "Chiang Kai-shek is demolished and Syngman Rhee is tumbling down," and accusing Rhee of turning to the Japanese imperialists to save himself.[39] On May 21 some minor incidents touched off a major assault by two KPA Border Guard battalions on the Ongjin Peninsula, in the Turak Mountains. The South brought in reinforcements by sea, raising their force levels to eight battalions within days. The North now occupied positions as much as five kilometers below the parallel, so the South launched an assault on T'aet'an, ten kilometers north of the parallel. On May 28 five hundred Korean People's Army (KPA) soldiers moved south of the parallel again, touching off fighting in which several tens of men died on each side. The southern side was badly flogged in this engagement, too: its units "proved unable to launch a coordinated large-scale attack." Kim Paek-il took up the general command of the Ongjin region on June 5; his deputy was Kang Yŏng-hun (who in 1989 was prime minister of the ROK). The Ongjin fighting continued through the end of June, often at rather heavy levels punctuated by minor battles elsewhere along the parallel. The North Korean press accused Rhee of provoking fighting to find a way to keep American troops in the South.[40]

The North also heated up a big campaign to welcome a "national" meeting of the Democratic Front for the Unification of the Motherland [*Choguk t'ongil minjujuŭi ŭi chŏnsŏn*] on June 25 in P'yŏngyang, a year to the day before the war began. On the last Sunday in June 1949, heavy fighting opened up in the dawn hours on the Ongjin Peninsula; three days later the South sent about 150 *Horim* (forest tiger) guerrillas on a long foray across the parallel; they roamed around causing problems in the area above and to the east of Ch'ŏlwŏn for a few days, but were wiped out by July 5.[41]

The Sunday, June 26 battle is important because UNCOK sent a delegation to Ongjin after hearing of "heavy fighting." It arrived courtesy of an ROK naval vessel and was guided around by ROKA personnel. UNCOK members remained on the peninsula for a day or so and then returned to Seoul on Monday evening, from which they then filed a report to the UN blaming "northern invaders" for the trouble.[42] It is quite possible that the North was to blame, but what is remarkable is UNCOK's failure to investigate and report upon provocations by the South as well, and instead publicly to take both the ROK and the American word as gospel; it thus became a partisan in the civil conflict.

It is also noteworthy that just before this incident, Kim Sŏk-wŏn gave UNCOK a briefing in his status as commander of ROKA forces at the thirty-eighth parallel: North and South "may engage in major battles at any moment," he said; Korea has entered into "a state of warfare." "We should have a program to recover our lost land, North Korea, by breaking through the 38th border which has existed since 1945"; the moment of major battles, Kim thought, is rapidly approaching.[43] Such southern threats resulted in the posting of UNCOK military observers (see chapter 15).

As if enough did not happen on the last Sunday in June, just past noon An Tu-hŭi, a member of the Northwest Youth and an officer in the ROKA, entered Kim Ku's home and assassinated him. Drumwright commented that military police "arrived within minutes of Kim's death, although there were no military installations nearby." Both American and British sources thought that Rhee was behind the murder, and the British cited rumors that Kim was plotting a coup against Rhee.[44]

After the war began a year later, the former ROK home minister, Kim Hyo-sŏk, who had by then defected to the North, said that Rhee had plotted a "northern expedition" to begin on July 15, 1949, with Kim Sŏk-wŏn attacking northward from the Ongjin Peninsula with the goal of occupying Haeju and then P'yŏngyang. Whatever the truth of this, it is documented that in mid-July American authorities worried that the South was readying an attack on the North. Captured documents in this period showed that the Democratic People's Republic of Korea (DPRK) had fully mined the roads leading into the North, and feared an amphibious landing at the port city of Wŏnsan.[45] This came just after the end of American operational control of the southern military, and was apparently a prelude to the near-war of early August.

As of August 1, if not earlier, southern forces were in occupation of Ŭnp'a Mountain (Ŭnp'asan), an important salient north of the thirty-eighth parallel on Ongjin which commanded much of the nearby terrain. KMAG dispatched an advisory group to Ongjin on the same date, probably to restrain the South Koreans. In the early morning hours on August 4 the North opened up great barrages of artillery and mortar fire, and then at 5:30 A.M. some four to six thousand North Korean Border guard soldiers attacked, seeking in Roberts's words "to recover high ground in North Korea occupied by [the] South Korean Army." The North claimed that Southern elements from the *paekkol* [white bone] unit attacked northward from Ŭnp'asan on August 4;[46] in any case the mountain was in northern territory and the North cannot be blamed for wanting to recover it. The southern side was "completely routed," according to Muccio; two companies of ROKA soldiers in the 18th Regiment were annihilated, leaving hundreds dead and the North in occupation of the mountain. The retrospective importance that the North placed on this battle is evident in a large, electronic mural devoted to the Ŭnp'asan fighting, which is located in their war museum.[47]

What happened next was related in Muccio's account of two conversations, with Defense Minister Shin Sŭng-mo on August 13, and with Rhee on August 16. Each deserve quotation nearly in full.

Captain Shin stated that the reports from Ongjin reaching military headquarters on the morning of August 4 were most alarming. These reports indicated that the [South] Korean forces on the [Ongjin] peninsula had been completely routed and that there was nothing there to stand against the northern onslaught. He went on that in studying the situation with the general staff . . . the military were insistent that the only way to relieve pressure on Ongjin would be to drive north. The military urged mounting an immediate attack north towards Charwon [*sic*—Ch'ŏrwŏn].

In line with the advice given by General Roberts, Captain Shin decided against attack and took immediate steps to send limited reinforcements into Ongjin.

Captain Shin went on that as soon as the Prime Minister [Yi Pŏm-sŏk] returned from the Rhee-Chiang meeting at Chinhae he called Captain Shin and remonstrated with him that he should have had more courage, should have attacked the North. That General Lee [Pŏm-sŏk] took this position does not surprise me especially. It did surprise me, however, when Captain Shin went on to say that upon his return from Chinhae the following day President Rhee also told him that he should not have decided against attacking Charwon.

On August 16, Muccio went on to relate that Rhee

threw out the thought that . . . he might replace [Chief of Staff] Chae [Pyŏng-dŏk] with General Kim Suk Wan [Kim Sŏk-wŏn]. . . . Kim Suk Wan has long been a favorite of President Rhee. Last fall prior to Yŏsu Rhee mentioned to General Coulter and myself that Kim had offered to "take care of the North" if he could be supplied with 20,000 rifles for Korean veterans of the Japanese Army who were burning with patriotism. The Minister of Defense, the Korean general staff and American advisors are all against General Kim. They do not consider him a good soldier but a blusterer. They have called my attention to his pro-

pensity for needling northern forces in his sector of the front, for re-
sorting to Japanese banzai attacks and for deploying all his forces in a
most hazardous manner right on the front without adequate reserves.
They particularly object to his ignoring headquarters and going direct
to President Rhee.[48]

This account is backed up by evidence that Roberts did indeed order
southern commanders not to attack and threatened to remove KMAG if
they did, and British statements that ROKA commanders' heads "are full
of ideas of recovering the North by conquest. Only the American ambassador's stern warning that all American aid would be stopped . . . prevented the Army from attempting to attack across the parallel at another
point when the Communists attacked at Ongjin." Roberts told General
Almond of MacArthur's headquarters that the ROKA Chief of Staff "saw
no other recourse, in case Ongjin were lost, except to make an attack due
north on Chorwon (20 miles in). We succeeded in talking him out of that,
as it could only cause heavy civil war and might spread."[49] This scenario
linking Ongjin and Chŏrwŏn should be kept in mind when we examine
what happened in June, 1950.

Although an attack in early August was aborted, by the end of the
month Muccio described the situation as follows:

There is increasing confidence in the Army. An aggressive, offensive
spirit is emerging. Nerves that were frayed and jittery the past few
months may now give way to this new spirit. A good portion of the
Army is eager to get going. More and more people feel that the only
way unification can be brought about is by moving North by force. I
have it from Dick Johnston [*New York Times* reporter] that Chiang Kai-
shek told Rhee that the Nationalist air force could support a move
North and that *they discussed the possibility of the Nationalists starting an
offensive move against Manchuria through Korea!* There is some feeling
that now is the time to move North while the Chinese communists are
preoccupied. I doubt whether Rhee would actually order a move
North in his saner moments. Captain Shin, I know, is dead against it.
Lee Bum Suk would love it. However, should we have another Kaesong
or Ongjin flare-up, a counter-attack might lead to all sorts of unpredictable developments [emphasis added].[50]

Several elements of these episodes deserve attention, when we reflect
back on them from the vantage point of June 1950: the centrality of Yi
Pŏm-sŏk and his longstanding ties to Chiang; the judgement that the
place to "drive north" was at Ch'ŏlwŏn after Ongjin gave way; the North's
placing of mines on roads leading north of the parallel; the role of the
defense minister, Shin Sŭng-mo, an American ally in seeking restraint;

and the hazardous deployment of the ROKA at the border, with lots of equipment and few reserves.

At about the same time the ROK sent six minesweepers to attack the military port of Monggŭmp'o, close to P'yŏngyang, sinking four North Korean ships of 35 to 45-ton class; Inch'ŏn harbor was reinforced in case of a counterattack (which did not eventuate). According to John Merrill, the commander of this assault was Yi Yong-un, who bypassed the naval chain of command "on direct orders of the Minister of National Defense." (On June 25, 1950, as we will see, Yi Yong-un may have led an assault on the port of Haeju.)

In early September, American intelligence reported several attacks by southern forces across the parallel. On September 1, the Korean commander of the Ongjin task force, part of the critical Capital Division, said he would "destroy two factories" in Yŏngdamp'o due south of the Haeju peninsula, which manufactured cement and did ordnance repair for the KPA; but the Americans on the scene ordered him not to destroy installations "above the parallel." On September 5 a South Korean patrol attacked the Changjŏn headquarters of the 157th Company of the DPRK Peace Preservation Corps (*poandae*), claiming to have killed 320 of them. Meanwhile the southern commanders continued to have severe morale problems in the ranks: from the time of the establishment of the ROK up to September 1949, 5,268 ROK deserters had gone North, ranging from 300 to almost 1,000 per month.[51]

Within a few days of the Ongjin fighting in early August, the director of military intelligence in the Pentagon, Maj. Gen. Leroy S. Irwin, issued a report saying the North might mount a "direct military invasion" of the South in late September, citing an August 9 DPRK radio report that urged an "all-out effort" to overthrow Rhee, and setting September 19 as the date for elections for a unified People's Republic. Such an invasion, he thought, would perhaps accompany the "indirect aggression" ongoing in myriad guerrilla actions. Irwin did not think such an invasion would have much success, unless it were joined by Chinese Communist or Russian forces. The report was sent to Louis Johnson on August 10, with a covering memo saying this "is a potentially dangerous situation which we are following closely and which may possibly require high level action."[52]

This must be the estimate that caused Col. Preston Goodfellow to fly to Seoul in anticipation of a war. When Wellington Koo later asked about the possibility of "civil war" in Korea, Goodfellow said "he had been hurriedly sent for by R[hee] early last September and arrived at Seoul to hear that the N. Koreans were scheduled to attack on [the] 19th." Goodfellow told Koo that now (January 1950), the momentum for attack had shifted.

It was the South Koreans anxious to go into N.K., because they were feeling sharp with their army of well-trained 100,000 strong [*sic*]. But U.S. Govt *was most anxious to restrain any provocation by the S.K. and Goodfellow had gone there lately to do just that.* I asked how great was the possibility or danger of war breaking out in Korea. G[oodfellow] said U.S. Govt. position is this: *avoid any initiative on S. Korea's part in attacking N.K.*, but if N.K. should invade S.K. then S.K. should resist and march right into N.K. with III World War as the result but in such a case, the aggression came from N.K. and the Am[erican] people would understand it (emphasis added).[53]

When Wellington Koo, years later, was asked by an interviewer to reflect on the outbreak of the Korean War, he referred first to this episode with Goodfellow.[54]

Not much happened in September, however. There was a pick-up of guerrilla activity at mid-month, and perhaps a slight increase in parallel fighting; but September 19–20 was one of the quietest periods since early August, with but one minor incident reported. On September 21 the pattern of little skirmishes began again. In the last ten days of September activity picked up a bit, and there were reports of southward deployments of KPA troops, especially in the area of Haeju.[55] But Irwin's report is odd. None of the intelligence files I have seen show evidence of impending fighting in late September. It is much more likely that the North Koreans would have pointed toward September 9, the anniversary of the DPRK's founding.

At the end of September Rhee again made clear his desires to march North. In a letter of September 30, 1949, from Rhee to Oliver (the authenticity of which the United States denied during UN debates in the fall of 1950, but which Dr. Oliver verified as valid), Rhee said,

I feel strongly that now is the most psychological moment when we should take an aggressive measure and join with our loyal communist army [*sic*] in the North to clear up the rest of them in Pyongyang. We will drive some of Kim Il-sung's men to the mountain region and there we will gradually starve them out. Then our line of defense must be strengthened along the Tuman and Yalu River [i.e., the Sino-Korean border].[56]

On October 14, 1949, the North again sought to dislodge South Korean forces from Ŭnp'asan on the Ongjin Peninsula. They began with an artillery and mortar barrage and then assaulted the mountain and overran southern positions. The next day the ROKA counterattacked and fighting continued heavy for several days. On October 19th the fighting spread to the Ch'unch'ŏn area, where a South Korean platoon attacked northern units. On October 24 the Korean crew of the naval ship USS Kimball Smith mutinied and took the ship to the North, one of the finest American-supplied patrol boats in the southern Navy. The next day the South lobbed artillery onto northern positions at Ŭnp'asan and then attacked. Hospital reports from Ongjin put casualties at 13 officers and 344 enlisted men for the southern side, with northern dead claimed over 400. During this period there were many reports of rapid KPA troop movements, with soldiers being deployed in from Manchuria, and heavy weapons shipments coming into Ch'ŏngjin from the USSR; tank units moved toward the parallel, and civilians were moved out of front line areas. During October the North also began major campaigns to solicit donations from the population to buy equipment, especially Russian tanks, for the Army.[57]

Defense Minister Shin abruptly flew to Tokyo in the middle of all this and met with MacArthur. According to Rhee's account in a letter to Goodfellow, MacArthur agreed to begin military training for thirty or forty Korean officers in Japan.[58] At just the same time, as we will see, the United States succeeded in its campaign to get Rhee to replace Kim Sŏk-won. The parallel then quieted down until mid-December when Col. Paek In-Yŏp, newly assigned commander at Ongjin "with orders to keep things quiet," made a surprise attack and briefly reoccupied Ŭnp'asan. The North hastily counterattacked, but one of their battalions was "badly mauled" in an ROK ambush, something that embarrassed the North.[59] No major Ongjin fighting occurred again until June 25, 1950.

Perhaps because of all this trouble, a U.S. naval task force put in at Korean ports in early November. Rhee chose the deck of the American heavy cruiser, the USS St. Paul, to liken America to Santa Claus, and then, in the embassy's words, to "intimate more emphatically than in press conference[s]" that "war might be necessary" for reunification—while assuring Santa that "we will do all of the fighting needed."[60]

The 1949 border fighting reinforced the necessity for a civil-war deterrent in the minds of Muccio and Acheson. As Muccio put it in November,

The problem before me now is recommending sufficient military assistance to enable the Koreans to defend this area and at the same time to keep them from getting over-eager on moving North. . . .

The situation here requires forceful, clear thinking. I have pointed out to [Rhee] directly and repeatedly that . . . he has the good will of 48 nations of the world but if he should embark upon aggression himself he would lose that good will. In this event the U.S. would have to review its position in light of developments at that particular time. I feel that he is governed by this. *I am confident that he will not move North openly.* However, there is the danger of having him lose his head under some moment of stress as *another real attack at Kaesong or Ongjin* (emphasis added).[61]

Roberts put it more bluntly in a little-noticed interview after the war began: the ROKA commanders, he said, "believed the best defense was to attack." This, he went on, "placed us in a skittish position . . . to prevent the South Koreans from attacking, we gave them no combat air force, no tanks and no heavy artillery."[62] In short, liberals like Acheson and Muccio wanted for Rhee what they wanted for the island of Taiwan: a leash on "positive action," and a containment defense should an attack come—something absolutely essential in the Korean case, given the American refusal to provide offensive armaments. But, of course, containment liberals were not the only actors in the situation.

The South was badly mauled in both the Kaesŏng and Ongjin fighting, except for Colonel Paek's attack in December. Roberts was particularly disquieted by this, since it was his job to train the Korean Army. It is therefore odd that Roberts should have touted the ROKA so highly, both at the time and just before the Korean War began, not simply to reporters but in classified accounts of discussions with Congressmen and others.[63]

There are other curious aspects to the 1949 fighting. Acheson, for example, was aware of the August and October Ongjin battles, writing in notes to himself, "North Korea raids in far at Ongjin Pen., repulsed."[64] Yet in both cases the raids were not "in far," but limited mostly to Ŭnp'asan; nor were they easily "repulsed." Strangest of all, however, is the failure to link this very recent experience up with the Ongjin fighting of June 1950—in Muccio's terms to wonder what Rhee might do covertly, if not openly, and also to fail to predict what might happen the next time there was "another real attack at Kaesong or Ongjin."

In 1987 I was able to interview Han Jin Hyong, a sincere and unpretentious man who had been a secretary and document keeper for a northern border unit in the summer of 1949. He thought that the 1949 fighting was "the beginning of the war," the 1950 war "had already started." Since this is not the official North Korean position, and it was blurted out in the heat of a television interview, I took it to be an earnest statement.[65] It is correct, except that the civil conflict had started in 1945, and 1949 inaugurated a phase of direct confrontation along the parallel by regular army units.

The Final Solution to the Guerrilla Problem

When the war that Army intelligence predicted for late September did not materialize, the Americans and their Korean charges heaved sighs of relief or dismay, as the case may be, and got on with the task of stabilizing Rhee's home front. As the parallel quieted and the talk of a *pukbŏl* or "Northern Expedition" died down, the Americans and their southern charges turned to the problem of the guerrillas. For the next six months the object was a consolidation of ROK control in the interior, and a suppression of the opposition in Seoul.

The veteran journalist A. T. Steele captured the flavor of the period in October 1949. "An unadmitted shooting war between the Governments of the U.S. and Russia is in effect today along the 38th parallel. . . . It is smoldering throughout the territory of the new Republic of Korea . . . only American money, weapons, and technical assistance enable [the Republic] to exist for more than a few hours." The ROK was "dedicated to liberty," he wrote, but it is "a tight little dictatorship run as a police state." Its jails overflowed with prisoners, thirty thousand according to his estimate; "torture of captured political antagonists is commonplace," and "women and children are killed without compunction" by both sides. Americans on the scene "are almost evangelical in their fervor for Korean revival," but, Steele thought, "once the American props are withdrawn, South Korea will fall beneath the weight of Communist Asia."[66] So, was the ROK to be "little China," in this case little Nationalist China? There was one difference. The South Koreans, at least in American eyes and with assumed American backing, had the will and the know-how to suppress communists in the interior. They were effective where the Nationalists were not, in this limited but very important sense.

At the end of September Roberts said that it was of the "utmost importance" that the guerrillas "be cleared up as soon as possible," and asked that the U.S. Army dispatch more infantry officers to work with the ROKA. Every division in the Army, he told MacArthur, was being diverted in part or in full from the parallel to the interior, and "ordered to exterminate guerrilla bands in their zones." Three task forces were designated: the T'aebaek, the Chiri, and the Honam. Col. Kim Paek-il was placed in charge of the critical Honam task force, responsible for the Chŏlla Provinces.[67]

Maj. Bennie W. Griffith, Jr., a KMAG officer, helped organize the suppression. He had been trained in mountain and jungle warfare, and knew that "constant pressure" by mobile, small units had to be brought to bear on the guerrillas. He had suggested to his Korean counterpart that the best trained troops be grouped into an antiguerrilla task force, which "would spend most of its time in the field as a highly mobile force, capable of moving to any given area. . . . My counterpart and I worked out entrapment maneuvers and tactics . . . and employed them against some of the bands quite effectively." He employed such methods in early 1949, but nonetheless acknowledged that by the spring and summer of

1949 "guerrilla bands had become a real problem," and that by the fall they had "broadened their bases of operations, expanded their number of bases, and increased their number of raids." Thus Griffith submitted a plan which called for "a major military counter-guerrilla effort"; this plan, however, lost out to a second plan, "developed by the KMAG staff." It was his recollection that Colonels Hausman and Reed, who organized the suppression of the Yŏsu rebellion, had developed it.[68] In any case Americans were the authors of the autumn-winter suppression effort in 1949–1950.

The Chŏlla and the Kyŏngsang Provinces, the Americans said, "have been noted for extensive leftist activities since the liberation." Here, "the People's Republic and its People's Committees were strongest. It was in those rich, rice-producing provinces that the Japanese had most exploited the peasants. It was in those provinces that the Communist-directed All Korea Farmer's Union [Chŏnnong] was able to organize swiftly and, apparently, well during the first years of the American Occupation."

The guerrillas in the Chŏllas and Kyŏngsangs, the sources continued, therefore were able to draw upon the resentments of local people, although they never achieved "a solid, Communist-dominated bloc." A Tokyo G-2 report demarcated an oval-shaped area running from Mokp'o in the east to Namwŏn in the north, around and through the Chirisan area to Sunch'ŏn, as "the guerrilla stronghold in the ROK, with the guerrillas in nearly complete control of South Chŏlla Province" until late 1949. Guerrillas in Kangwŏn Province came down from the North, the report said, "but almost 100 percent of the guerrillas in the Chŏlla and Kyŏngsang Provinces . . . have been recruited locally." North Korean sources estimated that in August there were upwards of forty-four thousand guerrillas active in the South, which was too high; an American estimate in September put the strength of the guerrillas at about three thousand, too low.[69]

KMAG intelligence reports show high levels of guerrilla engagement throughout the fall of 1949, and suggest a much higher total of active guerrillas than the three thousand figure of September.[70] The ROKA "body count" was always inflated, introducing a constant bias into the data. In October there were many clashes involving 100 or more guerrillas, as we have seen. Toward the end of November, a KMAG advisor reported that "relentless searching of all areas is keeping the guerrillas on the move," with progress being made in turning the people against the guerillas. A week later, Kim Paek-il "confidently predict[ed] that guerrilla resistance in his area will collapse not later than February 15, 1950," an estimate from which his American advisor dissented. The guerrillas did seem weaker in Kim's Honam region by this time, as we have seen, with higher rates of activity in the Kyŏngsangs.

In late December 1949 some twelve thousand ROK troops operated in Kangwŏn province alone, "assisted by the police and countless auxiliary forces," against about one thousand guerrillas. Local peasants generally refused information about the guerrillas to the ROK forces, leading to severe reprisals, of which denial or confiscation of grain rations was usually the least.[71] British sources said the Rhee regime had a "policy" of "destroying villages which had given food or shelter to the rebels." By the time the winter offensive got under way, the same source said ROK forces had been relocating people and "destroying villages" for over a year; yet now they were again "arranging to evacuate the inhabitants of several large areas in the southern provinces." John Merrill says that "more than ninety thousand persons along the western margins of Chirisan and about fifteen thousand in the T'aebaek mountain area were removed to . . . strategic villages, or simply forced from their homes, in the dead of winter." Orphans alone were estimated as high as twenty thousand; the government gave them no help of any kind. In October 1949, for example, ROK police took two thousand families out of Chech'ŏn, "destroyed all its houses and crops," and left the evacuees to live in caves, "in great distress."[72]

A National Assembly report asserted that "police, army and youth organizations" forcibly requisitioned grain, and that police often made "cruel assaults" on villages thought to harbor or succor guerrillas. Police and youth squads regrouped peasants into protected villages, and allocated village quotas for unpaid corvée labor, used to cut back trees and foliage in the hills. The report estimated that forty thousand peasant homes had been destroyed in South Chŏlla alone, through both guerrilla and subjugation raids.[73]

On November 2, 1949, shortly after the winter offensive got going, two truckloads of troops from the ROKA 22d Regiment, returning from suppression campaigns in the mountains, negotiated a narrow, rocky valley 800 yards wide and a mile long, near the village of Chich'ŏn-dong in Chŏngdo county, North Kyŏngsang. As they sought to ford a stream, guerrillas descended upon them and killed 18 soldiers. The remaining troops then burned many homes and killed many people in Chich'ŏn-dong, claiming that "the people had been cooperating with the guerrillas." An American advisor commented that this "disorderly" conduct was "typical" of other experiences.[74]

Americans documented a particularly grisly episode on December 24, 1949, in which the 7th company of the 25th regiment of the ROKA under 2d Lt. Yu Chin-gyu entered a remote mountain village named Sŏkdal (Mun'gyŏng county, North Kyŏngsang), assembled all the villagers, accused them of aiding the guerrillas, and then, in the words of the American account, "without provocation opened fire [on] civilians with carbines, rifles, grenades and bazooka. Total killed by trps [sic] 3 infants, 9 schoolboys, 43 men and 43 women . . . 23 of 27 houses in village were burned." The incident was then falsely reported as a "massacre perpetrated by 70 guerrillas."[75]

A KMAG advisor to the ROKA 19th Regiment, identified as one Major Painter, wrote that firefights with guerrillas on Chiri-san in the last week of 1949 had netted 64 dead rebels, and several tens of captives; 32 had become "reformed Reds" who promised to be good and had "joined the Reformed Communist Society." But he questioned the body counts turned in by ROK forces, since only about 15 rifles had been collected: "Either they are shooting anyone they find in the mountains or are killing some who wish to surrender."[76]

In late November, ROK forces killed the important guerrilla leader Ch'oe Hyŏn in a battle in Changhŭng, South Chŏlla. This was not Kim Il Sung's ally of the same name; his real name was Ch'oe Sŏng-u, born in 1915 in Ch'ungch'ŏng Province. In December 1949 there were almost daily incidents involving 100 guerrillas or more, clashes with the suppression forces and attacks on police and government officials. By one count, 402 people on all sides died during the month. In January the number of incidents declined, with only seven clashes involving 100 or more guerrillas. It was the dead of winter, and much of the guerrilla activity involved foraging for supplies. By the end of this month, Drumwright reported that the "work of exterminating the rebels" was largely completed in the South Chŏlla area, and Kim Paek-il was transferred to the North Kyŏngysang suppression forces, where he relieved Gen. Kim Ŭng-jun.[77]

In late January, the ROKA 25th Regiment hit 175 guerrillas in Chinbo, killing 57: "the friendly troops amputated parts (ears & penis's) of some dead guerrilla bodies [sic]" to prove that "someone had been killed." This report prompted a KMAG advisor to demand that the ROKA commanders not condone and let go unpunished such activity, but there is no record to indicate anything was done.[78] In late February guerrillas attacked a village in Yangsan-gun, South Kyŏngsang, burning down 96 houses and killing 8 people. When the suppression forces caught up with 36 of the guerrillas, they killed 29 and took 7 captives, 4 men and 3 women— to save them for newsmen, who could witness their beheading and disemboweling.[79]

The ROK claimed to have engaged a total of 12,000 KPA soldiers and guerrillas in January 1950, killing 813, and losing but 51. Roberts told a reporter that 6,000 guerrillas had been killed in the November 1949– March 1950 period, in what he called an "all-out mop-up campaign [that] broke the backbone of the guerrilla movement." Internal reports as of mid-April put the total guerrilla dead since October 1 at 4,996, so the Roberts figure seems plausible.[80]

Captured guerrillas and leftist suspects who were not executed found themselves under intense pressures to "convert" their political beliefs and affiliations; torture was widely used, and police threatened to "exterminate" those who refused to recant. According to a careful account by a group of American social scientists, at the local level all persons accused of leftist or communist leanings were required to join so-called *podo yŏn-maeng* (guidance alliance; see chapter 6) which were "organized and supervised locally by the police to get all suspect individuals under surveillance . . . so that an effort could be made to convert them from their previous views." When the war began many members were killed by Rhee's police, in spite of recantations; six such deaths occurred in one small village the social scientists studied.[81]

These were, of course, the methods that the *kempeitai* had used to create communist and nationalist apostates during the colonial period; they were the most hated of Japanese divide-and-rule techniques, fiendish by their very nature, but effective in creating bitter and enduring fissures in resistance groups. Before 1945, in Korea and areas of China under Japanese control, only resisters who were never arrested could be free of the suspicion that they had turned in their comrades. The North Koreans seemed especially incensed by this program, and of course linked it to Japanese methods.[82]

In March 1950 the North Koreans sought to infiltrate several hundred well-trained guerrillas to bolster the sagging fortunes of the southern partisans. Some sources said they hoped to expand base areas in the Kyŏngsang Provinces. Unlike the often desperately underequipped southerners, they came with medics and mortar platoons. The proximate reason for the DPRK reinforcement may have been the death on March 21 of Kim Tal-sam, the leader of the Cheju guerrillas, who was trying to cross into the North. A March 7 intelligence report on Kim's plan to make his way to the parallel caused all East coast units to go on alert; he and eighty comrades ran into an ambush southwest of Samch'ŏk and the whole unit was wiped out. At the same time a guerrilla group under veteran leader Yi Ho-jae was moving north, either planning to cross the parallel or to contact the reinforcements in the northern reaches of the T'aebaek range. The North sent two groups of 320 each across the parallel, the first led by Kim Sang-ho, the second by Kim Tu-hyŏn.

Kim Sang-ho was a former police sergeant in the southern town of Yŏnan, and he commanded a group including at least two hundred southern youths who had entered the Kangdong School a year earlier for two months of guerrilla training, followed by tactical exercises in the Chŏlwŏn area. They embarked from Yangyang and crossed the parallel on March 24. Kim Tu-hyŏn's group also included Kangdong trainees, and left Yangyang on the same date, crossing the parallel by a different route.

The 10th Regiment of the ROKA 8th Division destroyed the first group in two weeks of fighting east of Kangnŭng from March 25 to April 9, with 250 killed, wounded, or captured. On April 9 the ROKA 8th Regiment of the 6th Division clashed with the second group, killing 76; by April 22, this group was also destroyed, and Kim Tu-hyŏn killed.[83]

The American command was particularly happy with this result, lauding the 6th Division under Kim Paek-il and the 8th Division under Yu Chae-hŭng. The British also noted the South Koreans's increased capacity for anticommunist warfare, in contrast to the sorry performance the previous summer. In May and June, guerrilla incidents tapered off remarkably, reaching in early June "a new low." The last report filed before the war began said small guerrilla bands of fifteen to thirty still operated in various areas, but were generally quiet. The North sought to infiltrate sixty more guerrillas on June 10, with about half of them getting destroyed.[84]

North Korean materials bear out the sense that the guerrilla struggle was exhausted, if not destroyed by the spring of 1950. Yi Sŭng-yŏp wrote in January that the guerrilla movement was developing strongly and was the key to unification. The account had an optimistic tone, saying there was a "great expansion" of the struggle in the fall of 1949. His exaggerated figures showed 44,200 guerrillas in August and 89,900 in October, dropping to 77,900 in December, with the decline attributed to people making preparations "to tide over the winter." The guerrillas would go forward "to make 1950 the year of decisive victory."[85]

By March he was less ebullient, seeking to explain the guerrilla failure rather than laud their successes: winter was the toughest time for the guerrillas, with "indescribable cold, hunger and hardship," the Rhee clique mobilized five of eight divisions, terrorist groups destroyed villages, thousands of people were moved to protected areas, the strongest region, Honam, had few geographic advantages for guerrillas, and so on. His tortured logic lamented the loss of key guerrilla commanders, acknowledged "very big errors" in harming people and property, and yet claimed that the "winter offensive" had nonetheless failed. It was, in short, a defensive essay by a southern communist leader who had much riding on the fate of the guerrillas. At the same time, he noted that the KPA was "maturing and expanding as an indomitable force."[86]

Kim Sam-yong, another southerner, argued in March 1950 that the suppression forces were "incomparably better armed," and that Americans guided their efforts (he claimed that Roberts took direct command in the T'aebaeksan region in early February, which is plausible); Ameri-

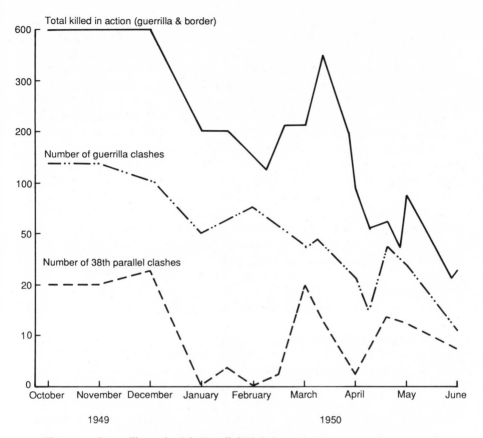

Figure 2. Guerrilla and 38th Parallel Fighting, October 1949–June 1950
SOURCE: KMAG G-2 (Intelligence) Weekly and Periodic Reports

can-supplied planes, ships, and heavy weapons were used, especially
along the coast from Pusan to Uljin, which he said was fully blockaded.
Kim claimed that with the spring coming, the guerrillas would again expand rapidly. Ch'oe Yong-gŏn, however, made only the briefest mention
of the southern partisans in a speech at the second anniversary of the
founding of the KPA, while going on about the Kim Il Sung guerrillas in
Manchuria, and lauding the growth of the KPA: "it is prepared to unify
the territory and liberate the compatriots in the southern part." From
March onward, the party newspaper seemed to grasp at straws in finding
guerrilla activities to write about in the South.[87]

There may well have been splits in the leadership on the meaning of
the apparent defeat of the southern partisans in the spring of 1950.
Southern communists would want to find some way to invigorate the

movement, and Kim Il Sung's group might decide that the time was ripe for a KPA liberation of the South—when the southern partisans were weak and could claim little credit for reunifying the peninsula. But it is most unlikely, as some have argued, that the decline in guerrilla fortunes would cause Pak Hŏn-yŏng to argue for a conventional attack. He had little power in the North, no military experience, and later it was precisely the Kim group that charged him with this, and then executed him, as part of the scapegoating over the results of the war.

It is more likely that a coalition would form behind a change in strategy, arguing that unconventional warfare was going nowhere and, with the efficient virtues of large-scale conventional warfare demonstrated in the devastating southward march of the Chinese Communists in 1948–1949, that this would be the preferred strategy in Korea as well. In comparing Korea with China and (later) Vietnam, it is so often forgotten that both civil wars in China and Vietnam, thought to be guerrilla wars in their essence, were ended by large-scale conventional battles.

At the same time, it is not evident that the guerrillas suffered an irremediable loss in the 1949–1950 "winter offensive." After all, it is standard procedure to melt away during the winter months, as Kim did in Manchuria, and return when the conditions are better. The levels of activity by local guerrillas after the war began suggest that the movement was by no means extirpated.

The extraordinary intensity of the "winter offensive" was possible because large elements of the southern army were diverted to antiguerrilla operations. This, in turn, deeply affected the disposition of forces defending against the regular armies of the North. Roberts told Jessup in January 1950 that many of the guerrilla bands "have been completely exterminated," which was possible "only by devoting to the campaigns overwhelming superiority," thus tying up large numbers of troops. Roberts said he now hoped to get the National Police to develop counterinsurgency units that could relieve the Army. In March, Roberts said that the antiguerrilla effort "took the bulk of five regiments," and that formal garrison training suffered as a result. He had detached ten thousand police from the Korean National Police (KNP) for antiguerrilla training, seeking about twenty battalions of five hundred men each, which he thought would be completed by May 1.[88]

CONCLUSION

A close inspection of events a year or so before the Korean War shows a stunning concatenation of events: the withdrawal of American combat forces from Korea, provocative assaults across the parallel by southern forces, a meeting between Rhee and Chiang sandwiched around Rhee and Yi Pŏm-sŏk calling for a march north, UNCOK observers who only observed one side's transgressions, the return of North Korean expeditionary forces from China and the southward deployment of heavy tank and artillery forces, a seemingly successful suppression of guerrillas in the southern interior, all ensuing as competing forces in Washington fought over containment and rollback in a broad review of Asia policy. This "decent interval" thus encompassed most of the people, events, and forces that interacted to produce war in June 1950. It would be enough to tax the faculties of any statesman; let us now look at what one statesman, Dean Acheson, did about this bubbling cauldron.

Chapter Thirteen

"THE SPEECH":
ACHESONIAN DETERRENCE AT
THE PRESS CLUB

"In those days I was fresh and eager and inexperienced," [I]
should have known that in speaking off the cuff from notes, and
in not consulting others, "you've left yourself open to a very serious misunderstanding."

Dean Acheson

It was a miscalculation by them, based upon a misrepresentation
by us.

Richard Nixon

IN THE YEAR before the Korean War, we have argued, American policy
toward East Asia underwent a profound transformation, embodied in
NSC 48, the new paper for Asia, and the process of decision behind it.
Beneath the formal policy documents were a host of new assumptions—
on containment and rollback, Japan's position in the world economy,
China's presumed expansionist tendencies. As these assumptions worked
their way through the bureaucracy and into established policy, most of
the decisions usually thought to have come as a result of the fighting in
Korea were already made or prefigured: the extension of containment to
East Asia, the provision of military aid to the French in Indochina, the
refusal to recognize the People's Republic of China, the hegemonic conception linking an Asian hinterland to the needs of the Japanese economy, and the containment/rollback dialectic of the Korean War.

But there is a fly in the ointment. The reader will already have had a
spasm: what about the Press Club speech? Acheson's "green light" to Kim
Il Sung hardly bespeaks a structure of containment deterrence, rather a
fatal lapse of credibility, hardly a globalism run amok, rather an ill-considered retreat—saved at the bell only by the courageous decisions of
June 27, 1950.

Acheson spoke on Asia policy at the Press Club in Washington, D.C.,
on January 12, 1950. Although few commented on the Korea portion of
the address at the time, after June 25 observers noted that he had
seemed to exclude South Korea from the American defense perimeter in
Asia. His Republican opponents, especially McCarthy, blasted him for
giving "the green light" to the communists to attack. Historians and po-

litical scientists determined that the speech was a classic failure of deterrence; one can open many texts on American foreign policy and find this argument.

The most sophisticated version of this position is in the important study of deterrence by Alexander George and Richard Smoke. They recognize much more subtlety in Acheson's position that did his Republican detractors, and nicely grasp the distinction between limited and general war strategies that had emerged before the Korean War. But they nonetheless view the Korean case as one of "failure to employ deterrence," with Acheson (and American policy) excluding South Korea from the defense perimeter, only to be stunned into awareness, by the North Korean attack, "of the *political* as against the 'strategic' importance of South Korea." They also write that the administration's position was not "unilaterally determined," but grew out of a policy debate on Korea that was "remarkably free of controversy."[1]

As we have seen in earlier chapters, Korea policy was quite rancorous, and after 1946, determined exclusively by Acheson and the State Department over military objections. Furthermore that determination rested precisely on the calculation that whatever Korea's military significance, it had great political-strategic value.

But of more interest is George and Smoke's concern about why policy makers did not do more to warn the North Koreans away. They cite three ways that one might respond, given evidence of increasing tension in Korea: promise direct military support to the ROK, maintain the existing commitment but increase indirect military and diplomatic support, or reduce the limited commitment and prepare to "cushion the costs" of failure. "What is curious," they find, is that the administration "did not respond in *any* of these three ways. . . . This was not a 'rational' response to the changing situation." They go on to deplore this failure, and suggest what lessons it might have for other such cases.[2]

Indeed it is a curiosity. Not that Acheson failed to employ deterrence: it was just a different deterrent, for a civil war, where he had to restrain both sides. The curiosity of this strategy is that you leave your ally vulnerable without telling him why, and you leave yourself vulnerable if you let your ally go down the drain without a defense. Therefore you must tacitly or secretly contemplate a defense, under specified conditions (the ally did not provoke the aggression, for example), if you do not in fact want the ally to fall. If you do not plan a defense, you take measure three in the George and Smoke scenario. And if you plan a defense but do not want an attack to occur, you take measure two. George and Smoke have the wrong logic but the right facts: Acheson did neither of the above. One is therefore left with two possibilities: he was not "rational," or he thought an attack under certain conditions would be in the American interest.

Beyond the political science accounts, the Press Club speech has entered a mysterious and impenetrable realm of frozen verdicts, received wisdom, and twitching viscera, impervious to fact and argument, such that if "who started the Korean War" is the first reflex question people like to ask, the second will usually be, "what about Acheson's speech?" History has rendered its august judgment: Acheson blundered. So has political science: he was irrational.

The verdict is wrong, and there is no wisdom here. Even the premise has always been stupefyingly improbable: that Stalin, of all people, or for that matter Kim Il Sung, would be misled by a public speech into thinking the United States would not defend South Korea. Stalin's usual modus operandi was probably to put negatives in front of Acheson's public statements, as a first cut at discerning enemy intentions. A dialectical logic of interacting opposites would immediately course through his mind on reading the speech: Acheson says he won't defend them, so probably he will; maybe he means it; in any case he's trying to mislead us; maybe by pretending to believe him we can suck the Americans into a stupid war, so on and so forth. Not to mention that Stalin was reading top secret American documents with his breakfast, courtesy the British spies—Philby, McLean, Burgess, Blake, and that lot.

Or, how about the premise that a man whom James Chace blessed as "the most gifted Secretary of State since John Quincy Adams,"[3] erred so badly, acted irrationally, failed to think it all through, could not get his signals straight? Yet these suppositions die hard: an historian who has worked on the Truman administration for a decade told me he thought Acheson was a person of profound, muddle-minded naiveté.

Acheson's reflections about the speech and the controversy it aroused are, in typical fashion, unhelpful. In his memoirs he says surprisingly little, except to dismiss his critics and to remark on the "stupidity" of the Russians in sponsoring the North Korean attack. In the retrospective Princeton seminars, Acheson told the willing ears of his friends, "in those days I was fresh and eager and inexperienced," one should have known that in speaking off the cuff from notes, and in not consulting others, "you've left yourself open to a very serious misunderstanding."[4]

ON THE APPREHENSION OF IMPONDERABLES

When a reader peruses the papers of a prominent individual, sitting astride the daily flow of policy papers, memos, notes, letters, and diaries, one forms judgments. Some people you like more, others less; some reputations are enhanced, others diminished; eventually you arrive at fairly certain conclusions about the person. Acheson's papers bring forth the unshakeable conviction that this was not a naive, nor an inexperienced man. Indeed, few secretaries of state have ever matched Acheson's grasp of world affairs, his vision, his Olympian self-confidence, his capacity to think things through, to discern logic in the welter of events, and to articulate that logic as policy. He was also a master at the retrospective construction of historical verdicts, which we may assume was behind his protestations of naiveté.

Acheson's executive credo may be read in his description of Secretary Marshall's greatness—more apt for Acheson than for Marshall: "All elements of the problem were held, as it were, in solution in his mind until it was ready to precipitate a decision. This is the essence and the method—or rather the art—of judgment in its highest form. Not merely military judgment, but judgment in great affairs of state, which requires both mastery of precise information and apprehension of imponderables."[5]

Acheson's method as an executive was to think through the logic of a problem on his own, say the problem of Taiwan. Next, he would relate Taiwan to larger regional and global concerns. These larger concerns, in turn, would be examined in the light of what was best for the world economy and what was best for the American state in its confrontation with the Soviets. The world was for Acheson like a set of city blocks; here was Europe, there was Asia; here was Korea, there was Japan; although he did not know the blocks intimately and rarely ruminated on a nation like Korea, and viewed everything through a prism of American and European interests, in one country and region after another Acheson was able to fit these blocks into the larger whole, as he saw it, and then devise appropriate policies for each. Only people who have never sought intellectually to order global events (and therefore think it impossible), or specialists who plumb the parts at the expense of the whole, could fail to find in Acheson a man who was the antithesis of the naive groper.

In some circles of foreign policy analysis it is de rigueur to see the imputation of a plan or strategy as either a misunderstanding of the policy process or a variety of conspiracy theory, even to deny that policy makers have plans at all. "Acheson never thought about Korea, he had no time to do so," one diplomatic historian remarked about an earlier version of my argument; "have you ever seen the daily appointment book of a Secretary of State?" But Acheson thought about his global city and its various blocks on a daily basis; he had visions, plans, and he knew how to keep a secret. Acheson rarely seemed to expect or to care that those around him would understand; he enjoyed his private vision and the exercise of a hidden-hand, secret power.

The recalcitrant reader who resists this characterization will have to confront not simply my own misapprehensions and imputations of design, but Acheson himself. For it was this man who began his memoir with a cherished and somewhat breathless account of how he, through careful thought and timely intervention, turned the screws on the Japanese just before Pearl Harbor. Acheson's "search for a function" in the State Department after he left Wall Street in 1941 was found in affairs that "touched off the big event of 1941."[6] This passage repays our attention, not for what Acheson may or may not have done, but for the intellectual structure, the intricate logic, of his argument.

At that time, as director of the Division of Controls, Acheson played a role in imposing so-called "freezing controls" on Japan (the West's "obstreperous offspring," in his words). It was a matter of the small filip given to events, to tip them this way and not that: the Japanese ship Tatutu Maru was the lever, which "like the USS *Maine* and Jenkins' ear, became the instrument of great events."[7]

The details of the affair are not important to us, but the structure of action is: the invocation of the Stimsonian tradition; the creation of a field or situation that channels and confines enemy behavior, and appears to leave the initiative up to him; policy expressed in language "intended to cloak ideas"; the use of football metaphors ("a near fumble due to a faulty pass"); the small act setting events in motion; the "stupidity" of the enemy in reacting; all this in the interest of an "ultimate truth too unformed for statement." Or as Acheson summed it up, "The inarticulate major premise was that whether or not we had a policy, we had a state of affairs."[8]

We do not know with certitude what this "state of affairs" was, since it was by definition unarticulated. It would appear to be one in which, in Acheson's reconstruction, Japan—a rising but weaker nation—would be presented with a field of power and a realm of choice which would inevitably defeat it: if it did not act, it would be relegated to a second-rank status in perpetuity; if it did act, war would be the result, the onus would be on the enemy, and the result of that would be defeat by the United States (and second-rank status in perpetuity).

Acheson's manipulation of freezing controls eventually brought forth, he wrote, "a great stillness" between the United States and Japan, as the statesman awaited the denouement. It so happened that Acheson was at his Sandy Spring farm on that sudden Sunday, clearing fallen timber and picnicking with Archibald MacLeish: "At last our enemies, with parallel stupidity, resolved our dilemmas, clarified our doubts and uncertainties, and united our people for the long, hard course that the national interest required."[9]

All this leads me to the assumption that Acheson knew what he was doing on January 12, rather than trying to squeeze Asia policy into his morning schedule of shaving, breakfasting, and meeting high school model UN groups. To do otherwise would be to deny the specific character of the man, to ignore his acumen, and to abdicate the essential task of judgment without which history becomes a nihilistic endeavor in which we flounder about aimlessly, beached on this misperception or that irrationality.

ACHESON'S ARCHITECTURE IN THE FAR EAST

When we examine the logic of the Press Club speech, it takes us far from Korea, back to the world system, and the Sino-Soviet question—the main thing Acheson wanted to talk about on January 12. The speech was an integral part of Acheson's Far Eastern architecture, and fully explicable in those terms. It stands up quite well on close reading; furthermore Acheson's private justifications of the speech, as opposed to his public admissions of naiveté, fit a thread of logic running through the whole episode.

Acheson's architecture partook of a conception in which several levels of analysis interact: the global, regional, national, and domestic, the latter an arena both of political and bureaucratic conflict. A theory of political economy underpinned all levels, one that assumed an interaction between power and plenty, or between the system of states and the world economy. At the global level, Acheson pursued a revival and flourishing of the world economy. The great antagonist to this was socialist control of the Eurasian land mass, stretching "from Berlin to Canton, from Murmansk to Tirhana," as the North Koreans put it; the feasible and practical remedy was therefore to draw lines of containment around its periphery, revive the industrial economies of West Europe and Japan, link up the underdeveloped hinterlands, and seek to split the Russians and the Chinese. The latter could not be done, Acheson thought, either by containment or rollback in China. The Nationalist regime had proved itself incontinent, and rollback would both open an endless running sore, and arouse elemental forces of nationalism and xenophobia—in China *and* America. Instead, Chinese nationalism could be used to split Moscow and Beijing, and the charms and enticements of the market might bring China out of isolation and render it dependent on the West and Japan.

From the standpoint of world-system theory, or simply the way an international banker looked at the world, China was little more than an agrarian political economy with a modern fringe stitched along its coast by the imperial powers; it could not industrialize on its own resources. The Soviet Union, however, was the biggest self-sufficient political economy in the world next to the United States, and was the one nation since

Japan to show itself capable of general industrialization on its own. The feasibility of enmeshing China was thus much greater.

Japan was to be the engine of growth in the Asian region, shorn of military and political power and reintegrated into a potent industrial position in the world economy, but one of the second rank. This necessitated, however, a hinterland providing raw materials and markets. Therefore, as we have seen, Acheson developed a "great crescent" strategy as the Asian expression of containment, linking an offshore island defense with a Japanese hinterland; the hinterland would include Japan's former colonies, to the extent that they were available, but above all it would encompass Southeast Asia and Indochina.

Korea occupied a contingent position in this architecture. Was it "little China" or "little Japan"? If it were little China, Rhee another Chiang, the economy corrupted and inviable, and North Korea an authentic revolutionary nationalist challenge, linked to China, then Korea would just be another domino. If it were "little Japan," however, with effective anti-communist leadership, a growing economy with the necessary links to Japan and the United States, and North Korea was "little Russia," an extension of Soviet power, the whole picture changed: it might be a place to reverse the tide of communist expansion. We have seen that in 1947 Acheson chose to include Korea in his containment strategy, even if he could not get Congress to foot the total bill he wanted.

Taiwan was a buzzing, irritating fly in this ointment—not the Nationalist regime itself, which Acheson thought was . . . just another domino. More worrisome were Taiwan's supporters in Washington. Without the bizarre influence of the "China" issue in American politics, Acheson might have gotten his way and a flourishing Sino-American relationship might not have had to wait the passage of a quarter-century. As always, distant foreign events interacted explosively with domestic conflicts, making foreign policy a matter of deft accommodation of a stubborn world *and* a recalcitrant American polity. As it happened, Acheson became the flypaper for a horde of Republican and right-wing horse flies, something that might well defeat the grandest architecture.

Like another shrewd internationalist, Roosevelt, the mote in Acheson's eye was Asian revolutionary nationalism. Nationalism he could understand; revolution he could not. His China policy rested on a reasonably apt grasp of Sino-Soviet relations, but an abominable reading of internal Chinese politics. His Korea policy simply assumed Soviet puppetry in P'yŏngyang; he had no idea of the nature of the North Korean leadership, nor the historical and revolutionary forces it drew upon. The same was true of his Indochina policy, where even in the late 1960s he retained the idea that Ho Chi Minh was not an authentic revolutionary, merely a creature of Soviet policy. People like Kim and Ho simply did not enter Acheson's mind as historical actors.

At any rate, Acheson's policy was a mix of containment and internationalism, the embodiment of the 1947 compromise. If a Sino-Soviet monolith emerged, it had to be prevented from expansion. If China could be split from the Soviet Union, it could perhaps be enmeshed in the world system.

With the complete routing of the Nationalists on the mainland predictable by late 1948 and accomplished by the summer of 1949, American policy toward China could be conceived simply. As Dean Rusk once put it, "our first choice in respect to Peiping [*sic*] was that it fall . . . our second choice was that, if it didn't fall, it could somehow be separated from Moscow." George Kennan supplied the geopolitical rationale for the second choice. The Soviet Union, he argued, had an enormous internal market yet to be developed, and its links to the Far East were stretched thin and rather primitive; he did not think the Soviets could give the Chinese what they needed, or "do much in the way of intertwining its economy with that of China." He recalled a meeting with Stalin, where the generalissimo had said "if anybody is going to give anything to the Far East, I think it's you."[10]

In early 1949 the CIA acknowledged that the Chinese Communist victory would change the balance of power in East Asia to the Soviets' favor, but China would still be heavily dependent on foreign aid, and "superior ability to provide such assistance belongs to the US, not the USSR." State Department internationalists tended to agree with British policy, that is, to maintain diplomatic recognition, continue trade, avoid military skirmishes with the Communists, and hope that at a later point China would turn to the West in search of its superior technology, financial resources, and expertise. Chinese industrialization "will require foreign capital, foreign capital goods, and foreign technical assistance," the British said, and will be "almost entirely dependent on non-Communist sources for supplies of rubber, oil, and fertilizers." Far East chief Walton Butterworth agreed, and emphasized the uses of oil to American policy in rendering China tractable, given U.S. dominance of the world oil regime; he and others in the State Department also wanted to continue Sino-Japanese trade, for similar reasons. This policy was thwarted by American domestic politics and destroyed by the Korean War, but it came back thirty years later, with energy resources again used in search of outer limits on Chinese action.[11]

The American desire to split China and the Soviet Union had an internal corollary in Chinese politics. That most adroit of Chinese internationalists, Chou En-lai, had seemed to hint in 1949 that the People's Republic of China (PRC) wanted a relationship with the United States because the

Soviets could not give China the help it needed, and to forestall dependency on Moscow. Furthermore, American intelligence assumed the existence of factional splits in the Politburo and Central Committee between pro-Stalin and anti-Stalin groups; American policy had responded quickly when Tito split with Moscow, and Americans searched for Titoism in China. The leaders of the pro-Soviet group were thought to be Liu Shao-ch'i, Li Li-san, Wang Ming, and Kao Kang, among others.[12]

During the NSC 48 final meeting on December 30, 1949, Acheson urged that China's "xenophobia" be deflected from the United States to the Soviet Union by charging the latter with "detaching" Manchuria, thus placing the United States "on the side of the nationalist movements." His colleague John C. Wiley, ambassador to Iran, went so far as to suggest to him, ten days later, direct American military intervention to split the Communists: the United States should look for an incident like the Boxer Rebellion "to present adequate justification for police intervention." He thought "a quick, clean thrust" would do the trick, and lamented that it was "most disadvantageous" that Japan had to be removed from Manchuria in 1945.[13]

Acheson's strategy was a bit less provocative. He chose instead to play a China card (the PRC's presumed fears of Stalin), by planting leaked intelligence information in the *New York Times*, thence to go public while Mao was sojourning in Moscow, blasting the Russians and seeking to split Moscow and Beijing. This was the main point he wished to make when he spoke at the Press Club, and it is what got most of the attention.

Mao had arrived in Moscow for negotiations with the Soviets in late December 1949, starting on a cold note and remaining far longer than expected. On his arrival TASS reporters asked him how long he intended to stay and got back this abrupt reply: "how long I stay depends on how long it takes to be able to solve the questions relating to the interests of the People's Republic of China."[14] It was hardly the auspicious note heralding the Eurasian monolith. As the visit dragged on intelligence agencies became more convinced of serious differences. Indeed, in early February the CIA director came running to Foggy Bottom with a Mukden dispatch citing a "rumor of a strong possibility of a state of war" between China and the USSR in Manchuria, with reports coming in about rapid movement toward the Northeast by the veteran New Fourth Army.[15] Although the veracity of this report cannot be known, it is easily conceivable that Mao moved divisions into Manchuria as a bargaining chip during his negotiations in Moscow. In any case, such news emboldened Acheson.

Like the hidden prompter in an opera, Acheson played his theme through voices in the *New York Times*. On December 30 he met with James Reston, after which readers were treated to a New Year lead article by Reston saying a new "Asia paper" (that is, NSC 48, which Truman signed December 30), in development since the past August, had just been approved; the United States had decided against "occupying Formosa" in favor of attempts "to widen the breach" between Moscow and Beijing "over Manchuria." Sino-Soviet difficulties had been "developing faster than expected"; the United States did not wish to create a "Spanish situation" in which the United States and the USSR would fight a civil war through proxies, but instead deflect Chinese anti-imperialist sentiments toward Moscow.[16]

Later in the same month, Acheson told the American embassy in France that intelligence information indicating that the Soviets were preparing an "unequal treaty" for China should be "planted as soon as possible," and suggested that C. L. Sulzberger would be a good "cut-out." Sulzberger dutifully wrote several columns in the *Times* based on this and other intelligence leaks about Sino-Soviet differences.[17] It is testimony to Acheson's skills at ventriloquy that he was so successful in getting key opinion leaders to reflect and repeat his views. The British called Reston his "mouthpiece," and indeed many of Reston's articles read as if they were scripted by Acheson; Senator Vandenberg's speeches in Congress often seemed activated by an Achesonian cadence.[18]

Acheson and the CIA knew little about the Chinese leadership at this time, however, and when the Sino-Soviet Treaty was concluded in February, Acheson had a lot of egg on his face. Chou En-lai was always loyal to Mao, even through the devastation of the Cultural Revolution; Liu Shao-ch'i may have had experience in urban underground politics that made him more Leninist than Mao, but an open breach between the two did not occur until the 1960s, and then over different issues. Li Li-san and Wang Ming had little influence with the high CCP leadership. Kao Kang was a different story, as we have seen; indeed, Kao Kang preceded Mao to Moscow in 1949, so here there was obvious sensitivity.[19] Nonetheless, Acheson's tactic of openly blasting the Soviets for imperial designs only tended to bring the PRC leadership together. Because he himself had little grasp of revolutionary nationalism, he grossly misjudged China's anti-imperialist sensibilities—which viewed the United States as little different than the European imperial powers, at least in the twentieth century, whereas the Soviets had maintained an anti-imperialist stance since 1917.

TAIWAN DECEPTIONS

Thus 1950 dawned with Acheson ostensibly waiting for "the dust to settle" from the Chinese civil war, meaning the occupation of Taiwan by the Communists, thereafter to get on with the manipulative business of sowing seeds of discord to orient China away from Moscow and toward the market economies. This would mean no American defense of Taiwan, to avoid looking like an imperialist, and recognition of the PRC. Now this was not really Acheson's policy toward Taiwan, but he seemed curiously content to let everyone think it was, through the venue of James Reston, a press statement in early January, and other means. He also touched off a firestorm of criticism from the Right. What, then, was his policy?

In essence Acheson wanted to keep Taiwan and the mainland separated, but not to tell anybody about it, least of all Chiang Kai-shek. He therefore constructed a deterrent much like that in Korea, in which he sought to hold a territory that the military said we could not afford to defend, to constrain both sides in a civil war situation, and to get the United Nations involved in implementing American policy.

In March 1949 Acheson responded to a Joint Chiefs of Staff (JCS) suggestion that maybe the United States should deploy force in or around Taiwan, by arguing that this would stimulate anti-imperialist sentiments, "just at the time we shall be seeking to exploit the genuinely anti-Soviet irridentist issue in Manchuria and Sinkiang." He went on,

> It is a cardinal point in our thinking that if our present policy is to have any hope of success in Formosa, we must *carefully conceal our wish to separate the island from mainland control*. . . . If we are to intervene militarily on the island, we shall, in all probability, do so in concert with like-minded powers, preferably using UN mechanism and with the proclaimed intention of satisfying the legitimate demands of the indigenous Formosans for self-determination either under a UN trusteeship or through independence (emphasis added).

In this period Acheson also told the National Security Council (NSC) that he "preferred to try to develop a spontaneous independent movement in Formosa which could then lead to an agreement in the UN for a new deal for Formosa. This way, he said, we could get international sanction for U.S. intervention."

Some days later he suggested "taking over the island under the front of international action, first by underground encouragement of a revolution and then by UN action to establish a trusteeship for the island." By June 1949 Walton Butterworth had prepared a paper recommending "an immediate committal of the problem of Formosa to the UN," complete with a draft statement which Acheson could make, citing principles of self-determination; the resonance with Korea a year later is remarkable.[20]

This is vintage Achesonianism, complete with the triumphant cynicism. As with his 1947 Korea policy, it is unilateral containment cloaked as multilateral internationalism, the microcosm of American interests structuring the macrocosm of UN and allied policy. The corollary of the policy was that Chiang Kai-shek and his regime evaporated from the analysis. Taiwan might get a UN trusteeship, or a native government, or a coup d'etat, but it would not get the Kuomintang. Why? Because the regime had proved its incontinence, because it was not effectively controlled by Americans, and because it had ridiculous pretensions to retake a mainland it had just lost, which could only materialize with full American backing. The policy was containment, not rollback. Chiang Kai-shek thus became Acheson's odd man out.[21]

Acheson could not agree to an open policy of Truman Doctrine–style containment, meaning a military advisory group and military aid as an earnest of American intentions, for three reasons. First, he had to restrain rollback forces in his own administration, and an open commitment to defend the island would only embolden them—as Warren Cohen puts it, he refused to "encourage Truman to play Teddy Roosevelt."[22] Second, his policy had to remain secret, so Beijing would not know. Third, he was containing the island, not the regime. This was the difference with Korea, where the United States had created the regime, where it had advisory groups and certain important controls, and, perhaps, where rollback might work. In the case of Taiwan, it is documented that he kept the essence of the strategy secret: the United States did, indeed, want the island kept from communist hands. This was also the case with the Korea deterrent, but it was part of the unarticulated "state of affairs."

George Kennan, surprisingly, *did* want Truman to play Teddy Roosevelt: the only sure way to deny Taiwan to the Communists, he said in July 1949, "would lie in the removal of the present Nationalist administrators from the island," followed by a regime that would invoke the principle of self-determination; such "intervention" would work if done resolutely, "the way Theodore Roosevelt might have done it."[23] From this point onward to the very weekend the Korean War broke out, a coup against Chiang was the minimax strategy that would realize Acheson's goal; it kept Chiang casting backward glances over his shoulder for a year.

Acheson could control Taiwan policy at the commanding heights, in the Oval Office, but not in the bureaucracy and the body politic, where his efforts were continuously subverted. On the day that Acheson informed Reston that Taiwan would not be defended, MacArthur went so far as to tell the *London Times* that Truman had adopted a new "positive" policy for containing communism in Asia (true), including the dispatch of military and civilian advisors to Taiwan (probably false).[24] This and other events in early January put the fat in the fire and "China" had even more weight in internecine American political struggles. Acheson was in the awkward position of being pregnant with an idea to which he could not give birth—that there was, all along, a commitment to defend the island. As he later put it in his typically bland and airy manner, so far as he knew since the fall of 1948, "the policy of this government has been that the control of Formosa by a power hostile to the U.S. . . . would be inimical to our interests."[25]

On January 5, 1950, Truman and Acheson both held news conferences on the Taiwan question, the president pledging no defense of the island "at this time," while Acheson masked his delicate condition with an equally bald statement that there would be no defense of Taiwan. The president's statement sent the British into a flurry, for they correctly saw in the timing contingency the possibility of an American commitment in the event of hostilities.[26] Acheson played a dual game, content to let the unwashed mass think what it would, eager to unbalance his antagonists both at home and abroad, in Taipei and Beijing, Moscow and Washington.

To the Press Club

Acheson labored on his Press Club speech right through this firestorm over Taiwan, and delivered it in the immediate aftermath. Its purpose was to present that portion of NSC 48 that Acheson wanted to get out to the public. He spent more time preparing this speech than he did on the June decision to intervene in Korea; for an allegedly overworked and harried secretary of state, he seemed to have time to burn. His appointment book illustrates his attention to East Asia and the crafting of what he wished to say.

December 14: "off-the-record discussion of F[ar] E[ast]"
December 24: "Far eastern meeting"
December 28: four-hour meeting on "Far Eastern paper"
December 29: NSC meeting "re Formosa"
January 3: "Meeting on Far East"
January 4: met Truman "re Formosa"
January 5: "meeting on FE speech"
January 8: "all day on FE speech"
January 9: "regular meeting—on speech."
January 10: after 4 pm, "worked on speech"
January 11: met Butterworth and Rusk of Far East Dept.
January 12: "all morning at home working on speech"[27]

State Department underlings also developed several drafts for Acheson, contrary to the received wisdom about his extemporaneous bumbling. Rusk had a draft done by January 3; on January 9 Acheson read a version to his aides, then gave it to them for further work. The next day Acheson worked over a thorough outline, and wrote comments on previous drafts. There were still other drafts by January 12. George Kennan added his own suggestions for Acheson, a typically arcane collection of turn-of-the-century ideas.[28]

Acheson did not like any of it. His marginal comments on the drafts offer vintage examples of his world view. For example, one Foggy Bottom scribbler wrote, "We have no grand objective. We proceed by looking around us and over our shoulders to be sure of what we are actually doing." To which Acheson responded, "*No!*" He later said that he had a draft that he thought was "terrible . . . I pretty well threw it away."

Korea was prominent in all the drafts, and was the first Asian nation mentioned in the last one readied for Acheson on January 10. This paper termed the ROK one of "a number of new states [that] have joined the family of free nations"; the Democratic People's Republic of Korea (DPRK), on the other hand, was run by "an obscure assortment of Communists, installed in office in P'yŏngyang by the Soviets in defiance of the UN." The existence of American military and economic missions in Seoul "demonstrated our intentions in Korea." But Acheson wrote at the end of the section, "CAUTION: Do not imply that Korea can count on our material assistance regardless of own efforts. We cannot extend unrequited aid." In none of these drafts did the idea of a defense perimeter appear. Acheson added this to his own version, along with the distinction between those nations automatically included, and those in which the first recourse would be to indigenous defense. But he did so in this context: in a draft dated January 8, Acheson scrawled out on a yellow legal pad that Japan and Korea were "the areas of our direct responsibility," followed by "South Korea is," and then a blank paragraph to be filled in later. So, the phrases allegedly "excluding" the ROK from the defense perimeter had to have been added, by Acheson, over the next few days.[29]

The copy that Acheson read from at the Press Club was destroyed, leading to a two-week hiatus between the record of his oral remarks and the publication of a written transcript by the State Department. But it should be clear that Acheson by no means spoke off the cuff, with minimal preparation. Instead he determined "not [to] work with these drafts and not [to] work with anybody," to do it all himself, something characteristic of his helmsmanship, thinking naturally that he knew better. He did not bother to discuss the defense perimeter idea with those who would implement it, the military agencies; he included in it the Aleutian Islands, Japan, Okinawa, and the Philippines.[30]

In the passage relevant to Korea, he said,

> So far as the military security of other areas in the Pacific is concerned, it must be clear that no person can guarantee these areas against military attack. . . . Should such an attack occur—one hesitates to say where

such an armed attack could come from—the initial reliance must be on the people attacked to resist it and then upon the commitments of the entire civilized world under the Charter of the United Nations, which so far has not proved a weak reed to lean on by any people who are determined to protect their independence against outside aggression.

As Acheson later put it, "that was the warning which I gave in January 1950. That was the warning which the aggressor disregarded."[31]

Thus South Korea was not pointedly excluded from the American defense perimeter, a common misconception. Certain nations (Japan) would be defended, and in other threatened nations (like the ROK), initial reliance would be on those attacked to defend themselves, and if they could not, the implication was, the situation would be reevaluated.

John Lewis Gaddis writes that Acheson's defense perimeter was not inadvertent, but rested on much previous planning; indeed, he believes, an offshore island strategy was the consensual position in 1950. Thus he is forced to conclude that the "abrupt turnabout" in June 1950 demonstrated "the gap between the intentions of statesmen and the consequences of their actions"; and later on he says, "Korea, of course, represented the most striking departure from the original 'defensive perimeter' concept."[32]

The idea of a defense perimeter was certainly not new. The CIA had discussed it as early as the summer of 1947, saying that "while US troops occupy Japan the US has a vital interest in maintaining a position in Korea which will protect its position in Japan and North China." However, once the Japan Occupation had ended, "Korea's indefensible position against attack from the north makes it of less interest to the US, since the US first line of defense near Korea is the US Pacific Islands Defense Base System."[33] To the extent that this represents Gaddis's "original concept," it *did* include Korea—if American troops were still in occupation of Japan, which of course they were in 1950.

MacArthur had similar ideas. In his important talks with Kennan in March 1948, he made explicit what his perimeter defense system meant: the United States would have a "U-shaped area" containing a "striking force," an area which would include Midway, the Aleutians, Clark Air Base in the Philippines, and Okinawa—"the key bastion." However, no bases or troops would be in Japan. In other words, Japan was to MacArthur what South Korea was to Acheson, a place that would be defended regardless of the presence or absence of troops. However for MacArthur, the perimeter had both a defensive and offensive function.[34]

But this was not what activated Acheson's thinking at the Press Club. There is no evidence that these previous references to a defense perimeter informed his logic, which in any case militated against strategic formulations smacking of "purely military" considerations. Gaddis errs in assuming that Acheson merely adopted this strategic concept without much thought, thus creating a gap between intent and consequence. In fact Acheson's perimeter had its base in political economy, in the "great crescent" that would, through political and economic means, both secure and develop a grand area from Japan around to India. Indeed, two days before his speech in secret testimony he described "the real center" of U.S. interest in Asia as a "crescent or semicircle which goes around . . . Japan at one end and India at the other," and remarked that Japan's economic needs must come first in East Asia.[35] The Press Club speech was therefore consistent with his conception of Korean containment in 1947, and with his world view: and so was the intervention in June 1950. Thus the gaps, unintended consequences, inadvertent off-the-cuff statements, failure to distinguish "political" from "strategic" considerations, not to mention striking departures and abrupt turnabouts, evaporate in a consistent logic.

ILLITERACY IN P'YŎNGYANG

Now, in spite of this evidence, let us assume that Acheson nonetheless unintentionally communicated the wrong signal, that the United States would do nothing in the event of an invasion—thus failing the first test of a credible deterrent, creating the appropriate image of risk or fear in the mind of the enemy. So what *was* the North Korean reaction to Acheson's speech?—something about which an entire literature has not paused to inquire, an odd thing since Kim Il Sung was supposed to have been fooled by it. It turns out that the North Koreans thought Acheson *included* the ROK in his perimeter, a bit of a daunting fact for Acheson's presumed failure of deterrence.

Of course, Acheson's preparation for the speech and other materials make it obvious that he could not conceive of the North Koreans—or perhaps any Koreans—as actors in their own right. A "tenth-rate stooge" of Moscow[36] could never be expected to grasp the subtlety of his grand design. Is it the case that they could not read, either?

The truth is a bit different. The North Korean press followed Acheson's words with close attention and sophistication throughout this period, and one may assume that internal materials circulated among the leadership were better. A week after the speech, the North ran an account of Jessup's visit to the ROK (he arrived in Seoul the day before Acheson's speech, and also took a Dulles-like tour of the thirty-eighth parallel), charging him with trying to construct an "East Asian defense line," which they also termed an "attack line," running through Japan, Okinawa, South Korea (Cheju Island), the Philippines, and Taiwan.[37]

This probably referred to the "defense perimeter" passage; in any case the first direct North Korean response to the Press Club speech was to run a Soviet account by Andrei Vyshinsky, which treated the "defense line" as a line of expansionism, but then dwelt extensively on Acheson's charges about the USSR trying to detach Manchuria. The next day the North Koreans ran their own treatment. According to press accounts, they said, Acheson had not prepared much in advance for the speech; but later it turned out he had practiced this "extemporaneous speech" eight or nine times. The article then said,

> Acheson's view was that those countries *inside* what he called a defense line, meaning those subjugated countries, Japan, the Philippines, and *South Korea*, such countries would be America's 'direct responsibilities' [for defense].
>
> It is clear that Acheson is saying that he intends to continue America's imperialist policy in Asia. This is a policy of subordinating Asian peoples, of opposing all those people who fight for their independence and freedom [and are] following the Soviet Union and the great Chinese people, and moreover, [those peoples who] follow the fraternal model of China (emphasis added).[38]

Why did they *include* the ROK in the defense perimeter? The answer is probably no more complex than to say they were reading the *New York Times*. The absence of a transcript for the reporters present on January 12 led them to rely on their notes, and indeed the *Times* did not even bother to refer to the Korea section of Acheson's speech in its account the next day; all the emphasis was on what he said about presumed Sino-Soviet differences. It treated the defense perimeter concept as nothing new or noteworthy—"it will continue to be held." But then in its Sunday review of the week's news, the *Times* said, "Second, there is the area of direct American responsibility—the 'defense perimeter' running *through* occupied Japan, *Korea*, Okinawa and the friendly Philippines. Mr. Acheson said: 'There we had direct responsibility and there we did act' (emphasis added). It is Southeast Asia where we are "only one of many nations . . . [and there] the direct responsibility lies with the peoples concerned."[39]

The British response was equally confused. Ambassador Franks initially cabled that South Korea was included in the area of "direct U.S. interest," along with Japan, Okinawa, and the Philippines, and then three days later said it was an area of direct interest, but was not included in the defensive perimeter, an accurate rendering of Acheson's intent.[40]

The South Korean reaction was also revealing. Ambassador Chang told Acheson of Rhee's "appreciation" for the Press Club speech, and British Ambassador Holt said it had "given considerable satisfaction to the Korean Government who find in [it] a comforting assurance of the intention of the U.S. Government to go on giving strong support to the Korean Republic." Muccio's monthly summary did not even mention it, dwelling instead on Rhee's jittery reaction to the House's temporary defeat of the Korean aid bill, by a narrow margin of two votes.[41]

A former secretary to Kim Kyu-sik whom I interviewed in P'yŏngyang in 1987, Shin Ki-ŏn, remarked that Acheson's speech is interpreted to mean that once the North Koreans heard it, they exclaimed, "Good, now let's go and invade South Korea." But in fact, Shin said, Acheson was "saying meow with his eyes closed," a Korean phrase meaning purposely to deceive. The speech was nothing more than "deception," and "the North Korean leadership knew all that."[42]

The defeat of the aid bill seemed a debacle much greater than anything said at the Press Club, since it was the first time since 1939 that Congress had turned down an administration foreign aid proposal. Yet it ended up merely reinforcing Acheson's position on the ROK. During the debate China lobbyist Walter Judd said that Korea was not essential to the security of the United States, citing Acheson's Press Club speech. Acheson had said the United States would not defend Taiwan, and Judd wanted to show that the State Department wanted to let Korea, too, fall without making it appear that it had been pushed.[43]

Acheson had been placed on the hot seat: Judd had called his bluff on the essential difference between his Korea and Taiwan policies; furthermore Senator Vandenberg told the secretary he was "shocked" by the bill's defeat: "as good a case could be made for our efforts in Korea—and probably a better one—as almost anything we had done in the foreign field."[44]

Acheson suddenly got very active on Korea. On January 20 he told the Cabinet that the House decision "has terrified nations in Europe and everywhere else—that we are pulling out [of Korea]." Acheson urged Truman to make a public statement, so the Koreans would understand that "we did not intend to write them off." Acheson thereupon drafted a memo for Truman to use, saying that the ROK "owes its existence in large measure to the U.S.," it is supported by the UN, and "we have not only given the ROK independence," but supported it with various sorts of aid.[45] But he could not reveal his hole card—that Korea was firmly on the containment line—because of Rhee's volatility. The House soon reversed itself, and voted $100 million for fiscal year 1951 (July 1, 1950–June 30, 1951).

The North Koreans followed this sequence closely, and did better than most American newspapers at analyzing what the House action really meant. Their first reaction was to highlight a congressman's statement that more aid to the ROK would be "pouring money down a rat hole," something the North heartily agreed with. At the same time, Rhee and his allies knew they could not last a day without American aid, and so they purposely "parade before the Americans their weakness." The article said that capitalists did not like to throw good money after bad, and therefore they might treat Rhee the way they had Chiang Kai-shek, and let him go down the drain. Nonetheless one should not conclude from the defeat of the aid bill that Washington was "abandoning South Korea." The Truman administration would find "other methods to continue aid."

The article then concluded as follows:

> The majority behind the "aid" cutoff were Republicans, and these are extreme reactionaries who talked about protecting their "rights and interests" in China and elsewhere, and even about war adventures . . . thus, we have to heighten our readiness even more, beat back the enemy, and bring the save-the-nation struggle for the unification and independence of the Motherland to an even higher level.[46]

Later, P'yŏngyang noted that the opponents of the aid bill were people who wanted the United States to back Taiwan, and that Acheson was "maneuvering skillfully" to get the aid restored: "in a word, the quarrel over Korean aid only came about because of the bankrupcy of American's China policy." It said Acheson linked aid to Korea with his plans for trying to construct a defense line between Japan and Southeast Asia. Thus it looked as if "Acheson has drawn no lessons from the failure of U.S. policy in China."[47]

At the same time, the North Koreans claimed that Rhee and Muccio had hammered out an agreement on mutual defense in Seoul on January 26, which, according to an Associated Press account, had a "secret" element in it. I have no other information on this, but it may have been some measure to give Rhee more assurances of support. The article rendered Acheson's statement to the House with considerable distortion, to the effect that "we have already obtained South Korea and will not let it out of our hands."[48]

In March P'yŏngyang termed Acheson's Press Club speech full of "lies" and "demagogy," a "noisy chorus" that, the implication was, masked his real intention to "prepare a war against the national liberation struggles in Asia." Acheson's Taiwan policy was part of his mendacity, they said, for he really intended to keep it for the United States. It noted that "several tens" of American military advisors had secretly been dispatched to Taiwan and that MacArthur was sending Japanese military officers, both of which were accurate.[49] With the propaganda discounted, the "tenth rate stooge" was closer to the reality of U.S. policy than most of the American press.

The Koreans also reprinted Chou En-lai's analysis of the speech, claiming that its main intent was to drive a wedge between China and the USSR, and to "destroy" the national liberation movements in Vietnam, South Korea, and the Philippines. On February 10 they finally got the defense perimeter straight, saying that the United States would "control" Japan, the Philippines, and the Ryukyus. It was silent on the ROK's position outside the perimeter. Yet within days of that presumably interesting discovery, another essay said that the speech *hides* rather than demonstrates American plans.[50] Later on, as we will see, Senator Connally did much more than Acheson to place South Korea in an exposed, undefended position. Does this mean that there was, even if at a later point, a North Korean belief that the ROK would be left on its own?

The answer is no. The evidence indicates that the North Koreans were doing precisely what I suggested at the beginning of this discussion, mulling Acheson's intent over in their minds, no doubt thinking through all the possibilities; they were not "stupid," and were unlikely to be fooled by a public statement. Moreover it is typically forgotten that the United States had its largest military advisory group in the world in the South, positioned at the parallel or running the daily combat with guerrillas. In my view P'yŏngyang always believed that the United States was committed to keeping the Rhee regime in power. The real effect of the speech was probably to keep them off balance, wary, unsure about what might come next—exactly Acheson's intent with regard to *both* Koreas.

The idea that Acheson naively gave the green light to Stalin or Kim, or that this was where American deterrence failed is, in short, a fantasy. The Korea portion of the address got little attention before June 1950. To my knowledge not a single Republican complained about Korea being "excluded" by Acheson before the Korean War; the flurry of attacks on him came after June 25 and was an artifact of domestic political struggles.

Yet the Republican attacks and the verdicts of "history" laid down a smoke screen that has yet to be penetrated; even someone as shrewd as George Kennan misconstrued what Acheson sought to do on January 12. He said later that Acheson failed to distinguish between areas we would ourselves defend in an all-out war, and areas not falling in that category, but nevertheless ones in which we "would not be able to permit a provocative communist military aggression." Yet this is exactly what Acheson did in the speech, effectively if quietly. Kennan also remarked, "I have always been puzzled at the beating Acheson has taken over this and his own failure to defend himself. It seems to me wholly clear that these statements of his were based on papers prepared in the Pentagon. Acheson would never have taken it upon himself to make such a decision individually.[51] As we have seen, the defense perimeter concept was *not* discussed with the Pentagon, and Acheson *did* take it upon himself to make such a decision (not to mention many others) on his own. This statement is merely an index of Kennan's failure to understand his boss, and his declining fortunes in early 1950; he was simply not privy to Acheson's thinking. So what was Acheson's thinking?

ACHESON FOR THE DEFENSE

By 1950, as we have seen, national security elites had a palpable sense of the Soviets pressing against the entire containment perimeter, from Iran to Indochina to Taiwan to Korea; the rollback current wanted to reverse this momentum, along the same fault lines. For Acheson, who favored containment, the limits to American power meant one could not guarantee defense of all these places; moreover even if one intended it, telegraphing this to the Soviets would be the height of stupidity. At the same time, it would be absurd to exclude Japan or Germany from such a perimeter. Everyone knew the United States would defend them. The conflict would come in Paul Nitze's "soft spots," the regions of contingency.

Furthermore, Acheson had other fish to fry. If he had extended a clear guarantee to South Korea, the China Lobby would immediately have demanded similar inclusion for Taiwan. The rollback constituency in the United States, Taiwan, and the ROK would immediately have been emboldened. Furthermore the record is clear that Acheson purposely sought to leash Rhee while deterring the North; one does neither by declaring a defense regardless of Korean behavior. At the Acheson Seminars in 1954, he said that had the ROK been given a firm guarantee, "You would in effect have given South Korea such an underwriting that their whole conduct would have been quite different and it would have been very provocative and very belligerent."[52]

If Acheson needed any further reinforcement on both the volatile situation in Korea and Rhee's unreliability, his confidant Philip Jessup supplied it after he returned from his extensive tour of Asia in March 1950 (coming back early to face McCarthy's charges). Jessup told Acheson he found in Korea "a situation of actual war existing in many areas"; Korea had moved from cold war to "hot war." At the same time, Rhee's undemocratic policies, were "about as bad in this respect as anyone we have had to deal with." But, he added the formulaic caveat, obligatory since 1945: "there is no substitute for Rhee." During their talks in Seoul Rhee had told Jessup that the South "would have a much better strategic defense line if their forces moved into North Korea"; although Rhee assured him that he was not planning to "embark on a conquest," Jessup thought Rhee "has not objected when the southern forces along the thirty-eighth parallel have from time to time taken the initiative."[53]

It is just as clear, however, that Acheson thought the South Koreans would fight and the Chinese on Taiwan would not; this and the absence of a "nationalist" issue for Acheson made Korea very different from Taiwan. Acheson told David Bruce a few days before the last American troops left Korea in 1949, "the all-or-nothing boys refuse to do what is possible in Korea, because we will not attempt what is impossible in China." At an earlier point he responded to a query as to why, if containment were the policy, we did not back the Nationalists: "policy the same; incidences are different."[54]

In other words you did not expect effective containment from incontinence, the United States did not wish to fight losing battles and wallow in quagmires. The "incidences" in Korea were such that Truman Doctrine containment could work, and if it did not work because of a Soviet-sponsored attack, then the United States would have a direct responsibility to defend the South.

Acheson's intent was to construct a *defense*. In May 1950, he said, the United States should "maintain [its] position in [the] East and be careful not to lose there while building in West." He told Congress in 1951 that his January speech had been designed not to abandon Korea, but to call attention to the United Nations' responsibility for it, and to those vulnerable nations who "will stand up and fight for their own independence." A year before the war in a top secret telegram to Muccio, he had instructed him "to avoid any possibility [of] jeopardizing U.S. objective of replacing unilateral U.S. responsibility for future [of] Korea with international responsibility through UN." This was very similar to his view on how Taiwan could ultimately be kept "separated from the mainland." Elsewhere he remarked that the policy was "defense," not "liberation."[55] The defense was not just in Korea, but against *four* dangerous constituencies: North Korea, South Korea, Taiwan, and pro-Nationalist rollback advocates in the United States.

ACHESON FOR THE OFFENSE?

The Press Club speech, thus, stands up well as an invocation of collective security in an inherently ambiguous situation, and as a way of handling Acheson's many antagonists. But in August 1950 when Acheson came under Congressional attack for the speech, he chose to explain his "defense" in somewhat different terms. In handwritten notes, he anticipated that China Lobbyist Senator Wherry would say he gave a " 'green light' for aggression." First, he recalled "our plan of 1947" for Korea, when he applied containment, only to be rebuffed by Congress and the Pentagon. Then,

What we have had to do is to construct a defense with inadequate means, trying to guess where each play would come through the line. . . . The charge regarding Korea is that we should have known that the attack was coming; that we should have announced that we would meet it. As to the first, the task of an opposition is to oppose and perhaps it is doing its best *with a situation which it itself created.* In August it is easy to foresee [sic] what happened in June. But the problem was not in June to know that Korea held the potential of attack. It was to foretell which of many such potential sources of attack would be the one where it developed (emphasis added).

He went on to ask which Congressman was ready to send the tanks, planes, and other materiel necessary for defense to the ROK, the Philippines, Greece, Turkey, Iran, and the like.[56]

Acheson is the linebacker and he knows they may come around the end, or throw a pass, or come off tackle. A properly constructed defense encourages the offense to choose one instead of another option; it creates a field of force that constrains enemy decision. It is interesting that the U.S. general war plan at this time was named "Offtackle." More noteworthy is Richard Nixon's rendering of Acheson's logic; he chose a metaphor from his favorite game, poker: "the North Koreans thought our intentions were face up on the board. . . . It [June 25] was a miscalculation by them, based upon a misrepresentation by us."[57]

Was Acheson saying that the best offense is a good defense? The speech, it will be remembered, came right after a big brouhaha over his Taiwan policies. Yet it paid no attention to his domestic critics, while potentially raising another charge against him: abandonment of South Korea. If, however, it were aimed at Stalin and the North Koreans, designed to keep them guessing, the ambiguity both in the speech and in its reception would be salutary. Indeed it worked almost perfectly, Acheson saying the ROK was out of a direct defense line and the *Times* saying it was in—if the intent were ambiguity.

But in early May Senator Tom Connally short-circuited Acheson's studied ambiguity. The Senate Foreign Relations Committee chairman gave an interview to *U.S. News and World Report* where he bluntly excluded South Korea, the magazine running a big map on May 5 to make the point perfectly clear. During the interview Senator Connally was asked if we would "abandon Korea." And he responded, "I'm afraid it's going to happen, whether we want it or not. I'm for Korea. We're trying to help her . . . [but Russia] can just overrun Korea just like she probably will overrun Formosa." But, the interviewer asked, "isn't Korea an essential part of the defense strategy?" Connally's answer: "No. Of course, any position like that is of some strategic importance. But I don't think it is very greatly important."[58]

U.S. News has often been used to place important leaks. But its May 5 issue was not seeking to depict an American retreat, or failure to stand up to the communists. Instead it might be called its NSC 68 issue. It carried a big article entitled, " 'Cold War' Crisis: Gunfire Next?", saying "it's the spring offensive," the cold war is warming up, moving toward "a new crisis." It will not mean World War III, the magazine averred, because the Soviets are not ready to fight. But it will mean "gunfire." If Korea were to be the place, it said, "military advisors from U.S. would be involved, but troops were not likely to be sent." The "Worldgram" in the same issue related that "Western officials look for a succession of crises"; "maybe Korea, or Indo-China, almost certainly Formosa." (Some weeks later its "Whispers" column noted that Acheson "enjoys a freer and freer hand in guiding this country's course in the world"; Truman "seldom interferes.")

Connally's remarks, and the articles in *U.S. News*, are not easy to figure. On the one hand were the palpable jitters about some sort of conflict breaking out, with Korea mentioned twice. On the other, he bluntly excluded a defense of Seoul. Connally was not a foreign policy official, but he was influential. Perhaps he represented established policy, or perhaps not; perhaps he just failed to grasp the distinction between defending the ROK in a general war, as opposed to a limited attack.

Acheson's reaction was more definite: the next day, he publicly refused to correct Connally's statement. He does not mention this episode at all in his memoirs, although he does praise and run pictures of Connally, "a staunch supporter" and bipartisan stalwart.[59] The reaction in Korea was panicky. South Korean newspapers headlined the interview for several days, and the embassy found it very damaging. Rhee told Drumwright it was an "open invitation to [the] Commies to come down." Most important, Muccio cabled back to ask why such statements were being made, since they clearly did not represent American policy.[60]

Now, Connally had another mouthful to disgorge in the interview, which most observers have overlooked. Speaking of policy makers in Washington, he said, "A lot of them believe this: They believe that events will transpire which *will maneuver around and present an incident which will make us fight.* That's what a lot of them are saying: 'We've got to battle sometime, why not now?' " (emphasis added). The senator was an experienced Washington hand. He was called to the White House on the evening of December 7, 1941, where he asked FDR, "How did they catch us with our pants down, Mr. President?"[61]

There is a beguiling subject that Americans do not find it comfortable to talk about: we might call it the American way of going to war. The pattern is to let (or make) the other guy jump first. The hand palsies just to write about it, sensing that critics are poised to wheel their guns in your direction, and in the face of the popular belief that America minds its own business, only going to war under outrageous provocation. Chou En-lai once said that the first principle of Mao's method for dealing with the enemy was, "control others by letting them have the initiative."[62] The Chinese have a long tradition of hegemonic statecraft. Leaving the initiative in the hands of the enemy is effective if you are stronger, and especially if you have (or think you have) a democratic polity that cannot be reasoned with, but needs to be stampeded. It is much more a second-rank or rising power that finds a surprise attack to be in its interests (rarely if ever would a tenth-rate stooge try it). Such behavior is also the way of the aristocrat, and passive-aggressive personalities: never indulge in messy and bossy interventions, but structure a situation so that a person does what you wish them to, without having to be told. Remote control, as it were.

Revisionist historians have attempted to show that every war since Polk went into Mexico began with some inveigling or maneuvering of the enemy. Charles Callan Tansill thought Lincoln tricked the South into bombarding Fort Sumter, the sinking of the Maine is still an issue, the role of arms merchants in World War I was the subject of Congressional inquiry, and some assert a purposeful sabotage of the Lusitania. The Tonkin Gulf incident in 1964 is another case in point. McGeorge Bundy, his brother William married to Acheson's daughter, gave us an example that perhaps shows familial learning: when a company of Viet Cong soldiers attacked an American base at Pleiku in February 1965, it precipitated a rapid escalation of the war, inaugurating the first phase of the bombing of North Vietnam. Bundy remarked that "Pleikus are streetcars," that is (in George Kahin's words), "you could expect one to come along presently, and you were ready to board it as soon as it did." During the 1980s the Reagan administration tried one provocation after another to get Qaddafi or the Sandinistas to provide an excuse for retaliation. These things happen; they are not concoctions of conspiracy theorists.[63]

The important and relevant case for Korea, however, is Pearl Harbor—as Matthew Ridgway immediately knew when an interviewer asked him to comment on the "revisionist" theory that Acheson and Truman were really "trying to tease the North Koreans to invade." He responded, "there's no scintilla of evidence known to me which would support that theory any more than there is that Franklin Roosevelt deliberately precipitated the Pearl Harbor crisis."[64]

Acheson was a student of Henry Stimson's policies (as was McGeorge Bundy).[65] About ten days before Pearl Harbor, Stimson entered in his diary a famous and much-argued statement—that he had met with Roosevelt to discuss the evidence of impending hostilities with Japan, and the question was "how we should maneuver them [the Japanese] into the position of firing the first shot without allowing too much danger to ourselves." Charles Beard quoted this in his Pearl Harbor book, and cited another statement by Forrest Davis and Ernest Lindley:

> The question perplexing high officials was how, in the absence of a direct Japanese attack on the American flag, to summon the nation, divided as it then was on questions of foreign policy, to the strong action which they believed essential. . . . It was commonly supposed that the Japanese were too smart to solve this problem for the President by a direct assault on the American flag.

Beard also cited Stimson's testimony before Congress in 1946, saying that it is dangerous to "wait until [the enemy] gets the jump on you by taking the initiative." Nonetheless,

> in letting the Japanese fire the first shot, we realized that in order to have the full support of the American people it was desirable to make sure that the Japanese be the ones to do this so that there should remain no doubt in anyone's mind as to who were the aggressors.
>
> It is axiomatic that the best defense is offense. It is always dangerous to wait and let the enemy make the first move. . . . On the other hand, I realized that the situation could be made more clean cut from the point of view of public opinion if a further warning [to the Japanese] were given.[66]

In 1941 Acheson saw himself turning the screws on Japan. In 1950, was Acheson "maneuvering the North Koreans"? We know that in spite of his goal "carefully [to] conceal" the American desire to detach Taiwan from the mainland, he said several times in 1950 that the United States would not come to Taiwan's defense. In late March 1950 he discussed with Christian Herter what he saw as the deteriorating American position in the balance of power in the past "six to nine months," and his sense that the American people would have to make "certain sacrifices in order to meet the problem of Soviet aggression." Herter then said the United States should do something to show Americans the gravity of the situation, to which Acheson responded that it was not necessary to do anything but wait: "the chances are too good that the Russians will do so themselves." (In this context, Acheson referred to the possibility of an attack on Taiwan.)[67]

In July 1950, after the war began, Louis Johnson suggested to Acheson that the United States should loosen controls on Chiang Kai-shek so he could pursue a more "active" defense of Taiwan. Acheson wrote back that he opposed unleashing Chiang:

If the enemy is clearly and unequivocally branded by our own and world opinion as an aggressor, the political and military advantages are obvious. Similarly, it seems to me that we should take considerable military risks rather than place ourselves in the role of an aggressor by launching an attack on our own initiative, unless there are overwhelming considerations of national security involved.[68]

In the light of what we now know, Acheson's testimony to the MacArthur Hearings in 1951 is most interesting. When told that General Roberts had said the South Koreans were not fully armed because some feared they might attack the North, Acheson said blandly, "I had not heard that idea." Then when Senator Byrd said, "leaving there an untrained and poorly equipped Army was simply an invitation for an attack," Acheson said, "You may be right about that."[69] *You may be right about that.* Here is the man who refused heavy offensive equipment to the South saying "he had never heard about that," then agreeing that a weak, exposed Army may be "an invitation for an attack." This sort of performance must have been in Acheson's memory when he said of his appearances before Congress, "I used to tell them lots, but never the whole truth"; after all, Congress "can be troublesome and do minor damage like boys in an apple orchard."[70]

Later in his testimony he called attention to Dulles's June 19, 1950, speech in Seoul, quoting his comment that despotism "has resumed the offensive," and saying that the United States had responded twice before to "unprovoked military aggression," even though "we were not bound by any treaty to do this."[71]

Acheson did not have to rally a mostly isolationist nation in 1950, but he did have to find a way to get Congress and the American people to support, for the first time in their history, a permanent global role, a national security state, and the enormous increases in spending for both envisioned in NSC 68. Let us look at his private account once again. "What we have had to do is to construct a defense with inadequate means, trying to guess where each play would come through the line . . . the task of an opposition is to oppose and perhaps it is doing its best with a situation which it itself created." A defense that encouraged an attack on an exposed position solved this problem—unless it was Taiwan, which would only hearten Acheson's bureaucratic and political enemies and lead to reliance again on the Nationalists. An attack in Korea would be different, and meeting it would defend something important (Japan), defuse opposition pressures on the administration, and rally support for NSC 68. So, one needed a particular exposed position. One proffers a menu of choices to the communists, and encourages a choice that would be preferable from the American standpoint.

Korea is like Pearl Harbor in another way: even a lifetime of research would not prove definitively that Roosevelt was either guilty or innocent of "maneuvering the Japanese," and the same is true of Acheson and Korea. We do not have signals intelligence that would suggest American advance knowledge of North Korean action, a major lacuna that we do have for Pearl Harbor. Anyway, if Acheson thought he was maneuvering Stalin or Kim Il Sung, it is the sort of thing a statesman rarely admits to, or commits to the documentary record. It goes with him to the grave, along with his language "intended to cloak ideas," his "inarticulate major premise" that whether or not there was a policy, there was "a state of affairs." So, this is not history, but an absorbing sort of speculation given license by Acheson's 1941 modus operandi and his own words about "the speech."

The important thing we have sought to bring forth is an interpretation of the Korea portion of Acheson's "speech" that refutes naiveté, indecision, or inexperience, and that sees him doing more than creating a passive, flawed, and ill-considered defense in Asia. His idea was that the best offense is a well-constructed defense. This was shrewd containment, but it was still containment, resting on the premise that if positive action were the order of the day in 1950, it was better if the communists acted first.

We may leave this controversy with one last speculation: what if the enemy is not "stupid," as Stimson said of the Japanese and Acheson said of the Soviets in retrospect? What if the purported quarterback of the offense is actually on the defense, too, and unlike the Japanese does not want war? In other words what if he is Stalin, whose cynical and shrewd diplomacy trumped Churchill and Roosevelt frequently during the Second World War? What if he has a similar policy toward those regions of contingency in the East-West struggle: support them, if they can fight and if Soviet interests are not hurt; abandon them (e.g., the Greek guerrillas) if it is the opposite; but in any case leave a realm of ambiguity that does not commit Soviet might and prestige. And then, make a mess here, make a mess there (Korea, Indochina) and hope that the Americans will be sucked in to hemmorhage blood and treasure in three decades of "stupid" wars?

More Speeches: Total Diplomacy and the Commitment to Indochina

"The speech" was Acheson's way of making public part of the new Asia policy called for in NSC 48, and its major goal was to sow conflict between Moscow and Beijing. The Korea portion, or what Acheson said about it in retrospect, is important to us for grasping his conception of containment, but it had little impact at the time. Only later did it get attention, as Republicans constructed a flawed historical verdict as an artifact of party politics. In February and March 1950, Acheson made more speeches, this time seeking to make public aspects of NSC 68. These got extraordinary attention at the time, far more than the Press Club speech, but have been forgotten in the wake of another flawed historical verdict: that the Korean War was the turning point in applying containment to Asia.

On February 16, 1950, Acheson spoke "off the record" to a meeting of the Advertising Council at the White House, calling for "total diplomacy" against the Soviets, his code word for the NSC 68 program, and pleading for the support of the American public. "We must be prepared to meet wherever possible all thrusts of the Soviet Union," he said; this remark filtered out to the press—as clear a warning to, say, the North Koreans as a statesman could give. Much like the earlier speech, Acheson vented his ideas through our newspaper of record, James Reston's lips moving but Dean Acheson speaking. On February 19, Reston wrote that the new State Department goal was "to organize a joint economic and security policy from Alexandria to Tokyo; to maintain at all times, as a deterrent to Soviet aggression the power of swift and terrible retaliation." That is, a great crescent uniting power and plenty, and the oil of the Middle East with the industrial base in Japan.

Soon the *Times* was calling this "the Acheson Doctrine," an extension of the Truman Doctrine, which, the editors noted, "was enunciated long after the cold war had started." In other words, "total diplomacy" was a policy to deal with events already thought to be under way. If the first phase of the struggle was in Europe, the second phase was in Asia: Acheson saw "the big weakness" in the Western position in Asia, and hoped to "strengthen lands on the southern rim of China."[72]

Acheson went public with "total diplomacy" in his March 15 address to the Commonwealth Club in San Francisco, likened by the *London Times* to the Marshall Plan speech. He dwelt for a time on the reasons for Asian revolution and its desires for national independence, saying that America's goals were identical. In China, however, this revolution had gone to the Communists "by default." Its rulers would "bring grave trouble on themselves and their friends" if they were to allow Moscow "to lead them into aggressive or subversive adventures beyond their borders," or if China were used "as a base for probing for other weak spots." And then he underlined the point: "I say this so that there may be no mistake about the attitude of the United States."

Reston chimed in with a column the next day, linking the Commonwealth address to the Press Club speech—and continuing to misinterpret it just as the *Times* had in January: Acheson had said at the Press Club, Reston wrote, that Japan *and Korea* were where "the U.S. had direct responsibilities to defend those areas, and was in a position to do so," but he had cited Southeast Asia as a place where "the direct responsibility . . . lay with many other peoples." Now, however, the emphasis was shifting; Washington was planning to do "whatever it can to discourage [the Communists] from trying to make a grab, directly or indirectly, for the rich rice-producing areas of Southeast Asia." Therefore, Acheson "directly warned the Chinese."[73]

This is fascinating. Perhaps Reston knew that Acheson privately backed containment in Korea, or perhaps he just read old issues of the *Times* and got the speech wrong. In any case he had Southeast Asia in Korea's position within Achesonian deterrence, then he goes on to say that this is changing, with direct attention to containment south of China's borders. Since, as we will see, the North Koreans were still poring over Acheson's words, they must have again scratched their heads about whatever it was Acheson had said in January.

On March 16 Acheson spoke at the University of California in Berkeley, saying that "total diplomacy" did not mean war, but peace—if the other side were to accept seven points: his very first called for a Soviet gesture, such as allowing the UN Commission on Korea (UNCOK) to enter North Korea. (This was two weeks after Rhee's March 1 speech, where he called for an attack on the North with UNCOK officials on the podium). Other points called for free elections in communist countries, an end to obstructionism in the UN, an end to subversion, and so on; Acheson was asking the Soviets to accept Washington's policies on a world scale, and then there would be peace. Meanwhile, internal documents made clear that Washington did *not* want a negotiation in the spring of 1950, for fear it would weaken the momentum for NSC 68.[74]

The *Times* editorialized that the Berkeley speech laid special emphasis on "final settlements with Austria and Korea," but noted that Acheson had in effect asked Moscow to give up on communism. When Acheson returned to Washington the two addresses were termed the most important of his tenure, and the Moscow embassy said no recent pronouncement had made a bigger impression on the Soviets.[75]

The North Koreans also paid close attention, the party newspaper admitting that they "could not but agree" with Acheson's points on Asian revolution and the demand for national independence: "If we only listen to his words, we would think that the Philippines . . . South Korea, Indonesia, and such countries, had already achieved national independence . . . Acheson talks loudly about national independence, but his policy is to destroy it." The answer to "total diplomacy," they said, was to deepen the movement for national liberation.[76]

Public evidence now underlined the dialectic between containment and rollback that was explicit in NSC 68 and "total diplomacy." Reston wrote that the speeches on the coast signaled an abandonment of the "caution" of the Press Club address, and an application of the Truman Doctrine to Southeast Asia. In another article Reston said that Acheson had created a "strategy committee" led by Nitze, to coordinate all aspects of American policy. Officials now realized that "operations must be conducted simultaneously, aggressively and consistently in all areas at once, and that a positive and more forceful strategy must be devised by the West if it is to regain the initiative in the 'cold war.' " Truman told the Federal Bar Association on April 24 that "the example we set for free men everywhere will help to roll back the tide of Communist imperialism in other parts of the world."[77] It appears, however, that Acheson and Truman were playing Dulles (who had just joined the administration): that is, wrapping the substance of containment in the rhetoric of rollback.

Few at the time caught the shifting dynamics of American global policy, but the reclusive iconoclast Scott Nearing got it right when he wrote that it was not the Soviets, but the Americans who were launching "a spring offensive"—"the most spectacular result [of which] was the decision to win the war in Indochina."[78] Nearing was correct: at the time of the "total diplomacy" speeches, Acheson recommended immediate military aid to the French in Indochina, "to help contain this pseudo-nationalist form of invasion" (that is, Ho Chi Minh's Democratic Republic of Vietnam and the Vietminh, presumably invading their own country); the aid started flowing in early May, well before the Korean War. The *Times* ran banner headlines when this was announced, terming it an application of containment to Southeast Asia, whether the American people knew it or not. The North Koreans also marked well this new departure in American strategy, linking it to "total diplomacy." The United States they said, wanted first to help France, second to grab its colonies, and above all to suppress the national liberation movement in Asia.[79]

Acheson remarked in May that the United States and France were agreed on the strategic importance of Indochina, and on the domino theory: "if [Indochina] goes, Southeast Asia goes." Momentarily overcome by this newfound American support, the French ambassador to England sought a joint statement on Indochina by "the three colonial powers": France, the United Kingdom, and the United States.[80]

Chapter Fourteen

NORTH KOREA ON
THE EVE OF THE WAR

There has been a great, historic change today in the international environment surrounding Korea from what it was forty years ago, when U.S. imperialism and Japan colluded to subjugate weak Korea . . . the Korean people have waked up and have united. After suffering thirty-six years under Japanese imperialism, they do not again plan to be slaves under another name.

Nodong sinmun, *January 19, 1950*

The Japanese since the time of Hideyoshi have called Korea the dagger pointed at Japan's heart. An abrupt American withdrawal [from Korea] . . . would mean the collapse of the free Korean state and the passage of the dagger once more into Russian hands. . . . What it comes down to is that if Japan is to be defended all of Japan has to be a base, militarily and economically.

New York Times *editorial, May 27, 1950*

O N THE SURFACE, North Korea in early 1950 seemed to be going about the business of economic development, with more emphasis perhaps on a military buildup than in 1948, but not much to distinguish this fateful year from the previous one. Kim Il Sung's New Year's address, an annual ritual something like a State of the Union message, was full of rhetoric about fulfilling the second two-year economic plan. In discussing four "foundations" for the Democratic People's Republic of Korea (DPRK)—political, economic, military and cultural—he placed the military first among those things to be strengthened in the coming year. The Rhee forces, he said were "openly colluding with the irreconcilable enemy of our nation, the Japanese imperialists, and openly intending to foment a fratricidal civil war." The people in the North, "more than at any [previous] time," must be vigilant in preparing themselves for anything the South might attempt; the Army "must always be ready" should "the enemy come."

He called for peaceful unification, and ended by saying, "as we greet the New Year in 1950, let us go forward to a new victory in uniting the homeland."[1] Read in a vacuum, the speech might seem bellicose. Examined in the context of his 1949 address—or indeed the sort of rhetoric that the North Koreans pour forth in the 1980s, about war breaking out "at any minute"—it was relatively mild.

Rumors circulated that Kim made a trip to the USSR around this time, either to help celebrate Stalin's seventieth birthday in December, or to meet with Stalin in January while Mao and Chou En-lai were in Moscow.[2] Except for one appearance at a *Chŏndog g'yo* gathering, he vanishes from the party newspaper during January, except for messages that could have been scripted by aides. It is possible that this is the meeting Khrushchev refers to in his memoirs, although it must be said that John Merrill's assiduous research has cast serious doubt on this source—which had enough problems before Merrill found out that many concise, declarative statements in the published memoirs are vague and indistinct in the original Russian.[3]

Other articles in January spoke of the socialist bloc being impregnable, as we have seen, and made vicious attacks on the Rhee regime, saying that some 149,000 of "our fine sons and daughters" had been slaughtered by this "clique"—which was now rejected by Left, Center, and Right in the South, given that Rhee had arranged the murder of Kim Ku. An account of the growth of the Korean People's Army (KPA) placed emphasis on the border fighting along the parallel, and said "homeland defense support committees" were sprouting up to gather money for the purchase of tanks, planes, and naval ships. "In the not distant days ahead," one article concluded, "the country-selling criminals, to be cursed for a thousand years, will be swept away," and finally Korea will be unified.[4] Still, this was not different in kind from earlier rhetoric.

For every bellicose article pledging to wipe out the Rhee clique, one could find two or three about raising production and fulfilling economic targets. The second session of the Supreme People's Assembly opened in late February, and much of the time was taken up with extended discussions of meeting the targets of the second two-year plan, if possible by the fifth anniversary of liberation in August, that is, ahead of schedule. A "construction battle" (*kŏnsŏl t'ujaeng*) was promoted widely in March and continued through June, with campaigns to raise money through bond drives both for the economy and the military. China was doing much the same thing in this period. The targets for the first year of the second two-year plan were completed in April 1950, well ahead of schedule.[5]

In the early months of 1950, one could sense a heightened emphasis on revolution, both at home and abroad: "Today, both internationally and domestically the struggle between democracy and reaction is becoming more and more acute, and the provocative methods of our class enemy are appearing in different types and forms." Yet in the spring of 1950 communist regimes on a world scale heated up the ideological struggle in response to the deepening Cold War and the sense of crisis in American circles, and North Korean rhetoric reflected this emphasis. At the end of March the party journal stressed the necessity to strengthen "military, political, and economic power," a reversal of priorities from 1948, perhaps, but not from the spring of 1949. It referred to "an intense class struggle" in Korea, yet also referred to cases of "spies" and "wreckers" in Bulgaria and Hungary, suggesting that the article was following the Kremlin line. It ended with hortatory calls to "overfulfill" the two-year plan.[6]

In late May Hong Nam-p'yo, a prominent southerner with close ties to Kim Il Sung, exemplified in his speech the curious formula for unification in this period: it was to be "peaceful unification"—through the guerrilla struggle in the South. A violent undermining of the Rhee regime would open the way to nonviolent reconciliation, or so this logic would suggest. Thus, he ended his speech by saying the Rhee clique would be swept away and peaceful unification would be accomplished "in the near future" (*kakkaun ap'nal*): but by the South Korean people, not the Korean People's Army.[7]

The North Koreans thus spoke about liberating the South in "the near future," emphasized the military and the class struggle, and called 1950 a year of decision. Yet if one were to take this as a harbinger of their intentions to attack the South, what is one to say about nearly identical rhetoric in China about liberating Taiwan? People's Republic of China (PRC) propaganda in the spring of 1950 was a mirror image of that of the Democratic People's Republic of Korea (DPRK), saying Chiang was on his last legs and therefore running amok, slaughtering "patriots"; the People's Liberation Army (PLA) was just like the KPA, it would seem, a "100 battles—100 victories" army, ready to move on a moment's notice; "the great task" for 1950 was "the liberation of Taiwan."[8] In mid-April there were rumors that Kim Il Sung and Pak Hŏn-yŏng were in China—but doing what? Preparing a war or celebrating Kim's thirty-eighth birthday?[9] (Kim was born April 15, 1912, the day the Titanic capsized.)

The ballast of meaning in the tons of propaganda emanating from P'yŏngyang and Beijing in the spring of 1950 was, nonetheless, weighted toward economic development and production. An important internal party document in mid-May placed both theoretical and practical emphasis on strengthening the material foundation of the North, citing Marx on the relationship between base and superstructure. Fundamental industrial development was necessary, "to build a rich and strong state that can guarantee our nation's independence (chajusŏng)." The "sacred duty" of party workers was to foster the economic base and surpass the targets of the two-year plan.[10]

We have cited this document earlier. Its emphasis was really on escaping Soviet domination rather than subduing the South. This could not be stated, but was implied over and over in the emphasis on *chajusŏng*. The document lauded the Soviets for their "friendly aid," while bracketing that with "the struggle of the people tightly united around Kim Il Sung" as the two essential reasons for DPRK successes. Long-term plans and the effective organization of economic development were "a means of guaranteeing the *chajusŏng* of a democratic state's economy and ensuring that it does not become subordinated (*yesŏk*) to a foreign economy."

The use of "foreign" rather than "imperialist" was precisely the kind of language that would cause an immediate narrowing of Soviet eyes, down to a tiny squint in the case of Koreans whom the Soviets knew to be inveterate nationalists. And if that were not enough, the document bluntly stated that the regime has been acting on such principles since 1949, that is, since Soviet troops were withdrawn. Thus it is clear that the "new environment" and "new conditions" and "new work methods" in the title refer to the period 1949–1950; Kim was quoted many times, saying things like Korea's economy must go forward using domestic resources exclusively, only such means will "guarantee the *chajusŏng* of our national economy." Like the months-long flurry of pro-China–model articles in 1947, this one used Chinese terminology like "rectification of work styles" [*saŏp pangsikŭl kaejo*]. Kim Il Sung was coming out of the closet again, as a communist far more influenced by China than by the Soviet Union, but ultimately a Korean revolutionary nationalist determined to have the Hermit Kingdom back again, Korea for the Koreans. Not a word about an impending unification can be found in this document.

Another indication of North Korean intentions up to May 1950 would perhaps strike the reader as farfetched, unless one knows how the regime operates. Invitations to noncommunist American visitors are treated with high priority, and always reflect the regime's estimate of whether relations with the United States are getting better or worse. In late 1949 Walter Sullivan, a *New York Times* correspondent whose fine, well-informed reporting on South Korea surpassed that of any journalist in the period, was told by a South Korean who must still remain nameless that the North might allow him to visit. In February 1950 Sullivan sent three letters to P'yŏngyang through a Korean courier, requesting a visit. His model was to be Edgar Snow's reporting from Yanan, he told the North Koreans, and therefore he wanted to be very thorough, spend several months, get Kim Il Sung's biography, and the like.

To his surprise, within one week he got a positive response from a high official in the the Interior Ministry. In March various discussions occurred through intermediaries on the arrangements and conditions of the visit. In early April Sullivan went off to Hong Kong; from there, Chinese traders with good contacts in Beijing were to arrange his passage to North Korea on a Soviet freighter.

On May 12, a Mr. Li from Canton said he would soon have the final arrangements ready, and on May 16 a letter from the Korean intermediary told him not to get discouraged. In early June, however, Mr. Li went off to Beijing for several months. On June 20 Sullivan cabled the Interior Ministry in P'yŏngyang, saying he needed final confirmation of the visit in order to get passage on a Soviet freighter scheduled to leave in a few days. Sullivan got no response, and was still in Hong Kong when the war began.

British intelligence knew about the planned trip, it turned out, even though Sullivan understood from the beginning that the South Koreans "would pull out all the stops" to keep him from going, and therefore treated the matter with great secrecy. Rumors that he would be "assassinated" if he tried to go might suggest that Seoul knew about it as well. This could account for the failure of the attempt. But the timing is also noteworthy, suggesting that the North Koreans were still interested in a months-long visit as late as mid-May, but not in June.[11]

SOVIET INFLUENCE IN THE DPRK IN 1950

The CIA's last summary report on the DPRK before the war started began with the following statement: "The 'Democratic People's Republic' of northern Korea is a firmly controlled Soviet Satellite that exercises no independent initiative and depends entirely on the support of the USSR for existence." It estimated that the KPA was "entirely the product of Soviet planning," and that some two thousand Soviet advisors filtered throughout the ranks of the KPA.[12] This was by no means an isolated judgment, but represented the thinking of almost all American agencies before June 1950. The Seoul embassy said in May 1950 that "Soviet power now blankets North Korea completely." In retrospective studies, the CIA maintained this position, asserting that the Soviets created "a strong indigenous regime responsive to Soviet control," continuing to manipulate Korean affairs after their troops withdrew through "covert control." Although they sponsored "the development of a strong national military establishment," they controlled this through the ubiquitous advisors. The KPA was said to be a virtual carbon copy of the Soviet Army.[13] To the extent that such judgments are valid, it is impossible to imagine the Koreans marching on Seoul in June 1950 without Soviet support and direction.

Other intelligence sources found a different picture, suggesting a far smaller Soviet effort than, say, Nicaragua in the 1980s or, proportionally speaking, China in 1950, and far smaller than the American presence in the South. The same sources that asserted total Soviet dominance would also link this to traditional Russian needs for a warm water port on the

Korean peninsula—which the Soviets never got.[14] Unlike the Americans, the Soviets also appear to have relinquished control of North Korean airports when their troops left. Those captured Russian documents that have thus far been declassified are quite mundane, mostly of a commercial nature. One made reference, however, to a certain "M" unit, saying that Soviet advisors "must not discuss among themselves personnel of 'M' unit or other problems" in the presence of Koreans, and refers to security problems with Korean technicians who had formerly served the Japanese. The CIA also seemed to suggest that Soviet agents dogged Kim Il Sung's heels, less to give him orders than to keep watch on his activities. None of this would be surprising; the Americans kept all top secret materials from Korean nationals, and paid extraordinary attention to the activities of Syngman Rhee, even mobilizing his wife to watch over him.[15]

There is surprisingly little evidence of a Soviet presence in the reams of captured North Korean documents. We can observe the presence of certain important Soviets, like Mikhail Ignatiev, who turned out to see off the new Korean ambassador to China in January 1950, or Terentii Shtykov, who was gone at the same time Kim Il Sung was, probably to China, in April 1950. Public statements by Korean leaders just before the war laud the Soviets for liberating Korea in typically slavish fashion, yet refer only to cultural and economic aid. In March 1950 Hŏ Hŏn said some five hundred Korean students were studying in the USSR, mentioned Soviet teachers and textbooks in DPRK schools, and "large-scale" aid to develop "an independent, national economy." Otherwise, when Soviet troops withdrew, the Soviets left the resolution of the problems of the peninsula "to the Koreans themselves."[16]

As for the numbers of Soviet military advisors, they seem quite low—much lower than the CIA's figure of two thousand. The South Korean Defense Minister put the total at only 120 before the war, which accords with intelligence estimates after the war began, saying the Soviets used "approximately fifteen advisory officers per NK division," there being less than ten divisions before June 1950. There were only fifteen Soviet advisors to the Korean Air Force. Advisors went down to the battalion level, the Americans liked to say, something that sounds impressive. But there were three regiments to each division, and three battalions to each regiment. If the total number were around 120, fifteen per division, then a battalion would have only one or two Soviet advisors.[17]

This evidence suggests that if the Soviets could "firmly control" and even "blanket" North Korea with a few hundred advisors, and just 120 for a KPA of one hundred thousand soldiers, we should all, including the CIA, study their techniques—not to mention explaining why the Soviets needed the maintenance of tens of thousands of troops in several Eastern European countries. Soviet interest in China was far greater, with thousands of advisors of all types visible in major cities by the spring of 1950, leading Americans evacuated from China to say that the Soviets have "invaded" all fields of endeavor, the PRC having "sold out to Russia lock, stock, and barrel."[18] Yet even that high apparent level of Soviet influence masked sharp Sino-Soviet differences, and considerable Chinese autonomy compared to East Europe.

Perhaps even more unlikely is the proposition that the Soviets could have ordered the North Koreans into a war that the North itself did not want, or that they would have launched a war with such apparently flimsy controls in the DPRK. The truth of the situation was much closer to the intelligence judgment Senator Smith heard when he journeyed to Tokyo and Seoul in late 1949: he was "advised that Russia has declined to help North Korea at the present time, on the theory that she does not want to use a relatively minor issue like Korea as the possible start of World War III."[19]

SOVIET MILITARY DELIVERIES TO THE NORTH

The literature on the Korean War assumes that the Soviets fully equipped the KPA, and made heavy shipments of tanks, planes, artillery, and other equipment in the spring months of 1950, precisely oriented toward what was presumably to come at the end of June. Meanwhile the Americans in their haphazard and ill-thought policies failed to equip the South with comparable equipment. This is usually considered to be the one irrefutable testimony to Soviet designs, to American benign intentions, as well as the cardinal explanation for the collapse of the southern army in the early days of the fighting.

Military historian Roy Appleman depicted the KPA as fully Russian-equipped, the Soviets making "particularly large shipments of arms and military supplies" in the spring of 1950. The CIA said the KPA was fitted out "almost entirely with Soviet equipment prior to the invasion," with heavy shipments of military vehicles in the first months of 1950, running at the rate of 150 or so per month.[20]

No full account of this and many other matters is possible without a collation of a variety of estimates and judgments. In spite of its bulk and general reliability, Appleman's account rested heavily on Colonel Willoughby's ATIS reports, military intelligence estimates, and internal studies by military historians that were heavily biased by the cold war.[21] The CIA, furthermore, rarely spoke with one voice in its reports. A perusal of several streams of intelligence on Soviet deliveries presents a different picture.

Within weeks of the opening of the fighting in June, the CIA reported that KPA equipment "appears to have been obsolete or obsolescent Soviet discards." Hanson Baldwin, with good intelligence contacts, reported at about the same time that the KPA had nothing beyond World War II vintage tanks, planes, and artillery.[22] The bulk of KPA equipment was turned over when Soviet forces left Korea. There were months of heavy delivery in 1949, just as there were in early 1950; heavily armed tank units were just north of the thirty-eighth parallel by October 1949, if not earlier. The Soviets also *sold* their weaponry to the North, before and through much of the war; they even exacted payment for the large stocks of equipment they left behind in 1948. Military historians later concluded that the Soviets had been reluctant to equip the North with their newer weaponry, even during the worst periods of the war, let alone before the war. The new Stalin tank, the heavy 152mm howitzer, and other advanced weaponry were never supplied, which "lessened the effectiveness of the North Korean enemy immeasurably." Artillery was a great weakness of the KPA against the Americans, yet "the USSR consistently abstained from supplying the NKPA with any of its excellent corps . . . or heavy artillery."[23]

One glaring difference between the South and North was in air capability, the North having propeller-driven fighters and light bombers. British intelligence thought the Soviets agreed to supply upwards of 150 "close support aircraft" to North Korea in secret agreements concluded at the time of the public cultural and trade agreements in March 1949. However, a detailed intelligence report on the northern air force, with information verifiable in other sources, said that when the Soviets departed in 1948 they left to the North ninety-three airplanes: forty YAK 9o trainers, fifteen YAK Ps, thirty IL-10 ground attack planes, and eight reconnaissance planes. In July 1949 another twenty-two YAK trainers were delivered. On April 15, 1950, Soviet pilots flew in fifteen more YAK Ps, eight YAK 11s, and forty more IL-10s. This is completely believable, since April 15 was Kim's birthday.[24]

All of these planes were of pre-1945 vintage, with no jet aircraft such as the Soviets delivered to the Chinese in the spring of 1950. The most numerous aircraft, the fearsome-sounding IL-10 ground attack bomber, was a single-engine prop plane, a bit bigger than a Piper Cub, capable of flying 195 miles per hour and carrying a bomb load of four 550 pound bombs and six 220 pound bombs.[25] Such planes were useful against the South alone, but the American Air Force destroyed the whole batch in a matter of days—and it was quite predictable that American airpower would join the South's battle.

Most interesting, perhaps, was the route for transferring military equipment. The great bulk of it came through Manchuria, with the remainder coming in through East coast ports. Given the high numbers of China veterans in the KPA, accounting for well over half of the total armed forces, it is likely that this "Soviet equipment" was actually World War II Soviet weaponry deployed in Manchuria against the Kwantung Army, and left behind for (more likely sold to) the PLA and the Northeast government of Kao Kang. Willoughby's intelligence reported heavy arms shipments from Manchuria to North Korea in April and May 1950, but coming in with several tens of thousands of Korean Chinese Communist Forces (CCF) veterans. This would also account for the presence of Japanese military equipment in the KPA, and American arms that had been captured from the Nationalists.[26] Was it the Soviets or the Chinese who were doing this? It is impossible to say; it was probably both.

The North was, therefore, by no means reliant solely on Soviet arms. The Japanese had arsenals in northern Korea, which gave the DPRK the capability to produce machine guns, mortar, and artillery shells; they manufactured a small tank-like car that was used to good effect in the early fighting; they had the technical capability to recondition obsolete Soviet and Japanese weapons, and to tailor the Japanese arsenals to provide ammunition for them. Volume production of machine guns of the PPSh type was begun in 1948, with up to seventy per day rolling off the lines. The North also made 120mm and 82mm mortars, gunpowder, and dynamite.[27]

Soviet arms shipments to the North consisted, then, of selling them obsolescent equipment, directly or through Chinese Communist auspices. The one exception would be the air force, which was obsolescent but which gave the North a distinct advantage over the South. The last shipments were birthday presents for Kim, just as were MIG-23s finally delivered to the DPRK in 1985, flown in by Soviet pilots on April 15. Was the reason the impending North Korean attack on the South? More likely it was for the same reason as in 1985: to compete with China for influence, by providing the Koreans with weapons the Chinese could not—at a time when thousands of China-linked veterans were streaming back to their homeland.

There is also no hard evidence that shipments were geared to an invasion in June 1950, as opposed to, say, October 1949 or for that matter any point in the summer of 1950 or thereafter. A detailed CIA report in September 1950 specifically examining Soviet weapons deliveries said that the major equipment of the KPA came from Soviet and Japanese World War II stockpiles; in 1950 "there has *probably* been a substantial flow of Soviet equipment" (emphasis added). However, and this is the critical point, "intelligence reports do not indicate a preinvasion stockpile of a magnitude required to support current operations," meaning the time when the KPA was pressing on the Pusan Perimeter.[28]

Charles Bohlen, in his memoirs, decried as "childish nonsense" the idea that the North Koreans might have started the war as an "independent act": "How could an army, trained in every respect by the Soviet Union, with Soviet advisors at every level, and utterly dependent on Moscow for supplies, move without Soviet authorization?"²⁹ What we have suggested above answers part of his question: the KPA was not trained just by the Soviets, Soviet advisors were not at every level, and the Koreans were by no means dependent only on Moscow for supplies. And why would the Soviets have authorized an attack? Bohlen's answer is itself nonsense: "I believe Stalin never dreamed the U.S. would intervene." If the Soviets "authorized" whatever happened on June 25, the rationale will have to be stronger than to suggest that Acheson duped Stalin.

WARNINGS OF NORTH KOREAN MILITARY ACTION

By June 1950, alarms about an invasion of the South were old hat, standard fare for intelligence officers. American intelligence sources first predicted a North Korean invasion in the spring of 1946, and available reports show many repetitions over the next four years, with no particular increase just before the war.

Gen. John R. Hodge had warned for years that the North Koreans would attack the South once American troops withdrew, and perhaps even before they left, leading to frequent invasion alerts during his tenure. John Muccio reported that American troops went on invasion alert six times between March 1 and August 25, 1948, and in October American intelligence sources drew up a two-page, single-spaced list of invasion threat reports received around the time of the Yŏsu Rebellion. Rumors and reports of imminent attack continued in November and December.³⁰

Throughout 1949 this situation persisted, particularly around times of intense border fighting. As we have seen, rumors of war were strong enough in September to send Preston Goodfellow scampering off to Seoul, although it was by no means clear whether this had to do with Northern instead of Southern threats. In February 1950, two G-2 reports cited invasion threats for May 1950 and another said it would come in June 1950; in March it was said that the ROK would be destroyed on July 14, 1950; and in early May the G-2 chief wrote, "the war of nerves is once more receiving its annual stimulant . . . reports during this period had the North Koreans invading South Korea on the 7th, 8th, and 9th of May. . . . Next reported invasion date is 12 May with a 'rain check' for the 20th of May."³¹ The weary tone was the best evidence that American intelligence officers thought the spring 1950 alarms were, as Yogi Berra once put it, "deja vu all over again."

Roberts said in March 1950 that invasion threats were far more numerous in 1948 and 1949 than in the previous six months, and that "[38th] parallel incidents had dropped off markedly." There was a quickening of border fighting in May and June 1950, with an average of about fifteen incidents per week from May 5 to June 16, but all of them were minor compared to the previous summer.³²

In the early months of 1950, Korean Military Advisory Group (KMAG) intelligence got frequent reports of the southward deployment of KPA troops and equipment. In January, it thought the KPA 2d Division headquarters displaced southward from Hamhŭng to Wŏnsan, along with an artillery regiment, and noted other indicators of southward movement of tanks and troop units. In February, it came to the conclusion that DPRK intelligence was deceiving ROK intelligence by reporting false southward troop movements; in March and April scattered evidence of southward deployments came in again, including reports of the arrival of more tanks at Chŏrwŏn, and then the materials grow thin, with little of note mentioned in May and June.³³

The evidence of southward deployment would seem to be the most significant sort of information, given that invasion alarms could easily be scare tactics by either P'yŏngyang or Seoul, whereas the new deployments enhanced invasion capabilities. Yet indications of southward deployment were if anything stronger in late 1949 than in the spring of 1950. There were many such reports in September, October, and November, combined with evidence of the receipt of Soviet heavy weapons through North Korean ports, and the movement of civilian families just north of the parallel, viewed by some as preparatory to an invasion (although it was standard Soviet procedure to clear civilians from tense borders). In late November 1949 half of the total number of tanks in the P'yŏngyang area were said to have been shipped to the vicinity of the parallel, one hundred tanks reportedly arrived in Chŏrwŏn a week later, another thirty-seven arrived in Pokkye from Wŏnsan the next week. In mid-December KMAG G-2 said that some three thousand soldiers thought to be in Hamhŭng were now near the parallel at Kaesŏng, and cited barracks construction to house thousands of new troops close to the border. KPA order of battle estimates were changed to reflect this southward deployment as early as September, 1949.³⁴

Once again, in other words, the events of previous years clearly shaped perceptions in 1950. Americans on the scene had lived with invasion threats since 1946; the South had "cried wolf" so many times that few bothered to listen; there was so much "noise" in five years of American intelligence reports in Korea that no one saw the war coming, or so it seems.³⁵ Furthermore, the battles in 1949 shaped immediate perceptions in 1950. War seemed so likely in the summer of 1949 that the intelligence evidence of 1950 paled by comparison; more important, in 1949 knowledgeable Americans knew that the South sought to provoke war, and therefore viewed North Korean threats and deployments *in that context,* finding them to be predictable, at times even understandable, defensive responses to southern activities.

Thus it was that both British and American intelligence estimated that an invasion would not come in the summer of 1950. A top secret British document said "it has always been our view that irrespective of [stated] strengths, the North Korean forces would have little difficulty in dealing effectively with the forces of South Korea should full scale hostilities break out," but the potential for bringing the ROK down from within was still so great that the North would probably not "resort to open aggression." Interestingly, the report said that whereas in the past Americans had disagreed about relative capabilities of the two sides, they were now "coming round to our way of thinking," that is, the North would sweep the ROKA away. The CIA noted one week before the war that the KPA had deployed new units, tanks, and artillery southward "in recent months," but argued that the North had far from exhausted the potential for internal war in the South.[36]

Yet the problem with all this intelligence is not really "noise" and "crying wolf"—which would suggest that the actual evidence of impending attack was ignored or dismissed. It is that even today the evidence of impending attack is simply not visible in the reams of intelligence reports and estimates now available. Post–Korean War KPA deployments have from time to time been far more threatening than in the period before June 1950. It may be that signals intelligence and electronic intercepts would show a different picture, but this is the one category of intelligence that the U.S. government has held back. The rest of the evidence of impending attack was as strong in the fall of 1949 as it was in the spring of 1950, but even then it was not strong enough to predict an attack, and of course none occurred anyway.

What the evidence does indicate is that the North had the capability to destroy the South by June 1949, not June 1950, and that it was on a virtual war footing from September 1949 onward, if not earlier. The result of the 1949 fighting underlined Northern capabilities, since they devastated ROKA units in the major battles. By the end of the year the North had placed near the parallel much of the men and equipment it would later use in the South, and added to this in the spring of 1950, but with no visible qualitative change in the equipment. In short, both sides confronted each other in June 1950 about the way they had in the fall of 1949. Both sides moved forces close to the parallel in the weeks and months preceding the war, and observers on all sides would have every reason to believe that 1950 would repeat 1949: more border clashes, more guerrilla war.

The one interesting caveat to this analysis is a growing awareness by the Americans that the North had the capability to achieve the limited goal of capturing Seoul, which would then probably lead to a collapse of the Rhee regime. This judgment was based both on the military capabilities of the North and the political inadequacies of the South. Muccio told the British ambassador in December 1949 that "he could not believe that the present regime could survive for more than a few days if the government abandoned the capital," and the CIA in June 1950 said that although the "combat effectiveness" of the KPA and the ROKA was "nearly equal," KPA superiority in tanks, heavy artillery, and aircraft gave it "a capability for attaining limited objectives in short-term military operations against southern Korea, including the capture of Seoul."[37]

Seoul was the core area both of regime support and its sinews of control in the form of elaborated bureaucracies and transportation and communication facilities; beyond Seoul and the surrounding Kyŏnggi Province, and with the exception of the sparsely populated Ch'ungch'ŏng Provinces, opened an abyss of poorly-controlled populations mostly sympathetic to the Left. Furthermore the Korean political perspective on both sides was that an elimination of the center would be the key to the collapse of the opposing regime: Rhee wanted to seize P'yŏngyang, and Kim wanted to seize Seoul. The difference, as ever since 1945, was that Kim's goal was far more feasible than Rhee's, expressing the relative political strengths of both sides. In any case, given the experience of the summer of 1949, it is entirely believable that important elements on both sides thought that an attempt to seize the other side's capital would mark the summer of 1950.

One change in KPA capabilities did reflect a qualitative augmentation, and probably had the most to do with the North Korean timetable: the return of the China veterans. As we have seen, large-scale transfers occurred in March and May 1950, with some 40,000 to 50,000 CCF Koreans crossing the border in March, and perhaps 20,000 in May, the latter involving troops of Lin Piao's Fourth Field Army. The last figure does not include still more Korean troops in the same field army that fought in the battle for Hainan Island in May of 1950; British sources estimated a total of 80,000 to 100,000 Korean veterans were still in China as of the end of 1949, meaning that several tens of thousands of Koreans were still there when the war began.[38]

Was this return part of a northern "buildup," oriented toward aggression against the South? The answer is yes, in the broad sense that when Kim Il Sung sent thousands of Korean youths to fight in China, he knew that one day they would return, battle-hardened and with a strong call on Chinese reciprocity. By 1950 the PLA had cleared the mainland of Nationalist troops, and so the Koreans came home. It is clear that the returnees gave the North Koreans an enhanced capability that they did not have in the summer of 1949. But the answer is also no, in that it is just as clear that several tens of thousands of Koreans remained in China as of June 25, and that there had been little time to integrate those forces that had returned in March, April, and May. So, the return of the CCF veterans might predict a war in the summer of 1950, but more in August or September than in June.

Estimates of the KPA order of battle just before the war varied considerably. The British in late April thought KPA forces totalled 66,670, including about 16,000 CCF veterans; another 80,000 CCF Koreans were thought to be in Manchuria. Along the parallel, northern and southern forces were arrayed in nearly equal numbers, with KPA units in both defensive and offensive deployments, depending on the unit.[39]

MacArthur's intelligence in early June 1950 firmly identified only five regular army divisions in the KPA, for a total of about 55,000 soldiers; many reports had come in of sixth and seventh divisions formed from recently-arrived CCF veterans, as well as indications of a North Korean intent to field thirteen divisions by September 1950, but these were not accepted as verified in early June. A map showing KPA order of battle information as of June 24, 1950, from the same intelligence sources shows a total of 74,370 soldiers compared to 95,000 for the ROKA; this indicates that in the interim, MacArthur's intelligence had accepted the existence of two more KPA divisions. Police and constabulary units boosted this to 139,820 for the North and 152,100 for the South.[40]

The deployment of KPA forces as of June 24 does not show sharp, recent southward movement. The order of battle placed 5,700 troops at Changdan, northeast of Ongjin; 3,300 at Haeju; 2,000 at Sariwŏn; 2,200 near Kumch'ŏn; 11,000 near Kunhwa and Yŏnch'ŏn (just above Ch'unch'ŏn), and 5,700 near Yangyang. In the interior were 9,000 at Chinnamp'o, 9,400 at P'yŏngyang, 6,000 at Wŏnsan, 2,800 at Hamhŭng, 6,000 near Nanam, 2,800 at Hoeryŏng, 2,800 at Kanggye, and fully 11,000 at the border town of Sinŭiju. In other words, of the total of 79,700 by this counting, only 29,900 troops were concentrated near the parallel, whereas nearly 50,000 were north of the line from Chinnamp'o to Wŏnsan.

The ROKA order of battle, by contrast, had 2,500 on Ongjin, 10,000 at Kaesŏng, 9,500 at Chajangni, 3,000 at Ch'unch'ŏn, and 7,500 at Chumunjin; in the interior were 28,000 in the Seoul area, 7,000 at Wŏnju, 4,500 at Pusan, 5,000 near Taegu, 5,500 near Kwangju, and 5,000 near Taejŏn, plus some smaller, inconsequential deployments. Thus of the ROKA total of 87,500, 32,500 soldiers were at the border, 35,000 within 35 miles or a day's march of the border at Seoul and Wŏnju, and only 20,000 in the more distant interior.[41]

Writing retrospectively, Appleman stated that by June 25 the KPA had eight divisions at full strength and two at half-strength; about one-third of these were CCF veterans, according to him. The border constabulary had an additional 13,000 men stationed along the parallel in defensive formations. More constabulary units were at P'yŏngyang (3,000) and another 5,000 or so were arrayed along the Sino-Korean and Soviet-Korean borders. Since a full-strength KPA division had 11,000 soldiers, if we accept this estimate we get a total of 88,000 in eight divisions and another two divisions at half strength (except that Appleman indicated that the latter two got most of their soldiers *after* the fighting began). But even if we count two more divisions, each at half-strength, the total would only be 99,000, compared to 94,808 for the ROKA, according to Appleman.[42]

This evidence is complex and somewhat contradictory, but it suggests that as of June 25, the KPA numbered not less than 87,500 and not more than 99,000, that about one-third of that strength was acquired in 1950 (mostly from CCF returnees), and that this build-up *only brought the KPA to the levels reached the previous summer by the ROKA.* Furthermore, the ROKA had more soldiers along the parallel, many more near the parallel, and the North had by no means concluded an expansion of its forces, available to it because of China returnees, when the war began. By September the North could have fielded upwards of five more divisions, and thus be in a far better position to make war.

NORTH KOREAN MOTIVES

What about DPRK intentions? Are there motives that can be established that would explain, first, why the North would choose to launch an invasion that carried a significant likelihood of American involvement, and second, why the North would choose to move in June 1950, and not later? The answer to the first question is that several motives can be established, some more important than others; the answer to the second is that none of these motives explain the timing of an attack in late June 1950—unless the attack was *preemptive*, timed to coincide with the Dulles and Johnson visits to Tokyo, a matter we will take up later.

We have deliberately excluded the question of *Soviet* motives for an attack in June 1950, for the following reasons: first, there is no good evidence one way or the other, even today, nor is there likely to be any; second, the Soviets did not have the capability to command an attack that the North Koreans themselves did not want; third, the Koreans did have the capability, with the return of their China soldiers, of launching an attack independently; and finally, the result of the war was to push through NSC 68, triple American defense spending, hasten the rearmament of Japan and Germany, and greatly heighten cold war tensions for years thereafter on a world scale—all significant setbacks to the USSR when compared to any potential gains that might come from a northern victory. Much of this would have been entirely predictable to a Kremlin that was well aware of American internal policy deliberations.

It is far more likely that the Soviet position was a general one arrived at in 1949 or earlier, to distance the Soviets from the volatility of the North Korean leadership, and reason as follows: a war in Korea is likely. There is a great possibility that either the North or the South will launch it. We do not want to involve our prestige in it, but it could bring benefits: if North Korea succeeds and swallows the South, this is a gain for the communist world. More likely they will fail, by bringing on American intervention: this will teach all communists a lesson about going against Moscow's wishes, or acting outside its directions; it will raise the distinct possibility of getting the Chinese into the war, blooding them against the Americans and making them more dependent on us; it may bog the United States down in a stupid peripheral war and exhaust their blood and treasure for no good purpose.

The great risk was that such a conflict might expand into a general war, one that the Soviet Union was certainly not ready for in 1950. Thus, a careful distance from the North Koreans had to be maintained. This is quite speculative, of course, as all discussions of Soviet decisions must be in the absence of internal documentation. But it does fit the evidence about Soviet-Korean relations before the war and Soviet behavior after the war. In any case none of this would explain the timing of an attack in June 1950, when, as we will see, the Soviets had been making diplomatic overtures to defuse the crisis-ridden atmosphere of early 1950.

One common argument is that the North attacked because of a factional conflict in the leadership. Pak Hŏn-yŏng and his allies were worried about the loss of their base in the South and argued that a frontal assault would touch off a popular uprising among the masses, leading to a quick communist victory. This hypothesis, as we will see, brings into rare agreement the CIA, the Kim leadership, independent Korean sources in Japan, and some important scholarship in the United States. Its virtue is that it would explain, in part, the timing of a June invasion. If we assume that the southern guerrillas were, indeed, exhausted by the spring of 1950, and factor into that the land question, it appears to be a cogent argument.

In January 1950 the Central Committee of the Democratic Front for the Unification of the Homeland, including many of Pak's supporters, said patriots cannot "quietly sit by" while the Rhee "country-selling clique" and the U.S. imperialists "create a situation of unbearable misery and wretchedness unprecedented in our nation's history." The statement accused Rhee of slaughtering 149,000 "patriots" since the Liberation, with 62,000 having died just since July 1949. It detailed allegations of brutal tortures of dissidents, leading the guerrillas "to answer reactionary terror with righteous terror" (a revealing admission for communists to make).

The authors paid particular attention to the intense thought-reform methods used to create communist apostates in the South, listing names of "turncoats" like Cho Pong-am, Chang Kŏn-sang, and Pak Il-wŏn. It said the obstacles to the overthrow of the Rhee regime were, in order, "the aggressive intervention of the American imperialists," the Rhee clique itself, and UNCOK, "a tool of American imperialism." These obstacles must be eliminated, it said, "by our own efforts." As if to underline that the guerrilla war was not going well, it named guerrilla heroes who had sacrificed their lives, such as Ch'oe Hyŏn and Yi Tŏk-ku. Then, it raised the land question. "Syngman Rhee is not giving land to the peasants and will never give land to the peasants. Never in human history have landlords given their land to peasants. Peasants must wrest the land from landlords with their own hands!"

Pak Hŏn-yŏng published an essay in the same issue, from which many phrases in the above document were lifted. He said Rhee's repression was worse now than ever before, and paid particular attention to the "winter offensive" against the southern guerrillas, detailing the extraordinary mobilization of ROK forces since the fall of 1949. The whole burden of this discussion was, by implication, to explain why the southern guerrillas were losing, even though he ritually claimed that they had, of course, defeated the offensive.

He went on to say, "we must model ourselves on the ardent patriotic and self-sacrificing spirit of the Soviet people in the great war to defend the fatherland"; only after that does he mention the Chinese example of how a people united could defeat Chiang Kai-shek and all the "plots" of U.S. imperialism. Then he said, "Can we sit idly by with arms folded while watching half of the national territory become a colony of a foreign country and the brethren in the southern part become slaves of U.S. imperialism? Don't we today possess all the conditions necessary for a common, united struggle? Hasn't our independent and democratic base in north Korea majestically developed and strengthened?"

As if to downplay the obvious bellicosity and immediacy of this statement, he then said the Korean people do not want to plunge their peninsula "into the flames of war," and urged everyone to join the guerrillas and expand the struggle for "peaceful unification."[43]

The land question was important not because it was the essence of the social question in the South; this had been true since 1945. What made it important in this context was the Rhee land reform program, promulgated in 1949. It is generally thought that land reform began to be implemented before June 1950, but in fact not a single acre had changed hands by June 25, as we will see; furthermore the summer grain harvest was just ripening and being brought in by peasants. The previous two harvests had been good ones, contributing to the perception that the southern economy was on the upswing and turning peasants away from the appeals of guerrillas. If land were distributed in July and August 1950, as planned, and if the South got a bumper harvest, as projected, the poor peasant base of the southern guerrillas would be severely undercut. Since the Korean countryside has been generally quiet in the decades since the consummation of the land reform, this is a cogent argument.[44]

As early as 1951 a centrist in Japan, Kim Sam-gyu, claimed that the attack came about because Pak and his allies wanted it. Robert Simmons picked this up, arguing that Pak Hŏn-yŏng "encouraged a drive south."[45] An important State Department account done in 1963, based on classified intelligence materials, said that the attack was decided upon "hastily and none too cautiously," and that the southerners "had unquestionably been instigators of the aggression" because of the success of ROK efforts against the guerrillas. In early 1950, the study asserted, discussions about an attack were reportedly held, in which Kim Il Sung sided with Pak Hŏn-yŏng and South Korean Worker's Party (SKWP) leaders, whereas Ch'oe Yong-gŏn opposed the idea, thinking the United States would enter the war. "Ch'oe disappeared from public life for a while and plans for war matured."[46]

This argument cannot be accepted, however. The 1963 study is interesting mainly because it implicitly suggested that the attack was the work of the DPRK leadership alone, without reference to Soviet machinations; otherwise it grossly overestimated Pak's importance within the DPRK leadership. To the extent that it reflects the American grasp of high DPRK politics—and it must—it suggested that as of 1963 the United States still did not know much about this leadership.

As early as 1947 internal DPRK materials show that the decades-long experience of Pak and other communists who remained in Korea during the colonial period was downplayed or eliminated in favor of Kim's version of Korean communist history, as we saw in chapter 9, which in any communist regime is an indication of who holds ultimate power. Pak was made Foreign Minister in the DPRK regime, a position that brought little influence. There is no other evidence of a breach between Kim and Ch'oe Yong-gŏn in this period, except hints that Ch'oe favored Soviet mechanized warfare over Maoist methods, much like Peng Te-huai in China; in fact Ch'oe appeared prominently at the February 8, 1950, anniversary of the founding of the KPA, and it was he who took the lead in the heretical declaration of Kim as *suryŏng* (Great Leader) of the Korean people. This was a term that Pak never uttered before the Korean War; no doubt he despised the usage and thought it reflected on Kim's puerile grasp of Marxism-Leninism as well as his inveterate nationalism. Furthermore

Pak was never a military man, and it is inconceivable that Kim Il Sung and Ch'oe Yong-gŏn, who were close in a way that Kim and Pak never were and who shared a common guerrilla background, could fall out over Pak's view that the United States would not intervene and the South was ripe for plucking.

The apparent defeat of the southern partisans and the impending land reform were good reasons for *any* Korean communist to back a conventional assault in the summer of 1950, not just southerners. Furthermore, as we will see, the KPA told southern citizens over and over that *it* was their liberator, not the southern guerrillas. Kim Sam-gyu, Robert Simmons, the State Department, and the North Koreans in their 1953 scapegoating of Pak are also wrong in alleging that no southern "uprising" occurred. In the early days of the war there was no need for an uprising, since the southern regime collapsed quickly; no one with any brains "rises up" in the face of army and police violence when armed help is on the way. But when the KPA arrived its efforts were greatly aided by activities of the southern people in the Chŏlla and Kyŏngsang Provinces, as we will see.

It may be that Kim Il Sung and his allies found it convenient to let Pak Hŏn-yŏng and the southerners dangle out front in promoting an assault that everyone wanted, which would be politically shrewd. But more likely the thesis about Pak's role became useful only in 1953, when he and the other southerners could be scapegoated for the debacle of the war, which brought a holocaust on the North. That Kim's leadership could both survive this horrendous outcome *and* brutally purge the southern communists (soon to be followed by the Soviet and Yanan factions) is merely one more testimony to Kim's embracing dominance of the northern system, and the tight unity of the Manchurian guerrillas.

Another thesis is that the North acted because of the division of the peninsula, seeking unification before Korea was irrevocably separated. By now this will seem utterly obvious to the reader. But there is an interesting element of timing here. For years the North claimed that Rhee wanted a forced unification of the peninsula, through a "northern expedition." The demands for a separate southern government in 1945–1946, the May 1948 elections, and the establishment of the ROK were always seen as predicated not on separatism but on laying the groundwork for an attack northward. In May 1950, for the first time according to my research, northern materials accused Rhee of seeking the *permanent division* of Korea.[47] This was a significant departure for DPRK rhetoric before the war, even if it became a litany after the war and down to the present. At a minimum the usage raises the question how the South could simultaneously want to divide Korea forever, and to attack the North.

The salience of the national division should need no emphasis by now, except that the literature in the United States still tends to ignore the unification issue, failing to grasp its importance in the Korean context, and treating the northern assault, implicitly or explicitly, as an attack across an "international boundary." No Korean accepted the division as permanent in 1950, just as no American in the civil war years of the 1860s would have accepted a foreign decision to divide the United States five years earlier.

This argument does not explain the June 25 timing, however. Unification was the critical issue, but there were still several possibilities for attaining it short of an all-out attack that might well bring American intervention; the rhetoric of May 1950 is important, but not decisive for events in June, as opposed to some later date in the summer—or the following year, for that matter.

The one motive for which the evidence is most abundant in early 1950 is the DPRK's growing concern with the revival of Japan and especially its economic and military relations with the Rhee regime. In spite of their incessant denunciations of American imperialism, the North Koreans have always seen this as a disease of the skin, Japanese imperialism as a disease of the heart (to borrow Chiang Kai-shek's metaphor). The formative maturation of Kim and his allies occurred in struggle against a vicious, unreconstructed imperial monster capable of wiping out whole populations in search of its goals, imbued with vulgar racial hatreds, and showing on its hands the blood of millions of Asians. When one finally grasps the carnage wreaked by the Japanese militarists—Koreans and Chinese put the total figure at 15 million dead—and learns of things like their bacteriological warfare programs in Manchuria, with gruesome experiments on living human beings (including American POWs), distinguishing them from the Nazis seems an arcane and pedantic exercise. The Manchurian guerrillas were reared in a harsh milieu of abject poverty and recalcitrant peasant populations whose common characteristic, by Japanese as well as Korean testimony, was an implacable hatred of the Japanese overlord. In 1950, so reams of verbiage in DPRK media had it, the United States sought to revive this monster and reintroduce it in Korea.

In the one public appearance he made in January 1950, Kim Il Sung told the Third Congress of the Friends Party (*Chŏng'udang*) that although the North had many achievements to its credit, "we still have not wiped out the Rhee country-sellers and we still have not liberated the people in the southern part." He then turned not to his usual subject, the role of American imperialism in prolonging the deathbed-wriggle of the Rhee clique, but to Japanese imperialists, to whom Rhee had gone begging to save himself. He likened Rhee to the national traitor Yi Wan-yong, who aided in the Japanese annexation, in discussing Rhee's dispatch of Defense Minister Shin Sŭng-mo to Tokyo "to make secret arrangements with the Japanese bastards (*Ilbonnom*)."[48]

At about the same time the party organ accused the United States of trying to knock together a "Pacific Pact" in the wake of the Chinese Communist victory and the ever-widening people's struggle in Southeast Asia, leading "the American ruling class" to make Japan "into a military base and source of armaments." The result of the "separate peace" the United States was planning would be the establishment of military bases in Japan, the article said, citing *Newsweek* in September 1949; all this was being done to oppose the USSR and the national liberation struggle in Asia— "and, it is said, to prepare a war against the DPRK and China."[49]

Three days later the same paper again likened Rhee to Yi Wan-yong, and warned that, "There has been a great, historic change today in the international environment surrounding Korea from what it was forty years ago, when U.S. imperialism and Japan colluded to subjugate weak Korea . . . the Korean people have waked up and have united. After suffering thirty-six years under Japanese imperialism, they do not again plan to be slaves under another name."[50]

Another lengthy article in January presented a litany of allegations about recent ROK-Japan ties: a trade agreement in April 1949 exchanged Japanese coal for Korean minerals; the Americans pushed for more trade in October 1949; Shin Sŭng-mo met secretly with MacArthur and Japanese militarists in the same month; Rhee sent the well-known collaborator Shin Hŭng-u (Hugh Heung-woo Cynn) to be his representative in Tokyo; the United States stated publicly that the ROK now recognized the value of mutual, reciprocal relations with Japan; Rhee openly stated that the ROK and Japan now had a "common enemy"; and so on. Lurking behind all this was the common interest of Wall Street capitalists and Japanese "profiteers," hiding behind slogans of "free trade," to make Korea, once again, a "dependency" (*yesŏk*) of Japan.[51]

In early February a signed commentary took up Acheson's Press Club speech again, terming him "the leader of American foreign policy" and saying the speech showed he wanted to redouble efforts to transform Japan and Okinawa into a military base for aggression in Asia, all to the benefit of "the Wall Street masters." Pak Ch'ang-ok's commentary on the Sino-Soviet Treaty a few days later quoted only that section dealing with the revival of Japanese militarism, and said the new alliance made for "a tremendous, unbeatable force" to defeat American "plots" in Asia, such as their desire to use Japanese militarists in a new war.[52]

Rhee traveled to Japan in mid-February, taking Ben Limb, Clarence Ryee, and Colonel Chŏng Il-gwŏn with him, sparking an eruption of propaganda in P'yŏngyang. Ever since, North Korean sources have asserted that it was during this visit that Rhee and MacArthur plotted war in Korea. At the time, the party newspaper said the basic purpose of the trip was to foster close relations, "especially military [relations]"; Rhee was colluding with Japanese militarists, "the sworn enemy of the Korean people." Rhee and his representative in Japan, Hugh Cynn, were talking of "forgetting the past" and cooperating with Japan now and "in the future," as part of "a plot to bring Japanese imperialism back to our land." Premier Yoshida, they said, looked forward to close economic relations with the ROK; the United States now pushed the ROK and Japan closer because of the defeat of its China policy and the bankruptcy of the same policy in Korea.[53]

A signed commentary some days later gave the following reasons for Rhee's visit: guerrillas would become active again, in the period of "thick foliage," necessitating Japanese help in suppressing them; the Sino-Soviet Treaty had brought "a blazing fighting spirit" to the movement to unify Korea; and defections within Rhee's own ranks had him badly worried. Rhee had said the ROK and Japan had to join hands to meet the common danger, and Foreign Minister Limb had urged everyone to forget the unfortunate past—prompting the North Koreans to say, this is what you get from a former salesman of *Ajinomoto*. The hidden goal, however, was to forge some sort of alliance with Japan, under American prodding.

Subsequent articles on his trip, which were daily fare for some weeks, ladled out a special stew of vicious epithets, terming Rhee "a traitor for all ages," calling Hugh Cynn a "Japanese police spy," claiming that Crown Prince Yi Ŭn had served as a go-between for Rhee to meet Japanese militarists, thus venting the North Korean spleen about a trip that they obviously took very seriously. The commentary reached a crescendo with charges that Rhee and MacArthur had plans to bring Japanese troops to Korea, as part of a plot "for fanning a fratricidal . . . large-scale civil war," hoping thereby to destroy "the rapidly developing democratic construction in the northern half." Therefore, "the day is not far off" when the Rhee forces will meet the judgment of the people.[54]

Perhaps the most interesting commentary came in articles linking Rhee's trip to American policies at the turn of the century, when Theodore Roosevelt blessed Japanese control of Korea. One author said the United States, while preaching "science and democracy" to Asians, had simply followed on the heels of the European imperialists in China, and had justified Japanese imperialism. Here the author quoted Theodore Roosevelt on the presumed perils of propinquity, causing Japan to find its natural sphere of influence in its near reaches, Korea and Manchuria. The United States supported the Nanking government in 1927–1937, while simultaneously supplying Japan with war materiel right up to the months before Pearl Harbor; the Americans then warred on Japan to weaken it, so the United States could substitute for Japan as Asia's leading imperialist. After the war, the United States hoped that China would become its great Asian ally, and thus sent huge amounts of aid to the Kuomintang (KMT). Now, with Chiang's regime in ruins, it was turning to Japan.[55] It was a sophisticated argument.

An emotional and utterly believable commentary remarked that courageous Korean revolutionaries had, to their great chagrin, failed to achieve their "sacred goal" of expelling the Japanese: "the faces of those who fell by the enemy's sword mortify us as they float up clearly in our remembrance." All the more reason, therefore, never again to allow this "sworn enemy" to "stretch its bloody hands to our territory again." Yet American policy, bankrupted by the Chinese victory, was now turning to the revival of Japanese militarism and ROK-Japan collusion. The Potsdam Declaration of demilitarization and democratization was being destroyed. "These facts cannot but pose a grave threat to the Korean people."

The article went on to cite the clause in the 1948 DPRK Constitution stating that any country that aids and abets the reestablishment of Japanese imperialism threatens the independence of Korea, and therefore becomes an enemy of Korea. Thus, the Korean people must unite ever more tightly around Kim Il Sung, "strengthen the alliance (*tan'gyŏl*) with the democratic countries led by the USSR, *and with the Chinese people*," and struggle ever more mercilessly to wipe out the Rhee clique.[56]

In April the party journal accused the United States of making Korea once again a source of raw materials, markets, and foodstuffs, thus "to destroy Korea's independent economy and make it a complete dependency of the U.S. and Japan." It quoted Rhee as saying on February 18, "Today in southern Korea, Korean soldiers are dying every day. This is to save the freedom of Japan and of the whole world . . . thus the two countries [Japan and Korea] must cooperate to meet the common threat." Citing a TASS account, the journal charged that secret agreements had been reached for Japan to provide the ROK with military supplies, and that Rhee and Yoshida had agreed with Chiang Kai-shek to base planes flown by Japanese pilots in southern Korea so they can attack cities in Northeast China and North Korea.[57]

Internal DPRK materials show these same emphases in the spring of 1950. Some lectures in May stated that the United States had turned its back on the Potsdam Declaration, was reviving the Japanese economy and the *zaibatsu*, and was turning it into a military base and war-materiel workshop; they cited a statement in early March by General Eichelberger about the necessity for Japan to rearm. Rhee and MacArthur (not Rhee and Truman) were scheming to bring Japanese militarists into Korea and plotted war in their February meeting. Again, the document concluded by pointing to the dire threat implied by all this, although the materials averred that Rhee will be defeated "through the partisan struggle in the South."[58]

Topic number one in lectures for KPA political officers dated in June stated, "the basic policy of the American imperialists is newly to militarize Japan." They referred to, among other things, the revival of *zaibatsu* groups like Mitsubishi, which previously owned many factories in northern Korea, American protection for biological warfare criminal General Ishii, Eichelberger's statement, and American plans to keep bases at Yokusuka and Sasebo. This external aspect was, of course, linked to the continuance of colonial social formations and bureaucracies, and pro-Japanese elements in the South. Because Korea was Japan's first victim "above all other nations," it must monitor these activities, which constitute "a threat and menace to the Korean people." The materials had a different emphasis than the previous ones, however, by suggesting that American plans for remilitarizing Japan were intimately connected with plans for making Korea a bridgehead for attacking China and the Soviet Union. "The U.S. imperialists are tying together the Rhee country-selling criminals and the Japanese militarists and getting them to provoke civil war in our country with the sinister [intention] of making Korea a military base for aggression in the Far East."

Although these June lecture materials said that the Sino-Soviet alliance was a great guarantee of peace in the Far East, and urged everyone to join the worldwide campaign for peace headed by the USSR, something that reads as if it were scripted in Moscow, the ending is distinctly Korean. "Our memories have not dimmed," it said, and again cited the DPRK Constitution; all soldiers must train harder, strengthen preparations for battle, get ready to "wipe out and smash the Rhee traitors at a single blow." "The Syngman Rhee country-selling traitors who are enticing the Japanese militarist elements back onto the soil of southern Korea must be wiped out and smashed and the homeland's unification must swiftly be accomplished."[59]

After the war began the same themes predominated. Just after the United States intervened, the party newspaper in a signed commentary called attention to the Americans' having "colluded with the eternal enemy of the Korean people, the Japanese militarists," and cited transfers of Korean rice and tungsten to Japan in return for war materials. Secret guidance documents for political workers in July 1950 dwelt on Rhee's February trip and the export of rice to Japan; Mun Hak-bong, who claimed to have been the servant of an American CIC official, said that in the February meeting Rhee and MacArthur agreed to put the ROKA under the latter's command in case of war, work together with former Japanese military officers, train ROKA officers in Japan, and have South

Korea play the lead role in touching off a war for all of East Asia. Other defectors to the North, like former Home Minister Kim Hyo-sŏk, also placed key emphasis on the February meeting.[60]

It is clear from all these broadsides, then, that the North Koreans feared the revival of Japanese militarism and its heavy-industrial economic base, and its reintegration with the South. But what elements of truth exist in all this propaganda? Syngman Rhee had a reputation for fierce hatred of the Japanese, and after the Korean War he was a key obstacle to American desires to reinvolve the Japanese and Korean economies. But that was not true before the war. The *Chicago Tribune* correspondent Walter Simmons wrote in November 1949 that South Korea remained "amazingly Japanized." The schoolkids looked Japanese in their black uniforms, the newspapers seemed like Tokyo replicas, it was common to hear Japanese spoken in the streets. Relatedly, "intelligent Koreans now concede that economic cooperation with Japan offers the only hope of developing any sort of foreign trade"; American tungsten engineers had doubled output in recent months, much of it going to Japan; 100,000 tons of Korean rice would be shipped by the end of 1949.[61]

In January 1950 the American embassy found "a trend toward rapprochement with Japan," with Hugh Cynn going to Japan as Rhee's representative in spite of a "reputation for Japanese collaborationism" that had kept him out of government service thus far; Rhee had told the embassy that "he was eager to move toward ending traditional ill will toward Japan . . . and had informed the Japanese of his desire to negotiate a *modus vivendi*," with Supreme Command, Allied Powers (SCAP) approval. In mid-January Rhee told newsmen, "it is not good to enlarge on our bad feelings toward Japan, forgetting the common enemy," and the same day told Jessup that he "is much interested in increasing trade relations with Japan," dwelling on the possibilities of ROK-Japan cooperation.[62]

Rhee left for Tokyo on February 16 and returned two days later. All that is known about his visit is what was publicly available at the time; MacArthur kept no records of this or any other meeting with Rhee. State Department and other internal materials are mostly silent about the trip, in spite of intense interest in what Rhee and MacArthur were doing on the part of embassy and other officials. Rhee met with MacArthur three times, Yoshida once, along with a variety of other government officials and Diet members. He made frequent reference to "the common enemy," communism, and urged Japanese economic and technical aid for the ROK. His press release upon his return did say, as the North Koreans charged, that when the ROKA "fights for Korean freedom . . . it also defends the freedom of Japan."[63] To my knowledge, no ROK president again referred publicly to a Korean role in Japan's front-line defense until the 1980s.

Gen. Robert L. Eichelberger did, indeed, call for the rearmament of Japan on March 3, and Rhee did, indeed, have plans for the training of ROKA officers in Japan, the first contingent of which left for Japan in April 1950. Even the most ridiculous of DPRK charges, that Shin Sŭng-mo and Rhee were involved with the ineffectual and mostly Japanized Prince Yi Ŭn, turns out to have been true. One is caught between wild North Korean charges and an implausible, provocative shamelessness in Seoul, which mocked the entire history of Korean resistance to Japanese imperialism.

Eichelberger, former commander of the Eighth Army in Japan and a charter member of the Japan Lobby, called for the rearmament of Japan in a speech at the Waldorf-Astoria, in the face of a "Red plan" to "couple" Japan's industrial capacity with tungsten, oil, and other raw materials "to the south." In fact, of course, this was what the United States was planning to do, but Eichelberger's interest in tungsten is worthy of note, since his brother's firm later won a big contract for Korean tungsten.[64]

Of greater interest, Willoughby was meeting with former Japanese militarists in this period, although no information seems to be available on the substance of their discussions. This takes on increasing significance because North Korean intelligence—not to mention Soviet or Chinese—was excellent in Japan before the war. A big Korean spy ring was broken in August 1950, and investigators found that the large Korean community, ease of entry to the country, and Japanese laxness had led to "high-level penetration into Japanese governmental agencies by [North] Korean agents."[65] They were presumably in a position to know about things like the Voorhees mission to Japan in April 1950, which as we have seen urged a revival of what was left of the Co-prosperity Sphere.

Meanwhile, some Americans began to paraphrase Itō Hirobumi in depicting Korea's relationship to Japan. Gen. Roberts said of South Korea in March, "This is a fat nation now with all its ECA goods, with warehouses bulging, with plenty rice [sic] from a good crop . . . an excellent prize of war; strategically it points right into the heart of Japan and in the hands of an enemy it weakens the Japanese bastion of Western defense." Now that the reader had dismissed this as the work of a military mind, let us listen to a New York Times lead editorial in late May, dealing with the Japanese Peace Treaty as the Dulles visit impended; it was titled "Japan's Perilous Position." "The Japanese since the time of Hideyoshi have called Korea the dagger pointed at Japan's heart. An abrupt American withdrawal [from Korea] . . . would mean the collapse of the free Korean state and the passage of the dagger once more into Russian hands. . . . What it comes down to is that if Japan is to be defended all of Japan has to be a base, militarily and economically."[66] It remains for a logician to explain how Hideyoshi's twin aggressions, not to mention the annexation, constitute a Korean dagger pointed at the Japanese heart.

Just before the war the Rhee regime continued to give every indication that it was willing and eager to follow the American and Japanese lead. In March Gen. Chae Pyŏng-dŏk was in Japan "trying to acquire machinery [for] the arsenal program"; the next month Rhee's Korean National Party said, "we shall reexamine our relations with the newly-born democratic Japan, and establish an anti-Communist front in cooperation with that nation," and new trade agreements were negotiated by Harold Lady after a joint Korean-Japanese commercial conference; in May the Bank of Korea opened offices in Tokyo, and the ROK agreed to ship $2.6 million worth of ores to Japan during the next year, including tungsten, cobalt, and manganese.[67]

In June 1950 the veteran industrialist Pak Hŭng-sik showed up in Japan and gave an interview to *The Oriental Economist*, published the day before the war began. Described as an advisor to the Korean Economic Mission, he was also said to have "a circle of friends and acquaintances among the Japanese" (a bit of an understatement). In the years after liberation a lot of anti-Japanese feeling had welled up in Korea, Pak said, owing to the return of "numerous revolutionists and nationalists." Today, however, "there is hardly any trace of it." Instead, the ROK "is acting as a bulwark of peace" at the thirty-eighth parallel, and "the central figures in charge of national defense are mostly graduates of the former Military College of Japan." Korea and Japan "are destined to go hand in hand, to live and let live," and thus bad feelings should be "cast overboard."

The Japanese should buy Korean raw materials, he said, of which there was an "almost inexhaustible supply," including tungsten and graphite; the Koreans will then buy "as much as possible" of Japanese merchandise and machinery. They will also invite Japanese technical help with Korea's textile, glass, chemical, and machine industries. Pak himself owned a company that was an agent for Ford Motors: "we are scheduled to start producing cars jointly in Korea before long."

The problem today, Pak said, was the unfortunate one that "an economic unity is lacking whereas in prewar days Japan, Manchuria, Korea and Formosa economically combined to make an organic whole."[68] If Polanyi was right to call the Rothschilds the microcosm of the internationalist vision, Pak Hŭng-sik was the embodiment of the Japanese colonial idea—having been born a Korean his only unfortunate, but not insurmountable, fate.

Chapter Fifteen

SOUTH KOREA ON
THE EVE OF THE WAR

There is a comical aspect to this, because the visits of these people
over there, and their peering over outposts with binoculars at the
Soviet people, I think must have led the Soviets to think that we
were on to their plan and caused them considerable perturbation.

Kennan

Yes, Foster up in a bunker with a homburg on—it was a very amusing picture.

Acheson

THE AMERICAN PRESENCE in South Korea is often thought to have diminished to a null point after the final removal of combat forces in
the summer of 1949, such that the question becomes, why did they return in June 1950? In fact American influence had reached new heights
by 1950, with Korea accommodating the largest American embassy in the
world, the biggest aid mission, and the most numerous military advisory
group.[1] As the war approached, furthermore, important dignitaries
sought to underline Korea's salience with well-publicized visits to the
peninsula.

A few weeks before the war broke out British Minister Vyvyan Holt
vividly sketched this new mise-en-scène: "Radiating from the huge ten-
storied Banto Hotel," American influence "penetrates into every branch
of administration and is fortified by an immense outpouring of money."
Americans kept the government, the army, the economy, the railroads,
the airports, the mines, and the factories operating; they supplied funds,
electricity, expertise, and psychological succor. American gasoline fueled
every motor vehicle in the country. American cultural influence was "exceedingly strong," ranging from scholarships to study in the United
States, to several strong missionary denominations, to "a score of traveling cinemas" and theaters that played mostly American films, to the
Voice of America, even to big-league baseball: "America is the dream-
land" to thousands if not millions of Koreans.[2]

In addition to the large Economic Cooperation Administration (ECA)
and Korean Military Advisory Group (KMAG) missions, the U.S. Information Service had, by its own testimony, "one of the most extensive
country programs that we are operating anywhere," with nine centers in

Korea, parlaying libraries, mobile units, and a variety of publications, films, and Americanism before the Korean people. American officials ran Kimp'o International Airport, and controlled the entry and exit of American citizens; by mid-1950 a CIA proprietary airline, Civil Air Transport, ran the Korean National Airline. Besides the official presence, unofficial Americans often advised or directed private industry.[3]

In spite of occasional Congressional delays, American aid continued to flow in comparatively great amounts. In March 1950 Congress finally approved a $100 million economic and military aid package for fiscal year 1951; after Muccio asked for tanks and planes for the Republic of Korea (ROK), Acheson sought an additional $10 million. Perhaps combining these figures with the value of military equipment left behind, U. Alexis Johnson put the total aid level in the year before the Korean War at $220 million.[4] To put American gratis aid in perspective, the entire ROK national budget for fiscal year 1951 was $120 million, with $27 million formally earmarked for defense (actually about 80 percent went for defense and internal security).[5] Analytically, American money subsidized a state policy in which Rhee and the social formation he represented used the strong colonial bureaucracy to beat down their enemies and perpetuate their class position; domestic state revenues paid for coercion, and the United States paid for everything else.

"Right Off Japan There":
Korea's Economic Telos

Sen. Elbert Thomas of Utah—considered by himself, if not by everyone, as the reigning Asia expert in the Congress—put this question to Edgar A. J. Johnson of the ECA in June 1949: "If you are going to restore the [Korean] economy you have to restore the economy in connection with the type of trade . . . that has been going on for the last 40 or 50 years. Is that not right?"[6] Unlike Thomas's theories about Chinese peasants and their little silver balls (chapter 4), this one elicited assent: "That is quite right," Johnson said, and went on to nail the point to the wall for the senator: "there will be a complementarity between Korea and Japan which will inure to the benefit of Japan." Thomas thought the Japanese empire (as he called it) had built and built well in Taiwan and Korea: the latter was "a glorious example" of what could be done to wrench a people out of benighted poverty. There were problems of exploitation, true; in order to reforest Korea ("one of the great things in history") the Japanese "had to shoot [Koreans] to let a tree grow," since peasants were always chopping them down. But these pecadilloes paled before the Japanese accomplishment. Why not continue this union?[7]

The ECA had hoped to sell the senators on a Korean aid package by lauding the politics of the Republic of Korea: Paul Hoffman testified that "it will be the bastion of democracy in Asia, and it will be a very bright and shining light in the midst of the great darkness on that continent." But that inflated currency passed badly even in the Senate; Hoffman coined a better theme when he said that the Korean and Japanese economies were "naturally complementary . . . in helping Korea we are also helping Japan, too."[8]

Americans who could call up anything about Korea and its thirty million people recollected that it had been a Japanese colony: in that context it had had some worth, and might again. In and of itself, Korea was unavailing. In a colloquy in the Senate in July 1949, after Sen. Tom Connally remarked that South Korea "is the last thing we have in the Far East," Sen. Henry Cabot Lodge responded, "It isn't much good, but it's ours." But later on in the discussion Connally explained its importance: "Right off Japan there, it is going to be tied in with Japan in its economy and its fiscal relations, and it seems to me that strengthening it would be a military asset in the event we have any military operations in that area."[9]

Standing behind the ubiquitous concern about the "viability" of the South was this question: what good was it, unless it were connected to something else of value—the struggle with the Soviets or the revival of Japanese industry. This prevailing American view reversed the traditional Korean assumption: what good was Korea, if it was only important to something else? The Korean "good" was a self-contained homeland, Korea for the Koreans. Above all else, it was the working out of these two contrary logics that produced the Korean War in June 1950.

In the months just before the war, Tracy Voorhees, undersecretary of the Army and a charter member of the Japan Lobby, pushed a plan to integrate the Korean and Japanese economies that was called the "Greater East Asia Co-Prosperity Sphere" plan by his detractors in the State Department. He urged that American aid to other East Asian nations "be explicitly tied to Japan," requiring trade with Japan. He said in March 1950 that he was disturbed by "the lack of coordination" between the Korea and Japan economic programs, but ECA officials wondered what he was talking about: the programs were already "well integrated"; ECA-Korea "was doing everything within its power" to increase coordination.[10]

The ostensible problems in Korea after the ROK was established were inflation and stagnation: the government printed a lot of money, and many enterprises functioned at less than half their capacity. The diplomatic record is full of discussion of these issues, especially in the months before the Korean War. The American remedy then, as in the 1960s, was to get the Koreans to export. "The Korean balance of payments cannot be solved unless Korea becomes once again a food exporter," Johnson told the assembled senators in June 1949;[11] the rice harvest was the one bright spot in the Korean economy at that point, and a surplus was available for export.

But this, too, meant a reintegration with Japan, since that was always Korea's market for rice exports. Indeed, we find the Americans making the same semiperipheral substitution that the Japanese did: rougher grains like millet for the white rice that Koreans equated with a proper meal. Under American prodding to popularize the detested export policy, Rhee told Koreans it was not healthy to eat rice alone: "We want other grains in exchange for the export of rice." The Americans were ready to provide them—flour, corn, wheat, and later on, even American rice—establishing a food dependency and a lucrative protected market for American grains that is now in its fourth decade.[12]

The other potential export items were tungsten, the most valuable mineral in the South, and cotton textiles—both industries that had rapid development from the mid-1930s, under the Japanese aegis. American experts installed new technology to mine tungsten in 1949, expecting a quick doubling of output. The textile industry had 315,000 spindles and 10,000 looms in 1949; it produced 5 million yards of cloth a month in the same year. "All the production curves are upward now since last August," the ECA said in June 1949.[13]

ROK representatives signed a new trade agreement with Japan on June 8, 1950; it provided for $35 million in trade, not counting rice exports. Japan agreed to import tungsten and other ores, fish products, animal hair, and the like; Korea would import wool, cotton, and rayon, as well as cement, sheet glass, radios, machinery, and transport equipment.[14]

South Korea was an early example of the hegemonic regulatory regime that many developing countries have been subjected to in recent years, especially since the debt crisis began in the late 1970s. In Korea's case, the regime was not that of the International Monetary Fund or the World Bank; this came later, as we have seen, because by 1947 Rooseveltian multilateralism had given way to American unilateralism, in part because the Bretton Woods mechanisms were too weak. What Korea got was a highly penetrative American regime, which left—or sought to leave—few important economic decisions just to the Koreans themselves.

The best place to examine this system is in the aid agreement signed on December 10, 1948, in Seoul.[15] In return for the flow of American dollars and goods, the Koreans agreed to balance their budget, keep a stable currency, an appropriate rate of exchange, and to closely regulate precious foreign exchange. The Americans also elicited pledges to open the country to foreign traders, reduce barriers to foreign exchange, fa-

cilitate "private foreign investment," and develop Korean export industries "as rapidly as practicable."

The United States added bite to the demands by placing ECA officials
in a supervisory capacity on American-supported projects (that is, almost
all projects), and by closely regulating the expenditure of foreign exchange—every last dollar of it. The agreement required that the "United
States aid representative" approve the Korean government's import-ex-
port program, concur in any allocation of foreign exchange, and be able
to inspect the distribution of American aid anywhere in the country. It
also required the ROK "to facilitate the transfer" of strategic materials
needed by the United States, which allowed the United States to take the
entire annual output of South Korean tungsten. Aid dollars were to buy
coal and other imports from Japan, American bottoms were to be used
for at least half the shipping, and so on.

The neocolonial aspects of this agreement would have been controversial, had its full content been revealed; Kim Il Sung predictably claimed
that it "transferred the south Korean economy to American hands." He
found especially reprehensible the "open door" passages that established
guarantees for foreign traders to travel through the interior at will.[16]
Rhee apparently kept from his cabinet the clauses requiring American
agreement on expenditures. An ECA official remarked later on that
"none of the high-ranking cabinet members" he met with seemed to be
aware of the clause requiring American concurrence in the allocation of
foreign exchange. When Rhee tried to terminate the agreement during
the Korean War, thinking that it gave Americans too much control over
the Korean treasury, John Muccio called it "organic": it could not be unilaterally abrogated without calling into question the entire American aid
program.[17]

It was, indeed, organic to the American-Korean relationship, denoting
a form of lateral, external penetration of the Korean state that expressed
the degree to which the ROK was a transnational construct. The oil regime into which the Americans organized South Korea would be another
good example. Although I discuss these matters in detail elsewhere,[18] we
may appreciate the dailiness of the mechanism in this one vignette, from
February 1950. "Minister of Commerce and Industry, Yun Po Sun, accompanied by Messrs. Lorean, Dawson and Kinney, called on the President [Rhee] . . . to discuss ways and means to expedite conclusion of the
contract to export 100,000 metric tons of rice to Japan." Rhee did not
like the price that Supreme Command, Allied Powers (SCAP) and ECA
set for the exported rice, nor the idea of importing barley from Japan or
wheat from the United States as a substitute in the Korean diet, but he
could do nothing about it. The agreement called for 100,000 tons of rice

for export to Japan in 1949, 285,000 in 1950, and the hoped-for level by 1954 was fully half a million tons.[19]

The fiscal and monetary pledges were honored in the breach by the Rhee regime, as anyone knowledgeable about the period would hasten to say; by June 1950 inflation was rampant, the budget was not balanced, and an overvalued currency hindered exports. How could this happen, given the high levels of American aid and close supervision?

In essence we may say that the liberal economic assumptions embodied in the 1948 agreement were isomorphic to the liberal political form of the 1948 Constitution. Each rested uncomfortably on a Korean society and political economy that emptied them of content. If the American demands in the 1948 agreement seem like the essence of sweet reason, it is only so from the standpoint of a power with nothing to fear from free trade. The modal Korean political economy, whether we speak of the right or the left versions of it, was almost the opposite: closure to the world economy, protectionist tariffs, a home market inaccessible to foreigners, and general industrialization for the nation, rather than partial industrialization for export to the world market.

In the spring of 1950, embassy and State Department officials were most worried not about the North Koreans, but about the viability of the Rhee regime. Rising inflation, combined with the political qualities of the ROK, evoked fears that the history of Republican China would be repeated.[20] Arthur Bloomfield and John P. Jensen of the Federal Reserve Bank journeyed to Korea in March 1950, and warned that inflation and deficit spending were out of control and might lead to an economic collapse. They urged a series of reforms based on previous work by the Fed in Paraguay, the Dominican Republic, Guatemala, and the Philippines: raise taxes, reduce deficits, use credit and monetary controls to stem inflation, and eliminate corruption.[21]

In 1950 the Korean economy presented a mixed, but not disastrous picture. Although inflation was bad, the 1949 summer grain harvest was the best ever, and the fall rice harvest was good. Industrial production in December 1949 was at 202, compared to 1947 figures indexed at 100; by March 1950 this was down to 163, then up to 218 in May. But levels of savings and investment were very low. The rural population was described in May 1950 as living "at a primitive level," with the average urban dweller "living at or near subsistence levels." The state still rationed rice, fixing the price and the amount each peasant family could buy. The labor movement was moribund, with most leaders dead or in jail, and "continued close Government control" of all unions. The state made heavy use of unpaid corvée labor, often dragooning people from politically-blacklisted families.[22]

The bellwether land question seemed to have been solved when a land reform bill finally passed the National Assembly in June 1949, placing a limit of three *chŏngbo* (about 7.5 acres) per family and providing for a system in which tenants made incremental, long-term payments for the land, while the state presented landlords with immediate payment in the form of rice bonds, which it hoped would be invested in industry. This reform applied to the roughly 80 percent of landlord-held land not owned by the Japanese. Americans always were the prime movers behind this gradualist redistribution, hoping to stimulate production and dampen peasant rebelliousness; the North Koreans also saw a strong relationship between the land problem and the guerrilla struggle.[23]

Unfortunately not a single paddy changed hands under the new law before the war—even though it is widely believed that the reform was implemented shortly after National Assembly passage. The ROK as of April 1950 had no administrative machinery for enforcing the land reform, and planned to use June and July 1950 to iron out landlord-tenant disputes and bureaucratic problems, and then carry out the distribution after the autumn rice harvest. In a secret memorandum in November 1950, an American official said, "at no point prior to the Korean hostilities, as far as can be determined, did the [ECA] Mission inform us that the distribution of a single parcel of land under this law had been completed; nor did we receive such information from any other source."[24] In October 1950 Rhee again sought postponement of land redistribution, which, the CIA reported, reflected pressures by the "landlord class" to delay or kill the reform, thus to "maintain their traditional controlling position in Korean political and economic life."[25]

AMERICAN-KOREAN MILITARY TIES

Nowhere was the American stamp more obvious than on the ROK Army, which was the most blessed of Korean institutions in American aid and support. Vyvyan Holt wrote that "the Korean troops all wear American uniforms, carry American arms, and move with American transport." Its eight divisions plus a First Cavalry Regiment recapitulated the American military model. The ROKA expanded from 50,000 in 1948 (when the Constabulary became the Army) to 75,000 in June 1949 to 100,000 a month later, with 95,000 enlisted men and 4,948 officers. The Capital Division, the elite corps of the ROKA, had three regiments, of which the best trained in the autumn of 1949 was the 17th—a regiment we will have much more to say about later. The Army did not expand significantly from that point until the war began.

The ROK also numbered 33,000 in the Army reserve, 51,000 in the National Police (which included combat battalions), and 6,700 in the Navy (*haegun*), or what the United States preferred to call the Coast

Guard. On paper the ROK thus had a total mobilizable armed strength of about 190,000, not counting the multitudinous youth groups. It had six artillery and three antitank battalions managing the heavier weapons. In June 1949 the ROK established an Air Academy and in October, an Air Force. Until the Korean War the pilots worked with training aircraft; by that time the strength of the Air Force was about 1,800 men. Although American sources emphasize the parallel development and expansion of the ROKA and the Korean People's Army (KPA), in fact the southern army grew much more rapidly in mid-1949, and the North played catch-up for months thereafter.[26]

KMAG advisors, numbering about 500, dominated the upper echelons of the Korean military. They were directly and continuously engaged in everything from suppressing guerrillas to training soldiers to administrative and budget matters, finally to exercising restraint on hotheaded Korean generals.[27] But this does not necessarily mean that the advisors controlled Korean action. It was more often a matter of running behind the Koreans, arms waving, while wringing a tourniquet around the necks of high officers by withholding offensive materiel.

When American combat forces withdrew in July 1949, they transferred without charge some $110 million in military equipment and supplies (again, about the size of the total ROK state budget), which included a lot of captured Japanese equipment, 128 antitank guns, 90 cannons, 20 liaison and reconnaissance aircraft, and the like. The Americans thought what they gave the Koreans was more than enough for a defensive army. Within the limits imposed by the American desire to leash Korean offensive capability, the United States did much more than the Russians. Muccio told Rhee in May 1949 that even if he were to take at face value G-2 estimates of what the Russians were doing for the KPA (which he thought were exaggerated), the United States was doing "considerably more."[28]

The Rhee regime put out farragoes of disinformation about American military deliveries, claiming for example that the ROKA had only been given enough ammunition to fight for two or three days; when General Roberts pointed out to Rhee that there was ammunition sufficient to last for five months, he did not relent, because he sought American backing for the offensive. That is the long and short of it, even if ROK spokesmen and their American advocates never tire of saying Acheson stupidly left the ROKA weak and exposed.

As always, it was the military that balked at the diversion of even more scarce American funds to Korea, not Acheson and the presumed appeasers in the State Department. KMAG officials sought to lower the fiscal year 1951 ROK defense budget by a full 25 percent. The Department of the Army worried in September 1949 that even the existing levels of military aid might either encourage the ROKA to attack, or provoke pre-emptive northern aggression. Muccio said in November 1949 that the problem was in getting sufficient military assistance "to enable the Kore-ans to defend this area and at the same time keep them from getting over-eager on moving North." Elsewhere he remarked bluntly, "We were in a very difficult position, a very subtle position, because if we gave Rhee and his cohorts what they wanted, they could have started to move north the same as the North started to move south. And the onus would have been on us."[29]

The one ROK weakness that seemed most striking in comparison to the North was air power,[30] and it is here that local American officials sought improvement in the months before the war, in spite of their wor-ries about giving the South offensive capabilities. Muccio, Roberts, and the ECA mission all recommended the provision of forty F-51 fighter planes to the ROK, to match the North's forty YAK fighters. But on March 11, 1950, Gen. Lyman Lemnitzer told Louis Johnson that an air force was not needed for the ROK, because it would not help hold the ROK against Soviet attack, was not needed to counter the northern threat, and might provide a "plausible basis" for allegations of a southern threat against the North. Muccio and the State Department also urged that Air Force advisors be detailed to Korea to train Korean pilots on ten AT6 trainers, which had been fitted out with machine guns at State De-partment request; this, too, was resisted by the Pentagon.[31] Yet even the airpower deficiency on the southern side is not odd, nor an indication of American unconcern: throughout the post–Korean War period the United States has also kept the ROK air force weak relative to the North's, preferring instead to substitute advanced airpower under its own control.

Pentagon opposition to aircraft for Korea was based both on general war plans, and on refusal to give the ROK weaponry that Acheson was denying to the Nationalists. Thus to obtain an air force Rhee, like Chiang Kai-shek, turned to MacArthur, Claire Chennault, and Civil Air Trans-port (CAT). The origin of this effort appears to have been Rhee's cable to MacArthur of September 19, 1949, where he said he was "feeling des-perate" about the strength of the DPRK's air force: "we approached Gen. Chennault who is deeply interested in our proposition and [he] recom-mended Brig. Gen. Russell E. Randall to come to help us as our advisor." Rhee asked that Randall, who was then on active duty, be "loaned" to the ROK. This cable was sent while Colonel Goodfellow was in Seoul and probably reflected his advice, since in early 1950 he was seeking aircraft for the ROK.[32]

Randall arrived in early November as an "employee" of the Rhee gov-ernment, even though Muccio and Roberts asked the Department of the

Army to deny him permission to enter Korea. Randall was a West Pointer with twenty-five years experience in air force activities; he led "Randall's Raiders" against the Japanese in Western China, and headed the Army Air Force liaison mission to the Chinese Nationalists in 1945. In 1948 he was assigned to a top intelligence post in Washington. He was known as a strong backer of Chiang Kai-shek.[33]

Randall toured Korea for about ten days. Little is known of the substance of his visit, but the North Koreans closely monitored his movements. When he returned to the United States he advocated an air force for the ROK. Randall was probably involved with Chennault's attempts to get CAT access to Korea in early 1950, which we discuss in the next chapter. Rhee's advisor Harold Lady was involved in all the aircraft negotiations, including Randall's visit and the purchase of the AT6 trainers, which he advised Rhee to buy from a private American company at prices "considerably in excess of the market," according to ECA records—which clearly implied that Lady was skimming the difference for himself. Although little is known about this purchase or how it came about, it probably proceeded much like Taiwan's purchase of military equipment from private American firms, such as the World Commerce Corporation.[34]

General Roberts was an avid salesman for the Korean Army, in spite of his private doubts about it. He told the Pentagon in March 1950 that it was underrating "the importance of the South Korean army of 100,000 trained men, trained to shoot for the West"; he told the Joint Chiefs of Staff (JCS) during their visit to Tokyo in March 1950 that "the Korean Army was making genuine progress and that he was confident that unless Russia furnished actual troops that the South Korean forces could handle any invasion by North Korean forces." The JCS were so impressed that they directed him to prepare a plan for the gradual reduction of KMAG.[35]

In some exuberant interviews with Marguerite Higgins a month before the war, Roberts said, "KMAG is a living demonstration of how an intelligent and intensive investment of 500 combat-hardened American men and officers can train 100,000 guys to do the shooting for you." The countryside had been "in a perpetual uproar" until recently, he indicated, but was now under control thanks to American advisors "at every level" who "live right there with [the Koreans] . . . and stay with them in battles." Higgins cited rumors that French officers had arrived to learn about KMAG counterinsurgency techniques for "export" to Indochina. In sum, Roberts thought, "the American taxpayer has an army that is a fine watchdog over the investments placed in this country and a force that represents the maximum results at minimum cost."[36]

Roberts's bluster remains a difficult thing to explain, since the fighting in 1949 made plain ROKA deficiencies, and internal materials as late as May 1950 depict the miserable state of various Korean Army units. Many were poorly trained, military equipment was constantly pilfered and cannibalized for other uses, personal rivalries were rampant, the Japanese-trained general staff was mostly incompetent. Roberts said in May that even the 6th and 8th Divisions, which had gained much experience in guerrilla fighting, had many weaknesses. They did not know how to use supporting weaponry, like artillery and mortar; signal equipment was neither maintained nor properly used.[37]

The training schedule of the Army is also interesting, as the war approached. The Koreans were to have completed the battalion phase of training by the end of March, and the regimental phase by June 30, a schedule well known to the North Koreans. Training timetables fell behind, however, because large units were still tied down by guerrillas in the interior. Thus on March 14, 1950, to speed up the timetable, the Army pushed "a concentrated, thirteen-week schedule to bring all units through the battalion phase by June 1 and the regimental phase by summer." By mid-June, fourteen police battalions had taken over internal security duties, freeing up some army units for regimental training.[38]

Still, according to Col. W.H.S. Wright of KMAG, in mid-June slightly more than 200 guerrillas (a ridiculously low estimate) were still tying down "three of the eight Divisions of the Korean Army"; he hoped that the Korean National Police (KNP) battalions could be phased in over the next eight months. Other sources indicated that Rhee hoped to replace 13,000 ROKA with the 10,000 KNP, but that progress was slow, and the new target date was August 1.[39]

These were American plans, however, sponsored by Roberts. They did not necessarily suit Rhee or his Korean commanders. From late April 1950 onward, several ROKA regiments did begin moving northward, deploying from Sunch'ŏn to Chŏnju, Andong to Onyang, Mach'ŏn to Wŏnju, and the like.[40] This movement ensued in spite of the absence of KNP replacements. By the time the war began, more than two-thirds of the ROKA was at or near the parallel. From Ongjin in the West to Chumunjin in the East, 32,500 troops were concentrated along the line, 28,000 were north of Seoul or in it, 7,000 were at Wŏnju, and 20,000 troops were in areas from Taejŏn southward.[41] In other words a substantial and fairly rapid redeployment northward occurred in the weeks before June 25.

In retrospect American authorities noted that within a few days of the start of the war, the South had lost 70 percent of its military equipment, all in fighting north of the Han River; MacArthur said that the southern army had not "developed any positions in depth. Everything between the

38th parallel and Seoul was their area of depot," that is, almost all their supplies were north of Seoul.[42]

How is this to be explained? Most likely because southern commanders thought the summer of 1950 would be like the summer of 1949, only more so. It was, as we have seen, Kim Sŏk-wŏn's plan to concentrate ROKA forces along the parallel in the summer of 1949, pending border battles with the North, and a march North. The ROKA deployed northward because Rhee thought fighting would again erupt at the parallel in the summer months; the absence of a defense in depth was probably because Rhee, Kim Sŏk-wŏn, and others thought the best defense was a good offense. That is one plausible explanation of the South's refusal to follow Roberts's plan, and it is noteworthy that this occurred after Roberts's wife became seriously ill and he began to wind down his affairs in preparation for early retirement.

Indeed, KMAG was the one American agency that lost most of its high command just before the war. In March Roberts wrote that "within the next three months KMAG loses all top officers," including himself. He left for Japan on June 15, with his replacement not scheduled to arrive until August; he accompanied Dulles back to Seoul, then returned and shipped off from Tokyo to the United States on June 23 after several days of talks with MacArthur, for which there appears to be no record. The acting chief of KMAG, Col. W.H.S. Wright, was also in Japan just before the war, returning to Seoul on June 26.[43]

Although some thoughtless writers, and especially the North Koreans, have sought to depict Roberts as a coconspirator in provoking the war, really the opposite is the case. Roberts had been clamping restraints on headstrong Korean generals for a year before the war began. A career soldier of limited capacities, with no pretensions or ambitions, he knew how to carry out Acheson's and Muccio's orders. For this he was loathed and reviled by Rhee and generals like Kim Sŏk-wŏn, whose head rolled in the fall of 1949 at Roberts's behest.[44] Therefore the extraordinary significance of Roberts's role on June 25 is not his presence, but precisely his absence. For the first time he was away in a moment of crisis, and so were many experienced KMAG officers.

The American military, however, had not forgotten Korea. In late March 1950 the aircraft carrier Boxer scrambled forty-two jets for flights over central Vietnam as a demonstration of American "military strength," and two weeks later it sent fifty planes roaring over Pusan and Taegu. The carrier Valley Forge left on a similar mission in mid-May, with an accompanying task force of twenty ships, to show the flag in "the troubled Orient." In May the United States also mounted near Puerto Rico the largest war games since 1945, involving 60,000 soldiers under the command of none other than Gen. John R. Hodge; insignificant in itself, it would still have given the North Koreans pause.[45]

"THE COMATOSE COMMISSION"

When war came in June, the United Nations Commission on Korea (UN-COK), and especially its military observers, played a critical role in legitimating the American and South Korean version of events, and in convincing the United Nations to condemn North Korea and join the battle. Most analysts have taken it for granted that UNCOK was a reasonably objective observer, and in a position to monitor the events that began the war. In fact, the use made of UNCOK was little short of scandalous.

UNCOK was an important component of the Western presence in South Korea, but unlike the United States its position had deteriorated almost to nonexistence in the months before the war. UNCOK barely functioned in late 1949 and early 1950, holding few meetings and even fewer with a quorum. A committee so crucial to the international legitimacy of ROK state formation in 1948 almost lapsed into oblivion. How this happened is of extraordinary import.

In the middle of the summer 1949 border battles, several commission members sought to call United Nations attention to the explosive situation in Korea. The man they wrote to, almost always, was Andrew Cordier, an American diplomat who later played a key role in the ouster of Patrice Lumumba in the Congo. In early July the French delegate, Henri Costilhes, called for American-Soviet negotiations on Korea, fearing the "imminent danger of internecine warfare." This in turn led to a report in the *New York Times*, saying that UNCOK would recommend to the UN that the Korea problem be turned back to the U.S. and the USSR, and that UNCOK be terminated.[46] This period also witnessed UNCOK's briefing by border commander Kim Sŏk-wŏn, which we treated in chapter 12.

UNCOK thought it was sandwiched between an indifferent United Nations and a bubbling civil war, and it wanted out. But it did not get out. It is of signal importance that the decision to install military observers grew out of worries about aggression emanating from the South, more than from the North. At the time of the September 1949 exodus, Egon Ranshofen-Wertheimer, an important and knowledgeable UNCOK staff member, wrote to Phillip Jessup urging that UNCOK be replaced by a UN High Commissioner, who would seek to open talks among all sides to prevent a unification by force. The North might "strike a decisive blow" against the South, he feared, although he did not think that was likely in September 1949:

On the other hand, the ROK might feel that its chances of absorbing the North are diminished from month to month in view of the growing strength of Kim Il Sung's armies. . . . The temptation for Rhee to invade the North and the pressure exerted upon him to do so might, therefore, become irresistible. The top military authorities of the Republic . . . are exerting continual pressure upon Rhee to take the initiative and cross the parallel.[47]

At the same time, Butterworth told the British that "there had been a good deal of fighting and that there was a hot-headed element in the South, possibly composed of northern Koreans"; thus he wanted UNCOK to have military men on the scene, the implication being that they, like Roberts, would restrain the *South* Koreans.[48] It is exceedingly doubtful that the Americans bothered to inform the United Nations of this fact, however. But it did not escape the attention of the North Koreans, who reported accurately that the decision to appoint military observers grew out of two months of private discussions in Seoul from September to November about the possibility of a war along the parallel. They said publicly that the observers were an American ploy to "legalize" interference in Korean affairs,[49] but it is clear that they understood that UNCOK was expected to restrain the South as well as monitor the North. As for the South, they would wish to influence, cajole, but above all corral and confine foreign military observers sent to watch for aggression, anticipated more from the southern side of the thirty-eighth parallel. UNCOK's fifteenth report in October 1949 reflected the southern logic:

The deterrents to unification by force have grown weaker of late . . . there is some hope that the Commission will not in all circumstances refuse to countenance the use of force in the settlement of the Korean question. The [military] observer teams are not looked upon as an impartial body, but as a means of making sure that responsibility for the initiation of military conflict is placed where it belongs.

There are indications that the [ROK] Army is restive. This lack of docility is not limited to the Army. . . . There seems also to be some confidence that in case of crisis the Northern regime will not receive strong support from outside.

Seoul's streets were "full of marching young men in and out of uniform . . . one has a sense of the growing mobilization of the population." One could not be entirely sure of the ROK's intentions; "they point, however, in the direction of military action."[50]

Note the logic of this passage: the UNCOK military observers were not to be impartial, but to place the blame for civil war "where it belonged."

Whereupon the passage indicates that it belonged with the South. Rhee wanted an UNCOK that would turn a blind eye to southern provocations, meanwhile getting ready to blame the North when hostilities began. Note also that these letters and reports filtered through the hands of a man named Zinchenko, a Soviet citizen on the UN staff; one assumes that they then filter to Stalin, and to Kim Il Sung.

In September 1949 most of the delegates departed, virtually closing up shop. Remaining UNCOK functionaries complained of their "enforced idleness"; a U.S. embassy memorandum of January 1950 referred contemptuously to "the comatose Commission." February brought hopes of a "rejuvenated" group, and in March it was announced that military observers would be added to UNCOK, but by the end of March it was again said to be "largely inactive."[51]

By late May 1950, UNCOK consisted of official delegates from Australia, Turkey, Taiwan (Nationalist China), and India. As in 1948, the observers often left much to be desired. The Indian delegate was hospitalized with a broken leg. Kasim Gulek, the Turkish delegate, got a degree in England and then in 1933 went to Berlin where he completed a law degree under the Nazis. He was notorious in Seoul for his insulting advances on Korean women.[52] A small staff assisted the delegates: its secretary was Tao-Kim Andre Hai from Vietnam (that part ruled by Bao Dai). A Salvadoran delegate and one Australian military observer arrived at the end of the month, to be followed by another military observer on June 6. No further additions occurred before the Korean War.[53]

The Australian military observer Maj. F.S.B. Peach arrived on May 29, his countryman Squadron Leader R. J. Rankin a week later, that is, less than three weeks before the war. Peach was an Australian Army officer, Rankin an Air Force man. They had no experience in Korean affairs, and had never visited the country. After thirteen weeks of intensive training by the Peace Corps, including heavy language study, I arrived in Seoul in 1967. It was at least two weeks before I had oriented myself in any fashion to a country that seemed far more complex, cluttered, alien, and overwhelming than I had been led to expect. Many of the other members of our group were sick or exhausted, and some returned home within days of their arrival. If someone had asked me to tour the DMZ and report on whether the South Korean Army was defensively or offensively arrayed, I might have responded that I was still trying to find my way back to the hotel.

UNCOK was, and perhaps had to be, little more than an adjunct of the American presence in Korea. MacArthur sent planes to fly the delegates around, KMAG provided jeeps, and the embassy shepherded them through their days, housing and feeding them, and putting up with their unending complaints about life in Seoul.[54] As in 1949, UNCOK visits called forth the full foreign visitor's treatment for which the ROK is justly famous. The UNCOK Secretariat went up to observe the parallel in early 1950, in a convoy headed by a machine-gun mounted jeep full of military police; they passed through towns and villages along the route up from Seoul where soldiers stood with rifles at 50-yard intervals; huge preparations had been made for their arrival at the parallel—a band played, children brought flowers, local officials turned out,[55] and any chance of independent inquiry vanished like the morning calm.

Five members of UNCOK went over to have a look at the east coast in late March, 1950. Stopping first in Kangnŭng, they were briefed by 8th Division ROKA commander Yi Hyŏng-gŭn, the swashbuckling officer who, as we saw in volume 1, had a bit too much of the Japanese Imperial Army about him for American tastes: Gen. Yi "recalled the thirteen-month control exercised by the People's Committee in 1945 and 1946 and admitted the continued existence of a leftist underground movement," hearkening back to the heyday of the committees. They interrogated a forty-five-year-old man who had been a member of the local peasant union since 1946, and had joined guerrillas in the summer of 1948—"at that time contacts existed between guerrillas in the hills and underground organizations" in Kangnŭng, but such contacts ceased in 1949, he related. The UNCOK group then traveled north to the parallel. The "entire population" of various villages along the way "were massed at the road side in greeting," and from time to time their transit was interrupted by "tremendous organized mass reception[s]."[56]

The Rhee forces, ever adept at the manipulative skills of "low determines high" diplomacy, managed to involve UNCOK directly in their version of civil war politics. UNCOK delegates were at the reviewing stand when Rhee urged an attack on the North on March 1, 1950, and the speech by the Turkish delegate, Gulek, demonstrated the degree to which UNCOK sided with the ROK. A week later Gen. Kim Sŏk-wŏn spoke at a ceremony honoring UNCOK. The Australian member, Arthur Jamieson, spoke at the May Day 1950 extravaganza welcoming the first anniversary of An Ho-sang's paramilitary Student Defense Corps; the youths shouted oaths of fealty to "the supreme leader of the nation," Syngman Rhee, and vowed to recover "the lost territories."[57]

UNCOK held some desultory meetings with South Korean leaders in the early months of 1950, sampling opinion; these consisted exclusively of Rhee stalwarts or the "opposition" figures with whom the Americans first consulted in September 1945.[58] No longer was UNCOK interested in listening to the moderates, or the tattered remains of the Left. The Rhee regime was also successful in prevailing upon the governments of Taiwan and the Philippines to appoint friendly delegates, and to bring pressure on other governments to do the same.[59]

The delegate from China (that is, Taiwan) was Liu Yu-wan, an important and trusted Nationalist diplomat. He was the first Nationalist ambassador to Korea in 1948. Liu often met Koreans in the company of Yi Pŏm-sŏk, a protégé of Chiang Kai-shek; UNCOK officials thought he was quite close to President Rhee.[60] He was the most active member of UNCOK in 1949–1950, serving as its rapporteur in the fall of 1949, and as its chairman during the writing of UNCOK's report on the important May 30, 1950, elections—something that greatly pleased the U.S. embassy, and that also happened to place him in this key position when the war broke out. In July 1950, he was appointed deputy chief of mission in Tokyo, an important post for the Nationalists since it involved frequent interaction with MacArthur.[61]

UNCOK was not composed exclusively of representatives from America's threatened dominoes or client states, however. The Australian and Indian delegates and several members of the administrative staff were far more responsible to the ideals of the United Nations, and in June 1950 they sought again to contact the North Koreans, for the first time since the May 1948 elections. This important demarche also had the backing of Trygve Lie and, apparently, Acheson and certain Russians.

It will be remembered that in his important Berkeley speech in March, Acheson suggested that if the Soviets wished to show good faith, they might allow UNCOK into North Korea. Acheson's daily intelligence summaries show an entry for May 2 saying that Lie "will take advantage of any opportunity while [in Moscow] to discuss the Korean question with Soviet leaders." A UN Secretariat official had related that the head of UNCOK, "rather mysteriously and surprisingly," had suggested to Lie that the assistant secretary-general of the UN, the Russian named Zinchenko, "might serve as liaison between North and South Korea and possibly act as 'a sort of mediator' between the two capitals." Shortly the United States informed Muccio that the UNCOK attempt to enlist Lie in "making contact with North Korea" would not contradict its "terms of reference." The embassy urged great secrecy, saying that should news of this gambit leak out in Seoul, it would have "explosive possibilities."[62]

After some weeks the North responded, through an unknown modality, that it would send three emissaries to meet with UNCOK representatives on June 10 at Yohyŏn Station on the thirty-eighth parallel, and invited South Korean political party leaders to come as well. The ROK said any who did so would be deemed traitors. John Gaillard, a member of the UNCOK staff, departed for Yohyŏn station with the two Australian military observers, Peach and Rankin, accompanied by some Western reporters, arriving at the parallel at 3:30 P.M. on June 10. He was told by Gen. Paek Sŏn-yŏp, the commander, that he could not proceed. At Paek's order, southern forces raked the opposing hills with automatic weapons fire, whereupon northern forces responded in kind.

The northern guns quieted at 5 P.M., the appointed time for Gaillard to traverse the parallel; ROK guns continued firing. But finally a stillness fell, and Gaillard went forward. He talked with the North Koreans for about two hours, whom he found to be thoroughly frightened: they had been hiding in holes, thinking that ROK guns would target them. He accepted from them copies of a unification appeal; they declined to receive UNCOK materials that Gaillard had brought for them, saying they had no authority to do so, and also questioned him as to his nationality—which was American, yet another stumbling block.[63]

As Gaillard sought to return across the parallel, blazing South Korean guns pinned him down again. Finally he was allowed back. The next day the three emissaries, Yi In-gyu, Kim Tae-hong, and Kim Chae-jang, crossed into the South, saying that they wished to see political party leaders that ROK authorities had prevented from meeting with them. They were arrested, and the first indications were that they would immediately be shot. Instead they were jailed and remanded to a military court, perhaps after American representations. All three, according to embassy sources, had "subversive records" in pre-1948 southern Korea; they would undergo interrogation to get "maximum information" and to get them to defect. The Americans urged "gentle handling" and their return across the parallel, "after intelligence or counterpropaganda usefulness [had] ended."[64]

By June 15, two of them had "defected," giving broadcasts into North Korea acclaiming Rhee as the "Father of the Country," recanting all their previous political beliefs, and lauding the "freedom and plenty" of the South. The third refused to speak, fearing for his family in the North. But by June 18, he had also been broken and began broadcasting.[65]

The Yohyŏn meeting heralded the first direct contact between UNCOK and North Korea since the United Nations became involved in the Korean question, and although little of note was transacted, it was an exceedingly important symbolic meeting that unquestionably had the approval of Kim Il Sung. It also would have established a precedent for further contacts and, with the result in from the May 30 elections, for newly-elected moderates to work around Rhee toward talks with the North. At this time it also appeared likely that China would be allowed into the United Nations under a Byzantine formula that the United States was not opposing (although not supporting, either); this would only promote the use of the UN for mediation between the Korean sides. It is, finally, most interesting that at this late date, Acheson was still apparently looking for some breakthrough on Korea.

THE MAY 30 ELECTIONS

A few weeks before the war began, the ROK held its second National Assembly elections. The result was a disastrous loss for the Rhee regime, bringing into the Assembly a strong collection of middle-roaders and moderate leftists, several of them associated with the Yŏ Un-hyŏng current in Korean politics, and most of them hoping for unification with the North.

The high politics of the ROK in 1950 consisted of a two-party system, the same one forged in the fall of 1945: the Rhee party and the Korean Democratic Party (KDP). Both agreed on everything except who should run the executive and control the police and the army. The Korean Democratic Party continued to be run by Kim Sŏng-su and his allies, and in February 1949 it got a few Rhee-aligned politicians to break off and join it. Thereupon its name was changed to the Democratic Nationalist Party (DNP). Rhee responded by trying to gather his old NSRRKI supporters into the Taehan Nationalist Party (TNP),[66] but in typical fashion the real struggle was within the coercive agencies of the state, not at the ballot box.

An important embassy political study completed in April 1950[67] could have been written in the fall of 1945. The DNP, it said, was "the largest and most powerful" party, backed by "industrialists and landlords." It had a "lightly veiled" opposition to land reform, and had no "political machine" in the rural areas, relying instead on police and bureaucrats to bring people to the polls. Indeed, "organization of all political parties is weak outside of Seoul, especially in the rural areas." Its newspaper, as always, was the *Tonga ilbo*. As in 1945, only the Left sought to organize peasants and workers, and almost all leftist organization was underground or destroyed by 1950.

Politicians from both parties agreed that there were "no great differences" between the positions of the two parties; the embassy commented that "ideological differences among the various groups are secondary to contests for power and prestige" and that there was "no longer any basic overt disagreement between Right and Center as to the fundamental character or desirability of the government of the ROK." Factional conflict was nonetheless intense, leading people "to bolt their party on very slight provocation." The system was paternalistic and flowed out from the center; in local areas the police kept order, and politicians saw no virtue in organizing big constituencies. Instead they sought penetration and control of the central bureaucracy, or as the embassy put it, "Korean groups which feel they are not receiving their share of the wealth or power direct their efforts not to carving out a greater field for private enterprise, or for individual liberty, but to attempting to gain control of the authoritarian governmental system."

Rhee's party was completely dominated by the executive, and had even less coherence than the DNP. As always, it was "a loose federation of factions" with little or no local leadership. Because of severe factional infighting over previous months, the embassy wondered if it could "hold together until election day." Parties that had some strength in the 1940s were moribund. Kim Ku's Korean Independence Party (KIP) was now "a very small group," moderate politicians aligned with Yŏ Un-hyŏng or Kim Kyu-sik ran "miniscule" parties of no weight. After all, politicians had to be careful since "an overly liberal-minded candidate" might say the wrong thing, and "it is a simple matter to jail him on suspicion of subversive activity." The Americans wrote about all this, of course, as if it fell from the sky at some point in the distant and misty past, instead of being integrally related to American-directed and supported actions over the previous five years.

Elections, for Rhee, were a vexing anathema conducted only to please the Americans. Almost as soon as the ROK was established in 1948, its top leaders worried about the next go-round of voting. Cho Pyŏng-ok confided to Wellington Koo in January 1949 that the Rhee regime faced "two big questions": the second was a northern invasion, and the first was this: "if the leftist politicians like Kim Koo [!] and Kimm Kiu Sic should get a majority in the legislative assembly, President Rhee's party would lose its present control, and [they] would certainly pursue a policy of appeasement with North Korea in the name of unification."[68] Rhee sought to postpone the elections several times, but under intense American pressure the date was finally set for May 30.

In many districts of Seoul, conservative clones ran against each other: Kim Sŏng-su against Pak Sun-ch'ŏn, Kim To-yŏn against Helen Kim, Yun Ch'i-yŏng against An Tong-wŏn. Election committees uniformly came from the thin stratum of wealthy and highly educated Koreans, working with government officials to register voters, herd them to the polls, and get helpful policemen to post handbills calling opposition candidates "Red dogs" and the like. Election brokers offered votes at 200,000 *wŏn* per thousand, while the myriad youth groups, described as quasi-governmental organizations, "campaigned" for either the DNP or TNP.[69] At least 9,000 people were under detention for violation of the infamous National Security Law at election time, 5,000 of whom had been held without trial for more than four months.[70] As we saw earlier, these included thirteen members of the National Assembly who were convicted of violating this law on March 14, 1950.

In spite of all this the Rhee system was incomplete, a shaky approximation of the total politics it sought. A major new element was injected when many former moderates and mild leftists ran as "independents" and got on the ballot. Most were allies of Kim Kyu-sik, Kim Ku, and the late Yŏ Un-hyŏng. These included Chang Kŏn-sang, Cho So-ang, Ŏm Hang-sŏp, Wŏn Se-hun, Yi Sun-t'aek, Ch'oe Tong-o, Paek Sang-gyu, An Chae-hong, Yŏ's brother, Yŏ Un-hong, and many more obscure figures. Rhee fretted mightily about such people, jailing thirty candidates and over one hundred campaign workers by the time of the election.

Those who trundled to the polls recalcitrantly voted against the government and elected about sixty independents and moderates, including most of those listed above, with only thirty-one members of the previous Assembly being returned. The mass of Koreans cast a vote against the incumbents, and often for the most left-leaning candidates available, most of whom were in favor of unification. Government officials were defeated, the embassy said, "almost to a man." Most sources thought the new assembly lineup would show 62 in the TNP, 48 in the DNP, 22 from pro-Rhee youth corps groups, 60 independents, plus another 24 from splinter parties and "middle-roaders" who might vote with the independents, giving them a distinct majority. The *Tonga ilbo* thought the independents would coalesce under the leadership of Wŏn Se-hun, Yŏ Un-hong, and Chang Kŏn-sang. Cho Pyŏng-ok's fears proved valid in general, but also in his own case: he lost to Kim Ku–aligned Cho So-ang.

Both Rhee's party and the DNP lost heavily. MacArthur's intelligence explained the losses by reference to the ruling politicians' "stigma" as pro-Japanese, and noted that Rhee's charges of procommunism against the moderates helped many of them to be elected. Rhee, however, mounted a rostrum a week after the elections and declared that "the people, it seems, are rather disturbed by the [results of] the election," and linked the moderates to the communist cause.[71]

Among Americans, pro-Rhee conservatives and anti-Rhee liberals were both discomfited. Roy Howard, the China Lobby figure, wrote Rhee that he was sorry to learn of "the apparent reduction in your control of the situation." The CIA, however, had hoped to see the reduction of Rhee's "autocratic control" by the DNP—described as "a relatively talented and well-organized group representing landed and business interests" that would be more likely to carry out economic policies urged upon Korea by the Americans. Liberals also fretted that the huge aid program would be jeopardized, since Congress had placed a rider on the Korean aid bill saying it would cease if a "coalition" or unified government emerged, defined as a government having one or more communists, or any members of the North Korean ruling party, in its midst. No real communists were elected, of course, but Rhee's supporters used that label for most of the moderates; the *New York Times* reported that Rhee thought many of those elected had a "Red tinge."[72]

Soon after the election returns the North Koreans agreed to meet with UNCOK representatives, as we have seen, and began a major new unification effort; although little is known about their contacts within the National Assembly, unquestionably they existed. The newly-elected independents subsequently remained in Seoul when KPA tanks rumbled in, "almost to a man," and many worked with the new administration.[73]

On June 7 the Democratic Front for the Unification of the Fatherland (DFUF) issued an appeal for joint North-South talks among political leaders, suggesting they meet on June 19 at the thirty-eighth parallel, and calling for peaceful unification through all-Korea elections in early August and the convening of a new unitary national assembly on the fifth anniversary of liberation. The proclamation made special appeals to southern independents, terming Yŏ Un-hyŏng "the Korean people's patriot who fought for the independence and democracy of the homeland," lamenting Kim Ku's assassination, and lauding Kim Kyu-sik for his attempts at North-South unity. It demanded restoration of the People's Committees. Muccio said the North had seized the initiative in the propaganda battle with this appeal; it had a "superficial reasonableness" that might be attractive to the "large body [of] South Korean public opinion which still yearns for elimination of the 38th parallel," and to the "confused liberal opinion" in the National Assembly. But the date for an all-Korea assembly also might serve "as a preliminary step for all-out civil war," Muccio said, although deeming this outcome improbable.[74]

ROKA Chief of Staff Ch'ae Pyŏng-dŏk said anyone who responded to the North's appeal would be considered a traitor (and therefore subject to execution); a Soviet newspaper published before the war claimed that Rhee reinforced the border from June 13 to 19 so no one could cross to the North.[75] On June 19 the meeting was held, but only those southerners already in the North participated.

At this time P'yŏngyang issued warrants for the arrest of nine "national traitors": President Rhee, Yi Pŏm-sŏk, Kim Sŏng-su, Shin Sŭng-mo, Ch'ae Pyŏng-dŏk, Cho Pyŏng-ok, Yun Ch'i-yŏng, Hugh Cynn, and Paek Sŏng-uk; a baleful "etcetera" dangled at the end of the list. The group that met on June 19 called for a North-South meeting of assemblymen two days later, to arrange the merger of the southern legislature with the DPRK's Supreme People's Assembly by August 15. For the first time, a northern statement used the official name of the National Assembly, and did not list any members as "traitors"—although the embassy noted that some, like Chang T'aek-sang, "would undoubtedly qualify."[76]

From hindsight this flurry of activity resembles not only a propaganda ploy but one that purposely masked the coming assault. Yet the North had done the same in June and September 1949, leading Americans at the time also to think it might herald an invasion.[77] The events of May and June 1950 do not prove that the North orchestrated a smoke screen to hide war plans; the election results would in fact embolden those who argued that the Rhee regime was ripe for more political activity leading to an internal collapse.

The North played one last political card at this time, an unprecedented offer to exchange Cho Man-sik, the Christian democrat still alive in a northern prison, for two top members of the South Korean Worker's Party (SKWP), Kim Sam-yong and Yi Chu-ha, who had been arrested by the KNP in late March. They had been confidants of Pak Hŏn-yŏng, operating from the SKWP base in Haeju. The North Korean press was extremely exercised about these arrests for weeks before the war, suggesting that the embassy was correct in believing that the action had smashed the SKWP underground in Seoul. About thirteen high SKWP members were rounded up in the aftermath, and at least two were "converted" by torture—leading Drumwright to exclaim that " 'conversion' has been of inestimable value to the Police" in getting information necessary to "wreck" the SKWP. It does not appear that Kim and Yi were broken, however.

According to ROK intelligence, after the "secret" merger of the North Korean Worker's Party (NKWP) and the SKWP in June 1949, Kim Sam-yong was made "directly responsible to Kim Il Sung," which they thought reduced Pak Hŏn-yŏng's influence and made Kim Sam-yong the key leader of communists in the South.[78] This is merely one more reason to reject the notion that Pak somehow started the war. But the breaking of the southern party apparatus decapitated underground activities which, combined with the sagging fortunes of the guerrillas, would make more salient the virtues of a conventional military assault.

Rhee did decide to respond to this proposal, saying Yi and Kim could be exchanged for Cho Man-sik if Cho's son were added to the deal; Rhee went against "vigorous opposition" by the military brass, who did not want to let such important communists loose. It may be that Rhee did not expect Kim Il Sung to give up the son, too, but on June 18 the North responded positively, rejecting only Rhee's suggested modality of exchange, which was UNCOK. On June 23 both sides were still disagreeing on how the exchange would occur; at 11 P.M. that day the North suggested the exchange be consummated at noon on June 26. The embassy reported on June 24 that the South had decided not to pursue the exchange, except on ROK terms. On June 26, after the war started, Yi and Kim were taken from the West Gate prison to a military command post on South Mountain in Seoul, where they were tied to a tree and shot. At some point in the summer or fall of 1950, Cho Man-sik and several of his relatives were executed in the North.[79]

BEDLAM: STRUGGLE FOR THE RHEE STATE

As if the Rhee regime did not have enough on its hands with the elections, the North Korean initiatives, and a variety of other pressing problems, in the weeks leading up to the war a murky factional struggle threatened to tear it asunder. Unlike the decline in Rhee's fortunes in the National Assembly, which was a mostly ineffectual body that could not threaten his rule, this fracas involved the coercive agencies of the state: the Home Ministry, the police, the army, and shadowy intelligence groups. In good Korean fashion the arena of strife was the commanding heights, pitting Rhee's forces against the conservative (DNP) opposition; the goal was control of the bureaucracy and the Seoul nerve center.

Ernst Fraenkel, the former USAMGIK Justice Department official, said that at "the roots" of the ROK system there were in effect two governments: "one official and open, and another unofficial, a 'shadow' organization." He thought the shadowy state-within-a-state was probably the more effective of the two.[80] South Korea was in this sense isomorphic to the conflict going on at the same time in the American state for control of foreign policy—but the dramatis personae were a bit different than Dean Acheson and Louis Johnson. The specific objects of this internal brawl were to compromise and purge the defense minister, Shin Sŭng-mo (who was also the acting prime minister at the time); the home minister, Kim Hyo-sŏk; the head of the Korean National Police; and other prominent officials, and to replace them with cronies of Yi Pŏm-sŏk, Yun Ch'i-yŏng, Louise Yim, and, of course, Syngman Rhee. If the reader asks, were not the existing officials also close to Rhee, the answer is that they were acceptable to Rhee but also, and critically, more acceptable to the Americans and to the DNP. Their suggested replacements, in every case, were not. The Home Ministry and National Police had been the bureaucratic preserve of the DNP/KDP since 1945, with many if not most of its members owing their positions to Cho Pyŏng-ok and Chang T'aek-sang, with Cho (if not Chang) being a great American favorite.

A particular goal, for example, was to place Gen. Kim Sŏk-wŏn in the position of chief of staff of the Army, something Shin and the Americans did not want. This Shin-Kim struggle is of more than passing interest, since Shin was pliable and pro-American, Kim was ornery and disliked Americans; he had been replaced as head of the 1st Division in the fall of 1949 under intense American pressure, because of his provocative behavior along the thirty-eighth parallel. The shadow cabinet of this dim conspiracy looked like this: defense minister, Chŏng Un-su; KNP director, Chang Sŏk-yun; home minister, Paek Sŏng-uk; Army chief of staff, Kim Sŏk-wŏn; deputy chief of staff, Yi Ŭng-jun; head of Seoul Police, Chang Yun-po; Louise Yim, the vastly corrupt crony of Rhee, would return to her mediating role in doling out Japanese vested properties to her friends, as minister of commerce and industry.[81]

Chŏng Un-su was the son of P'yŏn Tong-hyŏn, a long-time secretary and ally to Rhee in the United States; P'yŏn had advocated an attack on the North in correspondence with Rhee in 1949. His son was an American citizen who joined the U.S. Army, came to Korea, and carried out special investigations for Rhee. By 1950 Chŏng was close to Yi Pŏm-sŏk. Yun Ch'i-yŏng was one of the earliest confidants of the American command in September 1945, and was allied with perhaps the most notorious colonial police torturer in Korea, No Tŏk-sul; Yun prevailed upon Rhee to intervene personally to keep No from being imprisoned for his services to the Japanese. Yi Ŭng-jun we met in volume 1; he was the Japanized general who enjoyed parading in jackboots and riding crop.

Chang Sŏk-yun was well-known to Americans as "Montana Chang," that is to say notorious; he had lived in Montana and must have become an American citizen, because when he returned to Korea he was a sergeant in the U.S. Army. He worked in USAMGIK G-2 and the Counter-Intelligence Corps (CIC), where he did intelligence work for the Americans and his own private investigations for Rhee; he was the brother-in-law of Yun Ch'i-yŏng. He was also close to Yi Pŏm-sŏk. By 1950 Montana Chang was described as a "long-time Presidential special agent," and was reviled by the embassy as corrupt, obstinate, and a dangerous and perennial source of intrigue. He was also deeply implicated in a nauseating morass of extortion, arrests, brutal beatings, and the like, directed at Rhee's opposition.[82]

Paek Sŏng-uk was close to Yi Pŏm-sŏk, and sashayed around Seoul with an influential concubine named Son Chae-p'yŏn. Considered a " 'living Buddha' blessed with remarkable clairvoyant powers" by those who knew her charms (mainly Paek and Yi), Ms. Son conducted seances for high officials—including, it would appear, President Rhee himself. The ancient Yi Se-yŏng was also part of this conspiracy, using his remnant Sŏron-p'a faction from the Yi Dynasty as a conduit into the regime for supporters of Kim Ku, now lacking their factional leader.

It is important to note two qualities of this rogues' gallery: nationalism in regard to the Americans, or at least obstreperous resistance to embassy and KMAG meddling; ties to, respect for, and sometimes cringing obeisance toward, Generalissimo Chiang Kai-shek. Muccio said that when Chiang visited Chinhae in 1949, he had been struck by the "scurrying servile manner" of Yi Pŏm-sŏk and other Koreans in front of Chiang, for whom they have "awe and profound respect."[83]

The longest tradition in the long tradition of *sadae* was to serve China. Americans always considered Yi Pŏm-sŏk either too nationalistic or too pro-Chinese; he spoke Chinese better than he did Korean, and was widely regarded as the head of the pro-Nationalist group in Korea, which would also include the followers of Kim Ku. Yi had become quite powerful through his control of the Korean National Youth, as we have seen; the embassy wrote that Yi had "considerable influence in the Police and Army through former members of his USAMGIK-sponsored Korean National Youth Corps who are now members of those organizations." Anyway, a faction with links to China always has a high resonance in Korean politics. Yi's goal, the embassy thought, was to reduce the long-standing, considerable DNP influence in the state bureaucracy, then make Rhee dependent upon and manipulable by this group, "and thereby be in a position to control the Executive and Legislative (and therefore, the Judicial) branches of the Government."[84]

In late March the embassy reported that Rhee was more and more dependent on Yun Ch'i-yŏng and Louise Yim, who had set up the Tae-han Nationalist Party in December 1949 to try to build "a strong political following" for Rhee, with an eye cast toward the May 30 elections. Yun

11. Yi Pŏm-sŏk speaking in September 1949, with Syngman Rhee idly scratching his neck, in the rear

and Yim were also anxious to have Kim Sŏk-wŏn named chief of staff of the ROKA, since Kim was a key fund-raiser for the TNP: he had "given generously of funds . . . accumulated when [he was] Commander of the First Division."

KMAG and the embassy, however, thought the return of Kim would be "disastrous." Roberts, for example, reviled Kim's "speculations, dishonesty, corruption, misuse of public office and total disregard of the ethics and moral standards required of an officer"; he retained "all the worst features of the Japanese officer class and, as far as I can make out, practically none of its undoubted professional virtues." Kim's knowledge of military science and tactics was "extremely limited," Roberts thought, his capacity for corruption and military ineptitude correspondingly distended. But that was perhaps a lesser problem than this: "he consistently disregarded directives from Headquarters, Korean Army," to the point that Roberts "would have brought him to trial by general courts martial on several occasions." But this was impossible because of his close ties to Rhee. Kim Sŏk-wŏn always bypassed his superiors (meaning mainly Shin Sŭng-mo), "taking all his intrigues and disloyalties direct to President Rhee." If Kim were appointed chief of staff, Roberts said he would resign, return to Washington, and recommend that the United States reevaluate "the continued efficacy" of KMAG.[85]

At this same time, it was reported that Rhee feared Kim Hyo-sŏk, the home minister socked into the middle of this bedlam, who was one of the DNP opposition's allies. Kim later stayed in Seoul and made broadcasts on behalf of the DPRK, just like the middle-road assemblymen. He had been an organizer of the *Minbodan* in the 1948 elections, while holding a position in the Home Ministry. He also got himself elected to the National Assembly, from Hapch'ŏn County in South Kyŏngsang. Shin Sŭng-mo was both pro-American and close to the DNP, and had brought Kim Hyo-sŏk into the Home Ministry position. In the spring of 1950 Kim was "carefully building up a police organization" to help elect DNP candidates; he began using police power to support DNP people in the countryside.

In April Rhee fired Kim Hyo-sŏk, replacing him with the mystical Paek Sŏng-uk. At this time he also appointed Gen. Ch'ae Pyŏng-dŏk as Army Chief of Staff, leaving Kim Sŏk-wŏn fidgeting out in the cold. This unquestionably resulted from American pressure. Known as "Fatty Chai" to Americans, the corpulent general was ineffectual but, unlike Kim, knew how to take orders.[86]

After Paek Sŏng-uk arrived in office he promptly fired the director of National Police, Kim Tae-sŏn, and replaced him with Kim Pyŏng-wŏn, whom the embassy said was controlled by Yi Pŏm-sŏk and Yun Ch'i-yŏng. Kim Tae-sŏn had been an important National Police confidant of Americans in the Occupation. Several other high police officials were removed on April 27, because of Rhee's fears that they were supporters of Cho Pyŏng-ok and the DNP. In late April Shin Sŭng-mo took over as prime minister (he had been in an acting capacity), probably in deference to American pressure.[87]

Shin and Kim Hyo-sŏk also had an intelligence organization in the military, led by Lt. Col. An Ik-jo, who in KMAG's words "does nothing but collect political information" in the army and give it to Shin. An's rank had apparently not increased since 1941, when he was a Lt. Col. in the Japanese Kwantung Army. He was deputy chief of police in Ch'ungch'ŏng Province in 1948, and entered the army in 1949 "through the influence of Kim Hyo Suk."[88] Rhee's intelligence counterpart to An's group was something called the Political Action Corps, which was thought by the embassy to be at the center of this conspiracy. It was ostensibly a special intelligence agency giving Rhee "undistorted" information on Korean politics. Montana Chang now worked in this Corps, perhaps directing it, collecting intelligence for Rhee.[89]

In April An Ho-sang replaced Shin Sŭng-mo as the head of the ROK's key government-supported youth group, the Taehan Youth Corps (Shin had been doing triple duty, heading this Corps, as well as being minister of defense and acting prime minister). An, the former education minister whom liberal Americans thought to be a fascist incarnate, was close to Yi Pŏm-sŏk and Yun Ch'i-yŏng, and also to Mun Pong-je, the *Sŏbuk* leader, whom the Americans described as the real power in the Taehan Youth Corps.[90]

When we add An Ho-sang and Mun Pong-je to this involuted conspiracy, we add the most inveterate if furry-minded of Korean nationalists, and the most reactionary and provocative of the northern refugee leaders. Mun had been sending his Northwest Youth (*Sŏbuk*) squads up to the parallel and into North Korea for at least two years, provoking gun battles across the dividing line, and carrying out sabotage, setting fires, destroying homes, and the like in the North. In April 1950 Mun had been intent on having his *Sŏbuk* youths put in proper military uniforms and given a paramilitary or reserve role for the ROKA in the coming battles with the North—that is, those Northwest members not already enrolled in the police or army. At the end of March he claimed to have organized seventeen divisions of 10,000 youths each (between the ages of twenty-two and thirty-five, we should call them men), into the *Taehan Ch'ŏngnyŏn pangwidae* (Korean youth defense corps) and wanted them outfitted in uniforms identical to those of the ROK Army, that is, American uniforms. This was a bid for new respectability, which also would have pushed the textile mills toward full capacity. But the Americans refused to approve official uniforms for the group, and also demanded that the

Army cut its ties to the group's "officer's school," since it was "more a political machine than a defense unit."[91]

The final act in this Byzantine political drama, before the war, was the appointment of Montana Chang as director of National Police on June 19. The embassy viewed this as a defeat for the defense minister, Shin, who was now quite isolated in the commanding heights.[92]

It is not difficult to imagine what the North Koreans would think about this bizarre political intrigue in the spring of 1950, which they unquestionably knew much about.[93] With the return to power of several unruly nationalists, allied with Kim Sŏk-wŏn, they would be on high alert for the sort of incidents that happened in the summer of 1949. Furthermore Rhee continued to give them every reason for concern, with continuous fulminations about a march North, and at some levels, American and UNCOK encouragement or acquiescence in Rhee's threats.

When Rhee met with several American Congressmen in early December, 1949, for example, he averred that the people in the North "were as one man awaiting a signal from him to righteously arise and throw out the Soviets"; he wanted more American military aid "to defend the borders of the Yalu." When Sen. Allen Ellender interjected, "in other words, you would like the U.S. to give you the signal to move North," Rhee responded that he had given assurances to Muccio and others "that he would not move North without prior understanding"; he did not explain what that pregnant statement might mean. Sen. Homer Ferguson and Rep. Lemke piped up and encouraged Rhee to attack sooner rather than later: in Muccio's paraphrase, Ferguson and Lemke "reflected impatience at the delay in getting the Communist menace out of the way, implying that an armed struggle was inevitable and the sooner the better."[94]

At the March 1, 1950, independence anniversary celebrations, with American and UNCOK officials on the podium, Rhee exclaimed that despite advice of "our friends from across the seas . . . that we must not cherish the thought of attacking the foreign puppets," he could not ignore the cries of distress from the North: "to this call we shall respond."[95]

The war of nerves escalated considerably in early May, when both Rhee and Defense Minister Shin Sŭng-mo warned that the North was massing for an attack. They placed ROKA border troops on full alert; invasion scares came almost every day in the first two weeks of May. On May 10 Shin referred to an emergency situation, saying that an invasion was "imminent," with ROKA intelligence showing the arrival of large numbers of Korean Chinese Communist Forces (CCF) troops and deployments in force toward the border. Two days later Rhee held a news conference, telling foreign reporters that May and June were the "dangerous months," and that the ROK needed more weapons; he alluded to

"Korean [i.e., ROK] designs against North Korea"; he told Korean reporters that the North was about to invade.[96]

The Americans and the British thought Rhee and Shin were pulling a charade or "stunt" designed exclusively to scare more military aid out of Washington. American intelligence reports did not show a significant southward movement of troops in this period, and as we have seen KMAG intelligence officers discounted the invasion scares as an annual ritual.[97] However, both Koreans sides would recall that the fighting in 1949 began on May 4; the Shin-Rhee statements, and the alerts, are good evidence that they expected it to begin again in 1950. Furthermore, an ominous silence followed these alarms for the next six weeks, during which time evidence of KPA southward deployment did begin to appear.

What most impressed the North, one imagines, was less Rhee's threats and more the internal disintegration of the regime. By seeking to ally themselves with both the new National Assembly moderates, a majority, and with the losers in the factional struggle like Kim Hyo-sŏk, they might be able to split the executive and the legislature in two. There is no proof that Kim Hyo-sŏk and the Assembly moderates were in cahoots with the North, but the North unquestionably sought to woo the moderates, and their decision to stay in Seoul when the war began has a retrospective eloquence on this possibility.

SOUTH KOREA'S GROWING CHINA CONNECTION

It is unquestionable that the Americans thought Rhee's new appointments in May and June were disastrous, involving in every case people whom the United States had difficulty controlling; the regime seemed to be on the verge of bifurcating into two warring cliques. They were less concerned about the interconnection of the Political Action Corps rogues with Yi Pŏm-sŏk, but it is very important, because increasing ties with important Chinese Nationalist officials also mark this period of internal collision in the Rhee state. Here one may find the internal Korean mechanism for Chiang Kai-shek's desires, which may or may not have affected the outbreak of the war, but which in any case no one has isolated heretofore.

Yi Pŏm-sŏk is of particular interest. He had been a high officer in the Chinese Nationalist army and had modeled his youth group on the KMT "Blue Shirts," as we have seen; furthermore, he worked with Americans in OSS/SACO in China, and was flown back to Seoul by several American OSS operatives in August 1945. So he had connections both to Chiang Kai-shek, and presumably to the many former SACO officers trying to save Chiang's regime in 1950.

South Korean historiography emphasizes the strong nationalism of the

China-linked exiled Koreans like Kim Ku and Yi Pŏm-sŏk, and rightly so, if we contrast such people with those Koreans who served the Japanese. But we cannot thereby assume that such people were "nationalists" in relation to the Chinese; they often appeared merely traditional, that is, following the Yi Dynasty practice of taking the Chinese lead, modeling their politics on Chinese forms, and hoping to invoke Chinese support in their internecine struggles with other Korean leaders.

Their ally of preference for a march North was therefore Nationalist China. Yi Ch'ŏngch'ŏn, leader of the Taedong Youth and long an activist in China, startled General Hodge as early as September 1947 with a plan to invade the North, and then keep on going. If the Americans should give the command, "The Korean Army in South Korea shall be concentrated near the 38th parallel. Before the Communist army makes a raid over the line, the Korean Army will advance north of the 38th parallel, and march toward the Korea-Manchuria border, defeating the communistic armies everywhere." Once the North Koreans had been mopped up, the Koreans would join with "the Far East allied armies" across the Yalu River, "and continue marching northward." Elsewhere in the document, Yi defined the "allies" as the Chinese Nationalists, first, but if the United States would allow the Japanese to rearm, "the Japanese army shall take charge of the operation in the localities of Maritime Provinces [i.e., the Soviet Union] and Liaotung Peninsula, while the Korean army will take on the operations against the enemy front [on the] Yalu River." A force of 250,200 men would suffice for this crusade, he thought, plus a lot of money and weapons which would come, need it be said, from "the whole-hearted assistance of America."[98]

This document specifies just what the United States had on its hands in the South; it accentuates the volatile mix of far-fetched inanity and brazen aggressiveness that characterized the older nationalist elite. It measures the truly pathetic pretensions of this same elite, ready to fling the Japanese army yet again at mainland communists, and feigning to have an officer corps at their disposal (Yi listed 2,700 Korean officers available from the Japanese Army, a high total, 200 from the *Kwangbok* army, and 80 from the Yi Dynasty). Finally, this plan (if we may call it that) exemplifies their rigid conviction that despite their patent inadequacies, all other Koreans should fall in line behind them. But as soon as the snickering dies down, we may remember that the same sort of nonsense animated the Kuomintang (KMT) for three decades on Taiwan, that Syngman Rhee's plans were almost as implausible, and that Yi Chŏng-chŏn was not alone in wanting to draw the Nationalist Army into Korean battles.

Kim Hong-il, a former officer in the Chinese Nationalist army and often considered the founder of the ROK Navy, also favored a joint ROK-

ROC military thrust through the North and into Manchuria. Yi Pŏm-sŏk, the first defense minister, threatened unification "by war if statesmanship fails" at the time the ROK was established. The first foreign minister, Chang T'aek-sang, got his education in Edinburgh rather than Chungking, and so took a more legalist position: since the United Nations had recognized the ROK, "any Korean who resisted the Government's authority, even in north Korea, was a rebellious traitor," and thus South Korean forces would be justified in invading the North.[99]

Kim Ku, often thought to be the greatest of Korean nationalists, was close to the so-called "CC clique," Chen Li-fu and his brother Chen Kuo-fu; funding for his efforts and for the Korean Provisional Government came either from them, or from secret police chief Tai Li.[100] Kim Ku, of course, had been assassinated in July 1949, something "almost fatal to the China faction."[101] But this meant that Rhee feared the China group thereafter, worrying about coups or assassination plots taken in revenge (since Rhee was thought to be behind the murder of Kim Ku); this history also played into the Political Action Corps intrigues.

It will be remembered that it was precisely at the time of Chiang's visit to Korea in August 1949 that Rhee's generals, led by Yi Pŏm-sŏk and Kim Sŏk-wŏn, sought to march North and were restrained by Shin Sŭngmo, for which the latter got Rhee's opprobrium. In February 1950, Robert Strong heard from the Korean ambassador to Taipei, Shin Sŏk-u, "in utmost confidence" that Defense Minister Shin had a "military telephone line from his residence direct to [the] Gimo," and, furthermore, that Chiang had privately told the ambassador that the third world war would break out in July 1950, with one of the possible causes being an invasion of Taiwan.[102]

Two high Nationalist generals, Wu T'ieh-ch'eng and Chu Shih-ming, showed up in Seoul from April 19 to 22, 1950, reportedly seeking air and naval bases in South Korea "in exchange for air support for the 'little civil war' against the Communist forces in North Korea." Their trip would seem to be important, since the Nationalist Army was pulling out of Hainan at precisely this time, and thus one might expect one or both of them to be cloistered at military headquarters in Taipei. Air cover was also an element essential to any "northern expedition." Journalists quoted "responsible authorities" in Tokyo as saying the two came looking for airbases from which to bomb Manchuria; these press reports were later denied. Rhee received Gen. Wu, and he conferred with other high ROK officials. The British Chancery in Tokyo thought it "complete nonsense" that Rhee or KMAG would let the Nationalists have bases in Korea, but it is not so implausible for Rhee (it is for KMAG or the embassy) in a context where both regimes were deeply threatened.[103]

Wu T'ieh-ch'eng had been mayor of Shanghai and KMT commander in the important Kwangtung Province post; he had long been close to Tu Yüeh-sheng, head of the underground "Green Gang" in Shanghai, and was also part of what Parks Coble calls the "Soong group"—Wu was on several company boards with T. V. and T. L. Soong.[104] Chu Shih-ming was head of the ROC mission in Tokyo, and came in on an American military plane, indicating MacArthur's apparent support for his approach to Seoul. Interestingly, during the Occupation he had almost as many meetings with MacArthur as did his chief of staff, Gen. Almond. In the 1940s Wu and Chu were frequent associates of Milton Miles, head of OSS/SACO; indeed Miles claimed to have known Wu for twenty years.[105] Chu was mixed up in the autumn 1949 efforts by Pawley, Donovan, and others to get a military advisory group for Taiwan (see chapter 16).

The two Nationalist generals irked Rhee by spending much of their time with Yi Pŏm-sŏk, who had worked with Wu in China. The American embassy thought the purpose of the visits was to develop joint "intelligence underground activities" in Manchuria and North China. Strong, in Taipei, reported that Chiang urged General Wu to return home, since the use of South Korea by the Nationalists as "an intelligence and underground activities base" was "already well in hand" before the visit. This may be an allusion to Goodfellow's visit to Taipei for a fortnight in March; in Wellington Koo's account of Goodfellow's visit, Koo said he had met with Chu Shih-ming. The two generals returned to Tokyo on April 22, where they conferred with MacArthur, got back to Taipei on April 28 for meetings, and then continued on to the Philippines. When Wu returned to Taipei again, he was appointed vice-minister for national defense.[106]

Back in the British Foreign Office, Guy Burgess found this news worth a marginal highlight. This lover of the night and the good life was taking such unlikely interest in his work by then, as even to peruse local press reports from Taiwan. Someone, probably Burgess, drew a line next to the news on May 17 that Chu Shih-ming was not being returned to his Tokyo post, but would be replaced by Ho Shih-lai. On June 6–7, Vice-Minister for Defense Wu again returned to Seoul, a visit about which nothing is known. The U.S. embassy did not report it, an unusual lapse for such an important foreign visitor, especially since Muccio was trying to figure out what the Chinese were up to.[107]

Nationalist Ambassador Koo issued an odd statement on May 17, asserting that the security of South Korea was threatened, thus putting Japan in jeopardy; those who wanted to protect Korea and Japan ought therefore see Taiwan as integral to defense of the entire area. Meanwhile intelligence reports came in from Hong Kong saying that the formidable New Fourth Army, in the aftermath of the Hainan victory, was moving to Northeast China, "to watch developments in Korea." Two reasons for concern were cited: first, the Nationalists might bomb Peking, Tientsin, and industrial cities in the Northeast; China had charged that five air-fields had been constructed in Korea since January 1950, that the United States was spending $40,000 to repair Kimp'o airport near Seoul for use by B-29 bombers, and that Chiang had asked Rhee for the use of these bases "in attacks on North China." The other reason: "the Communists reportedly have these armies prepared to join with forces from North Korea in a drive through the Korean peninsula."[108]

The North Koreans charged in January 1950 that the United States had plans to make Cheju Island into an air base, for use against North Korea and North China. The United States, they said, was "preparing an aggression line (*chŏllyaksŏn*) from Taiwan through the Ryukyus to Cheju." They linked this to the November 1949 visit by General Randall, and also said that the head of the U.S. Far East Air Force and Shin Sŭng-mo had conducted an inspection of Cheju in late December. Rhee had agreed to "cede" (*haryang*) the island to MacArthur, and had made secret agree-ments with Chiang to base Nationalist aircraft in Korea. The same issue carried a *Hsinhua* article with much accurate information on the origin of Cooke's informal military advisory group for Taiwan, noting that since the loss of the mainland, "the U.S. imperialists have begun to display a special assertiveness (*chŏkkŭksŏng*) with respect to this island," a reference to its use for rollback schemes.[109]

Meanwhile from Tokyo the veteran *Le Monde* journalist Robert Guil-lain dispatched an article on "the revival of the Right," having talked with a shadowy Japanese kingpin who told him, "Chinese Communism is a redoubtable armed force. It should be faced with another armed force. It is high time that we learned who can furnish it." This dark figure was "in touch with China [Taiwan], with Korea, with the Philippines . . . he knows all about a project for an air base for the Chinese Nationalists on an island near Korea."[110] The informant was probably Kodama Yoshio, or an associate; Kodama, according to Anthony Sampson, was in Seoul with the American forces on the day the Korean War began.[111]

What makes the air base allegations plausible is that Rhee and Chiang did discuss basing Nationalist aircraft in Korea when they met in August 1949; Muccio said that Chiang wanted to use his airpower to attack Man-churia and to cover a South Korean attack against the DPRK. To my knowledge there is no evidence that the U.S. Air Force sought an air base on Cheju, but we know that Chiang and Rhee discussed this in the pre-cise context of a war against North Korea, and it is likely that Randall also was involved. U.S. military intelligence reported that as a result of Wu's visit, Cheju Island "is reported to become [*sic*] a Nationalist air base," but does not say whether American authorities accepted this re-port as fact.[112] In any case this background would make the North Koreans and the Chinese Communists pay careful attention to the May and June visits by Nationalist generals—as did Guy Burgess.

Two days before the Korean War, Muccio responded to a query by Niles Bond about whether Chiang Kai-shek, fearing an imminent invasion, had sought asylum in Korea. Muccio wrote, "there are indications that maneuverings have been going on but I have not been able to put my finger on anything concrete." He thought it was likely that the requests went not to Rhee but to Yi Pŏm-sŏk and other China-aligned Koreans.[113]

Foster Up in a Bunker with a Homburg On

After the Korean War, Herbert Feis in his best choir-boy manner queried Acheson on John Foster Dulles's well-marked visit to the thirty-eighth parallel on June 19, 1950: "Are you sure his presence didn't provoke the attack Dean? There has been comment about that—I don't think it did. You have no views on the subject?" Acheson's deadpan response: "No, I have no views on the subject." Kennan then interjected, "There is a comical aspect to this, because the visits of these people over there, and their peering over outposts with binoculars at the Soviet people, I think must have led the Soviets to think that we were on to their plan and caused them considerable perturbation." "Yes," Acheson said, "Foster up in a bunker with a homburg on—it was a very amusing picture."[114]

Yes, funny, amusing—and illogical: were Kennan right, Dulles was "on to their plan," why then would the attack have ensued? If Dulles's presence might have "provoked the attack," a presence *where*—at the thirty-eighth parallel, where all American dignitaries visit? Or in Japan, supping with the *zaibatsu* elite? And above all, *why*? Why would either the Russians or the Koreans take such a strong risk of American intervention, at this time? It is not a question likely to be answered without a full consideration of all the possible explanations. It is obviously not a question that interested Acheson, whose wonderful and well-tutored memory mysteriously dimmed. Suddenly Acheson had "no views" on a subject of critical import: whether Dulles's visit provoked a war.

So, why did Dulles go to Korea? He originally had no plans to visit the peninsula; instead he had thought of detouring to Taiwan, bird-dogging Louis Johnson should the latter run off to see the generalissimo and his Madame. But then Korea came up front and center during a dinner with the Korean ambassador to the United States, Chang Myŏn, on June 10, 1950. Present were Dulles, Rusk, Allison, and Niles Bond. Chang told them his regime was in crisis. Four days later, the CIA warned of the possibility of a North Korean attack, and on the same day Dulles told Wellington Koo he would "go to Korea for a look."[115]

The Korean ambassador reports that his regime is in crisis. The CIA reports that the North Koreans can attack at any moment. Dulles decides to have "a look." It will be remembered that Chang Myŏn was an American favorite, and that he was a leader of the opposition DNP/KDP, also an American favorite. The CIA was on record before the May 1950 elections hoping for a DNP victory, and it lauded Chang's qualities in its biographical sketches. In April and May Rhee's most provocative allies were rapidly undermining DNP stalwarts in the bureaucracy, and by early June it was clear that left-leaning and moderate politicians had scored a major victory over both Rhee and the DNP—even the Americans' *capo di tutti capi*, Cho Pyŏng-ok, had been voted out. At the same time, South Korean intelligence reported an impending attack and put the Army on full alert.

Chang knew Dulles as well as any Korean, having worked "very hard—hand in hand" with him at the United Nations in 1948, when the two interacted on a daily basis. He liked to call Dulles "the Father of the Republic of Korea."[116] Chang had returned to Korea in May, meeting MacArthur along the way; there is no record of the substance of their talks. He came back urgently to Washington in mid-June, seeking to convince American officials that the ROK was on the verge of collapse; after the fact he said that he had also warned that a North Korean attack was "imminent."[117]

A news account by Homer Bigart on June 14 reported that Chang had told officials that the Koreans "badly needed assurance from the U.S. that they will be given protection," and that Dulles would therefore journey to Seoul and make "an important statement of U.S. policy in relation to Korea, and other nations in the 'no-man's land' between Communism and the Atlantic Pact allies." This would be, of course, the netherworld of Achesonian indirect containment and deterrence, the exposed and contingent intermediate zone. Dulles would not "pledge the U.S. to go to war," but might "remind" threatened peoples that the U.S. had twice gone to war without treaty commitments. This would be "a solemn warning to Russia."

But Bigart had more to say. The State Department had "received disquieting reports that Communist propaganda is making some headway in South Korea," a different emphasis that points to the problems of the Rhee regime and the results of the May elections, rather than worries about the North Koreans.[118]

After the war began, Bigart wrote, "It may now be revealed that two weeks ago . . . Chang warned high officials that his country was on the verge of internal collapse owing mainly to fear that the U.S. would abandon her . . . he pleaded for some guarantee of armed intervention by the U.S. in the event of war." Chang had said an invasion might come "momentarily." Thus, Bigart wrote, Dulles went to Korea "to give a strong statement of reassurance."[119]

Chang wrote to Rhee on June 11, the day after the dinner, saying that he was confident that Dulles's visit "may bring about a change in the Department's policy with regard to the Far East." On June 17, Chang told Wellington Koo that he was "expecting a drastic change of U.S. policy toward the Far East in general and toward Korea, Japan and Formosa in particular" after the Dulles and Johnson visits. Just after the war began, Chang also told Koo of his previous warnings about the "imminence" of attack.[120]

There is, to my knowledge, no record in the State Department holdings of what transpired during the June 10 dinner. When I queried Rusk in an interview, he said he could remember nothing about it. It seems likely, however, that the focus was more on the struggle for the Rhee state and the potential for internal collapse, than on an impending attack, the evidence for which does not show up in intelligence materials in May or early June.

Chang's timing was impeccable, but he could not have known that his visit came in the midst of a building momentum for a reversal of Taiwan policy, with a Communist invasion impending, through an ouster of Chiang and a commitment of American force to defend Taiwan. Now, it appeared, the other American client was in deep trouble as well, thus bringing forth one problem after another. As in regard to Taiwan, Acheson wanted to contain the ROK's territory but not necessarily the regime. Chang Myŏn and the DNP were, in the beclouded American eye, isomorphic in Korea to Hu Shih and the "liberals" in Taiwan. The liberal element seemed to be losing out in Korea, either to Rhee's provocative allies like Kim Sŏk-wŏn or to waffling moderates who might favor unification—just as the United States hoped to install liberals or get a neutral regime in Taipei, as we will see in chapter 16.

What Rhee wanted was a direct American defense guarantee of his government and after that, no interference. This was the lietmotiv of Rhee's diplomacy. Without U.S. backing his hand palsied, for he knew better than anyone that his regime had clay feet. With it he was emboldened. In the summer of 1949 he was told repeatedly that he did not have it, and Acheson sought to underline this in his Press Club speech. At a minimum the regime had to be disciplined with questions about whether the United States would defend it. In the summer of 1950, several sources claim that Dulles told him he *did* have such a guarantee, and the North Koreans have ever since claimed that Dulles's visit provoked the war.

Dulles arrived in Seoul on June 18, to a *Tonga ilbo* article praising him as the "magical midwife" of the Republic of Korea. During his three-day visit he spoke to the National Assembly, visited the thirty-eighth parallel, held a news conference, attended an UNCOK meeting, got an honorary degree, met some Presbyterians (a predictable diversion), and chatted with Rhee a number of times.[121]

There is no full record of Dulles's conversations with Rhee. Muccio reported that Rhee emphasized to him the dangers of the loss of Taiwan, which would threaten the ROK from the north and south, but otherwise his account is uninteresting.[122] Dulles's speech to the National Assembly on June 19 was drafted with the help of Rusk and Jessup; in Jessup's recollection, it "dealt with what they could look forward to in the way of help in the event they were attacked." Dulles told Acheson his speech was designed to emphasize, for the benefit of the Japanese and the Russians, the American desire to "stand fast in these environs of Japan," among which he included Taiwan as well as the ROK.[123] The critical passage in the speech read,

> Already [in the 20th century] the U.S. has twice intervened with armed might in defense of freedom when it was hard pressed by unprovoked military aggression. We were not bound by any treaty to do this. . . .
> You are not alone. You will never be alone so long as you continue to play worthily your part in the great design of human freedom.[124]

With Dulles present in the National Assembly, Rhee asserted that "if we should lose the Cold War by default we will regain our free world in the end by a hot war regardless of cost—of that I am sure."[125] Koreans viewed Dulles's speech as, in Chŏng Il-gwŏn's words, evidence of "an absolute guarantee" to defend the ROK. Gen. Almond, MacArthur's chief of staff, also saw the speech as a reversal of previous policy, and just after Dulles left, Rhee cabled MacArthur that the results of the visit had been "wonderful," but saying nothing more. However, the embassy's internal cables show no sense that any policy breakthrough occurred, and the British did not even bother to mention the more controversial parts of the speech.[126]

Since the war began P'yŏngyang has never stopped blathering that Dulles did not visit the thirty-eighth parallel "to pick daisies," but plotted with Rhee to provoke a war. This allegation began with broadcasts by Mun Hak-bong, a former hanger-on in Seoul, that MacArthur wanted a war in Korea to begin in July so that Taiwan could be occupied before the end of the month, presumably to stave off a PRC invasion; Rhee, however, wanted the attack to begin earlier because of the political crisis of the ROK, and got Dulles to agree to this. Seoul, Tokyo, and Washington were thus "in continuous communication from June 20 on."[127]

The North Korean case does not get better than this as the years go on. A September 1950 North Korean article merely repeated common

12. "Foster up in a bunker with a homburg on," June 19, 1950

Soviet allegations about Dulles's Wall Street background and his alleged ties to the Nazis; it made no mention of his trip to Japan or the significance of his work on the peace treaty, simply saying that when he came into the Truman administration he called for "a foreign policy of strength."[128] Although Mun Hak-bong is probably right to relate the Taiwan issue and the internal crisis of the Rhee regime to the outbreak of the Korean War, it is extraordinarily implausible that Dulles would have agreed with MacArthur that Rhee should start a war, when Dulles and MacArthur were at odds about both Japan and Taiwan policy, when Acheson and Dulles were mainly concerned with watching Louis Johnson and restraining Rhee, and when such an outcome would merely play into the hands of Johnson and MacArthur, and the restive right-wing. Furthermore, there is no evidence before the war started that the North found Dulles's visit any more provocative than previous ones, such as Jessup's in January—who also visited the parallel with various military officers in tow, spoke to the National Assembly, met with Rhee, and who received his due load of North Korean abuse for it.[129]

There is no question that during the visit, Rhee not only pushed for a direct American defense, but advocated an attack on the North. Dulles invited along with him a favorite reporter, William Mathews, editor of the *Arizona Daily Star*. On June 19, Mathews met Rhee; this appears to have been a separate meeting, not the one on the same day when Rhee met Dulles. Mathews wrote this of Rhee, just after the meeting: "He is militantly for the unification of Korea. Openly says it must be brought about soon . . . Rhee pleads justice of going into North country. Thinks it could succeed in a few days . . . if he can do it with our help, he will do it." And Mathews noted that Rhee said he would "do it," "even if it brought on a general war."

Preferring to maintain his contacts rather than tell the truth, Mathews kept all this under his hat when he returned to the United States, thus not to "embarrass" Dulles. Some years later he blandly aped official mystifications for an historian, to the effect that when he and Dulles visited the parallel, "all of the military dispositions of the ROK Army were defensive"—despite KMAG information given to him at the time that the ROK had four divisions at the parallel and one in Seoul, not to mention Rhee's threats.

When Dulles visited the thirty-eighth parallel, according to Mathews's account, KMAG officers told him the ROKA was "the best army in Asia today," but that planes and tanks had been "deliberately withheld by American authorities, fearing possible offensive use." Col. W.H.S. Wright of KMAG told him that the forward echelon of "a Chinese division" was now twenty miles north of the parallel, a reference presumably to the southward displacement of the 6th Division, full of CCF Koreans. "All civilians have been cleared out of [an] area several miles wide" on the northern side of the parallel, Wright related, but he apparently did not say that this had happened in the fall of 1949 as well. Anyway, Wright had "absolute confidence" in his intelligence agencies: KMAG would have "twenty-four hours notice of any impending attack by the North Koreans."

Mathews also met with Floyd A. Stephenson, a marine colonel in World War II then with General Motors, who had just flown in from Taiwan and who told him all about Admiral Cooke's operation. It is not clear if Stephenson also met Dulles, nor is it known what he was doing in Korea.[130]

All this is yet more proof of Rhee's provocative behavior, but it is not different than his threats to march North made many times before, and directly to Jessup in January. The Dulles visit was vintage Rhee: but there is no evidence that Dulles was in collusion with him. It is most unlikely that this high-flying and politically ambitious legalist, on a mission to trade moral bombast for rollback praxis, would have dipped down to Rhee's level.

Another eyewitness to the Dulles visit was UNCOK delegate Arthur Jamieson. He later recalled a dinner he attended, with those present including Dulles, Rhee, Allison, Muccio, and Harold Noble.

> Throughout the evening Rhee pursued the twin topics of the possibility of a North Korean attack and how the U.S. would respond. . . . Dulles made unsuccessful attempts to turn the conversation. He then developed and stuck to the argument that North Korea would not attack except at Soviet instigation and that the existing balance of power was so much in favour of the U.S. that the Soviet Union would be deterred from acting along any such lines. Rhee kept asking, "But what if there is an attack?" Dulles refused to be drawn into any commitment, delivering instead a homily about American constitutional processes.
>
> When people have asked whether the war could not have been started by the ROK my mind still goes back to Rhee's look of dejection and disenchantment as he bade his guests good night.[131]

In itself, this is evidence of nothing. If Rhee and Dulles had an understanding, they would hardly have communicated it with so many people present, including perfect strangers and assorted wives. Nonetheless, the story rings true: Rhee's incessant demands and provocative urgings and Dulles's studied refusal to get involved, relying on his tried and true stock of lawyerly diversions. He was there to carry out Achesonian policy, not to detonate Rhee's war.

When he got to Japan Dulles called for "positive action" in the Far East, but hastened to qualify his meaning: the United States intended "to preserve international peace, security and justice in the world"; "well-informed people" did not expect a war, given the current balance of power.[132] He was, as ever, Foster Dulles the legalist, peacemaker, bipartisan accommodator, Republican centrist, trying to snatch rollback rhetoric from the jaws of the restless American Right. The funereal Mr. Dulles in a bunker with a homburg on, eyeballing Kim Il Sung: it was rather humorous, after all.

Chapter Sixteen

TELLTALE TAIWAN

The U.S. should inform Sun Li-jen in the strictest confidence through a private emissary that the U.S. Government is prepared to furnish him the necessary military aid and advice in the event that he wishes to stage a coup d'etat for the purpose of establishing his military control over the Island.

State Department, June 19, 1950

In May and June 1950 the Kuomintang (KMT) faced its *Götterdämmerung*, an impending Communist invasion that would take final revenge for the massacres of 1927 that set Chinese nationalism on two separate and irremediably hostile paths. Truman and Acheson still refused to commit to a defense of the regime. Worse, cold war internationalists were after Chiang's scalp, with plans for a coup d'etat. Even the rollback partisans, anxious about Chiang's future, seemed to draw back in May after the Nationalists failed to defend Hainan Island. Moderate allies of the rollbackers in Washington got cold feet, especially Senator Smith and Foster Dulles. Like the Rhee regime, the Chiang regime was gravely at risk in June 1950.

A successful invasion was not implausible, American officials knew, because Nationalist troop morale was low, the road and railway network was close to the Western shore and difficult to defend, and spare parts for tanks and other equipment were lacking. The longer the Communists waited, the better the defenses would become. Perhaps most important, to ferry invasion forces the Chinese Communists had ingeniously devised wooden-armored, motorized junks that were difficult to sink with naval or aircraft weaponry, having foot-square hardwood keels that could buckle the metal hulls of destroyers, should the junks be rammed. The junks carried 40mm guns that could disable "thin-skinned destroyers" and were also effective enough to keep Nationalist pilots flying high.[1]

The problem for Chiang was to square the circle by merging the internationalist backing for the island with the rollbackers' love for generalissimos. Airpower still seemed to be a panacea that might save the Nationalists, so they bombed China's coastal cities and sought airbases in Korea to hit Manchuria. But mostly Chiang sought to manipulate American politics to gain the backing that would save his regime; the U.S. Navy turned out to be the best bet.

The Navy thought Taiwan was in its territory, that is, the Pacific

Ocean; if the island was "an unsinkable aircraft carrier" to General Mac-Arthur, shouldn't the Navy control it, and keep the other services out? The logic was impeccable. But intelligence connections were the main reason for the strong ties between naval officers and the Nationalist regime. The Sino-American Cooperation League (SACO), the name of the OSS's operation in wartime China, had been run by Adm. Milton Miles, with much help from Adm. Charles Cooke, and they cultivated relations with the most powerful people in the KMT regime, those who ran the secret services. In 1949 and 1950 Americans beginning with William Donovan used these ties to try to save Chiang's regime.

Taiwan the island was a different story. It had strategic value for the American lake in the Pacific by 1948 if not earlier, and had economic utility too, through a revival on different terms of its relationship to Japan. The triangular capitalist structure we assessed earlier had its implementation before the war began, bringing Taiwan's sugar, bananas, and raw materials to Japan in return for machine tools, locomotives, and cloth for Taiwan's textile industry. Taiwan imported Korean bicycles, auto parts, simple machines, and fish, in exchange for agricultural cash crops. Another small army of American economic advisors rode herd on Taiwan's incipient developmental plans.[2]

An "FMAG" After All

In the fall of 1949 Chiang's supporters sought to circumvent Acheson and achieve de facto containment by bringing an informal group of "retired" military officers to Taiwan, along with a large boodle of military equipment, including enough tanks to make the Republic of China (ROC) tank corps among the more formidable in the world. This effort was secretly advanced by U.S. Army intelligence, and it may have had Acheson's tacit support.

On November 7, 1949, William Pawley sent a letter to Acheson suggesting that "a small group" of retired officers be dispatched to Taiwan as military advisors; the total, including additional civilian economic advisors, would be 130 to 150. Pawley asked for the "approval or acquiescence" of the U.S. government. The origins of this effort were complex, and some of the facts remain hidden. Philip Sprouse of the Far East office thought that Pawley's approach grew out of an earlier plan by the president of Reynolds Aluminum, "Mr. Reynolds," to get Gen. Albert Wedemeyer to head a military mission to Taiwan, for which Wedemeyer was to be paid $1 million per year. (Taiwan had an aluminum industry from the late 1930s, and Reynolds frequently lobbied on Chiang's behalf.) Reynolds approached T. V. Soong, H. H. Kung, and Pawley in trying to raise money and influence for this mission.[3]

Chen Chih-mai, the Nationalist embassy operative in Washington, saw Wedemeyer on September 14 and learned from him that Reynolds had secured $5 million for the effort from someone associated with the KMT (it must have been T. V. Soong or H. H. Kung, given the sizeable sum), and had urged Wedemeyer to leave the Army and help Chiang. Wedemeyer declined.[4]

Acheson's response to Pawley was curiously ambiguous. Instead of an outright prohibition or denial, he wrote that he did not object to a limited number of private American citizens going to Taiwan, if their services "were contracted directly by Chi Govt [*sic*] without responsibility on part of this Govt." He reiterated his opposition to an official military advisory group, which would be "widely interpreted as evidence American intention to underwrite mil[itary] defense of Island" and which, if the KMT nonetheless collapsed, would cause "very great" damage to U.S. prestige.[5] In short, Acheson appears to have given Pawley the "acquiescence" he requested.

A few days after Pawley's approach, a new figure entered the scene, trying to get around Acheson directly to the president through Truman's conservative aide, Adm. William Leahy (who was a good bit more sympathetic to the Nationalists than was his boss.) This was Adm. Charles Cooke, who met Leahy on November 10, urging that military advisors be sent to Taiwan. He wound up later as the leader of the informal group.[6]

On November 16, William Donovan met with Walter Mansfield, Philip Fugh, Gen. Cheng Kai-ming (vice-minister of ROC National Defense), and his associate Col. C. V. Chen; Mao Jung Fong, the head of ROC Secret Service, was expected to attend but did not. Cheng and Mao were with SACO in the mid-1940s. Nothing is known of the substance of their meeting, but it probably related to Pawley's advisory group.[7] Another Navy man, Adm. Oscar C. Badger, showed up in mid-November in Washington, meeting with Gen. Cheng Kai-ming and lobbying military agencies on Taiwan's behalf. In mid-December, when NSC 48 and its Taiwan provisions were the subject of hot dispute between Acheson and the Pentagon, Badger met with Wellington Koo and, in typical fashion for the China Lobby crowd, told him about "top level discussions" in government circles on the Taiwan question; Koo had prepared a memorandum to present to Acheson, also urging an American military advisory group, but Badger suggested that he bypass Acheson and go directly to Truman.[8] Although it is by no means easy to ferret out the genesis of this group, it is obvious that a number of regular and retired military officers were involved, including people in the navy, army intelligence and, according to Wellington Koo, a Col. Lawrence Ives who had approached Koo about supplying weapons to Taiwan as early as June 1949, and who claimed this had the "secret blessings" of the Marine Corps.[9]

At the beginning of January 1950 Truman and Acheson said once again that there would be no formal American backing for the Nationalists; China Lobbyists fluttered about, and then came up with a new plan. William Donovan was the fixer this time, it would appear. A subsidiary of his World Commerce Corporation, called Commerce International China, became the vehicle for informal military aid and advisors for Taiwan. It was said by Wellington Koo to have been directed by Col. David Li, who in March 1949 had led an anticommunist committee which had merged with pro-Chiang industrialist Frederick McKee's lobbying committee.[10] It may well have been a CIA proprietary company, but in any case it had definite ties with Army intelligence.

World Commerce was Donovan's vehicle for business and espionage ventures, set up in 1947. Nelson Rockefeller and John J. McCloy "took an interest in the corporation," according to Cave Brown, and most of its directors and associates had been involved with American or British intelligence. Its president was Frank T. Ryan, who had been with the Office of Strategic Services (OSS) in Spain; also involved were William Pawley, and W. T. Keswick, head of Matheon, Ltd., a big Far Eastern trading company. He had been the British SOE's (Special Operations Executive) chief for Asia during the war; he and Preston Goodfellow knocked out the basic agreeement dividing intelligence regions between the United States and England, as we have seen. World Commerce had representation in forty-seven countries, and became what Brown called a "commercial intelligence service." Commerce International itself was run by S. G. "Sonny" Fassoulis, who was indicted in the so-called "Guterma scandals" in 1959. Drew Pearson asserted that Fassoulis and a partner, Miran Aprahamian, received 12 percent commissions on sales of ammunition to Taiwan.[11]

Another of those involved in setting up the advisory group, Ambrose Cates, wrote that Commerce International first contracted to sell arms to Taiwan on July 4, 1949: five hundred pieces of military equipment, mostly tanks, went to the Nationalists for a bit over $2 million. This, he said, was done "through the assistance and help of the U.S. Army"; "we had to keep the sale as quiet as possible," given State's opposition ("the State Department called us warmongers").[12]

According to another principal in this business, Irving Ritchie Short, he heard about the idea of sending a volunteer force to fight for Taiwan from the Nationalist embassy, in the fall of 1949. When Sen. William Knowland, sometimes called "the Senator from Formosa," visited Taiwan in November 1949, Short toured military installations with him, getting photographed with Knowland several times. When he returned from Taiwan, according to Lt. Col. Carl M. Poston, many government agencies received Short warmly—although not the Department of State. The Intelligence Division of the Defense Department put him on temporary duty, and he met with Gen. A. R. Bolling, head of Army G-2, and later with Generals Bradley and Vandenberg. Poston also reported that Short "talked to some people in the office of The Secretary of Defense," presumably Johnson's staff members who were close to the Nationalists.

In December 1949 Short met with Alfred Kohlberg, top dog in the China Lobby, and William Bullitt, who had been raising private funding for the advisory "volunteers" through "Texas oil people," presumably including H. L. Hunt. A joint congressional committee had dispatched Bullitt to China in 1948, to see what could be done for the Nationalists once Dewey became president (he recommended an $800 million package of aid).[13] Bullitt, like many Republicans, had a strong desire for a reversal of the Dewey defeat, for which the "China" issue became a vehicle. When Bullitt returned from Texas he told Short to take a small group of people to Taiwan and announce the formation of the volunteer group: "then the money would be forthcoming from the people in Texas." Shortly thereafter one Col. Williams from the Army introduced Short to Sonny Fassoulis, who gave him $500,000 for a public relations campaign on Taiwan's behalf. It would be interesting to know Col. Williams's first name. Goodfellow's negotiations with British intelligence in 1942 were conducted with Col. Garland Williams at his side, and we have seen that Donovan was involved with the Englishman at the same meetings, W. T. Keswick. Interestingly, Fassoulis was said to have met with Acheson and Truman about Taiwan around this time. Part of this money was used to fund a trip to Taiwan in late May 1950 by a group of American correspondents, mostly from the Hearst press, and Short also made his way to Taiwan.[14]

Much more money, however, went from Commerce International and Fassoulis to buy arms for Taiwan. Fassoulis was the principal agent for Chinese Nationalist procurement of military supplies, especially large numbers of tanks; Wellington Koo's aide Chen Chih-mai linked Short and Fassoulis to China Lobbyists Frederick McKee and Alfred Kohlberg, but still wondered "why this company should devote such a large sum of money on our behalf."[15]

SPECIAL ACTIVITIES: DONOVAN

William Donovan's movements during this period are hard to track, but we do know the following. In November 1949, he met with high Kuomintang intelligence officials, as we noted above. A month later he turned up in London, lecturing Air Chief Marshal Sir John Slessor on the "folly" of recognizing Mao's regime, which the British were about to proceed with; instead, Donovan told him, "we should be organizing 'resistance' inside China," and suggested that General Claire Chennault be named minister of defense in a Chinese exile regime. Slessor worried that Donovan and others like him might be getting Truman's ear, and criticized "the inadequacy of our liaison with MacArthur." The British, he said, were nearly as "ignorant" about what the Americans were doing in China as about the Soviet bloc in general.[16]

Donovan then embarked on a seven-week visit to East Asia. His ostensible purpose was to help Chennault in a legal fight to retrieve a fleet of China National Aircraft Corporation (CNAC) planes that the British had seized in Hong Kong; he had State Department help in this, owing to fears that the sequestered planes would be returned to China and augment the PRC's (People's Republic of China) air force. Chennault wanted them on Taiwan as part of his arsenal for attacking the mainland. Donovan, Whiting Willauer, and Tommy Corcoran had developed by this time, according to William Leary, "an imaginative scheme to operate an airline for the CIA on the periphery of Communist China," from Korea down to Malaya.[17]

On February 8 Willoughby held a dinner for Donovan in Tokyo (a few days before Syngman Rhee showed up at MacArthur's headquarters). About thirty people attended, with the Kuomintang general Chu Shih Ming placed next to Donovan. In his public remarks Donovan said merely that he came to Asia to look after the CNAC airplane case. But Donovan and Chennault met privately with Willoughby about establishing spy networks in China, and a British diplomat related that Donovan had "visited all important countries between [Burma] and Japan," advocating covert action against the Chinese Communists. He quoted Donovan as saying, "given the oportunity I could have the whole show organised in eight months, I know the men to employ and I would complete the job [of overthrowing Mao] in less than three years." He deplored Truman's unwillingness to back the Chiang regime.[18] Some weeks later Donovan testified in Congress to the effect that MacArthur should be made "Supreme Commander in the Far East and Southeast Asia." Donovan met with Phillip Jessup at least twice during the latter's Far Eastern trip of the same period; he also met Karl Rankin, Hong Kong Consul-General and a backer of the Nationalists. I have no evidence that he visited Korea on this trip.[19]

Upon his return Donovan rejoined the battle with Acheson and the containment forces. As always the question was whether an aggressive offense was better than a good defense. In a letter to Acheson of February 12, drafted a day after his return, Donovan noted that leaders in East and Southeast Asia thought the United States had "written off that part of the world," said that Taiwan should be "denied to enemy occupation," and that "immediate action is necessary in this region because of expected Soviet moves." He urged the appointment of a "Supreme Commander," who would be authorized "to employ such countermeasures as he finds necessary to meet acts of subversion against this area." Donovan also held consultations with several other State Department officers.[20]

In late March Donovan again wrote to Acheson, saying that the Soviets had "imposed a subversive war upon us . . . a war we may lose unless we quickly take the initiative." He called for unorthodox warfare measures that would be "centralized in Washington for global use and direction," and for "a Commander" who would be given "decisive and central authority to plan, to dispose and to direct [operations] . . . a Committee of Action can assist him. . . . Let him exercise daring and initiative. It is not containment that we need, but positive and affirmative action." Acheson wrote back a perfunctory reply; Donovan circulated the entire correspondence to Wall Street friends like R. A. Wormser, to Sen. H. Alexander Smith, and others.[21]

Donovan developed a plan of action, much like the above, speaking about it at every opportunity. It included the designation of a Supreme Commander with discretionary authority, military missions in various Asian countries, sustained "affirmative action against the Soviets," open backing of the Chinese Nationalists, and so on. He argued that Formosa, Korea, Japan, and Southeast Asia were "all one theater," which must be defended against Russian plans to extend "their continental conquest" in Asia. In early April he circulated a paper criticizing "passive defense," which only allowed Stalin "to retain the initiative; if he is blocked on one front about his vast periphrey [sic], he is free to bulge out elsewhere." The United States "must wrest the initiative from him." The list of those to whom the paper was sent included Robert Wood and Jay Jerome Williams, cronies of MacArthur and Rhee, respectively.[22]

Donovan was not merely another crackpot advocate of rollback about whom Acheson could make his private jokes. His influence was great within intelligence circles. He was America's "master spy," a formidable politician of enormous prestige, who became after MacArthur the most important threat to Acheson's defensive strategy. Furthermore he was after Acheson's hide: in late March he told Senator Smith to start thinking about "a Democrat satisfactory to Truman" as Acheson's replacement.[23]

Sen. Alexander Smith was a mediocrity called upon to rise above his level of competence by the foreign policy crisis of 1950. But he loved Donovan. They exchanged many letters, with Smith underlining passages he found insightful (especially urgings of "positive and affirmative action"). Smith circulated Donovan's material among senators on the Foreign Relations Committee. When McCarthy's rantings got big headlines, Smith wrote in his diary, "it comes to me to call Bill Donovan and get him into this picture with a few of the clearest heads." As Hainan Island fell and Taiwan seemed next, Smith spoke with Donovan on April 25, 27, and 28; on the latter date he jotted down, Donovan "wants action," suggesting that the United States take Russian hostages as retaliation for the shooting down of an American plane over the Baltic. In mid-May he remarked that the State Department was now willing "to take a new look at the whole Formosa situation," and sought to get senators interested in the Far East to consult with Rusk, Dulles, and Donovan.[24]

In late May Donovan left for a European trip, presumably on business (perhaps we should say presumably Europe); he was returning on the Queen Elizabeth when the Korean War broke out.[25]

SPECIAL ACTIVITIES, GOODFELLOW: CHINESE FLAGS FLY KOREAN FLAGS

Just at the time when the Formosa issue was bubbling furiously in the United States, Preston Goodfellow became a critical go-between for the China and Korea Lobbies. Unlike China Lobby types who were fixated on Taiwan, he linked the fortunes of the Nationalists and the South Koreans together. Like Cooke, Cates, and Short, he was a classic expansionist, mixing narrow speculative activities with subversion and anticommunism. (The Irving Short case documents Alfred Kohlberg's knowledge of Goodfellow and his relationships in Korea. One document related that Kohlberg's backing for Short's plan "was to be similar to that carried out by H. P. [sic] Goodfellow in Korea 'thereby establishing himself [Kohlberg] with the Chinese Government whereby he might profit in the future.' ")[26] Unlike these other people, however, Goodfellow had important links to more general interests, as we have seen. From the fall of 1949 to the Korean War, Goodfellow used all his OSS techniques in clandestine efforts on behalf of the Rhee regime and, by February 1950 if not earlier, Chiang Kai-shek and the Kuomintang: subversion and unconventional warfare, business operations as a cover, connections with Army intelligence. Although I have by no means been able to get to the bottom of all his activities—like Donovan, he covered his tracks—enough is documented to suggest lines for further inquiry.

In September 1949 Goodfellow had rushed to Korea when it looked like a war might begin, as we saw in chapter 12. After leaving Korea he visited Tokyo, from October 11 to 17, MacArthur calling him a "special advisor" to Rhee and billeting him at the Imperial Hotel. He then went to Kyoto, which was under the occupation command of Gen. John B. Coulter. When Senator Smith flew from Tokyo to Seoul on MacArthur's plane, he stopped off in Kyoto to talk to Goodfellow. MacArthur had suggested this, telling Smith that *"Korea is a must for us [sic],"* that unlike

13. Col. M. Preston Goodfellow with Mr. and Mrs. Rhee, in the late 1940s

China, Supreme Command, Allied Powers (SCAP) did have responsibility for Korea (an interesting comment in the light of the June 1949 troop withdrawal and MacArthur and Willoughby's subsequent claims that it was a State Department responsibility), and that he thought the South Koreans "can hold their own against the North." All Smith records of the Goodfellow meeting is that the latter told him the State Department had tried to arrange a coalition government in Korea.[27]

Donovan apparently did not visit Korea during his 1949–1950 Asian trip, but Preston Goodfellow did and, like Donovan, sought to organize anticommunist guerrillas. After he returned from another Korea trip in December 1949, about which nothing is known, Goodfellow wrote to Herbert Hoover on January 3 that his "associates" in Taiwan wanted to send a delegation to the United States to get their views across.[28] To my knowledge this is the first evidence of Goodfellow's Taiwan involvement. The next day he showed up at the Nationalist embassy in Washington.

Accompanied by Col. Frank H. Collins, an obscure figure who appears to have been involved with the Korea Lobby in 1947, Goodfellow underlined his ties to Donovan and suggested to Ambassador Koo the "organization of a foreign legion for China to fight the Communists."[29] In the OSS he and Donovan had put many underground agents into Japanese-occupied China, he said; and now "he has put through an arrangement for S. Korea to train thousands of young Koreans for such service." He suggested that South Korea might be used as a channel to get U.S. military aid to the Nationalists—"for Chinese flags to fly Korean flags," as a disguise. Goodfellow and Collins returned again to Koo's embassy on January 12, the former saying that "he has been entrusted with having Koreans in South Korea for underground work in [the] North." He also said he had several thousand automatic pistols for sale (he had offered them to Kim Tae-sŏn of the Korean National Police as well). Koo related that the Generalissimo would like to hear about what Goodfellow could do for them, in "organizing underground work."

On January 24 Goodfellow wrote to Rhee, telling him he had seen Koo, and that "a number of things which Korea and Formosa might work out to their mutual advantage were discussed"; also, "I am writing Gen. MacArthur and sending him some information which will interest him."[30] After getting clearance from Taipei, on February 3 Koo invited Goodfellow back and said that Chiang wanted him to spend a fortnight in Taiwan, all expenses paid. The money came from a secret fund in the United States under the control of Yu Kuo-hua, a relative of Chiang's who was deputy executive director of the International Monetary Fund.[31]

Hollington Tong met Goodfellow at the airport when he arrived in Taipei, simultaneously with Admiral Cooke in mid-February; Goodfellow "emphasized his close relations with Korean Government, SCAP and Okinawa military authorities." (Goodfellow's son knew nothing about his father's East Asian visits, but did remember him saying Okinawa had been quite significant.) It is not clear if Cooke and Goodfellow traveled together, but the embassy and the State Department noted their arrival with unusual interest—although they were able to learn little about their subsequent activities. It is also worth noting that Donovan had been in Tokyo the previous week, and Rhee had just arrived there, for a meeting that the North Koreans have ever claimed as the point at which MacArthur and Rhee plotted war in Korea. Like Colonel David Girdwood (see chapter 4), Goodfellow described himself as working for a fertilizer company, which the State Department indicated was a cover.[32] State Department concern with all the informal actors coming to Taiwan was probably behind its advice that all elements of the American government could visit Taiwan only with Strong's consent. Occasionally Strong got a courtesy call from a CIA man, or one of Willoughby's intelligence people. But he could not enforce this rule, and before the Korean War "the island was probably crawling with CIA and military types."³³

After he returned to the United States Goodfellow told members of the Nationalist embassy that he had met with Chiang Kai-shek twice; Chiang asked him "to consult Gen. MacArthur and Pres. Syngman Rhee about various matters and report back which he did [*sic*]." Goodfellow visited Korea again on March 15, for what was publicly called a "short visit"; he later told Rhee that he had taken "messages" to Tokyo and Taipei. Goodfellow said he had discussed the creation of an underground in China with MacArthur, with the latter "all sympathetic"; with Rhee, he said he discussed trading relations with Taiwan. He remarked that General Wheeler of the SCAP staff had said MacArthur should be given responsibility for the whole China area, so that covert operations could be channeled through him, thus to bypass "the administration's deep-rooted objection to further aid to the G[eneralissimo]." At some point in March, Yu Kuo-hua gave Goodfellow a check for $20,000 for "special purposes," money said to have come directly from the Generalissimo.³⁴

On March 27, Koo got a cable directly from the Presidential mansion in Taipei asking him from then on to refer any "concrete proposal" from Goodfellow "to the G[eneralissimo] for consideration and approval, as no agreement has been made yet to engage him." From that point on, the embassy was bypassed in Goodfellow's communications with Taipei. (Louis Johnson also operated through back-channel communications with Taipei that bypassed the Nationalist embassy.)³⁵ The diary entry continued, "[the cable] mentioned Chu Shih-ming reporting [that] the Col. [Goodfellow] had suggested . . . the large funds necessary for carrying on guerrilla activities on the mainland should be [illegible word] raised by the Col. himself from Americans in U.S. H[wang] said the Col's trip to Tokio [*sic*] and Korea [here follow three illegible Chinese characters, and the entry ends]." This diary entry is confusing and incomplete. The reader has it as in the original.

Koo's diary entry for April 3, 1950, indicated that General Chu Shih-ming had an "apparently unfavorable impression" of Goodfellow's visit, and that Koo told T. V. Soong about his involvement with Goodfellow. Soong then resolved to cable Chiang directly to find out more about the situation, since the embassy was, from March 27 onward, cut out from information on the Chiang-Goodfellow arrangement.³⁶ That is the end of the Goodfellow trail in the Koo diaries. It is quite remarkable, however, to find Wellington Koo returning to his dealings with Goodfellow when asked many years later by an interviewer to reflect back on the Korean War; although the interviewer obviously knew nothing about it, it is the first thing Koo mentions, he recapitulates the story for several pages, and then refers to Goodfellow having told him in January 1950 about the State Department's desire to leash Syngman Rhee, so that "the aggression would come from North Korea." Koo then added, "that is strategy!"[37]

It may be that Goodfellow's activity with the Nationalists was also known to Sen. H. Alexander Smith. Smith wrote in his diary on February 26, "it comes to me to have a small dinner with Goodfriend [*sic*] and Barrett . . . and also for General Donovan to mobilize those forces that are available for (a) a positive anti-communist policy in Far East (b) a positive Voice of America program." The next day he again said, "arrange f[or] Goodfriend meeting and also Donovan." On March 7, Smith writes, "I feel that I need guidance to be more positive and aggressive with my whole approach. Build on Donovan's program. . . . Goodfriend pictures (Korea, Formosa, China & Far East program, Donovan, Short) I need vision and guidance." On March 17, he said, "went to State Dept. where Goodfriend showed his pictures and gave us his story of his approach to China and the Cold War generally."[38]

Was "Goodfriend" actually Goodfellow? Goodfellow was apparently in Seoul on March 15, so how could he be in Washington on March 17? This is possible since Korea was a day ahead in time, but unlikely; it is also possible that he covered his movements or sought to throw people off the track. It was a common mistake to call him "Goodfriend"; Averell Harriman did it in August 1950.[39] I have never come across a person named Goodfriend in any account from the period. Furthermore, the association with Donovan and Short, the latter working for a subsidiary of World Commerce, for which Goodfellow also worked, both trying to organize underground operations for Chiang, would seem to bear out the assumption that Goodfriend was Goodfellow. Interesting, therefore, that he held forth at the State Department, with "pictures." But what pictures?

By the end of April 1950, the American chargé d'affaires who had recently arrived, Robert Strong, reported from Taipei that "use of South Korea by Nationalists as [an] intelligence and underground activities base" was already well in hand.[40] Although he did not say if this resulted from Goodfellow's activities, it is likely that it did. In any case it was an important development, linking the fate of the ROK and the ROC. I do not know what Goodfellow did between the end of March and June 12, 1950—but by that later date, as we will see, he was back in the army.

SPECIAL ACTIVITIES: CHENNAULT

Airpower was not only a pet concern of rollbackers, but played an important but little-known role in events leading up to the Korean War. If the Chinese Communists were to obtain Soviet jets, Nationalist air superiority would end and its planes would no longer be able to fend off an invasion by bombarding the jerry-built troop landing flotillas, made up mostly of Chinese junks. If, on the other hand, the Nationalists got large numbers of jets and bases somewhere north of Taiwan, they could bomb not just the Chinese coast (which they did continually in early 1950), but hit the industrial heartland in Manchuria as well. Chennault led the attempt to get planes for the Nationalists, and to raise yet another volunteer air force for them in late 1949.

Given official American restrictions on military support to Taiwan, Chennault turned first to MacArthur and then to Rhee. In October 1949, British sources cited reports of Japanese flyers coming to fight for the Nationalists. A month later it was clear that Japanese aviators were "being allowed to slip out of Japan to Formosa."[41]

Chiang Kai-shek sought a Korean airbase during his visit with Rhee in August 1949, and in November Chennault and another pro-Taiwan aviator, Air Force general Russell E. Randall, showed up in Seoul. Chennault wanted to establish CAT links with Korea, and may also have pursued the air base issue. He wrote to MacArthur that Rhee was most anxious to have an air arm, "one or two squadrons of fighters" which, to be sure, "would not be sufficient for an offensive campaign against North Korea," but would be helpful in ground support if the North attacked. Chennault urged that his friend, Randall, be employed by Rhee and "be given authority to train all classes of aviation personnel and organize them into appropriate units." Chennault asked Randall to report the results of his survey to MacArthur or to Willoughby.[42]

In letters to Rhee after his November visit, Chennault urged him to develop commercial air links through CIA-funded Civil Air Transport, which would provide "an integrated air service" for South Korea, Japan, and Taiwan "to knit them together politically and economically into an effective bulwark against further Communist aggression" (at the time there was no overseas Korean air line, and the U.S. Air Force controlled Kimp'o airfield). CAT, he said, had "worked tirelessly" to make possible continued Nationalist resistance "to Communist aggression." Whiting Willauer came to Washington in January 1950 to raise funds for CAT, and by early March the CIA and other departments concluded that support of CAT was "in the national interest."[43]

In May 1950, CAT proposed a joint venture with Korean National Airlines, the domestic service, in which CAT would have the preponderant interest; according to American embassy sources Rhee was initially cool to the idea, but by mid-June he and sidekick Harold Lady wanted CAT to run an international service between Formosa and Korea, and proposed the purchase of DC-3 planes to get it going. The embassy refused to disburse foreign exchange for this purpose. At the outbreak of the

Korean War CAT was still "blocked" in Korea, except for providing air transport to a mission of Korean traders that went to Taiwan and Southeast Asia in April. Whiting Willauer said that an embassy employee, J. Franklin Ray, Jr., was responsible for obtaining CAT aircraft for this trip.[44]

In June 1950, in spite of its CIA backing, CAT was nearly insolvent. Rumors continued to fly that Chennault had organized American and Japanese flyers into a volunteer air force to fight for the Nationalists; although some Japanese and American flyers unquestionably came to Taiwan, the effort did not amount to much. In Taiwan and Korea Chennault was mainly trying to fight communists as a way to make money. When the Taiwan press reported, for example, that the nearly-bankrupt CAT had gotten a $300,000 subsidy from the KMT in mid-June, 1950, British sources commented, "I think it is a bit much for CAT, Inc. not only to mulct the refugee traffic of exorbitant fares for flying them out of China, but now to get even more solid cash out of the dwindling funds of the Formosan National Government."[45]

In spite of this subsidy, Willoughby's intelligence apparatus reported on June 22, 1950, that CAT was bankrupt, and had evacuated some planes from Taiwan in fear of an imminent invasion. The day after the Korean War began, however, Chennault wired MacArthur, saying CAT planes were ready to go. Soon CAT was flying transport jobs for the UN Command and carrying out unspecified intelligence assignments. Willauer sent Chennault a memo on July 10 referring to "the Korean break," implying that the war bailed CAT out after "the exhaustion of [cash] reserves over the last six months"; he later stated that "the Korean War gave [CAT] a very much needed assist . . . we finally got in there as CAT and also set up and operated Korean National [Air] until the Koreans could take it over by themselves."[46]

SPECIAL ACTIVITIES: COOKE

In March 1950 Ambrose Cates contracted with Admiral Charles Cooke to head the advisory group, clearing it with Commerce International headquarters in New York (presumably William Donovan) and with Chiang Kai-shek, the latter agreeing to pay a "service fee" of $750,000 per year. The generalissimo's son, Chiang Wei-guo, was "together constantly" with Cates when the latter visited Taiwan. Cates also related that he had three conferences with MacArthur, who "has really given us backing," and had been "constantly advised of what we're doing." By the summer of 1950 Cates claimed (it was an exaggeration) to have funneled 1,200 tanks to the Nationalist Army, giving it the fourth largest tank force in the world. He also contracted with Philco to provide radar and refurbish KMT mobile armored forces. Commerce International's contracts, signed in July 1949, and January, July, and November 1950, included the shipment of tanks, frigates for the Navy, surplus shells for naval guns, and unspecified air force equipment, rumored to include jet aircraft. All in all, it was a heady period for Cates: "when they go back to China [*sic*], then we are going to be a big company."[47]

The advisory group contract may have been signed in March, but the first contingent of American officers arrived in Taipei toward the end of January 1950. At about the same time, a Major Vanderpuyl of Willoughby's intelligence staff came to Taiwan. Cooke arrived on February 11, the same time that Colonel Goodfellow showed up in Taiwan. He carried Hearst International News Service credentials, issued by Hearst executive E. D. Coblentz, publisher of the *San Francisco Call-Bulletin*. The "retired" officers in this grouping were mostly people who resigned from the services as soon as Cooke hired them. By June 28, 1950, the group included Marine Generals O. T. Pfeiffer (from Tokyo) and R. L. Peterson, Air Force Gen. Byron Johnson, Rear Admirals H. L. Krosskopf and Walter C. Ansel, various naval captains, and Colonels Shaw and Poston (probably Lt. Col. Carl M. Poston), intelligence officers from Willoughby's command. The Marine and Air Force generals, and several others, arrived by mid-May. Cooke got help directly from the U. S. Navy in assembling his officers; Navy support for Chiang and for rollback would be anomalous, since the Navy tends toward internationalist strategies, but this case is explained by the close ties between Naval intelligence and the Nationalist government during World War II.[48]

Although little information on the Commerce International effort drifted into the American press at the time, the Chinese and the North Koreans were well aware of the genesis and purpose of the operation. The Chinese news agency seemed to have exaggerated the amount of military equipment sold to Taiwan (enough to equip five divisions), but most of their information was right and they correctly identified Cheng Kai-ming's role in meeting with Wedemeyer and others in the fall of 1949.[49] The State Department and the Joint Chiefs of Staff (JCS) both disapproved of the effort, but there is little evidence that either did much to block it.[50]

Cooke met with both MacArthur and Premier Yoshida on his way to Taipei. Within a week of his arrival Cooke was touring Chinese military establishments with Mme. Chiang, identifying himself as a correspondent for the Hearst International News Service; he went back and forth between Tokyo and Taipei frequently, and met with Bradley and Johnson during their trip to Tokyo just before the war started. By May 1950 Cooke took an active role in Nationalist strategy, recommending an abrupt withdrawal during the battle for Hainan; he also urged Chiang to give top command authority to Gen. Sun Li-jen. In a top secret letter Robert Strong, American chargé in Taipei, said that "Cooke is now more or less openly heading up planning for all Chinese forces." William R. Mathews, who traveled with Dulles on his June Far Eastern trip, wrote that Cooke and Marine Major General Francis "are in Formosa incognito planning Chinese Nationalist operations," and that Chiang hoped to reinvade the mainland within the next year, providing he got American air force help.[51]

Irving Ritchie Short showed up on Taiwan in mid-April 1950. Short had been in contact since November 1949 with a man in Taiwan named Eugene Hovans, "a Russian with a colorful background in China." Hovans was said to be involved in anti-Soviet espionage in Bangkok and elsewhere. Another contact was Terry Kwan of U.S. Naval intelligence, an aide to Admiral Cooke.[52]

In a letter of February 6, 1950, to Hovans, Short said he had become a consultant to the Department of Defense: "I cannot tell you what is cooking, but I can say that something is very much in the wind." Acheson was in trouble because of the Hiss case, he said, and "we are fighting him all the time"—the State Department was "an enemy of our true interests." Short said he would continue trying to organize a volunteer fighting group for the Nationalists, and "bypass" State; he would soon have jobs for Hovans and Kwan. Hovans, for his part, told American officials that Short was getting funding from Mme. Chiang and from H. H. Kung, and indeed Mme. Chiang arranged several guest houses for Short and his party. An American investigator also linked Short to the arrival of Colonel Vanderpuyl on Taiwan, something said to have been arranged after meetings with Generals Bolling, Bradley, and Vandenberg.

Short visited Hong Kong shortly after he arrived in Taiwan, accompanied by Carl Hess of *Pathfinder* magazine and one "Holtz." He also was in contact with someone named William Wee, "who associated with (Scott) George in gold traffic." The State Department treated this visit with top secret–eyes only sensitivity, Acheson saying at one point, "Prefer Short and his supporters believe his activities unknown." At a later point, however, Robert Strong indicated that the State Department knew little about the Short effort: on July 6, after the Korean War began, he wired, "Should we now use all possible means including Chinese sources to learn Short's connections?"[53]

Chinese Nationalist direction of Short's work was obvious. In mid-March Wellington Koo reported that Kohlberg returned from Taiwan and urged Short to send a small group of American military people to Taiwan; two weeks later Koo reported that Chiang Kai-shek himself had "ordered" Short to proceed to Taipei, and on April 10 Chen Chih-mai told Koo to have Short and his group screened "by the security agency of the American Legion."[54]

This is all that the available files show on this case. After the Korean War began, Short fell ill in Taiwan. He appeared to recover and departed for Japan, where he soon expired: "he was a very young man when he died, as a few local officials and newspapers pointed out." Hovans was tortured to death by the KMT secret police, also shortly after the war began.[55] It is not clear that the Short gambit amounted to much in itself. He was young, brash, and in over his head; by June 1950 he seems to have done little more than generate publicity for the KMT. The importance of Short, and perhaps Hovans, would derive from what they were in a position to know about other operations.

For our purposes the Short case is important because it documents the active involvement of Army intelligence, Louis Johnson's office, and perhaps even high officers like Generals Bradley and Vandenberg, in recruiting volunteer forces for the Nationalists. According to State Department documentation, it was an Army colonel who first put Short in touch with Donovan's firm, Commerce International. Furthermore Short was brought into an intelligence capacity with the Department of Defense, in spite of (because of?) his close ties to and partisanship for the Nationalist cause (he was the agent of a foreign government). It would not be unreasonable to assume that all of the above also applied to the Cooke case: in effect, an alliance between the Nationalists, the China Lobby, high officials in the Defense Department, and Donovan's Commerce International subsidiary.

In addition to Cooke's group, Japanese military advisors came to Taiwan as early as June 1949, about twenty of them training soldiers at a military branch of the Tsao Shan political school thereafter. Chiang Kai-shek had an ambitious plan to bring in a Japanese "foreign legion" numbering as many as 300,000 officers and soldiers, "for the purpose of spearheading a Nationalist invasion of the mainland." The plan may sound ridiculous, much like similar plans in Korea by Chinese-aligned leaders like Yi Pŏm-sŏk and Yi Ch'ŏng-ch'ŏn, but it was the origin of a significant Japanese participation in Nationalist military affairs—unquestionably supported by MacArthur and Willoughby.

Chiang also released some of Japan's worst war criminals from his jails in 1949, including Gen. Okamura Yasuji, famed for his "kill-all, burn-all, loot-all" campaigns against the Chinese people. With the communist threat to the island growing critical in April 1950, Chiang brought in some of the highest-ranking militarists of the prewar period as advisors: Admiral Hasegawa, former Governor-General of Taiwan, Gen. Okamura Reiji, a Japanese commander in China, and Mishimura Kokei.

Before they left Tokyo, an aide to MacArthur told them that although it was State Department policy not to defend Taiwan, MacArthur was responsible for the security of the Pacific and viewed Taiwan as integral to it. In late April an attaché on Taiwan reported that the former chief of staff of the Japanese 23rd Army was training ROCA field officers. Another forty Japanese advisors in government and industry were scheduled to arrive in mid-June. Chiang also sought to recruit German advisors, including Gen. Alexander von Falkenhausen, who headed the German military mission to China in the 1930s that built the blockades against the Kiangsi Soviet, occasioning the Long March. The pity was, he languished in a Brussels prison for crimes against humanity committed while he was the Nazi military governor of Belgium.[56] But militarist and Nazi war criminals could not save the regime if its place of exile were swamped by Communist-laden junks.

The American press at the time (and most scholars since) may have been unaware of the "special activities" I have just described, but the Chinese Communists monitored them closely in their press. On January 12, 1950, the *People's Daily* highlighted the arrival in Hong Kong of "the chief of American special services" (Donovan), allegedly to help the KMT with its spying; the *Hsinhua* news agency asserted on February 15, 1950, that the U.S. Government had decided to send a military advisory group to Taiwan, and the *People's Daily* frequently cited the presence of Charles Cooke and General Pfeiffer on Taiwan thereafter. In March the *People's Daily* accused MacArthur of sending many "Japanese war criminals" to give Chiang military advice, linking Wu T'ieh-ch'eng to that activity; finally, in April it said the U.S. was expanding air bases in Korea so that Chiang's planes could bomb Manchuria.[57]

THE INVASION

From the New Year onward, American and British intelligence agencies predicted that the "last battle" of the Chinese civil war would come in June 1950. In January British Foreign Office sources predicted an invasion of Taiwan "by the end of June"; Guy Burgess implied that this was the CIA estimate in remarking that "the U.S. technical estimate . . . has been 'by the middle of 1950.' " In April, Burgess said the invasion would come in May-June, or September-October.[58]

Burgess took time off from his sundry dalliances to follow the Taiwan issue attentively. By March 22, the news that MacArthur had arrested a Taiwan independence leader in Tokyo led him to "the logical deduction" that "SCAP is now bent on saving the Nationalists." Evaluating an April 14 memo saying that air power might be decisive in taking Taiwan, Burgess said, "we have been told even tho' we had never been entirely convinced that the State Department had written Formosa off so far as long term policy is concerned."[59] This was right on the money, and would also reflect his thoughts on Acheson's having appeared to place Korea outside the American defense perimeter.

The intelligence assumptions behind these predictions are not known: presumably they took into account the monsoons and high seas of July and August, which would make an invasion unlikely after late June. They might also have been based on a timetable for the conquest of the mainland, but even then, why would the invasion not come earlier, or later? The frequency of the June prediction suggests harder evidence than the merely circumstantial, some sort of "humint" or human intelligence penetration of the PRC leadership, so that the Communist timetable would be known.

In May the Nationalists appeared to have played out their string. T. V. Soong, then in the United States, broke with Chiang and quit the KMT Central Committee in early June, as dispatches reported "heavy Communist troop movement from central and south China toward . . . the invasion base" on the southwest coast. The American chargé, Robert Strong, reported from Taipei on May 17, "fate of Taiwan sealed, Communist attack can occur between June 15 and end July." He suggested to Acheson that the United States begin evacuation of dependents immediately, and recommended that the CIA be out by June 15. (Evacuation notices to nonessential American personnel went out on May 26.) The Taipei consulate said that the best guess from a meeting of all American representatives was that the island would be attacked before July 15. In mid-June Willoughby's intelligence spied masses of Chinese junks assembling off the Fujian coast.[60]

The State Department remained adamantly unwilling to back Chiang, and ostensibly disinclined to defend the island. Acheson told Johnson in March that he would not license the sale of tanks and jet fighters for Taiwan, citing British objections; this would appear to have signaled his willingness personally to obstruct the attempt by Johnson and other China Lobbyists to funnel advanced weaponry to Chiang.[61]

The immediate cause of this sense of impending doom for the KMT was its defeat on Hainan Island, a large and important territory full of minerals and other raw materials that the Japanese had just begun to develop before the war ended. In the midst of the January 1950 crisis over Taiwan policy in Washington, Senator Knowland visited Wellington Koo and said that to counter Acheson's line that the Nationalists would not fight, it was of "utmost importance" that they successfully defend Hainan against the Communists.[62]

But the CIA said in late February that the Nationalists were incapable of making the political and military changes necessary to defend Taiwan, and the Hainan debacle merely confirmed this view.[63] After extensive preparations for the island's defense, it fell in the third week of April without much of a fight. Two high ROCA generals were off in Korea on unknown business, as we have seen, instead of at their command posts. Supporters of the Nationalists in Washington wiped egg off their faces. By early June the British found "flagging interest" in Congress for Chiang's cause. Most important, the Hainan debacle undercut moderate Republican support for Taiwan.[64]

The Nationalist's plight was only deepened by the deafening silence from Washington after the Hainan defeat. Had the Chinese Communists attacked Hainan *after* June 25, it would have been condemned as heinous aggression; it would have made Quemoy and Matsu look like child's play. An administration wishing to stop a similar invasion of Taiwan would have been much more vociferous. From Taiwan came reports of "deep gloom and defeatism following Hainan," hemorrhaging capital flight, and the chartering of ships and airliners for escape. Some, however, pondered an alternative scenario.

Robert Strong warned in late April that "desperate measures may be attempted by [the] Nationalist Government to involve [U.S.] in [a] shooting war as [a] means of saving its own skin." A week later, on May 8, Chiang held a news conference where he said, "We must apply the maxim [that] the best defence is offence, to invade the mainland, in order that Communist forces may be contained in[side] China."[65] But after the Hainan debacle, this seemed like the terminal ranting of a madman.

There was an alternative reading of the Hainan defeat, offered by one of Chiang's American intimates, and by British observers. Whiting Willauer wrote on May 1, "I am damned certain that Hainan was deliberately surrendered to focus attention on the Far Eastern urgency [*sic*] prior to the big three [*sic*] conference. It was of no strategic value to those on Formosa."[66] British intelligence rightly believed that the decision to abandon Hainan was taken under strong advice from Admiral Cooke; they thought he was backed in this by MacArthur. They said the retreat from Hainan was orderly and disciplined, not the stampede depicted in the press.

Guy Burgess found Cooke "worth a passing glance. It is said to have been owing to his advice that Hainan was evacuated . . . Adm. Cooke is not now in U.S. employment. When he was, he was a nuisance in O.S.S." Again he remarked that whether the Nationalists can hold Taiwan or not was closely related to the "very vexed question of what U.S. assistance will be given and by who [*sic*]."[67]

Admiral Cooke had a different perspective, according to the available record. He told MacArthur that he got to Hainan just in time to see the Nationalists "completely defeated," calling it a "debacle." Just what had caused it, he did not know. But "the loss of Hainan will I fear have some adverse reactions in the U.S.—particularly the way it was lost." Cooke does not say if he ordered the withdrawal or not, but he thought the loss of an island so close to Vietnam also meant that the days of the Bao Dai regime were numbered. "One wonders what measures can be taken to wake up the U.S. to the seriousness of the debacle that it has allowed to descend upon itself."[68]

Whatever Cooke's role in the evacuation of Hainan, the defeat reflected so badly on the Nationalists that it is unlikely to have been a carefully considered withdrawal, even if it were to bolster defenses for a final stand on Taiwan. It cannot be emphasized enough that the Chiang regime had clay feet; it was doubtful that the army, much less so the people of Taiwan, would rally to its cause. This was, as Acheson and Kennan knew, a divulgate system that required someone else to fight its battles against both the Japanese and the Communists. Expansionists and rollbackers grossly overrated Chiang's potency, mostly out of ignorance, although they also benefitted from the regime's leakage by gaining access to its wealth and resources. For them this rickety ship of state was an opportunity. But for internationalists it signaled the impossibility of organizing Nationalist China in the world economy and in the American security structure.

The rollback current retained its fascination with airpower as a panacea for Chiang's plight. All through early 1950 Nationalist planes bombed cities and military installations along the China coast, aided by Americans in Chennault's CAT, and perhaps by Japanese pilots. But the problem in May and June 1950 was the emerging Communist dominance of the air. It was air supremacy that would guarantee success for an invasion of Taiwan. Intelligence agents spied swept-wing MIG jets over Chinese cities, proliferating ominously like the birds in Hitchcock's film by that title.

Admiral Cooke drew MacArthur's attention to the strategic implications of jet airpower deployed from what CINCFE (Commander in Chief, Far East) had called an unsinkable aircraft carrier: "the idea of permitting them [Communist jets] to be established on Formosa is fantastic. A rational man has difficulty accepting that fact." In a letter of May 2, Cooke told him, "the Russians are organizing airfields all up and down the coast of China . . . if Formosa is lost to the Communists, which means the Russians . . . World War III sooner or later becomes inevitable."[69] Such Soviet air capability would threaten Seventh Fleet ships and atomic-capable bombers on Guam and Okinawa.

MacArthur sent Cooke's May 2 letter on to Willoughby, whose intelligence organizations had been closely monitoring the air buildup in China. Gen. Omar Bradley wrote to Louis Johnson on May 5 that PRC airpower was "on a rapidly rising curve . . . a Russian-controlled air organization has been moving in since January." He urged immediate American countermeasures, saying MacArthur agreed with him. Bradley linked this to Taiwan by suggesting that qualified observers be dispatched to obtain "complete factual information" on the situation there. Later in May he met William Bullitt, who showed him a letter "from a Chinaman named Shah," who said the Nationalists urgently needed jets, since their prop planes were no match for MIGs.[70]

Gen. Chennault told Sen. Smith that the sighting of jets over Shanghai "looks like the turning point toward real trouble" (although he thought the planes looked more like Japanese Zeroes than MIGs). Smith had just obtained information to the effect that Chu Teh had promised the occupation of Taiwan before the end of June, using paratroopers to be dropped from Chennault's impounded transport planes. Shortly thereafter Senator Knowland told him of Cooke's judgment that Taiwan needed 300 jets, as quickly as possible. Knowland thought Congressional action on the planes was "vital" at "this critical juncture." On June 12, Smith sent to Dean Rusk a letter he received from Taiwan, saying the new airpower posed a threat "of the gravest kind," demanding "timely and positive action at once" by the U.S. In the *New York Times*, Hanson Baldwin wrote that the MIGs signified that "Formosa's end is near."[71]

The CIA and British intelligence agreed that a mainland air buildup ensued in the spring of 1950. The CIA documented large shipments of aviation gas coming into Manchuria, although it was not clear that they were sent southward. The British said the big increases in air power could be for an attack on Taiwan, but also might be a response to Nationalist bombing of the China coast, since Soviet anti-aircraft shipments also increased markedly. Burgess thought it made more probable an invasion of Formosa, but he did not think the Russians would let China have any high-technology jet fighters, or would only allow Russian pilots to fly them, a judgment concurred in by American intelligence.[72] To the extent that this were true, it either meant the jets would be held back in an invasion of Formosa, or would signal direct Soviet involvement.

For Chiang's American supporters, all this merely quickened their attempts to organize a Flying Tiger–like international air brigade to defend Taiwan. By mid-May rumors circulated that Japanese, American, and even Israeli pilots were in Taiwan, forming a brigade or working with the ROC Air Force.[73] These efforts were bound to be ineffectual without access to jet aircraft, however, which Acheson had denied to the Nationalists.

In early May 1950 the British reported that Chiang had intimated to visiting Hearst journalists that he might consider a SCAP defense of Taiwan if his sovereignty were not impaired. The first Foreign Office minute on the cover of this document asked if there was truth in reports that a volunteer brigade of aviators might be going to Taiwan, something that General Chennault and Irving Ritchie Short were trying to organize; Guy Burgess then commented (on May 24) that "a serious situation" would arise "when and if Formosa is attacked," which he thought might come "in a month or so." He thought a SCAP defense of Taiwan had "sensational implications," and remarked that "it is reasonably certain that in spite of the State Department, this is what elements of the U.S. War Department and SCAP's regime desire." He cited another telegram from the U.K. embassy in Washington, which "raises the *possibility* [*sic*] that the U.S. may extend military aid to Formosa under President's [Truman] sanction."

A few days before the Korean War, according to Nationalist cable traffic, Air Force General Vandenberg said "a turning point" might come with the Johnson-Bradley visit to Tokyo, making it possible to supply American jets or air cover to Taiwan; Far East Air Force Commander Stratemeyer on June 23 was said to want American jets, and already to have appointed American Air Force advisors, to help defend the Nationalists: "but the important point," the cables said, "is the decision of Washington."[74]

The threat of PRC air dominance did not diminish before the Korean War, but for a brief time in mid-June it seemed that an invasion had been put off, perhaps until 1951. On June 12, Dulles heard Wellington Koo say it would come in early July, but responded that the State Department thought the PRC would not attack until the following year, unless they came to believe that the Nationalists would not resist. Willoughby's intelligence on June 10 cited KMT Army Chief of Staff Chou Chih-jou to the effect that an invasion was not imminent, and that the Communists would concentrate on Indochina for the time being, apparently leading SCAP officials to tell Marguerite Higgins that the Communists had postponed their invasion plans, "at least beyond mid-summer" 1950. Perhaps most interesting, she was told that Russian advisors were pressing the Chinese to put the invasion off until the spring of 1951, so as not to provoke the Americans.[75] To the extent that this last were true, the Chinese might feel like the North Koreans when they heard that the Soviets wanted to keep Germany split.

Within a few days the estimates again changed, however, as reports came in of a massive invasion fleet forming along the southern China coast. On June 17 and 23, Willoughby's intelligence found "undeniable evidence" of this gathering flotilla of small ships, junks, and ersatz troop carriers, but was still not sure it heralded an imminent invasion. British intelligence cited reports in mid-June from Shanghai alone of the assembling of "an invasion fleet" of ten LSTs and nine LSMs capable of landing

20,000 troops. Other accounts documented this fleet buildup toward an invasion just as the Korean War began.[76]

The difficulty with all the May-June estimates of a Chinese Communist invasion, air buildup, fleet buildup, and the like is that the Nationalists' alarmist farrago masked their own threats to China, backed by powerful Americans. Airpower deployment, threat and counterthreat, was crucial to the delimiting of the Korean War once it got out of hand in late 1950, as we will see; it was important before the war began, too. Much that the Chinese and the Russians did might be interpreted as a response to Nationalist activities which, the other side would have reason to believe, had American support, either in Washington or Tokyo.

COUP D'ETAT: ONE LESS GENERALISSIMO

The Nationalists thus faced the distinct probability of a Communist invasion in the next few weeks, if not days. They had not succeeded in garnering the American commitment nor the airpower they needed to fend it off, thanks to Acheson. Their support in Washington was waning after Hainan fell, and ominously so among their usual supporters; even Henry Luce had been inactive, explaining to Wellington Koo on June 6 that "he had the lever but was in need of a fulcrum." The Nationalists even sought succor from the French, then embroiled in Indochina. But on June 8 the French ambassador to the United States, M. Henri Bonnet, informed Koo that France was "cold to the idea" of working together.[77]

Shortly thereafter Chiang sought asylum in the Philippines and Korea. American naval sources in Manila cabled that it was "highly probable" that Chiang and his entourage "may enter Subic Bay by ship or Sangley by plane unannounced."[78] The first among postwar dictators to look to the United States for conveyance from the presidential palace to exile and repose, after him came the deluge: the Shah of Iran, Battista, Rhee, Thieu and Ky, Somoza, the Shah again, "Baby Doc" Duvalier, Marcos. But some—Ngo Dinh Diem, Rafael Trujillo—got a bullet for their efforts, a more worriesome scenario.

Willoughby told MacArthur on June 15 that Maj. Gen. Ho Shih-lai had communicated in "absolute secrecy" Chiang's urgent request "to accept American high command in every category and hopes to interest Gen. MacArthur to accept this responsibility, preferably for the entire Far East but specifically for Formosa and places himself and his people in every governmental level at the disposal of Gen. MacArthur."[79]

There was a silver lining in the gathering clouds. As Taipei's Washington network well knew, bureaucratic momentum was building toward a reversal of the Acheson policy. Indeed, by late June, Acheson and Truman were the only high officials still balking at a defense of the ROC.

The reason, as always, was the nature of the Chiang regime. But perhaps something could be done to end the whole unfortunate China mess, with Louis Johnson and Dean Acheson at each other's throats, and Asia policy threatening to lurch out of control.

So, containment liberals came up with an Occam's razor, a minimax solution, to the generalissimo problem: a coup d'etat. That would solve just about every question facing American policy in East Asia in June 1950. It would make possible a defense of the island, and enhance Acheson's control of the policy process. It would remove the China Lobby cancer from inside the administration, undercut the growing opposition to Truman's policies, and satisfy moderates in Congress and the military who wanted Taiwan defended and who wanted a stand against communism through some kind of "positive action" short of war. It wouldn't please Joe McCarthy, but Dulles was the proper symbol of an opposition for which this would be the solution; a filip to events on Taiwan would make his role as bipartisan accommodator feasible.

A coup was, however, an unfortunate choice of means. Americans have the novel mix of ineptness in political intrigue and deep belief in its cure-all virtues (take Donovan, for example). It is the dementia of an apolitical people who do not think through political and social questions, settling instead on a technical fix, a possible act toward an impossible outcome. Every time the knife is wielded another sore appears, to paraphrase Arthur Koestler. But if Chiang Kai-shek had any forte it was a passion and skill for intrigue. His agents and friends had wormed their way into influence at the commanding heights of the American state, had they not? If people came looking for his scalp, he might have a riposte.

A coup was obviously not Taipei's solution, nor that of stalwart expansionists in the China Lobby, who would prosper only with someone like Chiang in the saddle. It would not have been Syngman Rhee's solution: "little Chiang Kai-shek" to many liberals, with his own regime crumbling he might be next. (The United States later concocted "Operation Everready," a scenario to depose Rhee when he resisted the armistice in 1953.) Finally, it would not have been MacArthur's solution, but an assault by Europe-firsters against his close ally; more importantly it would have enhanced Acheson's control of Asia policy.

Thoughts about a coup against Chiang had been floating around Washington since the Nationalist loss of the mainland heaved into view. In May 1949 Livingston Merchant wrote that the KMT was corrupt and incompetent, but its character could not be altered "short of the dangerous and risky effort to finance and support a coup d'etat." When George Kennan was feeling like Teddy Roosevelt in June 1949, he proposed that an emissary might be sent to Gen. Sun Li-jen, to suggest in effect that he take over the ROCA and put Chiang in the status of "a political refugee."

Sun was, he thought, perhaps the only KMT general with the will and experience to fight the communists.[80]

There may have been some activity toward a coup in the summer of 1949. Howard Hunt told an interviewer in 1975 that a man named Boris T. Pash was in charge of an "assassination unit" in the CIA, and the Senate Select Committee on Intelligence concluded that in the early days of the Agency such a unit did exist, headed by Pash. An army colonel, Pash was chief counterintelligence officer for the Manhattan Project, and served with MacArthur (whom he revered) in occupied Japan. He was assigned to the Office of Policy Coordination (OPC) in March 1949. He testified under oath before the committee that his duties included "contingency planning for the death of foreign leaders, such as Stalin."

No assassinations were carried out, it was said, but neither was the method ruled out of bounds. Two instances were "seriously suggested," but rejected at higher level; both involved "Asian leaders." One was to have been against Chou En-lai at the Bandung Conference, the other against an unnamed "Asian leader" in the summer of 1949.[81]

The OPC had a much bigger program on Taiwan than is generally known. A former member recalls being stunned to find that Truman had quietly "authorized massive support to the Chinat [*sic*] plan to retake mainland China"; by 1951, the OPC had more than six hundred people on the island, under the cover of a company called "Western Enterprises." They worked with Chinese Nationalist remnants in Burma under Li Mi, who mixed their opium trafficking with occasional forays across the border into China.[82]

A covert capability for a coup may have been in place on Taiwan by the fall of 1949. In late August Rusk said he was exploring the possibility of getting Col. Frank Merrill "to go out to Formosa and talk with General Sun," to see if there was "some plan" which would "save Formosa." Rusk had been Frank Merrill's deputy in Burma in 1943. One day Rusk mounted a mule and trekked into the northern Burmese wilderness, only to find Gen. Sun Li-jen, then division commander of a crack Chinese Nationalist army. At this time Goodfellow was a leader in OSS efforts to send guerrillas into Burma to fight the Japanese.[83]

In the fall of 1949 important Chinese defectors from Chiang's regime like Li Tsung-jen and Kan Chieh-hou showed up in Washington, Kan stating bluntly on September 16 that somebody ought to get rid of Chiang. During the behind-the-scenes efforts in the fall of 1949 to get some sort of military advisory group for Taiwan, Ward Canaday drew up a paper for Louis Johnson suggesting that Sun Li-jen should become commander in chief of the Nationalist armies, bolstered by an American military mission that could be paid for by Chinese tungsten and tin. Then "Western trained liberals" grouped around Hu Shih "should be given political power to form a new cabinet." "Whatever the U.S. 'indicates' as desirable can be arranged," Canaday reasoned, because "at this present juncture a 'revolution by consent' could be obtained from the Kuomintang so that these liberals will be installed." T. V. Soong had similar ideas about Hu Shih in 1949, although the earliest such suggestion that I have found came from Mrs. Ogden Reid, in May 1949.[84]

Robert Strong said that when he flew to Taipei in December 1949 with Kenneth Krentz (former consul general in Taipei), Krentz told him that Sun Li-jen was going to be approached and told that "if he would agree to take control" of the Nationalist government, the U.S. "would support him to the hilt." But Sun flatly refused to do so.[85]

At this point Chiang was no longer president, having stepped back in the wake of the debacle on the mainland, but he was very much in control. It beggars the imagination to think he or his close allies would consent to a Hu Shih-centered "revolution," if it meant that the liberals would be more than a figleaf. Such thinking merely reflects the eternal attempt by Americans to replicate themselves in exotic environs, to finger something known, in this case a third force between a Right that was not yet dead and a Left that they wish had never been born.

Hu Shih was a revered Chinese liberal, but of the sort whose durable function was to be the exception proving the rule. There were as many of his type in China in the 1940s as there were Confucians and Buddhists in America. Aged, politically ineffectual, and lacking any effective organized constituency on Taiwan, he was somewhat of a cross between Philip Jaisohn and Kim Kyu-sik. Sun Li-jen was a fine general, but so were others; the reason his name came round like clockwork in all the talk about coups was his training at Virginia Military Institute and his fluent English. He was one KMT general whose name the Americans could remember; furthermore he had OSS connections. Chiang knew this, of course, and probably had a small army keeping an eye on him.

With the Communists still consolidating their control of the mainland, the Chiang problem was not urgent in 1949. Its salience rose with the China policy crisis in the United States, and the growing threat of an invasion. Acheson got Hoover's opposition in January, McCarthy's in February, and the return of Chiang to the ROC presidency in March; there was the palpable threat of an invasion in June that might place Soviet naval and airpower in a position to surveil the Pacific outside the Vladivostok-perimeter "choke points."

Toward the end of March Harlan Cleveland, an internationalist with the ECA, confided to Nationalist sources that the administration would not give any military aid as long as the Gimo was in control. Rusk underlined this a month later. On the very day that Hainan was falling, Rusk listened patiently to Wellington Koo go on about how the Nationalists had reorganized parts of the Army and instilled "high spirit and will to resist," and the like. He then responded bluntly that the United States "had no intention as yet to review the policy" of no military aid for Taiwan.[86]

After the Hainan defeat David Barrett, the American military attaché in Taiwan, sent a top secret cable quoting a high-level Chinese official to the effect that Chiang and his cliques were "helpless and hopeless"; the source recommended "drastic measures to save [the] situation." Chiang gave bad orders to the Army through his crony Chou Chih-jou, while his two sons interfered with their own organizations; the chances of saving the situation with the Chiang clique's meddling were "extremely slight." Yet Barrett thought that the United States could not afford to yield even "one yard" to the Communists in Asia. Thus, "In this desperate situation I feel US Govt should not shrink from any measure to strengthen the defense of Taiwan even if it involves interference in internal affairs of a friendly nation to an extent hitherto unprecedented in our history."[87]

Other sources suggested that Barrett's key informant was none other than Sun Li-jen. Robert Strong wrote that Sun "brought up the problem of the Gimo" with Barrett around April 27; as if responding to a direct query, Strong remarked that the issue of whether Sun would "pull a *coup d'etat*" was an idea he thought had been "dead and buried these several months." (Strong did not think Sun was especially outstanding, having merely "a veneer of Americanization.")[88]

Barrett's cable was shown to Rusk on May 1. Two days later, none other than Paul Nitze brought forth a "hypothetical" plan to blast Chiang off the mark.[89] The object was a coup by Sun Li-jen, who had "confided" that he was ready to "assume full military control." The United States would then engage its prestige behind Sun and organize an effective defense of the island, while fomenting resistance on the mainland: trading Chiang for his policy, as it were.

Nitze wanted the whole hog. American criteria of "a successful coup," he said, would be the elimination from power of "all prominent members of the KMT" and the assumption of full military powers by Sun—all this to be done within forty-eight hours. A political vacuum would result, he wrote (anencephaly would be more apt), so the United States should be prepared with "a list of political leaders who can take over the civil administration in the immediate wake of the coup." Three days after that, "the most competent American officials that we can obtain" would arrive in Taipei. They would provide the regime guidance from that time on, through a "veiled but vigorous" American hand. Taiwan would then become a "show window for Asia," and "a base for clandestine propaganda and subversive activities directed at Soviet imperialism on the continent."

The United States should try to split rather than alienate the Chinese

Communists, since the latter might stir up a nasty nationalism. So, the new regime would declare itself "an autonomous provincial government." Meanwhile word would be gotten to Communist generals like Ch'en Yi and Yeh Chien-ying that Taiwan would never subvert their territory. Ch'en and Yeh would then have the mission "to conduct revolutionary activities in North China and Manchuria," presumably against the Russians; if they were to break with Moscow's puppets in Peking, Sun would give them air force support, aided by the United States.

If the Communists nonetheless attacked Taiwan, the United States would defend it with air and naval power—although "it must be realized that the USSR may be willing to make a Spain out of the Formosan situation and that American units committed to this operation might find themselves faced by the best of modern Soviet aircraft and submarines."

Nitze thought a new "synthetic ideology" would also be needed, the Three People's Principles having staled a bit over three decades, and everything would "have to be done at a forced pace because time may well be running out on us." Thus there would needs be a "forced draft" of "a large number of American covert operators," plus small submarines and surface vessels for smuggling agents into the mainland from small islands off the coast. "This Government should in no way be involved in Sun's coup d'etat," Nitze wrote, perhaps even with a straight face, thereby enunciating the principle of plausible deniability that has been used in one coup after another.

One hearkens already to a chorus of voices saying how silly this plan was, no one ever dreamed of implementing such a harebrained scheme. But apart from the stunning buffoonery of thinking the PLA general staff could be split off from Beijing to fight against the Russians while the United States occupied Taiwan, Nitze merely summed up plans by Canaday, Rusk, and others that went forward into May and June, and an enormous covert effort to overthrow the communists went forward on Taiwan and the coastal islands thereafter. Those who wish to get to the bottom of all this might assist scholars in obtaining the relevant documentation, including the still classified paper entitled "Draft: Coup d'etat in Formosa."[90]

On the May 30 holiday, Rusk met with Nitze, Jessup, and others and argued that "Formosa presents a plausible place to 'draw the line,' and is, in itself, important politically if not strategically." He said he had been drafting papers for Acheson on how to carry this out; besides himself and Acheson, only Dulles knew about the planning. The State Department Bureau of Intelligence and Research wanted the "green light" to go ahead with "a US move involving force to prevent the fall of Formosa." Rusk and the others agreed to discuss the following plan informally with Acheson on May 31:

The Gimo would be approached, probably by Dulles in the course of his trip to Japan on June 15, with the word that (a) the fall of Formosa in the present circumstances was inevitable, (b) the US would do nothing to assist Gimo in preventing this, (c) the only course open to the Gimo to prevent bloodshed of his people was to request UN trusteeship. The US would be prepared to back such a move for trusteeship and would ready the [Seventh] fleet to prevent any armed attack on Formosa while the move for trusteeship was pending.

Intelligence and Research, he said, worried that the Russians might be trying to push the United States into a commitment to defend Taiwan, "which would give them an opportunity for pushing the Chinese Communists into a clash with us." A UN trusteeship might avoid that outcome.[91] It was an interesting suggestion. A biographer reports another element of the scenario, gotten directly from Rusk, that in early June 1950 Rusk got "a secret, hand-delivered note" from Sun Li-jen, whom he knew well from Burma days: Sun proposed "to lead a military coup to oust Chiang Kai-shek." Rusk then destroyed the document.[92] This may be true, or Rusk may wish to place the onus for the coup on Sun, rather than where it belongs: in Washington.

In a memo for Acheson on May 30, Rusk acknowledged that the United States already had in place on Taiwan "covert activities directed against the Communists on the mainland," and in support of "certain elements in Formosa"; these included the capability for "some armed assistance on a covert basis." Later, Merchant referred to the covert capacity on the island by saying, "discreet contact should . . . be maintained on Formosa with Formosan leaders. At an early opportunity Frank should be given some guidance." This would be Frank Wisner, the OPC head. (Merchant had told Rusk about a meeting with General Carter Magruder and Robert Joyce who headed the State Department's liaison office with the CIA's operations section, in which reference was made to "Frank" using his funds to support CAT for a while longer, as it tries to get the planes back from Hong Kong; there were also references to Frank's "shop" and "Frank's people.")[93]

According to the scattered and insufficient documentation now available, Gen. John Magruder, an important OSS operative and Asia hand, suggested to Johnson in April 1950 that retaking the mainland through covert operations should have a "special urgency"; he thought "the initiative must be seized and retained" through "aggressive flank actions against the [China] base itself." He called for "emergency planning" and the establishment of a central agency to conduct operations against China. Magruder was well known to Donovan, and may have discussed this plan with him. In any case, on the same day Ray Peers wrote to Donovan saying that the OSS experience in raising anti-Japanese guerrillas in Burma would be a good model for anti-China activities. Peers was head of CIA training activities in 1949, and was CIA station chief on Taiwan by 1951, training guerrillas for raids on the mainland.[94]

Karl Rankin cabled MacArthur in late May, asking about a report that one Liu Lin-chuan had been contacting Chinese guerrillas in Anhwei and Honan, claiming that a representative of MacArthur "promised him $20 million for subsidizing anti-Commie guerrillas";[95] this might have been related to Goodfellow's efforts on Taiwan to raise guerrillas.

Rusk's May 30 memo went on to suggest a quid pro quo for an American defense of Taiwan, a defense defined as the Seventh Fleet putting itself "in control of Formosan waters," thus to prevent action "by or against Formosa." This would be for Chiang to leave the island, turn over control to its commander (Sun Li-jen), and then remand the Taiwan problem to the UN, which might establish a UN commission on Taiwan. After that, he suggested, Truman could reverse his January 5 statement and commit to a defense of Taiwan.

Memoranda attached to Rusk's document refer to an important conversation between Joseph Dodge and the Japanese Finance Minister Ikeda (see chapter 17), delivering "the personal views of Prime Minister Yoshida," to the effect that in Yoshida's judgment the United States seemed to be "writing off Formosa," communists were making strong gains in Indochina, and South Korea was "not strong and could, perhaps, easily be abandoned." The Japanese were "desperately looking for firm ground . . . they were skeptical on just what and when and where the U.S. would stand firm." Rusk bracketed this depiction of a shaken Yoshida with an unsigned memorandum that carried most of Dulles's phrases from his important May 18 call for a reversal of Taiwan policy. Dulles had etched an expanded "great crescent" strategy: should Taiwan fall, Japan and the natural resources of Indonesia would be threatened, "and the oil of the Middle East will be in jeopardy."[96]

British Ambassador Oliver Franks met Acheson after dinner on June 5, and found Acheson thinking of ways to deny Taiwan to the communists short of outright American military intervention in the island; the Foreign Office then commented, "There are the seeds of trouble here."[97] On June 9 Rusk's ideas matured, in a memorandum for Acheson entitled "Bi-partisan Policy on China-Formosa Problems." He recommended a "UN Commission" for Taiwan; the proposal he drafted for presentation to the United Nations would "call upon all governments and authorities concerned to cease hostile acts between Formosa and the mainland"; the UN commission might also recommend "a joint temporary trusteeship," with the knotty issues thereafter to be decided "on the principles of self-determination." He also wrote that it might be useful to resolve the issue of seating China at the UN, "since the free world expects to move to the counter-offensive and reduce Kremlin control over its present orbit."[98] (This last item, odd as it is, was meant to mollify Beijing by admitting it to the UN, thus neutralizing it while the U.S. moved to the "counter-offensive.")

The reader will again mark the assumptions of containment liberalism, desirous of cloaking American unilateralism in internationalist clothes. This is a plan for an internationalist's coup. But Rusk also intruded the telltale language of rollback, speaking of the "counter-offensive" and the *reduction* of the Kremlin sphere, the language used in NSC 48 and NSC 68. That is, this document is redolent of the new coalition and the new spectrum of acceptability created by the changed strategic assumptions of the summer of 1949, and the march into the administration of Foster Dulles.

Taken together, the May 30 meeting and the June 9 document are breathtaking. In the summer of 1950, knowledge that the United States had plans six weeks before the war to interpose the Seventh Fleet and utilize the UN in this manner—shall we say this *Korean-model* manner, of trusteeship and a UN commission—would have caused a sensation. And so State Department historians are anxious to tell us that there is no record that Acheson saw or "acted on" Rusk's June 9 memorandum, and that "no policy decision" was made before June 25.[99] What they do not tell us is that Acheson had wanted to separate Taiwan from the mainland for more than a year, and had etched this scenario for using the UN in his 1947 thinking about containment in Korea. It is hardly the case that he needed tutoring from Rusk to figure all this out. Anyway, the State Department's research was insufficient. Acheson's appointment book shows a meeting with Rusk, Nitze and Dulles on June 9; he also met with them on May 31.[100]

On June 6 Dulles, the only person aware of Rusk's plans besides Acheson and Nitze (and perhaps Jessup), asked to see Hollington Tong, an advisor to Chiang who had just come from Taipei and who had met Goodfellow there. According to Wellington Koo's account, Dulles said he wanted to correct "his previous pessimistic foreboding re Am[erican] military aid to Formosa. Tong was told that if the G[eneralissimo] would be a little humble, there might be a way of saving Formosa. Mr. D[ulles] did not say what plan there was." Koo accurately guessed that the plan might be to bring in the UN, or ask Chiang to step aside. If Chiang were somehow unaware of the coup plans before June 6, he would not have been after his ambassador figured out Rusk's plans.[101]

Warren Cohen wrote that Koo and Tong had talked with both Dulles and Rusk, and had gotten the impression that Acheson might be won over if Taiwan were "Chiang-less." The next day, June 7, Paul Griffith, the assistant secretary of defense and Johnson's key go-between with the Nationalists, turned up at the Chinese embassy. Griffith also met with Koo and Tong, and suggested how Washington might be won over if it were Acheson-less—and more than that.

Griffith had told Koo earlier that if enough anxiety could be raised over China policy, Acheson might "step out." As we have seen, a pack of rollbackers were after Acheson's scalp, with McCarthy in the lead, but Johnson, Donovan, Kohlberg, and others not far behind. On June 7 Koo and Tong heard Griffith reiterate the view that Acheson should go, also that Truman had told Johnson to stay out of the China question, it was State's business. That, however, applied to peacetime, when foreign policy was up to the diplomats. But, "if war should break out," Griffiths stated, "then it would be very different. Then the Secretary of Defense would take charge and have a great deal to say in relations with foreign countries." He proceeded to arrange for Hollington Tong to fly to Tokyo and meet Johnson during his visit.[102] Interestingly, Acheson wrote to Johnson the next day, telling him he should not visit Taipei on his Far East trip, as Madame Chiang had requested, and that he should make "no prior commitment" to meet any Chinese Nationalist representatives in Tokyo.[103]

One wonders what Griffith thought about his comments to Koo when war broke out a few weeks later. In the context of the coup planning, it is about as close as one can come to advocating war to save the KMT regime. But then, one wonders what they all thought on that sudden Sunday morning, knowing what they knew.

On June 10, T. V. Soong said he declined to return to Taiwan, as Chiang had requested, and articles in the press linked this to an impending invasion of Taiwan. Shortly thereafter Chiang removed him, his brother T. L. Soong, and his brother-in-law H. H. Kung from the board of directors of the Central Bank of China. At this time, H. H. Kung was in Tokyo visiting Willoughby.[104] This information suggests that the Soong group was at odds with Chiang just before the planned coup; it places H. H. Kung and Hollington Tong (the latter apprised of Rusk's hopes to depose Chiang), in Tokyo meeting with Willoughby and MacArthur just before Johnson and Dulles showed up.

Meanwhile, reports came to Acheson from sources inside the KMT saying that Chiang "will never agree" to an increase of power for Sun Li-jen, and had recently been "more bitter than ever" against the United States. Robert Strong also reported that Communist shelling had destroyed wharfs on Chinmen Island, making evacuation of the Americans there impossible for about twenty days. On June 13 Acheson asked if this would "have any special relationship to [the] situation beyond Chinmen," that is, to the evacuation of Americans from Taiwan: "answer yes or no for Rusk eyes only." The next day he answered in the negative, indicating that the evacuation could proceed.[105]

The generalissimo was not going to budge. On June 19 the coup plans gathered strength with a top secret review of Taiwan policy since January 1950. Truman had made his January 5 statement that Taiwan would not be defended, the document stated, because of the Joint Chiefs' judgment that the strategic importance of Taiwan did not warrant the use of American armed force. So, the policy continued to be "to seek to deny the Island to the Chinese Communists by diplomatic and economic means." But now, intelligence estimates indicated that the fall of the island was "a foregone conclusion." The Sino-Soviet treaty, moreover, "greatly reduced any prospect that a serious rift might develop between Moscow and Peiping [*sic*]." Thus the "nationalist" issue seemed impossible to exploit; meanwhile deteriorating conditions on the mainland had enhanced Taiwan's importance as a rallying point for anti-communist resistance.

Therefore, if the United States were now to defend Taiwan, Chiang and his close allies "must be willing to leave the Island and turn over civil and military administration to such Chinese and Formosan leaders as the U.S. may designate." Then the U.S. Navy would "prevent action by or against Formosa." Should Chiang resist, there was another alternative: "The U.S. should inform Sun Li-jen in the strictest confidence through a private emissary that the U.S. Government is prepared to furnish him the necessary military aid and advice in the event that he wishes to stage a coup d'etat for the purpose of establishing his military control over the Island." The latter alternative offered "better long-range possibilities" than the first (presumably because Chiang would not agree, or might find another place of exile and later try to return to Taiwan), but "it would have to be undertaken quickly with the greatest skill and finesse." Handwritten notes attached to this document refer to the interposition of the Seventh Fleet between Taiwan and the mainland.[106]

Who might have been the "private emissary," and was one sent? Rusk had earlier referred to Cooke's advisory group and the buying of arms through commercial channels as an ongoing category of covert "US assistance" to Taiwan (thus implying, as did Acheson in the fall of 1949, that the administration tacitly condoned the activity). During this period Rusk was talking to Capt. Howard Orem, assistant chief of Naval Operations, about "various angles" with respect to the "status" of Admiral Cooke. Merchant also brought up to Rusk someone called "Well Digger Gardner," urging that "we modify our position by withdrawing any objection to his departing for Formosa even tho he is only on official leave status."[107] One has no way of knowing who Well Digger Gardner might be, but here we have a hint that an emissary might have been sent, or that Cooke might have been approached about covert action against Chiang.

On the same day, June 19, Louis Johnson's office was seeking "a reversal of present U.S. policy [toward Taiwan] at the eleventh hour." According to a memo sent by civilian advisor Kenneth Young to Gen. John Burns, the JCS had recently stated that "China is the vital area in the Far East and that continued resistance on Formosa is in the military interest"; thus Johnson's people wanted the State Department "to make a public statement explaining [this] shift in U.S. policy." Young favored the appointment of former OSS-China head Milton Miles as a senior military advisor to Taiwan, plus an additional nine field-grade officers, resistance groups to penetrate the mainland, and the dispatch to Taiwan of a voluntary group of American fliers. Young also recommended "covert means to assure silver" to Nationalist troops, an eccentric item explicable only by the silver lobby's desire for rollback. Young also called for Chiang's removal, but not as an urgent matter. All of these expansionist ideas were hinged to a *public* reversal of Truman's January refusal to defend Taiwan.[108]

On June 22 or 23, Dulles wired from Tokyo MacArthur's important June 14 paper calling for a reversal of policy on Taiwan (this was subsequently read at the Blair House meetings, June 26, 1950), with Dulles expressing his agreement with it: "on receiving it, Acheson conferred with his top Asia policy advisors minus Dean Rusk, then out of Washington."[109] MacArthur's evolving viewpoint on Taiwan as the war approached was given in an extended interview with British Admiral Patrick Brind and American Admiral Radford on June 3. MacArthur unburdened himself of "his intense feeling regarding the value of Formosa to the Allies," saying that denial of military assistance to Chiang was "the greatest possible mistake." Brind learned from him that military aid to Chiang was now on the front burner in Washington, and that MacArthur thought it would go "in spite of statements to the contrary," thus showing his close feel for the efforts of Dulles and Rusk.

MacArthur and Radford both stressed Taiwan's value "as a means of entry into China." All the services were placing "great pressure" for a reversal of Acheson's policy, the military thinking that the line had to be drawn somewhere on Communist expansion, and Taiwan "would be a good opportunity." They both wanted military support for Chiang, but no "unilateral statement" saying Taiwan would be defended, because that would "involve intervening to stop Formosa being used as a base against Communists."[110] In short, as Acheson, Rusk, and Dulles moved toward containment through neutralization, MacArthur and others sought to keep Chiang in power and preserve Taiwan for rollback.

Friday, June 23 was to have been an important day in the coup planning. Livingston Merchant said that if the policy toward Taiwan were to change, the U.S. would have to "go the whole hog." He quoted Kennan as saying that before any change could come, "the Gimo must be effectively removed from control," and he said Acheson would be anxious to talk to Rusk upon his return. Where had Rusk gone? To the Plaza Hotel in New York, where on the evening of June 23 he approached Hu Shih about replacing Chiang and organizing a government. As Hu described the meeting, Rusk mentioned the Freedom League and the China Movement sponsored by Hu, as a potential "liberal" grouping to replace Chiang and the KMT. Hu responded that as a civilian he had little or no power, and blamed the United States for its lack of statesmanship in failing to back the KMT on the mainland; it had made "all the errors." But he did say that Chiang ought to "divest himself of the Presidency" in order to get American military aid. Hu Shih told Rusk he really had no power, and refused to "lead any movement or organize a government."

Frederick McKee had arranged this meeting, and when Hu Shih told Wellington Koo about it, T. V. Soong was present.[111] When I asked Rusk about his trip to the Plaza in an interview, his usually acute memory went blank: he could not recall a thing about it, even that it had happened. Frederick McKee was, after Kohlberg, Chiang's biggest backer in the United States. *His* minimax solution to the Taiwan problem was not likely to be a coup. He had earlier written to Rusk calling for covert actions "to start a rollback," quoting Teddy Roosevelt: "the best way to parry is to strike."[112] When Rusk met Hu Shih under McKee's auspices, he merely tipped his hand for nothing in return.

Did Hu's refusal to go along with Rusk mean the coup was off before the Korean War began? That is not the case. On June 29 Kennan told a top secret National Security Council (NSC) meeting that "Chiang might be overthrown at any time." Rusk told me in an interview that indeed, some elements of the Nationalist military were preparing to move against Chiang, but then the Korean War intervened. His biographer got a similar story: Rusk had taken the coup idea to Acheson, "who promised to take the matter up with Truman. But before any presidential decision could be made, North Korea mounted an invasion of the South, an event which probably saved Chiang's regime."[113]

Acheson did his part. On Friday afternoon, June 23, as Johnson departed Tokyo, as Rusk went up the Plaza, as the junks congregated off Fujian, as the Seoul embassy waited to see if Rhee would make the exchange for Cho Man-sik, as UN military observers returned from the Ongjin Peninsula, as T. L. Soong dumped soybeans in Chicago, he held a news conference to announce that Truman's January 5 statement was still American policy: no defense of Taiwan. He did not add: it is the policy unless Chiang were overthrown that weekend.

By early July Sun Li-jen was reported to be the subject of "growing suspicion" by Chiang, with MacArthur's intelligence citing "a move to subvert" him on July 2. A major reorganization of the KMT ensued, as allies of T. V. Soong and H. H. Kung were moved out in favor of those loyal to Chiang's son, Chiang Ching-guo. In September Karl Rankin remarked that coup planning had "been toyed with rather extensively in the past, even including reported efforts of cloak-and-dagger agencies to suborn certain of Chiang's generals." In 1955, Sun Li-jen was placed under detention by Chiang Kai-shek, from which he was not released until 1988.[114]

CONCLUSION

Decadent Guy Burgess read everything coming in from Taiwan in May and June 1950, it would appear, even unclassified press reports. The British Chancery in Moscow also found Soviet newspapers taking inordinate interest in any scraps of information on the Taiwan question.[115] The day before war broke out in Korea, Burgess judged that "the Soviets seem to have made up their minds that the U.S.A. have a finally decided policy [not to defend Taiwan]. This *we* [sic] have never quite come to believe." This was written on a document from the Moscow embassy, citing a public lecture on June 7 by F. N. Oleshchuk, deputy chief of the Central Committee's Agitprop Department, in which he said that the Americans were preparing the evacuation of Chiang Kai-shek to Tokyo.[116]

Burgess had a subtle appreciation of the evolution of American policy on Taiwan, and the departmental conflicts it aroused; indeed, it is hard to find another person who caught the nuances better, except perhaps for Robert Strong, the chargé on Taiwan. We may assume that Burgess communicated this to the Soviets, including his obvious suspicion (which we have now documented on two occasions) that the United States really intended to defend Taiwan. The same judgment would presumably apply to South Korea. The timing of Burgess's June 24 minute is also arresting, since by then he had probably read Acheson's June 23 statement. All this on a muggy weekend in June.

Chapter Seventeen

A QUIET WEEKEND IN JUNE:
TOKYO, MOSCOW, AND WASHINGTON
ON THE EVE OF THE WAR

> Be innocent of the knowledge, dearest chuck,
> Till thou applaud the deed.
>
> *Macbeth*

T HE LAST WEEKEND in June 1950 dawned on a torpid, somnolent, and very empty Washington. Harry Truman was back home in Independence; Acheson was at his Sandy Spring country farm; Rusk was in New York; Kennan had disappeared to a remote summer cottage without so much as a telephone; Nitze was salmon fishing in Nova Scotia; the Joint Chiefs were occupied elsewhere; the United Nations representative, Warren Austin, rested at his home in Vermont; the new Army Chief of Staff, Gen. J. Lawton Collins, puttered around his cottage on Chesapeake Bay; Matthew Ridgway, Collins's "general manager" at the Pentagon, honeymooned in Pennsylvania with his new bride; Secretary of the Air Force Thomas Finletter vacationed in New England; U. Alexis Johnson, Rusk's righthand man, was up in the Blue Ridge mountains, "hiking with a bunch of Boy Scouts."[1]

In Seoul no one minded the store, either, Harold Noble was anxious to report.

> The deputy chief of staff, Chŏng Il-gwŏn and the adjutant general were both in the United States preparing to return home. The chief of naval operations, Admiral Son Wŏn-il, was in the middle of the Pacific Ocean. . . . Fifty of the ablest officers of the ROK Army were in Japan. . . . Only the usual four divisions were disposed northward toward the parallel, and their main elements were well south of the border.[2]

The ROK Foreign Ministry arranged a picnic in the hills near Seoul for the entire foreign press contingent. The buses went off early Sunday morning, June 25; Jack James overslept and missed the bus, thus getting a scoop on the others. Ambassador John Muccio whiled away Saturday night playing strip poker with the embassy secretaries.

The reader will not be prepared for this account of a sleepy, languid early summer weekend like any other, with important people shuffling off to this or that summer repose. Amid a bubbling cauldron of conflict and intrigue, the languor will be unexpectedly anticlimactic. A right-wing summit was breaking up in Tokyo, Chiang Kai-shek might be over-thrown at any minute, and that might or might not come in time to stop a communist invasion, the CIA said the North Koreans could invade at any time, but those who were witting about MacArthur's willfulness and the coup and the invasion timing were all taking their ease. The South Korean Army had been on alert since at least May 10, its ambassador to Washington had said the regime was about to collapse and predicted an imminent attack, June 1949 had witnessed a major battle in Ongjin that began at dawn on the last Sunday of the month. Yet no one was watching.

Readers of weekend newspapers would learn that Louis Johnson arrived back on Saturday morning from his meeting with the Truman nemesis, MacArthur, the press full of speculation on highly secret meetings that might bring forth a new Taiwan policy; but he maintained a studied and uncharacteristic silence about what he had learned. They read that Acheson was not so silent, bestirring himself at Sandy Spring to tell reporters, just before Johnson returned, that the policy had not changed, it remained what it was on January 5, "no military assistance" for Taiwan. Dozens of professors were fired at the University of California for refusing to say they were not communists, while Arthur Schlesinger, Jr., gave a bellicose speech likening the Soviets to the Nazis, "a master race" seeking to enslave the world. But Sen. Tom Connally reassuringly told the *New York Times* that recent reports from Moscow and elsewhere "indicated an easing off in the international tension."[3]

But as always in this anxious period, no weekend was free from evidence of conflict and intrigue. Only close readers might attend to an errant counterpoint to the summery atmosphere, the buried news that "all combat units of the [U.S.] Army have been alerted for tests that will determine how quickly they could start moving toward ports of embarkation in an emergency," the tests to come after July 1.[4] That is, American combat units were on alert (for tests) in the United States and Japan before news of the war came. This probably was happenstance, but might be related to predictions that the PRC would invade Taiwan. Worldwide American troop strength was 591,000 in June, including ten combat divisions, with 360,000 in the United States and the largest contingent abroad in Japan: 108,500, compared to 80,000 in Germany. Four divisions were in Japan—the 7th, 24th, 25th, and the 1st Cavalry Divisions.[5]

In North Korea, some combat units were on alert and others were not, and some of its expeditionary soldiers were gathered near the parallel and others were still in China. The alert, as in Washington, was said to be for summer training maneuvers. Readers of their newspapers on a rainy weekend would perhaps have taken a start at Korean People's Army (KPA) broadsides against Rhee, charging that he had gathered five of eight divisions at the front and was planning to attack, but that he simultaneously wanted "national division more than unification" and hoped "to freeze the 38th parallel." There ensued a discussion of the recent unification proposals, followed by this:

> All soldiers: fight the enemy mercilessly! [The people] suffering miserably in the south are waiting to be saved with outstretched hands. . . . So, if the homeland or the people call you, be ready at any time to destroy the enemy and unify the territory . . . with belief in victory and hatred for the enemy, let us all march forward in struggle to strengthen our battle forces.[6]

The "struggle to strengthen our battle forces" referred to the war games about to begin, just above the parallel.

In South Korea, an Australian embassy representative sent in daily reports in late June, saying that

> patrols were going in from the South to the North, endeavouring to attract the North back in pursuit. Plimsoll warned that this could lead to war and it was clear that there was some degree of American involvement as well as the South Koreans wishing to promote conflict with American support.

The former Australian prime minister, E. Gough Whitlam, related the same story as follows:

> Less than a week before war erupted . . . the Australian Government had received reports of intended South Korean aggressions from its representative in South Korea. The evidence was sufficiently strong for the Australian Prime Minister to authorize a cable to Washington urging that no encouragement be given to the South Korean government. That cable cannot now be found among official papers in Australia.[7]

John Burton, who was secretary of the Australian Foreign Office, resigned over this issue (being replaced on June 19, 1950), and asserted that "all these telegrams have now vanished from the F[oreign] O[ffice]."

These accounts are obviously in error about Plimsoll, who was not in Korea until November 1950. But the mixing up of names is very common in the memory of diplomats. Burton could not add anything more in an interview, in the absence of records and, as he candidly acknowledged, with the mists of memory of what happened three decades ago. In my researches I found no evidence of such Australian cables, but also counted an unusual number of Australian documents that were removed (not declassified) in the State Department records of 1950. Dr. Burton told me that "there has been a high level attempt to cover all this up"; soon his career in the Foreign Service was over.[8]

Australians were prominent in another rendering of the last weekend in June, however, and this one stuck. Arthur Jamieson of the UN Commission on Korea (UNCOK), as we have seen, supped with Rhee and Dulles on June 19 and thought Rhee an unlikely aggressor (he also thought that Whitlam was mistaken about the mysterious cables).[9] The two itinerant UNCOK military observers, F.S.B. Peach and Ronald J. Rankin, both Australian, completed a survey of the entire parallel on the afternoon of June 23. When the United Nations committed itself to the Korean conflict, as we will see, their judgment that the Republic of Korea Army (ROKA) was entirely in defensive array was decisive. They returned to Seoul on Friday, and set about "the shaping up of the report" on Saturday, not out of a sense of urgency "but because it was something nice and tangible" to do on a lazy weekend.[10]

Jon Halliday recounted their military observation as follows: "They slept mainly in Seoul and went up to the parallel on 9 of the days between June 9 and 23rd. How much could they really see in this period of time? The terrain is extremely mountainous with deep valleys cut off from each other . . . they returned to Seoul from the parallel on June 17, stayed in Seoul until the 21st." But they were on the Ongjin Peninsula from June 21 to Friday morning of the 23rd, which is where the war began on Sunday.[11]

This is how Peach recalled a visit during the survey to a South Korean "intelligence nest" near Ŭijŏngbu, having about six separate intelligence-gathering agencies: "We went and saw every one of them and they knew nothing. They were supposed to have agents up in the north, but they had nothing, nothing at all. Information was terribly hard to get." He then added, "wherever we went it was the same story, no information." Gavan McCormack is right to find this odd,[12] as will the reader who has attended to the warnings of impending attack in May and June. As we will see later, the best evidence of North Korean movements indicating a possible invasion comes only after June 15, which should have turned the southern "intelligence nests" into beehives of activity by the time Peach and Rankin turned up. It is far more likely that Peach and Rankin, just arrived in the country, were handled like most other foreigners inquiring of Korean intelligence: told what they presumably wanted to hear.

AN UNLIKELY TRIANGLE:
DULLES, JOHNSON, AND MACARTHUR

In the days before the Korean War began, three men met in Tokyo, each representative of the troubled conflicts of the American state, and each a mix of the formidable and the comical. Dulles had extensive diplomatic experience going back to the Hague Convention in 1907, but he was also a moral posturer lacking the soft touch one would expect from an experienced statesman; his frothy bombast and legendary bad breath made for a rhetorical halitosis that wearied many an adversary. With his rimless glasses, badly-tailored black suit, ill-perched homburg, and riveted Calvinist visage, Foster cut a funny figure. He was the State Department man in this dissonant trio, Acheson having dispatched him to watch over Johnson; he did not share the world view of either Johnson or MacArthur.

No one ever thought Louis Johnson a formidable statesman, chasing after the presidency through most of his tenure as secretary of defense and delighting in purposeful, irresponsible obstruction of Truman and Acheson's goals. He seems the least persuasive and the least likely to sway the other two. But he had fought tooth and nail with the State Department for control of Asian policy, and had a network of clandestine ties to the Nationalists, subverting Acheson's studied unwillingness to commit to a defense of Chiang. Army intelligence, under his explicit or tacit authority, had connived in putting a military advisory group and a large boodle of weapons into Taiwan, conveyed through William Donovan's firm.

Japan's benign American emperor, MacArthur, had unilateral sway over an independent kingdom that mocked the bureaucratic struggles between State, Defense, and the CIA. He did not want any of them interfering with his suzerainty in the East. Like the other two he had presidential ambitions; unlike them he preferred to be anointed rather than to campaign. Of the three, he seemed the most serene in the midst of the crisis of Asia policy.

To speak in a shorthand that is artless but illustrative, Dulles was a Europe-firster internationalist, and by that logic, a Japan-firster. Johnson was an Asia-firster nationalist and thus, a China-firster. MacArthur had reason to agree with Dulles on some things, Johnson on others, but always charted his own course. He was an Asia-firster, a rollbacker, but much more—and above all, a MacArthur-firster.

General Omar Bradley also joined this group, a sincere, professional military man, with little involvement in the Asia policy debate. He was one of those few in the Pentagon who had fretted over the withdrawal of troops from Korea in 1949, and he wanted a reversal of the Taiwan policy. But even after the Korean War began he was reticent about committing American ground forces. His presence on the Johnson delegation might have drawn communist attentions, however, because of a speech toward the end of May, linked to NSC 68, where he had called for a defense mobilization plan covering the entire civilian economy, and legislation giving stand-by emergency powers to the president to cope with the Soviet threat.[13]

From almost any vantage point this Tokyo meeting held interest. On

Taiwan, Chiang hoped it would herald a commitment to his regime—
before a coup overthrew him. In Seoul, Rhee awaited Dulles's personal
visit, looking for a military alliance with the United States that would give
his regime the necessary backing to confront its northern and internal
enemies. In P'yŏngyang, Dulles's ties to prominent Japanese would raise
grave suspicions, and Johnson's ties to Taiwan would give them reason
for joint worries with Beijing. In Moscow, the Kremlin would herald the
journey to the East of the very personification of the "Wall Street master,"
and predict that a bilateral peace treaty would be the result.

And what of the reaction in Washington? Dulles was the secretary-of-
state designate in any moderate Republican administration. MacArthur
was the hero of the right-wing and the rollback current. Johnson was the
stalking horse for an army of China Lobbyists and right-wingers. For
Acheson, two of his worst antagonists were meeting with a man who was
the quintessential bipartisan accommodator—but would he accommodate to the Right or the Left? Which would prove stronger, the Wall
Street ties and internationalism that Acheson and Dulles shared, or partisan loyalties? From the vantage point of the Central Intelligence
Agency, military intelligence in Washington was meeting military intelligence in Tokyo, led by Willoughby who thought pinkos trod the halls of
the Agency and denied it access to his theater; the CIA knew him capable
of just about anything.

During this conservative summit a war breaks out. One might expect a
wary reaction, an intuition that Washington did not know everything
about the onset of this war, a head-scratching skepticism at this astonishing concatenation of events. But the record is bereft of such worries. Instead Washington committed to the war with lockstep efficiency and few
if any doubts.

The first word of Louis Johnson's visit came in the midst of NSC 68
conflicts in Washington. On April 24, Johnson stormed into Acheson's
office and squabbled with him over the peace treaty with Japan; Johnson
claimed that MacArthur's views had been distorted to make it seem as if
the general agreed with the State Department. Acheson said that American bases in Japan would cause difficulties with Japanese public opinion
and might stir up the communists, which led Johnson to say he was now
even more opposed to a peace treaty (elements in the Pentagon had worried that a quick peace treaty might draw down or even eliminate U.S.
military forces in Japan). According to Phillip Jessup, MacArthur had
told him in January that he supported Acheson's position on an early
peace treaty, and criticized Bradley and others on the Joint Chiefs of
Staff (JCS). So, Johnson blurted out that he and Bradley would go to
Tokyo to get SCAP's real view. Acheson responded that "he had not
known that Secretary Johnson was planning a trip to the Far East." Dulles

had just come into the Department, ostensibly to work on the peace with Japan, and supported Acheson's position on the need for a quick treaty. Like Acheson, he probably had contempt for Johnson. So, Dulles was, it appears, detailed to fly to Tokyo mainly to check up on Johnson, and to keep MacArthur on State's side in the peace treaty discussions.[14]

Japan was not the vexing problem for Johnson, however. His issue was China policy. His key subordinate Paul Griffith had made yet more pilgrimages to the Chinese embassy in early June to spill secrets, telling them that Johnson was their man; he had gone so far as to suggest that should war break out, Johnson would control China policy. Madame Chiang had invited him to visit Taipei, and Acheson had intervened to prevent it. This was an additional reason for Dulles to tag after Johnson.

On June 12 Dulles met with Wellington Koo, and told him there might be a possibility of military aid for Taiwan, if the Nationalists "would put up a heroic resistance to the Communist invasion . . . such a demonstration by deed was absolutely necessary." Dulles also told Hollington Tong that since Taiwan was not considered strategically vital, "if the people on the island would not defend themselves, the U.S. would certainly not go to the extent of fighting to save it." That is, he gave them nothing more than Acheson's policy. Dulles politely declined Koo's invitation to visit Taipei; given the State Department's position, a visit "might raise false hopes and do no good."[15] There was to be no help for the Kuomintang (KMT) from Dulles.

On the eve of his departure, Gen. Carter B. Magruder gave Johnson a briefing paper saying that if war erupts, Japan should be an "active ally" and should "assist in ending Russian [and communist] domination of Manchuria and China." MacArthur had already taken ominous measures toward this end in Japan, "strengthen[ing] air bases far beyond the normal requirements of the occupation," and extending runways allegedly to accommodate B-36 bombers; Japanese army and navy ammunition storages were "extended and improved" at Sasebo and Yokosuka.[16] Johnson and Bradley traveled separately from Dulles, arriving on June 18 and leaving for home Friday, June 23. As many as fifty people were present at SCAP (Supreme Command, Allied Powers) briefings for them, although there were some meetings lasting up to three hours just with MacArthur. Dulles hit Japan on June 17, then traveled to Korea, returned to Tokyo on June 20 and was there when the war began. He had several "long, intimate talks" with MacArthur, just between the two of them, during his visit.[17]

MacArthur had many members of his staff traveling back and forth to Taiwan in this period, as well as daily intelligence reports on the situation and close connections to Nationalist intelligence. On May 29, Generals Soule and Clubb returned from Taipei to say that the Soviets and the

Chinese were bringing in jet aircraft; MacArthur then cabled the Pentagon that if Taiwan fell, the Communists could threaten Okinawa, Clark Air Base in the Philippines, and the entire American military position in the Western Pacific; the island would become in Russian hands "an unsinkable aircraft carrier and submarine tender." On June 14, Adm. Charles Cooke came to Tokyo at MacArthur's request, "to set forth the Formosa situation" for Johnson and Bradley. The KMAG chief Roberts flew to Tokyo and guided Dulles to Korea and back; he then boarded a ship bound for the United States and retirement. His deputy Col. Wright also flew to Tokyo just before the war.[18]

In mid-June Chiang Kai-shek sent an urgent request through Willoughby in "absolute secrecy," saying he would be willing to place himself, his government and his army under MacArthur's "high command." That is, this generalissimo would step aside in deference to another, but not for Sun Li-jen. Shortly, reports came in that Chinese Communist troops opposite Taiwan had quadrupled.[19] On June 15 press reports surfaced through the well-connected Marguerite Higgins about "a formula for saving Formosa" to be discussed during the Johnson visit. Officers in SCAP headquarters said it was urgent "to take a strong stand in every place—including Formosa—where there is still a choice," likening the island to West Berlin, where a defense was offered in spite of its untenability from a military viewpoint. (The same reasoning would of course apply to South Korea.) She depicted SCAP officials as "reluctant to go into detail on the nature of this 'firm stand.' "[20]

Three days later Higgins said the Tokyo discussions would produce "an extensive and dynamic military-economic program to regain American initiative in the Communist-threatened Far East." This would be led by a "Far Eastern high commissioner" (read Generalissimo MacArthur), and would include "an early and benevolent Peace Treaty for Japan, and a reversal of American policy on Formosa." Johnson arrived on June 18 and supported a reevalution of "the entire Far Eastern American defense strategy," but lessened the sense of urgency by saying it should be ready by August. Higgins and other reporters emphasized the extraordinary secrecy of the talks.[21]

Dulles and MacArthur had a meeting of the minds on the Taiwan issue, with Dulles agreeing by June 21, if not earlier, to support MacArthur's important June 14 memorandum. (Johnson had given him a copy of the memorandum before Dulles got to Tokyo.) But it is not clear that Dulles agreed with MacArthur on defending the Chiang regime; the record shows his advocacy of a defense of the island, not necessarily the regime. As we have seen, Acheson knew by June 22 that Dulles had accommodated to his right on Taiwan.[22]

Johnson, of course, also backed MacArthur's position. Nonetheless he caviled at a presentation by Admiral Cooke on the Taiwan issue, and berated him for being disloyal to American policy and, by implication, to the United States Johnson was fully witting about Cooke's activities on Taiwan, and the role of Army intelligence and other agencies in supporting the effort (Cooke had told him he was reporting to MacArthur and the Chief of Naval Operations). In an interview, Cooke's son made a particular point of calling this incident to my attention, but he did not know what was behind it. I believe its meaning is the following: that Rusk had succeeded in using Cooke's operation as the covert channel for coup operations against Chiang, and that Johnson found out about it and flew into a rage, since he wanted Acheson out, not Chiang. But there is no proof for this, it merely fits the logic. Just as Johnson returned to the United States on June 24, before the news of the outbreak of fighting in Korea, he said "the U.S. must take positive action to prevent the fall of Formosa."[23]

PERILS OF PROPINQUITY

Dulles's goal was to make headway on the peace treaty and the revival of conservative Japan, which he did through personal contacts with the Japanese elite, Americans in the Japan Lobby, and even the emperor. Dulles's internationalism had always placed him on the side of close U.S.-Japan ties and an easy peace. As Robert Murphy put it, "I always found him thoroughly for a close association with the Japanese—a great hope that this would become the focus of American influence and power in Asia." Dulles had "a very reasonable attitude on the question of war crimes," Murphy thought, and was "very affirmative . . . on the question of rearming Japan."[24]

Dulles had crafted a noteworthy memorandum for Acheson before he left, fitting Japan into his favorite theme of rollback. Japan, he wrote on June 7, could become a shining example in Asia of "the free way of life," and therefore aid the effort "to resist and throw back communism in this part of the world," that is, rollback. Could Japan be saved, he wondered, if it were merely to adopt a defensive policy; "if defense can only succeed as supplemented by offense, what are the practical offensive possibilities?" He suggested "some counter-offensives of a propaganda and covert character" to prevent communist consolidation of "recently-won areas." But what Dulles really wanted to do, like Kennan, was to roll back the clock to an earlier conception of Japan's place in the world, before it went on the lamentable bender that ended with Pearl Harbor.

Mingling power and plenty with the flair of an American Itō Hirobumi, Dulles declared that "physical propinquity" linked Japan to the mainland, yet Japan was now "closely encircled" by communism. He went on, "There is natural and historic economic interdependence between Japan and now communized parts of Asia. These are the natural sources of raw material for Japan." Japan ought to be able to build its own ships, export capital goods and not just consumer goods, and develop armed forces able to resist "indirect aggression." He asked if there were other places in Asia, outside the realm of communist control, where Japan might find raw materials and markets; he ended with the redundant observation that the peace treaty was "merely one aspect of the total problem."[25]

Propinquity is such a rare term that it could not but conjure the original context: Itō, first resident-general in Korea, authored a "perils of propinquity" statement about Korea as a dagger at the Japanese heart.[26] Now the dagger was in communist hands, or very nearly so. Dulles's memorandum was penned after an extraordinary visit to Washington by Ikeda Hayato, Japan's finance minister, to deliver a personal message from Premier Yoshida. This was "so secret that Yoshida . . . did not inform his own officials of the aims of the mission." As we have seen, the main import was his expression of apprehension about where and when the United States might choose to take a stand against communism in East Asia, which Peter Lowe attributed to Yoshida's worries about Acheson's Press Club speech. Yoshida also put out a feeler suggesting the Japanese might desire American military bases after the Occupation ended, which was not, however, anything new—he had said about the same in 1948.[27]

Ikeda's meteoric rise from an obscure tax official to head of the finance ministry owed to his close support from Japanese big business,[28] and he had additional concerns beyond those of Japan's security. In conferences with Joseph Dodge, Ikeda proposed measures to fund a big leap in Japanese exports to Asia. Dodge told Congress at the same time that "Washington must inevitably rely on Japan as a 'springboard' supplying 'the material goods required for American aid to the Far East."[29] Shortly before Ikeda's arrival, Tracy Voorhees, also close to the Japan Lobby, had returned from a Far Eastern survey to urge a revival of what was left of the Co-prosperity Sphere. He backed a study by a member of his mission, Stanley Andrews, the director of Foreign Agricultural Relations, which urged the integration of production between Japan, the ROK, and Taiwan: "Japan is the biggest and most assured market for Korean rice in the same manner . . . [as] Formosan sugar." As if to leave little to the imagination, the report referred to all this as "a restoration" which would "gradually provide a market of almost universal magnitude." He urged an integration of Economic Cooperation Administration (ECA), World Bank, Point 4, and Export-Import Bank financing to launch this program of restoration and growth. As the contents leaked, the British connected such thinking to the revival of prewar relationships, and the Soviets charged that the United States was trying to reestablish the Co-Prosperity Sphere. Ikeda's mission brought sharp attention in Japan, the press speculating about its purpose and its unprecedented secrecy.[30]

Just before he embarked for Japan, Dulles told Acheson that Japan ought not be heavily armed, but that the United States should develop a positive program aimed at destabilizing China and North Korea, while developing "adequate sources of raw materials and markets" for Japan's industry outside the communized parts of Asia. He also urged a defensive guarantee for Japan, and a show of strength in the "environs of Japan." Michael Schaller writes that Dulles's recommendations "appear cryptic and somewhat sinister in light of the Korean War."[31]

Dulles was a friend of Harry Kern, the organizer of the Japan Lobby, who was invited to fly with him to Tokyo. On June 22 Kern organized a dinner for Dulles at the home of Compton Pakenham, with "a few well informed Japanese." These included Marquis Matsudaira Yasumasa, related by marriage to the head of the Mitsui *zaibatsu* group and a former secretary to Count Kido Koichi, Lord Keeper of the Privy Seal; the latter was convicted as a war criminal, but just before Pearl Harbor he and Matsudaira were part of an elite group opposed to a war policy. Matsudaira had "intimate contact with the court and access to the emperor." Present also was Sawada Renzo, related by marriage to the Mitsubishi group and connected to American intelligence; also Kaihara Osamu, a man involved in the rural police and constabulary who later became secretary general of Japan's Defense Agency; finally Watanabe Takeshi, a financial expert "close to the Chase Manhattan-World Bank group throughout the postwar period," and much later the chairman of the Japan branch of the Trilateral Commission. The theme of the dinner was Japan's changing role in American strategy.[32] Dulles also met with Yoshida that day, urging upon him Japan's rearmament. Yoshida responded with chuckles and parables, and did not evince a desire to rearm his country before the Korean War.[33]

A few days after the dinner Matsudaira brought back a message for Dulles from the emperor, an unprecedented event in the postwar period made more remarkable by its circumventing of the SCAP command. Dulles told Kern that this was "the most important development" in U.S.-Japan relations during his visit. The content was less stunning, Hirohito calling for an advisory group of wise men who could bypass SCAP and its "irresponsible and unrepresentative advisors" in the interests of better relations. There is some question about the authenticity of the message, but Kern thought it was the first step in setting up "the machinery for reaching those who really hold the power in Japan." He urged both Dulles and Averell Harriman to pursue this opening "as vigorously as possible."[34] By this time the Korean War had begun, sending the Tokyo stock market soaring and eventually reinvigorating the Japanese economy to the degree that some have termed the war "Japan's Marshall Plan."

This encounter with Japan's elite underlined Dulles's agreement with Acheson that Japan was the proper focus of American policy in Asia, and suggested that Dulles and MacArthur were somewhat at odds on Japan's role in Pacific security. When Dulles returned, according to Truman, he suggested that MacArthur ought to be "hauled back to the United States"[35] The main result of Dulles's visit in regard to Japan policy, and not necessarily his accomplishment, was MacArthur's June 23 memorandum, where he reversed himself (a maneuver he was beginning to master) and demanded that American forces be based in Japan.

In April MacArthur had said that "the real bastion of strength should be Okinawa," and that 95 percent of the Japanese opposed American bases. By June 14, however, he argued that military reverses on the mainland had raised the pressures "upon vital segments of our strategic island *frontier* off the Asian coast" (counterpoint to Acheson's notion of an island *defense* line). "We should proceed to call a peace conference at once," he said, "thereby Japan and all of Asia would witness the resurgence of our moral leadership and renewal of our initiative in the conduct of Asian affairs . . . it is in the pattern of Oriental psychology to respect and follow aggressive, resolute and dynamic leadership." MacArthur called for "a reassertion of positive leadership, [and] the regaining of forceful initiative." He did not, however, urge the rearming of Japan, saying the Japanese people would not stand for it. Two days before the Korean War, MacArthur said that American troops must be based in Japan, and indeed that Japan's "entire area . . . be regarded as a potential base for defensive maneuver with unrestricted freedom reserved to the United States." Now, it turned out, the Japanese "have come to hold as beneficent the presence of American troops in their midst.[36]

This brought closer the conclusion of a bilateral peace treaty, but this had been in the cards for some time and it seems unlikely that it would be a casus belli for the Soviets, as Kennan has suggested; in any case they would predict that a war would only hasten the process. The North Koreans, on the other hand, had good enough intelligence to pick up Dulles's involvement with elite figures who shared his imperial conception of Korea's relationship to Japan's political economy and who were connected to the prewar *zaibatsu* that had exploited the peninsula. This would have arrested their attentions far more than his hurried visit to the thirty-eighth parallel. It is another cardinal fact pointing toward a motive for ousting the Rhee regime in June 1950: to break the incipient international system of Northeast Asia, focused on a revival of Japan's industrial base.

SOVIET POLICY ON THE EVE OF THE WAR

For months before the Korean War, the Soviets and their allies sponsored a worldwide "peace" campaign, something that met with distrust and derision in Washington, and that cannot be taken as an earnest of Soviet intent. But in the spring of 1950 the public record, at least, would indicate several important Soviet concessions and attempts to get negotiations going, which were met with stony silence in Washington.

Georgy Malenkov was assumed to be a maker of important and aggressive speeches, and to have special interest in Asia, as we saw earlier. In March 1950 he gave a long speech, dwelling extensively on American imperialism in Western Europe; after some thirty paragraphs he finally got around to a single sentence about Asia, referring to the new alliance with China.[37] It is a minor example of the major tendency of Soviet policy: fixation on security in Europe.

The Soviet magazine *New Times* sought to soft-pedal Acheson's "total diplomacy" (and therefore NSC 68). His "spring diplomatic offensive"; was nothing new; although American media were calling it a "radical turn," it was just a continuation of "the same old warmongering policy." Foster Dulles was an old Soviet běte noire, but the magazine saw Dulles's entry into the administration merely as a matter of seeking bipartisan support for Truman's policies. Subsequent issues in May paid attention to his Wall Street background and his alleged dealings with the Nazis. But in issues for April, May and June 1950 there is little attention to East Asia, and nothing about Dulles's trip to Tokyo. The only reference to Korea in the spring of 1950 said that the "people's liberation movement" was growing in the South, threatening the Rhee regime and "American rule."[38]

But of course the Soviets did grasp the turning point that had been reached in the spring of 1950, with NSC 68. It is therefore significant that in late April the Soviet ideological journal *Bolshevik* brought forth and harped on statements that Lenin had made to a group of American reporters in 1920: "Let American capitalists not touch us. We will not touch them." He had called for trade and business-like relations; the article termed Lenin's remarks of "exceptional importance" and said the Soviet goal was peaceful coexistence. Soon all major Soviet organs published Lenin's statements, suggesting that war with capitalism was "not a fatal inevitability."[39]

In early May Moscow requested new four-power talks on the Austrian treaty, which the Austrian government termed "very surprising and very promising." At the same time UN Secretary-General Trygve Lie announced that he would fly to Moscow for talks on "the most critical situation since 1945." According to UN background briefings, Stalin told Lie that he had a "profound belief" in "the possibility of long-continued co-existence of the two systems, Communist and capitalist."[40]

A week before the Korean War began, a major story appeared saying that Moscow had told Walter Ulbricht, the East German leader, "to look upon the present division of Germany as permanent and alterable only by war or revolution"; thus, "under present circumstances," Germany will stay split.[41] This is merely yet more evidence of the Soviet desire to keep Germany divided, something unsurprising today. But looked at through Korean eyes, this is a very important statement for the time. Kim Il Sung would see this as proof of Soviet desires to *contain* the Korean goal of reunification. Evidence on what Soviet policy actually intended for Korea is of course unavailable, but it is not clear why the same logic would not apply to Korea, especially since the minor goal of gobbling up South Korea might wreck the major goal of preventing the rearmament of Japan, West Germany, and above all the United States.

Almost all internal American intelligence estimates in the spring of 1950, whether in Washington or Tokyo, said the Soviets would not risk global war in 1950. The idea was that the period of maximum danger would approach in 1953 or 1954. Soviet public statements in the spring of 1950 would seem to bear this out, and suggest a Soviet attempt to prevent, not stimulate, the NSC 68 program. Their expenditures for the 1950 defense budget, given out in mid-June, were "only slightly more than last year," according to Harry Schwartz; the public figure was 18.5 percent of the national budget, compared to 32 percent in 1940 and 24 percent in 1946. "Veteran American officials with years of experience in dealing with the Russians," Marguerite Higgins was told in Tokyo at this time, "are convinced the Soviet Union does not intend to provoke war at this time and will not permit the Chinese Communists to do so."[42]

Whatever one may think of the Soviet mood and its initiatives before the war, Washington was not interested in lessening tensions. When Lie told Truman about his talks with Stalin, the president insisted that the Soviets were to blame for the UN deadlock and the troubled state of the world; nor did Acheson welcome Lie's talks, acording to Arthur Krock; they diverted people from "the central thesis: East-West conflict." Washington officials, he said, wondered why Lie chose this time to visit Stalin, "when Mr. Acheson and his fellow-conferees [in London] were hammering out the defensive accords against Soviet aggression." Stalin might talk about peaceful coexistence, but Robert Strausz-Hupe and Stefan Possony had argued in a recent book, of which Krock heartily approved, that the Soviets believed in "the Marxian postulate that disarmament and the abolition of war are possible only with the fall of capitalism."[43]

If this is one measure of the American zeitgeist in mid-1950, another would be the hysteria about a "peace march" at the end of May in East

Berlin by communist youth groups. Administration sources told journalists on background that this march might be the signal for an invasion of West Berlin; troops went on alert in Europe. On May 28 half a million youths paraded peacefully through East Berlin, and the *Times* intoned that it would appear that they did not "follow their original plans and 'invade' Western Berlin."[44]

As always during this period, it was James Reston who brought Acheson's views before the public. In mid-March he said that American officials thought the Soviets wanted to arrange a deal with the United States to divide the globe, "a two-world settlement" in which each had its bloc, with hands off both. "Almost all recent [Soviet] statements or actions" seemed to bear this out. Stalin wanted a free hand to deal with Yugoslavia, and to exclude the West from China. All this is plausible and fits with our analysis above.

But American officials were not "even slightly interested in such a deal," according to Reston. The United States would not "wash its hands" of Soviet satellites, nor would it do anything to encourage the satellization of Yugoslavia or China. Furthermore, these officials were concerned with a bigger problem: "how to get reliable steady public support" for the new global policies, and the expenditures they would require.[45] This interpretation does not mean that Acheson wanted war, or was less interested in peace, by his lights, than Moscow. It does suggest that the Soviets had few reasons to start a war in Korea in June 1950.

THE DEREVYANKO CASE

Lt. Gen. Kuzma Derevyanko, the Soviet head of mission in Tokyo, had been a fixture in Japan since the surrender ceremony on the U.S.S. Missouri, when MacArthur buried him back in the crowd of dignitaries to show his disdain for the Soviet war effort in the Pacific. By 1950 he was thought to be the Soviet's top veteran of postwar Asian affairs. On May 27, he and his entire staff of forty-nine members packed up and abruptly returned home from Tokyo, seemingly for good, leaving in their place some very junior military officers. SCAP got "unusually short notice" of their departure. Some thought it might herald "a stronger Soviet drive in Southeast Asia," an interpretation that took on added force with the recall a few days later of the top Soviet representatives in Thailand. But SCAP officials were mostly "at a loss" to explain the Derevyanko exit to reporters; internal reports bear this out.[46]

This followed on the heels of abrupt movements by Premier Yoshida who, on May 23, suddenly cancelled a pre-election speaking tour to return to Tokyo and meet with Finance Minister Ikeda Hayato, who had just returned from Washington. Press accounts speculated that "an offer of a separate peace treaty with the United States might be imminent."[47] On May 26 newspapers announced that Dulles would visit Japan in June. High-level American reports at the time suggested that "urgent consultations may be getting under way in Moscow," but by July 8 the CIA had still discerned no clear pattern in the return of Soviet diplomats from Japan, Thailand, and other countries in the previous six weeks.[48]

In the William Donovan Papers is a document that is said to have come from a member of Stalin's Secretariat, through underground sources in Europe; it got to Donovan's hands in April 1953, and recounted a Kremlin meeting on June 10, 1950.[49] The participants included Stalin, Molotov, Malenkov, Bulganin, Voitinsky (a former Comintern operative, then head of the Soviet Council for Pacific Relations), General Derevyanko, ambasssador to P'yŏngyang Shtykov, Li Li-san of the Kao Kang regime, Kim Il Sung, and some stenographers. They convened in a small room across from Stalin's personal quarters.

Molotov opened the meeting by saying that the North Koreans had "petitioned" for Soviet approval of "their proposed action toward the unification of the Korean people." Shtykov said all Koreans wanted unification, and the Rhee regime was "making feverish preparations for an armed invasion of North Korea." Li Li-san said a northward attack "would be the initial step toward the reestablishment of a reactionary regime in China"; furthermore China could not tolerate the Rhee regime controlling the Yalu hydroelectric facilities. Derevyanko chimed in, to the effect that South Korea would not be able to resist the North, having no tanks or artillery—the only clear suggestion in the document that the North's "action" meant an invasion of the South.

The participants give this meeting plausibility. Li Li-san was on the first delegation of Chinese officials to P'yŏngyang after the war began, as we will see; it is also quite predictable that Shtykov would be present with Kim Il Sung. The timing and the accurate discussion of the issues between North and South in June also lends the account credibility.

It is more likely, however, that this account was forged, probably by the Chinese Nationalists. Just as one begins to think there might be something to it, Voitinsky is quoted as saying that Edward Carter of the Institute for Pacific Relations (IPR) and Owen Lattimore "have had numerous conferences with Voitinsky and Swanidse in Moscow," and have stated, presumably based on their privileged access to internal American secrets, that the United States had washed its hands of South Korea and will not defend it.

In fact, Lattimore had himself called for the removal of support from the Rhee regime in the fall of 1949, in State Department discussions having only low-level classification; for this he was criticized at the time, and openly in March 1950 by McCarthy. He had no access to top secret materials; if he had, he would easily have concluded that the United States *would* defend the South. That he and Carter met frequently in Moscow with Voitinsky is so implausible as to suggest the document was concocted not to show North Korean responsibility for the attack, but to smear Lattimore and the IPR. The idea that Li Li-san was Moscow's man was widespread in American intelligence circles, but it is absurd to imagine Mao and Chou En-lai allowing him to represent China on such an important matter. If a high PRC military officer or one of Kim's Chinese allies from the Manchurian guerrilla days had been at the meeting, one would have to credit the account. But it seems merely to be an artifact of the bad intelligence and the internecine American conflicts of the early 1950s.

Although there is some evidence in intelligence materials that Kim and Shtykov were out of the country in April, they were apparently in China, not Moscow. There is no evidence that Kim traveled to Moscow in early June. MacArthur's Counter-Intelligence Corps (CIC) reported that Derevyanko left Tokyo for a meeting of the Soviet Supreme Council to be held on June 12, for the purpose of studying the Far Eastern situation, but the main concern appeared to have been Southeast Asia. The contents of an intercepted Moscow letter dispatched to the Japanese Communist Party made no mention of Korea.[50]

The Derevyanko departure seems by the timing of it to have been related to the peace treaty issue; his head may have rolled because the Soviet effort to stop a bilateral American-Japanese peace was getting nowhere, and Dulles's impending visit suggested a treaty was closer to fruition. He was reported to have been demoted, ending up running the notorious Kolyma prison camp in the Gulag.[51] In any case he never was a powerful figure in Moscow.

If the Soviets wished to hide an upcoming North Korean attack, they could hardly have chosen a worse time for diplomats to throw together their belongings and disappear. Indeed, in the three weeks before the Korean War American forces in Japan were on alert, perhaps because MacArthur anticipated something happening after the Derevyanko departure.

WASHINGTON ON THE EVE OF THE WAR

As Dulles, Johnson, and MacArthur met in Tokyo, Truman administration East Asia policy moved toward a climax. The basic sinews of major policy change were already in place: containment in South Korea, a Seventh-Fleet separation of Taiwan from the mainland and the start of a quarter-century of hostility to the People's Republic of China, a bilateral peace treaty with Japan leaving American bases, military aid to the French in Indochina.

Louis Johnson testified on June 5 that Korea, Iran, Greece, and Turkey were areas where "our national interests are vitally involved," and cited Iran and Korea as "subject to varying degrees of external Communist aggression against which their present forces are inadequate." Meanwhile Marguerite Higgins reported from Korea that fighting was intense along the parallel, and the *Herald-Tribune* editorialized that just as a scare in Berlin (over the communist youth march) died down, Korea was "flaring up." Higgins said "observers" in Korea thought the maintenance of the ROK as an "anti-Communist bastion" was just as "important to the morale of Asia as is Berlin's fate to the morale of Western Europe."[52]

An American spy plane that entered Soviet territory near the Baltic was shot down, causing a momentary war scare.[53] The secretary of the Navy, Francis P. Matthews, said on Armed Forces Day that "we are left with no alternative than to assume that the fateful moment of final decision is close at hand." Although McCarthy's din was dying down at this point, Truman's attorney-general, J. Howard McGrath, delineated how far the United States had come from the wartime alliance with Russia: communists were "rodents," he said, committed to "international sadism."[54]

The Taiwan conflict in American politics was still completely unresolved, however, and if Rusk wanted Chiang's scalp, others wanted Acheson's. After losing his chance to be the bipartisan accommodator, Senator Smith told Louis Johnson in early June that "Acheson should go." By mid-June he and other Republicans, after speaking with Rusk and Dulles, thought "it looks now as though we might work out a plan to give aid to Formosa"; on June 20, "the Formosa situation looks very much better." Acheson gave a three-hour speech to the Governor's Conference on June 20, those present saying "he scared hell out of us," and "swept all of us," including critics of the administration.[55]

The strangest episode in June 1950 is related in Wellington Koo's voluminous and valuable papers, where one man linked together two efforts to cut the Gordian knot on America's Far Eastern policy. For the Acheson forces, it was the minimax strategy of eliminating Chiang Kai-shek. For the opposing side, it was "a trick" that remains to be explained.

Although Dean Rusk was out of town, he was not relaxing. On Friday evening, as we saw, he arrived at the Plaza Hotel to meet with Hu Shih, the goal being the formation of a "liberal" government to substitute for Chiang Kai-shek and his crew. Acheson was waiting for him to return from New York, according to Livingston Merchant, and it is in this precise context that, on Friday, Acheson said the policy on military aid to the

KMT had not changed. Frederick McKee, a major financial backer of the China Lobby, had arranged Rusk's New York meeting.

According to a top secret account of a June 15 meeting at the Nationalist embassy in Washington, Chen Chih-mai had lunch with a man identified as Dr. Raymond T. Shepard; later that day he also met Shepard's lawyer, Col. Michael Looney, and the latter's friend, John Megson. They suggested that the KMT might wish to retain Daniel Hanlon, a law partner of William Boyle, who had gotten an offer from Franco of $50,000 to represent the Spanish government, but Truman had told him to turn it down; Hanlon would be available as a lobbyist for the KMT for $30,000.

Looney then left, and Shepard and Megson said this, in Chen's recounting: " 'Time is of the essence,' that we must come to a decision no later than Saturday. The reason for the rush, as related to me, is that they want to 'pull the trick' immediately after the Johnson-Bradley visit, and leave the opposition no time to spoil the thing." The only other item in this document mentioned that "they talked about making immediate use of the $75 million earmarked for 'the general area of China,' to ship arms and ammunition to [Taiwan] soonest possible."[56]

Wellington Koo embellished this account a bit in his oral history, adding that a "Mr. Gratz" was also present, a lawyer to Shepard: "Gratz said he would tell Mr. Boyle, Chairman of the National Democratic Committee, to tell the President" about sending arms to Taiwan. He also appears to link another Ohio industrialist to the account, Carl W. V. Nix of Akron, who had been doing business in Japan for years, and with whom Koo spoke on June 16. Chiang Kai-shek had cabled that he had seen Nix in Taipei, that Nix was interested in military aid for the KMT, and that as a boyhood friend of Bess Truman, he would try to reach the president about aid for Chiang's regime. Koo thought this approach indicated that the Democratic Party was coming to see the importance of the Taiwan issue for upcoming Congressional elections.[57]

William M. Boyle, Jr., was chairman of the Democratic National Committee, a charter member of the Kansas City Pendergast machine, and a confidant of Harry Truman. He was widely thought to have arranged Truman's whistle-stop campaign in 1948 that won him the election, and would therefore have worked with Louis Johnson, Truman's key fundraiser in 1948.[58] Hanlon was a Washington lawyer associated with Boyle and the Democratic Party.

Raymond T. Shepard was identified as a Youngstown industrialist and close friend of Frederick C. McKee; McKee and one "Colonel Moody" had spoken highly of Shepard to the Nationalist embassy. Shepard was said to have been friends with Joseph Ku of the Chinese embassy, to have contributed funds to McKee's pro-KMT committee, and to have had

meetings with people in the State Department on behalf of the KMT.[59]
A Dr. Raymond T. Shepard did live in Youngstown in 1950; he was an
entomologist who subsequently ran a lucrative food concession in
Youngstown steel mills, which would account for the "Dr." and perhaps
the "industrialist." Both he and his wife are deceased, but his daughter
and a longtime lawyer friend told me they had no idea that Shepard had
any involvement with the Nationalists or any interest in East Asia policy;
he was a longtime Republican, so they could not explain his involvement
with Boyle and Hanlon; they had never heard of any friendship with
McKee. It is possible that an imposter used his name.

John Megson also cannot be located, but Chen described him as "working with the State Department on special assignments. He says he is a
friend of General Chennault and Mr. Willauer." He is the second person
allegedly working with the State Department to show up in the Koo files,
the first being the mysterious and very knowledgeable Captain Ross
Jung. Michael Looney was identified as a lawyer for Shepard, and as a
lawyer for the Democratic National Committee. In 1987 I located Col.
Michael Looney, a retired military officer; in a phone conversation with
his wife that was rather strained, she said her husband had had a recent
stroke, could not speak, would not see me, and that they had recently
"burned" his personal papers. She said he had known John Megson, but
she did not know Megson's current whereabouts. Various attempts to get
information on the people connected to this episode through the Freedom of Information Act have gone for nought, at this writing.

The association with Whiting Willauer is of more than passing interest,
since Willauer was then deeply involved with Chiang and had returned
to Washington, D.C., from Taiwan in mid-June, to meet with OPC/CIA
officials. At the time Willauer was close to Hans Tofte, who had arrived
in Japan in May to direct OPC (Office of Policy Coordination) efforts in
Japan, and to Richard Stilwell, head of Asia for the OPC. Until that point,
according to William Leary, the CIA had not been allowed entry to Japan
by MacArthur and Willoughby (although some agents were there anyway); the result of Willauer's meetings with OPC was that Frank Wisner
decided to acquire CAT for "authorized covert projects."[60]

William Boyle liked to claim that he would never stoop to using his
friendship with Truman to exert influence in Washington on behalf of
his clients, but Wellington Koo's papers record that, according to William
Pawley, Boyle personally interceded with Truman to get Pawley appointed for special missions in the State Department in 1951, over Acheson's objections; as we have seen, these assignments were mostly for the
CIA.[61]

McKee was a Pittsburg industrialist, scion of a wealthy family and a
casket maker; he was reclusive, never married, and left no papers. He

was second only to Kohlberg as a political and financial backer of the China Lobby. He had worked with Senator McCarran in ferreting out "pink cells" in the State Department, prompted by Chinese Nationalist emissaries; in the summer of 1949 he was in touch with Mme. Chiang, T. V. Soong, and Wellington Koo about ways to aid the Nationalists, including the Chennault Plan; he was involved with T. V. Soong's efforts in the spring of 1950 to save the KMT with some cryptic plan that attracted Congressional support; and he was involved with Donovan.[62] He had written to Rusk in late April advocating "rollback," as we saw, and saying "the best way to parry is to strike." McKee wrote to Donovan in the same month, saying a "High Commissioner" should be appointed for the Far East, and recommending military aid to the Nationalists so they could raid the mainland and thus "relieve the pressure on Indo-China"; this might also commence "a roll-back which might go to the Yangtza [River—*sic*] or Manchuria." In the spring of 1950 Donovan was working with Willauer on the CNAC planes held in Hong Kong; the American ambassador in Indonesia, H. Merle Cochran, wrote to William Donovan on May 8, 1950, saying that Willauer had visited him twice since early April: "he has discussed his plans and problems with me." Cochran does not explain for Donovan what they might be, but assumes he knows.[63]

The references to Boyle and Nix suggest an attempt to bypass Acheson and reach the president directly at the last minute, to save Taiwan; as we have seen, Truman usually took a harder line than his secretary of state. But the involvement of Looney, Shepard, and Megson is curious. Only the latter two referred to "pulling a trick" in private conversation with Chen, and the reference to "the opposition" seems to mean not the Republican opposition, but the opposition to American support for Chiang. Looney's career pattern suggests that he was in military intelligence, not the law profession, and whatever work Megson did for the State Department, it was unlikely to be in the Foreign Service if he was close to Willauer. Shepard is the hardest to explain; perhaps someone used his name as an alias, but it is interesting that Shepard, Nix, and McKee all hailed from the intertwined industrial structure of the Midwest, which historically had mixed its protectionist proclivities with distaste for the internationalism of New York investment bankers and lawyers, that is, Acheson's natural constituency.

Perhaps most important, McKee was the one who suggested that Chen meet with Shephard and the others on June 15, *and* he arranged the June 23 meeting between Rusk and Hu Shih. In other words this eccentric but stalwart backer of Chiang Kai-shek was aware of the critical issues between the KMT and the Truman administration, between Acheson and Johnson: a coup against Chiang versus a removal of Acheson or a change in American policy.

What was "the trick"? That cannot be answered. But the timing is suggestive. They want a "decision" no later than Saturday, which seems to refer to June 17, but it must mean June 24, because they want to "pull the trick" immediately after Johnson's return, which was scheduled for Saturday morning, June 24—thus "to leave the opposition no time to spoil the thing." Something is to happen on June 24 simultaneous with Johnson weighing in on behalf of a change in Taiwan policy, and before Acheson has a chance to thwart it. That, at any rate, is the implication.

The reader might now benefit from a brief chronology of the events covered in the past several chapters, to summarize our narrative before getting to the main event; all dates are in 1950.

January 4: Goodfellow meets Wellington Koo
January 5: Truman and Acheson, no defense for Taiwan
January 12: Press Club speech
February 8: Donovan in Tokyo
February 11: Goodfellow, Cooke met by H. Tong in Taipei
February 14: Rhee in Tokyo
February 15: Sino-Soviet Treaty announced
February 24: Phone link between Shin Sŭng-mo and Chiang
March 15: Goodfellow in Seoul
April 15: Irving Short in Taipei
April 19–22: Wu T'ieh-ch'eng and Chu Shih-ming in Seoul
April 22: Wu T'ieh-ch'eng and Chu Shih-ming in Tokyo
April 23: Hainan falls
June 6: Dulles sees Hollington Tong
June 6–7: Wu T'ieh-ch'eng returns to Seoul
June 7: Griffith visits Koo, sends Tong to Tokyo
June 10: Chang Myŏn dinner in Washington
June 10–12: Chiang cashiers Soong bros., H. H. Kung
June 11–12: H. H. Kung visits Willoughby
June 14: CIA warning about N. Korean invasion
June 15: Date for CIA evacuation from Taiwan
June 19: Dulles visits parallel; Johnson in Tokyo
June 19–20: State Dept. pushes coup against Chiang
June 20: Rusk assures Congress all is well in Korea
June 22–23: Dulles dispatches MacArthur's Taiwan paper
June 23: Rusk meets Hu Shih at Plaza Hotel
June 23: Acheson says January 5 policy still holds

Two final items adumbrate this quiet weekend: first, Preston Goodfellow had joined the Army. His secretary wrote on June 12, "Col. Goodfellow has been called back in the Army for a tour of duty."[64] Goodfellow was fifty-nine at the time, one would think a bit on in years for military obligations. According to Army intelligence documents obtained under the Freedom of Information Act and received while this book was in proof, Goodfellow was called to active duty in military intelligence on May 2, 1950, as an "executive officer" for an unknown assignment at Fort Eustis, Virginia. Although G-2 investigators sought to block his access to sensitive materials, on June 22 an unidentified individual backed up Goodfellow and urged that his case be brought to the attention of Gen. Lawton Collins. It is known that after the war began, many OSS and military intelligence operatives returned to service, using the Army as a cover. Goodfellow, a key representative of military intelligence interests in the OSS and a longtime associate of Donovan, beat the rush.

Donovan, however, was nowhere to be seen. He was, it is said, returning from Europe on the Queen Mary when the war began. It must then have been his wife who wrote in his diary from June 24 through 28 these items: "call Graham, re report"; "MacRae"; "Frank and Graham"; "Rubinstein." A man named Graham was known as "Mr. Korea" in the CIA in 1950, and told me in an interview that he had almost concluded that the North Koreans were about to attack, kicking himself thereafter for not telling his superiors. He said he never had contact with Donovan. Frank might be Frank Wisner. Rubinstein—who also appears twice in April diary entries—might be Serge Rubinstein, Korean gold magnate, spy, rogue, crook (his biography can be found in the Donovan Papers). Then again, these people might be Mrs. Donovan's bridge partners.[65]

Something did happen on June 24, around midday, Washington time. It happened on the isolated and remote Ongjin Peninsula, to which we now turn.

Chapter Eighteen

WHO STARTED THE KOREAN WAR?
THREE MOSAICS

No serious, honest scholar can ever have any question about it.
North Korean Communist forces attacked the Republic of Korea
without warning, with provocation and without justification.

Dean Acheson

W HO STARTED the Korean War? This question cannot be answered.
Instead, the reader is asked to consider three mosaics, each explaining how the war might have "started." All three are conspiracy theories, including the established American-South Korean position: that the Soviets and North Koreans stealthily prepared a heinous, unprovoked invasion. The first mosaic is this "official story," and especially the documentary evidence behind it. Mosaic Three is the North Korean account, which precisely reverses the first position: the South launched a surprise, unprovoked invasion all along the parallel. The most absorbing, perhaps, is Mosaic Two: the South provoked the war. Then there is a set of intelligence mosaics, of report and counterreport, which meander in and out and raise the question, who knew what, when?

INCIDENT AT ONGJIN: "I NEVER QUITE KNEW WHAT WENT ON"

Most accounts of the outbreak of fighting in June 1950 leave the impression that an attack began all along the parallel at dawn, against an enemy taken completely unaware. Both South and North Korean official histories assert this; they merely differ on which side attacked. But the war began in the same, remote locus of much of the 1949 fighting, the Ongjin Peninsula, and some hours later spread along the parallel westward, to Kaesŏng, Ch'unch'ŏn, and the East coast. As an official American history put it, "On the Ongjin Peninsula, cut off from the rest of South Korea, soldiers of the 17th Regiment stood watch on the quiet summer night of 24–25 June 1950. For more than a week, there had been no serious incident along the 38th parallel. . . . Then at 0400, with devastating suddenness . . . [artillery and mortar fire] crashed into the ROK lines." Attacking elements were said to be from the 3d Brigade of the Democratic People's Republic of Korea (DPRK) Border Constabulary, joined at 5:30

A.M. by the formidable 6th Division. One company of the 17th Regiment was annihilated, the other two retreated by sea.[1]

Roy Appleman's official account differed only a bit from this rendering. He wrote that "the earliest attack" hit Ongjin around 4 A.M., in a combined assault involving the 14th Regiment of the 6th Division, plus the 3d Brigade. Artillery and mortar began at 4 A.M., and soldiers crossed the parallel at 4:30, but "without armored support." Appleman got this information from an interview with long-time American intelligence operative James Hausman, who was not at Ongjin. Southern general Chŏng Il-gwŏn, head of the guerrilla suppression campaign, wrote soon after the war began that the "main attack" was at Ongjin, using the 6th Division; the mysterious Lim Ŭn has Ch'oe Hyŏn, Kim Il Sung's ally, leading the Ongjin charge.[2]

On the locus of the first attack, the North agreed. In his radio address shortly after noon on June 25, Kim Il Sung said that forces of the Republic of Korea Army (ROKA) 17th Regiment had attacked on Ongjin to the west of Haeju; according to Koreans who heard the broadcast, he added this aside: "Kim Sŏk-wŏn, I'm coming to get you, you won't escape me now!"[3]

The North's official radio said on June 26 that South Korean forces began shelling the Ŭnp'a-san area (scene of several 1949 battles, especially the big one on August 4), on June 23 at 10 P.M., and continued until June 24 at 4 A.M., using howitzers and mortars. A unit commanded by Kang To-gŏn was defending Turak-san on Ongjin in the early hours of June 25, it was said, when it was attacked by the "Maengho" or "fierce tiger" unit of the 17th Regiment, which it proceeded to destroy. By 2:30 P.M. on June 25, the unit had advanced below the parallel as far as Sudong; meanwhile partisans sprang forward to disrupt police stations and units in Ongjin.[4]

South Korean sources asserted, however, that elements of the 17th Regiment had counterattacked and were in possession of Haeju city, the only important point north of the thirty-eighth parallel claimed to have been taken by ROKA elements until after the Inch'ŏn landing. Ch'ae Pyŏng-dŏk announced this at 11:00 A.M. June 26, a timing that would account for numerous newspaper articles saying that elements of the ROKA had occupied Haeju, and which have since been used to suggest that the South might have attacked first.[5]

The Americans and the Soviets also quickly zeroed in on what happened in Ongjin. Although most observers missed it at the time, just after the war started the United States Information Agency drew especial attention to the 1949 Ongjin fighting in public information materials—especially "a large-scale invasion" at Ongjin on August 4, 1949—showing a curious sensitivity to something hardly anyone else had brought up in the

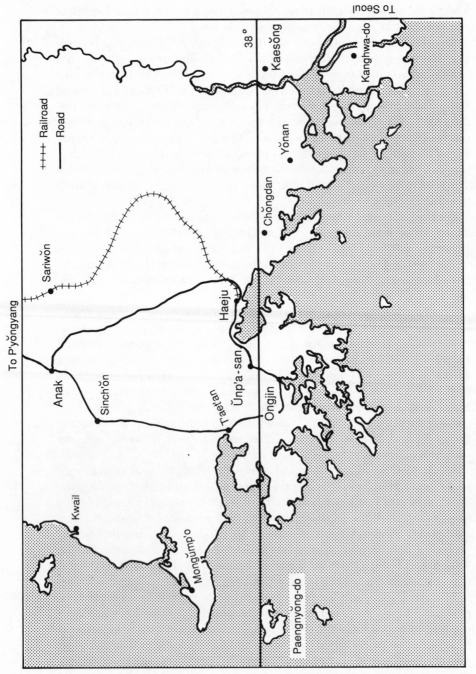

Map 7. Ongjin-Kaesong Region, 38th Parallel

first days of the war, and getting it out with an unaccustomed rapidity. It blamed all of the fighting in the summer of 1949 on the North Koreans, when internal materials showed that much of the fighting had been started by the South.[6]

This exercise in disinformation was widely assumed to be gospel truth; all the mendacity was thought to be emanating from the mouth of the Soviet UN representative, Adam Malik. When he rejoined the United Nations he charged that on June 24 Saturday leaves had been cancelled for the crack unit of the ROKA, the "twin tiger" outfit known officially as the 17th Regiment, and the next morning it attacked near Haeju. He said that his information had come from the North Koreans, and quoted a South Korean POW named Han Su-hwan.

According to the North Korean materials upon which Malik apparently based his account, Han said he was a political officer in the 17th Regiment. After the UN observers left Ongjin on June 23, Han alleged, officers were alerted and "stayed up" the night of June 24–25, and then "by daybreak of the 25th a secret order reached us from Headquarters to launch an attack" across the thirty-eighth parallel. The first and third battalions of the 17th Regiment attacked west of Haeju, penetrating one to two kilometers, he claimed.

This attack, Malik claimed, was first discussed concretely on June 20, the central figures being Shin Sŭng-mo, Ch'ae Pyŏng-dŏk, and Kim Sŏk-wŏn, "who divided among themselves the regions within which they would direct military action." He added darkly, "a particularly ominous and evil role is being played . . . by General MacArthur, who feels that he is the deputy of God in Asia."[7]

This is about the sum total of the public information on the origin of the Ongjin fighting, although it was embellished and written up in many ways thereafter. Neither I. F. Stone nor Karunakar Gupta go beyond it, although they do say a bit about the earlier fighting in the area. Mainstream critics, including academic specialists, have leaped to attack such "revisionists" with alacrity, but usually with a complacent unwillingness sincerely to assess the issue. Some have displayed a remarkable incapacity to evaluate reliable historical sources—citing the South Korean official history of the war, for example, which, like the northern histories, is a compendium of half-truths, distortions, and critical omissions.[8] It would be like asking scribes of the Confederacy what happened at Fort Sumter. But, is there any significance to this tale, and what do formerly classified materials show?

All sides agree that the war started at Ongjin. What no one saw fit to point out is that the Ongjin Peninsula is hardly the place to start an invasion if you are heading southward: it's a cul-de-sac, and the 17th Regiment could simply have been blocked near Haeju if Kim Il Sung feared a southern counterattack after his invasion. It is a good place to jump off if you are heading northward, since it commands transportation leading right to P'yŏngyang, and in June 1950 was remote from the Seoul-based American attempts to rein in southern army commanders.

One hypothesis we have entertained earlier is that both sides may have been set on city-grabbing in the summer of 1950. Threats and actions directed at seizing Haeju were made by Kim Sŏk-wŏn and others from May 1949 onward; some evidence suggests that the North in 1950 might have hoped merely to seize Seoul and bring about a unified government.[9] Haeju was several times the site of North-South leftist gatherings seeking unification. More important, it housed the SKWP headquarters and was the point from which the southern communist effort was directed and from which numerous agents were dispatched in the three years after the party was forced underground in the South.[10] It was also thought to be the headquarters for the southern guerrillas. Coming on the heels of the counterinsurgency campaigns, the breaking of the Seoul underground, and the seizure of Kim Sam-yong and Yi Chu-ha, capturing it would be a rallying point against communism and a distinct blow to Pak Hŏn-yŏng and his forces.

Haeju commanded a direct route to P'yŏngyang by both road and rail, making the movement of troops far easier and quicker in the rough terrain. ROKA possession of it would also backstop their precarious hold on the Ongjin Peninsula. (In the August 1949 Ongjin fighting, as we saw, ROK generals in desperation wanted to abandon the peninsula and move against Ch'ŏrwŏn.) Haeju was part of rice-rich Hwanghae Province, the main repository of southern-style society in the North: landlords, tenancy, quasi-feudal relationships. It was the prime region for underground penetration by pro-ROK guerrillas and spies before and during the war; it was about the only place where any anticommunist resistance was evident in 1950–1953.[11] Haeju was surrounded by little islands and peninsulas that could (and did) harbor southern agents. In other words people who have hastened to point out that Haeju was worthless do not know what they are talking about.

The 17th Regiment was not just another unit in the ROK Army. It was a key frontline force along a line from which two full companies of soldiers had defected to the North in May 1949, a mutiny that devastated ROK morale. The loyalty of the 17th thus had to be absolutely assured. It was directly commanded by one of two brothers who headed the Northwest or *Sŏbuk* faction in the Army, Paek In-yŏp, who had brought many *Sŏbuk* youth members into it; the other brother, Paek Sŏn-yŏp, commanded the ROKA 1st Division (formerly commanded by Kim Sŏk-wŏn). Both were born near P'yŏngyang, a few years after Kim Il Sung. Paek Sŏn-hwa, who may or may not be related, was ROKA intelligence chief in 1949–1950. Regional loyalties structured most units of the army and this one was full of northerners with virulent hatred of communism. And as we saw in chapter 12, Paek In-yŏp mounted an attack on Ŭnp'asan in December 1949, to boost morale.

The 2,500 men of the 17th were the best trained in the ROK Army, and although the regiment was officially part of the elite Capital Division, it was often listed by itself as if it were a separate, smaller division. It had been blooded against the southern guerrillas, operating out of the Nam-wŏn suppression headquarters until early 1950. There its commander was Kim Paek-il, another northerner who, like Kim Sŏk-wŏn, had been head of a special Japanese Kwantung Army detachment to hunt down Korean and Chinese guerrillas. (The defecting officers of the 18th Regiment in 1949 drew special attention to the baleful influence of Kim Sŏk-wŏn and Kim Paek-il.) Had Rhee not been blocked by Americans in making Kim Sŏk-wŏn chief of staff in May 1950, he would have commanded Paek In-yŏp as head of the Capital Division.

Probably the official command lines did not matter much. Paek In-yŏp was also a veteran of the Kwantung Army, and Yi Ch'ŏngch'an, the head of the Capital Division when the war began, had been a major in the Japanese Army. Since this was the elite guard of the president, Rhee's cronies like Kim Sŏk-wŏn would influence it whether they actually commanded it or not. Kim Paek-il, for example, was said to be functioning with the command of this division after the war began.[12] These officers came to maturity in a Kwantung Army that specialized in the provocation of "incidents" as prelude to war, the best known being the Mukden affair in 1932.

Also with the 17th was the infamous "Tiger Kim." Kim Chong-wŏn got the name "Tiger" for his service to the Japanese Army; after 1945 he liked journalists to call him "the Tiger of Mt. Paekdu." He volunteered for the Imperial Army in 1940 and rose to sergeant, "a rank which epitomized the brutality of the Japanese Army at its worst," in John Muccio's words; he served in New Guinea and the Philippines. He was with the Korean National Police (KNP) at the Eastgate Station in 1946, then for eight months in 1947 he was Chang T'aek-sang's personal bodyguard. He then entered the Army, where he rose quickly through the ranks in the guerrilla suppression campaigns. Americans remembered him for his brutality in the suppression (Muccio called it "ruthless and effective"), and for his refusal to take American orders. An American in 1948 termed him "a rather huge, brute of a man"—after witnessing Kim and his men "mercilessly" beat captured Yŏsu prisoners, including women and children, "with cot rounds, bamboo sticks, fists." He worked closely with Kim Paek-il and Chŏng Il-gwŏn, and by August 1949 he was a regimental commander.

After the war began, a KMAG advisor went "berserk with the idea of killing Kim," according to Muccio. The officer himself, named Emmerich, was not berserk: he said he would have to shoot Kim, "if no one else will get rid of him." Kim was berserk. He had killed some of his own officers and men for alleged disobedience, avoided the front lines of fighting like the plague, and had beheaded fifty POWs and guerrillas (said to be just "one group" among others that had received this treatment).

Emmerich was transferred; Kim was temporarily relieved of his command under American pressure. But Rhee soon promoted him to deputy provost marshal, and later sent him to assist in running the occupation of P'yŏngyang in the fall of 1950. He eventually commanded the martial law regime in Pusan, after distinguishing himself in the squalid terror of the "conscription" campaigns, which consisted of "shanghai-ing the required number of young men off the streets." He also prided himself on being a "one-man censor of the press," which he indeed was in one instance where he personally administered a beating to two reporters for the Yŏnhap sinmun. Although he was clearly, on this evidence, a war criminal in Korea if not necessarily in the Philippines, Tiger Kim was part of Rhee's bestiary of close and trusted confidants.[13]

With leadership such as this in the 17th Regiment the internecine Korean struggles of the 1930s would be recapitulated, but on dramatically reversed terms. Out of the same generation (something weighty in the Korean cultural context), in their nation's maximum point of trial these warriors had chosen opposite sides: the opportunists took on the color and status of the Japanese militarists, while the guerrillas were little more than rag-tag, poorly equipped bands, hunted down by Japanese/Korean forces with every advantage.

In 1950 this was not so. When in the spring the 17th redeployed from the interior to the parallel at Ongjin, led by colonial Quislings, the northern generals would have marked its approach with the riveted mix of alarm and relish of a cobra lying in wait for an oncoming mongoose. To counter the 17th, the North backed up its border soldiers with elements of the 6th Division, full of experienced China soldiers, placing them near Haeju. It was led by Pang Ho-san, the revolutionary who trained at Whampoa and had a long record of anti-Japanese fighting in China.

From May 1949 onward the North Korean press had paid close attention to Kim Sŏk-wŏn and Kim Paek-il, the former being chief of the thirty-eighth parallel in 1949 and the latter the overall commander of the counterinsurgency in the South. The North would know they retained substantial influence in an elite unit they had previously commanded. On May 18, 1950, the China-aligned head of the Ministry of the Interior, Pak Il-u, held an extraordinary news conference, responding to Shin Sŭng-mo's May 10 briefing where he claimed that an invasion was imminent. He began by saying that it was a "northern expedition," not an invasion of the South, that was at issue. He cited "dangerous and provocative" public statements by ROK leaders about marching north, including one by Kim Sŏk-wŏn, dated May 4, 1949, that when he attacked he would have "breakfast in Haeju, lunch in P'yŏngyang and dinner in Wŏnsan." Although he disparaged ROK capabilities, saying its leaders "would not know how to sell rice from inside a ricebag," he also said, "The authorities of the DPRK are paying deep attention to the dangerous war provocations of the southern puppets. Furthermore . . . according to accurate materials that have become known to us, the Rhee puppet government had concentrated five of its eight divisions along the thirty-eighth parallel." His first example of this was the Ongjin Peninsula where, he said, two infantry regiments had been added to the existing forces; he then listed other reinforcements along the parallel, saying that troops were being brought up from the interior guerrilla fighting. Why was this being done, he asked, just when the guerrillas would become active, benefitting from the spring foliage? The answer: Rhee was "impatient to provoke a civil war," but the United States and the UN Commission on Korea (UNCOK) were trying to hide this. He ended by urging "peaceful unification," and called on all the Korean people to "heighten their vigilance . . . always be prepared to control [Rhee's] dangerous war provocations."[14]

KMAG G-2 materials cite various border incidents in Ongjin just before the war. Although minor in comparison to the fighting of 1949, there were quite a few, with significant loss of life, and the majority occurred in the Ongjin-Haeju-Kaesŏng region. Of fourteen incidents in the week of May 18–25, seven were near Ongjin and Haeju; a total of thirty-two northerners and six southerners died in these border incidents. The next week there were twenty-five incidents, with a smaller number dead; five of these were near Ongjin, six near Kaesŏng. Of thirteen incidents, June 1–8, five were at the parallel just north of Ongjin; two were on the parallel just east of Haeju; one occured near Kaesŏng. The June 8–15 report showed fourteen border incidents, of which three were near Haeju and four near Kaesŏng; most were contacts with Ongjin-area southern guerrillas, not KPA soldiers. Another source for the same period, however, counted eight border incidents (not broken down geographically) in which the ROKA and the Korean People's Army (KPA) both lost twelve soldiers, a casualty total said to be higher than in recent weeks. No reports from either source could be located for the period June 16–25, but this evidence hardly suggests that the parallel was particularly quiet in the eastern reaches in the weeks before the war.[15]

An unusual source gives evidence that fighting was ongoing in this remote region through the last week of June. Captured North Korean documents include top secret "public opinion" reports from Haeju, where on June 21, 1950 a twenty-two-year-old student is quoted as saying, "there is a war almost every day along the 38th parallel."[16]

As in the fall of 1949, British sources in the spring of 1950 reported that KMAG advisors were "seeking the removal of over-aggressive officers in command positions along the parallel"; this was at the time of the attempt to bring Kim Sŏk-wŏn back into the ROKA, so it cannot have referred to him. In the interim until they were removed, the report said, "a border incident . . . could precipitate civil war." But the British thought this would not happen as long as American officers controlled the situation.[17] Thus the significance of the absence of Roberts, Wright, and other high KMAG officers in late June.

The UNCOK military observer, Ronald J. Rankin, told an interviewer that although everything was peaceful along the parallel when he and F.S.B. Peach made their survey, he recalled that something was different about the last place they visited, his memory was vague but there was something he could not put his finger on about this place: Ongjin.[18] The other observer, Peach, told an interviewer,

> I never quite knew what went on. There's a bit of mystery still about Haeju, I think it may have been Paek [In-yŏp] and his merry men, the 17th Regiment attacking it [Haeju]. It could have been some of them fighting their way to get back into South [Korea]. We didn't hear anything about it until the war had been going for a while and I never quite knew what went on.[19]

The observers returned from Ongjin to Seoul on the morning of Friday, June 23.

The first intelligence reports on the fighting that I have had access to are curiously inconclusive on who started the fighting in Ongjin. Interestingly, there are no extant reports from Willoughby's Korea Liaison Office for the last weekend in June. Air Force intelligence reported that "at 0400 engagement started between North and South Korean forces at Ongjin . . . by 0600 fighting had worked itself across to the East coast." The initial report to MacArthur merely said, "fighting with great intensity started at 0400, 25 June on the Ongjin Peninsula."[20]

A bizarre document,[21] consisting of captured Russian radio intercepts of South Korean Army communications, contained an intercept from Ongjin that had ROK sources saying, "at June 25 at 0300 hours, fighting began in the region of Ongjin. At the present time [June 25, 10:30 A.M.] the enemy is attacking fiercely." (Later intercepts refer to North Korean attacks, not an indeterminate beginning.) Furthermore, another intercept from the "General Staff" (presumably of the ROK Army) at 1845 hours, but not giving the day in question, referred to "a joint conference" at 0800 hours "for the planning of a night operation 25 June." This cannot but refer to the period before the fighting began; it would be a conference that must have been scheduled for 8:00 A.M. Saturday, June 24—some hours after Peach and Rankin left Ongjin, some hours after Rhee decided not to make the exchange for Cho Man-sik. It would have been intercepted at 6:45 P.M. on Friday evening, June 23, some thirty hours before anyone claimed that fighting began at Ongjin.

Like the Americans in the South, the Russians had units listening in on the other side's radio transmissions. These intercepts clearly indicated that the target was the ROKA communications system. For example, on June 25 at 0830 hours, Shin Sŭng-mo was quoted as saying "the enemy is conducting strong artillery fire and a general attack. The numbers are much greater than we anticipated . . . in almost all the regions the enemy has seized our contested points." At Ongjin at 0800 hours someone radioed, "the situation is very difficult. The enemy is continually attacking and bringing in new troops."

The intercepts also included an item saying that "ships nos. 509, 507, 501, and 506 have been dispatched, and engaged the enemy in battle. Enemy forces are eight times as great as ours, up to 10:50 hours, our ships suffered great losses." The time of this intercept is June 25, 0800 hours, meaning that the ships were dispatched the previous day—sometime before 10:50 P.M., June 24. Haeju was approachable by sea as well as by land. This information squares with an assertion by former ROK Admiral Lee Yong-un, who said that he was, on June 23, "in command of a small naval unit on a mission against Haeju districts." Agence France-Press is also said to have reported the shelling of the Haeju area by the ROKA, beginning at 10:00 P.M. on June 23. I have not located that report.

Lee himself had been court-martialed in the spring of 1950 on suspicion of involvement in communist smuggling operations, but he was cleared and returned to duty in June. Available evidence says that he was assigned to the Chinhae naval base on the southern coast, not the Haeju area. It may also be that, if Lee was involved in anything, it was small-scale naval shelling of the Haeju area, a fairly commonplace occurrence.[22]

The intercepts also included one from the commander of the First Front to the ROK minister of Defense, June 25 at 0600 hours, saying "the enemy started strong attacks on our front . . . in points 1, 2 and 3 we started a battle with a detached unit." This is inconclusive; it clearly demarks what is well known, that the North opened up with all barrels by 6 A.M., but by not identifying the points (1, 2, 3), it is not clear if the last statement refers to a counterattack or an attack. Nothing in this limited Soviet file suggested a general South Korean attack all along the parallel, as charged later by the North, and that alone implies its authenticity since a few weeks later the Soviets joined P'yŏngyang's chorus.

British sources, based on POW accounts that the North provided, said that, if these "are to be believed, the southern forces had some hours warning of the northern attack. Several southern units are reported from this source to have been alerted on the evening of the 24th of June and some are said to have been ordered to advance during the night."[23]

Another piece of evidence comes from a North Korean brigade perched across from the 17th Regiment on June 21. It was an operational order for reconnaissance, and said in what seems to be a poor translation, "in the future each reconnaissance unit should repel the enemy or capture them," and then later, "with the beginning of the attack, determine the route of enemy withdrawal and enemy concentrations."[24] This "attack" could be a counterattack in the context; or the document could merely refer to the kind of daily fighting that went on in the area. In any case, it offers no proof of a stealthy North Korean plan for an invasion, and implies that the unit was expecting an attack from the South.

In an interview with Thames Television in P'yŏngyang in 1987, Chun Sung Chol said that on June 24–25 he was a staff officer in a border garrison on the Ongjin Peninsula. Here is how he described the alleged South Korean attack:

> To be honest, at the time I thought it was another of the enemy's armed invasions. I did not yet know that it was an all-out war. While I was thinking it was another armed invasion, there came an order from our superiors to counter-attack [sic]. Then I realized that the enemy had started the war throughout our land. . . . I thought it was just a major armed provocation attempt.

Was Haeju ever occupied by South Korean forces? MacArthur reported on June 26 at 0355 that "South Korean forces on Ongjin Peninsula assumed offensive attacking in direction of Haeju"; he did not say when they did this. Top secret intelligence maps in Willoughby's headquarters show elements of the 17th Regiment in occupation of Haeju as of 0700 hours on June 26. This information came well before Chae Pyŏng-dŏk's announcement that Haeju had been occupied, which the ROK has always said was based on a journalist's mistaken report from Ongjin (they even offered to produce this journalist for the Thames Television documentary). The next day, Willoughby's intelligence reported, "one infantry batallion and one artillery battery [of the 17th] occupy Haeju"; it said that Ongjin itself was now occupied by North Korean forces, with 1,250 soldiers in the 17th Regiment having been evacuated by sea as of 1700 hours on June 26. Drumwright said that Paek In-yŏp got 60 percent of his troops out of Ongjin on June 26. Willoughby's intelligence maps carried elements of the 17th in occupation of Haeju on June 28 and 29, but on June 30 they disappear with no explanation.[25]

The North Korean press denounced Ch'ae's claims to have occupied Haeju as "a lying fabrication" and a "comedy," but this could perhaps be attributed to typical KPA bravado that it was an ever-victorious army, and because some commander would be in trouble for such a lapse. The South likewise rarely if ever admitted a defeat.[26]

If Paek got 1,750 of 2,500 soldiers out of Ongjin, what happened to the rest? Appleman says "most of two batallions" were evacuated, but "the other batallion was completely lost in the early fighting." The North Koreans claimed to have eliminated 2,000 soldiers in the 17th; it might be an exaggeration, but if it were not, that would make for almost 4,000 soldiers in the 17th, not the listed total of 2,500.[27]

It will be remembered that Pak Il-u charged on May 18 that *two* infantry regiments had been placed in Ongjin; we also know that in late 1949 KMAG had been trying to reduce the size of the Ongjin task force, over Korean objections.[28] What might the other one be? In the William Donovan Papers—so much of critical importance happens to turn up in these papers—is an account by Brig. Gen. C. E. Ryan, given to Donovan in March 1952. It related that elements of the 17th Regiment performed the "outstanding" feat of escaping north across the parallel. "With escape by the sea cut off, the regiment struck north across the Parallel, hacking its way through the Red division in its path. Using captured ammunition and vehicles, the ROK troops kept their integrity as a fighting force and turned south in a maneuver which rejoined them with their hard-pressed comrades near Seoul." The commander of this effort? Ryan identifies Kim Paek-il.[29] These sources, of course, say this was a counterattack.

Robert Oliver, Rhee's close advisor, has a similar account, although he says that Paek In-yŏp was in command: in the first hours of the war, he wrote, Paek "led his men in a bold counter-attack northward. They broke out of the [Ongjin] peninsula, captured the town of Haeju, and then fought their way out of the surrounding north Korean troops." We saw that Peach, also, thought Paek "and his merry men" might have attacked Haeju. Harold Noble had a similar account of the occupation of Haeju; he found the 17th Regiment "full of piss and vinegar" on June 30, just as they were entraining southward, apparently from Seoul or its southern suburbs. Troops routed a couple of days earlier with major casualties would not be so ebullient.[30]

Kim Paek-il and Kim Sŏk-wŏn did not have formal command positions, and their whereabouts on the last weekend in June is unknown to me.[31] However, by July 15 Kim Sŏk-wŏn had been rewarded with command of Rhee's favored Capital Division; Kim Paek-il commanded the entire 1st Corps of the ROKA in the fall of 1950, going around with his American advisor, Lt. Col. Edward Rowney.[32] Kim died in a plane crash in 1951.

The indeterminate beginning of the fighting was also implied in Muccio's famous cable on the start of the fighting, which said that, based on "Korean Army reports which [are] *partly confirmed* by KMAG field advisor reports," the North attacked in Ongjin. He later said, with perhaps some understatement, that continuous prodding and probing along the parallel by both sides "made it so difficult to determine what was going on . . . the morning of the 25th."[33] All this suggests, at a minimum, that the evidence of what happened on the morning of June 25 was a rather slim reed upon which to base American intervention and a United Nations commitment.

KAESŎNG ERUPTS

After its beginning on the Ongjin Peninsula at midnight to 4:00 A.M. (depending on the evidence), the fighting spread to nearby Kaesŏng two to four hours later. A pleasant urban leisure spot for Korea's landed aristocracy for centuries, and locus of its incipient but ultimately failed merchant class, it remained in 1950 a small museum of the cultured world of *yangban* repose. It was also a nodal pivot of conflict, with a small mountain (*Song'ak*) cleft by the thirty-eighth parallel on the northeast edge of town, and which even in 1987 still showed the residue of artillery bombardment.

The intrepid Marguerite Higgins visited Kaesŏng at the end of May, the day before the elections. North Korean radio blared forth provocative threats that election day would be a signal for an attack southward all along the parallel. "The next few days in Kaesŏng may be critical," she wrote, but 12th Regiment commander Song Ho-ch'an told her, "if the Communists attack us, we will whip them as usual. But we think they are bluffing." The next day Roberts also discounted an invasion, but said, "at this point we rather invite it. It will give us target practice."[34]

Kaesŏng was the only point on the parallel where an American officer was present on the morning of June 25. Joseph Darrigo, KMAG advisor to the 12th Regiment, was just below Song'aksan, sleeping in a KMAG compound. At 5:00 A.M. artillery fire jounced him out of bed; "the volume of fire indicated an enemy attack"—in other words, he did not know whose artillery he heard when he awakened. Shortly thereafter he hopped in a jeep and headed south, dodging bullets from a group of KPA soldiers disembarking from a train in the middle of town. He found ROKA 1st Division headquarters, where he soon met none other than Paek Sŏn-yŏp, its commander, with whom he remained the rest of that

Sunday. An American missionary heard Darrigo's jeep roar by, but it and the artillery were such common happenings that he rolled over and went back to sleep. When he awoke two hours later, KPA soldiers were staring into his room. He spent the next three years in a North Korean prison camp.[35]

The railroad from Kaesŏng ran to the west about six miles, then turned North and crossed the thirty-eighth parallel two miles later. The North Koreans had pulled up the tracks on their side of the parallel around the time of the Song'aksan fighting in 1949, to make an invasion more difficult. Apparently they relaid the tracks shortly before June 25. It would not take long for soldiers to entrain and go eight miles (perhaps an hour?). So again, at Kaesŏng, there is no proof that the North could not be responding to a southern provocation. Yet for the careful reader this railroad business will be telling: it is impossible to replace tracks from 3:00 A.M. to 5:00 A.M., in response to a provocation at Ongjin. It is our first piece of evidence (of which there will be much more shortly) that the North had made preparations for an assault against the South, even if we have not yet been willing to say that they launched the assault without provocation.

The careful reader will be equally attentive to this telling fact: the Army asked MacArthur on June 26, "were South Koreans able to execute previously planned mine field defensive operations? If so how were North Korean tanks able to penetrate the area?" Clay Blair described land mines placed in the road as "the most effective portable antitank weapon," better than bazookas. The United States had supplied the ROK with large numbers of such mines. But they were not placed on June 25.[36] In 1949, the North had pulled up the railway and placed mines all along the roads leading north from Kaesŏng. In 1950 they replaced the rails and removed the mines. But the South never placed its mines, and concentrated much of its army and its supplies forward near the parallel—not a defensive formation. So what does this structure of action suggest? That the North was not ready to fight in 1949 when the South was, and that the North was ready to fight in 1950 when the South also was.

It appears that the KPA lifted their mines just as the war began, not some weeks earlier as might be expected. A handwritten report dated June 29 says that four groups from the Second Company, an engineer's group, were dispatched to the Sixth Battalion (no division given), and removed mines from 10:00 P.M. on June 24 to 4 A.M. on June 25, "after receiving the attack order from the battalion commander and in order to assure passage through the road." But just above this entry, the author writes that all this occured "after the battle started" [*chŏnt'u kaesi hu*], which is consistent with preparations for a response to an expected night attack, or for a KPA invasion. The report also said the unit continued clearing mines from above the thirty-eighth parallel on June 26.[37]

It is also uniformly assumed in the literature on the Korean War that tanks are offensive weapons, and therefore ipso facto evidence of North Korean intent. But there is no agreement among military strategists on whether the tank is an offensive or defensive weapon.[38] And, of course, the literature dwells on the ROK having been left defenseless against tanks, in that it had few bazookas, while never probing the failure to place antitank mines.

There is a hint in the documentation that the 12th Regiment commander, Song Ho-ch'an, might have aided the North's attack on Kaesŏng. Muccio later said that he surrendered to the North "under suspicious circumstances." Another American source claimed that the North's initial assault and its quick seizure of Seoul was "aided by a native fifth column organized in advance by quislings." Neither source gives any details about this interesting but highly sensitive issue.[39] But it would fit with an interpretation that the May elections brought forward a middle-road group of leaders willing to unite with the North, leaving Rhee and his close allies isolated. Kaesŏng would be a good place for southern troops to fall away, since it commands a direct route to Seoul. In any case, the battle ended quickly with this historic town in northern hands. Elements of the ROKA First Division were able to organize a defense at Munsan, several miles south of Kaesŏng, and they held the KPA there for three days.

THE EASTWARD SPREAD OF THE FIGHTING

At the border town of Ch'unch'ŏn, further eastward from Kaesŏng, the South Koreans unquestionably had advance knowledge of fighting to begin on June 25, which southern and American sources say, of course, was warning of the North Korean attack.

Thomas D. McPhail was a KMAG intelligence officer, probably part of Willoughby's Korea Liaison Office, who got "a wealth of information" from South Korean agents that he dispatched into northern territory. On Thursday June 22 such information caused him to go down to Seoul from his position near Ch'unch'ŏn with the 6th ROKA Division, to warn G-2 officials that the North had moved citizens away from the parallel and had secreted camouflaged tanks and artillery in "the restricted area," the area just north of the parallel. Although the American G-2 "wasn't impressed," McPhail's information caused the 6th Division to cancel all passes "and fully man defensive positions for the week-end." Because of this "preparedness," "the initial attack was repulsed."[40] So much for the North Koreans mounting an unexpected surprise attack against an Army on leave for the weekend. It is highly implausible that this advance information, and the 6th Division alert, would not have been communicated to other elements in the ROKA.

Appleman has the attack at Ch'unch'ŏn beginning at 5:30 A.M., that is, two or three hours after fighting began at Ongjin, and after radio units had wired accounts back to Seoul and, presumably to other divisions. He gives a somewhat different account than McPhail's, agreeing that no passes had been issued and that "the positions were fully manned when the attack came." Appleman reports that McPhail went from Wŏnju to Ch'unch'ŏn on Sunday morning, whereas McPhail told Ridgway he was in Seoul when the fighting began; in any case he was not at the parallel.[41]

The 7th Regiment of the ROKA 6th Division faced the KPA 2d Division when this fighting commenced; no Americans were present. The North employed no tanks until Monday evening (June 26), suggesting that border security units did the early fighting. In very heavy fighting the 6th Division acquitted itself so well that Ch'unch'ŏn did not fall for three days (Drumwright says six days), and then only withdrew because Seoul had fallen and it was flanked by the enemy.[42]

On the East coast the ROKA 8th Division also gave a good account of itself. Here, too, no Americans were at the parallel; Koreans awakened KMAG advisor George D. Kessler in Samch'ŏk and told him the North had attacked. Official histories are unclear on when the fighting began, Appleman saying "about 5 A.M." Initially there were reports that the North had landed guerrillas as far south as P'ohang, which would be clear evidence of several days' premeditation; but these came from South Korean police and proved false, and may have been put out as disinformation by southern authorities.

Landings occurred around 5 A.M. near Samch'ŏk and "later" near Kangnŭng, that is, sometime on June 25; Kessler saw sampans and junks lying offshore, and several hundred men—but they "acted like guerrillas rather than regular units."[43] This was, however, a common occurrence, happening every week or so in March 1950. This was a strong leftist and guerrilla area, and most of the guerrillas were southerners; ROK authorities as a matter of policy identified all guerrillas as North Koreans. Fighting was not heavy on the East coast in the first days of the war, with Kangnŭng in southern hands until June 28; in any case the South controlled the information coming in from this isolated region, which even in the late 1960s had no direct rail or road routes from Seoul.[44]

Around 5:30 A.M., according to Appleman, KPA forces at the parallel south of Ch'ŏrwŏn assaulted the lst Regiment of the ROKA 7th Division, dealing it heavy casualties; it gave way and the 3d and 4th KPA divisions, with an armored brigade, crashed through and began a daunting march toward Seoul.[45] South of these KPA units was the Seventh Division, headquartered at the critical invasion-route town of Ŭijŏngbu; it had not committed its forces to battle even by Monday morning, probably because it was waiting to be reinforced by the 2d Division, which had entrained from Taejŏn; when the Second arrived on Monday, it collapsed and the troops panicked. It was through the gaping hole of the Ŭijŏngbu corridor that North Korean troops poured on the afternoon and evening of June 26, thus jeopardizing the capital. Drumwright later wrote that "the failure of the 2nd Division to fight" was the main reason for the quick loss of Seoul;[46] the collapse of 7th/2d Division defenses may also be an aspect of the "fifth column" activities that Americans refer to darkly, but with no details. Or, it may have been a function of ROK strategy.

Two divisions could not march down this strategic corridor without extensive preparations for attack. Unlike the fighting at Ongjin, Kaesŏng, and Ch'unch'on, this is excellent evidence of North Korean premeditation for an assault. It still is not evidence that the North started the fighting on June 25 at 4 A.M.; it is standard procedure when a commander is either expecting battle or exercising large numbers of troops in simulated battle to have a couple of divisions in top condition, ready for battle at a moment's notice. Remember that KMAG intelligence officers were confident that they would have twenty-four hours notice of an impending North Korean attack, which they thought would be enough time to alert and ready the necessary defenses. It is likely that at least two or three KPA divisions were kept in this kind of readiness from May 1949 onward. It would appear that the march down the Ŭijŏngbu corridor was caused more by southern collapse or retreat than northern preparedness; perhaps the North knew that the 2d Division would not resist them, or perhaps it did not want to resist them.

It is also known that the KPA was not fully mobilized on June 25, and that it faced numerically superior units. MacArthur's command reported through the UN at the end of July that at the Eastern and Western portions of the parallel the North attacked with reinforced border constabulary brigades, at Kaesŏng and Ch'unch'on with a division each (but as we have seen not at the start), and ran through the Ŭijŏngbu corridor with 8,000 to 10,000 troops and fifty tanks—a total force of about 38,000. Arrayed against them were five ROKA divisions located near Seoul or north of it, at least 50,000 troops.[47]

The evidence on the unfolding of the war from West to East in the early morning hours of June 25 thus does not support Mosaic One, the judgment that the North Koreans suddenly opened a general invasion all along the parallel against a sleepy, unprepared South. Joseph Darrigo was the only American military man at the parallel when fighting began; he awoke to the sounds of someone's artillery. All the other information on the early fighting came from ROK Army sources which, as the evidence from the summer of 1949 demonstrated, absolutely cannot be credited. But even on that evidence, the fighting rippled from West to East over several hours, and the 6th Division, at least, had a day or so of advance warning. The North was not particularly successful at Munsan or Ch'unch'ŏn or the East coast; it crashed through at Kaesŏng and Ŭijŏngbu when southern units put up suspiciously token resistance, or did not choose to fight.

The numbers of troops committed by the North also bear on a larger question of military strategy. In a closely-argued book, John Mearsheimer has shown that for the success of a blitzkreig strategy the attacker must assume a three-to-one force advantage to effect the "strategic penetration" that is the essence of the method.[48] The course of the fighting after June 25 does resemble a classic blitzkreig; but if so, it was carried forth against an enemy that was equal in size if we take static order of battle data, larger in size on the evidence we have just adduced.

SUNDAY IN SOUTH AND NORTH

In Seoul Drumwright got news of the invasion Sunday at 8:15 A.M., Muccio at 9:30; both got active sending cables back to Washington, with descriptions of the fighting based mostly on ROK Army accounts. Just before noon Muccio met Rhee and found him unperturbed enough to say, "perhaps the present crisis presented the best opportunity for settling the Korean problem once and for all"; he also likened the attack to "a second Sarajevo," an analogy that was rather better than Truman's to Munich. But it was also, of course, an analogy to the rapid engagement of already mobilized, prepositioned forces of war, a small incident touching off general conflagration with a clanking automaticity.[49]

Drumwright reported that KMAG got going quickly on Sunday morning, but that it "deeply missed the steady guiding hand" of Generals Roberts and Wright. Harold Noble, whose account of the early days of the fighting is assumed to be definitive, was still in Tokyo as late as June 26, having gone there on June 23, for reasons he does not make clear. Muccio also met with UNCOK at 3:00 P.M., a meeting requested by its chairman, Liu Yu-wan, the Nationalist diplomat.[50]

On the morning of June 25 Harold Lady, Korea Lobby stalwart and Rhee confidant, suddenly flew to Tokyo. Arthur Bunce, it will be remembered, thought that Lady had more influence on Rhee than anyone in his cabinet. He had been involved in particularly sensitive negotiations on trade between Japan and South Korea in the spring of 1950, going back and forth to Tokyo, personally negotiating an $80 million agreement. On the morning when the war broke out, John Allison later related, "Mr. Lady made private arrangements and flew to Japan." There is no record of why he did this, or who he met in Japan. But when he subsequently tried to return to Korea, Muccio declared him persona non grata and blocked his entry; eventually SCAP also refused to allow him to stay in Japan and he returned to the United States. A note scribbled on documents in the Lady case reads, "I'm sorry Muccio destroyed the evidence." Goodfellow later said to Rhee, "I have heard many queer stories about [Lady's] conduct at the time of the invasion. I would like to know the truth." There is no record of Rhee's reply.[51]

John Gunther was in Tokyo on the morning of June 25, talking to an Occupation officer who was suddenly called to the phone: "He came back and whispered, 'A big story has just broken. The South Koreans have attacked North Korea!'" Gunther later dismissed this inapposite tidbit, "so wildly inaccurate" about a North Korean attack that "achieved complete tactical and even strategic surprise. It was more disgraceful than Pearl Harbor."[52]

In P'yŏngyang, Koreans were being told that the South started the fighting, with few details but with some interesting language. On June 26 the military newspaper *Chosŏn inmin-gun* (Korean People's Army)[53] had two big announcements on its front page, from the Cabinet and the Interior Ministry. The Cabinet's brief statement said the South made a "surprise attack" (*purŭi chin'gong*) into territory north of the parallel, in the "early dawn" (*irŭn saebyŏk*) of June 25. (In the past, the KPA had used *irŭn saebyŏk* to mean as early as 1:00 A.M.) It said the Cabinet held a discussion of these "tense emergencies" on June 25.

The Interior Ministry used the same language, but said the surprise attacks "ranged along the thirty-eighth-parallel battle area," listing attacks "from the West [i.e, Ongjin] toward Haeju," and in the areas of Kŭmch'ŏn and Ch'ŏrwŏn. The southerners had advanced one to two kilometers. The northern authorities had ordered the Border Constabulary to "repulse" the invaders, thus opening a "fierce defense battle." The invaders were said to have been thrown back from the Angyang area.

The Interior Ministry then warned the South that if it did not stop "its adventuresome war activities," the North would take "decisive countermeasures to control the enemy." A later Interior Ministry report in the same issue said KPA units had been rushed to the aid of the Constabulary, and had "gone over to a counterattack," repulsing the enemy and pushing into the South "five to ten kilometers . . . in many areas."

The issue also reported a meeting of military brass at 10:00 P.M. on June 25, to discuss an appeal from Kim Il (not Kim Il Sung) to the effect that Rhee had opposed every effort at peaceful unification, and now had opened an attack. It said little else. Another article on the inside pages urged propagandists to take the message of unification to everyone, saying that Rhee's attack sought to destroy the growing success of the drive for peaceful unification. None of these appeals said anything about the Soviet Union, Stalin, socialism, or communism. One called for letting victory ring in the streets of Seoul by the fifth anniversary of liberation, perhaps suggesting that the North expected a much tougher battle than it got.

The lead editorial in this issue recited a litany of Rhee's abuses, most of them in opposition to unification, all the way back to the trusteeship imbroglio. It paid particular attention to his opposition to the June 19 proclamation, going against "the unanimous desire of the Korean people" to reunite the divided halves. It accused Rhee, under the direction of the American imperialists, of "going so far as to collude with the atrocious enemy of the Korean people, Japanese imperialism." It said the South began shelling the North on June 23, killing one and wounding twenty on the northern side. Thus, "we cannot bear the criminal activity of the country-selling traitors anymore," the day of reckoning is at hand, "the time for unifying the Homeland has come!" All Koreans should rise up for independence and unification, showing their love of the homeland, the people, and "the respected and beloved Great Leader (*suryŏng*) Kim Il Sung." "Toward the battle quickly to liberate the south Korean people!"

Apart from the strong emphasis on the unification issue, this editorial (and the other articles) are noteworthy for saying nothing about: (1) the southern guerrillas, (2) the suppression of the communist underground in the south, (3) Dulles's visit to the parallel. It is excellent evidence against two interpretations, first that Pak Hŏn-yŏng stimulated the attack, and second that the North seriously believed that Dulles was in Korea to provoke war (as they have said ever since). Otherwise, the themes were very similar to editorials on June 21 after Rhee's rejection of the June 19 statement; it does seem to have been an editorial written in haste for June 26, not one scripted in advance. Most of the other articles in the issue were clearly standard ones written before June 25; one lambasted yet again Acheson's March 16 "total diplomacy" speech, terming it another name for "atomic blackmail."

On June 26 Kim Il Sung spoke to the Korean people, and now accused the South of making "a general attack" (*chŏnmyŏnjŏk chin'gong*) across the parallel. Rhee had long sought to "provoke" a fratricidal civil war, he said, having "incessantly provoked clashes" at the front line; in preparing a "northern expedition" he had "even gone so far as to collude with our sworn enemy, Japanese militarism." The KPA had now gone over to the counteroffensive, he said, advancing ten to fifteen kilometers into the South, liberating Ongjin, Kaesŏng, and Yŏnan.

Kim called on all the Korean people to rise up, if they did not want again to be a dependency of imperialism; guerrillas must widen the movement, workers must strike, peasants must push the land reform, people must restore the people's committees. His statement gave no details on the alleged southern attack. Internal materials were little better in specifying the exact nature of Rhee's provocation.[54] Mosaic Three is thus barely worth talking about: there is no evidence of a general southern invasion all along the parallel, even in northern materials put out at the time.

"DOCUMENTARY EVIDENCE OF NORTH KOREAN AGGRESSION"

Almost a year after the outbreak of the war, the United States released captured North Korean documents that were said to prove that the North carefully planned and prepared an "unprovoked attack" timed for June 25. Since then most scholarly and official accounts have accepted the validity of these documents, which validate Mosaic One. A secret JCS history said they had been "authenticated as official attack orders," and Appleman also assumed their validity. The North claimed from the beginning that they were forgeries.[55]

The documents in question are "Reconnaissance Order No. 1," said to have been issued in Russian to the Chief of Staff of the KPA Fourth Division on June 18, and "Operations Order No. 1," June 22 in Korean from the commander of the division, Yi Kwŏn-mu. The first document was found in Seoul on October 4, 1950, the second in July, presumably on the battlefield.

Like so much else about the Korean War, this aperture on "whodunit" only dims as it is magnified. For reasons that are not revealed in archival materials, and that do not immediately pop to mind, the decision to declassify the documents (in translated English versions) was made at a high level just as MacArthur was being sacked in April 1951, over the objections of military security people who "have been against the release of this information."[56] We might speculate that the Truman administration wished to hang MacArthur for just one crime, insubordination, and not for others—such as the suspicion by I. F. Stone, then being circulated, that MacArthur had something to do with the start of the war.

The originals have never been found. I was told by two archivists that various agencies of the American government had sought them for many years, to no avail. When the North Koreans again claimed that they were forgeries in 1965, American authorities at P'anmunjŏm urgently contacted the chief of Military History, who could not turn them up. Therefore he turned to General Willoughby in search of the originals (both documents were vetted through Willoughby's Allied Translator and Interpretor Service):

> Extensive search in Depat of Army [sic] records collection and in appropriate retired record depositories has failed to locate these orders. English translations are available but the Military Armistice Commission desires the untranslated versions of these orders. Research revealed that in September 1950, Operation Order No. 1 was in the custody of the ATIS, G-2, GHQ, Far East Command. This is the last known record of location.

Willoughby replied, "the handling of enemy documents was almost routine" (whatever that might mean), and referred the inquiry to two Americans who were Japanese linguists.[57]

The two most important documents of the Korean War, declassified only on high level approval, are missing. The communists claim they are forgeries. Arch anticommunist Willoughby commanded the organization that processed the documents. An urgent request is made to him. Yet all he says is that they were handled routinely (almost), and directs the inquiry on materials in Russian and Korean to low-level employees who read Japanese (where it foundered).

"Reconnaissance Order No. 1"[58] originated with the intelligence staff of the KPA on June 18, and was issued to various military units—although when it was received is not clear. Different instructions went to different units. One to the 3d Border Brigade (the border constabulary, separate from the KPA) stationed near Haeju stated, "A strengthened [ROKA] 17th Regiment is in a defensive position on the Ongjin Peninsula, and in the direction of Enan [Yŏnan] one batallion of the 12th Regiment . . . is also on the defensive. The forward edge of the defense line is along the slopes of the heights at the thirty-eighth parallel." "During preparation for the attack and in time of artillery preparation," the document continued, the 3d Border Brigade should "define more accurately" various things—including surveilling the nearby sea to see if a fleet comes to support or evacuate the enemy.

Accompanying this document was "an intelligence plan of the North Korean army for an attack operation" at an unspecified date, issued in Russian on June 20. Although the North Koreans claimed it had to be a forgery because the Americans translated it as "North Korean army," in fact the Russian version says Korean People's Army (*Koreiskaia narodnaia armiia*). This long, complicated document cited as "objectives" (among others), to uncover what the enemy's "counteraction" would be against "our attack on the South," to "determine precise data on the defense system of the enemy," and the like, with the "period of execution" designated as "16 to 25 June 1950." Another section of the document speaks of a quick march on the South, seizure of Seoul within three days, and some general statements (not plans) about "mopping up operations" in the rest of the peninsula, which the document implied would take about a week after Seoul fell. Although much of the material seems plausible, especially the relative detail on the seizure of Seoul and the absence of detail on what comes next, some of the place names are given in Japanese rendering (but then Americans also used Japanese maps and renderings of place names), and the plan to seize Seoul in three days seems a bit pat (in fact the KPA occupied the capital unexpectedly quickly).

No original of this document is available. A photostat of the Russian-language text shows no departmental markings, signatures, or personal seals; everything is written in the same script. Thus it must be a transcription from the original; in any case it is unverifiable on its face. It is strange that the language is Russian. Few Korean officers could speak or read Russian (most of the generals had served in China and spoke Chinese), and in the multitude of captured Korean army documents I have seen, all were in Korean. (There is far more English interspersed with Korean in ROK documents than there is Russian in North Korean documents, and many southern documents were wholly in English.)

This document becomes less compelling when one knows what the South Koreans have done with it. Both South and North Korean official historiography on the war is composed of half-truths, critical omissions, rank embellishment, and outright lies. The reigning conception in both halves of Korea is to maintain the proper line, not to honor historical accuracy and truth. Anyone who deviates from the line is suspect; saying the other side did not start the war gains a jail sentence. The South is simply more sophisticated in pursuing this conception than the North, so they take in more people—including some American scholars.

If one observes what the South does over time, it first asserts the validity of "Reconnaissance Order No. 1" without question, since this fits its interests, and then goes on to weave one tale after another. A good example is an article in the Seoul press in 1979 on a defector from the North, Lt. Col. Chu Yong-bok. Only a handful of defectors of his middling rank or higher ever came out of the DPRK; nonetheless Chu just happened to be at the right place at the right time: he "personally translated a top secret 'Invasion Operational Order' from Russian into Korean." The article goes on to quote his account of the ten days before the war, weaving together existing documentation with gross falsehood. Some of this just happens to show up in captured materials declassified in Washington two years earlier, which Chu could hardly have seen since he was in Brazil. His account makes the claim that on June 23 "the entire armed forces of north Korea received a war directive from Kim Il-sung, instructing, 'Every member of the People's Army shall complete preparation for combat by today.' " Not only is such an order implausible on its face, but no official American source has ever made such a claim and no POW interviews say that such an order was given.[59]

The mysterious high-level defector Lim Ŭn also claims uncannily to have been critically placed, witnessing KPA shells flying during its attack in the early morning of June 25. A high official in North Korea, Hyŏn Chun-gŭk, tried to convince me in an interview that he had personally witnessed South Korean forces attacking on June 25.[60]

Yi Kwŏn-mu's operations order was said to have been captured in Taejŏn on July 16, 1950. An English translation and a photostat of the Korean version are available.[61] It was issued by the Operations Department of the 4th Infantry Division, at Okke-ri; it carries the classification "extremely secret" (*kŭngp'i*), a common designation in North Korean captured materials of much lesser presumed sensitivity. Although it is dated June 22, it was only received at 0500 hours on June 24. The "smoking gun" passage reads, "The 1st Infantry Regiment of the enemy's 7th Infantry Division is standing on the defensive against our attack"; attack is *konggyŏk*, which could easily mean the kind of assault that had been going on along the thirty-eighth parallel for more than a year. There is nothing to suggest, as Appleman does, that Yi Kwŏn-mu issued an order for an "attack down the Uijongbu corridor," to be joined by the first and third KPA divisions.

Was it an invasion disguised as a minor attack or as summer maneuvers, even from the soldiers themselves and in operational orders to officers? It also stretches credulity to assume that a carefully planned full-scale invasion would result from a document received less than twenty-four hours before the invasion was to begin. Appleman admits that 4th Division officers "told their men that they were on maneuvers,"[62] and furthermore convinced them of it. (POWs almost always believed that the ROK started the war.)

The Korean version of the order is in faint pencil and Yi's name is printed in the same style as the rest of the document. There is no signature or personal seal. Thus it appears to be a Korean transcription from an unavailable original, and as such is unverifiable. The verdict on this document, too, must be: not proved.

The most damning materials vetted by Willoughby's ATIS are not the two reconnaissance orders cited above. I have not seen the Korean originals of the ATIS translations, but the context and wording suggest more plausibility than the two reconnaissance orders. Some loose handwritten sheets in Korean, captured October 14, 1950, list orders and directives from the KPA 2d Division.[63] A combat order in this collection with no date, but obviously no later than June 22, signed by Hyŏn P'a, chief of staff, said the southern border town of Ch'unch'ŏn should be secured within one day. "Combat preparations in the area of concentration will be completed by 1800 hours," June 22, 1950. "The division will commence its march in accordance with the special order." Artillery firing preparations were to be completed by 2400 hours, June 22. Another order, dated June 21 and signed again by Hyŏn P'a, says the 2d Division "will penetrate the Myŏng'gyu-dong defense line, then will occupy Ch'unch'ŏn"; reconnaissance units were to establish observation posts from June 21 onward. This is convincing, except that according to American accounts it would appear that main force KPA units, with tanks, were not committed against Ch'unch'ŏn until the evening of June 26, and this is the one place acknowledged to have had advance warning, as we have seen.

Many POW accounts show that KPA units moved southward toward the parallel from June 20 to 24 (although they do not say that the North attacked first). For example, Yi Mun-uk, with an engineer batallion of the KPA 5th Division, said he left Nanam for Yangyang on June 20, and left Yangyang marching south on June 24; Hŏ Yŏng-guk of the same unit independently gave corroborating information.[64]

A dead soldier's diary recorded the following inconclusive but suggestive sequence: "25 June: arrived at thirty-eighth parallel at about 0100 hours. . . . At about 0515 hours simultaneously with the firing of a flare our army opened artillery fire. . . . At 1400 hours I saw fighting going on south of the thirty-eighth parallel."[65] A top secret reconnaissance order of June 22 called upon observation teams to determine the strength, positions, and firepower of ROKA units across the thirty-eighth parallel.[66] But presumably the same would have been asked of units in May 1949, during the Ongjin Peninsula fighting.

A June 29 "battle report" from three companies in the KPA 3d Battalion said the companies received an order to commence marching at 0330 on June 24: "Reaching the place of departure, [the unit] waited for the order to attack. Began attack at 0503 hours. When crossing *mansei* bridge, met enemy's mines and artillery fire." Some loose handwritten battle accounts signed by a KPA officer named Ok Chae-min included the following, in ATIS's translation:

> On order of the regimental commander of 2nd Battalion started from the concentration point at 0800 hours on the 23rd [of June], and occupied the starting line till 0330 hours on the 24th. The battalion occupied Yongpyong River region in front of Chomili hill . . . and waited for the signal for attack. Artillery firing began at 0440 hours on the 24th. Our troops . . . moved in the direction of Manseri. Then at the signal the infantry occupied the attacking line and all launched a charge.[67]

These are both excellent "smoking gun" documents, with one problem: the guns were smoking a day before the Korean War started (0330, June 24) and must describe some minor border engagements, if they are authentic.

A captured document from the 121st unit of the KPA, "Instruction for Advance in Defensive Action," says this:

> The atrocious traitor Rhee Syngman's puppet government . . . to carry out internecine [warfare] forced the concentration of the so-called "National Defense Army" and "Police" along the thirty-eighth parallel with the intention of invading the northern half, and they continued to attack that area with fire-power . . . [thus we] decided to beat [them] down by military force.

This proves that the North Koreans cynically termed their June aggression an "advance in defensive action," except for one problem: the document is dated January 10, 1950, and refers in the past tense to 1949.[68]

Another document has Ch'oe A-rim, commander of an artillery unit in the 825th KPA detachment, telling his superiors on June 12, 1950 that his unit was not combat-ready; he said they would need at least twenty days to repair weapons, find new sights for mortars, and the like.[69]

OTHER DOCUMENTARY EVIDENCE

The captured North Korean materials that I have used throughout this book include many military orders issued just before the war began. Because they were used by and vetted through American intelligence agencies, the North Koreans will never accept their validity. It is also true that South Korean intelligence had access to this collection just after it was released, if not before, and that archivists later barred unnamed South Korean individuals or agencies from using the collection because of the removal or disappearance of materials.[70] Some apparently crucial documents listed on the long manifest to the collection are missing, therefore; but the possibility also exists of additions to the collection.

For these reasons the scholar must use the collection with care. But short of spending my lifetime trying to validate every item, I can say that most of the materials are unquestionably authentic. They exist in original form in hundreds of archival boxes, and show no traces of any obvious cases of alteration or of much use. Nor do they have the crucial drawbacks of the aforementioned documents: they are not translated, nor are they photostated; one can finger the dusty originals.

It would appear that the highest-level documentation has been held back from declassification, because a State Department study cited central party records, which are not in the collection, in coming to a conclusion of critical importance: "Top secret work plans of the Standing Committee of the Labor Party headquarters dated January–June 1950 make absolutely no reference to the forthcoming invasion, although covering in some detail all other aspects of government policy." Furthermore, several highly placed North Korean officers, including the chiefs of staff of two KPA divisions, "stated that they had only the barest presentiment of the coming of hostilities, and that they were given no concrete indication of their onset until approximately one week before the invasion took place." (Note that this is only presentiment of "hostilities," not of a KPA invasion.) Nor did this official study say a word about captured attack orders, suggesting instead that "it is possible but not proven by current evidence that the Chinese were more massively involved in the preparations for war" than were the Russians.[71]

In general the materials make it obvious that the North Koreans were preparing for conflict in the summer of 1950, and that something important was to occur around June 25—in the best case, major military maneuvers using live ammunition in the immediate area of the thirty-eighth parallel, at worst an invasion. How extended the conflict would be, and who would initiate it, remain open questions. The documentation is not inconsistent with the interpretation that the KPA was kept in a high state of mobilization and readiness awaiting a first provocation by the South, on the experience of the border fighting in the summer of 1949. The collection offers little support to the official American position that the North Koreans stealthily prepared a full-scale and unprovoked invasion. There is no evidence that points to such an interpretation before June 18 or 19, one week before the war. And even on the weekend of June 25, some units were unmobilized and going through routine training.

Sometimes the most suggestive information is the most mundane: for example, a bunch of notebooks compiled by mechanics and technicians as they serviced the fighter planes of the KPA 3d Squadron in the period from April to June 1950. The entries for April show various inspections and servicing, whereas those of June 19, 20, and 22 show the exclusive entry, "airplane preparation" (pihaengi chunbi).[72] A similar set of materials, captured and translated by Willoughby's outfit, contains the following: "By June 20 each [air] group will have 10 fighter planes, completely maintained and satisfactorily prepared for flights at any time. All planes . . . will be fully armed between 12 and 20 June." This is for the purpose of making "the execution of the summer combat training a success," with 80 percent of the relevant personnel to be trained by the end of June. The same document has routine training plans through the end of June, and a summer maneuver schedule through September.[73]

If this seems damning (and the talk of summer training just a cover), air force people will not necessarily find it so. Planes are fully armed and prepared as if for battle in combat games. I have been told by former American pilots that in pursuance of realistic combat training, occasionally they were ordered on bombing runs against North Korea as if it were the real thing, with only a radio at the last minute countermanding the first order and returning them to base.

Large numbers of interview transcripts with North Korean POWs that are now available defy easy summary, but this much can be said: many of them document southward movement toward the parallel from the middle of June to June 22 or 23; most of the POWs believed this was for summer battle maneuvers and war games, although some suspected a war was about to begin; some of the POWs crossed the parallel on June 25 and some did not; the vast majority of the POWs captured in the summer of 1950 thought the South had started the war. That is, even their own experience of moving quickly toward the parallel, being issued live ammunition, being told to prepare as if real battle were in the offing, did not prove to them that the North started the war. A layman finds this hard to understand because laymen are not part of military units that are frequently exercised in the most realistic conditions possible, that is, when the troops are not themselves sure that the maneuvers are not for real.

The POW interviews also are internally contradictory, to the point of incessant negation of the negation. An example would be an unidentified member (no rank given) of the KPA 5th Division named Yi Yong-wŏn, who said he arrived in Yangyang just above the parallel on June 22, and who said that on that date his whole unit (which also is unidentified) "knew they were going to be at war with the South Koreans." Then here is Yi Wŏn-gu, also of the 5th Division, also unidentified as to rank or unit, who arrived in Yangyang and was given seventy rounds of ammunition and four grenades. His unit was told "they were going out on bivouac." At 4:00 A.M. on June 25, his unit "marched to the 38th Parallel and encountered South Korean troops."[74]

All too many similar examples could be cited; in any case the POW testimony, taken by South Koreans and Americans determined to pin aggression on the North, is less compelling than the subsequent judgment by State Department intelligence, discussed above, that most of the KPA general staff also seemed in the dark about the invasion war plan.

A highly classified document dated June 13, 1950, "Political and Cultural Work in Wartime"[75] seems at first to signal a coming assault, since it seeks to prepare troops for "the time of marching" (*haenggun*), with the basic task being "complete readiness"; officers should carefully keep military secrets, watch for spies, and the like. It gives instructions for "political thought" work and for smashing reactionary plots in the "occupied areas." But read as a whole, the document suggests merely that officers and soldiers give all this "deep study," with no indication of the timing or nature of the impending conflict. So, it documents KPA planning for an assault on the South, which is no surprise, but it does not prove that they attacked first, or indeed had plans to in June.

Another document dated June 16 and titled "Combat Bulletin no. 1," classified "absolutely secret," shows extensive preparation of soldiers for battle training which will be carried out "under the nose of the thirty-eighth parallel." Keeping military secrets will be "of the utmost impor-tance," and troops were forbidden to engage in making forecasts [yech'uk kosa] of what was likely to happen. But all this was for "bivouac training" and "strengthening our fighting power," that is, routine military training and maneuvers; one can imagine it happening frequently north of the DMZ today.[76]

Other military documents seem to provide conclusive proof that not all frontline KPA units were part of the invasion on June 25. Several docu-ments on political training of KPA soldiers in early June refer to various regimens—inspections, political training, physical exercise—to be com-pleted by June 30, to assure the success of "summer battle training" (which the context suggests will begin in early July).[77]

A collection of orders issued to the 855th detachment of the KPA in mid-June also embodies routine military training procedure. Only one item looks interesting from hindsight: a secret order of June 20, saying the training lectures scheduled for June 26–27 would not be held as orig-inally planned. But another routine order received on June 24 asked for four drivers to be sent to another unit by June 28.[78]

Reports in May from General Willoughby's Korea Liaison Office[79] picked up information that residents had been evacuated from the par-allel once again in 1950: but not in June, rather in late February, "in anticipation of the 'spring launching' of the South Korean Army into these districts." The North Koreans wanted an "empty zone" as a "first line of defense against South Korea."

The KLO circulated on May 15 an account of a mid-March, six-day meeting of KPA battalion commanders that surveyed the results of the 1949 border fighting. Claiming that the KPA had inflicted 25,000 casu-alties (killed and wounded) on the ROKA in 1949, the survey expected 1950 to be more of the same: "each unit commander must constantly study and prepare for an accidental war." Except, that is, for a reported address to the conference by Kim Il Sung, paraphrased as follows:

The [ROKA], which is supported by the Americans, has poor morale and is defending South Korea rather than intending to attack North Korea. Even [should the ROKA attack the North] . . . we shall easily repulse that puppet group.

In 1949, we defended North Korea only; however in 1950 we will begin the heroic struggle to merge the separated Korea and will achieve a glorious, complete independence.

A smoking gun, no? But then comes the last paragraph:

The only way to obtain a glorious victory is to cause disturbances on the 38th parallel line and have the South Korean Army devote all of its attention to that area while our guerrilla units attack the puppets from the rear. This is the only way to unify our separated country.

On May 25 the KLO G-2 commented that six regular KPA divisions had been garrisoned "roughly in a cross-country belt between the 38th and 39th parallel." But the G-2 thought an invasion would require at least a two-to-one advantage; he therefore thought the North Koreans were trying to build thirteen divisions, which meant waiting for all their China soldiers to return. An invasion was unlikely until the returned manpower was in hand.

Ultimately, this documentation illustrates just how hard it is to estimate the intentions of an army based on incomplete evidence, even four decades after the fact. Some scholars will find in the documents I have cited, or others, "smoking guns" beyond challenge. My reading is that there are some local documents indicating cap-guns going off; few documents are clearly different from what one would find along the parallel during the heavy engagements in 1949. Perspective is important here: scholars cannot get any central documents, to my knowledge, but internal analysts got no damaging evidence from them; and those that were released and claimed to be general orders cannot be trusted. It is quite amazing that this should be the case, given that the United States occupied the North; in that perspective, it is remarkable that the evidence is not better.

My good friend Frank Baldwin and many others have argued both empirically, and logically, to the point that "The coordinated movement of troops, preceded by artillery bombardment, could have been accomplished only after lengthy, careful planning. That such a movement of forces could have been an instantaneous [*sic*] response to a South Korean attack is patently implausible."[80] There is no question that lengthy, careful planning would be required—something that probably began in early 1949, just after Soviet troops left, in any case planning and training that any military commander would have done throughout the summer of 1949 or be relieved for dereliction, in the face of South Korean border assaults and threats to invade. Furthermore, much of the time since 1953 several divisions of the KPA have been poised in offensive formation with high military readiness just north of the DMZ, something the Pentagon never tires of pointing out when military appropriations are debated in Congress. Presumably the South, also, would need to plan its movement of forces toward the parallel in the spring of 1950 and the artillery and mortar that it routinely fired preparatory to its attacks, and that it appears to have poured into the Ŭnp'a-san area from the evening of June 23. That KPA troops were prepositioned, that civilians were moved out, that tank units were gathered, that China-linked divisions were near the parallel is all true: but the same was true in the autumn of 1949.

The evidence is also compatible with an interpretation linking the summer of 1949 to June 1950, that the North waited until it had the majority of its crack soldiers back from China, and then positioned them to take advantage of the first major Southern provocation. Furthermore, we have that tantalizing Soviet radio intercept, giving more than a day's advance warning of an ROKA assault planned for the night of June 25, which would give the North the necessary time secretly to fuse its artillery, gas up its planes and tanks (only fifty tanks were committed by late Sunday, remember), and prepare to settle Rhee's hash once and for all.

Still, the objective reader will now be troubled by Mosaic One, the official American story, and think it quite likely, if not proved. Then let us look at Mosaic Two, which in my view cannot but suggest that either side *could* have started it, which is precisely the tip-off of the civil character of the war and really all that I am interested in saying; ultimately a structural argument is better than this mandatory nitty-gritty empirical slog, and I am far from interested in blaming this old and terrible calamity on one side or the other.

Mosaic Two

Let us assume, for purposes of argument, that Kim Paek-il or Paek Inyŏp, or both, did not merely counterattack across the parallel toward Haeju, but attacked in the night of June 24–25, say about 1:00 or 2:00 A.M., seeking to seize Haeju. What would have been the purpose of such an action, which seems suicidal in retrospect? What possible logic could have motivated the South in attacking? Were South Korean officers capable of this?

First, of course, we have the incontrovertible evidence that Kim Sŏk-wŏn and other commanders did launch attacks across the parallel in the summer and fall of 1949, reportedly seeking to occupy Haeju, and wanted to do more. A document captured by the North Koreans and authenticated by its author, Gregory Henderson, quoted Kim Paek-il in late August 1949. "Col. Kim laid some emphasis on the great sentiment existing in the Army for invasion of the North. . . . Col. Kim stated that he felt 'that the troops needed about six months more training before being really prepared.' "[81] Several authors dismiss the possibility of a southern attack based on Rhee's demeanor in June 1950, but it is not critical to assume that Rhee was necessarily witting to the action; in the Korean context in May-June 1950, with the regime collapsing, such action could have been designed as the prelude to a putsch within the forces of order in the ROK by "nationalists," that is, aggressive officers who did not like American controls, and those like Yi Pŏm-sŏk aligned with Chiang Kai-shek, as a follow-on to the battle for the Rhee state beginning in April. Furthermore Rhee's executive was deeply penetrated by Americans and leaked like a sieve (even to the Apostolic Delegate via Francesca Rhee), and Koreans knew this better than anyone.

What would be the strategy behind an assault on Haeju? Perhaps it would have started what was hoped to be an engagement bigger than those in the summer of 1949, but not an all-out war; a city is seized, the North Koreans respond but in a containable way, and the top-level Americans then in Tokyo are presented with some fairly heavy fighting. Washington is confronted with yet more evidence of aggressive communist action in East Asia. Kim Paek-il, Paek In-yŏp, and Kim Sŏk-wŏn were young and headstrong, and full of confidence—however foolish that may seem in retrospect—after the suppression of the southern guerrillas; Kim Sŏk-wŏn may have proved inept as a commander thereafter, but this was the man whom the Americans sought to control from August through October 1949. And those Americans were absent in June 1950.

Or, perhaps southern intelligence knew that the North would respond by plunging into the South, trying to seize Seoul; perhaps the gathering tanks near the parallel suggested a blitzkreig being readied for later in the summer, and a plunge across the parallel would trigger it early, followed by a rapid pullback for ROK forces—the preferred strategy for dealing with a blitzkreig. In either case, the shrewder and more deniable the provocation the clearer the "aggression"; remote Ongjin was a perfect place to make the cut. The army can pull back quickly, suck the North deep into the South, and get the American commitment that the two Kims and Rhee knew was their only saving hope.

In this regard, furthermore, remember the visit of Capt. Ross Jung to Wellington Koo in June 1949, informing him that a secret understanding existed that American troops in Japan would join the battle if the North attacked and pushed into the South. Remember also John Burton's claim that in the weeks before the war the South was seeking to needle the North into attacking, and that a high-level cover-up then censored cables coming in from Korea. Remember Preston Goodfellow's rendering of his advice to Rhee about placing the onus on the North, and Wellington Koo's retrospective exclamation: "that is strategy!"

In the wider context, the Kim Sŏk-wŏn faction was linked to Yi Pŏm-sŏk, who was in turn the leader of the pro-Chiang faction in Korea; this was the man whom Nationalist emissaries preferred to talk to instead of Rhee, and he and others like him showed a fawning devotion to the generalissimo. The latter knew that an American coup was in the works against him, and that a communist invasion was likely at any time. Henry Luce remarked to Wellington Koo in May that he had been inactive on the China issue, he had the lever but he was looking for the fulcrum: Chiang may have found the fulcrum on the Korean peninsula, the provocation of a war that saved his regime for two more decades, and bid fair to bring Nationalist troops back to the mainland. The Korean War was, in fact, "the fluke that saved Formosa";[82] perhaps it was no fluke.

We have seen that Rusk talked to Hu Shih on the evening of June 23, at a meeting arranged by China Lobbyist Frederick McKee; Rusk thought a coup against Chiang would happen that week, or weekend; "but then the Korean War intervened." T.V. Soong's brother was part of a conspiracy to dump soybeans in Chicago timed for events that were to transpire on the last weekend in June. Hollington Tong had met with Goodfellow in Taipei, was knowledgeable about the coup attempt against Chiang, and flew to Tokyo to meet with Johnson and others after Griffith told Koo that a war would put Johnson in the driver's seat of American policy. The KMT had a key diplomat leading UNCOK, with exact knowledge of the military observation schedule of Peach and Rankin. In one of his last cables from Seoul before the war, Muccio was trying to put his finger on precisely what the Chinese were doing with the Rhee regime. The mysterious Americans who visited Wellington Koo—Shepard, Looney, and Megson—linked to McKee and Willauer, wanted to "pull the trick" on the day that Johnson returned from Tokyo, Saturday morning, June 24. When it was high noon in Washington, it was the dead of night on the Ongjin Peninsula. The candidate for an American intelligence operative who was in touch with Rhee, Chiang, and MacArthur is Preston Goodfellow, who had sped to Korea in September 1949 when Army intelligence indicated a war might begin, and who had reentered the Army by mid-June. This is, at any rate, one mosaic of what *might* have happened; it has the virtue of giving us the lineage of how it *could* have happened—which no previous accounts have ever done.

Sir John Pratt, an Englishman with four decades of experience in the China consular service and the Far Eastern Office, wrote the following in 1951: "The Peking Government planned to liberate Formosa on July 15 and, in the middle of June, news reached the State Department that the Syngman Rhee government in South Korea was disintegrating. The politicians on both sides of the thirty-eighth parallel were preparing a plan to throw Syngman Rhee out of office and set up a unified government for all Korea."

Pratt said that on June 23 Acheson reacted to news from Tokyo that the Taiwan policy had been reversed by denying that this was so, which got back to Tokyo on June 24. (This would refer to Dulles's dispatch from Tokyo, signaling his agreement with MacArthur on defending Taiwan.) Thus the only way out, for Chiang, was for Rhee to attack the North, which ultimately made Acheson yield and defend Nationalist China.[83] Pratt was an unlikely vehicle to convince anyone, however. Most Englishmen found him eccentric; the brother of Boris Karloff, and exhibiting a similar visage, he was a bit spooky and forbidding.

Americans, even fairly knowledgeable ones, are prey to what might be called the fallacy of insufficient cynicism. Muckraking investigative journalists, now and then exceptions to this rule, lack the patience of the scholar, are completely dependent on their sources, and do not usually understand the minds of politicians in high places. Thus I. F. Stone hinted that Dulles might have been involved in a conspiracy with MacArthur and Chiang to provoke war in Korea, and a gaggle of critics descend on this ridiculous conspiracy theory. It is, indeed unlikely that Dulles was anything more than Acheon's messenger in June 1950. But he and Acheson were structurally reconstituting a political economy that was a deadly threat to Korean revolutionaries. And conspiracies do exist, even if Foster Dulles was an implausible participant (his countenance was almost as unlikely as Sir John Pratt's).

Anyone who has read this text closely to this point, and does not believe that Willoughby, Chiang, Wu T'ieh-cheng, Yi Pŏm-sŏk, Rhee, Kim Sŏk-won, Tiger Kim, and their ilk were capable of a conspiracy to provoke a war, cannot be convinced by any evidence. Furthermore, the inadequate cynicism of Hartzian Americans leads to the curious consequence that well-established facts are swept from a memory that does not wish to believe them.

Fletcher Prouty, who for many years briefed the White House on intelligence operations, wrote that the clandestine operator "prepares the stage by launching a very minor and very secret, provocative attack of a kind that is bound to bring reprisal." Often third parties or mercenaries are chosen for this task; the first strike "takes place in deep secrecy . . . no one knows this hidden key fact." This, he says, "is the fundamental game of the secret team." The covert action, Prouty says, is "enmeshed with and enhanced by concealed drives of the special interest groups." (We might add that the early 1950s were more vulnerable to "special interests" than any other period, with military intelligence, the CIA, Tokyo G-2, Chiang Kai-shek, and many others scrapping for turf within the American state.)

Innocent and patriotic men come upon the scene "after the first provocations have been made," according to Prouty; the CIA will brief the
National Security Council (NSC) (without telling them about the first
deep cut, or perhaps they don't know about it either); the next step is to
declare that the enemy's response constitutes "aggression," and then
bring the nation in behind the administration's actions. Prouty says this
was first tried, amateurishly, in Greece in the late 1940s, and then again
in Vietnam—perhaps he refers to the Tonkin Gulf incident. He noted
Allen Dulles's definition of intelligence as "the catalytic element that trig-
gers response."[84]

The North Koreans, with their combination of unworldly solipsism
and short fuses, are perfect targets for this sort of provocation. Former
intelligence officers have remarked that when they have nothing better
to do, they try to dupe and pin something on North Korean diplomats.

Senatorial and other inquiries into the activities of American intelligence agencies have demonstrated that in several cases, agents provocateurs sought to get the other side (especially Castro in Cuba) to commit
some action which would then be used to justify an assault or invasion.
Two knowledgeable authors write that the CIA intended "to mount a
fake attack on Guantanamo that would make Castro look like an aggressor and justify direct American intervention"; within the CIA "the theme
was always the same: Get something started to overtly call in the military
and follow up with complete seizure and installation of a favorable government." The president was not to be witting, of course, but the principals also mulled over "how much [Allen] Dulles [Director of the CIA] was
to be cut in on the full extent of the provocation incident."[85]

Similar activity marked the 1980s rollback effort along the borders of
Nicaragua, with the Contra war, the mining of Nicaraguan harbors and
the like. One of the people involved in organizing the Contras was Gen.
Richard Stilwell, who in 1950 was the CIA chief for East Asia, and a close
associate of Whiting Willauer and Hans Tofte. When a Thames Television team approached him about an interview in 1986, he also recommended that they interview James Hausman and Paek Sŏn-yŏp—which
they did.[86]

All this is of more than passing interest in a tense situation in which
Rhee and Chiang were deeply threatened from within and without, and
wanted containment first and rollback later, whereas Acheson, committed in his own mind to defending both territories, wanted to remove
Chiang, and wanted the communists to strike first along the containment
periphery. In the summer of 1950, Henry Wallace wrote an angry letter
to Dean Acheson, citing evidence that Rhee might have started the war.
Acheson responded in vehement disagreement, but with one of the most
interesting Freudian slips in American history. "No serious, honest

scholar can ever have any question about it. North Korean Communist forces attacked the Republic of Korea without warning, with provocation [*sic*] and without justification."[87]

Ultimately, however, the new evidence still does not prove that South Korean elements attacked first in the early morning hours of June 25, 1950. If they did, two additional points must be made: first, this does not gainsay clear evidence of North Korean preparation to take advantage of such a provocation with an invasion of the South; it merely makes the North Korean action more justifiable in the Korean context. Second, if indeed there were attacks across the parallel by the South, given that two companies of ROKA soldiers deserted from the parallel a year earlier, one could not exclude the possibility that the provocation might have been engineered by fifth-column elements, thus to justify a North Korean invasion.

Now I can hear the chorus: too clever by half, you're around the bend now. So, listen to Dulles at an NSC meeting after the war ended, when he worried that the North might start it up again. "He thought it quite possible that the Communists would launch their attack by infiltrating ROK units and staging an attack on the Communist lines in order to make it appear as though hostilities had been started on ROK initiative."[88] One wishes not to be less incredulous than Foster Dulles, who peered across the parallel into the North on June 19, and who spent the rest of his life with unsettling whispers from that sudden Sunday, as if Banquo's ghost were shaking his gory locks. At several high-level meetings Dulles worried aloud that the United States would not know how a new war might start in Korea, and that Rhee might well start it. At the 168th meeting of the NSC in October 1953, Dulles said "all our efforts" must be to forestall a resumption of war by Rhee; in 1957 at the 332nd meeting he still worried that Rhee might "start a war"; two weeks later, "If war were to start in Korea . . . it was going to be very hard indeed to determine which side had begun the war." This time President Eisenhower had something to say in response: in such a circumstance the United States would do "what the French had said to the Russians at the outbreak of war in 1914, that is: 'France will do whatever is in its own best interests.' "[89] Ike had an impeccably Achesonian point.

The Intelligence Failure: A "Curious Set of Mosaics"

If we assume that there was no southern provocation on the night of June 24–25, just the start of the northern invasion, another question then arises. Did anyone see it coming? If so, why did they not attempt to stop it, blow the whistle against this atrocious act of aggression? As we have seen, American intelligence was split into several different tendencies, each with its own interests, each at odds with other agencies. In Tokyo, Willoughby claimed to have predicted the attack, while MacArthur told everyone within earshot how much it surprised him. In Washington Truman was outraged that no one had warned him, and everyone expressed amazement about the attack (one that several major newspapers, not to mention the ROK defense minister, had warned against in May)—except, it appeared at first, the CIA, which was said to have predicted an imminent invasion on June 19. South Korean intelligence is another matter; to my knowledge there is no reliable information on what they knew and when they knew it.

Louis Johnson had arrived back in the United States on the morning of June 24, uncharacteristically keeping his own counsel for the next few days; the only evidence I have found of his initial reaction to the news was to tell Arthur Krock of the *New York Times* that "no one had expected the Korean thing . . . our intelligence showed for weeks on weeks every Sunday morning North Koreans made forays southward across the parallel, raised a little ruckus and then withdrew back on their side of the line." Instead, in Tokyo Johnson had learned of MacArthur's "grave fears of a Communist attack on Formosa," his intelligence showing "150,000 Chinese commies" massed across from the island.[90]

When some senators later asked Johnson what Tokyo's intelligence looked like just before the war, he responded that "nothing was said about any immediacy of trouble in Korea," and repeated the story that the KPA came across the line every Sunday morning. In remarks deleted at the time and released in 1975, Johnson said that Willoughby had told them the Kremlin's next move would be in Iran, and had said nothing about trouble in Korea.[91]

This is a strange thing. No one expected anything to happen in Iran in mid-1950, and Willoughby never expressed the slightest interest in that country, nor had he any intelligence apparatus there. Furthermore, in a letter to Willoughby of June 29, 1950, Johnson lead off with the line that "I'm reminded now of your most accurate summation of the Korean intelligence . . ." (the ellipsis is in the French style, suggesting there is more to be said). His sidekick Paul Griffith left Wellington Koo with the impression, on June 28, "that the North Korean attack had not been unexpected."[92] Little more can be said here about this contradiction, however, given that Johnson's papers are so picked clean of usable information as to make one wonder if this was the same man who was once secretary of defense. Omar Bradley wrote that he, Acheson and Truman all wondered if Johnson might not be insane.[93] It seems that everyone who does not quite fit the scenario for what is supposed to have happened on June 25 is insane, senile, a communist, or Boris Karloff's brother.

What about Willoughby, another "lunatic" to liberals? Johnson's June 29 letter does not turn up in his papers. But he did say for the rest of his life that he had warned Washington about a North Korean attack in June. In a *mea non culpa* scripted in 1951, Willoughby wrote, "All aspects of the preparations for military operations under way behind the 'little iron curtain' in North Korea were under scrutiny by intelligence agencies under G-2 . . . few, if any, of the activities of the North Korean Government escaped the attention of intelligence gathering and reporting agencies."[94]

On March 10, 1950, Willoughby sent to Washington a weekly report warning that the North would invade the South in June 1950. On May 25, his G-2 reported that six regular KPA divisions were garrisoned between the thirty-eighth and thirty-ninth parallels. (Border Constabulary elements, however, were reported to be "of low strength on a peace footing.")[95]

In other accounts, including his later book on MacArthur, Willoughby continued the line that he had predicted the attack. It is clear, however, that he did not (at least not for Washington's consumption). The March 10 report, as Acheson later pointed out, had within it a notation that G-2 did not credit the invasion report. On March 25, Tokyo G-2 said it did not expect an attack in the summer of 1950.[96] The May 25 report had within it the judgment that successful offensive operations require a two-to-one advantage, and since by his estimate six KPA divisions faced five ROK divisions, they were not likely to attack. Willoughby made hash of the important distinction between capabilities and intentions, saying the North had the capability for an attack, then that it did not, then that intentionality and the decision on timing would come from the Kremlin, and Kremlin intentions were for Washington to figure out. No one reading his reports, as they are now available, would have predicted an attack on June 25, 1950.

Willoughby's vehemence on this issue is probably related to the experience of Pearl Harbor, when he and MacArthur left lots of planes huddled together on airfields in the Philippines, sitting ducks for Japanese aircraft to devastate them many hours after the attack at Pearl. Although Admiral Kimmel became the scapegoat for the "intelligence failure" at Pearl Harbor, many thought MacArthur's lapse was worse.[97] In this light it is interesting that MacArthur should have been so quick to express his "complete surprise" at the Korean attack, the second time in a decade he was caught with his pants down.

Willoughby's various accounts do, however, suggest something that never seemed to faze him: that *Tokyo and Seoul* expected an attack for weeks before it occurred, but chose to do nothing to head it off. Willoughby wrote, as for the "alleged 'surprise' " on June 25, "the entire South Korean Army had been alerted for weeks and was physically in position along the thirty-eighth parallel." Whereas the CIA had but four operatives in North Korea, he had sixteen, who presumably fed him information about the coming attack. He thought he was pilloried for this alleged "intelligence failure" only because he lacked political backing in Washington.[98] This bothered him much more than the contradictions involved in both the ROKA and the American forces in Japan being on alert for three weeks, his allegedly telling Johnson and Bradley that everything was fine in Korea, then claiming in retrospect that he saw it all coming.

G-2 intelligence summaries for May and June show evidence of the southward movement toward the parallel of China returnees, thought to be distinct units from the regular KPA. In mid-May, G-2 reported that some civilians had been moved from the thirty-eighth parallel area, but it thought this might have been done in February 1950; later it concluded that it was done in April and May, yet it was thought to be for defensive, not offensive purposes. G-2 also thought it might be a type of corvée for agricultural work during the spring rice-transplanting season (which was probably closest to the truth). Six months before the war, MacArthur's G-2 recorded similar arrivals of reinforcements along the parallel, "potentially offensive" in nature; but their assumption was that the troops were built up "to forestall any attacks by the [South] Korean Army."[99] American observers put themselves in the shoes of the North Koreans, knowing about southern aggressiveness, and found the military buildup understandable; after all, as we have seen, the North was just reaching the force levels that the South had accomplished by August 1949.

Many G-2 reports have much more information on Korea than on China, making a mockery of MacArthur's claim that his intelligence had no interest in the peninsula. But there is no evidence in the existing G-2 materials to suggest even *concern* about an impending invasion, let alone a specific prediction. There is absolutely nothing new in the June issues, nothing that was not reported as far back as the fall of 1949. The only prediction in the files is a Chinese Nationalist report supposedly issued on June 21, saying that the North was going to attack the South, but giving no timing. The Nationalist estimate was not reported until June 29, so it is anyone's guess whether it was actually made on June 21.[100]

Much more interesting is the evidence that the United States made electronic and perhaps visual or photographic reconnaissance flights along the Korean coast. Although reports from this source are still classified, the flights had resumed on June 10, after an unexplained moratorium in the spring of 1950. They were described as "electronic reconnaissance operations" and "aerial reconnaissance"; the aircraft were instructed to stay at least twenty nautical miles from the Soviet Union, China, and North Korea.[101] Although cloud cover just before the war would have inhibited such intelligence-gathering, it is implausible to imagine that the North Koreans could make hasty preparations in mid-June for an invasion by 50,000 troops without being detected by such methods.

It is known also that the United States had signals and electronic intelligence mechanisms on the ground in South Korea; one document mentions 352 personnel in Field Station 8609 AAU, "operational prior to the Korean War." The National Security Agency refuses to declassify signals intelligence from 1950, however, so there is no possibility of judging exactly what was known before June 25. But a well-informed former intelligence official has something interesting to say about signals intelligence. The North Korean communications deception plan, William Corson says, was "a conscious effort not to increase the volume of their radio traffic . . . [they] had disguised tactical orders and instructions in innocuous [*sic*] administrative messages. In essence, this produced a kind of 'radio silence.' " Well, in essence this produced not "radio silence," but *no evidence* of radio silence, just routine messages. Yet during the war it became clear that twenty-four to forty-eight hours of radio silence was the standard KPA procedure before an attack. This provides no evidence whatsoever about a North Korean invasion, only retrospective judgment on *why* no battle orders were picked up, why evidence of impending attack does not appear in the G-2 records that presumably filtered electronic intelligence upward.[102]

A close look at Tokyo's intelligence failure, in other words, turns up as many questions as it answers. What about MacArthur himself? William R. Mathews met MacArthur as Dulles left his office at 7:00 P.M. on June 25; MacArthur described the attack as "a complete surprise"; Roberts had just told him three days earlier that an attack was unlikely. He also called it "an act of international banditry; inexcusable, unprovoked aggression"; if we don't meet this one, he said, "there will be another and another."

MacArthur swore Mathews to secrecy and then said he had already dispatched two LSTs, "loaded with munitions." "I have done this on my own . . . I am ready to go to any length with my air power." He and Dulles, MacArthur said, "are in nearly complete agreement on everything." MacArthur also met Carl McCardle of the *Philadelphia Bulletin* on June 25, and told him, "Russians are Oriental, and we should deal with them as such . . . they are mongrels."

At 9 P.M. Mathews met Dulles, who said he had fired off a telegram urging the commitment of American ground forces to Korea, which had been held up for two hours by officers wondering if Dulles "had the right to send a telegram . . . equivalent to a declaration of war." Flying back to the United States with Dulles, Mathews learned that American forces in Japan "had been on alert for three weeks."[103] MacArthur's precipitate actions in sending weaponry and pledging air power on the evening of June 25 would support the assertion of Capt. Ross Jung that there was, after the June 1949 troop withdrawal, a secret understanding that American force would return should the South be attacked. They do not prove it, either. But MacArthur's behavior in the wake of the Sunday morning news is hardly that of a man taken completely unawares, in an existing situation where American policy allegedly had written South Korea off in the event of an attack.

Dulles had a different version of MacArthur's behavior, saying that, in John Allison's rendering, CINCFE went from "jaunty disdain" of the North Korean invasion, viewing it as a "reconnaissance in force," to "abject despair" by Tuesday, June 27. Allison probably referred to Dulles's memo of June 29, 1950, "Notes on Korea," where he said MacArthur was not promptly informed about the attack, and then did not take it seriously until the third day: "it seems to have been assumed that the attack was a purely North Korean adventure, carried out without the Soviet planning, preparation and backing which would assure its success." Truman told Eben Ayers on July 1 that he "should have heard" what Dulles said on his return from Tokyo.

> MacArthur knew nothing of [the news of war in Korea] and [Dulles] was unable to get any of the General's staff to call MacArthur. All of them were afraid to. So Dulles did it himself. Dulles, the President indicated, would like to have MacArthur hauled back to the United States but the President pointed out to him that the General is involved politically in this country . . . and that he could not recall MacArthur without causing a tremendous reaction.[104]

One wonders if this was Dulles's real view, or something said to ingratiate himself with Truman.

The usually reliable Alvary Gascoigne, with excellent access to MacArthur, lost his logic in his account of SCAP when the war broke. He related that the attack "came as a complete surprise to everybody both [in Tokyo] and Korea," but also that military intelligence had learned in April "that preparations were being made for such an attack." This meant that the Americans should have made up their minds about what to do "when the storm broke." Clayton James remarked that "the real MacArthur will always remain elusive," since the general "was a master at role-taking": elsewhere he caught "the streak of showmanship that is part and parcel of the man."[105]

All this is unquestionably true, but it makes the task of unpacking MacArthur's actions rather difficult: we now have him on June 25 alternatively unaware, completely surprised, determined to meet the attack, disdainful, terming the invasion a reconnaissance, calling it international banditry, sending munitions with no approval from Washington, desiring to settle with the Soviet "mongrels," ready to go to any length with air power, and, two days later, in abject despair.

In 1951 he merely chose to bamboozle Congress, telling them he "didn't have anything to do" with intelligence collection in Korea, and when pressed, "I fancy that it was the South Korean Government" which had intelligence responsibility. Without blinking he then went on to say, since Korea was adjacent to Japan, "I would have been vitally interested" in intelligence information. Only once did his dissembling skills escape him. When Sen. Wayne Morse asked him if General Lemnitzer had requested that MacArthur make "immediate shipment of military supplies to South Korea" just *before* the outbreak of the war, he responded in good Watergate fashion, "I have no recollection of it."[106]

In Washington, a controversy broke over whether there had, indeed, been any "intelligence failure." The head of the CIA, Roscoe Hillenkoetter, testified before the Senate Appropriations Committee in executive session on June 26, and left the impression with the senators, which was then leaked to several reporters, that the CIA was not only well aware of North Korean capabilities for invasion, but had predicted the timing as well. He referred in particular to a CIA report of June 19 that an attack on the South was immediately impending. This report is said to have cited the evacuation of civilians just north of the parallel; recent, heavy concentrations of troops and tanks; and rapid troop movements. The mystery deepens in that officials with the requisite clearances have not been able to find this report, and Hillenkoetter's June 26 testimony was not recorded.

The *New York Times* said that Senators Knowland and Bridges, who had immediately charged that the administration was caught "flatfooted" by the invasion, suddenly expressed satisfaction with the CIA after Hillenkoetter's testimony. Alisdair Cooke of the *Manchester Guardian* wrote that Hillenkoetter said that the CIA "was prepared for an invasion this week or next and had ships ready to evacuate [American] families" in South Korea.[107]

The *Times* had reported that Hillenkoetter "could offer no explanation why the receiving agencies had failed to interpret the indications he furnished as evidence of a move to be undertaken soon." Thus other Washington bureaucracies quickly leaped to the attack, for if this were true, then the Pentagon and the NSC were the culprits, not the CIA, for failing to act on the June 19 warning. Instead of an intelligence failure, there would be an implementation failure. Declassified top secret materials from the Defense Department say that, although officials were not sure precisely what Hillenkoetter said in the Senate, the CIA had really only reported a North Korean capability for an attack, not an estimation of intentions, and no timetable. After being accused by senators on June 27 of being "caught off guard," General Lemnitzer and Major General Burns asserted that no intelligence agency "had focused attention on Korea as a point of *imminent* Communist attack" (emphasis in original). Lemnitzer said, "the attack was a surprise to me." He then went on to review "all available CIA reports," none of which cited an impending attack. But these did not appear to include the June 19 warning; or if they did (the memo is not clear on this point), no one can find the report so that an independent assessment of it could be made.[108]

Part and parcel of this bureaucratic covering of the rear end was an attempt to paint Hillenkoetter as sadly incompetent, failing to grasp even the elementary distinction between capability and intentions; once again the official story on June 25 is contradicted only by the incompetent, the insane, and the Frankenstein look-a-likes. Hillenkoetter did not write the June 19 report, however—it was said to have come in from the field—and its disappearance is a bit of a problem.

George Kennan's analysis of the June 1950 situation also deserves quotation at length, conjuring yet more possibilities.

> In the staff [in early June] we got the distinct impression, from reading a series of intelligence reports, that the Russians did plan some sort of military initiative, somewhere. We examined the whole situation . . . reports from the satellite countries, that indicated meetings of satellite leaders, and a few cryptic things said by satellite people had been picked up that indicated something was going to happen. And we examined this from every angle . . . we convinced ourselves that they must be planning some sort of military action through satellite forces which would not commit the Red Army. And with that in mind, we held a series of briefings with our intelligence people in the Department, and went all around the periphery and the only place to which we did *not* [sic] give detailed attention was Korea, because the moment we mentioned that they said the intelligence from our own military people was that the South Korean Army was so strong that an attack . . . by the North Koreans was out of the question, that the question was rather the opposite one; whether we could restrain Rhee and the South Koreans from taking after North Korea. And on the basis of that, we left that and went on to the other places and came out completely baffled.

Acheson then interjected, "this intelligence did not come from Depart-mental sources, because we didn't have any sources there—it came from MacArthur's headquarters."[109]

Now, this gives a far different picture than what we have heard thus far. The CIA predicts, on June 14, a capability for invasion at any time. No one disputes that. Five days later, it predicts an impending invasion. Some dispute that judgment, but the report is missing. Kennan says that no one paid attention to Korea—except to worry about the South attack-ing—and Acheson says we had only MacArthur's intelligence, when there were fifteen committees collecting intelligence on Korea.

Kennan's staff was actually watching Eastern Europe on the last week-end in June, as ominous troop movements were reported in Bulgaria near the Yugoslav border. The *New York Times* on June 23 reported a Belgrade claim that Bulgarian troops, in full battle dress and with ar-mored support, were moving toward Yugoslavia; it said "armed provo-cations" along the border were more worrisome in the past month. A sanitized CIA report of June 27 noted the movement under blackout of special trains toward the same frontier.[110]

This information might suggest three scenarios: that the USSR sought to divert attention from Korea; that the Korean War saved Yugoslavia from invasion; or that the troops were moved because of fear of another rollback attempt in Albania, which was about one hundred miles away from Bulgaria through Yugoslav territory. Most likely, the movements were merely designed to intimidate Tito. In any case, they would account for Kennan's worries about Soviet military action, using satellite troops.

The knowledgeable William Corson has a fine discussion of the diffi-culties of predicting a military attack.

> Two basic streams of intelligence information, those from electronic and human sources, may be likened to two rivers starting from a trun-cated mountain with one (the electronic) rushing down the mountain's steep side and ending up in a stagnant pool, the other meandering down its gentle slope and emptying into the sea, where its meaning and character become lost as it merges with other extraneous streams of information.[111]

From this miasma comes "a curious set of mosaics," each predicting op-posite outcomes. Anyone who has waded through reams of periodic in-telligence reports knows the truth of this formulation. Another sterling analyst of intelligence flows, Ronald Lewin, wrote that the vast capabili-ties of modern intelligence collection, and the immense variety of enemy options and possibilities thereby revealed, put before the historian "the most stringent demands . . . to recall how things looked *at the time* [sic]."[112]

As an example, we can take an intelligence report from Hong Kong in early March 1950 that cited Chinese Communist sources to the effect that North Korea would try to organize a rebellion in the southwest of Korea in June, and after it develops, attack across the parallel. Prescient, no? But the G-2 discounted the prediction, because another source said the USSR had so far "curbed the North Korean determination to take drastic steps, so that the US may be kept from taking a firmer attitude." A good, pregnant comment (unless the USSR had no curbing powers on the North). This same source went on to relate, "With a view to retrieving their fortune [*sic*], the Chinese Nationalists may conduct intrigue activities to cause armed conflict between the US and the USSR . . . thus the situation in Korea may make a great change in 1950 [*sic*]." Knowing what the reader knows now, would one say scenario one is most likely, scenario two, scenario three, or all of the above, perhaps conjoining and commingling at the same time?[113]

So what Corson and Lewin have to say is well taken. But when Corson gets to the intelligence failure in Korea, he is no help. He begins by saying that "more than fifteen separate watch committees" were surveilling Korea, and were to sound the alarm "if hostile military actions were imminent." This unexpectedly extensive network of intelligence surveillance he dates from mid-1949, that is, the time of the troop withdrawal and Rhee's provocative behavior at the parallel. At the top, however, interdepartmental committees could not sort out all the incoming reports, owing in part to "the 'hole card' game which was played with intelligence information under the sole control of a given [intelligence] community member."

He cites the CIA's June 14 report, giving the North the capability to invade, but not addressing their intentions. He does not mention the June 19 report. He does say that Truman was furious with Hillenkoetter for failing to warn him, which might indicate that Hillenkoetter was also covering his rear in his June 26 testimony. But remember also Corson's judgment that Truman, unlike Roosevelt, took his intelligence in summarized form. Corson notes that Hillenkoetter was hardly "the master of America's intelligence house," usually being bypassed outright by Frank Wisner, head of covert operations in the Office of Policy Coordination. Since, as we have seen, electronic snooping seems not to have given an indication of North Korean intentions, Corson points out that this left the question of intentions to "human intelligence," that is, covert operators of which, according to Willoughby, the CIA had four in North Korea. One of them was James Kellis, as we have seen, a soldier-of-fortune type connected to "Wild Bill" Donovan. Another source cites the presence of one Mr. Yun, who is said to have given advance warning of an attack, perhaps through a southern liberal named Sŏl Chŏng-sik, who appeared to have cast his lot with P'yŏngyang and was later executed for treason.[114]

Now, Corson also says that the June 14 report leaked out to "informed circles," and thus "it was feared that administration critics in Congress might publicly raise the issue. In consequence, a White House decision of sorts was made to brief Congress that all was well in Korea." The reader once again will need help with such logic: the CIA says on June 14 that North Korean capabilities, in Corson's paraphrase, "had reached the point where its forces could invade South Korea at any time." Thus a decision is made "to brief Congress that all was well in Korea." Allegedly this was because Congressional critics might "raise the issue." (Then the attack comes, and Congressional critics do, indeed, "raise the issue.") Would it not be the expectation that Congress would be told that all was *not* well in Korea? That is, unless a surprised and outraged Congress is one's goal.

The logic gets more tenuous when we learn that Dean Rusk was chosen for this task, knee-deep in coup plots against Chiang Kai-shek, and that he did it on June 20, the day after the CIA's June 19 report (which Corson does not mention and which no one can find, but which Rusk, one of the top three decision makers in the administration by this time, would presumably see—although he told me in an interview that he did not see it). After lauding the ROKA for its commitment to "a free and independent Korea," and praising its success in reducing incidents along the parallel, he told the Congressmen in executive session, "We see no present indication that the people across the border have any intention of fighting a major war for that purpose [taking over South Korea]. I should inform the committee—could I have a minute off the record on this, Mr. Chairman?" Corson, who seems to know everything, asserts that in the unretrievable off-the-record testimony, Rusk "further waffled the details of the North Korean build-up mentioned in the CIA [June 14] estimate."[115]

Gen. Ridgway later said of Rusk's June 20 testimony, "I was shocked when I read that because it was so perfectly evident, we'd gotten a flow of warning messages through there [Korea] all the time, a lot of them emanating from Rhee, but [there were] constant probings by the North Korean forces across the border."[116]

Another piece in this puzzle is a letter from William Knowland (who heard Hillenkoetter's testimony) to Herbert Hoover, a year later, seeming to imply that there had been advance warning of an invasion.[117] Furthermore the day *before* Hillenkoetter's testimony, that is, the day the war broke out, Robert F. Whitney, a *New York Times* Washington correspondent, reported a statement from Hillenkoetter "that his agency was aware that conditions existed in Korea that could have meant an invasion this week or next," and furthermore, "At the Pentagon . . . an aide said privately that the United States expected the attack and had made all the preparations that could be made." The aide said in particular that ships had been readied to evacuate Americans, "as evidence that the invasion was not a surprise." Whitney went on to say, "The fact that the Government had taken no diplomatic steps was cited by some observers in the capital as evidence that the invasion was not specifically anticipated by intelligence sources."[118] That is, unless one does not want a diplomatic step, and wants a surprised and outraged United Nations.

Whitney also said that observers thought Truman would not have gone to Independence if he thought an attack was coming. We have seen that Truman was outraged because Hillenkoetter told him nothing. As Prouty noted, the best strategy is for the president himself to be unwitting, which is easier with one who takes his intelligence reports in digested form. Then you get the maximal outcome, a surprised president.

Close readers will remember that it was none other than General Lemnitzer whom Wayne Morse named in questioning MacArthur in 1951 about reports that military supplies were dispatched to Korea in advance of June 25: "I have no recollection of it" was MacArthur's response. And it is Lemnitzer and General Burns (the latter deeply involved in covert operations on Taiwan) who take upon themselves the task of discrediting Hillenkoetter. There are three other pieces of evidence indicating that Morse was on to something: first, about five days before the war began, General Ridgway requested information on naval aircraft "Hellcats," small gunboats, and other military aid items destined for Indochina which might be diverted to Korea.[119]

Second, Wellington Koo related a story told him by Gen. Ho Shih-lai in 1970, who replaced Chu Shih-ming in Tokyo in May, 1950. "He had never mentioned [it] to anybody else," Koo said. Ho told him,

> when war in Korea was approaching in June, with North Korea about to attack South Korea, Gen. MacArthur in Japan sent Admiral Cooke . . . to ask the Generalissimo for Chinese troops to be sent to South Korea to check the North Korean invasion. The Generalissimo accordingly designated General Chou Chih-jou to negotiate with Admiral Cooke. . . . The discussions were still going on, when the war in Korea actually broke out.[120]

Cooke was in Tokyo for the Johnson-Bradley meetings, and returned to Taiwan before June 25.

Most curious of all is the news that came creeping into the letters column of *Army* magazine in 1985, that in the week of June 19, 1950, the Pentagon "approved, printed, and distributed" a plan called SL-17, which assumed a KPA invasion, a retreat to and defense of a perimeter at Pusan, followed by an amphibious landing at Inch'ŏn. Clay Blair wrote soothingly that the Pentagon "produced war plans for every conceivable contingency,"[121] but this is the first time we have heard that it also specialized in clairvoyance—just when the CIA predicted an imminent invasion, with a request for war materiel to be diverted to Korea shortly after that.

Once again, conclusions cannot be drawn here, but must await declassification of materials that would shed more light on this particular part of the story. It makes legitimate, however, the speculation that a small group of officials in Tokyo and Washington saw the attack coming, prepared to meet it, and then let it happen—while keeping Congress in the dark, then and thereafter.

An alternative scenario, another mosaic, would question whether anyone saw the attack coming, whether the CIA's June 19 report (if there was such a report), was right in saying that the North was preparing an imminent invasion. Instead, the quickening of American support for and attention to Korea circa June 14 would be based on a coming southern provocation, with MacArthur or Chiang (or both) witting, but regular officials in the containment current (Ridgway, the Pentagon, maybe Rusk) supplied with disinformation about North Korean intentions; perhaps cowboys in the rollback current work with Tokyo or Taipei to thicken the stew. Some officials secretly prepare to contain the attack for Achesonian reasons; others prepare to provoke the attack to save the generalissimo's hide. The reader will want to refer back to chapter 15 to see why this timing is so suggestive. But it is just a scenario.

THE MOSAIC OF PREFERENCE

What is the *most likely* mosaic? There is no question now that movement toward war quickened in mid-June. Appleman rightly dates the rapid southward deployment of the KPA from June 15,[122] but was it for invasion or for summer war games? We have documented that the North carried out major military exercises just before the war. Corson says the following:

> The movement of war materiel was detected and traced as moving in ever increasing quantities from the Soviet Union via Manchuria into North Korea. Significantly, this logistical flow provided hard intelligence showing that the Soviets were building up the North Korean supplies of ammunition and petroleum products, the basic ingredients consumed in an attack. At the time, American intelligence about North Korean forces in terms of training hours, vehicle utilization, and ammunition authorizations for training purposes was quite good, and the

analysis of the build-up suggested in one example that the North Koreans had received in one three-week period the equivalent of twenty years' artillery shells (based upon the training level which had remained constant for the previous three years).

The invasion then came, Corson says, when the North Koreans, who "had been detected 'exercising,' turned south and crossed the thirty-eighth parallel."[123] That is unquestionably what happened. But what made them turn south, on June 25? The structure of action was in place, but what explains the timing?

OTHER sources do not agree with Corson that the logistical buildup pointed toward an invasion. MacArthur said on June 28 that "there is no evidence of a logistic buildup in northern Korea to support extensive operations"; the CIA said at that time that such a buildup "may have occured over the past year" (that is, not in the months just before the war). But subsequent CIA information was that "intelligence reports do not indicate pre-invasion stockpiling (of combat equipment) of a magnitude required to support current operations."[124]

By and large the only equipment the Americans captured that could clearly have been new equipment stockpiled for an invasion were trucks with low mileage on their odometers. In September 1950, MacArthur had "physical proof" of only ten military items delivered to the Koreans in 1949 and 1950—some machine guns, grenades, radio receivers, and the like. As we have seen, KPA military equipment included "surplus Soviet stocks" of World War II vintage, much of it left behind by departing Soviet troops, captured American weaponry gotten from the Nationalists in Manchuria, and stocks of Japanese equipment, both that left in place in 1945 and that manufactured in North Korea in former Japanese arsenals.[125] Soviet aviation gas did come into Manchuria in early 1950, but the CIA thought it was for Chinese air power, to cover the invasion of Taiwan.

The knowledgeable Walter Sullivan said the North's "feverish" mobilization, according to American intelligence officers, only began after the United States came into the war; it "had not carried out its mobilization plan at the time the war began." When Muccio telephoned Tokyo intelligence sources on the morning of June 25, he was told that there was nothing unusual showing up, anywhere in the world. The KMAG G-2 report flow also showed no evidence of an impending invasion, and KMAG officials went beyond that in telling reporters on June 25, "there had been no intelligence reports of troop movements or concentration of supplies."[126]

Corson's information does not acknowledge four things: a similar buildup in the summer and fall of 1949; the DPRK's substantial capability to manufacture its own ammunition; the flow of tens of thousands of Korean soldiers back through Manchuria from the Chinese civil war, carrying with them tons of ammunition and other equipment; and the inevitable change in "training schedules" that would come with the KPA nearly doubling in a few months. It is sophistry to present the North Korean buildup as an artifact merely of late spring 1950, when the same evidence existed in the fall of 1949, and to dwell on this while ignoring the rapid movement of ROKA troops from the interior to the parallel in the same period, which make the KPA actions understandable.

British sources noted that by the end of the summer, 1950, captured documents and POW interviews had still not shed light on how the invasion occurred; they also remained in the dark about the June 25 timing. The Soviets might have wanted to give the United States a slap in the face because of the peace treaty issue; M. E. Dening wrote, "this would account for the timing, which is otherwise a complete puzzle." One perspicacious reporter found it incredible that a military commander would choose to start a war at the beginning of the rainy season, and thought this indicated the North did not plan to push beyond Seoul.[127]

Again: the North was exercising large numbers of troops, and suddenly turned south. This would be consistent either with a closely-held plan for invasion, or a response to a southern provocation: but most likely both. In October 1987, during tough and often bitter negotiations with North Korean officials about letting a Thames film crew enter the country, and after being pressed time and again to answer the question, "who started the war," even though we had said that was not a proper "civil war" question (which elicited the response that it was not a civil war, but a war of aggression by American imperialism), at length I remarked that I thought the war in 1950 was intimately linked with the near-war in 1949, but that because crack soldiers were not back from China, the North did not want to fight in 1949, even if the South did. In 1950 the expeditionary force had returned, and perhaps then the North awaited the first southern provocation to settle the hash of the Rhee regime. This was met with a memorable, eloquent silence, as the officials exchanged glances and hard faces suddenly turned soft. They said nothing more about it.

Yi Pŏm-sŏk may have been close to the truth about what happened next, when he said that the North, in his view, had originally intended a limited campaign, but found the going so easy (with the collapse of the 12th Regiment and the 7th and 2nd Divisions) that they just kept on rolling.[128] From this we deduce that the goal was to grab and hold Seoul, and form a coalition government; the war plan was probably developed in stages over the period January 1949–June 1950, so that certain expecta-

tions and standard operating procedures entered the calculations, proliferated their own sets of interests, and imparted the machine-like automaticity and incipient rigor mortis characteristic of military
bureaucracies as they prepare for the decisive moment. I still think that
the North chose that moment at some point between June 15 and 25,
and that it was not their preferred moment, but one forced upon them
by the imbricated march of events in the last week of June.

So, what is left of Mosaic One, that the North launched an unprovoked
invasion? The evidence suggests considerable doubt, even today, that the
North launched a premeditated, carefully planned, full-scale invasion on
June 25. Mosaic Three is barely worth considering; there is no evidence
for the North's claim that the South launched a major invasion all along
the parallel; nor was this their claim when the war began. And what of
Mosaic Two? It still cannot be dismissed by honest historians. If one knew
the Korean situation for years, and one knew what happened in the summer and fall of 1949, and one was well connected with intelligence apparatuses that would know, or at least suspect, that the North Koreans
would wait, in the summer of 1950, for the first major southern provocation and then take off southward; and one understood that the United
States would respond only to an attack that could be presented as unequivocal and unprovoked, and one had journeyed to Seoul to tell this to
Rhee, and to Washington to tell it to Koo, and to Tokyo to tell it to Mac-
Arthur, and to Taipei to tell it to Chiang, in other words if one were
Colonel Goodfellow, one might have reason to join the army on June 12,
1950, at the age of fifty-nine. Then one makes a first, deep cut, "pulls a
trick" that will suck in the North Koreans. And, perhaps, a few days earlier someone draws up a report projecting an imminent invasion, and
then destroys the report, and lets an unwitting and sincere president stew
over Hillenkoetter instead of ask what happened.

This is the mosaic that will most outrage the complacent reader,
steeped in the American fallacy of insufficient cynicism. But it also fits
the logic and the evidence—in part. Here is, in fact, the rollbacker's scenario. It also happens to accord with Acheson's containment scenario,
although it is not necessary that he be witting for it to work—always in
the passive mode, leaving the initiative to the enemy. It is the one mosaic
bringing the containment current and the rollback current together: Korea came along and saved them both (for a while), as it did Rhee and
Chiang. At least the honest historian must retain some skepticism here,
pending further information; the evidence, I believe, renders I. F.
Stone's famous judgment both prescient and disturbing: as he put it, "the
hypothesis that invasion was encouraged politically by silence, invited
militarily by defensive formations, and finally set off by some minor

lunges across the border when all was ready would explain a great deal."[129] But who knows?

Let us return to Mosaic One, and assess sole responsibility to North Korea for the events of June 25, 1950. Let us assume, as Freud would not, that Acheson's slip was innocent: it was an attack "without warning, with[out] provocation." To leap from that to the official judgment that this was outrageous, unprovoked aggression across an international boundary against an innocent and unsuspecting enemy would be a specious brand of empiricism that lifts the invasion from the fighting in the summer of 1949, for which all sides had responsibility (the United States included), and from the South's provocations in 1949–1950, not the least being the American-directed subjugation campaigns against the guerrillas. Even without that, such judgments abstract from the milieu in which, just two years earlier, the United Nations was used to make the thirty-eighth parallel an "international" boundary (not that any Koreans, Rhee included, recognized it as such), and in which, five short years earlier, the United States initiated the division of an ancient nation's integrity, deepened (with much Soviet help) a premature "cold war," and sponsored reactionary and pro-Japanese forces that set up a separate southern regime against even existing State Department policy, let alone the desires of the Korean people. With all this accomplished, the ultimate irony became possible: Koreans invade Korea. The truth is, the very existence of the southern state was a provocation to the North, and vice versa. Americans who remember their civil war ought to be able to understand that.

Conclusion: "The Native Hue of Resolution"

Who started the Korean War? This question cannot be answered. We have only seen fit to present three mosaics, two of them partially supported and partially unsupported by the meandering streams of evidence. The vexed reader, discomfited by the author's innuendos and his unwillingness to commit himself to one interpretation or another (so that he may be hanged by his thumbs for it by one group or another), has gotten what he deserved for asking the wrong question. From the start of this project it has been our position that the question pregnant with ideological dynamite, "who started the Korean War," is the wrong question. That is why it will not be answered. It is not a civil war question, it only holds the viscera in its grasp for the generations immediately afflicted by fratricidal conflict. No one cares anymore that the South fired first on Fort Sumter; they may still care about slavery or the union. No one wants to know who started the Vietnam War, although some remain outraged by the manner in which it ended: but that is ideology.[130] A new generation has arisen in South Korea that wants to know who started the war, but with the political sensibility of the morally outraged youth opening fire on the old fogeys. Here is a sure sign that the viscera are weakening, prelude to a later generation that will extrude this question from its guts and cease being captive to "history" in the Nietzschean sense, so that they may be free to act in the present toward the reconciliation of the Korean people.

Old Korea hands, such as they were, intuited our position in the immediate aftermath of June 25. Col. Maurice Lutwak had been an Occupation provincial governor, remaining in Korea from 1945 to 1950. In July 1950 he said that the Russians "are like men who have a lion by the tail and can't let go"; he was convinced that the Russians did not plan the attack. If they had, they would have chosen winter when the roads and surfaces were hard, not the monsoon season. "The North Koreans are so individualistic," he said, "that I believe they began it themselves."[131] The Americans had tigers by the tail: ones like the Tiger of Mt. Paekdu and Kim Sŏk-wŏn. Perhaps they began it by themselves.

Someone took an off chance, someone risked their universe to gain an end in June 1950. And this is lost irretrievably to history, unavailable to any retrospective uncovering: the act of will, resolution, method, intended to shape history, give it a direction. The problem with our detailed empirical inquiry is, as Shakespeare put it, that

> The native hue of resolution
> Is sicklied o'er with the pale cast of thought,
> And enterprises of great pith and moment
> With this regard their currents turn awry,
> And lose the name of action.

Whichever "Tiger" made the cut, Korea's historical and peculiar dementia is to pull in foreigners, the whole world if needs be, to resolve Korean problems, without thinking through all the consequences. Whether it was some *yangban* emissary squinting at Hideyoshi's eyes to divine his intentions in 1590 and getting an invasion, or the *Ilchinhoe* aiding the Japanese and getting colonization, or Kim Il Sung hoping to suck in the Soviets or the Chinese, or Rhee or Kim Sŏk-wŏn or Yi Pŏm-sŏk seeking to suck in the Americans: this is a pattern. The phenomenon is a kind of implosion, a "black hole" whose vacuum no one governs. One way or another that is what happened in the early morning hours of June 25.

Imagine: that the Korean War should have started in remote and isolated Ongjin, within the realm of far-off, remote Korea; that the conflict was between the Kim Il Sungs and the Kim Sŏk-wŏns; that the United States and then China should have been drawn into this black hole; and that global war was at the doorstep six months later: it is still amazing, daunting, terrifying.

It became an unmitigated tragedy for all concerned, this war that began with an incident at Ongjin. Who caused the Korean War? No one and everyone, all who were party to the intricate tapestry of events since 1945. Who "caused" the Korean War? Placing that emphasis, we abandon history for politics, for philosophy, for the human terrain where there are not "facts."

Who started the Korean War? This question should not be asked. Koreans, especially, should stop asking this question, and instead develop that worldliness and disgust for narrow "fatherlandishness" that Nietszche demanded of Germans—that they should learn to "love the south in the north and the north in the south."[132] This is a condescending thing for an American to say. But Germans only learned this lesson in the hardest way possible. Koreans have still not learned it.

Part IV

EPILOGUE

Chapter Nineteen

THE WAR FOR CONTAINMENT

> Instead of doing what the enemy set out to do, the enemy has done
> the exact opposite. Nothing they could have done would be more
> calculated to defeat their own purpose. It is all their own stupidity.
> . . . It isn't a Korean War on either side.
>
> *Dean Acheson*

O N A QUIET Saturday night on the quietest weekend in June 1950,
Dean Acheson had repaired to his Sandy Spring farm in Maryland
after "one of his routine late nights at the State Department." At 9:26
P.M. that evening, June 24, John Muccio's first cable arrived; within an
hour Dean Rusk was at the State Department. John Hickerson phoned
Acheson immediately, who told him "to take the steps which were necessary" to have the Security Council meet the next day. At 11:30 P.M.
Hickerson made this request to Trygve Lie. The decision was, as Rusk
later acknowledged, based on this first telegram from Seoul.[1]

Acheson and Rusk were virtually the only high officials in Washington
at the time. Truman had left for Independence that morning, and paid
a quiet visit to his brother's farm on Sunday before returning to Washington. In succeeding days, Acheson dominated the decision-making
which soon committed American air and ground forces to the fight. Acheson (along with Rusk) made the decision to take the Korean question to
the UN, before he had notified Truman of the fighting; he then told
Truman there was no need to have him back in Washington until the
next day. At the Blair House meetings on the evening of June 25 Acheson argued for increased military aid to the Republic of Korea (ROK),
American air cover for the evacuation, and the interposition of the 7th
Fleet between Taiwan and the mainland; on the afternoon of June 26
Acheson labored alone on the fundamental decisions committing Amer-
ican air and naval power to the Korean War, approved that evening at
Blair House. Thus the decision to intervene was Acheson's decision, sup-
ported by the president but taken before United Nations, Pentagon, or
Congressional approval.[2]

George Kennan, who supported the June decisions, recalled from
notes taken at the time that Acheson broke off collegial discussions on
the afternoon of June 26:

14. Acheson and Rusk leave the White House on June 27, 1950

He wanted time to be alone and to dictate. We were called in [three hours later] and he read to us a paper he had produced, which was the first draft of the statement finally issued by the President, and which was not significantly changed by the time it finally appeared, the following day . . . the course actually taken by this Government was not something pressed upon [Acheson] by the military leaders, but rather something arrived at by himself, in solitary deliberation.

Acheson concurred with Kennan, saying, "that's as I recall it." That evening the Blair House group approved the commitment of air and sea power to the Korean War, and interposed the 7th Fleet between Taiwan and the mainland. Kennan noted that the decisions of June 26 were the key ones, and Acheson said they were taken before Congressional or United Nations consultations ("it wasn't until 3:00 in the afternoon [on June 27] that the U.N. asked us to do what we said we were going to . . . in the morning").[3] Much like the Press Club speech, the Korean decision was Acheson's, arrived at "in solitary deliberation."

These decisions followed on Acheson's logic of containment in Korea, elaborated first in 1947 and structuring his Press Club speech. When he cleared some time on Sunday afternoon to think through the events in Korea, he decided that to "back away" would destroy American power and prestige: "By prestige I mean the shadow cast by power, which is of great deterrent importance."[4] We can also recall again his words: "What we have had to do is to construct a defense with inadequate means, trying to guess where each play would come through the line." And again, "the task of an opposition is to oppose and perhaps it is doing its best with a situation which it itself created." Acheson was, as he said, present at the creation. He saw himself shaping a world from the standpoint of American hegemonic interests, with insufficient resources. In Asia he shaped a defense, and established a state of affairs, in which the offense would blunder. This logic does not require that Acheson anticipate the attack, nor that he necessarily wanted it to come in Korea. He wished to stand back, be patient, and structure environments: the two we have discussed in detail are Korea and Taiwan, but we might add Iran, Turkey, Greece, and Berlin as other potential trouble spots on the periphery of the Soviet empire.

Intimately aware of the thinking of Henry Stimson before Pearl Harbor, Acheson felt the same sense of catharsis when the attack came. Whether Stimson "maneuvered" the Japanese into attacking or not, in the aftermath he noted in his diary, "Now the Japs have solved the whole thing by attacking us directly in Hawaii"; he expressed "relief that the indecision was over and that a crisis had come in a way which would unite all our people." Acheson viewed Korea in the same light—Korea solved the problem of NSC 68 and united Americans behind a policy of resisting alleged Soviet aggression through historically unprecedented defense expenditures. Joseph Harsch caught this atmosphere just after the Korea decisions when he wrote, "Never before . . . have I felt such a sense of relief and unity pass through the city."[5]

Acheson's logic later led him to the conclusion that "it isn't a Korean war on either side," a revelatory comment that grew out of the following discussion:

> Korea is not a local situation. It is not the great value of Korea itself which led to the attack. It isn't that *they* [*sic*] wanted square miles in Korea. But it was the spearpoint of a drive made by the whole Communist control group on the entire power position of the West—primarily in the East, but also affecting the whole world. Surely their purpose was to solidify Korea—but it was also to unsettle Japan, South East Asia, Philippines, and to gain all of South East Asia, and to affect situation also in Europe. That is what the war in Korea is being fought about.

And he went on, "instead of doing what the enemy set out to do, the enemy has done the exact opposite. Nothing they could have done would be more calculated to defeat their own purpose. It is all their own stupidity." Korea was a "testing ground" for both sides, "that is the global strategy of the global purpose of both sides. It isn't a Korean war on either side."[6]

Such thinking extruded most of what I have discussed in this study, that is, it extruded Koreans and their history, deemed irrelevant to the real issues. That the war occurred in Korea was happenstance for Acheson. It was like Spain, a testing ground for the superpowers. The real history of Korea in this period fits what we now call a "North-South" conflict, the main agenda being decolonization and a radical restructuring of colonial legacies. Displacing this to an East-West framework renders it irrelevant, and an entire Korean War literature can be written with the barest knowledge of the internal Korean milieu.

Nevertheless, Acheson was wrong. It was a *Korean* war on the northern side, and for much of the southern population. It was an East-West problem for the United States, a result that Syngman Rhee had assiduously sought to bring about since 1944. And so it became a war of North Koreans against Americans, slaughtering each other for incommensurable and, to the other side, incomprehensible goals.

But it was still a war for containment, for the defense. Acheson's lofty and cold-blooded global logic had no place for a unification of Korea under Rhee's auspices, unless it could be done with minimal difficulty. "We have got to put in the force necessary to reoccupy to the 38th," he said in mid-July; "this means, I suppose, that if we are forced out, we have to come in again as quickly as possible." Were the Chinese to come in, the same would be true. "If the Soviets come in, I should think that we still have to fight it out in Korea unless and until the war becomes general."[7]

This was containment with a vengeance, but still containment. Truman accepted Acheson's ideas, and both were consistent thereafter—until rollback accumulated bureaucratic and political weight in Washington, and seemed to carry no cost. On June 26 Truman told an aide that Korea was "the Greece of the Far East,"[8] something much closer to the Achesonian logic, and to the truth of the Korean civil war, than his later analogies with Munich, Genghis Khan, and Tamerlane. Korea with its large Economic Cooperation Administration (ECA) and Korean Military Advisory Group (KMAG) contingents was part of the indirect containment network of the Truman Doctrine, but only acknowledged as such within the State Department. When it was obvious by June 26 that the ROK Army was collapsing, the logic moved toward direct containment with American military force.[9]

Acheson's first recourse was to the United Nations, not to the United States Congress. He had a confident, easy contempt for the opinions of those who disagreed with him, whether in the military, the legislature, or the public at large (public opinion was for him a cranky constraint on his autonomy of decision). He did not consult Congress on June 24–26, he said, because "you might have completely muddied up the situation which seemed to be very clear at the time," and because Congressmen might have "circumscribed the President's prerogatives" (no problem there from the UN). He later expressed some astonishment when told that as early as June 28, 1950, Senator Taft referred to the Acheson-Truman decisions as "a complete usurpation by the President of the authority to use armed forces."[10] It had not occurred to Acheson, perhaps, that warmaking is the Congress' prerogative.

Acheson dealt in secrecy not just at the level of the inarticulate premise, or to keep a noisy democracy at bay, but to the point of taking information bearing on his decisions with him to the grave, hiding it from the historical record.[11] He preferred the autonomy of private decisions taken mostly with his own counsel, the only one he really trusted, and then presented to an inexperienced president who so often deferred to Acheson.

American military leaders were more sober and measured about the limits to American power, and reticent about committing ground forces to the war in Korea, as the Blair House meetings make clear.[12] But Acheson had little use for their judgment, either. The Joint Chiefs of Staff (JCS), he said later, "do not know what they think until they hear what they say." But once they have spoken, "the Pope has spoken, and they are infallible." In National Security Council (NSC) meetings, according to Acheson, the JCS would present their viewpoint in an involved paper which no one usually read, "then a discussion, and then—in my experience, always—the President deciding in favor of what I thought was the sound view, which was the one I presented to him." If a controversy existed between Defense and State, the president almost always followed Acheson's position, "not because I presented it, but because the other view was so silly. There wasn't any sense to it. It hadn't been thought through."[13]

Acheson was right about the Joint Chiefs, if we speak of their capacity to chart global strategy for the United States. The Pentagon was used to the pulling and hauling of departmental prerogative and budget squabbles, or the sanctity of standard operating procedures, giving the JCS position papers the incoherent quality of Graham Allison's bureaucratic-politics "mosaic." Acheson's hegemonic guidance and global vision held sway above this flux inside the American state, good evidence that Graham Allison had given his "Model I" a premature burial.[14] As I have argued, the foreign policy apparatus in the early postwar period had a remarkable autonomy within the American state, and Acheson's acumen gave him a whip hand in one critical decision after another. But the inchoate mosaic nonetheless produced a better sense of the limits of American power, both in Korea and subsequently in Vietnam, than did the continuous expansionism of the internationalists.

"It hadn't been thought through." This was the ultimate insult from a man with a rigorous logical mind. It is painfully apparent that Acheson held even the mind of his own president in similar contempt, in spite of lavishing praise on him in public. His president was impatient with ambiguity, and possessed, as Robert Donovan delicately put it, "an appetite, too much of a one, really, for unhesitating decision."[15] His penchant for historical analogy usually left him wide of the mark, but it seemed to gird his loins and underpin his confidence, almost as if Walter Mitty sat in the oval office, plumbing "history" for guidance. The Blair House conferences have Acheson with all the good lines, Truman left mostly to make the historical asides that were his stock and trade. Acheson coached Truman all the way along, even to his memoirs: he told A. Whitney Griswold that as the president prepared them, he was trying to keep Truman from making "a total fool of himself." His correspondence with Truman betrays a palpable condescension.[16]

After Truman decided to commit American ground troops in Korea, he left to posterity a remark that makes one wish to drop to the knees and beg forgiveness: "We have met the challenge of the pagan wolves."[17] But Truman with all his limitations was a democrat with an abiding belief in the judgment of the common man, something that he himself exemplified. As I. F. Stone once put it, Truman was "as honorable and decent a specimen of that excellent breed, the plain small-town American, as one could find anywhere in the U.S.A."[18] Unassuming to a fault, he once told an admirer who called him a great president, "cut out that talk . . . you've got to have brains to be a great man."[19] Acheson had the brains of a great man, and the hubris to use them as he chose, in a raucous democracy that knew next to nothing about his agenda.

The Acheson decisions, however, committed the United States to a war whose dynamics he could not master—in the field or in the American body politic. As it lurched into its own dialectic, this war soon brought on a debacle threatening the peace of the world, and the only dog barking in Washington was the voice of principled Republican conservatism—a voice soon silenced for good by a bipartisan centrist coalition dedicated to supporting the interests of the national security state.

When the war began the State Department's Office of Intelligence Research prepared an extended study in remarkably short order that, unlike the military's position, was heavily loaded toward intervention. It was completed within eighteen hours of the first news of the fighting, and argued that the North Korean intention was to gain "a decisive victory" by seizing Seoul within a week; the South was "militarily inferior" and likely to collapse once Seoul was taken. Since P'yŏngyang was "completely under Kremlin control," the action must be "a Soviet move"—albeit one "unique among [Soviet] moves" in the postwar period. Since it was unique, the Kremlin must have concluded that Korea "was more important than we have assumed." Later it was suggested that the Soviets now saw Korea as having "great strategic value in neutralizing the usefulness of Japan as an American base."

It went on, "Considering the *apparent* [sic] US commitments to South Korea," Moscow would not take this risk unless it considered the "liquidation of the South Korean Government" as essential to its global strategy. If the United States did not oppose this result, "a severe blow would be dealt US prestige throughout Asia," with the consequences of greatest importance in Japan. The damage to American prestige would also be great in Europe, especially in Germany. But if the United States responded effectively, this would "enhance [Japanese] willingness to accept US protection and its implications." A prompt American response might also cause China to question its alliance with the Soviet Union, if the latter could be shown to be weak or inept in Korea.[20]

This report suggests that the intelligence failure was less one of effective fact-gathering and facile communication up and down the line, than a failure at the level of assumptions and logic. No evidence is given to prove that North Korea is under complete Soviet domination, this is merely assumed. This then leads to the judgment that the Soviets must now see great strategic value in southern Korea—something they could have had at little cost simply by continuing their march in August 1945—and be willing to risk global war to get it.

⌐ The immediate goal was to neutralize Japan: unasked is the question why that could not be done from bases near Vladivostok, or in Manchuria or North Korea, with no risk of war with the United States. Needless to say, nothing is said about the substantial border fighting that had ensued in Korea for a year, much of it caused by the South, or the South's oft-stated desire to do just what the North was then doing. But the real message is in the invocation of American prestige, which was the theme of the State Department's containment in Korea from 1947 onward. In its presentation of both Soviet and American policy, it agreed in effect with Acheson that "it isn't a Korean War on either side." In any case, a president would have had a hard time beating back the tide of intervention with a study like this in the file.

American air and naval power was committed to the conflict after the June 26 Blair House meeting, that is, during the afternoon of June 27 Korea time. The BBC monitored a South Korean broadcast, repeated at ten minute intervals on June 27, announcing the commitment of U.S. airpower, but adding that "American troops will gradually participate in the fighting" as well, with MacArthur setting up a command post in Seoul "immediately" to direct the fighting. SCAP (Supreme Command, Allied Powers) denied this, but it is a good indication of how the Republic of Korea (ROK) used and abused American military support. Their air-dropped propaganda leaflets routinely referred to the Americans as being part of the *Taehan min'guk-gun* (the South Korean army), when of course the reverse was the case; the United Nations Command was referred to similarly.[21]

Acheson's June 25–26 decisions prefigured the commitment of American ground troops, which came in the early morning hours of June 30. The Joint Chiefs remained "extremely reluctant" to commit infantry troops to the fighting right up to June 30, and were not consulted when Truman made his decision. The immediate precipitating factor, however, was MacArthur's judgment that the ROK Army had mostly ceased to fight. MacArthur wanted an American regimental combat team at first, and then two divisions. Within a week he cabled that the Korean People's Army (KPA) was "operating under excellent top level guidance and had demonstrated superior command of strategic and tactical principles." He wanted a minimum of 30,000 American combat soldiers, meaning more than four infantry divisions, three tank batallions, and assorted artillery.[22]

The reticence of the JCS was not simply because of the incoherent quality of their decision making. In June 1950 the total armed strength of the U.S. Army was 593,167, with an additional 75,370 in the Marines.[23] North Korea alone was capable of mobilizing perhaps 200,000 combat soldiers in the summer of 1950, not to mention the immense manpower reserve of the Chinese People's Liberation Army (PLA). Civilians like Acheson and Dulles were committing infantry forces with little or no consultation, except with MacArthur who also had contempt for the Joint Chiefs and for the limits of American power. All had only the barest knowledge of the fighting force that American soldiers would soon face. Within a few months nearly all American combat effectives ended up in Korea, a drastic diversion of American fighting strength to a peripheral area.

The North Korean reaction to the Acheson-Truman decisions gave no indication, in the available materials, that the leadership was caught by surprise when the Americans came into the war, underlining our previous judgment that they regarded the United States as already committed to the defense of the ROK, were not impressed by Acheson's Press Club speech, and instead acted to preempt a worsening situation. Their rhetoric did suggest that once the United States came in, the North tried to invoke similar Soviet help. On July 2, the party newspaper called their struggle "a just war for national unification," and went on to describe North Korea as liberated "by Soviet armed strength," the first people's democracy in the East, and now the East Asian promontory of the Soviet camp. Thus "Korea is not isolated," and therefore the United States will not be able to defeat the Korean people, "fighting for freedom and justice."[24]

A week later the Seoul-based *Haebang ilbo* (Liberation daily) announced a complete national mobilization, American intervention having created an "emergency situation." Pak Hŏn-yŏng went on to recount a litany of American crimes against Korea, going back to its support for the Japanese Annexation; he likened the current intervention to that against the Bolsheviks after their revolution won power. An editorial on Soviet aid to Korea referred, quite pointedly in the context, only to their diplomatic and "moral" support (*sŏngwŏn*); there is no reference to any material Soviet assistance. It went on to say, more than once and with a trace of posturing, that the KPA and the southern guerrillas were filled with confidence in their eventual victory.[25]

A few days later, Kim Ch'aek in an appeal to soldiers said that the war would already have been finished had it not been for American intervention, and referred again to the (Democratic People's Republic of Korea) DPRK's confidence in the final outcome. A lead editorial entitled "Marshal Stalin is the Lodestar of Korean Liberation and the Intimate Friend of the Korean People" nonetheless went on to argue for resistance to

foreign aggression "through our own efforts and our own strength," saying that the KPA could defend Korea by itself and did not require foreigners to fight their battles for them. It would expel the Americans with
Korean strength alone, and thus "eliminate the danger of a new war and
safeguard the right of national self-determination." Then Koreans could
build "a rich and powerful nation."[26]

At the end of July, Kim Il Sung gave an interview to a correspondent
from *L'Humanité*. "The Korean people did not want this war," he remarked, but it had been forced on them by the Rhee regime and the
United States. Interestingly, he said that documents captured in Seoul
showed that the war was instigated by the "Rhee clique," with KMAG
involvement in the planning—a rather different picture than their usual
one of U.S. imperialism and Dulles having done it at the behest of "Wall
Street masters." Without American help, the war would now be over.
With American intervention, he said, "we do not anticipate that victory
will be easy. However, the Korean people are determined to fight until
all the American invaders are expelled." United Nations backing for
American intervention, he thought, made for "a disgraceful page" in the
history of that body.[27]

The United Nations Acts

In the United States, by contrast, the United Nation's condemnation of
North Korean aggression and the establishment of a United Nations
Command (UNC) was thought to be its finest hour, invoking collective
security against a breach of the peace. Acheson himself remarked, as we
have seen, that the United States acted first and got the UN to ratify its
decisions later, just as he acted first in calling the Security Council together and told Truman later. At the UN Acheson operated through
Ernest Gross, his trusted legal confidant, who was acting in Warren Austin's stead until the latter returned to his post. Had the UN not backed
up the American decisions, Acheson and Kennan agreed, the United
States would have gone ahead anyway, but would have had more problems with that residual, nagging irritant—public opinion.[28]

Dulles shared these Achesonian assumptions, viewing American unilateralism in the name of the UN as the essence of internationalist legal-
ism. In July he referred back to his speech before the ROK National
Assembly on June 19, where he said, "the United Nations requires all
nations to refrain from any threat or use of force against your territorial
integrity or political independence." He was merely paraphrasing article
2 of the United Nations Charter, which calls upon all member nations to
"refrain in their international relations from the threat or use of force
against the territorial integrity or political independence of any state."

Earlier he had said that never had history witnessed a "more open and outrageous case of aggression" than that of the North Koreans.[29]

Koreans seek to unify their national territory, divided five years earlier, and it becomes a species of "international relations." It becomes a more atrocious aggression than that of Hitler or Tojo, this "challenge of the pagan wolves." The daunting aspect of these gross distortions is that Dulles believed them, and so did most Americans, including a largely silent Congress. In the United Nations on June 25, the allies had reacted with hesitancy to the American draft resolution referring to the North Korean "act of aggression," saying it was not clear which side had acted first; "they also took the general line that this was a fight between Koreans. In its essence . . . it was in the nature of a civil war." But they, too, were effectively silenced.[30]

The slim information upon which this United Nations commitment was based was none other than the June 26 report of the UN Commission on Korea (UNCOK), giving a shortened version of the judgments of the two Australian military observers described in chapter 15. Acheson remarked on July 1 that UNCOK's presence on the scene was "most fortunate and perhaps even [the] saving circumstance"; its June 26 report "almost without question determined immed[iate Security Council] vote"; it was "of invaluable assistance in confirming . . . ROK unprepared victim deliberate assault."[31]

UNCOK was under the chairmanship of the Kuomintang (KMT) diplomat, Liu Yu-wan, who led the commission in its various consultations with American and Korean officials on June 25, and who met with Muccio that evening to assure him that the committee would send the UN "all facts on [the] hostilities." But UNCOK fell considerably short of that standard.

Its report was drawn together on the morning of June 26, and then finalized in Japan on June 29, based exclusively on American and South Korean sources, and the Peach-Rankin oberver's report, on which some preliminary work had been done on June 24, before the hostilities commenced. Even on June 25 the two military observers reported that they "were having trouble getting information"; on June 27 all UNCOK members evacuated to Japan, covering the first leg to Suwŏn under the guidance of ROK foreign minister and Rhee crony Ben Limb, thence traveling on American military transport. Eight members arrived in Pusan from Tokyo on June 30. This means, of course, that UNCOK members woke up in Seoul on Sunday morning to a war, wrote a report based on the limited observations of two people and whatever the Koreans and Americans chose to tell them, and then were in the care of the American military for the next three days. They left all their archives behind in

Seoul, making it impossible to verify what facts UNCOK had at its disposal.[32]

Most of the allies were reluctant to commit troops to the effort, contrary to received wisdom. The British dragged their feet throughout the summer of 1950, more alarmed by the American escalation of the war and concerned about the Formosa issue than about resisting North Korean aggression. At the end of August two British batallions arrived, the first allied contingent to fight on Korean soil. Korea was little more than a sideshow for the British, from 1945 onward, but it had the virtue of being distant from the empire. As an RAF man once put the British position, with its considerable cycnicism, "I think we must make a stand with the Americans somewhere and the farther away from our own possessions the better the chance of holding them." Ultimately the British made more of a stand than anyone else; by the spring of 1951 the totals showed about 12,000 British soldiers, 8,500 Canadian, 5,000 Turks, 5,000 Filipinos, and other contingents below 1,000. The United States paid most of the bill for the allied troops.[33]

Among the obscure and anomalous events still resistant to explanation and logic in the Korean decision, not the least is the Soviet absence from the Security Council in June—thereby abjuring their much used and abused veto mechanism. Adam Malik was taking his ease on Long Island rather than saying *nyet* on the Security Council, a boycott conducted ostensibly because the UN had refused to admit China. He was planning to return to Moscow for consultations on July 6.[34]

Soviet intentions were high in the minds of State Department planners on Saturday evening, June 24: "would Malik attend," Acheson recalled. "Some of us bet that there was not enough time for his orders to be changed by Sunday P.M."[35] But if the Soviets sponsored the attack, they would have expected an American response in the UN, giving Malik plenty of advance warning. In any case there was enough time for him to motor in for subsequent resolutions. And so what do we make of his absence? Another Soviet "stupidity," Acheson besting Stalin yet again?

In an interview Dean Rusk related that in the 1960s he had asked Andrei Gromyko about this matter. The Soviet delegation to the UN had instantly wired Moscow for instructions, Gromyko related, and for the first time ever in its experience got back a message direct from Generalissimo Stalin: *nyet*, do not attend.[36] If we can trust this anecdote, what might it mean?

The logic would suggest one of two possibilities: Stalin wanted to suck the United States into a war in peripheral Korea, hoping ultimately to blood the Chinese against American soldiers; UN backing would greatly boost a policy of intervention. Second, Stalin may have hoped that cloaking American intervention in the UN flag would destroy this body, or at minimum reveal it to be an American tool. There was speculation in May 1950 that the Soviets might prefer to leave the United Nations, after Herbert Hoover's call for their expulsion. This, too, would suggest that Stalin thought Soviet purposes could no longer be served by the organization.[37] The Soviet invitation to Trygve Lie at about the same time militates against this interpretation, however.

The anecdote perhaps reveals more than Rusk would think: if it is true, it suggests the Soviets did *not* have advance knowledge of the attack. If the Soviets planned and sponsored the North Korean action, why would instructions—either to return or continue the boycott—not have been transmitted earlier? Why would Malik have not vetoed the UN resolutions? They would certainly have been able to anticipate that the United States would take the Korean question to the UN, since that had been part of American planning since 1947, and the Soviets were reading our plans.[38]

There would be a corollary benefit of the Soviet absence, to teach a recalcitrant ally a lesson about moving independently. In 1948 Kim Il Sung made a pointed reference to the Soviet delegation's absence from the "Little UN" meetings, allowing the United States to get United Nations sanction in setting up the Rhee government. Although he did not criticize the Soviets for this in the text, even to mention it carried an implicit censure, and from the Korean standpoint such behavior would raise questions about the Soviet commitment to the DPRK, as contrasted to what the United States did for the ROK.[39] Kim unquestionably resented the Soviets for not vetoing UN resolutions in 1950, although it was not politic for him to say so.

When Malik finally did return to his seat, on August 1, he declared that the resolutions on Korea had been illegal and should be rescinded. The *New York Times* called this "the ultimate arrogance of a power-maddened despotism which mistakes the UN for one of its zombie soviets and proposes to make it kowtow to the great Khan in Moscow.[40] The *Times* editorial aptly reflected the political atmosphere in the United States in mid-1950, to which we now turn.

THE AMERICAN REACTION TO THE WAR

When news of the Korean War broke on that quiet weekend, the press reported, "an atmosphere of tension, unparalleled since the war days, spread over the capital." Many commentators agreed with Kennan, who remarked that were the United States not to act, it would face "a drastic and catastrophic drop in world confidence."[41] Once American air and infantry power were committed, however, a cool breeze of relief passed through the steamy capital, and through the American political spectrum from one end to the other.

From 1945 to 1950, we have argued, political conflict between the extremes of globalism and rollback moved the consensual midpoint of the American political spectrum to the Right, including a James Burnham and excluding a Henry Wallace. The Korean War shoved it rightward again, while retrieving for the consensus Henry Wallace and, in the first months of the war, the iconoclast I. F. Stone, both of whom initially supported Truman's actions.[42] Hardly a voice was raised in protest in Congress, except for Republican conservatives who thought legislative prerogatives had been infringed.[43]

Liberal media sang administration tunes. *The Progressive* asserted that the North Koreans had violated the United Nations charter (i.e., Dulles's argument). "This aggression must be stopped," *The Nation* said; the North Koreans had "bluntly turned down" an UNCOK plea to discuss P'yŏngyang's plan for a general election, and then, "in the fashion made memorable by Adolph Hitler," rolled across the border.[44] Other liberal journals, like *The Reporter* and *The New Republic*, also supported American intervention.

The Daily Worker opposed the war, of course, but likewise showed little interest in probing at official sources of information, contenting itself mostly with repeating stories it got from the Soviet press. In the summer of 1950 about the only place one could go to find in the American media a principled, independent critical stance, and a sincere inquiry into what really had happened in Korea, was to three periodicals of miniscule circulation: *Monthly Review*, Scott Nearing's *World Events*, and George Seldes's *In Fact*.

Monthly Review called Korea a civil war, and implied that the utter collapse of the Rhee regime made it rather a people's war as well. "It is pretty clear that responsibility for the outbreak of full-scale warfare rests on the North," it said, but it saw no moral difference between this and Lincoln's offensive after the South shelled Fort Sumter. Alone among all commentary on Korea that I have seen, it argued that the real issue was not who attacked first. It predicted that the United States would suffer "a disastrous defeat" in Korea.[45]

Scott Nearing was an independent social democrat who cranked out his little magazine from a farm in New England, offering the best critical commentary on American foreign policy in 1950. As we have seen, he immediately caught the implications of Acheson's "total diplomacy" offensive in the spring; at that time he listed Korea with Indochina as places where wars were "in progress." The Korean War, he said later, was a civil war, but also a war for national independence; it had been a testing ground in the cold war since 1945, not since June 1950. George Seldes was also a voice of reasoned dissent until his magazine folded for lack of funds.[46]

It is not simply that such views were accurate, in the light of history. More daunting is that they recapitulated the private opinions of the Americans most knowledgeable about Korea. The CIA, as we have seen time and again, wrote with scarcely-concealed contempt about Rhee's police state, and found him volatile and dangerous, perfectly capable of launching a war of aggression. High officers in KMAG knew how close a war had come in the summer of 1949, launched from the South. And after the war began old Korea hand John Reed Hodge wrote that "we have been at war for several years [in Korea] in everything except the actual shooting and physical maneuver." Korea was always "the hot spot of the Orient." But, Hodge said, "I have kept my mouth shut" since the war began.[47] So did everyone else. I have not found a single serious dissent from Truman's decision within the available archival materials.

There was one public episode of official dissent, however. In mid-July, a labor advisor to the ECA on home leave from Korea, Stanley Earl, told *The Oregonian* that the Rhee regime was "rotten and corrupt," "a real police state" and not a democracy "by any stretch of the imagination." Shortly thereafter, *The Daily Worker* reprinted the dispatch. Earl was summoned to Washington, "presumably to answer questions" about his statements; Edgar Johnson of the ECA told him he had been "indiscreet." Earl thereupon sputtered to reporters that every Communist in the United States "should be put in jail as a security measure." Nonetheless, he still wondered "what has now happened to the arrogant, horse-riding South Korean officers who committed so many indignities against their fellow Koreans" (including one division commander who charged his troops one million *wŏn* per month to use the mess hall). A week later Stanley Earl resigned from the ECA, his remarks having "caused some furor" in the State Department. He continued to speak out, however, saying that the Rhee regime would have collapsed in a week without ECA support.[48]

George McCune's fine book, *Korea Today*, a sincere account by a principled liberal, was published by Harvard University Press just as the war began. Foster Dulles took time from his duties to write William Holland, secretary-general of the Institute for Pacific Relations (IPR) (which had sponsored the book), with this chilling admonition: "I question whether its publication at this time will serve to promote real insight into the issues which today so deeply engage our nation."[49] It was merely one more nail driven in the IPR's coffin, especially given Dulles's closeness to the Rockefeller Foundation, which withdrew IPR funding in the early 1950s.

The first demonstrations against the war occurred mostly in New York, and drew mostly communist support. Paul Robeson spoke at one rally in

Harlem in early July. The Fellowship of Reconciliation offered a mild protest shortly thereafter. In early August some peace demonstrators sought to march in New York, but police broke it up immediately; the *New York Times* was hostile to the very idea of a march.[50]

By this time the American spectrum of political acceptability had Acheson, the architect of American intervention, at its left pole. He had courageously risked his position to defend Alger Hiss a few months earlier; he had such towering prestige among liberals that he rarely if ever got a bad press in, say, the *New York Times* (more often it seemed that he helped script its articles). Furthermore within weeks of the opening of the war McCarthy opened up on him again, accusing him of inviting the communists to attack in Korea.[51] It was from this time, not from January 1950, that the Press Club speech became an issue. The now-intractable verdict that he erred, that his "deterrence failed," is really a ghost of McCarthy's attacks. But, of course, this merely welded liberals more strongly behind Acheson.

The curdling up of this cold war consensus rendered those who were part of it incapable of challenging Red-baiters at the level of assumptions; only means and methods were at issue. Reeves correctly points out that even during the climactic Army-McCarthy hearings, none of the senators "challenged any of the Red-Scare assumptions Joe freely repeated. Each of the Senators expressed his deepest hatred of all Communists." This would include even the liberal who symbolically interred McCarthy, but not McCarthyism: Joseph Welch. He told McCarthy, "I admire the work you do, when it succeeds." Richard Nixon, as usual, was the one who best exemplified the age. Some people thought communists should be shot like rats, he observed: "Well, I'll agree: they're a bunch of rats, but just remember this. When you go out to shoot rats, you have to shoot straight, because when you shoot wildly . . . you make it easier on the rat."[52]

Leading lights of academia were far more often to be found on the side of the state than on the side of independent critical judgment, or the First Amendment. The period inaugurated the harnessing of academic talent to fight the cold war. Harvard president James Conant, as one example among many, wrote a memorandum for a "confidential" meeting of seven college presidents in September 1950, calling for "mobilizing the youth of the nation in this unparalleled crisis." The Soviets may go to war in the period 1952–1954, he wrote, and millions of soldiers will be needed. Therefore, the United States should introduce "universal military service of two years for all able-bodied youth before they take their place in the industrial life of this country."[53]

In the atmosphere of McCarthyism, Godfrey Hodgson is right to say, "liberals were almost always more concerned about distinguishing themselves from the Left than about distinguishing themselves from conservatives." Thus they joined "the citadel of . . . a conservative liberalism." Liberal interventionism was both a cause and a result of such behavior. Like the matrix of decision in foreign policy, this 1950s citadel, if we may call it that, persists today, and indeed had an Indian summer in the 1980s—as anyone who is outside the citadel knows, through facing the same experience over and over again.

Hodgson's explanation of this persistence is a good one: "if the fear of being investigated had shown the intellectuals the stick" in the early 1950s, "the hope of being consulted had shown them the carrot" thereafter. Being an influential client meant accepting the confines of one's patronage.⁵⁴ But in 1950, it was the stick that counted, and a mighty one it was.

Let us say you think the United Nations was wrong to join the war in Korea. What might you have faced if you demonstrated militantly in favor of your position? Morris Amchan, the former deputy chief counsel for War Crimes at the Nuremburg trials, wrote that the UN saw the attack as a "breach of the peace," and therefore "aggressive and criminal." Thus, any person who was thereafter to "substantially participate" on the North Korean side "must be charged with knowledge of the fact that he is participating in the waging of an aggressive war and illegal aggression." All "high persons" doing this should be "held responsible before an international tribunal."⁵⁵ Would a militant pro-North Korean demonstration, on the model of the 1960s marches on Washington, constitute substantial participation? Probably not.

If you were a Korean or a communist, however, mere pro-North Korean sentiments or protest brought a harsh penalty. The FBI investigated and had deported several Koreans, permanent residents in the United States who took the northern side, or who were known as anti-Rhee leftists; the records are still classified on this, but it is alleged that some who were deported were subsequently executed in South Korea, and that others went to the North.⁵⁶

The McCarran Act, named for its sponsor, the ignorant and corrupt inquisitor of the China field, passed Congress on September 23, 1950, establishing among other things concentration camps for those thought to be a threat to American security. A week later, *U.S. News and World Report* published "rules for communists" under the Act. It reassured its audience that the government would not set up camps for communists "right away." But, once they existed, who would go into them? "Many Communists and fellow travelers. Others would be rounded up, too. Anybody could be held if considered dangerous to United States security." The Ku Klux Klan would not be included, however, because it lacked "connections with the Communists."⁵⁷ Readers who hasten to point out that no one was ever placed in the camps might recall that no one knew that in September 1950.

With a distinctly attenuated if not nonexistent Left, the way was open on the Right for almost anything, and some public officials felt unconstrained. The commandant of the Air War College, Maj. Gen. Anderson, said in late August, "Give me the order to do it and I can break up Russia's five A-bomb nests in a week. And when I went up to Christ—I think I could explain to Him that I had saved civilization." Not to be outdone, Navy Secretary Francis P. Matthews publicly called for preventive war, in a flourish of Orwellian logic: by becoming "an initiator of a war of aggression," the Americans "would become the first aggressors for peace." Both officials soon left the Truman administration, but less because of what they said then because of their closeness to the views of Louis Johnson.[58]

The United States during this period is not to be compared with authoritarian states like prewar Japan or Germany, or the Soviet Union. It remained open, over the long term, to a reversal of some of the worst excesses of 1950 (although by no means all of them); the press was not muzzled and dissenters were not confined, unless they were the leaders of the communist party, and the Supreme Court later overturned their convictions under the Smith Act. But this is not really the point. Judged by the ideals America established for itself, and its presumed fight for freedom on a world scale, the early 1950s were a dark period indeed, a maximization of the potential for absolutist conformity that Louis Hartz had the courage to explore in 1955. If critics were not shot or tortured, they nonetheless suffered loss of careers, ostracism, intense psychological pressures, and admonitions to change their thoughts or be excluded from the spectrum of political acceptability.[59]

The overwhelming influence of the United States blanketed critical opinion on a global scale. An enormous State Department file with hundreds of reports from all over the world shows how the American machine for massaging and manipulating allied opinion worked, its most frequent technique being to question the motives and political alignments of virtually anyone dissenting from the official version of what happened in Korea. When critical opinion did rear its ugly head, it almost always drew upon the same limited set of anomalous and contrary information mined by I. F. Stone and a literal handful of other critics.[60]

An epitaph for this period came from Charles Beard's great admirer, the fearless and independent historian Harry Elmer Barnes. In *Perpetual War for Perpetual Peace* (which might be a paraphrase of Matthews's program), Barnes wrote,

Fantastic political boundaries are set up carelessly and arbitrarily, but once they are established . . . they take on some mysterious sanctity. . . . Every border war becomes a world war, and world peace disappears from the scene. By this absurd policy, internationalism and interventionism invite and insure "perpetual war for perpetual peace," since any move which threatens petty nations and these mystical boundaries becomes an "aggressive war" which must not be tolerated, even though to oppose it may break the back of the world.[61]

It was a long and tortured path that both Korea and the United States trod, to get from 1945 to 1950.

"A REAL FANCY SOVIET BONER": MOSCOW'S REACTION TO THE WAR

In 1983 the United States accomplished a mini-rollback in Grenada, and in the aftermath it appeared that a major rollback against the Sandinistas in Nicaragua might be in the offing. Rather quickly Cuba, the communist nation providing Nicaragua's main military backing and most of its advisors, was forced publicly to say that in the event of an American invasion, it could do nothing for its ally. In 1986 an American naval task force entered the Gulf of Sidra, and shortly thereafter American jets bombed and strafed Libya, attempting to punish Libyan terrorism and to kill its author, Qaddafi. Readers of the fine print noted that the Soviets quietly withdrew their ships and submarines from Libyan waters and did nothing for their beleagured friend, in Libya or elsewhere.

What do such facts mean? They are critically important signals to the other side that indicate that communist realpolitik, even in the 1980s, will sacrifice certain allies rather than confront the might of America, and that there are distinct and predictable limits on those places where the Soviets will invoke the credibility of their very substantial armed deterrent. The record of the Korean War suggests that North Korea was not one of them: from day one, the Soviets made clear their determination to stay clear of the fighting. We are thus left to reconcile the ubiquitous American assumption that Stalin started the war with the unambiguous evidence that he distanced Soviet interests, prestige, and armed might from the conflict, allowing the United States ultimately to pulverize North Korea.

After the war started the Soviet information apparatus was silent for three days, except to repeat some of P'yŏngyang's statements verbatim and without comment. But in the early morning hours of June 26 Russian ships that had sailed from the Soviet-controlled port of Dairen, just opposite Korea, were ordered "to return to their own defense zone immediately." Soviet naval vessels also stayed clear of the war zone and their submarines never, from June 25 onward, interfered with American shipping. As Kennan later remarked, "it must be to them an intensely humiliating and irritating experience" to have to keep their naval forces "out of areas which seem to them almost part of their territorial waters."[62] But keep them out the Russians did, and religiously so.

On June 28 the Moscow press finally reacted, not to the war but to the American decision to intervene. *Pravda* called Truman's decisions "a direct act of aggression" against Korea *and* China. The CIA found it curious that the Soviets did not initially refer to or criticize the United Nations resolutions that sanctioned American intervention, but instead said the United States was "grossly trampling on the United Nations Charter, acting as though the United Nations Organization did not exist at all."[63]

On June 29 Roscoe Hillenkoetter reported that "he had no evidence that the USSR was prepared to support the North Koreans"; there appeared to be "little Soviet military activity anywhere in the Far East." The Moscow embassy and various reporters said there was no "war scare" in Moscow, with people going about their business as usual. In early July the Soviet press still devoted little space to the events in Korea. The Soviets also silenced the satellite press in Eastern Europe, and censors "quickly snuffed" resolutions calling for Soviet intervention in Korea. Kennan noted on June 29 that the Soviet response indicated it wished to be "unengaged," whereas Chinese statements had been "highly bellicose and inflammatory," near to "a declaration of war against us."[64]

Perhaps the most remarkable of early Soviet reactions to the fighting came on July 6, when Andrei Gromyko met in great secrecy in Moscow with the British ambassador, Sir David Kelly, and told him that "the USSR wished for a peaceful settlement of the Korean dispute." In a second meeting, after coordinating with the Foreign Office and the American embassy, Kelly asked that the Soviets persuade North Korea to pull back to the 38th parallel. Gromyko responded that the war had been "provoked" by the South, and resisted the supposition that Moscow had this sort of influence on North Korea. The American ambassador thought Gromyko's first demarche was sincere, reflecting "the Soviet view that the outcome in Korea cannot be favorable to the USSR."[65]

We are asked to believe that the Soviets would start an aggression thinking the United States would not respond; they would stupidly fail to veto UN action; then ten days later, at the first blush of United States involvement and before much Korean-American fighting, they would ask for a peaceful settlement because the outcome could not be favorable to the USSR. In fact, when looked at from P'yŏngyang's standpoint Gromyko's statement was more an act of treachery than one designed to support a beleagured ally.

In his famous "memoirs," Khrushchev revealed that when the war began, the Soviets pulled back their advisors with the KPA. But intelligence sources detected this quickly, through early POW interviews and other means. Daily field situation reports were generally negative on any direct participation by Soviet officers in the war, while occasionally citing evidence of Soviet advisors remaining in the North with air and naval units. POWs "consistently recall[ed] Soviet military advisors being with their units before the crossing of the 38th parallel, [but] almost to a man they have not seen them since."[66] This action may simply be more evidence of Soviet distancing from the war. But it could also have been a move similar to that threatened by General Roberts in August 1949, that is, to take the military advisors home if the South Koreans marched into the North. Regardless, the Russians left the Koreans to fight in the South on their own, and communicated a clear signal to Washington.

Moscow's studied distance from the Korean events solidified Washington's decision to intervene. Malik's absence from the Security Council and the Kremlin's three-day silence, along with episodes like the clearing of Soviet vessels from nearby waters, spoke volumes as to Soviet intentions. The Soviets might have put troops on alert, maneuvered them around, hiked up the tension in Berlin—routine cold war measures that the Soviets have used time and again to intimidate and deter the West. Instead, at best they did nothing and at worst showed their fear of American power. Thus they reinforced Washington's sense that it would get a free hand in Korea.

Once the United States was committed to the war and employed a formidable array of high-technology firepower, the Russians did little in response, denying their best equipment to the Koreans and making them pay for everything. Yet the Soviets had, by CIA estimates, an enormous army in the Far East of thirty-two divisions, 468,000 soldiers, and 5,300 aircraft, most of it concentrated near Korea (Vladivostok, Dairen, Sakhalin, the Kamchatka Peninsula).[67]

There is no evidence of an upturn in Soviet military shipments to North Korea after June 25; instead, if anything a decrease was registered. At about the same time intelligence sources told the *New York Times* that they had "no knowledge that the North Korean invaders actually received new supplies from the Soviet Union since the war began." KPA military equipment included captured American weaponry gotten from the South Koreans on the battlefield (the American materiel was substantial: when they retreated from the parallel, ROKA forces "abandoned almost all their supplies obtained from the U.S."; by the spring of 1951 Southern forces had left enough materiel on the battlefield to equip ten divisions). The best Soviet materiel, like the Stalin tank and their new 152mm howitzer, "was never turned over to the NKPA or the CCF"; after the first weeks of the war, the KPA "was never able to trade blows with the US Army on equal terms." American firepower easily destroyed or neutralized the obsolescent tanks and artillery deployed by the North.[68]

The North Koreans did purchase much military equipment from the Soviets in 1949 and 1950, something they made no secret about in the party newspaper, as we have seen, featuring on the front pages pictures of Soviet tanks purchased through various sorts of bond drives. The Soviets sold them pre-1945 vintage models, from stocks placed in the Soviet Far East in expectation of major land campaigns against the Japanese. Any northern leadership looking at what the South was getting from the United States would have done the same, especially since the South got its equipment gratis, whereas the North had to purchase everything. The first public aid going to the North Koreans after the war began came from funds raised in Hungary for a battlefield medical hospital. Two years into the war, POWs and refugees from the North related that "far greater material aid was coming from China than from the Soviet Union."[69]

At the celebrations in P'yŏngyang of the fifth anniversary of liberation, when the KPA was locked in battle with an ever-growing American army, Kim Il Sung lauded the Soviets for their help in liberating Korea and departed from his usual stance to praise Stalin as "the lodestar of the Korean people"; he may have been trying to wheedle more aid out of the Soviets. Still, there was very little reference to any Soviet help since the war began. He could refer only to Soviet "sympathy" and "moral support." Stalin's message to Kim was exceedingly brief, exactly two lines long, making no mention of American intervention in Korea. Ambassador Shtykov's address to a P'yŏngyang rally was similarly noncommittal, with tepid remarks like the following:

> The Soviet people . . . offer their sincerest congratulations and admire the brilliant struggle of the Korean people for freedom and independence. The Soviet people have always had friendly feelings for the Korean people and, moreover, have such feelings [now] . . . the Soviet people always delight in the achievements of the Korean people in *peaceful construction* and also take pleasure from their achievements in the struggle for the freedom and independence of the homeland (emphasis added).

Shtykov assured his audience that the Soviets and other progressive peoples were "demanding" that the United States stop its "armed intervention in Korea," and offered the Soviet experience in repelling the German invaders as a guide for the Koreans. It was a barely disguised way of telling the Koreans they were on their own, and quite unlike Chinese statements during the same period which we will come to shortly.[70]

It was not to be expected that the Soviets would have chosen to fight with everything they had in Korea, even though the United States came close to doing just that right up against the Soviet border; they were simply in no position to take on the full might of the United States, and certainly not over Korea. What is more remarkable is how very little the Soviets did. They could have protected North or South Korean ports and cities, provided newer tanks and artillery, up-to-date antiaircraft, jet fighters; if they had authored the war, a defensive Soviet role in the air war might also have been expected after the eradication of the small North Korean air force and a full commitment of the USAF. As Khrushchev suggested in his memoirs, more tanks might have put the KPA over the hump at the Pusan perimeter; if the USSR were ever to intervene decisively with air power, MacArthur noted, August would have been the time.[71]

Yet the Soviets did nothing, even about USAF bombing forays along their borders and, once or twice, into their territory. *US News and World Report* noted, at the critical moment of the war for the South, that Stalin was "passing up chances to be belligerent" by not firing on or interfering with American planes near Soviet borders; "the only Soviet reaction so far has been deep silence." When the Americans reoccupied Seoul, intelligence analysts were surprised to find that large numbers of Russians did not accompany the North Koreans to Seoul, and that the Russians apparently did not try to exploit secret documents left in the American embassy.[72]

American intelligence, as we have seen, had reached a consensus before June 25 that the Russians did not want war. Once the fighting began, of course, the question then became why *did* the Soviets want—or at least risk—war in 1950, after all? (No one took seriously the notion that North Korea could have acted alone.) George Kennan immediately, by June 30, elaborated the most cogent answer: the invasion was not about Korea, it was about Japan. The Kremlin's aim was "to acquire strategic control over South Korea probably for reasons mainly defensive." It sought either to get the United States involved "in a profitless and discreditable war of attrition" or to acquiesce in "the Communist seizure of South Korea," thus causing the United States to suffer "a tremendous prestige defeat and the loss of public confidence everywhere." Kennan also said that the Kremlin had kept itself "unengaged" and allowed its puppets to work their will; the Chinese Communists seemed to be more engaged and were perhaps "thereby committing certain political blunders" which could redound to United States advantage. He thought the Chinese might come into the war, something the United States *should* oppose militarily in Korea (and also in Taiwan if they invade), but not elsewhere.[73]

Somewhat later Kennan said the Soviets did not launch the Korean operation

> as a first step in a world war or as the first of a series of local operations designed to drain United States strength in peripheral theaters. They simply wanted control of South Korea; saw what looked to them like a favorable set of circumstances in which to achieve it; feared that if they did not achieve it now, time might run out on them. They did not think it likely that we would intervene militarily.[74]

This is a flawed conclusion. It had been clear since 1945 that the United States intended to have unilateral sway in Japan, since 1947 that a peace treaty excluding the Soviet Union and including limited Japanese rearmament was in the cards. The peace treaty was far from being concluded in June 1950; it was not even clear that American troops would be stationed indefinitely in Japan. Anyway, the Soviets had many ways short of war to influence Japan, and neither Japan nor the USSR was in any position to wage war in 1950, a mere five years after the devastation of World War II. Most important, a war in Korea was the one event most likely to bring into being permanent American bases and a rearmed Japan, yet possession of South Korea did not markedly enhance Soviet strategic capabilities vis-à-vis Japan. And if "they simply wanted control of South Korea," why did they not pursue that goal in 1945, and why was time running out in 1950, when even the CIA thought continued guerrilla war was the preferred communist strategy for achieving control of the South? Kennan's reasoning, one thinks, really mirrors his own deeply held belief that Japanese power should have been reintroduced into Korea, thus to balance Soviet power, and that the Soviets wanted a better strategic position to cope with that eventuality.

A formerly classified colloquy in Congress in July 1949 provided a military view of the value of South Korea to the Soviets. Maj. Gen. W. E. Todd, director of the JCS's Joint Intelligence Group, testified that Korea "would be at the bottom" of Soviet priorities for "armed aggression." When Tom Connally asked if the Soviets might take over South Korea to "gum up" the Japanese situation, Todd responded that "we do not believe" the Soviets would do so—it was possible, but not probable. The Soviets "would improve their strategic position very little in the Far East by occupying South Korea." Soviet positions in eastern Siberia, Vladivostok, and Sakhalin gave them "as favorable [a strategic position] as they would have if they took the rest of Korea." Japan, he said, was "almost under the guns of Mukden, Sakhalin, and the Kurils . . . the gain for the

Soviets would be small, we feel—very small indeed." And South Korea itself would be "a liability" for the Soviets, not a gain.[75]

Acheson pressed the assumption of Soviet responsibility to its logical conclusion in August 1950. Without assessing the reasons for their presumed authorship of the war, he said,

> The profound lesson of Korea is that, contrary to every action preceding, the USSR took a step which risked—however remotely—general war. Suppose, if you wish, and I do, that the Kremlin's best guess was that we would not pick up the glove. Nevertheless, the risk was there. Neither the Kremlin nor any other foreign office acts without understanding that the off chance may occur. Still they acted.[76]

If we change the declarative to the interrogative, Acheson had posed the central question: why *would* the Kremlin risk general war over southern Korea? What was so important in June 1950 as to cause a move "contrary to every action preceding," something that would override the terrible perils of the "off chance" coming true, from an attack based on a flimsy "best guess"? The answer is nothing. Nothing to be gained offset the risks.

If we ask the ulterior question, *qui bono*, the answer is the same. No benefits accruing to the Soviet Union from taking over South Korea by direct armed force would offset the predictable and inevitable consequence of spurring American, German, and Japanese rearmament, especially the trebling of defense expenditures called for in NSC 68. There is, in short, no good reason in the summer of 1950 why the Soviets should have been so deeply unhappy with the artifice that the tsars recommended at the turn of the century to counter Japan, that Stalin acquiesced to in 1945, and that the Soviets have been quietly content about since 1953: a divided Korea. So, to accept the American logic on the authorship of the war means to accept colossal blunders (what Reston called "a real fancy Soviet boner"[77]) on the part of Kremlin strategists.

But perhaps the Soviets merely miscalculated their timing. The British Foreign Office thought it "preposterous" that the DPRK could have acted alone, but thought "perhaps [the] timing somehow was wrong," because the Soviets had much to lose "in forcing [the] US hand at this time." Nor did the British think the Soviets wished to wreck the UN, but instead "had been searching for means of rejoining [the Security Council] without too much loss of prestige." *Time* magazine cited "plenty of evidence" that the Soviets miscalculated "the time of day in the U.S."; thus they were "mum" for thirty-six hours. "Had they expected the U.S. move," they would have gotten Malik to the UN in time to veto the American resolutions. "This was the Kremlin's worst blunder in years."[78]

In other words, Stalin stealthily plots aggression, takes the risk of global war with a superpower that towered over the Soviet Union materially, and makes one blunder after another at both the strategic and tactical level. He misjudges South Korea's value to Soviet strategy, the effect of the war on Japanese and Western rearmament, and the American willingness to fight in Korea. He even gets the time zones wrong. Acheson sits back and makes a fool of him.

Two scenarios fit the evidence and the logic of the situation. One is that Soviet involvement—promoting the war, but remaining in the background—had precisely the goal that Kennan suggested on June 30: "the first of a series of local operations designed to drain U.S. strength in peripheral theaters." A high official in Yugoslavia also held this view, that the Soviets did not care how the conflict ended for the Korean communists, but did want "to get the U.S. bogged down." Perhaps French military intelligence put this scenario best, in mid-July.

> Leading French military circles are convinced that the war in Korea will become a protracted affair, maintained primarily by Communist China . . . in view of the rapid North Korean successes, Communist aid to North Korea might be reduced in the near future so as to prevent any termination of the Korean War, even should it be an outright Communist victory. The Soviets distinctly wish to tie up the American military forces in the Far East . . . the Far East is slated to become the bottomless pit into which American might and wealth shall be poured . . . should the Americans succeed in launching a successful counter-offensive, "International Brigades" formed of Chinese and Manchurian troops can always be sent in superior numbers to the Korean battlefields to stave off an eventual defeat.[79]

For Stalin such a strategy would not necessitate direct involvement in starting the war. It might mean showing the Koreans intelligence that the United States would not join the battle, or merely giving the Koreans their heads. If the North Koreans win, it either presents the United States with another blow to its prestige in the Far East, or leads to a bigger effort to reinvade Korea (remember that Acheson said early on, if the United States were thrown out, it would have to come back in).

This reasoning fits Stalin's conspiratorial turn of mind and his blend of cynicism and conservatism, and fits the evidence on the low levels of Soviet involvement in the war. It is unquestionably something that would have occurred to Stalin once American and Chinese forces clashed: a way to drain American resources, obviate Sino-American détente, and make China dependent on the USSR. But, this scenario may be too clever by half. By the spring of 1950 it would not have been difficult for Stalin to predict that the United States would respond in Korea, and that it might try to pursue a rollback. But the chances were even better that the United

States and China were heading for a clash over Taiwan. It is more likely that, in the face of North Korean revolutionary nationalism and the volatility of the peninsula, a distancing from whatever might happen in Korea was the best Soviet policy.

The second scenario is that the war had a purely Korean authorship. There is still nothing in the existing evidence on Soviet behavior that is inconsistent with this alternative. This would explain why Malik was absent from the Security Council, why the Soviet propaganda apparatus was slow to respond, why Soviet submarines and advisors were pulled back, why weapons shipments decreased, why Gromyko was willing to talk about peace within ten days of the opening of the war, why the Soviets did so little, anywhere in the world, to help the Koreans.

The Soviets had plenty of intelligence in North Korea and cannot have been unaware of the disposition of KPA forces as late June approached. But what if the North Koreans lose? What if the Americans come in and occupy their territory? If the initial invasion was at Soviet prodding and then the Soviets do nothing, it is a terrible betrayal. But if the Koreans moved first without Soviet sanction—or indeed, against their wishes—and then the Americans come in, a lesson is taught to all Soviet allies. And if the Americans occupy the North, Chinese communist mettle and loyalty will be tested. In short, whether the North wins or loses, Stalin wins. If the reader remains unwilling to grant that the evidence and the logic points to this conclusion, the fact remains that it hardly points toward a collegial decision on war between Stalin and Kim Il Sung.

THE CHINESE REACTION

The Chinese response to the war was quicker than the Soviet, and less noncommittal. On June 26, the Hsinhua news agency released a North Korean statement on the fighting in Korea; the *People's Daily* published its first editorial on June 27, a day before the first Moscow editorial, and it said much more. The Chinese lambasted the Rhee regime as an American puppet, cited its many provocations of the North, and criticized American policy along the North Korean line. Syngman Rhee, it said, "lacked the political and military experience" of Chiang Kai-shek, thus being weaker at home and requiring more American support. Although the Chinese were naturally concerned with American intervention in the Taiwan straits, and promised no direct backing to the Koreans, their statements went a good bit beyond Moscow's muted position.[80]

The British attaché in Beijing, Hutchison, thought that the Russians had planned the invasion, although he noted that Chu Teh—close to Korean military leaders like Mu Jŏng—had been absent from Peking for some time before June 25; some thought he was planning an attack on

Taiwan, others that "he may have been in touch with North Korean leaders." Hutchison sought to argue that news about Korea had been thin in
the Chinese press in the weeks before the war, and thus that Beijing "may
not have been . . . previously advised of plans for invasion"; yet he found
fourteen articles on Korea from June 1 to 26, and the Soviet press was
less attentive than this. By the end of September, Hutchison had come to
think that "China was the prime mover in setting off the Korean War,"
and noted frequent statements by K. M. Pannikar that the Russians did
not instigate the attack. The Foreign Office commented that it was "quite
possible that the Korean conflict was started by the Koreans themselves
without Russian or Chinese prompting," although there might have been
Chinese involvement because of the large number of CCF Koreans transferred to the DPRK. (It is obvious that no one really knew what to
think.)[81]

The Americans were no better at gauging Beijing's involvement. Kennan rather reversed Hutchison, thinking at first that China was involved,
later that it was not. On June 30 he cited Beijing's greater backing for
the DPRK, relative to the Soviets, and said the Chinese might come into
the war—and the United States should resist this in Korea, but not elsewhere, especially not in China. Much later, he reflected that he thought
Moscow did not inform Mao about the impending war, and Mao had
"little, if any, prior warning when it occurred. We thought we could detect signs of considerable confusion and bitterness in the Chinese camp
over this fact."[82]

The existing evidence, even today, is quite mixed on China's possible
foreknowledge of the opening of the war. In the days before June 25,
Mao was continuously involved in party meetings, and publicly called for
a demobilization of the vast PLA. Yet this was the same time when huge
numbers of Chinese troops had mobilized opposite Taiwan, apparently
for an invasion. MacArthur's intelligence placed the important Chinese
military leader Nieh Jung-chen in P'yŏngyang on June 23, and in mid-
July asserted that Chinese and Korean leaders held a military conference
to coordinate operations in Korea and against Taiwan. But this information came from Nationalist sources and the British Foreign Office
found it "extremely hard . . . to assess." MacArthur hewed to the position
that the Chinese were more involved in the war than the Russians, something born out by the lack of Soviet military activity in the Far East from
June 1950 onward. Yet this judgment is impossible to separate from
MacArthur's desire to carry the war to the mainland, and therefore to
assure Washington that the Soviets would not respond.[83]

In July Willoughby's intelligence turned up a Japanese agent who said
he had been trained in Shantung (opposite Korea and home to most Chinese living in Korea) for many months in 1949, with some other Japanese

and many more Koreans. On June 1, 1950, he and the other agents left P'yŏngyang by boat, crossing the Yellow Sea and landing near Inch'ŏn on June 10. They were dispatched by a Chinese Communist intelligence specialist. They had been told, he said, that an attack on the South would come in mid-June, and apparently were supposed to coordinate with North Korean agents (said to blanket South Korea even down to the villages, where many sympathizers were local elders). He also reported that Soviet and Chinese leaders had met in early 1950 on the Korean problem, determining that the Chinese would send their Korean divisions to the North, while the Soviets would provide tanks. An invasion of Taiwan was to have occured, he said, but lacked the requisite naval vessels.[84] This report is plausible, but lacks any additional confirmation.

In the spring of 1950, of course, China transferred tens of thousands of Korean troops back to the DPRK. This also is inconclusive; it might merely reflect the end of the fighting on the mainland. In any case similar numbers had been transferred back in 1949, as we have seen. After China entered the war the United States charged it with abetting North Korean aggression by returning these troops, but China replied that it could hardly keep Korean troops in China if they wished to return home.[85]

None of this evidence is in any way conclusive. Just as in the Soviet case, we are left with no proof of Chinese involvement in the outbreak of the war. But if we examine the circumstantial evidence, it points more toward Chinese than toward Soviet advance knowledge, if not necessarily responsibility. Even if they were unaware of the timing, for leaders like Mao and Chu Teh, it would not be hard to imagine that the return of tens of thousands of Korean fighters to the North would lead to an early assault on the South. It is very difficult to believe that they thought the Soviets alone were responsible for the war, or that it came as a complete surprise to them. It is far more likely that they and the Koreans closely monitored the growing linkages between Chiang, Rhee, and various Americans in the early months of 1950, and decided to coordinate a response.

As the war and American involvement deepened, the Chinese took on a measure of responsibility for North Korea's fate that predated their actual intervention by months, and that went quite beyond the Soviet position. By July 10, various Chinese organizations had begun a movement to oppose American imperialism in Taiwan and Korea; at this time they spoke of "aid and support" (*sŏngwŏn*), but nothing about direct military involvement. Intelligence reports, however, marked a continued transfer to Manchuria of large numbers of troops from the New Fourth Army.[86]

On July 31 MacArthur arrived in Taiwan, acting as if he had plenipotentiary responsibilities to negotiate a military arrangement with Chiang

Kai-shek. August 1 was Armed Forces Day in China and Chu Teh used the occasion to lambast American imperialism, call the North Korean battle "completely just," and refer to the DPRK as "our good neighbor." Most important, a message to P'yŏngyang adopted at the meeting used the term *tan'gyŏl* to refer to the PRC-DPRK relationship. This word means unity or alliance, although not an alliance in the formal sense. But it was not used to refer to the DPRK-Soviet relationship, and the reference included pointed remarks on the "intimate unity" of Korea and China, going back to the joint struggle against Japan. In the context the term also had a pan-Asian flavor, calling on the Koreans, Chinese and Vietnamese to unite, and hailing Mao, Kim Il Sung, and Ho Chi Minh. A Korean report on the rally in Beijing characterized Chu Teh's statements on August 1 as "a solemn declaration" by one "who commands the great armed might of five million soldiers," and cited articles in the Chinese press by guerrillas who had fought with Kim Il Sung in Manchuria. The next day, Kennan came up with an intelligence report that China had offered military aid to the KPA, which the latter had turned down.[87]

In mid-August the Chinese sent a delegation to the Liberation Day ceremonies in P'yŏngyang, and their behavior contrasted with the tepid support of the Soviet representatives. This began with a message from the new ambassador to P'yŏngyang, Ni Chih-liang, highlighting the long-standing elder brother–younger brother relations of China and Korea, and their joint struggle against imperialism:

> China and Korea from long ago have been two brotherly states. In the great struggle to achieve independence and liberation, the Chinese and Korean peoples established intimate relations and common understanding. Today, when the U.S. imperialists are mobilizing land, sea, and air forces in attacking Korea, while at the same time through armed intervention intend to block the Chinese people's liberation of Taiwan, our two countries and peoples are completely united in the struggle to oppose American imperialism and to achieve national independence and liberation.
>
> Our two countries' unity (*tan'gyŏl*), friendship and cooperation, existing between our two peoples from long ago, are being further consolidated, and our common struggle for independence and liberation contributes to them, and to preserving peace in Asia and the world.[88]

Kuo Mo-jo led the twenty-one member Chinese delegation to North Korea, which was much larger than the Soviet representation; it included Li Li-san of the Northeast Government. At first glance it is odd that a cultural figure like Kuo should head the delegation. But Kuo was close to Chou En-lai, and both had taught at the Whampoa Academy—which several star Korean generals had gone through.[89] Kuo's statements frequently referred to the joint armed struggle against the Japanese, and now against the United States. In his Liberation Day address in P'yŏng-yang, Kuo also invoked pan-Asianism by citing China's "iron will" to come to the aid of the national liberation movement in Asia, and quoting Mao on how Asian problems must be solved by Asian peoples themselves. "The Korean people's victory is following that of the Chinese people, and other Asian peoples will follow them both." The *Far Eastern Economic Review* reported that when Li Li-san was in P'yŏngyang he had "acted as if there was a Sino-Korean alliance in operation."[90]

In mid-August American authorities picked up growing evidence of PRC backing for the North. At an NSC meeting on August 14, Averell Harriman suggested the time had come publicly to link China to the Korean fighting. Intelligence sources later claimed that the Chinese pledged to furnish 250,000 soldiers for Korea in a high-level Beijing meeting on August 14, and by the end of the month a huge Sino-Korean army was poised on the Chinese border with Korea. The deployment toward Korea seemed to wax as the chances of an invasion of Taiwan waned; there was still much evidence of the massing of necessary shipping and an impending invasion up to the end of July, but then the reports disappeared. On July 21 Chou En-lai assured Pannikar that the Chinese had every intention of staying out of the Korean hostilities, but by late August he inaugurated the steady drumbeat of warnings that, in retrospect, clearly foreshadowed the Chinese entry into the war.[91]

THE DRIVE ON PUSAN

In the summer months of 1950 the Korean People's Army pushed southward with dramatic success and, until the First Marine Division stiffened the defense, with one humiliating defeat after another of American forces. An army that had bested Germany and Japan found its back pressed to the wall by what they thought was a hastily-assembled peasant military, ill-equipped and, worse, said to be doing the bidding of a foreign imperial power. Kim Il Sung later said that the plan was to win the war for the South in one month, and by the last week of July he had nearly done so.[92] For a month the fighting stabilized at the Pusan Perimeter, then in early September a fierce push nearly broke through the American/South Korean lines. But a massive amphibious landing at Inch'ŏn dashed the North Korean calculus, and brought UN forces back to Seoul.

It was apparent within days that however the war started, the North Korean strategy was a tank-led infantry attack with the initial objective of taking Seoul: that is, a blitzkreig. Mearsheimer argues that the best defense against a blitzkreig is a mobile one of trading territory for time, hoping to stretch the attacker's lines (although he found no such cases of that). The "ideal" mobile defense, he continues, would occur "when the attacker is pursuing limited objectives," and the defender "actually encourages deep penetration." The more successful the blitzkreig in this special situation, the more likely that the attacker's limited goals will change to maximal ones, to his detriment.[93]

The disarray of the southern leadership argues against the notion that the ROKA premeditated such a defense; the North Koreans either demolished or bypassed the strong points of the ROK "forward defense" (a bit of a euphemism), and the army and regime unraveled. But Rhee is on record as telling MacArthur on August 12, "for tactical reasons we have been withdrawing from city to city in the hope that American reinforcements would arrive soon. . . . This plan has been followed strictly by our military leaders and it has helped the enemy gain ground too easily."[94]

This was surely MacArthur's strategy, once he took command. It is in the calamitous pause south of Seoul for more than a week that the seeds of the North Korean defeat were sown, according to both MacArthur and Kim Il Sung, and many military historians. When the attack resumed it was too late, and increasingly too removed from sources of resupply, for victory. Like a judo match, MacArthur drew the blitzkreig southward, ultimately extruding its momentum so it fell on its face. Bravo for MacArthur. In any case, this must reflect back on what the North Korean strategy actually was: a city-grabbing blitz, not one to envelope the whole peninsula. No commander who studied either Soviet or American manuals of strategy would launch a blitzkreig against approximately equal forces and the distinct likelihood of American involvement. But if you thought the other side would try to seize Haeju as prelude to a march on P'yŏngyang, the riposte would be to take Seoul. Whatever transpired in 1950, that was the South Korean plan in 1949 and, as they say, generals always prepare to fight the last war.[95]

This strategy is preemptive, and would fit a logic suggesting that the North Koreans took the risk of American involvement because they thought that over time things were likely to get worse rather than better from their point of view, with growing ties between the ROK and Japan, the distinct likelihood that some event (like the seizure of Taiwan) would stiffen the American commitment, and a much larger boodle of economic and military aid pouring into Seoul. So let us take a deeper look at this preemptive strategy.

In what Mearsheimer calls the Israeli "blitzkreig" during the 1967 "Six Day War," Moshe Dayan and his staff pursued a "defensive strategy, executed offensively" (in their words). The first sign of impending conflict came on May 14, when Israeli intelligence "detected Egyptian forces moving into the Sinai." A week later Nasser declared that he would block the Straits of Tiran; Israeli commanders worried that "if Israel did not strike soon, the Egyptians might strike first" and thus seize the initiative. The opposing forces were about equal in size. On June 1 Dayan joined the government and argued for "a military attack without delay." Dayan developed a classic blitzkreig strategy of penetration along four axes; on June 4 he said, "our best chance of victory [is] to strike the first blow." The next day the Cabinet decided to go to war, and it began the day after that.[96]

However outrageous some may find this comparison between Kim Il Sung and Moshe Dyan,[97] this analysis offers point-by-point correspondence to the June war in 1950. Noteworthy is the rapid sequence, from May 14 to June 6; in Korea it would be May 18 (Pak Il-u's news conference) to June 25. The sides were about equal in number, and both thought the other side might attack first, given their troop movements. Both justified their blitzkreig as defensive. Both cabinets were in the dark, and presented with a fait accompli (ergo the explanation for why party standing committee records show no evidence of the coming war). Finally, the Israeli decisions illustrate just how rapidly one can prepare a blitzkreig. A widened comparison to recent surprise attacks can be found in Table 2.

All of these involved assaults across national boundaries except for the Israeli attack, against an Egyptian force in the Sinai and a United Nations peace-keeping force (which, unlike UNCOK, quickly extruded itself), and the North Vietnamese assault in the central highlands of Vietnam, which is perhaps the best comparison to the Korean case (in the nature of the conflict, it being within the national boundaries, in the size of the forces, the suggestion that it was not meant to be the "final battle," and the unexpected pullback or collapse of the southern defenders—except that the United States chose not to resist North Vietnam in 1975). In each case, the attacker claimed that it was responding to previous extended provocations; the North Korean case was more ambiguous at its start (on June 25) than most of the others.

In the wake of the capture of Seoul and the KPA's unexplained delay, its next big push resulted in the capture of Taejŏn, in what most analysts thought was the KPA's finest battle. In early July American daily situation reports said KPA infantry was "first class," its armor and service "unsurpassed in World War II." Americans were especially impressed with the 6th KPA Division, formed entirely of CCF Koreans and led by Pang Ho-san, which participated in the initial fighting on Ongjin, swept southward along the coast through the Chŏllas, then abruptly turned east, occupying Chinju by August 1 and thereby directly menacing Pusan. But the delay south of the capital, probably occasioned by the necessity to bring

TABLE 2

COMPARATIVE DATA ON THE NORTH KOREAN ASSAULT

conflict	no. of troops	tanks	artillery	airpower
KPA dawn attack	40,000	80	opening barrage	a few sorties
Six Day War[a] dawn attack	36,000	250	opening barrage	major assault[b]
Cambodia[c] dawn attack	32,000 U.S. 48,000 ARVN	100s	opening barrage	fighter suport[d]
PRC-India[e] dawn attack	30,000	a few	opening barrage	none
PRC-DRV[f] dawn attack	150,000	100	opening barrage	none
DRV 1975 no dawn attack	200,000	100	opening barrage	none

SOURCE: Research assistance by Michael Robinson from: Allen S. Whiting, *The Chinese Calculus of Deterrence* (Ann Arbor: University of Michigan Press, 1975); Randolph S. Churchill and Winston Churchill, *The Six-Day War* (Boston: Houghton Mifflin, 1967); Hal Kosut, ed., *Cambodia and the Vietnam War* (New York: Facts on File, 1971); *New York Times*, May 1–10, 1970; July 10, 1978; December 3–10, 1978; January 18–25, 1979.

[a] Israeli attack on Egyptian forces
[b] 450 Israeli aircraft destroy 416 Egyptian planes in initial phase
[c] American-South Vietnamese invasion, May 1, 1970
[d] Air support combined with air attack on North Vietnam and a blockade of the Cambodia coast
[e] October 1962 Chinese assault on India
[f] Chinese invasion of Vietnam, February 17, 1979

up artillery and other supplies from the rear, and probably reflecting an initial plan only to seize Seoul, gave MacArthur the essential time necessary to organize a defense in the southeast.[98]

If the North Koreans were surprised by American intervention, one would not know it from their behavior. They did not flinch as their troops encountered American land, air, and sea power. In a radio broadcast of July 9, Kim said that if the Americans had not intervened, the war would now be over. He called upon the southern people to widen the partisan struggle, and ended the speech with references to heroes like Ulji Mundŏk and Yi Sun-shin who had defended Korea against foreign invaders. Internal materials called the war for the South a *namjin chŏnt'u* or "battle of southward advance" which had destroyed the Rhee regime, but which was now directed against American imperialism and the Rhee clique, in that order. Political officers told Army soldiers that they had the wherewithal to defeat the Americans because they were defending their homeland against the threat of recolonization, had officers who combined advanced Soviet military technique with the experience of the Kim Il Sung partisans, and had the support of the people through land reform and the restoration of the people's committees. "Will the war be long or short?" American intervention meant victory would be "a bit delayed."[99]

The KPA march threatened a full envelopment of the peninsula as early as July 26, when General Walker ordered a military withdrawal from Taegu. But the next day MacArthur flew over to Korea and demanded that further withdrawals cease, and shortly thereafter the 2d Infantry Division landed at Pusan and was rushed up to the line at Chinju. The 6th Division had just "beat hell out of us" there, an American officer related; the next day Masan was occupied and American forces retreated to the Naktong River, employing a "scorched earth" policy that led to the burning of many villages harboring guerrillas: "smoke clouds rose over the front from Hwanggan to Kumchon."[100]

By the beginning of August American and ROK forces outnumbered the KPA along the front, 92,000 to 70,000 (47,000 were Americans), but in spite of this the retreat continued. MacArthur hid this from other American officials, claiming that his forces were outnumbered two or three to one. In the first week of August, however, the First Marine Division went into action and finally halted the KPA advance. The front did not change much from then until the end of August.[101]

The Pusan perimeter had its northern anchor on the coast around P'ohang, its southern anchor in the Chinju-Masan region, and its center just above the major city of Taegu. The latter became a symbol of the American determination to staunch the KPA's advance; for Koreans it was even more important, as a major stronghold of the southern Left. But it was P'ohang in the northeast that was probably the key to stopping the KPA from occupying Pusan and throwing the Americans into the sea.

Appleman wrote that the "major tactical mistake" of the North Koreans was not to press their advantage on the east coastal road. The KPA 5th Division worried too much about covering its flanks, instead of moving quickly on P'ohang and thence combining with the 6th Division to threaten Pusan. This was also the verdict of the Korean high command. China veteran Mu Jŏng replaced (China veteran) Kim Kwang-hyŏp as head of the KPA II Corps, including the 5th Division, in mid-July; he commanded the east coast effort during August, when P'ohang was captured and then lost again; in early September his forces again captured P'ohang after ROKA General Kim Sŏk-wŏn, head of the 3d Division, panicked in the fighting. But this was too little and too late, and eventually Mu Jŏng was sacked and blamed for the failure to capture Pusan.[102]

15. KPA soldiers hold the line, South Korea, summer 1950

Had KPA forces marched as quickly in the east as they did along the southern coast, Pusan might well have been lost. It is doubtful, however, that this would have ended the war, for the KPA still lacked defenses against a major amphibious landing.

At the end of August KPA forces launched their last major offensive at the perimeter, making "startling gains" which in the next two weeks severely strained the American-Korean lines. On August 28 Pang Ho-san ordered his troops to take Masan and Pusan in the next few days; three KPA battallions succeeded in crossing the Naktong River in the central sector, P'ohang and Chinju were lost, and the perimeter was "near the breaking point" with KPA forces again pressing on Kyŏngju, Masan, and Taegu. Walker moved 8th Army headquarters from Taegu to Pusan, other high officials were evacuated from Taegu, and prominent Koreans began leaving Pusan for Tsushima Island. On September 9 Kim Il Sung said the war had reached an "extremely harsh, decisive stage," with the enemy being pressed on three fronts; General Walker two days later reported that the frontline situation was the most dangerous since the perimeter was established. Appleman wrote that by mid-September, "after two weeks of the heaviest fighting of the war [UN forces] had just barely turned back the great North Korean offensive." American casualties were the highest of the war to date, totaling 20,000, with 4,280 dead, by September 15.[103]

16. KPA nurses minister to the wounded

North Korea had brought its forces along the front to 98,000, but upwards of one-third of them were new, raw recruits. Guerrillas, including many women, were active in both the P'ohang and the Masan area fighting, however. Still, the North Koreans were by then badly outnumbered. MacArthur had succeeded in committing most of the battle-ready divisions in the American army to the Korean fighting; by September 8 he had been sent all available combat-trained Army units except for the 82d Airborne Division. Although many units were with the Inch'ŏn operation, some 83,000 American soldiers and another 57,000 Korean and British faced the North Koreans at the front; by this time, the Americans had five times as many tanks as KPA, and their artillery was "vastly superior."[104]

On September 15, of course, the United States carried out a massive amphibious landing at Inch'ŏn, thus relieving the pressure all along the front. Shortly thereafter a document was retrieved giving Kim Il Sung's epitaph on the southern fighting, four months after the war began. Although its authenticity is not proved, the analysis is plausible. "The original plan was to end the war in a month," he said, but "we could not stamp out four American divisions." The units that had captured Seoul disobeyed orders by not marching southward promptly, thereby giving "a breathing spell" to the Americans. From the beginning, "our primary enemy was the American soldiers," but he acknowledged that "we were taken by surprise when allied United Nations troops and the American Air Force and Navy moved in."[105] This suggests that the involvement of

American ground forces was anticipated, but not in such size, and not with air and naval units—a curious oversight, unless the Koreans thought that Soviet air and naval power would either deter or confront their American counterparts. It would have been hard for anyone, including the Joint Chiefs of Staff, to imagine that the vast majority of American battle-ready infantry would be transferred around the globe to this small peninsula, of seeming marginal import to U.S. global strategy.

The Inch'ŏn Landing: Capturing the Hub

In mid-September 1950 MacArthur masterminded his last hurrah, a tactically adroit amphibious landing at Inch'ŏn that brought American armed forces back to Seoul five years nearly to the day after they first set foot on Korean soil, again snatching the defeat of the Korean Left from the jaws of victory. Like Hodge's XXIV Corps, MacArthur's fleet weighed anchor under threat of a late summer typhoon, but this divine wind hewed away from the flotilla's main path.[106] Inch'ŏn harbor has treacherous tides that can easily ground a flotilla of ships if the wrong time is chosen, but the American passage through the shifting bays and flats was technically flawless. American marines landed almost unopposed, but then slogged through a deadly gauntlet before Seoul finally fell at the end of September.

The virtues of an amphibious landing behind North Korean lines were obvious once it was clear that Soviet forces would not challenge American control of the sea and air; indeed, as we have seen, they were obvious even before June 25. MacArthur had by mid-July begun planning for a landing at Inch'ŏn, Haeju, or Chinnamp'o, the latter two being north of the parallel and indicating MacArthur's early concern for rollback. But Inch'ŏn was the primary objective, signifying, as Almond had it, "the capture of the hub,"[107] the core region of Korea with its advanced bureaucratic, communications, and transportation facilities. With control of the state in Seoul, the Korean Right controls the South. Although much mythology has surrounded MacArthur's choice of Inch'ŏn (begun by the generalissimo himself [108]), depicting him standing alone in his clairvoyance against stodgy colleagues who thought "Operation Chromite" would surely fail, it was the logical point of entry for an America willing to muster overwhelming naval force.

Adm. Arthur Dewey Struble, the Navy's crack amphibious expert who led the landing operations at Leyte in the Philippines and who directed the naval operations off Omaha Beach during the Normandy invasion, commanded an enormous fleet of 261 ships in the Inch'ŏn operations, depositing the Marines with hardly a loss. As Blair puts it, "Inchon was a piece of cake, one of the easiest landings in the history of modern warfare." Against this the North Koreans could do nothing. They were not surprised by the invasion, as the American mythology has it, but could not resist it and so began what their historians call euphemistically "the great strategic retreat."[109]

Captured North Korean documents show that by July 31, if not earlier, the KPA developed defense plans for Inch'ŏn: the enemy has been driven back, the documents said, "but plans to invade Inch'ŏn and retake Seoul if given the opportunity." By August 17 some "comrades" were trying to leave the area because of fears of an Inch'ŏn landing "very soon"; on September 4 Pak Ki-su, commander of the KPA 226th unit on an island near Inch'ŏn harbor, said the enemy had landed advance units with the "ultimate purpose" of attacking Seoul.[110]

On September 6, the commander of the KPA 884th detachment at Inch'ŏn, Yi Kyu-sŏp, told his troops the following: "The enemy is planning a big military adventure when the opportunity is there, to launch a surprise amphibious attack at the port of Inch'ŏn for the purpose of capturing Inch'ŏn, and then Seoul. Our detachment . . . will have a fierce battle with them . . . with the important duty of protecting the capital city of our homeland." So, the troops were to heighten vigilance, watch for enemy ships and get all fishermen to do likewise, patrol outlying islands, and the like. On September 12, KPA commander Kim Yŏng-mu, in charge of strategic Kangwha Island and the nearby Kimp'o airfield area, ordered his troops to complete defenses "by September 15, as previously directed," since the enemy was planning a large amphibious landing on or about that date. The next day Kim Il Sung said the American fleet was approaching Inch'ŏn, Wŏlmi Island was being bombed, and all units should be ready to "throw back enemy forces when they attempt their landing operation."[111]

The CIA continued to think that tactical surprise had been achieved, because the North Koreans were preoccupied with the possibility of landings at other ports, although it reported "considerable attention" to building up coastal defenses at Inch'ŏn. But Operation Chromite was a badly kept secret; when American troops and correspondents departed Japan a week before the landing, Russian diplomats were seen waving and yelling, "happy invasion!"[112]

The odd and unexplained element in the invasion is the happy landings available to the Americans by virtue of a complete absence of Soviet aid to the North. Soviet naval and air power was, as usual, kept clear of the battle area. But more important, the Soviets had not helped the Koreans in mining Inch'ŏn Harbor. Later on, when Struble deposited 50,000 Marines in Wŏnsan, minesweeping operations greatly delayed the landing. Thirty Soviet advisors helped to assemble and place the Wŏnsan mines.[113] But few mines were found at Inch'ŏn.

Japan was more involved in taking Inch'ŏn than the Russians were in defending it. After the war began, according to Robert Murphy, "thousands of Japanese specialists who were familiar with [Korea]" worked there secretly with the Americans. Hundreds of Japanese participated in the Inch'ŏn and Wŏnsan landings, manning minesweepers and other support craft, something that SCAP sought mightily to keep secret. The North Koreans periodically publicized such Japanese participation, but no one believed them until Japanese participants wrote about their role many years later. Although Japanese leaders were wary during the KPA's drive on Pusan, Premier Yoshida declared the Korean War "an act of providence" at the time of Inch'ŏn, reflecting the enormous boost to the Japanese economy that had come with the war and, perhaps, hopes that Japanese industrial installations would be recovered for the "free world" after MacArthur's march north. Yoshida's callousness must have made Korean patriots wonder how many times Japan was willing to sacrifice its close neighbor to its own benefit.[114]

In any case the evidence seems to suggest that the Russians were willing to help the North Koreans protect ports north of the parallel, but not at Inch'ŏn. This might be in keeping with the Soviet sense that Korea had been divided in 1945 and their only responsibility was north of the parallel, or it might suggest that Stalin wanted to facilitate an American invasion that would shortly bring them into the North, and smack up against the Chinese border. The point may have been to open an aperture through which MacArthur could pour troops for an aleatory march to the northern frontier. Then again, it may have been inadvertence.

The Americans thus landed, with the 1st Marine Division as the spearhead, against surprisingly light resistance. They entered Inch'ŏn on the first day, encountering a sullen population that "certainly [did] not look happy"; "the people were not so much as glancing at the marines and sailors." South Korean leaflets dropped in the city proclaimed the reentry of the ROK Army, "with the support of United Nations naval forces." North Korean defenses in the area only stiffened on September 19, preparatory to the bloody battle for Seoul, which lasted ten days and ended only with vicious, hand-to-hand street fighting against pockets of "bitter resistance."[115] But this was just a delaying action to allow a massive retreat of officials and others from Seoul; in the end the North Koreans could do little in the face of massive American force. Even an occupation of Pusan could not have ended the war or prevented Inch'ŏn, for, as we have seen, the Americans were determined to come back in even if they were thrown into the Japan Sea, and they had the military capability to do it.

Willoughby exulted in MacArthur's triumph, likening it to Napoleon's campaigns and his "twenty-seven characteristic maneuvers against the enemy's rear." But Hideyoshi might prove the better analogy. MacArthur had regained the strategic initiative and the offensive, which he pursued with a vengeance. But he now had committed an American expeditionary army from all the services totaling 309,843, about half the total United States armed forces and including nearly all trained units in the world, to a land war in Asia on a narrow peninsula that most other strategists had declared peripheral if not indefensible.[116] The war for containment ended on September 30 as ROKA patrols crossed into the North, pressing a rollback in the face of an even larger combined army of Chinese and Koreans, sequestered in the mountain fastness of the Sino-Korean border.

Chapter Twenty

THE POLITICAL CHARACTER OF
THE WAR: PEOPLE'S COMMITTEES
AND WHITE PAJAMAS

The country at this time took ye Alarm and were immediately in
Arms, and had taken their different stations behind Walls, on our
Flanks, and thus we were harassed in our Front, Flanks, and Rear
. . . it not being possible for us to meet a man otherwise than behind a Bush, Stone hedge or Tree, who immediately gave his fire
and went off.

T HE QUICK collapse of the Rhee regime and its dependence on the
United States to succor it and fight its battles ultimately owed not to
the North Korean assault, but to the regime's political character and its
lack of rooted support in the broad reaches of Korean society. It continued to be the regime of Seoul, perched uneasily atop the powerful central state; the swift capture of the capital cast it adrift, much like its wan-
dering president. As the ruling group vacated southward, most Koreans
did not follow them.

A small percentage of the population consisted of propertied and educated Koreans, and most of these fled before the KPA's assault. A
smaller percentage of educated Koreans wanted a democracy as the
Americans define it; many were Christians, and many of them fled. But
many also remained in Seoul. The vast majority of Koreans, more than
90 percent, were a hardworking, unrewarded, very poor, and very disjointed people in 1950. They cared above all about the fortunes of their
families, then they wanted a regime that would not oppress them, and
some perhaps even conceived of a politics that might benefit them. They
knew little if anything about liberal democracy, no more than Americans
know about Confucian rectitude or peasant subsistence. They stayed in
place. Another vast majority of Koreans wanted a regime that could sustain itself independent of foreign intervention, and nearly all wanted a
unified nation.

They had two regimes to choose from, led by Kim Il Sung and Syngman Rhee, not by Karl Marx and Thomas Jefferson. North Korea might
have been Sparta, true, but Seoul was a far cry from Athens. In 1950
(not in 1910 or 1990), the regime of the people's republic offered more
of what Koreans wanted from their politics, and to more Koreans, than

did the Rhee regime. This was the basic source of the DPRK's strength. It is why American intelligence found, during the war for the South, that a "very small percentage of South Koreans in Communist held areas has fled south to friendly territory."[1]

There is a further question about the North Korean occupation of the South that returns us to the analytical and definitional questions with which we began this study: what were this war's origins, and what manner of war was it? The answer proffered was that it originated in the collapse of Japan's colonial empire, and that it was a civil and revolutionary war, to unify and transform the country. The proof of this is to be found in the three-month northern occupation, where Koreans came back to the questions of 1945: which regime rules, who owns the land? There is barely a single study of this facet of the war, because if the war is called foreign aggression, who cares? Yet in the midst of the massive push toward Pusan, thousands of Korean cadres, from North and South, set about restoring the people's committees disbanded in 1945–1946, and pushing through land redistribution on a revolutionary basis. Through it all they beat the drum of Korean unification and independence.

The Left in the South had been nearly destroyed in the interim five years, but the conditions in which it found support were substantially the same. Yet the second liberation of 1950 came under distinctly North Korean auspices. Nothing is more characteristic of the Kim system than a superordinate imposition of core leadership upon spontaneous or inchoate forces welling up from below, as we have seen, and 1950 was no different. From the beginning of the northern occupation, internal and published materials emphasized the passive tense: the South was being liberated *by* the Korean People's Army (KPA). With the merger of the southern and northern parties in 1949, the group of southern leftists and communists around Pak Hŏn-yŏng were relegated to an adjunct status, but this was particularly true of the Army, which traced its origins back to the Manchurian guerrillas, was the critical organ of Kimilsungist power (more so than the party or government apparatus), and had hardly any southern communists in its leadership.

A secret document issued early on by the Interior Ministry for cadres in the "liberated areas" told them to emphasize that this liberation came courtesy of the KPA. It was mostly silent on who started the war, instead linking the fighting to ending the threat that Korea might be permanently divided: "our war is a just war to unify the homeland and liberate the people in the southern part." The list of Hail Marys to be utilized in propaganda began, "long live the KPA, growing out of the guerrilla war against Japan"; then there were hosannas to "the eternally-unified Korean people," the DPRK, and "the peerless patriot and glorious leader," who by now needs no introduction. There was no mention of the Soviets, except for their leadership of the socialist camp, where, interestingly, they were paired in tandem with China.[2]

Another set of instructions to Interior Ministry cadres gave the Soviets "the decisive role" in liberating Korea (while mentioning that they started fighting in the East only on August 9), but placed the origin of the DPRK in the people's committees, which the creativity of the Korean people brought forth as "an unprecedented, new form of sovereignty." It linked this movement to that for land reform, both of which served "to sweep away" the effects of thirty-six years of Japanese rule, thus "to make our country rich and strong."[3]

Within the party apparatus the emphasis was also on northern tutelage. An article on "party life" said many southerners have little training in "organization life," and indeed could not have given the tough conditions of underground work in the South; but now, "for the first time [they] are receiving training in principles of inner-party democracy." Thousands upon thousands of party and government cadres were "sent down" to organize committees and land reform at the local levels; many of them were southerners previously trained in the North, but what is striking in internal materials is the virtual absence of anything diverging from Kimilsungist orthodoxy.[4]

Internal materials mention Yŏ Un-hyŏng, lauding him as a patriot, and occasionally there is use of the 1945 term "Korean People's Republic," instead of the DPRK. The people's committees that emerged under the aegis of the KPR were viewed as the origin and basis of the people's republic in North and South. But there is little if any reference to a communist tradition apart from that of Kim Il Sung.[5]

THE OCCUPATION OF SEOUL

In the early evening of June 27 the 9th Regiment of the KPA 3d Division entered Seoul, rumbling down the road from Munsan to the Independence Gate, where it then crashed tanks into the Sŏdaemun prison and released thousands of leftists jailed by the Rhee regime. Some sporadic resistance continued for the next several hours, but by noonday on June 28 the city was pacified. This inaugurated a three-month period of occupation—liberation to those who benefitted—that saw the reinstitution of the people's committees (PC) that first emerged in 1945.

The Seoul People's Committee was led mostly by southerners, beginning with its chief, Yi Sŭng-yŏp, and its vice-chairman, Pak Ch'ang-sik. Moderates and middle-roaders from the National Assembly and various political parties remained in Seoul, and lent their names to the new administration. By early July the administration had confiscated all Japanese property, and that of the ROK government, its officials, and "monopoly capitalists." The KPA distributed rice stocks to poor people, and left the administration of justice in the hands of local peace preservation groups, many of whom had just gotten out of prison.[6]

In the early days of the new regime, the released prisoners settled scores with their antagonists who had abused and jailed them, mainly members of the Korean National Police and the rightist youth groups. People's courts arraigned and denounced them, after which summary executions took place.[7] This experience has led to a general judgment, reinforced by the American propaganda apparatus, that the occupation of the south was a living hell for those who experienced it.[8] I myself seem always to be running into Koreans who say the experience was terrible, while also saying that they successfully hid out during the entire three months.

Evidence from the time, including interviews with ROK officials who fled Seoul, does not suggest that the occupation was politically onerous for the majority of Seoul's citizens, although generalized fear, food shortages and the American bombing made it an often hellish experience.[9] An account by Y. H. Chu, who remained in Seoul for the entire period, said that released prisoners and locally-recruited officials abused people early on, through people's courts and the like, but "the red police speedily countermanded such practices and proclaimed that no 'people's trials' shall be tolerated." The KPA troops who garrisoned the city were not seen much, and were "rather gentle and well behaved. They did not molest people, nor did they [do] any looting." "Cases of physical torture were rarely reported," he said, but there was a kind of mental torture, as those who were objects of the regime were required to attend group meetings and confess their sins. "Reactionaries" were arrested, but not generally executed; at the end, in September, leftist youths killed many who were on various "blacklists." High-ranking ROK officials and other prominent individuals who stayed behind were interned, including the novelist Yi Kwang-su; Ku Cha-ok, a former provincial governor; Chang In-gap of the *Tonga ilbo*; and Yi Chang-gun, a provincial governor under the Japanese; many went to the North in September, whether voluntarily or not.[10]

O Tae-sŏn, a Korean National Police (KNP) officer in Rhee's presidential detail, remained in Seoul for the first three weeks after the war began, and "had no knowledge of any general or large-scale executions." Some people were taken away in the night, to where he did not know. When leftists looted the Naija Apartments, an American billet, the Seoul PC required that all articles be returned, and said the looters would be "severely punished."[11]

Although we do not have internal North Korean instructions to cadres on the first occupation of Seoul, we do have them for the second in early 1951. They urged soldiers quickly to establish "revolutionary order" and "observe mass discipline," to "strictly prohibit arrests and killings without cause," to prohibit entry to citizen's homes without cause, to protect enemy property and prevent looting, respect and not interfere with churches and believers, and to protect foreigners under applicable international laws.[12]

After Seoul was retaken, American social scientists working for the forerunner of the RAND Corporation conducted interviews with about one hundred people who had remained in Seoul, sixty with officials of various ministries and the rest with various citizens, although none with "ardent cooperators" with the North Koreans.[13] Their summary of the three months suggests that it was vintage North Korean practice: a tight ship, disciplined behavior, and a thorough bath in Kimilsungist politics.

Officials who staffed the occupation were often of southern origin, and had been trained for as much as three years for their duties; they were aided by local leftists who "came crawling out of the underground." Tons of leaflets, posters, and propaganda materials "had been printed and stored in freight cars." Officials were "courteous and reasonable." "When orders were given, the reasons for them were patiently explained. When systematic confiscation of property took place, the new uses to which it was to be put were carefully indicated. When people were arrested it was done apologetically and always in terms of the necessity of locating some 'outside' enemy." Occupying officials and police had been "strictly briefed," the study found, and comported themselves politely and efficiently. "No action was ever taken without its well-reasoned explanation."

The regime, as in the North, embraced all but its outright enemies. Intellectuals and technicians were welcomed, as were ordinary state administrators; "to the great majority of workers, the Communists opened the door freely in return for [the] promise of cooperation." People's courts were held, the study found, but "in the majority of cases . . . the Reds were only too glad to give the accused 'another chance.' To be sure, the pressure to cooperate was great, but the typical story indicates that the arguments were reasonably assembled and that the much-feared and widely rumored systems of torture never materialized." Some former officials were arrested in the dead of night and interrogated, but most got put in a program of reeducation through study and, sometimes, manual labor.

Every soldier and official behaved like a political officer, using extensive face-to-face communications. Workers were quickly brought into mass organizations, and students held endless rallies to support the war and volunteer. Korea's long-abused women were a major target of the regime. The Women's League established organizations at every level, its workers distributing pamphlets door-to-door. Every PC had to have at least one woman; "women held jobs of honor, worked at employment usually denied them, [and] sometimes went around calling each other *tongmu* [comrade]." If a soldier met a woman in the street, he would lecture her on women's equality.

A huge number of political meetings at all levels, supplemented by periodic rallies and mass meetings, drummed in the regime's message. In early July a radio announcement said all those with something to confess should go to local police stations and do so, and thousands showed up. Criticism and self-criticism, both in oral face-to-face circumstances, and in written confessions, was a daily experience for government officials, school teachers, and anyone in a position of authority, used extensively "both for diagnosis and therapy." People got up to render their personal histories, and to reflect upon, repent from, and apologize for their past transgressions. The social scientists thought all this was akin to "a religious revival," and that it got quick results. (When the ROK authorities came back to Seoul, they found many of the confessions and used them to round up "communist sympathizers.") The schools at all levels were organs of political indoctrination, but also a means "to attack illiteracy and ignorance on the broadest basis."

In spite of the regime's discipline and vigor, its mass politics would suffocate a Western liberal. Yet many members of the tiny stratum of Korean liberal politicians stayed behind, worked with this regime, and then returned to the North with it—voluntarily, according to the evidence from the time. About sixty members of the National Assembly remained in Seoul, and toward the end of July, forty-eight of them held a meeting expressing their allegiance to the DPRK. These included moderate members of the Korean Democratic Party like Kim Yong-mu, Wŏn Se-hun, Kim Sang-hyŏn, and the "Brown University '05" graduate who dallied off Inch'ŏn in September 1945 waiting to greet the Americans, Paek Sang-gyu; people aligned with Yŏ Un-hyŏng like his brother and Chang Kŏn-sang; Kim Ku's close associate Cho So-ang, and two favorites of the Americans in the Occupation, Kim Kyu-sik and the South Korean Interim Government (SKIG) administrator, An Chae-hong. In late July Kim Kyu-sik and the venerable March 1st Movement participant, O Se-ch'ang, denounced Rhee in radio broadcasts. Wŏn Se-hun was on the Kyŏnggi Province People's Committee; No Il-hwan, one of the moderate legislators imprisoned by Rhee in 1949, was a "people's judge" in Kae-sŏng. Kim Kyu-sik, Cho So-ang, and the KPG-aligned Song Ho-sŏng were reportedly members of the Seoul PC, at least for a time.[14]

17. Student "volunteers" for the KPA drill in Seoul, summer 1950

Even one American did the bidding of the regime. "Seoul City Sue," the Tokyo Rose of the Korean War, broadcast appeals to American soldiers over the radio in an unmistakably native accent. She was Anne Suhr, a former Methodist missionary née Anne Wallace who left the service in the north during the 1930s to marry a Korean man named Sŏ. He later worked for the Military Government in the 1940s, and was jailed as a leftist by the Rhee regime in the spring of 1950.[15] She presumably returned to the North after Seoul was recaptured.

American G-2 sources found that "generally speaking, North Korean support in [the] Seoul populace comes from the working class and university and high school students including females. Merchants [were] classed as neutrals with ROK leanings. Intelligentsia [was] pro-ROK . . . estimate 60 percent [of] Seoul students [are] actively aiding NK." The CIA agreed with such judgments, while British sources found that, according to an informant, student and youth volunteering for the KPA was high, with three-quarters of those who volunteered (or were conscripted) "quite openly showing their sympathy with the Communists."[16] No one who lived through the occupation of Seoul could deny that students were among the most ardent supporters of the regime, which has sent chills up the spine of the Korean Right ever since.

18. A KPA officer holds a political meeting with South Korean peasants, summer 1950

The occupation ended amid the crisis of the Inch'ŏn landing and the vicious battle for Seoul. Discipline broke down and many killings occurred, which we will examine later. Many buildings were also burned, apparently by vagrants and children who were urged to do so by the KPA.[17]

THE REVIVAL OF THE COMMITTEES

Kim Il Sung called for the restoration of the people's committees in his first radio address after the war broke out, and American intelligence recognized the crucial importance to the North Koreans of this political form, "dissolved long ago by US Army Military Government." Propagandists referred to this history over and over again, and counterposed the committee form not to the politics of the ROK, but to the reimposition of "the ruling organs of Japanese imperialism."[18] In other words their point was to restore people's committees which predated the reimposition of the colonial state, not to impose on the South the North's political forms.

The first committee reinstated to power was in the county of Yŏnbaek just below the parallel. It had been among the first to be disbanded by American troops, in September 1945. On June 27 a mass meeting elected fifteen members to a provisional county PC. The chairman, Yi Tu-ch'ŏl, and the vice-chairman, Kim Nǔng-dae, were both veterans of the guerrilla struggle in the South. Many people arose to spit out their bitterness at the Rhee regime and American imperialism. When Seoul was captured, prisoners released from detention and other leftists set up self-defense groups (*chawidae*) operating from police boxes, and immediately organized PCs in various districts (*tong*) of the capital.[19] Restored PCs emerged all over the South after the KPA marched through; the North Koreans termed them "provisional" PCs, pending formal elections.

According to a former secretary to an ROK cabinet member, each *tong* PC had a staff of about ten, "selected by the leftists of each *tong* in open meeting"; they were responsible for a population of two to five thousand people. The PCs "were allowed to operate [by] themselves," without much surveillance by the North Koreans. Members of the National Guidance Alliance, the grouping of apostate communists, were also active in setting up Seoul commitees, which the secretary thought indicated that they had a prior arrangement with P'yǒngyang to feign commitment to the ROK before the war began. In Seoul and throughout the rural areas, activists from the outlawed *Chǒnp'yǒng* union and *Chǒnnong* peasant association worked on reviving PCs, and many were elected to PC posts.[20]

It is plausible that daily administration was left mostly to the newly-reemerging committees, but the North Koreans exercised sharp procedural controls to assure that PC membership would conform to North Korean practice and discipline. Top secret instructions to cadres on how to run PC elections in Anyang illustrate the process. Kang Yong-su, chief of the interior department for Sihǔng County, ordered the establishment of a broad patrolling network (*kyǒngbi-mang*) to guard the elections in wartime conditions during a ten-day period, July 20–30. The elections began at the village level on July 25, moving up to the township level two days later, and to the county level on July 28. Self-defense units were to guard election points against "impure elements, wreckers, and arsonists," and to send two or three people around to gather up public opinion and to deal with "evil" ideas and "impure" plots. Daily reports on such activity were to be dispatched to higher levels. Armed force was not to be displayed at the election places; otherwise, "it will look like the forcible elections held under the Rhee puppet regime." It was thought important "to raise [people's] political awareness to a high point."

Political and social organizations should be examined by cadres, and singled out were "the nominees for village, township and county PCs to see that individuals are recommended who are truly capable of serving the people." People who could not vote included the following, in order: "pro-Americans," defined as members of the ROK government or the National Assembly or "reactionary organizations"; "national traitors," members of terrorist groups, and people "who actively helped American imperialism through economic aid"; and the "pro-Japanese clique," including central, provincial, and county administrators and police during the colonial period, plus "people who actively helped Japanese imperialism through economic aid."[21]

The American social science/intelligence study of the occupation of the South found that village-level PCs would have a slate of three or four candidates, usually chosen from among younger members of very poor families (the voting age was eighteen and over); mass meetings would precede the voting, with KWP cadres getting people to discuss the candidates and urging everyone to vote. Usually there was one candidate whom the Labor Party favored; occasionally peasants missed the point and elected the wrong person, so the election would be held again. Local records show that KWP members made up one-third to one-half of village and township PCs.[22] None of this is surprising, especially for elections held during a vicious war, but it does indicate that committee elections were unlikely to spawn the complex social composition found in 1945.

Published regulations for the PC elections were a bit less forthright, but followed the general policy etched above. Those proscribed from voting were "pro-Japanese, pro-Americans, and national traitors." The bottom-up procedure was very much like that in 1945. A general meeting at the village level would elect PC members, and representatives who would form assemblies at the township level; then the townships would select representatives to the county level, and so on. The assemblies would then select PC members, twenty to fifty at the county level, fifteen to twenty-five at the township level, five to seven in the villages. The PCs would also employ clerks to do routine administrative work. A directive signed by Kim Tu-bong said that such procedures would "democratize the restored people's committees," after the reestablishment of interim PCs in the wake of the KPA march southward;[23] this probably means that an element of untoward spontaneity accompanied their initial revival.

Elections under these procedures began on July 25, starting at the village level in Kyŏnggi Province and finishing at the county level July 29. Most of the new PCs replaced provisional ones that had emerged after June 25. In the previous ten days voter registration and propaganda teams had spread through the province. In Koyang elections, the regime claimed that 100 percent of the people participated in "a free atmosphere" (a reference to the May 1948 elections), singing songs about "the people's guerillas" and "General Kim Il Sung." News of elections and the onset of land reform crowded out the war dispatches in this period.[24]

It is obvious even from published materials that anyone opposing the Kim regime would not dare run for election, and the frequent claims of 100 percent participation betray either a stunning naïveté about what ordinary common sense would suggest, or a high level of coercion. But, as in the North, the PCs provided participation to people who had never occupied a political post or been asked a political opinion in the past. The PCs brought an entirely new class of people to power.

Many members were women, and almost all, in the countryside, were poor peasants; they were also remarkably young. In elections in nine villages in Koyang County, for example, 86 percent of the eligible voters participated (a low count), electing fifty-seven people of whom ten were women, nineteen were workers, and twenty-nine were poor peasants. In a nearby township election, of seventeen people elected, ten were under thirty years of age; only two were over forty. In Poŭn County, for which we have rather complete data, nearly all the PC members were poor peasants; in some case as many as half were Korean Worker's Party (KWP) members, and the vast majority were under forty years of age. Elections for the forty-one-member PC in Yangju County brought forth ten women, twenty-seven poor peasants, and nine workers. Of some 6,100 village PC members elected by August 6 in Kyŏnggi, about 5,800 were peasants and workers; the remainder were *samuwŏn*, students, intellectuals, and businessmen.[25]

According to the official newspapers of the period, PC elections were completed in the provinces of Kyŏnggi, Kangwŏn, and southern Hwanghae by August 6. Of the more than 15,000 people elected at all levels in Kyŏnggi, women constituted 14 percent of the total, peasants 86 percent, workers 8 percent, and all the rest 6 percent—figures that correspond to previous North Korean experience. The elections in the Ch'ungch'ŏng Provinces were done by mid-August, those in the Chŏllas by August 25. In the latter case, it was emphasized more than usually that the PCs were restored and elected through the work of the local people themselves, which stands to reason given the leftist character of this region.

It is also noteworthy that the elections proceeded quickly in South Chŏlla, whereas in North Chŏlla, a less leftist province, for unexplained reasons elections had been held in only seven counties by August 25. At all levels in the Chŏllas the vast majority of PC members—often 90 percent—were poor peasants. Workers only approached 10 percent participation at the county level. Elections also proceeded in Kyŏngsang Province counties occupied by the KPA, mostly the mountainous eastern counties away from the fighting front.[26]

North Korean leadership of the restoration of the PCs did not mean that North Koreans staffed them; the members were local people, including many who had first joined the committees in 1945. The provincial PC in South Chŏlla was led by Kim Su-p'yŏng, a leader of the 1948 Yŏsu rebellion; Yi Ch'ang-su, a close friend and participant in the 1948 events, ran the Yŏsu county PC.[27]

LAND REFORM

The restoration of the committees was relatively easy compared to the attempt to carry through revolutionary land reform in the midst of a war. But a confrontation with Korea's landed class, which had succeeded in blocking the reformist redistribution pushed on the ROK by the Americans, was taken to be the essence of the antifeudal, anticolonial character of the Korean revolution. Internal party materials had argued for years that the Japanese maintained a significant Korean landlord class to facilitate control of peasants and extraction of rice, and therefore "the anti-Japanese struggle was organically connected to the people's struggle against reactionary landlords." Without the support of "new foreign aggressors," they would have no power.[28] In June 1950 they temporarily lost their foreign backing, and met with a revolution that cleared away class structures and power that later made possible Rhee's land redistribution program—because the Americans would not fight merely to restore land to this class that had ruled Korea for centuries. Thus, paradoxically, the northerners did the Americans a favor, if violently, by breaking the back of landlord obstructionism.

The land reform law of July 4, 1950, called for expropriation of landlord-held land without compensation, and limited the amount of land peasants could keep to five *chŏngbo* (about twelve acres); but it allowed richer peasants who worked their own land to keep up to twenty *chŏngbo*, a rather large farm in Korea, and also did not touch Oriental Development Company land that had been redistributed to tenants in 1948 by USAMGIK. Although people's courts and attacks on landlords occurred sporadically, it seems that most landlords had fled before the KPA and so it was not a particularly violent campaign, compared to those in China and Vietnam. It was more akin to the Yanan land program, which sought to win over the vast majority of those working in agriculture, and to downplay sharp class struggle. In villages intensively studied by Americans later on, they found that no farmer lost all his holdings, and no land was taken merely because the owner was a rightist, if his holdings fell under the ceilings. As in the North, peasants were given deeds making the land their "permanent property," heritable by their offspring, but the land could not be sold or rented out; newspapers were predictably full of peasants proclaiming their eternal gratitude to "the great leader" for getting land, just as in the 1946 reform.[29]

Local PCs had the responsibility for organizing the redistribution, but decisions on who got what land, in terms of size and quality, were dealt with by five to nine member land reform implementation committees, also called village committees, composed of poor peasants, tenants, and agricultural laborers—with KWP cadres usually presiding. These committees were to investigate and register all landlord property, including tools and grain stocks, gather statistics on tenancy, draw up lists of peasants to get land, and submit their results to the next highest level. Just as in the 1946 reform, families received land according to a "labor point" system, in which one point was allowed for each fully productive laborer, whether male or female, and fractions for teenagers, children, and people over sixty; a determination was also made on the quality of particular plots of land. Although peasants later said the reform was conducted impartially, they thought the better quality lands went to the poorest peasants, and to the most ardent supporters of the North. Anyone defined as using land "parasitically," meaning they did not work it with their own hands, had it confiscated. Participation was required of peasants, particularly in identifying pro-Japanese individuals. Falsification of records, or hiding land, could bring stiff prison terms. The reform abrogated all existing debt, including repayment for the ODC (Oriental Development Company) land redistributed in 1948. A tax of about 25 percent was then imposed on peasant production.[30]

Much like the situation with the people's committees, once the KPA marched through an area, peasants (usually tenants) would occupy or claim their lord's land, the latter usually having fled behind the Pusan perimeter. The North dispatched thousands of cadres to impose regularity and procedure on these actions. American intelligence sources noted that land reform came immediately on the heels of military victories: "obviously this program was crucial to them." Internal materials show that Interior Ministry cadres got extensive preparation prior to carrying out the reform; interestingly, these materials appear to have been prepared after June 25, 1950, that is, they were not readied before the war broke out.[31]

Although little is known about land reform in the first weeks after the war began, on July 20 Pak Mun-gyu, DPRK agriculture minister and Yŏ Un-hyŏng's old political associate, told southern peasants to prepare for land reform, while indicating that it might not be concluded before the war ended.[32] This timing changed once the war bogged down, however, and the cadres quickly pushed through a radical redistribution, hoping to win peasants to their side with a tangible gain of land. Although the North had plenty of experience with a quick land reform, having done it in March 1946, the evidence suggests that the program in the South was hasty and lacking the careful political preparations of Chinese-style campaigns.[33]

Captured records from Poŭn County show that village land reform committee members were sent up to the county level to get a "short course" in implementing the reform. The county land reform committee was headed by the local KWP chief, and composed of leaders of the county PC, the local peasant association, the women's group, and the leftist youth organization. All but one gave their class background as poor peasant. In the villages, poor peasants and party activists predominated on some sixty-nine land reform committees, with five to eleven members each.[34]

Published reports on nine villages in Koyang County said that the reform process began in mid-July and ended on August 9, when a "settling accounts" mass meeting was held in the local township. The next day congratulatory celebrations went on in the villages. There was nothing said about attacks on landlords, people's courts, or the like, but "settling accounts" usually meant divvying up landlord property. A total of 1.5 million *p'yŏng* of land was confiscated from landlords (1.4 million *p'yŏng* of the total), the ROK state, businesses, schools, and churches (the last holding 21,620 *p'yŏng*). It was redistributed to 814 households, 450 of whom were landless tenants, 346 land-poor peasants, with the remainder made up of hired laborers. They all thanked Kim Il Sung, and pledged to "raise production to support the front and build a rich and powerful country."[35]

In Shindo township, in a region of rich rice paddies and much tenancy, twelve landlords, including the wealthiest one, Yi Tong-u, had 1.8 million *p'yŏng* confiscated; it was divided among about 1,200 peasant households, one-third of whom were pure tenants, most of the rest being part-owners, part-tenants. Information on North Ch'ungch'ŏng, where smallholding was much more common, shows that in one village only 57,298 *p'yŏng* was confiscated from all sources, and given mostly to land-poor peasants rather than tenants. A general meeting in the village decided to give a peasant named Yi Chang-ha a special award of land because he had participated in the autumn uprisings in 1946.[36]

An investigation of records on one hundred peasants in Anyang shows that cursory listings were made of the amount of dry and paddy fields each peasant worked, and what part of it they owned and what part of it they worked as tenants. Most were smallholders who owned most of the land they farmed, while renting an additional plot and working it as tenants to feed their families. Only four were pure tenants, but only seven worked no tenanted land at all. Most held very small plots, only one owning more than 6,000 *p'yŏng*; this was one of those who worked no tenant land. Two people owned more than 5,000 *p'yŏng*, and still they both worked additional land as tenants. The average holding was about 2,000 *p'yŏng*.[37]

Documents like land titles, called *chŭngmyŏngsŏ*, recorded only the lo-

cation, type, and amount of land, with the locations often vaguely described, nothing like Western land titles. Written on the cheapest sort of
paper, perhaps all that was available, they were given to peasants during
the redistribution. Most of the time it appears that little land changed
hands; it was more a matter of tenants having squatter's rights, getting to
keep the land they had been working.[38]

By the end of August, newspapers claimed that land reform was complete in the provinces of Kyŏnggi, the Ch'ungch'ŏngs, Kangwŏn, and
North Chŏlla; it was still going on in South Cholla, but was complete in
the counties around Kwangju. By the time of the Inch'ŏn landing, the
reform was complete in South Chŏlla, with some 58,675 *chŏngbo* having
been redistributed. Preliminary investigation work had been done in a
couple of counties in North Kyŏngsang and a few land reform committees had been formed by September, mostly in the northeastern counties
of Yech'on, Mun'gyŏng, Yŏngju, and Andong.[39]

POLITICS IN THE PROVINCES

Thousands of cadres entered towns and villages and sought in short order to revive the revolutionary organizations of the period just after liberation, as we have seen. As ever, the political complexion of the South
shaped and skewed this activity, just as it did the war, making it easier
here, harder there: directly imposed by the North in those regions lacking a strong Left, but merging with the indigenous forces in provinces
like the Chŏllas.

North Korean materials demonstrate that little was left to chance, even
at the village level. A top secret July 16 directive to cadres at the township
level from the Sihŭng County police read as follows:

(1) Rapidly, after a few days of concrete examination of the local
situation, organize an intelligence network, and widely begin the work
of voluntary confessions (*chasu*); get reactionaries voluntarily to surrender hidden weapons; arrest the ringleaders of reactionary political parties, social organizations, and police organs, giving them no opportunities [for resistance].

(2) Collect important documents from the reactionary police, study
and analyze them for help with your work.

(3) Punish spies who are from the North first.

(4) All government officials, spies for south Korea and the United
States, officials of the National Guidance Alliance, cadres of the Korean National Youth, responsible officials of political parties led by
Rhee, Kim Sŏng-su, Shin Sŏng-mo, and Yi Pŏm-sŏk should be purged
and arrested; then get in touch with this office [the county level].

(5) For the lower-ranking officials of the above groups, use voluntary confessions to find out about the local situation.

(6) In investigating crimes, never forget political awareness and an attitude of vigilance.

(7) Enemy property is to be confiscated and reported according to the DPRK Constitution; keep a precise accounting; absolutely no confiscated property may be used just as you please.

The township authorities were also told to organize small numbers of youths for village security, "communication networks" of four or five people, and "defense committees" to repair war damage and the like.[40]

An indication that these matters did not proceed so swiftly is provided by another set of documents, from mid-August, urging police in Poŭn County to remedy defects in their work, including failure to mobilize themselves and members of the local PCs to secure confessions, failure to collect and maintain records, allowing wrangling and factional infighting. One directive urged police "to set in motion each [police] branch and mass organization to sweep out the fear and dread among the people who groaned under Rhee's despotism, by proper administration of justice, putting people at ease, and [thus] actively promoting the lending of support to the army."[41]

The "voluntary confession" (*chasu*) was the prime method used all over the South to ascertain local political information and assess the loyalties and tendencies of citizens. Original examples of confession documents from villages in Iksan County illustrate the thorough, detailed, and sometimes remarkably petty pattern of inquiry into the thoughts and behavior of ordinary citizens. Chŏng Mun-gyu, a man of thirty, confessed that he had joined Kim Ku's youth group in 1947, working as a section chief in the local organization; he pledged to "cleanse my spirit," and to devote himself to the DPRK from then on. Hong Sun-yŏng, a peasant also thirty, admitted to having made "tricky propaganda for the police, saying that when the KPA came, all property will be taken and all the people will be slaughtered." But having seen "what liberation really means," he wanted to devote his life to the DPRK. A policeman from Kunsan, Sŏ Pyŏng-du, age twenty-five, who had been in the Japanese navy, said he had "to a small extent" been involved in "evil atrocities," which he left undescribed. But he pledged to do better.

A tenant farmer named Yi Pong-yong had been mobilized in 1942 to work in a hydroelectric plant in Japan; when he returned to his village in 1945 there was little chance of reclaiming his tenanted land, and so he had no choice but to help the police in his village. He was detailed to watch peasant rebels kept in the village jail, or posted as a village guard to look out for guerrillas. He had also captured peasant rebels from time

to time. But being a "propertyless person" (*musanin*), he was "won over
to the side of the revolution." So he brought food to the families of imprisoned peasants and helped them in other ways; he acknowledged that
although he knew he should work for the revolution, his resolve had not
been strong, he "could not wipe out his bad political line." At the end of
his confession, he said, "if you forgive my crimes I will fight with zeal for
the People's Republic."

In Korean traditional fashion, good leftists were found through guar-
antors who provided documents akin to recommendations. Kim Su-
bong, twenty-four, was said to be a poor peasant—"and therefore his
character is excellent." He joined the South Korean Worker's Party
(SKWP) in 1947, frequently setting signal fires in the hills to call people
to demonstrations. In early 1948 he was ordered to attack a nearby township office; later on the SKWP required him to join his village police, and
from there to provide information on imprisoned comrades and other
matters. A policeman won a guarantor who was willing to write that he
had "repented of his past" after confessing voluntarily to various sins; the
guarantor appealed for leniency, saying he would take responsibility for
any crimes or reactionary behavior the man might do in the future.[42]

Scattered lists of those detained by the police indicate that the North
Koreans were particularly on the lookout for people who had fled the
North; on one list of fourteen criminals, mostly former officials and reactionary political types who had opposed the Left in various ways, two
people merely have the entry that they went to the South.[43]

Such methods seem to be the essence of how a totalitarian regime goes
about its work, yet there was space for resistance. For example, documents on volunteers for the KPA from several villages in Sihŭng County
show widely variant rates of voluntarism; from July 10 to September 3,
149 of 942 youths in eight villages volunteered, the highest rate being 47
of 120 in Pangbae village, the lowest being 7 of 173 in Sŏch'o village. This
data, incidentally, also suggests that it was a matter of voluntarism rather
than conscription.[44]

North Korean internal materials dealing with "public opinion" also offer some candor. Reports from Sihŭng in early August said that the local
people do not like Americans, and wonder why they are fighting in Korea. Peasants were happy to get land, and were not upset about the crop
collection program. However, "our principles are not yet rooted among
the majority of the people. Many people still don't understand the significance and seriousness of this war. They do not willingly volunteer for
the army."

Another report said that the KPA was "supported and highly admired
by the people," but some KPA soldiers had regrettably gotten into alter-
cations caused by "drinking wine and making love to strange girls in the-

aters," including prostitutes who used to serve the American army. Therefore "indiscreet behavior, especially in low-class theaters, is strictly prohibited." Wartime conditions also aggravated public peace, with the food shortage causing "constant fighting with rifles and swords" among youths in Inch'ŏn; air raids terrified people and caused mass exoduses from urban areas.[45]

The social science/intelligence study of the occupation examined two communities near Taejŏn: Kŭmnam, a township of 14,000 made up mostly of smallholding peasants, few possessing more than three *chŏngbo*, engaged in irrigated rice farming; and Kach'ang,[46] a village of 600 surrounded by very productive land, about half of which had been owned by absentee Japanese landlords. Most residents were very poor tenants. Within Kŭmnam the researchers studied one neighborhood village, run by a single, but very divided, clan.[47]

KPA units who had fought in China passed through the area and garrisoned it, followed by civil officials who arrived in late July. All the North Koreans emphasized that they were fighting the war with their own resources, with no help from the Soviets; the Soviet role in fact was "passed over with almost no mention," and the Americans were also "dismissed very lightly." Instead, great emphasis was placed on "the reputed self-sufficiency of the North Koreans," along with the three major themes of the occupation: reunification, land reform, and the restoration of the people's committees.

The communists retained the basic administrative divisions of local government, while replacing the existing offices with people's committees as "the sole governing bodies." All PC officials were selected through elections, which the authors noted was unprecedented in previous local experience. Mass organizations of women, peasants, workers, and youths were formed, and *Chŏnp'yŏng* unions were reactivated in local factories. All sorts of other groups came into being, exemplifying the remarkable North Korean emphasis on placing everyone in an organization: self-defense groups, construction units, crop-estimation teams. The American authors found the result at the local level to be "a nearly autonomous administration, answerable to the community through elections"; it provided services "on a scale never attempted before."

Responsible police officers were all North Koreans, but were small in number and were limited mostly to the county and township level; they rarely appeared in the villages. Instead, an informal communist system existed at the village level, with county-level specialists coming down to set various kinds of organizations in motion (just as we saw earlier). A KWP branch was organized at the neighborhood and village level, but citizens were less aware of it than an informal grouping of leaders within the party: "the villager tended to see power resident in persons," less than in formal institutions like the KWP. In Kŭmnam, about nine people were thought to be powerful: seven outsiders, including northerners and southerners, and two villagers, the chiefs of the PC and the KWP branch. Top authority was thought to reside in a North Korean who remained behind the scenes and kept aloof, another pattern of North Korean politics. The authorities sought to keep old administrators in their positions, if they were not top-level, and reemployed neighborhood chiefs who had not fled.

The most interesting pattern that emerged in this was a parallelism between subordinated clans and communist politics. Kinship cleavages often recapitulated distinctions between those who supported the North and those who remained passive, or pro-South. We discussed this in chapter 7, and suggested that this experience was probably general throughout southern Korea in villages afflicted by political strife. Kŭmnam was a one-clan village, but the clan was split between the richer descendants of the founder's first wife, and the disadvantaged descendants of his second wife. The latter enthusiastically supported the new regime, while the leader of the advantaged side of the clan was executed as an avidly pro-Rhee reactionary—the one person to be executed in Kŭmnam. The village PC leader was head of the disadvantaged lineage. A man in his late thirties of *yangban* descent, with a primary school education, he had won his position because his infant son had died during a time when he and his wife were being beaten by Rhee's police for allegedly allowing a man who had attacked a police box during the autumn 1946 uprisings to take refuge in his home. Therefore he was a "martyr" of the Rhee regime.

The other local influential headed the KWP branch, and was a lifelong friend of the PC leader. His family was the only one in the village not a member of the split clan, but instead had been the only hereditary slave and *ch'ŏnmin* family in the village. He was not known to be a leftist before the North Koreans came; villagers thought he got his position through personal connections. When the Rhee regime returned, the two men fled; the police proceeded to beat up their wives.

Other categories of people that supported the North Koreans, according to this study, included the young, having some education (communists sought them out because they were respected in the village for their education). A pattern developed of getting the educated, *yangbans*, and even rightists, "to give the new regime an air of continuity and respectability." The second category included those who were disadvantaged compared to other villagers, whether through relative poverty, or because of previous political run-ins with the police; most of these were the poorest peasants in the village. The last comprised those who won position through personal connections, especially clan connections—this happened "on a formidable scale." One man who cooperated was an extreme rightist, but he did so to save his uncle, who was in custody. The uncle then protected him from retribution when the Rhee forces returned.

The other village did not have the profound cleavages found in Kŭmnam, and traditional leaders provided a buffer between the new regime and the people. The village people's committee "was in every particular directed by the traditional leaders of the community as a superficial compromise necessary in order to insure the security of the settlement." PC leaders included several prominent farmers who worked their own land, led by the owner of the local rice-cleaning mill. This same group had selected the village chief in the past. They instructed villagers to cooperate with the outsiders. The study concluded that this "evasion" was "completely successful," but was highly dependent on village solidarity. Had there been one dissenter, the villagers thought, the evasion would not have worked. In the end, the communists "found no way to gain control over the community."

Both villages had rates of illiteracy over 50 percent, and only one or two radios; most communication was by word of mouth and by wall newspapers and posters. ROK and American broadcasts barely penetrated during the occupation. As in Seoul, women were particular targets of the new regime. All those interviewed remembered strong attacks on concubinage and prostitution; women were given free prenatal care, and were encouraged to run in PC elections. The Women's League was largely a failure, however, attracting few members.

Little evidence of North Korean brutality and torture came to the attention of the researchers. The forces of order were uniformly thought to be better than their ROK counterparts: "they never struck a villager or inflicted personal punishment upon him, even at the end of the occupation when they engaged in other forms of questionable behavior." What villagers hated most was the constant exaction of a kind of corvée labor, where peasants would repair bridges or roads that had been bombed, without being given pay or extra rations. This was usually considered the worst thing that the North Koreans ever did.

This valuable study both confirms the structure of the North Korean occupation discussed earlier, and indicates that at the village level leadership patterns were varied and complex, that PC composition could occasionally be quite diverse, and that the occupation had some of the problems penetrating the isolated, self-contained villages that had always bedeviled the central administration in Korea. The total character of North Korean rule seems to give way, at least at the village level, to a much more common pattern of administrative command and local resistance, of central orthodoxy and village complexity, of formal unity and substantive pluralism.

THE GUERRILLA WAR IN THE SOUTH

In most of the literature, the war for the South resembles a simple game of positional warfare: the North "struck like a cobra," in MacArthur's phrase, rolled rather quickly to the Pusan perimeter, tried but failed to punch through American lines, and then was defeated by MacArthur's brilliant landing at Inch'ŏn. The KPA is thought to have used tank warfare exclusively, Soviet blitzkreig tactics, running into trouble when its supply lines got too long, and ultimately being swept up in MacArthur's trap. Those who speak at all about the role of the southern population in the summer of 1950 generally comment on their passivity; nobody "rose up" to greet the KPA armies, yet another reason for failure. Even the Kim Il Sung leadership has indulged in aspects of this tale, scapegoating Pak Hŏn-yŏng and other southern communists for failing to produce an uprising, as if the North had a Bay of Pigs calculus of attack and popular explosion.

That is not the way the war for the South appeared at the time, or in internal accounts by official analysts. A major study by 8th Army historians in 1951 emphasized that the majority of KPA units had been trained in China and took their military doctrine from Maoist principles of warfare. Most soldiers were equipped with little more than a bag of millet and a rifle, requiring little resupply, and merged Soviet tank and artillery tactics with Chinese guerrilla and double-envelopment strategies. Throughout the summer of 1950 they were aided by guerrillas, most of them local but some coming from the North. During the weeks of the Pusan perimeter, "large tactical units, division [size] or larger," had to be diverted to secure rear areas infested with guerrillas. From June 25 to August 31, total guerrilla casualties were 67,228 killed, 23,837 captured, and 44,154 surrended. That is more than double the total number of Americans killed in action during the entire war.[48]

The battle for the South was shaped by the political complexion of different provinces. This was most marked in the Chŏllas, where the ROK offered next to no defense because it was confronted with rapidly advancing CCF (Chinese Communist Forces) Korean units at the front, and a guerrilla upsurge in its rear. The Chŏllas were conquered in a mere forty-eight hours of fighting. In the southeastern Kyŏngsangs, the other major leftist area, guerrillas were active, but so were countermeasures including massive burning of villages and the evacuation of large numbers of civilians whose loyalty was suspect; this was also, of course, the point of maximum deployed American force—including the use of B-29s for massive tactical bombing forays that turned battle areas into seas of fire.

Kim Il Sung called on the southern people to "rise up in rebellion" in his June 26 broadcast, but for the next two weeks there was very little, if any, guerrilla activity in the South;[49] this does not connote that the events of June 25 were coordinated with southern partisans. The pattern seems instead to have been one of general quiescence as long as ROK or American forces of order remained formidable, followed by a quick emergence of guerrillas as KPA troops approached.

Americans first felt the combination of frontal assault and guerrilla warfare in the battle for Taejŏn. Local peasants, including women and children, would come running along the hillsides near the battle lines, as if they were refugees. "At a given signal, the 'refugees' snatched rifles, machine guns, and hand grenades from their bundles and brought down withering fire on the troops below." The retreat from Taejŏn ran into well organized roadblocks and ambushes, often placed by local citizens. From this point onward, American forces began burning villages suspected of harboring partisans; in some cases they were burned merely "to deny hiding places to the guerrillas."[50]

As the Americans worked their way southward they soon came to Yŏngdong, one of the most thoroughly leftist counties in the South. North Koreans sources had it "liberated" by guerrillas before the KPA arrived; Walter Sullivan reported that some three hundred guerrillas in Yŏngdong harassed retreating American forces, and that they would take over local peacekeeping once the KPA passed through. "The American G.I. is now beginning to eye with suspicion any Korean civilian in the cities or countryside. 'Watch the guys in white'—the customary peasant dress—is the cry often heard near the front." The diary of a dead Korean named Ch'oe Sŏng-hwan, either a KPA soldier or a guerrilla, noted on July 26 that American bombers had swooped over Yŏngdong and "turned it into a sea of fire."[51]

While American forces were getting badly mauled in the battle for Taejŏn, Gen. Pang Ho-san, commander of the KPA 6th Division, made up exclusively of China veterans, captured the key port city of Kunsan at the northern border point of the Chŏllas without resistance on July 23, and then gobbled up the rest of the southeast in just two days—what Appleman called "a spectacular triumph in [KPA] enveloping maneuvers." They had the town of Hadong in South Kyŏngsang by July 26, causing Americans to realize they would have to withdraw all the way to a beachhead near Pusan. ROK forces in the Chŏllas offered next to no resistance: most of them fled well before the KPA arrived.[52]

This was the stronghold of the Korean left, a region of blanketed people's committees in 1945 and guerrillas in the years before the war. American informants told the press that "guerrillas rose before [the] Army came" in the southwest, especially in the cities of Mokp'o and Kwangju; the latter, the Americans said, "has long been one of the principle centers of Communist activity." In Kwangju 4,000 workers quickly struck the Chŏnnam Spinning Mill and stoned the owner; many police boxes were attacked in outlying areas. Students at the local Chosŏn College were heavily involved in disorders. The pattern indicated that "the Red underground and rural guerrillas had orders to lay low until the main Communist forces were drawing near."[53]

The diary of a captured guerrilla recorded that he entered Kwangju on July 27, only to be "ashamed" to find that Chirisan guerrillas "had occupied Kwangju city and were performing their respective duties while our unit was always following behind the others." The next day his unit learned that defeated ROK soldiers and police "were raiding people's committees and slaughtering people" near Naju. Several former ROK police and officials were caught by the guerrillas, who shot four of them, then held a people's court and executed eight more. The ROK officers were then buried next to the PC members that they had previously killed (a common practice that made it difficult to determine the authorship of atrocities).[54]

North Korean sources reported that Chirisan guerrillas were active in Sunch'ŏn and Kwangyang counties by July 3; in Sunch'ŏn they were said to have attacked KNP and Minbodan people. In the radical mining town of Hwasun, guerrillas attacked "evil elements" and then divided up their property with local people. Seoul newspapers called upon peasants to protect grain stocks, and join the partisans: "only then will you get land." According to the *New York Times*, lightly armed guerrillas drove ROK police battalions out of Iri and several other towns in South Chŏlla around July 19.[55]

The guerrillas and the swath of the 6th Division collected the summer grain harvest in the fertile Chŏllas before it could be destroyed, dealing a harsh blow to the South. The battlefield effect was even worse. Willoughby's G-2 called the 6th Division's sweep very bold and "extremely hazardous" in the way it stretched lines of supply for the KPA; they lunged forward without obvious backup forces. Later, however, the G-2 determined that supplies were provided locally, with garrisoning and public order left to guerrillas and leftists. By July 25, this combined movement constituted "an immediate menace" to American operations: "A tactically skilled and strategically war-wise enemy has recognized the 'soft spot' in the Allied disposition and has made a complete and sweeping envelopement, at practically no expense . . . [it can now] turn east and advance on a broad front."[56] Hanson Baldwin said "the flanking drive . . . down the West coast to the southern coastlands of Korea was greatly underestimated. It has become a major threat." Within days Pang Ho-san's forces threatened Pusan, and Gen. Walton Walker issued a "no retreat" order to his troops: in this "critical" situation, "we aren't going to give up one more inch."[57]

The Chŏllas remained under full communist control until late September, when guerrilla forces, now much stronger, retreated to the hills again. At the end of October, when MacArthur proclaimed the war virtually finished, a report on South Chŏlla found at least 20,000 guerrillas in the province, holed up in nine mountainous areas; villages flew the ROK flag by day, the DPRK flag by night. Rhee's police held all but one of the county stations, but only 80 of 338 substations. The ROK province governor estimated that the majority of guerrillas were natives of South Chŏlla.[58]

By early August, Gen. John H. Church, commander of the 24th Infantry Division and a veteran of the Anzio campaign, concluded that Korea was not like the European battles of World War II: "It's an entirely different kind of warfare, this is really guerrilla warfare." It was "essentially a guerrilla war over rugged territory," according to British sources; American troops were "constantly exposed to the threat of infiltration by guerrillas sweeping down from the hills into and behind its positions." Willoughby told Ridgway on August 7 that the partisans "are well organized, and are at present the single greatest headache to U.S. forces."[59]

As the fighting spread to the southeast, guerrillas became active in the Kyŏngsangs. At the time of General Walker's "no retreat" order, guerrillas struck at Kŭmhae, only ten miles north of Pusan; Americans had also begun worrying about the strategic city of Taegu. "Like Kwangju, it has been a scene of extensive Red organization and one abortive uprising. As the chief rail and highway center behind the front, its security is vital. The Korean National Police have reportedly made numerous arrests in the city in addition to those prior to the beginning of the war."[60] Daily situation reports listed incidents with small numbers of guerrillas in Tonghae, Miryang, Ulsan, Haman, Hadong, and Kŏchang in mid-July, along the belt of left-wing counties leading west from Pusan; somewhat later reports of guerrilla activity from several counties in North Kyŏngsang came in, mostly attacks on police and local notables.[61]

By late July guerrillas fought in the northern counties and along the upper east coast of North Kyŏngsang, in Andong, Yŏngju, Yongyang, and just north of P'ohang; some 1,200 guerrillas were observed near Ŭisŏng on July 27, boldly entering nearby towns. Another 2,000 were said to be in mountains northeast of Taegu. The Kyŏngsang partisans included guerrillas coming down from North Korea through the ports of Samch'ŏk and Yongdŏk. Kim Il Sung's Manchurian ally O Chin-u (defense minister through much of the 1980s), commanded about 1,500 guerrillas who landed south of Kangnŭng some days after the war began; included were some 400 China veterans with extensive guerrilla experience. Their mission was to penetrate into the Kyŏngsangs, avoid contact with enemy forces, and wait for the KPA to arrive before going into action.[62]

This threat continued to bedevil the defenses of the Pusan perimeter, and accounted for the majority of guerrilla casualties in the summer of 1950. The Americans allowed Korean National Police battalions to deal with real and suspected guerrillas with their customary brutality, while adopting draconian methods of their own. Virtually any village suspected of harboring or supporting guerrillas was burned to the ground, usually from the air. Furthermore, cities and towns thought to be leftist in inclination were simply emptied of their population through forced evacuations. All but 10 percent of civilians were moved out of Sunch'ŏn, Masan was emptied of tens of thousands of citizens, "all civilians" were moved out of Yech'ŏn. Amid a threat that "the leftists and Fifth column, living in Taegu, are conspiring to create a big disturbance," and with the perimeter under great strain, vast numbers of Taegu citizens were evacuated for fear of "an uprising." By mid-August, many of these removed citizens were concentrated on islands near Pusan, forbidden to leave.[63]

Meanwhile the war barely affected Cheju Island, scene of the strongest guerrilla movement in the late 1940s. Although a few minor incidents in mid-August caused an Irish priest to inform the embassy that "the communists were beginning to run rampant," only one hundred or so partisans were left on the island. At the start of the war the ROKA commander, Japanese-aligned Gen. Yi Ŭng-jun, put some 1,100 suspects in prison and placed the island under martial law; those arrested included Cheju's chief judge, the chief procurator, the chief of administration, the chief of agriculture, the mayor of Cheju city, and several businessmen and lawyers. (They were charged with conspiring to arrange a welcome for KPA soldiers.) General Yi maintained a 9:00 P.M. curfew throughout the summer, confiscated all radios, and censored all news in advance; understandably, the islanders knew little about the course of the fighting. The chief of the Cheju police force was a former "youth leader."[64] It was business as usual on Cheju.

"WHITE PAJAMAS": PEOPLE'S WAR AND THE QUESTION OF RACISM

The prevalence of guerrillas in the South meant that Americans found themselves in a new kind of war in Korea, in which the enemy and the people became indistinguishable. A People's Army soldier might doff his uniform for the characteristic white raiment of the peasantry and dissolve into the mass; someone's grandmother or a ten-year old kid might pull a gun from a bundle and kill you. The result was a very dirty war.

The average G.I. arrived in Korea with the barest knowledge of where he was, who he was fighting, and why; he was thrown into battle in the steaming humidity, frequent rain squalls and muddy terrain of midsummer; he slogged through rice paddies fertilized with human waste, something common in peasant societies but overwhelming at the first scent; if he slaked his thirst with paddy water he got amoebic dysentery. In this UN "police action" he faced an enemy who fought a total war, using every resource to turn Korean weakness into strength. Sometimes this meant using little kids to ferry ammunition; sometimes it meant driving weeping refugees into American lines to cover an infantry assault. The average G.I. also came from an American society where people of color were subjugated and segregated, and where the highest law officer in the land, Attorney General McGrath, had called communists "rodents." It thus did not take long for soldiers to believe that Koreans were subhuman, and act accordingly.

This element of the Korean War has been lost from the collective memory, as if Vietnam were the only intervention where "Mylais" occurred. But in 1950, the people in "white pajamas" and what they provoked in Americans was as accessible as the neighborhood barbershop reading table. Military historian Walter Karig, writing in *Collier's*, likened the fighting to "the days of Indian warfare" (a common analogy); he thought Korea might be like Spain—a testing ground for a new type of conflict, which might be found later in places like Indochina and the Middle East. "Our Red foe scorns all rules of civilized warfare," Karig wrote, "hid[ing] behind women's skirts." He then presented the following colloquy:

> The young pilot drained his cup of coffee and said, "Hell's fire, you can't shoot people when they stand there waving at you." "Shoot 'em," he was told firmly. "They're troops." "But, hell, they've all got on those white pajama things and they're straggling down the road." . . . "See any women or children?" "Women? I wouldn't know." "The women wear pants, too, don't they?" "But no kids, no, sir." "They're troops. Shoot 'em."[65]

John Osborne told the readers of *Life* that G.I.s were ordered to fire into clusters of civilians by their officers, quoting one of them: "it's gone too far when we are shooting children." This was a new kind of war, he said, "blotting out of villages where the enemy *may* be hiding; the shelling of refugees who *may* include North Koreans."[66]

Eric Larrabee, writing in *Harper's*, began by quoting an English captain who subdued the Pequot Indians in 1836: "the tactics of the natives . . . far differ from Christian practice." He recalled the reflections of a British officer at Lexington during the American revolution: "The country at this time took ye Alarm and were immediately in Arms, and had taken their different stations behind Walls, on our Flanks, and thus we were harassed in our Front, Flanks, and Rear . . . it not being possible for us to meet a man otherwise than behind a Bush, Stone hedge or Tree, who immediately gave his fire and went off." A Marine in Korea told the author, "in Tarawa you could at least see the enemy. Here the gooks hide in the bushes." Larrabee argued that what was a limited war for Americans was a people's war for Koreans (much like the American war against the British), and said it could not be fought with a "brutal and senseless display of technical superiority"—instead, without using the terms he called for the development of rapidly-deployable special forces to fight the people's wars of the future, where the object would be winning the people over to our side.[67] This was the liberal response to people's war, embodied in the decisions a decade later of the Kennedy administration.

The modal American response, however, came out of the expansionist current in American history, and in this sense the Indian Wars were indeed the place to start to guage the meaning of the Korean War. (It is worth remembering that General Custer began his final battle on June 25.) Expansionists thought that they moved into regions that were empty of civilization, bereft of people who demanded respect. Indians were not even adults, but "eternal children . . . too immature themselves to launch a campaign of resistance"; the child-like imagery carried over to the Pacific War, and to the axiomatic thought of a MacArthur.[68]

What had been possible against Native Americans proved inoperable against East Asian peoples. The westward path that encountered tribes of people and destroyed them, crossed the Pacific and met civilizations of people, now in anti-imperial revolt. But the revolt and the civilization were in the realm of unapprehended imponderables. In the long, dark night of expansionist ignorance about Asia, Koreans (and Chinese) were people without history, people who could not act in history—"could not strike a blow in their own defense," in the turn-of-the-century rendering. If the first injunction for a soldier should be to know your enemy, Americans in Korea failed it from the top brass down to the privates, and they paid dearly for their ignorance and underestimation of the people they faced.

The disastrous misjudgment of Koreans began right at the top, the day the war began. "I can handle it with one arm tied behind my back," MacArthur said; the next day he remarked to Dulles that if he could only put the 1st Cavalry Division into Korea, "why, heavens, you'd see these fellows scuddle up to the Manchurian border so quick, you would see no more of them."[69] A few days later, the generalissimo thought he would turn the KPA around at Suwŏn, just south of Seoul. On June 29 it now appeared that two full divisions would be required, and two weeks into the war he called for "the equivalent of not less than four to four and-a-half full strength infantry divisions." By mid-July he had developed respect for the Koreans:

> The North Korean soldier must not be underestimated. He is a tough oppponent, well-led, combines the infiltration tactic of the Japanese with the tank tactics of the Russian of World War II. He is able to march and maneuver and to attack at night with cohesion which [Mac-Arthur] has never been able to do. These are the troops who served in China . . . [the] tank work is extremely efficient and skillful.[70]

American G.I.s were told, and believed, that as soon as Korean soldiers saw the whites of Yankee eyes, they would turn tail and run. Press commentary from around the world expressed absolute shock that the KPA was still rolling in early August; Arthur Krock found it difficult to believe that "the weakest of the satellites is licking hell out of us."[71]

There was the added, troubling postulate that these were puppet troops, fighting Stalin's battles. A puzzled Dulles found the North Koreans "fighting and dying, and indeed ruining the whole country, to the end that Russia may achieve its Czarist ambitions." Rusk thought it important to find out how the Russians get the satellites "to fight their actions" for them—"here was a technique which had been very effective and it was not obvious how the success had been achieved." There appeared to be a "nationalist impetus," too, so it would be well to figure out how the Russians "stimulate this enthusiasm."[72]

Then there was an even more troubling fact: our Koreans would not fight. As late as 1969 General Ridgway was still vexed by this conundrum, even though, as he said, "My acquaintance with Orientals goes back to the mid-1920s." (He might have added that his experience included chasing Sandino in Nicaragua.)[73] The North Koreans were more "fanatical" fighters than the Chinese, he learned, yet the South Koreans were not good soldiers: "I couldn't help asking why. Why such a difference between the two when they were the same otherwise." He speculated that perhaps the KPA was using "dope," but never found evidence of it.[74]

In the summer of 1950 basic knowledge about the KPA and its leaders was treated as a revelation—for example, that the majority of its soldiers had fought in the Chinese civil war. At the beginning of September the *New York Times* found big news in a biography of Ch'oe Yong-gŏn released by MacArthur's headquarters: it discovered that he had fought with the Chinese Communists, placing him in Yanan in 1931 (no mean feat, three years before the Long March). Also unearthed was the information that he was in overall command of the KPA, which appeared to suggest that international communism was allowing the locals to run things. Two days later the *Times* turned up the news that Mu Jŏng had also fought in China, and that most of the KPA's equipment had been sold to it by the Russians in 1948. Ergo, "With its peculiar combination of fanaticism, politics and just plain rudimentary fighting qualities of Orientals . . . [the KPA] is a strange one. Some observers believe that, in the absence of good pre-war intelligence, we have just begun to learn about it."[75]

Early on the *Times* had found a queer tone in North Korean statements to the United Nations: they "had a certain ring of passion" about them, as if they really believed what they were saying about American imperialism. The *Times*'s own rendering of the "imposter" Kim Il Sung read as follows:[76]

> The titular leader of the North Korean puppet regime and ostensible commander of the North Korean armies is Kim Il Sung, a 38-year old giant from South Korea, where he is wanted as a fugitive from justice. His real name is supposed to be Kim Sung Chu, but he has renamed himself after a legendary Korean revolutionary hero . . . and many Koreans apparently still believe that it is their "original" hero and not an imposter who rules in North Korea.

If that is "all the news that is fit to print," the *Times* might as well have had its editorials scripted by Syngman Rhee. The ordinary reader would believe that KPA soldiers were trouncing Americans and dying by the thousands, all for a poseur with a hyperactive pituitary, a John Dillinger on the lam from august organs of justice in Seoul.

One thing that never seemed to cause cognitive dissonance for Americans, however, was the juxtaposition of a widely-assumed Korean barbarism against the KPA's superior morale and fighting skills. By the Vietnam War blatant racism was mostly the province of blowhards like Curtis LeMay, who enjoyed giving vent to his spleen about an Asia he could not control; in Korea it suffused the political spectrum, from the hard noses of the expansionists to the polite society of liberalism. Consider the judgment of the military editor of the *Times*, Hanson Baldwin, three weeks into the war: "We are facing an army of barbarians in Korea, but they are barbarians as trained, as relentless, as reckless of life, and as skilled in the tactics of the kind of war they fight as the hordes of Genghis Khan. . . . They have taken a leaf from the Nazi book of blitzkreig and are employing all the weapons of fear and terror." Chinese communists were reported to have joined the fighting, he erred in saying, and not far behind might be "Mongolians, Soviet Asiatics and a variety of races"—some of "the most primitive of peoples." Elsewhere Baldwin likened the Koreans to invading locusts; he ended by recommending that Americans be given "more realistic training to meet the barbarian discipline of the armored horde."[77]

A few days later Baldwin remarked that to the Korean, "life is cheap. Behind him stand the hordes of Asia. Ahead of him lies the hope of loot." What else "brings him shrieking on," what else explains his "fanatical determination?"[78] Mongolians, Asiatics, Nazis, locusts, primitives, hordes, thieves—one would think Baldwin exhausted his bag of analogies to capture a people invading their homeland and defending it against the world's most powerful army. But he came up with another for dealing with "the problem of the convinced fanatic." "In their extensive war against Russian partisans, the Germans found that the only answer to guerrillas . . . was 'to win friends and influence people' among the civilian population. The actual pacification of the country means just that." (A pacification, perhaps, like that in the Ukraine.) Somewhat uncomfortable with North Korean indignation about "women and children slain by American bombs," Baldwin went on to say that Koreans must understand that "we do not come merely to bring devastation." Americans must convince "these simple, primitive, and barbaric peoples . . . that we—not the Communists—are their friends."[79]

Lest the reader think that I single out Baldwin, whose military reporting on the war was often superb, listen to Telford Taylor, chief counsel for war crimes at the Nuremberg Trials. "The traditions and practices of warfare in the Orient are not identical with those that have developed in the Occident . . . individual lives are not valued so highly in Eastern mores. And it is totally unrealistic of us to expect the individual Korean soldier . . . to follow our most elevated precepts of warfare."[80] MacArthur opined that "the Oriental dies stoically because he thinks of death as the beginning of life" (utterly baseless in the secular Korean context); "the Oriental when dying folds his arms as a dove does its wings."[81]

Matthew Ridgway, a man of character who often spared precious time to write poignant letters to American mothers who lost sons in Korea, was no less afflicted by this ubiquitous racism. When he first got to Korea and visited a POW camp, he remarked, "these prisoners are in appearance but a shade above the beast. It is by the use of such human canaille that the Soviets are destroying our men while conserving their own." He hoped a film would be made to show Americans "these creatures in their natural state," with close-ups "of their facial expressions." The "evil genius" behind the war, he thought, was "some type of Eastern mind and whether Russian or Chinese, we shall inevitably find many of the same methods applied on major scales, if and when we confront the Slav in battle."[82]

Perhaps these are people with no experience in Korea. Edgar Johnson, former Economic Cooperation Administration (ECA) administrator in Korea, lambasted the "wild, adolescent chauvinism" of the North Koreans in their "shocking, shameful, criminal invasion" of June 25; these were "half-crazed automatons" in the orbit of "a monolithic slave-and-master world." An American who had worked in the Occupation told the *Far Eastern Economic Review* that Koreans were "a hard, fierce and cruel people," possessed of "a ferociousness and wildness." Korea was a "hotbed of scoundrels, wildmen, semi-barbarians." American missionaries in Korea thought that too much inbreeding had led to "an arrested mental development." British sources said that it was precisely the foreigners living in Korea (meaning mainly Americans) who "entertain the lowest opinion of Korean intelligence, mores, ability, and industry."[83]

It is, of course, to General Willoughby that we may turn for a vintage *übermentsch* line on Koreans, different only in degree from the above. He later reflected that Americans faced an "Oriental brutality" that plumbed "satanic depths" in the Korean War.

> These simple coolies, in uniform, were social as well as military expendables to their masters. One cannot help reflecting that the worst feature of the Korean War was the utter waste of highly civilized material . . . American highschool boys and university graduates, expensive social and moral investments who had to face a mob of half-men with blank faces who killed prisoners after tying their hands behind their backs.[84]

This nauseating stew of racial stereotypes had the effect, for Americans high and low, of stirring diverse peoples into what Anderson calls "a nameless sludge," or accumulating them under just one name ("gook"), as a way of "erasing nationness"—and thus erasing a people from one's consciousness: "nationalism thinks in terms of historical destinies, while racism dreams of eternal contaminations . . . outside history."[85]

In contrast to the war in Vietnam, barely a voice was raised against such racism. In the summer of 1950, I found but a single article that found virtue in Koreans (other than that the ROK was staunchly anti-communist, another mistaken stereotype if we speak of the majority) and vice in the ingrained racism of Americans in Korea and the "absolute contempt" in which most of them held Koreans.[86] Furthermore, the same American society that fought for freedom in Korea prohibited Koreans from entering the country to reside in 1950 under existing racial quotas, and denied naturalization to 3,000 Koreans who came to the United States before 1924; fifteen states prevented Korean-Caucasian marriages, eleven states refused to allow Koreans to buy or own land; twenty-seven occupations in New York City were proscribed to Koreans.[87]

One hastens to "give the other side," to recite Korean virtues, to call up their long history, high achievement and love of moral virtue, to mitigate the unrelieved crudity of it all. But any American who today drives a

Korean auto, uses a Korean computer, shops at the ubiquitous fruit and vegetable stores in New York, the produce perfectly arranged and shined to brilliance, or watches his son or daughter lose out at Harvard to a Korean applicant, will presumably not need didactic aid. It was in fact the Americans quoted above, tabula rasa on everything Asian but sure they were right, who were the barbarians.

Such attitudes shaped the battle, pitting young American soldiers by the thousands against an enemy that they were unprepared to fight, one which fought with rare courage, tenacity, and cunning. And these attitudes shaped the behavior of the enemy, who commonly remarked that "the Americans do not recognize Koreans as human beings,"[88] and who needed nerves of steel to cope with an American army that, as the war ground on, increasingly seemed capable of anything.

THE QUESTION OF ATROCITIES

Wild charges about satanic barbarism encourage the suspicion that if there was all that smoke, there must have been fire. Growing up on comic books depicting North Korean and Chinese soldiers as rabid, bloody-fanged beasts, for years I could not purge from my mind the notion that fighting such people must have made the Korean War a horror. Yet all testimony points to the very same "Red Chinese" as the most disciplined and correct army in the war. That could be verified a thousand times, however, before it would erode the residual Orientalism infecting the Western mind, from the simplicity of comics to the august judgments of contemporary advocates of "the West."

There is also a matter of expectations. Since the French Revolution liberals and progressives have tended to accept, at a gut level, that violence in service to a revolution is somehow more justifiable than violence in service to a counterrevolution, even if neither can be justified in the abstract. One rather expects that the South Koreans will execute communists, and has one's judgment confirmed when they do. One expects that the North Koreans will execute landlords, and is surprised if they do not. In this sense, neither the North nor South Koreans give much surprise. The North had a more discriminate political terror, because of its doctrine and because its enemies were fewer. The KPA was more disciplined in its treatment of the general civilian population than the ROKA. But the North's political operatives committed frequent executions that mocked the magnanimous claims of its "Great Leader." To the extent that the North may look "better" in a narrow and repugnant empiricist sense, this difference ultimately traces to the strength and weakness of the social formations each represented.

I recognize and admire the deep shame that Koreans feel when the subject of atrocities is mentioned at all; I believe it must be discussed, but I also wish Americans could feel a kindred shame. What does one expect from Americans? How does one think about their violence? The reflex response to a report that American soldiers shot civilians or airmen burned a village is to say, war is hell, Korea was so alien, one couldn't tell friend from foe. But I think that both North and South Korean atrocities are far more understandable in a civil war and revolutionary circumstance—one has only to remember the American civil war—than the atrocities committed by Americans, foreign to Korea's conflicts and there on a UN-sanctioned "police action" to bring freedom and democracy. Also, is it less atrocious to kill several hundred peasants in a village from the air, using napalm, then to line them up and shoot them? The carnage is more removed from the purview of the author, and so less sickening, but it is no different on a moral scale. Once this is said, it is not clear to me that Americans were better than the "Oriental" combatants—that we "follow[ed] our most elevated precepts of warfare," in Telford Taylor's words. Now let us look at the evidence on which I base this judgment.

The information is not terribly good—after all, these are prima facie cases of war crimes, so people and governments have much to hide. It is unfortunately necessary to say that if American or British or United Nations internal documents investigate an atrocity and lay it at the door of the South Koreans, and keep such discoveries secret, this is better evidence than ROK denials that such atrocities occured or claims that the North Koreans really did them, especially since the Americans, at minimum, were not happy to find such evidence. None of this evidence was ever tested in a court of law or an international tribunal, however, and therefore must be considered, in a legal sense, inconclusive.

Then there are quantitative and qualitative questions that defy easy answer. If one side slaughters ten thousand noncombatants and another side five hundred, it is not comforting to say that the first is worse: both sides commit atrocities. The numbers game is nauseating. All sides in the Korean War were guilty of unforgiveable atrocities (although none held a candle to the Germans or Japanese in the just-concluded world war).[89]

Existing evidence suggests that the Rhee regime massacred political prisoners as it retreated from Seoul, Inch'ŏn, and Taejŏn. Australian sources referred to "the stupid order of the Rhee Government to execute about 100 communists in Seoul before it evacuated," which would include the murders of the two North Korean emmissaries, Kim Sam-yong and Yi Chu-ha. UPI stated that ninety to one hundred had been executed, including "the beautiful 'Mata Hari' " of Korean communism, Kim Su-in.[90]

The North Koreans claimed to have found eyewitnesses to the slaughter of one thousand political prisoners and alleged communists in Inch'ŏn, perpetrated in the period June 29 to July 1. They alleged that this was done on the order of an American KMAG advisor. An attempt at a prison break happened at this time, aided by outside forces in Inch'ŏn; Tokyo G-2 sources said that a "guerrilla riot" occured in Inch'ŏn on June 30, resulting in the arrest of three hundred people. The State Department's Office of Intelligence Research noted the North Korean charges, but dismissed the affair as "nothing more than an ROK police action against rebellious elements attempting a prison break and other dissidents aiding them."[91]

In early August Alan Winnington published an article in the London *Daily Worker* hyperbolically titled "United States Belsen in Korea," alleging that ROK police under the supervision of KMAG advisors had butchered seven thousand people in the village of "Yangwul," near Taejŏn, during the period July 2–6. Accompanying KPA troops, he found twenty eyewitnesses who said that on July 2, truckloads of police arrived and made local people build six pits, each two hundred yards long. Two days later political prisoners were trucked in and executed, both by bullets to the head and sword decapitation, and layered on top of each other in the pits "like sardines." The massacres continued for three days. The witnesses said that two jeeps with American officers observed the killings.[92]

North Korean sources said four thousand had been killed (changing it some months later to seven thousand), comprised mostly of imprisoned guerrillas from Cheju Island and the T'aebaek-san area, and those detained after the Yŏsu-Sunch'ŏn incident. They located the site differently, placing the events at Chango village in Sanae township, Taedŏk county; official gazateers show no such village near Taejŏn. There is a Nangwŏl village in the vicinity of Taejŏn, however, often written or pronounced as Yangwŏl.[93]

American internal sources reported that southern authorities imprisoned most known leftists when the war began; as towns fell to the KPA, "our information is that these prisoners are considered as enemies of South Korea and disposed of accordingly, before the arrival of North Korean forces."[94]

The American embassy in London called the Winnington story an "atrocity fabrication" and denied its contents. However, British officials in Tokyo who talked to SCAP officers said that "there may be an element of truth in this report," but SCAP thought it was a matter to be handled between London and Washington. Gascoigne said that reliable journalists have "repeatedly" noted "the massacre of prisoners by South Korean troops"; but J. Underwood of the U.S. prisoners of war mission told British sources that he doubted seven thousand prisoners could even have been assembled in Taejŏn, as not more than two thousand were in the city's prisons.[95]

Army intelligence on July 2 rated as "probably true" a report that the KNP in Taejŏn were "arresting all Communists and executing them on the outskirts of the city." The CIA stated the next day that "unofficial reports indicated that Southern Korean police are executing Communist suspects in Suwŏn and Taejŏn, in an effort both to eliminate a potential 5th column and to take revenge for reported northern executions in Seoul." Neither report gave numbers, however.[96] The American internal evidence suggests that the executions Winnington discovered did occur, although it might have been two to four thousand instead of seven thousand.

There is unimpeachable evidence of South Korean massacres on a lesser scale. A *New York Times* reporter observed an ROK policeman with forty civilians in his retinue, alleged guerrillas, as he "crashed the butt of his rifle on the back of one after another." "We bang-bang in the woods," the policeman happily said, meaning that the prisoners "would be taken into the groves and executed after their backs had been broken." An Australian witnessed a similar incident, where in Kongju twenty civilian prisoners were kneeling and being beaten by guards "on [the] least movement." On inquiry, the guards responded, "guerrillas, bang bang." A *Manchester Guardian* correspondent saw a truckload of sixty prisoners taken to the Kŭm River on July 12 and executed by ROK authorities. "Tiger" Kim had fifty POWs beheaded, as we saw in chapter 18, but when the Red Cross made representations about it, KMAG officers said they "would not like to see it get in the hand of correspondents."[97]

The head of the KNP, Kim Tae-sŏn, acknowledged on July 14 that his forces had executed twelve hundred suspected Communists since June 25. In an interview the journalist Keyes Beech, who got the story, said that Kim was under a cloud for admitting atrocities to a reporter. A week later, as KPA forces approached the Chŏllas, Gen. Yi Ŭng-jun declared martial law and authorized capital punishment for subversive and sabotage activities, and for "anyone considered a political criminal by the commander." On July 26 the ROK government announced that any civilian "making enemy-like action" would be shot; all civilians now had to travel by special trains, and people in the battle area would only be allowed to leave their homes for two hours each day. "All those found violating these regulations will be considered enemies and will be executed immediately." In essence this meant that a free-fire zone now surrounded the front-lines.[98]

By August reports circulated widely about South Korean atrocities. At some undetermined point 120 civilians were killed in Taegu in a "single mass execution." John Osborne wrote in *Life* that the brutality of the southern police was so terrible that "the means cannot be described"; villagers "leap at every command with a livid and unmistakeable fear."

Americans sought out North Korean POWs for interrogation, but could rarely find them. Osborne described one American captain "screaming for live prisoners." American officials routinely denied the reports of atrocities, but the British made representations to the United States about them, and Prime Minister Nehru took an UNCOK member aside, saying that the South Koreans "had been guilty of very many excesses," including the shooting of "left wing sympathizers on a large scale." According to his information, by contrast, "the North Koreans were behaving with relative moderation and making themselves popular."[99]

Most reporters were afraid to print what they witnessed in Korea, given the cold war atmosphere of the time. One who sought to do so was James Cameron of London's *Picture Post*, who took pictures of and wrote about what he termed "South Korean concentration camps" in Pusan in the late summer of 1950.

> I had seen Belsen, but this was worse. This terrible mob of men—convicted of nothing, un-tried, South Koreans in South Korea, suspected of being "unreliable." There were hundreds of them, they were skeletal, puppets of string, faces translucent grey, manacled to each other with chains, cringing in the classic Oriental attitude of subjection, the squatting foetal position, in piles of garbage. . . . Around this medievally gruesome market-place was gathered a few knots of American soldiers photographing the scene with casual industry. . . . I took my indignation to the [U.N.] Commission, who said very civilly: "Most disturbing, yes; but remember these are Asian people, with different standards of behavior . . . all very difficult." It was supine and indefensible compromise. I boiled, and I do not boil easily. We recorded the situation meticulously, in words and photographs. Within the year it nearly cost me my job, and my magazine its existence.

The *Picture Post* never published Cameron's story, causing a "mini-mutiny" on the magazine; shortly thereafter the *Post* "withered away, as it deserved."[100]

As the ROK authorities swept back up the peninsula in the wake of the Inch'ŏn landing, they took vicious and deadly retribution against collaborators with the North. British sources cited "a medieval witchhunt" by the police, and a Korean from the South later likened it to "the killing fields" in Cambodia. One American described South Korean officers forcing some one hundred alleged collaborators, including children, pregnant women, and old men, to dig their own graves before being massacred—"This kind of thing happened all over the front."[101]

Other sources witnessed many truckloads of "political" cases arriving at Seoul's West Gate prison; of the four thousand people that it held, twelve hundred were women, some with infants. Each ten-foot square cell held twenty-four people. A *New York Times* reporter witnessed the execution of one woman at the prison who carried a four-month-old baby on her back. Drumwright cabled the State Department that by mid-November, 16,115 "collaborators" had been arrested; 6,588 had been released, the rest were still being held; military courts had given death sentences to 451, civil courts to 131, with many cases pending.[102] It was an underestimate, referring only to those executed with some measure of judicial procedure. But, by now, the reader can fill in these details.

A secret account by North Korean authorities, for internal consumption, detailed South Korean atrocities committed in Seoul after it was retaken: nearly 29,000 people were said to have been "shot" by ROK authorities, with 21,000 executions occurring in prisons and the rest perpetrated by police and "reactionary" organizations. Entire families of people's committee leaders were slaughtered, it said. The document accused the ROK and the United States of "slave labor" treatment of those collaborators with North Korea (and their families) who were not executed. They were not allowed to carry ROK citizenship cards, and were used for various corvée labor projects. The report detailed gruesome tortures, and alleged that three hundred female communists and collaborators were placed in brothels where they were raped continuously ("day and night") by South Korean and American soldiers. This report may be false, but then why would DPRK officials lie to their superiors in secret internal materials?[103] I would hope the report could be proved false, for it strikes heaven on the face, differing only in scale from Nazism.

NORTH KOREAN ATROCITIES

From the start of the war there were reports that the North Koreans executed former ROK officials, KNP officers, leaders of rightist youth groups, and former Korean employees of the United States.[104] We saw in our discussion of the occupation of Seoul that this was true, with the early executions often resulting from released prisoners settling scores; later on the North Koreans tried to stop executions. A DPRK Interior Ministry document stated that the KNP included many colonial police who fled the North, sons of northern landlords who had joined the Northwest Youth, sons of landlords and capitalists in the South, and people who were relatively high up in the colonial regime. It thus declared that their crimes "cannot be forgiven."[105] Although the document said nothing about executing such people, one can imagine that this provided the basis for the executions, after a kangaroo "people's court." There is no evidence on the numbers involved, but they must have been substantial.

There is evidence of KPA executions of captured American soldiers. This first surfaced in early July, and in the wake of the Inchŏn landing it got worse: several groups of thirty to forty executed American POWs were found, and one group of eighty-seven was retrieved just as their hands were being tied. MacArthur and Willoughby frequently referred to such behavior in demands that North Korean leaders be tried for war crimes. Internal materials, however, show that MacArthur had documents indicating that KPA leaders had ordered against such practices, and that therefore war crimes trials would not be appropriate.[106] According to POWs, these executions appear to have occurred when it became onerous or impossible to take American prisoners to the North, and they were done in the traditional battlefield "humane" manner: one bullet behind the ear. Treatment of ROKA POWs was considerably worse, but there is little evidence on this.

Internal North Korean evidence verifies that many POW killings occurred, and that KPA officers sought to stop the killings. On July 25, the high command said,

> Wrong treatment of men surrendering by certain units on our side has been inviting great losses in the thought campaign. For example, certain units shot the men who were surrendering instead of capturing them. Therefore the following orders should be strictly observed. (1) Every surrendering man should be taken prisoner. (2) Shooting is strictly prohibited.

On August 16, KPA officer Ch'oe Pong-ch'ŏl said, "Some of us are still slaughtering enemy troops that come to surrender . . . the responsibility of teaching the soldiers to take POWs and treat them kindly rests on the political section of each unit."[107]

American POWs who were liberated after Inch'ŏn reported generally good treatment by their captors (given existing conditions), good discipline by KPA troops, and some executions. An UNCURK (UN Commission on the Unification and Rehabilitation of Korea) group later reported that in spite of many reports of political executions and atrocities against rightists, "few cases came to the notice" of their survey team that visited Kangwŏn Province in early November, interviewing ROK and American officials and speaking to local people. G-2 sources also found that thousands of political prisoners were moved out of Seoul to the North, including many KNP officers, rightist youth leaders, and others who were thought to have been eliminated.[108]

In the crisis of the Inch'ŏn landing several major massacres of political prisoners occurred. In Mokp'o five hundred were slaughtered, another five hundred were killed in Wŏnsan when the North Koreans withdrew, and many mass graves, presumably containing those executed by the North Koreans, were found by advancing troops. An UNCURK file documents, with photographs and interviews of survivors, the massacre of political prisoners in Chŏnju and Taejŏn, done by KWP cadres and local political agents. Most of the victims were made to dig a large pit, then shot and tossed into it; the majority were ROK policemen and youth group members.

Based on American and South Korean inquiries, the total massacred in the South was placed at 20,000 to 22,000.[109] I do not know how the figure was arrived at. UNCURK reports suggest a significantly lower figure; furthermore the UNCURK investigations were balanced, whereas the Americans and South Koreans never mentioned ROK atrocities.

The official history by Appleman alleged that the North Koreans perpetrated "one of the greatest mass killings" of the war in Taejŏn, with between five thousand and seven thousand people slaughtered and placed in mass graves. Some Americans were included; in one incident six survivors, including two Americans, were found alive, feigning death under the light soil thrown on top of them. Mass burial graves, he writes, were also found at many points in South Chŏlla, and he says that the North Koreans "ran amok" in Wŏnju on October 2, killing between one and two thousand civilians.[110]

Seoul's West Gate prison held seven to nine thousand prisoners, most of them imprisoned in the last month of the northern occupation; they consisted mostly of ROK police, army, and rightist youths. From September 17 to 21 all these prisoners were moved to the North by rail, except for those who could not walk, who were shot. American sources counted two hundred in graves, and estimated the total killed at one thousand. Reginald Thompson saw "the corpses of hundreds slaughtered in the last days by the Communists in a frenzy of hate and lust." When P'yŏngyang was occupied, American sources reported finding thousands of corpses in a wide trench near the main prison. Seven hundred people were said to have been executed as the North Koreans left Hamhŭng.[111]

In archival materials I have found no other evidence of such large massacres in Taejŏn, Wŏnju, and South Chŏlla, and Appleman does not balance his account with the hard evidence of southern massacres. I have not seen any account of a North Korean massacre of thousands at Taejŏn. The figure of seven thousand was also used for the alleged South Korean atrocity at Taejŏn in early July. Perhaps the North Koreans used the same pits in which to throw the bodies of executed people. Other official sources say the North Koreans held about seventeen hundred people in South Chŏlla jails by September; when they pulled out, ten of these were killed and the rest went free.[112]

One incident of a mass killing was properly and fully investigated, with equivocal results. A KMAG advisor reported that in the last week of September seven hundred civilians had been "burned alive, shot or bayoneted by [the] Commies before leaving Yangp'yŏng," in Kangwŏn Province; pictures of the victims were taken, and witnesses said most of the dead were members of the KNP and rightist youth groups. When an UNCURK team investigated the massacre, they found about forty civilian bodies, and a nearly equal number of executed KPA soldiers, still in uniform. An investigation by the embassy vice-consul, Philip Rowe, turned up only nine bodies. Local people said the rest had been carried off by the victim's families. Rowe was willing to believe this, but he was nonetheless unable to verify the KMAG account. He did not mention the murdered KPA soldiers.[113]

As allied forces moved into the North, little evidence of atrocities by the retreating communists was found. A November 30 UN Command document stated that "no reports of any [enemy] atrocities have been received from the areas recently taken by UN troops."[114] The evidence of North Korean atrocities in the south is nonetheless damning. For what it is worth, captured documents continued to show that high-level officials warned against executing people. Handwritten minutes of a KWP meeting on December 7, 1950, apparently at a high level, said "do not execute the reactionaries for [their] wanton vengeance. Let legal authorities carry out the purge plan."[115] It wouldn't be much solace for the victims and their families.

AMERICAN ATROCITIES

Reginald Thompson, an Englishman, authored *Cry Korea*, a fine, honest eyewitness account of the first year of the war. War correspondents found the campaign for the South "strangely disturbing," he wrote, different from World War II in its guerrilla and popular aspect. "There were few who dared to write the truth of things as they saw them." G.I.s "never spoke of the enemy as though they were people, but as one might speak of apes." Even among correspondents, "every man's dearest wish was to kill a Korean. 'Today,' . . . 'I'll get me a gook.' " Americans called Koreans gooks, he thought, because "otherwise these essentially kind and generous Americans would not have been able to kill them indiscriminately or smash up their homes and poor belongings."[116]

Charles Grutzner, who reported the war for the *New York Times*, said that in the early going, "fear of infiltrators led to the slaughter of hundreds of South Korean civilians, women as well as men, by some U.S. troops and police of the Republic." He quoted a high-ranking U.S. officer who told him of an American regiment that panicked in July and shot "many civilians."[117] Keyes Beech wrote in the *Newark Star-Ledger*, "It is not the time to be a Korean, for the Yankees are shooting them all . . . nervous American troops are ready to fire at any Korean." General Willoughby, livid with rage over Seymour Hersh's disclosure of the Mylai massacre and the subsequent prosecution of Lt. William Calley during the Vietnam War, said such things happened all the time in Korea, and quoted a letter from a man named Harry McDaniel: "I was a captain in front-line combat in Korea, with orders to shoot anything that moved after dark."[118]

The North Koreans claimed that American forces massacred large numbers of civilians in the "red" county of Yŏngdong. According to a KPA detachment that got to Yŏngdong on July 20 and spoke with ten eyewitnesses, American troops herded some two thousand civilians from two villages in Yŏngdong county into the mountains in this guerrilla-infested county, and then when Taejŏn fell, slaughtered them, apparently mostly from the air, although the account also said women were raped before being shot.[119] There is no other confirmation, but reference to such American atrocities is rare in North Korean materials from the summer of 1950, most of the accounts referring to South Korean behavior. Usually they merely recounted stories about American soldiers dragging women off and raping them,[120] a common occurrence according to many Korean informants with whom I have spoken.

Original KMAG materials show that on August 6, 1950, a request was made "to have the following towns obliterated" by the Air Force: Chŏngsŏng, Chinbo, and Kusu-dong. Ten days later, five groups of B-29s hit a rectangular area near the front, full of towns and villages, creating an ocean of fire with hundreds of tons of napalm. Another such call went out on August 20. On August 26 is the single entry, "fired eleven villages."[121]

In 1950 the North Koreans had next to no defenses against air attacks. Soviet and Chinese pilots and planes provided no air cover in the summer and fall of 1950. Ridgway acknowledged shortly after he arrived in Korea that the United States was opposed "by an enemy whose only advantage is sheer numbers, whose armament is far inferior quantitatively and qualitatively, who has no air support whatever, meager telecommunications and negligible armor." An Air Force general termed bombing runs "a free ride," with serious antiaircraft only in the P'yŏngyang area. When he shot his jet up the coast to "Indian Country" near the Yalu, Sen. John Glenn said he had to give "Pingpong" (the capital) a wide berth, but that elsewhere antiaircraft fire was thin.[122]

Complete control of the skies produced a certain air of indulgence, which no doubt contributed to Korean casualties. As I. F. Stone put it, the raids and the sanitized reports "reflected not the pity which human feeling called for, but a kind of gay moral imbecility, utterly devoid of imagination—as if the flyers were playing in a bowling alley, with villages for pins."[123] For example, even though pilots were told to bomb targets that they could see to avoid hitting civilians, they often bombed major population centers by radar, or dumped off huge amounts of napalm on secondary targets when the primary one was unavailable. In a major strike on the industrial city of Hŭngnam on July 31, 500 tons of ordinance was delivered through clouds by radar; the flames rose two or three hundred feet into the air. The Air Force dropped 625 tons of bombs over North Korea on August 12, a tonnage that would have required a fleet of 250 B-17s in the Second World War. By late August, B-29 formations were dropping 800 tons a day on the North.[124]

Much of the tonnage was pure napalm. From June to late October, B-29s unloaded 866,914 gallons of napalm; Air Force sources took delight in the virtues of this relatively new weapon, introduced at the end of the previous war, joking about communist protests and misleading the press about their "precision bombing." They also liked to point out that civilians were warned of the approaching bombers by leaflet, when all pilots knew these were ineffective.[125]

The agony of those thousands of innocent civilians hit by napalm may be approximated in this account of a mistaken drop on a dozen American soldiers (by PFC James Ransome, Jr.): "Men all around me were burned. They lay rolling in the snow. Men I knew, marched and fought with begged me to shoot them. . . . It was terrible. Where the napalm had burned the skin to a crisp, it would be peeled back from the face, arms, legs . . . like fried potato chips."[126]

Reginald Thomson wrote that in September 1950, "handfuls of peasants defied the immense weight of modern arms with a few rifles and carbines and a hopeless courage . . . and brought down upon themselves and all the inhabitants the appalling horror of jellied petrol bombs." In such warfare, "the slayer needs merely touch a button, and death is on the wing, blindly blotting out the remote, the unknown people, holocausts of death, veritable mass productions of death, spreading an abysmal desolation over whole communities."[127]

When American forces came back to Seoul, Maj. Gen. Frank E. Lowe was outraged that retreating KPA forces had torched the capitol building (yielding but partial damage): for this act of "wanton pillage," he urged "immediate retalitation in the form of complete destruction of Pyon-yang [*sic*] by aerial bombing after due notice to civilian population to evacuate." Perhaps one capital city is worth one capitol building for General Lowe, but he might have been less indignant if he knew that the building was the former headquarters of the colonial regime, its architecture arrayed to represent the first character of Nippon.[128]

The war for the South ended with 111,000 South Koreans killed, 106,000 wounded, and 57,000 missing; 314,000 homes had been destroyed, 244,000 damaged. American casualties totalled 2,954 dead, 13,659 wounded, and 3,877 missing in action. North Korean casualty figures are unknown, but combat losses alone ran to perhaps 70,000.[129]

Chapter Twenty-One

THE WAR FOR ROLLBACK

And let me speak to the yet unknowing world
How these things came about. So shall you hear
Of carnal, bloody, and unnatural acts,
Of accidental judgements, casual slaughters,
Of deaths put on by cunning and forc'd cause,
And, in this upshot, purposes mistook
Fallen on the inventors' heads: all this can I
Truly deliver.

Horatio in Hamlet

A S THE DOG DAYS of August drew to a close in Washington, President Truman and his secretary of state decided to transform their undeclared war into a campaign to liberate North Korea. Just as victory for the containment thesis glimmered over the horizon of the bloody Pusan Perimeter, high liberals reached beyond to its antithesis. The incremental changes of the previous year came to an imperceptible climax, creating a new synthesis: "limited" rollback. But from that unnoticed point, the momentum of the battlefield and of American politics gathered a strength that carried the administration quickly onward, creating an irreversible watershed in American anticommunist strategy.

The American memory and much scholarship remain wedded to two propositions: the first is that rollback really was a Dullesian policy, an artifact of the Eisenhower years; the particular amnesia here is to forget that only the Truman administration executed an actual rollback. When this memory is jogged, the second proposition weighs in: rollback was MacArthur's policy, and MacArthur's fault. Acheson's Princeton seminars were animated by a tangible desire to blame MacArthur for the debacle in North Korea, and as usual Acheson's historical constructions and polished ventriloquy entered the mainstream interpretations.

Both propositions are wrong. Dulles in 1953 traded rollback rhetoric for containment policy, which was a direct result of the critical turning point in 1950–1951 and which structured eight years of comparative peace-and-quiet containment praxis amid all the bumptious, bellicose rhetoric of the Eisenhower years. Dulles was an advocate of rollback—but in the Truman years, not the Eisenhower years. The Korean rollback broke the incipient containment system: then its failure placed enduring limits on containment.[1] Dulles was a keeper of that grail.

Second, rollback was not MacArthur's policy, nor his fault (even though he favored it). The march north stimulated the broadest coalition in Washington behind any Korea policy in the postwar period. It stretched from unreconstructed anticommunists on the Right to liberals like John Vincent and O. Edmund Clubb, thus healing breaches between internationalists and nationalists. In late summer 1950, rollback had arrived at the consensual midpoint of the spectrum of American possibilities. Yet this was a follow-on to the logic emerging in the previous year, partaking of the same dialectic between containment and rollback found in NSC 48 and NSC 68, and in some cases using the same rhetoric. We will establish this link between prewar planning and the actualized progression of the conflict.

The Korean decision was, for Acheson, a defensive one to throw back the North Korean assault,[2] pursuing the containment logic he had elaborated three years earlier. But it occurred in 1950, not in 1947, after nearly a year of internecine conflict that had placed a new option on the agenda, rollback. By June 1950, Acheson was one of the few Truman administration officials who remained opposed to rollback. As rollback momentum waxed, however, Acheson's control of foreign policy waned. He had his hand tightly on the tiller until June 25, but as the battle unfolded in Korea he tacked to a strong wind, a force-ten typhoon, that carried events over the precipice toward a foreign policy Götterdämmerung that, in his words, demolished the Truman administration.

The Widening Gyre

The North Korean thrust southward seemed immediately to stimulate American thinking of a thrust northward, or should we say, Foster Dulles's thinking. Alvary Gascoigne has Dulles in late June saying, "in a desultory way," that the Korean incident might be used to go beyond the parallel. By mid-July Dulles was a key advocate of rollback, assisted by Dean Rusk, John Allison, and the early backer of the policy in the Far East, John Paton Davies.[3]

Within three weeks of the war's start, key decision makers had turned containment logic on its head, a sleight-of-hand not without some black humor, in which the heretofore inviolable "international" boundary at the thirty-eighth parallel, which when crossed by Koreans of the northern persuasion had evoked Hitler-style aggression, now was deemed permeable from the south. Americans for the first, last, and only time evinced a touching regard for Korean reunification. Cold warrior Everett Drumwright wrote Allison on July 10 that "once the rout starts it would be disastrous and stupid of us to stop at the 38th parallel. . . . Our goal and the UN goal is unification." Allison was stimulated to prepare a top secret memo, arguing that unlike the boundaries in central Europe, the parallel had no de jure significance (after all). The record, he said, showed "that this line was agreed upon only for the surrender of Japanese troops and that the United States had made no commitments with regard to the continuing validity of the line for any other purpose."[4] In other words the parallel bisecting Korea was an internationally-recognized boundary if Koreans cross it, but not if Americans do.

Dulles quickly gave Allison's paper to Rusk, and the next day, July 14, penned a memo to Paul Nitze, arguing explicitly for a march north. When the Policy Planning Staff (PPS), still under the Kennan influence, worried that the Kremlin might intervene against this, Allison wrote an "emphatic dissent." Three days later, Allison was heading up the National Security Council (NSC) study of rollback that resulted in the enabling document that appeared in September, NSC 81, embodying much of the language of Rusk, Allison, and Dulles in July. The Defense Department weighed in with its own paper, arguing for rollback and showing a poignant regard for Korean aspirations for unification. The course of the war had now provided "the first opportunity to displace part of the Soviet orbit," thus linking the march north to the realm of feasibility pointed to in NSC 48; the paper was unusually frank in noting that "Manchuria, the pivot" of the Soviet Far East strategic complex "would lose its captive status."[5]

It was in Allison's top secret paper of August 12, however, that the NSC 48–NSC 68 syllogism was patent: "Since a *basic policy* of the United States is to *check and reduce* the preponderant power of the USSR in Asia and elsewhere, then UN operations in Korea can set the stage for the non-communist penetration into an area under Soviet control" (emphasis added). John Davies and others also wrote memos in August explicitly linking rollback in Korea to the "check and reduce" goals of previous policy.[6]

The problem that remained was not whether to roll back the North, but who should control it: no one wanted Rhee in the saddle, and he had called publicly for rollback at about the time Allison did, causing the latter to say John Muccio ought to "caution him about premature statements."[7] The liberal internationalists-manqué who now supported rollback retained a vestigial reformism: the North would get ROK rule, but only if the ROK were liberalized, through an all-Korea, UN-supervised election. Failing that, it would get that still untested internationalist device: an allied trusteeship.[8] As we will see, Rhee was able to avoid this fate in 1950 just as he had in 1945, lurching into the North with his usual entourage of national police, rightist youths, and dispossessed landlords. But this was a minor matter compared to letting MacArthur and the China Lobby run the rollback.

Acheson was the executive who had to think about controlling foreign policy through the oval office and not somewhere else. But at precisely the time his advisors were settling on liberating the North, so were his key antagonists. MacArthur called for a rollback on July 17, and three days later Louis Johnson again sent his aides scurrying off to the Nationalist embassy to spill secrets of the highest sensitivity: that the Government had already decided to march north ... at Johnson's instance. (Those conservatives who howl about the Philby-Burgess-Michael Straight perfidy in "tipping off" the Russians to American plans to go to the Yalu, like William Safire, ought to ponder how long it took Moscow or Beijing to read Louis Johnson's mind, courtesy the Nationalists' leaky ship: by July 21, I would suspect.)[9] In any case Acheson could not have MacArthur and Johnson steering the course of events, with the China Lobby and the Nationalists trundling along behind. For then rollback meant a war for China. If Acheson went for rollback, it had to be "limited," just as he wanted a "limited" war.

Truman approved a march north, according to the best evidence, at the end of August.[10] The decision was embodied in NSC 81, written mostly by Rusk, which authorized MacArthur to move into North Korea if there were no Soviet or Chinese threats to intervene. It explicitly called for "a roll-back"; the enabling order to MacArthur, sent on September 16, referred to "the pursuance of a rollback." MacArthur was to use only Korean units in operations near the Chinese border.[11]

Nothing illustrates the highly charged politics of rollback more than Truman's dismissal of hardliners in his administration simultaneously with his decision to buy their line, thus trading policy for people. Louis Johnson was relieved in early September; although Robert Donovan and others link this to Johnson's waffling on Truman's order to MacArthur to retract his inflammatory message to the Veterans of Foreign Wars,[12] that came on August 26, yet Truman decided on September 1 that Johnson had to go for reasons that have yet to be revealed,[13] just after he determined on rollback. It is likely that Acheson prevailed upon Truman to replace him, given Johnson's unreliability and his attempt to wrest foreign policy initiative from Acheson, and, perhaps, his potentially treasonable relations with the Nationalists. Truman also removed Navy Secretary Matthews for publicly advocating preventive war on the Russians.[14] High politics in Washington increasingly bore the earmarks of a Chinese "two-line struggle": competing doctrines, high officials dismissed from office and blamed for advocating what the incumbents wished to do, reversals of historical verdicts.

MacArthur had from the beginning taken the rollback momentum in Washington and shaped it to his own purposes, in which the Korean War became the spark and the prelude for rollback on the mainland, using

Nationalist forces and American airpower. He backed the introduction of thirty thousand Nationalist troops as soon as the fighting began; in late July he led an imperial procession to Taipei, like the chieftain of an independent kingdom. He kept State Department representatives in the dark about his discussions with Chiang Kai-shek, leading Acheson to wire William Sebald for information on their discussions, and to become "increasingly disturbed" at MacArthur "taking foreign policy in his own hands." Johnson was ordered to cable MacArthur that "no one other than the President . . . has the authority to order or authorize preventive action against concentrations on the mainland . . . the most vital national interest requires that no action of ours precipitate general war or give others excuse to do so."[15]

Truman and Acheson also sent Averell Harriman to tell MacArthur that the war had to be limited to Korea. MacArthur responded that the United States ought to be "more aggressive in promoting dissension within China," and that if Chiang's forces landed and did not do well, that wouldn't be all bad: the United States might "get rid of him that way." Strong later wrote that MacArthur "played a lone hand with the National Government to the complete exclusion of the Embassy in Taipei"; Chiang, for his part, was "playing the Tokyo end of the United States Government for all it is worth."[16]

MacArthur was undaunted. He told Ridgway that China would not come into the war. But if it did, "I would go there and assume command, and deliver such a crushing defeat [that] it would be one of the decisive battles of the world—a disaster so great it would rock Asia, and perhaps turn back Communism."[17] After Inch'ŏn Gascoigne found the general "supremely pleased with himself," but disgusted with Washington for "unwarranted interference in the conduct of the war." MacArthur seemed ready "to take on the Chinese or even the Russians," brushing aside worries about global war; he "spat blood at Dean Acheson." Gascoigne thought him flushed with success and "pretty dangerous."[18]

Once the first troops crossed the parallel, rollback was on everybody's lips. War dispatches routinely referred to the "liberated areas" in the North. Charles Murphy remarked in early October that the United States should redouble its efforts "to look for ways to wrest the initiative from the Soviets and to roll them back." O. Edmund Clubb wrote that "our problem is to begin to roll up the satellites by positive action and not simply to remain in a defensive posture," and hoped that if the Chinese came into the war, they would get a good bloodying. John Carter Vincent weighed in from his exile in Bern, saying "personally, I believe we should cross the 38th parallel when set to do so irrespective of whether Chou En-lai is bluffing or not."[19]

MacArthur was correct in telling senators in 1951 that the crossing of the parallel "had the most complete and absolute approval of every section of the American government,"[20] if we grant him the license of mild exaggeration owed to a person who had been badly blindsided by liberal reconstructions. But there were different types of rollback. There was MacArthur's, which resembled a locomotive with no brakes. And there was Acheson's, a controlled rollback limited to Korea. It was the grand bipartisan accommodator, Dulles, who joined Acheson in trying to apply the brakes.

Some Republicans were "beating the drums for reckless action," Dulles wrote to MacArthur in mid-November, "which would involve us deeply in war on the mainland of Asia. You produced a miracle on the land in Korea. But I doubt whether you would feel that that proves that we should make the Asian mainland the area for the testing of the relative strength of the Free and Communist world."[21] But by then it was too late for Washington to apply the brakes, as all eyes focused on the first big defeat for communism in the postwar period. Amid a widening gyre the political middle had held, but had stretched and distended to accommodate political rivalry at home and the dialectic of battle in far-off Korea. The joining of the containment and rollback currents added a perverse momentum to Washington's policy, like a roller coaster car that climbs upward, jerks onto a track and abruptly gathers a quickened energy as it crests the summit. A process of incremental revision in the logic of containment, animated by a two-line struggle, now reached that point where quantity changes into quality, and a new reality dawns.

Who stood against this conjoined momentum? After the fact, nearly everyone on the left of General MacArthur. Generals Albert Wedemeyer and Omar Bradley may be taken as representative, the former saying that if the policy was to deter aggression, "we had no business going North," the latter calling the crossing of the parallel "a bold and aggressive step" and "extremely dangerous"—the decisions were "drastically wrong."[22]

At the time, however, one needed a high-powered microscope to discover serious opposition. Herbert Feis found Rhee's talk about occupying the North rather horrifying in mid-July, but he was not influential and was not heard from again. The prospect of a parallel crossing appalled America's British allies in July (they called it an "invasion"); but by the autumn they acquiesced in the rollback, while caviling about letting Rhee's regime—which the Foreign Office termed one of "black reaction, brutality, and extreme incompetence"—run the North.[23] It was only George Kennan who stood against the rollback juggernaut—idiosyncratically, as always.

In mid-August as he prepared to leave the State Department, Kennan set down his thoughts on "Far Eastern Policy" for Acheson. He began,

"The course upon which we are today moving is one, as I see it, so little promising and so fraught with danger that I could not honestly urge you to continue to take responsibility for it." Among the problems, he said, were a lack of "clear and realistic" objectives in Korea, MacArthur's "wide and relatively uncontrolled latitude" ("we do not really have full control"), and the obvious fact that American policy was only solidifying the Moscow-Beijing axis. And then he gave his recommendation, a mouthful: "First of all, we should make it an objective of policy to terminate our involvements on the mainland of Asia as rapidly as possible on the best terms we can get." This included getting out of the "hopeless" mess the French had made in Indochina—and a pullout in Korea, too, if the United States could arrange

> a Korea nominally independent but actually amenable to Soviet influence, provided this state of affairs were to be brought about gradually . . . and were accompanied by a stable and secure situation in Japan. . . . It is beyond our capabilities to keep Korea permanently out of the Soviet orbit. The Koreans cannot really maintain their own independence in the face of both Russian and Japanese pressures. From the standpoint of our own interests it is preferable that Japan should dominate Korea than that Russia should do so.*

As ever, the asterisk was to Teddy Roosevelt's defense of Japanese ascendancy in Korea.

Japan was "the most important single factor in Asia," but at the moment it was "too weak to compete." However, "with the revival of her normal strength and prestige," Japan would be able to regain her influence in Korea. "It is important that the nominal independence of Korea be preserved, for *it provides a flexible vehicle* through which Japanese influence may someday gradually replace Soviet influence without creating undue international repercussions" (emphasis added). He urged negotiations with the Russians for "a termination of the Korean War" and the retreat of KPA forces north of the parallel. Kennan closed by acknowledging a bit of a problem with public opinion should his policy be adopted: "violent and outraged opposition" would ensue. Nonetheless, "there is a clear problem of responsibility involved, which begs for clarification."[24]

Rarely has such prescience accompanied such triumphantly bad timing. From 1961 onward every American administration sought, if secretly, the partial substitution of Japanese economic and, ultimately, military influence for the American in the "flexible vehicle" of the regimes running South Korea. Kennan's callousness about Japan's record in Korea was unfortunate. But Japan was the only factor in Asia that held his attention because it was the only industrial power, something far closer to reality than the morbid fear of China that ensued for two decades. Kennan seemed always in the position of being right for the wrong reasons, setting out a private and eccentric logic. It is doubtful that Acheson paid his paper a second thought, and Kennan did not aspire to become what he called "a floating kidney" by pushing his views too much, so he shuffled off to Princeton. But he was the only one who took the measure of the impending calamity—and when it came, he gave Acheson wise and affecting counsel.[25]

THE OCCUPATION OF THE NORTH

On the day before Republic of Korea Army (ROKA) units crossed over to the North, Acheson said the parallel no longer counted: "Korea will be used as a stage to prove what Western Democracy can do to help the underprivileged countries of the world."[26] All this would pale if the Rhee regime ruled in its usual manner, however. The ROK saw itself as "the only legal government in Korea," signaling its intention to incorporate northern Korea under its aegis on the basis of the 1948 Constitution. The UN, however, had made no commitment to extending the ROK mandate into the North, and the British and French were positively opposed to the idea—even suggesting that ROK weakness and corruption, and the possibility that it might "provoke a widespread terror," raised questions about whether it should be allowed to reoccupy *the South.*[27]

American ideas for the occupation of the North called for the "supreme authority" to be the United Nations, not the Republic of Korea; failing that, a trusteeship or an American military government. The United States may also have had secret plans to remove Rhee: Preston Goodfellow cabled his friend on October 3, saying, "Some very strong influences are at work trying to find a way to put some one in the presidency other than your good self."[28] It was as if the conflicts between Rhee and State in 1945 were to be rerun; the department categorically rejected the ROK claim to a mandate over the North and instead called for new UN-supervised elections. (The South wanted elections only for one hundred northern seats in the ROK National Assembly.) On October 12 the UN resolved to restrict ROK authority to the south for an interim period. In the meantime, the existing North Korean provincial administration would be utilized, with no reprisals against individuals merely for having served in middle or low-level positions in the Democratic People's Republic of Korea (DPRK) government, political parties, or the military. (DPRK) land reform and other social reforms would be honored; an extensive "re-education and re-orientation program" would show Koreans in the North the virtues of a democratic way of life.[29]

In the event the northern occupation recapitulated the pattern of

1945: State Department plans were undone by local occupiers, no UN-supervised administration or trusteeship emerged, and influential Koreans got the ear of the Americans. Thus we find Cho Pyŏng-ok, the National Police director so useful to Hodge in October 1945, flying into P'yŏngyang on October 25 with Naval intelligence personnel, before noncombatant Americans arrived.[30]

Within a week of the parallel crossing the people of Kaesŏng, according to the *New York Times*, were among those who "got their first peek at democracy at work."[31] But the ostensible government in the North had nothing to do with United Nations trusteeships or State Department civil affairs plans. It was the southern system imposed on the other half of the country. The civil conflict pitted one state structure and social system against another.

The evidence is that MacArthur and Rhee planned the occupation themselves, and that American intelligence agencies worked closely with ROK forces. The State Department was in the dark, seeking to find out what commitments had been made between the two; one report had Rhee promising to MacArthur that he would amnesty criminals, hold elections to fill the one hundred "northern" seats in the National Assembly, and then "set up a single government for all of Korea." MacArthur told British authorities that he agreed with this electoral procedure, because anything else would hurt South Korean morale.[32]

The effective politics of the occupation consisted mostly of the National Police and the rightist youth corps that shadowed it. Cho Pyŏng-ok, by then home minister, announced on October 10 that the Korean National Police (KNP) controlled nine towns north of the parallel, with a special force of thirty thousand in recruitment for occupation duty. Shortly Drumwright cabled that Washington's idea that there should be only a minimum of ROK personnel was "already outmoded by events" with some two thousand police across the parallel; but he thought some local responsibility might result if police who originally came from the North could be utilized. (Thousands of police who had served the Japanese in northern Korea had fled South at the liberation, and Rhee had always seen them as the vanguard of his plans for a "northern expedition.") By October 20, if not earlier, An Ho-sang had his youth corps conducting "political indoctrination" across the border.[33] ROK occupation forces were on their own and unsupervised for much of October.

An American observation team reached Wŏnsan on October 15, finding about 70 percent of the dwellings in the city demolished by aerial bombing, and only 20,000 of 150,000 residents still around. Nearly all DPRK officials were gone, reportedly after having shot several hundred political prisoners. "Pinched faces and ragged clothing" were the norm, the population having suffered badly since June 1950. Cho Pyŏng-ok addressed the bedraggled and desultory citizenry on October 15.[34]

American units encountered heavier fighting on the western side of the peninsula, the 1st Cavalry Division entering P'yŏngyang only on October 19 after stubborn resistance, no doubt occasioned by the DPRK leadership's emptying the city of all officials, most records, all moveable factory equipment, even bicycles. Rhee placed "Tiger" Kim in charge of the initial occupation, naming him deputy provost marshall general for the capital. On the day American forces moved into the city, Rhee announced the abrogation of the northern land reform, prompting the CIA to comment that this "reflects recent pressure by the landlord class to nullify . . . land reform in order to maintain their traditional controlling position in Korean political and economic life." P'yŏngyang's new mayor chose United Nations Day to announce that land would be returned to its "rightful owners."[35]

American intelligence teams, including Richard Sneider of State's Bureau of Intelligence Research, combed through the Soviet embassy (which, neighbors said, had been vacated right after the Inch'ŏn landing, an interesting tidbit) and the homes and offices of high DPRK officials, apparently getting little of value. Drumwright deplored the lack of trained personnel for what was, after all, "the first communist capital taken in history." He was surprised to find that the DPRK capitol was a well-appointed building constructed "on land belonging [*sic*] to the American Northern Presbyterian Mission, right in the middle of a missionary compound." The homes of American missionaries stood as they had in 1945, with their furniture intact.[36]

19. South Korean interrogation of peasants, North Korea, fall 1950

Counter-Intelligence Corps (CIC) investigators found from interviewing North Korean citizens that they had many complaints about low pay, evening study groups, and "constant harassing for increases of production." The CIC estimate was that about half of them were still sympathetic to communism. Land reform had made 70 percent of the peasants "ardent supporters" of the regime, even though their taxes were often higher than the stipulated 25 percent of the crop. Perhaps 20 percent of students in the North secretly supported the South. The majority (70 percent) of those interviewed still "felt that the Communists were right, that we [the U.S.] had no right to 'invade' South Korea and their homeland." The interviewers attributed this in part to the "intense nationalism" of education in North Korea.[37]

A *London Times* reporter motored up to P'yŏngyang through "a countryside as trim and carefully husbanded as any in Asia," observing the carefully placed rice mounds drying in the fields, preparatory to being bound and marketed, and remarking on the absence of a North Korean "scorched earth" program. Peasants were grateful that the Korean People's Army (KPA) retreat "remained unmarred by any attempt . . . to destroy his crops or paddy bunds. Stocks of rice were removed, but the earth was not scorched."

In the city things were different. A state of anarchy existed, with no effective administration, police reprisals against suspected collaborators (including many assassinations), and rightist youths roaming the streets, looting what little property was left. Stores were shuttered and much of the population had departed; citizens who remained appeared in "much better condition than did those in Seoul." The new city council included older businessmen who had remained in P'yŏngyang since 1945: U Che-sŏn, a former tungsten mine owner and associate of Cho Man-sik, who ran a large soy sauce factory until 1949; O Chin-hwan, who had owned two firms in Manchuria before 1945 and who still retained two large homes in P'yŏngyang; Yun To-sŏng, a banker with the *Shokusan Ginko* who ran textile and leather firms in the DPRK. They were fig leafs with no power. But it would appear that some members of the "class enemy" fared well in the North until 1950. American Civil Affairs officers were "pathetically few," and barely experienced:

> The recruitment of a provisional city council for Pyongyang would have been farcical, if the implications were not so obviously tragic. It was rather like watching an Army sergeant selecting men for fatigue duty. As a result, weeks after the fall of the city there were no public utilities, law and order was evident only on the main streets during the hours of daylight, and the food shortage due to indifferent transport and distribution had assumed serious proportions.[38]

People tended to remain close to their homes, according to UN Commission on the Unification and Rehabilitation of Korea (UNCURK) observers, because of the "pillaging and looting and general violence of ROK troops." Troops entering a village were witnessed demanding "the first thousand bags of rice" from the fall crop; officers confiscated houses "without any authority." Reprisals were threatened against any citizen reporting such activity to Americans.[39] If this account of the occupation appears one-sided, the evidence does not support an alternative: nary a good word is spoken about ROK behavior. Furthermore, there is worse to tell.

Many correspondents remember Syngman Rhee's speech in the hollow capitol building in Seoul on September 29, shards of glass occasionally tinkling to the floor, MacArthur gazing on benignly and Rhee at his impressive best, evoking tears and pathos throughout the audience. The text, written by Harold Noble, evoked Korea's long history and thanked the Allies with heartfelt warmth for the liberation of Seoul. It also included the following pledge: "The ROK is a signatory to Article IV of the Geneva Conventions, and will treat surrendered and captured enemy accordingly. . . . In victory we must and we shall show magnanimity . . . we must not betray ourselves into using the harsh methods which the enemy has used." Reginald Thompson listened to the address and later wrote, "He promised justice, mercy and forgiveness to all who surrendered. It was a noble speech. . . . I am far from hard-boiled. These words moved me deeply. . . . Even now it is as impossible to believe them to have been uttered in a spirit of the most appalling cynicism as it is equally impossible to believe that they were not."[40]

This was written after Thompson witnessed the rule of the ROK in the North, where according to internal intelligence reports and the highest levels of the American government, the ROK perpetrated a nauseating reign of terror and called it liberation, in the name of democracy and the United Nations.

State Department officials had sought some mechanism for supervision of the political aspects of the rollback, "to insure that a 'bloodbath' would not result. In other words . . . the Korean forces should be kept under control."[41] But occupation forces in the North were under no one's control. The social base of the DPRK was broad, enrolling the majority poor peasantry, so potentially almost any northerner could be a target. Furthermore, the South's definition of "collaboration" was incontinent, spilling over even to old women caught washing the clothes of People's Army soldiers.[42]

The British had evidence by the end of October that the ROK as a matter of official policy sought to "hunt out and destroy communists and collaborators"; the facts confirmed "what is now becoming pretty notorious, namely that the restored civil administration in Korea bids fair to become an international scandal of a major kind." The Foreign Office urged that immediate representations be made in Washington, because this was "a war for men's minds" in which the political counted almost as much as the military. Ambassador Franks accordingly brought the matter up with Dean Rusk on October 30, getting this response: "Rusk agrees that there have regrettably been many cases of atrocities" by the ROK authorities, and promised to have American military oficers seek to control the situation.[43]

Cho Pyŏng-ok announced in mid-November that 55,909 "vicious red-hot collaborators and traitors" had been arrested by that date alone, a total that was probably understated. Internal American documents show full awareness of ROK atrocities; for example, Korean Military Advisory Group (KMAG) officers said the entire North might be put off limits to ROK authorities if they continue the violence, and in one documented instance, in the town of Sunch'ŏn, the Americans replaced marauding South Korean forces with American 1st Cavalry elements.[44]

Once the Chinese came into the war and the retreat from the North began, newspapers all over the world reported eyewitness accounts of ROK executions of people under detention. United Press International estimated that eight hundred people were executed from December 11 to 16 and buried in mass graves; these included "many women, some children," executed because they were family members of Reds. American and British soldiers witnessed "truckloads [of] old men[,] women[,] youths[,] several children lined before graves and shot down." A British soldier on December 20 saw about forty "emaciated and very subdued Koreans" being shot by ROK military police, their hands tied behind their backs and rifle butts cracked on their heads if they protested. The incident was a blow to his morale, he said, because three fusiliers had just returned from North Korean captivity and had reported good treatment. Elsewhere British troops intervened to stop the killings, and in one case opened a mass grave for one hundred people, finding bodies of men and women, but in this case no children. There were many similar reports at the time, from soldiers and reporters. The British representative in northern Korea said that most of the executions occurred when KNP officials sought to move some three thousand political prisoners to the South. "As threat to Seoul developed, and owing to the destruction of the death-house, the authorities resorted to these hurried mass executions by shooting in order to avoid the transfer of condemned prisoners South, or leaving them behind to be liberated by the Communists. However deplorable their methods one can readily grasp the problem."[45]   Rhee defended the killings, saying "we have to take measures," and arguing that "all [death] sentences [were] passed after due process of law." Muccio generally backed him up, defending the ROK against the atrocity charges. He was aware of ROK intentions by October 20 at the latest, cabling that ROK officials would give death sentences to anyone who "rejoined enemy organizations or otherwise cooperated with the enemy," the "legal basis" being the ROK National Security Law and an unspecified "special decree" promulgated in *Japan* in 1950 for emergency situations—something that may indicate SCAP (Supreme Command Allied Powers) involvement in the executions. CIA sources commented with bloodcurdling aplomb that ROK officials had pointed out to UNCURK that "the executions all followed legal trials," and that MacArthur's UN Command "has regarded the trial and punishment of collaborators and other political offenders as an internal matter for the ROK." The legal instrument the CIA had in mind was "Emergency Law Number One," a special decree that, the CIA seemed to suggest, justified the murder of POWs and political criminals (after trial, of course). Many of the witnessed murders in fact had no legal procedure whatsoever, and were carried out not just by police but by rightist youth squads. A Japanese source, cited by a conservative scholar, estimated that the Rhee regime executed or kidnapped some 150,000 people in the political violence of the North's "liberation."[46]

This sad record does not owe to some putative "Korean brutality," as most Americans thought. Civil wars, not to mention revolutions, have witnessed comparable political violence everywhere in the world. The forces of order in the ROK were mostly trained in Japanese colonial institutions; collaborators with Japan in the ROK police and military lacked legitimacy, and knew so themselves. In such circumstances people have little recourse other than force to maintain their rule. Far more troubling is the complicity and involvement of Americans in the atrocious character of the northern occupation, going beyond the shameless justifications for ROK behavior discussed above.

We find chilling American instructions to political affairs officers on the ground in the North, at odds with the benign, magnanimous occupation envisioned by the State Department, or Acheson's messianic call to show the world the democratic way. Counterintelligence personnel attached to the 10th Corps were ordered to "liquidate the North Korean Labor Party and North Korean intelligence agencies," and to forbid any political organizations that might constitute "a security threat to X Corps." "The destruction of the North Korean labor Party and the government" was to be accomplished by the arrest and internment of the following categories of people: all police, all security service personnel, all officials of government, and all current and former members of the North Korean Worker's Party (NKWP) and the South Korean Worker's Party (SKWP). The compilation of "black lists" would follow, the purpose of which was unstated. These orders are repeated in other 10th Corps documents, with the added authorization that agents were to suspend all types of civilian communications, impound all radio transmitters, even to destroy "[carrier] pigeon lofts and their contents."[47] The Korean Worker's Party (KWP) was a mass party with as much as 14 percent of the entire population on its rolls; such instructions implied the arrest and internment of upwards of one-third of North Korean adults. Perhaps for this reason the Americans found that virtually all DPRK officials, down to local government, had fled before the onrushing troops.[48]

Instructions are unavailable for the other major occupying Army in the western sector, the Eighth. The evidence merely points to the establishment of a Civil Assistance Command to carry out civil affairs; British sources said most personnel were untrained, and that "all UN troops, from Generals down, were bitter against all Koreans, whether from North or South. They loathed and despised them. This did not make it easy to run the 'C.A.C.' " The predictable result was "an appalling chaos."[49]

Other internal materials document odious connivance in South Korean atrocities. Counter-Intelligence Corps detachments, accompanied by KNP investigators, were instructed from the occupation of Inch'ŏn onward to draw up "white" and "black" lists of Koreans; members of people's committees were particular targets for blacklisting. "Team agents [also] made use of rightist organization[s]," including getting them "to assist in establishing order." American CIC personnel were present with many ROK police and intelligence units in the North. KMAG advisors also accompanied ROK military units, and stated on October 2 that the KNP would be used "to control civil population and maintain order as soon as possible after liberation"; perhaps anticipating what would happen next, KMAG recommended a "method [of] silencing" reporters following in the ROK wake.[50]

Original ROK blacklists exist in the archival collection of "captured enemy documents"; apparently American investigators thought they were North Korean blacklists. One shows that the South Korean "White Tiger" unit listed sixty-nine residents of Hyesan County, North Ham'gyŏng Province as "reactionaries" [pandongja], of which nine were designated as "spies" [milchŏng], nineteen as "incorrigibly bad" [akjil], and twelve as "both"; the rest had no designation other than reactionary. The charges against them were: cooperating with the army, being members of the party, jailing "patriots," and spying on ROK units or agencies.[51]

During firefights with guerrillas in October 1950, a memorandum from an Army intelligence officer named McCaffrey to Maj. Gen. Clark Ruffner suggested that, if necessary, the Americans could organize "assassination squads to carry out death sentences passed by ROK Government in 'absentia' trials to guerrilla leaders," and went on to say, "if necessary clear the areas of civilians in which the guerrillas operate," and "inflame the local population against the guerrillas by every propaganda device possible." (The ROK was, by all allied testimony, lax in distinguishing between guerrillas and their supporters in such "trials.") In the aftermath of the Chinese intervention, a staff conference with Ridgway, Almond, Coulter, and others in attendance brought up the issue of the "enemy in civilian clothing." Someone said, "we cannot execute them but they can be shot before they become prisoners." To which Coulter replied, "We just turn them over to the ROK's and they take care of them."[52]

After they reoccupied P'yŏngyang, North Korean sources claimed that fifteen thousand people had been massacred in that city alone. Some two thousand were said to have been found shot in the courtyard of the main prison, and thousands more bodies were piled in twenty-six air raid shelters.[53] The major atrocity always alleged by DPRK authorities, however, was said to have occurred in the town of Sinch'ŏn, between the capitol and Kaesŏng, where hundreds of women and children were kept for some days in a shed without food and water, as Americans and Koreans sought information on their absconded male relatives; later they were doused with gasoline and roasted alive. This atrocity has never been verified by independent sources, but neither have the charges and the photographic evidence been sincerely investigated or refuted. In November 1987, together with a Thames Television crew I visited the charnel house and the tombs, looked at original photos and newspaper stories, and spent the day with the only survivor; we came away convinced that a terrible atrocity had taken place, although the evidence on its authorship was impossible to document.[54]

THE YAWNING TRAP:
"WE HAVE FLUSHED THE COVEY"

On the day that Marines landed at Inch'ŏn, MacArthur's formidable publicity apparatus began a farrago of releases claiming that the main forces of the Korean People's Army had been caught in a giant pincer movement, that it had few if any reserves left, and that it was on the verge of defeat. Gen. Walton Walker was "a quail-shooting Texan," and after Inch'ŏn he exulted: "We have flushed the covey, and we are now kicking up the singles."[55] The drumbeat went on for weeks as American and South Korean forces rolled up to the Yalu, lasting until a final offensive in late November that was to bring the boys home by Christmas. At that point Chinese forces intervened and threw the allied forces back, causing "a new war" in MacArthur's eyes, a terrible and avoidable defeat in Truman's eyes.

Two verdicts arose from this crisis, the conservative one that MacArthur was stabbed in the back and that there was "no substitute for victory," and the liberal one that Truman and Acheson courageously limited the war to the Korean peninsula after MacArthur grossly misjudged Chinese intentions and then threatened a worse disaster by carrying the war to the China mainland. Recent literature has shown both verdicts to have been false, both in the general American failure, whether in Washington or Tokyo, accurately to gauge Chinese intentions, and the frequent, active consideration given by Truman and his advisors to extending the war to the mainland.[56]

What remains, however, is the assumption that Inch'ŏn was a brilliant operation that destroyed the North Koreans, leaving China to bail Kim Il Sung's chestnuts out of a very hot fire. For many years I believed this myself, and thought North Korean constructions of the post-Inch'ŏn period as "The Great Strategic Retreat," a defeat for MacArthur, and the like, were sheer fantasies, and that MacArthur kicked their singles into a general KPA rout. But primary evidence does not support such a conclusion. Instead it suggests that the Inch'ŏn victory was Pyrrhic, that the KPA was out of the fight for only about three weeks, and that MacArthur and his advisors, fighting a guerrilla war as a conventional war, were drawn into a trap. Willoughby, it will be remembered, likened Inch'ŏn to Napoleon's generalship. But when American soldiers again met KPA main force units head on, the snows, the howling, horrifying winds, and a temperature of twenty-two degrees below zero mocked this analogy, as if the Russian winter had migrated to Korea to defeat another great but tragically grandiose general.

MacArthur told Gascoigne on September 19 what his acolytes had already been telling the press, that he did not think the KPA had significant forces left north of the parallel; large "pockets" of bypassed enemy forces would easily be mopped up later on. A week hence UN Command (UNC) headquarters had the KPA fleeing northward in disarray, "thoroughly routed and disorganized," and unable to defend the parallel, which ROK troops shortly crossed against no resistance.

ROKA units moved into the North on September 30, Washington time, the spearhead patrols of the 3d Division crossing over in the East near Yangyang. The honor of being the first commander to cross the parallel went to Gen. Yi Chŏng-ch'an, who had just replaced Kim Sŏk-wŏn as head of the 3d—thus denying Kim his chance to chase after Kim Il Sung yet again. Yi was a member of a prominent family; his grandfather was Korean consul to Washington in 1887–1889, and later governor of Kyŏnggi Province. After the annexation, the Japanese bestowed the honor of "Count" upon him. General Yi's father, a businessman during the colonial period, owned the first factory to produce rubber shoes in

Korea. Yi Chŏng-ch'an graduated from the Japanese Military Academy in 1934, and rose to the rank of major in 1945.[57]

The ROK termed the new phase "a holy war for the restoration of the lost territory," with "our National Army counterattacking"; the allied role was typically left unmentioned.[58] Rhee's plans were to unify the North, but not necessarily to stop there: he wrote MacArthur in August that the Allies would have "firm bases of operation established on the Eastern side of the Manchurian border," a great advantage "when the global conflict begins." In early October South Korean units swept up the peninsula with next to no resistance. They were twenty-five miles above the parallel within two days, had four divisions in the North within a week, and captured the eastern port city of Wŏnsan on October 10. Thereafter they kept on rolling toward the Yalu—an odd and heady new reality for an army that, a few weeks earlier, had been judged continuously to "break" under North Korean pressure.[59] After a week of marching in the North, an ROK major kept repeating that he could not understand why the KPA "had been giving up beautiful natural defenses," causing a reporter to comment that the North Koreans "have not been fighting," and that the quality of their soldiers had clearly been overrated.[60]

UNC headquarters announced "spectacular gains" in mid-October; the Red capital was seized, leading SCAP officers to claim that the war was over. The *New York Times* also thought the final phase of the war was at hand: a banner headline trumpeted, "UN Troops Race Unopposed Toward the Manchurian Border." Hanson Baldwin thought the Russians must have decided to "cut their losses"; others proclaimed a "smashing North Korean defeat," and cigars were lit all over Tokyo and Washington.[61]

Battlefield reports, however, did not show the capture of large regular units, or even a single ranking KPA officer. MacArthur thus sought to tighten the noose with another amphibious landing at Wŏnsan on the East coast, but harbor mines slowed it down so that ROK soldiers were well past Wŏnsan when the Marines hit the shore. Subsequent airborne landings behind North Korean lines also failed to roll up significant forces. This meant that composing and uniting Korea and destroying the KPA would require covering the entire northern territory.[62]

British reporters were more discerning (or perhaps freer to report the truth) than Americans, and immediately understood what had happened: MacArthur's pincer trap had closed, and inside was little more than the green soldiers recently recruited for the final push against the Pusan perimeter. Thompson wrote, "The North Korean Army had disappeared like a wraith into the hills. . . . The trap had closed, and it was empty." The *London Times* penned a phrase that would seem incomprehensible in the received wisdom on the post-Inch'ŏn fighting: "The aggressiveness of the rearguard suggests that there is a future Korean Mao Tse-tung in Kanggye." A "dangerous complacency" had overtaken American officers, it said. "The enemy's forces were declared to have been destroyed when elements of 12 divisions were identified . . . the intrinsic strength and pliability of Communist armies were forgotten. . . . Fears that large numbers of Communists and their followers withdrawing into the northern hills would wage a partisan war had been realized."

Among American reporters, only Asia hand Walter Sullivan understood that many KPA leaders had fought with the Chinese, and were now following "Chinese Communist" strategies of withdrawal and retreat, with preparations for it having been made over the previous three months.[63] The North Koreans had left tens of thousands of guerrillas in the American wake, regrouped and replenished existing divisions, and brought in fresh troops from reserves in Manchuria. While Willoughby assured the press that no more than twenty thousand KPA effectives remained, by late November line units and left-back guerrillas may have been six or seven times that figure.

There was a veteran Korean Mao Tse-tung in Kanggye—several of them. The high leadership had retreated to the wild mountain fastness where it had been in the 1930s, following tried and true methods of guerrilla war filtered from Sun Tzu to Mao to Kim and his allies, and waiting for reconstituted divisions, the weather, the Chinese, and the hubris of Americans to become their allies. Their forte in the 1930s, lamented so often by the Japanese, was their capacity to attack and disappear without a trace. In 1946 in important interviews that had done so much to explain North Korean practice, a high member of Kim's guerrillas had said their first principle was "fight when it profits you, watch and wait when it does not . . . fight only when you know the situation; if you don't, take another opportunity. This is how a small army beats a big army."[64]

A top secret order from Pak Il-u on September 30 stated that the American "blood-sucking vampires" had made an "adventurous attack" at Inch'ŏn, occasioning an "extremely serious military and political situation, decisive for the fate of the homeland." "A protracted war" was now unavoidable. This would require "a rapid transition" to new fighting methods: "the entire people must rise up in a righteous war to oppose US agression." People should "ambush and destroy the enemy wherever he is," with leaders "taking the initiative and setting an example."[65]

Just after UN forces crossed the parallel, Chinese People's Liberation Army (PLA) commander Yeh Chien-ying reportedly gave a secret speech in Canton, saying that American forces had achieved only "superficial superiority" as a result of Inch'ŏn, and were now being lured northward.

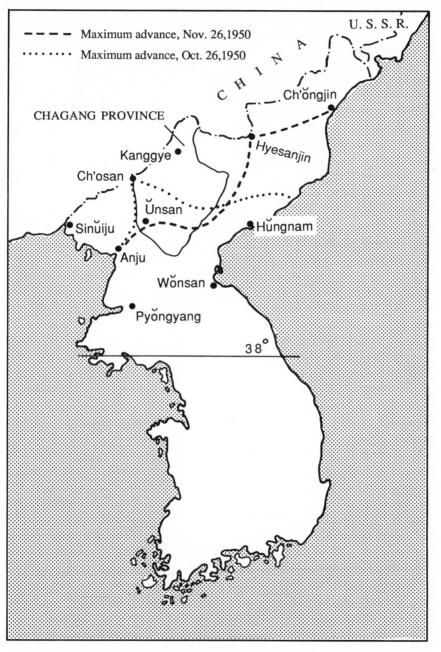

- - - - Maximum advance, Nov. 26, 1950
.... Maximum advance, Oct. 26, 1950

U. S. S. R.

CHINA

CHAGANG PROVINCE

Ch'ŏngjin

Kanggye

Hyesanjin

Ch'osan

Ŭnsan

Sinŭiju

Hŭngnam

Anju

Wŏnsan

Pyŏngyang

38°

Map 8. UN Advances to the Yalu and the Chagang-do Redoubt

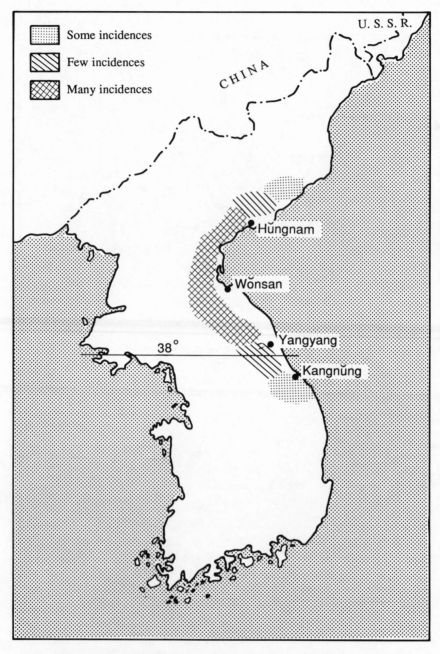

Map 9. Guerrillas in the 10th Corps Area, November 1950

The extensive mountainous areas are being fully exploited to induce the enemy to penetrate deep into the interior where more than three divisions of the enemy's main strength have been surrounded through mobile fighting tactics. It may be likened to the first stage of the liberation war in China when the Chiang bandits released their whole strength for an assault on Yenan and Kalgan and the main tactics pursued by us then consisted of the preservation of our strength to await the opportunity for encirclement and annihilation of the enemy.

Another report paraphrased a Chinese directive of October 3, saying that the KPA had compiled a "splendid record" in defeating the Rhee forces; with American intervention the war had now reached "a new stage." The KPA, however, was "unbeaten and remains [a] powerful force gaining recruits at home and abroad. Although it has abandoned certain territory it has gained enormously in strength." It could afford to let Korea's cities fall, the report said: "PLA abandonment [of] Yenan is precedent for this sort of action."[66]

A captured notebook quoted Pak Ki-sŏng, chief of political intelligence in the KPA 8th Division: "The main force of the enemy still remained intact, not having been fully damaged. When they were not fully aware of the power of our forces, they pushed their infantry far forward . . . to the Yalu River. This indicated that they underestimated us. All these conditions were favorable to lure them near."

A KPA officer captured at the time of the joint Sino-Korean offensive said that until late November, the KPA had been "continuously withdrawing."

One may think that going down all the way to the Pusan perimeter and then withdrawing all the way to the Yalu River was a complete defeat. But that is not so. That was a planned withdrawal. We withdrew because we knew that UN troops would follow us up here, and that they would spread their troops thinly all over the vast area. Now, the time has come for us to envelope these troops and annihilate them.

He said that combined KPA and Chinese forces striking from the front would be aided by "eight strong corps which will harass and attack the enemy from the rear." KPA forces had moved back as far south as Andong and Sangju in North Kyŏngsang Province to envelop UN troops.[67]

After the Chinese came into the war, William V. Quinn, intelligence chief for the X Corps, grasped what had happened after Inch'ŏn. The enemy had "taken to the hills," he said, fighting necessary delaying actions while "relentlessly continu[ing] their northward withdrawal." Several different routes led to "the mountainous redoubt of Chagang-do." During the colonial period, he said, Kim Il Sung had acquired a reputa-

tion "as a skillful and ruthless guerrilla chief . . . his base of operations
. . . was an area in the rugged terrain north and northwest of Hamhung."
It may have been foresight, Quinn said, "or a safeguard against what has
become inevitable." In any case in the spring of 1950 Kim carved out a
new province in his old haunt, calling it Chagang. Natural boundaries,
mountains and rivers, made it almost impregnable from the south, but
"an adequate road grid laces the area together and provides access to
Manchuria."

The North Koreans had established a system that, unlike the ROK, did
not rely on control of the capital, but penetrated to the villages in a way
no previous Korean state ever had, giving it political strength to go with
the guerrilla tactics. Around October 10 DPRK party, state, and military
leaders began to withdraw toward the Chagang area, taking with them
local civil officials and "confirmed Communists." "Changjin and Kapsan
were repeatedly mentioned as the assembly areas for withdrawing
forces"; the East coast was left completely exposed, allowing the ROKA
to cruise unassisted to the border. So rapid was the withdrawal that in
many cases "the enemy completely broke contact" with UN forces (mostly
ROKA forces in the east). On the western side, delaying resistance was
heavier to evacuate the capital; the assembly point was Kanggye, which
they rapidly withdrew toward—while bombers blasted the escape route
that Americans expected a conventional army to take, toward Sinŭiju on
the Chinese border. Quinn thought that with Manchurian resupply
routes, guerrillas would be able to fight "for an indefinite period of time,"
inaccessible to amphibious or air attack. When Chinese and Korean
troops came into the war from Manchuria, major forces crossed the Yalu
at Manp'ojin and moved through Kanggye, dealing the Americans their
terrible defeat at the Changjin (Japanese name, Chosin) Reservoir. Another large army crossed at Antung, eventually linking up with regrouped KPA units in the vicinity of Kapsan.[68]

In October and November, the People's Army fought a guerrilla war
in North and South. As we have seen, KPA forces maintained heavy pressure in the southeast in spite of their advance knowledge of the Inch'ŏn
landing, and for some ten days after it. This was done to pin as many
UN forces down in the southeast as possible, and to delay the operation
of MacArthur's pincer, in combination with KPA resistance in the Seoul
area. On September 25 there was a general break-and-withdrawal all
along the perimeter. KPA forces doffed their uniforms for peasant dress
and headed into the hills, the majority as organized units. Pang Ho-san
was able to lead much of his 6th Division through the mountains all the
way back to Chagang, where his forces again joined the battle in late November. Some forty thousand KPA and local guerrillas stayed in the
Chŏlla area. Kim Ch'aek organized about ten thousand guerrillas in the

area between Ch'unch'ŏn and Wŏnsan from among retreating KPA units; Kim Il commanded what Americans called "a small but efficient fighting force" near Ch'orwŏn, and former mayor of Seoul Yi Sŏng-yŏp reportedly commanded a guerrilla detachment in the same area.

A long listing of guerrilla activities south of the parallel for the last two weeks of October included the following: 15,000 guerrillas in possession of Yangyang; "strong concentrations" at Samch'ŏk, Ulchin, and Kangnŭng; guerrillas in occupation of Kŭmhwa, Hwach'ŏn, and Koesan; 1,000 near Kwangju; 300 engaged near Mun'gyŏng; 300 attacked at Changsu by UN troops; 2,000 near Chŏngŭp; two to three thousand near Mokp'o; and so on.[69]

As always, the strongest guerrilla province was South Chŏlla, and most of the guerrillas were local people. Guerrillas controlled the province from the Inch'ŏn landing to the Chinese entry. They also extended into the southern part of North Chŏlla; an American survey estimated that only 30 percent of both provinces was secure in early November. Only 1 percent of the fall rice harvest was collected in "the guerrilla infested, heavy rice-producing area of southwest Korea," according to the CIA. In late November it reported Kwangju under ROK control, but "overland routes into [the] city are cut and conditions are uncertain in outlying areas." The area south of Chŏnju could be traveled "only in an armed convoy"; rail and road lines were cut time and time again. ROKA action against the guerrillas was ineffective: they sweep through the hills, "and the bandits move out ahead of them like pheasants in a corn field." The governor of South Chŏlla, Pak Ch'ŏl-su, told Americans who thought the guerrillas were from the North that "most of [the] guerrillas are [local] civilians who were active Communists while the Reds were in power and had to flee to the mountains."[70]

Guerrilla activities caused the general collapse of ROK county governments in Kangwŏn Province in late October. British sources said that "there are still a vast number of guerrillas at large . . . one gets sniped at even in the Seoul Inch'ŏn area." An official history estimated that a "minimum" of forty thousand guerrillas remained in South Korea in November; "numerous partisan bands . . . operated throughout the western part of South Korea." Many were "disguised" as peasants. Intelligence estimates at the time suggest a much larger total; as we have seen, forty thousand were thought to be in South Chŏlla alone; daily reports in October and November also listed twenty thousand in the T'aebaeksan area, and groups of one to two thousand in the Chinju-Hadong-Kŏch'ang region. Various regiments of the ROKA 11th Division were in daily action against large concentrations of guerrillas throughout South Chŏlla Province, and in the southern counties of North Chŏlla—in other words, precisely the counties of PC strength in 1945–1946. ROK police could not occupy the towns of Muju, Changsan, Chŏngŭp, and Koch'ang in late October because guerrillas controlled them.[71]

A captured diary from a Sŏbaeksan guerrilla listed Yun T'al-wŏn as the commander of a detachment said to be 130 strong, and recorded several attacks on police boxes in mid-October. Local bandits were recruited into their ranks: those who "plunder the property of rich farmers and capitalists shall be taken as guerrillas and trained to fight against the enemy." The unit had drill regimens that were heavy on criticism and self-criticism sessions, as inoculation against what some people like to call the "free rider" problem: "Have you inflicted any losses on your country or your fellowmen through [following] your own interests?" "Let us bear each other's agony and show more love toward our fellowmen with whom we live and die . . . never damage anything belonging to the people." As for the opposition, "kill unconditionally all those who work for the enemy. Confiscate their property, dividing it among the poor."[72]

In early November Kim Il's guerrilla detachment struck south of the parallel, seizing Ch'unch'ŏn and then marching toward Seoul; it took two ROK divisions to drive them back. His forces kept the ROKA continuously engaged in the Ch'orwŏn-Hwach'ŏn area. His group, or another in the vicinity, threatened a major hydroelectric plant north of Seoul in the third week of November. Kim Ch'aek's group was much larger, at least ten thousand strong, and mounted continuous guerrilla attacks "from the very moment [American] troops came ashore" in Wŏnsan. Destructive attacks on rail and highway routes between Wŏnsan and Hŭngnam were common, and the Wŏnsan-Majŏnni road (Majŏn is twenty-eight miles along the road between Wŏnsan and P'yŏngyang) was "one of the worst centers" of guerrilla attacks. By late November, X Corps counted twenty-five thousand guerrillas in the area south and west of Hŭngnam. Appleman wrote that in November, "virtually all of North Korea west or northwest of the X Corps front . . . was in enemy hands"; the same was true of large areas to the south and southwest.[73]

As the closing of the Sino-Korean trap drew near, the KPA infiltrated an entire division (the 10th) through the mountains to within twenty miles of Taegu, where it kept the American 1st Marine Division and assorted ROKA units occupied for many weeks in tough mountain fighting; American sources described this as "a remarkable military feat." Ridgway estimated total guerrilla strength in South Korea at the end of 1950 at sixty thousand operating almost down to Pusan.[74]

The centrally-positioned KPA guerrillas also were a factor in MacArthur's famous and calamitous decision to split his columns for the march to the Yalu. Appleman argued that the main reason for the decision was the forbidding terrain, with high mountain ridges splitting the peninsula and an underdeveloped East-West transportation and communications network (he also did not think it was bad strategy). Other military historians said the split was not just because of geography, but because East-West communication and transport "was unsafe because of guerrilla activity."[75]

MacArthur may have had his measure taken by Korean and Chinese generals, but Willoughby zealously sought to hide it, shamelessly shaping intelligence reports and public briefings to make MacArthur look like his glorious leader instead of Napoleon on the way to Moscow. Shortly after Inch'ŏn, UNC headquarters claimed that there were few if any KPA reserves north of the parallel, and only twenty thousand KPA effectives left in all of Korea; Willoughby continued to use this figure until mid-November. Ninety-five thousand POWs were said to have been captured, the impression being that most of the KPA had been killed or rolled up.[76] On October 13, the CIA estimated that the KPA had 132,000 soldiers ready for combat north of the parallel, including eighty thousand in "fairly cohesive" line divisions; this figure does not seem to include guerrillas. Yet Willoughby maintained the twenty thousand estimate.[77]

When the major Sino-Korean offensive came, overnight the KPA was said to have eleven divisions and about 120,000 troops. By December 3 there were 150,000, by December 20, 200,000, and these figures did not count guerrillas in the south numbering at least 40,000: "MacArthur raised the North Korean Army, like Lazarus, from the tomb."[78] KPA forces must have gone to rear areas for regrouping, Willoughby now explained; the twenty thousand figure had been based on how many soldiers were "reported in contact with UN forces." Reginald Thompson commented that "the intelligence estimate of 20,000 enemy had been a minimum of 80,000 on the wrong side."[79]

Of course, Inch'ŏn was still a bad defeat for the KPA. Entire units in the 3d Division panicked and collapsed, according to Appleman, and the 8th Division lost four thousand casualties; the 12th was completely destroyed after fighting "stubborn delaying actions." Huge quantities of equipment were lost; the morale of troops and civilians was badly hurt.[80] The retreat, however, squeezed the best out of a bad deal that North Korea could not control, an enormous amphibious invasion.

"A Glut of Chinamen": The PRC Enters the War

When KPA commanders "lured the enemy in deep," they also had a web of reciprocal ties with China to call upon, by virtue of their common struggle against Japanese imperialism and their having dispatched more than 100,000 Koreans to the fight for the China mainland. They also had mutual interests served by a joint Sino-Korean destruction of the American rollback: protection of the Chinese border and the jointly-exploited hydroelectric resources of the Yalu and, more generally, prevention of a revived U.S.-Japanese "Co-Prosperity Sphere"; the substitution for it of a communist pan-Asianism; and destruction of Nationalist schemes to join the war or invade the mainland, which threatened both China and North Korea. Plans for a joint campaign were most likely laid when the Pusan perimeter proved impermeable, although it is possible that the Chinese agreed to guarantee the North against an American invasion before June 25. But the immediate causes are in a sense beside the point. Anyone with an intuitive feel for Sino-Korean relations running back to antiquity could have predicted the Chinese response when a modern-day Hideyoshi swept up the peninsula.[81]

A hard-pressed Chou En-lai was unflagging in warning Americans that China would come in, but no one listened to him, or to his famous conduit, the astute bon vivant Sardar Pannikar. A hard-nosed realpolitik might predict that China would not allow American troops to camp across a poorly-protected river border, whose energy output fueled so much of Manchurian industry. Yet even that simple judgment, which the CIA arrived at when it was too late, was controversial: it was to be "liberal" in the American context to assert that China came into the Korean War to defend its borders. This is by now the consensus position of national security strategists.[82] But it was only part of the puzzle, and few understand the other, equally important reasons for the Chinese entry.

Throughout the spring and summer of 1950, intelligence operatives and journalists monitored the northward movement toward Manchuria of the crack New 4th Army, containing many Korean and Sino-Korean units. In August it began a period of intensive drilling and maneuvers across the Korean border. Willoughby's outfit counted thirty-seven divisions and noted that "many Koreans have served in these Manchuria units"; some worried that the activity might be "preliminary to entering the Korean theater." But the conclusion was that "infiltration might take place but no organized participation." MacArthur told Harriman in August that the Soviets were likely "to try to get the Chinese involved in the present conflict . . . they will get the northern Chinese armies to send units if they can." But, he said, "we can win now and if we do he [the Soviet] will not risk involvement." Shortly thereafter he told Collins and Almond that "If we win, the Chinese will not follow the USSR . . . the Oriental follows a winner."[83]

The CIA, on the available evidence, was little better. On September 20 it envisioned a possibility that Chinese "volunteers" might enter the fighting; a month later it had "a number of reports" that Manchurian units would be sent to Korea. However, it said "the odds are that Communist China, like the USSR, will not openly intervene in North Korea." Chinese intervention might have turned the tide at an early point, but that time had passed. After the first phase of Chinese involvement, the CIA still thought the People's Republic of China (PRC) was acting at Soviet behest, continuing the "war-by-proxy" experiment it launched on June 25. On November 1 Bedell Smith accurately wrote that the Chinese "probably genuinely fear an invasion of Manchuria," and that they would seek to establish a cordon sanitaire for border security "regardless of the increased risk of general war." But on November 24 as MacArthur lunged forward in his last great offensive, the CIA found insufficient evidence to suggest a Chinese plan for "major offensive operations."[84]

The British were deeply apprehensive about MacArthur's northward sweep. They had reports from the Mukden consulate that the best People's Liberation Army (PLA) units, many with Koreans in them, had begun dawn-to-dusk training in August; officials had requisitioned sewing machines from tailor shops to stitch new uniforms. On October 5 British armed services chiefs were convinced that China would intervene, and in a meeting electric with "great uneasiness" they urged representations to Washington for a two-week halt at the parallel, and immediate negotiations with the PRC. By mid-October the families of high Chinese officials had removed southward, Mukden was placed under martial law, air raid drills shook the city, the price of gold skyrocketed amid "considerable panic," and entire factories were dismantled, with the machinery shipped northward. But in the end the British government decided only to urge Washington that MacArthur not be allowed to take action outside the boundaries of Korea; their intelligence predictions were no better than Washington's, persisting in the belief that China would not act. They discounted Pannikar's warnings. Their attaché in Tokyo, Bouchier, was a complete creature of MacArthur's fantasies, predicting in mid-November of the approaching final offensive, "I am wholly confident of successful outcome . . . it will not take very long."[85]

This intelligence analysis flowed from bad assumptions, not bad information. The CIA hewed closely to the established policy line, not wishing to make waves; often its reports were inferior to the coverage of journalists, and frequently less objective. In the middle of the worst foreign policy crisis of the postwar era, Acheson and Truman wrangled with Clement R. Attlee and his advisors, saying they were completely wrong to see the PRC as in independent actor: "all they do is based on the Moscow pattern," Acheson said, "and they are better pupils even than the Eastern European satellites." He and the president defended MacArthur against British criticism, saying he always acted under UN orders. Truman went on, "[the Chinese] are satellites of Russia and will be satellites as long as the present Peiping regime is in power . . . the only way to meet communism is to eliminate it." "The Russians only understand the mailed fist," he said, "and that is what we are preparing for them." Were the

20. Gen. Charles Willoughby, Gen. Mathew Ridgway, and Walter Bedell Smith

United States to quit Korea, "all the Koreans left behind would be murdered. The Communists care nothing about human life."[86] With hysteria like that, "intelligence" analysis is quite beside the point.

Years after the fighting ended, George Kennan remained wedded to the assumption that the Koreans were Soviet- rather than Chinese-aligned, saying that Mao could not have been "wholly pleased" to see the ROK "dramatically conquered not by Mao's Koreans but by Stalin's"; therefore, "China must, one would think, have been compensated in some way" for their intervention by the Russians.[87] Yet the South was conquered precisely by "Mao's Koreans," to use yet another expression showing Kennan's incapacity to imagine Koreans as historical actors.

The best-informed media in America were strongly behind the march to the Yalu, and just as incapable of judging Chinese intentions. The *New York Times* editorialized that it was incredible for China to feel threatened by "a free and united Korea"; as the final offensive began, Reston assured his readers that Washington sources did not think the Chinese would intervene, and an editorial lauded American forces for refusing "to be deterred by Chinese Communist threats."[88]

Perhaps the best proof that evidence counted less than assumptions is the experience of Indian ambassador to the PRC Sardar Pannikar, who consistently warned that the Chinese would not tolerate a march to the Yalu. On September 26 the PLA chief of staff, Nieh Jung-chen, told him that China would have no option but to resist if the Americans continued to provoke them; when Pannikar said the experience of Korea had shown that the Americans would not spare "a single industrial establishment" in China from bombing, Nieh said that could not be helped. Chou En-lai and the Polish ambassador to Beijing said similar things, convincing Pannikar that the PRC "had decided on a more aggressive policy, regardless of [the] consequences." A week later Chou called him in and told him China could not tolerate American soldiers crossing the parallel.[89]

But no one was listening, because Pannikar was thought unreliable. The CIA thought him an unwitting "medium" for a Chinese attempt to deter American forces from unifying Korea with empty bluff; Jessup and Rusk thought him "temporarily following the Party line for ulterior motives." His "Mephistophelian quality," they wrote, "was not limited to his spade beard." They recommended ways of countering his influence in New Delhi.[90]

An Indian correspondent had these observations from China in mid-November:

> During an 80-mile railway trip from Peking to Tientsin last week, this correspondent saw seven trains, each about two furlongs long, loaded

with Japanese tanks, American armoured cars, and Soviet artillery pieces, together with hundreds of petroleum wagons . . . [a] feverish movement of troops to Manchuria had been going on for nearly six weeks . . . [foreigners said] the whole of Northeast China "bristled with war preparations, reminiscent of Japanese days."

He even heard rumors that the PRC leadership was preparing to abandon coastal cities and retreat to Yanan for a protracted war. But Reuters chose to treat this dispatch as a secret, and not publish it.[91] What this correspondent could see, American intelligence apparently could not.

A crestfallen Pannikar lamented that all his warnings had been ignored, and as the prospect of Sino-American war dawned, he cast his eyes across China's capital in late autumn:

From the coal hill the entire city looks as if overlaid with molten gold. The autumn tints melt naturally into the yellow tiles of the Forbidden City. [The] Government has done marvellous work in restoring Peking. The Palace seas . . . with fresh running water and new embankments with the gardens and the great Dajoba restored. Peking looks really magnificent.

What is the use of thinking of a worldwide war, he said,

in order to put Bao Dai or Syngman Rhee in power? . . . I feel miserable and frustrated. To contemplate with equanimity a war today is, I think, a crime: but the leaders everywhere seem, at least unconsciously, to have resigned themselves to the catastrophe.[92]

A Principle of Reciprocity

Just as Pannikar's warnings wandered back to the West in late September, the PRC conspicuously placed another reason for defending Korea on the front page of the *People's Daily*: Korean "volunteers" had shed blood by the thousands for China's revolution; just as "the Korean people have stood on the side of the Chinese people during the past decades," China "will always stand on the side of the Korean people." They specifically cited the contributions of the Korean Volunteer Army (KVA) and the Yi Hong-gwang Detachment. At the same time Mao Tse-tung asked a wealthy Hong Kong capitalist, Lu Tso-fu, to bring the following to the attention of the Americans:

In view of the long association of North Korean Communists with the Chinese Communist Party . . . and because of the military assistance given the Chinese Communists by Korean volunteers in fighting the Japanese and later the Nationalists in Manchuria the Chinese Communist Party owed a debt of gratitude to the Korean Communists which they could not ignore. . . . [Mao] did not wish war with the United States but . . . if American forces crossed the 38th parallel he would be under very heavy pressure to send Chinese forces.[93]

When the first contingents of volunteers entered Korea, Chinese sources again lauded the Korean volunteers in China, likening them to LaFayette and his French soldiers in the American revolution, and the Abraham Lincoln Brigade in the Spanish Civil War. "We can never forget the Korean people . . . [who] not only participated in the war of liberation but also in the Northern expedition of 1925–27, in the land reform war of 1927–37, and in the anti-Japanese war of 1937–45." Captured Chinese POWs said they had joined the war because Koreans had fought in China; it was also common for Korean units to come across the border with the Chinese. An intelligence report dated October 9 stated,

> Chinese Communist aid will go to North Koreans if the UN cross [*sic*] the 38th parallel because: A. Chinese Communist indebtedness to North Korea, specifically for aid from Yi Hong Kwang to Lin Piao in the fight against KMT. B. UN occupation of North Korea would be a threat to Chinese Communist territory. C. USSR ordering the Chinese to participate.

Willoughby's G-2 people deemed this report "false" and unreliable.[94]

In spite of their bluster about a wholly new war and taking on the whole Chinese nation, MacArthur and Willoughby knew, or should have known, who they were fighting. Their order of battle on the PLA's 4th Field Army, dated November 7, estimated that 145,000 Koreans, either from Korea or Manchuria, had been integrated into it during the mainland campaigns. The Korean forces had originally been based, the report said, on the old Northeast United Army and the Yi Hong-gwang "column"; the principle of integration was two Chinese for every one Korean.[95] They also knew that the KPA had held elements of this force in reserve in Manchuria; as we have seen earlier in this study, Koreans who fought in the 4th Field Army in the Hainan "last battle" were not back to Korea when the war began.

There is also evidence that the ROK government knew that China would intervene to defend the North Koreans. The Korean representative in Tokyo, Kim Yong-ju, waited until early December to inform the British that in his view the PRC joined the war because "there existed . . . an agreement whereby in return for the services of North Korean soldiers in the liberation of North China . . . the Peking Government was under an obligation in certain circumstances (e.g., if there was an attack across the thirty-eighth parallel), to come to the aid of North Korea."[96]

This is plausible, as we saw earlier, and suggests that Kim Il Sung may have had a rather powerful ace in the hole before June 1950, which would lead him not to fear the intervention even of large American ground forces.

A hierarchy of causality for the Chinese involvement, in my view, would place reciprocity first, and the defense of the border and the prevention of an integration of the region with Japan second; of course the two would mingle inextricably for both Chinese and Koreans, reinforcing each other. A third important consideration would be the decisive supplanting of Soviet influence in North Korea. In my view this happened in 1949, as I have said, but it was congealed by Chinese blood that soaked Korean soil beyond measure.

Stalin would expect this to happen. Some therefore thought he was lukewarm about Chinese involvement. A Yugoslav vice-minister for foreign affairs told the British that the Soviets had sought to get an Eastern European volunteer brigade to fight in Korea, but that Budapest and Prague had been cold to the idea. The Soviets feared the effects of Chinese involvement on the power structure of the Far East, he said; the Soviets "had not wanted to see Chinese interference in Korea . . . but regarded it as a lesser evil than a complete occupation of Korea by U.N. troops."[97] Finally, MacArthur had plans to introduce Chinese Nationalist forces at the Yalu and in southern China in the event of PRC participation in the war; the Chinese would have suspected this from June 1950 onward, giving them another reason to resist MacArthur's march North.

The Chinese decision directly to aid North Korea probably came in the last week of September, coordinated with the KPA break from the Pusan perimeter, rather than after Allied forces crossed the parallel (which the Chinese and Koreans expected to happen). ROK forces crossed the parallel October 1, and two days later British intelligence sources observed long convoys of 150 trucks, thought to carry troops and supplies, in "bumper to bumper" traffic moving down from Antung to points as much as eighty miles inside Korea; "the scale of movement . . . would appear to point to Chinese intervention." POW interviews later showed that Chinese Communist Forces (CCF) units began crossing the border no later than October 14.[98]

It appears that the first Chinese volunteers joined the battle right after direct negotiations between the DPRK and PRC at the highest level. A special train brought Kim Il Sung to Beijing around October 25, moving under cover of darkness and blanketed security. He was accompanied by three other uniformed Koreans, and the Northeast leader, Kao Kang. High PRC leaders, including Chou En-lai and Nieh Jung-chen (the two besides Mao most closely linked to the Korean decision) were not seen in

Beijing in the same period, reappearing for the funeral of Jen Pi-shih on October 27.[99]

On October 22 KMAG advisors had thought that the KPA was no longer capable of "an organized defense." But within a few days, "fresh, newly equipped North Korean troops" struck the UN front lines savagely, with tanks and air support. Strong Sino-Korean forces attacked the ROKA II Corps, causing its "complete collapse and disintegration," and crippling the right flank of the 8th Army. The attackers were "fresh, well organized and well trained units, some of which were Chinese Communist Forces."[100]

Ŭnsan may have been home to the North Koreans and familiar to the Chinese, a good spot for Herbert Hoover to have a few drinks in 1909, but it was horrible for Americans in 1950. On November 2, eight hundred American soldiers were enveloped and slaughtered just short of the Ŭnsan gold/monazite mines, as combined Sino-Korean units plunged out of the mountains. War correspondents wrote that it looked like an "Indian-style massacre." The temperature was frigid, the darkness seemed interminable, and all through the night scouts circled the American lines, tooting bugles and eerie horns to disorient troops who, after all, were not quite sure where they were or what they were fighting for. A captured Chinese critique of these first engagements said that American soldiers had "fatal weaknesses."

> Their infantry men are weak, afraid to die, and haven't the courage to attack or defend. They depend on their planes, tanks and artillery . . . they are not familiar with night fighting or hand to hand combat . . . without the use of their mortars they become completely lost . . . dazed and completely demoralized . . . at Unsan they were surrounded for days yet they did nothing.[101]

The general assault continued through November 6, with about 27,000 Chinese soldiers joining a KPA now estimated at about 160,000. The allies were pushed well back from the Yalu border, and then the enemy slipped away. The battlefront stilled, the enemy forces grew "strangely quiet"; once more, curious withdrawals ensued in front of Allied troops. The Chinese *and* the Koreans intended this as a warning not to resume the march North,[102] but the Americans discounted the October feint and prepared for a major offensive. As the CCF broke contact and disappeared, allowing large numbers of trapped American soldiers to "filter out," on November 12 the Allies resumed pushing toward the border.[103]

MacArthur sent U.S. Marines toward the Changjin Reservoir and the American 7th Division north of the Ŭnggi River, in spite of temperatures ranging to 22 degrees below zero. Once again UN forces were able to run north unimpeded.[104] Within a week the American 7th Division had secured Kim Il Sung's heartland of Kapsan, and reached Hyesanjin on the Yalu against no resistance. Among the American units occupying the Changjin Reservoir area was the 27th Infantry, which had a history of fighting Moros on Mindanao in 1902 in the American campaign against the Philippine insurrection, and which as "The Wolfhounds" had been part of the American expeditionary forces against the Bolsheviks in Siberia.[105]

This time CIA daily reports caught the pattern of enemy rearward displacement, arguing that such withdrawals had in the past preceded offensive action, and noting warily that there were "large, coordinated and well-organized guerrilla forces in the rear area" behind the Allied forces, along with guerrilla occupation of "substantial areas in southwest Korea." But as late as November 20 the estimate was mixed, with some arguing that the communists were simply withdrawing to better defensive points, and others that the pattern of "giving ground invariably in face of UN units moving northward" merely meant "a delaying action," not preparation for all-out assault.

On November 24 MacArthur launched his "reconnaissance in force," a general offensive all along the line. He described it as a "massive compression and envelopement," a "pincer" movement to trap remaining KPA forces. On November 25 he flew up to the the Yalu, dipping the wings of his "SCAP" plane at American troops in Hyesanjin. The offensive rolled forward for three days against little or no resistance, with ROK units entering the important city of Ch'ŏngjin. Lost amid the hoopla of American victory were reports from spotter pilots that enemy troops were "swarming all over the countryside," and the retrieval of Chinese POWs from six different armies.[106]

Strong enemy attacks began on November 27, executing a "deep envelopement" that chopped Allied troops to pieces.[107] American forces were badly chewed up, the ROK II Corps collapsed again, and within two days a general withdrawal ensued. On December 4 the Joint Chiefs of Staff (JCS) cabled MacArthur that "the preservation of your forces is now the primary consideration"—that is, the utterly overexposed core of the entire American expeditionary force, now battered and surrounded.[108] Two days later communist forces occupied P'yŏngyang, and the day after that the Allied front was only twenty miles above the parallel at its northernmost point. The combined Sino-Korean offensive cleared North Korea of enemy troops in little more than two weeks from its inception. Almond wrote that "we are having a glut of Chinamen"; he hoped he would have the chance later "to give these yellow bastards what is coming to them." By the end of December, Seoul was about to fall once again.[109]

MacArthur described the first Sino-Korean feint as "one of the most offensive acts of international lawlessness of historic record"; the KPA, he told Washington, was completely defeated, having suffered 335,000 casualties with no forces left. Thus, "a new and fresh [Chinese] army now faces us." In fact, KPA forces far outnumbered Chinese at this point. When large Chinese units entered the fighting at the end of November, he radioed back that he faced "the entire Chinese nation in an undeclared war."[110]

The North Korean press placed big pictures of its *suryŏng*, Kim Il Sung, on the front page of newspapers announcing the entry of the fraternal Chinese "volunteer army," and the ousting of UN forces from the North. Kim credited this to the KPA, guerrillas behind the front, and the Chinese volunteers, in that order. He announced that "the path to final victory has opened." Meanwhile Kim's group met in a secret plenum and sacked Mu Jŏng for his putative failure to reach Pusan on the eastern front, and atrocities committed under him in the North; unmentioned was his closeness to Chu Teh and other Chinese leaders, just as the PLA flooded in.[111]

Americans sought first to blame this debacle on South Korean divisions. MacArthur's headquarters told the British that they "melt away like butter" under any serious pressure; "history repeats itself and once again our march to the Yalu River has been halted by our right flank." Soldiers complained that "an orderly, dependable military front" had cracked "under the cowardice of those who supposedly had been fighting for their homes and their future." Indeed, the ROKA had not fought well. It had been sucked into a freewheeling march through the eastern part of the peninsula against forces that it had done badly against only weeks before; when the attack came, entire units panicked and left their equipment in place. By the end of the first year of the war, they had lost on the battlefield enough armaments and supplies to equip ten divisions. Tito was one of the few also to point out that the ROK failed to generate effective guerrillas behind enemy lines, as the North had done so often.[112]

But it is hardly to be expected that young conscripts would fight for an officer corps with poor leadership skills, and with patriotic credentials so tainted by Japanese colonial service. Far more damning was MacArthur's repeated failure to grasp what kind of a war he was fighting, and what manner of enemy. He fought a guerrilla war as a conventional war, letting history "repeat itself" from the battle for Taejŏn onward, but especially in his failure to gauge the meaning of the North's rapid retreat.

Behind the allied lines, guerrillas coordinated actions with the Sino-Korean offensive. Kim Il's guerrillas, now estimated at 20,000 strong, occupied the strategic city of Ch'unch'ŏn on November 21. Kim Ch'aek, demonstrating "a shrewd ability as an organizer and tactician," put his more numerous guerrilla units into "a well-coordinated and determined battle to block our freedom of movement to the north and northeast of Seoul." The guerrillas showed "marked cooperation" with the front-line forces, making "repeated forays, striking UN elements on the flanks and rear."[113] The guerrilla actions forced MacArthur to take large numbers of troops out through the port of Hŭngnam. From December 3 to 10, G-2 sources noted many reports of guerrilla flanking and envelopment movements south of Hŭngnam. The "intense guerrilla activity which has occurred in these localities in the past three months" by regrouped KPA units and guerrillas in the rear areas was now coordinated with attacks by Chinese forces, their thorough knowledge of the countryside being "invaluable to attacking CCF units." They would thus "effectively neutralize a substantial number of UN troops." If these forces were to seize Yangyang, Wŏnju, and other communication points, it "would virtually block immediate movement of Eighth Army forces."[114]

In mid-December Allied forces encountered few Chinese, but Korean guerrillas were forcing troops "to fight their way back to take up new positions well behind existing front lines." On December 18, a British military attaché wrote that "for several weeks now Eighth Army have only contacted North Korean forces along their front." In these same days, guerrillas in central Korea appeared to be converging on Seoul.[115]

By early January, American military sources estimated that KPA armed strength, including active guerrillas, was probably about 200,000; the Chinese total was overestimated at almost 300,000. In fact North Korean and Chinese troops were about equal in total numbers, and American commanders thought the Koreans were "better troops" than the Chinese.[116]

It would be foolish to discount the importance of the Chinese intervention in destroying the American rollback into North Korea. But the Korean contribution to the outcome, both in strategy and in fighting power, has been ignored in the literature.[117] The primary, day-to-day evidence makes the indictment of MacArthur's generalship all the more devastating. He not only dismissed the palpable Chinese threat, but got badly outmaneuvered by Korean generals who operated with a fraction of MacArthur's materiel: especially Kim Ch'aek, who died of "paralysis of the heart" in February 1951, leading the North Koreans to rename the port city of Sŏngjin for him.[118]

MacArthur later suffered a spasm of the Id, remarking that he had always been able "to take care of the enemy in my front—but have never been able to protect myself from shafts from the rear."[119] In fact he had coveys of Koreans "in his rear." But the rear he surveilled was in Washington—saboteurs of his brilliant generalship who thought there was "a substitute for victory." Yet each MacArthur victory called forth a new war, until his final offensive which did, indeed, turn out to be the disaster "that rocked Asia," as he had predicted in August—but the other way round.

But what remains so stunning is Washington's full knowledge of MacArthur's willfulness and irresponsibility, well before the war began, and its simultaneous backing for him until the debacle in November. Some directives he interpreted loosely, of course, but the JCS gave him a commander's discretion to fight the battle as he saw fit.[120] The basic condition of this support was the broad coalition behind rollback. The *Manchester Guardian* wrote that the more MacArthur sought to explain himself, the worse it got: "the ashes of his plans would be better left unraked."[121] Instead they were combed through and through, while another pile of glowing embers faded almost unnoticed in Washington.

The Rhee leadership panicked before the Sino-Korean onslaught. The president was at his senile worst, "rambling on" before Americans that if he would only be given more weapons, he would equip Korea's youth and fight the Chinese hand-to-hand in the streets of Seoul. Meanwhile Rhee, Chang Myŏn, and even the nationalist Yi Pŏm-sŏk sought exile in Japan, or a stopgap measure to mimic the Nationalists and establish a "little Taiwan" on Cheju Island if the Americans would allow it; tons of machinery, strategic materials, and documents were moved to Cheju during this period. A jittery Muccio sought to replace Rhee with a "Junta" led by Chang Myŏn, or with, of all things, a "governing commission."[122] American policy toward Korea had come full circle, beginning in apparent innocence in late 1945 with the return of Rhee and the "governing commission" and ending in utter ruin, with what appeared to be world war unfolding on a peninsula always deemed to be among the worst of places to make a stand.

THE PANIC IN WASHINGTON

It is commonly remarked that the Cuban Missile Crisis was the most perilous of postwar crises. But the defeat of the rollback in northern Korea occasioned by far the greater danger, because it bore down upon two axes: the grand global conflict between socialism and capitalism, and the internal struggle for the American state between nationalists and internationalists. Whether they knew it or not, China and North Korea had perfect aim, decisively reversing the first and greatest attempt to displace a socialist state, and simultaneously exploding a temporary and unstable coalition between two currents in America. As 1950 drew to a close, panic gripped the highest levels of government in Washington, and the leaders sought to reverse their crushing defeat by invoking nearly every weapon in the vast American arsenal.

The minutes of Truman's cabinet meetings are laced with the grave tension of the moment. The day after the Sino-Korean offensive began, the situation was thought capable of developing into "complete involvement in total war." By December 9 Truman wrote, "I've worked for peace for five years and six months and it looks like World War III is here. I hope not—but we must meet whatever comes—and we will." Three days later he told the Cabinet that "we are faced with an all-out situation," with "total mobilization" and the declaration of national emergency under consideration. National Security Council minutes show a similar alarm, Truman stating that the United States "would not surrender to these murderous Chinese Communists."[123]

On November 29 Acheson saw an "unparalleled danger" in China's action, calling it "a fresh and unprovoked aggressive act even more immoral than the first" (back in June). The next day Truman rattled the atomic bomb at a news conference, saying the United States might use any weapon in its arsenal;[124] it was a threat based on contingency planning to use the bomb, rather than the faux pas so many assumed it to be. It prompted Attlee to bolt to Washington, probably without finishing his evening meal.

American elites were united, temporarily, on the strongest response to China. James Conant, Julius Ochs Adler of the *New York Times*, Vannevar Bush, Tracy Voorhees, and others formed the Committee on the Present Danger, calling for war mobilization on a grand scale; twenty-five years later the committee was revived after elite consensus had again been destroyed, that time over Vietnam. General Bradley thought that global war "could erupt at any hour"; Bernard Baruch privately informed Acheson that the bomb should be used, "if it can be used effectively"; Stuart Symington, chairman of the National Security Resources Board, was ready to attack China and present the Soviets with an ultimatum that any further aggression "would result in the atomic bombardment of Soviet Russia itself." Nitze was game to blow the dams on the Yalu, old Manchuria-hand Harriman seconding him by saying that this would cripple Manchuria's industry, and therefore Soviet war-making capacity. The Joint Chiefs suggested "full mobilization" at home, preparations for "global conflict" (which included withdrawing American forces from Korea), and holding atomic bomb capabilities "in immediate readiness." Kennan was in an uncharacteristically moral repose, stating that "the Chinese have now committed an affront of the greatest magnitude" that the United States would not be able to forget for years; the Chinese would have to worry about "righting themselves with us not us with them."[125]

Truman gave vent to his penchant for bad historical analogy, calling for global mobilization against "the inheritors of Genghis Khan and Tamerlane, the greatest murderers in the history of the world." The leader of the other American party was not better. Herbert Hoover mingled a reviving isolationism with hand-wringing about "Asiatic hordes" that had swept the globe twice before; the Sino-Soviet sphere made for a third wave, "a congeries of thirty different races that will someday go to pieces . . . meanwhile they are cannon fodder." *Commonweal* found the crisis reflective of "the days of Augustine and 'The City of God,' written as the Roman Empire fell about him before the onslaught of the barbarians."[126]

If this crisis did not herald the recrudescence of the Golden Horde, it was the genesis of a new global empire, a national security state, and, finally, the means to pay for it. The Sino-Korean defeat of rollback did more than anything else to bring the NSC 68 process to conclusion, a crisis that finally pushed the cash through Congress. Neither the North Korean nor the Inch'ŏn invasions had prompted Congress to cough up, especially in an election year.[127] After an NSC report stating that "our military build-up must be rapid because the period of greatest danger is directly before us," Truman on December 15 declared a national emergency, created an Office of Defense Mobilization with "sweeping powers" under General Motors chief Charles Wilson (another bipartisan accommodator, who became Eisenhower's defense secretary), and authorized defense spending to increase by $18 billion to $49 billion, almost quadrupling the level in June 1950.[128]

Through this crisis McCarthy and his allies were curiously quiet. Perhaps it was because of MacArthur's palpable failure, or the enormous increases for defense spending happening under crypto-pink Democratic rather than patriotic Republican auspices. Or, it may simply have been that McCarthy was occupied with other matters. Drew Pearson had once again surfaced innuendoes about McCarthy's manhood, stirring an important but subterranean sexual politics that animated the capital. On December 13, Pearson's fifty-third birthday, McCarthy cornered him in the cloak room of the Sulgrave Club, kneed him twice in the groin in good Tailgunner-Joe fashion, and slapped him to the floor. Richard Nixon thereupon intervened, ejaculating, "let a Quaker stop this fight."[129]

NOVEL WEAPONS

Another result of the December crisis was the threat to use what Washington liked to call "weapons of mass destruction": atomic, chemical, and biological weapons. This was entirely bipartisan, by no means limited to the right-wing "crazies" like Curtis LeMay; the Truman administration deployed a palpable atomic diplomacy for the next two years, quite in contrast to the received verdict that it was only Eisenhower and Dulles in 1953 who contemplated such means. Short of atomic weapons, America rained a fiery destruction from the air with another novel weapon, napalm, and later broke massive dams to flood Korea's northern valleys.

This is the most disturbing aspect of the Korean War, difficult to write and to read about; it is what accounted for the remarkable civilian death toll of more than two million people. It remains somehow amazing that the United States was willing to go to such lengths to defeat the Korean revolution, far beyond what it did in Vietnam.

The evidence is sketchy, and much of it remains classified. I have done my best to put together what I can document, but much more will someday be known. MacArthur, of course, wanted to bomb Manchurian airfields, blockade the coast of China, and insert nationalist forces into southern China—rollback with a vengeance. He wanted air, naval, and logistical support for "an initial lift" of 100,000 Nationalist soldiers, with Shanghai the principal landing target. The result, he hoped, would be "the domination of South China behind the protection of a defensive line along the Yangtze River." This would be prelude to "larger operations" aimed at the overthrow of communist rule throughout China. This may well have been MacArthur's plan from the beginning of the war. What is interesting is that after the Chinese intervention it won the support of Ridgway and the Joint Chiefs, in general if not in all the details mentioned above. On January 23, the JCS "tentatively agreed" to prepare an immediate naval blockade of China, and to "remove restrictions on operations of Chinese Nationalist forces and give such logistic suppport to these forces as will contribute to effective operations against the Communists." They agreed to bomb Manchuria and China proper if China were to attack American forces outside of Korea, presumably meaning airpower directed against the Japan or Okinawa staging areas.[130]

On November 30, the day of Truman's news conference threatening use of the atomic bomb, General Stratemeyer sent an order to General Vandenberg that the Strategic Air Command be put on warning, "to be prepared to dispatch without delay medium bomb groups to the Far East . . . this augmentation should include atomic capabilities." Curtis LeMay remembered correctly that the JCS had earlier concluded that atomic weapons would probably not be useful in Korea, except as part of "an overall atomic campaign against Red China." But, if the orders were now to be changed, LeMay wanted the job: he told Stratemeyer that his headquarters was the only one with the experience, technical training, and "intimate knowledge" of delivery methods; the pyromaniac who directed the firebombing of Tokyo was again ready to proceed to the Far East to marshall the attacks.[131]

Prime Minister Attlee sensed that Truman was serious about using the bomb, and amid "grave perturbation" in London he departed posthaste for Washington. He knew that the United States possessed a strong advantage in atomic weaponry over the Soviets at this time, the United States having about 450 weapons and the Soviets perhaps 25. There was general disagreement between the British and American representatives in several days of meetings; according to Foreign Office records the Americans pushed for a "limited war" against China, including air attacks, a blockade of the coast, and covert introduction of anti-communist forces in southern China; General Marshall was one who was doubtful about the "efficacy and success" of such a program. Attlee sought a written promise that the bomb would not be used in Korea, but Truman would only give him oral assurances. Attlee told the French prime minister that he thought American threats to use the bomb would sugggest that "Europeans and Americans have a low regard for the value of Asiatic lives," and that such weapons should be reserved only for times when "desperate measures" were warranted—"certainly not [in] a conflict in which the U.S. were confronted with a Power like Korea."[132]

Use of the atomic bomb had been discussed since the early days of the war. On July 7 the JCS Division of Plans asked for a study of "utilization of atomic bombardment" in Korea, and on July 9—a mere two weeks into the war—MacArthur sent Ridgway a "hot message" that prompted the JCS "to consider whether or not A-bombs should be made available to MacArthur." Ridgway said that American troop movements to the Far East already were having "a crippling effect" on the general reserve, and markedly reducing "our capacities to carry out ... Emergency War Plans." Atomic bombs, by implication, might relieve some of the burden on American ground troops.[133]

General Bolte, chief of operations, was asked to talk to MacArthur about using atomic weapons "in direct support [of] ground combat"; some ten to twenty bombs could be spared without "unduly" jeopardizing the general war plan. Bolte got from MacArthur an early indication of his extraordinary ambitions for the war, which included occupying the North and handling potential Chinese—or Soviet—intervention: "I would cut them off in North Korea. In Korea I visualize a cul-de-sac. The only passages leading from Manchuria and Vladivostok have many tunnels and bridges. I see here a unique use for the atomic bomb—to strike a blocking blow—which would require a six months repair job. Sweeten up my B-29 force." General Vandenberg of the Air Force responded obligingly that the B-29s would be kept up to strength.[134]

The JCS planning group determined, however, that atomic bombs were not warranted in the war for containment in the summer of 1950, when the Americans faced only the North Koreans; the reasons were mainly technical, in that suitable targets did not present themselves, and conventional bombing was obliterating most North Korean objectives. Nonetheless, good targets might appear if the Chinese came in, the study concluded. Use of the bomb "would [also] fill fundamental gaps [in] our knowledge re tactical use" of the weapons. So, even though the bomb was not needed now, "necessary preparations should be made to insure [its] operational readiness."[135]

According to British sources, on December 9, 1950, MacArthur requested commander's discretion to use atomic weapons. On December 24 he submitted "a list of retardation targets" for which he needed twenty-six atomic bombs. He also wanted four to drop on the "invasion forces" and four more for "critical concentrations of enemy air power." In interviews published posthumously, he said he had a plan that would have won the war in ten days: "I would have dropped between 30 and 50 atomic bombs . . . strung across the neck of Manchuria"; then he would have introduced half a million Nationalist troops at the Yalu, and then, "spread behind us—from the Sea of Japan to the Yellow Sea—a belt of radioactive cobalt . . . it has an active life of between 60 and 120 years. For at least 60 years there could have been no land invasion of Korea from the North." He expressed certainty that the Russians would have done nothing: "my plan was a cinch."[136]

Cobalt 60 has 320 times the radioactivity of radium. One 400-ton cobalt H-bomb, Carroll Quigley wrote, could wipe out all animal life on earth. MacArthur sounds like a warmongering lunatic in these interviews, but if so he was not alone. Before the Sino-Korean offensive, a committee of the JCS had said that atomic bombs might be the "decisive factor" in cutting off a Chinese advance into Korea; initially they could be useful in "a 'cordon sanitaire' [that] might be established by the U.N. in a strip in Manchuria immediately north of the Manchurian border." A few months later Rep. Albert Gore complained that "Korea has become a meat grinder of American manhood," and suggested "something cataclysmic" to end the war: a radiation belt dividing the Korean peninsula. Although Ridgway said nothing about a cobalt bomb, in May 1951 he renewed MacArthur's request of December 24, this time for thirty-eight atomic bombs.[137]

The United States came closest to using atomic weapons in early April 1951, precisely the time that Truman removed MacArthur. Although the documents are sketchy on this episode, it would appear that, as with the removal of rollback-advocate Louis Johnson, Truman nearly traded MacArthur for his atomic policies. On March 10, 1951, MacArthur asked for something he called a " 'D' Day atomic capability" to retain air superiority in the Korean theater (meaning he would hit Manchurian airfields with atomic weapons). On March 14 Vandenberg wrote, "Finletter and Lovett alerted on atomic discussions. Believe everything is set." At the end of March Stratemeyer reported that atomic bomb loading pits at Kadena air base on Okinawa were operational; the bombs were carried there unassembled, and put together at the base. It is not clear from this memorandum whether the bombs were assembled and ready for use. But on April 5 the JCS ordered immediate atomic retaliation against Manchurian bases if large numbers of new troops came into the fighting, or, it appears, if bombers were launched against American forces from there; and on April 6 Truman issued an order approving the JCS request, and the transfer of a limited number of complete atomic weapons "from A[tomic] E[nergy] C[ommission] to military custody." However, "in the confusion attendant upon General MacArthur's removal," the order was not executed.[138]

In 1950 atomic bombs were heavy, unwieldy devices necessitating big sand loading pits and time-consuming assembly; the core of nuclear material was the last item to be shipped to military custody. As the best symbol of executive power in foreign policy, the cores were kept under presidential control in the Atomic Energy Commission. At the time of MacArthur's removal, Truman gave the military custody of the fissionable cores, sans MacArthur. Professor Roger Dingman, who has done the best research on this question and who knows much more about it than I do, showed me an operational atomic target list in his possession, which included Shanghai city center among several other industrial cities, and four cities in North Korea that were to be hit in preliminary atomic attacks, designed to perfect the method before hitting China.[139]

One of the contingent circumstances for the use of atomic weapons was if the Chinese were to commit heavy air power from Manchuria. The Soviets moved two hundred bombers into Northeast China, and through Pannikar issued a warning that they would respond if Manchuria were attacked; it was about the first time in the war that the Soviets sought to deter American escalation. Although MacArthur's backers squawked mightily about communist "sanctuaries" in Manchuria, the real sanctuaries were in Pusan, where vast quantities of American war materiel sprawled throughout the city, and Japan, which had become part of the war theater with incessant American bombing runs originating there. American commanders recognized that they were terribly vulnerable to air strikes in Pusan and Japan, and therefore thought they had to deter or meet this threat with escalation to nuclear bombardment.[140] But it would appear that the Soviet airpower move stayed the American hand, since Korea was not worth the distinct risk of world war.

The Joint Chiefs again considered the use of nuclear weapons in June 1951, this time in tactical battlefield circumstances, and there were many more such suggestions as the war continued to 1953. Robert Oppenheimer went to Korea as part of "Project Vista," designed to gauge the feasibility of tactical use of atomic weapons; in early 1951 a young man named Samuel Cohen, on a secret assignment for the Defense Department, observed the battles for the second recapture of Seoul, and thought there should be a way to destroy the enemy without destroying the city. He became the father of the neutron bomb.[141]

Perhaps the most daunting and terrible of America's atomic blackmail, however, was Operation Hudson Harbor. It appears to have been part of a larger project involving "overt exploitation in Korea by the Department of Defense and covert exploitation by the Central Intelligence Agency of the possible use of novel weapons"; other memos in the file suggest that these "novel weapons" are tactical atomic bombs, although that is not entirely clear and may refer to other types of weapons of "mass destruction."[142]

This project sought to establish the capability to use atomic weapons on the battlefield, and in pursuit of this goal lone B-29 bombers were lifted from Okinawa in September and October 1951 and sent over North Korea on simulated atomic runs, dropping "dummy" A-bombs or heavy TNT bombs. The project called for "actual functioning of all activities which would be involved in an atomic strike, including weapons assembly and testing, leading, ground control of bomb aiming," and the like. The bombers took off from Okinawa, but everything was commanded from Yakaota Airbase in Japan. The project indicated that the bombs were probably not useful, for purely technical reaons: "timely identification of large masses of enemy troops was extremely rare."[143] No one knew this in P'yŏngyang, where leaders needed nerves of steel as their radar tracked B-29s simulating the attack patterns that had resulted in the devastation of Hiroshima and Nagasaki just five years earlier.

American leaders were callous to the implications of threatening the use of atomic weapons on Asian peoples. In 1954 Nitze and Oppenheimer had a colloquy about the warmth and nobility of the Japanese people, "even in Hiroshima." Oppenheimer continued, "Oh, especially in those towns . . . they were fantastic." Nitze remarked that "There was a kind of feeling: 'My goodness, we survived this; we had . . .' " And Oppenheimer supplied the conclusion: "We had it coming."[144]

The record also shows that Ridgway asked for chemical weapons to staunch the Sino-Korean offensive in December. In pencilled diary notes written on December 16, Ridgway referred cryptically to a subcommittee on "clandestine introduction [of] wea[pon]s of mass destruction and unconventional warfare"; I know nothing more about this item, but it may refer to his apparent request of MacArthur that chemical weapons be used in Korea. The original of Ridgway's telegram is unavailable, but MacArthur's reply on January 7, 1951 read, "I do not believe there is any chance of using chemicals on the enemy in case evacuation is ordered. As you know, U.S. inhibitions on such use are complete and drastic." The next day, in a conference with Almond and others, the transcript says, "If we use gas we will lay ourselves open to retaliation. This question has been taken up with General MacArthur for decision. We have requested sufficient quantitites to be shipped immediately in the event use of gas is approved."[145]

Without the use of "novel weapons"—although napalm was very new at the time, introduced just at the end of World War II—the air war nonetheless leveled North Korea and killed hundreds of thousands over the next two years. As soon as Chinese troops hit Korean soil MacArthur ordered that a wasteland be created between the front and the border, destroying from the air every "installation, factory, city, and village" over thousands of square miles of North Korean territory. On November 8, 70 B29s dropped 550 tons of incendiary bombs on Sinŭiju, "removing [it] from off the map"; a week later Hoeryŏng was hit with napalm "to burn out the place"; by November 25, "a large part of [the] North West [sic] area between Yalu River and southwards to enemy lines . . . is more or less burning"; soon the area would be a "wilderness of scorched earth."[146]

This was all before the major Sino-Korean offensive. With that, the Air Force on December 14–15 hit P'yŏngyang with 700 500-pound bombs, napalm dropped from Mustang fighters, and 175 tons of delayed-fuse demolition bombs, which land with a thud and then blow up at odd moments, when people are trying to rescue the dead from the napalm fires. Again at the beginning of January, Ridgway ordered the Air Force to hit P'yŏngyang "with the goal of burning the city to the ground with incendiary bombs," in two strikes on January 3 and 5. At about the same time American B29s dropped "tarzon" bombs on Kanggye; this was an enormous new 12,000-pound bomb never tried before Korea. As Americans retreated below the parallel, the scorched-earth policy of "torching" continued, burning Ŭijŏngbu, Wŏnju, and other small cities in the South as the enemy got near them.[147]

From Wŏnsan southward guerrillas had established themselves in many places, as we have seen, and the air war was extended to root them out through the creation of free fire zones. Ridgway on January 5 "desired that consideration be given to the napalming of villages" on the axis of the enemy advance. Almond put the rationale as follows on January 16: "We know that guerrilla bands with which we are now contending are going to be in our flanks and rear continuously, and we must fight them by every means available. Air strikes with napalm against those guerrilla bands wherever found is a most effective way to destroy not only the bands themselves, but the huts and villages in the areas they retire to."

The guerrillas holed up in villages in the day, he said, "and come out at night." Thus, "I have instituted a campaign of burning these huts."[148]

General Barr flew over the vicinity of T'anyang on January 18, giving the following description:

> Smoke from flaming villages and huts has filled valleys [in the] vicinity [of] Tangyang [*sic*] with smoke three thousand feet deep and blinded all my observations and created [a] flying hazard. . . . Methodical burning of dwellings is producing hostile reaction. . . . People cannot understand why US troops burn homes when no enemy present. . . . Methodical burning out poor farmers when no enemy present is against the grain of US soldiers. From house burning we already have estimated 8000 refugees and expect more. These are mostly the old, crippled, and children.

Thus Barr recommended to Almond "selective" rather than "methodical" burning. Almond understood that Barr's orders were not to burn indiscriminately, but "to select and burn out those villages in which guerrillas or enemy forces were being harbored, willingly or unwillingly . . . and those habitations forward of front line positions or in isolated mountain fastnesses from which guerrillas could not otherwise be barred."[149] Almond did not seem to understand that his orders amounted precisely to what Barr had observed, a free fire zone against anything that moved.

21. Children try to aid their mother, North Korea, late 1950

In any case, on January 25 he continued to defend the firing of villages, carrying the logic through to its conclusion: the local population was being killed, true, but "the meager population remaining appears sympathetic to and harbors the enemy."[150]

A bit later George Barrett of the *New York Times* found "a macabre tribute to the totality of modern war" in a village north of Anyang:

> The inhabitants throughout the village and in the fields were caught and killed and kept the exact postures they held when the napalm struck—a man about to get on his bicycle, fifty boys and girls playing in an orphanage, a housewife strangely unmarked, holding in her hand a page torn from a Sears-Roebuck catalogue crayoned at Mail Order No. 3,811,294 for a $2.98 "bewitching bed jacket—coral."

Acheson wanted censorship authorities notified about this kind of "sensationalized reporting," so it could be stopped.[151]

Ridgway later had second thoughts about the firing of towns:

> I have been struck by those areas I have visited which had formerly been occupied by the CCF. There appeared to have been little or no vandalism committed. . . . You have my full authority [to safeguard your troops] . . . this does not, however, extend to the wanton destruction of towns and villages, by gun-fire or bomb, unless there is good reason to believe them occupied.[152]

This did not seem to make much difference in policy. By 1952 just about everything in northern and central Korea was completely leveled. What was left of the population survived in caves, the North Koreans creating an entire underground society, in complexes of dwellings, schools, hospitals, and factories. In spite of World War II bombing studies showing that such attacks against civilian populations only stiffened enemy resistance, American officials sought to use aerial bombing as a type of psychological and social warfare. As Robert Lovett later put it at a cabinet meeting, "If we keep on tearing the place apart, we can make it a most unpopular affair for the North Koreans. We ought to go right ahead."[153] The Americans did go right ahead, and in the final act of this barbaric air war hit huge irrigation dams that provided water for 75 percent of the North's food production. Agriculture was the only major element of the economy still functioning; the attacks came just after the laborious, back-breaking work of rice transplantation had been done. The Air Force was proud of the destruction created: "The subsequent flash flood scooped clean 27 miles of valley below, and the plunging flood waters wiped out [supply routes, etc.]. . . . The Westerner can little conceive the awesome meaning which the loss of [rice] has for the Asian—starvation and slow death." Many villages were inundated, "washed downstream," and even P'yŏngyang, some twenty-seven miles south of one dam, was badly flooded. Untold numbers of peasants died, but they were assumed to be "loyal" to the enemy, providing "direct support to the Communist armed forces." That is, they were feeding the northern population. The "lessons" adduced from this experience "gave the enemy a sample of the totality of war . . . embracing the whole of a nation's economy and people."[154] This was Korea, "the limited war."

We may leave as an epitaph for this genocidal air war the views of one of its architects, Gen. Curtis LeMay. After the war started, he said,

> We slipped a note kind of under the door into the Pentagon and said, "Look, let us go up there . . . and burn down five of the biggest towns in North Korea—and they're not very big—and that ought to stop it." Well, the answer to that was four or five screams—"You'll kill a lot of non-combatants," and "It's too horrible." Yet over a period of three years or so . . . we burned down *every* [sic] town in North Korea and South Korea, too. . . . Now, over a period of three years this is palatable, but to kill a few people to stop this from happening—a lot of people can't stomach it.[155]

Chapter Twenty-Two

CONCLUSION: THE SETTING SUN

How little the world would look moral without forgetfulness! A poet might say that God made forgetfulness the guard he placed at the threshold of human dignity.

Nietzsche

Who knew what they might find beyond this new horizon? The children of the sun would keep to their westward bearing . . . "We ever held it certain that going toward the sunset we would find what we desired." In four centuries no one ever said it more fully.

Bernard DeVoto, The Course of Empire

THE KOREAN WAR ended in the spring of 1951, about where it began. For the next two years giant conventional armies slaughtered each other along a shifting front in the middle of the peninsula, thus to get a suspension of the fighting, an armistice, on July 27, 1953, along the same lines at which an agreement could have been gotten in 1951. A complex mutual deterrence of airpower threat and counterthreat, atomic diplomacy, secret negotiation, and Chinese restraint reestablished the status quo ante of late September 1950. The Chinese had taught their lesson, had limited the war for an America that could not do so; they had no appetite for uniting the peninsula, nor for suffering the atomic bombardment that was predictable should they push the United Nations expeditionary forces into the sea. The Americans, in turn, were deterred from the latter course by the positioning of formidable fleets of Soviet bombers in Manchuria, and settled for a barely digestible containment victory.

All that is beyond the scope of this study. The 1951–1953 fighting loses the stuff of the *Korean* war that we were interested in, the one that began in the ruins of the Japanese empire and ended in early 1951, a war pursued through political strife, rebellion, unconventional insurgency, border fighting, and conventional assault. The origins of that war had "laws of motion" at different "levels of analysis," or to put it simply, to figure it out we needed to know what made a peasant in Chŏlla-do tick, and what made the Americans tick, and what made the global system tick. We started with a few seemingly inconsequential decisions in August and September 1945, and ended up discovering the world of the late 1940s, and the crucible of American strategic decision ever since.

The events of the early liberation period pushed us back in search of an explanation, back to "late development," Japanese-style, a defensive, forced-pace industrialization that loosed Korean peasants from the land by the millions, scattering them through the regional political economy that fueled the Japanese attempt at upward mobility within the world system. When the empire broke up in 1945, these were now worker-peasants, and as they returned to their homes they became the restless raw material for a gathering explosion, going under the name revolutionary nationalism, and led by Koreans with decades of experience in the Asian turbulence of the first half of this century.

This aspect of the Korean dialectic met its opposite in ambitious, upwardly mobile elements who had prospered under the Japanese, usually in close connection to the massive colonial state: bureaucrats, military and police officers, entrepreneurs and even industrialists, and a landlord class that had begun the slow process of transforming itself toward capitalist production. When these elements inherited the Japanese state, they got a formidable ally in the intense class conflict marking Korea in the postliberation period.

Koreans encountered an America that, under Roosevelt, wanted to channel and confine their nationalism but open the Korean door, and to accommodate a Soviet Union that bordered Korea and that would therefore require Soviet-American cooperation if it were to remain unified. The enlightened internationalist device was trusteeship, which sought to govern policy from 1943 to 1946; this was probably the only way postwar Korea could have remained united. It failed ultimately because, like all other American policies toward Korea in our period, it did not consult Koreans, take them seriously, or find their desires for unitary nationhood and independence acceptable. The Soviets, for their part, wanted a friendly regime on half the peninsula; they had their own desires to channel and confine Korean nationalism. The North Korean invasion in 1950 sought to break the American *and* the Soviet embrace, and come up with a unified nation that could resist them both.

Until early 1947 Korea and its local conflicts drove the course of events; the cold war started there in 1945 as did premature containment, spawned by local Soviet-American tension and the American response to Korean social and political movements; by mid-1946 two effective states competed, each reinforced and expanded by the requisites of manning the bulwark at the solidifying thirty-eighth parallel. The movement toward a separate southern state that was wholly the charge of the United States became the critical turning point in the first year after liberation, giving American policy a stake from which it never turned back.[1] The suppression of the autumn harvest uprisings showed the formidable coercive qualities of the colonial state, and gave a breath of life to its Korean staff. The southern Left, which had governed events theretofore, saw its strength dissipate and its center of gravity move off to P'yŏngyang. By mid-1947 Yŏ Un-hyŏng was dead and Pak Hŏn-yŏng was subordinate to Kim Il Sung.

The Truman Doctrine and the revival of Japanese industry shifted a larger center of gravity in early 1947, and for the next three years external forces commanded events in Korea. The local containment policy prefigured Acheson's decisions, winning high-level sanction with his "drawing the line" not just in Greece and Turkey, but in Korea as well. Behind this was not John Hodge's fear of communism, however, so much as the political economy of the great crescent, a regional expression of the world view that brought the Marshal Plan to Europe and, even more generally, the United States to its status as global hegemone, an increasingly unilateral role in a second-best world, but still costumed in the Rooseveltian rhetoric of internationalism. As Korea's salience rose for the United States, the Soviets withdrew their combat forces and Kim Il Sung dispatched his legions to the Chinese civil war.

Just as containment won approval its opposite emerged, a rollback strategy with a law of motion emanating from an older, declining political economy, one appropriate to the entrepreneur or the national industrialist rather than the multinational corporation; expansionism was its general expression and rollback was its preferred strategy. "Foreign policy" was so new to the American superpower that the agencies of the state responsible for it had near-complete autonomy from the broader society; those interested in it had been the Ivy League–educated blue bloods in the Foreign Service, carrying out what were really the regional policies of the Northeastern quadrant and the South: New England traders, southern planters, and Wall Street investors had been the "special interests" behind foreign affairs. But in the 1930s a new hegemonic bloc of industrial exporters formed, and in the late 1940s, one after another, new institutions of hegemonic maintenance proliferated, subject to internecine power struggles that were mostly outside the purview of the average American. Thus the sequence of the first and second Korean wars was prefigured a year earlier, in the bubbling up of rollback inside the American state—just as the last United States combat troops left Korea.

This convergence on rollback we explained both by the superordinate mechanism of "China," an interpretation of the Chinese revolution that enabled conservatives to refight the 1948 election and the New Deal, and by the truly important instrument of a recrudescent Japan, hinged to a regional political economy much of which was in communist hands. Liberals and conservatives within the American oval could unite behind Dean Acheson's June decisions and then merge on a march north, for different reasons. The first tendency wanted the brakes applied at the Yalu, while the latter wanted to career into an unknown wilderness called

China. The coalition broke apart when it confronted the real China; the rollback strategy and its historic constituency then drifted toward the oblivion of crackpot surrealism and nostalgic reminiscence, and containment became the modal choice of foreign policy elites.

Meanwhile there was a law of motion within Korea, as Koreans tried to wrest back the wherewithal to govern events. Syngman Rhee was bolstered by American backing, the United Nations imprimatur, and a mass mobilization of youths in the streets, but the truncated economy festered. Kim Il Sung forged a strong army with Soviet equipment and Chinese tempering, and brought it home in the year before the war; the North Koreans put a great effort into reviving colonial heavy industries for their preferred strategy, import-substitution (communist-style) that would provide a base to resist foreign encroachment. In 1949–1950 the South Koreans showed that they knew how to fight guerrillas, at least with American backing; the economy began to move as harvests improved and revived links to Japan were forged. Still, the war that broke out on June 25 was a local affair, the denouement to struggles going back to the colonial period: the Kim Il Sungs against the Kim Sŏk-wŏns.

That war, however, transformed South Korea; it was the partial equivalent of the revolution its social structure demanded but did not get in the previous five years. The revolution was capitalist and the war foreshortened and hastened it, above all by ending landlordism and by relieving the state of its obsession (80 percent of the budget) with coercive ministration.

Landed wealth deeply penetrated and hamstrung the Korean state, immobilizing the bureaucracy. The National Assembly, which landlords dominated, acted as an external check on executive power; stalwarts like Cho Pyŏng-ok and Chang T'aek-sang populated the coercive agencies with their supporters. Nothing better expressed the twilight power and the ineffably recalcitrant backwardness of Korea's landlords, and the basic character of the class conflict in Korea, than their obstinate determination to get back what they took to be their birthright, their holdings in both South and North, even in the midst of a devastating war being fought for them by the world's premier power. To them, this is what the war was about, and they were right. Only the clearing of this class from the land by the North Koreans in the summer of 1950, cutting them loose and placing them at the mercy of the Americans, finally made the redistribution possible.[2]

In the space of my coming to maturity, from when I was a little boy putting together plastic models of Sabre jets and MIG-15s and reading comic books about howling Koreans to the present, both Koreas have moved from a demolished, desperate condition on a peninsula full of thoroughly aggrieved and disjointed people to a position among the "modern" nations of the world. The splendid resilience and vitality of its people expressed itself in massive drives to regroup and rebuild; at first the North did better than the South, reconstructing quickly and then realizing the highest industrial growth rates in the world for about two decades. P'yŏngyang today is a modern phoenix, risen from the ashes to a lovely city of grand promenades, verdant parks, and stunning Korean architecture in a contemporary mode.

After the April 1960 student revolution gave the final coup de grace to the Rhee regime and the colonial remnants in the forces of order, the South Korean state was able to turn its attention to development with a vengeance, and in the past two decades has itself had the premier industrial growth rate in the world, opening outward to the world while the North reaps the diminishing returns of self-reliance. Seoul, too, is a vast energetic city and the country is among the most productive nodes in the world economy.

If one asks, what about the future, "which Korea will win out," I do not know; the last four decades proffer two answers, but I have no answer except the one the witches gave in Macbeth:

> If you can look into the seeds of time,
> And say which grain will grow and which will not,
> Speak then to me, who neither beg nor fear
> Your favors nor your hate.

Let us merely record the revival and florescence of a great civilization.

MAKING AND REMAKING OF HEGEMONY: NOT A KOREAN WAR AT ALL

If the Korean War became a total war for Koreans, it was for Americans a moment in the making and remaking of American hegemony; as Acheson said, from this standpoint it was not a Korean War, it could have happened anywhere. Acheson also blurted out something else, in retrospective seminars in 1954 held to aid him in writing his memoirs and to cook MacArthur's goose: "Korea came along and saved us."[3]

The reference is to NSC 68, the most important cold war document of our time, and to Korea as a necessary *crisis* that enabled the enormous defense expenditures called for in the document. More generally, Korea was a crisis enabling the second great wave of American state-building in this century. The New Deal was the first, and the National Security state was the second, with its bureaucracies growing exponentially from the early 1950s. The Korean War thus propelled hegemony outward, and state-making inward. But this is now commonplace in the literature, at least the competent literature; Korea was an instance in the making of

American hegemony. The standard argument is that Korea occasioned the globalization of containment, stretching Kennan's limited containment to Nitze-Dulles unlimited commitments.

But we said making and *remaking*, and "remaking" does discover some new history. NSC 68 also had within it not just a globalization of containment, but our dialectic between containment and rollback. NSC 48 signaled the end of a thorough revaluation of United States policy toward Asia, to account for the Chinese revolution and the incipient reappearance of Japanese industry; it had the same dialectic between containment and rollback. In late August, Truman and Acheson decided to march into North Korea, thus giving MacArthur's thrust its broad backing in Washington. An unstable compromise on containment from 1947 to 1950, lacking bipartisanship on Asia but above all lacking the funds to underpin the new hegemony, was brought together via the march North—for about two months, from late August to late October. Rollback met a regrouped People's Army and two hundred thousand Chinese "volunteers," causing the greatest crisis in the postwar period and limiting a war that could not be limited in Washington. In the winter of 1950, foreign policy centrists like Acheson and Nitze discovered belatedly that containment was the policy.

Centrist rollback had failed, but it was blamed on Asia-first rollbackers. And so MacArthur slowly faded from the scene, but not without some uproarious pulling and hauling in domestic American politics, as the rollback constituency fought back against this reversal of correct verdicts. In the interests of bipartisan consensus a revisionist history had to emerge: MacArthur, the lone wolf, would be blamed for the rollback failure; Dulles would merge with the comfortable broad middle, while using rollback rhetoric to sate the outraged appetites of the right-wing. Most important, the failure of Korean rollback put decisive outer limits on "positive action" for the next several decades. Containment was the real Eisenhower policy, vastly preferable to the centrist elites then in control of foreign policy.

It was Foster Dulles, putative architect of rollback, who placed these limits (following on the Chinese, that is). In 1953, for example, he suggested the ultimate civil war deterrent: placing the American army smack in front of the ROK Army, if required to keep the latter from marching north; and just like Truman and Acheson, Dulles learned that the United States could not carry the war to China, but must limit it to the Korean peninsula.[4] More illustrative, however, was the search for a place where a mini-rollback might be accomplished, its feasibility defined by getting in and out unscathed, and not provoking the Chinese or the Russians. The paltry place of choice for Dulles, which he brought up frequently, was Hainan Island, off the Sino-Vietnamese coast.[5] But of course, it was never tried. Like another rollbacker, Ronald Reagan at Grenada in 1983, Dulles was reduced to an "island" strategy, an irony given his purported opposition to Acheson's island perimeter. Well before the Hungarian rebellion in 1956 (usually thought to spell the end of his rollback fantasies), Dulles criticized "preventive war" doctrines and rollback: trying to "detach" satellites from the USSR, he said, "would involve the US in general war." Secretary of the Treasury Humphrey seconded Dulles: "an aggressive course of action to roll back Communism" was out; it was "not worth the risks it entails."[6]

Containment thus became the preferred strategy, a system with historically-forged boundaries within which choices were made, and it has been the modal preference of every administration since 1950. Kennedy's unwillingness to follow through with a big invasion at the Bay of Pigs expressed the difference between rollback in Cuba and Korea. The 1950 episode also explains why there was no invasion of North Vietnam; the fear of provoking China animated national security elites until Nixon's opening to Beijing made it irrelevant in 1971. No American administration could risk blowing itself apart by invading North Vietnam and getting another "glut of Chinamen."[7] China understood that the wars in Korea and Vietnam were proxy wars, with the Chinese revolution being the real issue. Through its bloody sacrifices in Korea and its deft deterrence in Vietnam, China placed definitive limits on American expansionism in these, its two most important former tributary states. In any case, the boundaries on containment explain the stalemate (indeed, what Daniel Ellsberg has called "the stalemate machine") between conservatives and liberals over the Bay of Pigs in 1961, the Vietnam War, and Nicaragua throughout the 1980s.

We can now understand how the anticommunist strategy of successive administrations was forged. But that does not fully explain the remaking of American hegemony. Hegemony implies something more than a strategy, more than a global division into spheres of influence in realpolitik terms. It implies a political economy. In its American internationalist mode, the essence of hegemony was to draw outer limits demarcating a grand area for free trade and economic growth. Such a system favors the automaticity of economic exchange over the necessities of spheres of influence or the use of military force. The lines for this in East Asia were drawn mostly in 1947, with the reverse course in Japan and the "great crescent" in the rest of Asia; here we see both the origins of containment in the region, and grasp how containment was subordinate to the hegemonic conception, just one among several possible strategies. This political economy suggested to some Americans and some Japanese the virtues of rollback, recovering a place, North Korea, where the Japanese had built heavy industries and had important mineral resources: this would be liberal rollback, limited rollback. This was not the operative *reason* for rollback in Korea, but it would have been an important result. In any case, this incipient "restoration" gives us the motive for the North Korean assault: It was an attempt to *break* the developing Northeast Asian political economy, predicated on American hegemony and Japanese regional dynamism. This was what the North Koreans fought about. They and the Chinese succeeded in keeping the neo–co-prosperity sphere within its post-1945 boundaries.

Still, there is a begged question throughout the argument on American foreign policy thus far: what, after all, explains a critical shift like that in 1950? We have analyzed two sides, based in differing social forces and interests, that struggle within the state for power and as they do so, shape a middle position which becomes a foreign policy output. But that is endemic; it occurs daily. We have suggested that the crisis of 1949–1951 was the most important, reflecting a victory that lasted a generation. What was the force behind that victory?

The victory went to a coalition of internationalists and containment advocates, shaped by a conflict with expansionism/rollback. It was a costly struggle, but Dean Acheson and John Foster Dulles held the whip hand when it was over. The power behind the internationalists was a new "hegemonic bloc" coming to power in the 1930s, based in new productive forces: advanced, high-technology industries and incipient multinational corporations that did not fear world market competition, and that were sufficiently labor-insensitive to accommodate unions and therefore to help build a business/labor party. In the final analysis, as we must say to avoid being labeled mechanical determinists, the basis that shaped and conditioned the political position of the internationalists in the American state was a vibrant new set of productive forces.

But by 1950, the internationalists did not have a world—a grand area—in which to expand effortlessly and infinitely. The rise to great power status of the Soviet Union meant that the socialist bloc occupied regional sections of the world market (as did declining European empires, a more temporary problem). Had internationalism been sufficiently rooted in American politics, it might have succeeded in bringing the USSR and its allies into this world market. But the domestic struggle in the US made that impossible, the opposing side was strong enough to exercise a veto on that option; internationalist autonomy in foreign policy was held hostage by American democracy, because most of the internationalist leaders were appointed and not elected, and most of those who were elected could not figure out what they were talking about. Furthermore it is by no means clear that Stalin preferred an accommodation with Western capital and its world economy to the neomercantilist strategy of withdrawal, isolation, and a go-it-alone, heavy-industry–first industrialization that marked "socialism in one country" since the early 1930s. So, we got a world of two blocs for a generation. Secondly, as the Korean War demonstrated, postcolonial "Third World" states had emerged and had deployed stunning force in their attempts to break the postwar American-dominated world system. The crisis of 1950 thus stabilized the bipolar system visible in 1947, while leaving certain regions in the Third World contingent, an intermediate zone where superpower conflict could ensue without threatening global war.

We thus have the following elements in our explanation of critical shifts in America's foreign orientation: (1) most basic, the rise (or decline) of new productive forces; (2) the emergence of socialist power in the world system; (3) the emergence of revolutionary nationalism in the colonial areas. The first is the breath of life; the second and third elements condition and limit expansion into the world market, or may cause expansion to fall back upon itself.

RAVELED AND UNRAVELED THREADS

If we recall Perry Anderson's words from the introduction, "there is merely that which is known—established by historical research—and that which is not known: the latter may be either the mechanisms of single events or the laws of motion of whole structures," I have satisfied myself, if not the reader, in establishing causation at the structural level. But there is a law of motion to the single event (the "smoking gun"), or the single person—the mechanism of the individual moment, we can call it. That moment often occurs at the intersection of force fields produced by the combining laws of motion. Here no one can be satisfied with the evidence presented in this book; we can only say that we now can ask better questions than we could before.

The questions pour forth like a torrent: if M. Preston Goodfellow could speak, what would he now say? And Guy Burgess, and Kim Philby, and Frederick McKee, and Admiral Cooke, and William Pawley? And what would George Blake have to say, still living in Moscow? Not to mention Kim Il Sung in P'yŏngyang, Sun Li-jen in Taipei, Paek Sŏn-yŏp in Seoul, Richard Stilwell in Washington? What was William Donovan's part in Asian events in 1950? How can we unpack the role of T. V. Soong and his money in American politics in the decade after 1945? Who murdered Serge Rubinstein, and why?[8] Was Goodfellow known to Acheson?—for here we have an intersection of the individual moments of internationalism and expansionism, the latter playing its historic role in pushing *both* forward.[9] To say these are matters for further research is a bit jocose; the individual moments tumbled forth noisily, but slipped silently into the murky depths of archives held closely, or archives "deep-sixed," or events unplumbed even by their authors.

One retrospective remark may provoke more rumination about that enticing if irrelevant question, "who started the Korean War?" When Acheson was in Missouri helping Truman with his memoirs, the President stated emphatically that he wanted "to state conditions as they were" before he made decisions, not as they looked in retrospect. On Korea, for example, the steps he and Acheson took in June 1950 "must be based on the facts as we had them—not on what we had later."[10] What they had later, of course, remained unexplained.

Two clear winners emerged from the Korean War: Japan and China. We know next to nothing about the role either may have played in the war's genesis. But under the ancient principle *qui bono*, it therefore is worth asking, did they have a role in starting it?

Premier Yoshida described the war as "a gift of the gods,"[11] and the Tokyo stock market fluctuated for three years according to "peace scares" in Korea. Perhaps nothing so pleases conservative Japanese elites as to sit back, pat their full tummies, and watch Koreans tear themselves to pieces. It was this war and its manifold procurements, not the "great crescent," that ultimately pushed Japan forward along its march toward world-beating industrial prowess. North Korean war motives, we believe, derived from American/Japanese plans for industrial revival and for a restoration of prewar economic patterns. But we know little or nothing about what Japan's militarists and colonial specialists were doing after 1945, except that the United States protected one of the worst, General Ishii, and Robert Murphy tells us several thousand of such specialists worked on or in Korea during the Korean War. As for the individual moment, we would still like to know what Kodama Yoshio was doing in Seoul on June 25, as part of the American army (according to Anthony Sampson). Stockpiler of black sands and precious metals, bankroller of high Japanese politicians, rumored to be close to the CIA, his presence demands explanation.

China emerged from the Korean War with its control at home consolidated, its economy leaping forward, and its international standing rising (as evidenced at Bandung in 1954); much of this owed to its participation in the war, its having fought the United States to a standstill. China transferred its Korean fighters by the tens of thousands to Korea in the year before the war, and could not have been unaware of the developing tension in Korea. Another China, the Nationalist variety, got from this war a guarantee of American defense and backing for the KMT for a generation; it also benefitted from war procurements. The dangling threads here are Nieh Jung-chen's rumored presence in P'yŏngyang on the last weekend in June 1950, and a veritable tapestry of raveled and unraveled threads in the comings and goings from Taiwan in the months before the war.

At this writing we can even hope that the most sequestered archive will speak, Moscow's, and speak honestly, instead of trying to claim itself as the great liberator, to bury and belittle Korean strivings, to project original innocence about its occupation of Korea—all the false indulgences it has put forth thus far amid its general silence.

We began this project by remarking that all parties to the war have a conspiracy theory about how it began. We now understand that multiple conspiracies intersected on the last weekend in June 1950. But if conspiracies exist, they rarely move history; they make a difference at the margins from time to time, but with the unforeseen consequences of a logic outside the control of their authors: and this is what is wrong with "conspiracy theory." History is moved by the broad forces and large structures of human collectivities, and the Korean War is no exception.

History and Memory

The Korean War is called "the forgotten war" in America, because it is forgotten. This condition explains the experience of a North Korean official who came to New York on Olympic business, finding that people could barely recall when the Korean War occurred, that cab drivers thought communists ran South Korea (since human rights were so violated), and that Americans were friendly and innocent of the antagonism he expected to find. He rightly called it a form of amnesia, but thought it very useful in starting a new relationship.[12]

Clay Blair's "call"[13] is a way to think about the Korean War. By calling the Korean conflict a "forgotten war," we both name it, and we remember it—a paradox: what is it that we are remembering to forget?

Forgetting, Nietzsche said, is no mere result of inertia: "It is rather an active and in the strictest sense positive faculty of repression." This human animal *needs* to be forgetful, he says; forgetfulness is "like a doorkeeper, a perserver of psychic order, repose and etiquette. . . . there could be no present without forgetfulness."[14] So it is not for nothing that the Korean War is called the Forgotten War. There is more than a little wisdom in the penultimate episode of the television show "M.A.S.H.," where Hawkeye opens a bottle of cognac and remarks, "We drink to forget."

For Americans the war started with a thunderclap in 1950; most memories dim about anything before that. For Koreans, it began in 1945 and had its climax in 1950. That climax was a blow struck in the Korean defense, "an act of a new quality against the repetitive examples of . . . past weakness." Designed to give the future a direction, it also had a retrospective eloquence on a long, lamentable, but ultimately transient history of Korean mendicancy. It was an act that instantly rendered that humiliation contingent, "in the past," a temporary condition from, shall we say, 1600 to 1950 (or perhaps only 1876 to 1950). It was a new thing that suddenly revalued this history "from top to bottom." It was an act that said, Koreans have stood up. But this act of invasion also invades our thought, our assumptions; it makes us think "how uncommon and how unlikely is this spectacle of a man getting himself killed for an interpretation of history."[15]

Once it is done, once "the cut" is made, "the instant of the act . . . rushes wordlessly into the past," and the world closes up.[16] The world renders its judgment, but stripped from the act is its subjectivity, its audacity, its very presumptuousness in thinking this act can make a difference.

What happens when the world closes up, and renders its judgment? Martin Heidegger asserts that there is an intimate connection between memory, the naming of things, and that process we call thinking. By naming we locate or "call" something for the memory, rescue it from oblivion, retain it and keep it for thought. We war against "that passing away which allows what has passed only to be in the past, which lets it freeze in the finality of this *rigor mortis*."[17] If that finality is buried, we should dig it up and think about it, even if it shocks us.

We do not remember history, but particular verdicts, integral to and shaped by the raucous domestic politics of the 1950s. What is the *epitaph* on the American tombstone—what does the rigor mortis say? The tombstone has two messages: for the Truman liberal, Korea was a success, "the limited war." For the MacArthur conservative, Korea was a failure: the first defeat in American history, more properly a stalemate, in any case it proved that there was "no substitute for victory." The problem for MacArthur's epitaph is that if MacArthur saw no substitute for victory, he likewise saw no limit on victory: each victory begged another war. The problem for the Truman liberal is that the limited war got rather unlimited in late 1950.

So we need another verdict: a split decision—the first Korean War, the war for the south in the summer of 1950, was a success. The second war, the war for the North, was a failure. Thus Dean Acheson produced a schizophrenic epitaph: the decision to defend South Korea was the finest hour of the Truman presidency; the decision to march to the Yalu occasioned "an incalculable defeat to US foreign policy and destroyed the Truman administration"; this was "the worst defeat . . . since Bull Run"[18] (another interesting analogy). Acheson's psychic repose was uninterrupted, however, because he assumed that the latter happened not to him but to his bête noire: Acheson squares the circle by blaming it all on

MacArthur, and much mainstream historiography has squared the circle in the same way.[19]

Michael Walzer, in his book *Just and Unjust Wars*, written to examine the question in the light of Vietnam, finds the war for containment to be just, the war for rollback unjust. He cleanly splits the difference and gives to the Achesonian position its most sophisticated liberal defense, and illustrates the grip that the Korean verdicts still have on the American mind. But Walzer's usually impeccable logic falls down at a key point in his presentation. In justifying the march into North Korea the American ambassador to the UN called the thirty-eighth parallel "an imaginary line." Walzer comments, "I will leave aside the *odd notion* that the thirty-eighth parallel was an imaginary line (how then did we recognize the initial aggression?)" (emphasis added). Walzer leaves this mouthful without further thought, yet it is basic to his argument on the war.[20] Had he probed its meaning, examined the origin of this "imaginary line," he might have come to the critical paradox in Acheson's (and Walzer's) position, which we may simply state: "June 25, 1950: Koreans invade Korea."

In the midst of the December crisis Richard Stokes, British minister of works, intuited this paradox. The thirty-eighth parallel decision, he wrote to Bevin, was "the invitation to such a conflict as has in fact arisen."

> In the American Civil War the Americans would never have tolerated for a single moment the setting up of an imaginery [*sic*] line between the forces of North and South, and there can be no doubt as to what would have been their re-action if the British had intervened in force on behalf of the South. This parallel is a close one because in America the conflict was not merely between two groups of Americans, but was between two conflicting economic systems as is the case in Korea.[21]

The schizophrenic epitaph accompanies and interprets a two-line conflict in America, but confuses "the call," the naming of this war, and thus confuses our thought. Memory reaches back and finds a void, or a politically determined, received wisdom. Even on the Left, there is mostly a silence—Korea is rarely included in the panoply of American postwar interventions from Greece to Nicaragua, and tiptoeing in on cat's feet, one senses the judgment: it was a just war—even for the Left. It is this that explains Walzer's illogic. The implicit assumption seems to be that Korea was not a people's war, like Vietnam. (This becomes stranger still when one realizes that American military officers saw Vietnam as another Korea, often confused the two countries, and in curious ways, still do.[22]) The Korean Left and its leader, Kim Il Sung, are too unknown, too alien; and the American Left is too liberal (Acheson and Truman are too close), to live with the truth of the Korean War: it was the worst of American postwar interventions, the most destructive, for more genocidal than Vietnam. The civilian toll in North Korea was about two million, or 20 percent of the prewar population. This is a proportion higher than the horrendous losses suffered by the Soviet Union and Poland in World War II; Japan suffered a total of about two million military and civilian deaths, or 3 percent of its population. Because the Korean War occurred at a time of repression in America and was so *unseen*,[23] almost anything was possible.

"Better a mended sock than a torn one," said Hegel; not so for self-awareness. The American split verdict on the Korean War is an agreement to disagree, a stitched-together mending of a torn national psyche. Above all it is a compact to forget—a selective forgetting that preserves psychic order. You remember one verdict, and forget or condemn the other. Each verdict implies a corresponding amnesia. What we have done is to unravel the stitching. But what of the active forgetting? What does not pass by the doorkeeper of memory? What is repressed?

There is something Nietzsche calls "historia abscondita," concealed, secret, or unknown history: "perhaps the past is still essentially undiscovered!" he exclaims; "there is no way of telling what may yet become a part of history." This is from *The Gay Science*,[24] but it harks back to Tacitus: arcana of empire, empire as something veiled and mysterious. In other words all history, not just I. F. Stone's work on the Korean War, may be *hidden history*.

Thus, to properly name the Korean War, we needed to discover it, to uncover it: we needed an *excavation*. We needed to be one of those Acheson hated: the "reexaminationists," always pulling carefully nurtured plants—in his case policies—up by the roots to have another look.

The Korean War needed then and still needs the light shed by the ancient tool of Chinese philosophers, a rectification of names. Can we call it an international aggression across established boundaries? Can we liken Kim Il Sung to Hitler or Tojo? Can we place the United States or South Korea in a position of innocence, like Czechoslovakia or Poland in 1938–1939? Was Korea American territory, like Pearl Harbor? No one who has perused the record of 1945–1950 could plausibly draw such analogies. No Korean ever would, because no Korean recognized the thirty-eighth parallel as permanent; this is what made Rhee think Sarajevo rather than Munich. It is a most revealing analogy: a small incident touches off a world war, the Armageddon in which both Rhee and Chiang thought they could recover the "lost territory." Yet, fortunately, it was not Sarajevo (although no one knew that for almost a year). America gets us closer: a civil war. Spain and Vietnam get us even closer: a revolutionary civil war.

What is the final meaning of the North Korean invasion, that blitzkreig which, however it started, shattered the peace of a Sunday morning calm? No foreign office, Acheson said, acts without consideration of the "off chance." But this decision was not made in a foreign office: it was made in a Korean mind that mingled cold calculation with a youthful, undaunted bravado that gave itself over to an unknown future in the way that only youth can. In its indifference to the likely result (a rearmed America, the turning of the cold war into a glacier, but who cares if Korea is unified), there was a solipsism and supercharged chauvinism that tells us that its authorship was local, and that renders its failure less than tragic and less than noble,[25] a Faustian wager that went awry. There was something "early," prevenient, insistently parvenu about it, something ineffably "Korean" about it, if by that we mean the Korea of our century that lives so impatiently with the categories the rest of the world prepares to define, encapsulate, and (thereby) control it. It was a way of saying, the twentieth century has pinned us to a wall and we refuse it.

Can there be a moral justification for the North Korean attack even if the thirty-eighth parallel is not "an imaginary line," and even as the attack is rendered by Mosaic One, the official story? From this standpoint we would need to argue that

> The general, non-pacifist public seems to feel that a "defensive" war is morally superior to an "offensive" war. The distinction here, however, is not based on objective fact but only on subjective sentiment. . . . In terms of historical causation, everyone recognizes that modern wars do not start with the firing of the first shots, but have their source in a whole series of events that mark the developing conflict. . . . The question of who fired the first shot could not possibly answer the deeper question of who was, historically speaking, the "aggressor."

This author remarked that "it is no longer a problem of starting a war, but of winning it, or losing"; the "question of when to shoot is a matter of expediency." He continued, "If there is good reason to believe that a sudden, massive armed blow would in the net result, as compared with waiting for such a blow from the enemy, save many lives and goods . . . then to strike such a blow, far from being morally wrong, is morally obligatory." The reader who wishes to know who said this—Kim Il Sung? Mao Tse-tung? Stalin?—may find out in the note.[26] It tells us what our enemies were dealing with in early 1950, but it abstracts from the full meaning of the war.

The June invasion was part of an ongoing dialectic beginning in 1945; shortly after it happened, when the first Americans entered the fighting, the early, pristine verdict declared that it was a civil war, and a people's war—evidence for which we found in mass magazines like *Collier's* and *Life*. This act of discovery was simple, as close as the neighborhood barbershop in 1950. But in the free democracy of the United States in 1950, hardly a soul drew this conclusion, or could do so without running a gauntlet of repression. For Americans, it is this history that, upon reexamination, is most shocking. This discovery leads to a different name: but to make that name stick in the 1980s required two volumes, not a copy of *Collier's*. We have now rectified the name: it was a civil and revolutionary war, a people's war.

FACING WEST: THE END OF EXPANSIONISM

The Korean War did not end proxy conflict in the Third World, but it did draw a line in Asia beyond which traditional American expansionism could no longer venture. East Asian revolutionary nationalism had filled the imaginary empty vessel in the American mind known as "China." This conclusion was intuited by a certain Dr. Sontagg, to whom Bedell Smith (in an NSC meeting at the end of the war) attributed the observation that "for the first time in a thousand years the East has successfully stood up to the West and secured a stalemate."[27]

Richard Drinnon's *Facing West* is a marvelous recreation of the motive forces driving Americans "from the rising to the setting sun," in John Fiske's words; hardier Americans like that veteran of the Civil and Indian Wars, Arthur MacArthur, spoke of westward currents having swept "this magnificent Aryan people across the Pacific." William Seward thought Western civilization must move "westward until the tides of the renewed and of the decaying civilizations of the world meet on the shores of the Pacific Ocean." Other woolly quotations could be adduced, muffling the prophetic counterdiscourse uttered by a Mark Twain: "We cannot maintain an empire in the Orient and maintain a republic in America."[28] But what is so remarkable about Drinnon's book is that not a single index entry exists for the Korean War. He rightly links frontier expansionism to the suppression of the Philippine insurgency, but then leapfrogs Korea to end the book with the Indochina War. But it was Korea that put the brakes on the expansionist impulse; Vietnam was a containment liberal's war that never could transcend the logic of the Korean lesson.

Drinnon's unsparing account of the fate of native peoples unfortunate enough to be caught in the wake of expansionism makes for unsettling reading, perhaps like my own on the atrocious character of the Korean War. It is not just that expansionists thought they were carriers of civilization; the other side of that coin was a genocidal impulse toward the "nameless sludge" under which they grouped the races and peoples standing in their way—people without civilization, people without history. "War and torture have the same two targets, a people and its civilization," Elaine Scarry writes. "In both war and torture, there is a destruction of 'civilization' in its most elemental form."[29]

It pains me deeply that my own country should so divert itself from its proper path, as to find its enemies among small countries fighting for their survival and dignity, and to celebrate those paltry victories (Guatemala, Libya, Grenada, etc.) as an earnest of American patriotism, or to indulge in so much self-pity about the defeat in Vietnam. If you wish to say that the Soviets are worse, my response is that I judge my country by its own standards. A fundamental incommensurability of the enemy has placed the American soldier (usually against his will) in conditions where he violated time-honored rules of warfare, and thereby lost his soul as a fighter.[30]

The shock of being fired on by women in white pajamas in Korea's "Indian country" was fearsome but unsurprising. What shocks is the unrestrained American bombardment in Korea, which sought both to torture a people and destroy a society, by the testimony of its makers. A minor commitment in 1945 grows to the point where atomic weapons are brandished to intimidate and terrorize, five years after Hiroshima; for technical reasons they are not used and oceans of napalm are substituted, thus to get "Korea, the limited war." The unconscious interior intent of the war was to destroy the historically self-contained Korean civilization, to "open" old Korea. But it did not consciously occur to American planners to destroy a civilization, because from Acheson and Kennan on down they thought none existed.

Yet Korean resistance and rennaissance, during and since the war, is testimony to the clash between settler expansionism and rooted civilization. The impulse that on the American continent encountered tribes of people and destroyed them, in East Asia faced an enduring civilization in open anti-imperial revolt, and met its match.

For American expansionists, Asia was a wilderness akin to the frontier, where one could escape the confining grid of Europe, the city, the bureaucracy, and cavort freely among people who did not count. The United States was itself a fragment of European civilization, understanding part but not all of what it meant to sustain such a civilization over time. The fragment spins out its telos in a continent empty of people capable of resisting it, but also unbounded by knowledge of the historical sources of its freedom, or the reality or imaginative presence of its modern alternative, socialism. This is of course Louis Hartz's point:

There is more than a touch of irony in the fact that circumstances of national power should have made of America the leader of the resistance to the Bolshevik revolution. It is as if history actually had an interest in the vivid [*sic*] doctrinal contrast. For a fragmented liberalism is of course the most powerful manifestation of the bourgeois tradition that can be found.[31]

The Korean War put an end to the extension of the frontier in Asia, for American expansionists and their great hero, Douglas MacArthur, who had his back broken there. The Korean War began a process, which was then hastened by the Vietnam War because it was a "seen" war, a closely-observed war, in which those facing West were turned round finally to face themselves, and to face up to their responsibility for what will be seen, after all the special pleading and extenuating circumstances are accounted for, a few generations hence, as an American holocaust visited upon the Korean and Vietnamese peoples. The way to face that and to atone for it is to think through why it happened, to reckon with it: a reckoning instead of a forgetting.

THE ROTATION OF THE EPICENTER

In a remarkable, eloquent speech in Seattle in 1951, MacArthur said,

> To the early pioneer the Pacific Coast marked the end of his courageous westerly advance. To us it should mark but the beginning. To him it delineated our western frontier. To us that frontier has been moved across the Pacific horizon. . . . Our economic frontier now embraces the trade potentialities of Asia itself; for with the gradual rotation of the epicenter of world trade back to the Far East whence it started many centuries ago, the next thousand years will find the main problem the raising of the sub-normal standards of life of its more than a billion people.[32]

Since the end of the Korean War, as we have seen, both Koreas have rebounded and South Korea, in particular, has brought itself forcefully to the world's attention by selling it what it wants at a good price. In the same few decades, the country I love, which my ancestors came to from Scotland in 1632 (a bit after the Hideyoshi invasions, to put it in Korean context), in a series of stupid and senseless wars has frittered away its world-bestriding position and the immense moral authority garnered by the defeat of the Nazis. The requisites for maintenance of the containment system grow exponentially; meanwhile a relatively small group of investors and industrialists continue to export the sinews of its strength and its very dynamism abroad, pursuing Polanyi's "glorious fiction," Crowther's "strange dementia," or Beard's "aleatory quest."

Capitalism moves forth in great cascades of creation and destruction,[33] waves of uneven development which distribute plenty here and poverty there; from the standpoint of the promise of 1950, the American political economy is an empty husk with vast reaches of the old industrial heartland in varying states of decay and disintegration, and its people now know the meaning of the Biblical phrase, what profits a man to gain the world and lose his soul? The solution to this problem is the same one Beard gave fifty years ago, a "nationalism of the commonweal" that would entail "the withdrawal of public support from private interests engaged in making outward thrusts perilous to security," the assertion of democratic controls on corporate might and wealth, and an end to empire.[34]

Behind the bipolar boundaries forged in 1950, Japan, South Korea and Taiwan revived and today exercise a powerful gravity upon their communist neighbors. Call it a great crescent or the Pacific Rim, the Achesonian hegemony proved its staying power. In our time it now appears that the Koreans and the Chinese merely succeeded in delaying for two decades the dynamism of this regional economy; both China and North Korea could contain classic expansionism, but neither could contain the automaticity of the economic mechanisms of a dynamic regional capitalist economy, once it got going again in the mid-1960s. Instead this political economy is lapping at their shores and carrying before it the heretofore impregnable bulwarks of the communist containment system. So perhaps it was the "natural economy" after all; perhaps here is a kind of rollback that works; perhaps this is how you achieve the "grand area" that was the midcentury goal of the internationalists. And now, as the capitalist mechanism is wedded to resurgent and resourceful East Asian civilizations, things have come full circle, long before MacArthur's millennium: the rotation of the epicenter puts the American heartland at risk in a way inconceivable in 1950.

But this unfolds before our very eyes; we needn't be "historians" to see this, and make a judgment about it. Meanwhile the Korean War recedes from our memory for the right reasons: it is now a thing seen and a thing known, it is time for it to be in and of the past, so that we may act in the present toward the reconciliation and reunion of the Korean people. For beyond the good historian, as Nietzsche knew, is the good citizen, and there is much to be done:

A historical phenomenon, known clearly and completely and resolved into a phenomenon of knowledge, is, for him who has perceived it, dead: for he has recognized in it the delusion, the injustice, the blind passion, and in general the whole earthly and darkening horizon of this phenomenon, and has thereby also understood its power in history. This power has now lost its hold over him insofar as he is a man of knowledge; but perhaps it has not done so insofar as he is a man involved in life.[35]

PREFACE

1. *FR* (1950) 1, pp. 393–95, Acheson notes for Congressional testimony, circa August 1950.

CHAPTER ONE

1. James Gleick, "Snowflake's Riddle Yields to Probing of Science," *New York Times*, January 6, 1987.
2. "Against positivism, which halts at phenomena—'There are only *facts*'—I would say: No, facts is precisely what there is not, only interpretations. We cannot establish any fact 'in itself': perhaps it is folly to want to do such a thing." Friedrich Nietzsche, *The Will to Power*, trans. Walter Kaufmann and R. J. Hollingdale (New York: Vintage Books, 1968), p. 267.
3. Jean-Paul Sartre, *Critique of Dialectical Reason*, trans. Alan Sheridan-Smith (London: New Left Books, 1976), pp. 100–101.
4. For a cogent and systematic essay explicating similar themes for the academic study of international relations, see Alexander Wendt, "The Agent-Structure Problem in International Relations Theory," *International Organization* 41, no. 3 (Summer 1987), pp. 335–70, esp. pp. 355–69.
5. Sartre, *Critique*, pp. 35–37.
6. Sartre, *Critique*, pp. 53–58.
7. Friedrich Nietzsche, "Schopenhauer as Educator," in *Untimely Meditations*, trans. by R. J. Hollingdale (New York: Cambridge University Press, 1983), p. 127–28.
8. Friedrich Nietzsche, *The Gay Science*, trans. Walter Kaufmann (New York: Vintage Books, 1974), pp. 172–73.
9. Eric R. Wolf, *Europe and the People Without History* (Berkeley, Calif.: University of California Press, 1982), pp. 3–13; Perry Anderson, *Lineages of the Absolutist State* (London: New Left Books, 1974), pp. 7–9.
10. Jean-Paul Sartre, *Search for a Method*, trans. Hazel E. Barnes (New York: Vintage Books, 1968), pp. 164–65.
11. See Shlomo Avineri, *The Political and Social Thought of Karl Marx* (Cambridge, England: Cambridge University Press, 1968), pp. 65–95.
12. Karl Polanyi, *The Great Transformation* (Boston: Beacon Press, 1957), p. 27.
13. For a delightful account of reading Marx for his literary merits (among other merits), see Robert Paul Wolff, *Moneybags Must Be So Lucky: On the Literary Structure of Capital* (Amherst: University of Massachusetts Press, 1988).
14. Sartre, *Critique*, pp. 61–62.
15. Karl Marx, *Grundrisse: Foundations of the Critique of Political Economy*, trans. Martin Nicolaus (New York: Penguin Books, 1973), pp. 100–101.
16. Quoted in Ian Buruma, "Korea: Shame and Chauvinism," *New York Review of Books* (January 29, 1987), p. 25.
17. Edmund Wilson, *To the Finland Station* (New York: Doubleday, 1940, 1953), pp. 2–4.
18. For example, Glenn Paige, *The Korean Decision* (Glencoe, Ill.: The Free Press,

1968); Graham Allison, *Essence of Decision: Explaining the Cuban Missile Crisis* (Boston: Little, Brown, 1971); Morton H. Halperin, *Bureaucratic Politics and Foreign Policy* (Washington, D.C.: The Brookings Institution, 1974); Robert Jervis, *Perception and Misperception in International Politics* (Princeton, N.J.: Princeton University Press, 1976); Alexander George and Richard Smoke, *Deterrence in American Foreign Policy: Theory and Practice* (New York: Columbia University Press, 1974).

19. Otto Hintze, *The Historical Essays of Otto Hintze*, ed. Felix Gilbert (New York: Oxford University Press, 1975), p. 283.

20. For an excellent discussion of Polanyi's theory and method, see Fred Block and Margaret R. Somers, "Beyond the Economistic Fallacy: The Holistic Social Science of Karl Polanyi," in *Vision and Method in Historical Sociology*, ed. Theda Skocpol (New York: Cambridge University Press, 1984), pp. 47–84.

21. Robert Cox, "Gramsci, Hegemony, and International Relations: An Essay in Method," *Millenium* 12 (Summer 1983), pp. 162–75.

22. Franz Schurmann, *The Logic of World Power: An Inquiry into the Origins, Currents, and Contradictions of World Politics* (New York: Pantheon Books, 1974) (hereafter, *Logic*). For an application of Schurmann's theory to Vietnam, see Paul Joseph, *Cracks in the Empire: State Politics in the Vietnam War* (Boston: South End Press, 1981).

23. See Bruce Cumings, "Chinatown: Foreign Policy and Elite Realignment," in *The Hidden Election*, ed. Thomas Ferguson and Joel Rogers (New York: Pantheon Books, 1981), pp. 196–231; also an early sketch of my argument in Cumings, "From Internationalism to Containment to Rollback and Back Again: The Course of US Policy toward Korea, 1943–50," in my *Child of Conflict: The Korean-American Relationship, 1943–1953* (Seattle: University of Washington Press, 1983), pp. 3–55.

24. That is, the scuttling of SALT II and the eventual ending of strategic arms talks; the major defense buildup; the formal adoption of new nuclear war–fighting strategies (PD-59 for Brzezinski, the 5-year "Defense Guidance" for Secretary Weinberger); bases and a conventional buildup in the Middle East; hostile attacks on Nicaragua and aid for the government of El Salvador. See Cumings, "Chinatown," *Child of Conflict*.

25. Louis Hartz, *The Liberal Tradition in America* (New York: Harcourt, Brace and World, 1955).

26. Daniel Chirot and I worked this conception out one day over lunch; I cannot say if it is original.

27. Benedict Anderson, *Imagined Communities: Reflections on the Origin and Spread of Nationalism* (New York: Verso, 1983), p. 16.

28. Louis Hartz, *The Founding of New Societies* (New York: Harcourt, Brace and World, 1964), p. 119.

29. Thomas Ferguson, "From Normalcy to New Deal: Industrial Structure, Party Competition, and American Public Policy in the Great Depression," *International Organization* 38, no. 1 (Winter 1984), pp. 41–94; Schurmann, *Logic*, p. 140; Alan Wolfe et al., "Political Parties and Capitalist Development," *Kapitalistate* 6 (Fall 1977), pp. 27–28.

30. See Nico Poulantzas, *Political Power and Social Classes* (London: New Left Books, 1973); also Bruce Cumings, "Reflections on Schurmann's Theory of the State," *Bulletin of Concerned Asian Scholars* 8, no. 4 (October-November 1976), pp. 55–64.

31. Ferguson, "From Normalcy to New Deal."

32. Laurence H. Shoup and William Minter, *Imperial Brain Trust* (New York: Monthly Review Press, 1977), pp. 135–48.

33. Welles was forced out of the Roosevelt administration when he was caught in flagrante delicto in a Washington men's room by FBI agents.

34. Gerard Zilg, *DuPont: Behind the Nylon Curtain* (Englewood Cliffs, N.J.: Prentice-Hall, 1974), pp. 292–95; Charles Higham, *Trading with the Enemy* (New York: Delacorte Press, 1983).

35. Carter is the best example of Schurmann's point that "any chief executive who fails to fight the interests soon finds himself at their mercy" (*Logic*, p. 185). No president was pushed, pulled, and mauled by "the interests" more than Carter; he deployed his office as if it were just another part of the bureaucracy.

36. See Benedict Anderson, *Imagined Communities: Reflections on the Origin and Spread of Nationalism* (New York: Verso, 1983).

37. Allison, *Essence of Decision*.

38. Polanyi, *Great Transformation*, p. 132.

39. *New York Times*, March 16, 1987.

40. Richard Drinnon, *Facing West: The Metaphysics of Indian-Hating and Empire-Building* (New York: New American Library, 1980), p. xiii.

41. Maurice Meisner, *Li Ta-chao and the Origins of Chinese Marxism* (New York: Atheneum, 1970).

42. Godfrey Hodgson, *America in Our Time* (Garden City: Doubleday, 1978), p. 123.

43. See Charles P. Kindleberger, *The World in Depression, 1929–1939* (Berkeley: University of California Press, 1973); Ferguson, "From Normalcy to New Deal."

44. Daniel Yergin's distinction between Yalta accommodators and Riga containers, in *Shattered Peace* (Boston: Houghton Mifflin, 1978), p. 11.

45. Richard J. Barnet is especially good on this point, in *The Roots of War: The Men and Institutions Behind U.S. Foreign Policy* (Baltimore, Md.: Penguin Books, 1973).

CHAPTER TWO

1. See Charles Maier, "The Politics of Productivity," in *Between Power and Plenty*, ed. Peter Katzenstein (Madison: University of Wisconsin Press, 1978); also Joan Spero, *The Politics of International Economic Relations*, 2d ed. (New York: St. Martin's Press, 1981), pp. 37–41.

2. Immanuel Wallerstein, *Historical Capitalism* (New York: Verso, 1983), p. 58.

3. See Bruce Cumings, "The Political Economy of Chinese Foreign Policy," *Modern China* (Summer 1979), pp. 1–29.

4. See Cumings, "Chinatown: Foreign Policy and Elite Realignment," in *The Hidden Election*, ed. Thomas Ferguson and Joel Rogers (New York: Pantheon Books, 1981), pp. 196–238.

5. Kim Ch'aek led 10,000 soldiers into China in March 1947; see chapter 11 infra.

6. Truman, quoted in Eben Ayers Papers, box 26, diary entry for April 17, 1947.

7. Eben Ayers Papers, box 26, diary entry of March 11, 1947; Arthur Krock, *New York Times*, September 24, 1948, quoting Eugene Rostow, who said that Acheson was the chief force behind the Bretton Woods agreements. William Clayton was undersecretary of state for Economic Affairs, and had been head of Anderson, Clayton & Co., "world's largest seller of cotton." (Lynn Eden, "The Diplomacy of Force: Interests, the State, and the Making of American Military Policy in 1948," [Ph.D. diss., University of Michigan, 1985], p. 87.)

8. Thomas J. Schoenbaum, *Waging Peace and War: Dean Rusk in the Truman, Kennedy and Johnson Years* (New York: Simon and Schuster, 1988), p. 142.

9. See Richard M. Freeland, *The Truman Doctrine and the Origins of McCarthyism* (New York: Schocken, 1974), p. 142 and passim.

10. Arthur Schlesinger, Jr., *The Vital Center: The Politics of Freedom* (Boston: Houghton Mifflin, 1949); Reinhold Niebuhr, *Moral Man and Immoral Society* (New York: Charles Scribner's Sons, 1932); James Burnham, *The Struggle for the World* (New York: John Day, 1947).

11. Joseph M. Jones, *The Fifteen Weeks* (New York: Harcourt, Brace & World, 1955), p. 151; Leahy quoted in Matthew Connelly Papers, box 1.

12. *FR* (1950) 1: Acheson notes for Congressional hearings, circa August 1950, pp. 393–95.

13. This is ably discussed in Walter LaFeber, *America, Russia and the Cold War 1945–1984*, 5th ed. (New York: Alfred A. Knopf, 1985). The key "turn" came on February 21, 1947, when a British embassy official informed Acheson that England could not give Greece and Turkey $250 million in military and economic aid (p. 51). See also Stephen E. Ambrose, *Rise to Globalism*, 3d ed. (New York: Penguin Books, 1983), ch. 5.

14. Ambrose, *Rise to Globalism*, p. 147, citing Kennan's famous "X" article.

15. LaFeber, *America, Russia and Cold War*, pp. 51–54; see also Freeland, *Truman Doctrine and McCarthyism*, pp. 98–100; also Joyce and Gabriel Kolko, *The Limits of Power: The World and U.S. Foreign Policy, 1945–1954* (New York: Harper and Row, 1972), p. 341–45. Richard J. Barnet emphasizes the importance of Mideast oil in the Truman Doctrine, in *The Roots of War*, p. 163.

16. Isolationist criticism of the Truman Doctrine noted that "the loud talk was all of Greece and Turkey, but the whispers behind the talk were of the ocean of oil to the South." (Justus Doenecke, *Not to the Swift* [Lewisburg, Pa.: Bucknell University Press, 1979], p. 77, quoting *Time*, March 24, 1947.)

17. Charles Prince, memorandum of September 1947, in Donovan Papers, box 73B, item 751. At that time, the United States controlled 42 percent and England 52 percent of known oil reserves in the Middle East, according to Prince.

18. *Barron's*, March 17, 1947; *The Commercial and Financial Chronicle*, June 5, 1947.

19. *Fortune*, June 1947; the same issue carried a detailed, well-informed article on Korea, which we will treat later.

20. *Fortune* (February 1950); see also W. A. Swanberg, *Luce and His Empire* (New York: Charles Scribner's Sons, 1972), p. 183.

21. Charles A. Beard, *President Roosevelt and the Coming of the War* (New Haven, Conn.: Yale University Press, 1948), pp. 580, 592–93, 597; the figures are from Godfrey Hodgson, *America in Our Time*, p. 32.

22. David S. McLellan, *Dean Acheson: The State Department Years* (New York: Dodd, Mead, 1976), pp. 4–13.

23. Aristotle, *Nichomachean Ethics*, in *The Basic Works of Aristotle*, ed. Richard McKeon (New York: Random House, 1941).

24. Charles Higham, *Trading with the Enemy*, pp. 60, 68, 123–28, 161.

25. Dean Acheson, *Present at the Creation: My Years in the State Department* (New York: W. W. Norton, 1969, 1987), p. 7, 10; also Barnet, *Roots of War*, ch. 3, "The Education of a Governing Class," where Barnet sees the ascendancy of this class beginning with Stimson's appointment (p. 53).

26. Robert Patterson Papers, box 19, cabinet meeting minutes, March 7, 1947.

27. Foster Dulles Papers, box 35, Arthur Krock column of September 24, 1948; see also Forrest C. Pogue, *George C. Marshall: Statesman 1945–1959* (New York: Viking Press, 1987), pp. 163, 207–8. Pogue has Acheson playing a key role in the Marshall Plan, but Charles Bohlen doing most of the writing (p. 210).

28. Acheson, *Present at the Creation*, pp. 29, 81, 102–3.
29. In 1960 he lumped together communism, revolutionary nationalism, and Islamic radicalism as species of mass "fanaticism." See Acheson, *Among Friends: Personal Letters of Dean Acheson*, ed. Acheson and David McClellan (New York: Dodd, Mead, 1980), p. 189. Acheson labeled the section on McCarthyism "the attack of the primitives" in his *Present at the Creation*.
30. I. F. Stone, *The Hidden History of the Korean War* (New York: Monthly Review Press, 1952, paperback 1970), pp. 203–4.
31. RG335, Secretary of the Army file, box 3, "Meeting of the Secretaries of State, War, and Navy," January 29, 1947.
32. RG353, SWNCC-SANACC, box 86, folder 334, "334 Committee, Interdepartmental, Korea." Acheson's approval is documented in 740.0019 file, box C-213, Martin to Wood, March 31, 1947. Participants in the interdepartmental committee included Benninghoff, Hodge and Arnold from the Occupation, Hugh Blakeslee, John Hilldring and Edwin Martin. At the same time, a draft paper for the Policy Planning Staff referred to "programs such as Greek, Turkish, Korean." (Policy Planning Staff file [hereafter PPS file], draft paper, March 28, 1947.)
33. See in particular 740.0019 file, box 3827, Vincent to Hilldring, March 26, 1947, and Hilldring to Vincent, April 7, 1947. The latter includes this statement: "Will you please prepare a statement for the Secretary regarding our proposal for taking control of Korea under a U.S. Commissioner."
34. Gardner, in Cumings, *Child of Conflict*, pp. 61–62; Bevin quoted in Harold Nicolson, *Diaries and Letters*, vol. 3 (London: Collins, 1966), pp. 107–8.
35. U.S. Congress. Senate Committee on Foreign Relations, Historical Series, *Legislative Origins of the Truman Doctrine* (Washington: U.S. Government Printing Office, 1973), p. 22; see also Lloyd Gardner, "Commentary," in Cumings, ed., *Child of Conflict*, p. 61–62.
36. On Sunday afternoon, June 25, 1950, Acheson cleared time to think, and decided that to back away from the Korean challenge would destroy American power and prestige: "By prestige I mean the shadow cast by power, which is of great deterrent importance" (*Present at the Creation*, p. 405).
37. RG335, Secretary of the Army file, box 3, "Meeting of the Secretaries of State, War, Navy," March 19, 1947. Forrestal said the strategic importance of Korea had been "overemphasized," which was not Acheson's point. On Marshall's concurrence, see also Pogue, *Marshall: Statesman*, p. 444.
38. A particularly good example of State's conception of the political-strategic value of Korea is to be found in John Allison's memorandum of September 9, 1947 to Kennan, in 740.0019 (Control) Korea, box C-214.
39. HST, Acheson Papers, box 65, handwritten note by Acheson to "Jim" (presumably James Webb), dated "August ?, 1950," and carrying the number 1063-b; also Acheson's memo of NSC meeting, July 27, 1950.
40. William Borden and Michael Schaller have done original and path-breaking work on the "great crescent" program (Acheson and the State Department used the term several times in 1949–1950). See William S. Borden, *The Pacific Alliance: United States Foreign Economic Policy and Japanese Trade Recovery, 1947–1955* (Madison: University of Wisconsin Press, 1984) and Michael Schaller, *The American Occupation of Japan: The Origins of the Cold War in Asia* (New York: Oxford University Press, 1985). John Lewis Gaddis finds an early use of the "great crescent" term in a PPS study of March 1949 (*The Long Peace* [New York: Oxford University Press, 1982], p. 89). I have set out my ideas at greater length in "The Origins and Development of the Northeast Asian Political Economy: Product Cycles, Industrial

Sectors and Political Consequences," *International Organization* (Winter 1984), pp. 1–40; and *Industrial Behemoth: The Northeast Asian Political Economy in the 20th Century* (Ithaca, N.Y.: Cornell University Press, forthcoming).

41. Schaller, *American Occupation of Japan*, p. 78; Hoover Presidential Library, Post-Presidential Individual File, box 462, Hoover to Patterson, May 7, 1947. As Borden points out (*Pacific Alliance*, pp. 65–66), Pauley did support reparations from Japan, urging that colonial industries be revived for the benefit of Asian nations that Japan had exploited, and that limits be placed on Japanese industry, so that its living standards were no higher than neighboring countries. His remarks on Korea indicate that he thought Americans should control Korean industries, rather than Korean leftists or Japanese—that is, the typical expansionist position one would expect from an independent oil man.

42. 740.0019 file, box 3827, Marshall's note to Acheson of January 29, 1947 attached to Vincent to Acheson, January 27, 1947; RG335, Secretary of the Army file, box 56, Draper to Royall, October 1, 1947. I do not know what gave Marshall this idea, so shortly after he had assumed his new position.

43. Borden, *Pacific Alliance*, p. 15.

44. John Roberts dates the influence of his "Japan crowd" from January 1947 onward (John G. Roberts, "The 'Japan Crowd' and the Zaibatsu Restoration," *Japan Interpretor* 12 [Summer 1979], p. 390).

45. Schaller, *American Occupation of Japan*, pp. 83–97.

46. Marshall Papers, box 3, "Meetings of Secretaries of State, War, Army, Navy," xerox no. 2327; see also an earlier document where an interdepartmental meeting brought "general agreement" on, but "no definite decisions in respect to," a three-year program for Korea as delineated in the interdepartmental report on Korea. (RG319, P & O Division, 319.1 Section IV, box 51, T. W. Parker memo to General Norstad, March 10, 1947, Marshall Papers xerox no. 2779.)

47. No author, "Korea," *Fortune*, June 1947, pp. 99–103. The only departure from the State Department position in the article is to laud Rhee as "the most American ideologically" of all Korean leaders.

48. Yi Ch'un-sik, *Sŏn'gŏ tokbon* [Election reader] (Seoul: Sinhŭng ch'ulp'an-sa, 1948), pp. 51–61, 94–95. After discussing Truman's historic speech to a joint session of Congress, formally declaring the containment policy, *The Seoul Times* cited an Associate Press report saying that Korea and Hungary "loomed biggest on the list of potential candidates for extension" of the Truman Doctrine's "declaration of support for free peoples." Ten days later the same paper included a Washington report that after the Greek and Turkish aid proposals were dealt with by Congress, officials would submit an aid package for Korea, here said to be in the range of $200 million. The article related that should such a new program eventuate, "it would seem to be a sweeping victory for Dr. Syngman Rhee who . . . has been in Washington urging [similar] changes" (*Seoul Times*, March 13, 24, 1947).

49. Kennan's memo to Lovett, June 30, 1947; and to Marshall, PPS file, box 33, July 21, 1947.

50. RG335, Secretary of the Army file, box 335, "T.N.D. Memo for General Draper," March 5, 1948, formerly top secret. Russell D. Buhite argued that declassified documentation merited a revaluation of Korea's importance to American foreign policy in the late 1940s, and therefore developed a conception of "major" interests, to explain those cases like Korea which are less than "vital" and more than "peripheral" (" 'Major Interests': American Policy Toward China, Taiwan, and Korea 1945–1950," *Pacific Historical Review* 47, no. 3 [August 1978], pp. 425–51). My

distinction, however, is between political-strategic and military-strategic conceptions, the former much harder to weigh than the latter.

51. RG218, JCS 383.21 file, box 33, section 17D, JCS 1776, "Action by Commanding General, U.S. Armed Forces in Korea in Event of an Invasion by North Korean Army," May 9, 1947; box 130, section 12, Hodge to JCS, August 30, 1947. In a cable of May 11, 1947, MacArthur said, "I place little credence in General Hodge's fear of a possible 'invasion.' " (Ibid., box 33, MacArthur to War Department, May 11, 1947.)

52. USFIK 11071 file, box 62/96, minutes of conference between Hodge and Wedemeyer, August 27, 1947.

53. RG218, JCS, 383.21 Korea, box 25, section 18, JCS to CINCFE, December 30, 1948.

54. 895.00 file, box C-945, memo of conversation, Dean Rusk and Lt. Col. T. N. DuPuy, August 18, 1949.

55. Koo Papers, box no. 124, 1947 interview notes. On April 26, Vandenberg informed Koo that a $300 million aid bill for Korea would soon come before Congress (Ibid.).

56. Matthew J. Connelly Papers, cabinet meeting minutes, March 7, 1947.

57. See especially his remarks in CP, 1977, item 316B, "Transcript of Roundtable Discussion on American Foreign Policy toward China," October 6, 7, 8, 1949.

58. Kennan Papers, box 23, "China," February 1948.

59. PPS file, box 2, PPS-39, "US Policy toward China," September 7, 1948; 82d Congress, Senate Committee on Internal Security, *Hearings on the Institute of Pacific Relations*, vol. 10, pp. 3986–87.

60. PPS, box 32, 99th meeting, June 13, 1949.

61. "So far as my limited observation qualifies me to judge, the average town Korean spends more than half his time in idleness, and instead of cleaning up his premises in his long intervals of leisure, he sits contentedly on his threshold and smokes, or lies on the ground and sleeps, with his nose over an open drain from which a turkey-buzzard would fly and a decent pig would turn away in disgust." George Kennan, "The Land of the Morning Calm," *Outlook* (October 8, 1904), pp. 366–67; see also Kennan, "The Korean People: The Product of a Decayed Civilization," *Outlook* (December 21, 1905), pp. 409–16.

62. See Cumings, *Industrial Behemoth*.

63. PPS file, box no. 13, Kennan to Rusk and Jessup, September 8, 1949. Earlier on Kennan had simply written off Korea. In establishing priorities for American aid to Asia in September 1947, he thought Korea would become a Soviet satellite, and knew the American military did not wish to make a stand there. So, "unless the United States takes military, political and economic measures far beyond the limits of practicability," Korea should be "eliminated or at best put at the bottom of the list, excepting for interim assistance in the immediate future." But, this also drew upon his assumption that Japan should have responsibility for Korea, not the United States.

64. Ibid., box 32, "U.S. Policy Toward a Peace Settlement with Japan," September 22, 1947. This document was the basis for NSC 13/2 of October 1948, the instrument governing the reverse course. See HST, NSC file, box 206. See also Roberts, "Japan Crowd," p. 399, who notes Max Bishop's prominent role in developing NSC 13/2 along with Kennan.

65. CP, 1977, item 316B, "Transcript of Roundtable Discussion on American Foreign Policy toward China," October 6, 7, 8, 1949. For a brilliant account of Japan's postwar position in the world economy see Jon Halliday, "The Specificity of Ja-

pan's Re-integration into the World Capitalist Economy after 1945: Notes on Some Myths and Misconceptions," *Rivista Internazionale di Scienze Economiche e Commerciali* 28, no. 7–8 (July-August 1981), pp. 663–81.

66. Harry Kern, "American Policy toward Japan," 1948, a privately-circulated paper, in Pratt Papers, box 2. "Remote control" was in Kern's quotation marks because it was George Sansom's term.

67. PPS, box 33, unsigned memo of April 29, 1949, probably by Kennan; the paper was quickly leaked to the *New York Times*.

68. Kennan Papers, box 24, "Assessment of Foreign Policy," June 23, 1950, originally top secret.

69. See for example his prescient analysis in 1950 of how atomic weapons had changed world politics, where he nonetheless likens these "weapons of mass destruction" to the concepts of warfare "once familiar to the Asiatic hordes." *FR* (1950) 1, pp. 22–44, "International Control of Atomic Energy," January 20, 1950.

70. Kennan Papers, box 24, speech draft dated January 9, 1950.

71. Eden, "The Diplomacy of Force," p. 39 and passim. John Lewis Gaddis does not distinguish between these three forces in American foreign policy, and thus conflates world view, world economy, and military doctrine into a single national strategy. See *The Long Peace*.

72. RG335, Secretary of the Army file, box 22, packet Ous 400.38 Korea, and Ous 121 Korea. The term "graceful exit" is used in a memo from Brig. General C. V. Schuyler, Chief of Plans and Operations in the War Department, to "Mr. Blum," January 2, 1948, in RG218, JCS, 383.21 Korea (3-19-45), box 130.

73. RG319, 091 Korea file, G-3 Operations, box 38A, Chamberlin to Director of Plans and Operations, February 11, 1947. General Wedemeyer, while arguing that American troops had to come out of Korea, nonetheless compared its strategic position to Austria's: a communist Austria would threaten Germany, and a communist Korea would threaten Japan. Koo Papers, box 124, interview notes, Koo interview with Wedemeyer, November 17, 1947.

74. Cumings, "Introduction," in *Child of Conflict*, p. 20; see also 740.0019 file, box C-213, "Summary of Conclusions at Staff Meeting," April 8, 1947.

75. 740.0019 file, box no. 3827, Hilldring to Vincent, April 7, 1947, and Vincent to Acheson, April 8, 1947.

76. RG218, JCS, box 130, Section 2, JCS 1483/44, September 22, 1947, and Memo for the Chief of Staff, same date; see also James F. Schnabel and Robert J. Watson, *History of the Joint Chiefs of Staff* (Wilmington, Del.: Michael Glazier, Inc.), vol. 3, pp. 13–14 (hereafter JCS, *Korean War*).

77. PPS file, box 33, Kennan to Butterworth, September 24, 1947; box 32, "U.S. Policy Toward a Peace Settlement with Japan," September 22, 1947; Cumings, "Introduction," *Child of Conflict*, pp. 23–24.

78. *FR* (1947) 6, p. 814.

79. Richard Robinson, "Betrayal of a Nation," unpub. manuscript (Massachusetts Institute of Technology), pp. 188–90; CIA, "National Intelligence Survey, Korea," NIS 41, compiled in 1951 and 1952, in Carrolton Retrospective Collection (CRC), 1981, item 137 B, C, D; item 138 A to E; item 139, A to C.

80. Johnson first met Rhee in Harris's church. (Thames Television interview with Johnson, February 1987.)

81. *Korean Survey* (April 1955).

82. RG319, entry 47, box 3, Rhee to Richards, Nov 21, 1949; Rhee to Richards, December 9, 1949; Jane Towner to Richards, June 3, 1950; Richards to Clarence

Ryee, June 24, 1950. These would appear to be letters intercepted by U.S. intelligence.

83. Goodfellow Papers, box 1.

84. Acheson worked closely with Hoover on the reorganization of the executive branch in 1947–1948 (Acheson, *Present at the Creation*, p. 242).

85. Oliver interview, August 1985.

86. 895.00 file, box 5693, E. Allen Lightner, Jr., memo of Nov 11, 1952. Oliver told me he doubted that Rhee ever took much for himself from the ventures of the Staggers group and its like, preferring to use their narrow interests to help his broader goals. (Interview, Robert Oliver, August 1985.) This is probably true, since it corresponds to Rhee's manipulations of wealthy backers in Korea.

87. Ibid.

88. "Excerpts from Conference at Korean Commission," November 18, 1946, Goodfellow Papers, box 1. Those present included Goodfellow, Williams, Staggers, and Ben Limb.

89. Patterson's appointment book shows a meeting scheduled for March 26 with Rhee, described as "President of Korea"; apparently the meeting was later canceled. Patterson met with Roy Howard in January 1947, before Howard left on a visit to Korea with his editors, then met again with members of the party in March 1947, after their return, to discuss revisions of American policies in Korea (Patterson Papers, box 20, box 98).

90. HST Official File, box 1304, George Maines to Matthew Connelly, April 30, 1947; Goodfellow Papers, box 1, letter of March 26, 1947, Harris to Vandenberg; Oliver Papers, letter from Oliver to his wife, February 19, 1947. Professor Chong-sik Lee provided me with limited access to the Oliver collection, which he controls. All references to this collection come from a computer printout that he sent to me.

91. Robert Oliver, *Syngman Rhee and American Involvement in Korea, 1942–1960* (Seoul: Panmun Books, 1978), pp. 56, 63, 95–98; he quotes a letter from Hilldring to Oliver.

92. Oliver interview, August 1985.

93. RG335, Secretary of the Army file, box 22, memo for General Norstad, Oct 2, 1947, "Report on visit to Korea with Under-Secretary of the Army."

94. Goodfellow Papers, box 1, Hodge to Goodfellow, January 15, January 23, 1947.

95. An example is Leon Gordenker, *The United Nations and the Peaceful Unification of Korea* (The Hague: Martinus Nijhoff, 1959).

96. RG353, SWNCC-SANACC, box 86, folder 334, "Interdepartmental, Korea." In January 1947 MacArthur suggested "submission of the entire Korean problem to UN," but this remained within the context of existing policy predicated on the Joint Commission discussions. 740.0019 file, box 3827, Vincent to Secretary, January 27, 1947, citing MacArthur's cable no. CX69369.

97. 895.00 file, box 7124, May 9, 1947, "Possible UN Assistance in the Conduct of Elections to Establish a Provisional Government in Southern Korea," prepared by the Division of International Organization Affairs.

98. HST, Acheson Papers, box 81, Princeton Seminar transcripts, February 13, 1954; RG353, SWNCC-SANACC, box 29, "Enclosure 'B' to SWNCC 176/27," "U.S. Policy toward Korea," July 25, 1947.

99. NSC 8, "The Position of the U.S. with Respect to Korea," March 22, 1948, is to be found *FR* (1948) 6, pp. 1164–69. Although Truman finally approved NSC 8 in April 1948, it was the culmination of a stream of documents in 1947, including SWNCC 176/30 of August 4, 1947, which argued that the United States could not withdraw from Korea, because if the communists came to dominate it would "se-

riously damage U.S. prestige"; SWNCC 176/30 also noted Congressional unwill-
ingness to fund a big program for Korea. It recommended that when the second
Joint Commission broke down, a letter be sent to the Foreign Minister of the
USSR suggesting various measures to resolve the impasse on Korea, which, if the
Soviets refused them, as was expected, would be the occasion for turning the
Korea problem over to the UN. The paper continued to argue that there was an
"urgent need for the positive program recommended by the Special Interdepartmental Committee" on March 22, 1947, and urged more pressure for congressional approval. The drafters thought if the policy won UN backing, Congress would be more likely to provide the necessary funds.

100. FO371, piece no. 69939, Allison communication to British Embassy, in Embassy
to Foreign Office, February 21, 1948.; piece no. 69941, Tomlinson minute on
Franks to FO, June 4, 1948.

101. 740.0019 file, box C-215, memo of May 23, 1949, enclosing a long study of Korean policy, untitled and undated, by David E. Mark.

102. Warren I. Cohen, *Dean Rusk* (New York: Cooper Sqaure Publishers, 1980), pp.
8–12; Lloyd Gardner, *Architects of Illusion: Men and Ideas in American Foreign Policy,
1941–1949* (Chicago: Quadrangle Books, 1970), p. 225.

103. 895.01 file, box no. 7125, Hodge to Secretary of State, November 21, 1947. William Langdon, author in late 1945 of the first plan for a separate southern regime, predicted in January 1948 that "a monolithic rightist regime will emerge
from UN elections in South Korea" (501.BB file, box 2173, Langdon to State,
January 10, 1948).

104. G-2 Weekly Report no. 100, August 3–10, 1947; see also RG43, U.S.-USSR Joint
Commission on Korea file, boxes 1 and 2, including official minutes of the Second Joint Commission; also RG332, G-2 Weekly Report no. 104, August 31-Sep-
tember 7, 1947; also no. 105, September 7–14, 1947; also USFIK 11071 file, box
62/96, transcript of a meeting between Hodge and Congressman R. Hebert, undated but it came at the end of the summer in 1947; also *Tonga ilbo*, October 22,
1947.

105. G-2 Weekly Report no. 93, June 15–22, 1947; no. 94, June 22–29, 1947; no. 98,
July 20–27, 1947. G-2 noted that Kim Ku had called for major demonstrations
against the Soviets and trusteeship on June 23, but "the masses did not rally to
the call" and the action fizzled.

106. *FR* (1947) 6, 771–73.

107. 740.0019 file, box C-213, Hilldring to Vincent, November 8, 1946, enclosing
Bunce's memorandum on his discussions in the north; RG59, Wedemeyer Mission, box 3, Hodge radio to Navy Department, July 8, 1947.

108. *Seoul Times*, September 27, 1947.

109. During the summer the CIA had predicted that an impasse at the Second Joint
Commission might produce "a dangerous possibility . . . the unilateral withdrawal
of Soviet troops in order to try to force a withdrawal of U.S. troops," which would
leave the South open to an attack by Korean units in the North. American intelligence estimated that Soviet forces had been drawn down to two divisions in
north Korea, and that they could be sent home in a month (Central Intelligence
Group, "Korea," SR-2; RG335, Secretary of the Army file, box 57, Jacobs to Secretary of State, October 8, 1947).

110. Schoenbaum, *Waging Peace and War*, p. 158.

111. *The Christian Science Monitor*, July 7, 1948, in John Foster Dulles Papers, box 38.

112. Townsend Hoopes quotes Elliott Bell: "Foster was not a man with a great deal of
come-hither" (*The Devil and John Foster Dulles* [Boston: Little, Brown, 1973], p. 6).

113. Koo Papers, box 124, Interview Notes, meeting between Wang Shih-chieh and C. E. Saltzman, October 2, 1947; Charles Bohlen said a 4-power conference was less in the U.S. interest than putting the Korea problem to the UN, in a meeting between Bohlen and Koo, October 10, 1947 (ibid.).

114. Shirley Hazzard, "The Betrayal of the Charter," *Times Literary Supplement,* September 17, 1982; the Fulbright quote is herein. I am indebted to Jon Halliday for alerting me to this article. See also Peter Lowe, *The Origins of the Korean War* (New York: Longman, 1986), p. 37.

115. Hazzard, "Betrayal of the Charter."

116. G-2 Weekly Report no. 106, September 14–21, 1947.

117. Kim Il Sung, 1948 New Year's speech, *Sun'gan t'ongsin,* January 1948.

118. Hoo was born in Washington, D.C., in 1894; he received a doctor of laws degree in Paris, and was vice-minister of Foreign Affairs, 1942–1945 (*China Handbook* [New York: Rockport Press, 1950], p. 752).

119. FO317, piece no. 69338, Kermode to FO, February 16, 1948; piece no. 69940, Kermode to FO, February 12, 1948; piece no. 69337, Kermode to FO, December 22, 1947, and January 25, 1948. See also *Seoul Times,* March 17, 1948.

120. Lowe, *Origins of the Korean War,* p. 44.

121. FO317, piece no. 69337, Kermode to FO, January 17, 1948; piece no. 69939, Kermode to Bevin, February 28, 1948; *Seoul Times,* January 16, 1948; HST, PSF, box 253, CIA, "Implementation of Soviet Objectives in Korea," ORE 62, November 18, 1947.

122. USFIK 11071 file, box 64/96, Weckerling to Hodge, March 8, 1948; and Weckerling to Hodge, April 24, 1948; FO317, piece no. 69337, Kermode to FO, January 17, 1948; piece no. 69939, Kermode to FO, January 21, 1948. Also *Seoul Times,* January 13, 1948.

123. 895.00 file, box 7125, Jacobs to State, April 1, 1948; USFIK 11071 file, box 62/96, SKIG Executive Order no. 23, June 22, 1948.

124. USFIK 11071 file, box 64/96, Weckerling to Hodge, March 13, 1948; "National Election Committee Action No. 2," April 21, 1948.

125. *Seoul Times,* January 23, 1948; USFIK 11071 file, box 62/96, "UNTCOK packet"; box 64/96, April 27 memo, Milner to Weckerling; 895.00 file, box 7125, Jacobs to State, April 14, 1948, enclosing an extensive "Report on Activities of the Office of Civil Information, USAFIK, and Department of Public Information, USAMGIK, in Publicizing Elections in South Korea," dated April 2, 1948.

126. USFIK 11071 file, box 64/96, Weckerling to Hodge, March 15, 1948, relating his "conversation" with Mughir; Weckerling to Hodge, March 8, 1948.

127. Ibid., Weckerling to Hodge, April 27, 1948.

128. Lowe, *Origins of the Korean War,* p. 44.

129. USFIK 11071 file, box 64/96, Weckerling to Hodge, "Daily Report of UNTCOK Activities," March 8, 10, 1948; Patterson's address is paraphrased in 501.BB file, box 2173, Langdon to State, March 16, 1948.

130. USFIK 11071 file, box 64/96, Weckerling to Hodge, "Daily Report of UNTCOK Activities," March 8, 10, 15, 1948; RG335, Secretary of the Army file, Royall to Secretary of Defense, March 16, 1948.

131. USFIK 11071 file, box 64/96, Weckerling to Hodge, memos of March 8, 9, and April 24, 1948.

132. Lowe, *Origins of the Korean War,* p. 46.

133. USFIK 11071 file, box 64/96, Weckerling to Hodge memos of March 8, 9, 1948.

134. Interview with Maj. Bennie W. Griffith, Jr., conducted by John Merrill. I am indebted to Dr. Merrill for this reference.

135. USFIK 11071 file, box 64/96, Fraenkel to Weckerling, April 23, 1948; Weckerling to Hodge, "Daily Report of UNTCOK Activities," April 24, 28, May 1, 1948. The description of Manet in Kyŏngju is in Hugh Deane Papers, "Notes on Korea," May 4, 1948.

CHAPTER THREE

1. Peter Viereck, "The Revolt Against the Elite—1955," in *The Radical Right*, ed. Daniel Bell (New York: Doubleday, 1955, 1963), pp. 135–54. Hofstadter's article in the same volume, "The Pseudo-Conservative Revolt—1955" (pp. 63–80), presented rollback constituencies as pathological, and later of course he penned a famous and influential article entitled "The Paranoid Style in American Politics." In the Bell volume Hofstadter wrote that those Americans who supported Hitler represented "almost all that was despicable—anti-Semites, fascists, Europe-haters, the bigoted and the crackpot" (p. 98). Yes, but "Europe-haters?" This most favorite pastime of generations of Americans is despicable like fascism? Furthermore rollbackers did not despise Germany, Italy, or Spain; Hofstadter's conception of Europe is England and France, the enlightened northern Europeans. (For an excellent critique of Hofstadter see Lawrence Goodwyn, *The Populist Moment* [New York: Oxford University Press, 1978], pp. 314–15.)
2. Thomas C. Reeves quotes this apt characterization of McCarthy by William Schlamm, in *The Life and Times of Joe McCarthy* (New York: Stein and Day, 1982), p. ix.
3. Charles Beard, *The Open Door at Home: A Trial Philosophy of National Interest* (New York: Macmillan, 1935), p. 197. This is still a brilliant book, written by a progressive historian who did not share the liberal-internationalist consensus of the post-1935 era. Roosevelt forged that consensus, of course, and was unappreciative: on the inside cover of Beard's *A Foreign Policy for America*, he wrote, "40 years' hard and continuous study has brought forth an inbred mouse" (quoted in Thomas C. Kennedy, *Charles A. Beard and American Foreign Policy* [Gainesville: University of Florida Press, 1975], p. 98). See also Ronald Radosh, *Prophets on the Right* (New York: Simon and Schuster, 1975), p. 39; and Harry Elmer Barnes, who sharply criticized the historians of the postwar consensus, Samuel Eliot Morison and Arthur Schlesinger, Jr., for their attacks on Beard and for their support of an imperial foreign policy. See his *Perpetual War for Perpetual Peace* (Caldwell, Idaho: The Caxton Printers, 1953), pp. 22–23, 65.
4. Karl Marx, "Bastiat and Carey," in *Grundrisse: Foundations of the Critique of Political Economy*, trans. Martin Nicolaus (New York: Vintage Books, 1973), pp. 883–88.
5. Lynn Eden, "The Diplomacy of Force: Interests, the State, and the Making of American Military Policy in 1948" (Ph.D. diss., University of Michigan, 1985), pp. 177–88.
6. Samuel Crowther, *America Self-Contained* (New York: Doubleday, Doran and Co., 1933), passim.
7. Polanyi, *Great Transformation*, pp. 3, 68–76.
8. George N. Peek and Samuel Crowther, *Why Quit Our Own* (New York: D. Van Nostrand Co., 1936), p. 12 and passim. Peek had been a Roosevelt advisor in the "first New Deal," before the triumph of internationalism.
9. See *The National Republic*, any issue from the late 1920s onward; the board of patrons is given in a letter from Walter Steel (the editor) to Willoughby, September 21, 1959, in Willoughby Papers, box 8.

10. See Zilg, *Behind the Nylon Curtain*, p. 369; good information is also available in Higham, *Trading with the Enemy*, pp. 162–64. See also Jules Archer, *The Plot to Seize the White House* (New York: Hawthorn Books, 1973); George Seldes, *One Thousand Americans* (New York: Boni & Gaer, 1947), pp. 287–89.

11. The Father Coughlin reference is in D. Clayton James, *The Years of MacArthur*, vol. 1, 1880–1941 (Boston: Houghton Mifflin, 1970), p. 442 (hereafter, *MacArthur*).

12. Gardner, *Economic Aspects*, pp. 85–86.

13. Gareth Stedman Jones, "The History of US Imperialism," in *Ideology in Social Science*, ed. Robin Blackburn (London: New Left Books, 1972), pp. 216–17.

14. Richard Drinnon, *Facing West*, pp. xiii–xiv, 278; Walter LaFeber, *The New Empire: An Interpretation of American Expansion 1860–1898*. (Ithaca, NY: Cornell University Press, 1963), pp. 69–71. LaFeber also notes that Alfred Thayer Mahan linked the navy with free trade, and to an America with an industrial complex that produced vast surpluses (pp. 85–95).

15. Bell, *Radical Right*, p. 47; Alan Westin, "The John Birch Society: 'Radical Right' and 'Extreme Left' in the Political Context of Post–World War II—1962," in Bell, *Radical Right*, pp. 201–26. Hofstadter wrote in the same volume that John Birchers "are in our world but not exactly of it"; their politics is "essentially pathological," and they speak a "private language" (p. 83).

16. Bernard Fensterwald, Jr., "The Anatomy of American 'Isolationism' and 'Expansionism,'" *Journal of Conflict Resolution* 2, nos. 2 and 4 (June and December 1958). For other interpretations of isolationism that abjure political economy, see Norman Graebner, *The New Isolationism: A Study in Politics and Foreign Policy Since 1950* (New York: The Ronald Press, 1956); Robert A. Divine, *Second Chance: The Triumph of Internationalism in America During World War II* (New York: Atheneum, 1967); LeRoy N. Rieselbach, *The Roots of Isolationism* (New York: Bobbs-Merrill, 1966).

17. Seymour Martin Lipset, "The Sources of the 'Radical Right,'" in Bell, *Radical Right*, pp. 259–312. Lipset found McCarthy's attacks on Eastern liberals as susceptible to communist infiltration "unique" in American politics (p. 329). Yet this was standard practice on the Right in the 1930s.

18. Justus D. Doenecke, *Not to the Swift*, pp. 12, 22–26, 43–46, 78, 120, 164; also Doenecke, *The Literature of Isolationism* (Colorado Springs: Ralph Myles, 1972), esp. p. 23; also Doenecke, "Power, Markets, and Ideology: The Isolationist Response to Roosevelt Policy, 1940–41," in *Watershed of Empire: Essays on New Deal Foreign Policy*, ed. Leonard P. Liggio and James L. Martin (Colorado Springs: Ralph Myles, 1976), pp. 132–61; also Wayne S. Cole, *Roosevelt and the Isolationists, 1932–1945* (Lincoln: University of Nebraska Press, 1983), esp. pp. 7–8, 37–38, 51–55, 103–9.

19. See for example Immanuel Wallerstein, "McCarthyism and the Conservative" (Master's thesis, Columbia University, 1954), pp. 4 and passim; Wallerstein also noted the ethnic German and Catholic constituencies for McCarthyism. I am indebted to Professor Wallerstein for providing me with a copy of his thesis. See also Martin Trow, "Small Businessmen, Political Tolerance, and Support for McCarthy," *American Journal of Sociology* 64 (November 1958), pp. 270–81.

20. Dean Acheson, *Among Friends*, p. 201.

21. Thomas Ferguson, "From Normalcy to New Deal: Industrial Structure, Party Competition, and American Public Policy in the Great Depression," *International Organization* 38 (Winter 1984), pp. 41–94; Ferguson, "Party Realignment and American Industrial Structure: The Investment Theory of Political Parties in Historical Perspective," *Research in Political Economy* 6 (Greenwich, Conn.: JAI Press

Inc., 1985), pp. 1–82. See also Michael Hogan, "Corporatism: A Positive Appraisal," and John Lewis Gaddis's attempt to understand what Hogan, Ferguson, and others are talking about ("The Corporatist Synthesis: A Skeptical View"), both in *Diplomatic History* 10, no. 4 (Fall 1986), pp. 357–72.

22. Beard, *Open Door at Home*, pp. 38–44, 64–65, 70–72, 149.

23. Ibid., pp. 130–31.

24. Carroll Quigley, *Tragedy and Hope: A History of the World in Our Time* (New York: Macmillan, 1966), pp. 880–82, 1245–47.

25. David M. Oshinsky, *A Conspiracy So Immense: The World of Joe McCarthy* (New York: The Free Press, 1983), pp. 160, 303–5. Studebaker, an innovative if smaller firm in the home market, sold cars abroad—for example, police cars to South Africa.

26. Cole, *Roosevelt and the Isolationists*, p. 109. Kohlberg thought that America would be saved by "small business men, by the veterans, and by the farmers." *New York Times*, September 5, 1950.

27. On DuPont see Zilg, *Behind the Nylon Curtain*.

28. The best statement of this point is to be found in Alisdaire McIntyre, *After Virtue* (South Bend, Ind.: University of Notre Dame Press, 1981).

29. John T. Flynn, *The Road Ahead* (New York: Devin-Adair, 1952), pp. 10–11, 59, 92, 139, 156.

30. See various letters from 1946–1948 in Robert Wood Papers, box 42; Frazier Hunt, *The Untold Story of Douglas MacArthur* (New York: Devin-Adair, 1954), p. 506; Anthony Kubek, *How the Far East Was Lost* (Chicago: Henry Regnery, 1963), pp. 446–47; Joseph P. Kamp, *We Must Abolish the United States: The Hidden Facts Behind the Crusade for World Government* (New York: Constitutional Education League, 1950), p. 27; MA, VIP file, box 5, H. L. Hunt to MacArthur, June 6, 1951.

31. Willoughby Papers, box 5, Willoughby to Austin B. Taylor, November 29, 1966; box 2, William F. Clarke to Willoughby, September 8, 1970; John T. Flynn, *While You Slept: Our Tragedy in Asia and Who Made It* (New York: Devin-Adair, 1951), pp. 27–38; Herbert Hoover Library, Post-Presidential File, Wedemeyer entry, copy of Ivan D. Yeaton to General Albert Wedemeyer, no date.

32. See David C. Martin, *Wilderness of Mirrors* (New York: Ballantine Books, 1980), pp. 199–200.

33. Polanyi, *Great Transformation*, pp. 9–12; Quigley, *Tragedy and Hope*, p. 52.

34. Hodgson, *America in Our Time*, pp. 113–14, 116–17. Hobson was probably the first to link internationalists and the concept of interdependece. See Giovanni Arrighi, *The Geometry of Imperialism: The Limits of Hobson's Paradigm*, trans. Patrick Camiller (New York: Verso, 1983), p. 104.

35. Acheson thought Japan an "obsteperous child," spawned by the West (*Present at the Creation*), p. 4.

36. MacArthur Papers, RG10, VIP file, box 5, Hoover to MacArthur, October 23, 1947.

37. Ibid., box 11, Wedemeyer to MacArthur, October 21, 1952.

38. Drinnon, *Facing West*, pp. 315–18.

39. See MacArthur's posthumous interview, *New York Times*, April 9, 1964; Willoughby, "Aid and Comfort to the Enemy," 1951, in Willoughby Papers, box 13; James, *MacArthur*, vol. 2, pp. 179, 717.

40. Richard Norton Smith, *Thomas E. Dewey and His Times* (New York: Simon and Schuster, 1982), p. 561.

41. Cole, *Roosevelt and the Isolationists*, pp. 55, 94, 111, 130–31; Goodwyn, *Populist Moment*, pp. 215–17, 234. See also Arthur F. Sewall, "Key Pittman and the Quest for the China Market, 1933–1940," *Pacific Historical Review* 44, no. 3 (1975), pp. 351–

71; and Partha Sarathy Ghosh, "Passage of the Silver Purchase Act of 1934: The China Lobby and the Issue of China Trade," *Indian Journal of American Studies* 6, no. 1/2 (1976), pp. 18–29.

42. Alfred Steinberg, "McCarran: Lone Wolf of the Senate," *Harper's*, November 1950, pp. 88–95. According to Peter Dale Scott, McCarran helped the Mafia obtain casino licenses in Las Vegas; he was apparently the model for the senator in the film, *Godfather II* (Scott, *The War Conspiracy* [New York, Bobbs-Merrill, 1972], p. 198; Oshinsky, *A Conspiracy So Immense*, p. 207).

43. U.S. Senate, Committee on Foreign Relations, Historical Series, *Economic Assistance to China and Korea: 1949–1950* (Washington, D.C.: U.S. Government Printing Office, 1974), p. 3. Blum notes that in 1949 McCarran wanted $1.5 billion in aid for Taiwan, of which $500 million would be for silver currency (Robert M. Blum, *Drawing the Line: The Origin of the American Containment Policy in East Asia* [New York: W. W. Norton, 1982], p. 43).

44. Wayne S. Cole, *Roosevelt and the Isolationists*, p. 55; Clark was associated with Tommy Corcoran and T. V. Soong. See Office of Chinese Affairs, box 4198, information in "descriptive entry," 793.00/6-2851. Thomas's remarks are in *Economic Assistance to China and Korea*, ibid., p. 36; also U.S. Senate, Committee on Foreign Relations, Historical Series, *Foreign Relief Assistance Act of 1948* (Washington, D.C.: U.S. Government Printing Office, 1973), p. 343. Acheson somehow was able to contain himself and sit quietly during Senator Thomas's monologue. When William Pawley conjured with "roll back" on the mainland, he thought invading forces should take silver coin with them ("minted in the U.S."), in case they ran into trouble (William D. Pawley Papers, box 2, "Russia Is Winning," p. 281).

45. Wellington Koo Papers, box 175, "Outline of Military and Economic Aid for China Recently Proposed to U.S. Government," September 1, 1949; box 124, conversation with McCarran, March 31, 1949; box 180, Chen-chih Mai to Koo, February 26, 1949. See also *FR* (1949), 9: p. 683, Koo to Acheson, August 15, 1949. Production of silver coins for Taiwan began at the Philadelphia and Denver mints in June 1949; Senator Clark of Idaho was involved along with McCarran. See Koo papers, box 159, folders E.1 and E.3.

46. Pawley Papers, box 2, "Russia Is Winning," p. 366.

47. See Willoughby Papers, box 7, folder "Mexico," including information on the Compania Exploradora Mineral Nacional S.A., and a letter from O'Crotty to Willoughby, August 13, 1956.

48. Ferdinand Lundberg, *Imperial Hearst: A Social Biography* (New York: Equinox Cooperative Press, 1936), pp. 174–76, 191, 193, 256, 310, 337. Lundberg said J. P. Morgan interests were third-ranking behind Mills and Hearst in the Cerro de Pasco mine. He noted that the Hearst-aligned National City Bank "dominated the economic and financial life of the Philippines," and that Hearst ranches in California were the state's biggest employers of cheap Chinese labor.

49. Seldes, *One Thousand Americans*, pp. 223–25; Robert Wood Papers, box 43, Wood to Courtney Whitney, September 7, 1951. Wood described Hunt as "not an educated man," but nonetheless "interesting."

50. Gardner, *Economic Aspects*, p. 271.

51. Herbert Hoover Presidential Library, Post-Presidential File, box 328, Fellers to Hoover, February 3, 1943; Fellers memorandum of January 1, 1953; Fellers to Hoover, November 8, 1955.

52. William Pawley Papers, box 2, draft manuscript "Russia is Winning," "prologue," and pp. 1–2; also Pawley, *Americans Valiant and Glorious* (New York: n.p., 1945); also William Pawley file, HST.

53. Whiting Willauer Papers, box 1, biographical file.
54. Thus Ben Anderson chooses MacArthur as his first, best example of American nationalism—his benedictory West Point speech in 1962 full of "ghostly *national* imaginings" (Benedict Anderson, *Imagined Communities: Reflections on the Origin and Spread of Nationalism* [New York: Verso, 1983], p. 17).
55. James, *MacArthur*, vol. 3, pp. 365–68.
56. James, *MacArthur*, vol. 1, pp. 57–58, 94.
57. PPS file, box 1, Kennan memos of conversation with MacArthur, March 5 and 21, 1948; *FR* (1949), 9, pp. 544–46, Moreland to State, memo of conversation between MacArthur and Huber Congressional Committee, September 5, 1949; MacArthur Archives, RG5, SCAP, box 1A, MacArthur, "Memorandum on the Peace Treaty Problem," June 14, 1950.
58. See James, *MacArthur*, vol. 1, pp. 383–84; vol. 2, p. 251; the last quote is from Robert Smith, *MacArthur in Korea: The Naked Emperor* (New York: Simon and Schuster, 1982), p. 231.
59. James, *MacArthur*, vol. 2, p. 406; see also W. A. Swanberg, *Citizen Hearst* (New York: Charles Scribner's Sons, 1961), pp. 516, 521; Cole, *Roosevelt and the Isolationists*, pp. 542–43; abundant information on Wood's backing for a MacArthur presidential run is in the Robert Wood Papers; for Hunt's backing of MacArthur in 1952 see MacArthur Papers, RG10, VIP file, box 5.
60. Biographical information from MacArthur Archives, Willoughby papers, box 1; also James, *MacArthur*, vol. 2, pp. 80, 90. Willoughby told Allen Dulles that he had excellent entree in Germany, because his father's family was "unimpeachable in Wilhelmian society." Willoughby to Dulles, March 17, 1955, Willoughby Papers, box 1.
61. Willoughby Papers, box 11, Willoughby to Sen. T. F. Green, April 30, 1958; transcript of Willoughby's testimony in the U.S. Senate, May 5, 1958; Willoughby, "Franco and Spain," *The American Mercury* (January 1960), pp. 23–32. The same issue carried a viciously anti-Semitic article entitled "Termites of the Cross." Willoughby apparently helped the World Anti-Communist League, then headquartered in Seoul, to obtain funds from the Billy James Hargis Crusade. See the letters from Jose Hernandez, Secretary-General of the WACL to Willoughby, Willoughby Papers, box 12. From the 1950s to the 1980s this League has brought together anticommunists in Seoul, Taipei, and other threatened right-wing regimes, with Japanese and American ultra-rightists. When *The Reporter* published its famous two-part study of the China Lobby, Willoughby wrote MacArthur that Max Ascoli, the editor, was "an Italian Jew" and that *The Reporter* had "Rosenwald money" behind it. MacArthur Papers, VIP file, box 12, Willoughby to MacArthur, August 7, 1952.
62. Willoughby to MacArthur, May 27, 1952, MacArthur Papers, VIP file, box 12; the diatribe about Johnson and Scalapino is in Willoughby Papers, box 10. The reference is to Johnson, *An Instance of Treason: Ozaki Hotsumi and the Sorge Spy Ring* (Stanford, Calif.: Stanford University Press, 1964).
63. Willoughby wrote to MacArthur on November 22, 1951, that Prange perhaps possessed internal histories of the Southwest Pacific Campaigns: "unfortunately, while I controlled all copies of your manuscript there were one or two intermediate working galleys that I have not been able to trace. I have certification of destructions [*sic*], by one of my henchmen; however . . . I am not certain that one set . . . could not have slipped through the dragnet? [*sic*]." MacArthur Papers, VIP file, box 12.
64. See Willoughby's letter to Sen. Owen Brewster, December 21, 1949, which Brew-

ster sent to Louis Johnson, Johnson Papers, box 103; Willoughby Papers, box 2, Willoughby to General Theodore D. White, February 17, 1956; box 5, Willoughby to Franco Noguira, Portuguese Foreign Minister, December 15, 1966; Herbert Hoover Presidential Library, PPI file, box 559, Willoughby to Hoover, October 21, 1948, where Willoughby advocated adding Franco's thirty-three divisions to the "Western front" against communism. There is some evidence of close contacts between the Spanish ambassador to Tokyo and MacArthur in FO317, piece no. 84092, Gascoigne to FO, July 18, 1950. Col. McCormick agreed with Willoughby about Franco, describing him as "the originator of war as we have known it for the last fifteen years." See a speech by McCormick, February 25, 1950, in Willoughby Papers, box 2.

65. One example of his ties to Japanese militarists is his offer to Ridgway of the services of "Col. Hattori" of Japan's "old officer corps," Willoughby to Ridgway, July 22, 1951 (misdated as 1950 in the original), Ridgway Papers, box 19. Willoughby wrote to Allen Dulles in 1955 that he had recently spoken with "certain Junker circles," and Dulles invited him to the CIA for a briefing, since Dulles also "had two very interesting meetings with them." (Willoughby to Frank Wisner, October 30, 1955; Dulles replied to the letter instead of Wisner, on November 20, 1955, in Willoughby Papers, box 1); on his ties to Gehlen and other anticommunist Germans, see Willoughby to Dean Rusk, October 20, 1961, ibid., box 10; Willoughby to Sen. Spark Matsunaga, January 1, 1968, ibid., box 10.

66. Willoughby Papers, box 5, Willoughby to Nelson Bunker Hunt, letters of December 2, 6, 1966, March 3, 11, 1968; the March 11 letter acknowledges a contribution to the *comité* from N. B. Hunt; Willoughby to Franco Nogueira, December 15, 1966.

67. On Willoughby's exclusive access to MacArthur, see the testimony of General Almond, Chief of Staff, Oral History Interview transcript, March 25, 1975, Almond Papers; Almond said he "knew very little about the details of [intelligence] information," and that Willoughby "had more access [to MacArthur] than any other staff member" in reporting intelligence information to the chief. On Willoughby being "very close" to MacArthur, see the observation of a British attaché in FO317, piece no. 84074, Bouchier sitrep, December 9, 1950; the quotations by Willoughby are from MacArthur Archives, VIP file, box 11, Willoughby to MacArthur, "1947" (no more specific date); also Willoughby to MacArthur, January 25, 1950; elsewhere Willoughby described MacArthur as having "the faith which moves mountains," lauded his "Scottish breed[ing]," and said his military moves "were like lightning." See MacArthur Archives, RG6, box 15, packet no. 2; Charles A. Willoughby and John Chamberlin, *MacArthur, 1941–1951* (New York: McGraw-Hill, 1954), pp. 356–58.

68. In this context Nietzsche wrote, "we who were children in the swamp air of the [eighteen] fifties are of necessity pessimists concerning the concept 'German'; we simply cannot be anything but revolutionaries—we shall not come to terms with any state of affairs in which the *bigot* is at the top" (*Ecce Homo*, trans. Walter Kaufmann [New York: Vintage Books, 1969], p. 247).

69. Quoted in *In Fact* 19, no. 23 (September 5, 1949), p. 2.

70. *In Fact*, April 17, 1950; the *New York Times* put Kohlberg's business at $1 million per year, and listed Goodwin and McKee as key members of the Lobby. Goodwin admitted being on a retainer of $25,000 per annum from Taipei, a princely sum in 1950, but the fee reportedly went as high as $40,000 a year. Describing him as "a Wall Street operator" and an advisor to Robert Young of the Chesapeake and Ohio Railroad, *The Times* also noted Goodwin's involvement with Father Coughlin

and the Rev. Gerald K. Smith, together with whom he had extolled Hitler and Mussolini in 1941. He was a well-known opponent of Roosevelt and the New Deal (April 11, 30, 1950). See also RG59, Office of Chinese Affairs, box 4198, "Notes on Alfred Kohlberg," July 23, 1951; and correspondence in Wellington Koo Papers, box 180, especially Chen Chih-mai to Koo, October 28, 1948. For additional details see Ross Koen, *The China Lobby in American Politics* (New York: Octagon Books, 1974), and Joseph Keeley, *The China Lobby Man: The Story of Alfred Kohlberg* (New Rochelle, N.Y.: Arlington House, 1969); on p. 24 Keeley refers to the "army of Chinese women."

71. John Foster Dulles Papers, box 35, Dulles to Walter Judd, February 2, 1948; box 42, Kohlberg to Dulles, February 15, 1949.

72. Koo Papers, box 180, Chen Chih-mai to Koo, October 28, 1948.

73. On the Pawley group see Pawley Papers, "Russia is Winning," pp. 80, 289–92. In December 1950 the group met and urged a "strategy of offense" against China, thus "to launch armies of Asians to fight Asians." On Howard, see various memos and letters in Roy Howard Papers, box 251, "China file" and "Asia file," including a January 5, 1950, letter to T. V. Soong, correspondence with Louise Yim and Syngman Rhee in June and July 1950; see also Willoughby to Howard, June 22 and September 16, 1950; Howard described K. C. Li as "an old friend of mine" in a letter of March 24, 1949 (box 243); Truman's characterization is in Walker Stone to Howard, December 1, 1950 (box 251).

74. *The Christian Science Monitor* discussed T. V. Soong's bankrolling of the China Lobby, in early April 1950. See Wellington Koo Papers, box 217, Koo Diary, entry for April 3, 1950; see also box 180, Joseph Ku to W. Koo, August 11, 1949 and September 15, 1950; Koo to J. Ku, June 9, 1949; box 217, Koo Diary, entry for October 12, 1949, where Koo says he "handed one thousand dollars to Utley for her research work." Robert Wood provided Utley with $2,000 to subvene the publication of her *Bungled Into War: From Yalta to Korea* through the Henry Regnery Company. Wood introduced her to H. L. Hunt, who apparently also funded her work. See Robert Wood Papers, box 18, Utley file. Peter Dale Scott asserts that the Bank of America was a "leading institutional backer" of the China Lobby; see Scott, *The War Conspiracy*, p. 222 n. This may involve California bank deposits by T. V. Soong estimated to have run into the hundreds of millions of dollars.

75. Tyler Abell, ed., *Drew Pearson: Diaries, 1949–1959* (New York: Holt, Rinehart and Winston, 1974), p. 212. The diary refers only to "Johnson," but it obviously refers to Louis A. Johnson.

76. Willoughby Papers, box 6, Willoughby to Kohlberg, February 8, 1950; see also box 2 for correspondence between Kohlberg and Willoughby in the early 1950s. By February 1949 if not earlier, Willoughby was feeding classified information to Kohlberg on alleged spying by Agnes Smedley and Guenther Stein, no doubt most of which Willoughby had collected to feed his personal fantasies. See Koo Papers, box 180, Chen Chih-mai to W. Koo, February 23, 1949.

77. David Oshinski quotes the "sockful" line in *A Conspiracy So Immense*, p. 111; the Soviet comment from *Izvestia* is in *New York Times*, March 27, 1950; "Communists and queers" and "egg-sucking liberals," ibid., April 21, 1950.

78. Or what one did not look like: Thomas F. Murphy, Federal prosecutor in the Hiss case, said

> The Communist does not look like the popular conception of a Communist. He does not have uncropped hair, he does not wear horn-rimmed glasses nor carry the Daily Worker. He doesn't have baggy trousers (*New York Times*, March 13, 1950).

79. Richard Rovere, *Senator Joe McCarthy* (New York: Harcourt, Brace, 1959); Vierick in Bell, *The Radical Right*, p. 150, see also pp. 137–39. Talcott Parsons is much fairer to this "gullible mass," viewing its broadest preference as isolationism, with nostalgic longing for simpler days of individualism and the frontier. See "Social Strains in America—1955," in Bell, *Radical Right*, pp. 175–99.

80. Viereck, in Bell, *Radical Right*, p. 150; Rovere, *The American Establishment and Other Reports, Opinions, and Speculations* (New York: Harcourt, Brace and World, 1962), pp. 9, 11, 13. On McCarthy's attack on the establishment see also Wallerstein, "McCarthyism and the Conservative," pp. 3, 18.

81. On McCarthy's German and Catholic ties, see Wallerstein, "McCarthyism and the Conservative," p. 22; Capehart is quoted in Hodgson, *America in Our Time*, p. 34. In 1951 a constituent wrote to Sen. Tom Connally, "The people of Texas are tired of this British Appeasement, that is being loaded on this country by the British, and the Britisher whose Title is Secretary of State [*sic*]." Elmer Adams to Connally, May 21, 1951, Tom Connally Papers, box 45.

82. Dirksen's statement is quoted in Wallerstein, "McCarthyism and the Conservative," p. 50.

83. On McCarthy's alleged homosexuality, see Drew Pearson, *Diaries, 1949–1950* (New York: Holt, Rinehart and Winston, 1974), pp. 188–89. Such rumors may explain why McCarthy was said deeply to fear J. Edgar Hoover. On McCarthy's fear of Hoover, see William R. Corson, *The Armies of Ignorance: The Rise of the American Intelligence Empire* (New York: Dial Press, 1977), p. 378.

84. Michael Paul Rogin, *The Intellectuals and McCarthy: The Radical Specter* (Cambridge, Mass.: MIT Press, 1967), pp. 103, 217; see also Mary Sperling McAuliffe, *Crisis on the Left: Cold War Politics and American Liberals, 1947–1954* (Amherst: University of Massachusetts Press, 1978), p. 81.

85. On Hoover, Willoughby, Whitney, and Smith helping McCarthy, see Thomas C. Reeves, *The Life and Times of Joe McCarthy* (New York: Stein and Day, 1982), pp. 318, 502; for the 1953 episode see Willoughby Papers, box 23, John W. Jackson letters, written on Justice Department stationery to Willoughby and to Ho Shih-lai, both dated October 16, 1953. The faked files (on Lattimore, John Service, and others) are discussed in Robert P. Newman, "Clandestine Chinese Nationalist Efforts to Punish Their American Detractors," *Diplomatic History* 7, no. 3 (Summer 1983), pp. 205–22.

86. The investigations of Grajdanzev and others are in Willoughby Papers, box 18, "Leftist Infiltration into SCAP," January 15, 1947 and thereafter; Willoughby supplied his 1947 studies to Benjamin Mandel of the McCarran Subcomittee after Mandel solicited them, and also stated that he had given them to McCarthy, box 23, Mandel to Willoughby, February 19, 1954. See also Willoughby to W. E. Woods of HUAC, May 1, 1950, Willoughby Papers, box 10.

87. Lindsay Chaney and Michael Cieply, *The Hearsts: Family and Empire* (New York: Simon and Schuster, 1981), pp. 130–31.

88. Reeves, *Joe McCarthy*, pp. 197–98; Oshinsky, *Conspiracy So Immense*, pp. 303–4.

89. *New York Times*, March 14, 22, 27, 31, 1950. For an excellent account of the Lattimore case see Stanley I. Kutler, *The American Inquisition: Justice and Injustice in the Cold War* (New York: Hill and Wang, 1982), pp. 183–214.

90. *New York Times*, April 4, 1950.

91. *New York Times*, May 16, 1950.

92. "Transcript of Round Table Discussion on American Policy toward China," State Department, October 6–8, 1949, CRC 1977, item 316B. Someone, apparently a State Department official, placed a big question mark on the original transcript,

next to Lattimore's point about collaborators in the Rhee regime. The transcript quotes Taylor as saying "cold prosperity sphere," obviously a transcriber's error which I corrected in the quotation. On Lattimore's support for the U.S. role in the Korean War, see *New York Times*, August 1, 1950.

93. See *New York Times*, April 8, 1950, on Kohlberg and McCarthy; Willoughby's role is obvious in Willoughby Papers, box 6, packet of correspondence with Kohlberg. Willoughby said that "Lattimore is only listed as a name in the French police section; the file is *empty*." In a letter of May 16, 1950, to Kohlberg, Willoughby said his own file was empty on Lattimore—files developed by combing Japanese secret police (*kempeitai*) reports from Shanghai—where in the 1930s, Willoughby opined, "were sown the dragon's teeth that have ripened in the Red harvest of to-day." Frank Wisner of the CIA visited Willoughby in May 1950, returning with his files on Soviet spy networks in the Far East; no State Department people, including Lattimore, were part of it (Papers of the Office of the Executive Secretariat, Summaries of Acheson's Daily Meetings, box 4, entry for May 2, 1950). O'Kelliher saw Wellington Koo on Lattimore, April 28, 1950 (Koo Papers, box 217, Koo Diary).

94. *New York Times* editorials, April 5, 19, 1950. Other responsible officials who held this "shocking view" were for example, most of the high Army Department officials in 1948–1949, who were ready to write off the ROK even if it meant a communist takeover; General Lawton Collins told the MacArthur Hearings in testimony deleted at the time, that Korea "has no particular military significance," and if the Soviets were fully to occupy the peninsula, Japan would be in little greater jeopardy than it already was from Vladivostok and the Shantung Peninsula.

95. At least in business circles. *American Affairs*, the journal of the National Industrial Conference Board, ran Utley's laudatory review of Burnham's *Coming Defeat of Communism* (12, no. 2 [April 1950], pp. 121–24); also another article entitled "The Soviet Worm in our School Libraries." Yet this was a centrist journal of opinion.

96. McAuliffe, *Crisis on the Left*, p. 147.

97. Perhaps the best example is John Paton Davies, a hard-line cold war liberal, who was just beginning a plan to build up the academic field of "area studies" and bring enormous amounts of government and foundation funding into American universities, through what was originally to be an institute of Slavic studies, but which subsequently became a model for the organization of studies of the communist world, and threatened Third World areas. Wild Bill Donovan was at the center of this effort, working with Davies and helping him to get foundation funding. The government was not to be involved, thus to allay suspicions that such institutes were little more than "an intelligence agency." Their work should be "impartial and objective," etc. However, a letter to Donovan from Clinton Barnard of the Rockefeller Foundation, dated October 28, 1948, says "the most compelling aspect of this proposal is the intelligence function which the Institute could perform for government." See the extensive documentation on this project in Donovan Papers, box 73a. Others involved included Evron Kirkpatrick, Robert Lovett, Richard Scammon, and many more. But Donovan described it to Davies as "your project."

98. On the role of White and Currie during World War II, see Higham, *Trading with the Enemy*, p. 223.

99. Isaac Don Levine, editorial in *Plain Talk* 2, no. 9 (June 1948), pp. 36–37; see also the editorial in 3, no. 1 (October 1948), pp. 32–34. Chinese Nationalist sources reported that Levine's "main concern is to drive the Communists out of North China and Manchuria." (Chen Chih-mai to Wellington Koo, October 28, 1948, "top secret," in Koo Papers, box 180.) It is not clear if Nationalist sources funded

Plain Talk, as many critics thought, but certainly they supported Levine's rollback policies in Northeast China.

100. Burnham, *Struggle for the World*, pp. 4–14, 48–55, 134–64, 181–83, 203, 228–36, 239; Schlesinger in John P. Diggins, *Up From Communism: Conservative Odysseys in American Intellectual History* (New York: Harper and Row, 1975), pp. 163–64, 322.

101. Burnham's involvement with the Office of Policy Coordination (see chapter 4) is documented in Bradley F. Smith, *The Shadow Warriors: O.S.S. and the Origins of the C.I.A.* (New York: Basic Books, 1983), p. 367.

102. Burnham, *Coming Defeat of Communism*, pp. 16–25, 135–40, 206–30, 256–66. See also "Our Spineless Foreign Policy," *The American Mercury* 70, no. 313 (January 1950), pp. 3–13, where Burnham again mentions Albania as an opportunity for rollback. The best study of the national security state is Barnet, *The Roots of War*.

103. Hoopes, *The Devil and John Foster Dulles*, p. 118; also *FR* (1950) 1: pp. 140–41, McFall to Webb, January 26, 1950; *Life*, February 27, 1950.

104. R. A. Wormser to A. A. Berle, Dana C. Backus, Joseph L. Broderick, and Donovan, February 20, 1950, Donovan Papers, box 76B. The committee is not identified, but seems to be a subcommittee of the New York Bar Association. All those named were prominent Wall Street lawyers.

105. Harry Elmer Barnes, "Introduction," in Barnes, ed., *Perpetual War for Perpetual Peace* (Caldwell, Idaho: The Caxton Printers, 1953), pp. 22–23, 62–65. The book was dedicated to Charles Beard.

CHAPTER FOUR

1. Quoted in Corson, *Armies of Ignorance*, p. 42.

2. L. Fletcher Prouty, *The Secret Team* (Englewood Cliffs, N.J.: Prentice-Hall, 1973), pp. x–xiii; Corson, *Armies of Ignorance*.

3. Corson, *Armies of Ignorance*, pp. 19–20.

4. Christopher Simpson, *Blowback: America's Recruitment of Nazis and Its Effects on the Cold War* (New York: Weidenfeld and Nicholson, 1988), pp. 90–96. For the OPC's budget, see Leonard Mosely, *Dulles: A Biography of Eleanor, Allen, and John Foster Dulles and Their Family Network* (New York: Dial Press, 1978), p. 245. On Stilwell, see Joseph Burkholder Smith, *Portrait of a Cold Warrior* (New York: Ballantine Books, 1976), p. 66, and Thomas Powers, *The Man Who Kept the Secrets: Richard Helms and the CIA* (New York: Pocket Books, 1979), p. 415.

5. Corson, *Armies of Ignorance*, pp. 303–315.

6. Ambrose noted that during Allen Dulles's days on Wall Street, he "worked on a daily, intimate basis with the political and industrial elite of Europe and the U.S."; both he and Foster came from the firm of Sullivan & Cromwell. Stephen E. Ambrose, *Ike's Spies: Eisenhower and the Espionage Establishment* (New York: Doubleday, 1981), p. 172.

7. Hoover Presidential Library, PPI file, box 328, Fellers to Hoover, January 11, 1953; Allen Dulles Papers, box 58, McCarthy to Dulles, July 16, August 3, 1953.

8. Donovan Papers, box 1, Kellis to Donovan, July 24, 1954. Kellis had been accused of being an American agent by the Chinese Communists, having been in the OSS in China in 1944–1945; he was active in collecting intelligence on the North Koreans, as we will see; he went on a mission to Greece with Donovan in June 1952. See ibid., Kellis to Donovan, December 3, 1952.

9. Ambrose, *Ike's Spies*, p. 170.

10. Corson writes that McCarthy "damaged the intelligence community so profoundly that one can only hope it will ultimately recover" (*Armies of Ignorance*, p. 378).

11. See Allen Dulles Papers, box 57, Ascoli to Dulles, April 8, 1952. See also Jon Halliday and Bruce Cumings, *Korea: The Unknown War* (New York: Pantheon Books, 1988), p. 72. The quotation on the CIA as a liberal refuge is from Corson, *Armies of Ignorance*, p. 27. Although he could not in the end prove it, Stanley Bachrach was convinced that the CIA funded the "Committee of One Million," another arm of the China Lobby (see his *The Committee of One Million: 'China Lobby' Politics* [New York: Columbia University Press, 1976], p. 55). In any case the CIA funded Chennault's airline.

12. Donovan Papers, box 120A, Carleton S. Coon to Conyers Read, "Wild Bill and Mac the God," February 8, 1945.

13. Corson, *Armies of Ignorance*, p. 205.

14. CRC, item 247a, JCS2106, March 13, 1950, notes by secretaries W. G. Lalor and J. H. Ives, on JCS visit to Far East, formerly top secret. SCAP also approved the entry into Japan of individual CIA people, on a case-by-case basis. For example, on June 2, 1950, it approved the entry of CIA employees Robert A. Stricklin and Raymond F. McClelland.

15. HST, PSF, CIA file, box 250, CIA memo of August 3, 1950.

16. Most of the information on this episode is still classified. But see Corson, *Armies of Ignorance*, pp. 319–23; Allen Dulles Papers, box 49, Dulles to Willoughby, January 22, 1951, where he says the recent agreements "will afford a real basis for effective cooperative action, and I am eagerly looking forward to working most closely with you *from here on*" (emphasis added). The Almond Papers document a meeting between Willoughby and Smith, January 17, 1951, in "Korean War Diaries"; a G-3 Operations Staff report wrote in awkward prose, "At the outbreak of the Korean War the relationship between the CIA and the Commander of an active theater had not previously been applied [*sic*]. Consequently there was some difficulty in arriving at a coordinated effort in covert and guerrilla activities. A recent agreement between General MacArthur and General Smith, CIA, provides for coordinated action." G-3 Operations file, box 37, "Utilization of Korean Manpower," January 29, 1951.

17. See Willoughby Papers, box 13, "Aid and Comfort to the Enemy," done in Tokyo in early 1951 by Willoughby or his staff; see also Willoughby's letter of May 22, 1964, to unnamed "editors," and Willoughby to Maj. General A. J. Trudeau, G-2, Department of the Army, October 8, 1954, box 5. In the latter document, Willoughby says that the entry of the CIA into the Far East meant that "the issue of central authority of G-2 (for which I have always fought) was at issue." The indications that Army historians charged Willoughby with destroying documents are in "War Department Correspondence, 1961–67," box 12. In unprecedented fashion for someone who was not an American president, MacArthur's papers and intelligence documents were deposited in Norfolk, Va., where for years archivists took it upon themselves to protect the general's place in history. Although this is no longer the case, it is true that the collection is surprisingly thin and spotty; it appears also that MacArthur never deposited even in this protected archives, the papers he used for his memoirs. See an article in *The Virginia Pilot*, December 5, 1971, included in Willoughby Papers, box 6. Willoughby never mellowed; in the right-wing *Herald of Freedom*, no. 47 (July 1971), he described the Center for International Studies at MIT as both "CIA-financed" (accurate) and "a hotbed of subversion" (ridiculous) (box 4).

18. Committee on Armed Services and Committee on Foreign Relations, U.S. Senate,

Military Situation in the Far East (Washington, D.C.: U.S. Government Printing Office, May-June 1951), pp. 123, 241 (hereafter, *MacArthur Hearings*).

19. *MacArthur Hearings*, p. 239; James, *MacArthur*, vol. 3, p. 416; Willoughby Papers, box 1, Leonard J. Abbott to Willoughby, May 15, 1951; box 6, Willoughby to Dan Catlin, October 29, 1969. An unpublished official study described the KLO as a small, covert, but "very active" intelligence agency. See "The North Korean Invasion of South Korea," no author, no place, file no. 228.03 HRC G.V. Korea 370.03, Center for Military History.

20. Donovan Papers, box 1, item 10, James Kellis to Donovan, August 31, 1950.

21. Thomas F. Troy, *Donovan and the CIA: A History of the Establishment of the Central Intelligence Agency* (Frederick, Md.: Alethia Books, 1981), pp. v, 23–28. This was originally an in-house CIA study, for the tutoring of new recruits. See also Corey Ford, *Donovan of OSS* (Boston: Little, Brown, 1970); also Anthony Cave Brown, *The Last Hero: Wild Bill Donovan* (New York: Times Books, 1982), pp. 35, 75, 103.

22. Biographical notes and 1919 trip diary, in Donovan Papers, box 132C; Walter Pforzheimer to Allen Dulles, January 11, 1965, citing Donovan's 1919 diary, Allen Dulles Papers, box 6.

23. Cave Brown, *Last Hero*, p. 13.

24. Ibid., pp. 76, 728, 735, 830. In February 1945 Donovan left Washington "suddenly and very secretly—he went to unusual lengths to cover his tracks" (p. 130). Smith is much less impressed with Donovan's *mystère*, but notes the same itinerant pattern. Bradley F. Smith, *The Shadow Warriors: O.S.S. and the Origins of the C.I.A.* (New York: Basic Books, 1983), pp. 32–33, 418.

25. Cave Brown, *Last Hero*, p. 821, quoting Whitney Shepardson, former chief of secret intelligence in the OSS; Smith, *Shadow Warriors*, p. 418. See also Troy, *Donovan*, p. 145, who remarks upon Donovan's distaste for research and analysis and his love of action.

26. Corson, *Armies of Ignorance*, pp. 182–83, quoting a Donovan memo dated October 24, 1942.

27. Extensive information on the foreign areas institute is to be found in Donovan Papers, box 73A; scattered information on Donovan's involvement in the University of Washington case is in box 75A, item 889, handwritten notes dated February 3, 1949; in these Donovan wrote, "communism is a disease of society—it needs quarantining."

28. Lynn Eden makes this point effectively, and rightly says that Wall Street corporate internationalists saw themselves as the universal class—"that the *special* conditions of its emancipation are the *general* conditions within the frame of which alone modern society can be saved" (quoting Marx; Eden, "The Diplomacy of Force," p. 286; see also pp. 84–87).

29. Transcripts of these talks are available in Dean Acheson Papers (Yale), box 17.

30. Christopher Robbins, *Air America* (New York: G. P. Putnam's Sons, 1979), pp. 27, 36, 43.

31. Willauer says Smith told him in 1953 that the communists were threatening in Guatemala, and Smith "wanted someone who had face to face experience with Communism." Willauer Papers, box 1, tape transcription of December 1, 1960; see also p. 72 of the guide to the Willauer Papers. Willauer was born in 1906, graduated from Princeton and from Harvard Law School, was a cofounder of the Flying Tigers, and later ambassador to Honduras and to Guatemala. On Willauer's role in the Bay of Pigs, see Scott, *War Conspiracy*, p. 9.

32. Willauer Papers, box 1, "secret" report on CAT dated in early 1951 (no exact date is on the document).

33. Drew Pearson reported that, according to Treasury Department information, the Nationalists had given Chennault $250,000 during World War II (*Diaries*, p. 60).

34. Robbins, *Air America*, pp. 48–49, 56–57, 70; the dummy corporation was known first as The Pacific Corporation, then as the Airdale Corporation; Whiting Willauer's papers indicate that Corcoran helped reorganize CAT in New York in the first three months of 1950 (Willauer Papers, box 1, packet, "CAT, 1948, 1949, 1951"); see also Koo Papers, box 161, packet on Civil Air Transport, listing Corcoran as secretary of CAT; also Ambrose, *Ike's Spies*, p. 250; also Scott, *War Conspiracy*, pp. xvii.

35. Pawley Papers, box 2, Pawley, "Russia is Winning," pp. 1–4, 250, 257–58, 280, 293–318, 330–48, 366–71, 443–44. Pawley claimed to have had "many dozens" of meetings with Truman in 1945–1950; the Pawley file at the Truman Library shows only a handful, based on Truman's official appointments book, but many may have been secret. Castillo Armas made his headquarters in Tegucigalpa, where Willauer was ambassador, before the attack on Arbenz. For Pawley's friendship with Nixon and his alleged ties to the Mafia, see Anthony Summers, *Conspiracy* (New York: McGraw-Hill, 1980), pp. 449–50.

36. *New York Times* obituary, December 25, 1970; Milton E. Miles, *A Different Kind of War* (New York: Doubleday, 1967), pp. 577–78. Miles was another pro-Chiang rollbacker who had ties to Central America; in the 1950s he enjoyed vacations in the Dominican Republic, reveling in the glamour of having *el jefe* pull up to his hotel, tooting the fancy fender horns of his Cadillac limousine. See the papers of Mrs. Miles, Naval War College, for these vignettes.

37. *New York Times*, August 26, 1935. I could not learn the outcome of the charges, but Goodfellow's son still remembered the incident clearly half a century later (Interview, August 1987).

38. *New York Times*, September 8, 1929; *Brooklyn Eagle*, August 1, 1938.

39. *War Report of the Office of Strategic Services*, pp. 26, 72–74; William Corson, *Armies of Ignorance*, pp. 178–80.

40. Corson, *Armies of Ignorance*, pp. 189–90, 195–96.

41. Philip Knightly et al., *The Philby Conspiracy* (New York: Ballantine Books, 1981), pp. 97, 121–26, 152.

42. Roosevelt, *War Report of the OSS*, pp. 73, 80, 83; Smith, *Shadow Warriors*, pp. 91–92, 171, 196; Corson, *Armies of Ignorance*, pp. 189–98. Roosevelt and Corson identify Goodfellow's office as "Special Activities/Goodfellow," but Smith calls it "Special Operations/Goodfellow." See also Goodfellow Papers, box 3, Memorandum of May 14, 1942.

43. Goodfellow Papers, box 1; *New York Times* obituary, September 6, 1973. In a letter to Hodge on July 21, 1946, Goodfellow mentioned that he had just returned from South America, where he found "the same Soviet pattern everywhere," something which he had communicated to "Mr. Hoover," on July 19, presumably J. Edgar given the FBI's responsibilities for intelligence in Latin America; but it might have been Herbert Hoover (box 1). China lobby people were connected to "operatives serving dictator Rafael Trujillo" in the late 1950s, according to Peter Dale Scott, but he doesn't name any (*Crime and Cover-up: The CIA, the Mafia, and the Dallas-Watergate Connection* [Berkeley, Calif.: Westworks Publishers, 1977], p. 8).

44. Hoover Presidential Library, PPI file, box 341, Goodfellow to Hoover, September 24, 1947.

45. Oliver, *Rhee and American Involvement*, p. 224; Oliver says Goodfellow wanted urgently to set up a Korean purchasing mission, presumably in the United States.

46. Goodfellow Papers, box 1, Rhee to Goodfellow, October 26, 1949, and December

1, 1949; Goodfellow to Chey Soon Ju, December 27, 1949; Chey to Goodfellow, February 3, March 8, May 10, 1950; Goodfellow to Chang Kee Young, April 4, 27, 1950; letter to E. A. Dockery, November 30, 1950; Goodfellow to Rhee, August 7, 1951; Goodfellow to Chey Soon Ju, March 11, 1953; Firth Sterling, Inc., to Goodfellow, July 21, 1954; Goodfellow to Rhee, October 16, 1956, and January 30, 1957. See also Roy Howard Papers, box 259, Shingoro Takaishi to Howard, December 19, 1951, discussing Goodfellow's plan to import automatic baking equipment to Japan; also reference to "the Japanese project" in which he was involved with Alan Goldsmith, in Hoover Presidential Library, PPI file, box 341, Goodfellow to Hoover, May 6, 1952. Goldsmith was a conservative businessman in New York who was involved with *The Freeman* and with business deals in Korea in late 1950. See box 341, ibid., Goldsmith file.

47. Far East 890.00 file, box 1863, Embassy to State, February 22, 1950. In 1944 Shoemaker was Lt. Commander for U.S. Air Combat Intelligence, and later was a SACO "intelligence officer." See Miles, *Different Kind of War*, pp. 318, 528.

48. *The Marine Digest* (Seattle), July 11, 1942, October 2, 1943, January 28, 1950, April 6, 1950, June 3, 1950, and June 28, 1952; Goodfellow Papers, box 1, Goodfellow to Rhee, April 12, 1950; Goodfellow to W. P. Kim, April 12, 1950; Bunce to Goodfellow, April 29, 1950.

49. Goodfellow Papers, box 1, Bunce to Goodfellow, January 28, 1950; Goodfellow to Rhee, January 31, 1950; Chang Kee Young to Goodfellow, September 2, 1949. Shoemaker was with Standard Electronics in 1950.

50. Quoted in Martin, *Wilderness of Mirrors*, p. 63.

51. *The Observer* (London), March 27, 1983; also *International Herald-Tribune*, January 3–4, 1981; I am indebted to Jon Halliday for providing me with these articles. See also Corson, *Armies of Ignorance*, p. 239, on MacLean's passing of Manhattan Project and later atomic bomb secrets.

52. Fitzroy MacLean, *Take Nine Spies* (London: Weidenfeld and Nicolson, 1978), pp. 253; see also Knightly, *Philby Conspiracy*, pp. 175–88, which is the fullest and best account of the still-classified Albanian operations, and Powers, *Helms and CIA*, p. 53. According to Leonard Mosely, 500 Albanian émigrés were "sent across the border" in April 1950 (*Dulles*, p. 278). Former CIA operative Harry Rositzke describes the Albanian operations as "a 'positive intervention' designed to unseat a Communist regime," and places the timing of the operations in 1949 and the spring of 1950 (Rositzke, *The CIA's Secret Operations* [New York: Reader's Digest Press, 1977], pp. 171–72).

53. Knightly, *Philby Conspiracy*, pp. 20, 40–41.

54. FO317, piece no. 83314, Burgess comments on FC10338/31, February 2, 1950.

55. Burgess's comments on FO317, piece no. 83313, January 30, 1950.

56. MacLean, *Nine Spies*, p. 232.

57. Michael Straight, *After Long Silence* (New York: W. W. Norton, 1983), p. 250.

58. Knightly, *Philby Conspiracy*, pp. 178–79.

59. The first view and the quotation are to be found in Corson, *Armies of Ignorance*, p. 327; the best example of the second view is Martin, *Wilderness of Mirrors*. Knightly et al. do not believe Philby was discovered before 1952, since they met another "bloody Albanian debacle" in that year (*Philby Conspiracy*, p. 240).

60. Alf Welhaven, "Gold Mining in Korea," unpub. ms., 1933; Spencer J. Palmer, "American Gold Mining in Korea's Unsan District," *Pacific Historical Review* 21, no. 4 (November 1962), quoting the Arab traveler on p. 380. I am indebted to Laurance Rand for providing me with the Welhaven essay.

61. T. P. O'Connor, quoted in Leigh S. J. Hunt Papers, biography by Jessie Noble

Hunt, written in 1947. Hunt also had interests in the first railway concession, the Inch'ŏn line, and Yalu timber forests.

62. Fred Harvey Harrington, *God, Mammon and the Japanese* (Madison: University of Wisconsin Press, 1961).

63. Herbert Hoover, *Memoirs. Vol. 1: Years of Adventure, 1874–1920* (New York: Macmillan, 1951), pp. 29, 38–40, 100, 107–8. Mrs. Janet Bosworth, whose husband worked at the Ŭnsan mines in the early 1930s, told me that everyone talked of how Hoover left an unpaid liquor bill in 1910 (Letter, July 21, 1985).

64. Palmer, "American Gold Mining," pp. 387–88, 390–91; see also Welhaven, "Gold Mining in Korea." Welhaven wrote, "my opinion is that the Korean is by far the best miner in the world for the money, and that Korean labor is the only really cheap labor."

65. Fred Harvey Harrington, *God, Mammon*, p. 161; Palmer, "American Gold Mining," pp. 383–87; Laurance B. Rand, "American Venture Capitalism in the Former Korean Empire," Columbia University Seminar on Korea, May 1984.

66. Ferdinand Lundberg, *America's Sixty Families* (New York: Vanguard Press, 1937), pp. 27, 269–70, 276; Lundberg, *Imperial Hearst*, preface by Charles Beard, pp. 19–20, 174–82, 191–93, 256, 310, 337. Lundberg noted Hearst's early praise for Hitler, and his audience with him in 1934 (pp. 343–44). Lists of the OCMC, Cerro de Pasco, Insular Lumber, and Homestake Boards of Directors are available in annual editions of *Moody's Industrials*. The 1919 edition shows that Hearst associate L. T. Haggin was second vice-president of OCMC, president of Cerro de Pasco, and on the Homestake board; Ogden Mills was on the OCMC and Cerro de Pasco boards. L. T. Haggin died in 1929, survived by a sister, Mrs. George B. DeLong, and a daughter, Ella Haggin McKee. OCMC later came to be dominated by Fassett and Mills interests, including a number of businessmen in Elmira, New York, who populated the OCMC and Insular Lumber boards. Five or six of them were on the OCMC board from 1925 to 1939, and in the 1950s they were still on the Insular board. Ogden Mills died in 1937, at which time he was on the OCMC and Cerro de Pasco boards. He was the grandson of Ogden Darius Mills, who returned from the gold rush a wealthy man, thereafter establishing himself on Wall Street, and making his family one of the wealthiest in the country; Ogden ran against Al Smith for governor of New York in 1926, was Hoover's treasury secretary and close friend, and was described in his obituary as "a bitter foe of the New Deal" (*New York Times*, October 12, 1937). The Mills-Reid family interest in OCMC continued up to Pearl Harbor, too; the 1940 edition of *Moody's*, for example, shows the Mills representative Roy C. Gasser, a Wall Street lawyer, on the boards of OCMC and Cerro de Pasco; he looked after Mills' financial interests (on Gasser see Hoover Presidential Library, PPI file, box 440, correspondence with Mrs. Ogden Mills; also Reid Family Papers, box C25). On Donovan and Mills and the founding of the American Legion, see Rodney G. Minott, *Peerless Patriots: Organized Veterans and the Spirit of Americanism* (Washington, D.C.: Public Affairs Press, 1962). Adolph Coors was director of the Seoul Mining Company, a Colorado firm, in 1914. It had capital of $500,000, and reserves estimated at $12 million. Its mines were located near P'yŏngyang, and several OCMC associates were involved with it as well, including H. E. and A. H. Collbran. (Hoover Presidential Library, Pre-Commerce file, box 65, Annual Report of the Seoul Mining Company for 1914.) Insular Lumber Company was managed by Harvey Pope in the late 1940s, and was described as "the largest" lumber company in the Philippines. (See Adm. William V. Pratt Papers, box 2, Adm. Berkey to Adm. Pratt, January 29, 1950.) On Whitney and Insular, see LBJ Library, Drew Pearson Papers, file G237, Douglas Mac-

Arthur, undated, unsigned memo. It is not clear from this file what the relationship was. The review of Lundberg's book is in *Kŭlloja*, no. 8 (August 1947).

67. Foster Bain, "Problems Fundamental to Mining Enterprises in the Far East," *Mining and Metallurgical Society of America* 14, no. 1 (January 1921), pp. 1–34. Also Boris P. Torgasheff, *The Mineral Industry of the Far East* (Shanghai: Chali Co., Ltd., 1930), p. 131. North Korea requested Japanese technological help for reopening Ŭnsan in April 1987, according to Economist Intelligence Unit, *Country Report: China, North Korea*, no. 2 (1987), p. 46. This report said the Ŭnsan mines were thought to contain up to 1,000 tons of gold, but that recent production had only been some 300 kilograms per year, worth about $4 million—"apparently because most shafts are flooded and hence unworkable."

68. Palmer, "American Gold Mining," p. 389; letter from Laurance Rand, January 15, 1984.

69. John D. Littlepage and De Maree Best, *In Search of Soviet Gold* (New York: Harcourt, Brace, 1937), pp. 26–29.

70. Reel 28, Shanghai Municipal Police File, report of January 19, 1940; also newspaper *Shanghai Zaria*, December 31, 1936, ibid. I am indebted to Kevin Marchioro for calling this file to my attention.

71. *New York Times*, February 8, 1939, April 22, 1941, April 24, 1947, February 8, 1949, January 28, 1955; Reel 28, Shanghai Municipal Police File, report of January 19, 1940; Donovan Papers, box 141, "Personal History of Serge Rubinstein." Drew Pearson linked Rubinstein to Boeing Aircraft, and thought his murder arose from a blackmail case (*Diaries*, p. 345). On Dmitri Rubinstein and Rasputin, see Alex de Jonge, *The Life and Times of Grigorii Rasputin* (New York: Coward, McCann and Geoghegan, 1982), pp. 265–66.

72. Laurence Rand letter, January 15, 1984; letter from Fred Hodgson, August 27, 1985.

73. The State Department said in a release of January 25, 1950 that the Soviets operated "several coal and gold mines" along the Yalu (*New York Times*, January 26, 1950); gold output in all Korea for 1944 was 16,636 kilograms; in 1947 it was 5,281 kilograms in north Korean state-operated mines (MA, RG6, box 79, intelligence summaries, no. 25, February 21, 1951). In 1949, 1.8 tons of gold were mined at Munp'yŏng in three months alone, and exchanged for Soviet "weapons, chemicals and machines" (MA, RG6, box 58, intelligence summary no. 2831, June 10, 1950).

74. See the diary of his trip in Reid Papers, no. 626, container C1.

75. RG332, XXIV Corps file, box 87, newspaper translations, *Chosŏn inmin-bo* [Korean people's news], June 1, 1946; *Chungang sinmun* [Central news], May 29, 1946. The *Chosŏn inminbo*, May 28, 1946, quoted Rhee on May 27 as follows: "I organized the US-Korean Economy Co[mpany] with Mr. Oliver, Mr. Goodfellow and other friends. This company is mostly concerned with gold and silver. The gold will be mined from [the] Unsan mine which is one of the two great gold mines in the Orient . . . when the government is established I will give this company the monopoly rights." Articles on the Ŭnsan mines had appeared in the press since March 1946, when the garbled name of Samuel Dolbear ("Samuel Dolbin") appeared, accurately stating that he had been appointed a mining advisor with USAMGIK through Rhee's intercession, and was then a representative of OCMC. See RG218, JCS, box 129, Hodge to War, March 18, 1946; this document mentioned an article that appeared in the *Chosŏn inminbo* in mid-March. It is also discussed in RG43, Joint Commission, box 9, US Military Mission in Moscow to State,

March 31, 1946. Since the U.S. Military Mission picked this item up, it may suggest awareness of Soviet sensitivities about North Korean gold.

76. Conversation with Kye Trout, nephew of Arick, April 10, 1982; letter from Janet Bosworth, July 21, 1985. On Cho Pyŏng-ok, see CRC 1981, item 138C, CIA, NIS 41 "Biographies of Key Personalities"; Herbert Kim was a graduate of the Colorado School of Mines who was employed by the Soviets in gold-mining in Siberia in the mid-1930s; he later worked in the USAMGIK Bureau of Mines (see Prostov to Davies, September 2, 1948, Donovan Papers, box 73A).

77. Jonathon Marshall, "Some Notes on the Secret History of Tungsten, 1940–52," unpub. ms. I am indebted to Dr. Marshall for sharing his manuscript with me. See also Office of Chinese Affairs, box 4210, Peking to State, March 21, 1950, where it is said that all Hunan and Kiangsi tungsten is going to the USSR under a ten-year contract; the figures are from the *New York Times*, December 27, 1950.

78. Marshall, "Secret History of Tungsten," quoting G-2 reports on Kodama and the *Los Angeles Times*, February 6, 1976.

79. Goodfellow Papers, box 1, May 14, 1942.

80. 895.00 file, box 5696, December 5, 1949, report by Pitt Hyde, enclosed in "Minerals, ROK," February 18, 1950; also Strong to State, September 10, 1952; also FO317, piece no. 76259, F17232, November 9, 1949, reprinting a *Chicago Tribune* article of November 6, 1949; also Robert B. Hall and Lewis G. Nonini, "Mining and Mineral Resources in the Republic of Korea as of 1961," unpub. ms. I am very grateful to Mr. Nonini for providing me with a copy of this report, and other helpful information.

81. 895.00 file, box 5696, Muccio to State, April 2, 1951; State to Muccio, April 21, 1951; Acheson to embassy, September 10, 1951; Willard Thorp and others, memo of telephone conversation, October 4, 1951; Acheson to embassy, October 16, 1951; 895.00 file, box 5696, Strong to State, September 10, 1952.

82. 895.00 file, box 5696, see a host of cables in September and October 1951, also Strong to State, September 3, 1952; Pusan to State, July 12, 1953; Seoul to State, October 7, 1953; the information on Crampton is in 895.00 file, box 5697, Chappelear to Young, September 24, 1953.

83. 895.00 file, box 5696, Thorp to Secretary of the Army, November 23, 1951; Gordon Strong to State, September 3, 1952. Muccio remarked that the Koreans "have endless reserves of the ore and perhaps feel they can afford to sign a contract disadvantageous to themselves as long as production is increased and more dollars can be earned" (Muccio to State, September 8, 1952).

84. 895.00 file, box 5696, Embassy to State, May 15 and July 12, 1953.

85. See Goodfellow Papers, box 1, Goodfellow to Francesca Rhee, December 5, 1951; Kenneth Mann to Goodfellow, July 21, 1954. Very little documentation is available on this deal, but Mann's background is interesting. He had been with Republic Steel in Youngstown in the 1930s, then joining the OSS and serving on Donovan's staff in 1943; as chief of one of four OSS divisions in 1944, he served with Wedemeyer in Chungking. In 1948 he was operating vice-president of Reynolds Aluminum, which had strong interests in Taiwan, and he then became chairman of the board and president of Firth Sterling in Pittsburgh, in 1949. Under his leadership, Firth became a major contractor for high-temperature alloys for jet engines and missiles (895.00 file, letter, Staggers to Mann, June 11, 1954, in 895B.2547; see also *National Cyclopedia of American Biography*, vol. J, p. 73).

86. *New York Times*, April 2, 1976, quoted in Marshall, "Secret History of Tungsten."

87. Marshall, ibid.

88. Jonathan E. Helmreich, *Gathering Rare Ores: The Diplomacy of Uranium Acquisition,*

1943–1954 (Princeton, N.J.: Princeton University Press, 1986), pp. 45–48, 160, 164, 174, 249–56. "Experiments in 1942 indicated that thorium . . . when subjected to bombardment in a cyclotron would decay into a fissionable 233 isotope of uranium." Further success with thorium in 1944—thought to be ten times as plentiful as uranium—meant that thorium "immediately became of strategic value" (p. 267n). Gregg Herken wrote that "because of thorium's relative abundance, its postwar control was more difficult than that of uranium," and says that General Groves particularly targeted supplies in India and Brazil (Herken, *The Winning Weapon* [New York: Vintage Books, 1982], pp. 14, 101–2, 108–10). On Pawley see ibid., and Pawley Papers, "Russia is Winning," pp. 317–19. Pawley does not give the date of his monazite mission to India, but he joined the State Department to do special missions in early 1951, and he says that "the American supply position for monazite sands had eased" by 1952. He writes that he was also directed to get India "to prevent ore and compounds of uranium and thorium from reaching Iron Curtain countries." Nehru said he would not ship it to the Soviet bloc, but refused Pawley's request to ship monazite to the United States; Pawley says he still got 500 tons out of India for "medical research."

89. Robert K. Wilcox, *Japan's Secret War* (New York: William Morrow, 1985), pp. 25, 35–38, 151–52, 166. This book is generally unreliable. I have sifted from it information that I consider factual and plausible. On Kodama's involvement with securing fissionable materials, see Murray Sayle, "A Patriot Passes," *The Spectator* (January 28, 1984), pp. 8–9. I am indebted to Jon Halliday for calling this article to my attention.

90. Intelligence Summary-North Korea, No. 38, June 15, 1947; see also no. 12 (May 1, 1946); no. 14 (June 22, 1946); G-2 Weekly Report, no. 42 (August 1–15, 1947).

91. KMAG G-2 Periodic Report no. 285, March 23–24, 1950; also Far East Office, box 1863, Taiwan to State, April 22, 1950; also MA, RG6, box 58, Intelligence Summary no. 2831, June 10, 1950.

92. Knightly, *Philby Conspiracy*, p. 194.

93. FO317, piece no. 83014, Dening notes on talks with Rusk, July 22, 1950; Hoyt S. Vandenderg Papers, box 86, Vandenberg to Stratemeyer, August 25, 1950; see also HST, PSF, CIA file, box 248, report for August 28, 1950, where it is stated, "this plant reportedly processed monazite which is a primary source of thorium and other elements used in atomic energy production."

94. RG349, FEC G-2 Theater Intelligence, box 465, November 23, 1950, G-2 report.

95. RG349, FEC G-2 Theater Intelligence, box 462, G-2 reports, August 6 and November 1, 1951.

96. *MacArthur Hearings*, vol. 3, p. 2187; *New York Times*, June 9, 1951.

97. *New York Times*, July 6, 1951.

98. *Far Eastern Economic Review*, September 28, 1950.

99. *New York Times*, May 23, 1950. On Grew's involvement with World Commerce, see RG335, Secretary of the Army file, Sam Duncan to William Draper, September 7, 1948. See also Agriculture Department, RG16, box 1942, Correspondence file of Secretary of Agriculture, and box 2041, "Investigations," both of which show no reference in 1950 or 1951 to these investigations. Archivists could find nothing about the soybean investigation.

100. Blum says Madame Chiang's group of Chinese in the United States in 1948–1950 included Chen Li-fu, H. H. Kung, Chen Chih-mai of the embassy, UN ambassador T. F. Tsiang, and T. V. Soong. See Blum, *Drawing the Line*, p. 21. Dean Rusk reported to Acheson in July 1949 that a broker on the West coast held T. V. Soong's $200 million account, and that total holdings by Soong and other wealthy

Chinese ran to $1.5 billion (Office of the Executive Secretariat, daily meetings, box 4, entry for July 5, 1949). On Corcoran's handling of some of T. V.'s accounts, see Office of Chinese Affairs, box 4198, information on China Lobby attached to 793.00/6-2851, terming Corcoran T. V.'s "chief representative." T. V. and T. L. met with Congressman Boykin of Alabama and with Sidney Souers of the NSC on March 21, 1950, T. V. suggesting that "in due time" the Nationalists would land 250,000 soldiers to retake the mainland, and urged American support for this; in early April Boykin said he had "drawn up a plan" with Soong and had met with Acheson aide James Webb about it on April 3 (HST, Sidney Souers Papers, box 1, Souers letter for file, March 21, 1950; Boykin to Souers, April 4, 1950).

101. *New York Herald-Tribune*, June 10, 1950; *New York Times*, June 10, 16, 1950; on Kung's visit to Willoughby, see Roy Howard Papers, box 251, Willoughby to Howard, June 22, 1950; the information on Wen is in Office of Chinese Affairs, box 4195, Hong Kong to State, June 22, 1950.

102. *New York Times*, June 16, 1950; the table is also drawn from daily soybean futures in the *Times*.

103. *New York Times*, June 19, 25, 26, 27, 1950.

104. I. F. Stone, The *Hidden History of the Korean War* (New York: Monthly Review Press, 1952; paperback, 1970), p. 352.

105. Office of Chinese Affairs, box 4223, Anne B. Wheeler to A.G. Hope, July 25, 1950; Hope to Magill, August 1, 1950. Hope drew up a full list of those involved in the speculation, document no. 793.521/7-2250, but it is not to be found in these materials. T. L. is termed "the worst of the Soongs" in Far East 890. file, box 4124, Barnett memo of conversation with Stuart, April 16, 1951. See also Stone, *Hidden History*, p. 350.

106. Far East 890. file, box 5647, Clubb to Merchant, August 3, 1950.

107. Pearson, *Diaries*, p. 250; Stone, *Hidden History*, p. 349. Pearson also refers to more Chinese soybean speculation in 1953, naming Dyke Cullum and one Li Kung. See also Sterling Seagrave, *The Soong Dynasty* (New York: Harper and Row, 1985), p. 489n.; and Scott, *War Conspiracy*, p. 196, who says, "McCarthy himself took part in the profitable soybean speculations, on the advice of a Pepsi-Cola lobbyist."

108. Hoover Presidential Library, box 341, Hoover to Goodfellow, May 17, 1951, acknowledging the soybean meal sent to him earlier. Goodfellow's letter is unavailable.

CHAPTER FIVE

1. This includes even the newest work. Robert Blum, for example, wrote an entire book on NSC 48 with but the barest mention of the rollback dialectic. See Blum, *Drawing the Line*.

2. Louis A. Johnson Papers, biography in the University of Virginia guide to the collection.

3. See Johnson Papers, box 102, for a thick packet of correspondence about the 1949 Bohemian Grove retreat. See also William Domhoff, *The Bohemian Grove and Other Ruling Class Retreats* (New York: Harper and Row, 1974). Johnson personally invited Dean Acheson to the summer encampment in 1949; others present included J. Edgar Hoover, Herbert Hoover, Mark Clark, and various and sundry oil and banking executives. The Korean War caused Johnson to miss the summer

1950 encampment, to his great regret; but California lumberman S. Orie Johnson later informed him that, in Herbert Hoover's camp at Bohemian Grove, "I got pretty well acquainted with a young chap, Richard Nixon, who is running for Senator from California. He is all right. I sincerely hope he beats the Left-Wing gal he is opposing, Googins, sometimes known as Helen Gahagen Douglas" (box 105, S. Orie Johnson to Louis Johnson, August 14, 1950).

4. Quoted in Blum, *Drawing the Line*, p. 17.

5. Robert J. Donovan, *Tumultuous Years: The Presidency of Harry S. Truman, 1949–1953* (New York: W. W. Norton, 1982), p. 61.

6. The Koo Papers are full of evidence backing up these points. On December 29, 1949, Griffith informed Koo about recent high-level discussions, including presumably the NSC 48 decisions; on January 16, 1950, O'Kelliher told him Johnson was about to resign because Truman had told him China policy was up to the State Department; Leslie Biffle transmitted highly secret Pentagon information in November 1950. See Koo Papers, box 217, diary entries for December 29 and January 16; box 180, Joseph Ku to Koo, November 3, 1950.

7. See for example Johnson's belief that he had kept MacArthur's June 23 memo on the Japan peace treaty secret from State, *FR* (1950) 6, pp. 1264–65, memo of telephone conversation, Johnson to Dulles, August 3, 1950. On March 17, 1950, Sidney Souers got a call from Johnson saying that Soong "had some startling information about Russian intentions" and Souers should immediately see him; this was part of a scheme worked out by Soong and Congressman Boykin to reverse American policy on Taiwan, discussed elsewhere. On March 21 Souers met with Soong and found he had no such "startling" information. See HST, Souers Papers, box 1, memo of March 17, 1950.

8. Cohen, "Acheson, His Advisors, and China," in *Uncertain Years: Chinese-American Relations, 1947–1950*, ed. Dorothy Borg and Waldo Heinrichs (New York: Columbia University Press, 1980), p. 21; Kennan Papers, box 24, Kennan memo on differences with the State Department, September 1951.

9. Louis Johnson, "US Policy toward Asia," June 10, 1949, in HST, PSF, NSC files, box 206. For the JCS judgment see Schnabel and Watson, JCS, *Korean War*, p. 36.

10. Dulles told Wellington Koo about his June conversation with Acheson on August 18, 1949. Koo Papers, box 130. See also minutes of the 41st Meeting of the NSC, June 2, 1949, HST, PSF, NSC files, box 220; RG59, Policy Planning Staff files, box 2, PPS53, "US Policy toward Formosa and the Pescadores," July 7, 1949.

11. *FR* (1949) 7, pt. 2, pp. 1046–57.

12. CIA, "Implications for US Security of Developments in Asia," July 25, 1949, National Archives, Judicial, Fiscal, Social Branch, Records of the National Security Council, NSC 48 file (hereafter, NSC 48 file).

13. Rusk, Memo for Acheson, "US Policy and Action in Asia," July 16, 1949; Yost to Jessup, July 18, 1949, where Yost says Rusk also intended an American defense of Taiwan; Acheson to Jessup, July 18, 1949; and Jessup to Rusk, July 21, 1949, all in RG59, 1945–1949 Confidential File, box C-846.

14. Michael Schaller, *The American Occupation of Japan*, p. 200; Blum, *Drawing the Line*, pp. 89–92.

15. 890.00 file, box C-846, November 18, 1948.

16. Schaller, *American Occupation of Japan: The Origins of the Cold War in Asia* (New York: Oxford University Press, 1985), pp. 182, 203–4; also Cumings, "Introduction," *Child of Conflict*, p. 47.

17. *FR* (1949) 9, pp. 519–23, account of Chennault's plan and his visit to the State Department on May 11, 1949.
18. Schaller, *American Occupation of Japan*, p. 183.
19. *FR* (1949) 9, pp. 556–58, Johnson to NSC, October 18, 1949. His comments came in reaction to the JCS's negative judgment.
20. NSC 48 file.
21. Davies to Kennan, August 24, 1949, PPS Files, box 13.
22. 795.00 file, box 4267, "Tentative Findings on US Policy in the Far East," September 2, 1949, given to Acheson by Jessup, Fosdick, and Case; it is not clear if they authored the document.
23. The October 14 draft is in NSC 48 file. The next draft was dated October 26; see James S. Lay, Jr., memo for Rusk, J. H. Burns, and Daniel C. Fahey on NSC 48, October 26, 1949, a "sanitized" version of which was declassified in 1981. This was not written by Lay, who was the NSC secretary; the authors are not identifiable (HST, PSF, NSC files, box 207).
24. *FR* (1949) 9, Bishop to Rusk, October 21, 1949. It is not clear if Bishop actually wrote this memo.
25. October 25, 1949, draft, NSC 48 file.
26. Office of Chinese Affairs, box 15, S. C. Brown to Philip Sprouse, October 24, 1949, formerly top secret.
27. John Allison to Butterworth, October 19, 1949, NSC 48 file; Schaller, *American Occupation in Japan*, p. 206.
28. CIA, "The Strategic Importance of Japan," ORE 43-48, May 24, 1948, HST, PSF, box 255.
29. CIA, "Consequences of US Troop Withdrawal from Korea in Spring 1949," February 28, 1949, HST, PSF, CIA file, box 256.
30. *FR* (1948) 6, pp. 1337–41, Bishop to Butterworth.
31. HST, Acheson Papers, box 27, "U.S. Policy in China," November 3, 1948, sent to Acheson by someone named "Joe" in the ECA, who was not necessarily the author. This was probably Joseph Jones, who at the same time proposed that the United States take the lead in "clearing China of communism on Japan's behalf," in Schaller's words (*American Occupation of Japan*, p. 142).
32. Quoted in Schaller, *American Ocupation of Japan*, p. 157.
33. Schaller, *American Occupation of Japan*, pp. 143–44.
34. HST, PSF, NSC files, box 20. NSC 41 was approved on March 3, 1949.
35. HST, CIA file, box 249, CIA, "Relative US Security Interest in the European-Mediterranean Area and the Far East," ORE 69-49, July 14, 1949. Another CIA memorandum from the period referred to "the US objective of containing communism in Asia" and linked Southeast Asia to the Japanese economy, saying, "the single most important factor in stabilizing [it] . . . is the procurement of low-cost raw materials and the recovery of markets" (Judicial, Fiscal, and Social Branch, Records of the NSC, NSC 48 file, CIA, "Implications for US Security of Developments in Asia," July 25, 1949). For other planning along these lines, see Schaller, *American Occupation of Japan*, pp. 213–45.
36. In NSC 48 file. The document has markings indicating it was coordinated with a CIA draft, if it was not itself drafted in the CIA; it also shows that Max Bishop, not an NSC member, checked it out on September 15, 1949.
37. Unsigned October 14, 1949, draft of NSC 48, in NSC 48 file.
38. See for example the October 14, 1949, draft, in NSC 48 file.
39. *Manchester Guardian*, April 1, 29, 1950. Willard Thorp thought the British feared Japanese competition, and wanted trade to go on within the Sterling group; they

blocked most-favored nation status for Japan and its adherence to GATT in 1949 (*FR* [1949] 1, pp. 666–69, Thorp to Acheson, April 22, 1949; pp. 715–26, report on 3d GATT session, November 10, 1949). In 1949 the British exported 940,000 yards of textiles, the United States 880,000; in spite of war devastation the Japanese were already up to 750,000, and this was only 30 percent of Japan's prewar average, when in the 1930s it became the world's most efficient producer of textiles.

40. Textile unions protested tariff reductions by the State Department in May 1950, saying that the industry was "the sacrificial goat" to American free trade policies. They recognized that low tariffs would benefit Japan most of all, and said the industry had lost 124,000 jobs since 1948 (*New York Times*, May 28, 1950).

41. At the 139th meeting of the NSC, April 8, 1953, "The President expressed the belief that there was no future for Japan unless access were provided for it to the markets and raw materials of Manchuria and North China." Secretary of Treasury Humphrey wanted the United States to be "aggressive" in providing Japan and West Germany with a secure position where they could "thrive, and have scope for their virile populations. In some respects, it seemed to him, we had licked the two wrong nations in the last war." Whereupon, "Mr. Cutler [Special Assistant to the President] inquired whether the Council wished to go further than this and adopt a policy which would look to the restoration of Japan's lost colonial empire." Ike said no, probably not (Eisenhower Library, Eisenhower Papers [Whitman file], National Security Council Series, box 4).

42. Howard Schonberger, "The Japan Lobby in American Diplomacy," *Pacific Historical Review* 46, no. 3 (August 1977), pp. 327–59; John G. Roberts, "The 'Japan Crowd,' " pp. 384–415.

43. See Jon Halliday, *A Political History of Japanese Capitalism* (New York: Pantheon, 1975), pp. 185–88. Roy Morgan of Ford Motor Company, long having a market in Japan, urged in 1952 a "general amnesty" for Japanese war criminals and an end to the purge, saying that "in the group of zaibatsu we find some of our most pro-American friends." Ridgway Papers, box 20, Morgan to Ridgway, January 23, 1952.

44. For example, Kern wrote to J. F. Dulles in 1951, saying that W. R. Castle had learned that the Japanese were willing to offer for American use in Korea "some of their intelligence agents, who formerly operated in China." See Kern to Dulles, January 15, 1951, John Foster Dulles Papers, box 53; he also wrote periodically to Allen Dulles. See the Kern file in the Allen Dulles Papers. Schonberger and Roberts also suggest that he may have had intelligence connections.

45. Walter Isaacson and Evan Thomas, *The Wise Men: Six Friends and the World They Made* (New York: Simon and Schuster, 1986), p. 21.

46. See various letters in 1937, Castle to Mills, Ogden Mills Papers, box 49; also Hoover Presidential Library, Post-Presidential Individual File, box 469, Pratt to Hoover, June 11, 1947; also several letters between Kern and Hoover, box 391.

47. James, *MacArthur*, vol. 3, p. 234.

48. Harry Kern, "American Policy toward Japan," no date, but sometime in 1948, Adm. William V. Pratt Papers, box 2. See also Kern to Eichelberger, October 30, 1948, in Robert L. Eichelberger Papers, box 22. Some members of the Japan Lobby also imbibed typical Japanese prejudices about Koreans. General Eichelberger, for example, a high officer in the Occupation, remarked to Kenneth Roberts that "I have 500,000 Koreans living in Japan ... potentially most of them are as red as one of your lobsters"; the half-million Koreans are "mostly bastards." A month later he suddenly found 700,000 Koreans in Japan, who were "the most

dangerous element from my standpoint" (see Eichelberger to Roberts, March 18 and April 19, 1948, and Eichelberger to Roy Howard, May 4, 1948, in Eichelberger Papers, box 19).

49. Bishop accompanied Royall, Dodge, and others on an important mission in February 1949; Alvary Gascoigne described Bishop as in agreement with Kennan on Japan, including a liberalization of the Occupation and a lessening of demands for reform. See FO317, piece no. 76215, Gascoigne to Dening, February 4, 1949.

50. Patterson Papers, box 35, address by Draper, "The Rising Sun of Japan," October 31, 1950.

51. R. C. Kramer, "Japan Must Compete," *Fortune* (June 1947); Felix Morely, "A Solution for Korea," *The Freeman* (October 30, 1950), pp. 81–82; Koen, *China Lobby*, p. 186; Kern to Pratt, February 15, 1950, Pratt Papers, box 2; Schaller, *American Occupation of Japan*, pp. 37–38. Kubek alleged that Grew and Dooman were forced out of the State Department for supporting the preservation of the Japanese emperor, in *How the Far East was Lost*, p. 282; for McGovern's views see *Seoul Times*, March 4, 1948, quoting Congressional testimony where he said, Japan is "a bastion of pro-American sympathy and ideology in the Far East," and "a bulwark against communism."

52. Acheson later remarked that "the whole period of NSC 68 came from the fall of 1949 to the spring of 1950"; he termed it "really one of the great documents in our history." Acheson Seminars, October 10–11, 1953, sessions.

53. Acheson wrote in 1961 that Nitze "is one with whom I find myself in agreement about 99 percent of the time" (*Among Friends*, p. 212).

54. *FR* (1950) 1, pp. 153–59, Yost, "Basic Negotiations with the Soviet Union," February 15, 1950; ibid., pp. 176–82, "Meeting of the State-Defense Policy Review Group," March 2, 1950.

55. *FR* (1950) 1, pp. 196–200, "Meeting of State-Defense Policy Review Group," March 16, 1950. Lovett had gone back to Wall Street, identified here merely as a "banker." See also Isaacson and Thomas, *Wise Men*. Like Acheson, Lovett was also deeply influenced by the diplomacy of Henry Stimson (pp. 28–29).

56. Michael Hogan, "Corporatism: A Positive Appraisal," *Diplomatic History* 10:4 (Fall 1986), pp. 370–71; see also Fred Block, "Economic Instability and Military Strength: Paradoxes of the 1950 Rearmament Decision," *Politics and Society* 10, no. 1 (1980), pp. 35–58; and Kolko and Kolko, *Limits of Power*, pp. 471–75.

57. *FR* (1950) 4, pp. 1168–84, Joint Intelligence Committee, U.S. Embassy Moscow, "Soviet Intentions," April 25, 1950.

58. NSC 68 is available in Thomas H. Etzold and John Lewis Gaddis, eds., *Containment: Documents on American Policy and Strategy, 1945–1950* (New York: Columbia University Press, 1978).

59. *New York Times*, March 12, 1950; *Barron's*, January 2, 1950.

60. For the Schaub and Thorp dissents see *FR* (1950) 1, pp. 218–20, 298–306; see also CIA, "Comparison of Selected Items in US and USSR Military Strength and Industrial Production," RR MP-35, formerly top secret, HST, PSF, CIA file, box 250. The study is undated, but carries figures for 1949, 1950, and 1951. See also Matthew A. Evangelista, "Stalin's Postwar Army Reappraised," *International Security* 7, no. 3 (Winter 1982–1983), 110–39.

61. *FR* (1950) 3, pp. 1007–13, Acheson to Acting Secretary of State, May 8, 1950.

62. PPS file, box 2, "U.S. Ojectives with Respect to Russia," August 18, 1948.

63. Acheson wrote that NSC 68 "became national policy" in April 1950, even though Truman had not signed it; I would agree. However, he goes on to relate, "it is doubtful whether anything like what happened in the next few years could have

been done had not the Russians been stupid enough to have instigated the attack against South Korea" *(Present at the Creation,* p. 374).

64. PPS, box 32, memorandum of discussion, June 13, 1949. Reinold Niebuhr sat through this exchange silently.

CHAPTER SIX

1. 895.00 file, box 7124, Maj. Gen. Albert Brown to Hodge, "Political Program for Korea," February 20, 1947.

2. See the following CIA studies: "Korea," SR 2, Summer 1947; "The Current Situation in Korea," ORE 15-48, March 18, 1948; "Communist Capabilities in Korea," ORE 32-48, February 21, 1949; CRC, 1981, items 137 B, C, D, 138 A to E, 139 A to C, "National Intelligence Survey, Korea," NIS 41 (compiled in 1950 and 1952).

3. RG59, Lot File 55 D150, "Records of the Wedemeyer Mission to China," various memoranda in box 3 and box 10; see especially box 3, "Korean Interim Government Briefing." Hereafter, "Wedemeyer Mission."

4. RG335, Secretary of the Army file, box 56, Osgood to Draper, November 29, 1947.

5. Tokyo despatch no. 80, July 14, 1949, courtesy of Gavan McCormack; FO317, piece no. 69939, Kermode to FO, February 7, 1948. Kermode also noted that the clear desire of most Koreans was for reunification; he thought them insufficiently fearful of communism.

6. Hodge told Wedemeyer in 1947 that he would not remove Cho Pyŏng-ok and Chang T'aek-sang, because if he did so leftists might get control of the police; yet an American police advisor said in 1947 that one "could not begin to reform [the] police without their removal." Cho and Chang were also "personal friends of General Lerche's." William Maglin, American director of the KNP, thought he had "never met a man more mature and a more true patriot" than Cho; "we differ on many things, but we have never differed on the question of fairness or what is good for the Korean people or country in relation to the police." If there were to be no reforms in the police, than few if any collaborators could be brought to justice. When SKILA finally passed a tepid anticollaborator bill in 1947, the police served notice on Hodge that they would "oppose the administration of the law" if Hodge did not veto the bill, so of course he vetoed it (RG332, XXIV Corps Historical File, box no. 21, Memorandum for Wedemeyer, no date, but circa August 1947; ibid., "History of Korean Department of National Police," which has the Maglin quotation; ibid., box 10, interview with Major Broom, Inspector, KNP, March 2, 1947; Richard Robinson, "Betrayal of a Nation," Manuscript, Massachusetts Institute of Technology, p. 146).

7. See the fine study by Carter Eckert, "The Origins of Korean Capitalism" (Ph.D. diss., University of Washington, 1986).

8. For a fine exegesis of just what I am talking about, see Roberto Mangabeira Unger, *Knowledge and Politics* (New York: The Free Press, 1975).

9. USFIK 11071 file, box 62/96, Hodge monologue to visiting Congressional delegation, October 4, 1947.

10. Juan Linz, "Some Notes Toward a Comparative Study of Fascism in Sociological Historical Perspective," *Fascism: A Reader's Guide,* ed. Walter Laquer (Berkeley: University of California Press, 1976), pp. 3–121.

11. Yi Ch'un-sik, *Son'go tokbon,* p. 63.

12. USFIK 11071 file, box 65/96, Brown to Hodge, November 20, 1946; G-2 special

report on the Northwest Youth, June 3, 1947, attached to G-2 Weekly Report no. 90, May 25-June 1, 1947; G-2 Weekly Report no. 105, September 7–14, 1947; no. 108, September 28-October 5, 1947.

13. G-2 Weekly Report; no. 108, September 28-October 5, 1947; no. 113, November 2–9, 1947; RG334, box no. 18371, 971st Counter-Intelligence Corps Detachment (CIC), "CIC Monthly Information Report no. 7, December 20, 1948; 895.00 file, box 7127, Muccio to State, January 10, 1949.

14. RG94, USAMGIK Special Reports, "Biographic Reports on the Cabinet of the Korean Republic," August 11, 1948, compiled from State Department Intelligence and Research Department files.

15. Louise Yim, *My 40-Year Fight for Korea* (Seoul: Chungang University, 1951), p. 282; Yi Pŏm-sŏk, *Minjok kwa ch'ŏngnyŏn* [Nation and youth] (Seoul: Paeksu-sa 1947), p. 68. See also Lloyd Eastman, *Seeds of Destruction: North China in War and Revolution, 1937–1949* (Stanford, Calif.: Stanford University Press, 1984).

16. 740.0019 file, box 3828, Jacobs to State, August 12, 1947, enclosing a memo by Vivian L. Parker, a USAMGIK advisor who had gone to Shanghai, dated April 5, 1947. Another MG official, Clyde Sargent, an apologist for the KNY who likened it to the American Boy Scouts, doubted that Yi had worked for Tai Li, although he said that Yi admitted that Tai Li had requested his services in May 1945, and Sargent did not know if he had accepted the offer or not. See ibid., memo by Clyde Sargent, May 8, 1947. On Miles and Tai Li, see Michael Schaller, *The U.S. Crusade in China, 1938–1945* (New York: Columbia University Press, 1979); on Yi's OSS foray in 1945, see *Minjok kwa ch'ŏngnyŏn*, p. 252.

17. CIA, "National Intelligence Survey, Korea."

18. Yi, *Minjok kwa ch'ŏngnyŏn*, pp. 28–34, passim.

19. 740.0019 file, box no. 3827, Langdon to State, January 21, 1947; RG94, USAMGIK Special Reports, Hodge to the Adjutant General, "Report on the Occupation of South Korea," September 1947.

20. Wedemeyer Mission, box 3, Ernest Voss, Semi-annual report on the KNY, September 2, 1947; G-2 Weekly Report no. 108, September 28-October 4, 1947; Hugh Deane Papers, "Notes on Korea," May 23, 1948.

21. Hugh Deane Papers, "Extracts from KNY Quarterly Report for Period Ending March 31, 1948"; also Wedemeyer Mission, Voss's Semi-annual report, September 2, 1947.

22. G-2 Weekly Report no. 117, November 30-December 7, 1947, where the G-2 refers to the group as "club-wielding, youthful terrorists"; G-2 study of Northwest Youth, June 3, 1947, attached to Weekly Report no. 90, May 25-June 1, 1947; Weekly Report no. 85, April 24-May 1, 1947.

23. Ibid., G-2 study of Northwest Youth; Robert Scalapino and Chong-sik Lee cite interviews with Mun Pong-je in regard to the September 1945 assassination of Hyŏn Chun-hyŏk, blaming it on communists; Army intelligence linked the crime to right-wing death squads (*Communism in Korea* [Berkeley: University of California Press, 1972], vol. 1, p. 321). The KNY propaganda organ, *Yibuk t'ongshin* [News from the North], is available at the Hoover Institution; various examples of southern and *Sŏbuk* leaflets are in RG242, SA2010, item 2/76, DPRK documents on "public opinion" in Haeju, marked "absolutely secret."

24. G-2 Weekly Report no. 95, June 29-July 6, 1947; G-2 Periodic Reports nos. 515 and 518, April 1, 23, 1947.

25. On this group see G-2 Weekly Report no. 98, July 20–27, 1947; also *Seoul Times*, May 10, 1947.

26. *Seoul Times*, May 28, 1947; *Minjung ilbo*, June 3, 1947; CIA, "National Intelligence

Survey, Korea"; G-2 Weekly Report no. 105, September 7–14, 1947; see also G-2 no. 97, July 13–20, 1947, which quotes Yi as saying that the Taedong Youth would be the "nucleus" for the southern army; on Rhee's control over the NWY, see G-2 Periodic Report no. 537, May 22, 1947.

27. RG334, CIC file, box no. 18343, 441st CIC Detachment, Semi-monthly Report, March 1, 1948; 895.00 file, box no. 7127, Drumwright to State, February 23, 1949.

28. William C. Bradbury, Samuel M. Meyers, and Albert D. Biderman, eds., *Mass Behavior in Battle and Captivity* (Chicago, University of Chicago Press, 1968), pp. 247–76, 284–90, 306–9. The volume concluded that Koreans in the camps were more procommunist than the Chinese: "The evidence of this study does support the belief that spontaneous anti-Communist sentiment was significantly more widespread and intense among the Chinese—and probably also among the South Koreans—than among the North Koreans." About one-fifth of POWs with domiciles in the South chose to go to the North when the war ended (p. 329; see also p. 216).

29. *Seoul Times*, June 5, August 17, 1948; RG335, Secretary of the Army file, box 56, Coulter to State, November 12, 1948.

30. USFIK 11071 file, box 62/96, "Labor Problems and Policies in Korea," June 18, 1946; this was the report of an official Labor Advisory Mission to USAMGIK. See also information on Chŏn Chin-han and *Noch'ong* in Wedemeyer Mission, box 3, "Korean Minutes."

31. RG332, XXIV Corps Historical File, box 10, Bunce to State, April 24, 1947; G-2 Weekly Report no. 94, June 22–29, 1947.

32. Deane Papers, "Notes on Labor in South Korea," July-August 1947, and "Notes on Korea," May 4, 1948.

33. G-2 Weekly Report no. 102, August 17–24, 1947; Hugh Deane Papers, "Notes on Labor in South Korea," July-August 1947; RG335, Secretary of the Army file, box 22, "Report on a Visit to Korea with Under-Secretary of the Army," October 2, 1947; Wedemeyer Mission, box 3, "Korean Minutes," report on Chŏn Chin-han.

34. HST, PSF, Daily CIA Summaries, box 255, February 21, 1949; ibid., NSC file, box 3, daily CIA reports on Korea, June 6, 1951; 895.00 file, box 5691, Drumwright to State, May 6, 1950; ibid., box 5694, Strong to Embassy, July 22, 1952.

35. Roger Baldwin Papers, box 11, "Report to Friends," May 23, 1947; "Civil War," May 16, 1947; "More Civil War," May 17, 1947; "Interview with Lyuh Woon Hyung," no date.

36. Edgar A. J. Johnson, *American Imperialism in the Image of Peer Gynt* (Minneapolis: University of Minnesota Press, 1971), p. 168.

37. G-2 Weekly Summary no. 97, July 13–20, 1947. This source said Yŏ was on his way to visit his friend Hwang Chin-nam, not Edgar Johnson.

38. The North Koreans acknowledged in 1984 that a grenade was thrown at the podium where Kim spoke on March 1, 1946; a Soviet soldier lost his arm in shielding Kim.

39. G-2 Weekly Summary no. 98, July 20–27, 1947; *Seoul Times*, August 30, 1947. See also USFIK 11071 file, box 62/96, Hodge's monologue with some visiting American congressmen, October 4, 1947, where Hodge said, "we happen to know that Kim Koo has a murder factory in North Korea, in South Korea, in China, and in Japan, so Kim Koo might have been behind the killing [of Yŏ]." Leonard Bertsch told me flatly that Kim Ku was responsible, but also said that he had first gotten Rhee's agreement (Interview, May 19, 1973). Seoul police said that Han had intended to kill Kim Il Sung, but could not do so because of his police protection. It

would be interesting to know if Han or members of his group were involved in the attempt on Kim's life on March 1, 1946.

40. Richard Robinson, "Betrayal of a Nation," pp. 222–30; *Seoul Times*, July 19, 1946, and October 10, 1946; RG332, box 21, handwritten notes from Korean-American conference, entry for November 12, 1946.

41. RG332, box 21, Bureau of Public Opinion, report of Bertsch's investigation, March 4, 1947; 895.00 file, box 7124, Langdon to State, April 14, 1947.

42. G-2 Weekly Summary no. 90, May 25-June 1, 1947; G-2 Periodic Report no. 624, June 30, 1947; Periodic Report no. 575, July 8, 1947.

43. CIA, "Prospects for the Survival of the Republic of Korea," October 28, 1948; Thames Television interview with Yŏ Yŏn-gu, P'yŏngyang, November 1987.

44. Hodge's eulogy at Yŏ's funeral was distant and tepid; the general delivered himself of but one line of praise: that Yŏ was a man of "moderation, tolerance, and understanding" (USFIK 11071 file, box 62/96). Shortly after his death Kim Il Sung called Yŏ "one of the fine patriots of the Korean people, sacrificed at the hands of the pro-Japanese and national traitors" (RG242, SA2005, item 1/34, Kim Il Sung, "Report on the 2nd Anniversary of Liberation," August 14, 1947).

45. FO371, piece no. 69937, Kermode to FO, December 1, 1947.

46. 895.00 file, box 7126, Jacobs to State, August 16, 1948.

47. G-2 weekly report, no. 117, November 30-December 7, 1947; FO317, piece 69937, Kermode to FO, December 19, 1947; piece no. 69939, Kermode to FO, January 26, 1948; Deane Papers, "Notes on Korea," March 20, 1948; *Seoul Times*, December 4, 5, 1947, January 17, March 8, 18, 1948. Kermode discussed Chang's collaboration with the Japanese, but also thought him "the most intelligent politician on the right."

48. 895.00 file, box 7128, Jacobs to State, July 24, 1948, enclosing the text of Rhee's inaugural of the same day.

49. Rhee first began using *Ilminjuŭi* during a speaking tour in April 1949. See 895.00 file, box 7127, Drumwright to State, May 17, 1949; on the doctrine itself see Syngman Rhee, *Ilminjuŭi kaesul* [Outline of the One People Principle] (Seoul: Ilminjuŭi po'gŭp-hoe, 1949), pp. 2–10; also Koh Kwang-il, "In Quest of National Unity and Power: Political Ideas and Practices of Syngman Rhee" (Ph.D. diss., Rutgers, 1962), pp. 63–65.

50. "Round Table Conference on the Philosophy of Ilminjuui," *Yŏnhap sinmun*, January 21, 1949; text in 795.00 file, box 4262, Embassy to State, February 1, 1950. I have not been able to locate the Korean original, so the translation is the Embassy's.

51. 795.00 file, box 4262, Embassy to State, January 18, 1950; ibid., Drumwright to State, March 15, 1950.

52. Robinson, "Betrayal of a Nation," pp. 249–50; Gregory Henderson, *Korea: The Politics of the Vortex* (Cambridge, Mass.: Harvard University Press, 1968), p. 141; 795.00 file, box 4262, Drumwright to State, March 25, 1950; see also ibid., box 4299, Embassy to State, May 12, 1950, where An is termed "Nazi-like." Barrington Moore, Jr.'s, fine passage on "Catonism" includes this judgment: "Reactionary social theories are liable to flourish in a landed upper class that manages to hang onto political power successfully although it is losing out economically or perhaps is threatened by a new and strange source of economic power" (*Social Origins of Dictatorship and Democracy* [Boston: Beacon Press, 1966], p. 490).

53. "Round Table Conference"; see also An Ho-sang, *Minjok ŭi chuch'esŏng kwa hwarangŏl* [The subjectivity and Hwarang spirit of the nation] (Seoul: Paedal munhwa

yŏn'gu-wŏn, 1967); in English see An Ho-sang, *The Ancient History of the Korea-Dong-I Race: Creator of East Asian Culture* (Seoul: Institute of Paedal Culture, 1974).

54. 895.00 file, box 5691, Drumwright to State, January 7, 1950.

55. 895.00 file, box 7127, Drumwright to State, March 14, 1949.

56. Yung Myung Lhee, "The Policies of Syngman Rhee and the U.S. (1945–1950)" (Master's thesis, University of Chicago, 1962), pp. 64–66; 895.00 file, box 7127, Muccio to State, April 18, 1949; ibid., Drumwright to State, May 17, 1949.

57. 895.00 file, box 7128, Drumwright to State, August 25, 1949; CIA, "National Intelligence Survey, Korea."

58. 795.00 file, box 4299, Drumwright to State, May 1, 1950, enclosing a translation of An's speech; ibid., Drumwright to State, June 15, 1950.

59. This was my impression from a number of interviews for the Thames Television documentary. It also is unfortunately common to hear Americans say that Koreans are brutal bastards. The late Richard Sneider, former U.S. ambassador to the ROK, addressed a small group at the University of Washington in 1979, which I attended. After the one Korean present left the room, he blithely remarked, "You know the Koreans; they like to beat each other up."

60. CIA, "National Intelligence Survey, Korea." This study noted "an almost complete absence at the top levels of young, reliable and trained Korean administrators"; those Koreans with administrative experience were "all of pro-Japanese sympathies." Administrative talent was mainly to be found in departments charged with "the maintenance of order."

61. 895.00 file, box 7127, Muccio to State, November 7, 1949; ibid., Muccio to State, December 2, 1949; ibid., Embassy to State, November 21, 1949; the originals of the oaths may be found in RG242, "Captured Enemy Documents," SA2009, Item 7/67.

62. HST, PSF, NSC file, box 205, CIA, "Review of the World Situation," December 16, 1948; HST, PSF, NSC file, box 257, CIA, "Communist Capabilities in South Korea," ORE 32-48, February 21, 1949; 895.00 file, box 7124, Langdon to State, December 12, 1947; 895.00 file, box 7128, Muccio to State, December 10, 1949; 895.00 file, Embassy to State, December 10, 1949. In another memo (Muccio to State, December 9, 1949), the rate of arrests in early December is put at two thousand in a three-day period.

63. 895.00 file, Muccio to State, December 20, 1949; *Tonga ilbo*, December 16, 1949; Muccio's praise of Kim is in Muccio to State, September 27, 1949; FO317, piece no. 84053, Holt to FO, May 1, 1950, "Annual Political Report for the Year, 1949"; Rios-Mont quoted in *New York Times*, December 6, 1982.

64. 795.00 file, box 4262, Embassy to State, January 18, 1950; 895.00 file, box 7128, Embassy to State, December 10, 1949; FO317, piece no. 76259, Holt to FO, October 13, 1949.

65. RG319, entry 47, box 3: letter, "Angela" to Ray Richards, January 27, 1950. I do not know who she was.

66. CIA, "Prospects for the Survival of the Republic of Korea," ORE 44–48, October 28, 1948; CIA, "National Intelligence Survey, Korea."

67. CIA, "Prospects for the Survival."

68. *New York Times*, March 14, 1950; 795.00 file, box 4299, Drumwright to State, March 22, 1950, enclosing Fraenkel's analysis of the trial; additional information on this case may be found in 895.00 file, box 7128, memo on the trials, December 2, 1949.

69. The listing of provincial officials is attached to 895.00 file, box 7127, March 17, 1949, trip by McDonald and Rozier through the provinces.

70. G-2 Weekly Report no. 122, January 9–16, 1948.

71. CIA, "The Current Situation in Korea," ORE 15–48, March 18, 1948.

72. RG335, Secretary of the Army file, box 57, Jacobs to State, March 30, 1948.

73. 895.00 file, box 7127, Embassy to State, June 29, 1949; also Thames Television interview with Kim's former secretary, Shin Ki-ŏn, P'yŏngyang, November 1987.

74. Deane Papers, "Notes on Korea," June 9, 1948.

75. *Seoul Sinmun*, March 16–23, 1950, enclosed in 795.00 file, box 4299, Drumwright to State, April 3, 1950; CIA, "National Intelligence Survey, Korea."

76. CIA, "National Intelligence Survey, Korea."

77. *Seoul Times*, July 3, 1947; Hodge reported in April 1948 that Jaisohn refused to be "a candidate for President," because "another Korean winter will kill him" (RG335, Secretary of the Army file, box 57, Hodge to State, April 1, 1948). Channing Liem, an associate of Jaisohn's who graduated from Lafayette College, held a Ph.D. from Princeton, was an ordained Presbyterian minister, and who taught political science at Princeton in the late 1940s, joined Jaisohn as an assistant in Korea in 1948. Shortly after the Korean War began, Liem and Col. J. W. Fraser, a former military attaché in Seoul, sought again to utilize Jaisohn's services, this time in a propaganda and public affairs capacity. See 795.00 file, box 4267, Fraser to Weckerling, July 26, 1950, attached to 795.00/8-250.

78. Chang's CIA biography describes him (and Hŏ Chŏng) as more reasonable and less nationalistic than other Korean politicians (CIA, "National Intelligence Survey, Korea"); Muccio's communication to Rusk described Rhee as senile, and compared him to Chiang Kai-shek: "we have the same danger here that exploded in our face in China." It is not clear whether Muccio wanted Chang to "guide" Rhee, or in effect to replace him, which would seem to be the outcome of getting him to "head the War Cabinet" (795.00 file, box 4300, Muccio letter to Rusk, January 1, 1951). Peer de Silva was the CIA chief in Seoul in 1960–1961, and describes his relations with Chang in *Sub Rosa: The CIA and the Uses of Intelligence* (New York: Times Books, 1978), pp. 151–71.

79. R. H. Tawney, *Land and Labor in China* (New York: Octagon Books, 1932, 1964), p. 177. Yu's advice is in U.S. Air Force, Air University, "A Preliminary Study of the Impact of Communism on Korea," Appendix C.

80. G-2 Weekly Report no. 96, July 6–13, 1947.

81. For example, William Bullitt wrote, "To describe [Rhee] as 'a stubborn old man' is to display a total ignorance of his character and moral courage. He is in fact a gentleman unafraid, and a great Christian leader" ("The Story of Syngman Rhee," *Reader's Digest*, September 1953, p. 37).

82. He was hardly less scathing than Rhee in referring to a principled liberal like Stewart Meacham as being "from the group of American liberal-pinko crowd that the communists penetrated during the war, almost all of [those] whom we had here [having been] reformed by realities or removed because undesirable" (RG335, Secretary of the Army file, box 22, Hodge to DuPuy, March 28, 1948).

83. Harold Noble Papers, "Hodge of Korea," 1949; RG335, Secretary of the Army file, box 57, Hodge to Army, August 18, 1948; MacArthur Papers, RG10, VIP file, box 5, Hodge to MacArthur, May 17, 1948; the Capone Gang reference is in CP, 165F, Hodge to War Department, January 3, 1948, referring to Kim Ku's and Rhee's involvement in the Chang Tŏk-su assassination; Bertsch interview; Francesca Rhee to "Mrs Frye," Lee/Oliver Papers, May 4, 1947.

84. CIA, "Prospects for the Survival of the Republic of Korea," ORE 44–48, October 28, 1948, Appendix A, "Personality of Syngman Rhee"; CIA, "National Intelligence Survey, Korea."

85. Oliver interview, August 1985.
86. Ibid.; Koreans used to apologize to Oliver for having to work for a Korean with a foreign wife.
87. Nixon was quite taken with Rhee during a visit to Seoul in 1953, regaling the Eisenhower cabinet with this and other insights on the old man's personality (Eisenhower Library, Eisenhower Papers [Whitman file], National Security Council Series, 175th Meeting, December 15, 1953).
88. Oliver interview, August 1985.
89. CIA, "National Intelligence Survey, Korea."
90. CIA, "National Intelligence Survey, Korea"; HST, Muccio Oral History, Interview no. 177, dated December 12, 1973, p. 15; Oliver interview, August 1985.
91. RG335, Secretary of the Army file, box 57, Hodge to Army, August 9, 1948; Oliver, *Rhee and American Involvement*, pp. 143, 224, 419–20; *Chicago Daily News* account in *The Daily Worker*, July 7, 1950; 895.00 file, box 5695, Allison to Rusk, March 30, 1950, enclosing Bunce's comments.
92. 895.00 file, box 7128, "895.001 Rhee" file, 1949; Lasher was a promoter of rightist youth groups during the Occupation, who later worked with Rhee's *Taehan* Youth, apparently with embassy status or sanction (895.00 file, box 5691, Drumwright to State, February 4, 1950).
93. Oliver, *Rhee and American Involvement*, p. 99; Ben Limb, *Hoegorok* [Reminiscences] (Seoul: Yŏwŏnsa, 1964), pp. 243–44, and *Imjŏng eso indo kkaji* [From Imjong to India] (Seoul: Yŏwŏnsa, 1966), pp. 123–24, and biography; CIA, "National Intelligence Survey, Korea." The CIA said Limb was in "private business" in Hawaii, and an acquaintance from Hawaii who went to North Korea later said that he had sold Japanese products the whole time he was in the United States, working for Ajunimoto, a Japanese foodstuffs company, as a salesman and broker. See *Nodong sinmun*, February 14, 1950, Yi Sa-man, "What Kind of Person is Im Pyŏng-jik?"
94. USFIK 11071 file, box 62/96, "Biographies of ROK Cabinet Officials"; RG94, USAMGIK, "Biographic Reports on the Cabinet of the Korean Republic," August 11, 1948, compiled by the State Department Bureau of Intelligence and Research. The CIA reported that the Department of Commerce has been "a chronic center of mismanagement and corruption" (CIA, "National Intelligence Survey, Korea"). See also a detailed embassy report by Gregory Henderson on the Korean investigation of Yim that led to her dismissal, which included attempting to collect bribes totaling 50 million wŏn, supposedly to present to Rhee on his seventy-fifth birthday; it would also appear that on January 6, 1949, "she was bribed with two dozen undershirts" by a man from Taejŏn (895.00 file, box 7128, Embassy to Seoul, April 9, 1949).
95. Oliver, *Rhee and American Involvement*, pp. 191, 206; CIA, "National Intelligence Survey, Korea."
96. Rhee offered a naval base on Cheju Island to the United States in his talks with Army Under-Secretary Draper in a discussion of April 10, 1948, and wanted in return U.S. help to "drive the Soviets from Korea" (RG335, box 22, top secret account of Draper's talks with Rhee, April 10, 1948).
97. CIA, "National Intelligence Survey, Korea."
98. HST, Muccio Oral History, December 27, 1973, p. 29.
99. 895.00 file, box 5691, see the statement at a meeting of high ROK officials held December 19, 1949, Drumwright to State, January 7, 1950.
100. HST, Muccio Oral History, December 27, 1973, p. 29.
101. Goodfellow Papers, box 1, Hodge to MPG, January 28, 1947; MacArthur's August 15 statement is in several sources; see Oliver, *Rhee and American Involvement*,

p. 186. MacArthur's other trip was to Manila on the granting of independence to the Philippines. On Rhee's October 1948 meeting see 895.00 file, box 7126, Muccio to State, November 11, 1948; G-2 Periodic Report, October 22–23, 1948, USFIK 11071 file; on the October trip see also RG332, XXIV Corps Historical File, loose material for "XXIV Corps Historical Journal," dated October 19–23, including an Associated Press dispatch from Tokyo dated October 22, 1948, saying MacArthur told Rhee he would defend Korea; FO317, piece no. 69944, Gascoigne to FO, October 30, 1948. Archivists responsible for the MacArthur Papers say no transcripts of Rhee-MacArthur talks exist; one told me that MacArthur never kept minutes or transcripts of private meetings. When one day early in the Japan Occupation an officer drew up a transcript of a mundane meeting and asked MacArthur what to do with it, he was told to burn it.

102. 895.00 file, box 7127, Drumwright to State, June 13, 1949; ibid., Muccio to State, September 13, 1949; RG338, KMAG file, box 5412, Ch'ae Pyŏng-dok to KMAG Executive Officer, December 29, 1948. Ch'oe Tŏk-shin, a division commander, was one of those who had fought with the Chinese Nationalists.

103. Kim Se-jin wrote that a power struggle between Rhee and Kim Ku led Rhee, in the fall of 1948, to bring into the Army "young and more malleable officers," and leaving out those with Chinese experience. Rhee personally appealed to former officers in the Japanese Army, including Kim Sŏk-wŏn, to come into the Army in 1948. After the Yŏsu rebellion, Rhee paid special attention to bringing in officers of North Korean origins, who would give him "blind and unswerving loyalty" (*The Politics of Military Revolution in Korea* [Chapel Hill: University of North Carolina Press, 1971], pp. 44–56).

A typical biography of a lesser officer, Lt. Col. An Ik-jo: "Commissioned as Lt. Col., Manchurian Army (Kwantung) in 1941 ... Vice-Chief of Police, Ch'ungch'ong Namdo, 1948; Provost Marshal of 3rd Division, August 1949 ... entered the Army through the influence of Kim Hyo-sok [then Home Minister]" (795.00 file, box 4262, January 18, 1950; RG338, KMAG file, box 5417, Secor to Deputy C/S, June 7, 1950).

104. *Seoul Times*, August 25, 28, 1948; the Deane Papers contain an anonymous, long memorandum on "The Pro-Japanese," which documents from the *Maeil shinbo* appalling support for Japanese war and mobilization policies by important members of the South Korean elite.

105. *Seoul Times*, August 27, 1948.

106. 895.00 file, box 7127, Drumwright to State, March 14, 22, 1949; FO317, piece no. 76259, Holt to Bevin, June 10, 1949.

107. 895.00 file, Muccio to State, October 7, 1949; ibid., November 7, 1949; HST, PSF, NSC file, box 3, Daily Intelligence Summaries, February 2, 1952. On Rhee's political finances, see volume 1 and, as one of many pieces of evidence, G-2 Weekly Report no. 105, September 7–14, 1947, where the G-2 comments that Rhee was really the only politician with the finances necessary for political success, garnered by protecting collaborators.

108. 895.00 file, box 7127, Drumwright to State, May 17, 1949; on the 1945 levy, see *Seoul Times*, June 24, 1948; Wedemeyer Mission, box 3, "Korean Minutes"; *Seoul Times*, November 15, 1947, for Kim's appointment.

CHAPTER SEVEN

1. RG242, SA2012, item 8/37, *Haebang-hu Chosŏn (yŏn'gu chaeryo)* [Korea after Liberation (materials for study)], pp. 37–38. This is a handprinted document put out

by the South Chŏlla branch of the SKWP in early 1950, for the use of cadres. The North also traced the SKWP origins to the autumn uprisings. See RG242, SA2005, item 1/6, *Podo* [report], no. 4 (April 1947), pp. 46–47.

2. CIA, "Communist Capabilities in South Korea," February 21, 1949.

3. G-2 Weekly Summary no. 100, August 3–10, 1947, and no. 104, August 31-September 7, 1947.

4. CIA, "Communist Capabilities in South Korea," February 21, 1949.

5. RG332, box 18343, 441st CIC detachment, monthly report, August 18, 1948. Acceptance of the Kim Il Sung line is clear in *Haebang-hu Chosŏn (yon'gu chaeryo)*, pp. 10–28.

6. U.S. State Department, Office of Intelligence Research, Evelyn McCune, "Leadership in North Korea" (1963), p. 19. The study also noted that Pak dropped from sight at the time of Stalin's death.

7. In January 1948 the Kwangju branch sent a message to SKWP headquarters that was full of nationalist rhetoric: "We will go through fire and water without fearing death or [bullets] for complete independence of our fatherland . . . we will fight to the last man with the pro-Japanese and traitors for the benefit of the general laborers" (RG94, Central Intelligence, entry 427, box no. 18343, 441st CIC detachment, monthly report, January 15, 1948).

8. See for example the DNF document signed by Pak Hŏn-yŏng, Hŏ Hŏn, Yŏ Un-hyŏng, and others on January 22, 1947, in 895.00 file, box 7124, attachment to a letter to Secretary of State Marshall from the American Committee of the Korean Federation of Trade Unions, dated November 27, 1947.

9. 895.00 file, box 7124, Langdon to State, April 14, 1947.

10. G-2 Weekly Summary no. 99, July 27-August 3, 1947, no. 100, August 3–10, 1947, and no. 103, August 24–31, 1947; 895.00 file, box 7124, Jacobs to State, September 9, 1947; October 20, 21, 1947. (Jacobs put the total arrested at two thousand; in justifying the action he said that the police had discovered "plans for seditious action." G-2 sources claimed that the North Koreans had called for power to be turned over to the people's committees on August 15.) See *Seoul Times*, August 3–22, 1947; also Clyde Sargent, "Political Developments in South Korea, 1947," (Seoul, USAMGIK Public Opinion Bureau, January 1948), in RG332, XXIV Corps Historical File. Yi Ch'un-sik puts the total number arrested at twenty thousand, in *Sŏn'gŏ tokbon* [Election reader], p. 66.

11. G-2 Weekly Summary no. 102, August 17–24, 1947.

12. *Seoul Times*, August 20, 1947; G-2 Weekly Summary no. 103, August 24–31, 1947.

13. Hugh Deane Papers, "Trip to Chonju," August 13–17, 1947.

14. Wedemeyer Papers, box 3, Hŏ Hŏn to Hodge, August 29, 1947; this letter was accompanied by an MG biography describing Hŏ as "a mild-mannered, almost diffident, individual of scholarly bearing," who always denied he was a communist. See also 895.00 file, box 7124, Jacobs to State, October 21, 1947.

15. RG332, XXIV Corps Historical file, box 10, CIC report, June 14, 1947. This report said the police chief in Pusan had been assassinated in retaliation for the March 1, 1947, deaths.

16. Ibid., G-2 Weekly Summary no. 90, May 25-June 1, 1947; Roberts in *Seoul Times*, August 29, 1947.

17. Ibid., G-2 Weekly Summaries nos. 96, 97, July 6–20, 1947.

18. Special G-2 study attached to G-2 Weekly Summary no. 90, May 25-June 1, 1947.

19. Ibid., G-2 Weekly Summary no. 98, July 20–27, 1947.

20. Ibid., G-2 Weekly Summary no. 99, July 27-August 3, 1947.

21. Ibid., G-2 Weekly Summary no. 100, August 3–10, 1947.

22. Ibid., G-2 Weekly Summary no. 102, August 17–24, 1947.

23. Ibid., G-2 Weekly Summary no. 103, August 24–31, 1947. There are many, many other such incidents of violence reported in this issue and subsequent ones through September 1947.

24. See ibid., G-2 Weekly Summaries nos. 106–109, September 14-October 12, 1947. For example, on September 18, twenty-six members of the NWY came into Tae-sŏng village, near Haman in South Kyŏngsang, looking for leftist leaders: "The villagers attacked them. The result was one rightist killed and three injured." The Samgil account, based on interviews with American officers, is in Hugh Deane Papers, "Trip to Chonju, August 13–17, 1947."

25. Langdon wrote that disorders in July occurred "over wide areas [and were] growing in intensity and frequency"; he said that much of it was rightist-instigated. See 895.00 file, box 7124, Langdon to State, July 24, 1947. Many incidents of Left-Right village fighting in September 1947 were laid at the door of rightists by the American G-2. See ibid., G-2 Weekly Summary no. 109, October 5–12, 1947.

26. Linz, "Notes Toward a Comparative Study of Fascism," p. 93; see also Frank M. Snowden, "On the Social Origins of Agrarian Fascism in Italy," *European Journal of Sociology* 13, no. 2 (1972), pp. 268–95. The Korean village struggles also seem analogous to the peasant anarchist attacks on the Guardia Civil that Jerome R. Mintz describes in 1930s Spain (*The Anarchists of Casas Viejas* [Chicago: University of Chicago Press, 1982]).

27. U.S. Air Force, Air University, "A Preliminary Study of the Impact of Communism Upon Korea," p. 128; see Eric J. Hobsbawm, *Primitive Rebels*, 2d ed. (New York: W. W. Norton, 1965), and Elizabeth Perry, *Rebels and Revolutionaries in North China* (Stanford, Calif.: Stanford University Press, 1982).

28. U.S. Air Force, Air University, "Preliminary Study," no. 99. After noting that the NKC tenants had anted up 104 percent of the grain quota in North Chŏlla, the G-2 commented, "this fear of losing his land is the important factor to the farmer, and may provide the key for future grain collection programs." In late August the G-2 cited "a wave of open hostility" from peasants over the grain collection program (G-2 Weekly Summary no. 103, August 24–31, 1947). See also the survey of the collection and rationing system in RG332, box 10, SKIG National Food Administration, "History of the National Food Administration," Appendix C, "Food Report for South Korea as of March 1948"; also Appendix E, "Survey of Food Distribution in South Korea" (Seoul, 1947, 1948).

29. RG332, XXIV Corps Historical File, G-2 Weekly Summary no. 99, July 27-August 3, 1947.

30. U.S. Air Force, Air University, "Preliminary Study," pp. 123–28, 151–52. We will come back to this interesting study when we discuss the North Korean occupation.

31. HST, PSF, CIA file, box 257, CIA, "Communist Capabilities in South Korea," ORE 32-48, February 21, 1949.

32. This information came from a questionnaire that the G-2 gave to CIC officials (G-2 Weekly Summary no. 104, August 31-September 7, 1947). The CIC was said to have fifty separate lists of organization and leadership rosters for PCs throughout the South.

33. 895.00 file, box 7124, Jacobs to State, October 21, 1947. He does not say who conducted this survey.

34. "Political Survey of Kyongsang Pukto," in G-2 Weekly Summary no. 106, September 14–21, 1947.

35. USAMGIK Office of Civil Information survey, in G-2 Weekly Summary no. 103, August 24–31, 1947.

36. USFIK 11071 file, box 62/96, transcript of Hodge monologue to visiting congressmen, October 4, 1947; RG332, XXIV Corps Historical file, box 20, "Report of Special Investigation—Cheju-Do Political Situation," March 11, 1948, conducted by Lt. Col. Lawrence A. Nelson. Nelson was on Cheju from November 12, 1947, to February 28, 1948. On the guerrilla insurgency on Cheju and the mainland, and the Yŏsu Rebellion, see also John Merrill's important study, "Internal Warfare in Korea, 1948–1950: The Local Setting of the Korean War" (Ph.D. diss., University of Delaware, 1982), pp. 115–30, 172–78, 206–47, 253–67, 296–317, 321–60.

37. *Seoul Times*, June 18, August 6, 11, 1948; G-2 Intelligence Summary no. 144, June 11–18, 1948; *HUSAFIK*, vol. 2, pt. 2, "Police and National Events, 1947–48." In a report to the National Assembly on the origins of the insurgency, Yi Pŏm-sŏk traced it to "the propaganda and plots of the so-called People's Republic which sprang up right after Liberation," which were "still in existence" on Cheju (895.00 file, box 7127, Drumwright to State, enclosing Yi Pŏm-sŏk's December 1948 report). But the usual Rhee line was to blame it on the North Koreans.

38. G-2 Weekly Summary no. 116, November 23–30, 1947; *Seoul Times*, June 15, 18, 1950. These issues reported the results of a survey by a team of journalists from Seoul.

39. G-2 Intelligence Summaries nos. 134–42, April 2-June 4, 1948; *Seoul Times*, April 7, 8, 1948; *HUSAFIK*, "Police and National Events, 1947–48."

40. Rothwell Brown Papers, Brown to Hodge, "Report of Activities on Cheju-Do Island [*sic*] from 22 May 1948, to 30 June 1948."

41. *NDSM*, February 11, 1950. Cheju leftists and communists never had effective relations with the North Koreans, and even today the remnant survivors of the Cheju insurgents in Osaka remain independent, publishing accounts of the rebellion without taking a pro–Kim Il Sung line. A secret report on South Korea by the Organization Department of the NKWP said that "the current leader" of the insurgency "is not from SKWP cadre, like before the [April 3] incident"; this would suggest that SKWP leaders touched off the incident, but that the insurgency developed on its own momentum. The report said that the guerrillas "are in an extremely difficult situation" because of the blockade of the island, which shut off resupply from the mainland *and* from "Korean brethren in Japan." The report also claimed that the former Japanese head of the Kyŏnggi Province police had returned to Seoul in early June at Hodge's request, to advise the National Police on "establishing order" (RG 242, SA2006, item 14/31, *Chŏngse sunbo* [situation report], July 15, 1948. This appears to be Kim Tu-bong's personal copy).

42. RG94, Central Intelligence, entry 427, box no. 18343, 441st CIC detachment, report from Cheju of June 18, 1948.

43. *Seoul Times*, May 18, June 5, 7, 1948; see also Orlando W. Ward Papers, "Cheju Task Force," January 1947.

44. 1949 census figure in 795.00 file, box 4271.

45. USFIK 11071 file, box 33, "Opinion on the Settlement of the Cheju Situation," July 23, 1948, by Ko Pyŏng-uk, KNP superintendent.

46. Rothwell Brown Papers, Brown to Hodge, "Report of Activities on Cheju-Do Island [*sic*] from 22 May 1948, to 30 June 1948"; *Seoul Times*, June 5, 7, 1948. I have found no evidence of the return of Japanese officers, but that does not mean it did not happen.

47. *Seoul Times*, August 6, 11, 1948; G-2 Intelligence Summary no. 146, June 25-July 2, 1948.

48. G-2 Intelligence Summary no. 154, August 21–27, no. 159, September 24-October 1, no. 163, October 22–29, 1948; RG94, Central Intelligence, entry 427, box

no. 18343, 441st CIC detachment monthly report, October 21, 1948; 895.00 file, box no. 7127, Drumwright to State, January 7, 10, 1949.

49. RG338, KMAG file, box 5412, Roberts, "Weekly activities," November 8, 15, December 6, 1948. Roberts also said that rebels were burning villages, but it seems to have been the official authorities who did most of the burning.

50. 895.00 file, box no. 7127, Drumwright to State, March 14, 1949; Muccio to State, April 18, 1949.

51. FO317, piece no. 76258, Holt to Bevin, March 22, 1949.

52. 895.00 file, box no. 7127, Drumwright to State, May 17, 1949; Muccio to State, May 13, 1949. Chang had lost his bid for a seat from Seoul.

53. "The Background of the Present War in Korea," *Far Eastern Economic Review* (August 31, 1950), pp. 233–37; this account is by an anonymous but knowledgeable American who served in the Occupation. See also Koh Kwang-il, "In Quest of National Unity," p. 149; *Hapdong t'ongshin*, June 27, 1949, quoted in *Sun'gan t'ongshin*, no. 34 (September 1949), p. 1. (I could not find the original of this report.) Also RG349, FEC G-2 Theater Intelligence, box 466, May 23, 1950, G-2 report on Cheju, which has the governor's figures. He put the preinsurgency island population at 400,000, which I think is high. For a detailed North Korean account, see Yi Sŭng-yŏp, "The Struggle of the Southern Guerrillas for Unification of the Homeland," *Kŭlloja*, no. 1 (January 1950), p. 18.

54. 895.00 file, box 7127, Embassy to State, June 16, 1949; RG338, KMAG file, box 5413, KMAG weekly activities, June 27, 1949. The North Koreans cited some minor skirmishes on Cheju in early 1950. See *NDSM*, January 7, March 31, 1950.

55. Merrill, "Internal Warfare," p. 265.

56. 895.00 file, box 7127, account of a survey of Cheju by Capt. Harold Fischgrund of KMAG, in Drumwright to Muccio, November 28, 1949. Fischgrund thought all members of the NWY should be removed from the island, but of course they were not.

57. 795.00 file, box 4299, Drumwright to State, June 21, 1950; box 4268, Drumwright to Allison, August 29, 1950, enclosing a survey, "Conditions on Cheju Island." See also *Korean Survey* (March 1954), pp. 6–7. The Americans put Yi's death in June, but in awarding him a posthumous medal the North Koreans said he died in a guerrilla skirmish on the mainland in August 1949. See *NDSM*, February 11, 1950.

58. USFIK 11071 file, box 65/96, XXIV Corps G-3 section, "History of the Rebellion of the 14th Regiment and the 6th Regiment of the Korean Constabulary," November 10, 1948.

59. Ibid.; also RG332, XXIV Corps Historical file, box 35, translation of *Kukje sinmun* article of October 26, 1948; also report by "Special Agent no. 9016," October 28, 1948; also *Seoul Times*, October 25–30, 1948.

60. G-2 Weekly Summary no. 91, June 1–8, and no. 100, August 3–10, 1947; RG94, Central Intelligence, entry 427, box no. 18343, 441st CIC detachment, May 31, 1948, report.

61. "History of the Rebellion"; also RG332, XXIV Corps Historical file, box 35, report by "Special Agent no. 9016"; also USFIK 11071 file, box 77/96, "223rd report on Yŏsu," October 27, 1948.

62. Box 35, ibid., report by "Special Agent no. 9016"; RG332, box 21, "History of Korean Department of National Police for Period from 1 July 1948" (no other date given); USFIK 11017 file, box 77/96, G-2 flash report no. 152, October 22, 1948; G-2 Weekly Summary no. 164, October 20-November 5, 1948; also no. 166, November 12–19, 1946; FO371, piece no. 69948, Holt to FO, November 2, 1948.

The *Seoul Times* also reported that crowds cheered when policemen were attacked (October 26, 1948).

63. See RG332, XXIV Corps Historical file, box 35, for translation of the Yŏsu *Inmin ilbo*, October 24, 1948; also FO371, piece no. 69948, Holt to FO, November 2, 1948; USFIK 11071 file, box 76/96, message from Iri railroad police, October 22, 1948. An internal communist document says the Yŏsu mass meeting on October 20 pledged loyalty to the DPRK, and does not use the term KPR. It may be that the terms were used interchangeably, but it is more likely that "KPR" was altered to "DPRK" in this text, written in March 1950, so as not to offend the North. See RG242, SA2012, item 8/37, handprinted item from the South Chŏlla branch of the KWP, "*Haebang hu Chosŏn (yŏn'gu chaeryo)*" [Korea after liberation (materials for study)], March 1950.

64. 895.00 file, Muccio to State, November 4, 1948; *Seoul Times*, October 27, 1948; USFIK 11071 file, box 76/96, "Report on Yŏsu Event no. 164," October 23, 1948; also message from Kwangju railroad police chief, October 22, 1948.

65. RG242, SA2005, item 1/7, inaugural issue of *Sŏnjŏnja* [The propagandist] (1949, probably January), pp. 42–43; this was apparently something given to KWP activists to guide their work. The item held in RG242 would appear to have been Pak Hŏn-yŏng's own copy. See *NDSM*, January 30, 1950, for the later account; on the dispatched guerrillas see G-2 Weekly Summary no. 166, November 12–19, 1948. (The information is based on interrogations of four guerrillas captured in Kangwŏn Province, i.e., very distant from Yŏsu.) American attention to the quiescent thirty-eighth parallel is recorded in RG332, box 22, staff conference minutes for October 26, 29, November 5, 1948. The North Koreans initiated no violent incidents along the parallel from October 12 to November 5.

66. 895.00 file, box 7126, Muccio to State, November 4, 1948; USFIK 11071 file, box 65/96, "The Yŏsu Operation, Amphibious Stage," an undated report by Capt. Howard H. Darrow; also "History of the Rebellion."

67. "History of the Rebellion"; USFIK 11071 file, box 77/96, packet of documents in "Operation Yousi [*sic*]."

68. USFIK 11071 file, box 77/96, "Operation Yousi," "G-3 to C/S," October 20, 1948; "W. L. Roberts to CG, USAFIK," October 20, 1948; "Capt. Hatcher to G-3," October 21, 1948; "History of the Rebellion"; USFIK 11071 file, box 77/96, KMAG HQ to Gen. Song Ho-sŏng, October 21, 1948. The message is unsigned, but was presumably from Roberts. This file contains numerous original messages from Korean military and police units to and from USAFIK headquarters; also many daily intelligence reports. On the C-47s see 740.0019 file, box C-215, Muccio to State, May 3, 1949. KMAG was at that time called PMAG, since it was still "provisional."

69. USFIK 11071 file, box 77/96, "134th report on Yŏsu," October 23, 1948; G-2 flash reports no. 179 and no. 202, October 24, 25, 1948; report on Yŏsu no. 191, October 25, 1950; G-2 flash report no. 130, October 21, 1948; flash report, 6th Division G-2 to XXIV Corps G-2, October 23, 1948; G-2 flash report no. 158, October 23, 1948. See also box 65/96, "History of the Rebellion."

70. USFIK 11071 file, box 76/96, road patrol report on Posŏng and Changhŭng, October 24, 1948.

71. "History of the Rebellion"; also USFIK 11071 file, box 77/96, G-2 flash report no. 238, October 27, 1948; box 76/96, message from Col. Paek Sŏn-yŏp, October 26, 1948.

72. Keyes Beech, *Tokyo and Points East* (Garden City, N.Y.: Doubleday, 1954), p. 139.

73. "Yŏsu Operation, Amphibious Stage," report by "Special Agent no. 9016," G-2

Intelligence Summary no. 166, November 5–12, 1948; USFIK 11071 file, box 76/
96, Roberts to PMAG, October 25, 1950; "Message from Hausman," October 25,
1950. Carl Mydans witnessed the execution of twenty-two rebels in Sunch'ŏn, writing that loyal troops "were as savage as the Communists had been" (*Time*, November 8, 1948).

74. 895.00 file, box 7127, Drumwright to State, December 10, 1948, giving Yi Pŏm-
sŏk's official ROK figures as of December 7; G-2 Intelligence Summaries nos. 166,
167, November 12–26, 1948; RG332, box 22, staff conference, October 26, 1948;
FO317, piece no. 76258, Seoul Embassy to FO, January 7, 1949; RG338, KMAG
file, box 5412, Roberts's weekly report for November 22, 1949. The North Koreans claimed to have captured an American CIC document, detailing the execution
of sixty-three Yŏsu military rebels at Camp Taejŏn on January 27, 1949, South
Korean authorities being observed and aided by KMAG officers at the scene. The
document comes from the 971st CIC detachment, but does not appear in archival
files from that unit. It seems authentic. See *NDSM*, August 11, 1950.

75. "Major Pak Chung Hi" is included in a list of field grade officers in the ROKA
"confined for subversive activities," November 11, 1948. This was done at the order of Chai Pyŏng-dŏk. See RG338, KMAG file, box 5412, W. H. Secor to PMAG
Chief of Staff, November 12, 1948.

76. RG332, box 21, staff conference, October 26, December 24, 1948.

77. 895.00 file, box 7126, Muccio to State, November 16, 1948.

78. Ibid., Muccio to State, November 4, 11, 16, December 3, 17, 1948; box 7128, November political summary, December 10, 1949.

79. RG94, Central Intelligence, entry 427, box no. 18371, CIC Monthly Information
Report no. 7, December 20, 1948.

80. Ibid.

CHAPTER EIGHT

1. G-2 Weekly Summary no. 123, January 16–23, 1948.

2. RG94, Central Intelligence, entry 427, box no. 18343, monthly reports dated August 18, September 22, and October 21, 1948. USFIK 11071 file, box 21, "Situation Map and Estimate," September 22, 1948; also "Police Comments on Guerrilla
Situation," August 6, 1948, by Millard Shaw, an advisor to the KNP; also G-2 Intelligence Summary no. 149, July 16–23, 1948.

3. Yi Sŭng-yŏp, "Struggle of the Southern Guerrillas," pp. 16–17; Pak Hŏn-yŏng, in
NDSM, January 14, 1950; RG242, SA2005, item 1/7, Min Pyŏng-ŭi, "The Full
Story of the Southern Guerrillas," *Sŏnjŏnja* [The propagandist] (P'yongyang)
(1949). It is interesting that Yi uses the term *inmin hangjaeng* or people's war of
resistance for the uprisings in 1946; *inmin t'ujaeng* or people's resistance for Cheju;
and *ŭigŏ sakŏn* or something like "righteous incident" for the events in Yŏsu—thus
placing the latter in the category of a more minor event, an incident compared to
a movement. Another article referred to Yŏsu as merely a "riot" (*p'okdong*), and
said that protracted guerrilla resistance began after it. See Kim Yŏng-t'aek, "The
Courageous Armed Resistance of the South Korean People," *Sun'gan t'ongshin*, no.
14 (March 1949), p. 3.

4. 895.00 file, box 7127, Muccio to State, enclosing G-2 summary for December 1948.

5. RG335, Secretary of the Army file, box 78, packet of documents given Kenneth
Royall during his trip to Korea in February 1949; CIA, "Communist Capabilities
in South Korea," ORE 32–48, February 21, 1949; see also Hŏ Hŏn's article in

HGND NDSM, June 27, 1949. Hŏ Hŏn said guerrillas were strongly organized on Cheju and Chiri mountain, in bases in Odae mountain and the T'aebaek and Sŏbaek mountains, in the South Chŏlla counties of Naju, Posŏng, and Kohŭng, in Hadong and Kŏch'ang in South Kyŏngsang, and in the North Kyŏngsang counties of Kyŏngju, Ulsan, Andong, and Yech'ŏn.

6. 895.00 file, box 7127, Drumwright to State, enclosing report of a two-week tour by vice-consuls John W. Rozier and Donald S. MacDonald, March 17, 1949. Drumwright added his judgment that North Kyŏngsang province "was a hotbed of terrorist action, mob attacks, and communist activity"; in Taegu, "Communists were reportedly so strong that the police hesitated to cause undue incidents." See 895.00 file, box 7127, Drumwright to State, March 14, 1949.

7. Kim Yŏng-t'aek, "Courageous Armed Resistance," pp. 3–5. Many other incidents are listed here, including ones in Yŏngdong, and various counties in North Kyŏngsang.

8. See RG242, SA2005, item 1/7, Min Pyŏng-ŭi, "Full Story of the Southern Guerrillas," pp. 41–48. Min lists only Ongjin and Yŏnbaek, near the thirty-eighth parallel in eastern Kyŏnggi; American G-2 sources agreed that guerrillas operated there. He lists only four counties in North Ch'ungch'ŏng. He claims to cite guerrilla and underground newspapers from the South in arriving at these totals. See also the article by O Hong-t'aek in *HGND NDSM,* April 3, 1949, which places guerrillas in eighty-one counties as of March 1949. This author described the goals of the guerrillas as expelling American troops, overthrowing the Rhee regime, and restoring the people's committees. See also Yi Sang-buk, "The People's Guerrillas Launch a New Offensive, Holding High the Banner of the Patriotic Front," *Sun'gan t'ongshin,* no. 34 (September 1949), pp. 1–3. Yi said the guerrillas were now operating close to Taegu, "glorious capital of the October people's resistance"; they were active in all of South Chŏlla, but only "part" of North Chŏlla. In Kyŏnggi he mentions only two counties. Still, he claimed that guerrillas were "active" in 118 of 131 counties.

9. Yi Sŭng-yŏp, "Struggle of the Southern Guerrillas," p. 21.

10. 895.00 file, box 7127, Muccio to State, September 23, 1948, enclosing a report by Donald MacDonald on his recent visit to Kwangju; *Chŏlla Namdo-ji* [History of South Chŏlla] (Kwangju: Munhwa kongbo-shil, 1969), p. 215.

11. G-2 Weekly Summary no. 108, September 28-October 5; no. 109, October 5–12; no. 111, October 19–26, 1947; no. 123, January 16–23, 1948.

12. Roy Appleman, *South to the Naktong, North to the Yalu.* (Washington, D.C.: Office of the Chief of Military History, 1961), p. 577 (hereafter *Naktong/Yalu*); KMAG G-2 Periodic Report no. 260, February 7–8, 1950; for Yu Il-sŏk's life, see *NDSM,* March 7, 1950.

13. RG335, Secretary of the Army file, box 78, Yi Pŏm-sŏk, "Status of National Defense Forces," February 7, 1949, in packet of documents given to Secretary Royall during his trip to Korea.

14. Chronology, *Sun'gan t'ongshin,* no. 14 (March 1949); Central News Agency reports in *HGND NDSM,* April 3, 21, 26, May 15, 21, 28, June 9, 11, 19, 1949; RG242, SA2005, item 1/7, Min Pyŏng-ŭi, "Full Story of the Southern Guerrillas," pp. 47–48. Incidents reported in North Chŏlla counties such as Muju, Imsil, and Changsu merely said something like "bad elements were wiped out," with no casualty figures.

15. Min Pyŏng-ŭi, "Full Story of the Southern Guerrillas," pp. 45–47; RG338, KMAG file, box 5413, report on Hwasun mines by L. S. Chang, August 25, 1949; KMAG G-2 Periodic Reports nos. 164–176, August 12-September 6, 1949. North Korean

accounts of these incidents are very close to the KMAG G-2 reports, which were in turn based on KNP and ROKA reports; South Korean accounts, however, often distort the nature of the incidents. See for example *Chŏlla Namdo-ji*, pp. 753–54. They always use the term *kongbi* to refer to guerrillas; although this term usually is translated as "communist bandit," it literally means communist nonperson.

16. KMAG G-2 Periodic Reports nos. 183–260, September 16, 1949-February 8, 1950. These reports are full of accounts of guerrilla fighting in South Chŏlla, too numerous to mention.

17. *NDSM*, January 7, 1950. Most of the guerrilla activity reported in the North Korean press in early 1950 is from North Kyŏngsang.

18. RG94, Central Intelligence, entry 427, box no. 18371, CIC monthly report no. 6, November 20, 1948.

19. Kim Yŏng-t'aek, "Courageous Armed Resistance," pp. 3–5; *HGND NDSM*, April 3, 8, 21, 22, 29, May 12, June 11, 12, 1949.

20. KMAG G-2 Periodic Report no. 231, December 15–16, 1949. The North Koreans also referred to the "Ilwŏl-san guerrillas," led by Kim Tal-sam. See for example *NDSM*, January 6, 1950.

21. 895.00 file, box 7127, Drumwright to State, July 26, 1949, enclosing an account of a trip to the province by two ECA officials.

22. 895.00 file, box 7127, Drumwright to State, July 11, 1949; Muccio to State, August 10, 1949; see also FO317, piece no. 76259, Holt to FO, July 28, 1949. British sources said guerrilla incidents occurred all over North Kyŏngsang in mid-July.

23. 895.00 file, box 7127, Drumwright to State, July 11, 1949; also Drumwright to State, July 26, 1949; also KMAG G-2 Periodic Reports nos. 165–170, August 12–25, 1949.

24. KMAG G-2 Periodic Reports nos. 168–184, August 19-September 20, 1949; Min Pyŏng-ŭi, "Full Story of the Southern Guerrillas," p. 46.

25. KMAG G-2 Periodic Reports nos. 191–208, September 30-November 3, 1949; FO317, piece no. 76259, Holt to FE, November 5, 1949; also 895.00 file, Muccio to State, November 7, 1949; also Yi Sŭng-yŏp, "Struggle of the Southern Guerrillas," p. 13.

26. KMAG G-2 Periodic Reports nos. 211–220, November 7–28, 1949; FO317, piece no. 76259, Holt to FE, November 5, 1949.

27. KMAG G-2 Periodic Report, no. 233, December 19–20, 1949; no. 237, December 27–29, 1949.

28. *NDSM*, January 6, 7, 8, 1950; KMAG G-2 Periodic Reports nos. 221–241, November 28, 1949-January 6, 1950.

29. 695.00 file, box 4262, Drumwright to State, January 25, 1950.

30. KMAG G-2 Periodic Reports nos. 239–289, December 30, 1949-March 30, 1950; *NDSM*, February 4, 7, 15, 18, 26, March 2, 3, 12, 13, 20, 22, 24, 26, 30, April 3, 5, 8, 20, 21, 22, 26, 1950; many daily incidents are listed, with most of them in North Kyŏngsang counties.

31. We already cited evidence of a guerrilla training base near Sŏsan; a guerrilla attack in T'aechŏn county is cited in KMAG G-2 Periodic Report no. 184, September 19–20, 1949. Some sixty-five guerrillas attacked the T'aechŏn police station, killing nine civilians. On the North Korean treatment of guerrillas in the Ch'ungch'ŏngs, see for example Kim Yŏng-t'aek, "Courageous Armed Resistance," p. 5; he cites few incidents, and admits that even they are "new."

32. 740.0019 Control (Korea) file, box 3829, Jacobs to State, January 31, 1948, enclosing a field report by the USAMGIK Office of Civil Information.

33. *New York Times*, August 2, 1950.

34. See for example *HGND NDSM*, June 9, 12, 19, 1949; on Yŏngdong, see for example *HGND NDSM*, April 20, 1949, which lists several incidents in the county.
35. G-2 Weekly Summary no. 117, November 30-December 7, 1947.
36. G-2 Weekly Summary no. 167, November 19–26, 1948; 895.00 file, box 7127, Drumwright to State, January 10, 1949.
37. See North Korean discussions of various incidents in *HGND NDSM*, June 1, 4, 1949; see also KMAG G-2 Periodic Reports no. 228, December 9–12, 1949; nos. 284–289, March 21–30, 1950.
38. Bennie Griffith, answers to questionnaire by John Merrill, courtesy of Professor Merrill.
39. 695.00 file, box 4262, Drumwright to State, "Guerrilla Strength and Activity," April 15, 1950.
40. 895.00 file, box 7127, Drumwright to State, March 17, 1949, enclosing report of a provincial tour by John W. Rozier and Donald S. MacDonald.
41. Yi Sŭng-yŏp, "Struggle of the Southern Guerrillas," pp. 23–24; see also KMAG G-2 Periodic Reports nos. 207–211, October 31-November 8, 1949. Suppression forces claimed very heavy guerrilla losses in the same region in early November—463 KIAs in one case alone; this suggests that many peasants were being killed, and labeled guerrillas.
42. Hŏ Hŏn, eight-page speech in *HGND NDSM*, June 27, 1949. In the context, he referred to an incident in which South Korean police allegedly slaughtered a family of eight in Posŏng because one member had joined the guerrillas. The guerrilla's name was given as Chŏn Pi-ho.
43. Bennie Griffith, answer to questionnaire.
44. Hugh Deane Papers, "Notes on Korea," March 20, 1948.
45. During a memorable seminar at Thames Television in London, I remarked that the official South Korean point of view was that "not even one ROK citizen was ever a guerrilla," whereupon Kim Chong Hwi, who had been sent to London by the Seoul authorities, responded that indeed, all the guerrillas in the South were North Koreans.
46. RG332, box no. 18371, 971st CIC Monthly Information Report no. 7, December 20, 1948; KMAG Periodic Report no. 213, November 10–14, 1949.
47. CIA, "Communist Capabilities in South Korea," February 21, 1949; 795.00 file, box 4262, Drumwright to State, April 15, 1950, enclosing a report on "Guerrilla Strength and Activity." See also box 4299, Drumwright to State, May 4, 1950, "Estimate of Soviet Intentions toward South Korea." Captured documents from the Kangdong school list spies but not guerrillas. See MA, RG6, box 79, ATIS issue no. 15, January 3, 1951, translating a handwritten list of North Korean agents, most of whom came from the Kangdong school.
48. 795.00 file, box 4262, Drumwright to State, April 15, 1950.
49. A poem about the Chiri-san guerrillas published in the party press depicted them wishing long life to Kim Il Sung (*NDSM*, February 15, 1950). The inaugural issue of *Sŏnjŏnja* [The propagandist], issued in 1949, had a long article on the southern guerrillas by Min Pyŏng-ŭi, from which the "warm encouragement" quote is taken (RG242, SA2005, item 1/7, *Sŏnjŏnja*, p. 48).
50. RG332, box 18371, 441st CIC detachment, monthly report, December 20, 1948.
51. Interview with Thames Television, February 1987. I did not attend this interview, but made notes in the immediate aftermath on what Hausman told the Thames crew both during the filmed interview, and in off-camera discussions. Hausman did not request confidentiality for the off-camera statements, for which there were three witnesses.

52. Goodfellow Papers, box 1, draft of letter to Rhee, no date but late 1948.
53. 895.00 file, box 7127, Drumwright to State, February 11, 21, 1949. In March 1949 Drumwright urged two vice-consuls to solicit political information from American missionaries:

> Emphasize, at all times, that the Mission is fully aware that the Missionaries' work is fully understood to be non-political. Intimate, however, that their integration into the local scene and their business throughout the countryside both make it inevitable (especially with their command of the Korean language) that considerable "political" information come [*sic*] to their attention even without conscious effort. In the work of the U.S. Government to fight Communism and keep the Korean Government strong, it must know what is going on outside of Seoul, and just this miscellaneous Missionary information is invaluable.

See 895.00 file, box 7127, Drumwright directive included in Drumwright to State, March 17, 1949. See also ECA official Edgar A. J. Johnson's testimony to Congress on June 13, 1950, to the effect that the ROKA had killed five thousand guerrillas in the past year, and that it was "prepared to meet any challenge by North Korean forces," quoted in *New York Times*, July 6, 1950.
54. National Archives, Army Chief of Military History manuscripts, box 601, "Military Studies on Manchuria." The officers gave this as the reason why "Kim Il Sung and Choe Hyon went to the Soviet Union about February and returned to Manchuria about May or June."
55. Ibid.; for a longer discussion of Japanese methods, with documents, see also Chong-sik Lee, *Counterinsurgency in Manchuria: The Japanese Experience* (Santa Monica, Calif.: The RAND Corporation, 1967).
56. "Military Studies on Manchuria" and Chong-sik Lee, *Counterinsurgency in Manchuria*.
57. For biographical information on Kim Paek-il and Chong Il-gwŏn see Harutaka Sasaki, *Han'gukjŏn pisa* [Secret History of the Korean War], trans. Kang Ch'ang-gu (Seoul: Pyŏnghak-sa, 1977), Vol. 1, pp. 446, 508–11, 529, 567–68.
58. Yi Sŭng-yŏp, "On the Present Tasks of the Courageous Southern People's Guerrillas, Who Have Completely Defeated the Enemy's 'Winter Subjugation,' " *Kŭlloja*, no. 6 (March 30, 1950), pp. 9–22. Yi said that the suppression was aided by "our sworn enemy, the Japanese militarist clique," in "Struggle of the Southern Guerrillas," p. 25. For a similar account of the winter suppression by Pak Hŏn-yŏng, see *NDSM*, January 14, 1950. Pak also names Kim Paek-il. For a contemporaneous account discussing Japanese counterinsurgency techniques, including the establishment of fortified villages (*chipdan purak*) to separate guerrillas from peasants, see the article by a Manchurian partisan, Ch'oe Yong-jin, in *NDSM*, January 28, 1950. Another Japanese counterinsurgency officer told the Americans that Koreans were "known to be most susceptible to Communism among the nations of the Far East"; the Japanese had learned that Korean guerrillas should be dealt with "resolutely and thoroughly . . . destroy the enemy by utilizing every possible means." This meant prohibiting residence "in areas difficult to subjugate," and compelling the people "to reside as a group in designated areas." It was "absolutely necessary . . . to utilize [the] winter season to thoroughly suppress and mop up the enemy." Compared to China and Indochina, "Korean land features appear to be unsuitable for guerrilla warfare." Suppression forces can obtain "sea superiority," and barren hills offer no concealment "as compared to jungle areas." RG349, box 462, Intelligence memo, October 18, 1950, interview with an unnamed Japanese

with the code "Yok no. 5," who was obviously a counterinsurgency expert with Manchurian experience.

59. 895.00 file, box 7127, Embassy to State, March 25, 1949, transmitting a report on the guerrillas by Col. J. W. Fraser; Muccio to State, April 18, 1949; Muccio to State, May 13, 1949; Drumwright to State, May 17, 1949. In the latter dispatch, Drumwright said that "underpaid soldiers and policemen . . . fell back to the old pattern of oppression of hapless villager[s]." The documents do not name Kim Chi-hwi's wife.

60. *New York Times*, March 6, 15, 1950.

CHAPTER NINE

1. Wlodzimierz Brus, "Stalinism and the 'People's Democracies,' " in *Stalinism: Essays in Historical Interpretation*, ed. Robert C. Tucker (New York: W. W. Norton, 1977), pp. 239–41, 252–53.

2. Robert C. Tucker, "Communist Revolutions, National Cultures, and Divided Nations," *Studies in Comparative Communism* 7, no. 3 (Autumn 1974), pp. 235–45.

3. See for example Chong-sik Lee, "Stalinism in the East: Communism in North Korea," in *The Communist Revolution in Asia*, ed. Robert Scalapino (Englewood Cliffs, N.J.: Prentice-Hall, 1969).

4. Leon Trotsky, *Stalin*, 2d ed. (New York: Stein and Day, 1967), pp. 1–2, 358. See also Stephen Cohen, *Bukharin and the Bolshevik Revolution* (New York: Vintage Books, 1974), p. 291, for Bukharin's depiction of Stalin as "a Genghis Khan"; also Isaac Deutscher, *Stalin: A Political Biography* (London: Oxford University Press, 1949), p. 472: Stalin was "primitive, oriental, but unfailingly shrewd."

5. Shortly after the Rangoon bombing in 1983, in which the North Koreans apparently sought to eliminate much of the South Korean cabinet, a high Soviet official in Japan told me, "We have *nothing* to do with those people. *Nothing!*"

6. Brus, "Stalinism," p. 241.

7. See for example KWP, *Malksŭ chuŭi tang ŭi chojikjŏk kich'o* [The organized foundation of a Marxist party] (P'yŏngyang: Nodongdang ch'ulp'an-sa, 1949); also a handprinted text, *Ich'a taejŏn kwa Ssoryŏn ŭi widaehan choguk chŏnjaeng kwamok* [The second world war and the lessons of the Soviet Union's great fatherland war] (both are in RG242).

8. RG242, SA2009, item 6/76, NKWP Central Party School, *Tang Kŏnsŏl (kangŭi yogang)* [Party building (lecture outline)] (P'yŏngyang, no date, but probably late 1948); the first ninety-four pages deal with Marxism-Leninism and the Soviet experience, and the remaining fifty or so cover Korea.

9. See the text of PC regulations contained in Intelligence Summary—North Korea, no. 41, August 2, 1947.

10. See for example Kim's speech on the first anniversary of the founding of the Worker's Party, *Kŭlloja*, no. 8 (August 1947), pp. 27–44. See also my "Kim's Korean Communism," *Problems of Communism* (March-April 1974), for more on this aspect of "Kimilsungism" and contrasts with Maoism; and Merle Fainsod, *How Russia Is Ruled* (Cambridge, Mass.: Harvard University Press, 1957), pp. 128–31, 183.

11. Among the best critiques on this point is Mao's, in his *Critique of Soviet Economics*, trans. Moss Roberts (New York: Monthly Review Press, 1977).

12. RG242, SA2006, item 51/15, "Yuil dangjŭng suyŏ e kwanhaya" [On the distribu-

tion of uniform party identity cards], NKWP organization department, November 1946, top secret.

13. I. V. Kukushin, "The Comintern and the East," in *The Cominterm and the East*, ed. R. A. Ulyanovsky (Moscow: Progress Publishers, 1979), p. 396.

14. CRC, 1975 13C, State Department Office of Intelligence Research, Evelyn Mc-Cune, "Leadership in North Korea: Groupings and Motivations," 1963; RG242 SA2006, item 14/25, Chu Yong-ha, *Puk Chosŏn nodongdang ch'angnip ilchunyŏn kwa Chosŏn ŭi minjuhwa rŭl wihan t'ujaeng esŏ kŭŭi yŏkhal* [The first anniversary of the founding of the North Korean Worker's Party and its role in the struggle for Korea's democratization] (P'yŏngyang: KWP ch'ulp'an-sa, 1947).

15. Ch'oe Hak-so, *Nongmin chohap chojik-ron* [On the organization of peasant unions] (P'yŏngyang: Sahoe Kwahak-sŏ, 1946).

16. RG242, SA2009, item 6/76, NKWP Central Party School, *Tang Kŏnsŏl (kangŭi yogang)* [Party building (Lecture outline)] (P'yong yang, no date, but probably late 1948), pp. 97–98.

17. MA, RG6, ATIS Issue no. 31, April 3, 1951, based on captured KWP records; see also Kim Il Sung's figures in his report to the Second KWP Congress, *Kŭlloja*, no. 4 (14), (April 1948), p. 34. Data on KWP members in the Yŏngbyŏn County People's Committee showed that of a total of 126, all but thirteen were poor peasants (95), middle peasants (10), or hired laborers (8). Only fourteen had gone beyond elementary school. The average age was thirty-three, with some as young as twenty-one. Only eight were females. Among teachers at local elementary schools, one batch of data from Sŏnch'ŏn County shows that of 298 teachers, 195 were of poor or middle peasant backgrounds. See RG242, SA2005, item 4/45, party identification sheets from Yŏngbyŏn County; ibid., item 4/44, handwritten "Kyowŏn myŏngdan" [Teacher rosters].

18. Data from RG242 courtesy Pang Sun-joo. Internal evidence on the people's committees demonstrates a similar pattern in the governmental network. Peasants constituted 36 percent of those elected in the fall of 1946, workers 15 percent and *samuwŏn* 31 percent. Provincial data on the 1949 elections for North Hamgyŏng Province show that about 40 percent of those elected to provincial, city, and county posts were peasants, about 30 percent were workers. On the provincial PC itself, 38 percent were peasants and 25 percent workers; 16 of 108 members were women. See *HGND NDSM*, April 5, 14, 1949.

19. Fainsod, *How Russia Is Ruled*, pp. 211–13, 221.

20. RG242, SA2010, item 3/107, *Kanbu iyŏksa* [Cadre biographies], most of which were dated in early 1950.

21. See some handwritten personal statements from Ch'ŏlsan County in RG242, SA2006, item 6/20. One respondent says he "forgot to be politically conscious" and allowed his parents to arrange a marriage for him, "according to village custom" and without proper checking on the bride's "sŏngbun." Thus he ended up with Miss Kim Suk-hyŏn of unfortunate (i.e., high) class background.

22. Ibid.

23. See for example Wilbur Schramm et al., "Notes on the Pattern of Sovietization in North Korea," in U.S. Air Force, Air University, "Preliminary Study," pp. 206–64; also 695.00 file, box 3025, Lightner to State, June 13, 1951.

24. G-2 Weekly Summary no. 99, July 27–August 3, 1947; "General Kim Il Sung is the Leader of the Korean people," *Podo*, no. 3 (August 1947), pp. 18–21. As Yŏ Unhyŏng's followers moved in the wake of his bier in July 1947, they held up signs paying tribute to their dead leader as "the Sun of the Nation" (*minjogŭi t'aeyang*).

25. National Archives, Army Chief of Military History manuscripts, box 601, "Military

Studies on Manchuria," book 4, ch. 9, "Bandits and Inhabitants" (Tokyo: FEC, 1952).

26. To my knowledge only one source in all the published and unpublished literature on North Korea grasps the central importance of Kim's peculiar style of leadership, and that is the formerly classified study done in the early 1960s by Evelyn McCune for the U.S. State Department Bureau of Intelligence and Research ("Leadership in North Korea: Groupings and Motivations," 1963). She correctly terms the relationship between Kim and his close allies "a semi-chivalrous, irrevocable and unconditional bond . . . under iron discipline." It is a "deeply personal" system, "fundamentally hostile to complex bureaucracy." Kim and his allies were generalists, jacks-of-all-trades who could run the government or command the army, show a peasant how to use new seeds or cuddle children in a school; Kim would dispatch them as loyal observers of officials and experts or specialists outside the inner core, that is, in the realm of impersonal bureaucracy. McCune thought correctly that the powerful glue holding the Kim group together made it much more formidable than typical Korean political factions, based on weaker patron-client relations and given to splintering in power struggles and personal competition; thus it was able to assert dominance over rival groups rather easily. She also understood the concentric circle metaphor, providing a chart of the leadership radiating outward from Kim.

27. See for example E.M.W. Tillyard, *The Elizabethan World Picture* (New York: Vintage Books, 1942). On the statue, set up in Hŭngnam, see *Sun'gan t'ongshin*, no. 3 (46) (January 1950), daily record for December 1949.

28. *Kŭlloja*, no. 11 (January 1948), pp. 12–22.

29. Trotsky, *Stalin*, p. 18.

30. Peter Lowe located a British Foreign Office study of the DPRK Constitution, which found predictable similarities with the 1936 Soviet constitution, but quite unexpected parallels with Japan's Meiji constitution (*Origins of the Korean War*, p. 50).

31. Mao, *Critique of Soviet Economics*, p. 112. For an excellent discussion of doctrines of essence, see Unger, *Knowledge and Politics*.

32. "Conversation of the Great Leader Kim Il Sung with the south Korean delegates to north-south high-level political talks," Korean Central News Agency, July 4, 1982.

33. Kim's speech at the Moranbong theater, *Kullŏja* no. 8 (August 1947), pp. 2–26; Kim Il Sung, "Speech to the Youth of Korea," *Podo*, no. 3 (August 1947), pp. 11–17; Kim, "What Are the Demands of the Various Political Parties and Social Organizations Concerning the Establishment of a Democratic Provisional Government?" *Kŭlloja*, no. 6 (June 1947), pp. 2–15; Min Chu (pseud.), "Several Problems in Leadership Work in Economic Construction," *Kŭlloja*, no. 7 (July 1947), p. 20.

34. KWP Agit/Prop Department, "Se hwan'gyŏng kwa se chogŏn," pp. 1–3, 6, 16–18, 32–35.

35. See Cumings, "Corporatism in North Korea," *Journal of Korean Studies*, no. 3 (1983), p. 280; also Philippe Schmitter, "Reflections on Mikhail Manoilescu and the Political Consequences of Delayed Development on the Periphery of Western Europe," in *Social Change in Romania, 1860–1940*, ed. Kenneth Jowitt (Berkeley, Calif.: Institute of International Studies, 1978).

36. Schmitter, "Reflections," p. 120.

37. *HGND NDSM*, April 1, 29, May 11, 1949; the newspapers were full of similar accounts. Handwritten documents on small-group meetings in the youth organs

of the regime are in RG242, SA2005, item 9/278, "Records and Statistics of General Meeting," *Puk-Chosŏn minju ch'ŏngnyŏn tongmaeng*, September 18, 1948.

38. Kim Tu-bong, "The Results of the Elections and the Tasks Facing the Worker's Party," *Kŭlloja*, no. 2 (November 1946), p. 34.

39. Kim's speech to the Second Plenary Session of the NKWP, January 24, 1948, quoted in G-2 Weekly Summary no. 125, January 30-February 6, 1948.

40. RG242, SA2005, item 7/81, CDP, "Ch'oe Yong-gŏn ŭi kyŏllon," 6th Enlarged Central Committee Meeting, December 25, 1946.

41. RG242, SA2012, item 8/70, secret investigation of Namp'o CDP branches by Kim Kyŏng-sŏk, who was head of the Namp'o branch of the KWP. This file includes detailed background accounts of many CDP members. In 1948, one woman was elected to the ROK National Assembly, Louise Yim—and she through a special procedure (Kyung Jo Lee, "Social Origins and Backgrounds of Representatives of National Assembly in South Korea 1948–1961" [Ph.D. diss., Claremont Graduate School, 1975], p. 115).

42. See *Kaebyŏk sinbo*, May 24, 25, 1950, carrying articles on things like the "Lenin-Stalin theory" on colonial revolutions.

43. RG242 carries large numbers of the *Hamgyŏng Namdo nodong sinmun*, a few copies of the *Kangwŏn inminbo* and other newspapers, all reflecting this pattern. See also Hiroshi Sakurai, "Why Did the Korean War 'Break Out' on June 25, 1950?" seminar paper, May 1983.

44. Haruki Wada, "The Soviet Union and North Korea," seminar paper, University of Washington, 1984.

45. U.S. CIC agents found that "the North Korean Government never closed the churches"; it tried to use persuasion, and did not "smear" Christianity. Interviewees estimated that there were about 200,000 Christians in North Korea when the war began (RG349, box 464, 181st CIC detachment, November 30, 1950).

46. RG242, SA2009, item 9/113, North Korean people's committee, *To, si, kun, inmin wiwŏn-hoe chigu chŏngwŏn mit samu punjang* [District administrative staff and duties in province, city, and county people's committees], "extremely secret," no place, no date.

47. RG242, SA2005, item 6/11, *saŏp kwan'gye sŏryu* [work documents], "secret."

48. RG242, SA2009, item 6/72, DPRK Naemusŏng, *Haksŭp chaeryojip* [Materials for study], no date.

49. RG242, SA2010, item 4/46, Yi Min-yŏng, head of the North Ch'ungch'ŏng People's Committee, directive on "The collection of views and the organization of an inspection network for public opinion," August 5, 1950.

50. RG242, SA2010, item 2/76, documents from the Haeju area, most dated in 1949 and 1950.

51. RG242, SA2010, item 8/106, data on clerks in the county government.

52. RG242, SA2012, item 8/16, raw data on people under surveillance by the Ch'ŏrwŏn police.

53. RG242, SA2010, item 3/145, report on Meng Mun-ok, June 1948.

54. MA, RG6, box 81, POW interrogation reports, especially Interrogation Report no. 612, August 19, 1950; there are many others that could be cited. See also Wilbur Schramm's findings in "Notes on the Pattern of Sovietization in North Korea" in U.S. Air Force, "A Preliminary Study of the Impact of Communism Upon Korea" (Maxwell Air Force Base, Ala.: Air University Human Resources Research Institute, 1951).

CHAPTER TEN

1. Zbigniew Brzezinski, *The Soviet Bloc: Unit and Conflict*, rev. ed. (Cambridge, Mass.: Harvard University Press, 1971), p. 67. Recent scholarship is less certain of the changes in Soviet policy in 1947. William Taubman agrees that the Zhdanov speech symbolized a big shift and was a response to containment; later on he links Stalin's position to a conception of "two parallel world markets" confronting each other, one capitalist and the other socialist (*Stalin's American Policy: From Entente to Detente to Cold War* [New York: W. W. Norton, 1982], pp. 172–77, 223–24). William Mc-Cagg, however, finds mixed evidence on the 1947 changes, and notes that Zhdanov and his followers were out of favor in 1948, before and after Zhdanov died; he dates the end of "separate roadism" for the satellites from early 1949 (*Stalin Embattled, 1943–1948* [Detroit: Wayne State University Press, 1978], pp. 109, 263–64, 268–70, 308–9). I think the North Korean case shows that the 1947 changes were important for the world confrontation, and I agree with Taubman's characterization of Stalin's conception of two world systems in conflict; but I also think that Soviet attempts at dominating Korea in 1947–1948 were half-hearted. If "separate-roadism" was out by 1949, so were Soviet troops from Korea, leaving weak reinforcement mechanisms; McCagg (p. 309) notes Stalin's indifference to Asian communism in 1948–1949. For a well-researched study that I believe overestimates Soviet influence in North Korea, see Erik Van Ree, "Socialism in One Zone: Stalin's Policy in Korea, 1945–1947" (Ph.D. diss., University of Amsterdam, The Netherlands, 1988).

2. In Soviet–Nationalist Chinese negotiations in 1945–1946, the Soviets sought to preserve classic big power concessions in the form of outright control of the port of Dairen, recognition of the independence of Outer Mongolia, some 154 Soviet-controlled joint stock companies running 80 percent of Manchurian industry, and the like. In negotiations with the Soviets in January 1946, Chiang Ching-guo came away thinking Manchuria was almost a matter of national defense for the Soviets (Koo Papers, box 175, "A Historical Note on Chinese-Soviet Relations," November 13, 1949). These demands, of course, presupposed a weak Nationalist regime, and even then were not pursued exclusively (industry was looted, troops were withdrawn) but seem to have been an attempt to get what could be had and let it go at that.

3. Willoughby's G-2 picked this up during the Korean War; see the translation into English, dated March 5, 1951, in MA, RG6, box 14; MA, RG9, box 110, Military Attaché Weekly Report, April 21, 1950; representative Chinese Nationalist views are available in *FR* (1949) 8, p. 167, Stuart to State, March 9, 1949.

4. On the Kao Kang affair see Franz Schurmann, *Ideology and Organization in Communist China* (Berkeley: University of California Press, 1968); for representative samples of the American intelligence estimates, see CIA reports from 1949 in HST, PSF, box 259; *FR* (1949) 8, pp. 639–41, Shanghai Consulate to State, December 21, 1949.

5. See for example RG59, Office of Chinese Affairs, box 4210, Peking to State, February 11, 1950, giving a detailed analysis of the CCP Central Committee.

6. No author, "Land Reform in China's Liberated Areas," *Puk-Chosŏn t'ongshin* [North Korea news], no. 1 (July 21-October 21, 1947), pp. 14–15; also Kim Chŏng-yong, "The Recent Situation in China," *Kŭlloja*, no. 6 (March 1949), pp. 57–61; on industrial production see Sŏl San, "Economic Development in China's Northeast," *Sun'gan t'ongshin*, no. 3 (46) (January 1950), pp. 9–13.

7. CIA, "The Situation in Korea," ORE 5/1, January 3, 1947. The CIA also said that

although "a socialistic program is favored by the large majority of Koreans," the Soviet-style program had not "won majority support."

8. FO317, piece no. 69945, R. S. Milward, "Communism in Korea," June 7, 1948.

9. HST, PSF, Intelligence File, box 249, CIA, "Relative US Security Interest in the European-Mediterranean Area and the Far East," ORE 69–49, July 14, 1949; 795.00 file, box 4299, "Estimate of Soviet Intentions toward South Korea," May 4, 1950.

10. Kim Yŏn-hun, "Patriotism in the Democratic State," *Kŭlloja*, no. 8 (August 1947), pp. 60–65; Paek Il, "The Theory of Dialectical Materialism is the World View of the Marxist-Leninst Party," *Kŭlloja*, no. 8 (August 1947), pp. 66–80. In 1946 French films still played in P'yŏngyang, but by 1948 theaters screened only Korean and Soviet films. In 1946, according to U.S. intelligence, the Soviets confiscated all short wave radios, and in 1948 they required that 60 percent of all films shown be Soviet-made (CP, 1981, "National Intelligence Survey, Korea").

11. Kim Il Sung, "Report on the Second Anniversary of Liberation," pp. 2–9.

12. H. de Galard, "Sept Ans de Politique Etrangere Sovietique," *L'Observateur*, October 9, 1952 (copy in Donovan Papers, box 8B(1), item 3089).

13. RG242, SA2009, item 7/195, soldier's notebook. The soldier's name is not given, but he was born into a tenant-farming family in Haeju, went to Manchuria in 1927, and joined the Korean Volunteer Army in November 1945; subsequently he served in the PLA Fourth Field Army. At the end of April, his unit was integrated with the KPA.

14. Dae-sook Suh, *The Korean Communist Movement, 1918–1948* (Princeton, N.J.: Princeton University Press, 1967), p. 317; 740.0019 file, box C-215, Muccio to State, January 6, 1949, reporting an interview with Father Hopple of the Benedictine monastery in Wŏnsan. It is known from secret documents that sixty-one Germans, mostly missionaries, lived in Wŏnsan and Kangwŏn Province in 1947. See RG242, SA2005, item 6/11, various secret Interior Ministry documents, most signed by the Interior Minister, Pak Il-u, November and December 1947.

15. CIA, "National Intelligence Survey: Korea"; U.S. State Department, McCune, "Leadership in North Korea."

16. Wada, "The Soviet Union and North Korea."

17. Lim Ŭn, *The Founding of a Dynasty in North Korea* (Tokyo: Jiyu-sha, 1982), p. 112.

18. Brzezinski, *Soviet Bloc*, pp. 16, 52, 122, 123n.

19. Wada, "The Soviet Union and North Korea."

20. *FR* (1949) 8, pp. 405–6, Stuart to State, July 6, 1949; ibid., p. 515, Embassy to State, September 1, 1949; ibid., pp. 586–93, Shanghai Consul to State, November 14, 1949; also Smith Papers, David Baird to Smith, July 25, 1950, enclosing the views of George Beswick.

21. CIA, "National Intelligence Survey: Korea"; U.S. Air Force, Air University, "Preliminary Study," Wilbur Schramm, "Notes on the Pattern of Sovietization in North Korea," p. 214.

22. See chapter 4.

23. Daniel Chirot, *Social Change in the Twentieth Century* (New York: Harcourt Brace Jovanovich, 1977), pp. 109–14.

24. U.S. State Department, McCune, "Leadership in North Korea"; G-2 Weekly Summary no. 100, August 3–10, 1947; RG349, box 462, G-2 report on Hŭngnam explosives plant, December 29, 1950. Army intelligence intercepted many letters in 1947 from Japanese technicians; see for example G-2 Weekly Summary no. 99, July 27-August 3, 1947.

25. G-2 Intelligence Summary—North Korea, no. 36, May 18, 1947; Kim Il Sung,

"1949 New Year's speech," *Sun'gan t'ongsin*, no. 8 (January 1949), p. 4. The Korean phrase he used was *wanjŏnhan chaju tongnip kukka*.

26. Deane Papers, "North Korea," August 1947.

27. MA, RG6, box 79, ATIS Issue no. 24, February 21, 1951. (Defense is assumed to be included in the budget line for "other expenditures.") See also a published copy of the plan in G-2, Intelligence Summary—North Korea, no. 36, May 18, 1947; also 895.00 file, box 5693, Muccio to State, December 3, 1950, enclosing an ECA study of the northern economy.

28. 895.00 file, box 5691, Drumwright to State, March 25, 1950.

29. Kim Il Sung, "Speech at the Meeting of Enthusiasts From the Industrial Branches of the Economy," November 19, 1949, in *Sun'gan t'ongshin* 42 (December 1949).

30. *Sae hwan'gyŏng*, pp. 40–41.

31. Anderson, *Imagined Communities*, p. 142.

32. *NDSM*, September 7, 1964.

33. On one-man management see Min Chu (pseud.), "Several Problems in Leadership Work," pp. 20–23; also *Sae hwan'gyŏng*, pp. 35–37, where it says that everyone in a plant must carry out the will of the *chibaein*, or master, after having held discussions to assure that everyone understands the reasons for his orders; see also *NDSM*, February 5, 1950; on the innovation of piece-rates in 1947 see G-2 Intelligence Summary—North Korea, no. 48, November 18, 1947. On one-man management in China, see the excellent discussion in Schurmann, *Ideology and Organization*; on the Soviet application of this system, see Fainsod, *How Russia Is Ruled*, pp. 425–29.

34. MA, RG6, box 78, ATIS Issue no. 14 dated December 29, 1950, translating Ko Hŭi-man to Kim Ch'aek, January 10, 1950, top secret.

35. Ibid., Issue no. 29, March 17, 1951.

36. Ibid., Issue No. 23, February 15, 1951, quoting documents captured in Wŏnsan; see also G-2, Intelligence Summary—North Korea, no. 48, November 18, 1947.

37. MA, RG6, box 78, ATIS Issue no. 31, April 3, 1951; the full title of Mortrans was the Joint Soviet-Korean Sea Transport Share Company; on O Ki-sŏp's role see also Issue No. 28, March 11, 1951.

38. *NDSM*, February 28, March 15, 1950; RG242, SA2005, item 1/2, *Chosŏn minjujuŭi inmin konghwaguk ch'oego inminhoeŭi chae sam ch'a hoeŭi hoeŭirok* [Records of the third session of the DPRK SPA], April 1949, pp. 223–25, 320.

39. MA, RG6, box 78, ATIS Issue no. 25, February 21, 1951.

40. FO317, piece no. 69940, Milward to Crossley, March 17, 1948; KMAG G-2 Periodic Report no. 274, March 3–6, 1950; RG349, box 462, G-2 report on Hŭngnam explosives plant, December 29, 1950; on military advisors see CIA, "Prospects for the Survival of the ROK," ORE 44–48, October 28, 1948; G-2, Intelligence Summaries-North Korea, no. 39, June 30, 1947; KMAG G-2 Periodic Report no. 176, September 2–6, 1949, all of which agree that Soviet advisors are not below the batallion level; see finally Kim Il Sung, "Report on the Development of the North Korean People's Economy, 1947," *Kŭlloja*, no. 4 (April 1947), pp. 22–24.

41. Kim's speech at the Moscow railway station is in Kim Il Sung, *Choguk ŭi t'ongil tongnip kwa minjuhwa rŭl wihayo* [For the unification, independence, and democratization of the motherland], vol. 1 (P'yŏngyang: KWP ch'ulp'an-sa 1949), pp. 335–36; information on the delegation and the specifics of the visit, as well as Kim's report on the visit, is in RG242, SA2005, Item 1/2, Records of the third session of the DPRK SPA, pp. 221–36. The comparison of this agreement to previous unequal treaties, including the 1882 U.S.-Korean Treaty, is in Pak Tong-ch'o, "The Meaning of the Korean-Soviet Agreement on Economic and Cultural Coopera-

tion," *Kŭlloja*, no. 8 (April 30, 1949), pp. 16–25; speeches by Kim Ch'aek and Ch'oe Yong-gŏn are carried in *HGND NDSM*, April 9, 1949.

42. Robert R. Simmons, *The Strained Alliance: Peking, P'yŏngyang, Moscow and the Politics of the Korean Civil War* (New York: The Free Press, 1975), p. 72.

43. See MA, RG6, box 79, for several translated documents dealing with Korean-Soviet relations in 1948 and 1949; apparently the Soviets failed to ship some 290 ZIS-150 trucks that had been promised in 1948, causing Kim Ch'aek to say that "our work is greatly hampered."

44. Brzezinski, *Soviet Bloc*, pp. 108–10.

45. KMAG G-2 Periodic Report no. 183, September 16–19, 1949; also RG319, G-3 file, box 36, Bolte to Army Chief of Staff, September 20, 1950; on the question of terminology, see *NDSM*, February 18, 1950, on the Sino-Soviet treaty.

46. Saburo Iyenaga, *The Pacific War* (New York: Pantheon Books, 1976).

47. Intelligence Summary—North Korea, no. 37, May 31, 1947.

48. National Archives, Army Chief of Military History manuscripts, box 601, "Military Studies on Manchuria."

49. RG242, SA2010, item 5/116, lectures for "political education," KPA Cultural Training Department, May 1950; SA2010, item 3/73, lecture notes by an unknown person dated January 16, 1950; SA2009, item 6/8, Kyŏnggi-do Interior Ministry branch, *Haebang chigu inmindŭl ŭi taehan haesŏl sŏnsan chegang* [Material for explanation and propaganda toward the people in liberated areas], July 15, 1950; Ch'oe Ch'ang-ik, "People are the Motive Force of History," *Kŭlloja*, no. 9 (September 1947), p. 20. McCagg notes that the Soviets also insisted that they, not Tito's guerrillas, liberated Yugoslavia (*Stalin Embattled*, pp. 59–60).

50. Kim Il Sung, "Report to the Second Congress of the KWP," p. 12; RG242, SA2009, item 6/76, NKWP Central Party School, *Tang Kŏnsŏl (kangŭi yogang)* [Party building (lecture outline)] (P'yŏngyang, circa late 1948), p. 99.

51. *NDSM*, January 24, 1950. Toward the end of the 3d SPA in April 1949, one stooge after another got up to call Stalin "the great genius leading mankind," "the supreme leader of the world's working people," "the saviour of the Korean people," and the like (RG242, SA2005, item 1/2, Records of the third session of the DPRK SPA, April 1949, pp. 400–402, and passim).

52. Mao's speech, quoted in *NDSM*, February 20, 1950; on Stalin's picture in China see *FR* (1949) 7, Stuart to State, July 6, 1949, quoting Chu Teh as telling Youth Congress leaders that pictures of Marx, Stalin, and Mao "are to be displayed from Left to Right in all public meeting places, government offices, factories, schools," and so on.

CHAPTER ELEVEN

1. CIA, "Current Capabilities of the Northern Korean Regime," ORE 18–50, June 19, 1950.

2. MA, RG6, box 17, "Communist Far Eastern Ring," February 6, 1948, enclosing intercepted Strong letter to Hugh Deane, August 15, 1947. Among other interesting observations, Strong said large numbers of Koreans came to the North after the fall 1946 uprisings, some 215,000 in the first five months of 1947, according to border quarantine stations; that the people were accustomed to "slave-teaching" and thought that "all government comes from above," not having to fight for their freedom or reforms: "they have a land reform in twenty days. No, that's not life . . . there ain't no class struggle and no talk of one . . . I have a feeling that people

here live in a kind of fool's paradise, building industry, farming and schools and a 'People's Republic' with perhaps a civil war around the corner." The first but not the last Western leftist to run afoul of Korean isolationism and solipsism, she complained about being told that everything in the country was "100% successful." Sad to say, in her published account of the visit she left out these criticisms. The original of the letter is available in the Hugh Deane Papers; see also her pamphlet, *North Korea* (New York: 1947).

3. RG242, SA2009, item 8/32, *Ch'ŏngch'i kyomun* [Political lectures], no place, no date but, before the Korean War.

4. RG242, SA2005, item 2/72, *Pan-Il t'usa yŏnsŏljip* [Speeches of the anti-Japanese fighters] (P'yŏngyang, August 1946), pp. 55–64. Another example of Chinese influence is a pamphlet, SA2013, item 1/145, *Chungguk kongsandang kwa minjok t'ongil chŏnsŏn* [The CCP and the national unification front], put out by the Hamhŭng City branch of the KCP in February 1946; it asked, among foreign countries, "Who is the very best at fighting for the Korean nation . . . who most actively works . . . for Korea's complete independence?" The implied answer was the Chinese Communists, not the Soviets (p. 1).

5. Han, Chae-dŏk, *Kim Il Sung Changgun* (P'yŏngyang: Minju Chosŏn-sa, 1947), pp. 26–28; *Puk-Chosŏn t'ongshin* [North Korea news], no. 1 (July-October 1947), pp. 24–27.

6. MA, RG6, box 68, Interrogation Report no. 3015, interviews with former professors at Kim Il Sung University and officers in the KPA; see also Wada, "The Soviet Union and North Korea."

7. U.S. State Department, McCune, "Leadership in North Korea."

8. Kim, "Greeting the First Anniversary of the Founding of the NKWP," pp. 27–44.

9. See the lead editorial, and articles by Kim Ch'ang-man and Chang Ha-il in *Kŭlloja*, no. 10 (December 1947), pp. 1–35.

10. See *Kŭlloja*, no. 11 (January 1948), pp. 2–22, for the lead editorial and Kim's article.

11. Mao Tse-tung, "On Methods of Leadership," in *Selected Works* (New York: International Publishers, 1954), pp. 113–14.

12. Kim, "Report to the Second Congress of the KWP."

13. See for example the lead editorials in *NDSM*, January 1, 1950, and February 28, 1950. Provincial newspapers frequently quoted the 2d Congress speech and the mass line emphases. See for example *HGND NDSM*, May 17, 1949.

14. Ch'oe Ch'ang-ik, "People Are the Motive Force of History," pp. 13–23. Again, as with Kim Ch'ang-man's articles in this period, Ch'oe's followed the lead editorial; he began by linking Kim Il Sung's guerrilla struggle to that by Koreans in Yanan, went on to discuss the domestic movement in Korea without ever mentioning Pak Hŏn-yŏng's KCP, distinctly slighted the Soviet effort in liberating Korea, and ended with a paean of praise to Kim. In other words, Ch'oe articulated the Kim Il Sung line throughout, except to bring in the Yanan Koreans.

15. Kennan, in CP, 1977, item 316B, "Transcript of Round Table Discussion," October 1949.

16. 895.00 file, box 7127, Drumwright to State, January 10, 1949; MA, RG6, box 14, G-2 Flash Report, July 4, 1950.

17. Ch'oe's statement is in RG242, SA2005, item 1/2, Record of the third session of the DPRK SPA, April 1949, p. 18; Chŏng's is in *NDSM*, February 27, 1950.

18. *Sae hwan'gyŏng*, May 1950, p. 16.

19. R. A. Ulyanovsky, ed., *The Comintern and the East* (Moscow: Progress Publishers, 1979), pp. 204–6, 223.

20. See my discussion in volume 1, and RG242, SA2009, item 8/32, *chŏngch'i kyomun*, where the 1941 date is given. See also Intelligence Summary—North Korea, nos. 30, 42, and 46, February 16, August 18, and October 18, 1947. Interestingly, a translation of Mao's "On Coalition Government," published in Seoul in February 1946, has inserts by the translator referring to Kim Il Sung's detachment, and the KVA, as having fought with the Chinese; these are the only resistance groups mentioned. See RG242, SA2006, item 15/32, Mao, *Yŏnhap chŏngbu* (Seoul: Uri sŏwŏn, February 1946), pp. 3, 6.

21. William W. Whitson, *The Chinese High Command: A History of Communist Military Politics*, with Chen-hsia Huang (New York: Praeger, 1973), pp. 87–88.

22. FO317, piece no. 69945, R. S. Milward, "Communism in Korea," June 7, 1948.

23. RG349, box 462, December 29, 1950, G-2 report on Hŭngnam explosives plant.

24. USAMGIK G-2, Intelligence Summary—North Korea, no. 37, May 31, 1947. See also FO317, piece no. 69940, Milward to Crossley, March 17, 1948, enclosing a secret study of North Korea in 1947; also piece no. 69945, R. S. Milward, "Communism in Korea," June 7, 1948.

25. See FO317, FK10310/4, July 7, 1950, BBC monitoring of Radio Taipei. On the March 1949 alleged pact, see *Han'guk chŏnjaeng-sa*, I, p. 711; Simmons, *Strained Alliance*, p. 32. Simmons cited a tantalizing Kyodo News report dated May 11, 1950: it said that North Korea concluded "a bilateral defense pact" secretly with the PRC, and that in the spring of 1949, Kim Il Sung told Shtykov that his forces would attack the south: "If the attack failed, by the intervention of a third country, there would be a temporary retreat to Manchuria, and they would attack again at a favorable time. Therefore, he proposed a military alliance with the Chinese communists." This report may well be true, but unfortunately Kyodo is notoriously unreliable.

26. G-2 Weekly Summary no. 113, November 2–9, 1947; also RG59, Wedemeyer Papers, box 3, statement by T. Y. Yun to the RDC, August 29, 1947; also G-2 Intelligence Summary—North Korea, nos. 36, 37, 38, and 39, May 18, 31, June 15, June 30, 1947; Ch'oe's statement is in no. 38.

27. RG59, Wedemeyer Mission, box 1, "China—Current Situation," July 11, 1947; also F. J. Dau, Asst. Military Attaché, Nanjing Embassy, to Lt. Col. Hutchin, July 7, 1947, citing American military attaché reports from Manchuria. See also Wellington Koo Papers, box 108, an "extremely secret" cable in Chinese from the Nationalist Foreign Ministry to Koo, dated June 23, 1947, which discusses the Korean participation, and also says large numbers of Japanese soldiers have joined or been impressed into the CCF.

28. Wellington Koo's papers, box 175, contain a document, "Historical Note on Chinese-Soviet Relations," November 13, 1949, which refers to 65,000 Korean troops in Manchuria commanded by "Li Hung-kwang"; a Chinese Nationalist intelligence report of August 22, 1950, cites a meeting held in early July in Mukden, allegedly participated in by Molotov, Mao, Kim Il Sung, and "Li Hong Kwan," the latter said to be the commander of the "North Korean People's Liberation Army." See RG59, Office of Chinese Affairs, box 4211. On the incorporation of the YHD into the KPA, see Intelligence Summary-North Korea, no. 132, March 19–26, 1948. The YHD training book is to be found in RG242, SA2009, item 8/73, *Sasang chinam* [Thought guidance], no place or date, but published by the Political Department of the YHD.

29. MA, RG6, box 58, intelligence summary no. 2803, May 13, 1950; no. 2805, May 15, 1950; no. 2821, May 31, 1950; no. 2840, June 19, 1950; no. 2880, July 29, 1950. This latter report placed the entire 6th Division at Haeju. See also KMAG

G-2 Weekly Report no. 2, April 7–13, 1950. See also Almond Papers, Korean War general file, periodic intelligence report no. 190, April 4, 1951, and "North Korean Military Personalities," April 25, 1951. Whitson listed Pang as commander of the 166th Division of the 17th PLA Army (Whitson, *Chinese High Command*, p. 322, chart H).

30. Appleman, *Naktong/Yalu*, p. 394; MA, RG6, box 58, intelligence summary no. 2817, May 27, 1950. Also Koon Woo Nam, *The North Korean Communist Leadership, 1945–1965: A Study of Factionalism and Political Consolidation* (University, Ala.: University of Alabama Press, 1974), pp. 46–47.

31. Information on backgrounds of KPA officers may be found in Intelligence Summary—North Korea, nos. 132, 134, 152, and 156, March 19–26, April 2–9, August 6–13, and September 3–10, 1948; they reported that Mu Chŏng and Kim Il Sung were "at odds most of the time," with Mu Chŏng particularly opposed to a separate government in the North (much like Kim Ku in the south) and said to be "threatening" Kim. It also said Mu had a Chinese wife whom he divorced upon his return to Korea. Several of the KVA leaders had trained at Whampoa Academy, including Pang Ho-san, Han Kyŏng, and Yi Ik-sŏng. Pang's father-in-law was a rightist who ran the Samsan Hotel in Sinŭiju, but his wife became a communist. See information in Almond Papers, "Korean War General Files," X Corps Periodic Report, April 25, 1951, "North Korean Military Personalities."

32. James F. Schnabel puts his emphasis on Soviet training of the KPA, grossly underestimating the CCF returnees at about 30,000. See *Policy and Direction: The First Year* (Washington, D.C.: Office of the Chief of Military History, 1972), p. 37. Appleman shows more awareness of the role of CCF veterans, but never emphasizes their importance; yet he puts the total number of Koreans in the CCF 4th Field Army alone at 145,000 (*Naktong/Yalu*, pp. 332, 523, 567, 750).

33. In addition to Schnabel, *Policy and Direction* and Appleman, *Naktong/Yalu*, see: KMAG G-2 Periodic Reports nos. 165, 200, 205, 240, 278, 280, and 285, August 12–16, October 18–20, and October 27–28, 1949; January 3–5, March 10–13, March 14–16, and March 23–24, 1950; also *FR* (1949) 8, pp. 573–74, Muccio to State, November 1, 1949; also 795.00 file, box 4271, Army study of Chinese aid to North Korea before June 25, 1950, December 29, 1950; FO317, piece no. 83238, E. T. Biggs political summary for August, including Chinese Nationalist intelligence estimates, September 13, 1950; Office of Chinese Affairs, box 4222, Freeman to Rusk, July 6, 1950, including Nationalist intelligence estimates. Whitson's information backs this intelligence up. In March 1950, he says, troops from the 167th, 169th, 170th and 171st Divisions of the PLA 17th Army returned and were reorganized as the KPA 10th Division (*Chinese High Command*, p. 322, chart H).

34. MA, RG6, box 14, "Order of Battle, Chinese Communist Fourth Field Army," November 7, 1950; see also MacArthur's top secret report of September 1, 1950, in 795.00 file, box 4269, MacArthur to Army, September 13, 1950.

35. See the diary in RG242, SA2010, item 5/188; also Kim Ho-il's diary translation in MA, RG6, box 79, ATIS no. 15, January 3, 1951; also the interrogation report on Chŏn, MA, RG6, box 80, Report no. 612, August 19, 1950. It is noteworthy that most of the interrogations were done by Japanese, then translated into English.

36. The translation of Sun Tzu is in RG242, SA2012, item 8/118; see also "Several Documents from the Chinese Civil War" [*Chungguk naejŏn e kwanhan che munhŏn*], RG242, SA2010, item 3/54 (KPA, 1950); Maoist texts on guerrilla war with fake covers, translated into Korean, are in SA2009, item 6/114, and SA2010, item 3/155; on Kim's "seven points for attention," see MA, RG6, box 78, ATIS item no. 8, translating a captured KPA notebook.

37. Kim's speech on February 8, 1948, is in *Choguk ŭi t'ongil tongnip kwa minjuhwa rŭl wihayô* [For the unification, independence, and democratization of the homeland] (P'yŏngyang: Nodongdang ch'ulp'an-sa, August 1949), pp. 73–87.
38. Han, *Kim Il Sung*, pp. 47–64.
39. *HGND NDSM*, June 1, 8, 1949.
40. See Kim Il's articles in *NDSM*, January 12, 19, 1950.
41. Kang Kŏn's article on the KPA is in *NDSM*, February 6, 1950; Ch'oe Yong-gŏn's is in *NDSM*, February 8, 1950; Ch'oe Hyŏn's, *NDSM*, January 20, 1950; Mu Chŏng's appeared on February 5, 1950; other articles cited in the text came from *NDSM* in January and early February 1950. Kang Kŏn died in Korean War fighting in September 1950. His obituary is in *NDSM*, September 11, 1950. His son was then reared in a Man'gyŏngdae school for orphans of patriots, and reportedly directed the 1983 terrorist attack on South Korean leaders in Rangoon, Burma.

    Ch'oe Yong-gŏn, according to the CIA, had "an outstanding reputation" as an officer in the CCF, but was thought during the Korean War to be an officer "of mediocre ability." His wife had also been a guerrilla in Manchuria (CIA, "National Intelligence Survey: Korea").

    Ch'oe Hyŏn was among Kim's closest intimates, retreating with him to the Khabarovsk border area with Manchuria in 1941 after a decade of guerrilla war. See Almond Papers, Korean War General Files, "North Korean Military Personalities," April 25, 1951.
42. *NDSM*, February 8, 1950. For other references to Kim as *suryŏng* see *NDSM*, February 5, 1950, March 4, 1950.
43. RG242, SA2010, item 5/116, lecture outlines for "political education" (*chŏngch'i sanghak*) to take place during planned "summer 1950 battle training," 855th unit of the KPA.
44. P'yŏngyang has a Korean history museum with exhibits that end in 1919; the visitor then moves to the Revolutionary Museum, which begins in 1919 with a portrait of seven-year-old Kim Il Sung in the van of the March First Independence Movement. The rest of the museum tells the story of Korean history from 1919 to the present through the life of Kim.
45. "Thank you, Kim Il Sung" messages always appeared in the newspapers, written by peasants and workers; the examples of soldier oaths are to be found in *HGND NDSM*, May 15, 1949, and in MA, RG6, box 78, ATIS translation item no. 8, from a captured KPA soldier's diary; examples of questions put to recruits are in RG242, SA2005, item 5/44. Of 102 recruits in this sample, 94 were of poor peasant class, 8 middle peasant. It is interesting to note the purely nationalist appeals used in these recruit interviews. When asked, "who must build the People's Republic," the correct answer was, "we must build it with our own hands."
46. Kim Chŏng-yong, "The Recent Situation in China," *Kŭlloja*, no. 6 (March 1949), pp. 50–71; *HGND NDSM*, May 6, 19, 1949.
47. *NDSM*, January 1, 14, 1950; *Sun'gan t'ongshin*, no. 5 (January 1950), pp. 1–2.
48. On the appointment of Yi Chu-yŏn, thought to be a confidant of Kim Il Sung, see *NDSM*, January 19, 1950; on the recognition of the DRV see *NDSM*, February 1, 1950. The response to Acheson's speech is in the issue of Jan 26, 1950.
49. Yi Sŭng-yŏp, "On the Present Tasks of the Southern People's Guerrillas," pp. 9–22.
50. Nitze, in *FR* (1950) 1, pp. 145–47, "Recent Soviet Moves," February 8, 1950; Kennan in Acheson Seminars, February 13, 1954; Acheson letter to Alan Bullock, April 27, 1955, Acheson Papers (Yale), box 4. Charles Bohlen also highlighted the

Malenkov speech in a letter to Kennan of November 9, 1951 (Bohlen Papers, box 36).

51. Walter LaFeber, *America, Russia and the Cold War*, p. 90.

52. For the October reference see *Sun'gan t'ongshin*, no. 37 (October 1949), p. 14; Kim's December speech is in *Nodong-dang chungang wiwŏnhoe chŏnggi hoeŭi munhŏnjip* [Documents on the general meeting of the KWP Central Committee], December 15–18, 1949 (P'yŏngyang: KWP, 1950), pp. 3–46.

53. Kirk quoted Soviet New Year's editorials in Kirk to State, January 4, 1950, *FR* (1949) 4, pp. 1075–77; the other references are from *NDSM*, January 1, 1950.

54. Articles in *NDSM*, January 6, 20, and March 30, 1950.

55. See Kim's "report to the Second Congress of the NKWP," pp. 11–12; "1949 New Year's Speech," *Sun'gan t'ongshin*, no. 8 (January 1949), pp. 1–6.

56. Speeches on June 25, 1949, quoted in *HGND NDSM*, June 27, 1949; see also the editorial in *HGND NDSM*, May 10, 1949.

57. *NDSM*, January 15, 24, 1950.

58. 795.00 file, box 4262, State to Embassy, January 31, 1950. For an editorial criticizing the "one-world" idea that "nationalism is dead," as well as Henry Luce's "American Century," see *HGND NDSM*, "What is Cosmopolitanism?" June 14, 1949. On the Chinese view of Korean nationalism, see "Intelligence Summary-North Korea," no. 36, May 18, 1947.

59. Drumwright to State, 795.00 file, box 4262, January 7, 1950; "The Background of the Present War in Korea," pp. 233–37; FO317, piece no. 69337, Kermode to FO, December 22, 1947.

60. Buss's memo of October 13, 1948, is in 895.00 file, box C-945, Muccio to Bond, October 21, 1948.

CHAPTER TWELVE

1. RG335, Secretary of the Army file, box 77, Royall to Secretary of Defense, March 17, 1948; HST, PSF, NSC meetings, summary of 9th NSC meeting, April 12, 1948. Royall was for withdrawal in spite of his doubts that the ROK could even maintain internal security, let alone defend against the North: "the Koreans have never had internal security and probably never will have, because of the dissident elements" (9th NSC meeting).

2. RG335, Secretary of the Army file, box 22, memo of conference between Muccio, Draper, and others, August 9, 1948; ibid., box 22, Almond to Mueller, January 11, 1949.

3. 895.00 file, box 7126, Muccio to State, November 16, 1948; 740.0019 file, box C-215, Muccio to Secretary of State, May 11, 1949; Muccio frequently called for additional armaments for the ROKA in 1949–1950.

4. 740.0019 Control (Korea) file, box C-215, Royall to Secretary of State, January 25, 1949; memo of conversation between Rhee, Royall, and Muccio, February 8, 1949, in Butterworth to Webb, March 3, 1949; also memorandum of conversation, Royall, Draper, and Muccio, February 25, 1949; also HST, PSF, NSC file, box 220, summary of the 34th meeting of the NSC, February 18, 1949.

5. RG330, Secretary of Defense file, box 33, Gray to Johnson, May 4, 1949.

6. The JCS estimate was discussed earlier in connection with the NSC 48 deliberations; the CIA estimated in February 1949 that "withdrawal of US forces from Korea in the spring of 1949 would probably in time be followed by an invasion"; later on in the document it deemed such an invasion "highly probable." See HST,

PSF, CIA file, box 256, CIA, "Consequences of US Troop Withdrawal from Korea in Spring, 1949," ORE 3–49, February 28, 1949. See also MA, RG9, Blue Binder, "Korea Planning and Withdrawal Documents," Colonels Levy and Maris, CINCFE, to Department of the Army, January 19 and June 12, 1949.

7. 740.0019 file, box C-215, Acheson to Seoul, May 9, 1949; Muccio to Acheson, May 11, 1949.

8. 895.00 file, box 7127, Drumwright to State, July 11, 1949.

9. Enclosed in Gordon Gray to Sidney Souers, June 30, 1949, a paper declassified by the National Security Council in 1981 and given to me by Michael Schaller, to whom I am grateful.

10. 740.0019 file, box C-215, Muccio to State, April 15, 1949; Muccio to State, May 7, 10, 1949; Acheson to Seoul, May 7, 1949; 895.00 file, box 7127, Muccio to State, September 13, 1949.

11. See 890.00 file, box C-846, Dean Rusk, memo for the Secretary, July 16, 1949, and Yost to Jessup, July 18, 1949; also *FR* (1950) 6, pp. 19–20, Thai Embassy to State, February 18, 1950.

12. Australian Tokyo Embassy to Canberra, June 15, 1949, courtesy Gavan McCormack (I am indebted to Professor McCormack for this document and other references herein from the Australian archives, which I did not visit); HST, PSF, NSC file, box 206, CIA, Review of the World Situation, June 15, 1949 (the CIA said that in spite of Rhee's panic, "the Republic's armed forces are at least equal in number and superior in equipment to those of North Korea"); Muccio's view is in 740.0019 file, box C-215, Muccio to State, May 31, 1949, the full statement being "Clamor and fear aroused by troop withdrawal have far exceeded my expectations. It now appears sense of crisis bordering on panic has enveloped higher circles [of] Korean Government"; the North Korean view is in *HGND NDSM*, June 4, 1949, terming Rhee a "country-selling criminal" who is "prostrating himself before his American masters" to get the troops to stay.

13. 895.00 file, box 946, Muccio letter to Butterworth, August 27, 1949.

14. In a secret Interior Ministry message to front-line units, dated November 27, 1947, Pak Il-u cited Korean National Police and Northwest Youth forays across the border, saying that with the announcement of the Soviet troop withdrawal, the South Koreans want to "provoke disorders" so that U.S. troops will not withdraw. See this document in RG242, SA2005, item 6/11, *Samu gwan'gye soryu*. A signed article in the June 24, 1949, issue of *HGND NDSM* said that Rhee wants "to start a civil war" to get the U.S. Army to stay in Korea.

15. Koo Papers, box 217, diary entries, February 8, June 28, 29, 1949; oral history, vol. 6, pt. 1, pp. 1–367; see the cable in box 147, cable no. 222, June 29, 1949. Wing Fook Jung is listed in *Army Register*, 1950. See a "Lt. Col. Jung" of Army G-2 listed in NA, Lot 55D128, box 381, Korean Log, June 24–25, 1950. Koo's Chinese-language cable to the Foreign Ministry in Taipei was dispatched on June 29, 1950, and reads as follows: "According to a secret source, the American Government is reviewing and examining the situation in Korea. The source predicts that since the American troops have withdrawn, the North Korean army will invade the South and South Korean government will be unable to resist the invasion. . . . At that time, General MacArthur will have an excuse to send the Seventh Division, which has been withdrawn, back to South Korea. . . . We should pay attention to this development."

16. ON ECA and KMAG as the largest such missions in any country, see 795.00 file, box 4299, Drumwright to Embassy, May 10, 1950; the Greek figure is from Army data in Knowland to Hoover, January 23, 1950, Herbert Hoover PPI file, box 395;

there were 37 officers and enlisted men in 1947, 330 in 1948. On military advisory groups as substitutes for American forces, see Omar H. Bradley and Clay Blair, *A General's Life* (New York, Simon and Schuster, 1983), p. 475.

17. *FR* (1949) 9, pp. 428–31, Acheson to Taipei, November 18, 1949. In February 1950, Acheson told Truman that "there will inevitably continue to exist special situations (e.g., Greece, Austria, Turkey) whose independent survival may depend upon support from us" (*FR* [1950] 1, pp. 838–41, Acheson to Truman, February 16, 1950). In April 1950 Truman linked together "Greece, Turkey, and Korea," in a public statement discussing countries getting aid "to strengthen their economies against communist subversion or aggression" (HST, Official file, box 1304, press release of April 3, 1950). Senator Knowland acknowledged the difference between Acheson's Korea and Taiwan policies by telling him in May 1950 that the United States should develop a program for Taiwan "in the same way that our assistance to Greece and to Korea has been handled" (Smith Papers, box 100, Knowland to Acheson, May 15, 1950).

18. U.S. Senate, Committee on Foreign Relations, Historical Series, *Economic Assistance to China and Korea: 1949–1950* (Washington, D.C.: U.S. Government Printing Office, 1974), pp. 148, 157, 170.

19. Far East confidential file, box C-846, meeting of the Secretary and consultants on the Far East, October 26, 1949 (emphasis added); HST, CIA file, box 255, CIA, "Governmental Programs on National Security and International Affairs for Fiscal Year 1951," ORE 74-49, September 22, 1949, top secret, sanitized copy declassified June 12, 1980. See also Kennan's testimony on June 20, 1949, where he said "there is a good deal of similarity" between US policies in Greece and Korea. "In Greece, too, we have not sent American Armed Forces." And, "I doubt if we would have chosen the Greek Peninsula as a place to fight the Russians with armed forces. . . . If there had been a war, that would not be the place we would have cared to tangle with the Russians." (U.S. Congress, House, Committee on International Relations, *United States Policy in the Far East, Part 2: Korea Assistance Acts, Far East Portion of the Mutual Defense Assistance Act of 1950* [Washington, D.C.: U.S. Government Printing Office, 1976], pp. 101–2.)

20. See Foreign Minister Pak Hŏn-yŏng's detailed listing of visits from October 29 to December 28, 1949, *NDSM*, January 14, 1950.

21. MA, RG9, box 40, Army to KMAG Chief, October 27, 1949.

22. Ibid., box 149, CINCFE to Army, December 27, 1948. MacArthur meant "ultimate responsibility" as long as American ground forces remained in Korea.

23. Reston spoke openly about this strategy in June 1950, noting that some opposed it, wanting to present the Soviets with a two-front war (*New York Times*, June 18, 1950).

24. *FR* (1950) 6, pp. 949–54, JCS, Joint Strategic Survey Committee, analysis of Indochina, November 17, 1950.

25. *New York Times*, letters column, April 30, 1950; Patterson Papers, box 45, Schlesinger to Patterson, July 11, 1950.

26. HST, Acheson Papers, box 65, Kennan's off-the-record speech to the National Defense Committee of the U.S. Chamber of Commerce, January 23, 1947, enclosed in Kennan to Acheson, August 21, 1950.

27. PPS file, box 32, 148th meeting record, October 11, 1949.

28. Acheson Seminars, July 23, 1953.

29. Roberts to Bolte, "Personal Comments on KMAG and Korean Affairs," August 19, 1949, xeroxed document held by archivist Robert Taylor, National Archives, room 13W. The South's official study, *Han'guk chŏnjaeng-sa* [History of the Korean

War] has extended accounts of the border fighting (Vol. 1, pp. 506–44), but I have relied instead on primary sources from the time, since this study blames all the battles on the North and has so many obvious distortions as to make it unreliable. The same is true of its treatment of the guerrilla fighting, and the outbreak of the war in June 1950.

30. USFIK 11071 file, box 62/96, G-2 "Staff Study," February 1949, signed by Lt. Col. B. W. Heckemeyer of Army G-2. The North Koreans sent a host of captured documents to the United Nations in photostatic copy in late 1950, but UN archival authorities seem to be unable to find them. The reference in the text is to *The Daily Worker*, December 4, 1950. I saw a photostat of this document in the North Korean war museum, and it bore the same markings and signatures as other KMAG materials that I have used, and did not seem to have been altered.

31. Robert K. Sawyer, *Military Advisors in Korea: KMAG in Peace and War* (Washington, D.C.: Office of the Chief of Military History, 1962), p. 58.

32. Kim, *Military Revolution in Korea*, pp. 46–63.

33. RG335, Secretary of the Army file, box 56, Hodge to JCS, January 14, 1948; Hodge also said, "it is safe to assume that some of the North Korean attacks are in retaliation for South Korean attacks." In a listing of various incidents in December 1947 and January 1948, Northwest Youth members were involved in nearly all of them. See also G-2 Intelligence Summary no. 142, May 28-June 4, 1948; RG334, 971st CIC detachment, box no. 18371, "Annual Progress Report for 1948," December 31, 1948; ibid., CIC Monthly Information Report no. 8, January 12, 1949.

34. 895.00 file, box 7127, Muccio to State, May 13, 1949; Drumwright to State, June 13, 1949.

35. *NDSM*, February 6, 1950. Because *Nodong sinmun* issues for May 1949 are not available, I do not know if they charged Kim with attacking at the time. With a Thames Television crew I interviewed a brigade leader in the KPA border constabulary, who fought at Sŏng'ak-san. He said the battle began on May 4 with a dawn attack across the parallel by the southern forces, in which they took Hill 291, part of Sŏng'ak-san. The North brought up reinforcements, and after four days of fighting they retook the hill. He claimed that four hundred ROKA soldiers were killed or wounded. He also asserted that another big battle at Sŏng'ak-san began with a dawn attack by ROKA elements on July 25, touching off five more days of heavy fighting (Interview with Chon Hi Sup, November 1987, P'yŏngyang).

36. Deane Papers, "Notes on Korea," June 2, 1948.

37. RG349, box 699, Roberts to General Almond, August 5, 1949. For additional information suggesting southern authorship, see *FR* (1949) 6, pp. 987–88, 1016–18.

38. *HGND NDSM*, May 7, 11, 1949.

39. Ibid., May 15, 1949. Chun Sung Chol, who participated in the May fighting at Ongjin, told a Thames Television crew that elements of the 2d Battalion of the ROKA 12th Regiment, together with combat police and elements of the Northwest Youth, attacked across the parallel east of Haeju on May 24, and again on May 27. He did not mention the North's attacks south of the parallel (Interview, November 1987, P'yŏngyang).

40. Merrill, "Internal Warfare," pp. 311–12; 895.00 file, box 7127, Drumwright to State, June 11, 1949; FO317, piece no. 76259, Holt to Bevin, June 21, 1949; *HGND NDSM*, June 23, 25, 1949; *Han'guk chŏnjaeng-sa*, Vol. 1, p. 508.

41. *HGND NDSM*, June 23, 1950; *New York Times*, June 28, 1949; Thames Television interview with Han Jin Hyong, P'yŏngyang, November 1987. Han was a secretary in the operations division of one of the North Korean border units, and showed

me original documents on the Horim unit. See also Kim Han Gil, *Modern History of Korea* (P'yŏngyang: Foreign Languages Publishing House, 1979), pp. 266–67.

42. *New York Times*, June 29, 1950 (the story of the Ongjin fighting was carried on the front page).

43. UN Archives, BOX DAG-1/2.1.2, box 3, account of briefing on June 15, 1949.

44. 895.00 file, box 7127, Drumwright to State, July 11, 1949; FO371, piece no. 76262, Holt to FO, June 28, 1949.

45. Kim Hyo-sŏk quotes Rhee as saying on July 15, 1949, that "he intended to start a northern expedition" (*Haebang ilbo*, July 8, 1950). See also MA, RG9, box 40, KMAG Chief to Department of the Army, July 22, 1949, where Roberts worries about lower levels in the ROKA provoking an attack; also MA, RG6, box 79, intelligence summaries, issue no. 26, February 28, 1951, translating a top secret report of July 15, 1949, by the North Korean 383rd Coastal Defense Unit, saying that an enemy force of Marines and infantry left Chinhae, and will attempt to land at Wŏnsan. On the mining of *all* roads into the North, "in preparation for an invasion by South Korean Armed Forces," see KMAG G-2 Periodic Report no. 174, August 30-September 1, 1949.

46. MA, RG9, box 43, Roberts to Department of the Army, August 1, 9, 1949; *New York Times*, August 5, 1949; *NDSM*, February 6, 1950.

47. Kim Han Gil also stresses the importance of the Ŭnp'a fighting, and the earlier fighting at Sŏng'aksan (*Modern History of Korea*, p. 266). At this time, Roberts sought to cut down on ROKA ammunition supplies, fearing an attack on North Korea: "it seems advisable to retain maximum degree of control over SKSF [S. Korean security forces] in this way" (RG349, box 747, Roberts to Dept of Army, top secret, August 2, 1949).

48. 895.00 file, box 946, Muccio, memos of conversation on August 13, 16, 1949.

49. Niles Bond told Australian officials that Muccio and Roberts "were constantly warning the Koreans that such a step [an attack northward] would result in the stoppage of American aid, the withdrawal of the Military Mission," and other measures. See Washington to Canberra, memorandum 953, August 17, 1949; also FO317, piece no. 76259, Holt to FO, September 2, 1949. Roberts's letter to Almond is in RG349, box 699, August 5, 1949. At this time, Roberts still thought the North Korean goal had been to seize all of Ongjin. (Roberts told Bolte similar information about the South's desire to invade Ch'ŏrwŏn; see Roberts to Bolte, "Personal Comments on KMAG and Korean Affairs," August 19, 1949.)

50. 895.00 file, box 946, Muccio to Butterworth, August 27, 1949.

51. Merrill, "Internal Warfare," p. 315; RG338, KMAG files, box 5414, Hansen to Roberts, September 1, 1949; also Bartosik to Capitol Division KMAG Advisor, September 1, 1949; also MA, RG9, box 43, U.S. Naval attaché, Seoul, to Washington, August 23, 1949; KMAG G-2 Periodic Report no. 176, September 2–6, no. 177, September 6–8, 1949.

52. RG330, Secretary of Defense file, box 2, Irwin, "Estimate of North Korean Objectives," August 9, 1949; *New York Times*, August 10, 1949.

53. Koo Papers, box 217, Koo Diaries, entry for January 4, 1950. Goodfellow arrived in Seoul on September 27, 1949 (895.00 file, box 7127, Muccio to State, October 7, 1949).

54. Koo, Oral History, Columbia University.

55. KMAG G-2 Periodic Reports no. 184, September 19–20, no. 187, September 23–26, no. 188, September 26–27, no. 189, September 27–29, 1949.

56. Quoted in Lhee Yung Myung, "The Policies of Syngman Rhee and the U.S. (1945–1950)," pp. 77–78.

57. KMAG G-2 Periodic Reports no. 198, October 14–17, no. 200, October 18–20, no. 201, October 20–21, no. 203, October 24–25, no. 204, October 25–27, no. 205, October 27–28, 1949.

58. Goodfellow Papers, Rhee to Goodfellow, October 26, 1949; *NDSM*, January 5, 1950. This issue discusses the campaign, and says it began in October 1949.

59. Merrill, "Internal Warfare," p. 334. KMAG G-2 Periodic Report no. 234, December 20–22, 1949, probably referred to this fighting in listing seventy KPA and five ROKA dead from an Ongjin battle on December 9–10, without mentioning that Paek started it. See also 895.00 file, box 7128, Embassy to State, summary for November, December 10, 1949.

60. 895.00 file, box 7128, Embassy to State, November 7, 1949.

61. 895.00 file, box 946, Muccio to Butterworth, November 1, 1949.

62. *New York Times*, July 15, 1950.

63. A former secretary to Rhee who defected to the North, and whose book contains much accurate information on the 1949 fighting, says the Ongjin and Kaesŏng fighting convinced Roberts of the strength of the KPA and the weakness of the ROKA, causing MacArthur to conclude that if the North were to attack, American troops would have to be used to defend the ROK. Mun Hak-bong, *Mije ŭi Chosŏn ch'imnyak chŏngch'aek ŭi chŏngbon wa naeran paep'oja ŭi p'ongno ham* [A true account of American imperialism's aggressive Korea policy and an exposure of the instigators of civil war] (P'yŏngyang: Chung'ang t'ongshin, September 1950), p. 70.

64. HST, Acheson Papers, box 81, "Notes on Korea."

65. Thames Television interview, P'yŏngyang, November 1987.

66. *New York Herald-Tribune*, October 30, 1949.

67. MA, RG9, box 43, Roberts to Department of the Army, September 23, 1949; Roberts to MacArthur, September 30, 1949; KMAG G-2 Periodic Report no. 221, November 28–29, 1949.

68. Major Bennie W. Griffith, Jr., response to a questionnaire submitted by John Merrill, courtesy Dr. Merrill.

69. 795.00 file, box 4262, "Guerrilla Strength and Activity," in Drumwright to State, April 15, 1950; MA, RG6, box 60, intelligence summary no. 2873, July 22, 1950.

70. The following section is taken from daily reports in RG319, G-2 file, box 873, KMAG G-2 Periodic Reports nos. 191–226, September 29-December 8, 1949.

71. 895.00 file, box 7128, Muccio to State, December 27, 1949.

72. FO317, piece no. 76258, Holt to Far East, January 18, 1949; piece no. 76259, Holt to Far East, October 14, 1949; Holt to Far East, October 27, 1949; Holt to Far East, November 16, 1949; Merrill, "Internal Warfare," p. 354.

73. 795.00 file, box 4303, Embassy to State, May 19, 1950, enclosing a recent National Assembly report—judged "valuable and reasonably accurate" by the Embassy.

74. KMAG Periodic Report no. 209, November 3–4, 1949, and no. 211, November 7–8, 1949.

75. MA, RG6, box 40, Daily Intelligence Summaries, no. 2686, January 16, 1950; a similar account is in MA, RG9, box 43, U.S. Military Attaché to Department of the Army, January 11, 1950. The North Koreans ran a similar acccount of the incident, but gave the name of the village as Sŏkbong-ni, and said that rightist youths under ROK protection were responsible. Their casualty figures were the same as the internal American account. See *NDSM*, January 3, 1950.

76. RG338, KMAG file, box 5417, raw notes, Major Painter to Advisor of KNP, "Activities 25 Dec to 1 Jan," 1950; "Notes on Col. Kang's Trip to Chiri San Area," January 5, 1950.

77. 795.00 file, box 4262, political summary for December, January 18, 1950; sum-

mary for January, February 11, 1950; Drumwright to State, February 15, 1950. See also *NDSM*, January 29, 1950, which admits Ch'oe's death and gives his real name, but no other details.

78. RG338, KMAG file, box 5417, B. J. Hussey to KMAG G-2, January 28, 1950.

79. 795.00 file, box 4262, Drumwright to State, March 15, 1950.

80. MA, RG9, box 43, KMAG cables to MacArthur and to Department of the Army, November-December 1949; *New York Times*, February 3, 1950; *New York Herald-Tribune*, June 5, 1950; 795.00 file, box 4262, Drumwright to Muccio, enclosing a KMAG G-3 report, April 20, 1950.

81. U.S. Air Force, Air University, "Preliminary Study"; see also 795.00 file, box 4262, Muccio to State, January 18, 1950. On December 2, 1949, the *T'aeyang sinmun* quoted police sources on a new campaign for "extermination of Reds not converted."

82. See RG242, SA2010, item 8/87, *Nodong-dang chungang wiwŏnhoe chŏnggihoe ŭi munhŏnjip* [Records of the general meeting of the KWP Central Committee], December 15–18, 1949 (P'yŏngyang: Nodong-dang ch'ulp'an-sa, 1950) p. 42; also *NDSM*, January 14, 1950. The latter accused Rhee of "resurrecting Japanese fascist techniques"; it said the program gets only "broken people," "splittists," and "trembling elements" who cannot undergo hardship. By giving in, such wobblers "consign themselves to eternal oblivion." But in fact the methods could break hardened communists, as the North Koreans well knew.

83. RG338, KMAG file, box 5417, KMAG G-3 report; also box 4262, Drumwright to State, April 15, 1950; RG338, KMAG file, box 5417, "Digest of Operations," March 31-April 3, 1950, and Schwarze to Roberts, March 28, 1950; RG319, G-3 Operations file, box 126, Operations report no. 39, March 17–24, 1950; KMAG G-2 Weekly Summary no. 1, March 31-April 6, 1950; no. 4, April 20–27, 1950. American sources identify the second leader as Kim Mu-hyon, but North Korean sources give it as Kim Tu-hyŏn (see *NDSM*, May 17, 1950).

84. 795.00 file, box 4299, Drumwright to State, April 25, 1950; also Muccio to State, June 23, 1950, enclosing a military attaché report; FO317, piece no. 84078, Holt to FO, April 22, 1950; MA, RG6, box 60, intelligence summary no. 2873, July 22, 1950.

85. Yi Sŭng-yŏp, "Struggle of the Southern Guerrillas for Unification of the Homeland," pp. 15–26.

86. Yi Sŭng-yŏp, "On the Present Tasks of the Southern People's Guerrillas," pp. 9–22.

87. Kim Sam-yong, *NDSM*, March 22, 1950; Ch'oe Yong-gŏn, *NDSM*, February 8, 1950. Ch'oe gave the southern guerrillas five short, vague paragraphs in a speech that ran over three pages. See additional references to the southern guerrillas in *NDSM*, March 16, 21, May 17, 1950. This latter article was particularly revealing, seeking to claim that the Kim Tu-hyŏn detachment killed one thousand enemy in the period April 1–20, while neglecting to mention that it ceased to exist after April 24.

88. Office of Chinese Affairs, box 4218, Jessup to Butterworth, January 18, 1950; RG319, G-2 operations file, box 121, Roberts to Bolte, March 8, 1950.

CHAPTER THIRTEEN

1. Alexander George and Richard Smoke, *Deterrence in American Foreign Policy*, pp. 146–49 (emphasis in original).

2. Ibid., pp. 163–64 (emphasis in original).
3. *New York Times*, October 2, 1986.
4. HST, Acheson Seminars, box 81, February 13, 1954.
5. Acheson, *Present at the Creation*, p. 141.
6. Ibid., pp. 17–27.
7. Ibid., pp. 4, 26.
8. Ibid., pp. 25–27.
9. Ibid., pp. 35–37.
10. Rusk, in Acheson Seminars, March 14, 1954; Kennan, CP, 1977, 316B, "Transcript of Roundtable Discussion," October 1949.
11. HST, NSC file, box 206, CIA, "Review of the World Situation," April 20, 1949; *FR* (1949) 9, pp. 826–42, draft of NSC 41, February 28, 1949, and UK Embassy to State, April 5, 1949; Warren Cohen, "Acheson, His Advisors, and China, 1949–1950," in *Uncertain Years*, ed. Borg and Heinrichs, p. 33; Bruce Cumings, "The Political Economy of China's Turn Outward," in *China and the World*, ed. Samuel Kim (Boulder, Colo.: Westview Press, 1984).
12. On Chou's approach to the United States, or at least what O. E. Clubb, David Barrett, and others thought to be an approach, see *FR* (1949) 8, pp. 357–60, Clubb to Secretary of State, June 1, 1949; American intelligence files are full of speculation on a pro-Stalin clique in Beijing; see for example Office of Chinese Affairs file, box 4210, Peking to State, February 11, 1950; Hong Kong to State, November 15, 1950.
13. HST, NSC file, box 220, summary of the 50th meeting, December 30, 1949; Office of Chinese Affairs, box 4193, Wiley to Acheson, January 10, 1950.
14. TASS dispatch quoted in *NDSM*, January 5, 1950.
15. Office of Chinese Affairs, box 17, Howard Furnas, memo for the record, February 7, 1950; the information came directly from the CIA Director and was delivered orally.
16. *New York Times*, January 1, 1950; Acheson's handwritten "notes on meetings" has an entry for December 30, 1949, reading, "Reston in New York" (HST, Acheson Papers, box 81).
17. *FR* (1950) 6, pp. 294–96, Acheson to Paris Embassy, January 25, 1950.
18. Reston was Paul Nitze's neighbor in Washington for more than three decades after World War II, and Nitze was very close to Acheson. See Reston's column on Nitze, *New York Times*, January 10, 1982; also FO317, piece no. 83013, Franks to FO, March 6, 1950.
19. In November 1950 Chang Kuo-t'ao, Mao's old comrade and later his Long March antagonist, told interviewers that Li Li-san and Wang Ming were not even close to Stalin, let alone powerful in China; he did not think there were coherent factions within the CCP, and said Liu Shao-ch'i and Mao got along well, although Liu "opposed Chinese intervention in Korea," an interesting fact. Mao, he said, wanted a good relationship with Moscow and agreed with Stalin on "almost all matters at present." Chang did think that Peng Teh-huai had little respect for Mao, and fought with him frequently. Office of Chinese Affairs, box 4211, Hong Kong to State, November 15, 1950, and January 31, 1951.
20. HST, NSC file, box 205, NSC 37/5 deliberations, March 3, 1949; box 220, summary of 33rd NSC meeting, February 4, 1949; summary of 35th NSC meeting, March 4, 1949; *FR* (1949) 9, pp. 346–350, Butterworth to Rusk, June 9, 1949.
21. Ronald Steel is right to say in regard to this issue that the United States was "hostile to any form of nationalism not subject to U.S. control." See his commentary in *Uncertain Years*, ed. Borg and Heinrichs, p. 54.

22. Cohen, "Acheson, His Advisors, and China," in *Uncertain Years*, ed. Borg and Heinrichs, p. 38.

23. *FR* (1949) 9, pp. 356–59, PPS 53, "Memo on US Policy Toward Formosa," July 6, 1949.

24. *London Times*, December 30, 1949; the dateline was Washington, but the source was MacArthur. See FO317, piece no. 84037, which deals entirely with this issue.

25. CP, 1979, 439B, "Notes on Meetings in Secretary's Office in re Testimony on MacArthur Hearings," May 16, 1951.

26. FO317, piece no. 83013, Franks to FO, January 16, 1950; Franks said the words "at this time" indicate that Taiwan's facilities would probably be taken over in time of war.

27. HST, Acheson Papers, box 45, appointment books. On the speech as a public rendering of NSC 48, see Judicial, Fiscal and Social Branch, Records of the NSC, NSC 48 file, Webb to Lay, February 24, 1950 (NSC 48 file).

28. Office of the Executive Secretariat, box 4, Summaries of Acheson's daily meetings, entries for January 3, 9, 1950; Acheson Papers (Yale), box 47, typed outline dated January 10, and various earlier drafts dated January 3, 8, 10; Butterworth Papers, box 3, January 12, 1950, draft; see also Acheson Seminars, July 23, 1953, session.

29. Acheson Papers (Yale), box 47, typed outline draft of January 10; Acheson's rough draft of January 8, 1950.

30. Acheson Seminars, February 13, 1954. In his preparation for the seminars, Acheson wrote that it was probably a mistake to do the speech "alone, at home"; "I was much more innocent in those days. I have found since that every draft should be filtered through many minds" (HST, Acheson Papers, box 81, "Notes on meetings," "Korea"). The truth was that he "filtered through" many drafts and many minds, and did not like what he read. Several long sections from earlier drafts were incorporated by Acheson, however; he just decided to write the defense perimeter portion himself.

31. Acheson, *Present at the Creation*, pp. 357, and 764n.

32. John Lewis Gaddis, *The Long Peace*, pp. 72–73, 94.

33. Central Intelligence Group, "Korea," SR2, Summer 1947.

34. PPS file, box 1, record of conversation between Kennan, MacArthur, and others, March 5, 21, 1948.

35. U.S. Senate, Committee on Foreign Relations, *Reviews of the World Situation: 1949–50, Hearings Held in Executive Session*, 81st Congress, 1st and 2d sessions (Washington, D.C.: U.S. Government Printing Office, 1974), pp. 105–71, January 10, 1950; see also Schaller, *American Occupation*, pp. 193, 213–15.

36. HST, Acheson Papers, box 81, notes on meetings, p. 17.

37. *NDSM*, January 19, 1950.

38. Ibid., January 25, 26, 1950.

39. *New York Times*, January 13, 1950; "News of the Week in Review," January 15, 1950.

40. FO317, piece no. 83013, Franks to FO, January 13, 16, 1950.

41. HST, Acheson Papers, box 65, memo of conversation with Chang Myun, January 28, 1950; FO317, piece no. 84077, Holt to FO, January 19, 1950; 795.00 file, Muccio to State, March 18, 1950. Rhee's worries are related in 795.00 file, box 4262, Drumwright to State, Feb 15, 1950. After the House defeated the aid bill, Ambassador Chang remonstrated with the State Department about that, and about Acheson apparently having left South Korea "on the other side" of the defense perimeter (*FR* [1950] 7, p. 12).

42. Thames Television interview, November 1987.

43. See the interesting account in FO317, piece no. 83013, Franks to FO, February 15, 1950; someone in the Foreign Office (Guy Burgess?) highlighted in this three-page memo only that part saying State wanted the ROK to fall, without being pushed. Franks also drew special attention to the fact that when the aid bill was finally passed, it still extended no monies past June 30, 1950.
44. HST, Acheson Papers, box 65, memo of conversation with Vandenberg, January 21, 1950.
45. Acheson's comments in Matthew Connelly Papers, box 1, Cabinet meeting minutes for January 20, 1950 (misdated as 1949); Office of the Executive Secretariat, box 4, summaries of Acheson's daily meetings, entry for January 20, 1950; Acheson to Truman, January 20, 1950, CP, 1979, 311B. See also his testimony on January 30, 1950, where he said that "the U.S. has a very considerable responsibility [for Korea]. . . . We have participated in a very leading way in setting up this nation" (U.S. Congress, House, Committee on International Relations, *United States Policy in the Far East, Part 2: Korea Assistance Acts, Far East Portion of the Mutual Defense Assistance Act of 1950* [Washington, D.C.: U.S. Government Printing Office, 1976], p. 405).
46. *NDSM*, signed commentary, January 31, 1950.
47. Ibid., signed commentaries, February 2, 11, 1950.
48. Ibid., February 2, 1950.
49. Ibid., March 3, 10, 1950.
50. Ibid., March 23, February 10, 1950; also Kang Ch'ol-su, "U.S. Imperialism is the Enemy of the Chinese People," ibid., March 10, 1950.
51. Kennan Papers, box 31, letter to Allen Whiting, October 20, 1960.
52. Acheson Seminars, February 13–14, 1954.
53. Office of Chinese Affairs, box 18, record of Jessup's account of his trip, Acheson and others present, March 23, 1950; box 4218, Jessup to Butterworth, enclosing minutes of his talk with Rhee, January 18, 1950. During his tour Jessup met with a number of right-wing supporters of Taiwan. He requested meetings with Admiral Cooke and General Wedemeyer; he met with Wedemeyer on December 20, but it is not clear if he met with Cooke. Jessup told Hartley Dodge on March 22, 1950, that he also "saw [Wild Bill] Donovan a couple of times on my trip." He met Knowland on December 20, the latter telling Jessup first off how much progress was being made in Korea (Jessup Papers, box A47; Far Eastern file, box 4122a, Jessup memo of conversation with Knowland, December 20, 1949). There is no evidence that Jessup, a mild-mannered, scholarly professor of international law and a vintage internationalist, differed from Acheson and other officials in viewing communism as monolithically controlled from Moscow and, in the spring of 1950, turning toward Southeast Asia; nonetheless McCarthy on March 7 described him as having "an unusual affinity for Communist causes," and went on to try to paint him as the key link between Lattimore and Acheson (*New York Times*, March 9, 1950). Jessup's usefulness was at an end, and soon Dulles replaced him.
54. HST, Acheson Papers, box 64, Acheson to Bruce, July 26, 1949; Cumings, "Introduction," *Child of Conflict*, pp. 33–35.
55. *FR* (1950) 3, pp. 1033–40, transcript of Acheson's remarks to European allies on May 11, 1950; *MacArthur Hearings*, vol. 3, pp. 1681, 1741; 895.00 file, box C-947, Acheson to Muccio, April 15, 1949; HST, Acheson Papers, "Notes on meetings," p. 17.
56. HST, Acheson Papers, box 65, handwritten note to "Jim," presumably James Webb, dated "August ?, 1950"; it has the number 1063-b written at the top. Peter Novick called my attention to the particularity of the phrase, "the task of an opposition is to oppose," arguing that this parliamentarian's locution could only refer

to Acheson's congressional opposition, not to the Soviets. That may be so, but the context seems rather to be a follow-up to the football metaphor. In any case, Acheson clearly discusses a situation (or "state of affairs") of defense that the administration created.

57. Richard Nixon, *The Real War* (New York: Warner Books, 1980), p. 254. When I wrote to Nixon about this passage, he said my letter "raises some very interesting but I fear unanswerable questions. Whatever American policy was in fact, Acheson's statement unfortunately left the impression the U.S. would not react if North Korea invaded the South. It could well be that Dean Acheson did not expect, let alone intend, that his statement be so interpreted by the enemy." Letter from Richard Nixon, November 4, 1981. This, of course, avoids my question—why Nixon suggested that Acheson had made a purposeful misrepresentation.

58. *US News and World Report*, May 5, June 9, 1950.

59. D. F. Fleming, *The Cold War and Its Origins*, vol. 2 (Garden City, N.Y.: Doubleday, 1961), p. 597; also Acheson, *Present at the Creation*, p. 415, picture overleaf. Connally was close on Acheson's heels re: NSC 48, chiming in on December 29, 1949, that the United States should not recognize the PRC (p. 349).

60. 795.00 file, Drumwright to State, May 2, 10, 1950; Muccio's cable, *FR* (1950) 7, May 25, 1950.

61. John Toland, *Infamy: Pearl Harbor and Its Aftermath* (New York: Berkley Books, 1983), p. 14.

62. Office of Chinese Affairs, box 15, "Two Talks with Mr. Chou En-lai," no date, attached to document no. 350.1001.

63. See among other sources, Glenn W. Price, *Origins of the War with Mexico: The Polk-Stockton Intrigue* (Austin: University of Texas Press, 1967), I am indebted to Robert A. Divine for calling this book to my attention; Charles C. Tansill, *Back Door to War: The Roosevelt Foreign Policy, 1933–1941* (Chicago: Regnery, 1952); George McT. Kahin, *Intervention: How America Became Involved in Vietnam* (New York: Alfred A. Knopf, 1986), pp. 277–80.

64. Ridgway Papers, Ridgway Oral Interview, March 5, 1982.

65. Stimson was a role model for many Eastern Establishment activists (Isaacson and Thomas, *The Wise Men*, pp. 28–29).

66. Beard, *Roosevelt and the Coming of the War*, pp. 244–45, 418, 519, 526–27. Toland cites a telegram from Gen. George Marshall and Adm. Harold Stark to MacArthur, November 27, 1941, saying, "if hostilities cannot, repeat cannot, be avoided the U.S. desires Japan commit the first overt act" (*Infamy*, pp. 6–7). See also Richard N. Current, "How Stimson Meant to 'Maneuver' the Japanese," *Mississippi Valley Historical Review* 40, no. 1 (1953), pp. 67–74.

67. HST, Acheson Papers, box 65, Memo of conversation with Herter, March 24, 1950.

68. *FR* (1950) 6, pp. 401–4, Johnson to Acheson, July 29, 1950; Acheson to Johnson, July 31, 1950.

69. *MacArthur Hearings*, vol. 3, pp. 2010–11, 2020.

70. Acheson Papers (Yale), box 9, Acheson to William Elliott, August 11, 1960.

71. *MacArthur Hearings*, vol. 3, p. 2020.

72. *New York Times*, February 19, March 10, 12, 1950; the British noted the importance of the *Times* articles and Reston's role, and we may assume the Soviets did as well (FO317, piece no. 83013, Franks to FO, March 6, 1950).

73. *New York Times*, March 16, 1950.

74. Ibid., March 17, 1950. A paper drawn up for Acheson's negotiations with the Allies said, "broad negotiations with the Soviets are undesirable at the present time,"

and during the meetings Americans said there was "no prospect" of fruitful negotiations, and instead the West should "build up situations of strength" (*FR*
[1950] 3, p. 863n, citing a paper of late April not included in the text; also pp.
1078–82, memorandum of tripartite meetings, May 9, 1950).

75. *New York Times*, March 17, 19, 1950; *FR* (1950) 4, p. 1185, Kirk to State, April 27,
1950. Wellington Koo paid no attention to the Press Club speech, but wrote in his
diary that the West coast speeches are "of great interest and importance," terming
them "a mild extension of the Truman Doctrine to Asia" (Koo Papers, box 217,
entry for March 17, 1950).

76. *NDSM*, March 28, 1950, signed commentary by Kim Ki-ho.

77. *New York Times*, March 19, April 14, 30, 1950.

78. *World Events* 7, no. 3 (Summer 1950); this was in press when the Korean War
began.

79. *FR* (1950) 3, pp. 43–44, "Military Assistance for Indochina," submitted to Truman
by Acheson on March 9, 1950; *New York Times*, May 9, 13, 1950; *NDSM*, May 17,
1950. Sulzberger wrote in the May 13 issue that whether the American people
know it or not, the United States was now "pretty well committed" to containment
in Southeast Asia.

80. *FR* (1950) 3, pp. 1007–13, Acheson to State, May 8, 1950; p. 901, record of the
Tripartite meetings for May 1, 1950.

CHAPTER FOURTEEN

1. *Kŭlloja*, no. 1 (January 15, 1950), pp. 3–7.

2. A State Department press release of June 30, 1950, says in its "chronology" that
Kim Il Sung went to Moscow to celebrate Stalin's birthday on December 14, 1949,
giving no date for his return. A copy is in Smith Papers, box 100.

3. Nikita Khrushchev, *Khrushchev Remembers*, intro. Edward Crankshaw, trans. and
ed. Strobe Talbott (New York: Little, Brown, 1970), pp. 367–68; John Merrill,
"Review of Khrushchev Remembers," *Journal of Korean Studies* 3 (1981), pp. 181–
91.

4. See the lead editorial, and Yi Chŏng-su, "Let's Strengthen the True Armed Force
of the Korean People, the KPA," both in *Sun'gan t'ongshin*, no. 5 (January 1950),
pp. 1–6.

5. *NDSM*, February 26, 27, March 26, May 15, 1950; on China see a long report on
mainland life in March 1950 by a former UNNRA official, in Smith papers, box
100. The embassy noted in April 1950 that the DPRK had gone past its targets for
the first year of the plan, "and had raised its objectives" for the second year. It also
said, without apparent sense of the contradiction, that the DPRK had developed
"a relatively self-sufficient, viable, expanding economy, geared and subservient to
that of the Soviet Union." See 795.00 file, box 4299, Drumwright to State, April
17, 1950.

6. Lead editorial, "Heightening Political Consciousness in the Production Process,"
Kŭlloja, no. 6, March 31, 1950.

7. *NDSM*, May 22, 1950.

8. Hsinhua message, in *NDSM*, March 3, 1950.

9. MA, RG9, box 110, weekly military attaché report, April 21, 1950. It referred to
the "return" of Kim and Pak, but does not say from where. Later intelligence
reports suggested a meeting in China in April, however.

10. RG242, SA2006, item 15/65, KWP Agitprop Department, "New work methods for

a new environment and new conditions," materials for party workers dated May 10, 1950.

11. Interview with Walter Sullivan, New York, May 21, 1983; I am indebted to Mr. Sullivan for sharing with me his letters and notes relating to the visit. There is, in my view, no question that the letters from P'yŏngyang were authentic and sincere.

12. CIA, "Current Capabilities of the Northern Korean Regime," ORE 18–50, June 19, 1950.

13. 795.00 file, box 4299, Drumwright to State, May 4, 1950; CIA, "National Intelligence Survey: Korea."

14. Willoughby later claimed that the Soviet Far East 5th Fleet had exclusive use of the port of Ch'ŏngjin (Willoughby Papers, box 10, "The North Korean Pre-Invasion Build-up," circa early 1951). Yet there was no such naval base, unlike, for example, the Soviet base at Camh Ranh Bay in Vietnam today. As we have seen, the Soviet military ran some ports directly until 1948, and established joint-stock companies for other ports. According to captured documents, a Korean-Soviet Sea Transportation Company, a joint-stock venture, signed an agreement with the North Hamgyŏng People's Commmittee for a thirty-year lease on the port and its facilities, in July 1947. But this was for commercial purposes, and there is no indication of a military component to the agreement. A top secret, voluminous intelligence estimate for the Far East put out in December 1949 carried no Soviet "major naval base" or "naval base" in North Korea. Air force intelligence estimates after the war began also showed no naval base. There is one top secret document citing a Soviet submarine base at Ch'ŏngjin, six months after the war began, but no such base seems to have existed before June 25. No Soviet military vessel, including submarines, entered Wŏnsan, the other major East coast port, after 1948. A July 16, 1947, document on the Ch'ŏngjin lease is translated in MA, RG6, box 78, ATIS issue no. 11, December 13, 1950; also ibid., box 98, "Intelligence Estimate Far East," December 1, 1949; this map does show a Soviet naval base just north of the Korean border at Posyet, and shows Soviet naval bases at Port Arthur and Dairen in China. A map showing a Soviet submarine base at Ch'ŏngjin, but no other bases, is in ibid., box 1, map no. SGS1282, marked top secret, no date but probably January 1951. Captured North Korean naval personnel said that no Soviet military vessel, including submarines, had entered the Wŏnsan harbor since 1948, in ibid., box 14, G-2 periodic intelligence report no. ZJY1061, July 4, 1950.

15. Captured documents indicated that the Soviets turned over control of the Wŏnsan airport to the DPRK on January 19, 1949; it had been taken from the Japanese in 1945 by a Soviet Naval Air unit. See MA, RG6, box 79, ATIS issue no. 17, January 10, 1951. Materials are not available on the P'yŏngyang airport. Many translations of captured Russian documents are in ibid., ATIS issue no. 22, February 8, 1951. On the Soviets watching Kim, see U.S. State Department, McCune, "Leadership in North Korea."

16. NDSM, January 19, 1950; Shtykov's absence in mid-April is noted in 795.00 file, box 4299, chronology for April, May 8, 1950; Hŏ Hŏn, NDSM, March 18, 1950.

17. CP, 1978, 52A, Shin Sŭng-mo to Collins, October 20, 1949; see also Ridgway Papers, box 16, memo to General Willoughby on query by Ridgway on the number of Soviet advisors, August 7, 1950. An interrogation of a North Korean pilot put the number of Soviet advisors at fifteen; he said that the head of the Air Force advisory group was replaced on June 27, 1950, an interesting detail (MA, RG6, box 14, G-2 periodic report, July 2, 1950). Although Stalin pulled Soviet advisors back when the war began, in the fall of 1950 there were Soviet advisors in northern cities, directing and sometimes manning antiaircraft guns. See Australian del-

egation to UNCURK, Memorandum no. 25, December 8, 1950, copy given to me by Gavan McCormack.

18. *New York Times*, May 4, 1950.

19. Smith Papers, box 98, Smith to Knowland, October 24, 1949. It would be interesting to know if it was perhaps Willoughby or Goodfellow who gave him this analysis.

20. Appleman, *Naktong/Yalu*, p. 12; HST, PSF, CIA file, box 250, CIA, "Military Supplies for North Korea," September 13, 1950.

21. Especially the "History of the North Korean Army," which is full of misinformation and propagandistic broadsides.

22. HST, PSF, CIA file, box 262, joint daily sitrep no. 16, July 12–13, 1950; *New York Times*, July 5, 1950; Walter Sullivan reported that the KPA had no post-1945 weaponry, except for all-purpose trucks, *New York Times*, July 27, 1950.

23. Willoughby Papers, box 10, Korea Liaison Office file, report of November 5, 1949; CP, 1975, 9D, Army Headquarters, Historical Section, staff study of weaponry of KPA and CCF. Dean Rusk said the Soviets had "shown a marked disinclination to render assistance to the North Korean and Chinese Communists without exacting payment therefore." See no. 605, Carrollton, p. 18 of notes; also *New York Times*, September 3, 1950, citing information from MacArthur's staff.

24. FO317, piece no. 84076, RAF squadron leader A. G. Lawrence to Scott, December 30, 1949; MA, RG6, box 58, intelligence summary no. 2827, June 6, 1950. The KLO reported that on April 15, three Soviet-made fighter planes landed at an airfield in South Ham'gyŏng Province, with a Soviet colonel on the reviewing stand. But it does not say that the planes were then given to Kim Il Sung (although that is quite likely) (Willoughby Papers, box 10, Korea Liaison Office file, report of May 8, 1950).

25. MA, RG6, box 59, intelligence summary no. 2853, July 2, 1950.

26. MA, RG6, box 9, Seoul Embassy attaché to CINCFE, December 7, 1950.

27. RG349, FEC G-2 Theater Intelligence, box 462, file on North Korean industry, no date, but after U.S. Occupation of North.

28. HST, PSF, NSC file, box 2, CIA, no. 326, "Military Supplies for North Korea," September 15, 1950.

29. Charles Bohlen, *Witness to History, 1929–1960* (New York: W. W. Norton, 1973), p. 294–95.

30. RG218, JCS file, box 130, Hodge to MacArthur, October 22, 1947; 895.00 file, box 7126, Muccio to State, September 14, 1948; G-2 Weekly Report no. 163, October 22–29, 1948. In November Muccio reported that the situation was "grave," with the North having the capability to destroy the ROKA even without getting its soldiers back from China; some reports said an invasion would follow the withdrawal of U.S. troops, while others said it might come before they leave; an "incompetent government without strong public support" meant that only the American Army was capable of maintaining the security of the ROKA (RG335, Secretary of the Army file, box 56, Coulter for Muccio to State, November 12, 1948). The deputy director of Army Intelligence said in December that "rumors continue to be reported from North Korea of an imminent attack on the South" (ibid., Carter W. Clarke to Chief of Staff, December 14, 1948).

31. KMAG G-2 Periodic Reports nos. 258, 260, 261, 277, February 3-March 10, 1950; G-2 Weekly Report no. 6, May 4–11, 1950 (KMAG intelligence switched from "periodic" to "weekly" reports on April 1, 1950).

32. G-3 Operations file, box 121, Roberts to Bolte, March 8, 1950; also G-3 Operations Reports nos. 46–50, May 5-June 16, 1950.

33. KMAG G-2 Periodic Reports nos. 246, 254, 256, 257, 258, 260, 261, 268, 269, 277, 282, 287, 288, January-April, 1950. KMAG G-2 Weekly Reports nos. 1–11, April 1-June 15, 1950.

34. KMAG G-2 Periodic Reports nos. 204, 205, 206, 208, 225, 226, 229, 230, 233, 234, 238, October 25-December 30, 1949.

35. On "noise," etc., see Roberta Wohlstetter, *Pearl Harbor: Warning and Decision* (Stanford, Calif.: Stanford University Press, 1962).

36. FO317, piece no. 84076, Major Ferguson-Innes of War Office to FO, top secret, December 30, 1949. Ferguson-Innes said that American intelligence gave to the British "the greater part of whatever intelligence they get on North Korea." For similar conclusions by British intelligence in April 1950, see ibid., piece no. 84079, Tokyo Chancery to FO, April 19, 1950. See also CIA, "Current Capabilities of the Northern Korean Regime," ORE 18–50, June 19, 1950.

37. FO317, piece no. 84078, Holt to FO, December 22, 1949; Holt said he agreed with Muccio's assessment. See also CIA, "Current Capabilities of the Northern Korean Regime," ORE 18–50, June 19, 1950.

38. KMAG G-2 Periodic Report no. 285, March 23–24, 1950; MA, RG6, box 9, Embassy to CINCFE, December 7, 1950. The latter information is based on POW interviews; see also box 16, Order of Battle for the PLA 4th Field Army, November 7, 1950; also FO317, piece no. 84076, Lawrence to Scott, December 30, 1949. Appleman's figures are more conservative, estimating that CCF veterans made up about one-third of the KPA as of June 1950, or about 32,000 troops. He thought about 12,000 transferred to the North in April 1950, the others coming over in 1949. His sources are mostly POW interviews; he did not make use of a variety of other intelligence sources, suggesting much higher totals. For example, he acknowledged that most of the soldiers in the 5th, 6th, and 7th KPA divisions were China veterans, which would amount to over 30,000 soldiers without reference to the other divisions, which included many China veterans who crossed back to Korea in 1948 and 1949 (*Naktong/Yalu*, p. 9).

39. FO317, piece no. 84079, Tokyo Chancery to FO, April 19, 1950. This was the estimate of a British military attaché who had recently returned from a survey in Korea.

40. MA, RG6, box 58, intelligence summary no. 2829, June 8, 1950; no. 2830, June 9, 1950; no. 2847, June 26, 1950.

41. Ibid., no. 2847, June 26, 1950.

42. *Naktong/Yalu*, pp. 8–18. Appleman also says the KPA had 85,000 "combat effectives" on June 25, compared to only 65,000 for the ROKA, but it is not clear how he arrived at this judgment.

43. *NDSM*, January 14, 1950.

44. The best version is in Hiroshi Sakurai, "Why Did the Korean War 'Break Out' on June 25, 1950?"

45. Simmons, *Strained Aliance*, pp. 104–110.

46. U.S. State Department, McCune, "Leadership in North Korea."

47. On May 17, in an editorial about the southern guerrillas, the party newspaper asserted that Rhee "opposes peaceful unification and wants to divide Korea permanently." A week later, an article said the May 30 elections would forward "the permanent division of the homeland" (*NDSM*, May 17, 23, 1950). In both cases the phrase is *punhal ŭl yŏn'guhwa*, literally the "fixing" or "permanentizing" of the division.

48. *NDSM*, January 20, 1950. The rest of the speech underlined his version of the

"East is Red" theme, discussed earlier, about the waxing of communist power and the waning of American power.

49. *NDSM*, January 16, 1950.

50. *NDSM*, January 19, 1950.

51. Han Ch'ŏl-ho, "The Rhee Clique's Strengthening Ties with Japanese Imperialism, under Directions from U.S. Imperialism," *Sun'gan t'ongshin* 48, no. 5 (January, 1950).

52. *NDSM*, February 10, 18, 1950.

53. *NDSM*, February 19, 1950.

54. *NDSM*, February 22, 23, 24, 25, 1950; each issue carried several articles on the trip, many of them signed commentaries. Some issues claimed that Rhee met with General Utsonomiya, former resident-general of Hong Kong and the organizer of the suppression of the March 1 Movement in 1919.

55. Kang Ch'ŏl-su, "U.S. Imperialism is the Enemy of the Chinese People," *NDSM*, March 10, 1950; this article also shows knowledge of Admiral Cooke's informal military advisory group on Taiwan. See also *NDSM*, February 25, 1950, for other references to Theodore Roosevelt.

56. *NDSM*, lead editorial, March 3, 1950. The emphasis in the quotation is added, since ordinarily China would be included in "the democratic countries"; this is an extraordinary usage.

57. Song Sŭng-ch'ŏl, "The Rhee Country-Selling Clique and the Japanese Militarists Are Colluding under the Direction of American Imperialism," *Kŭlloja*, no. 8 (April 1950), pp. 42–52.

58. RG242, SA 2010, item 3/55, "*Mijenŭn Ilbonŭl kunsa mohŏmul wihan pyŏnggigoro mandŭlgo ittda*" [American imperialism is making Japan into an arsenal for military adventurism] (P'yongyang: KWP ch'ulp'ansa, May 8, 1950), p. 64.

59. RG242, SA2009, item 8/33.3, *Ch'ŏngch'i sanghak kyojae* [Materials for political lessons], unpub., Cultural Training Department of DPRK Ministry of Defense, June 1950.

60. O Sŏng-hwa, "The US Imperialists Cannot Save the Rhee Clique, Now Facing Destruction," *NDSM*, July 5, 1950; *NDSM*, August 9, 1950; see also RG242, SA2012, item 6/122, Mun Hak-bong, *Mije ŭi Chosŏn ch'imnyak chŏngch'aek ŭi chŏngbon wa naeran paep'oja ŭi chinsang ŭi p'ongno ham* [A true account of American imperialism's aggressive Korea policy and an exposure of the instigators of civil war] (P'yŏngyang: Chung'ang t'ongshin, 1950), pp. 71–72; also Kim Hyo-sŏk in *Haebang ilbo*, July 8, 1950. Many similar articles from this period could be cited.

61. Walter Simmons, "The Truth About Korea," *Chicago Tribune*, November 6, 1949, in FO317, piece no. 76259, Holt to FO, November 9, 1949. Americans so often use the term "intelligent Koreans" to indicate those who agree with American policies; the rest, presumably, disagree and therefore must be stupid.

62. 795.00 file, box 4262, Embassy to State, January 18, 1950 (summary of events in December 1949); ibid., Drumwright to State, January 21, 1950; Office of Chinese Affairs, box 4218, Jessup to Butterworth, January 18, 1950.

63. 795.00 file, box 4299, Tokyo to State, February 19, 1950; Seoul Embassy to State, March 18, 1950; Hugh Deane Papers, Rhee's press release of February 18, 1950.

64. Shin met with Yi Ŭn during his visit in November 1949, causing some to report that a "monarchist" movement had begun in the ROKA (FO317, piece no. 76259, November 16, 1949). Eichelberger's provocative speech, said to have been cleared with the Defense Department, was discussed in *New York Times*, March 3, 1950; documents on the dispatch of ROK officers for training in Japan—apparently on American bases, but with the aid of Japanese officers—are in RG338, KMAG file,

box 5417. One of them was Captain Lee Hu-rak (Yi Hu-rak), later to be the director of the KCIA and a powerful figure in the Park regime.

65. *US News and World Report* stated in its August 4, 1950, issue that Willoughby had been trying "for months" to set up a Japanese "constabulary," and "has kept in touch with the most capable former officers"; one official said that the officer corps of a new Japanese Army "could be mobilized in 24 hours." On the Korean spy ring, see National Archives, manuscripts of the office of the Chief of Military History, box 625, FEC, Military History Section, "Intelligence and Counterintelligence Problems during the Korea Conflict [*sic*]" (1955), p. 49.

66. G-3 Operations file, box 121, Roberts to Bolte, March 8, 1950; *New York Times*, May 27, 1950.

67. G-3 Operations file, box 121, Roberts to Bolte; 795.00 file, box 4299, "Developments Concerning the 1950 General Election," in Embassy to State, April 24, 1950; also Embassy to State, May 12, 1950; also Drumwright to State, June 15, 1950; also box 5696, ECA to State, May 12, 1950.

68. *The Oriental Economist*, June 24, 1950, pp. 636–39. At about this time Shirasu Jirō, a close personal advisor to Premier Yoshida, told Walton Butterworth that "He thought that the best way to deal with the 600,000 Koreans still living in Japan was to deport them to Korea. In his opinion the Koreans in Japan were almost to a man engaged in illegal or non-gainful pursuits and that it was grossly unfair that the Japanese Government . . . assume obligations on behalf of this parasitic group." Butterworth said this reflected Yoshida's views (795.00 file, box 3006, Butterworth to Acheson, May 3, 1950).

CHAPTER FIFTEEN

1. Eisenhower Library, Ellis Briggs Oral History, June 19, 1970. Briggs, Eisenhower's ambassador to Korea, says the U.S. embassy in Seoul in June 1950 had a staff of more than two thousand, "numerically the largest embassy in the world."

2. FO317, piece no. 84053, Holt to FO, May 1, 1950.

3. CP, 1977, item 316B, "Transcript of Round Table Discussion," October 1949; MA, RG9, box 43, various KMAG cables to Tokyo, March 1950; the agreement to operate Kimp'o, signed January 14, 1950, is available in RG338, KMAG file, box 5415; see also Willauer Papers, box 1, Memo for Chennault, July 10, 1950; tape transcript, December 1, 1960. The Korea Shipbuilding Corporation, as an example, was run by an American yard foreman, employed by the American-based Pomeroy Company. See 795.00 file, box 4299, Drumwright to State, April 27, 1950.

4. U. Alexis Johnson, *The Right Hand of Power*, with Jef Olivarius McAllister (Englewood Cliffs, N.J.: Prentice-Hall, 1984), p. 97.

5. Bertil Renborg (principal secretary to UNCOK) said that 80 percent of the national budget was spent on the national police and the army (UN Archives, BOX DAG-1/2.1.2, box 3, report of March 31, 1950).

6. U.S. Senate, Committee on Foreign Relations, Historical Series, *Economic Assistance to China and Korea: 1949–1950* (Washington, D.C.: U.S. Government Printing Office, 1974), p. 159 (hereafter *Economic Assistance*).

7. Ibid., pp. 159–63.

8. Ibid., pp. 129, 134. Hoffman also described Rhee as "the George Washington of Korea," and said Yi Pŏm-sŏk was "an outstanding man" (p. 149).

9. Ibid., pp. 181, 191.

10. 895B. file, box 5695, Allison to Rusk, March 30, 1950, enclosing memorandum of meeting between Bunce, Allison, Voorhees, and others, March 15, 1950. E.A.J. Johnson accused Voorhees of trying "to make the Japanese economy viable at Korea's expense." See also Andrew J. Rotter, *The Path to Vietnam: The Origins of the American Commitment to Southeast Asia* (Ithaca, N.Y.: Cornell University Press, 1987), pp. 132–34.

11. Rotter, *The Path to Vietnam*, p. 136.

12. 795.00 file, box 4262, Drumwright to State, January 25, 1950, citing Rhee's January 20 press conference. In 1940–1944, Korea imported an annual average of 150,000 metric tons of millet and soya to substitute in part for rice shipped to Japan; in 1946 south Korea imported 179,000 metric tons of American wheat, corn, and flour. By 1948 the figure had reached 480,000, and continued rising thereafter. See USAMGIK, "History of the National Food Administration," Appendix C, "Food Report for South Korea as of March 1948," in XXIV Corps Historical file, box 10.

13. Senate Committee on Foreign Relations, *Economic Assistance*, pp. 133, 138, 144.

14. FO317, piece no. 83883, Gascoigne to FO, June 19, 1950.

15. "Agreement on Aid Between the United States of America and the Republic of Korea," December 10, 1948, Senate Committee on Foreign Relations, *Economic Assistance*, pp. 276–280.

16. RG242, SA2005, item 1/2, *Chosŏn Minjujuŭi Inmin Konghwa'guk ch'oego inmin hoeŭi chae sam ch'a hoeŭi hoeŭirok* [Record of the 3d session of the DPRK Supreme People's Assembly] (P'yŏngyang, April 19–20, 1949), Kim Il Sung's speech, p. 231.

17. 895B. file, box 5693, Lightner to State, October 16, 1951.

18. Bruce Cumings, *Industrial Behemoth: The Northeast Asian Political Economy in the 20th Century* (Ithaca, N.Y.: Cornell University Press, forthcoming).

19. Minutes of Joint Korean Government-American Mission Stabilization Committee, various meetings February 10–17, 1950, in 895.00 file, box 5693, February 22, 1950. See also FO317, piece no. 84141, Holt to FO, June 20, 1950, enclosing ECA report for May 1950.

20. Butterworth said just this to Acheson and others on April 5. See Office of the Executive Secretariat file, box 4, summary of the secretary's daily meeting, April 5, 1950.

21. 795.00 file, box 5696, report dated March 18, 1950. See also the book that Bloomfield and Jensen later wrote, *Banking Reform in South Korea* (New York: Federal Reserve Bank of New York, 1951).

22. 895.00 file, box 5692, J. Franklin Ray, Jr., monthly economic report for March 1950; also Ray to State, summary of basic economic information, May 9, 1950; Ray, monthly economic report for May, June 14, 1950. In April twenty thousand individuals were doing "concripted (unpaid) labor" building an airstrip in Pusan. See 795.00 file, Robert M. Berry report on Pusan, in Drumwright to State, April 27, 1950.

23. On the North Korean view, see for example Hong Nam-p'yo in *NDSM*, May 22, 1950, and Yi Sŭng-yŏp in *Kŭlloja*, no. 6 (March 30, 1950), p. 20. Hong explicitly refers to the Rhee reform measures as an attempt to "weaken" the guerrillas.

24. 895.00 file, box 5691, William Jones to Cyrus Peake, November 15, 1950, orig. classification "secret"; see also box 5696, Drumwright to State, November 28, 1950, which also says no land changed hands before June 25, 1950. See also FO317, piece no. 84053, Holt, annual report for 1949, May 1, 1950.

25. 895.00 file, box 5692, Drumwright to State, January 16, 1950; HST, PSF, NSC file, box 3, CIA memorandum of October 19, 1950.

26. RG319, Plans and Operations file, 091 Korea, KMAG study of ROKA, October 15, 1949. The 17th had a higher percentage of basic, squad, platoon, company, and battalion tactical training than any other infantry regiment. On ROK strength in June 1950, see KMAG G-3 Operations Report no. 51, June 9–16, 1950. A British military observer said that "by calling present reservists to active duty, a fairly well-trained army of 131,000 can be mobilized despite shortages of arms and equipment" (FO317, piece no. 84079, Tokyo to FO, enclosing report by military advisor Figgess, April 19, 1950). See also Robert K. Sawyer, *Military Advisors in Korea*, pp. 95–106.

27. See for example 795.00 file, box 4299, Embassy to State, June 19, 1950, which shows heavy KMAG involvement in the ROK defense budget.

28. HST, PSF, NSC file, box 205, Webb to Lay, February 10, 1950; *New York Times*, July 15, 1950; 740.0019 Control (Korea) file, box 3829, Muccio to State, May 21, 1949; Sawyer, *Military Advisors in Korea*, p. 96.

29. MA, RG9, box 40, Army to CINCFE, September 2, 1949; 895.00 file, box 5693, Drumwright to State, February 10, 1950; 895.00 file, box 946, Muccio to Butterworth, November 1, 1949; HST, Muccio oral history interview no. 177, December 27, 1973. The Department of the Army document demonstrated worry about the political implications should deliveries be so slow that they would leave to the North the "initiative on decision to invade," and deprive the South of material "necessary to withstand prolonged at[tack]."

30. Lowe, *Origins of the Korean War*, pp. 67–68.

31. Roberts and Muccio asked for seventeen Air Force advisors in September 1949 (MA, RG9, box 43, Roberts to Army, September 21, 1949); Roberts asked for forty F-51s in October 1949 (Butterworth Papers, box 1, Allison to Butterworth, November 2, 1949); Lemnitzer's decision is in RG330, Secretary of Defense file, box 33, Lemnitzer to Johnson, March 11, 1950; the State Department urged that nine Air Force advisors be assigned to Korea in March 1950, only to be turned down by the Air Force (RG330, Secretary of Defense file, box 82, Martin to Burns, March 10, 1950); KMAG and ECA requested forty F-51s and three C-47 transports in May, with no apparent result before the war started (MA, RG9, box 43, Seoul military attaché to CINCFE, May 24, 1950).

32. MA, RG10, box 9, Rhee to MacArthur, September 19, 1949; on Goodfellow's attempts to get aircraft for Rhee in early 1950, see Goodfellow papers, box 2.

33. MA, RG9, box 43, Roberts to Department of the Army, November 10, 1949; *New York Times*, September 1, 1945, February 18, 1946, July 13, 1948. The latter issue said Randall was "assigned to the office of director of intelligence," which presumably means the CIA director.

34. 995.00 file, box 6175, Ray to State, June 15, 1950; *New York Times*, November 27, 1949; also *Sun'gan t'ongshin*, no. 42 (December 1949), entry for November 17, 1949.

35. G-3 Operations file, box 121, Roberts to Bolte, March 8, 1950; CRC, 247A, JCS 2106, "Notes by Secretaries W. G. Lalor and J. H. Ives, on JCS Visit to the Far East," March 13, 1950.

36. *New York Herald-Tribune*, May 30, June 5, 1950.

37. RG338, KMAG file, box 5415, which has numerous memos in April 1950 about defects in the ROKA; see also box 5418, Roberts to Gerald E. Larsen, May 4, 1950 (Larsen was senior advisor to the ROKA 8th Division).

38. Sawyer, *Military Advisors in Korea*, pp. 76–78. Clay Blair notes that training patterns for the ROKA and for U.S. 8th Army in Japan, by coincidence, ran on similar tracks—and that both were behind schedule in June 1950 (*Forgotten War*, p. 51).

39. 895.00 file, box 5693, Ray to State, June 8, 1950; 795.00 file, box 4262, Drumwright to State, April 15, 1950; MA, RG6, box 58, intelligence summary no. 2833, June 12, 1950.

40. RG319, G-3 operations file, box 121, Operations Report no. 44, April 21–28, 1950, and no. 45, April 28-May 5.

41. MA, RG6, box 59, intelligence summary no. 2847, June 26, 1950, giving the ROKA order of battle. Apparently some smaller clusters of troops were not counted, since the total listed is 87,500, and the ROKA total was said to be 95,000.

42. Manuscript collection of the Office of the Chief of Military History, National Archives, "History of the Korean War," vol. 3, pt. 14, "Special Problems in the Korean Conflict," p. 9; MacArthur, *MacArthur Hearings*, vol. 1, p. 231.

43. G-3 Operations file, box 121, Roberts to Bolte, March 8, 1950; MA, RG9, box 43, KMAG to Tokyo, June 6, 1950; *New York Times*, June 26, 1950.

44. Kim Sŏk-wŏn was replaced as head of the 1st Division, and General Ch'ae Pyŏng-dŏk was relieved of his position as chief of staff, both on October 6, 1949. The intelligence report on this said that Kim "may be tried for alleged involvement in highjacking and smuggling operations across the parallel." Ch'ae is said to have learned of Kim's smuggling operation, and planned to court-martial him; "Rhee learned of Chae's intentions and relieved both officers." Rhee was said to have disliked Ch'ae (see RG349, box 699, "spot intelligence report," October 6, 1949). What the report does not say is that Rhee knuckled under to American pressure to relieve Kim, but took the American favorite Ch'ae with him.

45. *New York Times*, March 17, April 5, 29, May 11.

46. UN Archives, BOX DAG-1/2.1.2, box 3, Egon Ranshofen-Wertheimer to "Andy" (Andrew Cordier), July 5, 1949; *New York Times*, July 13, 1949. Throughout 1950, Andrew Cordier, executive assistant to the Secretary-General, was the point man in UN dealings with UNCOK—his name is on just about every letter from the UN, and most UNCOK correspondence was directed to him. (See for example UN Archives, Box DAG-1/2.1.2, box 16.) For Cordier's key role in deploying United Nations troops against Lumumba in 1960, see Jonathan Kwitny, *Endless Enemies* (New York: Congdon and Weed, 1984), pp. 65–66.

47. 895.00 file, box 7127, Ranshofen-Wertheimer to Jessup, September 22, 1949.

48. FO317, piece no. 76259, conversation between Butterworth and Dening, September 14, 1949.

49. *NDSM*, February 15, 1950; it cited an undated UPI report on the discussions in Seoul. Earlier the party newspaper had said UNCOK's military observers would help Rhee with his plans to touch off a war and called it an "aggressive tool" of the United States (*NDSM*, January 24, 1950).

50. UN Archives, BOX DAG-1/2.1.2, box 3, Sanford Schwarz to Lie and Zinchenko, October 31, 1949, enclosing the 15th report of UNCOK, October 8–28, 1949.

51. 895.00 file, box 7127, Muccio to State, September 13, 1949; Seoul Embassy to State, March 30, 1950; 357.AD file, UNCOK, box 1375, State Department to San Salvador Embassy, January 24, 1950.

52. UN Archives, BOX DAG-1/2.1.2, box 3, Renborg to Cordier, April 28, 1950.

53. 357.AD file, UNCOK, box 1375, Embassy to State, May 24, 29, June 6, 1950. Australia appointed its two observers on May 21; two military observers from El Salvador were appointed on May 22, and were on their way to Korea when the war began (795.00 file, box 4299, Drumwright to State, June 15, 1950).

54. See for example MA, RG9, box 43, KMAG to CINCFE, February 18, 1950.

55. UN Archives, BOX DAG-1/2.1.2, box 3, Renborg to Secretary-General, January 20, 1950.

56. UN Archives, BOX DAG-1/2.1.2, box 16, account of a visit to Kangnŭng on March 27, 1950.

57. 895.00 file, box 5697, Muccio to State, March 11, 1950; UNCOK file, box 1375, Embassy to State, March 11, 1950; 795.00 file, box 4299, Drumwright to State, May 1, 1950.

58. UNCOK file, box 1375, Embassy to State, May 25, 1950. Twelve meetings were held from February through April; the full list of those consulted was: Ben Limb, Kim Sŏng-su, Kim To-yŏn, Chon Yŏng-sun, Yun Po-sŏn, Helen Kim, Yi Pŏm-sŏk, Ch'i Chŏng-sun (Yi Ch'ŏng-ch'ŏn), Shinicky (Shin Ik-hŭi), and Pak Sun-ch'ŏn, editor of the pro-Rhee *Puin sinmun* [wives' news].

59. Koo Papers, box 130, record of conversation with Cho Pyŏng-ok, August 26, 1949; UNCOK file, box 1375, Seoul to State, May 9, 1950, saying that Chang Myŏn had prevailed upon Philippine President Quirino to have Rafael Luna appointed to UNCOK.

60. UN Archives, BOX DAG-1/2.1.2, box 3, Sanford Schwarz to Cordier, Oct 10, 1949.

61. *Seoul Times*, August 14, 1948; Koo Papers, box 217, diary entry for October 26, 1949; UNCOK file, box 1375, Muccio to State, May 24, 1950; FO317, piece no. 83236, FC1016/8, China summary for June 1950, July 12, 1950. UNCOK adopted a rotating chairmanship, three weeks at a time, from May 29 onward. Muccio commented, "this will put Liu, Chi[na], [in] key position [for] preparation [of the election] report," and the Salvadoran delegate would be chairman for its completion. The Americans were seeking to avoid any Australian meddling, preferring to leave the report up to delegates from countries with well-known traditions of democratic elections. Since the Australian delegate was to assume the post on May 29, with Taiwan to follow, that put Liu in the chairmanship when the war broke out (UNCOK file, box 1375). Willoughby's intelligence also reported that the May 30 election report would be "written largely under" Liu's direction (MA, RG6, box 58, intelligence summary no. 2831, June 10, 1950).

62. Office of the Executive Secretariat, box 31, daily secret summaries, May 2, 11, 1950; UNCOK file, box 1375, Drumwright to State, May 5, 1950. The latter includes a copy of the UNCOK letter to Lie asking him to use his "good offices" in appealing to Zinchenko and other Russians to arrange "a visit to the North" or a meeting in a neutral place.

63. 795.00 file, box 4299, Muccio to State, June 11, 1950; *New York Times*, June 11, 1950; UN Archives, BOX DAG-1/2.1.2, box 4, cables, June 10, 1950, Renborg to UN; June 12, report by Gaillard on the incident. UNCOK press releases on the meeting said nothing about the ROKA machine-gun fire.

64. 795.00 file, box 4299, Muccio to State, June 11, 12, 1950.

65. Ibid., Muccio to State, June 16, 23, 1950. The embassy claimed that no violence was used against the three emmissaries.

66. 795.00 file, box 4262, Drumwright to State, February 15, 1950; see also Embassy to State, April 3, 1950, carrying a long translation of a *Seoul Sinmun* account of party politics.

67. 795.00 file, box 4299, "Developments Concerning the 1950 Election," April 24, 1950; this study ran to fifty pages.

68. Koo Papers, box 130, record of conversation with Cho Pyŏng-ok, January 5, 1949.

69. "Developments Concerning the 1950 election," citing *Chayu sinmun*, April 12, 1950; also 795.00 file, box 4299, Embassy summary for May, June 19, 1950; see the occupations of the seventy election committee members in 795.00 file, box 4299, Drumwright to State, June 9, 1950.

70. *Tonga ilbo*, March 9, 1950.
71. HST, PSF, NSC file, box 208, CIA, "Review of the World Situation," May 17, 1950; MA, RG6, box 58, intelligence summary no. 2825, June 4, 1950; 795.00 file, box 4299, Drumwright to State, June 9, 1950; Muccio to State, June 9, 1950, citing an undated *Tonga ilbo* article.
72. Howard Papers, box 251, Howard to Rhee, June 9, 1950; *New York Times*, June 1, 1950. On the aid bill rider, see 895.00 file, box 5693, Webb to Seoul, March 17, 1950. The bill was passed with the rider in early May.
73. Muccio's words, in 795.00 file, box 4299, Muccio to State, July 6, 1950; see also HST, PSF, NSC file, CIA memorandum, July 7, 1950. About sixty National Assemblymen stayed in Seoul, and nearly all went to the North after the Inch'ŏn landing.
74. 795.00 file, box 4299, Muccio to State, June 9, 1950. The original appeal is in RG242, SA2009, item 4/9.
75. MA, RG6, box 59, intelligence summary no. 2834, June 13, 1950; this has a detailed treatment of the North's unification proposal. See also FO317, piece no. 84056, Moscow Embassy to FO, June 26, 1950, quoting a *Red Star* article of June 17.
76. 795.00 file, box 4299, Embassy to State, June 23, 1950; the embassy commented that the continued use of the August 15 date suggested that the North might "attempt some new action, such as renewal of guerrilla warfare or border incidents." See the original of the June 19 statement in RG242, SA2009, item 4/9.
77. Northern newspapers printed special issues in honor of a unification demarche on May 12, 1949, and the DFUF was set up with much fanfare a few days later; in early June the papers were full of articles about the DFUF and its various proclamations. See *HGND NDSM*, May 15, 21, June 9, 1949.
78. 795.00 file, box 4262, Muccio to State, April 4, 1950; box 4299, Drumwright to State, April 10, 1950; *NDSM*, May 23, 25, 27, 1950. Yi had been often described as Pak Hŏn-yŏng's "deputy," and the Seoul Metropolitan Police disagreed with other agencies in asserting that Yi was still Pak's deputy after 1949, and was the real hand controlling the southern communists. Both Yi and Kim had been staunch anti-Japanese resisters. Yi helped organize a major strike in 1929, and spent all but two years of the period 1931–1945 in jail. He became vice-chairman of the People's Committee in Wŏnsan in 1945, and then came to Seoul in 1946, where he joined the KCP Central Committee; he went underground after a warrant for his arrest was issued during the general strike in September 1946. Kim was born in 1908, and was arrested and tortured in 1933 and imprisoned until 1936; he was jailed again from 1941–1945. He was the chief of organization for the SKWP, and was reportedly decorated by Kim Il Sung in 1948 for his underground activities.
79. 795.00 file, box 4299, Muccio to State, June 20, 23, 24, 1950; Embassy to State, June 23, 1950. See also *Haebang ilbo*, July 30, August 6, 1950. On Cho Man-sik's fate, see 795.00 file, box 4269, Drumwright to State, November 13, 1950. Embassy sources thought that he was "surely killed," because there was proof that "almost all his relatives" were executed (one of his sons, however, turned up later in Seoul).
80. 895.00 file, box 5694, Ray to State, April 3, 1950. Fraenkel was one of the rare Americans with a few years' experience in Korea; he made this statement in response to a KMAG officer who was raging over the diversion to political purposes of "voluntary contributions" for national defense. Fraenkel said such funds were often collected through blackmail and the utilization of terror. The embassy reported that internal inspection reports in the National Assembly, kept back from

public view, found a "deep public resentment against police shakedowns and brutality" (795.00 file, box 4299, Embassy to State, February 18, 1950).

81. 795.00 file, box 4299, Drumwright to State, May 26, 1950. In South Korea this
episode is known as the "Korean Political Action Corps" (*Taehan chŏngchi'i kongjak-
dae*) scandal, and accounts of it may be found in Han'guk kwangbok samsip p'allyŏn-sa p'yŏnch'an wiwŏn-hoe, *Taehan Min'guk kwangbok samsip p'allyŏn-sa* [Thirty-
eight year history of Korean restoration] (Seoul: Samsŏn ch'ulp'an-sa, 1983), pp.
334–41; also Kim Kyo-sik, *Kwangbok isimnyŏn* [Twenty years of restoration], vol.
10 (Seoul: Kyemong-sa, 1972), pp. 19–92. These accounts go into remarkable detail about not just the plot, but a hundred little conspiracies; although the main
lines of the discussion parallel my account, I have no way of checking whether the
authors are right or wrong, and prefer to rely on the embassy accounts.

82. Ibid.; see also box 4299, Muccio to Secretary of State, June 20, 1950; Embassy to
State, June 23, 1950; also MA, RG9, box 110, military attaché reports for April
15, 21, 1950.

83. 795.00 file, box 4262, Muccio to Bond, June 23, 1950.

84. Ibid. Most of this information was provided by former KNP director Kim Tae-
sŏn.

85. 795.00 file, box 4299, Seoul Embassy, "Activities of Brig. Gen. Kim Suk Won,"
March 25, 1950.

86. Ibid., box 4299, Drumwright to State, April 17, May 2, 1950, Chronology for
April, May 8, 1950. For background information on Kim see *Haebang ilbo*, July 6,
1950.

87. 795.00 file, box 4299, Drumwright to State, May 1, 1950; Drumwright to State,
May 26, 1950; chronology for April, May 8, 1950.

88. RG338, KMAG file, box 5417, William Secor to KMAG Deputy COS, June 7,
1950.

89. MA, RG9, box 110, military attaché reports for April 15, 21, 1950.

90. 895.00 file, box 5691, Drumwright to State, January 7, May 19, 1950.

91. RG338, KMAG file, box 5415, Wright to Shin Sŭng-mo, May 13, 1950; Drumwright to KMAG, April 10, 1950. KMAG also demanded that the ROKA remove
its advisors from the group.

92. 795.00 file, box 4299, Muccio to Acheson, June 20, 1950; Embassy to State, June
23, 1950.

93. The intrigue was discussed in Seoul newspapers; the North also positioned many
effective spies in the South. See MA, RG6, box 58, intelligence summary no. 2831,
June 10, 1950.

94. 895.00 file, box 946, Muccio, memo of Rhee's conversation with American representatives, December 5, 1949.

95. 895.00 file, box 5697, Muccio to State, March 11, 1950; *New York Times*, March 2,
1950.

96. *New York Times*, May 11, 1950; 795.00 file, box 4299, Drumwright to State, June
15, 1950.

97. 795.00 file, box 4299, Embassy to State, June 19, 1950 ("in its eagerness to impress
the U.S. with its need for arms, the Republic had distorted its intelligence estimates of northern strength"). See also FO317, piece no. 84061, minute by Scott,
June 30, 1950, which says Holt reported that "the whole thing is just a stunt to
squeeze more military equipment out of the Americans." On the alerts along the
parallel, see FO317, piece no. 84078, Holt to FO, May 23, 1950; he cited two in
May as of that date. Another alert occurred in early June (795.00 file, box 4299,
Muccio to State, June 9, 1950). After the war began, UNCOK took up the ROK's

cudgel in a published report in September. It said that ROKA intelligence chief Chang To-yŏng had validated the intelligence that Shin cited on May 10. Chang said returned CCF soldiers moved southward from January 1950 onward, as did tank regiments; he said two officers from Roberts's staff essentially confirmed the information, but did not agree on "the imminence of any danger." He also said he told Roberts about this intelligence on May 12. Roberts responded that Shin did not talk to him on May 12, and said UNCOK was guilty of "hindsight observation" (*New York Times*, September 15, 1950). As we have seen, much of the movement of tanks and troops toward the parallel occurred in the fall of 1949.

98. RG332, XXIV Corps Historical File, box 10, G-2 Weekly Summary no. 105, September 7–14, 1947, enclosing Yi's proposal.

99. G-2 Weekly Summary no. 158, September 17–24, 1948; FO371, piece no. 69946, *Stars and Stripes*, September 8, 1948; 895.00 file, box 7127, Drumwright to State, January 10, 1949, quoting Chang's news conference of December 18, 1948.

100. Clarence Weems, "American-Korean Cooperation (1941–1945): Why Was It So Little and So Late?" (Seminar paper, Columbia University, 1981); Lim, *Founding of a Dynasty*, p. 135.

101. Kim, *Politics of Military Revolution in Korea*, p. 46.

102. Office of Chinese Affairs, box 4194, Strong to State, February 24, 1950.

103. FO317, piece no. 84125, Holt to FO, April 25, 1950; Tokyo Chancery to FO, May 2, 1950. The American embassy told the British that talk of airbases was only "conjecture." See also NA, 1950–54, box 6173, 994A.61, dispatches of April 20, 22, 1950.

104. Parks M. Coble, Jr., *The Shanghai Capitalists and the National Government, 1927–1937* (Cambridge, Mass.: Harvard East Asian Monographs, 1980), pp. 100, 229; also Wu T'ieh-ch'eng, *Wu T'ieh-ch'eng hui-i-lu* (Memoirs of Wu T'ieh-ch'eng) (Taipei, 1969).

105. Clayton James remarked on how few people ever got to talk with MacArthur directly; in an appendix of meetings with MacArthur, 1945–1951, he shows that Gascoigne had 128, Yoshida 75, Willoughby 51, Almond 40, and Chu Shih-ming, 36 (*Years of MacArthur*, vol. 3, p. 693). Also, Milton Miles Papers, box 2, Milton Miles to Mrs. Miles, April 3, 1947; box 3, Milton Miles to Wu Te-chen (the usual spelling of Wu T'ieh-ch'eng), March 9, 1947.

106. 795.00 file, box 4299, chronology for April, May 8, 1950; political summary for April, May 12, 1950; Office of Chinese Affairs, box 4195, Drumwright to State, April 19, 1950; Strong to State, April 22, 1950; FO317, piece no. 83234, Formosa summary for April, May 11, 1950. See also Koo Papers, box 217, Diary, entries for March 27, April 3, 1950. The North Koreans claimed to have captured documents in Seoul showing joint ROK-ROC intelligence efforts in Northeast China and North Korea, using Koreans who had fled to the South. Their goal was to establish small cells of spies. They recopied these documents in native Korean, which makes it impossible to make any judgment about their authenticity. It said the spies were to make contact with "HID," apparently an intelligence group (*NDSM*, August 7, 1950).

107. FO317, piece no. 83234, Taipei to FO, May 18, 1950, carrying a highlight in Burgess's pen, the only one on the document. On Chu Shih-ming, see Formosa summary for May, June 15, 1950; Wu's June 6 visit is reported in piece no. 83236, Formosa summary for June, July 11, 1950.

108. Smith Papers, box 100, Koo press release, May 19, 1950; Office of Chinese Affairs, box 4210, Hong Kong to State, June 6, 1950, citing an intelligence report from North China marked "C-3," which means it could be true.

109. *NDSM*, January 6, 1950. The term literally means "positiveness."
110. *Manchester Guardian*, May 8, 1950.
111. Anthony Sampson, *The Arms Bazaar: From Lebanon to Lockheed* (New York: Bantam Books, 1978), p. 253. Sampson gives no other information on what Kodama was doing in Seoul. Elsewhere he remarks that "Korea was, above all a Lockheed war," with Lockheed Shooting Stars flying 40 percent of all combat missions, and its Super Constellations ferrying troops across the ocean (p. 105).
112. RG349, FEC G-2 Theater Intelligence, box 466, G-2 report on Cheju, May 23, 1950.
113. 795.00 file, box 4262, Muccio to Bond, June 23, 1950. Bond said he thought the report plausible, since Chiang had made previous attempts to get asylum from Rhee.
114. Acheson Seminars, February 13–14, 1954.
115. Koo Papers, box 217, diary entry for June 12, 1950.
116. J. F. Dulles Papers, Chang Myŏn Oral Interview, September 1964. Chang had many virtues from the American standpoint, but for Korean revolutionaries he was exemplary of the worst Korean vice: *sadae* as a guiding principle.
117. MA, VIP file, box 2, Chang to MacArthur, July 1, 1950; FO317, piece no. 84061, minute by E.J.F. Scott on document no. FK1015/115, June 30, 1950; see also *London Times*, June 26, 1950.
118. *New York Herald-Tribune*, June 14, 1950.
119. Ibid., June 26, 27, 1950.
120. Chang's letter to Rhee appeared in a cache of documents the North Koreans captured, and was published in *The Daily Worker*, December 4, 1950. It seems authentic, being rather innocuous compared to what Chang told Koo. See Koo Papers, box 217, diary entries for June 17, 26, 1950.
121. *Tonga ilbo*, June 17, 1950; 795.00 file, box 4299, Embassy to State, June 23, 1950.
122. 795.00 file, box 4299, Muccio to Acheson, June 19, 1950.
123. Acheson Seminars, February 13–14, 1954; *FR* (1950) 6, pp. 1222–23, Dulles to Acheson, June 15, 1950. Dulles cleared the speech with Muccio after he arrived.
124. Dulles's June 19 speech is reprinted in Donald G. Tewksbury, *Source Materials on Korean Politics and Ideology*, vol. 2 (New York: Institute of Pacific Relations, 1950).
125. FO317, piece no. 84092, Foreign Office account of Rhee's provocative statements, July 20, 1950.
126. J. F. Dulles Papers, Chŏng Il-gwŏn Oral Interview, September 1964. Chŏng also referred in Korean to the "Dulles proclamation" and a Dulles "pledge" in which he said that "the U.S. absolutely would not abandon Korea and would protect it to the end"; but the context appears to be a retrospective contrast of Dulles's love for Korea with Acheson's exclusion of the ROK from the defense perimeter. See also Almond papers, "Korean War, Historical Commentary," Almond to H. C. Pattison, March 7, 1969, where Almond twice referred to Dulles having reversed Acheson's policy and "committed the U.S. to the defense of the Korean Republic." This, too, is part of a commentary on muddle-headed diplomats like Acheson. Rhee's cable to MacArthur of June 20, 1950, is in MacArthur Papers, VIP file, box 9. In it Rhee asks MacArthur to send one Admiral Dacker to Korea. Holt's report on Dulles's speech and his visit is very bland, with no hint of anything new. See FO317, piece no. 84059, Holt to FO, June 20, 1950.
127. *Minju Chosŏn*, undated account of allegations by Mun Hak-bong, included in 795.00 file, box 4266, Kirk (Moscow) to State, July 31, 1950; see also Mun's account in *NDSM*, August 9, 1950.

128. In Ch'ŏl, "What sort of Person is this Dulles, Who Provoked a War in Korea?" *Sun'gan t'ongshin*, no. 19/62 (September 1950), pp. 12–14.
129. *NDSM*, January 19, 1950: "The behavior of Jessup, who inspected the 38th parallel with the goal of encouraging the slaughter of the people and fratricidal civil war, exposed his own sinister plot, and the entire patriotic Korean people cannot hold back their hatred and indignation at this."
130. Mathews Papers, box 90, "Korea with the John Foster Dulles Mission," June 14–29, 1950; see also Mathews to Gabriel Kolko, September 24, 1964. Elsewhere Mathews said he found Koreans full of "much vitality and ambition" instead of the apathetic, exhausted people he expected; he was convinced that "within a year," Rhee would "launch the offensive to take over North Korea." Rhee insisted that since it was Korean territory, it "was not aggression." J. F. Dulles Papers, box 49, Mathews to Dulles, June 20, 1950.
131. Letter, Jamieson to Gavan McCormack, March 18, 1983, courtesy Gavan McCormack.
132. *New York Times*, June 22, 1950. Alvary Gascoigne got a similar private rendering of the results of the visit from Dulles. It shows Dulles's knowledge of Rhee's aggressiveness, before the fighting began, but also his own penchant for nonmilitary forms of rollback:

> [Dulles] did express to me his great satisfaction with the present situation in South Korea . . . Rhee and his men were not, he said, as many people thought, waiting for the day when they would be invaded by the North: they were looking forward, and with optimism, to the time when they themselves would invade North Korea and bring about the unification of their country.
>
> While on this theme Dulles said, speaking generally, that we all of us ought to be thinking now not only of arresting the red [*sic*] infiltrations all over the world, but of rolling the reds back, not by the use of force but by countering . . . them in political, social and economic fields by our own retaliatory moves (FO371, piece no. 83831, Gascoigne to FO, June 24, 1950; I am indebted to Jon Halliday for bringing this cable to my attention).

CHAPTER SIXTEEN

1. Robert Strong to Bruce Cumings, June 2, 1989. Strong said that Dean Rusk told him, after the loss of Hainan, that the Navy "bought a junk, bombarded it with everything that a destroyer and a cruiser had and could not sink it. When a shell holed the junks it left a neat circle which could be filled by plugs of wood wrapped in rags." Thus Rusk agreed to the sale of napalm to Taiwan in May, thinking it would take care of the sails. But the motors kept the junks going, anyway.
2. Koo Papers, box 175, memo of June 8, 1950. In fiscal year 1951 Taiwan was scheduled to export about $40 million in goods to Japan, of which fully $26 million was sugar from the colonially-developed industry, which had been second only to Cuba in the late 1930s. Bananas constituted another $3.6 million; the rest consisted of salt, alcohol, ethyl, and raw foodstuffs. Taiwan would import from Japan $40 million: $15 million of sulphate of ammonia; $3.2 million in kakhi cloth for the textile mills and the ROCA; $5.5 million in machine tools; and the rest in locomotives, iron and steel products, and chemicals. Taiwan would sell $6.6 million in goods to the ROK, including sugar, coal, soda, and bananas; it

would import $5.6 million: $1 million in bicycles, the rest in auto and bicycle parts, gunny bag machines, fish, and vegetables.

3. Office of Chinese Affairs, box 14, Pawley to Acheson, November 7, 1949, with an attached analysis by Philip D. Sprouse. Sprouse noted that Wedemeyer "did not deny" this account when Sprouse asked him about it. See also Pawley Papers, box 2, "Russia is Winning," pp. 269–70.

4. Herbert Hoover Presidential Library, Bourke Hickenlooper Papers, Foreign Relations Committee file, "China Lobby, evidence," 1949–1950, citing a top secret Nationalist cable of September 15, 1950, signed by Chen Chih-mai.

5. FR (1949) 9, pp. 428–31, Acheson to Taipei, November 18, 1949. Blum cited circumstantial evidence that Acheson also "may have decided" around September 9 to back the "Muslim generals" with military aid as per the "Chennault plan"; Truman was even more favorable toward covert action in China (Blum, Drawing the Line, pp. 101, 153, 161).

6. William D. Leahy Papers, box 6, Diary, entry for November 10, 1949. Leahy's response is not available, nor is it known if he discussed Cooke's visit with Truman. On Leahy's support for the Nationalists, see ibid., entry for October 1, 1948.

7. Donovan Papers, box 75A, Item 893. The text has the name as Chiang Kai-ming, but Cheng Kai-ming was vice-minister of National Defense, and no one named Chiang Kai-ming was prominent at this time. Cheng's properly romanized name was Ch'eng Chieh-min, but like Chiang Kai-shek he changed "chieh" to "kai." Cheng took over the Chinese secret service after Tai Li's death, according to Milton Miles. "Mao Jung Fong" was Mao Jen-feng, an associate of Miles in the OSS/SACO group (Milton Miles Papers, box 2, Miles to Karb Kunjara, February 2, 1947).

8. Koo Papers, box 130, Conversation with Admiral Badger, December 20, 1949; box 217, Koo Diaries, entries for December 9, 20, 1949. Koo sent his memo to Acheson anyway: see FR (1949) 9, pp. 457–60, Koo to Acheson, December 23, 1949.

9. Koo Papers, box 217, diary entry for June 23, 1949.

10. Wellington Koo oral history, vol. 6, p. J-463; Koo Papers, box 217, diary entry for March 18, 1949.

11. Cave Brown, Last Hero, pp. 795–800; on Fassoulis, see Scott, War Conspiracy, p. 210. On Fassoulis and Cates, see also 795.00 file, box 5687, Fassoulis to M. Hamilton, January 3, 1950; Pearson's column on Fassoulis is in Cooke Papers, box 26.

12. 795.00 file, box 4214, Commerce International letter of April 4, 1951, signed by M. A. Couvaras; Nicholson to Bushong, memo of August 9, 1951; Office of Chinese Affairs, box 4215, legal documents on Commerce International, dated March 12, 1952, including a long letter from Ambrose Cates to his parents, dated August 22, 1950.

13. 795.00 file, box 4257, Poston to Strong, August 14, 1950; also Blum, Drawing the Line, p. 41.

14. 795.00 file, box 4257, Poston to Strong, August 14, 1950.

15. Koo Papers, box 180, Chen Chih-mai to Koo, April 10, 1950.

16. FO317, piece no. 83008, Slessor to FO, December 30, 1949.

17. The planes included seventy-one DC3s, five Convairs, five 4-engine Skymasters, the total worth $30 million (Smith Papers, box 100, Chennault to Smith, March 13, 1950). See also Rankin Papers, box 14, Rankin to Rusk, April 14, 1950, where Rankin refers to the "rear-guard action we have been fighting" to keep the PRC from getting CNAC planes; also Schaller, American Occupation of Japan, p. 251; also William M. Leary, Perilous Missions: Civil Air Transport and CIA Covert Operations in Asia (University, Ala.: University of Alabama Press, 1984), p. 102.

18. FO317, piece no. 83013, Gascoigne to FO, February 11, 1950, enclosing notes by Ferguson on his conversations with Donovan, February 8, 1950; Schaller, *American Occupation of Japan*, p. 251.

19. MA, VIP file, box 3, Donovan to MacArthur, March 14, 1950; Jessup Papers, box A47, Jessup to M. Hartley Dodge, March 22, 1950; Karl Rankin Papers, box 14, H. Alexander Smith to Rankin, May 1, 1950; Donovan speech of February 16, 1950, included in Smith Papers, box 114.

20. Donovan Papers, box 5B, Donovan to Acheson, February 12, 1950; Acheson to Donovan, February 28, 1950.

21. Ibid., Donovan to Acheson, March 23, 1950; Acheson to Donovan, March 27, 1950; Whitney H. Shepardson to Donovan, April 27, 1950; Donovan to H. Alexander Smith, March 23, 1950; Donovan to Russell C. Leffingwell, July 6, 1950.

22. Ibid., box 7, Donovan memorandum of March 2, 1950; also box 3A, Donovan, "The Global War of Subversion," *Vital Speeches* (March 1, 1950), pp. 295–97; also box 76A, "Preface to a Basic Plan for a Psychological Campaign (Peacetime) Against the Kremlin Military Dictators," April 4, 1950, unsigned but probably authored by Donovan or an aide. See also an account of his congressional testimony in the *New York Times*, March 8, 1950, which quoted Donovan as saying the United States should "take the initiative in arresting aggressive communism" in Asia.

23. Donovan Papers, box 5B, Donovan to H. A. Smith, March 23, 1950.

24. Smith Papers, box 282, diaries, entries for April 4, 5, 22, 25, 27, 28; May 14, 15, 16, 1950.

25. Donovan Papers, box 76A, item 1042, May 26, 1950; *New York Times*, June 30, 1950.

26. Sheeks, "Activities of Irving Short," quoting Lt. Col. Carl M. Poston's account, who was relating a story he heard from "Col. Tally," who must have been Colonel Tally of Army intelligence (in 795.00 file, box 4257, Poston to Strong, August 14, 1950).

27. MA, RG9, box 43, KMAG cables, KMAG to CINCFE, October 8, 1950; CINCFE to KMAG, October 10, 1949. Smith met Goodfellow in Kyoto on October 15. See Smith Papers, box 98, Smith to William Knowland, October 24, 1949; box 282, Smith Diaries, entries for October 10, 15, 1949.

28. Hoover Presidential Library, PPI file, box 341, Goodfellow to Hoover, January 3, 1950. Goodfellow writes, "I have just returned from Korea." On January 2 Hoover's letter to William Knowland about Formosa had hit the press.

29. Koo Papers, box 217, Koo Diaries, entry for January 4, 1950; Koo oral history, vol. 6, p. J-392.

30. Goodfellow Papers, box 1, Goodfellow to Rhee, January 24, 1950. One surmises that the "Col. Collins" whom Goodfellow was with in February 1947 is the same man. He is referred to in Oliver Papers, Oliver to his wife, February 11, 1947. Collins was working with Goodfellow, Oliver, and Jay Williams in lobbying efforts for Rhee on Capitol Hill.

31. Koo Papers, box 217, Koo Diaries, entries for January 12, February 3, 1950; Koo oral history, vol. 6, pp. J-393–96; Nancy Tucker, *Patterns in the Dust: Chinese-American Relations and the Recognition Controversy 1949–1950* (New York: Columbia University Press, 1983, p. 77. Goodfellow wrote Kim Tae-sŏn on January 26, 1950, "Here is the picture I promised. Most police carry 38 caliber pistols not 45 caliber." Goodfellow Papers, box 1; he misspelled the name as Kim Sae Sun.

32. Koo oral history, vol. 6, p. J-398–99; 795.00 file, box 4255, Strong to State, February 24, 1950; Goodfellow is described as a "private businessman purportedly selling fertilizer." Back in Washington, someone drew attention only to this pas-

sage in this long weekly report. The report does not indicate whether Cooke and Goodfellow traveled together, only that they arrived at the same time. Also, interview with M. Preston Goodfellow, Jr., August 1987.

33. Robert Strong to Bruce Cumings, June 2, 1989; the State Department ruling came in March or April 1950, Strong thought.

34. Koo Diary, entry for March 23, 1950; Koo oral history, vol. 6, pp. J-396, J-399.

35. On back-channel communication to Taipei, see Nancy Tucker, "Nationalist China's Decline and its Impact on Sino-American Relations, 1949–1950," in *Uncertain Years*, ed. Borg and Heinrichs, p. 150. Louis Johnson's papers show no trace of this activity.

36. Koo Diary, entries for March 27, April 3, 1950; Goodfellow's March 15 arrival in Seoul is documented in 795.00 file, box 4262, Embassy to State, April 17, 1950. The *Tonga ilbo* recorded his visit on March 16, 1950. See also Goodfellow Papers, box 1, Goodfellow to Rhee, March 27, 1950. "Hwang" in the text must be Huang Shao-ku, Chiang's personal secretary. See Koo oral history, vol. 6, p. J-404.

37. Koo oral history, vol. 6, pp. A-2–4.

38. Smith Papers, box 282, Smith Diaries, entries for February 26, 27, March 7, 17.

39. In discussing personnel available for psychological warfare in Korea, Harriman "referred to the possibility of Col. Goodfriend, a former Army colonel who was in Korea when Harriman visited there in 1946." Office of the Executive Secretariat, box 4, summaries of Acheson's daily meetings, August 1, 1950.

40. Office of Chinese Affairs, box 4195, Strong to State, April 22, 1950. The China specialists in the Foreign Service "did not want one of their own in the line of fire," so Strong, not a Chinese language officer, "was picked to sit on the hot lid." He wrote that "he paid a high price for having occupied that hot seat, endured a lot of insults, was separated from my family, was harassed by the John Birchers even long after I retired. . . . Even the Saudis hired an American agent to try to stop my appointment to Iraq as Ambassador" (Robert Strong to Bruce Cumings, June 2, 1989).

41. FO317, piece no. 83233, Summary of events in Formosa, October 1949, January 19, 1950; see also the sanitized account of Chennault's meeting with MacArthur, November 21, 1949, in HST, PSF, CIA file, box 249.

42. MA, VIP file, box 2, Chennault to MacArthur, November 20, 1949.

43. 995.00 file, box 6175, J. Franklin Ray, Jr., to State, January 28, 1950, citing Chennault's letter to Rhee of December 5, 1949; Leary, *Perilous Missions*, pp. 103–4.

44. 995.00 file, box 6175, Ray to State, May 16, 1950; Willauer Papers, box 1, Willauer to L. K. Taylor, April 25, 1950.

45. FO317, piece no. 83235, Graeme Chivers to FO, June 29, 1950.

46. MA, RG6, Intelligence Summaries, box 59, no. 2843, June 22, 1950; RG9, box 12, SCAP to Chennault, June 27, 1950, referring to Chennault's cable of June 26 (MacArthur at that point declined CAT assistance); Willauer Papers, box 1, Memo for Chennault, July 10, 1950; tape transcript, December 1, 1960. Willauer in the latter source said that CAT was kept out of Korea before the war "due to the hatred of the Koreans for the Chinese and because we flew the Chinese flag." But, as we have seen, Rhee and Lady were ready to work with CAT by mid-June, and it was the embassy that blocked the joint venture.

47. 795.00 file, box 4214, Commerce International letter of April 4, 1951, signed by M. A. Couvaras; Nicholson to Bushong, memo of August 9, 1951; Office of Chinese Affairs, box 4215, legal documents on Commerce International, dated March 12, 1952, including a long letter from Ambrose Cates to his parents, dated August 22, 1950. For additional documentation, see 795.00 file, box 4254, S. G. Fassoulis

to M. Hamilton, January 3, 1950; Smith Papers, box 100, Burton Crane to Smith, October 13, 1950; Tucker, *Patterns in the Dust*, pp. 91, 187.

48. Robert Strong wrote that all copies of classified reports sent to Washington from Taiwan by State Department representatives and military attachés went through Vanderpuyl; he routinely gave them to Gen. Ho Shih-lai, the Nationalist representative on the Far East Commission in Tokyo. Truman found out about this and tried to fire Vanderpuyl, but since he "was a protégé of Louis Johnson and was very active in the American Legion," Truman dropped the matter (Robert Strong to Bruce Cumings, June 2, 1989). FO317, piece no. 83233, Taipei to FO, February 4, 11, 18, 1950; Office of Chinese Affairs, box 4195, Taipei to State, April 22, May 18, 1950. See also 795.00 file, box 4255, Taipei to State, June 3, 1950. Also, Charles M. Cooke Papers, box 6, Cooke to ROCA Chief of Staff Chow Chih Jou, July 1, 1950; box 26, Rear Adm. F. I. Entwhistle to Cooke, January 30, 1950; box 26, Gen. O. T. Pfeiffer to Cooke, May 6, 1950.

49. See the *Hsinhua* report, January 3, 1950, translated in *NDSM*, January 6, 1950.

50. State Department disgust with Cates and Cooke is obvious in most of the documentation cited above; JCS opposition is evident in *FR* (1950) 6, p. 413n, citing a JCS telegram to MacArthur of August 8, 1950.

51. Cooke Papers, box 2, Cooke to E. D. Coblentz, February 20, 1950; Office of Chinese Affairs, box 17, Strong to Sprouse, May 26, 1950; William R. Mathews Papers, box 90, "Korea with the John Foster Dulles Mission, June 14–29, 1950"; J. F. Dulles Papers, box 49, William R. Mathews, memo for Dulles, June 20, 1950; Smith Papers, box 100, Taiwan diary by Entwhistle and Twitchell, April 27, 1950, entry; MA, RG6, box 58, Intelligence Summary no. 2808, May 18, 1950. On Cooke's meetings with MacArthur, which occurred in February, May, and June 1950, see MA, RG9, box 12, Cooke to Fortier, June 9, 1950. Cooke was also prominent among those who welcomed MacArthur to Taiwan in August 1950.

52. 795.00 file, box 4257, Poston to Strong, August 14, 1950; Cooke Papers, box 4, Terry Kouan to Cooke, March 11, 1959. It would be interesting to know Colonel Williams's first name. Goodfellow's negotiations with British intelligence in 1942 were conducted with Col. Garland Williams at his side (Corson, *Armies of Ignorance*, pp. 189–90).

53. See Office of Chinese Affairs, box 4198, Robert B. Sheeks, "Activities of Irving Short and History of the Volunteer Composite Ground Force Group," June 14, 1951, which includes Short's own version, given to Colonel Poston on July 20, 1950; box 4194, Strong to Sprouse, March 2, 1950, enclosing letter from Short to Hovans; Special Agent S. L. Evans interview with Don Edgar, April 13, 1950; box 4195, Acheson to Rankin, top secret, eyes only cables of April 18, 19, 1950; box 4196, Strong to State, two cables on July 7, 1950; also box 4195, Strong to State, April 23, 1950.

54. Koo Papers, box 217, Koo Diary, entries for March 16, April 5, 1950; box 180, Chen Chih-mai to Koo, April 10, 1950.

55. Office of Chinese Affairs, box 4198, Sheeks, "Activities of Irving Short."

56. 795.00 file, box 4255, Taipei Embassy to State, July 20, 1953; box 4258, Strong to State, June 6, 1950; Office of Chinese Affairs, box 4219, Sebald to Allison, March 20, 1950, quoting information given Sebald by an unnamed G-2 officer; box 4195, Barrett to State, April 27, 1950; John W. Dower, "The Eye of the Beholder: Background Notes on the U.S.-Japanese Military Relationship," *Bulletin of Concerned Asian Scholars* 2, no. 1 (October 1969), p. 20. The information on the high officers came from the Taipei Consulate, and Acheson asked MacArthur to confirm or deny it (795.00 file, box 4195, Acheson to MacArthur, June 9, 1950). I could not

find MacArthur's answer, if any. On the dispatch of forty advisors in June, see Smith Papers, box 98, Basil R. Entwhistle to Smith, May 11, 1950; Entwhistle had just returned from Tokyo and Taipei. In January 1950, two Nationalist agents visited von Falkenhausen in his Belgian jail; he wrote at the time, "They agreed with my opinion. Something could still be saved. . . . As early as 1947 Chiang Kai-shek had urgently invited me [to come to Formosa as an advisor], but I was and am a prisoner" (Allen Dulles Papers, box 45, von Falkenhausen to Eric M. War-burg, January 12, 1950). In 1950 Gen. Sun Li-jen had a German advisor named Bodo Stein, who came to China with von Falkenhausen's military mission. When the mission returned to Germany in 1938, Stein stayed on in reconnaissance work. It is interesting to note that, according to Karl Rankin, later ambassador to Taipei, Chiang's second son, Chiang Wei-guo, was sent to Germany for military training in the 1930s, and stayed on long enough to participate in the 1938 Anschluss (see 795.00 file, box 4195, Taipei Embassy to State, July 20, 1953).

57. *Jenmin Jihpao* [People's Daily], January 12, March 23, 25, April 24, May 24, 1950; see also *Hsinhua Jihpao* [Hsinhua Daily], February 15, 1950.

58. FO317, piece no. 83297, comment or "minute" on Gascoigne to FO, January 13, 1950; piece no. 83243, memo on invasion of Formosa, January 25, 1950, minute by Burgess; piece no. 83247, report on Formosa, April 14, 1950, minute by Burgess.

59. Burgess's comments on FO317, piece no. 83243, FC1019/16, January 25, 1950; FC1019/11, March 22, 1950; FC1019/123, April 14, 1950.

60. *FR* (1950) 6, pp. 340–42, Strong to Secretary, May 17, 1950. On T. V. Soong, see *New York Times*, June 10, 1950, which reported that he was in New York with H. H. Kung. See also Office of Chinese Affairs, box 4195, Taipei to State, May 18, 1950. Evacuation notices were issued in the last week of May (795.00 file, box 4255, Taipei weekly report, May 26, 1950). Discussions with American military attachés prompted Strong's evacuation proposal; after it was sent, "there was practically no follow-up" by the State Department, and Strong "was not informed of what was cooking in Washington" (Robert Strong to Bruce Cumings, June 2, 1989).

61. In March Acheson refused to issue licenses for the sale of twenty-five M-4 tanks and twenty-five F-80 jets to Taiwan, citing in particular British fears that they would fall into PRC hands (RG330, Secretary of Defense file, box 115, Acheson to Johnson, March 7, 1950).

62. Koo Papers, box 217, diary entry for January 5, 1950.

63. CP, 1980, item 339C, CIA intelligence memos, ORE 7–50, February 20, 1950, and no. 292, May 11, 1950.

64. FO317, piece no. 83013, Franks to FO, June 5, 1950; Senator Smith told K. C. Wu that Hainan's loss had "very much concerned" Taiwan's friends in Washington. At the same time, Smith got a report from two friends, saying "action must be immediate to save the situation" on Formosa (Smith Papers, box 100, Smith to Wu, May 1, 1950; Basil R. Entwhistle and H. Kenaston Twitchell to Smith, May 11, 1950).

65. 795.00 file, box 4255, Taipei to State, April 28, 1950; Smith Papers, box 100, text of Chiang's news conference, May 8, 1950. Willoughby's intelligence reports contain criticism of Chiang's ineptness and his desire for a world war to bail him out in this period. See, for example, MA, RG6, box 58, intelligence summary no. 2819, May 29, 1950.

66. Willauer Papers, box 2, Willauer to Louise Willauer, May 1, 1950.

67. FO317, piece no. 83234, Formosa summary for April, May 11, 1950, Burgess minute on cover; piece no. 83235, Formosa summary for May, June 15, 1950.
68. MA, VIP file, box 3, Cooke to MacArthur, April 27, 1950. See also Charles M. Cooke Papers, box 1, Cooke to Rear Adm. W. F. Boone (U.S. Seventh Fleet Commander), April 26, 1950. Here Cooke defends the evacuation, but does not say he ordered it; in fact he writes, "Hainan did not need to be lost . . . the invasion . . . could have been defeated."
69. Ibid., Cooke to MacArthur, April 27, May 2, 1950.
70. MA, RG6, box 58, intelligence summaries no. 2803–2817, May 1950; most of the issues have information on growing PRC air capabilities. See also RG330, Secretary of Defense file, box 37, Bradley to Johnson, May 5, 1950; box 30, Bradley to Johnson, May 29, 1950. "Shah" was probably K. C. Shah, an aid to Chiang.
71. Smith Papers, box 100, undated Chennault note to Smith, apparently late March 1950; Francis Shen to Smith, March 31, 1950; Knowland to Smith, April 26, 1950 (Cooke told Knowland both MIGs and Zeroes had been spotted over Shanghai); "Commander Liu" et al. to Smith, June 12, 1950, enclosed in Smith to Rusk, June 16, 1950; *New York Times*, June 1, 1950.
72. HST, PSF, CIA file, box 250, situation summary for October 27, 1950. The CIA said there was no proof that the aviation gas was transferred south of Manchuria before the Korean War. Also FO317, piece no. 83316, Hutchison to FO, March 30, April 5, 1950; Burgess minutes on both. See also piece no. 83317, Hutchison to FO, May 18, 1950, Burgess minute. By this time Burgess said the presence in China of swept-wing jet fighters, that is, MIGs, was "established."
73. 795.00 file, box 4255, Taipei to State, May 12, 1950; see also William R. Mathews Papers, box 1, "Korea with the John Foster Dulles Mission, June 14–29, 1950." Mathews says Floyd A. Stephenson, field representative for General Motors, told him that a group of Flying Tiger airmen were in Taiwan.
74. Hickenlooper Papers, "China Lobby, evidence," cable signed by Kung Chi, June 23, 1950.
75. Koo Papers, box 180, conversation with Dulles, June 12, 1950; MA, RG6, box 58, intelligence summary no. 2831, June 10, 1950; similar reports came in on June 12; Higgins, *New York Herald-Tribune*, June 10, 15, 1950.
76. MA, RG6, box 58, intelligence summaries no. 2838 and 2844, June 17, 23, 1950; FO317, piece no. 83236, Formosa summary for June, July 11, 1950; piece no. 83249, Formosan consul to FO, June 19, 1950. Walter Sullivan reported from Hong Kong on June 29, 1950, that the fleet was assembled and ready to commence an invasion (*New York Times*, June 29, 1950).
77. Koo Papers, box 217, Diary, entries for June 6, 8, 1950.
78. MA, RG9, box 40, Naval Commander in the Philippines to Washington, May 29, 1950. This document stated, "information discloses Taiwan may fall in near future and Nats have been negotiating [with] high official Phil Govt and South Korea relative [to] asylum. Understand negotiations former have failed."
79. MA, RG6, box 1, Willoughby to MacArthur, June 15, 1950.
80. *FR* (1949) 9, pp. 337–41, Merchant to Butterworth, May 24, 1949; ibid., pp. 359–64, "A Possible Course of Action with Respect to Formosa and the Pescadores," June 23, 1949. Kennan was probably the author of this PPS paper, although it does not bear his signature.
81. Corson, *Armies of Ignorance*, pp. 360–66, which includes Senate testimony and reports. All documentation on the two cases was destroyed. On Pash's background see also Simpson, *Blowback*, pp. 152–53.
82. Joseph Burkholder Smith, *Portrait of a Cold Warrior* (New York: Ballantine Books,

1976), pp. 66–67. It is not clear what years Smith speaks of—certainly 1951, but perhaps 1949–1950 as well. An informant who wishes to remain unidentified said that Li Mi was working for the CIA by May 1950, if not earlier.

83. Executive Secretariat file, box 4, summaries of secretary's daily meetings, August 31, 1949. On Rusk and Merrill in Burma, see Schoenbaum, *Waging Peace and War*, pp. 80–84, 106.

84. Kan Chieh-hou told Rusk and others that he was "desirous of getting rid of the Generalissimo" (*FR* [1949] 9, pp. 719–20, September 16, 1949; see also Louis Johnson Papers, box 103, Canaday to Johnson, October 20, 1949). This would presumably be the Ward Canaday who was chairman of Willys-Overland Motors from 1936–1946, a company that was crucial to the war effort with its jeeps and trucks. T. V. Soong discussed having Hu Shih "head a cabinet to impress Americans" on several occasions, beginning in July 1949. See Koo oral history, vol. 6, pp. I-251, I-255, J-97-101. On the Reid approach, see Koo Papers, box 217, diary entry for May 16, 1949, quoting Mrs. Reid as saying that the KMT needs new faces, like Hu Shih.

85. Robert Strong to Bruce Cumings, June 2, 1989. Strong commented to me, "no explanation was offered by Krentz as to how Sun might be expected to gain control when all the mainlanders who had come to the island had been handpicked by Chiang and all the secret services were intact and operating."

86. Koo Papers, box 217, Diary, entries for March 25, April 20, 1950. Cleveland spoke to Lee Kan, who told Koo this was the first time anyone had said this "so plainly."

87. Office of Chinese Affairs, box 4195, Barrett to State, originally top secret, April 27, 1950. Notations on the original cable say it was shown to Rusk on May 1.

88. Office of Chinese Affairs, box 17, Strong to Sprouse, May 11, 1950, originally top secret. Strong says Sun talked to Barrett "two weeks ago."

89. Office of Chinese Affairs, box 4195, doc. no. 793.00/5-350, "Hypothetical Development of the Formosan Situation," May 3, 1950, originally top secret. The document is signed with the initials PHN, which could be none other than Paul H. Nitze. The copy I saw was number one of only four that were made. Otherwise there are none of the usual markings on it. It was not filed until June 29, 1956.

90. Declassification censors refused my request to release this document in 1987. It is in Office of Chinese Affairs, box 17, February 20, 1950. Robert Strong wrote that Nitze's proposals were "fatuous, extremely broad-brush, and full of pious generalities which the US had no means of attaining"; he said that Kennan, whom Strong served with in Prague, was "a true expert on the USSR, but on China he was a babe in the woods. . . . Sun Li-jen could not have gained control of the Kuomintang and the other levels of power without the elimination of at least 100 officials and officers" (Robert Strong to Bruce Cumings, June 2, 1989).

91. 795.00 file, "For P.A. only," May 31, 1950, relating the content of the May 30 meeting, formerly top secret. See also *FR* (1950) 6, pp. 347–49. P.A. was Park Armstrong.

92. Schoenbaum, *Waging Peace and War*, p. 209.

93. Office of Chinese Affairs, box 18, Merchant to Rusk, date unclear but March 1950. An informant who wishes to remain indentified said "Frank" had to be Wisner, and gave me Joyce's position. Rusk was atypically rash in arguing in October 1949 that the United States "should employ whatever means were indicated" in causing discomfort to the Chinese Communists: "arms here, opium there, bribery and propaganda in the third place" (Far East 890.00 file, box C-846, Meeting of the Secretary and Consultants on the Far East, October 26, 1949, in 890.00/11-

1749). Acheson told MacArthur in late 1949 that support for "self-reputed anti-communist guerrilla forces would be unprofitable and politically dangerous. Nationalist guerrillas during the Sino-Jap War regularly turned over to enemy. USA has given enough munitions to Nationalists to meet any guerrilla needs if they were desirous [of] fighting" (MA, RG9, box 145, Acheson to SCAP, December 24, 1949). This may merely mean that Acheson was opposed to Nationalist covert action, not to American.

94. RG330, Secretary of Defense file, box 30, Magruder to Johnson, April 7, 1950; Donovan Papers, box 1, Peers to Donovan, April 7, 1950; R. Harris Smith, *OSS: The Secret History of America's First Central Intelligence Agency* (Berkeley: University of California Press, 1972), pp. 265, 265n. Peers was an OSS veteran who commanded forces in Burma; it is worth remembering that Goodfellow also served in Burma. Peers later gained fame as the author of an official report on the My Lai massacre in Vietnam. In 1951 the CIA sponsored several invasions of China from Burma, using remnant Nationalist forces; the results were disastrous.

95. MA, RG9, box 40, Rankin to SCAP, May 27, 1950.

96. Office of Chinese Affairs, box 18, Rusk to Acheson, "U.S. Policy Toward Formosa," May 30, 1950. See also box 17, Merchant to Rusk, "Condensed Checklist on China and Formosa," June 29, 1950.

97. Lowe, *Origins of the Korean War*, p. 153.

98. Office of Chinese Affairs, box 17, Rusk to Acheson, June 9, 1950, formerly top secret.

99. *FR* (1950) 6, p. 348n.

100. HST, Acheson Papers, box 45, appointment books, entries for May 1, June 9, 1950. Rusk's memorandum of the meeting with Nitze, Jessup, and others on May 30 is actually dated May 31, which suggests it was probably drawn up to show to Acheson that day.

101. Koo Papers, box 217, diary entry for June 6, 1950; Koo oral history, vol. 6, p. J-448. Later on, in November 1950, Clubb told Merchant that contact with Chinese Nationalist military leaders should only be made "at the eleventh hour," because prior to that it would leak to Chiang. He refers back to a memo of July 14, 1950, which is probably about the failed coup attempt. I do not know why Clubb was talking about an "eleventh hour" again in November 1950, but this was the time when Chinese Communist forces entered the Korean War. Office of Chinese Affairs, box 17, Clubb to Merchant, November 22, 1950.

102. Koo Papers, box 180, memo of conversation, June 3, 7, 1950; Cohen, "Acheson, His Advisors, and China," in *Uncertain Years*, ed. Borg and Heinrichs, p. 32.

103. Koo Papers, box 180, June 7, 1950; Office of Chinese Affairs, box 17, Acheson to Johnson, June 8, 1950. Acheson was responding to Johnson about an invitation by Madame Chiang to visit Taipei, and to save the regime in its hour of crisis.

104. *New York Herald-Tribune*, June 10, 1950; *New York Times*, June 10, 16, 1950; on Kung's visit to Willoughby, see Roy Howard Papers, box 251, Willoughby to Howard, June 22, 1950.

105. 795.00 file, box 4254, Strong to Acheson, June 7, 1950; Acheson to Strong, June 13, 1950; Strong to Rusk, June 14, 1950.

106. Office of Chinese Affairs, box 18, "Summary of Principal Elements Underlying Present U.S. Policy toward Formosa, as Set Forth in President's Statement of January 5, 1950," June 19, 1950.

107. Office of Chinese Affairs, box 17, Merchant to Rusk, "Condensed Checklist on

China and Formosa." For Rusk's reference to Cooke's operation, see box 18, Rusk to Acheson, May 30, 1950.

108. RG330, Secretary of Defense file, box 37, Kenneth Young to General Burns, June 19, 1950. Chiang Kai-shek should be removed from power, Young said, but as a "long-range matter," and indeed this Pentagon document did not share the general sense of urgency about an impending invasion.

109. Schaller, *American Occupation of Japan*, p. 278.

110. FO317, piece no. 83008, Brind to FO, June 3, 8, 1950. General Almond later said, MacArthur always wanted to support Chiang, not just on Taiwan but in "getting back to the mainland as soon as possible" (Almond Papers, Oral History interview, March 25, 1975).

111. 795.00 file, box 3006, Merchant to Rusk, June 23, 1950; Koo Papers, box 217, diary entry for July 24, 1950; Koo oral history, vol. 6, pp. A-72–73.

112. Office of Chinese Affairs, box 4195, McKee to Rusk, April 27, 1950.

113. Schoenbaum, *Waging Peace and War*, p. 209.

114. Cohen, "Acheson, His Advisors, and China," in *Uncertain Years*, ed. Borg and Heinrichs, p. 32. This apparently came from an interview with Rusk. It is ironic that Rusk, the key actor in the coup planning, should say he got a "hint" of a coup. He also suggested to me that the coup planning was all the work of Chinese on Taiwan. See also MA, RG6, box 59, intelligence summary no. 2853, July 2, 1950; and Koo oral history, vol. 6, p. A-121. Rankin, a knowedgeable insider on China policy, suggested a coup against Chiang again in September 1950, and this is the context in which he made the remark quoted in the text (Rankin Papers, box 14, Rankin to Rusk, September 4, 1950). On Sun's 1955 arrest, see Koo Papers, box 170, Sun Li-jen case. Sun was allegedly arrested for doing nothing about a rebellion planned by a trusted subordinate, Kuo Ting-liang, whom the regime claimed was a communist agent. However, a recent article claimed that "the real circumstance leading to Sun's disgrace is still shrouded in mystery," and noted that the affair "is still seen as a textbook illustration of the 'US' unreliability as an ally' and its propensity to use generals favored by it to topple a leader unpopular with the Americans" (Shim Jae Hoon, "A Question of History," *Far Eastern Economic Review*, April 14, 1988).

115. Burgess's comments on FO317, piece no. 83234, FC1016/54, May 11, 1950, and on ibid., FC1016/59, May 11, 1950. See also FO317, piece no. 83297, Moscow Chancery to FO, January 10, 1950.

116. Ibid., piece no. 83250, Burgess comments on FC1019/198, June 20, 1950.

CHAPTER SEVENTEEN

1. Robert J. Donovan documents some of these summer activities (*Tumultuous Years*, p. 189). See also Blair, *Forgotten War*, p. 69; U. Alexis Johnson, *Right Hand of Power*, p. 94; Stueck, *Road to Confrontation*, p. 177.

2. Harold Joyce Noble, *Embassy at War*, ed. Frank Baldwin (Seattle: University of Washington Press, 1975), p. 219.

3. *New York Times*, June 23, 24, 25, 1950.

4. The combat alert is reported on June 25 (*New York Times*), but the dateline is June 24, before the news of war in Korea. Gen. Mark Clark was in overall command of the alert, with General Bolte responsible for supervision and coordination.

5. Joseph C. Goulden, *Korea: The Untold Story of the War* (New York: Times Books), p. 97.

6. RG242, SA2006, item 16/103, *Chosŏn inmin-gun* [Korean people's army], June 21, 23, 1950. Only a few copies of this army newspaper are available in RG242. There is some evidence that its editors were close to Pak Hŏn-yŏng's group, the June 23 issue containing an article that brings up the 1946 KCP counterfeiting case, refers to the KCP as the "precursor" of the KWP, dwells on the Kim Sam-yong/Yi Chu-ha case, and states that those who took up arms against the Japanese "at home and abroad" were only "the proletarian internationalist communists." This is a different historiography and emphasis from organs controlled by Kim Il Sung, and uses the terms communism (*kongsanjuŭi*) and in transliteration, proletariat (*p'ŭro-ret'aria*), rarely found in KWP publications. This, combined with the provocative rhetoric about an imminent battle, might be more evidence of Pak's involvement in the decision to go to war. But it is hardly enough to contradict the argument that Kim Il Sung, Ch'oe Yong-gŏn, and the others would never have agreed to the wishes of Pak, had they been strongly opposed to a war policy.

7. Gavan McCormack, *Cold War/Hot War* (Sydney, Australia: Hale and Iremonger, 1983), p. 97; E. Gough Whitlam, *A Pacific Community* (Cambridge, Mass.: Australian Studies Endowment and Council on East Asian Studies, Harvard University Press, 1981), pp. 57–58.

8. Letters, J. W. Burton to Bruce Cumings, November 25, 1981, February 3, 1982; also McCormack, *Cold War/Hot War*. Also, Interview with Burton, February 1987. Dr. Burton now teaches international politics at George Mason University.

9. Letter, Jamieson to McCormack, November 24, 1983, courtesy Gavan McCormack.

10. Ibid.

11. Jon Halliday, "The Korean War," *Bulletin of Concerned Asian Scholars* (July-September 1979).

12. McCormack, interview with Peach on August 13, 1982, in *Cold War/Hot War*, p. 81.

13. *New York Times*, May 20, 1950. Bradley's dissent from the troop withdrawal and his support of military aid to Taiwan is mentioned in Schnabel and Watson, JCS, *Korean War*, vol. 3, pt. 1, pp. 25–26, 61.

14. HST, Acheson Papers, box 65, memo of conversation on Japanese peace treaty, April 24, 1950; *FR* (1950) 6, pp. 1175–82, memo of conversation, Acheson, Rusk, Johnson, and others. See also *FR* (1956) 6, pp. 1109–16, Jessup talks with MacArthur, January 9, 1950; Jessup to Acheson, January 10, 1950. Reston represented Acheson's view in the *New York Times*, June 18, 1950, remarking that Acheson wanted Dulles to go along with Johnson to Tokyo.

15. Koo Papers, box 180, memo of conversation with Dulles, June 12, 1950.

16. Schaller, *American Occupation of Japan*, pp. 269–70; Lowe, *Origins of the Korean War*, p. 79.

17. Johnson Papers, box 138, itinerary for Johnson-Bradley visit; see also MA, RG6, box 9, schedule for Johnson-Bradley and Dulles visits; RG10, VIP file, box 3, Dulles to MacArthur, July 4, 1950. This letter, thanking MacArthur for his hospitality, shows no particular sign of warmth. Chinese Nationalist sources said that William Bullitt would accompany Johnson to Tokyo. See Chen Chih-mai to Taipei, May 31, 1950, translated cable in Wayne Morse Papers, box 22a, "China Lobby." I have no other evidence that Bullitt, then actively lobbying for arms for Taiwan, went along with Johnson. Allison accompanied Dulles, and noted that Dulles "had several private conversations" with MacArthur, no one else present (J. F. Dulles Papers, John M. Allison Oral Interview, April 20, 1969). William Sebald thought the

private meetings were about "politics," presumably meaning the 1952 election (Ibid., Sebald Oral Interview, July 1965).

18. MA, RG6, box 8, MacArthur to Department of the Army, May 29, 1950; RG9, box 12, Cooke to Fortier, June 9, 1950; Cooke had been in Tokyo in late May. Col. W.H.S. Wright, KMAG chief of staff, was given travel orders for Tokyo on June 19, arriving on June 24 (RG338, KMAG file, box 5420, KMAG officers' travel documents).

19. MA, RG6, box 1, Willoughby to MacArthur, June 15, 1950. Chiang communicated his request through Gen. Ho Shih-lai. Johnson said later that PLA troops for an invasion grew from 40,000 to 156,000 during his visit, according to Willoughby's information. See *MacArthur Hearings*, vol. 4, p. 2621.

20. Higgins, *New York Herald-Tribune*, June 15, 1950. She also said officers had told her an invasion of Taiwan was unlikely before at least midsummer, which does not reflect what internal reports said.

21. Ibid., June 18, 19, 1950. She said it was learned that MacArthur "would be willing" to become High Commissioner; this was a plan, as we have seen, suggested in the spring of 1950 by Donovan and others. See also *New York Times*, June 20, 1950, emphasizing the secrecy of the talks, which indicated that they were "of rather greater importance" than the publicly-stated purposes.

22. 795.00 file, box 4254, Sebald for Dulles to Acheson, June 22, 1950. Here Dulles reports the gist of MacArthur's memorandum, and says Johnson gave it to him on June 14. He also reports MacArthur's desire to make a personal survey of Taiwan's military, economic, and political requirements "to prevent the domination of Formosa by a Communist power." Sebald refers to a June 22 meeting where "there was general agreement as to the Formosa paper" (J. F. Dulles Papers, Sebald interview). Mathews says Dulles told him on June 21 that he and MacArthur agreed on "the necessity of holding Formosa" (Mathews diary, entry for June 21).

23. *New York Herald-Tribune*, June 25, 1950; RG330, Secretary of Defense file, box 73, Cooke to Johnson, June 20, 1950. Johnson gave this memo to Bradley, "eyes only and return." Cooke said here that he was "dedicated to the defense of the interests of the U.S.," and referred to Johnson not wanting to hear Cooke's June 19 presentation.

24. J. F. Dulles Papers, Robert D. Murphy Oral Interview, May and June, 1965.

25. 695.00 file, box 3006, Dulles to Acheson, June 7, 1950.

26. Note that the *New York Times* editorial cited at the beginning of chapter 14 and emphasizing the same theme was dated May 27, 1950.

27. Lowe, *Origins of the Korean War*, pp. 86–90. Lowe writes that Yoshida had indicated to the British in October 1948 that Allied (read American) troops would remain in Japan even after the treaty. According to Dower, Yoshida "took the initiative in formally broaching the possibility of post-treaty bases"; he did not confide his thoughts on this even to his closest associates and told Ikeda at the last minute (John W. Dower, *Empire and Aftermath: Yoshida Shigeru and the Japanese Experience, 1878–1954* (Cambridge, Mass.: Council on East Asian Studies, Harvard University, 1979), p. 374.

28. Chitoshi Yanaga, *Big Business in Japanese Politics* (New Haven, Conn.: Yale University Press, 1968), pp. 141–43.

29. Schaller, *American Occupation of Japan*, pp. 229–31.

30. Stanley Andrews, with Robert R. West, "Coordination of American Economic Aid in South and Southeast Asia," in RG335, Secretary of the Army file, box 77, Voorhees to Pace, April 4, 1950; Voorhees also sent this classified report to Herbert Hoover (Hoover Presidential Library, PPI file, box 545, Voorhees to Hoover,

April 4, 1950). See also *New Times*, May 10, 1950. This refers to an American economic mission to Japan in April, and quotes the *London Times* to the effect that what the U.S. hopes to do with Japan is reminiscent of prewar colonial relationships.

31. Dulles to Acheson, June 7, 1950, *FR* (1950) 6, 1207–12; Dulles memo, June 15, 1950, *FR* (1950) 6, 1222–23; Schaller, *American Occupation of Japan*, p. 271.

32. Pratt Papers, box 2, Kern to Pratt, September 8, 1950; Roberts, "The 'Japan Crowd,' " pp. 401–2; Howard Schonberger, "The Japan Lobby in American Diplomacy," *Pacific Historical Review* 46, no. 3 (August 1977), pp. 352–54. See also Dower, *Empire and Aftermath*, p. 217.

33. Dower, *Empire and Aftermath*, pp. 380–83.

34. Pratt Papers, box 2, Kern to Pratt, September 8, 1950; the message from the emperor is also in box 2. For more on this, and questions about its authenticity, see Roberts, "The 'Japan Crowd,' " pp. 402–3.

35. Ayers Papers, box 26, diary entry for July 1, 1950. Premier Yoshida later said that Dulles had favored rearmament, while he and MacArthur had a "secret understanding" not to do so (J. F. Dulles Papers, Yoshida Shigeru Oral Interview, September 1964).

36. *FR* (1950) 6, pp. 1170–71, Memo of conversation, Sebald and MacArthur, April 6, 1950; pp. 1213–21, MacArthur, memorandum on Japan peace treaty, June 14, 1950; pp. 1227–28, MacArthur, memorandum on the security of Japan, June 23, 1950.

37. *NDSM*, March 12, 1950, reprinting Malenkov's speech of March 9.

38. *New Times*, April 5, 12, 19, May 1, 10, 31, all June and July issues, 1950.

39. *New York Times*, April 21, 23, 1950.

40. Ibid., May 3, 4, 17, 1950.

41. *New York Herald-Tribune*, June 19, 1950.

42. *New York Times*, June 14, 1950; *New York Herald-Tribune*, June 15, 1950.

43. *New York Times*, May 30, June 1, 1950.

44. Ibid., May 29, 1950.

45. Ibid., March 13, 1950.

46. *New York Times*, May 28, 29, 1950; the State Department advisor in Tokyo on May 31 was "as yet uncertain as to what deductions are to be drawn from [Derevyanko's] sudden departure." Office of the Executive Secretariat, box 31, daily secret summaries, May 31, 1950. The Tokyo press gave a very big play to this story. See newspaper articles in MA, RG10, box 19.

47. *New York Times*, May 24, 1950.

48. Office of the Executive Secretariat, box 31, daily secret summaries, June 5, 1950; CP, 1978, item 22A, CIA report, July 8, 1950.

49. Donovan Papers, box 9A, item 4050, "Digest of Conference Transcript," June 10, 1950, received April 22, 1953.

50. MA, RG6, box 105, CIC District Field report, no. 12, July 12, 1950.

51. Conversation with Prof. Haruki Wada, November 1984. Nationalist intelligence sources said Derevyanko was the top Soviet military advisor in Changchun, in Manchuria, in late 1950, and part of a joint Sino-Soviet-Korean military command. See *New York Times*, December 13, 1950.

52. Louis Johnson Papers, box 111, testimony before the House Foreign Affairs Committee, June 5, 1950; *New York Herald-Tribune*, May 30, June 4, 1950.

53. Drew Pearson said the plane was spying on a Soviet testing ground for rockets; the plane was loaded with "secret electronics equipment" (*Diaries*, p. 117, 121).

54. *New York Times*, May 21, 1950, April 20, 1950.

55. Smith Papers, box 282, diaries, entries for June 1, 13, 20, 1950; *New York Times*, June 21, 1950.
56. Koo Papers, box 180, top secret account of June 15, 1950, meeting, apparently by Chen Chih-mai for Koo.
57. Koo oral history, vol. 6, p. J-464.
58. *Current Biography*, 1949, pp. 65–66.
59. Koo Papers, box 180, top secret acount of June 15, 1950, meeting; Koo oral history, vol. 6, p. I-246, p. J-464. The transcriber got the name down as "Russell Sheperd," or "Shippard," but it is the same man.
60. After the Hainan battle, Willauer wrote that "everyone out here, including myself . . . seems to conclude that we are rapidly losing the cold/hot war in the Far East." Shortly thereafter he went to the Philippines, while Chennault went to Korea. Willauer then returned to Washington from Taiwan in mid-June. Tofte knew Korea and Manchuria, having worked for the Danish East Asiatic Company in Manchukuo in the 1930s (Leary, *Perilous Missions*, pp. 109–10, 124–25).
61. *Current Biography*, 1949, p. 66; Koo Papers, box 218, diary entry for August 29, 1951.
62. Donovan Papers, box 75B; Koo oral history, vol. 6, p. I-239, I-268–70; on McKee and McCarran, see Blum, *Drawing the Line*, p. 67. McKee was involved with Donovan in the Committee to Defend America by Aiding Anti-Communist China; McKee was the first officer on the letterhead, Donovan the third, in a communication sent to Sen. Wayne Morse about the CNAC planes detained in Hong Kong, dated March 22, 1950 (Morse Papers, box A/22).
63. Donovan Papers, box 75B.
64. Goodfellow Papers, box 1, Ellen Dockery to David Namkong, June 12, 1950. She does not explain why he did so, and this is the only such reference in the Goodfellow Papers. Immediately after the war began, Goodfellow cabled Rhee, saying in full, "Tell Gen. Chae to hold fast. Help is coming. This is your hour. The prayers of the Democratic world are for you. Wish I were with you." On July 28 Goodfellow told S. T. Ryang the following: "I have been working on the Korean situation and expect to hear more on my assignment very soon" (box 1).
65. Donovan Papers, box 132C, appointment diary for 1950. These are Donovan's wife's diaries, it would appear, but they clearly carry entries for some, if by no means all, of Donovan's meetings.

CHAPTER EIGHTEEN

1. NA, manuscripts of the Office of the Chief of Military History, box 620, "History of the Korean War," vol. 1, pt. 2, ch. 2, "The Initial Attack"; see also the information on the 6th Division and Pang Ho-san in Almond Papers, periodic intelligence report no. 190, April 4, 1951, and an unnumbered report of April 21, 1951.
2. Appleman, *Naktong/Yalu*, pp. 21–22. Hausman was then an advisor to Chief of Staff Chae. Five American advisors were said to have been in Ongjin, but they sent no messages until 6:00 A.M., when they said the peninsula was about to be overrun. This makes it doubtful that the advisors were with Korean troops; they may have been sleeping, or recently returned from a Saturday night visit to Seoul or a camptown. See Sawyer, *Military Advisors in Korea*, pp. 114, 118. See also RG338, KMAG file, box 5415, "General Survey of Enemy Situations," Chŏng Il-gwŏn, undated but probably August 1950; Lim Ŭn, *Founding of a Dynasty*, p. 174.

3. Appleman, *Naktong/Yalu*, p. 21. Prof. Dae-sook Suh told me the story, which may be apocryphal, about Kim threatening Kim Sŏk-wŏn.

4. MA, RG6, box 78, ATIS translation issue no. 2, October 5, 1950, translating an article from the KPA newspaper *Powi* [Defense], July 2, 1950; also DPRK radio broadcast, noted in ibid., box 59, intelligence report no. 2848, June 27, 1950.

5. *New York Times, New York Herald-Tribune,* and *Washington Post* reported on June 26 that two companies of the 17th Regiment had occupied Haeju. The UK military attaché in Tokyo cabled on June 27 that two battalions of the 17th regiment occupied Haeju (FO317, piece no. 84057, Gascoigne to FO, June 27, 1950).

6. U.S. Information Agency, "The Communist Invasion of the Republic of Korea," July 12, 1950, a copy of which is in Smith Papers, box 100. On the very first page it refers to "a large-scale invasion" at Ongjin on August 4, 1949, and a "renewal" of the offensive on October 14, 1949. (The August 4 attack, as we have seen, was against a South Korean position north of the parallel.) The attached chronology, which also cites the above battles, strangely refers to "extremely heavy guerrilla warfare commenc[ing] across the 38th parallel," September 9–20, 1949; the parallel was mostly quiet in this period, as we have seen.

7. *New York Times,* August 12, 1950. Malik appears to have based his presentation on North Korean materials sent to the United Nations (see DPRK Ministry of Foreign Affairs, *Documents and Materials Exposing the Instigators of the Civil War in Korea* [P'yŏngyang: Ministry of Foreign Affairs, 1950], pp. 133–36). In any case that is what I used for the information in the text. Han's use of the term "daybreak" does not square with assertions elsewhere in the same North Korean materials that the attack began just after midnight, except that the North Koreans use words translated as daybreak or "early dawn" to mean as early as 1:00 A.M., as we will see, and on p. 122 in this same collection of documents, the text reads "at midnight, June 24th, Rhee Syngman [*sic*] in carrying out the orders of his American masters started the invasion."

8. Karunakar Gupta, "How Did the Korean War Begin?" *China Quarterly* 52 (1972); see also commentary by Chong-sik Lee, William Skillend, Robert K. Simmons, and Gupta's reply, *China Quarterly* 54 (1973), pp. 354–68. Note that the official history is content to say that a journalist in Ongjin put out the first account, misleading Shin Sungmo. John Merrill also points out that the second edition of the *Han'guk chŏnjaeng-sa* "omits all references to [1949] border clashes since they were regarded as being too 'political' " (John Roscoe Merrill, "Internal Warfare in Korea, 1948–1950: The Local Setting of the Korean War" [Ph.D. diss., University of Delaware, 1982], p. 149).

9. The Kolkos were among the first to suggest that the North Korean aim might have been limited to Seoul, and to argue that Soviet strategies avoided direct attacks on cities (as did Chinese strategies, we might add). Kolko and Kolko, *Limits of Power,* pp. 578–79, 586.

10. *Seoul Times,* October 14, 1947; HST, PSF, CIA file, box no. 255, CIA, "Communist Capabilities in South Korea," ORE 32–48, February 21, 1949.

11. On the attempt to penetrate Hwanghae see NA, OCMH manuscripts, box 620, "UN Partisan Forces in the Korean Conflict," 1952; also the Vanderpool Papers; also reports of anticommunist resistance, CIA file, NA, OCMH manuscripts, box 248, CIA daily intelligence summary for January 18, 1951; this and other CIA reports in the period put the resistance "north of Haeju."

12. Kim, *Military Revolution in Korea,* pp. 57–63. Yi Ch'ŏng-ch'an headed the Capitol Division only from June 15 to July 15, 1950; later, as commander of the Third Division, his troops were the first to cross the parallel into the North in the fall of

1950 (Ridgway Papers, box 19, Van Fleet to Ridgway, February 17, 1952, enclosing Yi's biography). On Kim Paek-il and the Capital Division in the summer of 1950, see RG338, KMAG file, box 5418, "KMAG Journal," entry for August 5, 1950. On the 17th Regiment in Namwŏn, and its superior training, see Plans and Operations file, 091 Korea, U.S. Military Advisory Group to the ROK, October 15, 1949. It is apparent that the 17th was treated as a separate unit, not under a particular division, in periodic intelligence reports from the ROKA headquarters in RG338, KMAG file, box 5418, July 9-November 7, 1950.

13. Most of the information and quotations are in Muccio's report, 795.00 file, box 4267, "'Tiger' Kim vs. the press," May 12, 1951. Muccio wrongly placed Kim in Pusan when the war began, and got the date of his removal wrong (saying it was July 7, 1950, when it was definitely after August 2). See also USFIK 11071 file, box 65/96, Yŏsu Rebellion packet; also "The Yosu Operation, Amphibious Stage," by Howard W. Darrow. At Yŏsu, Kim refused to follow the orders of two American advisors who told him not to try to land the 5th Regiment at Yŏsu; he tried to do so anyway, and failed. On the beheading incident, see RG338, KMAG file, box 5418, "KMAG Journal," entries for July 26, August 2, 1950. On Rhee and Tiger Kim, see Ridgway Papers, box 20, draft of a message Muccio planned to present to Rhee, May 3, 1951, chiding Rhee for relying on Tiger Kim, Montana Chang, and No Tŏk-sul for intelligence information, rather than the established agencies.

14. *NDSM*, May 19, 1950. Pak's statement was given extraordinary, front-page treatment. Articles on the 18th Regiment defection in the North emphasized the Kwantung Army experience of Kim Sŏk-wŏn and Kim Paek-il, and said all soldiers under them were required either to fight southern guerrillas, or to prepare for a "northern expedition" (*HGND NDSM*, May 11, 1949).

15. KMAG G-2 Weekly Summaries nos. 8–11, May 18-June 15, 1950; G-3 Operations file, box 121, operations report no. 51, June 9–16, 1950.

16. RG242, SA2010, item 2/76, Haeju materials from the KWP agit-prop department, marked "absolutely secret." The student also said, "soldiers from the Rhee side are being seized, they say, but everyone knows it isn't so." It is not clear what this refers to; it could mean he does not believe the South is attacking, or that he does not believe that the North is winning the engagements.

17. FO317, piece no. 84079, Tokyo Chancery to FO, enclosing the report of a military attaché's trip to Korea, April 19, 1950. This report said a civil war was not likely in the summer of 1950, however, because American advisors "have in the past successfully discouraged such an invasion" (i.e., by the ROKA), and the North Koreans would not move, they thought, pending the outcome of the current communist drive in Southeast Asia.

18. McCormack, *Cold War/Hot War*, p. 83. Rankin later indicated he did not mean he thought the South might be ready to attack, but merely that something was afoot.

19. Interview with Thames Television, 1987. Peach went on to say that he still did not think that the 17th Regiment had attacked, followed by a North Korean response.

20. MA, RG9, box 38, Far East Air Force Commanding General to other units, June 26, 1950; Schnabel, *Policy and Direction*, p. 66. See also George Howard Poteat, "Strategic Intelligence and National Security: A Case Study of the Korean Crisis (June 25-November 24, 1950)" (Ph.D. diss., Washington University, 1973), p. 12.

21. MA, RG6, box 80, ATIS Supplement, Issue no. 3, December 5, 1950: "Full translation of a file, dated 25 June to July 9, handwritten in Russian, containing radio communications, copies of interrogations, and intelligence summaries, presumably kept by Soviet military liaison interpretor, Lt. Murzin, whose signature appears." These were captured in Seoul on October 4, 1950; it could be that the

documents constitute a disinformation plant, but then why would they be so sketchy and inconclusive, and also so damaging to the North Korean position that the South launched an attack all along the parallel?

22. Committee for a New Direction for U.S. Korea Policy, *Conference for a New Direction in U.S. Korea Policy* (New York: 1977), p. 100. Admiral Lee's full remarks are as follows:

> I believe it's time to reconsider the cause of the outbreak of the Korean War. I can definitely declare, to judge by my own experience in naval engagements under my own command, that that view is entirely wrong.
>
> On June 23, two days before the outbreak of the war, the Korean army chief of staff issued "Combat Order No. 2." All the Korean army units were alerted and ordered to "go into action at 5, June 25." From 10 P.M., June 23, partial attacks were started to divert attention from the up-coming full-force invasion of the North. This was reported throughout the world by AFP wire services.

On Lee's court-martial, see MA, RG6, box 58, Intelligence Report no. 2833, June 12, 1950. Another source says that when Lee was cleared he was transferred to Chinhae, and was in late June commander of a "Training Task Group" (795.00 file, box 4299, Embassy to Seoul, June 23, 1950). It is possible, of course, that he might still have been in the Haeju area on June 23, since these reports do not give the dates of his court-martial or his assignment to Chinhae.

I must say also that I participated in this 1977 New York conference, but came to think later that it had been somehow influenced by the North Koreans, even though many anticommunist Koreans attended. A very garbled transcription of my remarks was published in the conference volume without my editing or approval.

23. FO317, piece no. 84097, "Draft Brief for the U.K. Delegation New York: on Korea," no date but probably September 1950.

24. MA, RG6, box 78, ATIS issue no. 1, September 26, 1950. I have not found the Korean original.

25. MA, RG6, box 9, MacArthur's second teleconference with Washington, June 26, 0355 hours; box 59, intelligence reports nos. 2847–2851, June 26–30, 1950; Drumwright, July 20, 1950, account, Smith Papers, box 100.

26. *Haebang ilbo*, July 8, 1950.

27. The casualty report is cited in MA, RG6, box 79, ATIS translation issue no. 15, January 3, 1951, from *NDSM*, June 28, 1950 (I have not found an original of this issue).

28. Merrill, "Internal Warfare," p. 149.

29. Donovan Papers, box 8B, Ryan to Donovan, March 8, 1952.

30. Oliver, *Rhee and American Involvement*, p. 290; Noble, *Embassy at War*, p. 87; Noble Papers, "Activities Log," June 30, 1950, entries for 1833 and 2130.

31. Keyes Beech met Kim Paek-il on the night of June 27 in Seoul, at KMAG headquarters (see his *Tokyo and Points East* [Garden City, N.Y.: Doubleday, 1954], p. 112).

32. Ridgway Papers, box 16, memorandum of August 9, 1950; Appleman, *Naktong/Yalu*, p. 324. It would appear that Kim Sŏk-wŏn cammanded the Capital Division from July 15 to mid-August, when he switched to the 3d Division. Kim Paek-il was accompanied in the fall of 1950 by Colonel Edward Rowny (the Reagan administration's key arms negotiator with the Russians in the early 1980s) (see Almond Papers, "Korean War Diaries," entries for November 1950). In a Thames

Television interview in February 1987, Rowny told me he could not remember Kim Paek-il.

33. HST, Muccio Oral History, December 1973 (emphasis added).

34. *New York Herald-Tribune*, May 29, 30, 1950.

35. Appleman, *Naktong/Yalu*, pp. 22–23; Sawyer, *Military Advisors in Korea*, p. 115. Blair's account differs a bit in the details. He gives the time Darrigo awoke as 3:30 A.M., whereas Appleman, Sawyer, and the missionary give a time of 5:00 or 5:30. According to an internal history, the 13th and 15th Regiments of the 6th KPA Division opened their main attack at 5:30, and the town fell by 9:30 A.M. (NA, Manuscripts of the OCMH, box 620, "History of the Korean War, vol. 1, pt. 2, ch. 2, "The Initial Attack"). Blair says that "at first [Darrigo] believed it to be the South Koreans firing their 105-mm snub-nosed 'infantry cannons,' but as the noise increased in fury, he realized it was not South but North Korean artillery." This account, of course, is not inconsistent with it being ROK artillery at first, the KPA in response (*Forgotten War*, p. 59). Lawrence Zellers, an American missionary living in Kaesŏng in June 1950, told me that there was no sign of any military activity that he could see on June 24, when he returned to his home just below Sŏng'aksan from a wedding in Seoul; he had witnessed "repeated and sometimes prolonged border skirmishes" during the summer and fall of 1949 ("mortar and artillery fire would almost always arch over our heads from both sides"). He frequently heard artillery early in the morning, and then Darrigo's jeep would take off down the road to ROKA 12th Regiment headquarters. On the morning of June 25 at a bit past 4:00 A.M. he heard artillery and small arms fire. As usual Darrigo jumped in his jeep and headed south. Zellers rolled over and went back to sleep; at about 7:30 he awoke to see People's Army soldiers "moving around and past our house." They left him alone until June 29 when all the local missionaries were questioned at length by North Korean police. They threatened him with execution, but later imprisoned him in the North (Letter, Lawrence A. Zellers to Bruce Cumings, August 24, 1987).

36. MA, RG6, box 9, Army to CINCFE, June 26, 1950; Blair, *Forgotten War*, p. 99. The mines were not placed, as MacArthur later acknowledged in his congressional testimony. See also Appleman, *Naktong/Yalu*, p. 7. A year before the war Roberts wrote that the area between Seoul and the parallel had been "loaded" from January 1949 on: "Three divisions are on the line . . . all the 'Artillery' [*sic*] and Anti-tank guns (91 and 127) are in Seoul vicinity or to the North thereof. The Engineers are prepared to do a demolition-delay job on all roads leading into Seoul" (RG 319, box 548, Roberts to Bolte, July 4, 1949). The absence of defensive demolitions in June 1950 would suggest a southern plan for a march into the North, or for a rapid withdrawal.

37. RG242, SA2010, item 3/43, *"Pogosŏ"* [Report], signed by Yu Pyŏng-jun, June 29, 1950. Yun was the unit commander of the second engineering company of the 241st Army. Parts of this report are illegible. Blair says the North "mysteriously removed" the railways in May 1950, but many other sources place it in 1949 (*Forgotten War*, p. 58).

38. John J. Mearsheimer, *Conventional Deterrence* (Ithaca, N.Y.: Cornell University Press, 1983), pp. 25–27.

39. 795.00 file, box 4267, "Tiger Kim vs. the Press," May 12, 1951; Schnabel and Watson, JCS, *Korean War*, vol. 3, pt. 1, p. 98.

40. Ridgway Papers, box 19, Thomas D. McPhail to Ridgway, April 15, 1965.

41. Appleman, *Naktong/Yalu*, p. 26.

42. Ibid., pp. 26–27; Smith Papers, box 100, Drumwright account, July 5, 1950.

43. Sawyer, *Military Advisors in Korea*, p. 117.
44. Appleman, *Naktong/Yalu*, pp. 27–28; Army G-2 said on June 28 that the reports of landings at P'ohang were erroneous (HST, PSF, CIA file, box 262, joint daily summary no. 3, June 28, 1950). The *New York Times* reported on March 6, 1950, that guerrilla landings on the East coast, said to originate in North Korea (although it is just as likely that the points of origin were in the South), were a weekly affair.
45. Appleman, *Naktong/Yalu*, p. 24; NA, manuscripts of the OCMH, box 620, "The Initial Attack." No details on this attack are given, except the units involved and the time the 1st Regiment was hit.
46. Smith Papers, box 100, Drumwright account of July 5, 1950. Col. James S. Gallagher, advisor to 2d Division, got word of an invasion at 8:00 A.M. Sunday morning, when the 2d Division got orders to move north from Taejon (Sawyer, *Military Advisors in Korea*, pp. 116, 120). They left at 1430 by train. Blair says the 7th Division gave way because the 2d did not arrive in time (*Forgotten War*, p. 60).
47. *MacArthur Hearings*, vol. 5, p. 3385.
48. Mearsheimer, *Conventional Deterrence*, pp. 36, 47.
49. See Laurence Lafour, *The Long Fuse*, 2d. ed. (New York: J. B. Lippincott, 1971), pp. 196–204, 254–64; also 795.00 file, box 4262, Muccio to State, June 25, 1950, two cables, one sent at 2:00 P.M. and the other 6:00 P.M., Seoul time.
50. Smith Papers, box 100, Drumwright account of July 5, 1950; Noble Papers, Harold Noble letter to "Bell" Noble, June 26, 1950; also 795.00 file, box 4262, Muccio to State, June 25, 1950, two cables.
51. 895.00 file, box 5695, Bunce, Allison, and others, meeting at the State Department, March 15, 1950; box 5692, Allison to Secretary of State, October 31, 1953; Drumwright to Robertson, December 10, 1953; box 5693, Ray to State, April 7, 1950; MA, RG9, box 43, KMAG to SCAP, March 25, 1950; Goodfellow Papers, box 1, Goodfellow to Rhee, October 3, 1950. Lady tried to go back to Korea in late July in spite of official opposition, but was blocked by Sebald (MA, RG6, box 80, SCAP to State, July 20, 1950).
52. John Gunther, *The Riddle of MacArthur* (New York: Harper and Brothers, 1950), pp. 165–66.
53. *Chosŏn inmin-gun*, June 26, 1950. On the use of the term *saebyŏk*, see an article in *NDSM*, May 22, 1950, saying the Odaesan guerrillas entered Ch'unch'ŏn on May 1, "at 1 a.m. dawn (*saebyŏk*)."
54. RG242, SA2005, item 2/67, broadcast transcript of Kim's "Appeal to All the Korean People," June 26, 1950. Lecture notes belonging to a KPA soldier, captured in August 1950 (RG242, SA2010, item 1/62), say this: "In the course of five years, Rhee became a lickspittle [of the imperialists] and prepared to provoke [*tobal*] a civil war. Through the night and morning of June 24–25, Rhee's army touched off the war* [*sic*]." The asterisk then noted, "The provocateur was American imperialism."
55. Schnabel and Watson, JCS, *Korean War*, vol. 3, pt. 1, p. 55n; Appleman, *Naktong/Yalu*, p. 20. The two documents were first released on May 2, 1951; the text and various statements about them by American representatives are in State Department, *The Conflict in Korea* (Washington, D.C.: U.S. Government Printing Office, 1951). The DPRK denounced the materials as false two weeks later (*KCNA*, May 16, 1951).
56. Office of the Executive Secretariat, box 5, daily summaries, April 20, 23, 1951. The declassification had been done, and a decision made to make use of them, by April 23.

57. MA, Willoughby Papers, box 12, Brig. Gen. Hal C. Pattison to Willoughby, August 5, 1965; Willoughby to Pattison, August 10, 1965.
58. MA, RG6, box 78, ATIS issue no. 6, November 8, 1950.
59. *Korea Herald*, June 27, 1979.
60. Lim takes it upon himself to refute every anomaly in the record, from the Haeju business to T. L. Soong's soybean scam. This is the surest evidence of any that the book was ghost-written in Seoul (*Founding of a Dynasty*, pp. 173–74 and ch. 5). Also interview with Hyŏn Chun-gŭk, August 1981.
61. MA, RG407, entry 429, box 350, ATIS Issue no. 2, October 30, 1950, "Order no. 1, dated 6/22/50, issued by Lee Kwon Mu, CO, 4th Infantry Division, Captured in Taejon area, 16 Jul 50."
62. Appleman, *Naktong/Yalu*, p. 20.
63. MA, RG6, box 79, ATIS issue no. 15, January 3, 1951.
64. MA, RG6, box 81, "Interrogation Reports, North Korean Forces," ATIS, August 25, 1950, interrogation reports nos. 603 and 605.
65. MA, RG6, box 61, intelligence summary no. 2883, August 1, 1950.
66. Ibid., box 78, ATIS issue no. 4, October 21, 1950.
67. Both are in ibid., ATIS issue no. 1, September 26, 1950. The first document said that ROKA losses included "one Japanese advisor."
68. Ibid., ATIS issue no. 1.
69. Ibid.
70. I was told this by an archivist at the Suitland National Records Center on September 5, 1984. After this episode, South Korean nationals were placed in plain view of archivists when they used the collection. Another individual who worked with the National History Compilation Committee, forwarding copies of the captured materials and other archival documents to Seoul, told me that the Committee refuses even to accept, let alone to publish, anything from the collection that departs from the South Korean line on the war, or its version of national history in the period. This, of course, makes the South's war histories of little use; but it also makes the captured materials one of the only collections of primary Korean documentation not tampered with by Seoul or P'yŏngyang.
71. U.S. State Department, *North Korea: A Case Study in the Techniques of Take-over* (Washington, D.C.: U.S. Government Printing Office, 1961), pp. 113, 117. Even Gen. Yi Sang-jo, deputy chief of staff of the KPA, was left in the dark about the war plan and was surprised when the war broke out, according to recent testimony. He nonetheless still believes that Kim Il Sung started the war, with Stalin's approval. See the report of an interview of General Yi, who now lives in the USSR, by Prof. Choi Pyong-kil, in *Korea Times*, June 18, 1989.
72. RG242, SA2005, item 4/75.
73. MA, RG6, box 78, ATIS issue no. 14, December 29, 1950.
74. MA, RG6, Box 81, ATIS issue no. 834, August 21, 1950; ATIS issue no. 423, August 7, 1950.
75. RG242, SA2009, item 10/58, "*Chŏnsi chŏngch'i munhwa saŏp*," issued by the Cultural Department of the KPA 655th detachment.
76. RG242, SA2008, item 10/56, "*Chŏnt'u sokbo*," no. 1, June 16, 1950. Issue number two, which I have not seen, was translated in ATIS issue no. 3, October 12, 1950 (MA, RG6, box 78). Dated June 18, it says much the same thing, in the available translated extracts: "A large-scale military exercise will be held near the 38th parallel. Therefore, no soldier should communicate with people outside. Everyone should be cautious, in order that this top secret not be disclosed to the enemy."

77. RG242, SA2006, item 20/28, handwritten record of a meeting on June 4, 1950, of the KPA 3d technical detachment, 6th beginning group.

78. RG242, SA2010, item 3/81, various orders in Korean issued to or by the 855th KPA unit.

79. Willoughby Papers, box 10, Korea Liaison Office file, report nos. 475-C (May 2, 1950), 498-C (May 15, 1950), and 518 (May 25, 1950). The very few reports from the KLO file in June show nothing of particular import about an impending invasion.

80. Baldwin, *Embassy at War*, p. 315. Gen. Richard Stilwell told a Thames Television interviewer in 1987 that North Korea still had "an extraordinarily large military force offensively postured bellied up against the [DMZ], and capable of launching a direct attack with, er, without warning, any strategic warning, perhaps within 24 hours of the first indication one might receive."

81. Reproduced in McCormack, *Cold War/Hot War*, p. 58. Henderson also quoted Col. Min Ki-sik as saying that one usually hears that the North was always attacking the South: "This is not true. Mostly our Army is doing the attacking first and we attack harder." Min had recently returned from training at the Infantry School, Fort Benning.

82. The reference is to a reported outbreak of schistosomiasis among PLA forces gathering to invade Taiwan.

83. FO317, piece no. 92804, FK1075/1, July 5, 1951, including Pratt's 1951 pamphlet, "Rearmament and the Far East," and excerpts from his speeches.

84. Prouty, *Secret Team*, pp. viii–xiii, 34–36, 67.

85. Warren Hinckle and William W. Turner, *The Fish Is Red: The Story of the Secret War Against Castro* (New York: Harper and Row, 1981), pp. 80–81. I am indebted to Kevin Marchioro for calling this book to my attention.

86. *New York Times*, June 8, 1984; a Public Broadcasting System consultant to the documentary, Austin Hoyt, told me about the interview with Stilwell in February 1987.

87. HST, Acheson Papers, box 65, Wallace to Acheson, July 26, 1950, enclosing a copy of the *China Weekly Review*'s article, "Background to the Civil War in Korea"; Acheson's letter to Wallace, August 10, 1950, contains the quotation in the text, verbatim.

88. Eisenhower Library, Anne Whitman file, NSC, 179th Meeting, box 5, January 8, 1954.

89. Ibid., boxes 4 and 9.

90. Arthur Krock Papers, box 1, notebooks, Book II, entries for July 1950. Johnson telephoned Krock on June 25, 26, 1950 (Johnson Papers, box 141, appointment book, June entries).

91. *MacArthur Hearings*, vol. 4, pp. 2572–84; RG46, *MacArthur Hearings*, deleted testimony, box one, Johnson testimony of June 14, 1951.

92. Johnson Papers, box 138, Johnson to Willoughby, June 29, 1950; Koo Papers, box 180, memo of meeting with Griffith, June 28, 1950; Koo oral history, vol. 6, p. A-24. Griffith apparently did not elaborate on what he meant.

93. Bradley, *General's Life*, p. 503.

94. Military History Institute, Carlisle, Willoughby Papers, box 10, "The North Korean Pre-Invasion Build-up," circa early 1951. Willoughby may not have written all of this, but it represents his views.

95. Ibid.

96. *MacArthur Hearings*, vol. 3, pp. 1991–92.

97. James, *Years of MacArthur*, vol. 2, pp. 5–14.

98. MA, Willoughby Papers, box 13, "Aid and Comfort to the Enemy," early 1951. See also Charles A. Willoughby and John Chamberlin, *MacArthur, 1941–1951* (New York: McGraw-Hill, 1954), pp. 352–54. The North Korean attack came "as a jolt to Washington," he says, but not to Tokyo.

99. MA, RG6, box 40, daily intelligence Summary, no. 2684, January 14, 1950.

100. MA, RG6, box 58, intelligence summaries no. 2803–2850, May 13-June 29, 1950.

101. MA, RG9, box 40, Commanding General, Far East Air Force, to other units, May 20, 1950; ibid., June 10, 1950. Both formerly top secret.

102. Little is known about signals intelligence capabilities in Korea, but unit 8609 of the Army Security Agency is mentioned in G-3 Operations file, box 34A, CINCFE to Army, September 4, 1950, attachment. See also Corson, *Armies of Ignorance*, p. 318. On KPA radio silence procedures, see NA, OCMH manuscripts, box 616, "History of the Korean War," vol. 3, "Enemy Tactics," p. 4.

103. Mathews Papers, box 90, diary, "Korea with the J. F. Dulles Mission, June 14–29, 1950." Bradley also says Roberts, his "old friend," reassured him that an invasion would not occur and, if it did, the South would be able to handle it (*General's Life*, p. 530).

104. Acheson Papers (Yale), box 1, Allison to Acheson, November 7, 1969; Ayers Papers, box 26, diary, entry for July 1, 1950; Far East file, box 4123, Dulles, "Notes on Korea," June 29, 1950.

105. FO317, piece no. 84060, Gascoigne to FO, July 5, 1950; James, *Years of MacArthur*, vol. 1, p. 572; vol. 2, p. 196.

106. *MacArthur Hearings*, vol. 1, pp. 235–241.

107. *New York Times*, June 27, 1950; *Manchester Guardian*, June 27, 1950. Sen. Leverett Saltonstall said that, acording to Hillenkoetter, the CIA gave a "final warning" about the attack on June 17; it is not clear if this was a separate report from that of June 19 (see *MacArthur Hearings*, vol. 1, p. 436).

108. RG218, JCS, file 383.21, box 25, section 21, "Memorandum for the Secretary of Defense," through Maj. Gen. J. H. Burns, signed by Maj. Gen. Lyman Lemnitzer, June 29, 1950. On the missing June 19 CIA report, see Schnabel and Watson, JCS, *The Korean War*, vol. 3, pt. 1, p. 52. Here they identify it as a CIA "field agency" report, presumably meaning it was sent in from Korea. The Joint Chiefs are at pains to say in another part of this Korean War study that they had no warnings of imminent attack, either from American or South Korean agencies. See JCS, "The Korean Conflict," manuscript in NA, vol. 4, ch. 2, Wilber W. Hoare, Jr., "The Week of Decision," pp. 1–2.

109. Acheson Seminars, June 23, 1953. Kennan clearly knew little about Korea. In the same session, he said that Soviet puppets were in charge in P'yŏngyang, not Mao's people, and that the Russians trained several divisions of Koreans from Kazakstan and moved them in to fight the war. If so, none was ever captured in three years of fighting.

110. *New York Times*, June 24, 1950; CP, 1977, item 175D, CIA report, sanitized, signed by Hillenkoetter, June 27, 1950.

111. Corson, *Armies of Ignorance*, pp. 154, 315–21.

112. Ronald Lewin, *The American Magic* (New York: Penguin Books, 1982), p. 65. His book, on signals intelligence in World War II, illustrates how important the same intelligence would be to Korea, should it come available. Roberta Wohlstetter did a careful study of Pearl Harbor, showing the difficulty of separating "intelligence" out from raw reports, or signals versus "noise" (*Pearl Harbor: Warning and Decision*, 1962).

113. RG 338, box 5417, March 6, 1950, G-2 HQ intelligence report, grade C-4.

114. Koo Woo Nam, *The North Korean Communist Leadership, 1945–1965: A Study of Factionalism and Political Consolidation* (University, Ala.: University of Alabama Press, 1974), pp. 92–93. Sŏl was purged in August 1953; he had been in the Political Administration section of the KPA Supreme Command. A Korean who wishes to remain unidentified told me that "Yun" was probably Yŏn Chŏng, a man who worked for Willoughby's KLO and who claimed to have given the KLO advance information on the North Korean invasion, and that the source of this information was probably Sŏl Chŏng-sik. Yŏn later undertook a risky mission for Willoughby, seizing patients from a Wŏnsan Hospital to see if they were sick with bubonic plague.

115. *United States Policy in the Far East, Part 2: Korea Assistance Acts, Far East Portion of the Mutual Defense Assistance Act of 1950* (Washington, D.C.: U.S. Government Printing Office, 1976), p. 464; Corson, *Armies of Ignorance*, pp. 315–21.

116. Ridgway Papers, Oral Interview, March 5, 1982; Rusk's June 20 testimony is in Selected Executive Session Hearings of the House Committee on International Relations, vol. 7, "U.S. Policy in the Far East," Part 2 (Washington, D.C.: U.S. Government Printing Office, 1976), p. 464. Hanson Baldwin reported a CIA warning of June 9, describing "a marked buildup" along the parallel; "capabilities of an invasion at any time were mentioned." This must refer to the June 14 report. About four KPA divisions, plus Constabulary units, had been in position for a long time at the parallel, he said. "But commencing in early June, light and medium tanks probably of Japanese manufacture, about 30 122-mm Soviet-type field guns and other heavy equipment were assembled at the front, and troop concentrations became more noticeable" (*New York Times*, June 28, 1950).

117. On June 17, 1951, Hoover sent to Knowland "a note from a reliable friend," unnamed; the content of the note is not known. On June 19, 1951, Knowland responded: "Your friend's information is substantially correct. I do know that Admiral Hillenkoetter appeared before the Senate Appropriations Committee for I was present at the time" (Hoover Presidential Library, PPI file, box 395).

118. *New York Times*, June 26, 1950. Whitney's dateline was June 25 from Washington.

119. G-3 Operations file, box 121, Bolte to Ridgway, June 20, 1950. Bolte refers to Ridgway's request, but does not say when it was made, and I have not been able to find it.

120. Koo oral history, vol. 6, p. A-116.

121. Blair, *Unknown War*, p. 87; Col. Donald McB. Curtis drafted SL-71, and discussed it in a letter to *Army*, July 1985.

122. Appleman, *Naktong/Yalu*, p. 19.

123. Corson, *Armies of Ignorance*, pp. 316, 318.

124. HST, PSF, CIA file, box 248, memo of June 28, 1950; box 250, CIA, "Military Supplies for North Korea," September 13, 1950.

125. 795.00 file, box 4269, MacArthur to Army, September 1, 1950 (MacArthur was responding to Soviet claims in the United Nations that all Soviet weaponry used by the KPA was from stocks left behind in 1948; the ten items were stamped as manufactured in the USSR in 1949 and 1950, but could have come via China); *New York Times*, September 7, 1950.

126. Walter Sullivan, *New York Times*, July 31, 1950; 795.00 file, box 4262, Muccio to State, June 25, 1950, cable no. 933; *New York Times*, June 25, 1950, quoting United Press accounts; Hanson Baldwin, *New York Times*, June 30, 1950.

127. FO317, piece no. 84064, Sawbridge to FO, August 17, 1950; piece no. 84130, Dening minute on no. FK10338/4, July 7, 1950; *Manchester Guardian*, June 26, 1950.

128. 795.00 file, box 4262, Muccio to State, June 26, 1950, cable sent at midnight, quoting Yi Pŏm-sŏk.
129. Stone, *Hidden History*, p. 44.
130. See for example Harry Summers, *On Strategy* (New York: Presidio Press, 1982), and my critique, "Parades of Remembering and Forgetting: Korea, Vietnam, and Nicaragua," *The Nation* (October 1986).
131. United Press account of Lutwak's July 20, 1950, speech in Charleston, S.C., *New York Times*, July 21, 1950.
132. Friedrich Nietzsche, *Beyond Good and Evil*, trans. Walter Kaufmann (New York: Vintage, 1966), p. 195.

CHAPTER NINETEEN

1. Alisdair Cooke, *Manchester Guardian*, June 27, 1950; *FR* (1950) 7, pp. 125–28, containing Muccio's telegram no. 925, an editorial note, and an interview with Rusk on August 7, 1950. The "editorial note" does not say who called Acheson, but Acheson says it was John Hickerson. See Acheson Seminars, transcript for February 13–14, 1954.
2. The "editorial note" (*FR* [1950] 7, pp. 125–28) says that Truman ratified the decision to go to the UN at 11:20 P.M. June 24, and that Lie was then called at 11:30, but Acheson says that he instructed Hickerson at 10:30 P.M. to call the Security Council together, which would be almost an hour before he called Truman; he is most explicit in saying Hickerson was told he should "proceed at once," and "if the President had a different idea, it would be perfectly possible to change what [Hickerson] was doing." When he called Truman, he told him "what I had authorized Hickerson to do," and the president "approved." Acheson related that on July 19, 1950, Truman sent him a note saying in part that Acheson's initiative in "immediately calling the Security Council of the U.N. on Saturday night and notifying me was the key to what developed afterwards. Had you not acted promptly in that direction, we would have had to go into Korea alone." Acheson also says that Truman wanted to return at once, but Acheson suggested he wait until the next day. See Acheson's account in Acheson Seminars, February 13–14, 1954. On the Blair House discussions, see *FR* (1950) 7, pp. 157–61 and 178–83.
3. Acheson Seminars, transcript of February 13–14, 1954. Kennan quoted from remarks he put down in a notebook in late June 1950. Bradley also noted Acheson's domination of the decision process, in *A General's Life*, p. 536. Kennan supported Acheson's decisions in a memo written on June 26, saying that "we should react vigorously in S. Korea" and "repulse" the attack. If the United States failed to defend the ROK, he thought, Iran and Berlin would then come under threat (Kennan Papers, box 24, Kennan to Acheson, June 26, 1950). For Acheson's discussion of the decisions, see *Present at the Creation*, pp. 405–7.
4. Acheson, *Present at the Creation*, p. 405.
5. Stimson's diary, quoted in Beard, *Roosevelt and the Coming of the War*, p. 553. See Acheson's notes for the Acheson Seminars (HST, box 81), where on p. 12 he writes, "June 25 removed many things from the realm of theory. Korea seemed to—and did—confirm NSC 68." Harsh is quoted in Hodgson, *America in Our Time*, p. 46.
6. CP, 1979, item 439B, "Notes on Meetings," May 16, 1951.
7. Ibid, p. 16 of notes.

8. HST, George M. Elsey Papers, "President's Conversation with George M. Elsey," June 26, 1950. I am indebted to Barton Bernstein for bringing this quotation to my attention. On June 30 in an NSC meeting, Truman made clear his desire to limit the war to Korea, and to the restoration of the 38th parallel—that is, containment. HST, PSF, NSC file, box 220, summary of the 59th meeting, June 30, 1950. In its "Review of the World Situation," July 19, 1950, the CIA said that "a failure to draw this line would have seriously discredited the whole US policy of containment" (HST, PSF, CIA file, box 250).

9. This sequence is clear, for example, in Glenn Paige, *The Korean Decision.*

10. Acheson Seminars, transcript of February 13–14, 1954. Robert Donovan notes that Taft was not the first to protest, others having spoken on June 27, but his was the "big gun" (*Tumultuous Years*, p. 220).

11. Acheson told Lucius Battle, in regard to a conversation with Army Secretary Frank Pace on July 13, 1950, "We have agreed to make no record of it. Repeat nothing" (HST, Acheson Papers, box 45, Appointment book entry for July 14, 1950). On the secret meeting regarding MacArthur, see Acheson Seminars, transcript for February 13–14, 1954.

12. General Bradley supported Achesonian containment at the first Blair House meeting, remarking that "we must draw the line somewhere." But he questioned "the advisability" of introducing American ground troops in large numbers, as did Frank Pace and Louis Johnson. At the second meeting on June 26, Generals Bradley and Collins again expressed the view that committing ground troops would stretch American combat troop limits, unless a general mobilization were undertaken. Louis Johnson now supported Acheson, however, while falsely leaking to the press that he, not Acheson, had advocated a defense of Taiwan (*FR* [1950] 7, pp. 157–61, 178–83). This led Truman to think once again of dismissing Johnson; Truman said that, contrary to press reports, "they had trouble getting the defense department to move," and "if this keeps up, we're going to have to have a new secretary of defense" (Ayers Papers, box 26, Diary entry for June 29, 1950).

13. Acheson Seminars, transcript for February 13–14, 1954.

14. Allison, *Essence of Decision*, pp. 10–38.

15. Donovan, *Tumultuous Years*, p. 202.

16. Acheson, *Among Friends*, pp. 185, 192. Truman always defended Acheson with no trace of the humiliation he must have felt from time to time.

17. Quoted in Donovan, *Tumultuous Years*, p. 256.

18. Stone, *Hidden History*, p. 105.

19. Eben Ayers Papers, box 26, Diary entry for November 7, 1948. Truman's fascinating and often humorous notes to himself during the Korean War nonetheless betray the mind of a sophomore history student, complete with numerous misspellings ("Isenhower," "Atcheson," always "Chiang Kai Chek"). In April 1952 he fulminated that "Genghis Khan, Tamerlane, Attilla and the cut throats of history were gentlemen beside the Bolshevic [*sic*]"; this and many similar remarks make the point that a little history can be a bad thing. The notes also show courage, determination, a deep patriotism, and a simple belief in the greatness of the United States. See HST, PSF, box 333, "Longhand Notes" file, 1945–1955.

20. *FR* (1950) 7, pp. 148–54, "Intelligence Estimate," Office of Intelligence Research. Hillenkoetter's CIA report for the president on June 25 said the action was a Soviet probe to test our resolve, but that if the United States intervenes, the Soviets will "either disclaim or otherwise localize the Korean conflict" (HST, PSF, CIA file, box 248, Hillenkoetter's daily summary for the president, June 25, 1950; there is no date on this report, but it clearly was done on June 25, from the context). In

general, the intelligence reports coming across Truman's desk from several different sources were poorly informed and heavily biased toward deepening the American commitment in Korea; he would have been much better off reading the *New
York Times*.

21. FO317, piece no. 84080, BBC monitor of Seoul broadcast, June 27, 1950; original
ROK leaflets are in MA, RG6, box 16; they were usually in Sino-Korean, which
the majority of Korean peasants could not read.

22. See the transcript of a teleconference with MacArthur in *FR* (1950) 7, pp. 250–52;
see also MacArthur's cable in MacArthur Papers, RG6, box 9, CINCFE to Army,
top secret, June 30, 1950; also CINCFE to Army, July 7, 1950. On the June 29–
30 combat troops decision, see also Acheson Seminars, transcript of February 13–
14, 1954. This validates the JCS's position that they were not consulted on the
decision, and indeed had resisted it right up to June 30. It also quotes Nitze as
asking if MacArthur "had already started to move the forces before he got the
permission," to which Acheson responded, "I have no record of that." See also
JCS, "The Korean Conflict," vol. 4, section VI, ch. 2, p. 11.

23. Schnabel and Watson, JCS, *The Korean War*, vol. 3, pt. 1, p. 46.

24. *NDSM*, July 2, 1950. Top secret internal materials for the use of party cadres said
much the same thing from late June, describing the conflict as "our all-people war
for national independence [*minjokjŏk tongnip*] and independent state sovereignty"
directed at Rhee and the Americans, a war to be won by Koreans which "will
arouse the complete spiritual support [*chŏngsinjŏk chiji*] of the world's anti-imperialist, democratic camp led by the great Soviet Union." (That is, don't count on
anyone else to help us.) See RG2009, SA2009, item 7/26, *Chŏnch'e tangdanch'edŭl kwa
tangwŏndŭl ege ponaenŭn Chosŏn Nodongdang chungang wiwŏnhoe ŭi p'yŏnji* [Letter
from the KWP Central Committee to all Party branches and members], June 27,
1950, "absolutely secret."

25. *Haebang ilbo*, July 9, 1950.

26. Ibid., July 19, 22, 1950.

27. Ibid., July 29, 1950.

28. Acheson Seminars, transcript for February 13–14, 1950.

29. *New York Times*, July 30, July 6, 1950.

30. *FR* (1950) 7, pp. 144–47, Memo of conversation, June 25, 1950.

31. UNCOK file, box 1375, Acheson to SCAP, July 1, 1950. See also McCormack, *Cold
War/Hot War*, pp. 77–84.

32. Ibid., Muccio to State, June 25, 1950; Seoul to State, June 27, 1950; Tokyo to
Secretary of State, June 27, 1950; Tokyo to State, June 30, 1950. See also 795.00
file, box 4262, Muccio to State, no. 933, June 25, 1950.

33. FO317, piece no. 83298, Dening meeting with Chiefs of Staff, July 12, 1950; also
piece no. 83299, with many items on US-UK disputes over Formosa in the summer
of 1950; also piece no. 84076, RAF squadron leader A. G. Lawrence to FO, December 30, 1949. The arrival of the British batallions is documented in HST, OIR
daily reports, August 25–28, 1950. The allied troop totals are from *MacArthur
Hearings*, vol. 5, p. 3586.

34. HST, PSF, CIA file, box 250, CIA daily report, July 8, 1950.

35. HST, Acheson Papers, box 81, "Notes on meetings."

36. Thames Television interview, Athens, Georgia, September 1986. See also Schoenbaum, *Waging Peace and War*, p. 211.

37. *New York Times*, May 8, 1950. The suggestion came in Hoover's letter to Knowland,
which was released to the press.

38. The East German press also claimed that the United States had alerted its allies to

be ready for UN action before the war began, something that cannot be verified, but that again would indicate Soviet time for advance planning. HST, State Department OIR pamphlet, "World Reactions to Korea Developments," no. 1, June 28, 1950.

39. Kim Il Sung's speech to the P'yŏngyang North-South Conference, *Puk Chosŏn t'ŏngshin*, no. 29 (May 1948), pp. 9–10.

40. *New York Times* editorial, August 30, 1950.

41. *New York Times*, June 26, 1950; Kennan Papers, box 34, draft memorandum, "Possible Further Danger Points," June 30, 1950.

42. Wallace resigned from the Progressive Party over its position on the Korean War in early August, and gave his support to Truman. See J. Samuel Walker, *Henry A. Wallace and American Foreign Policy*, Westport, Conn.: Greenwood Press, 1976), p. 209. Wallace said on July 15 that it was "insanity" for the United States to fight "for Syngman Rhee and his cruel government," but said the war must be supported because the UN had "sanctioned" it (HST, Acheson Papers, box 65, Wallace to Acheson, July 26, 1950, and enclosure). I. F. Stone's distanced but still supportive position is recorded in *The Compass* in June and July 1950; he shortly began questioning the official version, however, and began to work on his *Hidden History*.

43. In consultations on the afternoon of June 25 with Sen. Elbert Thomas, a member of the Far East subcommittee of the Foreign Relations Committee, Merchant reported that Thomas was "inclined to the view that legally this is civil war and not an act of aggression." Thomas also thought "that there is widespread sympathy for communism in South Korea." But Thomas, to my knowledge, did not speak out on the issue (795.00 file, box 4262, Merchant to Rusk, June 25, 1950).

44. *The Progressive*, August 1950; *The Nation*, July 1, 1950.

45. *Monthly Review*, lead editorial, 2/4 (August 1950), pp. 110–17.

46. *World Events* 7, no. 2 (Spring 1950); 7, no. 4 (Fall 1950).

47. Hoover Presidential Library, Kenneth R. Colegrove Papers, box 32, Hodge to Colegrove, July 6, 1950.

48. *The Oregonian*, July 19, 21, 23, 25, 29, 1950. This moderate newspaper, like so many others at the time, was chock-full of attacks on communists, people who are said to be communists, professors who will not sign loyalty oaths, and students who want the bomb banned; meanwhile any exiled anticommunist from Eastern Europe got a sympathetic hearing.

49. Dulles Papers, box 48, Dulles to Holland, August 17, 1950. Dulles slandered McCune, who died before his book appeared, by saying he was one of those "who contrast the perfection of communist words with the inevitable imperfection of our fallible deeds."

50. *New York Times*, July 4, 10, August 3, 1950.

51. *New York Times*, July 3, 1950.

52. Reeves, *Life and Times of Joe McCarthy*, pp. 578, 632.

53. Ridgway Papers, box 16, Conant memorandum of September 28, 1950.

54. Hodgson, *America in Our Time*, pp. 89, 97.

55. Letter to the *New York Times*, July 10, 1950.

56. Interview with a Korean-American who still wishes to remain nameless. This person also alleges that at least one mildly liberal, anti-Rhee Korean professor on the West Coast lost his position after an FBI investigation, narrowly avoided deportation to Korea, and was stateless and prevented from getting a passport for many years. Several of the deported Koreans were connected with the leftist Korean newspaper published in Los Angeles, *Korean Independence*.

57. *US News and World Report*, September 29, 1950.

58. *New York Times*, August 26, September 1, 2, 1950. Hanson Baldwin asserted that Johnson had also been talking about preventive war.

59. Among the best accounts along these lines is Victor Navasky, *Naming Names* (New York: Viking Press, 1980).

60. See the materials in 795.00 file, box 4263 and box 4269.

61. Barnes, ed., *Perpetual War for Perpetual Peace*, p. 657.

62. FO371, piece no. 84059, Gascoigne to FO, July 4, 1950, citing intelligence reports of "unknown reliability"; see also Chinese Nationalist intercepted messages placing the timing of this Soviet order at 0300 hours on June 26, in Office of Chinese Affairs, box 4222, Freeman to Rusk, July 6, 1950; *FR* (1950) 1, p. 363, Kennan to Acheson, August 8, 1950. The Italian embassy in Washington reported that a member of the Soviet embassy had stated on June 30, "apparently under instructions," that "not one Russian soldier will be sent into Korean territory" (795.00 file, box 4267, "Record of Actions in the Korean Crisis [June 30, 1950]," in 795.00/8-2550).

63. HST, PSF, CIA file, box 250, Foreign Broadcast Information Service (FBIS) translations of Radio Moscow, June 26–28, 1950. As late as July 6, FBIS had picked up no appeals by the USSR or its satellites for more than moral support to the North Koreans.

64. *FR* (1950) 1, p. 329, Memo of NSC consultant's meeting, June 29, 1950; also HST, PSF, State Department Office of Intelligence and Research, "World Reactions to Korea Developments," no. 5, July 2, 1950; 795.00 file, box 4264, Acheson telegram to all missions, July 3, 1950; on the East European press, see *New York Times*, July 1, 1950; Kennan quoted in Acheson Seminars, February 13–14, 1954.

65. 795.00 file, box 4265, "Kelly-Gromyko Talks," top secret, July 15, 1950.

66. MA, RG6, box 61, intelligence summary no. 2885, August 8, 1950; see also HST, PSF, "Army Intelligence—Korea," box 262, daily situation reports nos. 5–15, July 1–2–July 11–12, 1950. Army intelligence noted in early September that the joint daily situation reports had "constantly carried the statement 'Negative' " in regard to Soviet participation in the war (795.00 file, box 4268, Memo for the Chief of the Intelligence Division of the Army, September 8, 1950). State Department OIR summarized the question of Soviet advisors as follows:

> Interrogation of 250 NK POWs indicates pre-invasion presence of Soviet advisors with all NK units. All POWs agreed, however, that Soviet advisors departed from NK units before or at the time that the units crossed the 38th parallel. Normally five advisors were present with each division, two at division headquarters and one at each regiment. Presence of advisors also reported with NK naval, airforce, and military training schools. Advisors at no time physically commanded NK units but acted through NK army officers. (HST, PSF, "Selected Records Relating to the Korean War," box 3, OIR report no. 5299.51, August 30, 1950).

67. HST, PSF, CIA file, box 250, report of July 7, 1950. Soviet heavy TU-4 bombers and big naval ships were absent in the region, however, which meant there was little threat of an air and amphibious invasion of Japan.

68. The CIA reported in early August that Soviet arms shipments to North Korea "decreased somewhat since June 25" (HST, PSF, CIA file, box 250, daily summary for August 3, 1950; the CIA did register increased shipments to Manchuria, however, but was not sure if they were destined for Korea or to aid in an invasion of Taiwan). Also *New York Times*, September 7, 1950; NA, OCMH manuscripts, box

617, "History of the Korean War," vol. 3, pt. 13, "Enemy Materiel," pp. 1–2. On American materiel left on the battlefield by the ROKA, see *New York Times*, July 26, 1950. The CIA thought the Soviets were resupplying the North via rail and sea lines from Vladivostok, but went on to say that the majority of KPA equipment was from Soviet and Japanese stocks left behind; in 1950 "there has *probably* been a substantial flow of Soviet equipment" (emphasis added). See HST, PSF, NSC file, box 2, CIA, intelligence memo no. 326, September 15, 1950.

69. MacArthur told Sebald in November 1950 that both the Koreans and the Chinese paid for their Soviet materiel, in cash or in kind. 795.00 file, box 4269, Sebald to Acheson, November 15, 1950; HST, PSF, "Selected Records Relating to the Korean War," box 3, OIR report no. 5299.18, July 18–19, 1950; 895.00 file, box 5692, Embassy to State, June 18, 1952.

70. *Nodong sinmun*, August 15, 1950; *Haebang ilbo*, August 17, 18, 1950.

71. Nikita Khrushchev, *Memoirs, 1950–1953* (New York: Pantheon Books, 1977); Ridgway Papers, box 16, Memo of meeting with MacArthur, August 8, 1950. Peter Fleming noted in mid-August that the Soviets "have not troubled to detach any [air force] squadrons" to give the cities of North Korea "some sort of defence" (*The Spectator*, August 11, 1950, pp. 170–72). During a major battle for the port of P'ohang, the *New York Times* editorialized, "It should not go without notice that although the Russians had submarines in the waters through which our fleet went, they did nothing" (July 20, 1950). See also Drew Middleton's interesting commentary on Soviet passivity, *New York Times*, July 26, 1950.

72. *US News and World Report*, August 25, 1950; *New York Times*, October 11, 1950. The latter reported that embassy documents were still strewn around offices, as if a cyclone had hit. Highly classified documents were, of course, burned by embassy officials before they left.

73. Kennan Papers, draft memorandum, "Possible Further Danger Points," June 30, 1950, top secret.

74. *FR* (1950) 1, pp. 361–67, Kennan to Acheson, August 8, 1950, top secret.

75. U.S. Senate, Committee on Foreign Relations, Historical Series, *Economic Assistance to China and Korea: 1949–1950* (Washington, D.C.: U.S. Government Printing Office, 1974), pp. 175–79.

76. *FR* (1950) 1, pp. 393–95, Acheson notes for congressional hearings, circa August 20, 1950.

77. Reston's full point was that if all the Russians would get from the Korean War was "a $20 billion rearmament of the Western world, it will certainly go down in history as a real fancy Soviet boner" (*New York Times*, July 23, 1950). The actual figure went to $50 billion by the end of 1950 in American defense expenditures alone.

78. G-3 Operations File, box 121, London Embassy to State, June 26, 1950, reporting conversations with the Foreign Office; *Time*, July 17, 1950 (this article cited the views of "Western experts"). Simmons notes that the Soviets held no mass meetings in support of North Korea for ten days after the war broke out (p. 123); in chapter 5 he offers a cogent argument that the Soviets did not know the timing on the invasion, and that it probably came earlier than planned for the North Koreans (Simmons, *Strained Alliance*).

79. *US News and World Report*, July 28, 1950, carrying an interview with an unnamed "top Yugoslav official"; 795.00 file, box 4267, report of July 20, 1950, on French military intelligence thinking enclosed in Jack D. Neal, "China's Role in Korea," August 21, 1950.

80. FO317, piece no. 84057, Hsinhua June 26, 1950, report; piece no. 83278, Hutchison to FO, July 14, 1950; *Renmin Ribao*, June 27, 1950.

81. FO317, piece no. 83250, Hutchison to FO, June 29, 1950; piece no. 83278, Hutchison to FO, July 14, 1950; piece no. 84109, Hutchison to FO, September 28, 1950, with FO commentary.

82. Kennan Papers, box 24, "Possible Further Danger Points," June 30, 1950; box 31, Kennan letter to Allen S. Whiting, October 20, 1960.

83. MA, RG6, box 59, intelligence summary no. 2841, June 20, 1950, and no. 2852, July 1, 1950; FO317, piece no. 83251, Gascoigne to FO, July 18, 1950; MacArthur told Marshall in November that "I have from the beginning believed that the Chinese Communist support for the North Koreans was the dominant one" (MA, RG6, box 1, MacArthur to Marshall, November 8, 1950). In 1951 he told senators that "the linking of the Soviet to this Korean War has paled out as the events have progressed" (*MacArthur Hearings*, vol. 1, p. 250).

84. MA, RG6, box 60, intelligence summary no. 2882, July 31, 1950, with attached ATIS interrogation report no. 219.

85. In late December Rusk charged the PRC with a conspiracy against South Korea well before June 1950; the evidence was that "a large portion" of the KPA had fought in China, and that most KPA military equipment, including Soviet weaponry, was shipped from Manchuria. He also said (correctly) that the PLA's Fourth Field Army had begun moving north toward Manchuria before June 25 (*New York Times*, December 30, 1950). The Department of the Army had prepared a study, dated the day before, for the State Department on the large numbers of CCF Koreans transferred back to the DPRK before the war began, to prove Chinese aggressive intent against the ROK (795.00 file, box 4271, Army study of Chinese aid to North Korea, December 29, 1950).

86. *NDSM*, July 14, 1950; Office of Chinese Affairs, box 4196, Hong Kong to State, July 15, 1950; the *Hong Kong Standard* of July 15 noted that the New 4th Army was the "Mother" of North Korean troops, and the logical army for aiding the DPRK.

87. *Haebang ilbo*, August 6, 7, 1950; *NDSM*, August 11, 1950; 795.00 file, box 4267, Kennan to Armstrong, August 2, 1950.

88. *Haebang ilbo*, August 18, 1950.

89. I am grateful to David Roy for pointing this out to me. The DPRK has a big statue of Chou En-lai in Hamhŭng. A recent account by Nieh Jung-chen also highlights early August as a period of sharp change in China's attitude toward the war. According to Nieh, Teng Hwa was placed in charge of a standby strategic unit and sent to northern Honan, and on August 5 the PLA ordered full preparations to be completed by the end of August for a possible involvement in the war. See Nieh Jung-chen, *Nieh Jung-chen hui i lu* [Memoirs of Nieh Jung-chen] (Beijing: Chieh-fangchün ch'upanshe, 1984), vol. 2, p. 734.

90. *Haebang ilbo*, August 18, 1950; *Far Eastern Economic Review*, September 28, 1950. This journal thought that Li Li-san was "the real power behind the scenes in Peking," a common (and mistaken) judgment of intelligence officers at the time.

91. Office of the Executive Secretariat, box 4, NSC meeting summary, August 14, 1950; Willoughby Papers, box 10, "The Chinese Communist Potential for Intervention in the Korean War," no date; on August 26 the *New York Times* reported that two large Chinese armies totalling 160,000 to 200,000 soldiers were massed along the border near Antung. On Taiwan invasion reports, see FO317, piece no. 83236, report of July 27, 1950; also piece no. 83299, Paris to FO, July 26, 1950, citing French intelligence reports of an imminent invasion; also the *New York Times*, July 23, 1950, in which Burton Crane reported the massing of 700,000 naval vessels along the Chinese coast, and charges of an imminent invasion. On

Chou's July 21 conversation with Pannikar, see FO317, piece no. 83306, Hutchison to FO, July 25, 1950.

92. Lindsay Parrott wrote that most of the Korean peninsula had been won by the KPA in thirty-one days (*New York Times*, July 26, 1950).

93. Ibid., pp. 51–57.

94. Quoted in McCormack, *Cold War/Hot War*, p. 94.

95. It might be argued that if Kim Il Sung did have a maximal strategy of enveloping all of the South, it probably was to poke through the core area of Seoul and link up with the regions of leftist strength, in the Chŏllas and the Kyŏngsangs (succeeding in one but not the other, as we will see).

96. Mearsheimer, *Conventional Deterrence*, pp. 135–37, 142–53. In 1982 Prime Minister Menachem Begin of Israel made the following remarks in a lecture at the National Defense College: "In June 1967 . . . the Egyptian Army concentrations in the Sinai approaches [*sic*] do not prove that Nasser was really about to attack us. We must be honest with ourselves. We decided to attack him. This was a war of self-defense in the noblest sense of the term" (quoted in *New York Times*, August 21, 1982).

97. I frequently encounter academics who liken the North Korean assault to Hitler's attack on Poland, so I sense that a comparison with Israeli actions will offend.

98. See MacArthur's testimony, *MacArthur Hearings*, vol. 1, p. 232; also HST, PSF, "Selected Records Relating to the Korean War," box 3, OIR daily report no. 5299.9, July 8–9, 1950; on the 6th Division, see Almond Papers, Korean War general files, periodic report for April 21, 1951. On the Taejon battle, see Appleman, *Naktong/Yalu*, p. 179.

99. RG242, SA2005, item 1/30, transcript of Kim Il Sung's radio broadcast of July 9, 1950; SA2010, item 3/81, secret military order from the Cultural Department of the 715th KPA detachment, July 26, 1950; SA2010, item 1/62, captured lecture notes from a KPA soldier, circa July 1950.

100. *New York Times*, August 1, 3, 1950; Appleman, *Naktong/Yalu*, pp. 206–7.

101. Appleman, *Naktong/Yalu*, pp. 263–64; MacArthur Papers, RG6, box 1, MacArthur conference with Harriman, Ridgway, and others, August 8, 1950. MacArthur said "the North Koreans are among the best soldiers I've seen in any Army," stronger than enemy forces in Africa, Italy, or Okinawa during the Second World War. Part of this was hyperbole to secure more American soldiers for his theater, of course. On the front in August, see HST, PSF, "Army Intelligence—Korea," box 262, joint daily situation reports nos. 42–66, August 7–8 to August 31-September 1, 1950.

102. Appleman, *Naktong/Yalu*, pp. 104–6, 399–400, 404–5. See also *New York Times*, August 27, 1950, which placed Mu Jŏng at the P'ohang front in late August.

103. HST, PSF, CIA file, box 248, daily reports for September 1–10, 1950; Kim Il Sung's speech at the second anniversary of the founding of the DPRK, in *NDSM*, September 10, 1950; MacArthur quoting Walker on September 11, in Ridgway Papers, box 20, Ridgway memo of conversation with MacArthur, December 26, 1950; Appleman, *Naktong/Yalu*, pp. 404–7, 415–17, 438, 487, 547.

104. Appleman, *Naktong/Yalu*, pp. 319, 321, 394–95, 477, 545–47; James, *Years of MacArthur*, vol. 3, p. 451. The JCS told MacArthur he had everything but the 82nd Airborne on September 8, and that it would take four months before partially trained National Guard divisions could reach Korea; the JCS worried that nearly all the reserves of the Eighth Army had been committed to the fighting. See MacArthur papers, RG6, box 9, JCS to MacArthur, September 8, 1950.

105. HST, PSF, CIA file, box 248, daily reports, September 20–25, 1950; MA, RG6,

box 80, ATIS issue no. 30, March 21, 1951, translating two handwritten sheets, undated, giving Kim's summary on the first four months of the war.

106. James, *Years of MacArthur*, vol. 3, p. 474.

107. Almond Papers, Korean War diaries, diary entry for September 14, 1950; Almond makes explicit reference to Seoul's strategic position on communications and transportation routes. For MacArthur's mid-July scenario, see Department of the Army, "Memo for Gen. Bolte," July 17, 1950, held in NA, room 13W.

108. MacArthur told Gascoigne on September 27 that he decided on Inch'ŏn by himself, against all opinion (FO317, piece no. 83008, Gascoigne to FO, September 28, 1950).

109. *New York Times* obituary, May 4, 1983; Blair, *Forgotten War*, pp. 270–71 (see also pp. 238–42 for an excellent discussion of Inch'ŏn). Almond acknowledged that "the enemy had little capability of opposing our landing," lacking artillery and mobile forces (not to mention a navy; Almond Papers, oral history interview, March 26, 1975).

110. MA, RG6, box 78, ATIS issue no. 4, October 21, 1950, translated document from the KPA 317th artillery staff, July 31, 1950; issue no. 12, December 19, 1950, entry for August 17, 1950; issue no. 1, September 26, 1950, translated document signed by Pak Ki-su, September 4, 1950.

111. RG242, SA2009, item 7/133, document from the KPA 884th detachment, signed by commander Yi Kyu-sŏp, September 6, 1950; SA2009, item 7/84, orders of the KPA 107th infantry detachment issued by its commander, Ch'oe Han, and a higher KPA officer, Kim Yŏng-mu, September 12, 1950, marked "extremely secret." Kim Il Sung's radio transmission was issued in the clear on September 13, with Willoughby intercepting it and giving it to Almond on the same day (Almond Papers, "General Files, X Corps," X Corps radio log, September 13, 1950). The North Koreans did not inform their own people of the landing until September 18, when the *Nodong sinmun* referred matter-of-factly to the sinking of an American ship off of Inch'ŏn (*NDSM*, September 15–18, 1950).

112. HST, PSF, CIA file, box 250, CIA reports of September 15, 22, 1950; *Philadelphia Inquirer*, October 3, 1950; *New York Times*, September 14, 1950.

113. Appleman, *Naktong/Yalu*, p. 635.

114. Robert Murphy, quoted in Roberts, "The Japan Crowd," p. 406; on Japanese participation in the landings, see FO317, piece no. 83243, memo by J.H.S. Shattuck, October 28, 1950; Yoshida was quoted in *US News and World Report*, September 15, 1950. Seoul's *Haebang ilbo* reported on July 12, 1950, that KPA units encountered thirty Japanese officers as early as the fighting for Suwŏn.

115. *New York Times*, September 17, 1950; Daniel Doyle Papers, box 5, original ROKA leaflets in Korean; HST, PSF, CIA file, box 248, CIA daily reports, September 19–29, 1950. Bert Hardy graphically captured the dismal expressions of Inch'ŏn's people in his fine photographs. See Jon Halliday and Bruce Cumings, *Korea: The Unknown War* (New York: Pantheon Books, 1988). It would appear that Rhee was unaware of the impending Inch'ŏn landing as late as September 8, 1950, when he wrote to MacArthur asking for a landing at Inch'ŏn or north of Taegu (MacArthur Papers, VIP file, box 9, Rhee to MacArthur, September 8, 1950).

116. Willoughby wrote that Inch'ŏn "was much closer to Napoleon than to Wolfe and Montcalm." Napoleon's campaigns, he said, "contain at least twenty-seven characteristic maneuvers against the enemy's rear"; "the Napoleonic maneuver in northern Italy, in 1813, was successfully repeated in Korea, in 1950" (Willoughby Papers, box 13, "Aid and Comfort to the Enemy," p. 29). See also Ridgway Pa-

pers, box 16, Bolte, "Estimate of UN Forces Commited in Korea," September 29, 1950. At this time ROK forces totaled 79,253, and all other allied ground forces, 3,750, of which most were British.

CHAPTER TWENTY

1. HST, PSF, "Selected Records Relating to the Korean War," box 3, Office of Intelligence Research (hereafter, OIR file), report no. 5299.1, June 30–July 1, 1950. This was several days after the occupation of Seoul, and continued to be true as the KPA moved southward. The received wisdom that millions of Koreans fled before communist armies is an artifact of early 1951 and the second seizure of Seoul. Many of these OIR reports were compiled by Richard Sneider, later U.S. ambassador to Korea.

2. RG242, SA2009, item 6/8, Kyŏnggi-do Interior Ministry, *Haebang chigu inmindŭl e taehan haesŏl sŏnjŏn chegang* [Propaganda and explanation for people in the liberated areas], July 15, 1950.

3. RG242, SA2009, item 6/72, DPRK Interior Ministry, Cultural Section, *Haksŭp chaeryojip* [Materials for study], no date but post–June 25, 1950. Another document for party activists asked the question, "what are the people's committees?" and said they were popular organs "set up by the people with their own hands, spontaneously, through their own originality" (SA2009, item 6/7, *Chuganbo*, no. 1, August 13, 1950). Many other materials show the emphasis on the KPA's role in liberating the South. See an article in *Haebang ilbo* on the people's committees by Han Yun-nam (July 27, 1950); see also Kim Il Sung's speech on the fifth anniversary of Liberation, *NDSM*, August 16, 1950.

4. *Haebang ilbo*, August 13, 1950; many issues of this newspaper contained *kamsa ŭi messeji* or "message[s] of thanks" to Kim Il Sung. At all levels higher cadres were sent down to lower levels to direct work: from P'yŏngyang to Seoul, from Seoul to the provinces, from provincial cities to the counties, and from the counties to the villages. See for example RG242, SA2010, item 4/43, handwritten directive to county people's committee and party leaders from Kim Hak-yŏng, head of the cultural department of the South Ch'ungch'ŏng people's committee, September 15, 1950, directing them to conduct lectures in nearby villages explaining various policies.

5. Yŏ is termed "a patriot of the Korean people" who "fought for the independence and democracy of the homeland" in a unification appeal included in RG242, SA2009, item 9/4, *Choguk ŭi t'ong'il tongnip kwa chayu rŭl wihan chŏngŭi ŭi chŏnjaeng e kwanhan che munhŏnjib* [Selected documents on the just war for unification, national independence and freedom of the homeland], issued by the cultural department of the Korean People's Volunteer Army (*Chosŏn inmin ŭiyong-gun*, referring to southerners who volunteered to serve with the KPA), July 4, 1950. The term KPR was used twice instead of DPRK, for example, in *Haebang ilbo*, July 22, 1950.

6. OIR file, report no. 5299.3, July 3, 1950; 795.00 file, box 4265, interrogation of Kim Myŏng-ch'ŏl by Donald McDonald, July 9, 1950 (Kim had just left Seoul for Taejŏn).

7. OIR file, report no. 5299.17, July 16–17, 1950; no. 5299.30, July 31-August 1, 1950, reporting the public trials of about 160 police and youth group members on July 15–16, after which they were executed; another intelligence report of July 17, however, said that people's courts had not begun yet, after a report on July 12 saying that the courts "were operating day and night" (MA, RG6, box 14,

G-2 flash report for July 17, 1950; also G-2 periodic report, July 12, 1950). None-theless, the evidence is sufficient to document the existence of people's courts, perpetrating many executions. Im Tae-jŏng, secretary to an ROK cabinet member who left Seoul after two weeks, said that each Seoul district had a people's court, "operating day and night"; they arraigned ROK soldiers, KNP policemen, and rightist youth group members and usually killed them on the spot (795.00 file, box 4265, Donald McDonald interview with Im, July 11, 1950). A Seoul policeman who was interrogated by the American embassy said that "the worst excesses" were committeed by prisoners released from jail. (795.00 file, box 4265, Muccio to State, July 18, 1950).

8. See especially John W. Riley, Jr., and Wilbur Schramm, *The Reds Take a City*, with translations by Hugh Heung-wu Cynn (New Brunswick, N.J.: Rutgers University Press, 1951), the only English-language account of the occupation, which was based on the first part of the massive U.S. Air Force, Air University study, "A Preliminary Study of the Impact of Communism on Korea." This was done by a team of social scientists led by Schramm, and is generally a useful and well-done study. *The Reds Take a City*, however, is a considerably more negative portrayal than that in the original manuscript, and seems to fit the psychological warfare category more than the scholarly category. Documents from Truman's Psychological Strategy Board, having close ties to the CIA if it was not actually part of it, show that the Schramm study was coordinated by Evron Kirkpatrick, then with the State Department, and by the Air University and the fledgling RAND Corporation, as a model of social science research done for the government. The Schramm study was, indeed, the first such study produced by this group. (See HST, Psychological Strategy Board file, box one. This box has many memos indicating the close ties between well known social scientists, the CIA, and the foundations in the Truman era.)

9. American intelligence reported on July 10–11 that "Seoul has become [an] increasingly dead city following heavy US bombing" (OIR file, report no. 5299.11, July 10–11, 1950).

10. Y. H. Chu, "Ninety Days Under Red Rule," Noble Papers.

11. Memo for the record, July 16, 1950, Noble Papers.

12. RG242, SA2011, item 7/43, "On the Observance of Military Discipline by Those Units Entering Seoul," order signed by Kim Yong-su, chief of the political department in the KPA 8th Division, January 4, 1951.

13. U.S. Air Force, Air University, "Preliminary Study," pt. 2, pp. 35–95.

14. See the list of these and many more in *Haebang ilbo*, July 26, 1950; also OIR file, report nos. 5299.8, July 7–8, 1950; 5299.9, July 8–9, 1950, and 5299.24, July 23–24, 1950. A policeman who left Seoul in late July said he thought the moderates definitely were in support of the regime, and were not clearly coerced to do so (795.00 file, box 4265, Muccio to State, July 18, 1950). The CIA said on July 7 that the moderates "are believed to have remained in Seoul voluntarily" (HST, PSF, CIA file, box 248, report of July 7, 1950).

15. *New York Times*, August 28, 1950.

16. MA, RG6, box 14, G-2 report no. ZJY 1164, July 15, 1945; HST, PSF, NSDC file, box 3, CIA report of July 19, 1950; FO317, piece no. 84066, Korea mission to FO, September 9, 1950. The G-2 report also said that "feeling exists that ROK Army will return and majority would welcome this," but the report does not make clear who said this, or to which groups it applies. In 1951, the CIA said that a "large percentage" of the most prominent labor leaders in the South joined the North

Koreans within ten days of the beginning of the war. See HST, PSF, NSDC file, box 3, CIA, report of June 6, 1951.

17. U.S. Air Force, Air University, "Preliminary Study"; daily CIA summaries do not report any torching of the city from September 26 to September 29, when it was secured. See HST, PSF, CIA file, box 248, CIA reports September 26–29, 1950. Some of the burned out buildings were unquestionably caused by American bombing and the fight for the city, while others were just as clearly destroyed by fires set as the KPA left the city. In general, the destruction in Seoul was much less than that in northern cities.

18. Kim Il Sung, "Appeal to All the Korean People," June 26, 1950; HST, PSF, "Selected Records Relating to the Korean War," box 3, OIR file, report no. 5299.17, July 16–17, 1950; no author, "On the Second Anniversary of the Establishment of the DPRK," *Sun'gan t'ongshin*, no. 19 (62) (September 1950), p. 1.

19. *NDSM*, July 4, 1950; 795.00 file, box 4265, interview with Im Tae-jŏng by Donald McDonald, November 7, 1950.

20. Interview with Im Tae-jŏng by Donald McDonald, November 7, 1950; see also *Haebang ilbo*, July 21, 1950.

21. RG242, SA2010, item 5/121, top secret instructions to lower levels on PC elections, signed by Kang Yong-su, chief of the Sihŭng County interior department, July 20, 1950.

22. U.S. Air Force, Air University, "Preliminary Study," pp. 159–60.

23. See the official regulations for PC elections in the South and Kim Tu-bong's directive (signed also by Kang Yang-uk), in *NDSM*, July 15, 1950.

24. *Haebang ilbo*, July 19, 20, 22, 26, 1950.

25. *Haebang ilbo*, July 29, 31, August 9, 1950. RG242, SA2010, item 4/74, table on the political affiliations and class backgrounds of PC members in Poŭn County, no date but probably August 1950. The data showed that of 22 villages with 120 PC members, 56 were in the Labor Party; all 120 were poor peasants. All but four members were under 40 years of age. However, in 18 villages in Hoenam, with 106 PC members, only 16 were KWP members; 102 were poor peasants and 80 were under 40 years of age. Usually 15 to 20 percent were women.

26. *Haebang ilbo*, August 13, 14, 1950; *NDSM*, September 7, 11, 12, 18, 1950; *Sun'gan t'ongshin*, no. 19 (62) (September 1950), pp. 3–4; Yi Kyu, "The People's Committees are Being Restored and Strengthened in the Southern Part," *Kŭlloja*, no. 15 (August 15, 1950), pp. 51–58. The Kyŏngsang elections were said to have been completed in ten counties by September 1, and to be in process in another six counties by September 7.

27. MA, RG6, box 14, G-2 daily report, September 7, 1950.

28. RG242, SA2009, item 6/76, NKWP Central Party School, *Tang kŏnsŏl (kangŭi yogang)* [Party building (lecture outline)] (P'yŏngyang, no date, but probably late 1948), p. 97.

29. U.S. Air Force, Air University, "Preliminary Study," p. 181; peasants later reported that in the small set of villages studied, there was no serious violence or resistance to the reform. See also *Haebang ilbo*, July 20, 1950, on land reform procedures and on Kim Il Sung giving the land to peasants.

30. See an English version of the law in Noble Papers; the Korean text is available in RG242, SA2009, item 10/66; see also U.S. Air Force, Air University, "Preliminary Study," pp. 183–85; also *NDSM*, July 8, 1950. The comparison with the 1946 land reform law is very close; a copy of it is available in RG319, "Intelligence Summaries-North Korea," intelligence summary no. 42, August 18, 1947.

31. U.S. Air Force, Air University, "Preliminary Study," pp. 177–81; also RG242,

SA2009, item 6/72, *Haksŭp chaeryojip* [Materials for study], put out by the DPRK Interior Ministry for cadres in the liberated areas. It has no date, but information inside this 102-page document shows that it is post–June 25.

32. OIR file, report no. 5299.22, July 21–22, 1950.

33. U.S. Air Force, Air University, "Preliminary Study," p. 182. The haste of the reform was marked in the general lack of knowledge most peasants had about the reform procedures, which had been decided upon by the agricultural committees.

34. RG242, SA2010, item 4/74, tables of data on the land reform implementation committees in Poŭn County and Hoenam township, circa August 1950; also item 4/80, directive of August 17, 1950, signed by Pak Ki-sŏl, head of the Suhan-myŏn land reform committee.

35. *Haebang ilbo*, August 12, 1950.

36. *NDSM*, September 3, 7, 1950.

37. RG242, SA2009, item 5/142.2, tables compiled in Anyang, Suwŏn County, summer of 1950.

38. See examples of these rudimentary titles in RG242, SA2009, item 7/53; also SA2010, item 4/41.

39. *NDSM*, September 1, 16, 1950.

40. RG242, SA2010, item 5/121, Sihŭng County police memo to township police, top secret, July 16, 1950; also documents signed by the Sihŭng County interior department chief, Kang Yong-su, August 22, 1950.

41. RG242, SA2010, item 4/49, document of August 11, 1950, signed by Cho Hŭm-sŏn and Kim Myŏng-sun.

42. RG242, SA2009, item 10/55, collection of *chasuja myŏngbu* [list of confessions], Iksan County, August 1950; those in the text are merely samples from this collection.

43. RG242, SA2009, item 8/29, *1950, kuryuin myŏngbu* [list of those detained, 1950], from a police blotter in Kwangju County.

44. RG242, SA2009, item 6/17.2, list of volunteers for the KPA, summer 1950. The vast majority of those who volunteered were classified as poor peasants.

45. MA, RG6, box 78, ATIS issue no. 10, December 12, 1950; issue no. 12, December 19, 1950. Both carry translated documents from July and August 1950.

46. Given the Chinese spelling Kachiang in the text, it must be Kach'ang.

47. U.S. Air Force, Air University, "Preliminary Study," pt. 3, pp. 106–85. The primary writers of this portion were John Pelzel and Clarence Weems.

48. NA, OCMH manuscripts, box 616, "History of the Korean War," vol. 3, pt. 12, "Enemy Tactics," pp. 1–2, 90–91.

49. OIR file, report no. 5299.9, July 7–8, 1950.

50. MA, RG6, box 60, G-2 report no. 2872, July 21, 1950; *New York Times*, July 21, 1950.

51. *Haebang ilbo*, July 29, 1950; *New York Times*, July 22, 1950. The diary is translated in MA, RG6, box 78, ATIS issue no. 2, October 5, 1950. On the Yŏngdong battle, see also Appleman, *Naktong/Yalu*, pp. 199–200.

52. Appleman, *Naktong/Yalu*, pp. 210, 234; see also HST, PSF, Army intelligence file, box 262, joint daily sitreps nos. 24–29, July 20–26, 1950.

53. *New York Times*, July 25, 1950, quoting the director of "a U.S. Government Agency," and others.

54. MA, RG6, box 78, ATIS issue no. 1, September 26, 1950, translating the diary of Yi Kun-jang, a young guerrilla from Kangjin captured on August 25, 1950.

55. *NDSM*, July 4, 5, 10, 1950; *Haebang ilbo*, July 11, 12, 1950; *New York Times*, July 20, 1950.

56. MA, RG6, box 60, G-2 report nos. 2874, July 23, 1950, 2876, July 25, 1950, and 2878, July 27, 1950.

57. *New York Times*, July 26, 30, 1950.

58. 795.00 file, box 4269, Muccio to State, October 25, 1950, enclosing a report by Donald McDonald on a trip through South Chŏlla.

59. *New York Times*, August 5, 1950; FO317, piece no. 84065, Sawbridge to FO, August 17, 1950; Ridgway Papers, box 16, Willoughby to Ridgway, August 7, 1950.

60. *New York Times*, July 25, 30, 1950.

61. MA, RG6, box 14, G-2 daily reports, July 10–21, 1950. The *NDSM* also reported attacks in some of the same counties, July 5, 14, 1950.

62. MA, RG6, box 60, daily G-2 reports, July 20, 24, 31; August 2, 1950; OIR file, report no. 5299.31, August 1–2, 1950.

63. RG338, KMAG file, box 5418, "KMAG Journal," entries for July 24, August 8, 1950; handwritten "G-3 Journal," July 1950; Appleman, *Naktong/Yalu*, p. 478; *New York Times*, August 17, 1950; RG349, box 465, CIC report of Aug 17, 1950.

64. 795.00 file, box 4268, Drumwright to Allison, enclosing a report on an inspection of Cheju by Donald McDonald, accompanied by George Paik, August 29, 1950.

65. Walter Karig, "Korea—Tougher Than Okinawa," *Collier's*, September 23, 1950, pp. 24–26. Gen. Lawton Collins remarked that Korea saw "a reversion to old-style fighting—more comparable to that of our own Indian frontier days than to modern war" (*New York Times*, December 27, 1950).

66. John Osborne, "Report from the Orient—Guns Are Not Enough," *Life*, August 21, 1950, pp. 74–84.

67. Eric Larrabee, "Korea: The Military Lesson," *Harper's* (November 1950), pp. 51–57.

68. Drinnon, *Facing West*, p. 96; also John Dower, *War Without Mercy: Race and Power in the Pacific War* (New York: Pantheon Books, 1986).

69. Dulles Papers, John Allison oral history, April 20, 1969; Dulles Papers, William Sebald oral history, July 1965. Sebald quotes from his diary "words to that effect" from MacArthur.

70. Schnabel and Watson, JCS, *The Korean War*, pt. 1, p. 178–81; "Memo for General Bolte," July 17, 1950, giving MacArthur's remarks on July 13 in Tokyo. Other commanders were little better. General Church thought in the first week of the war that two American combat teams would turn the tide (MA, RG6, box 4, Church to Almond, June 28, 1950).

71. Appleman, *Naktong/Yalu*, p. 70; Arthur Krock Papers, box 1, notebooks, vol. 2, p. 222, entry for July 1950; see many press articles in late July and early August in 795.00 file, box 4267. Some French officers said they were thinking of moving to North Africa, since the American army obviously could not hold the line in Western Europe. General Bradley told senators in 1951 that "no one believed that the North Koreans were as strong as they turned out to be," and acknowledged that the military had "underestimated their ability to fight." When asked what he had learned from Korea, he said he learned a new type of warfare, "the guerrilla type" (*MacArthur Hearings*, vol. 2, p. 948).

72. *FR* (1950) 6, pp. 128–30, Dulles to Acheson, August 4, 1950; FO317, piece no. 83014, notes on talk between Dening and Rusk, July 22, 1950.

73. Thomas McPhail, KMAG advisor who finished his career as head of the U.S. Military Advisory group to Nicaragua under Somoza, wrote to Ridgway in 1965, "the old Guardia [National Guard] members who fought with the Marines against Sandino still talk about General Ridgway" (Ridgway Papers, box 19, Thomas D. McPhail to Ridgway, April 15, 1965).

74. Ridgway Papers, oral interview, August 29, 1969. His interviewer, a Vietnam veteran, told him the North Koreans sounded "about the same" as the Vietcong.
75. *New York Times*, September 1, 3, 1950.
76. *New York Times* editorial, July 5, 1950; *New York Times*, July 27, 1950. The CIA at this time also listed Kim as an imposter, who stole the name of an heroic guerrilla who died in Manchuria about 1940. See CP, "National Intelligence Survey, Korea."
77. *New York Times*, July 14, 1950.
78. *New York Times*, July 19, 1950.
79. *New York Times*, August 21, 1950. See Simpson's searing acount of the Nazi bloodletting in the Ukraine and the USSR proper, which he considered "without equal in history" (*Blowback*, pp. 13–26).
80. Letter to the *New York Times*, July 16, 1950. Taylor noted that these precepts have not always been followed, even by Western armies.
81. Ridgway Papers, box 16, Notes on conference with MacArthur, August 8, 1950.
82. Ridgway Papers, box 20, Ridgway to MacArthur, January 9, 1951; Ridgway to Collins, January 8, 1951.
83. FO317, piece no. 84130, enclosing Johnson's address of August 20, 1950, in Lenox, Massachusetts; he also said that the ROK was a "healthy" democracy, and anyone who suggests differently was either repeating the communist line, or "duped by their own ignorance." See also *Far Eastern Economic Review*, August 31, 1950. The informant went on to say that "we had various and numerous riots and insurrections constantly going on" during the American Occupation; occasionally the people would turn on the police who had served the Japanese with acts "that put to shame the acts of the most primitive barbarians." He also thought that "nothing mechanical ever works good in Korea," something that would come as a surprise to American workers in the textile, steel, electronics, and automobile industries today. See also FO317, piece no. 84070, Adamson to FO, October 5, 1950.
84. Willoughby and Chamberlin, *MacArthur, 1941–1951*, p. 312; draft chapter not used in ibid., Willoughby Papers, box 10.
85. Anderson, *Imagined Communities*, pp. 135–36.
86. See P. C. Tullier, "The Oriental Mind," *The New Yorker*, July 15, 1950.
87. *The Nation*, August 26, 1950.
88. See for example *Haebang ilbo*, July 24, 1950.
89. Japanese atrocity victims in the Philippines alone numbered 60,000 to more than 100,000—about half of whom were "murdered, wounded, or raped" during the two-month battle for Manila in 1945 (James, *MacArthur*, vol. 3, p. 94).
90. *New York Times*, July 1, 1950; Tokyo Australian mission to FO, July 10, 1950 (courtesy Gavan McCormack).
91. *NDSM*, July 6, 1950; MA, RG6, box 60, G-2 report of July 22, 1950; OIR file, report no. 5299.17, July 16–17, 1950.
92. London, *Daily Worker*, August 9, 1950.
93. RG242, SA2009, item 6/70, KPA HQ, *Chosŏn inmin ŭn tosalja Mije wa Yi Sŭng-man yŏkdodŭl ŭi yasujŏn manhaeng e pukssu harira* [The Korean people will avenge the beastly atrocities of the American imperialist butchers and the Syngman Rhee traitors], no date, but late 1950, pp. 40–41. The *Haebang ilbo* of August 10, 1950, put the figure at 4,000. See also U.S. Board on Geographic Names, *South Korea, Official Standard Names*, gazeteer no. 95 (Washington, D.C.: Department of the Interior, 1965).
94. RG349, box 465, CIC report, Aug 17, 1950. This also said that ROK officials

thought "approximately 80 percent of the South Korean population would offer no resistance to North Korean forces."

95. 795.00 file, box 4267, London Embassy to State, August 11, 1950; FO317, piece no. 84178, Tokyo Chancery to FO, August 15, 1950; Gascoigne to FO, August 15, 1950; Chancery to FO, August 17, 1950. Another British report said that when reporters photographed brutal beatings of prisoners by ROK police, American and ROK authorities prohibited publication of the photos (Chancery to FO, September 13, 1950).

96. HST, PSF, "Army Intelligence—Korea," box 262, joint daily sitrep no. 6, July 2–3, 1950; NSC file, box 3, CIA report of July 3, 1950. According to Callum MacDonald, a French priest witnessed South Korean killings at Taejŏn and sought to intervene (*Korea: The War Before Vietnam* [London: Macmillan, 1986], p. 41).

97. *New York Times*, July 11, 1950; FO317, piece no. 84178, Sawbridge to FO, July 25, 1950; *Manchester Guardian*, July 13, 1950; RG338, KMAG file, box 5418, report of August 2, 1950.

98. *New York Times*, July 14, 1950; interview with Keyes Beech, Thames Television, February 1987; OIR file, report no. 5299.22, July 21–22, 1950; *New York Times*, July 26, 1950.

99. *New York Times*, September 30, 1950; Osborne, "Report from the Orient"; FO317, piece no. 84094, U.K. High Commissioner to India to FO, August 17, 1950.

100. See "Cameron's Wars," *The Guardian* (London), September 5, 1982; also Halliday and Cumings, *Unknown War*, which has some of the censored photos.

101. Donald Knox, *The Korean War, Pusan to Chosin: An Oral History* (New York: Harcourt Brace Jovanovich, 1985), p. 295.

102. FO317, piece no. 84074, report by J. W. Swire, November 7, 1950; *New York Times*, October 28, November 3, 1950; 795.00 file, box 4269, Drumwright to State, November 17, 1950. By August 10, 1950, the North Koreans had compiled the following list of those executed, which I merely reproduce here; there is no way of verifying it: Yongdŭngp'o (Seoul working class suburb), 600; Inch'ŏn, 700; Suwŏn, 1,000; Puyŏ, 2,000; Taejŏn, 4,000; Ch'ŏngju, 2,000; Kunsan, 400. (*NDSM*, August 10, 1950).

103. RG242, SA2012, item 5/18, *Sŏul Si wa kŭ chubyŏn chidae esŏ ŭi chŏkdŭl ŭi manhaeng* [Enemy atrocities in Seoul city and its vicinity], two secret reports compiled by the Seoul branch of the KWP after the second recapture of Seoul, no date but early 1951.

104. See for example HST, PSF, CIA file, box 248, daily report for July 8, 1950.

105. RG242, SA2009, item 6/72, *Haksŭp chaeryojip*.

106. 795.00 file, box 4269, MacArthur to Army, September 1, 1950; this report mentioned but two incidents: one on July 10, where two Americans were found, and one on August 17, where 41 were killed. On the post-Inch'ŏn killings see *New York Times*, September 30, 1950. In circumstances of unconventional warfare the KPA behaved better than the Japanese during World War II; the latter frequently beheaded American POWs, and executed a minimum of 2,000. See 695.00 file, box 3026, G. T. Hagen to Mrs. Dunning, September 12, 1953.

107. MA, RG6, box 78, ATIS issue no. 2, October 5, 1950, document signed by Kim Ch'aek; issue no. 9, November 27, 1950, document of August 16, 1950. On July 26, the 715th KPA detachment also issued orders to stop incidents in which soldiers stole people's property and used it for themselves. See RG242, SA2010, item 3/81, secret military order of July 26, 1950.

108. UNCURK, "Report on a Visit to Chunchon, Capital of Kangwon Province, Re-

public of Korea," November 30, 1950; I am indebted to Gavan McCormack for this reference. See also *New York Times*, September 29, 1950. On the movement northward, see MA, RG6, box 14, G-2 report of October 16, 1950; RG349, CIC, November 6, 1950, report. The latter said that hundreds and sometimes thousands of South Korean civilians moved north with the retreating KPA.

109. HST, PSF, NSC file, box 3, CIA report of October 4, 1950; *New York Times*, October 6, 14, 1950.

110. Appleman, *Naktong/Yalu*, pp. 587–88, 599.

111. 795.00 file, box 4299, Drumwright to State, October 13, 1950; box 4269, Emmons to Johnson, November 13, 1950; Reginald Thompson, *Cry Korea* (London, MacDonald and Co., 1951), p. 92; *New York Times*, October 20, 1950.

112. 795.00 file, box 4269, Muccio to State, October 25, 1950.

113. RG338, KMAG file, box 5418, KMAG journal, entry for October 3, 1950; Noble Papers, Philip Rowe account of October 11, 1950.

114. RG319, G-3 Operations file, box 122, UNC operations report for November 16–30, 1950.

115. Handwritten minutes of a KWP meeting, apparently at a high level, December 7, 1950, translated in MA, RG6, box 80, ATIS issue no. 29, March 17, 1951.

116. Thompson, *Cry Korea*, pp. 39, 44, 84, 114.

117. *New York Times*, September 30, 1950.

118. Keyes Beech, *Newark Star-Ledger*, July 23, 1950. Willoughby Papers, box 7, "Foreign Intelligence Digest" (a publication of the Billy James Hargis Crusade), March 1971.

119. *Haebang ilbo*, August 10, 1950; RG242, SA2009, item 6/70, KPA HQ, "The Korean People Will Avenge," p. 47.

120. See for example *NDSM*, September 4, 1950, which claimed that American soldiers sometimes kept Korean women with their units for days, raping them at will.

121. RG338, KMAG file, box 5418, KMAG journal, entries for August 6, 16, 20, 26, 1950.

122. Ridgway Papers, box 20, Ridgway to Collins, January 8, 1951; note that this is after the Chinese came in, and the KPA's situation was even worse in the summer of 1950. See also the testimony of USAF Maj. Gen. Emmett O'Donnell, *MacArthur Hearings*, deleted testimony, box 1, p. 8046; John Glenn, interview with Thames Television, February 1987. Hanson Baldwin wrote that the United States faced "no air opposition, very little anti-aircraft" (*New York Times*, September 1, 1950).

123. Stone, *Hidden History*, p. 258.

124. *New York Times*, July 31, August 11, September 1, 1950.

125. See "Air War in Korea," *Air University Quarterly Review* 4, no. 2 (Fall 1950), pp. 19–40; "Precision Bombing," *Air University Quarterly Review* 4, no. 4 (Summer 1951), pp. 58–65, and other articles on the air war in Korea in the 1951 volume; also J. Townsend, "They Don't Like Hell Bombs," *Armed Forces Chemical Journal* (January 1951), pp. 8–11; "Napalm Jelly Bombs Prove a Blazing Success in Korea," *All Hands* (April 1951), p. 17; also E. F. Bullene, "Wonder Weapon: Napalm," *Army Combat Forces Journal* (November 1952), pp. 25–28.

126. Quoted in Blair, *Forgotten War*, p. 515.

127. Thompson, *Cry Korea*, pp. 39, 42, 54, 143, 150–51.

128. Almond Papers, "General Files, X Corps," 1 Mar Division to X Corps, September 28, 1950.

129. 895.00 file, Box 5693, Embassy to State, November 11, 1950, giving official ROK

figures; Ridgway Papers, box 16, memo on official Department of Defense count of American casualties, October 5, 1950.

CHAPTER TWENTY-ONE

1. Leslie Gelb has a good analysis of the containment system and its decision rules, and how it "worked" to produce stalemate and defeat in Vietnam. But he thinks, within that system, and therefore does not grasp how it originated. The rules to pursue it, the limits upon it, the money to pay for it, and the bureaucratic requisites of system maintenance were all forged in 1950–1951, not 1947—when containment was a doctrine, not an ongoing system. His analysis should really say that in Vietnam "the system" played out the logic of the Korean stalemate. See Leslie Gelb, with Richard K. Betts, *The Irony of Vietnam: The System Worked* (Washington, D.C.: The Brookings Institution, 1979).
2. On July 12 Acheson said the United States had to fight back up to the parallel, no matter what. If it were pushed off the peninsula, it would have to "come back in." But the United States should not widen the fighting to China. After reoccupying southern Korea, the United States would have to garrison it and support it in the future. "As the Virginians say, we have bought a colt." But the colt was named containment (HST, Acheson Papers, box 65, Acheson memo for "Paul," July 12, 1950).
3. FO317, piece no. 84093, memo by F. S. Tomlinson, July 9, 1950, referring to Dulles's discussions with Gascoigne when he was in Tokyo; on July 12 Davies suggested that the United States might take "naval and air action against military objectives contributing to Chinese aggression in Korea" (Rosemary Foot, *The Wrong War: American Policy and the Dimensions of the Korean Conflict, 1950–1953* [Ithaca, N.Y.: Cornell University Press, 1985], p. 83). See also Cohen, "Acheson, His Advisors, and China," in *Uncertain Years*, ed. Borg and Heinrichs, p. 46; also Bradley and Blair, *General's Life*, p. 558. (Bradley adds Acheson to those who were "hawkish" on crossing the parallel.)
4. 795.00 file, box 4265, Drumwright to Allison, July 10, 1950; Allison, "The Origin and Significance of the 38th Parallel in Korea," July 13, 1950. Although this memo is unsigned, Dulles's memo to Rusk the same day refers to "Allison's memorandum with reference to the 38th parallel" (in ibid).
5. *FR* (1950) 7, Dulles to Nitze, July 14, 1950, pp. 386–87; PPS draft memo, July 22, pp. 449–54; Allison to Nitze, July 24, pp. 458–61; Defense Department draft memo, July 31, 1950, pp. 502–10. See also 795.00 file, box 4266, "Future US Policy With Respect to North Korea," July 22, 1950.
6. *FR* (1950) 7, Allison draft memo of August 12, 1950, pp. 567–73.
7. 795.00 file, box 4265, Allison to Rusk, July 13, 1950.
8. 795.00 file, box 4267, Sandifer to Allison, August 23, 1950. Here it was stated that elections would probably "bring about extensive changes" in the ROK government, thus avoiding charges that a "police state" would be imposed on the North.
9. MacArthur told Bolte and others in a teleconference on July 17 that "the problem is to compose and unite Korea." He said once the front was stabilized, "it is then my purpose to infiltrate to the North—to follow any North Korean withdrawal." He acknowledged that all this was "speculative" at the time, but his intentions are clear ("Memo for Bolte," July 17, 1950, held in NA, room 13W). On July 20, O'Kelliher told J. Chiang of the Nationalist Embassy that the U.S. gov-

ernment had "decided to go right into North Korea to settle the Korean question once and for all"; Acheson had opposed this decision, but Johnson "had succeeded in persuading President Truman to authorize campaign into North Korea with U.S. troops alone" (Koo Papers, box 218, diary entry for July 20, 1950). By giving the Nationalists such information, Johnson probably opened it to PRC eyes as well, since the Communists had excellent intelligence on the Nationalists, including sophisticated communications spying. If so, the Chinese would have had two months to prepare for the American rollback. See also Straight, *After Long Silence*.

10. Foot, *Wrong War*, p. 74. Bradley puts the date of Truman's approval at September 7 (Bradley and Blair, *General's Life*, p. 560), but I agree with Foot's judgment, which is based on diligent research.

11. See NSC 81 and the various drafts leading up to it in *FR* (1950) 7. For Bolte's order, see Almond Papers, Korean War General Files, X Corps, Bolte to MacArthur, September 16, 1950. Bolte told him that UN forces now had "a legal basis" for operating in the North, and "it would be expected" that he would be given authorization to go North, but final decisions could not be made, pending USSR and PRC actions. This was consistent with the language of NSC 81, and MacArthur would of course fix on the "legal" authorization and take things from there.

12. Donovan, *Tumultuous Years*, pp. 264–66.

13. Pogue gives the September 1 date in *Marshall: Statesman*, p. 422; the JCS history by Schnabel and Watson stated that the reasons for Johnson's removal "have never been officially revealed" (*Korean War*, vol. 3, pt. 1, p. 218n).

14. *US News and World Report*, September 8, 1950.

15. 795.00 file, box 4254, F.H. to P.A., August 3, 1950; *FR* (1950) 6, Acheson to Sebald, August 1, 1950; Strong to Acheson, August 3, 1950; Johnson to MacArthur, August 4, 1950; Strong said he and military attachés had gotten "absolutely no information" on "decisions made by MacArthur" while he was on Taiwan. Sebald was similarly excluded in Tokyo: Gascoigne said Sebald found himself "completely 'smacked down' by the U.S. military, who would tell him nothing at all and treated him like dirt. His interviews with MacArthur elicited no information on the war" (FO317, piece no. 84044, Gascoigne to FO, August 9, 1950).

16. *FR* (1950) 6, Harriman memorandum of conversations with MacArthur, August 6, 8, 1950; Harriman comments at Acheson Seminars, February 13–14, 1950; Strong to Clubb, September 6, 1950.

17. Ridgway Papers, box 16, notes on conference with MacArthur, August 8, 1950.

18. FO317, piece no. 83008, Gascoigne to FO, September 28, October 4, 1950.

19. On "liberated areas," see many documents in 795.00 file, box 5696; Murphy quoted in HST, PSF, NSC file, box 220, 68th NSC meeting, October 2, 1950; Clubb quoted in 611.93 file, box 2860, Clubb to Rusk, October 26, 1950; *FR* (1950) 7, Vincent to State, October 7, 1950, p. 902; Clubb to Rusk, November 4, 1950, pp. 1038–41.

20. *MacArthur Hearings*, vol. 1, p. 245.

21. *FR* (1950) 6, pp. 1349–52, Dulles to MacArthur, November 15, 1950.

22. See Wedemeyer's remarks in *MacArthur Hearings*, vol. 3, p. 2378; Bradley and Blair, *General's Life*, pp. 561, 594. Unlike many of Truman's liberal advisors, however, Bradley readily admits to his own mistaken role in backing these decisions.

23. FO317, piece no. 84093, Tomlinson memo of July 9, 1950; Moscow Embassy to FO, July 26, 1950; piece no. 84099, "Korea: The 38° Parallel," October 2, 1950; see also various documents in piece nos. 84097, 84098, and 84099, autumn 1950. See also 795.00 file, box 4265, Feis memo attached to Dulles's July 14, 1950, memo.

24. HST, Acheson Papers, box 65, memoranda, Kennan to Acheson, August 21, 1950.

25. "In international, as in private, life what counts most is not really what happens to someone but how he bears what happens" (see Kennan's letter in Acheson, *Present at the Creation*, p. 476).

26. HST, Matthew Connelly Papers, box 1, Acheson remarks in cabinet meeting minutes for September 29, 1950.

27. FO317, piece no. 84100, John M. Chang to Acheson, September 21, 1950, relayed to the FO by the State Department; see also *FR* (1950) 3, pp. 1154–58, minutes of preliminary meetings for the September Foreign Minister's Conference, August 30, 1950.

28. A sixteen-page diary on American plans for military government in the North is available in Hoover Institution, Alfred Connor Bowman Papers. American officers sought specifically to keep ROK officials out of this administration. (Bowman was then chief of the Army's Military Government Division.) See also Goodfellow Papers, box 1, Goodfellow to Rhee, October 3, 1950.

29. FO317, piece no. 84072, Washington Embassy to FO, November 10, 1950, enclosing State Department paper on the occupation. Allison told the British that Ben Limb's claim that the ROK government was "the only legitimate government of all Korea" was "in direct conflict with the position taken by the US Government" and by the UN, both of which saw the ROK as having jurisdiction only in those areas where UNCOK observed elections (795.00 file, box 4268, Allison to Austin, September 27, 1950). On the UN resolution, see also *London Times*, Nov 16, 1950.

30. Noble Papers, "Conditions in Pyongyang," October 27, 1950. Noble reports that Naval intelligence personnel "had certain intelligence targets" in the northern capital, which he does not specify.

31. *New York Times*, October 7, 1950.

32. 795.00 file, box 4269, U. Alexis Johnson to Mathews, top secret, September 14, 1950. What the Department knew, according to this cable, had come from the JCS; but the JCS later chose not to elaborate to State on what it knew about the agreement (see RG218, JCS, 383.21 Korea file, Sec. 34, box 28, Kreps to JCS, September 29, 1950; FO317, piece no. 84075, Plimsoll memo on MacArthur meeting with UNCURK, November 21, 1950).

33. 795.00 file, box 4268, Acheson to Muccio, October 12, 1950. Acheson wanted Muccio to assure that the KNP would operate under the UN Command. See also box 4299, Drumwright to State, October 14, 1950; *New York Times*, October 20, 1950.

34. 795.00 file, box 4299, report on a visit to Wŏnsan by Donald McDonald, October 15–16, 1950.

35. HST, PSF, CIA file, box 248, daily summaries for October 19, 25, 1950; ibid., NSC file, box 3, CIA report for October 25, 1950; 795.00 file, box 4267, Muccio to State, May 12, 1951. The ECA prepared a news release on the North Korean land reform, based on a survey by Robert Kinney, an ECA employee and intelligence officer; the release was a propagandistic broadside calling the reform a fraud, deeming the DPRK agricultural system worse than the colonial one, and the like. Sabin Chase criticized this report within the ECA, saying that the reform had had "a favorable acceptance" among northern peasants, so why should the ECA be putting out such nonsense? (see 895.00 file, box 5691, Chase to Emmons, January 19, 1951).

36. HST, PSF, CIA file, box 248, daily summaries for October 30, November 14, 1950; 795.00 file, box 4299, Drumwright to State, October 27, 1950. Muccio mentions

Sneider's presence, along with Richard Scammon, as part of an intelligence team, in 795.00 file, box 5696, Muccio to State, November 20, 1950.

37. RG349, FEC G-2 Theater Intelligence, box 464, 181st CIC report on North Korean sympathies, November 30, 1950.

38. *London Times*, November 16, 1950.

39. H. W. Bullock, UNCURK Memo no. 2, "Conditions in Pyongyang," November 16, 1950, courtesy of Gavan McCormack.

40. The speech is enclosed in FO317, piece no. 84073, October 25, 1950; Noble said he wrote the speech in a letter to his wife, October 1, 1950 (Noble Papers). See also Thompson, *Cry Korea*, p. 88.

41. 795.00 file, box 4268, Durward V. Sandifer to John Hickerson, August 31, 1950, top secret.

42. British sources encountered the elderly woman charged with washing soldier's clothes in late November; she was among knots of "emaciated, dirty, miserably clothed" people tied in ropes and being herded through the streets (FO317, piece no. 84073, Korea to FO, November 23, 1950).

43. Ibid., handwritten FO notes on FK1015/303, U.S. Embassy press translations for November 1, 1950; piece no. 84125, FO memo by R. Murray, October 26, 1950; piece no. 84102, Franks memo of discussion with Rusk, October 30, 1950; Heron in *London Times*, October 25, 1950.

44. *Manchester Guardian*, December 4, 1950; RG338, KMAG file, box 5418, KMAG journal, entries for November 5, 24, 25, 30, 1950.

45. 795.00 file, box 4270, carrying UPI and AP dispatches dated December 16, 17, 18, 1950; FO317, piece no. 92847, original letter from Private Duncan, January 4, 1951; Adams to FO, January 8, 1951; UNCURK reports cited in HST, PSF, CIA file, box 248, daily summary, December 19, 1950. See also *London Times*, December 18, 21, 22, 1950.

46. *London Times*, UPI, December 16, 1950; 795.00 file, box 4299, Muccio to State, October 20, 1950; HST, PSF, CIA file, box 248, daily summaries for December 19, 20, 21, 1950. The CIA also reported that UNC officials had made representations to ROK officials about the atrocities, but "appear to have had little effect." The *Manchester Guardian* reported that American infantry elements saved one woman after arriving in the midst of executions carried out by members of An Ho-sang's Korean Youth Defense League; twenty-six others, including three women, a nine-year-old boy, and a thirteen-year-old girl, were already murdered: "when they grow up, they too would be Communists," the murderers said (December 18, 1950). The Japanese figure is in Nam, *North Korean Leadership*, p. 89.

47. Almond Papers, General Files, X Corps, "Appendix 3 Counterintelligence," November 25, 1950; William V. Quinn Papers, box 3, X Corps periodic intelligence report dated November 11, 1950 (Quinn was the X Corps G-2 chief).

48. FO317, piece no. 84073, Tokyo to FO, November 21, 1950.

49. Ibid.

50. MA, RG6, box 61, intelligence summary no. 3006, December 2, 1950; this document refers back to operations in Inch'ŏn in September, and suggests that such methods were standard. See also RG338, KMAG file, box 5418, KMAG journal, entry for October 2, 1950.

51. RG242, SA2010, item 2/99, *pandongja myŏngbu* [list of reactionaries], no date, but autumn 1950.

52. William V. Quinn Papers, box 3, X Corps HQ, McCaffrey to Ruffner, October 30, 1950; Ridgway Papers, box 20, highlights of a staff conference, with Ridgway and Almond present, January 8, 1951.

53. FO317, piece no. 92847, containing a TASS report of December 29, 1950.
54. Most able-bodied men had fled or taken to the hills as guerrillas, leaving their relatives in Sinch'ŏn. Since the atrocity occurred under enemy occupation, it is not surprising that the North Koreans have few names of the people involved. I was told that an American supervised the burning of women and children, whose name in their transliteration was "Vumaden (?) Harrison," said to be the commander of the area.
55. Quoted in John Edward Wiltz, "The Korean War and American Society," in Francis H. Heller, ed., *The Korean War: A 25-Year Perspective* (Lawrence: The Regent's Press of Kansas, 1977), p. 127.
56. Rosemary Foot's *The Wrong War* is the best account.
57. RG338, KMAG file, box 5418, KMAG journal, entry for October 1, 1950; periodic intelligence report, October 1, 1950. See General Yi's biography in Ridgway Papers, box 19, Van Fleet to Ridgway, February 17, 1952.
58. See, for example, *Tonga ilbo*, October 21, 1950; also FO317, piece no. 84073, U.S. Embassy press translations, November 1, 1950.
59. HST, PSF, CIA file, box 248, CIA daily reports, October 3–10, 1950; 795.00 file, box 4268, Drumwright to Allison, August 30, 1950; MacArthur Papers, VIP file, box 9, Rhee to MacArthur, August 12, 1950.
60. FO317, piece no. 83008, Tokyo to FO, September 28, 1950, enclosing Gascoigne's memo of conversation with MacArthur on September 19; for the press releases and commentary generated by MacArthur's command, see *New York Times*, September 16, 28, 29, October 2, 1950; the unnamed ROKA major is quoted in *New York Times*, October 9, 1950.
61. *New York Times*, October 15, 18, 22, 23, 1950; on the atmosphere in UNC headquarters when P'yŏngyang was seized, see *London Times*, November 16, 1950.
62. Blair, *Forgotten War*, pp. 318–19, 351.
63. Appleman, *Naktong/Yalu*, p. 658; Thompson, *Cry Korea*, p. 79; *London Times*, November 16, 1950; Sullivan in *New York Times*, October 2, 1950. In my view Sullivan's reporting from Korea in 1949 and 1950 should have won him a Pulitzer Prize; instead it got him a reputation as a leftist. Appleman fails to grasp KPA strategy, joining the chorus about the "virtual collapse" of the KPA after Inch'ŏn (p. 600). Rhee wrote to MacArthur on September 8 expressing fears about all the guerrillas left in the South, which "will be a cause of great danger after the main forces have passed by" (MA, RG10, VIP file, box 9, Rhee to MacArthur, September 8, 1950).
64. Interview with a member of Kim Il Sung's group, in Han Chae-dŏk, *Kim Il Sung*, p. 62.
65. RG242, SA2010, item 3/117, Interior Ministry directive no. 520, September 30, 1950, marked top secret. A CIC report placed Kim Il Sung in Beijing as early as October 6, and quoted him as instructing his commanders "to protect their routes of withdrawal by making a pretext of fighting a determined stand wherever possible" (RG 349, box 465, CIC report, October 6, 1950). For Kim Il Sung's own speech at the time, the authenticity of which I cannot verify, see Kim, "Temporary Strategic Retreat and the Tasks of Party Organizations," September 27, 1950, *Works*, vol. 3 (P'yŏngyang: Foreign Languages Publishing House, 1981), pp. 107–14. The American archives has a curious top secret document dated October 14, 1950, in which Kim Il Sung and Pak Hŏn-yŏng instruct troops to stop relaxing or throwing away their weapons after they cross the parallel, thinking that the enemy will not come North. It read, "The trend of thought on the part of officers was that the enemy would not cross the 38th parallel." But two weeks earlier the enemy

had crossed the parallel, and in mid-September the Soviet embassy evacuated P'yŏngyang. The fact that this top secret order was captured may suggest that it was a plant, designed to make the Americans think that the rollback caught the North by surprise and threw the KPA into confusion. See the English translation in MA, RG6, box 79, ATIS issue no. 19, January 30, 1951.

66. A text of the October 6 speech became available in Hong Kong in late December 1950. See *New York Times*, December 24, 1950. A paraphrase of the October 3 directive is in 795.00 file, box 4269, Hong Kong to State, October 17, 1950. An unnamed "veteran guerrilla campaigner" who had hunted guerrillas in Manchuria (probably a Japanese) predicted to American intelligence on July 19, 1950, that the KPA would resort to guerrilla warfare when U.S. forces built up to the point where they could take the initiative and force a retreat (MA, RG6, box 60, intelligence report no. 2870, July 19, 1950).

67. MA, RG6, box 80, ATIS issue no. 28, March 11, 1951, translating a notebook that is identified as belonging to Ch'oe Pae-yun, an intelligence officer, and apparently quoting Pak Ki-sŏng. It was captured on February 4, 1951. The other document is in Quinn Papers, box 3, periodic intelligence report no. 120, no date but probably January 1951.

68. Quinn Papers, box 3, "The Chagang-do Redoubt," annex no. 2, periodic intelligence report no. 37, no date but post–November 1950. The CIA said on October 18 that "There has been no evidence of any breakdown in the internal discipline of the North Korean communists. Their leaders have been through many years of adversity in China and Japanese-occupied Korea, and they probably will continue fighting in one way or another" (HST, PSF, CIA file, box 250, "Review of the World Situation," October 18, 1950). Acheson later said that MacArthur should have stopped at the "narrow neck" between P'yŏngyang and Wŏnsan, because the Japanese "never really reduced" the northern regions bordering China: "This was an area of guerrilla warfare almost all through the Japanese occupation" (Acheson Seminars, February 13–14, 1954).

69. MA, RG6, box 68, intelligence report no. 3005, December 1, 1950; see the laudatory account of Pang's exploits in *NDSM*, December 6, 1950; see also Almond Papers, "Korean War Command Report," X Corps "War Diary," November 1–30, 1950; also 795.00 file, box 4299, report by Army attaché Robert E. Edwards, enclosed in Emmons to Johnson, December 14, 1950; also Donovan Papers, box 5a, packet 2002, "By-passed Enemy Troops and Guerrilla Activities Below 38th Parallel for period 18 Oct—31 Oct 1950," no agency of origin, but originally classified "secret." See also HST, PSF, CIA file, box 248, daily report, October 17, 1950.

70. HST, PSF, CIA file, box 248, daily report for December 22, 1950; ibid., NSC file, box 3, CIA daily report for November 22, 1950; 795.00 file, box 4299, report on an inspection of the Chŏllas by Army attaché Robert E. Edwards, in Emmons to Johnson, December 14, 1950. This last source gives the 40,000 figure; the CIA put the total number of guerrillas in South Chŏlla at 8,000 to 10,000 in late October (HST, PSF, CIA file, box 248, daily report, October 27, 1950).

71. Almond Papers, "Korean War General Files," X Corps HQ operations report, October 16-December 31, 1950; FO317, piece no. 84074, report by J. K. Swire, November 7, 1950; NA, OCMC manuscripts, box 616, "History of the Korean War," vol. 3, pt. 12, "Enemy Tactics," pp. 88–89; RG338, KMAG file, box 5418, KMAG journal entries for October 9, 12, 26, 28, November 4, 9, 19, 1950; also box 5419, various briefing reports for an unnamed Commanding General, October and November 1950.

72. MA, RG6, box 80, ATIS issue no. 29, March 17, 1951, translating a diary of one "Major Chung," captured in October 1950.

73. 795.00 file, box 4299, report by Army attaché Robert E. Edwards, enclosed in Emmons to Johnson, December 14, 1950; Appleman, *Naktong/Yalu*, pp. 721–27, 745–46; HST, PSF, NSC file, box 3, CIA report of November 22, 1950; MA, RG6, box 14, FEC intelligence report no. 2224, December 19, 1950.

74. NA, OCMH manuscripts, box 615, "History of the Korean War," vol. 3, pt. 12, "Enemy Tactics," p. 82. The ROKA 2d Division was still fighting this force as "a full time concern" in February 1951. See also Ridgway Papers, box 18, Ridgway to Van Fleet, November 13, 1951.

75. Appleman, *Naktong/Yalu*, pp. 745–46; NA, OCMH manuscripts, box 617, "History of the Korean War," vol. 3, pt. 14, "Special Problems in the Korean Conflict," p. 42.

76. See for example *New York Times*, September 16, October 22, 28, 1950.

77. HST, PSF, CIA file, box 250, CIA report for October 13, 1950.

78. Stone, *Hidden History*, p. 217.

79. MA, RG6, box 61, intelligence summaries nos. 3008–3010, December 4–6, 1950; box 68, intelligence summaries nos. 3011–3016, December 7–12, 1950; *New York Times*, November 28, December 3, 19, 1950; Thompson, *Cry Korea*, p. 201. Bouchier indicated that Willoughby's figures did not include guerrillas. See Fo317, piece no. 84073, Bouchier to FO, December 8, 1950.

80. Appleman, *Naktong/Yalu*, pp. 565–67.

81. Sino-Korean diplomacy during the Hideyoshi invasions of the 1590s is a particularly instructive historical example; on this see Gari Ledyard's essay from which I have learned much, "The Korean Security Crisis of 1598: National Security, Confucian Style," presented to the Columbia University Faculty Seminar on Korea, December 12, 1980.

82. Largely because of Allen S. Whiting's *China Crosses the Yalu: The Decision to Enter the Korean War* (Stanford, Calif.: Stanford University Press, 1960).

83. 795.00 file, box 4268, teleconference of August 30, 1950; MA, RG6, box 1, MacArthur conference with Harriman, Ridgway, and others, August 8, 1950; conference with Collins, Almond, and others, August 24, 1950.

84. HST, PSF, CIA file, box 250, "Review of the World Situation," September 20, October 18, 1950; box 248, CIA report of November 1, 1950; CIA report of November 24, 1950, cited in Willoughby Papers, box 10, "The Chinese Communist Potential for Intervention in the Korean War."

85. Fo317, piece no. 83271, Mukden Consulate to FO, November 23, 1950; Office of Chinese Affairs file, box 4224, London to State, October 31, 1950, quoting a British-American Tobacco representative who had just left Mukden; piece nos. 84069, 84070, with many documents predicting that China will not enter the war; piece no. 84100, memo of conversation with British chiefs of staff, October 5, 1950; piece no. 83015, FO to Washington Embassy, October 11, 1950. Even the observant Hutchison thought from his Beijing vantage point that China would not come in (piece no. 83306, Hutchison to FO, September 28, October 12, 1950). On Pannikar see piece no. 83306, High Commissioner to India to FO, September 29, 1950, and the October 2 FO minute saying Pannnikar is too sympathetic to the PRC, and has "no real appreciation of Sino Soviet relations." Bouchier cabled on the eve of MacArthur's last offensive that UNC headquarters knew what it was doing, and had a better grasp of the situation than did agencies in other parts of the world (ibid., piece no. 84072, Bouchier to FO, November 13, 1950).

86. *FR* (1950) 3, pp. 1706–09, minutes of Truman-Attlee discussions, December 4, 1950.
87. Kennan Papers, box 31, Kennan to Allen Whiting, October 20, 1960.
88. *New York Times*, October 2, November 19, 21, 1950.
89. FO317, piece no. 83306, High Commissioner to India to FO, September 29, 1950. In a long conversation with British sources in Hong Kong in October 1951, Pannikar said it was "rubbish" to think that the Russians started the Korean War over American policies toward Japan. Neither the Chinese nor the Russians feared Japan, he said; the war was "a purely internal Korean affair." He thought the Chinese were more eager to enter the war "than the Russians were to have them intervene," citing China's proud nationalism and its interest in being a great power. See Office of Chinese Affairs, box 4199, Hong Kong to State, October 19, 1951.
90. HST, PSF, CIA file, box 250, CIA report of October 6, 1950; Office of Chinese Affairs file, box 18, McConaughy for Jessup and Rusk, October 12, 1950; FO317, piece no. 84109, FO minute on Hutchison to FO, September 28, 1950.
91. See the dispatch in FO317, piece no. 84121, Peking to FO, November 24, 1950; the dispatch was dated November 19.
92. FO317, piece no. 84121, Pannikar to Guy Wint, November 5, 1950.
93. FBIS no. 186, September 25, 1950; no. 187, September 26, 1950, citing editorials in *Renmin Ribao*; Canadian Archives, Department of External Affairs, War in Korea files, vol. 10, memo for the minister, September 26, 1950. I am indebted to William Stueck for giving me a copy of this document.
94. *New York Times*, November 12, 1950, quoting a PRC statement of the same day; RG338, KMAG file, box 5418, periodic intelligence report, November 6, 1950; MA, RG6, box 14, G-2 memo of October 9, 1950.
95. MA, RG6, box 16, Order of Battle, "Chicom 4th Field Army," November 7, 1950.
96. FO317, piece no. 84108, Tokyo to FO, December 4, 1950.
97. FO317, piece no. 84121, Belgrade Embassy to FO, December 2, 1950; Hutchison wrote from Beijing in late September that Chinese participation in the war "may prove to be [a] safeguard against extension and permanency of Russian influence in Korea" (piece no. 84109, September 28, 1950).
98. FO317, piece no. 84110, Tokyo military liaison to FO, October 4, 1950; see also Appleman, *Naktong/Yalu*, pp. 670–75, 717.
99. Office of Chinese Affairs file, box 4211, Hong Kong to State, October 26, 1950; FO317, piece no. 83271, FO minute on Mukden to FO, November 23, 1950. Nieh Jung-chen was close to Chou En-lai, having worked in Berlin in 1924 under Chou's direction; he entered Whampoa in 1925, again helping Chou to recruit communists, including Lin Piao. Nieh played "a key role" in getting Russian weapons to troops getting ready for battle in staging areas near Korea. Under Lin Piao's overall command, Li T'ien-yu led crack 13th Army troops into Korea between October 14 and 20; interestingly, Li had commanded a 100,000-soldier column in fierce battles in the crisis period of May 1947 in Manchuria, when large numbers of Koreans had joined the battle (see William W. Whitson, *The Chinese High Command*, pp. 93–95, 307, 338–39). Whitson estimates that some 400,000 Chinese soldiers were fighting in Korea by the end of November, which is at least 100,000 too high, and perhaps reflects Chinese desires to take credit for pushing the Americans out of the North.
100. See MA, RG6, box 9, Walker to CINCFE, November 6, 1950 (emphasis added).
101. MA, RG6, box 78, ATIS issue no. 11, December 13, 1950, translating PLA 66th Army, "Primary Conclusion of Battle Experience at Unsan."

102. Pak Il-u said some months later that the Americans did not learn their lesson from the numerous Chinese warnings issued by Chou En-lai, or the initial Sino-Korean offensive. This is interesting, for it suggests that not just the Chinese but also the Koreans might have been ready to negotiate at that time, had the Americans stayed at their new lines. If so, they probably would have demanded an American retreat below the parallel. See RG242, SA2012, item 6/57, Pak Il-u, *Chosŏn inmin'gun kwa Chung'guk inmin chiwŏn'gun ŭi kongdong chakjŏn* [The joint strategy of the KPA and the Chinese People's Volunteer Army] (P'yŏngyang: KWP ch'ulp'an-sa, 1951), pp. 13–18.

103. *New York Times*, November 6, 7, 11, 12, 1950.

104. RG338, KMAG file, box 5418, periodic intelligence report, October 22, 1950; *New York Times*, November 1, 2, 3, 1950; HST, PSF, CIA file, box 248, daily reports, November 1, 3, 4, 6, 7, 9, 10, 11, 1950.

105. Joseph B. Longuevan Papers, box 4, "History of the 27th Infantry."

106. HST, PSF, CIA file, box 248, daily reports, November 9–27, 1950; *New York Times*, November 24, 25, 26, 1950.

107. HST, PSF, CIA file, box 248, daily reports, November 15–21, 1950; RG338, KMAG file, box 5418, periodic intelligence report, November 26, 1950.

108. MA, RG6, box 9, JCS to MacArthur, December 4, 1950.

109. HST, PSF, CIA file, box 248, daily reports for November 27-December 16, 1950; Almond Papers, "Korean War, Historical Commentary," Almond letters to H. E. Eastwood, December 27, 1950, and W. W. Gretakis, December 27, 1950. Hŭngnam was shielded for several days while Allied troops were evacuated; there is a suggestion that the Chinese did not wish to interfere with this departure, when they could have inflicted even heavier losses.

110. MA, RG6, box 9, MacArthur to Army, November 6, 1950; MacArthur to JCS, December 4, 1950. Gascoigne thought Willoughby probably sought "to cook figures" on how many Chinese were in the North, noting that the total mushroomed overnight from 17,000 to 200,000 (FO317, piece no. 84119, Gascoigne to FO, November 24, 1950).

111. *NDSM*, December 9, 1950. The December 3 issue referred to Kim as *suryŏng*, Mao as the *yŏngdoja* [leader] of the Chinese people. See also Nam, *North Korean Communist Leadership*.

112. Ridgway Papers, box 17, Almond to Ridgway, February 14, 1951; FO317, piece no. 84073, Bouchier to FO, November 28, 1950; piece no. 84075, Bouchier to FO, December 16, 1950; *New York Times*, January 4, 8, 1951; *MacArthur Hearings*, deleted testimony by General Marshall, May 11, 1951, and by General Bradley, May 24, 1951; Ridgway Papers, box 22, Ridgway to Bradley, January 16, 1952. Ridgway said that by early 1952, the ROKA had lost enough heavy machine guns to equip thirty-four divisions, enough rocket launchers to equip twenty-five, and enough light machine guns to equip ten.

113. RG338, KMAG file, box 5418, periodic intelligence reports, November 21, 26, 29, 1950; NA, OCMH manuscripts, box 617, "History of the Korean War," vol. 3, pt. 14, "Special Problems in the Korean Conflict," p. 104.

114. MA, RG6, box 68, intelligence summaries no. 3007–3014, December 3–10, 1950.

115. FO317, piece no. 84074, Adams to FO, December 12, 1950; piece no. 84075, Bouchier to FO, December 13, 18, 1950; HST, PSF, NSC file, box 3, CIA reports for December 12, 13, 1950.

116. 795.00 file, box 4271, "Briefing of Ambassadors on Korea," January 17, 19, 1951.

117. For a recent (and badly misinformed) example, see Russell Spurr, *Enter the Dragon: China's Undeclared War Against the U.S. in Korea, 1950–1951* (New York:

New Market Press, 1988). British military attachés said in early December that the numbers of Chinese were quite exaggerated, with "very few confirmed contacts with the Chinese"; furthermore, it was often impossible to judge the nationality of enemy units. The number of Chinese POWs being taken did not indicate huge numbers of troops. Bouchier said the war was "becoming more and more baffling to report upon"; no one seemed to know where the "main bulk" of the Chinese were. (The FO commented that Bouchier had the Chinese "sprawling about everywhere" on one day, and absent the next.) An American observation pilot was quoted as saying that the Marines were never really surrounded at the Changjin Reservoir, but "had only been attacked at night" by small units that withdrew during the day. He had not seen marks in the snow indicating large numbers of troops. See Fo317, piece no. 84074, Adams to FO, December 6, 7, 17, 1950; Bouchier to FO, December 5, 11, 12, 1950; piece no. 84075, Bouchier to FO, December 13, 14, 16, 1950; also J. S. Schattuck minute on the December 16 report.

118. HST, PSF, CIA file, box 248, daily report for February 2, 1951.

119. Willoughby and Chamberlin, *MacArthur*, p. 403.

120. At a joint meeting of JCS, State, and other representatives on November 21, the conferees "unmistakeably, though indirectly, authorized MacArthur to launch his planned offensive." By this point the British chiefs of staff were beside themselves: they thought Acheson had "very little control over General MacArthur," that the offensive "can only lead to a clash with Communist China," and that the opposition forces "may well prove much stronger than Gen. MacArthur appreciates." They recommended in "the most forceful and unequivocal terms" that an approach be made to the United States forthwith to instruct MacArthur to remain at his present lines. But the British government declined, thinking it would not be "expedient" to make further representations at this point. See Schnabel and Watson, JCS, *The Korean War*, vol. 3, pt. 1, pp. 327–29; and FO317, piece no. 84104, memo on British chiefs of staff meeting, November 20, 1950; Cabinet meeting minutes, November 24, 1950.

121. *Manchester Guardian*, December 4, 1950.

122. 795.00 file, box 4271, "Use of Cheju Island as a Seat for the Government of the ROK," top secret, December 29, 1950; Dulles conversation with Chang Myŏn, January 4, 1951; Rusk conversation with Chang, January 17, 1951; HST, PSF, NSC file, box 3, CIA report for December 21, 1950; HST, CIA file, box 248, report for December 29, 1950. Yi Pŏm-sŏk also mentioned Taiwan as a place of exile, but Japan was his first choice. In the memos suggesting removal of Rhee, Muccio hoped that Chang would return quickly "and make the War Cabinet under his chairmanship an effective 'Junta' " (795.00 file, box 4299, Muccio to State, December 10, 1950). Expecting Chang to run a junta was like thinking Philip Jaisohn would make a good ROK president. See also box 4299, top secret memo signed by Jessup, December 28, 1950, saying that if Rhee sought to set up an exile regime on Cheju, the United States should consider "inducing President Rhee to withdraw in favor of a governing commission." This suggestion probably also came from Muccio; I do not know if it referred to the governing commission planning in late 1945.

123. HST, Connelly Papers, box 1, cabinet notes, November 28, December 12, 1950; Truman, "Longhand Notes" file, box 333, note for December 9, 1950; PSF, NSC file, box 220, 74th NSC meeting, December 12, 1950.

124. *New York Times*, November 30, December 1, 1950.

125. Bradley and Blair, *A General's Life*, p. 581; HST, Acheson Papers, box 65, Baruch

to Lovett to Acheson, December 2, 1950; Symington quoted in Barton Bernstein, "The Korean War and Containment" Acheson Papers, box 65, memo of conversation between Nitze, Harriman, Kennan, and Acheson, December 5, 1950; CRC, 1975, item 67A, JCS for Army Chief of Staff, December 3, 1950.

126. *New York Times*, December 13, 21, 24, 1950; Burton I. Kaufman, *The Korean War: Challenges in Crisis, Credibility, and Command* (Philadelphia: Temple University Press, 1986), pp. 121–23.

127. I am indebted to Gabriel Kolko for an interesting conversation on these issues.

128. *FR* (1950) 1, pp. 468–74, NSC report to the President, December 14, 1950; *New York Times*, December 16, 1950.

129. Oshinsky, *Conspiracy So Immense*, p. 180.

130. MA, RG6, box 9, CINCFE to JCS, February 7, 1951; see also a less ambitious plan in Ridgway Papers, MacArthur to JCS, December 30, 1950; Ridgway thought the logic of landing Nationalists in south China was "convincing to me and I feel I would be negligent were I not to state my full concurrence at once" (ibid., box 22, December 29, 1950). This was apparently in response to MacArthur's December 26 statement at a conference with Ridgway, that China was "wide open in the South," and that forces on Taiwan should be allowed to attack there. The JCS January 23, 1951, document, to the Secretary of Defense, is in MA, RG6, box 1. Just after MacArthur was removed, Ridgway asked for authority to send his troops across the Chinese *and* Soviet borders if he thought it necessary—"a surprising proposal coming from General Ridgway, considering what he had said to his subordinates about the dangers of enlarging the war" (Schnabel and Watson, JCS, *The Korean War*, vol. 3, pt. 2, p. 490).

131. Vandenberg Papers, box 86, Stratemeyer to Vandenberg, November 30, 1950; LeMay to Vandenberg, December 2, 1950. Paul Nitze had asked Gen. Herbert B. Loper on November 4 "to discuss the question of dropping atomic bombs on Chinese troops" in Korea. "Nitze speculated that a few bombs so aimed would not inflict heavy casualties but might deter further Chinese intervention." But after the conference, according to Robert Donovan, he concluded that using the bomb was infeasible (Donovan, *Tumultuous Years*, p. 308).

132. FO317, piece no. 84104, Cabinet discussion, November 30, 1950; piece no. 83109, minutes of meeting between Attlee, Pleven, and the Foreign Secretaries, December 2, 1950; Franks to FO, December 7, 1950. See also Schnabel and Watson, JCS, *The Korean War*, vol. 3, pt. 1, p. 376; on the number of atomic weapons in 1950–1951, see Donovan Papers, box 7A, item 2025, no date but apparently 1951.

133. The JCS study and various associated documents are available in RG319, G-3 Operations file, box 34, C.V.R. Schuyler to Lieutenant Colonel Lawler, "Utilization of Atomic Bombardment to Assist in Accomplishment of the US Objectives in South Korea," July 7, 1950. MacArthur's "hot message" is not available, but Ridgway discusses it in a memo of July 9, 1950 (Ridgway Papers, box 16).

134. RG319, ibid., box 34A, Bolte to Collins, July 13, 1950; see also Department of the Army, General Staff, "Memo for General Bolte," July 17, 1950, in Room 13W, National Archives; this includes the transcript of a teleconference with MacArthur on July 13, 1950.

135. RG319, Ibid., box 34A, Bolte to Collins, July 13, 1950; also Bolte memo of July 25, 1950. Such preparations took an ominous turn in late July, when the Air Force transferred two medium bomb groups to bases in England, targeted not on Korea but on the Soviet Union. The planes were atomic-capable and carried all the bomb components except the nuclear cores. This caused the British to

wonder precisely what the United States had in mind, and whether its actions in Korea might lead to a wider conflict. The Soviets had no effective delivery capability to the United States (the best they might do was in situ placement of bombs delivered by merchant ships to US ports). Thus Western Europe would be the prime Soviet target. See Hoyt S. Vandenberg Papers, box 86, July 1950 folder of top secret messages, Norstad to LeMay, July 9, 1950. The number of Soviet bombs and the possibility of in situ placement is discussed in HST, PSF, CIA file, box 250, CIA, "Soviet Preparations for Major Hostilities in 1950," August 25, 1950.

136. FO317, piece no. 84073, Bouchier to FO, December 9, 1950; G-3 Operations file, box 38-A, "Actions Necessary to Conclude the Korean Operations," July 6, 1951, Annex A, July 5, 1951; Willoughby Papers, box 8, interviews by Bob Considine and Jim Lucas in 1954, printed in *New York Times*, April 9, 1964.

137. Quigley, *Tragedy and Hope*, p. 875; G-3 Operations file, box 34A, Bolte memo of November 16, 1950, with attached memo of conclusions; Gore quoted in mid-April 1951 in Barton Bernstein, "The Korean War and Containment," paper prepared for a Woodrow Wilson Center conference on the Truman period, September 1984; see also G-3 Operations file, box 38-A, "Actions Necessary."

138. G-3 Operations file, box 38-A, "Actions Necessary"; Vandenberg Papers, box 86, Vandenberg to Norstad, March 14, 1951; MA, RG6, box 1, Stratemeyer to MacArthur, March 31, 1950; Walter S. Poole, *History of the JCS*, vol. 4, *The Joint Chiefs of Staff and National Policy* (Washington, D.C.: U.S. Government Printing Office, 1983), pp. 151–52.

139. Dingman has shown that the nuclear cores were transferred to military custody, even though David Rosenberg says the first such transfer for deployment overseas did not occur until June 1953 (Rosenberg, "The Origins of Overkill: Nuclear Weapons and American Strategy, 1945–1960," *International Security* 7 [Spring 1983], p. 27). Professor Dingman wrote (in a paper prepared for the American Historical Association Annual Meeting in December 1985) that Truman "sent two squadrons of B-29s carrying complete Mark IV atomic bombs to Guam and Okinawa." The bombers picked up their atomic cargo within hours of the White House announcement that MacArthur had been relieved. The best account of Dingman's fine research, which came out too late for incorporation in this book, is in his "Atomic Diplomacy During the Korean War," *International Security*, 3 (Winter 1988–1989), pp. 50–91.

140. Rusk told the British on November 29, 1950, that the Soviets had moved 200 twin-engine bombers to Manchurian airfields, and on December 6 the British Ministry of Defense noted that MacArthur had now had "a plain warning that to bomb across the frontier would bring the Soviet Air Force into action." Although MacArthur harped on his inability to attack Manchuria, "he apparently entirely disregards the fact ... that his own bases and communications ... also enjoy virtual immunity" (FO317, piece no. 84119, memo of conversation, Rusk and Franks, November 29, 1950; piece no. 84108, Chiefs of Staff to Bouchier, December 7, 1950). The Pannikar warning is mentioned in the Rusk-Franks discussions.

141. For more discussions of the use of nuclear weapons, 1951–1953, see Schnabel and Watson, JCS, *The Korean War*, vol. 3, pt. 2, pp. 613–14, 931–33, 954, 960–61. Samuel Cohen was a childhood friend of Herman Kahn; see Fred Kaplan, *The Wizards of Armageddon* (New York: Simon and Schuster, 1983), p. 220. On Oppenheimer and Project Vista, see G-3 Operations file, box 38, "Tactical Employment of the Atomic Bomb in Korea," December 22, 1950; also David C. El-

liot, "Project Vista and Nuclear Weapons in Europe," *International Security* 2, no. 1 (Summer 1986), pp. 163–83.

142. HST, Psychological Strategy Board file, box 33, Walter B. Smith to Gordon Gray, October 12, 1951; atomic weapons are referred to as "novel weapons" in ibid., RAND Corporation, "Study on Atomic Weapons," July 23, 1952.

143. G-3 Operations file, box 38-A, "Actions Necessary"; memo by S. V. Hasbrouck, November 7, 1951; memo for the Chief of Staff, Army, November 20, 1951; also Schnabel and Watson, JCS, *The Korean War*, vol. 3, pt. 1, p. v, also pt. 2, p. 614; RG349, FEC G-2 Theater Intelligence, box 752, Sept 30, 1951, CINCFE to CG SAC ("Requests SAC to execute simulated atomic strikes on tgts. vic. CT402453 and CT576484"); Oct 1, 1951, CG FEAF to 98th Bomb Wing commander, Okinawa; Oct 13, 1951, resume of operation ("need for a clear-cut definition of what is meant by tactical use of atomic weapons *in support of ground operations [sic]*)." Most of the documents on Hudson Harbor are still classified.

144. Acheson Seminars, March 14, 1954. The above evidence makes it difficult to understand how John Gaddis can publish a book in 1987 arguing for Truman's "self-imposed restraint" in not using or threatening to use atomic weapons in the Korean War. A close reading of this evidence, and what Gaddis has to say about the "very different attitude" of the Eisenhower administration, suggests that Truman and Eisenhower had about the same policy, and both gave serious consideration to the use of atomic bombs in the Korean War. Gaddis is right that Dulles was louder in talking about it (like his rollback rhetoric), but there was no "Hudson Harbor" equivalent under Eisenhower, according to the available record (see Gaddis, *Long Peace*, pp. 115–29).

145. Ridgway Papers, box 20, MacArthur to Ridgway, January 7, 1951; memo of Ridgway's conference with Almond and others, January 8, 1951.

146. Bradley and Blair, *A General's Life*, p. 584; MA, RG6, box 1, Stratemeyer to MacArthur, November 8, 1950; FO317, piece no. 84072, Bouchier to Chiefs of Staff, November 6, 1950; ibid., piece no. 84073, November 25, 1959, sitrep. Napalm is a mixture of naphthenic and palmitic acids, ignited by phosphorous to make it burn slowly and into the skin, a combustion that sometimes lasts up to fifteen days inside the wounds. It was invented during World War II by Professor Louis Fieser of Harvard, who said in 1966, during protests over its use in Vietnam, "we certainly had no thought of use of napalm against non-military personnel." See J. B. Nielands, "Chemical Warfare," in *The Social Responsibility of the Scientist*, ed. Martin Brown (New York: Free Press, 1971), pp. 82–83. Dr. Fieser's response to the far wider use of the weapon against Korean civilians is not recorded.

147. HST, PSF, CIA file, box 248, report of December 15, 1950; FO317, piece nos. 84074 and 84075, Bouchier situation reports, December 5, 17, 1950; *New York Times*, December 13, 1950, January 3, 1951; Blair, *Forgotten War*, p. 603.

148. Ridgway Papers, box 20, highlights of conference with Ridgway, January 5, 1951; box 17, Almond to Ridgway, January 16, 1951.

149. Almond Papers, "General Files, X Corps," Barr to Almond, January 18, 1951; Almond to Barr, January 19, 1951.

150. Ridgway Papers, box 17, Almond to Ridgway, January 25, 1951.

151. 895.00 file, box 6175, George Barrett dispatch of February 8, 1951; Acheson to Pusan Embassy, February 17, 1951.

152. Ridgway Papers, box 20, Ridgway discussion with unnamed commanding officers, no date but probably March 1951.

153. HST, Connelly Papers, "Notes on Cabinet Meetings," September 12, 1952. I am indebted to Barton Bernstein for calling this reference to my attention.

154. "The Attack on the Irrigation Dams in North Korea," *Air University Quarterly* 6, no. 4 (Winter 1953–1954), pp. 40–51. For an excellent account of the breaking of the dams, see MacDonald, *War Before Vietnam*, pp. 241–42.
155. J. F. Dulles Papers, Curtis LeMay oral history, April 28, 1966.

CHAPTER TWENTY-TWO

1. George Kahin's discussion of the American commitment to a separate southern state in Vietnam closely parallels the Korean experience, with the turning point in South Vietnam coming in 1954 (*Intervention*, pp. 66–92).
2. With the war on the Americans had enormous pressures that could be brought to bear on Rhee, were well aware of the revolutionary redistribution carried out by the North Koreans in the summer of 1950, and were determined not to let southern landlords regain their holdings. Thus, finally, implementation of the reformist redistribution began in the spring of 1951. See 895.00 file, box 5692, Drumwright to State, January 16, 1951; HST, PSF, NSC file, box 3, CIA memorandum of October 19, 1950. In March 1951 the CIA reported that ECA officials were pressing for redistribution, "despite the lack of enthusiasm" of "authorities with strong landlord sympathies [who] have been able to thwart implementation of the distribution schedule in some individual counties" (HST, PSF, NSC file, box 3, CIA memorandum of March 8, 1951).
3. In discussions on July 9, 1953, an unidentified person says, "we were having a hell of a time figuring out how we were going to get the NSC 68 program," whereupon another person says, "Korea came along and (saved?) us—do the job for us." Acheson replied, "I think you can say that" (HST, Acheson seminars, box 82).
4. See Eisenhower Library, NSC series, box 4, 168th meeting, October 29, 1953; at the 173rd meeting (box 5, December 3, 1953), after Eisenhower and Admiral Radford discuss atomic attacks on China from Shanghai northward, should it resume the war, Dulles said that the United States must limit its responses to inside Korea, keep its allies on board, and not extend the war to China. At the 177th meeting (December 23, 1953), Richard Nixon said "we must settle for a divided Korea" . . . a united, independent Korea "is simply not possible."
5. Eisenhower Library, NSC series, box 4, 144th meeting, May 13, 1953; for other Hainan references, see the 157th meeting, July 30, 1953; the 168th meeting, October 29, 1953; and the 179th meeting, January 8, 1954.
6. Ibid., box 6, 229th meeting, Dec 21, 1954.
7. See especially Kahin, *Intervention*, pp. 396–400; see also Summers, *On Strategy*, who does not begin to understand how Korea shaped the way the Vietnam War was fought, in spite of that being one of his major themes.
8. Drew Pearson thought Rubinstein "was a great blackmailer"; in 1955 Pearson linked him to Boeing Aircraft, and cited one Lee Brooke, involved with Rubinstein in the Stanwell Oil Company, in saying Rubinstein may have been murdered when someone ransacked his apartment looking for documents used in blackmail (*Diaries*, p. 345). But the murder remains unsolved.
9. Walter LaFeber, *New Empire*, pp. 407–8. Acheson's papers at the Truman Library and at Yale show no contact with Goodfellow, but Goodfellow said he often talked with Acheson, when the latter walked to work at Foggy Bottom.
10. HST, PSF, memorandum of discussion on February 16, 1955 between Truman and Acheson, xerox copy courtesy of John W. Powell.

11. Dower, *Empire and Aftermath*, p. 316.

12. Conversation in P'yŏngyang, August 1981.

13. *Korea: The Forgotten War*. Thames Television producers wanted to call our documentary "Korea: The Forgotten War"; Jon Halliday and I prevailed upon them to call it "Korea: The Unknown War" (like so much else about that documentary, it was a partial victory).

14. Nietzsche, *The Genealogy of Morals*, trans. Walter Kaufmann and R. J. Hollingdale (New York: Vintage Books, 1969), pp. 57–58.

15. I am indebted here to Frederic Jameson's discussion of the character Garcin in Sartre's *No Exit*, and also to numerous passages in Nietzsche's work. See Jameson, *Sartre: The Origins of a Style* (New York: Columbia University Press, 1984), pp. 3–18; the quotation is on p. 16.

16. Ibid., p. 13.

17. Martin Heidegger, *What Is Called Thinking?*, trans. J. Glenn Gray (New York: Harper Colophon Books, 1968), pp. 103, 138–41, 151–52. I am indebted to Gayle Turner for calling this book to my attention. Jameson writes, "The past always is assumed: we are not free to have no attitude toward it. It cannot be changed; but we always lend the changeless facts a meaning in terms of the lives we lead and even the forgetting of them" (*Sartre*, p. 13).

18. Acheson, *Among Friends*, pp. 99, 103–4.

19. In February 1987 I found myself in an academic meeting with MacGeorge Bundy, not a common experience. Historian Charles Maier introduced me and my work, whereupon Bundy said, "what do you think about the march North?" Before I could answer, he remarked that it was a combination of absent-mindedness in Washington and MacArthur's "craziness."

20. Michael Walzer, *Just and Unjust Wars: A Moral Argument with Historical Illustrations* (New York: Basic Books, 1977), pp. 117–23. The argument that the war for containment was just, the war for rollback unjust, is integral to the passage; in speaking of the June invasion, for example, Walzer writes, "it was the crime of the aggressor to challenge individual and communal rights," and the proper American response (carried out in the summer of 1950) was a "just war" that was "conservative in character," that is, a limited sort of police action on behalf of the international community. But if we cannot "recognize the initial aggression" how then do we assign "individual and communal rights"? The answer is, we cannot. George Kennan got many things Korean wrong at the time, but in his memoirs he finally got the nature of the war right: "This was, finally, a civil conflict, not an international one; and the term 'aggression' in the usual international sense was as misplaced here as it was to be later in the case of Vietnam" (*Memoirs, 1925–1950*, p. 490).

21. FO317, piece no. 83008, Stokes to Bevin, December 2, 1950.

22. For the view that Vietnam was (or should have been perceived as) another Korea see especially Summers, *On Strategy*. In a published book Curtis LeMay referred to "the invasion of South Vietnam" in 1950 (*America Is in Danger* [New York: Funk and Wagnalls, 1968], p. 109); General Almond wrote of the Tet offensive in 1968, "when the VC and North Koreans made their all-out attack" (Almond Papers, Almond to W. J. McCaffery, February 15, 1968).

23. See H. D. Harootunian, *Things Seen and Unseen: Discourse and Ideology in Tokugawa Nativism* (Chicago: University of Chicago Press, 1988), pp. 115–22. In trying to refute charges of genocide in Vietnam, arch-revisionist Guenter Lewy blithely remarks that whereas civilian casualties were but 28 percent of the total casualties in Vietnam, the figure for World War II was 40 percent, and for Korea 70 percent.

Therefore, presumably, he would agree that Korea was genocidal, even if by his empiricist tally Vietnam was not. See Lewy, *America in Vietnam* (New York: Oxford University Press, 1978), p. 451. I am indebted to Robert Divine for this citation. See also Dower, *War Without Mercy*, p. 298.

24. Nietzsche, *The Gay Science*, trans. Walter Kaufmann (New York: Vintage Books, 1974), p. 104.
25. The reference is to Ivan Morris, *The Nobility of Failure*.
26. James Burnham, *The Coming Defeat of Communism* (New York: John Day Co., 1951), pp. 145–47.
27. Eisenhower Library, Eisenhower Papers (Whitman file), NSC series, box 4, 144th meeting, May 13, 1953.
28. Drinnon, *Facing West*, pp. 241, 315–18; Seward quoted in LaFeber, *New American Empire*, p. 26; Mark Twain quoted in Gore Vidal, "Requiem for the American Empire," *The Nation*, January 11, 1986. Teddy Roosevelt thought that before the power of "the mightily civilized races," "the barbarians recede or are conquered" (Drinnon, *Facing West*, p. 232); Vidal has Teddy Roosevelt saying that "every argument that can be made for the Filipinos could be made for the Apaches . . . every word that can be said for Aguinaldo could be said for Sitting Bull"—much as Acheson responded to a critic of the Vietnam War by saying, "Everything you say could have been said of Korea" (Acheson Papers [Yale], Acheson to Prof. E. A. Burtt, October 14, 1965).
29. Elaine Scarry, *The Body in Pain: The Making and Unmaking of the World* (New York: Oxford University Press, 1985), p. 61.
30. "Equality before the enemy: the first presupposition of an *honest* duel. Where one feels contempt, one *cannot* wage war; where one commands, where one sees something beneath oneself, one has no business waging war" (Nietzsche, *Ecce Homo*, trans. Walter Kaufmann [New York: Vintage Books, 1969], p. 232).
31. Hartz, *Founding of New Societies*, p. 119.
32. Speech in Seattle, late 1951, quoted in Michael W. Miles, *The Odyssey of the American Right* (New York: Oxford University Press, 1980), p. 170. I find much to agree with in this book.
33. Joseph Schumpeter's point, of course.
34. Beard, *Open Door at Home*, pp. 301–2. The nationalism of the commonweal "assumes that foreign policy and domestic policy are aspects of the same thing . . . and that control over international relations can begin effectively with control over domestic policies and forces at home."
35. Friedrich Nietzsche, "On the Uses and Disadvantages of History for Life," in *Untimely Meditations*, trans. by R. J. Hollingdale (Cambridge: Cambridge University Press, 1983), p. 67.

I. Official Sources

Unpublished

Carrollton Press, Retrospective Collection.
Carrollton Press. 1975–1985.
England, Public Record Office, Foreign Office 371 File. 1948–1951.
Dwight D. Eisenhower Library, Eisenhower Papers (Whitman file), National Security Council Series.
Lyndon Baines Johnson Library, Drew Pearson Papers.
Gen. Douglas MacArthur Archives. Record Groups 6, 9, 10 (VIP). 1945–1951.
National Archives, Manuscripts of the Office of the Chief of Military History.
———. Record Group 43, US-USSR Joint Commission on Korea.
———. Record Group 94, Central Intelligence.
———. Record Group 165, Plans and Operations Division, ABC Decimal File.
———. Record Group 330, Entry 199, Office of the Secretary of Defense File.
———. Record Group 335, Office of the Secretary of the Army File.
———. Records of the National Security Council.
———. United States Army. Record Group 319, G-3 Operations Section. 1950–1951.
National Records Center, "History of the North Korean Army." Tokyo: G-2 Section. 1952.
———. United States Armed Forces in Korea. Record Group 332, XXIV Corps Historical File.
———. USFIK 11071 File.
———. United States Army. Record Group 319, "Intelligence Summaries-North Korea" (Army staff). Intelligence (G-2) Library. "P." File. 1946–1951.
———. United States Army. Record Group 407, "World War II Operations Reports." Entry no. 427, Counter-Intelligence Corps Reports. 1947–1951.
———. United States Army Military Government in Korea. Record Group 319, G-2 (intelligence) weekly and periodic reports.
———. United States, Far East Command. Record Group 242, "Captured Enemy Documents" (source of North Korean materials).
———. United States, Far East Command. RG 349, Far East Command G-2 Intelligence File.
———. United States Military Advisory Group to the Republic of Korea. Record Group 338, KMAG File.
———. KMAG journal. 1950.
Harry S. Truman Library. Official File; Presidential Secretary's File: Central Intelligence Agency File, National Security Council Meetings File, Daily Korean Summaries File.
Harry S. Truman Library. Psychological Strategy Board File.
Harry S. Truman Library. Presidential Secretary's File. "Selected Records Relating to the Korean War," Office of Intelligence Research File.
U.S. Air Force. "A Preliminary Study of the Impact of Communism Upon Korea." Maxwell Air Force Base, Ala.: Air University Human Resources Research Institute, 1951.

U.S. Central Intelligence Agency. "Communist Capabilities in South Korea." ORE 32–48, February 21, 1949.
———. "Current Capabilities of the Northern Korean Regime." ORE 18–50, June 19, 1950.
———. "The Current Situation in Korea." ORE 15–48, March 18, 1948.
———. "Implementation of Soviet Objectives in Korea." ORE 62, November 18, 1947.
———. "Korea." SR 2. 1947.
———. "Prospects for the Survival of the Republic of Korea." ORE 44–48, October 28, 1948.
———. "The Situation in Korea." ORE 5/1, January 3, 1947.
U.S. Joint Chiefs of Staff. Record Group 218, 383.21 Korea (3-19-45).
U.S. State Department. Office of Intelligence Research, Evelyn McCune, "Leadership in North Korea: Groupings and Motivations," 1963.
U.S. State Department. Record Group 59, Decimal Files, 501.BB category. 1947–1948.
———. 695.00 category. 1947–1954.
———. 740.0019 (Control) Korea category. 1945–1949.
———. 795.00 category. 1948–1954.
———. Far East 890.00 File. 1950–1954.
———. 895.00 category. 1948–1954.
———. Record Group 353, State-War-Navy Coordinating Committee. 1946–1947.
———. Record Group 353, "SWNCC-SANACC." 1946–1947.
———. Office of Chinese Affairs, 1944–1950 Subject File.
———. Office of the Executive Secretariat File.
———. Policy Planning Staff File.
———. United Nations Commission on Korea File.
———. Wedemeyer Mission File.
U.S. War Department. Record Group 319, Plans and Operations Division Decimal File, "Korea 1946–1950, 091 Korea." 1947–1950.

Published

Appleman, Roy. *South to the Naktong, North to the Yalu.* Washington, D.C.: Office of the Chief of Military History, 1961.
Chu Yong-ha, *Puk Chosŏn nodongdang ch'angnip il chunyŏn kwa Chosŏn ŭi minjuhwa rŭl wihan t'ujaeng esŏ kŭŭi yŏkhal* [The first anniversary of the founding of the North Korean Worker's Party and its role in the struggle for Korea's democratization]. P'yŏngyang: KWP ch'ulp'an-sa, 1947.
Chwaik sakŏn sillok [Record of the left-wing incidents]. Seoul: Tae'gŏmch'al-ch'ong, susa-guk, 1964.
DPRK Ministry of Foreign Affairs. *Documents and Materials Exposing the Instigators of the Civil War in Korea.* P'yŏngyang: Ministry of Foreign Affairs, 1950.
Kim Il Sung. *Choguk ŭi t'ongil tongnip kwa minjuhwa rŭl wihayo* [For the unification, independence, and democratization of the homeland]. P'yŏngyang: Nodongdang ch'ulp'an-sa, August 1949.
———. *Works*, vols. 1–7. P'yŏngyang: Foreign Languages Publishing House, 1981.
Korean Worker's Party Agit-Prop Department. *Sae hwan'gyŏng kwa sae chogŏn saeroun saŏp pangsik* [New work methods in a new situation and new conditions]. P'yongyang: Nodongdang ch'ulp'an-sa, May 1950.
Korean Worker's Party. *Nodongdang chungang wiwŏnhoe chŏnggi hoeui munhŏnjip* [Documents on the general meeting of the KWP Central Committee], December 15–18, 1949. P'yŏngyang: KWP, 1950.

Mun Hak-bong. *Mije ŭi Chosŏn ch'imnyak chŏngch'aek ŭi chinsang ŭl chŏngbon wa naeran paep'oja ŭi p'ongno ham* [A true account of American imperialism's aggressive Korea policy and an exposure of the instigators of civil war]. P'yŏngyang: Chung'ang t'ongshin, September 1950.

Republic of Korea. Kukbang-bu p'yŏnch'an wiwŏn-hoe. *Haebang kwa kŏn'gun* [Liberation and the establishment of the army]. Vol. 1 of *Han'guk chŏnjaeng-sa* [History of the Korean War]. Seoul: Kukpang-bu, 1967.

———. Kuksa p'yŏnch'an wiwŏn-hoe. *Taehan Min'guk-sa* [History of the Republic of Korea]. Seoul: 1970.

———. Naemu-bu ch'ian'guk. *Minjok ŭi sŏnbong* [Spearhead of the Nation]. Vol. 1 of *Taehan kyŏngch'al chŏn-sa* [Military History of the Korean National Police]. Seoul: Hŭngguk yŏn'gu hyŏp-hoe, 1952.

Sargent, Clyde. "Political Developments in South Korea, 1947." Seoul: USAMGIK Public Opinion Bureau, January 1948.

Sawyer, Robert K. *Military Advisors in Korea: KMAG in Peace and War.* Washington, D.C.: Office of the Chief of Military History, 1962.

Schnabel, James F. *Policy and Direction: The First Year.* Washington, D.C.: Office of the Chief of Military History, 1972.

Schnabel, James F., and Robert J. Watson. *The Korean War.* Vol 3 of *History of the Joint Chiefs of Staff.* JCS Historical Division. Wilmington, Del.: Michael Glazier, Inc., 1979.

South Korean Interim Government, National Food Administration. "History of the National Food Administration." Appendix C, "Food Report for South Korea as of March 1948," and Appendix E, "Survey of Food Distribution in South Korea." Seoul: 1947, 1948.

U.S. Board on Geographic Names. *South Korea, Official Standard Names.* Gazeteer no. 95. Washington, D.C.: Department of the Interior, 1965.

U.S. Congress. *The Military Situation in the Far East.* 2 vols. Washington, D.C.: U.S. Government Printing Office, 1951; NA, Deleted Testimony.

U.S. Congress. *Selected Executive Session Hearings of the House Committee on International Relations,* vol. 7. "U.S. Policy in the Far East," part 2. Washington, D.C.: U.S. Government Printing Office, 1976.

U.S. Congress. House. Committee on International Relations. *United States Policy in the Far East. Part 2: Korea Assistance Acts, Far East Portion of the Mutual Defense Assistance Act of 1950.* Washington, D.C.: U.S. Government Printing Office, 1976.

U.S. Congress. Senate. *Executive Sessions of the Senate Foreign Relations Committee (Historical Series),* vol. 5. Washington, D.C.: U.S. Government Printing Office, 1977.

U.S. State Department. *Foreign Relations of the United States.* Washington, D.C., 1947–1951.

———. *The Conflict in Korea.* Washington, D.C.: U.S. Government Printing Office, 1951.

———. *North Korea: A Case Study in the Techniques of Take-over.* Washington, D.C.: U.S. Government Printing Office, 1961.

II. Books

Abell, Tyler, ed. *Drew Pearson: Diaries, 1949–1959.* New York: Holt, Rinehart and Winston, 1974.

Acheson, Dean. *Present at the Creation: My Years in the State Department.* New York: W. W. Norton, 1969, 1987.

Acheson, Dean, and David McClellan, eds. *Among Friends: Personal Letters of Dean Acheson*. New York: Dodd, Mead, 1980.

Allison, Graham. *Essence of Decision: Explaining the Cuban Missile Crisis*. Boston: Little, Brown, 1971.

Ambrose, Stephen E. *Ike's Spies: Eisenhower and the Espionage Establishment*. New York: Doubleday, 1981.

————. *Eisenhower. Vol. 1, 1890–1952*. New York: Simon and Schuster, 1983.

————. *Rise to Globalism*. 3d ed. New York: Penguin Books, 1983.

An Ho-sang. *The Ancient History of the Korea-Dong-I Race: Creator of East Asian Culture*. Seoul: Institute of Paedal Culture, 1974.

————. *Minjok ŭi chuch'esŏng kwa hwarangŏl* [The subjectivity and Hwarang spirit of the nation]. Seoul: Paedal munhwa yŏn'gu-wŏn, 1967.

Anderson, Benedict. *Imagined Communities*. New York: Verso, 1983.

Anderson, Perry. *Lineages of the Absolutist State*. London: New Left Books, 1974.

Archer, Jules. *The Plot to Seize the White House*. New York: Hawthorn Books, 1973.

Arrighi, Giovanni. *The Geometry of Imperialism: The Limits of Hobson's Paradigm*. Translated by Patrick Camiller. New York: Verso, 1983.

Bachrach, Stanley D. *The Committee of One Million: 'China Lobby' Politics, 1953–1971*. New York: Columbia University Press, 1976.

Barnes, Harry Elmer, ed. *Perpetual War for Perpetual Peace*. Caldwell, Idaho: The Caxton Printers, 1953.

Barnet, Richard J. *The Roots of War: The Men and Institutions Behind U.S. Foreign Policy*. Baltimore, Md.: Penguin Books, 1973.

Beard, Charles A. *The Open Door at Home: A Trial Philosophy of National Interest*. New York: Macmillan, 1935.

————. *President Roosevelt and the Coming of the War, 1941: A Study in Appearances and Realities*. New Haven, Conn.: Yale University Press, 1948.

Bell, Daniel, ed. *The Radical Right*. New York: Doubleday, 1955, 1963.

Blair, Clay. *The Forgotten War: America in Korea 1950–1953*. New York: Times Books, 1987.

Blum, Robert M. *Drawing the Line: The Origin of the American Containment Policy in East Asia*. New York: W. W. Norton, 1982.

Bohlen, Charles. *Witness to History, 1929–1960*. New York: W. W. Norton, 1973.

Borg, Dorothy, and Waldo Heinrichs, eds. *Uncertain Years: Chinese-American Relations, 1947–1950*. New York: Columbia University Press, 1980.

Boyle, Andrew. *The Fourth Man*. New York: Dial Press, 1979.

Bradbury, William C., Samuel M. Meyers, and Albert D. Biderman, eds. *Mass Behavior in Battle and Captivity*. Chicago: University of Chicago Press, 1968.

Bradley, Omar H., and Clay Blair. *A General's Life*. New York: Simon and Schuster, 1983.

Brzezinski, Zbigniew. *The Soviet Bloc: Unit and Conflict*. Rev. Ed. Cambridge, Mass.: Harvard University Press, 1971.

Burnham, James. *The Struggle for the World*. New York: John Day Co., 1947.

————. *The Coming Defeat of Communism*. New York: John Day Co., 1951.

Cave Brown, Anthony. *The Last Hero: Wild Bill Donovan*. New York: Times Books, 1982.

Chaney, Lindsay, and Michael Cieply. *The Hearsts: Family and Empire*. New York: Simon and Schuster, 1981.

Chirot, Daniel. *Social Change in the Twentieth Century*. New York: Harcourt Brace Jovanovich, 1977.

Cho Pyŏng-ok. *Naŭi hoegorok* [My recollections]. Seoul: Min'gyo-sa, 1959.

Ch'oe Hak-so. *Nongmin chohap chojik-ron* [On the organization of peasant unions]. P'yŏngyang: Sahoe kwahak-sŏ, 1946.

Chŏlla Namdo-ji [History of South Chŏlla]. Kwangju: Munhwa kongbo-shil, 1969.

Churchill, Randolph S., and Winston Churchill. *The Six Day War*. Boston: Houghton Mifflin, 1967.

Cohen, Stephen. *Bukharin and the Bolshevik Revolution*. New York: Vintage Books, 1974.

Cole, Wayne S. *Roosevelt and the Isolationists, 1932–1945*. Lincoln: University of Nebraska Press, 1983.

Corson, William R. *Armies of Ignorance: The Rise of the American Intelligence Empire*. New York: Dial Press, 1977.

Crowther, Samuel. *American Self-Contained*. New York: Doubleday, Doran and Co., 1933.

Cumings, Bruce, ed. *Child of Conflict: The Korean-American Relationship, 1943–1953*. Seattle: University of Washington Press, 1983.

Dallin, David J. *Soviet Foreign Policy After Stalin*. New York: J. B. Lippincott, 1960.

Deutscher, Isaac. *Stalin: A Political Biography*. London: Oxford University Press, 1949.

DeVoto, Bernard. *The Course of Empire*. Lincoln: University of Nebraska Press, 1952.

Diggins, John P. *Up from Communism: Conservative Odysseys in American Intellectual History*. New York: Harper and Row, 1975.

Divine, Robert A. *Second Chance: The Triumph of Internationalism in America During World War II*. New York: Atheneum, 1967.

Doenecke, Justus D. *The Literature of Isolationism*. Colorado Springs: Ralph Myles, 1972.

———. *Not to the Swift: The Old Isolationists in the Cold War Era*. Lewisburg, Pa.: Bucknell University Press, 1979.

Domes, Jürgen. *Peng Te-huai: The Man and the Image*. Stanford, Calif.: Stanford University Press, 1985.

Domhoff, William. *The Bohemian Grove and Other Retreats: A Study in Ruling Class Cohesiveness*. New York: Harper and Row, 1974.

Donovan, Robert J. *Tumultuous Years: The Presidency of Harry S. Truman, 1949–1953*. New York: W. W. Norton, 1982.

Drinnon, Richard. *Facing West: The Metaphysics of Indian-Hating and Empire-Building*. New York: New American Library, 1980.

Dower, John W. *Empire and Aftermath: Yoshida Shigeru and the Japanese Experience, 1878–1954*. Cambridge, Mass: Council on East Asian Studies, Harvard University, 1979.

———. *War Without Mercy: Race and Power in the Pacific War*. New York: Pantheon Books, 1986.

Eastman, Lloyd. *Seeds of Destruction: North China in War and Revolution, 1937–1949*. Stanford, Calif.: Stanford University Press, 1984.

Etzold, Thomas H., and John Gaddis. *Containment: Documents on American Policy and Strategy, 1945–1950*. New York: Columbia University Press, 1978.

Fainsod, Merle. *How Russia Is Ruled*. Cambridge, Mass.: Harvard University Press, 1957.

Fleming, D. F. *The Cold War and Its Origins*, vol. 2. Garden City, N.Y.: Doubleday, 1961.

Flynn, John T. *While You Slept: Our Tragedy in Asia and Who Made It*. New York: Devin-Adair, 1951.

———. *The Road Ahead*. New York: Devin-Adair, 1952.

Foot, Rosemary. *The Wrong War: American Policy and the Dimensions of the Korean Conflict, 1950–1953*. Ithaca, N.Y.: Cornell University Press, 1985.

Ford, Corey. *Donovan of OSS*. Boston: Little, Brown, 1970.

Freeland, Richard M. *The Truman Doctrine and the Origins of McCarthyism*. New York: Schocken, 1974.

Gaddis, John Lewis. *The Strategy of Containment*. New York: Oxford University Press, 1982.

———. *The Long Peace: Inquiries into the History of the Cold War*. New York: Oxford University Press, 1987.

Gardner, Lloyd C. *Economic Aspects of New Deal Diplomacy*. Boston: Beacon Press, 1964.

———. *Architects of Illusion: Men and Ideas in American Foreign Policy, 1941–1949*. Chicago: Quadrangle Books, 1970.

Gelb, Leslie, with Richard K. Betts. *The Irony of Vietnam: The System Worked*. Washington, D.C.: The Brookings Institution, 1979.

George, Alexander, and Richard Smoke. *Deterrence in American Foreign Policy: Theory and Practice*. New York: Columbia University Press, 1974.

Goodwyn, Lawrence. *The Populist Moment*. New York: Oxford University Press, 1978.

Goulden, Joseph C. *Korea: The Untold Story of the War*. New York: Times Books, 1982.

Graebner, Norman. *The New Isolationism: A Study in Politics and Foreign Policy Since 1950*. New York: The Ronald Press, 1956.

Gunther, John. *The Riddle of MacArthur*. New York: Harper and Brothers, 1950.

Haebang-hu samnyŏn'gan ŭi kungnae chuyo ilgi [Chronology of important events within Korea after liberation]. Seoul: 1946.

Halliday, Jon. *A Political History of Japanese Capitalism*. New York: Pantheon, 1975.

Halliday, Jon, and Bruce Cumings. *Korea: The Unknown War*. New York: Pantheon Books, 1988. London: Penguin Books, 1988.

Halperin, Morton H. *Bureaucratic Politics and Foreign Policy*. Washington, D.C.: The Brookings Institution, 1974.

Han Chae-dŏk. *Kim Il Sung Changgun* [General Kim Il Sung]. P'yŏngyang: Minju Chosŏn-sa, 1947.

Han T'ae-su. *Han'guk chŏngdang-sa* [A history of Korean political parties]. Seoul: Sin t'aeyang-sa, 1961.

Han'guk kwangbok samsip p'allyŏn-sa p'yŏnch'an wiwŏn-hoe. *Taehan Min'guk kwangbok samsip p'allyŏn-sa* [Thirty-eight year history of Korean restoration]. Seoul: Samsŏn ch'ulp'an-sa, 1983.

Harootunian, H. D. *Things Seen and Unseen: Discourse and Ideology in Tokugawa Nativism*. Chicago: University of Chicago Press, 1988.

Hartz, Louis. *The Founding of New Societies*. New York: Harcourt, Brace and World, 1964.

———. *The Liberal Tradition in America*. New York: Harcourt, Brace and World, 1955.

Heidegger, Martin. *What Is Called Thinking?* Translated by J. Glenn Gray. New York: Harper Colophon Books, 1968.

Helmreich, Jonathan E. *Gathering Rare Ores: The Diplomacy of Uranium Acquisition, 1943–1954*. Princeton, N.J.: Princeton University Press, 1986.

Henderson, Gregory. *Korea: The Politics of the Vortex*. Cambridge, Mass.: Harvard University Press, 1968.

Herken, Gregg. *The Winning Weapon: The Atomic Bomb and the Cold War, 1945–1950*. New York: Vintage Books, 1982.

Higham, Charles. *Trading with the Enemy*. New York: Delacorte Press, 1983.

Hinckle, Warren, and William W. Turner. *The Fish Is Red: The Story of the Secret War Against Castro*. New York: Harper and Row, 1981.

Hobsbawm, Eric J. *Primitive Rebels*. 2d ed. New York: W. W. Norton, 1965.

Hodgson, Godfrey. *America in Our Time*. Garden City, N.Y.: Doubleday, 1978.

Hong Sŭng-myŏn et al. *Haebang isimnŏn* [Twenty years of liberation]. Seoul: Semun-sa, 1965.

Hoopes, Townsend. *The Devil and John Foster Dulles*. Boston: Little, Brown, 1973.

Hunt, Frazier. *The Untold Story of Douglas MacArthur.* New York: Devin-Adair, 1954.

Isaacson, Walter, and Evan Thomas. *The Wise Men: Six Friends and the World They Made.* New York: Simon and Schuster, 1986.

Iyenaga, Saburo. *The Pacific War.* New York: Pantheon Books, 1976.

James, D. Clayton. *Years of MacArthur. Vol. 1: 1880–1941.* Boston: Houghton Mifflin, 1970.

————. *The Years of MacArthur. Vol. 3: Triumph and Disaster 1945–1964.* Boston: Houghton Mifflin, 1985.

Jameson, Frederic. *Sartre: The Origins of a Style.* New York: Columbia University Press, 1984.

Jervis, Robert. *Perception and Misperception in International Politics.* Princeton, N.J.: Princeton University Press, 1976.

Johnson, Edgar A. J. *American Imperialism in the Image of Peer Gynt.* Minneapolis: University of Minnesota Press, 1971.

Johnson, U. Alexis. *The Right Hand of Power.* With Jef Olivarius McAllister. Englewood Cliffs, N.J.: Prentice-Hall, 1984.

Joseph, Paul. *Cracks in the Empire: State Politics in the Vietnam War.* Boston: South End Press, 1981.

Jowitt, Kenneth, ed. *Social Change in Romania, 1860–1940.* Berkeley, Calif.: Institute of International Studies, 1978.

Kahin, George McT. *Intervention: How America Became Involved in Vietnam.* New York: Alfred A. Knopf, 1986.

Kamp, Joseph P. *We Must Abolish the United States: Hidden Facts Behind the Crusade for World Government.* New York: Constitutional Education League, 1950.

Kaplan, Fred. *The Wizards of Armageddon.* New York: Simon and Schuster, 1983.

Katzenstein, Peter, ed. *Between Power and Plenty.* Madison: University of Wisconsin Press, 1978.

Kaufman, Burton I. *The Korean War: Challenges in Crisis, Credibility, and Command.* Philadelphia: Temple University Press, 1986.

Keeley, Joseph. *The China Lobby Man: The Story of Alfred Kohlberg.* New Rochelle, N.Y.: Arlington House, 1969.

Kennedy, Thomas C. *Charles A. Beard and American Foreign Policy.* Gainesville: University of Florida Press, 1975.

Kennan, George F. *Memoirs, 1925–1950.* New York: Pantheon Books, 1967.

Khrushchev, Nikita. *Khrushchev Remembers,* trans. Strobe Talbott. Boston: Little, Brown, 1970.

————. *Memoirs, 1950–1963.* New York: Pantheon Books, 1972.

Kim Han Gil. *Modern History of Korea.* P'yŏngyang: Foreign Languages Publishing House, 1979.

Kim Kyo-sik. *Kwangbok isimnyŏn* [Twenty years of restoration]. Seoul: Kyemong-sa, 1972.

Kim Pong-hyŏn, and Kim Min-ju. *Cheju-do inmindŭl ŭi '4.3' mujang t'ujaeng-sa* [History of the Cheju Island people's 'April 3' armed struggle]. Osaka: Munu-sa, 1963.

Kim Sam-gyu. *Minjok ŭi yŏmyŏng* [Dawn of the nation]. N.p., 1949.

Kim, Se-jin. *The Politics of Military Revolution in Korea.* Chapel Hill: University of North Carolina Press, 1971.

Kim Yong-jin, ed. *Pan-minja tae kongp'an-gi* [Court record of the traitors]. Seoul: Hanp'ung ch'ulp'an-sa, 1949.

Kindleberger, Charles P. *The World in Depression, 1929–1939.* Berkeley: University of California Press, 1973.

Knox, Donald. *The Korean War, Pusan to Chosin: An Oral History*. New York: Harcourt Brace Jovanovich, 1985.

Ko Yŏng-hwan. *Kŭmil ŭi chŏnggaekdŭl* [Today's politicians]. Seoul: Tonga ilbo-sa, 1949.

Koen, Ross. *The China Lobby in American Politics*. New York: Octagon Books, 1974.

Kolko, Joyce, and Gabriel Kolko. *The Limits of Power: The World and U.S. Foreign Policy, 1945–1954*. New York: Harper and Row, 1972.

Kŏn'guk simnyŏn-ji [Ten years of independence]. Seoul: Kŏn'guk simnyŏn-ji kanhaeng-hoe, 1956.

Kosut, Hal, ed. *Cambodia and the Vietnam War*. New York: Facts on File, 1971.

Kubek, Anthony. *How the Far East Was Lost*. Chicago: Henry Regnery, 1963.

Kutler, Stanley I. *The American Inquisition: Justice and Injustice in the Cold War*. New York: Hill and Wang, 1982.

Kwitny, Jonathan. *Endless Enemies*. New York: Congdon and Weed, 1984.

LaFeber, Walter. *The New Empire: An Interpretation of American Expansion 1860–1898*. Ithaca, N.Y.: Cornell University Press, 1963.

———. *America, Russia and the Cold War 1945–1984*. 5th ed. New York: Alfred A. Knopf, 1985.

Lafour, Laurence. *The Long Fuse*. 2d ed. New York: J. B. Lippincott, 1971.

Langley, Michael. *Inchon: MacArthur's Last Triumph*. London: B. T. Batsford Ltd., 1979.

Laquer, Walter, ed. *Fascism: A Reader's Guide*. Berkeley, Calif.: University of California Press, 1976.

Leary, William M. *Perilous Missions: Civil Air Transport and CIA Covert Operations in Asia*. University, Ala.: University of Alabama Press, 1984.

Lewin, Ronald. *The American Magic*. New York: Penguin Books, 1982.

Liggio, Leonard P., and James L. Martin, eds. *Watershed of Empire: Essays on New Deal Foreign Policy*. Colorado Springs: Ralph Myles, 1976.

Lim, Ŭn. *The Founding of a Dynasty in North Korea*. Tokyo: Jiyu-sha, 1982.

Limb, Ben. *Hoegorok* [Reminiscenses]. Seoul: Yŏwŏnsa, 1964.

———. *Imjŏng eso indo kkaji* [From Imjong to India]. Seoul: Yŏwŏnsa, 1966.

London, Kurt, ed. *The Soviet Union, A Half-Century of Communism*. Baltimore, Md.: John Hopkins University Press, 1968.

Lowe, Peter. *The Origins of the Korean War*. New York: Longman, 1986.

Lundberg, Ferdinand. *Imperial Hearst: A Social Biography*. New York: Equinox Cooperative Press, 1936.

McAuliffe, Mary Sperling. *Crisis on the Left: Cold War Politics and American Liberals, 1947–1954*. Amherst: University of Massachusetts Press, 1978.

McCagg, William O., Jr. *Stalin Embattled, 1943–1948*. Detroit: Wayne State University Press, 1978.

McCormack, Gavan. *Cold War/Hot War*. Sydney, Australia: Hale and Iremonger, 1983.

MacDonald, Callum A. *Korea: The War Before Vietnam*. London: Macmillan, 1986.

MacLean, Fitzroy. *Take Nine Spies*. London: Weidenfeld and Nicolson, 1978.

McLellan, David S. *Dean Acheson: The State Department Years*. New York: Dodd, Mead, 1976.

Maier, Charles S., ed. *The Origins of the Cold War and Contemporary Europe*. New York: New Viewpoints, 1978.

Mao Tse-tung. *Selected Works*. New York: International Publishers, 1954.

———. *Critique of Soviet Economics*. Translated by Moss Roberts. New York: Monthly Review Press, 1977.

Martin, David C. *Wilderness of Mirrors*. New York: Ballantine Books, 1980.

Mearsheimer, John. *Conventional Deterrence*. Ithaca, N.Y.: Cornell University Press, 1983.

Meisner, Maurice. *Li Ta-chao and the Origins of Chinese Marxism*. New York: Atheneum, 1970.

Miles, Michael W. *The Odyssey of the American Right*. New York: Oxford University Press, 1980.

Moore, Barrington, Jr. *Social Origins of Dictatorship and Democracy: Lord and Peasant in the Making of the Modern World*. Boston: Beacon Press, 1966.

Morris, Ivan. *The Nobility of Failure: Tragic Heroes in the History of Japan*. New York: Holt, Rinehart and Winston, 1975.

Mosely, Leonard. *Dulles: A Biography of Eleanor, Allen, and John Foster Dulles and Their Family Network*. New York: Dial Press, 1978.

Murphy, Robert. *Diplomat Among Warriors*. Garden City, N.Y.: Doubleday, 1964.

Nam, Koon Woo. *The North Korean Communist Leadership, 1945–1965: A Study of Factionalism and Political Consolidation*. University, Ala.: University of Alabama Press, 1974.

Navasky, Victor. *Naming Names*. New York: Viking Press, 1980.

Niebuhr, Reinhold. *Moral Man and Immoral Society*. New York: Charles Scribner's Sons, 1932.

Nieh, Jung-chen. *Nieh Jung-chen hui i lu* [Memoirs of Nieh Jung-chen]. 3 vols. Beijing: Chiehfangchün ch'upanshe, 1984.

Nietzsche, Friedrich. *The Genealogy of Morals*. Translated by Walter Kaufmann and R. J. Hollingdale. New York: Vintage Books, 1969.

———. *The Gay Science*. Translated by Walter Kaufmann. New York: Vintage Books, 1974.

———. *Untimely Meditations*. Translated by R. J. Hollingdale. Cambridge: Cambridge University Press, 1983.

Noble, Harold Joyce. *Embassy at War*. Edited by Frank Baldwin. Seattle: University of Washington Press, 1975.

Oliver, Robert. *Syngman Rhee and American Involvement in Korea, 1942–1960*. Seoul: Panmun Books, 1978.

Oshinsky, David M. *A Conspiracy So Immense: The World of Joe McCarthy*. New York: The Free Press, 1983.

Paige, Glenn. *The Korean Decision*. Glencoe, Ill.: The Free Press, 1968.

Paterson, Thomas G., ed. *Cold War Critics: Alternatives to American Foreign Policy in the Truman Years*. Chicago: Quadrangle Books, 1971.

Pawley, William. *Americans Valiant and Glorious*. New York: n.p., 1945.

Pearson, Drew. *Diaries, 1949–1950*. New York: Holt, Rinehart and Winston, 1974.

Peek, George N., and Samuel Crowther. *Why Quit Our Own?* New York: D. Van Nostrand Co., 1936.

P'eng Te-huai. *P'eng Te-huai tzu-shu* [P'eng Te-huai—his story]. Beijing: People's Publishing House, 1981.

Pogue, Forrest C. *George C. Marshall: Statesman 1945–1959*. New York: Viking Press, 1987.

Polanyi, Karl. *The Great Transformation*. New York: Beacon Press, 1957.

Prouty, L. Fletcher. *The Secret Team*. Englewood Cliffs, N.J.: Prentice-Hall, 1973.

Pruessen, Ronald W. *John Foster Dulles: The Road to Power*. New York: The Free Press, 1982.

Quigley, Carroll. *Tragedy and Hope: A History of the World in Our Time*. New York: Macmillan, 1966.

Radosh, Ronald. *Prophets on the Right*. New York: Simon and Schuster, 1975.

Reeves, Thomas C. *The Life and Times of Joe McCarthy*. New York: Stein and Day, 1982.

Rhee, Syngman. *Ilminjuŭi kaesul* [Outline of the One People Principle]. Seoul: Ilminjuŭi po'gŭp-hoe, 1949.

Rieselbach, LeRoy N. *The Roots of Isolationism*. New York: Bobbs-Merrill, 1966.

Riley, John W., Jr., and Wilbur Schramm. *The Reds Take a City*. With translations by Hugh Heung-wu Cynn. New Brunswick, N.J.: Rutgers University Press, 1951.

Robbins, Christopher. *Air America*. New York: G. P. Putnam's Sons, 1979.

Rogin, Michael Paul. *The Intellectuals and McCarthy: The Radical Specter*. Cambridge, Mass.: MIT Press, 1967.

Rotter, Andrew J. *The Path to Vietnam: The Origins of the American Commitment to Southeast Asia*. Ithaca, N.Y.: Cornell University Press, 1987.

Rovere, Richard. *Senator Joe McCarthy*. New York: Harcourt, Brace, 1959.

————. *The American Establishment and Other Reports, Opinions, and Speculations*. New York: Harcourt, Brace and World, 1962.

Sasaki, Harutaka. *Han'gukjŏn pisa* [Secret history of the Korean war], trans. Kang Ch'ang-gu. 3 vols. Seoul: Pyŏmghak-sa, 1977.

Scalapino, Robert, ed. *The Communist Revolution in Asia*. 2d ed. Englewood Cliffs, N.J.: Prentice-Hall, 1969.

Scalapino, Robert, and Chong-sik Lee. *Communism in Korea*. 2 vols. Berkeley: University of California Press, 1972.

Scarry, Elaine. *The Body in Pain: The Making and Unmaking of the World*. New York: Oxford University Press, 1985.

Schaller, Michael. *The American Occupation of Japan: The Origins of the Cold War in Asia*. New York: Oxford University Press, 1985.

Schlesinger, Arthur, Jr. *The Vital Center: The Politics of Freedom*. Boston: Houghton Mifflin, 1949.

Schoenbaum, Thomas J. *Waging Peace and War: Dean Rusk in the Truman, Kennedy and Johnson Years*. New York: Simon and Schuster, 1988.

Schurmann, Franz. *Ideology and Organization in Communist China*. Berkeley: University of California Press, 1967.

————. *The Logic of World Power: An Inquiry into the Origins, Currents, and Contradictions of World Politics*. New York: Pantheon Books, 1974.

Scott, Peter Dale. *The War Conspiracy*. New York: Bobbs-Merrill, 1972.

Seagrave, Sterling. *The Soong Dynasty*. New York: Harper and Row, 1985.

Seldes, George. *One Thousand Americans*. New York: Boni and Gaer, 1947.

Silva, Peer de. *Sub Rosa: The CIA and the Uses of Intelligence*. New York: Times Books, 1978.

Simmons, Robert R. *The Strained Alliance: Peking, P'yŏngyang, Moscow and the Politics of the Korean Civil War*. New York: The Free Press, 1975.

Simpson, Christopher. *Blowback: America's Recruitment of Nazis and Its Effects on the Cold War*. New York: Weidenfeld and Nicholson, 1988.

Skocpol, Theda, ed. *Vision and Method in Historical Sociology*. New York: Cambridge University Press, 1984.

Smith, Richard Norton. *Thomas E. Dewey and His Times*. New York: Simon and Schuster, 1982.

Smith, Robert. *MacArthur in Korea: The Naked Emperor*. New York: Simon and Schuster, 1982.

Stone, I. F. *The Hidden History of the Korean War*. New York: Monthly Review Press, 1952; paperback, 1970.

Straight, Michael. *After Long Silence*. New York: W. W. Norton, 1983.

Stueck, William. *The Road to Confrontation*. Chapel Hill: University of North Carolina Press, 1983.

Suh, Dae-sook. *The Korean Communist Movement, 1918–1948*. Princeton, N.J.: Princeton University Press, 1967.

Summers, Harry. *On Strategy*. New York: Presidio Press, 1982.

Swanberg, W. A. *Citizen Hearst*. New York: Charles Scribner's Sons, 1961.

———. *Luce and His Empire*. New York: Charles Scribner's Sons, 1972.

Taubman, William. *Stalin's American Policy: From Entente to Detente to Cold War*. New York: W. W. Norton, 1982.

Tawney, R. H. *Land and Labor in China*. New York: Octagon Books, 1932, 1964.

Thompson, Reginald. *Cry Korea*. London: MacDonald and Co., 1951.

Tilton, Timothy Alan. *Nazism, Neo-Nazism, and the Peasantry*. Bloomington: Indiana University Press, 1975.

Tillyard, E.M.W. *The Elizabethan World Picture*. New York: Vintage Books, 1942.

Trotsky, Leon. *Stalin*. 2d ed. New York: Stein and Day, 1967.

Troy, Thomas F. *Donovan and the CIA*. Frederick, Md.: Alethia Books, 1981.

Truman, Margaret. *Harry S. Truman*. New York: William Morrow and Company, 1973.

Tucker, Nancy. *Patterns in the Dust: Chinese-American Relations and the Recognition Controversy, 1949–1950*. New York: Columbia University Press, 1983.

Tucker, Robert C., ed. *Stalinism: Essays in Historical Interpretation*. New York: W. W. Norton, 1977.

Ulyanovsky, R. A., ed. *The Comintern and the East*. Moscow: Progress Publishers, 1979.

Unger, Roberto Mangabiera. *Knowledge and Politics*. New York: The Free Press, 1975.

Wales, Nym. *Song of Ariran: A Korean Communist in the Chinese Revolution*. San Francisco: Ramparts Press, 1973.

Walker, J. Samuel. *Henry A. Wallace and American Foreign Policy*. Westport, Conn.: Greenwood Press, 1976.

Wallerstein, Immanuel. *Historical Capitalism*. New York: Verso, 1983.

Walzer, Michael. *Just and Unjust Wars: A Moral Argument with Historical Illustrations*. New York: Basic Books, 1977.

West, Nigel. *A Matter of Trust: MI5, 1945–72*. London: Coronet Books, 1982.

Whiting, Allen S. *China Crosses the Yalu: The Decision to Enter the Korean War*. Stanford, Calif.: Stanford University Press, 1960.

———. *The Chinese Calculus of Deterrence*. Ann Arbor: University of Michigan Press, 1975.

Whitlam, E. Gough. *A Pacific Community*. Cambridge, Mass.: Harvard University Press, 1981.

Whitson, William W. *The Chinese High Command: A History of Communist Military Politics*. With Chen-hsia Huang. New York: Praeger, 1973.

Wilcox, Robert K. *Japan's Secret War*. New York: William Morrow, 1985.

Willoughby, Charles A., and John Chamberlin. *MacArthur, 1941–1951*. New York: McGraw-Hill, 1954.

Wohlstetter, Roberta. *Pearl Harbor: Warning and Decision*. Stanford, Calif.: Stanford University Press, 1962.

Wolff, Robert Paul. *Moneybags Must Be So Lucky: On the Literary Structure of Capital*. Amherst: University of Massachusetts Press, 1988.

Yanaga, Chitoshi. *Big Business in Japanese Politics*. New Haven, Conn.: Yale University Press, 1968.

Yang U-chong. *Yi taet'ongnyŏng t'ujaeng-sa* [History of President Rhee's struggle]. Seoul: Yŏnhap sinmun-sa, 1949.

Yergin, Daniel. *Shattered Peace: The Origins of the Cold War and the National Security State.* Boston: Houghton Mifflin, 1978.

Yi Ch'un-sik. *Sŏn'gŏ tokbon* [Election reader]. Seoul: Sinhung ch'ulp'an-sa, 1948.

Yi Pŏm-sŏk. *Minjok kwa ch'ŏngnyŏn* [Nation and youth]. Seoul: Paeksu-sa, 1947.

Yim, Louise. *My 40-Year Fight for Korea.* Seoul: Chungang University, 1951.

Yŏ Un-hong. *Mongyang Yŏ Un-hyŏng.* Seoul: Ch'ongha-gak, 1967.

Zilg, Gerard. *DuPont: Behind the Nylon Curtain.* Englewood Cliffs, N.J.: Prentice-Hall, 1974.

III. Articles and Periodicals

"Air War in Korea." *Air University Quarterly Review* 4, no. 2 (Fall 1950), pp. 19–40.

Akio, Yamakawa. "Lockheed Scandal." *Ampo* (April-September 1976), p. 3.

"The Background of the Present War in Korea." *Far Eastern Economic Review* (August 31, 1950), pp. 233–37.

Block, Fred. "Economic Instability and Military Strength: Paradoxes of the 1950 Rearmament Decision." *Politics and Society* 10, no. 1 (1980), pp. 35–58.

Brus, Wlodzimierz. "Stalinism and the People's Democracies." In *Stalinism: Essays in Historical Interpretation*, edited by Robert C. Tucker, pp. 239–58. New York: W. W. Norton, 1977.

Bullene, E. F. "Wonder Weapon: Napalm." *Army Combat Forces Journal* (November 1952), pp. 25–28.

Bullitt, William. "The Story of Syngman Rhee." *Reader's Digest*, September 1953, p. 37.

Ch'oe Ch'ang-ik. "People are the Motive Force of History." *Kŭlloja*, no. 9 (November 1947), pp. 13–23.

Cumings, Bruce. "Kim's Korean Communism." *Problems of Communism* (March-April 1974).

———. "Corporatism in North Korea." *Journal of Korean Studies*, no. 3 (1983).

———. "Parades of Remembering and Forgetting: Korea, Vietnam, and Nicaragua." *The Nation* (October 1986).

Current, Richard N. "How Stimson Meant to 'Maneuver' the Japanese." *Mississippi Valley Historical Review* 40, no. 1 (March 1953), pp. 57–76.

Elliot, David C. "Project Vista and Nuclear Weapons in Europe." *International Security* 2, no. 1. (Summer 1986), pp. 163–83.

Evangelista, Matthew A. "Stalin's Postwar Army Reappraised." *International Security* 7, no. 3 (Winter 1982–1983), pp. 110–39.

Fensterwald, Bernard, Jr. "The Anatomy of American 'Isolationism' and 'Expansionism.' " *Journal of Conflict Revolution* 2, nos. 2 and 4 (June and December 1958).

Ghosh, Partha Sarathy. "Passage of the Silver Purchase Act of 1934: The China Lobby and the Issue of China Trade." *Indian Journal of American Studies* 6, no. 1/2 (1976), pp. 18–29.

Halliday, Jon. "The Korean War." *Bulletin of Concerned Asian Scholars* (July-September 1979).

Han Ch'ŏl-ho. "The Rhee Clique's Strengthening Ties with Japanese Imperialism, under Directions from U.S. Imperialism." *Sun'gan t'ongshin* 48, no. 5 (January 1950).

Hofstadter, Richard. "The Pseudo-Conservative Revolt—1955." In *The Radical Right*, edited by Daniel Bell. pp. 63–80. New York: Doubleday, 1963.

Karig, Walter. "Korea—Tougher Than Okinawa." *Collier's*, September 23, 1950, pp. 24–26.

Kim Il Sung. "What Are the Demands of the Various Political Parties and Social Organizations Concerning the Establishment of a Democratic Provisional Government?" *Kŭlloja*, no. 6 (June 1947), pp. 2–15.

———. "Report on the Development of the North Korean People's Economy, 1947." *Kŭlloja*, no. 4 (April 1947), pp. 22–24.

———. "Greeting the First Anniversary of the Founding of the NKWP." *Kŭlloja*, no. 8 (August 1947), pp. 27–44.

———. "Report on the Second Anniversary of Liberation." *Kŭlloja*, no. 8 (August 1947), pp. 2–9.

———. "Speech to the Youth of Korea." *Podo*, no. 3 (August 1947), pp. 11–17.

———. "Report to the Second Congress of the KWP." *Kŭlloja*, no. 4 (14) (April 1948), pp. 2–12.

———. "1949 New Year's Speech." *Sun'gan t'ongshin*, no. 8 (January 1949), pp. 1–4.

Kim Tu-bong. "The Results of the Elections and the Tasks Facing the Worker's Party." *Kŭlloja*, no. 2 (November 1946), p. 34.

Kim Yŏng-t'aek. "The Courageous Armed Resistance of the South Korean People." *Sun'gan t'ongshin*, no. 14 (March 1949), p. 3.

Kim Yŏn-hun. "Patriotism in the Democratic State." *Kŭlloja*, no. 8 (August 1947), pp. 60–65.

Korean Survey.

Kramer, R. C. "Japan Must Compete." *Fortune*, June 1947.

LaFeber, Walter. "Crossing the 38th: The Cold War in Microcosm." In *Reflections on the Cold War: A Quarter-Century of American Foreign Policy*, edited by Lynn H. Miller and Ronald W. Pruessen. Philadelphia: Temple University Press, 1974.

"Land Reform in China's Liberated Areas." *Puk-Chosŏn t'ongshin* [North Korea News], no. 1 (July 21–October 21, 1947), pp. 14–15.

Larrabee, Eric. "Korea: The Military Lesson." *Harper's*, November 1950, pp. 51–57.

Linz, Juan. "Some Notes Toward a Comparative Study of Fascism in Sociological Historical Perspective." In *Fascism: A Reader's Guide*, edited by Walter Laquer, pp. 3–12. Berkeley: University of California Press, 1976.

Lipset, Seymour Martin. "The Sources of the 'Radical Right.'" In *Radical Right*, edited by Daniel Bell, pp. 259–312. New York: Doubleday, 1963.

Mao Tse-tung. "On Methods of Leadership." In *Selected Works*. New York: International Publishers, 1954.

Marx, Karl. "Bastiat and Carey." In *Grundrisse: Foundations of the Critique of Political Economy*, trans. Martin Nicolaus. New York: Penguin Books, 1973.

Merrill, John. "The Cheju-do Rebellion." *Journal of Korean Studies*, no. 2 (1980), pp. 139–98.

———. "Review of *Khrushchev Remembers*." *Journal of Korean Studies* 3 (1981), pp. 181–90.

Min Chu (pseud.). "Several Problems in Leadership Work in Economic Construction." *Kŭlloja*, no. 7 (July 1947), pp. 20–23.

Min Pyŏng-ŭi. "The Full Story of the Southern Guerrillas." *Sŏnjŏnja* [The propagandist] (P'yongyang) (1949).

Monthly Review 2, nos. 4 and 11 (1950–1951).

Morely, Felix. "A Solution for Korea." *The Freeman* (October 30, 1950), pp. 81–82.

"Napalm Jelly Bombs Prove a Blazing Success in Korea." *All Hands* (April 1951), pp. 17–19.

Newman, Robert P. "Clandestine Chinese Nationalist Efforts to Punish Their American Detractors." *Diplomatic History* 7, no. 3 (Summer 1983), pp. 205–22.

Osborne, John. "Report from the Orient—Guns Are Not Enough." *Life*, August 21, 1950, pp. 74–84.

"Our Spineless Foreign Policy." *The American Mercury* 70, no. 313 (January 1950), pp. 3–13.

Paek Il. "The Theory of Dialectical Materialism is the World View of the Marxist-Leninist Party." *Kŭlloja*, no. 8 (August 1947), pp. 66–80.

Pak Tong-ch'o. "The Meaning of the Korean-Soviet Agreement on Economic and Cultural Cooperation." *Kŭlloja*, no. 8 (April 30, 1949), pp. 16–25.

Plain Talk.

Podo [Report]. P'yŏngyang.

Puk-Chosŏn t'ongshin [North Korea News]. P'yŏngyang.

Roberts, John J. "The 'Japan Crowd' and the Zaibatsu Restoration." *The Japan Interpreter* 12 (Summer 1979), pp. 384–415.

Rosenberg, Ron. "The Shadow of the Mole." *Harper's*, October 1983, pp. 45–54.

Schmitter, Philippe. "Reflections on Mikhail Manoilescu and the Political Consequences of Delayed Development on the Periphery of Western Europe." In *Social Change in Romania, 1860–1940*, edited by Kenneth Jowitt. Berkeley, Calif.: Institute of International Studies, 1978.

Schonberger, Howard. "The General and the Presidency: Douglas MacArthur and the Election of 1948." *Wisconsin Magazine of History* 57, no. 3 (Spring 1974), pp. 201–19.

———. "The Japan Lobby in American Diplomacy." *Pacific Historical Review* 46, no. 3 (August 1977), pp. 327–59.

Sewall, Arthur F. "Key Pittman and the Quest for the China Market, 1933–1940." *Pacific Historical Review* 44, no. 3 (1975), pp. 351–71.

Simmons, Walter. "The Truth About Korea." *Chicago Tribune*, November 6, 1949.

Snowden, Frank M. "On the Social Origins of Agrarian Fascism in Italy." *European Journal of Sociology* 13, no. 2 (1972), pp. 268–95.

Sŏl San. "Economic Development in China's Northeast." *Sun'gan t'ongshin* 46, no. 3 (January 1950), pp. 9–13.

Song Sŭng-ch'ŏl. "The Rhee County-Selling Clique and the Japanese Militarists Are Colluding under the Direction of American Imperialism." *Kŭlloja*, no. 8 (April 1950), pp. 42–52.

The Spectator (August 1950).

Sun'gan t'ongshin [Periodic news]. P'yŏngyang.

Townsend, J. "They Don't Like Hell Bombs." *Armed Forces Chemical Journal* (January 1951), pp. 8–11.

Trow, Martin. "Small Businessmen, Political Tolerance, and Support for McCarthy." *American Journal of Sociology* 64 (November 1958), pp. 270–81.

Tucker, Robert. C. "Paths of Communist Revolution, 1917–1967." In *The Soviet Union, A Half-Century of Communism*, edited by Kurt London. Baltimore, Md.: John Hopkins University Press, 1968.

———. "Communist Revolutions, National Cultures, and Divided Nations." *Studies in Comparative Communism* 7, no. 3 (Autumn 1974), pp. 235–45.

Tullier, P. C. "The Oriental Mind." *The New Yorker*, July 15, 1950.

US News and World Report (1950).

Viereck, Peter. "The Revolt Against the Elite—1955." In *The Radical Right*, edited by Daniel Bell, pp. 135–54. New York: Doubleday, 1963.

Westin, Alan. "The John Birch Society: 'Radical Right' and 'Extreme Left' in the Political Context of Post-World War II—1962." In *Radical Right*, edited by Daniel Bell, pp. 201–26. New York: Doubleday, 1963.

Willoughby, Gen. Charles, "Franco and Spain." *The American Mercury* (January 1960), pp. 23–32.

World Events 7, no. 2 (Spring 1950); 7, no. 4 (Fall 1950).

Yi Chŏng-su. "Let's Strengthen the True Armed Force of the Korean People, the KPA." *Sun'gan t'ongshin*, no. 5 (January 1950), pp. 1–6.

Yi Sang-buk. "The People's Guerrillas Launch a New Offensive, Holding High the Banner of the Patriotic Front." *Sun'gan t'ongshin*, no. 34 (September 1949), pp. 1–3.

Yi Sŭng-yŏp. "The Struggle of the Southern Guerrillas for Unification of the Homeland." *Kŭlloja*, no. 1 (January 1950), pp. 15–26.

———. "On the Present Tasks of the Southern People's Guerrillas, Who Have Completely Defeated the Enemy's 'Winter Subjugation.' " *Kŭlloja*, no. 6 (March 30, 1950), pp. 9–22.

IV. Unpublished Dissertations and Studies

Eckert, Carter. "The Origins of Korean Capitalism." Ph.D. diss., University of Washington, 1986.

Eden, Lynn. "The Diplomacy of Force: Interests, the State, and the Making of American Military Policy in 1948." Ph.D. diss., University of Michigan, 1985.

Flint, Roy Kenneth. "The Tragic Flaw: MacArthur, the Joint Chiefs, and the Korean War." Ph.D. diss., Duke University, 1976.

Koh, Kwang-il. "In Quest of National Unity and Power: Political Ideas and Practices of Syngman Rhee." Ph.D. diss., Rutgers University, 1962.

Ledyard, Gari. "The Korean Security Crisis of 1598: National Security, Confucian Style." Columbia University Faculty Seminar on Korea, 1980.

Lee, Kyung Jo. "Social Origins and Backgrounds of Representatives of National Assembly in South Korea 1948–1961." Ph.D. diss., Claremont Graduate School, 1975.

Lhee Yung Myung. "The Policies of Syngman Rhee and the U.S. (1945–1950)." Master's thesis, University of Chicago, 1962.

Merrill, John Roscoe. "Internal Warfare in Korea, 1948–1950: The Local Setting of the Korean War." Ph.D. diss., University of Delaware, 1982.

Poteat, George Howard. "Strategic Intelligence and National Security: A Case Study of the Korean Crisis (June 25-November 24, 1950)." Ph.D. diss., Washington University, 1973.

Robinson, Richard. "Betrayal of a Nation." Manuscript, Massachusetts Institute of Technology.

Sakurai, Hiroshi. "Why Did the Korean War 'Break Out' on June 25, 1950?" Seminar paper, University of California, Berkeley, May 1983.

van Ree, Erik. "Socialism in One Zone: Stalin's Policy in Korea, 1945–1947. Ph.D. diss., University of Amsterdam, 1988.

Wada, Haruki. "The Soviet Union and North Korea." Seminar paper, University of Washington, 1984.

Wallerstein, Immanuel. "McCarthyism and the Conservative." Master's thesis, Columbia University, 1954.

Weems, Clarence. "American-Korean Cooperation (1941–1945): Why Was It So Little and So Late?" Paper. Columbia University Faculty Seminar on Korea, 1981.

V. NEWSPAPERS

Chinese Language

Renmin Ribao [People's Daily]. Beijing. June-November, 1950.
Ta Kung Pao. Hong Kong. June, 1950.

Korean Language

Chayu sinmun [Free News]. Seoul. 1947.
Chosŏn inmin-gun [Korean People's Army]. P'yŏngyang. 1950.
Haebang ilbo [Liberation Daily]. Seoul. 1950.
Hamgyŏng Namdo nodong sinmun [South Hamgyŏng Province Worker's News]. 1949–1950.
Kaebyŏk sinbo [Creation News]. Seoul. 1950.
Kangwŏn inminbo [Kangwŏn Province People's News]. 1949.
Kukje sinmun [International News]. Seoul. 1948.
Minjung ilbo [The Masses Daily]. P'yŏngyang. 1947.
Nodong sinmun [Worker's News]. P'yŏngyang. 1948–1950.
Puin sinmun [Wives' News]. Seoul. 1950.
Seoul Sinmun [Seoul News]. Seoul. March 1950.
T'aeyang sinmun. Seoul. 1949.
Tonga ilbo [East Asia Daily]. Seoul. 1950.
Yibuk t'ongshin [News from the North]. Seoul.
Yonhap sinmun. Seoul. January 1949.
Yŏsu Inmin ilbo [Yŏsu People's News]. Yŏsu. 1948.

English Language

The Christian Science Monitor. Boston. 1950.
Daily Worker. London. 1950.
Hong Kong Standard. Hong Kong. 1950.
Korea Herald. Seoul. June 1979.
Korean Independence. Los Angeles. 1949.
London Times. London. 1950.
Manchester Guardian. Manchester. 1950.
New Times. Moscow. 1950.
New York Herald-Tribune. New York. 1949–1950.
New York Times. New York. 1947–1951.
The Oregonian. Portland. July 1950.
Philadelphia Inquirer. Philadelphia. 1950.
Seoul Times. Seoul. 1946–1948.
Washington Post. Washington, D.C. 1950.

VI. PAPERS

Dean Acheson Papers, Harry S. Truman Library.
Dean Acheson Papers, Yale University Library.
Gen. Edward M. Almond Papers, Carlisle Military Barracks.
Eben Ayers Papers, Harry S. Truman Library.

Roger Baldwin Papers, Princeton University.
Haydon L. Boatner Papers, Hoover Institution.
Charles Bohlen Papers, Library of Congress.
Alfred Connor Bowman Papers, Hoover Institution.
Rothwell Brown Papers, Carlisle Military Barracks.
W. Walton Butterworth Papers, George C. Marshall Research Center.
William R. Castle Papers, Hoover Presidential Library.
Claire Chennault Papers, Library of Congress.
Kenneth R. Colegrove Papers, Hoover Presidential Library.
Sen. Tom Connally Papers, Library of Congress.
Matthew Connelly Papers, Harry S. Truman Library.
Charles M. Cooke Papers, Hoover Institution.
Hugh Deane Papers, University of Chicago.
William Donovan Papers, Carlisle Military Barracks.
Daniel Doyle Papers, Carlisle Military Barracks.
Allen Dulles Papers, Princeton University.
John Foster Dulles Papers, Princeton University.
Robert L. Eichelberger Papers, Duke University.
George M. Elsey Papers, Harry S. Truman Library.
M. Preston Goodfellow Papers, Hoover Institution.
Bourke Hickenlooper Papers, Hoover Presidential Library.
Herbert Hoover Post-Presidential Individual File, Hoover Presidential Library.
Roy Howard Papers, Library of Congress.
Joseph E. Jacobs Papers, Hoover Institution.
Phillip Jessup Papers, George C. Marshall Research Center.
Edgar A. Johnson Papers, Harry S. Truman Library.
Louis A. Johnson Papers, University of Virginia.
George F. Kennan Papers, Princeton University.
Wellington Koo Papers, Columbia University.
Korea Liaison Office Papers, Carlisle Military Barracks.
Arthur Krock Papers, Library of Congress.
William D. Leahy Papers, Library of Congress.
Joseph B. Longuevan Papers, Carlisle Military Barracks.
Gen. Douglas MacArthur Papers, MacArthur Memorial, Norfolk, Va.
William A. Mathews Papers, University of Pennsylvania.
Milton E. Miles Papers, Hoover Institution.
Ogden L. Mills Papers, Library of Congress.
Wayne Morse Papers, University of Oregon.
Harold Noble Papers, University of Chicago.
Robert Oliver Papers, selections from Chong-sik Lee, University of Pennsylvania.
Robert Patterson Papers, Library of Congress.
William D. Pawley Papers, George C. Marshall Research Center.
Adm. William V. Pratt Papers, Naval War College.
William V. Quinn Papers, Carlisle Military Barracks.
Karl Rankin Papers, Princeton University.
Gen. Matthew Ridgway Papers, Carlisle Military Barracks.
Clyde Sargent File, Hoover Institution.
Sen. Alexander Smith Papers, Princeton University.
T. V. Soong Papers, Hoover Institution.
Sydney W. Souers Papers, Harry S. Truman Library.
Charles W. Thayer Papers, Harry S. Truman Library.

Arthur Vandenberg Papers, Library of Congress.
Hoyt S. Vandenberg Papers, Library of Congress.
William Vanderpool Papers, Carlisle Military Barracks.
Orlando Ward Papers, Carlisle Military Barracks.
Whiting Willauer Papers, Princeton University.
Gen. Charles Willoughby Papers, Carlisle Military Barracks.
Gen. Charles Willoughby Papers, MacArthur Memorial, Norfolk, Va.
Robert Wood Papers, Hoover Presidential Library.

VII. Interviews

Interview with Leonard Bertsch, May 1973.
Interview with J. W. Burton, February 1987.
Interview with M. Preston Goodfellow, Jr., August 1987.
Interview with Robert Oliver, August 1985.
Interview with Walter Sullivan, May 1983.
Miscellaneous interviews with Thames Television, 1986–1987.